FISKE
GUIDE TO
COLLEGES

2020

Also by Edward B. Fiske

Fiske Guide to Getting Into the Right College with Bruce G. Hammond

Fiske Real College Essays That Work with Bruce G. Hammond

Fiske Countdown to College with Bruce G. Hammond

Fiske WordPower with Jane Mallison and Margery Mandell

Fiske 250 Words Every High School Freshman Needs to Know with Jane Mallison and David Hatcher

Fiske 250 Words Every High School Graduate Needs to Know with Jane Mallison and David Hatcher

Smart Schools, Smart Kids: Why Do Some Schools Work?

Using Both Hands: Women and Education in Cambodia

Decentralization of Education: Politics and Consensus

When Schools Compete: A Cautionary Tale with Helen F. Ladd

Elusive Equity: Education Reform in Post-Apartheid South Africa with Helen F. Ladd

Handbook of Research in Education Finance and Policy, ed. with Helen F. Ladd

FISKE GUIDE TO COLLEGES 2020

EDWARD B. FISKE

**former Education Editor of
the *New York Times***

**with Michelle Lecuyer
and
the *Fiske Guide to Colleges* staff**

 sourcebooks

Published by Sourcebooks
P.O. Box 4410
Naperville, Illinois 60567-4410
(630) 961-3900
sourcebooks.com

Thirty-Sixth Edition

**Your comments and corrections
are welcome. Please send them to:**

Fiske Guide to Colleges
Email: editor@fiskeguide.com

Printed and bound in the United States of America.

DR 10 9 8 7 6 5 4 3 2

To Sunny

Contents

Index by State and Country

The colleges in this guide are listed alphabetically and cross-referenced for your convenience. Below is a list of the selected colleges grouped by state. Following this listing, you will find additional listings that categorize the colleges by their yearly costs of attendance and by the average debt accrued by students during their tenure at each school.

University of North Carolina at Chapel Hill, 506
University of North Carolina Wilmington, 508
North Carolina State University, 511
Wake Forest University, 745
Warren Wilson College, 748

OHIO
Antioch College, 25
Case Western Reserve, 126
University of Cincinnati, 144
University of Dayton, 205
Denison University, 212
Hiram College, 323
Kenyon College, 405
Miami University, 457
Oberlin College, 521
Ohio State University, 529
Ohio University, 532
Ohio Wesleyan University, 534
Wittenberg University, 796
The College of Wooster, 800

OKLAHOMA
University of Oklahoma, 536
University of Tulsa, 718

OREGON
Lewis & Clark College, 419
University of Oregon, 541
Oregon State University, 544
Reed College, 584
Willamette University, 786

PENNSYLVANIA
Allegheny College, 12
Bryn Mawr College, 85
Bucknell University, 88
Carnegie Mellon University, 123
Dickinson College, 222
Drexel University, 227
Franklin & Marshall College, 266
Gettysburg College, 283
Haverford College, 315
Juniata College, 395
Lafayette College, 410
Lehigh University, 417
Muhlenberg College, 484
University of Pennsylvania, 548
Pennsylvania State University, 551

University of Pittsburgh, 556
Susquehanna University, 684
Swarthmore College, 687
Ursinus College, 723
Villanova University, 735
Washington and Jefferson College, 753

RHODE ISLAND
Brown University, 82
Providence College, 570
University of Rhode Island, 589
Rhode Island School of Design, 591

SOUTH CAROLINA
College of Charleston, 138
Clemson University, 164
Furman University, 268
Presbyterian College, 559
University of South Carolina, 651
Wofford College, 798

TENNESSEE
Rhodes College, 593
University of the South (Sewanee), 649
University of Tennessee Knoxville, 692
Vanderbilt University, 728

TEXAS
Austin College, 45
Baylor University, 57
University of Dallas, 197
Rice University, 596
Southern Methodist University, 656
Southwestern University, 659
University of Texas at Austin, 694
University of Texas at Dallas, 697
Texas A&M University, 699
Texas Christian University, 702
Texas Tech University, 704
Trinity University, 709

UTAH
Brigham Young University, 79
University of Utah, 725

VERMONT
Bennington College, 62
Champlain College, 133
Marlboro College, 437
Middlebury College, 465

Saint Michael's College, 628
University of Vermont, 733

VIRGINIA
George Mason University, 270
Hampden–Sydney College, 303
Hollins University, 330
James Madison University, 390
University of Mary Washington, 442
Randolph College, 579
University of Richmond, 598
University of Virginia, 737
Virginia Tech, 741
Washington and Lee University, 755
College of William and Mary, 788

WASHINGTON
The Evergreen State College, 248
Gonzaga University, 285
University of Puget Sound, 572
Seattle University, 642
University of Washington, 750
Whitman College, 781

WASHINGTON, D.C. (SEE DISTRICT OF COLUMBIA)

WEST VIRGINIA
West Virginia University, 772

WISCONSIN
Alverno College, 18
Beloit College, 59
Lawrence University, 414
Marquette University, 440
Ripon College, 601
University of Wisconsin–Madison, 793

CANADA
University of British Columbia, 357
McGill University, 359
Queen's University, 361
University of Toronto, 363

GREAT BRITAIN AND IRELAND
University of Aberdeen, 368
University of Edinburgh, 371
University of Glasgow, 374
University of St Andrews, 376
Trinity College Dublin, 380

Index by Price

	PUBLIC	PRIVATE
$$$$	More than $15,000	More than $54,000
$$$	$12,001–$15,000	$50,001–$54,000
$$	$10,000–$12,000	$44,000–$50,000
$	Less than $10,000	Less than $44,000

Price categories are based on current tuition and fees and do not include room, board, transportation, and other expenses.

PUBLIC COLLEGES AND UNIVERSITIES

INEXPENSIVE—$
University of Arkansas, 32
The Evergreen State College, 248
University of Florida, 254
Florida State University, 261
University of Iowa, 383
Iowa State University, 385
University of Mississippi, 476
University of Missouri, 478
University of Nebraska–Lincoln, 486
New College of Florida, 489
University of New Mexico, 498
University of North Carolina at Asheville, 503
University of North Carolina at Chapel Hill, 506
University of North Carolina Wilmington, 508
North Carolina State University, 511
Purdue University, 574
SUNY–University at Albany, 666
SUNY–Binghamton University, 668
SUNY–College at Geneseo, 673
SUNY–Purchase College, 675
SUNY–Stony Brook University, 677
Truman State University, 711
University of Utah, 725
West Virginia University, 772

MODERATE—$$
University of Alabama, 5
Arizona State University, 29
Auburn University, 42
University of Cincinnati, 144
Colorado State University, 178
University of Georgia, 278

University of Hawaii at Manoa, 318
Indiana University, 352
University of Kansas, 400
Louisiana State University, 422
University of Maine–Orono, 433
University of Maryland, 445
University of Maryland Baltimore County, 447
Ohio State University, 529
University of Oklahoma, 536
University of Oregon, 541
Oregon State University, 544
SUNY–University at Buffalo, 671
University of Texas at Austin, 694
Texas A&M University, 699
Texas Tech University, 704
University of Washington, 750
University of Wisconsin–Madison, 793

EXPENSIVE—$$$
University of Arizona, 27
UC Berkeley, 95
UC Davis, 98
UC Los Angeles, 103
UC San Diego, 107
UC Santa Barbara, 110
UC Santa Cruz, 112
College of Charleston, 138
Clemson University, 164
University of Colorado Boulder, 171
University of Delaware, 210
George Mason University, 270
Georgia Institute of Technology, 280
James Madison University, 390
University of Kentucky, 402

University of Mary Washington, 442
Michigan State University, 462
University of Minnesota, 472
University of Minnesota, Morris, 474
Ohio University, 532
University of Rhode Island, 589
Rutgers–The State University of New Jersey, 612
St. Mary's College of Maryland, 625
University of South Carolina, 651
University of Tennessee Knoxville, 692
University of Texas at Dallas, 697
Virginia Tech, 741

VERY EXPENSIVE—$$$$
UC Irvine, 100
UC Riverside, 105
Colorado School of Mines, 176
University of Connecticut, 183
University of Illinois at Urbana–Champaign, 345
University of Massachusetts Amherst, 449
Miami University (OH), 457
University of Michigan, 460
University of New Hampshire, 491
The College of New Jersey, 494
New Jersey Institute of Technology, 496
Pennsylvania State University, 551
University of Pittsburgh, 556
University of Vermont, 733
University of Virginia, 737
College of William and Mary, 788

PRIVATE COLLEGES AND UNIVERSITIES

* These colleges are public institutions, but Americans and other non-Europeans should compare them in cost and academic quality to top U.S. privates.

Index by Average Debt

$$$$	More than $33,700
$$$	$28,501–$33,700
$$	$24,000–$28,500
$	Less than $24,000

Debt categories are based on the average amount of principal accumulated by each undergraduate who borrowed during their tenure as a student. Public and private institutions have been rated using the same criteria. Institutions for which data on average borrowing was unavailable have been omitted.

LOW AVERAGE DEBT—$

Amherst College, 22
Antioch College, 25
University of Arizona, 27
Arizona State University, 29
Barnard College, 52
Bates College, 55
Boston College, 69
Bowdoin College, 74
Brigham Young University, 79
UC Berkeley, 95
UC Davis, 98
UC Irvine, 100
UC Los Angeles, 103
UC Riverside, 105
UC San Diego, 107
UC Santa Barbara, 110
UC Santa Cruz, 112
California Institute of Technology, 115
Carleton College, 120
University of Chicago, 140
Claremont McKenna College, 147
Clemson University, 164
The Cooper Union, 188
Dartmouth College, 199
Davidson College, 202
Deep Springs College, 207
DePauw University, 220
Duke University, 230
Emerson College, 241
The Evergreen State College, 248
University of Florida, 254
Florida State University, 261
Georgetown University, 275
University of Georgia, 278
Grinnell College, 293
Hamilton College, 300
Harvard University, 311
Haverford College, 315

The College of Idaho, 343
Kenyon College, 405
Massachusetts Institute of Technology, 451
Middlebury College, 465
Mount Holyoke College, 481
University of Nebraska–Lincoln, 486
New College of Florida, 489
University of New Mexico, 498
University of North Carolina at Asheville, 503
University of North Carolina at Chapel Hill, 506
Northwestern University, 516
Olin College of Engineering, 539
University of Pennsylvania, 548
Pitzer College, 152
Pomona College, 154
Princeton University, 563
Principia College, 568
Reed College, 584
St. John's College, 618
Saint Louis University, 623
St. Mary's College of Maryland, 625
Sarah Lawrence College, 639
Scripps College, 157
Skidmore College, 644
Stanford University, 661
SUNY–University at Albany, 666
Swarthmore College, 687
University of Tennessee Knoxville, 692
University of Texas at Dallas, 697
Texas A&M University, 699
University of Utah, 725
Vanderbilt University, 728
Vassar College, 730
University of Washington, 750
Washington and Lee University, 755

Washington University in St. Louis, 761
Wellesley College, 764
Wesleyan University, 769
Whitman College, 781
Williams College, 791
Xavier University of Louisiana, 805
Yale University, 807

MODERATE AVERAGE DEBT—$$

University of Arkansas, 32
College of the Atlantic, 40
Bard College, 49
Beloit College, 59
Bennington College, 62
Brown University, 82
Bryn Mawr College, 85
Centre College, 131
Chapman University, 136
College of Charleston, 138
University of Cincinnati, 144
Clarkson University, 161
Colgate University, 168
University of Colorado Boulder, 171
Colorado College, 173
Colorado State University, 178
Columbia University, 180
University of Connecticut, 183
Cornell University, 193
Denison University, 212
Dickinson College, 222
Drew University, 225
Earlham College, 234
Emory University, 243
Florida Southern College, 259
Franklin & Marshall College, 266
Hampshire College, 305
Harvey Mudd College, 150
University of Hawaii at Manoa, 318

The Best Buys of 2020

Following is a list of 20 colleges and universities that qualify as Best Buys based on the quality of their academic offerings in relation to the cost of attendance.
(See page xxi for an explanation of how Best Buys were identified.)

Public   Private

Public	Private
Arizona State University	Centre College
University of Florida	Drew University
University of Iowa	Earlham College
New College of Florida	Mount Holyoke College
University of North Carolina at Chapel Hill	Oglethorpe University
Purdue University	Olin College of Engineering
SUNY–Binghamton University	Rice University
Texas A&M University	St. Olaf College
Truman State University	Vanderbilt University
University of Wisconsin–Madison	Warren Wilson College

Introduction

FISKE GUIDE TO COLLEGES—AND HOW TO USE IT

The 2020 edition of the *Fiske Guide to Colleges* is a revised and updated version of a book that has been a bestseller since it first appeared over three decades ago and is universally regarded as the definitive college guide of its type. Features of the new edition include:

- Updated write-ups on more than 300 of the country's best and most interesting colleges and universities

- An index that categorizes the colleges according to how much debt, on average, students accumulate during their tenure at each school

- A list of schools that no longer require the SAT or ACT of all applicants

- A "Sizing-Yourself-Up" questionnaire that will help you figure out what kind of school is best for you

- "A Guide for Preprofessionals," which lists colleges and universities strong in nine preprofessional areas

- A list of schools with strong programs for students with learning disabilities

- Designation of the 20 schools that constitute this year's Best Buys

- Statistical summaries that give you the numbers you need, but spare you those that you do not

- Authoritative ratings of each institution by academics, social life, and quality of life

- The unique "If You Apply To" feature, which summarizes vital information about each college's admission policies—including admissions plans and test requirements

- A section on top Canadian, British, and Irish universities that offer first-rate academics and are easily the equivalent of the flagship public institutions and elite privates in the U.S.—but much less expensive than the latter

Picking the right college—one that will coincide with your particular needs, goals, interests, talents, and personality—is one of the most important decisions any young person will ever make. It is also a major investment. Tuition and fees alone now run at least $10,000 per year at a typical public university and close to $44,000 per year at a typical private college, and the overall tab at the most selective and expensive schools tops $70,000 per year. Obviously, a major investment like that should be approached with as much information as possible.

That's where the *Fiske Guide to Colleges* fits in. It is a tool to help you make the most intelligent educational investment you can.

WHAT IS THE *FISKE GUIDE TO COLLEGES?*

Fiske Guide to Colleges mirrors a process familiar to any college-bound student and his or her family. If you are wondering whether to consider a particular college, it is logical to seek out friends or acquaintances who go there and ask them to tell you about their experiences. We have done exactly that—but on a far broader and more systematic basis than any individual or family could do alone.

In using the *Fiske Guide*, you should keep some special features in mind:

- The guide is **selective**. We have not tried to cover all four-year colleges and universities. Rather, we have taken more than 300 of the best and most interesting institutions in the nation—the ones that students most want to know about—and written descriptive essays of 1,000 to 2,500 words about each of them.

- Since choosing a college is a matter of making a calculated and informed judgment, this guide is also **subjective**. It makes judgments about the strengths and weaknesses of each institution, and it contains a unique set of ratings of each college or university on the basis of academic strength, social life, and overall quality of life. No institution is a good fit for every student. The underlying assumption of the *Fiske Guide* is that each of the colleges chosen for inclusion is the right place for some students but not a good bet for others. Like finding the right spouse, college admissions is a matching process. You know your own interests and needs; the *Fiske Guide* will tell you something about those needs that each college seems to serve best.

- Finally, the *Fiske Guide* is **systematic**. Each write-up is carefully constructed to cover specific topics—from the academic climate and the makeup of the student body to the social scene—in a systematic order. This means that you can easily take a specific topic, such as the level of academic pressure or the role of fraternities and sororities on campus, and trace it through all of the colleges that interest you.

HOW THE COLLEGES WERE SELECTED

How do you single out "the best and most interesting" of the more than 2,200 four-year colleges in the United States? Obviously, many fine institutions are not included. Space limitations simply require that some hard decisions be made.

The selection was done with several broad principles in mind, beginning with academic quality. Depending on how you define the term, there are about 200 "selective" colleges and universities in the nation, and by and large these constitute the best institutions academically. All of these are included in the *Fiske Guide*. In addition, an effort was made to achieve geographic diversity and a balance of public and private schools. Special efforts were made to include a good selection of four types of institutions that seem to be enjoying special popularity at present: engineering and technical schools, those with a religious emphasis, those with an environmental focus, and those located along the Sunbelt, where the cost of education is frequently less than at their Northern counterparts.

Finally, in a few cases, we exercised the journalist's prerogative of writing about schools that are simply interesting. The tiny College of the Atlantic, for example, would hardly qualify on the basis of a superior academic program or national significance, but it offers an unusual and fascinating brand of liberal arts within the context of environmental studies. Likewise, Deep Springs College, the only two-year school in the *Fiske Guide*, is a unique institution of intrinsic interest.

HOW THE *FISKE GUIDE* WAS COMPILED

Each college or university selected for inclusion in the *Fiske Guide to Colleges* was sent a questionnaire to be filled out and returned online. This questionnaire covered topics ranging from their perception of the institution's mission to the demographics of the student body. Administrators were also asked to recruit a cross section of students to complete another electronic questionnaire with questions relating to what it is like to be a student at their particular college or university.

The questions for students, all open-ended and requiring short essays as responses, covered topics ranging from the accessibility of professors and the quality of housing and dining facilities to the type of nightlife and weekend entertainment available in the area. By and large, students responded enthusiastically to the challenge we offered them. The quality of the information in the write-ups is a tribute to their diligence and openness. American college students, we learned, are a candid lot. They are proud of their institutions, but also critical—in the positive sense of the word.

Other sources of information were also employed. Administrators were invited to send us any in-house research or other documents that would contribute to an understanding of the institution, and they were invited to comment on their write-up in the last edition. Also, staff members have visited many of the colleges, and in some cases, additional information was solicited through published materials, such as the Common Data Set, telephone interviews, and other contacts with students and administrators.

The information from these various questionnaires was then incorporated into write-ups by staff members under the editorial direction of Edward B. Fiske, former education editor of the *New York Times*.

THE FORMAT

Each essay covers certain broad subjects in roughly the same order. They are as follows:

Campus setting	**Housing**
Academics	**Food**
Student body	**Social life**
Financial aid	**Extracurricular activities**

Certain topics are covered in all of the essays. The sections on academics, for example, always discuss the departments (or, in the case of large universities, schools) that are particularly strong or weak, while the sections on housing contain information on whether the dorms are co-ed or single sex and how students get the rooms they want. Other topics, however, such as class size, the need for a car, or the number of volumes in the library, are mentioned only if they constitute a particular strength or weakness at that institution.

We paid particular attention to underage drinking on campus and efforts by colleges to deal with growing concerns about sexual assault. Also, we noted efforts that schools' administrations have been making to change or improve campus social and residential life through such measures as creating learning communities, restricting fraternities, and constructing new recreational facilities.

BEST BUYS

In the face of today's skyrocketing tuition rates, students and families in all economic circumstances are looking for ways to get the best value for their education dollar. To help out, the *Fiske Guide* has an "Index by Price" that groups public and private institutions into four price categories, as well as an "Index by Average Debt" that indicates how much debt students who borrow typically incur by the time they graduate.

We also designate 20 colleges and universities—ten publics and ten privates—as this year's Best Buys, institutions where it is possible for students to enjoy a quality academic experience at a relatively low cost. Most of these schools fall into the low/moderate categories for price and average debt, and their academic ratings range from 3 to 5. Many qualify to be Best Buys because of innovative financial aid policies or a commitment to enroll a socioeconomically diverse student body. Look for the Best Buy graphic next to the college name. (A list of all 2020 Best Buys appears on page xviii).

STATISTICS

At the beginning of each write-up are basic statistics about the college or university—the ones that are relevant to applicants. These include the address, type of location (urban, small town, rural, etc.), enrollment, male/female ratio, and the SAT or ACT score ranges of the middle 50 percent of the students. We report the relative cost of the school, the percentage of students receiving financial aid of any kind (including loans), the percentage of students who procure loans, and the average debt incurred by students. The percentage of incoming freshmen receiving Pell Grants is listed as an indication of the extent of socioeconomic diversity among the student body. Other statistics show the number of students who apply and the percentage of those who are accepted, the percentage of accepted students who enroll, the percentage of freshmen who graduate within six years, and the percentage of freshmen who return for their sophomore year. For convenience, we include the telephone number of the admissions office, the school's website, and email and mailing addresses.

Unlike some guides, we have intentionally not published figures on the student/faculty ratio because colleges use different—and often self-serving—methods to calculate the ratio, thus making this particular statistic virtually meaningless.

Within the statistics, you will sometimes encounter the letters "N/A." In most cases, this means that the statistic was not available. In other cases, however, such as schools that do not require standardized tests, it means "not applicable." The write-up should make it clear which meaning is the relevant one.

SAT AND ACT SCORES

A special word needs to be said about standardized test scores. Some publications follow the practice of giving the median or average score registered by entering freshmen. Such figures, however, are easily misinterpreted as thresholds rather than averages. Many applicants forget that if a school reports average SAT–Critical Reading scores of 500, this means that, by definition, about half of the students scored below this number and half scored above. An applicant with a 480 would still have lots of company.

To avoid such confusion, we report the range of scores of the middle half of freshmen—or, to put it another way, the scores achieved by those in the 25th and 75th percentiles. For example, that college where the SAT–Critical Reading average was 500 might have a range of 440 to 560. So if you scored within this range, you would have joined the middle 50 percent of last year's freshmen. If your score was above 560, you would have been in the top quarter and could probably look forward to a relatively easy time; if it was below 440, you would have been struggling along with the bottom quarter of students.

Keep in mind that score ranges (and averages, for that matter) are misleading at the growing number of colleges that no longer require test scores from all applicants (see the section on SAT and ACT Optional Schools on pages xxxviii–xxxix). The ranges given for these colleges typically represent the range of scores of students who choose to submit their test scores, despite not being required to do so.

Unfortunately, another problem that arises with SAT and ACT scores is that, in their zeal to make themselves look good in a competitive market, some colleges and universities have been known to be less than candid in the numbers they release. They inflate their scores by not counting certain categories of students at the low end of the scale, such as athletes, certain types of transfer students, or students admitted under affirmative action programs. Some colleges have gone to such extremes as reporting the relatively high math scores of foreign students, but not their relatively low verbal scores. Aside from the sheer dishonesty of such practices, they can also be misleading. A student whose own scores are below the 25th percentile of a particular institution needs to know whether his profile matches that of the lower quarter of the student body as a whole, or whether there is an unreported pool of students with lower scores.

Even when indicating a range rather than a single score, standardized tests are an imprecise measure of academic ability. Comparisons of scores that differ by less than 50 or 60 points on a scale of 200 to 800 are virtually meaningless. According to the laws of statistics, there is one chance in three that the 550 that arrived in the little envelope from ETS should really be at least 580 or no more than 520. On the other hand, median scores offer some indication of your chances to get into a particular institution and the intellectual level of the company you will be keeping—or, if you prefer, competing against. Remember, too, that the most competitive schools have the largest and most sophisticated admissions staffs and are well aware of the limitations of standardized tests. A strong high school average or achievement in a field such as music will usually counteract the negative effects of modest SAT or ACT scores. The imprecise, even misleading, nature of standardized tests is one reason that hundreds of colleges and universities have moved away from requiring or even considering them.

Note that the College Board launched a revised SAT exam in 2016. Thus, the SAT scores published in the 2020 edition of the *Fiske Guide* represent scores that applicants achieved on the "new" version of the exam.

COLLEGE COSTS

Tuition and fees are constantly increasing at American colleges, but for the most part, the cost of various institutions in relation to one another does not change. Rather than put in specific cost figures that would immediately become out of date, we have classified colleges into four groups ranging from inexpensive ($) to very expensive ($$$$) based on estimated costs of tuition and fees for the 2019–2020 academic year. The results for each college can be found in the "Index by Price" on pages xii–xiv. Separate scales were used for public and private institutions, and the ratings for the public institutions are based on the cost for residents of the state; out-of-staters should expect to pay more. If a public institution has a particularly low or high surcharge for out-of-staters, this is noted in the essay. The categories are defined as follows:

	PUBLIC	PRIVATE
$$$$	More than $15,000	More than $54,000
$$$	$12,001–$15,000	$50,001–$54,000
$$	$10,000–$12,000	$44,000–$50,000
$	Less than $10,000	Less than $44,000

In assessing the relative costs of various colleges and universities, it is important to keep in mind that the posted charges for tuition and fees are, in effect, "sticker prices." Every American who has ever walked into an automobile showroom knows that the price on the car window is not necessarily the amount he or she will end up paying, but rather the starting point for negotiations over matters such as trade-ins, financing terms, and so forth. The same rule applies to posted tuition and fee levels, especially at private colleges. Your cost at a particular college depends on a variety of factors, including your family's financial situation and how much the school wants you to enroll. Some wealthy students will pay the full sticker price, but many others—often a substantial majority of others—will receive "discounts" in the form of merit- or need-based scholarships, loans, and other concessions. Likewise, students from disadvantaged backgrounds who manage to gain admission to expensive Ivy League or other elite universities can expect virtual free rides. Bottom line: don't write off a school that you really like simply because the published sticker price looks too expensive. You might end up paying less at an expensive school seeking to lure you with a generous financial aid package than you would at a school with lower tuition and fees but a smaller financial aid budget.

FINANCIAL AID

Since the first edition of the *Fiske Guide to Colleges* appeared, the problems of financing college have become increasingly complex, mainly because of the seemingly relentless rise in the cost of education and some significant trends in financial aid. There has been a gradual shift from need-based to merit-based scholarships that favor middle class students, as well as a tendency for schools to build higher loans and smaller outright grants into their financial aid packages. On the other hand, partly in response to public pressure to increase socioeconomic diversity among their student bodies, a number of both public and private universities have begun to substitute grants for loans and even to eliminate tuition for low- and some middle-income students. Some colleges advertise that they are "need-blind" in their admissions, meaning that they accept or reject applicants without reference to their financial situation, and also guarantee to meet the "demonstrated need" of all students whom they accept. "Demonstrated need" is itself a slippery term. In theory, the figure is determined when students and families fill out a needs-analysis form (e.g., the FAFSA and/or CSS Profile), which leads to an estimate of how much the family can afford to pay, otherwise known as the "expected family contribution" (EFC). Demonstrated need is then calculated by subtracting that figure from the cost at a particular institution.

In practice, however, what seems rather straightforward can be misleading. For one thing, colleges may make their own independent calculations about what families can afford to pay. Five different colleges may each give the same student a different figure for what their EFC/demonstrated need is, and the differences can be significant. Some colleges say that they are need-blind in their admissions decisions but do not guarantee to provide the full financial aid required of all those who are accepted. Still others agree to meet the demonstrated need of all students, but they package their offers so that students they really want receive a higher percentage of their aid in the form of outright grants and a lower proportion in repayable loans. For example, if a school with a $50,000 annual price tag offers a financial aid package that includes $25,000 of grants and scholarships and $25,000 of "self-help" (institutional loans, Federal loans, a parent loan, or work study), that school can claim that it has met 100 percent of the student's demonstrated need, but at the end of four years, the student will still graduate with $100,000 of debt.

In order to test the sincerity of a school's promise to "meet 100 percent of demonstrated need," students might ask whether it has backed up that claim with other initiatives, such as replacing loans with grants in all financial aid packages or reducing or capping the amount of loans that families are expected to assume. Our write-ups often call attention to such initiatives. To get an idea whether the average student at a college graduates with a high amount of debt, check out our statistics on loans and debt (see below).

Students and parents should not assume that their family's six-figure annual income automatically disqualifies them from some kind of subsidized financial aid. In cases of doubt, they should fill out a needs-analysis form to determine their eligibility. Whether they qualify or not, they may be eligible for a variety of awards made without regard to financial need.

Inasmuch as need-based awards are universal at the colleges in this guide, the awards generally singled out for special mention in the write-ups in the *Fiske Guide to Colleges* are the merit scholarships. We have not mentioned awards of a purely local nature—restricted to residents of a particular county, for example—but college applicants should search out these awards through their guidance offices and the bulletins of the colleges that are of interest to them. Similarly, we have not duplicated the information on federally guaranteed loan programs that is readily available through both high school and college counseling offices, but we do cite novel and often less expensive variants of the federal loan programs that are offered by individual colleges.

For more information on the ever-changing financial aid scene, we suggest that you consult the companion book to this guide, the *Fiske Guide to Getting into the Right College*.

STUDENT LOANS AND AVERAGE DEBT RATING

In today's academic climate, it is common for students and/or their families to borrow funds to assist with paying tuition and other college expenses. Therefore, a potentially useful piece of information is the proportion of students at each school who find it necessary to procure loans to finance their education. The student loan percentage considers any loan program used by students at any time during their tenure at an institution. Included are institutional, state, Federal Perkins, Federal Direct Subsidized and Unsubsidized student loans, Federal Family Education Loans, and private loans certified by an institution, excluding parent loans. To ensure the most accurate information, schools submitted this data for students comprising their last graduating class. When available, this data was confirmed using the Common Data Set.

For a variety of reasons, the average debt carried by graduating seniors varies greatly from college to college as well as from student to student. Nevertheless, when considering a particular school, many prospective students will find it useful to know how much debt is typically incurred by students at that school. Thus the 2020 *Fiske Guide* lists the Average Debt Rating (ADR) for each school as reported in each institution's Common Data Set. The ADR is based on the average amount of principal accumulated by each undergraduate who borrowed during their tenure as a student. Using $28,500 as the median, we have organized the schools into four categories from low average debt ($) to very high average debt ($$$$). Both public and private institutions were rated using the same criteria.

DEBT RATING	AVERAGE CUMULATIVE PRINCIPAL PER UNDERGRADUATE BORROWER
$$$$	More than $33,700
$$$	$28,501–$33,700
$$	$24,000–$28,500
$	Less than $24,000

As previously noted at the end of the discussion of college costs on page xxiii, it is important when thinking about the cost of college to keep in mind your particular financial situation. Even if a school has high average debt levels, students who qualify for substantial financial aid packages may end up with little or no debt.

RATINGS

Much of the fierce controversy that greeted the first edition of the *Fiske Guide to Colleges* more than three decades ago revolved around its unique system of rating colleges in three areas: academics, social life, and quality of life. In each case, the ratings are done on a system of one to five, with three considered normal for colleges included in the *Fiske Guide*. If a college receives a rating higher or lower than three in any category, the reasons should be apparent from the narrative description of that college.

Students and parents should keep in mind that these ratings are obviously general in nature and inherently subjective. No complex institution can be described in terms of a single number or other symbol, and different people will have different views of how various institutions should be rated in the three categories. They should not be viewed as either precise or infallible judgments about any given college. On the other hand, the ratings are a helpful tool in using this book. The core of the *Fiske Guide* is the essays on each of the colleges, and the ratings represent a summary—an index, if you will—of these write-ups. Our hope is that each student, having decided on the kind of configuration that suits his or her needs, will then thumb through the book looking for other institutions with a similar set of ratings. The three categories, defined as follows, are academics, social life, and quality of life.

Academics ✍

This is a judgment about the overall academic climate of the institution, including its reputation in the academic world, the quality of the faculty, the level of teaching and research, the academic ability of students, the quality of libraries and other facilities, and the level of academic seriousness among students and faculty members.

Although the same basic criteria have been applied to all institutions, it should be evident that an outstanding small liberal arts college will by definition differ significantly from an outstanding major public university. No one would expect the former to have massive library facilities, but one would look for a high-quality faculty that combines research with a good deal of attention to the individual needs of students. Likewise, public universities, because of their implicit commitment to serving a broad cross section of society, might have a broader range of curriculum offerings but somewhat lower average SAT scores than a large private counterpart. Readers may find the ratings most useful when comparing colleges and universities of the same type.

In general, an academics rating of three pens suggests that the institution is a solid one that easily meets the criteria for inclusion in a guide devoted to the top 10 percent of colleges and universities in the nation.

An academics rating of four pens suggests that the institution is above average even by these standards and that it has some particularly distinguishing academic feature, such as especially rich course offerings or an especially serious academic atmosphere.

A rating of five pens for academics indicates that the college or university is among the handful of top institutions of its type in the nation on a broad variety of criteria. Those in the private sector will normally attract students with combined SAT scores of at least 1300 on Critical Reading and Math, and those in the public sector are invariably magnets for the top students in their states. All can be assumed to have outstanding faculties and other academic resources.

In response to the suggestion that the range of colleges within a single category has been too broad, we have introduced some half-steps into the ratings.

Social Life ☎

This is primarily a judgment about the amount of social life that is readily available. A rating of three telephones suggests a typical college social life, while four telephones means that students devote an above-average amount of time to socializing. It can be assumed that a college with a rating of five is something of a party school, which may or may not detract from the academic quality. Colleges with a rating below three have some impediment to a strong social life, such as geographic isolation, a high percentage of commuting students, or a disproportionate number of nerds who never leave the library. Once again, the reason should be evident from the write-up.

Quality of Life ★

This category grew out of the fact that schools with good academic credentials and plenty of social life may not, for one reason or another, be particularly wholesome places to spend four years. The term "quality of life" is one that has gained currency in social science circles, and, in most cases, the rating for a particular college will be similar to the academic and/or social ratings. The reader, though, should be alert to exceptions to this pattern. A liberal arts college, for example, might attract bright students who study hard during the week and party hard on weekends, and thus earn high ratings for academics and social life. If the academic pressure is cutthroat rather than constructive, though, and the social system is manipulative of women, this college might get an apparently anomalous two stars for quality of life. By contrast, a small college with modest academic programs and relatively few organized social opportunities might have developed a strong sense of supportive community, have a beautiful campus, and be located near a wonderful city—and thus be rated four stars for quality of life. As in the other categories, the reason can be found in the essay to which the ratings point.

OVERLAPS

Most colleges and universities operate within fairly defined "niche markets." That is, they compete for students against other institutions with whom they share important characteristics, such as academic quality, size, geographic location, and the overall tone and style of campus life. Not surprisingly, students who apply to College X also tend to apply to the other institutions—often referred to as "peer institutions"—in its particular niche. For example, "alternative" colleges such as Bard, Bennington, Hampshire, Marlboro, Oberlin, Reed, and Sarah Lawrence share many common applications, as do those with an evangelical flavor, such as Calvin, Gordon, and Wheaton (IL).

As a service to readers, we ask each school to give us the names of the colleges or universities that they consider to be their closest peer institutions and those with which they share the most common applications, and these are listed in the "Overlaps" section at the end of each write-up. We encourage students who know they are interested in a particular school to check out its peer institutions—and perhaps then check out the "overlaps of the overlaps." This method of systematic browsing should yield a list of 15 or 20 schools that, based on the behavior of thousands of past applicants, would constitute a good starting point for the college search.

IF YOU APPLY TO

Another helpful feature is the "If You Apply To" section at the end of each write-up. This is designed for students who become seriously interested in a particular college and want to know more specifics about what it takes to get in.

This section begins by listing the admissions plans that the school offers: early decision, early action, and/ or regular decision. If the college operates on a rolling-admissions basis—making decisions as the applications are received—this is also indicated.

Next, this section describes what standardized tests—SAT, ACT, or Subject—are required, and whether applicants are asked to submit scores for the optional essay portion of the SAT or for the ACT writing test.

Additionally, we indicate whether the school accepts the Common Application and include information on any special instructions or unique components of the application that may be pertinent for students to know about.

For additional details about the application process, students should consult the websites of individual schools, which will always contain the most complete and up-to-date information.

MOVING FORWARD

Students will find the *Fiske Guide* useful at various points in the college selection process—from deciding whether to visit a particular campus to selecting among institutions that have accepted them. To make it easy to find a particular college, the write-ups are arranged in alphabetical order in the indexes. An "Index by State and Country," the "Index by Price," and the "Index by Average Debt" can be found on pages ix, xii, and xv, respectively.

While most people are not likely to start reading at Adelphi and keep going until they reach Yale (though some tell us they do), we encourage you to browse. This country has an enormously rich and varied network of colleges and universities. There are dozens of institutions out there that can meet the needs of any particular student. Too many students approach the college selection process wearing blinders, limiting their sights to local institutions, the pet schools of their parents or guidance counselors, or ones they know only by possibly outdated reputations.

But applicants need not be bound by such limitations. Once you have decided on the type of school you think you want—a small liberal arts college, an engineering school, or whatever—we hope you will thumb through the book looking for similar institutions that might not have occurred to you. As already noted, one way to do this is to look at the overlaps of schools you like and then check out those schools' overlaps. Many students have found this worthwhile, and quite frankly, we view the widening of students' horizons about American higher education as one of the most important purposes of this book. Perhaps the most gratifying remark we hear comes when a student tells us, as many have, that she is attending a school that she first heard about while browsing through the *Fiske Guide to Colleges*.

Picking a college is a tricky business. But given the current buyer's market, there is no reason why you should not be able to find the right one *for you*. That's what the *Fiske Guide to Colleges* is designed to help you do. Happy college hunting.

Sizing Yourself Up

The college search is a game of matchmaking. You have interests and needs; the colleges have programs to meet those needs. If all goes according to plan, you'll find the right one and live happily ever after——or at least for four years. It ought to be simple, but today's admissions process resembles a high-stakes obstacle course.

Many colleges are more interested in making a sale than they are in making a match. Under intense competitive pressure, many won't hesitate to sell you a bill of goods if they can get their hands on your tuition dollars. Guidance counselors generally mean well, but they are often under duress from principals and trustees to steer students toward prestigious schools regardless of whether the fit is right. Your friends won't be shy with advice on where to go, but their knowledge is generally limited to a small group of hot colleges that everyone is talking about. National publications rake in millions by playing on the public's fascination with rankings, but a close look at their criteria reveals distinctions without a difference.

Before you find yourself spinning headlong on this merry-go-round, take a step back. This is your life and your college career. What are you looking for in a college? Think hard and don't answer right away. Before you throw yourself and your life history on the mercy of college admissions officers, you need to take some time to objectively and honestly evaluate your needs, likes and dislikes, strengths and weaknesses. What do you have to offer a college? What can a college do for you? Unlike the high school selection process, which is usually predetermined by your parents' property lines, income level, or religious affiliation, picking a college isn't a procedure you can brush off on dear ol' Mom and Dad. You have to take some initiative. You're the best judge of how well each school fits your personal needs and academic goals.

We encourage you to view the college selection process as the first semester in your higher education. Life's transitions often call for extra energy and focus. The college search is no exception. For the first time, you'll be contemplating a life away from home that can unfold in any direction you choose. Visions of majors and careers will dance in your head as you sample various institutions of higher learning, each with hundreds of millions of dollars in academic resources; it is hard to imagine a better hands-on seminar in research and matchmaking than the college search. The main impact, however, will be measured by what you learn about yourself. Piqued by new worlds of learning and tested by the competition of the admissions process, you'll be pushed as never before to show your accomplishments, clarify your interests, and chart a course for the future. More than one parent has watched in amazement as an erstwhile teenager suddenly emerged as an adult during the course of a college tour. Be ready when your time comes.

DEVELOP YOUR CRITERIA

One strategy is to begin the search with a personal inventory of your own strengths and weaknesses and your "wish list" for a college. This method tends to work well for compulsive list-makers and other highly organized people. What sorts of things are you especially good at? Do you have a list of skills or interests that you would like to explore further? What sort of personality are you looking for in a college? Mainstream? Conservative? Offbeat? What about extracurriculars? If you are really into riding horses, you might include a strong equestrian program in your criteria. The main problem won't be thinking of qualities to look for—you could probably name dozens—but rather figuring out what criteria should play a defining role in your search. Serious students should think carefully about the intellectual climate they are seeking. At some schools, students routinely stay up until 3:00 a.m. talking about topics like the value of deconstructing literary texts or the pros and cons of free trade. These same students would be viewed as geeks or weirdos on less cosmopolitan campuses. Athletes should take a hard look at whether they really want to play college ball and, if so, whether they want to go for an athletic scholarship or play at the less-pressured Division III level. Either way, intercollegiate sports require a huge time commitment.

Young women have an opportunity all to themselves—the chance to study at a women's college. The *Fiske Guide* profiles 11 such campuses, a vastly underappreciated resource on today's higher education scene. With small classes and strong encouragement from faculty, students at women's colleges move on to graduate study in significantly higher numbers than their counterparts at co-ed schools, especially in the natural sciences. Males seeking an all-male experience will find four options in the *Fiske Guide*.

Students with a firm career goal will want to look for a course of study that matches their needs. If you want to major in aerospace engineering, your search will be limited to schools that have the program. Outside of specialized areas like this, many applicants overestimate the importance of their anticipated major in choosing a college. If you're interested in a liberal arts field, your expected major should probably have little to do with your college selection. A big purpose of college is to develop interests and set goals. Most students change their intentions regarding a major at least two or three times before graduation, and once out in the working world, they often end up in jobs bearing no relation to their academic specialty. Even those with a firm career goal may not need as much specialization as they think at the undergraduate level. If you want to be a lawyer, don't worry yourself looking for something labeled "prelaw." Follow your interests, get the best liberal arts education available, and then apply to law school.

Naturally, it is never a bad idea to check out the department(s) of any likely major, and occasionally your choice of major will suggest a direction for your search. If you're really into national politics, it may make sense to look at some schools in or near Washington, D.C. If you think you're interested in a relatively specialized field, say, oceanography, then be sure to look for some colleges that are a good match for you and also have programs in oceanography. But for the most part, rumors about top-ranked departments in this or that should be no more than a tie-breaker between schools you like for more important reasons. There are good professors (and bad ones) in any department. You'll have plenty of time to figure out who is who once you've enrolled. Being undecided about your career path as a senior in high school is often a sign of intelligence. Don't feel bad if you have absolutely no idea what you're going to do when you "grow up." One of the reasons you'll be paying megabucks to the college of your choice is the prospect that it will open some new doors for you and expand your horizons. Instead of worrying about particular departments, try to keep the focus on big-picture items, such as: What's the academic climate? How big are the freshman classes? Do I like it here? and Are these my kind of people?

KEEP AN OPEN MIND

The biggest mistake of beginning applicants is hyperchoosiness. At the extreme is the "perfect-school syndrome," which comes in two basic forms.

In one category are the applicants who refuse to consider any school that doesn't have every little thing they want in a college. If you're one who begins the process with a detailed picture of Perfect U. in mind, you may want to remember the oft-quoted advice, "Two out of three ain't bad." If a college seems to have most of the qualities you seek, give it a chance. You may come to realize that some things you thought were absolutely essential are really not that crucial after all.

The other strain of perfect-school syndrome is the applicant who gets stuck on a "dream" school at the beginning and then won't look anywhere else. With those 2,200 four-year colleges out there (not counting those in Canada and Great Britain), it is just a bit silly to insist that only one will meet your needs. Having a first choice is OK, but the whole purpose of the search is to consider new options and uncover new possibilities. A student who has only one dream school—especially if it is a highly selective one—could be headed for disappointment.

As you begin the college search, don't expect any quick revelations. The answers will unfold in due time. Our advice? Be patient. Set priorities. Keep an open mind. Reexamine priorities. Again, be patient.

To get the ball rolling, move on to the Sizing-Yourself-Up Survey.

FISKE'S SIZING-YOURSELF-UP SURVEY

With apologies to Socrates, knowing thyself is easier said than done. Most high school students can analyze a differential equation or a Shakespearean play with the greatest of ease, but when it comes to cataloging their own strengths, weaknesses, likes, and dislikes, many draw a blank. But self-knowledge is crucial to the matching process at the heart of a successful college search. The 30-item survey on page xxix offers a simple way to get a handle on some crucial issues in college selection—and what sort of college may fit your preferences.

In the space beside each statement, rate your feelings on a scale of 1 to 10, with 10 = Strongly Agree, 1 = Strongly Disagree, and 5 = Not Sure/Don't Have Strong Feelings. (For instance, a rating of 7 would mean that you agree with the statement, but that the issue is a lower priority than those you rated 8, 9, or 10.) After you're done, read on to "Grading Yourself" to find out what it all means.

FISKE'S SIZING-YOURSELF-UP SURVEY

Size

___9___ 1. I enjoy participating in many activities.

___6___ 2. I would like to have a prominent place in my community.

___7___ 3. Individual attention from teachers is important to me.

___10___ 4. I learn best when I can speak out in class and ask questions.

___8___ 5. I am undecided about what I will study.

___7___ 6. I want to earn a Ph.D. in my chosen field of study.

} 37

___5___ 7. I learn best by listening and writing down what I hear.

___6___ 8. I would like to be in a place where I can be anonymous if I choose.

___5___ 9. I prefer devoting my time to one or two activities rather than many.

___4___ 10. I want to attend a college that most people have heard of.

___5___ 11. I am interested in a career-oriented major.

___10___ 12. I like to be on my own.

} 35

Location

___5___ 13. I prefer a college in a warm or hot climate.

___5___ 14. I prefer a college in a cool or cold climate.

___5___ 15. I want to be near the mountains.

___5___ 16. I want to be near a lake or ocean.

___5___ 17. I prefer to attend a college in a particular state or region.

___1___ 18. I prefer to attend a college near my family.

___5___ 19. I want city life within walking distance of my campus.

___7___ 20. I want city life within driving distance of my campus.

___7___ 21. I want my campus to be surrounded by natural beauty.

Academics and Extracurriculars

___10___ 22. I like to be surrounded by people who are freethinkers and nonconformists.

___2___ 23. I like the idea of joining a fraternity or sorority.

___8___ 24. I like rubbing shoulders with people who are bright and talented.

___6___ 25. I like being one of the smartest people in my class.

___5___ 26. I want to go to a prestigious college.

___10___ 27. I want to go to a college where I can get an excellent education.

___5___ 28. I want to try for an academic scholarship.

___10___ 29. I want a diverse college.

___10___ 30. I want a college where the students are serious about ideas.

Grading Yourself

Picking a college is not an exact science. People who are total opposites can be equally happy at the same college. Nevertheless, particular types tend to do better at some colleges than others. Each item in the survey is designed to test your feelings on an important issue related to college selection. "Sizing Up the Survey" (below) offers commentary on each item.

Taken together, your responses may help you construct a tentative blueprint for your college search. Statements 1–12 deal with the issue of size. Would you be happier at a large university or a small college? Here's the trick: Add the sum of your responses to questions 1–6. Then make a second tally of your responses to 7–12. If the sum of 1–6 is larger, you may want to consider a small college. If 7–12 is greater, then perhaps a big school would be more to your liking. If the totals are roughly equal, you should probably consider colleges of various sizes.

Statements 13–21 deal with location. The key in this section is the intensity of your feeling. If you replied to number 13 with a 10, does that mean you are going to look only at schools in warm climates? Think hard. If you consider only schools within a certain region or state, you'll be eliminating hundreds of possibilities. By examining your most intense responses—the 1s, 2s, 9s, and 10s—you'll be able to create a geographic profile of likely options.

Statements 22–30 deal with big-picture issues related to the character and personality of the college that may be in your future. As before, pay attention to your most intense responses. Read on for a look at the significance of each question.

SIZING UP THE SURVEY

1. **I enjoy participating in many activities.** Students at small colleges tend to have more opportunities to be involved in many activities. Fewer students means less competition for spots.

2. **I would like to have a prominent place in my community.** Student council presidents and other would-be leaders take note: it is easier to be a big fish if you're swimming in a small pond.

3. **Individual attention from teachers is important to me.** Small colleges generally offer more one-on-one with faculty in both the classroom and the laboratory.

4. **I learn best when I can speak out in class and ask questions.** Students who learn from interaction and participation would be well-advised to consider a small college.

5. **I am undecided about what I will study.** Small colleges generally offer more guidance and support to students who are undecided. The exception: students who are considering a preprofessional or highly specialized major.

6. **I want to earn a Ph.D. in my chosen field of study.** A higher percentage of students at selective small colleges earn a Ph.D. than those who attend large institutions of similar quality.

7. **I learn best by listening and writing down what I hear.** Students who prefer lecture courses will find more of them at large institutions.

8. **I would like to be in a place where I can be anonymous if I choose.** At a large university, the supply of new faces is never-ending. Students who have the initiative can always reinvent themselves.

9. **I prefer devoting my time to one or two activities rather than many.** Students who are passionate about one activity—say, writing for the college newspaper—will often find higher quality at a bigger school.

10. **I want to attend a college that most people have heard of.** Big schools have more name recognition because they're bigger and have Division I athletic programs. Even the finest small colleges are relatively anonymous among the general public.

11. **I am interested in a career-oriented major.** More large institutions offer business, engineering, nursing, etc., though some excellent small institutions do so as well (depending on the field).

12. **I like to be on my own.** A higher percentage of students live off campus at large schools, which are more likely to be in urban areas than their smaller counterparts.

13. **I prefer a college in a warm or hot climate.** Keep in mind that the Southeast and the Southwest have far different personalities (not to mention humidity levels).

14. **I prefer a college in a cool or cold climate.** Consider the Midwest, where there are many fine schools that are notably less selective than those in the Northeast.

15. **I want to be near the mountains.** You're probably thinking Colorado or Vermont, but don't zero in too quickly. States from Maine to Georgia and Arkansas to Arizona have easy access to mountains.

16. **I want to be near a lake or ocean.** Oceans are only on the coasts, but keep in mind the Great Lakes, the Finger Lakes, etc. Think about whether you want to be on the water or, say, within a two-hour drive.

17. **I prefer to attend a college in a particular state or region.** Geographical blinders limit options. Even if you think you want a certain area of the country, consider at least one college located elsewhere just to be sure.

18. **I prefer to attend a college near my family.** Unless you're planning to live with Mom and Dad, it may not matter whether your college is a two-hour drive or a two-hour plane ride.

19. **I want city life within walking distance of my campus.** Check out the neighborhood(s) surrounding your campus. Urban campuses—even in the same city—can be wildly different.

20. **I want city life within driving distance of my campus.** Unless you're a hard-core urban dweller, a suburban perch near a city may beat living in the thick of one. Does public transportation or a campus shuttle help students get around?

21. **I want my campus to be surrounded by natural beauty.** A college viewbook will take you only so far. To really know if you'll fall in love with the campus, visiting is a must.

22. **I like to be surrounded by people who are freethinkers and nonconformists.** Plenty of schools cater specifically to students who buck the mainstream. Talk to your counselor or browse the *Fiske Guide to Colleges* to find some.

23. **I like the idea of joining a fraternity or sorority.** Greek life is strongest at mainstream and conservative-leaning schools. Find out if there is a split between Greeks and non-Greeks.

24. **I like rubbing shoulders with people who are bright and talented.** This is perhaps the best reason to aim for a highly selective institution, especially if you're the type who rises to the level of the competition.

25. **I like being one of the smartest people in my class.** If so, maybe you should skip the highly selective rat race. Star students get the best a college has to offer.

26. **I want to go to a prestigious college.** There is nothing wrong with wanting prestige. Think honestly about how badly you want a big-name school and act accordingly.

27. **I want to go to a college where I can get an excellent education.** Throw out the *U.S. News* rankings and think about which colleges will best meet your needs as a student.

28. **I want to try for an academic scholarship.** Students in this category should consider less-selective alternatives. Scholarships are more likely if you rank high in the applicant pool.

29. **I want a diverse college.** All colleges pay lip service to diversity. To get the truth, see the campus for yourself and take a hard look at the student-body statistics in the *Fiske Guide*'s write-ups.

30. **I want a college where students are serious about ideas.** Don't assume that a college necessarily attracts true intellectuals merely because it is highly selective. Some top schools are known for their intellectual climate—and others for their lack of it.

A Guide for Preprofessionals

The lists that follow include colleges and universities with unusual strength in each of nine preprofessional areas: architecture, art/design, business, communications/journalism, engineering, film/television, dance, drama, and music. We also offer lists covering two of today's hottest interdisciplinary majors: environmental studies and international studies. In compiling the lists, we drew on data from the thousands of surveys used to compile the *Fiske Guide*. We examined the strongest majors at each college as reported in student and administrative questionnaires, and then weighed these against the selectivity and overall academic quality of each institution. After compiling tentative lists in each subject, we queried our counselors advisory group, listed on page 816, for additional suggestions and feedback. To make the lists as useful as possible, we have included some schools that do not receive full-length write-ups in the *Fiske Guide*. Moreover, while the lists are suggestive, they are by no means all-inclusive, and there are other institutions in the *Fiske Guide* that offer fine programs in these areas. Nevertheless, we hope the lists will be a starting place for students interested in these fields.

If you are planning a career in one of the subjects below, your college search may focus largely on finding the best programs for you in that particular area. But we also recommend that you shop for a school that will give you an adequate dose of liberal arts. For that matter, you might consider a double major (or minor) in a liberal arts field to complement your area of technical expertise. If you allow yourself to get too specialized too soon, you may end up as tomorrow's equivalent of the typewriter repairman. In a rapidly changing job market, nothing is so practical as the ability to read, write, and think.

ARCHITECTURE
Private Universities Strong in Architecture

Carnegie Mellon University
The Catholic University of America
Columbia University
The Cooper Union
Cornell University
Drexel University
Hobart and William Smith Colleges
Howard University
Lehigh University
Massachusetts Institute of Technology
University of Miami (FL)
Northeastern University
University of Notre Dame
Princeton University
Rensselaer Polytechnic Institute
Rice University
University of Southern California
Syracuse University
Temple University
Tuskegee University
Tulane University
Washington University in St. Louis

Public Universities Strong in Architecture

University of Arizona
UC Berkeley
California Polytechnic State University–San Luis Obispo
University of Cincinnati
Clemson University
University of Florida
Georgia Institute of Technology
University of Illinois at Urbana–Champaign
University of Kansas
Kansas State University
University of Maryland
Miami University (OH)
University of Michigan
University of Nebraska–Lincoln
New Jersey Institute of Technology
University of Oregon
Pennsylvania State University
SUNY–University at Buffalo
University of Texas at Austin
Texas A&M University
Virginia Tech
University of Washington

A Few Arts-Oriented Architecture Programs

Barnard College
Bennington College
Pratt Institute
Rhode Island School of Design
Savannah School of Art and Design
Wellesley College
Yale University

ART/DESIGN
Top Schools of Art and Design

Art Center College of Design
School of the Art Institute of Chicago
California College of the Arts
California Institute of the Arts
The Cooper Union
Kansas City Art Institute
Maryland Institute College of Art
Massachusetts College of Art and Design
Moore College of Art and Design
School of the Museum of Fine Arts (MA)
North Carolina School of the Arts
Otis College of Art and Design
Parsons School of Design
Pratt Institute

Rhode Island School of Design
Ringling College of Art and Design
San Francisco Art Institute
Savannah College of Art and Design

Major Universities Strong in Art or Design

American University
University of the Arts (PA)
Boston College
Boston University
Carnegie Mellon University
University of Cincinnati
Cornell University
Drexel University
Harvard University
University of Michigan
New York University
University of Pennsylvania
Syracuse University
University of Washington
Washington University in St. Louis
Yale University

Small Colleges and Universities Strong in Art or Design

Alfred University
Bard College
Brown University
Centre College
Champlain College
Cornell College
Dartmouth College
Furman University
Hollins University
Kenyon College
Lake Forest College
Lewis & Clark College
Manhattanville College
Mills College
Randolph College
Sarah Lawrence College
Scripps College
Skidmore College
Smith College
Southwestern University
SUNY–Purchase College
Vassar College
Wheaton College (MA)
Willamette University
Williams College

BUSINESS
Major Private Universities Strong in Business

American University
Baylor University
Boston College
Boston University
Carnegie Mellon University
Case Western Reserve
University of Dayton
Emory University
Fordham University
Georgetown University
Howard University
Lehigh University
Massachusetts Institute of Technology
New York University
University of Notre Dame
University of Pennsylvania
Pepperdine University
Rensselaer Polytechnic Institute
University of San Francisco
Santa Clara University
University of Southern California
Southern Methodist University
Syracuse University
Texas Christian University
Tulane University
Villanova University
Wake Forest University
Washington University in St. Louis

Public Universities Strong in Business

University of Arizona
UC Berkeley
University of Cincinnati
University of Connecticut
University of Florida
University of Georgia
University of Illinois at Urbana–
    Champaign
Indiana University
James Madison University
University of Kansas
University of Maryland
University of Massachusetts Amherst
Miami University (OH)
University of Michigan
University of Minnesota
University of Missouri

University of North Carolina at
    Chapel Hill
Ohio State University
Ohio University
University of Oregon
Pennsylvania State University
University of Pittsburgh
Rutgers–The State University of
    New Jersey
University of South Carolina
SUNY–University at Albany
SUNY–Binghamton University
SUNY–University at Buffalo
SUNY–College at Geneseo
University of Tennessee Knoxville
University of Texas at Austin
Texas A&M University
University of Vermont
University of Virginia
University of Washington
College of William and Mary
University of Wisconsin–Madison

Small Colleges and Universities Strong in Business

Agnes Scott College
Babson College
Bentley University
Bucknell University
Butler University
Calvin College
Claremont McKenna College
Clarkson University
Eckerd College
Fairfield University
Franklin & Marshall College
Furman University
Gettysburg College
Guilford College
Hendrix College
Ithaca College
Lafayette College
Lake Forest College
Lewis & Clark College
Millsaps College
Morehouse College
Muhlenberg College
Oglethorpe University
Ohio Wesleyan University
Presbyterian College
Rhodes College

University of Richmond
Ripon College
Skidmore College
Southwestern University
Stetson University
Susquehanna University
Trinity University (TX)
Washington and Jefferson College
Washington and Lee University
Whittier College
Wofford College
Worcester Polytechnic Institute
Xavier University of Louisiana

COMMUNICATIONS/ JOURNALISM
Colleges and Universities Strong in Communications/Journalism
American University
Arizona State University
Boston University
UC Los Angeles
UC San Diego
University of Florida
Fordham University
University of Georgia
University of Illinois at Urbana–
   Champaign
Indiana University
Ithaca College
University of Kansas
University of Maryland
University of Michigan
University of Missouri
University of Nebraska–Lincoln
University of North Carolina at
   Chapel Hill
Northwestern University
Ohio University
University of Oregon
Pepperdine University
St. Lawrence University
University of San Francisco
University of Southern California
Stanford University
Syracuse University
Texas Christian University
University of Utah
University of Wisconsin–
   Madison

ENGINEERING
Top Technical Institutes
California Institute of Technology
California Polytechnic State
   University–San Luis Obispo
Colorado School of Mines
The Cooper Union
Florida Institute of Technology
Georgia Institute of Technology
Harvey Mudd College
Illinois Institute of Technology
Massachusetts Institute of
   Technology
Michigan Technological University
New Jersey Institute of Technology
New Mexico Institute of Mining and
   Technology
Rensselaer Polytechnic Institute
Rochester Institute of Technology
Rose–Hulman Institute of Technology
Stevens Institute of Technology
Worcester Polytechnic Institute

Major Private Universities Strong in Engineering
Boston University
Brigham Young University
Brown University
Carnegie Mellon University
Case Western Reserve
The Catholic University of America
Columbia University
Cornell University
Drexel University
Duke University
The George Washington University
The Johns Hopkins University
Northeastern University
Northwestern University
University of Notre Dame
University of Pennsylvania
Princeton University
University of Rochester
Santa Clara University
University of Southern California
Southern Methodist University
Stanford University
Syracuse University
Tufts University
Tulane University
Vanderbilt University

Villanova University
Washington University in St. Louis

Public Universities Strong in Engineering
University of Arizona
UC Berkeley
UC Davis
UC Los Angeles
UC San Diego
University of Cincinnati
Clemson University
University of Connecticut
University of Delaware
University of Florida
University of Illinois at Urbana–
   Champaign
Iowa State University
University of Kansas
University of Maryland
University of Massachusetts Amherst
McGill University (Can)
University of Michigan
Michigan State University
University of Missouri
University of New Hampshire
The College of New Jersey
North Carolina State University
Ohio State University
Oregon State University
Pennsylvania State University
Purdue University
Queen's University (Can)
University of Rhode Island
Rutgers–The State University of
   New Jersey
SUNY–Binghamton University
SUNY–University at Buffalo
University of Texas at Austin
Texas A&M University
Texas Tech University
University of Toronto (Can)
University of Virginia
Virginia Tech
University of Washington
University of Wisconsin–Madison

Small Colleges and Universities Strong in Engineering
Alfred University
Bradley University

Bucknell University
Butler University
Calvin College
Clarkson University
Dartmouth College
Lafayette College
Lehigh University
Loyola University Maryland
Olin College of Engineering
University of the Pacific
Rice University
Smith College
Spelman College
Swarthmore College
Trinity College (CT)
Trinity University (TX)
University of Tulsa
Tuskegee University
Union College

FILM/TELEVISION
Major Universities Strong in Film/Television
Arizona State University
Boston University
UC Los Angeles
University of Cincinnati
DePaul University
Drexel University
University of Florida
Florida State University
University of Kansas
Loyola Marymount University
Memphis State University
University of Michigan
New York University
Northwestern University
Pennsylvania State University
Quinnipiac University
University of Southern
   California
Syracuse University
University of Texas at Austin
Wayne State University

Small Colleges and Universities Strong in Film/Television
Bard College
Beloit College
Brown University
California Institute of the Arts

Chapman University
Champlain College
Columbia College (CA)
Columbia College (IL)
Emerson College
The Evergreen State College
Hampshire College
Hofstra University
Hollins University
Ithaca College
Occidental College
Pitzer College
Pomona College
Sarah Lawrence College
SUNY–Purchase College
Wesleyan University

PERFORMING ARTS—DANCE
Major Universities Strong in Dance
Arizona State University
UC Irvine
UC Los Angeles
UC Riverside
Case Western Reserve
Florida State University
The George Washington University
Howard University
Indiana University
University of Iowa
University of Minnesota
New York University
Ohio University
Southern Methodist University
University of Texas at Austin
Texas Christian University
University of Utah
Washington University in St. Louis

Small Colleges and Universities Strong in Dance
Amherst College
Barnard College
Bennington College
Butler University
Connecticut College
Goucher College
Hollins University
Juilliard School
Kenyon College
Middlebury College

Mills College
Muhlenberg College
North Carolina School of the Arts
Princeton University
Sarah Lawrence College
Smith College
SUNY–Purchase College

PERFORMING ARTS—DRAMA
Major Universities Strong in Drama
Boston College
Boston University
UC Los Angeles
Carnegie Mellon University
The Catholic University of America
University of Chicago
DePaul University
Florida State University
Fordham University
Indiana University
University of Iowa
University of Minnesota
New York University
University of North Carolina at
   Chapel Hill
Northwestern University
University of Southern California
Southern Methodist University
Syracuse University
Texas Christian University
University of Washington
Yale University

Small Colleges and Universities Strong in Drama
Beloit College
Bennington College
Centre College
Colorado College
Columbia College (IL)
Connecticut College
Drew University
Emerson College
Ithaca College
Juilliard School
Kenyon College
Lawrence University
Macalester College
Middlebury College
Muhlenberg College

Occidental College
Otterbein University
Princeton University
Rollins College
Sarah Lawrence College
Skidmore College
SUNY–Purchase College
Vassar College
Whitman College
Wittenberg University

PERFORMING ARTS—MUSIC
Top Music Conservatories
Berklee College of Music
Boston Conservatory
California Institute of the Arts
Cleveland Institute of Music
Curtis Institute of Music
Eastman School of Music
Juilliard School
Manhattan School of Music
New England Conservatory
  of Music
North Carolina School of the Arts
Peabody Conservatory of Music
San Francisco Conservatory of Music

Major Universities Strong in Music
Baylor University
Boston College
Boston University
UC Los Angeles
Carnegie Mellon University
Case Western Reserve
University of Cincinnati
University of Colorado Boulder
University of Denver
DePaul University
Florida State University
Harvard University
Indiana University
University of Miami (FL)
Miami University (OH)
University of Michigan
University of Nebraska–Lincoln
New York University
University of North Texas
Northwestern University
University of Oklahoma
University of Southern California

Southern Methodist University
Vanderbilt University
Yale University

Small Colleges and Universities Strong in Music
Bard College
Bennington College
Bucknell University
Butler University
DePauw University
Furman University
Gordon College
Illinois Wesleyan University
Ithaca College
Knox College
Lawrence University*
Loyola University New Orleans
Manhattanville College
Mills College
Oberlin College*
University of the Pacific
Rice University
St. Mary's College of Maryland
St. Olaf College
Sarah Lawrence College
Skidmore College
Smith College
SUNY–College at Geneseo
SUNY–Purchase College
Stetson University
Wesleyan University
Wheaton College (IL)

* These two schools are unusual
  because they combine a world-
  class conservatory with a top-notch
  liberal arts college.

ENVIRONMENTAL STUDIES
Allegheny College
Antioch College
College of the Atlantic
Bowdoin College
UC Davis
UC Santa Barbara
University of Chicago
Clark University
Colby College
University of Colorado Boulder
Dartmouth College

Deep Springs College
Eckerd College
The Evergreen State College
Hampshire College
Hiram College
Hobart and William Smith Colleges
McGill University (Can)
Middlebury College
University of New Hampshire
University of New Mexico
University of North Carolina at
  Asheville
Oberlin College
Prescott College
St. Lawrence University
University of the South (Sewanee)
Tulane University
University of Vermont
University of Washington
Williams College
University of Wisconsin–Madison

INTERNATIONAL STUDIES
American University
Austin College
Brandeis University
University of British Columbia (Can)
Brown University
Bucknell University
University of Chicago
Claremont McKenna College
Clark University
Colby College
Connecticut College
Dartmouth College
Davidson College
Denison University
University of Denver
Dickinson College
Earlham College
Eckerd College
The George Washington University
Georgetown University
Goucher College
Hiram College
The Johns Hopkins University
Kalamazoo College
Lewis & Clark College
University of Mary Washington
University of Massachusetts Amherst
Middlebury College

Mount Holyoke College
Occidental College
University of the Pacific
University of Pittsburgh
Pomona College
Princeton University

University of Puget Sound
Randolph College
Reed College
Rhodes College
University of Richmond
St. Olaf College

Scripps College
University of South Carolina
Tufts University
Wesleyan University
College of William and Mary

Learning Disabilities

Accommodation for students with learning disabilities is one of the fastest-growing academic areas in higher education. Colleges and universities recognize that a significant segment of the population may suffer problems that qualify as learning disabilities, and the range of support services offered to such students is increasing. Assistance ranges from counseling services to accommodations such as tapes of lectures or extended time on exams.

Following are two lists—the first of major universities, the second of smaller colleges—that offer particularly strong services for LD students. If you qualify for such support, you should be diligent in checking out the services at each college on your list. If possible, pay a visit to the LD support office or have a phone conversation with one of the administrators. Since many such programs depend on the expertise of one or two people, the quality of the services can change abruptly with changes in staff.

Keep in mind also that many colleges are becoming increasingly skeptical of requests for LD services, especially when the initial diagnosis is made on the eve of the college search.

STRONG SUPPORT FOR STUDENTS WITH LEARNING DISABILITIES

Major Universities
American University
University of Arizona
Clark University
University of Colorado Boulder
University of Connecticut
University of Denver
DePaul University
Fairleigh Dickinson University
University of Georgia
Hofstra University
Northeastern University
Purdue University
Rochester Institute of Technology
Syracuse University
University of Vermont

Small Colleges
Bard College
Beacon College
Curry College
Landmark College
Lesley University
Loras College
Lynn University
Manhattanville College
Marist College
Marymount Manhattan College
Mercyhurst College
Mitchell College
Muskingum College
New England College
University of New England
St. Thomas Aquinas College (NY)
West Virginia Wesleyan College
Westminster College (MO)

SAT and ACT Optional Schools

Many years ago a small number of pioneering U.S. colleges and universities, most notably Bates and Bowdoin, decided that they would no longer require all applicants to submit SAT or ACT scores. They reasoned that there is a significant pool of bright students who can do quality academic work but who for one reason or another do not test well. A "test-optional" policy would allow schools to tap into this market.

Over the years the number of "test-optional" or, in some cases, "test-flexible" schools has grown dramatically. The National Center for Fair and Open Testing (FairTest), a Cambridge, Massachusetts–based advocacy organization that is critical of standardized testing in general, has tracked this growth, and at press time its website (www.fairtest.org) listed more than 1,000 such colleges and universities. Reasons for this growing aversion to college admissions tests are many. The early test-optional schools have been happy with the way the policy has worked out. The SAT has been a focus of repeated controversy, especially around incidents of scoring errors. In a parallel development, a number of schools and a national commission headed by William Fitzsimmons, the dean of admission and financial aid at Harvard University, have begun to argue that SAT Subject Tests, AP exams, and International Baccalaureate exams—tests that are closely tied to curriculum—are more useful than regular SAT and ACT scores. And perhaps most importantly, the whole field of "test prep" has spiraled out of control. Students and parents alike are tired of the anxiety surrounding prep courses—not to mention the financial cost of helping bolster the coffers of Kaplan or Princeton Review.

Until recently there was not much that students could do—especially if they hoped to be able to choose among a range of quality colleges. Over the last few years, however, a critical mass has emerged of quality liberal arts colleges and major state universities, many of which are described in the *Fiske Guide*, that are test-optional or test-flexible in the sense that they offer applicants a range of options for the tests they take. For the first time, students who wish to avoid getting involved in the admissions-test rat race can do so while still enjoying a range of colleges and universities from which to choose.

Accordingly, we now publish a list of those colleges and universities in the guide that are test-optional. We are not recommending that any particular student eschew college admissions tests and apply only to these schools. As a resource designed to help students and parents, we are simply pointing out that applicants now have that option.

In looking over the list below of test-optional or test-flexible colleges and universities described in the *Fiske Guide*, please keep a couple of things in mind. First, most of the schools are large state universities or small liberal arts colleges. You won't find many other types, including the Ivies or flagship publics. Second, keep in mind that there are different ways of being test-optional or test-flexible. Some schools, for example, only exempt students who meet certain GPA or class-rank criteria, while others on the list may require other types of tests or supplemental components, like extra essay questions. At some schools, test-optional policies come with certain conditions, such as disqualifying students who choose not to submit test scores from consideration for merit-based scholarships. **Since the test-optional field is changing daily, go to www.fairtest.org for updated information and, above all, confirm current policy with any school to which you are thinking of applying.**

Agnes Scott College	Beloit College	Champlain College
Allegheny College	Bennington College	University of Chicago
American University	Birmingham–Southern College	Clark University
Antioch College	Boston University	Colby College
University of Arizona	Bowdoin College	Colorado College
Arizona State University	Brandeis University	Connecticut College
College of the Atlantic	Bryn Mawr College	Cornell College
Austin College	Bucknell University	Denison University
Bard College	Calvin College	University of Denver
Bates College	The Catholic University of America	DePaul University

DePauw University
Dickinson College
Drew University
Drexel University
Earlham College
Emerson College
Eugene Lang College of Liberal Arts
Fairfield University
Franklin & Marshall College
Furman University
George Mason University
The George Washington University
Gettysburg College
Goucher College
Guilford College
Gustavus Adolphus College
Hamilton College
Hampshire College
Hartwick College
Hiram College
Hobart and William Smith Colleges
Hofstra University
College of the Holy Cross
Hood College
Houghton College
The College of Idaho
Ithaca College

James Madison University
Juniata College
Kalamazoo College
Knox College
Lake Forest College
Lawrence University
Lewis & Clark College
Loyola University Maryland
Manhattanville College
Marlboro College
University of Mary Washington
Middlebury College
Mills College
Mount Holyoke College
Muhlenberg College
New York University
Ohio Wesleyan University
Pitzer College
Presbyterian College
Prescott College
Providence College
University of Puget Sound
Quinnipiac University
Ripon College
University of Rochester
Rollins College
St. John's College

St. Lawrence University
Saint Michael's College
Sarah Lawrence College
Skidmore College
Smith College
University of the South (Sewanee)
Southern Methodist University
SUNY–Purchase College
Stetson University
Stevens Institute of Technology
Susquehanna University
Trinity College (CT)
Union College
Ursinus College
Wake Forest University
Warren Wilson College
Washington and Jefferson College
Washington College
Wells College
Wesleyan University
Wheaton College (MA)
Whitman College
Whittier College
Willamette University
Wittenberg University
Wofford College
Worcester Polytechnic Institute

A Note to the Reader

It seems like only yesterday that a small band of journalists gathered each evening in the back of the newsroom of the *New York Times*—where I was the Education Editor—to create the first edition of the *Fiske Guide to Colleges*. Now we've been in publication for more than 35 years!

The higher education scene was quite different in the early 1980s. Tuition and room and board averaged only $3,200 at public universities and $7,000 at private institutions. Stanford had just emerged as a national university, and hardly anyone outside the South had heard of Duke. AP exams and the Common Application were in their infancy, and Columbia still had not gotten around to admitting women. Division I university presidents still had some control over their athletic directors, and *U.S. News & World Report* was little more than a mediocre newsweekly. The Internet was still a distant vision.

But important changes were on the way. By the early 1980s the last of the baby boomers had worked their way through college. Admissions directors were losing sleep over whether they could fill their classrooms, so they responded with aggressive marketing campaigns. The methods they used seem quaint by current standards: telephone calls, videotapes (remember them?), and lavish four-color brochures that overflowed the mailboxes of any students whose ACT scores were larger than their shoe size.

The aggressive marketing of colleges produced a backlash—and an opportunity. Someone needed to wade in on the side of students and parents and cut through all the hype that was coming from the colleges. Thus was born the *Fiske Guide to Colleges*. Our vision was to use basic journalistic techniques to create a college guide that would provide reliable information on what it was like to be a student at the "best and most interesting" colleges and universities in the country. Since then we have done just that for millions of students, parents, and school counselors.

Consistent with changes in the culture of higher education over the last three decades, the content of the school profiles in the *Fiske Guide* has evolved. Given the impact of globalization, we have documented the proliferation of study abroad programs, and we have added write-ups on universities in Canada, Britain, Scotland, and Ireland. The write-ups reflect colleges' increased sensitivity to issues of campus safety, alcohol and drug abuse, and, more recently, to challenges surrounding sexual assault. Colleges today talk more about racial, ethnic, and socioeconomic diversity than they did in the early 1980s, although the numbers do not always show much progress. Many large universities have created "living/learning" communities in order to offer more intense learning environments within the context of a large institution. Perhaps most importantly, colleges, for better or worse, have seen it to be in their competitive interest to invest huge amounts of resources in student centers, fitness facilities, and other amenities designed to make the undergraduate experience more comfortable.

But one thing that has not changed over the last three decades is the importance of institutional cultures. When we started out to create the *Fiske Guide*, the big editorial risk was: Will numerous descriptions of small liberal arts colleges where "the faculty often invite students to their homes for dinner," make all liberal arts schools begin to sound alike—creating a pretty dull reading experience? But it turned out not to be a problem. The schools in the *Fiske Guide* are just as diverse as the students who apply to them. Even schools that look the same on paper have their own distinctive institutional cultures and personalities. The task of the *Fiske Guide* has been to capture those cultures and personalities of the "best and most interesting" colleges in the country. Students can then decide which schools are the best match for their own interests and learning styles.

In the age of the Internet, information is abundant and cheap. Endless facts and opinions about any particular college or university are just a few clicks away, but to know everything is to know nothing. The real challenge for college-bound students—the same challenge that faced an earlier generation in the early 1980s—is to cut through the mass of information that is being thrown at them and figure out what is really important. That's what the *Fiske Guide to Colleges* has been doing with authority for more than three decades. That's what we pledge to continue to do in the decades to come.

Edward B. Fiske
Durham, NC

University of Aberdeen: See page 368.

Adelphi University

One South Avenue, Garden City, NY 11530

Situated in a comfortable Long Island suburb within shouting distance of Manhattan, Adelphi lets you taste urban life without being overwhelmed. Long established as an innovator in public health and the arts, Adelphi's strengths are professional programs grounded in the liberal arts. Almost all undergrads are New Yorkers, two-thirds are women, and 93 percent get some financial aid. Compare to Fairfield and Quinnipiac.

Think of Adelphi as a Gen Y of higher education. After going through a tumultuous time in the late 1990s, Adelphi began coming of age in 2002 thanks to new leadership and a revamped mission. The campus has seen well over $250 million of new construction and the renovation of 500,000 square feet of facilities. Enrollment has grown by 66 percent, and more than 400 new faculty have been hired. Student financial aid has been expanded, and Adelphi has a policy of keeping tuition lower than peer institutions. At the same time, the school has focused on offering smaller class sizes and more hands-on learning experiences. Students say that, as a result, there is a palpable sense of energy among students and faculty.

Founded in 1863 as a prep school in Brooklyn, Adelphi morphed into a coeducational college in 1896 and in 1928 moved to Garden City, where it occupies 75 acres in an attractive residential suburb replete with Gothic cathedrals and stately homes. The campus is registered as an arboretum. The $76 million Nexus Building, home to the College of Nursing and Public Health, recently opened, and a $25 million renovation of the Harley University Center is underway.

General education requirements include a 24-credit distribution in several liberal arts areas, as well as courses in communication, quantitative reasoning, global learning and civic engagement, information literacy, and a foreign language. First-year students take part in a four-credit seminar that introduces them to life at Adelphi. All students are required to complete a capstone course or project. Adelphi's most popular majors have a decidedly preprofessional bent: nursing, business, psychology, and biology. Communication sciences and disorders, exercise science, and social work are other traditional strengths. The fine and performing arts are also notable, especially the theater program. Joint degree programs have been established in a number of disciplines, including dentistry, law, physical therapy, and environmental studies. The combined degree program in engineering with Columbia University allows students to earn a B.S. in physics from Adelphi and a B.S. in engineering from Columbia in five years.

> **"It's easy to form relationships with the instructors and network with them for future opportunities."**

Adelphi has "a relaxed but still serious environment," says a communications major. "The students are generally working hard, but it never feels too intense." Forty-eight percent of all classes have fewer than 20 students. Despite an increase in faculty hiring, students complain that it can be hard to find open courses come registration time and the quality of teaching can be hit or miss. Still, a criminal science major says, "It's easy to form relationships with the instructors and network with them for future opportunities." Adelphi's Learning Resource Program, for students with learning disabilities, is said to be well-staffed and effective, and Bridges

Website: www.adelphi.edu
Location: Suburban
Private
Total Enrollment: 6,304
Undergraduates: 4,858
Male/Female: 32/68
SAT Ranges: ERW 530–620, M 530–620
ACT Ranges: 22–27
Financial Aid: 93%
Pell Grant: 34%
Expense: Pr $
Student Loans: 61%
Average Debt: $ $ $
Applicants: 11,851
Accepted: 73%
Enrolled: 13%
Grad in 6 Years: 68%
Returning Freshmen: 80%
Academics: ✍ ✍ ✍
Social: ☎ ☎
Q of L: ★ ★ ★
Admissions: (516) 877-3050
Email Address: admissions@ adelphi.edu

Strong Programs:
Nursing
Business
Psychology
Biology
Communication Sciences and Disorders
Exercise Science
Social Work
Fine and Performing Arts

to Adelphi is an award-winning program offering career development and academic support to students with autism spectrum disorder.

Adelphi has increased its emphasis on experiential learning and student engagement in recent years. The Levermore Global Scholars program, open to students in all majors, takes an interdisciplinary approach to addressing global issues through special seminars, cultural excursions, activities at the UN headquarters in New York City, and opportunities for internships, study abroad, and service projects. Overall, 14 percent of students study abroad, choosing from more than 100 programs. The Honors College offers a rigorous liberal arts program for exceptional students.

Ninety percent of undergraduates hail from New York, while 4 percent arrive from foreign countries. The student population reflects the university's proximity to the Big Apple: 9 percent are African American, 17 percent are Hispanic, 11 percent are Asian American, and 2 percent are multiracial. Minority representation is growing among Adelphi's faculty as well. School-sponsored series like Diversity Dialogue and Common Ground encourage students to share their experiences with diversity and respond to national events, but a sophomore says, "Students tend to keep their political opinions to themselves." Thirty-four percent of current freshmen qualify for Pell Grants. Adelphi offers merit scholarships, worth an average of $15,500 each, to qualified students, and 264 athletic scholarships are available in 21 sports.

Despite several "comfortable and well-maintained" residence halls, a mere 22 percent of all undergrads (including 40 percent of first-years) live in campus housing. Gender-inclusive options are available, as are two first-year living/learning communities that draw about a quarter of incoming students each year. Many students reside in university-arranged off-campus apartments in Garden City. Campus dining gets mixed reviews. Students report feeling safe on campus, and a sophomore says, "The school provides us with the resources we need to support one another and not be afraid to talk about sexual assault."

> **"Many students choose to go [to the city] and adventure."**

Adelphi has been bolstering on-campus social life with an increase in free weekend and late-night programming aimed at encouraging students to stick around on weekends, and students are active in more than 80 clubs and organizations. Greek life does play a role in the social scene, with 11 fraternities and sororities that attract 9 percent of the men and 10 percent of the women, respectively. Adelphi is a dry campus, and students say that the policy is strictly enforced. In the fall, students look forward to Spirit Weekend, while spring brings Pantherfest and the Spring Concert. One student describes Garden City as "a very safe, low-key residential neighborhood," if not a college town. Sixty percent of students get involved in community service. A junior says, "Adelphi is very close to the city, so many students choose to go there and adventure." The Center for Student Involvement offers discounted tickets to movies, Broadway shows, and professional sporting events.

Adelphi fields several competitive Division II teams (the Panthers). Women's lacrosse is a powerhouse, having won national titles in 2014, 2015, and 2017. Recent conference champions include men's and women's soccer, men's lacrosse, and women's basketball, softball, bowling, volleyball, and tennis. Among the school's 13 club sports, ultimate Frisbee, hip-hop dance, Bollywood dance, soccer, and fencing are the most popular; more than a dozen intramural sports are also available.

At Adelphi, signs of renewal are everywhere, from the campus facilities to the burgeoning enrollment. Although the university's lingering commuter heritage can leave some wanting for more social opportunities, most welcome the chance to play an active role in shaping not just their education, but the community as a whole. Says a senior, "I really feel that all of our departments, as well as our students, work together to collaborate on new ideas, classes, events, and opportunities for the campus community."

The Levermore Global Scholars program offers special seminars, cultural excursions, and activities at the UN headquarters.

Adelphi has been bolstering on-campus social life with an increase in free weekend and late-night programming.

Overlaps

Fordham, Hofstra, St. John's University (NY), SUNY–Stony Brook, Molloy, CUNY–Hunter, SUNY–Binghamton, CUNY–Queens

If You Apply To ›

Adelphi: Early action, rolling admissions. SATs or ACTs: required. No Subject Tests. Accepts the Common Application with supplement. Application includes optional question regarding gender identity.

Agnes Scott College

141 East College Avenue, Decatur, GA 30030

Combines the tree-lined seclusion of Decatur with the bustle of Atlanta. More money in the bank per student than most Ivy League schools, and enrollment is up. Recent physical plant additions give ASC exceptional facilities for a college of its size. Small classes, sisterhood, a richly diverse student body, and a more exciting location than some of its cohorts. Big emphasis on leadership and global learning.

Agnes Scott College, founded by Presbyterians in 1889, offers a small-town campus atmosphere and provides women with an intellectually challenging institution—absent the distractions of men. The college is known for its science and math programs, but it also produces skilled writers and artists and continues to be one of the South's leading women's schools. It has become increasingly focused in recent years on designing a curriculum that cultivates globally aware women leaders. ASC's climate as a small, single-sex institution leads to close relationships with the faculty and very involved students—both academically and socially. "We believe in the power of women, of deep thinking, of honor, of social justice, of learning for the sake of learning," asserts one senior.

The Agnes Scott campus sits on 100 acres in the historic district of Decatur, just outside of Atlanta. The well-maintained Gothic and Victorian buildings are surrounded by gardens filled with rare shrubs, bushes, and trees—all evidence of thriving alumnae support. The $36.5 million Bullock Science Center includes an X-ray spectrometer, nuclear magnetic resonance imaging equipment, and a scanning tunneling microscope. The LEED Gold–certified Campbell Hall Living and Learning Center houses more than 80 beds and semi-suite style rooms, along with two learning centers.

> "We believe in the power of women."

In addition to outstanding instruction in the sciences, Agnes Scott provides students with solid grounding in the liberal arts, leadership, and global learning through an approach called SUMMIT. As part of SUMMIT, all first-year students participate in a two-day leadership immersion experience following orientation in the fall, and then in the spring semester embark on a weeklong, faculty-led, global study tour to places like Ghana, Iceland, and Peru. Each student also assembles her own board of advisors with faculty and staff members, a peer advisor, and a career mentor, and documents her progress throughout her four years with a digital portfolio. A junior praises Summit for connecting students with "a group of people totally committed to making sure you get where you want to be." Just before spring break, sophomores and upperclassmen participate in Peak Week, a series of leadership experiences that includes daylong visits with local employers, grad school boot camps, and lectures on topics such as "Adulting 101."

Academically, Agnes Scott delivers strong programs in biology, math, and astrophysics. The school also offers a top-notch German program, a rarity these days in U.S. higher education. Popular majors include psychology, business management,

Website: www.agnesscott.edu
Location: City Center
Private
Total Enrollment: 885
Undergraduates: 885
Male/Female: 0/100
SAT Ranges: ERW 580–690, M 530–610
ACT Ranges: 24–30
Financial Aid: 99%
Pell Grant: 42%
Expense: Pr $
Student Loans: 64%
Average Debt: $ $ $
Applicants: 1,534
Accepted: 66%
Enrolled: 25%
Grad in 6 Years: 67%
Returning Freshmen: 87%
Academics: ✍ ✍ ✍
Social: ☎ ☎
Q of L: ★ ★ ★ ★
Admissions: (404) 471-6285
Email Address: admission@agnesscott.edu

Strong Programs:
Psychology
Business Management
Neuroscience
Public Health
English Literature/Creative Writing
Biology

neuroscience, public health, and English literature/creative writing. Aspiring engineers may complete their degrees through a 3–2 program with Georgia Tech, while nurses benefit from a dual-degree program with Emory.

The overall academic climate at ASC is rigorous but collaborative, and students are focused on learning first. "We are encouraged to find our own paths instead of competing for the same one," says a public health major. Adds a senior, "In every course, there is a cross-curricular approach. You will, at the end of your four years, be an excellent writer, speaker, and critical thinker." An honor system, enforced by a student judiciary, allows for self-scheduled and unproctored exams. Seventy-eight percent of classes have fewer than 20 students, which encourages close student/faculty interactions in the classroom. A sophomore says, "I cannot emphasize enough how invested Agnes Scott professors are in their students."

> "We are encouraged to find our own paths instead of competing for the same one."

For those students wishing to leave Agnes Scott's idyllic campus behind for a time, there are study abroad options available at more than 150 universities in more than 50 countries. The Hubert Scholars Program combines experiential learning with humanitarian service either at home or abroad. Past Hubert scholars have mentored refugee girls in the local community and developed gender-equality education programs in Bangladesh. Sixty-eight percent of students participate in research and may attend or present results at an annual conference held in the spring.

Sophomores and upperclassmen participate in Peak Week, which includes grad school boot camps and lectures on topics such as "Adulting 101."

Agnes Scott students "recognize the value of two very simple things: the value of diversity and the value of women's education," says a sophomore. Fifty percent of ASC students are Georgia natives, 7 percent are international, and most of the rest hail from the Southeast. Despite the school's small size, its denizens are quite diverse; 30 percent of students are African American, 12 percent are Hispanic, 7 percent are Asian American, and 7 percent are multiracial. The school has made socioeconomic diversity a priority as well—an impressive 42 percent of current freshmen are eligible for Pell Grants. Ample support is available for students of diverse backgrounds, and the school has implemented initiatives like the Transgender 101 Workshop and Diversity and Racial Justice programs to educate the campus community. A business management major comments, "I am challenged every day to think about the world from perspectives that I could never think about myself." Most Scotties are liberal-leaning, and national issues of equal rights, immigration, and combating Islamophobia have attracted attention on campus recently. Agnes Scott awards merit scholarships averaging $27,600 annually, based on academic performance, leadership, or musical ability.

Eighty-four percent of students live in Agnes Scott's six dorms, which are linked by tree-lined brick walks. "The residence halls are pretty nice. They have walk-in closets, lots of storage, and all but one of them have air-conditioning," says a student. Juniors and seniors can live in Avery Glen, the college-owned apartment complex, while incoming students are assigned to one of two first-year dorms. Students say that dining services staff is friendly and receptive to student feedback, and the food is usually decent but options can be limited. They report feeling safe on campus too, and one student says, "Campus security is very tight. There are always officers around keeping watch."

> "I am challenged every day to think about the world from perspectives that I could never think about myself."

As for the ASC social scene, there are no sororities, but the college itself is a close-knit sisterhood. During the week, socializing tends to revolve around study groups, student club activities, and events planned by the campus programming board ("ProBo"), but when the weekend comes, social life moves off campus. "Parties at other colleges, nightclubs, bars, and off-campus restaurants are common places to find Agnes Scott students," says a senior. Enforcement of drinking policies falls

An impressive 42 percent of current freshmen are eligible for Pell Grants.

under the honor code; students of legal age can enjoy alcohol in their dorms and at certain functions. Every October, students celebrate Black Cat week, ASC's version of homecoming, during which classes compete in various activities to win the coveted Black Kitty prize ("an ancient stuffed cat," explains a studio art major) and students attend a formal dance. Other quaint traditions survive too, such as the ring ceremony where sophomores receive the black onyx class rings that make them part of the ASC "Black Ring Mafia," and throwing recently engaged classmates into the alumnae pond. And seniors who get into grad school or find jobs ascend to the top of the college bell tower, ringing the bell to share the good news.

Decatur itself is not really a college town, but there are some attractions for Agnes Scott students. "There are nice little venues and coffee shops; very hip and fun," a student says. Convenient public transportation serves cultural landmarks and provides access to the social scene in nearby Atlanta. Many ASC students get involved with community service both on and off campus, with Habitat for Humanity, the DeKalb Rape Crisis Center, Girl Scouts, Hands Across Atlanta, and Best Buddies. Popular road trips include Stone Mountain and Six Flags, or New Orleans for Mardi Gras.

Agnes Scott is a member of the Division III USA South Athletic Conference. Scottie tennis has been the most successful of the school's six varsity teams, winning multiple conference championships, and softball and soccer are also competitive. About 13 percent of students participate in intramural activities, such as Zumba, self-defense, and flag football.

Small but mighty, ASC stands out for the little touches that make students feel they're part of an intimate community, starting with pine-scented brochures sent to accepted applicants. One Scottie Sister reflects, "Agnes Scott builds women who are fearless, who change the world, who question things and inspire others."

During Black Cat week, ASC's version of homecoming, classes compete in various activities to win the coveted Black Kitty prize.

Overlaps

Georgia State, Spelman, Kennesaw State, University of Georgia, Mercer, Emory, Mount Holyoke, Smith

If You Apply To ›

Agnes Scott: Early decision, early action I and II, regular decision. SATs or ACTs: optional (required for homeschooled applicants. Test-optional applicants must either have an evaluative admissions interview or submit a graded writing sample). No Subject Tests. Accepts the Common Application.

University of Alabama

Box 870132, Tuscaloosa, AL 35487

"Roll, tide, roll" still says a lot—but not everything—about Alabama, which is one of the fastest-growing public flagships in the country. Passion for the Crimson Tide is as strong as ever, but also look for strong honors programs, emphasis on undergraduate research, and pockets of professional excellence. Though its football team is among the nation's elite, 'Bama still pales academically in comparison with rivals University of Georgia and University of Florida.

Although the University of Alabama earned its national reputation on the gridiron, the state's first university is committed to making an academic name for itself as well. In an effort to attract the South's best and brightest, UA has increased its emphasis on global perspectives, computer-based technologies, freshman learning communities, and undergraduate research and adopted a generous policy of merit scholarships.

Website: www.ua.edu
Location: City Center
Public
Total Enrollment: 33,191
Undergraduates: 29,822

(continued)

Male/Female: 45/55
SAT Ranges: ERW 530–640,
 M 520–640
ACT Ranges: 23–32
Financial Aid: 42%
Pell Grant: 18%
Expense: Pub $ $
Student Loans: 46%
Average Debt: $ $ $ $
Applicants: 38,129
Accepted: 56%
Enrolled: 35%
Grad in 6 Years: 68%
Returning Freshmen: 87%
Academics: ✍ ✍ ✍
Social: ☎ ☎ ☎
Q of L: ★ ★ ★
Admissions: (205) 348-5666
Email Address: admissions@
 ua.edu

Strong Programs:
Business/Marketing
Engineering
Communication Studies
Journalism
Health Professions
Management Information
 Systems
Food and Nutrition
Visual and Performing Arts

Consistent with its efforts to lure strong students from outside of Alabama, the school spends more than $135 million on merit aid.

'Bama's thousand-acre campus combines pristine brick, classical, revival-style buildings (a few of which survived the Civil War) with modern structures. One of the most stunning in the South, the campus boasts an expansive lawn and majestic trees and wraps around a shaded quadrangle, the home of the main library and "Denny Chimes," a campanile carillon that rings the Westminster Chimes on the quarter hour. Recent construction includes the $60 million Performing Arts Academic Center and a $10 million facility for the Adapted Athletics program, featuring a regulation wheelchair basketball court and accessible training and locker rooms.

> **"[Professors are] thorough and diligent with their classes and lectures."**

The only course Alabama requires students to take during their first year on campus is a two-term English composition sequence. Before graduation, students must also complete courses in natural sciences, math, humanities, and social sciences, and either two semesters of a foreign language or one of computer science. Optional Freshman Learning Communities allow students to take two or three academic courses together, and a one-credit seminar taught by a full professor that ties the other courses together. All students may also enroll in the two-credit Academic Potential Seminar, which covers skills like personal responsibility, time management, and test preparation. Incoming freshmen who are at the low end of UA's admissions requirements may participate in the Crimson Edge Program, which requires an academic support class and includes specialized academic advising.

The university is organized into eight undergraduate colleges and schools, which together offer more than 80 undergraduate degree programs. The Culverhouse College of Commerce offers strong programs in marketing and management information systems. The College of Communication and Information Sciences is one of the country's top communication schools, while respected programs in the College of Human Environmental Sciences include food and nutrition and athletic training. Among STEM fields, metallurgical and materials engineering is noteworthy. The School of Music is a regional standout, attracting guest artists such as Itzhak Perlman and Wynton Marsalis, and the studio art and art history programs are well regarded. New College allows students to work with faculty to design their own interdisciplinary major. The most popular majors include business, engineering, communication studies, journalism, and health professions. Full professors occasionally teach freshman courses, and one student describes them as "thorough and diligent with their classes and lectures."

> **"Something is always going on in the mansions we call Greek houses."**

The Honors College serves 9,800 students and houses UA's three university-wide honors programs: computer-based honors, international honors, and university honors. "Honors classes can include a Habitat for Humanity course, Peer Mentoring, or the one that takes the cake: the chocolate-tasting class," says one participant. Honors students also get early registration privileges and the opportunity to write a senior thesis. The University Scholars Program provides gifted undergraduates whose objectives include master's or doctoral degrees an opportunity to begin graduate work during their senior year and become eligible for graduate fellowships and scholarships. About 2,000 undergraduates conduct research each year, and other offerings include the May interim term, when students spend three weeks focusing on one course in depth. Seven percent of students study abroad through more than 50 faculty-led programs, as well as reciprocal exchanges and third-party affiliate options around the world.

Just 41 percent of 'Bama's undergraduates are Alabama residents, and 2 percent are international students representing more than 60 countries. UA students are "warm and welcoming," says a marketing major. Ten percent of UA students are African American, 1 percent are Asian American, 5 percent are Hispanic, and 3 percent are multiracial.

The biggest social and political issues on campus include free speech and race relations, and although UA traditionally leans right, a senior points out that "the influx of out-of-state students has brought a lot more political attention and representation to our school." 'Bama awards 272 athletic scholarships in 21 sports and has expanded the number of merit scholarships, which now average $16,000. Consistent with its efforts to lure strong students from outside of Alabama, the school spends more than $135 million on merit aid—twice what it allocates to students with financial need.

Although UA requires freshmen to reside on campus, most Alabama students live in off-campus apartments in the Tuscaloosa area; only 24 percent remain in campus residence halls. "UA has the best dorms around!" cheers a public relations major. "Seventy-five percent of the dorms are suite-style, which means students get their own bedroom." A freshman gives high marks to the living/learning communities for their tight-knit atmosphere. Students report that some campus dining halls are better than others, and one recommends the made-to-order fare at Bryant Dining, adding, "I would gladly eat at Bryant for the rest of my life." A senior notes that sexual assault awareness is "not something that's swept under the rug."

Much of 'Bama's social life revolves around the Greek system and athletic events. Twenty-eight percent of men pledge fraternities and 44 percent of women join sororities, and a sophomore says, "Something is always going on in the mansions we call Greek houses." Partying has remained a staple of the social scene in recent years, despite administrators' efforts to weaken it by prohibiting fraternities and sororities from having parties on campus, but students say alcohol policies are well enforced. Those looking for alternatives will find everything from dance crews to Bible study groups among the school's 500-plus student clubs. A modern trolley service connects the 'Bama campus to the city's thriving downtown. Tuscaloosa is described as "an awesome college town," that is "mostly centered around the university." Road trips to New Orleans (for Mardi Gras and Greek weekend formals), Atlanta, Nashville, and the Gulf Coast and Florida beaches are popular, but "many people never leave UA!" says a sophomore.

'Bama football remains the cornerstone of the university's competitive Division I athletic programs and is a perennial powerhouse, having won five national championship titles since 2009. The annual Auburn–Alabama game—the Iron Bowl, one of the most intense rivalries in the nation—is the highlight of the school year. "Any Alabama football game is a festival," a sophomore says. Men's golf has claimed two national championships in the last six years, and women's golf is a recent Southeastern Conference title winner. 'Bama sports a number of solid nonathletic teams as well, including the Alabama Forensic Council, which consistently places in the top 10 in national competition. Intramurals draw a third of the students.

Although sports are still an integral part of the UA experience, the university's declared emphasis is now on technology, merit scholarships, global perspectives, and undergraduate research. It's an approach that's bringing in more serious, cosmopolitan students. Best of all, says one finance and marketing major, "The students are so friendly, if you pass someone on the quad and say 'Roll Tide,' you've pretty much made a friend for life."

> 'Bama football is a perennial powerhouse, having won five national championship titles since 2009.

> "If you pass someone on the quad and say 'Roll Tide,' you've pretty much made a friend for life."

Overlaps

University of Alabama at Birmingham, Auburn, University of Mississippi, University of Georgia, University of Tennessee Knoxville, Florida State, University of Florida

If You Apply To ›

Alabama: Rolling admissions. SATs or ACTs: required. Subject Tests: optional. Does not accept the Common Application.

Albion College

Albion, MI 49224

Nestled between evangelical Hope and Calvin and out-there Kalamazoo, Albion is Michigan's middle-of-the-road liberal arts college. Think Gerald Ford, the moderate Republican president who is the namesake of Albion's signature institute for public service. Future doctors, lawyers, and businesspeople are well served.

Website: www.albion.edu
Location: Small Town
Private
Total Enrollment: 1,552
Undergraduates: 1,552
Male/Female: 47/53
SAT Ranges: ERW 510–610,
M 500–590
ACT Ranges: 20–26
Financial Aid: 99%
Pell Grant: 51%
Expense: Pr $ $
Student Loans: 64%
Average Debt: $ $ $ $
Applicants: 3,884
Accepted: 71%
Enrolled: 19%
Grad in 6 Years: 57%
Returning Freshmen: 79%
Academics: ✍ ✍ ✍
Social: ☎ ☎
Q of L: ★ ★ ★
Admissions: (517) 629-0321
Email Address: admission@
albion.edu

Strong Programs:
Public Policy
Economics and Management
Communication Studies
Biology
Psychology
Accounting
Finance
Exercise Science

Albion College is a small, private college in Michigan that emphasizes the importance of mixing learning with hands-on experience, particularly when it comes to citizenship and service. Albion helps students achieve their goals through personal attention from professors, internships, and a devoted alumni network. "Students at Albion College are not here to get an education and get out," says a public policy major. "They are here to build relationships and form lifelong connections with fellow students, faculty, and staff."

Founded in 1835 by the Methodist Church, Albion is located near the banks of the Kalamazoo River. In addition to its newer Georgian-style architecture, the college has retained and restored several of its 19th-century buildings. The campus is spacious, with statuesque oaks and a beautiful nature center. Robinson Hall, the campus centerpiece, houses myriad departments, including the Gerald R. Ford Institute for Leadership in Public Policy and Service, the Gerstacker Institute for Business and Management, and the Shaw Women's Center. The college is also home to one of the largest indoor riding arenas in the United States, which was recently expanded to host regional and national equestrian events.

Albion has a rich academic history and was the first private college in Michigan to have a Phi Beta Kappa chapter (1940). Students are required to take core courses distributed among humanities, natural sciences, social sciences, fine arts, and math. They must also satisfy requirements in environmental science and gender and ethnicity studies. Freshmen take a first-year seminar designed to provide a "stimulating learning environment" in a small-class setting; one recent offering, "To Sleep or Not to Sleep," included a trip to Europe to study firsthand the effects of jet lag. In their final year, students participate in a capstone experience.

> **"Students at Albion College are not here to get an education and get out."**

Consistent with Albion's interest in developing civic leaders, the Ford Institute takes a unique approach: students participate in a simulation of city government in which they play the roles of community leaders. Visiting speakers include senators and congresspeople, governors and state legislators, and interest-group representatives. The premed and prelaw programs draw dedicated undergrads, and the economics and management and communication studies departments are well respected. Other popular majors include biology, psychology, accounting, finance, and exercise science.

The academic climate at Albion is described as competitive in certain departments, but not cutthroat. One student says, "Because of the small-school setting, it is easy to talk to anyone in my class to work together or ask questions." Top-notch academic and career counseling and low student/faculty ratios keep students on track and motivated. Fifty-nine percent of classes have fewer than 20 students, and teaching assistants are used for tutoring, not teaching. Professors are said to be interested in students' academic performance and their emotional well-being. "They have additional office hours on Sundays, come in for review sessions at 10 o'clock at night, and give out their personal phone numbers for questions," according to a junior.

For those looking to expand their educational experience, Albion offers roughly 120 study abroad programs in 40 countries (11 percent of students go abroad), as well as an honors program for highly motivated students. The Foundation for Undergraduate Research, Scholarship, and Creative Activity, which pairs students from all disciplines with faculty mentors, is highly commended by students. One participant, a biochemistry major, says, "My professor walked me through new and old techniques individually, so I feel much more independent in the lab than most."

In the Ford Institute, students participate in a simulation of city government in which they play the roles of community leaders.

Albion attracts an ambitious, involved group of students. "Very few students at Albion just want to blend into the crowd," says a senior. Michigan residents make up 76 percent of the student population, and just 1 percent hail from abroad. "Since my first semester here, the school has evolved in a big way in terms of diversity," says a junior; currently, 13 percent of students are African American, 9 percent are Hispanic, 3 percent are Asian American, and 3 percent are multiracial. Additionally, 51 percent of freshmen are now Pell-eligible.

"[Professors] have additional office hours on Sundays [and] come in for review sessions at 10 o'clock at night."

A senior describes the student body as a mix of liberals and conservatives who are "concerned about current issues," including immigration and racial politics. There are a number of merit scholarships available, averaging $24,000, but no athletic scholarships.

Since Albion is a residential college, 95 percent of students call the co-ed residence halls home, and the general consensus is that the "overpriced" accommodations are "not great, but not terrible," and the Wi-Fi service can be unreliable. The majority of the freshman class inhabits Wesley Hall. During their sophomore year, many students move to the suite-style rooms in Whitehouse Hall or Mitchell Towers; seniors occupy apartment-style housing called The Mae. Other housing options include apartment annexes and fraternity houses. Sororities do not have houses; they hold their meetings in lodges. Meals are served in the centrally located dining hall, and a junior says, "It's amazing how many options we have for being such a small college." Students rate campus security staff and counseling services—including efforts to prevent sexual assault—highly.

Twenty-six percent of Albion men and 23 percent of the women belong to one of the school's six national fraternities and six sororities. Greek parties draw large crowds, composed of Greeks and non-Greeks, making them a primary part of many students' social lives. "Campus Safety monitors every party and there is a curfew in place," notes a sophomore. Students 21 and older may consume alcohol in certain campus residence areas. A well-run union board organizes all sorts of activities—films, lectures, plays, comedians, and concerts—to keep students occupied in their spare time. Road trips are a big part of weekends for many students; Ann Arbor, East Lansing, and Chicago are frequent destinations.

New developments in the downtown area include a brewpub, a bookstore/ coffeehouse, and a community theater.

Students report that, although there is not much to do in the town of Albion, its annual Festival of the Forks is fun, and the movie theater offers "free movies if you show a valid student ID!" According to an economics major, "The school has partnered with the city of Albion to help bring more business and entertainment into the city."

"Since my first semester here, the school has evolved in a big way in terms of diversity."

New developments in the downtown area include a brewpub, a bookstore/coffeehouse, and a community theater. Students focus some of their energy by working for groups supported by the Student Volunteer Bureau; in fact, half of the students volunteer in the community on a regular basis, participating in "city clean-up day, Habitat for Humanity, and volunteering at nursing homes and schools." Some traditional events that offer a nice break from academics are the Big Show, which brings a major artist or comedian to campus, and the Day of Woden, which is a picnic held in the spring on the last day of class.

The Britons football team competes in the Division III Michigan Intercollegiate Athletic Association and has won 36 conference championships—the most in MIAA history. Other strong teams include men's and women's lacrosse, men's swimming, women's basketball, and women's track and field. Hope College is a bitter rival, as is Alma College. Recreational and intramural sports attract roughly one-third of the students, and some of the most popular include canoeing, disc golf, basketball, volleyball, and indoor soccer.

At Albion College, professors are accessible and interested, academics are challenging without being overwhelming, and students feel supported and motivated. In the words of one senior, "Even though Albion is a small school in a rural town in Michigan, we want to make a big impact on the world and make our school known."

If You Apply To ›

Albion: Early action, rolling admissions. SATs or ACTs: required. Subject Tests: optional. Accepts the Common Application with supplement.

Alfred University

Alumni Hall, 1 Saxon Drive, Alfred, NY 14802

Talk about an unusual combination: Alfred combines a nationally renowned and state-supported college of ceramics, a school of art and design, an engineering program, and a business school wrapped up in a university of 1,600 undergraduates. The Finger Lakes is a region full of natural beauty, but it takes elbow grease to pry coastal types to the hinterlands of western New York.

Website: www.alfred.edu
Location: Rural
Private
Total Enrollment: 1,769
Undergraduates: 1,586
Male/Female: 52/48
SAT Ranges: ERW 490–610, M 500–600
ACT Ranges: 21–26
Financial Aid: 99%
Pell Grant: 45%
Expense: Pr $
Student Loans: 82%
Average Debt: $ $ $ $
Applicants: 3,566
Accepted: 63%
Enrolled: 19%
Grad in 6 Years: 53%
Returning Freshmen: 68%
Academics: ✏ ✏ ✏

With 1,600 undergraduate students, Alfred University isn't a bustling academic factory; it's a quiet, cloistered, self-described "educational village" in a tiny town wholly dedicated to the "industry of learning." The university boasts highly respected programs in art and design, as well as ceramic engineering. Innovation not only shapes the curriculum, but also has a profound effect on campus life. Small classes and friendly competition support this diversity while encouraging individuals to succeed. Along with being able to handle the academic rigors of the college, students also have to weather brutal winters that dump snow by the foot on the region.

Alfred's campus consists of a charming, close-knit group of modern and Georgian brick buildings, along with a stone castle. The Kanakadea Creek runs right through campus, and the town of Alfred consists of two colleges (the other is Alfred State College) and a main street with one stoplight. There are a few shops and restaurants, but certainly no malls, parking lots, or tall buildings. Notable campus facilities include the 36 kilns in Harder Hall and the five telescopes at the Stull Observatory. Recent additions to campus include a health and wellness center and a center for academic success.

> "Most teachers have high expectations, resulting in greater student performance."

The university and its students share a no-nonsense approach to education. Although prospective students apply directly to one of four colleges and declare a tentative major, half of all requirements for a bachelor's degree are earned in the liberal arts college. Requirements are quite different in each school. However, the mix usually includes coursework in oral and written communication, foreign language and culture, social sciences, history, literature, philosophy, and religion.

Alfred, though private, is actually the "host" school for the New York State College of Ceramics, which is a unit of the state university system and comes with a modest public university price tag. Ceramic engineering (the development and refinement of ceramic materials) is the academic cornerstone and the program that brings Alfred international recognition. All engineering programs are found within the Inamori School of Engineering, and there are degrees in renewable energy engineering and glass engineering science. The School of Art and Design's art department, with its programs in ceramics, glass, printmaking, sculpture, video, and teacher certification, is also highly regarded. The College of Business gets good reviews from students and provides undergraduates with work experience through a small business institute where students have real clients. Art and design majors are the most popular, followed by mechanical engineering, psychology, business administration, and accounting. The Track II program enables students to design their own interdisciplinary majors with personal guidance from top faculty members.

"I would say that Alfred is pretty competitive," says a junior. "The studio courses are challenging," adds a sophomore. Whatever their major, all students enjoy small classes, and the quality of teaching is reported as high. Most classes are taught by full professors, with graduate students and teaching assistants helping out only in lab sessions. "Most teachers have high expectations, resulting in greater student performance," says one junior. Alfred's academic advising and career planning services stress the university's commitment to helping undergrads plan their future. Through the new APEX (Applied and Experiential Learning) program, juniors and seniors can apply for up to $1,000 in funding to help offset costs associated with pursuing hands-on experiences like internships, apprenticeships, study abroad, and research positions. Faculty-led study abroad programs are offered during the May term and spring break, in addition to hundreds of exchange and affiliate programs, but only 2 percent of students study internationally. About 75 percent do research, many with the support of Alfred Research Grants for Undergraduate Students.

Alfred students are "creative and like to be challenged," says a business administration major. Eighty-two percent of the students at Alfred are from New York State, and 2 percent are international. African Americans comprise 10 percent of the student body, Hispanics 8 percent, Asian Americans 2 percent, and multiracial students 3 percent. Forty-five percent of freshmen are Pell-eligible, a notable number for a school of Alfred's size. Outstanding students can apply for many merit scholarships, averaging $12,100. There are no athletic scholarships.

"Alfred University will prepare you to go into the real world."

Eighty-five percent of students live on campus, and no one seems to mind the three-year residency requirement because the rooms are large and comfortable, and the dorms are equipped with lounges, kitchens, and laundry facilities. Upperclassmen have a choice of dorms that are co-ed by floor with single rooms, suites, or apartments. Freshmen enjoy their own housing divided into doubles. The school has two dining halls, and students say the offerings include plenty of selections for vegetarians and vegans. "The dining facilities are very nice and well equipped, and the food is both diverse and edible," says a junior. Campus security is good, according to most students. "AU security will provide rides or walking escorts if you feel unsafe walking alone," a biology major says.

Alfred's location in the Finger Lakes region, almost two hours from Buffalo and an hour and a half from Rochester, is isolated. The other chief complaint is the chilly, snowy weather. Social life is difficult due to the rural atmosphere and lack of Greek organizations, but the Student Activities Board brings many events

(continued)

Social: ☎ ☎ ☎
Q of L: ★ ★ ★
Admissions: (800) 541-9229
Email Address: admissions@ alfred.edu

Strong Programs:
Ceramic Engineering
Art and Design
Mechanical Engineering
Psychology
Business Administration
Renewable Energy Engineering
Glass Engineering Science

Ceramic engineering is the academic cornerstone and the program that brings Alfred international recognition.

Juniors and seniors can apply for up to $1,000 in funding to help offset costs of hands-on experiences like internships and study abroad.

to campus, including musicians, comedians, lecturers, and movies. Alfred is a dry campus, and students say the alcohol policy is largely respected and enforced in the dorms. "Alfred doesn't have too many problems with drinking that I have heard of," a student says. Because the university shares the town with Alfred State College, the dominant student population makes Alfred a good college town and "a very close community," observes a biology major. About a quarter of Alfred students volunteer in the community. The downtown scene provides students with an adequate number of movie theaters and eateries. Every spring brings the annual Hot Dog Weekend, a big carnival-like event that fills Main Street with game booths, bands, and lots of hot dog stands.

Alfred's Division III Saxons are ominous opponents on the football, soccer, and lacrosse fields. The equestrian team is competitive too. Many Alfred students are skiing, hunting, camping, and rock-climbing enthusiasts, and favorite road trips include Letchworth and Stony Brook state parks, as well as Ithaca, Rochester, Buffalo, and Toronto. Intramurals and club sports draw about a third of the students, with soccer, basketball, and handball being most popular.

"Alfred University will prepare you to go into the real world," says a freshman. Although small and somewhat secluded, Alfred University is a good choice for those students who want to concentrate on the ABCs of arts, business, and ceramic engineering—just be sure to bundle up for the long, snowy winters.

Overlaps

St. John Fisher, Hartwick, Nazareth, Clarkson, Elmira, SUNY–Buffalo, Rochester Institute of Technology, SUNY–Geneseo

If You Apply To ›

Alfred: Early decision, regular decision. SATs or ACTs: required. Subject Tests: optional. Accepts the Common Application with supplement. Applicants to School of Art and Design must submit portfolio.

Allegheny College

520 North Main Street, Meadville, PA 16335

An unpretentious cousin to more well-heeled places like Dickinson and Bucknell. Draws heavily from the Buffalo-Cleveland-Pittsburgh area. The college's powerhouse athletic teams feast on Division III competition. A robust Greek system gives Allegheny a strong traditional college life. If you've ever wondered what lake-effect snow is, you'll find out here.

Website: www.allegheny.edu
Location: Small City
Private
Total Enrollment: 1,748
Undergraduates: 1,748
Male/Female: 46/54
SAT Ranges: ERW 580–670, M 560–650
ACT Ranges: 23–29
Financial Aid: 99%
Pell Grant: 37%
Expense: Pr $ $
Student Loans: N/A

Allegheny College is a down-to-earth Eastern liberal arts school boasting a rich history of academic excellence in an intimate setting. Administrators here understand the importance of providing students with real-world experience to complement their classroom work, and the school places a special emphasis on the development of oral communication skills. A May term offers time for internships or other off-campus work and study, and a commitment to civic responsibility has spurred several new programs. Allegheny's small size means students don't suffer from lack of attention, and despite the heavy workload, anyone struggling academically will get help before the situation becomes dire.

> "[Professors] understand that my learning is different from other students'."

Allegheny's 80-acre campus is tucked away in Meadville, Pennsylvania, 90 miles north of Pittsburgh. Founded in 1815 and nestled in the Norman Rockwell–esque rolling hills of northwestern Pennsylvania, the campus is home to traditional architecture and redbrick streets, as well as newer additions such as apartment-style housing for upperclassmen. A nationally acclaimed science complex supports already strong programs, and the college also owns a 283-acre research reserve and an 80-acre protected forest. The 40,000 square-foot Vukovich Center for Communication Arts is home to rehearsal and instructional areas, video production facilities, and a large performance space.

Allegheny offers 30 majors and 41 minors, and all students are required to complete at least one minor in addition to their major. The college operates on two 15-week semesters each year, and each features an Academic Programming Day: classes do not meet and students participate in a variety of college-sponsored programs, including open houses and advising and career counseling workshops. Allegheny's curriculum requires all students to complete at least one course in each of eight distribution areas: civic learning; human experience; international and intercultural perspectives; modes of expression; power, privilege, and difference; quantitative reasoning; scientific process and knowledge; and social behavior and institutions. Freshmen take two first-year seminars that help them transition to college-level work and develop writing and speaking skills. Sophomores take a communication-focused seminar, juniors take a seminar in their major field, and seniors complete an intensive capstone project in their major, where they are required to orally defend a work of independent research.

> **"People stay on campus on the weekends to hang out, since we all live here."**

The school's strongest programs include environmental science and sustainability, economics, physical and biological sciences, and international studies (which offers a track in Middle Eastern and North African studies). Biology, economics, psychology, and communication enroll the most students. There is a major in biochemistry, a minor in environmental writing, and a new major in business. Co-op programs include 3–2, 3–3, and 3–4 options leading to degrees in engineering, public policy and management, nursing, physician assistant studies, occupational therapy, medicine, pharmacy, and dentistry.

The workload at Allegheny can be tough, but a senior says, "You are surrounded by deeply motivated students who make academics fun and interesting, and that takes off some of the intensity." Students praise Allegheny's faculty for their passion, knowledge, and accessibility. "All the professors I've had take my success very seriously, and understand that my learning is different from other students'," comments an economics major. You won't find a TA at the lectern in any Allegheny classroom, and 73 percent of courses have fewer than 20 students. The college's honor code allows students to take unproctored exams.

The Allegheny Gateway works with students to coordinate internships, study abroad, community service, and undergraduate research, and the school encourages students to have multiple experiences in these areas. "The people working in the Gateway offices are helpful and have a great network established," says a junior. Off campus, Allegheny offers study in several U.S. cities and more than 20 countries, as well as semester internships and field-based research opportunities. Twenty-four percent of students partake in some type of international experience. There's also an on-campus independent study option, and a three- or four-week Experiential Learning term in May that allows students to pursue short-term study abroad programs and internships that aren't available during the year. More than 100 students receive funding each summer to participate in faculty-guided research. In addition to a fledgling honors program, there are 14 national honor society chapters on campus.

Forty-six percent of Allegheny's students hail from Pennsylvania, and sizable contingents come from nearby Ohio, New York, and New England. Three percent

(continued)

Average Debt: N/A
Applicants: 5,114
Accepted: 68%
Enrolled: 14%
Grad in 6 Years: 75%
Returning Freshmen: 81%
Academics: ✍ ✍ ✍
Social: ☎ ☎ ☎
Q of L: ★ ★ ★
Admissions: (800) 521-5293
Email Address: admissions@ allegheny.edu

Strong Programs:
Environmental Science and
    Sustainability
Economics
Physical Sciences
International Studies
Biology
Psychology
Communication
Biochemistry

All students are required to complete at least one minor in addition to their major.

of students are international. "Students at Allegheny are not only very friendly, but willing to learn and to take chances," says one senior. African Americans make up 9 percent of the student population, Hispanics 9 percent, Asian Americans 3 percent, and multiracial students 4 percent. Politically, the school "veers heavily left," says a sophomore, and while there are occasional demonstrations for social justice, they're "nothing too extreme." Merit scholarships averaging $21,600 are available but there are no athletic awards. An impressive 37 percent of incoming first-years are eligible for Pell Grants.

The Experiential Learning term in May allows students to pursue short-term study abroad programs and internships.

Allegheny students live on campus for all four years, a requirement that a senior says "helps build community but also means that people live in a dorm room longer than they may want to." Options include all-freshman dorms, co-ed and single-sex halls, small special-interest houses, and apartment-style housing for juniors and seniors. Students are mostly satisfied with their on-campus food choices and note that the school is working to provide more vegetarian and vegan options. "Students have really been the driving force behind educational programming on sexual assault," says a sophomore.

According to a senior, "People stay on campus on the weekends to hang out, since we all live here"—and because school policies allow alcohol on campus for those of age. Greek organizations draw 26 percent of the men and 24 percent of the women, and provide a great deal of nightlife, but students don't characterize

"Students are encouraged to explore their unusual combinations of interests, skills, and talents."

Allegheny as a party school. There are two campus theater series, free movies in the quad, and comedians, hypnotists, slam poets, and live bands provided by the Office of Student Leadership and Involvement. Homecoming, Greek Sing, Wingfest in the fall (featuring free wings), and Springfest (a day full of bands, activities, and food) break up the monotony of studying, and midnight breakfasts served by faculty help ease end-of-semester stress. As for Allegheny traditions, there's the somewhat suspect "13th Plank" ritual, which states that all freshman women must be kissed on the 13th plank of the campus bridge by an upperclassman, in order to be considered "true Allegheny co-eds." Of course, a group of freshman men steal the plank every year at the beginning of the first semester to prevent that from happening.

Large-scale philanthropic events like Make a Difference Day and the Month of Service, in March, are particularly popular.

Downtown Meadville is a 10-minute walk from campus and worlds away from a college town, although a junior points out that "there are some hidden gems, including great restaurants, a movie theater, and a bowling alley." It also has several community playhouses, as well as schools, hospitals, children's homes, animal shelters, and other organizations that benefit from the more than 60,000 hours of service students contribute each year. "We've really gotten to know the local businesses and take pride in supporting our local community," says an English major. Large-scale philanthropic events like Make a Difference Day and the Month of Service, in March, are particularly popular. When students hit the road, they usually venture to factory outlets in nearby Grove City, Pennsylvania, or toward the bright lights of Pittsburgh, Erie, or Cleveland. Nearby state parks, Conneaut Lake, and Lake Erie offer waterskiing and boating in warm weather and cross-country skiing in the winter.

Overlaps

College of Wooster, Denison, Dickinson, Franklin & Marshall, Gettysburg, Penn State, University of Pittsburgh, Juniata

Athletics play a big role in Allegheny life, and the Wise Sport and Fitness Center gives students looking to break a sweat reason to cheer. About a quarter of Allegheny students compete in Division III athletics, and the Gators field 21 varsity teams, including new field hockey and men's lacrosse teams debuting in the 2019–20 season. Women's soccer is competitive, and men's and women's cross-country are recent conference champions. Fifteen percent of students participate in club and intramural sports, with rugby, ice hockey, basketball, and soccer drawing the most interest.

Allegheny boasts a rich history of academic excellence in an intimate setting, augmented by a growing emphasis on extracurricular experiences designed to produce well-rounded alumni. The campus's natural beauty and the genuine affection students feel for it and for each other remain unchanged. What's more, students appreciate the value placed on individuality and involvement. "Students are encouraged to explore their unusual combinations of interests, skills, and talents," says one junior. "The word 'no' is not often used here."

If You Apply To ›

Allegheny: Early decision I and II, early action, regular decision. SATs or ACTs: optional. Subject Tests: optional. Accepts the Common Application with supplement.

Alma College

Alma, MI 48801-1599

The college that put the "Alma" back in "alma mater." As friendly a campus as you'll find, Alma savors its Scottish heritage and combines the liberal arts with distinctive offerings in health and preprofessional fields. Students are socioeconomically diverse, but few out-of-staters enroll. If central Michigan eventually makes you stir-crazy, join the hordes who go abroad. Bring your bagpipes.

A tiny gem on Michigan's lower peninsula, Alma College was founded in 1886 by Presbyterians with an ambitious fourfold mission: "To prepare graduates who think critically, serve generously, lead purposefully, and live responsibly as stewards of the world they bequeath to future generations." Located in the city dubbed "Scotland, USA," the college puts its strong Scottish heritage on display. "Every spring, the city of Alma holds an annual Highland Festival that draws participants from all over the world," explains an environmental health major. "Our marching band also wears traditional Scottish kilts to every football game." Alma has a wide array of choices for its undergraduates, including distinctive offerings in health and preprofessional fields, as well as plenty of opportunities to learn abroad.

Alma's campus features 27 Prairie-style buildings of redbrick and limestone surrounding a scenic central mall. Although Alma was founded more than 130 years ago, most of the buildings have been built or renovated in recent years. There are lots of trees and open places to sit, at least in the warmer months. A recent upgrade to the Hogan Center added 12,000 square feet of fitness space and a new lab for the integrative physiology and health science department.

The Alma experience begins with Orientation Week, a freshman-only week of activities that help students get to know each other and ease the transition into college; students also begin their First-Year Seminar classes during this week. A peer mentoring program places successful upper-class students in contact with new students to help them adapt to the opportunities and expectations of the Alma community. To graduate, students must satisfy general education requirements, including the First-Year Seminar and 12 credits in each of three divisions: humanities, social sciences, and natural sciences. Students must also demonstrate proficiency in a second language or international awareness. Students accepted to the

> "The city of Alma holds an annual Highland Festival that draws participants from all over the world."

Website: www.alma.edu
Location: Small Town
Private
Total Enrollment: 1,371
Undergraduates: 1,371
Male/Female: 43/57
SAT Ranges: ERW 520–630, M 510–600
ACT Ranges: 20–27
Financial Aid: 99%
Pell Grant: 34%
Expense: Pr $
Student Loans: 80%
Average Debt: $ $ $
Applicants: 4,728
Accepted: 64%
Enrolled: 13%
Grad in 6 Years: 68%
Returning Freshmen: 77%
Academics: ✑ ✑ ✑
Social: ☎ ☎ ☎
Q of L: ★ ★ ★
Admissions: (800) 321-2562
Email Address: admissions@alma.edu

(continued)

Strong Programs:
Integrative Physiology and
    Health Science
Education
Biology
Psychology
Business Administration
Nursing
Communication
New Media Studies

four-year Presidential Honors Program complete a two-credit honors seminar for each of their first two years, followed by an honors thesis or research project their junior and senior years.

The college offers 41 majors, of which biology, nursing, communication, and new media studies are some of the strongest. Alma's most popular majors, by student enrollment, are integrative physiology and health science, education, biology, psychology, and business administration. A number of health-related preprofessional tracks are available, ranging from dentistry and optometry to physical therapy and sports medicine, in addition to preprofessional programs for engineering and law. A major in neuroscience was recently added. Students interested in the Scottish arts find a range of opportunities to work with nationally known instructors of bagpipe and Highland dance, or to join in seminars offered by award-winning Scottish authors.

According to a psychology major, the academic atmosphere is "relaxed, but the workload is busy." Another student adds, "The Counseling and Wellness Center at Alma is a great resource for anyone who may need extra support, especially in times of stress." Two-thirds of classes have fewer than 20 students, and many of them incorporate service-learning opportunities. During the one-month spring term, students enroll in a single intensive course, many of which involve off-campus study; in recent courses, students have studied social change in China, explored marine organisms in Hawaii, and volunteered in schools and hospitals in Peru. Undergraduate research is big at Alma too, and 41 percent of students pursue an independent project under a professor's guidance or join faculty projects. "Your professors double as your advisors, which allows you to build great relationships with them," explains a communication major.

> **"Your professors double as your advisors, which allows you to build great relationships with them."**

Alma's student-centered philosophy is exemplified by the Alma Commitment, which offers a promise that students will graduate on time (within four or four and a half years, depending on the major) and a pledge that each interested student can undertake an experiential learning opportunity, such as an internship, research fellowship, or study abroad. Participating students receive up to $2,500 in Alma Venture funding. Despite Alma's small size and rural surroundings, the terms "provincial" and "insular" just don't apply here. International study is highly encouraged, and 34 percent of students go abroad. Fittingly, Alma has a study abroad partnership with the University of Aberdeen in Scotland, along with programs in 15 other countries, such as Austria, India, Italy, and New Zealand. Additionally, the Posey Global Leadership Initiative funds 15 fellowships each year for students to participate in international internship, research, and leadership experiences. "I've been on five continents in the past four years thanks to this program, and each time I was able to give back to the community I went to," enthuses an environmental science major.

"Alma students are extremely involved, hardworking, dedicated to helping others, and caring," says one junior. The campus is largely homogeneous, with 91 percent of the student population coming from Michigan and 2 percent from abroad. African Americans account for 3 percent, Asian Americans 2 percent, Hispanics 5 percent, and multiracial students 3 percent of the student population. There is more to be said for socioeconomic diversity: 34 percent of freshmen are eligible for Pell Grants. While not an overly political campus, Alma does have its fair share of activists; personal rights and diversity concerns top the list of hot issues. Brainy types can vie for merit scholarships worth an average of $21,800; there are no athletic scholarships.

Eighty-eight percent of Alma's students reside on campus, and the college has invested $21 million in remodeling and modernizing the residence halls. Freshmen

Students can work with nationally known instructors of bagpipe and Highland dance or award-winning Scottish authors.

are assigned rooms in co-ed halls, while upperclassmen play the lottery and usually get suites; students report that with larger incoming classes, overcrowding is starting to become a concern. Other options include an international house, a Model UN house, and a Women's Resource Center. For meals, students go to the all-you-can-eat Commons or Joe's Place, a snack bar, but the food gets poor reviews. "If I don't have to, I don't eat it," says a biology major. Students say they feel safe on campus, but a senior notes that there has been "a strong push for greater emphasis on and enforcement of Title IX."

When it comes time to socialize, the Alma College Union Board provides plenty of on-campus fun. "We offer music performances, movie nights, speakers, student panels, and tons of events in the dorms," says a senior. Twenty-two percent of the men and 18 percent of the women go Greek. Parties at Greek houses are registered and monitored by security officers who scan IDs and distribute wristbands; students say these policies help keep underage drinking in check.

Alma's Model UN team has received top recognition at the National Model UN Conference in NYC for a record 22 consecutive years.

Town/gown relations at Alma are strong, with the vast majority of students volunteering, taking part-time jobs, and otherwise getting involved in the community. One student says, "Alma is a very small city, and does not offer too much to do outside of campus," other than a movie theater and a few restaurants. The annual Highland Festival features traditional Scottish games, bagpipers, and dancing; for members of the Alma marching band, who strut in kilts stitched from the school's own registered Alma College tartan, every performance might as

"I've been on five continents in the past four years thanks to [the Posey Global Leadership Initiative]."

well be a festival. Students with wheels will find diversions within easy reach, as Mount Pleasant, Saginaw, and the East Lansing campus of Michigan State are less than an hour away, and ski slopes are just a bit farther. In the warmer months, the beaches of two Great Lakes, Huron and Michigan, are two hours away.

The Alma Scots compete in Division III as a member of the Michigan Intercollegiate Athletic Association, the oldest existing athletic conference in the nation. Alma offers 25 varsity sports—12 each for women and men, plus competitive cheer—and the most popular include football, wrestling, women's soccer, and softball. For nonvarsity types, there is an active intramural program—about half of the students participate. Alma's Model United Nations team has received top recognition at the National Model UN Conference in New York City for a record 22 consecutive years (1997 through 2018), the longest streak of any college or university.

Alma challenges students to take their learning beyond the classroom and around the globe, and with caring faculty—and ample funding for off-campus experiences—students feel supported every step of the way. While students enjoy their school's warm, inviting atmosphere, they're also eager to venture out, explore, and pursue their goals. But no matter where their futures take them, for Alma alumni, bagpipes will always sound like home.

Overlaps

Hope, Kalamazoo, Albion, Augustana (IL), Gustavus Adolphus, College of Wooster, Grand Valley State, Michigan State

If You Apply To ›

Alma: Rolling admissions. SATs or ACTs: required. Subject Tests: optional. Accepts the Common Application with Alma supplement.

3400 South 43rd Street, P.O. Box 343922, Milwaukee, WI 53234

At last, a college that evaluates students on what they can do rather than how well they can memorize. Forget oval-blackening; students here show mastery in their chosen fields. Practical and hands-on, Alverno gives its all-female and economically diverse students the real-life experience necessary to succeed beyond graduation.

Website: www.alverno.edu
Location: City Outskirts
Private
Total Enrollment: 1,324
Undergraduates: 1,026
Male/Female: 0/100
SAT Ranges: N/A
ACT Ranges: 17–22
Financial Aid: 99%
Pell Grant: 72%
Expense: Pr $
Student Loans: 89%
Average Debt: $ $ $ $
Applicants: 610
Accepted: 78%
Enrolled: 42%
Grad in 6 Years: 42%
Returning Freshmen: 71%
Academics: ✍ ✍ ✍
Social: ☎
Q of L: ★ ★ ★ ★
Admissions: (414) 382-6100
Email Address: admissions@
  alverno.edu

Strong Programs:
Business and Management
Nursing
Psychology
Biology
Professional Communication
Education
Music Therapy

If you're the type of student who obsesses over your GPA, take heed: at Alverno College, you can forget about earning an A. That's because this Roman Catholic, women's liberal arts college emphasizes ability-based learning instead of letter grades. While its roots go back to 1887, Alverno came into its own in the 1970s with its distinctive approach to learning and, unlike other educational innovations of that era, has found a continuing niche. The student body is diverse—in age, background, and religion—and the learning environment is highly collaborative, though the ability-based method can "create a lot of work requiring much thought," says a professional communication major.

Alverno is located in a quiet residential area of Milwaukee. The parklike 46-acre campus is just 15 minutes from downtown and a 10-minute walk from shops and restaurants. The Sister Joel Read Center houses 73,000 square feet of science labs, multimedia production space, and computer facilities. Alexia Hall features a high-tech nursing simulation center, art and dance studios, classrooms, private study rooms, and a student commons area.

Alverno students are required to show mastery in eight key abilities: communication, analysis, problem solving, valuing in decision making, social interaction, developing a global perspective, effective citizenship, and aesthetic engagement. Students move through interdisciplinary progressive levels toward a degree by being "validated" in these areas. For example, a course in sociology might contribute to validation in communication and social interaction, as well as in

> "Students are extraordinarily driven, and they know what it takes to succeed in the real world."

making independent value judgments. The college offers detailed feedback rather than traditional letter grades, and faculty find innovative, "real-life" ways to assess students' mastery of subject matter and specific abilities. First-year students take an orientation seminar and introductory courses in the arts and humanities, science, psychology and social science, communication, and math. Religious studies aren't required, but for those who seek it, a Catholic liturgy is available. Students are also required to participate in off-campus, credit-bearing internships through one of the country's longest-standing, highly acclaimed internship programs.

"The level of professionalism that Alverno students have compared to those at other colleges or universities is amazing," one junior says. Alverno's business and management program is well established and among the most popular majors, along with nursing, psychology, and biology. Students praise the professional communication, teacher education, and music therapy programs as well. New majors are available in biomedical sciences, health education, and social work. Many professors at Alverno teach all levels of classes, so the quality of teaching is consistent throughout a student's college career, and regular academic advising keeps students on track. With an average class size of under 20 students and a low student/faculty ratio, students have easy access to faculty. "The faculty and staff really care whether you are successful," says a social science major. "They want to see you achieve and are willing to go [above] and beyond to make sure you do." Alverno also boasts a dedicated Career and Professional Development Center that provides career planning and job search assistance to students and alumnae, including frequent networking and on-campus recruiting events with employers. "We couldn't have more help," one junior says. Seventeen percent of Alverno students study abroad, often heading out on short, 10- to 14-day trips that complement a semester-long course.

"Students are extraordinarily driven, and they know what it takes to succeed in the real world," says a junior. Ninety-three percent of Alverno undergraduates hail from Wisconsin, and more than a quarter are above the age of 24; there are few international students. Alverno is one of the most inclusive and diverse colleges in the state, particularly socioeconomically: 72 percent of freshmen are eligible for Pell Grants. African Americans comprise 13 percent of the student body, Hispanics 27 percent, Asian Americans 6 percent, and multiracial students 4 percent. One-third of students are Catholic. Students and faculty often engage in roundtable discussions to look at political or social issues, according to a sophomore. Merit scholarships are awarded based on a personal evaluation of each incoming student.

Students are required to participate in off-campus internships through one of the country's longest-standing internship programs.

A three-day orientation program serves freshmen, transfer, resident, and commuter students. The majority of students are commuters, though dorm rooms house 16 percent of students, who say the residence halls offer clean, spacious rooms with fully equipped lounges, laundry, and cooking facilities available on each floor. "Dorms are comfortable and well maintained every day, including weekends," says one junior. Male visitors are allowed, but they must sign in and be out by midnight on weekdays. Events like Love Your Body Week and Denim Day promote student wellness and prevention of sexual violence.

"Milwaukee is a thriving city of the arts."

Dozens of cultural, dance, theater, and other student groups are active on campus, and the school has an on-site childcare center and a fitness center. But most of the social life takes place off campus at local clubs, bars, restaurants, coffee shops, and nearby colleges. "Milwaukee is a thriving city of the arts—visual, theatrical, and performance—not to mention the festivals that go on every year," says one art education major. In addition to a Performing Arts Center, free outdoor concerts, and ethnic festivals, the city also offers professional sports teams, parks, and shopping centers. Students look forward to Alverno's annual homecoming festivities, and Community Day, which allows students and faculty to participate in an annual day of service.

More than a quarter of Alverno undergraduates are above the age of 24.

Alverno competes in Division III athletics, including basketball, cross-country, golf, soccer, softball, tennis, and volleyball. The Inferno tennis and basketball teams have been the most successful programs, having set school records for wins. An informal intramural program occasionally offers activities like kickball and board-game tournaments.

Attending a school like Alverno promises an experience far afield in some ways from the traditional college world. The emphasis on real-world applications builds confidence in one's actual ability to perform, rather than the ability to score an A. Students and faculty are often on a first-name basis from the start and build relationships that help students find their "own unique style of learning," one senior says. It's a method that obviously works.

Overlaps
UW–Milwaukee, Mount Mary University, Carroll University, Cardinal Stritch

If You Apply To ›

Alverno: Rolling admissions. SATs or ACTs: required (ACT preferred). No Subject Tests. Does not accept the Common Application.

4400 Massachusetts Avenue NW, Washington, D.C. 20016-8001

If the odds are against you at Georgetown and you can't see yourself on GW's ultra-urban campus, welcome to American University. The allure of AU is simple: Washington, D.C. American has a nice campus in a nice neighborhood with easy access to the Metro and endless internship opportunities. American is smaller—and now more selective—than GW.

Website: www.american.edu

Location: City Outskirts

Private

Total Enrollment: 10,296

Undergraduates: 7,169

Male/Female: 37/63

SAT Ranges: ERW 610–690, M 570–660

ACT Ranges: 26–30

Financial Aid: 80%

Pell Grant: 18%

Expense: Pr $ $

Student Loans: 61%

Average Debt: $ $ $ $

Applicants: 18,699

Accepted: 29%

Enrolled: 32%

Grad in 6 Years: 79%

Returning Freshmen: 90%

Academics: ✍ ✍ ✍ ½

Social: ☎ ☎ ☎

Q of L: ★ ★ ★

Admissions: (202) 885-6000

Email Address: admissions@american.edu

Strong Programs:

Political Science and Government

International Studies

Business Administration

Communication Studies

Journalism

Public Health

Politics, Policy, and Law

Located just a few miles from our country's seat of power, American University is a breeding ground for the next generation of reporters, diplomats, lobbyists, and political leaders who will shape domestic and international policy. Alongside these eager buzzhounds is a host of students who take advantage of AU's strong programs in the arts, sciences, and business, and who recognize that Boston and New York City are not the only good urban destinations for college students. "American University is a diverse, pulsing, and dynamic school driven by some of the best faculty, staff, scholars, and students in the world," a senior says. Thanks to phenomenal internships, a comfortable location, and a strong international focus, AU continues to attract students from around the world.

AU's 84-acre residential campus is located in the northwest corner of Washington, D.C., in an upscale (and safe) area that's just minutes from downtown; free shuttle buses transport students to the nearby Metro (subway) station. There's a mix of classical and modern architecture. Flower gardens line the parking lots, and the quad has numerous sitting areas for reflection and study. The 70,000-square-foot, environmentally friendly School of International Service building is LEED Gold–certified. In 2018 AU became the first university in the United States to achieve carbon neutrality.

AU's core curriculum, introduced in 2018, aims to develop students into "effective citizens" and lifelong learners. First-years begin by taking Complex Problems, a small-group seminar focused on analyzing a special topic, and a yearlong AU Experience sequence that acclimates them to university life. In addition to coursework in writing, math or statistics, and diversity, students fulfill Habits of Mind requirements that cover five areas, ranging from ethical reasoning to creativity and aesthetics. Finally, all students complete a capstone course or project in their major. The core still leaves plenty of time for students to study abroad—choosing from more than 150 programs in more than 40 nations—or participate in an internship or co-op facilitated by the school's relationships with hundreds of private, nonprofit, and government institutions. The school also uses these connections in its Washington Semester program, which combines academic seminars with internships and career guidance, attracting a wide range of majors. Fifty-five percent of AU students study abroad and 91 percent complete internships.

> **"AU is more of an academic community, rather than a pressure cooker."**

In the classroom, says a public health major, the atmosphere is supportive: "AU is more of an academic community, rather than a pressure cooker." AU has outstanding programs in political science and government, international studies, business, communication studies, and journalism. In all, students may choose from nearly 70 programs and have the option to design their own interdisciplinary major. Three-year bachelor's degree programs are available in international studies, public health, and politics, policy, and law. Half of all classes taken by undergraduates have fewer than 20 students, and teaching assistants do not teach classes. "Professors are more than willing to help you and are open to questions and available for office hours," cheers one sophomore. An honors program offers a select group of about 25 entering students small seminars, special sections of many courses, and designated floors in the residence halls, plus specialized research or creative work in their major.

"Students at AU are smart, compassionate, politically aware, and driven to make the world a better place," a senior says. AU prides itself on drawing students from every state and approximately 125 foreign countries: 89 percent of undergrads are from states outside D.C. and another 8 percent hail from outside the U.S. "AU is a very international campus," observes one senior. Seven percent of undergraduates are African American, 14 percent are Hispanic, 7 percent are Asian American, and 4 percent are multiracial. A relatively high proportion—nearly two-thirds—are women. Not surprisingly, AU is politically active—after all, this is Washington, D.C. "If you aren't into politics in the slightest, it can be a bit frustrating to navigate the school socially," cautions a senior. The university offers hundreds of merit scholarships averaging $14,200 and has reallocated much of its financial aid to assist more financially needy students; 160 athletic scholarships are available as well.

More than two-thirds of AU students live in campus housing, which is guaranteed for the first two years. Students report that the quality of housing varies, but three new residence halls, Congressional, Continental, and Federal, opened in 2017. Living/ learning options are available for first-years and come highly recommended, including the two-year Community-Based Research Scholars program, which involves opportunities for service-oriented research. Campus dining receives mixed reviews, but one student comments, "It's really easy to eat healthy here." A journalism major says, "Campus police are present, friendly, productive, and trustworthy," and educational programming on personal wellness and preventing sexual assault is extensive.

"If you aren't into politics in the slightest, it can be a bit frustrating to navigate the school socially."

A good deal of the social life at AU revolves around campus-related functions, many of which are organized by the student government. A student says, "From political speakers to comedy groups and musical performances, students can always find something to do." Nine percent of the men and 11 percent of the women go Greek, and a psychology major notes, "Greek organizations are the only source of parties." The AU campus is officially dry, and most students take that seriously. The immediate area around AU has restaurants and shops, but you need to get a bit farther away for true nightlife over in Dupont Circle or Georgetown. D.C. offers ample entertainment, much of it free—the art house movie theaters, gallery openings, pro soccer games, museums and monuments, and funky live music. "You just jump on the Metro to get anywhere in the city," says a communication major. Each year, Family Weekend brings games, rides, and popular bands to campus, along with a carnival on the quad. Another annual favorite is the Founder's Day Ball, a formal dance held at a museum or other location in downtown D.C. Popular road trips include Baltimore, Williamsburg, Richmond, and the Ocean City shore.

Although there's no football, the American University Eagles compete in Division I athletics. Students are particularly enthusiastic about the men's basketball team, which has won the Patriot League conference championship multiple times, as have women's basketball, volleyball, and field hockey. Games against Bucknell, Holy Cross, and the Naval Academy highlight the schedule. Roughly 28 percent of students take part in 22 intramural and 28 club sports, ranging from flag football and badminton to cycling and sailing, which are divided into different levels of competitiveness.

First-years take Complex Problems, a seminar focused on analyzing a special topic, and a yearlong AU Experience sequence.

Ninety-one percent of AU students complete internships with hundreds of private, nonprofit, and government institutions.

Overlaps
Boston College, Johns Hopkins, Georgetown, Syracuse, Fordham, Boston University, George Washington, Northeastern

AU is heaven on earth for C-SPAN junkies. But even if you are not addicted to following current events, AU and Washington, D.C., are still a top combo for a rich college life. The opportunities for real-world experience—in fields ranging from business to international studies to political science—are outstanding. But AU is small enough to keep students from feeling lost in the fast-paced world inside the Beltway. As a junior explains, "We are a small campus, which gives the feeling of being out of the city, yet the city is at our fingertips."

If You Apply To ›

American: Early decision I and II, regular decision. SATs or ACTs: optional. No Subject Tests. Accepts the Common Application with supplement.

Amherst College

Amherst, MA 01002

Original home to the well-rounded, superachieving, gentle-person jock. Compare to Williams, Middlebury, and Colby. Not Swarthmore, not Wesleyan. Amherst has always been the king in its category—in part because there are four other major institutions in easy reach to add diversity and depth. Among the few liberal arts colleges with as many men as women. Leader among elite privates in seeking socioeconomic diversity.

Website: www.amherst.edu
Location: Small Town
Private
Total Enrollment: 1,836
Undergraduates: 1,836
Male/Female: 51/49
SAT Ranges: ERW 720–770, M 710–790
ACT Ranges: 32–34
Financial Aid: 57%
Pell Grant: 20%
Expense: Pr $ $ $ $
Student Loans: 29%
Average Debt: $
Applicants: 9,285
Accepted: 13%
Enrolled: 39%
Grad in 6 Years: 95%
Returning Freshmen: 96%
Academics: ✍ ✍ ✍ ✍ ✍
Social: ☎ ☎ ☎
Q of L: ★ ★ ★ ★
Admissions: (413) 542-2328
Email Address: admission@amherst.edu

Amherst offers a dynamic curriculum in the traditional academic disciplines and in numerous interdisciplinary fields. There are no core curriculum or distribution requirements, so students choose their program based on their own individual interests and plans for the future. Indeed, students' focus isn't on racking up high grade point averages, but rather on becoming people who base their thinking on a strong foundation in the liberal arts. Emphasizing "freedom to explore," the spotlight here is on learning. "If your education is really your first priority," says a sophomore, "then I don't think there's a better school."

Amherst's 1,000 acres overlook the picturesque town of Amherst and the Connecticut River Valley and offer a panoramic view of the Holyoke Range and the Pelham Hills. On campus, a plot of open land housing a wildlife sanctuary and a forest shares space with academic and residential buildings, athletic fields, and facilities. Amherst looks like a college is supposed to look, with trees and paths winding through the buildings to offer long, contemplative walks. While Amherst's predominant architectural style remains 19th-century academia—redbrick is key—everything from a "pale yellow octagonal structure to a garish, modern dorm" can be found here. The college recently completed a $242 million makeover of the east side of campus that included the construction of four new residence halls and the 255,000-square-foot, interdisciplinary Science Center.

> **"Amherst professors are what gives this place its life."**

To graduate, students must take a first-year seminar, declare a major at the end of sophomore year, and satisfy all major program requirements. First-year seminars, limited to 15 students and occasionally taught by two or more professors, help foster interdisciplinary approaches across topics and are offered in several subject areas. Thirty-nine percent of students choose to undertake a yearlong senior honors thesis in their major.

The most popular of Amherst's 40 majors include economics, mathematics, psychology, English, and history. More than a third of students pursue double majors, and a few overachievers even triple major. Students may create their own courses of study from Special Topics classes if the subject of their interest is not available. Amherst's unique Law, Jurisprudence, and Social Thought program is not a prelaw major; instead, it's an interdisciplinary study of the law, drawing on fields as diverse as psychology, history, philosophy, and literature, with a strong theoretical focus. New majors include Latinx and Latin American studies and classical civilization. Amherst's membership in the Five College Consortium means that students can also take courses from partner schools Hampshire, Mount Holyoke, UMass Amherst, and Smith, a benefit that significantly expands students' options.

The academic climate at Amherst is intense, but on such a small campus, the classroom environment is supportive and interaction with faculty is encouraged. "Amherst professors are what gives this place its life," says a computer science and environmental studies major. "They will play a huge part in your time here." Students also praise the college's robust career services. "The career center has a program called Pathways where students are matched by interests with alumni for mentor relationships," says a sociology major.

Amherst's commitment to academic flexibility extends beyond traditional coursework. "There's an initiative going on called Being Human in STEM, where students and faculty are looking at reconfiguring the way STEM courses are taught to students from marginalized cultural and socioeconomic backgrounds, to best meet their needs," says a senior. Students report that, with no graduate students around, it's easy to get involved with faculty research as early as your first semester. Forty-eight percent of students spend a semester or year abroad, choosing from 250 programs in dozens of countries. Amherst also has a sister university in Göttingen, Germany, and another in Kyoto, Japan, where one of the college's colonial-style buildings has been duplicated.

Emphasizing "freedom to explore," Amherst has no core curriculum or distribution requirements.

"Everyone at Amherst is a motivated go-getter," says an economics major. Only 12 percent of Amherst students hail from Massachusetts, and 9 percent are international. The student body is notably diverse; 14 percent are Asian American, 13 percent are Hispanic, 11 percent are African American, and 5 percent are multiracial. A linguistics major says, "Amherst is a politically active campus with **"Everyone at Amherst is a motivated go-getter."** the loudest voices being liberals. While other views are not silenced, they are sometimes drowned out." Admissions is need-blind, and all financial aid is awarded based on need, meaning no merit or athletic scholarships. Amherst guarantees to meet 100 percent of admitted students' demonstrated financial need with loan-free financial aid packages, which has helped attract a substantial number of low-income and Pell-eligible students. Financial aid extends to study abroad programs as well.

Housing at Amherst is guaranteed for four years, and 97 percent of students live on campus. "First-year students live together in seven dorms on the First-Year Quad, which is really good for community-building," says a sophomore. Those who don't want to take their chances with the room draw can participate in a lip-synch competition; the winner receives the top room pick for his or her class. Everyone who lives on campus, and anyone else who wants to, eats in Valentine Hall, which includes a buffet-style central serving station and five dining rooms. Much of the produce comes from Book and Plow, the on-campus farm, but students give the meals lukewarm reviews. Students agree that the campus feels safe, and a Black studies major comments, "There is definitely a culture here of sexual respect, and in instances where that culture is breached, the college takes swift action."

Although frats are nothing more than a faint memory, social activities are conducted almost entirely on campus. They range from dorm study breaks to club

Amherst has a sister university in Göttingen, Germany, and another in Kyoto, Japan.

events to low-key gatherings. Students report a sizable rift in the social landscape: "We have a pretty notorious athlete/nonathlete divide on campus that does have an effect on the social scene here," says a history major. Sports teams host most of the parties, but one student says a ban on hard alcohol and other restrictions have made the party scene "somewhat lacking." The Powerhouse, a building that originally served as a campus steam plant at the turn of the century, was recently converted into a nightlife venue for live performances, dances, movie screenings, art exhibits, pub nights, and other special events. Although some students bemoan the lack of campus traditions, seasonal festivals including Spring Weekend and Farm Fest are popular. Students also take advantage of the Five Colleges membership for social life and cultural events.

The town of Amherst is "small but charming," says a sophomore, with a few coffee shops, bars, and late-night dining options. The nearby city of Northampton offers more in the way of restaurants, concerts, and nightlife. Students take part in community service projects, such as Big Brothers Big Sisters and Habitat for Humanity, and the college funds roughly 150 summer public service internships every year. For the many outdoorsy types, good skiing in Vermont is not far, and Boston (an hour and a half) and New York (a little over three hours) are close enough to be convenient road-trip destinations.

> "First-year students live together in seven dorms on the First-Year Quad, which is really good for community-building."

Sports are taken seriously, both varsity and intramurals, and "impact" athletes are said to get favored treatment from the admissions office. The school has removed its century-old unofficial mascot, "Lord Jeff," due to controversy surrounding its historical associations and introduced a new mascot, the Mammoth. Amherst competes in Division III, but the strong baseball team takes on Division I opponents as well. Women's basketball won back-to-back national championships in 2017 and 2018, and men's cross-country and baseball have brought home recent New England Small College Athletic Conference titles. Any showdowns with "Little Three" archrivals Williams and Wesleyan are inevitably the biggest games of the season, drawing fans from all corners of campus. Amherst's intramural and club programs are also well supported.

"People carry themselves very seriously here, and that in itself creates a culture of pressure to succeed and achieve," remarks one sophomore. Yet the lack of restrictive requirements, a cadre of professors who are focused on teaching, and a devoted alumni network make it clear why most students love their institution. Says a junior, "The Amherst community goes far beyond your years on campus."

Overlaps

Williams, Middlebury, Colby, Yale, Brown, Harvard, Princeton, Stanford

If You Apply To ›

Amherst: Early decision, regular decision. SATs or ACTs: required (SAT essay or ACT writing recommended). Subject Tests: optional. Accepts the Common Application with supplement.

Yellow Springs, OH 45387

Part social activist, part granola, and part anarchist with plenty of none-of-the-above mixed in, Antioch is a haven for square pegs. After shutting its doors for three years, Antioch is now back in business and offering its signature co-op program: academic study interspersed with 11-week work experiences. March and protest to change the world, then get a job. Cool.

Antioch has long been the poster child for the funky diversity that characterizes U.S. higher education. Since its founding in 1852 by abolitionist and social reformer Horace Mann, this small liberal arts college in the Ohio boondocks has nurtured outspoken and socially aware students who thrive under the rigors of refreshingly nontraditional education. In 1902 Antioch pioneered the concept of co-op education, in which students alternate time in the classroom with jobs in the "real world."

The college was forced to shut its doors in 2008 because of inept management, but in 2011 it reopened, phoenix-like, thanks to loyal alumni and others unwilling to allow Antioch's signature approach to education to become a footnote to history. As it grapples with inevitable enrollment and financial challenges, Antioch is relying on a new generation of pioneers—students included—to reinvent the college for the 21st century.

Antioch is located in the progressive village of Yellow Springs (population 3,700), which has grown up around the college and become a popular destination for weekend tourists, thanks to its restaurants, art, and music. The campus is a mixture of traditional and eco-friendly buildings in various states of repair, including the giant Main Hall that looks like Hogwarts. The campus includes

"Our shared governance is pivotal to Antioch."

a working farm and dozens of geothermal wells and abuts the 1,000-acre Glen Helen Nature Preserve that serves both hikers and science students looking for field experience. The Wellness Center, which boasts a six-lane swimming pool and is open to the public, was recently renovated to the tune of $8.5 million as part of Antioch's new business strategy of generating revenue by leasing land and building rental units.

The academic climate is informal and collaborative, with most everyone called by their first name, but the overall atmosphere is hardly laid-back. "Because we are on an 11-week quarter system, we do the same amount of work that most people do in a semester," explains a psychology major. "Then there's the workload of helping to run a new college. That can be very mentally taxing."

Classes tend to be discussion-based, and take-home tests are common. The faculty is highly regarded but small, which means that turnover can be a problem. "A department can go from rock solid to extremely fragile in a matter of weeks," says a junior. Antioch's general education program includes a core curriculum with distribution requirements and two capstone experiences, starting with a series of major-related courses that culminate in original research or some sort of creative work or performance. Seniors also write a Senior Reflection Paper integrating their educational experiences in and out of the classroom over the previous four years.

Rather than selecting preset majors, all Antioch students design their own degree plans, picking and choosing courses from broad areas that suit their academic interests and needs. Environmental science is Antioch's strongest academic area, and students also praise the biomedical and other sciences. "We have well-equipped labs and do a lot of sustainability projects, such as learning about climate change,

Website: www.antiochcollege.edu

Location: Small Town

Private

Total Enrollment: 133

Undergraduates: 133

Male/Female: 38/62

SAT Ranges: N/A

ACT Ranges: 23–29

Financial Aid: 99%

Pell Grant: 59%

Expense: Pr $

Student Loans: 24%

Average Debt: $

Applicants: 152

Accepted: 97%

Enrolled: 13%

Grad in 6 Years: 56%

Returning Freshmen: 58%

Academics: ✍ ✍ ✍

Social: 🍺 🍺 🍺

Q of L: ★ ★ ★

Admissions: (937) 319-6082

Email Address: admission@antiochcollege.edu

Strong Programs:
Environmental Science
Biomedical Science
Political Economy
Media Arts
Psychology

recycling, composting, and other things that would help save our planet," says a sophomore. Everyone agrees that political economy is both strong and demanding. Media arts and psychology are also popular. A peer mentoring program supports first-year and first-generation students, while Early Alert and First Watch programs ensure that students do not fall through the cracks. Career and other counseling services are said to be caring but understaffed. Antioch, which views itself as a laboratory for democracy, is governed by a Community Council. "Students, staff, and faculty get elected and make important decisions for our school. Our shared governance is pivotal to Antioch," says one denizen.

In 1902 Antioch pioneered the concept of co-op education, in which students alternate time in the classroom with jobs in the "real world."

Under Antioch's flagship co-op program, students engage in full-time cooperative education experiences, generally off campus, for three or four quarters throughout their time at the college. "By the time you graduate, you have four amazing jobs on your résumé," gushes a sophomore. Each student is assigned a co-op advisor to help with the nearly continuous job hunt, which is eased by Antioch's extensive network of alumni. The downside: with students constantly coming and going, it is sometimes hard to maintain friendships and engage in extracurricular activities. Antioch has no study abroad program, but about 10 percent of students do co-ops in foreign countries.

Antioch students tend to be independent spirits. "We're all self-motivated and driven," says a freshman. "We're weirdos and proud." Sixty-two percent of students are women, and a hefty 59 percent of freshmen are eligible for Pell Grants. Hispanics make up 14 percent of the student body, African Americans 10 percent, Asian Americans 4 percent, and multiracial students 10 percent. The student body is geographically diverse, with 63 percent coming from out of state, but rural Ohio is an unlikely destination of choice for many minority students, and there are no international students. "It's an adjustment, especially if you're coming from a diverse area," says a junior, who adds, "Our campus is almost entirely 'liberal' with a mixture of Marxists, Democrats, and Socialists. There are maybe two Republicans in the student body." The college offers a handful of merit scholarships, but most financial aid is need-based.

> **"We're all self-motivated and driven. We're weirdos and proud."**

Rather than selecting preset majors, all Antioch students design their own degree plans.

Antioch operates a single dining facility with an all-or-nothing meal plan—19 meals a week or cook for yourself—and much of the food is supplied by local farmers and the student-staffed campus farm. That means, as a junior points out, that "Students can work on the farm and later eat their work." Students are required to live on campus in one of two residence halls or apartments until they are within a year of graduation. "There is no trouble finding housing," says a freshman. "Everything is very comfortable." Antioch was the first college to have a Sexual Offense Prevention Policy (SOPP) mandating verbal consent at every step of a sexual encounter, and entering students receive SOPP training during orientation. "We were famously mocked for it on SNL, but the rest of the country has slowly been following along," notes a political economy major.

In the absence of Greek organizations, social life tends to be rather low-key. "There's hiking, movies, two bars, and plenty of art and music events to attend both on campus and off," says a history major. Other diversions include the Camelot bike ride and quarterly dances before students head off on their co-ops. Dayton is 30 minutes away, Columbus and Cincinnati one hour. All sports at Antioch are intramural.

Antioch College is happily back on its feet but showing some growing pains. "We lose a lot of students due to the stressful environment," says a junior. "I think once we understand our institutional personality and promote it we will have better retention rates." For many students, however, Antioch's search for an updated

Overlaps

Hampshire, Marlboro, Warren Wilson, Evergreen State, Bennington, Earlham, College of the Atlantic, New College of Florida identity for the 21st century is part of what makes the place exciting. "Almost every person here has a different idea of what Antioch needs to be," observes a psychology major. "A perk of coming here is that you get to lend your hand in deciding what that will be."

If You Apply To ›

Antioch: Early decision I and II, rolling admissions. SATs or ACTs: optional. No Subject Tests. Accepts the Common Application. Application includes option to indicate gender identity.

University of Arizona

1200 East University Boulevard, Tucson, AZ 85721

Tucson is an increasingly popular academic destination, and it isn't just because of the UA basketball team. A large and highly regarded honors college attracts top students, as do excellent programs in the sciences, engineering, and business. Generally viewed as a cut above ASU in academic quality. Now offering tuition discounts to out-of-staters. Bring plenty of shorts and sunscreen.

With a campus that's encircled by mountain ranges and the beautiful Sonoran Desert, lined with palm trees and cacti, and set against a backdrop of stunning Tucson sunsets, it's no surprise that students at the University of Arizona love to hang out at the Mall. Not the shopping center, mind you—but a huge grassy area in the middle of campus where 36,000 Wildcats gather between classes. Judging by numbers alone, that's enough people to fill a medium-sized town. But students are quick to point out that the UA has a strong sense of community. "I always see familiar and friendly faces around the Mall," says a senior. With all the natural beauty that surrounds them, many Wildcats simply purr through four satisfying years.

Architecturally, the UA campus distinguishes itself from the city's regiment of adobe buildings with a design that seems a study in the versatility of redbrick. Old Main, the university's first building, is into its second century, but others verge on high-tech science facilities. A $28 million aerospace and mechanical engineering building has a state-of-the-art subsonic wind tunnel and rocket-combustion test facility. Eager shutterbugs can pore through photographer Ansel Adams's personal collection at the first-rate Center for Creative Photography. The Student Recreation Center is LEED Certified, and the recently completed Environment and Natural Resources 2 Building, featuring sustainable solutions like rainwater harvesting and low-flow faucets, is designed to look like a desert slot canyon.

> **"I always see familiar and friendly faces around the Mall."**

Arizona has 20 colleges and more than 100 undergraduate majors. Under the general education curriculum, students take 10 courses, one of which must have a diversity emphasis, that fall under the broad categories of arts, humanities, traditions and cultures, natural sciences, and individuals and societies. Almost everyone gets a healthy dose of freshman composition, math, and foreign language. Sciences are unquestionably the school's forte—the astronomy department is among the nation's best, helped by those clear night skies. Students have access not only to leading astronomers, but also to the most up-to-date equipment, including a huge

Website: www.arizona.edu
Location: City Center
Public
Total Enrollment: 36,263
Undergraduates: 29,701
Male/Female: 47/53
SAT Ranges: ERW 540–650, M 560–690
ACT Ranges: 21–28
Financial Aid: 85%
Pell Grant: 26%
Expense: Pub $ $ $
Student Loans: 54%
Average Debt: $
Applicants: 33,608
Accepted: 84%
Enrolled: 21%
Grad in 6 Years: 64%
Returning Freshmen: 83%
Academics: ✍ ✍ ✍ ½
Social: ☎ ☎ ☎ ☎
Q of L: ★ ★ ★ ★
Admissions: (520) 621-3237
Email Address: admissions@ arizona.edu

Strong Programs:
Astronomy
Architecture

(continued)

256-inch telescope operated jointly by the university and the Smithsonian. The small but rigorous College of Architecture, Planning, and Landscape Architecture is a national leader in sustainable planning for arid regions. Programs in biomedical engineering, optical sciences, nursing, entrepreneurship, business management, and retailing and consumer science are particularly well regarded, and the English and history departments are also standouts. Additionally, Arizona offers the nation's first undergraduate B.A. in law degree.

Academic competition, according to most students, is left up to both the individual and the specific course or area of study. "Our courses can be rigorous and give us a tough workload, but those are the classes that serve us best because we gain the most hands-on experience," comments a retailing and consumer science major. Some freshman courses are taught by graduate students, and 43 percent of all classes enroll fewer than 20 students. "Most of my professors are very well versed in their fields and continue to do research," says one student. Students also praise the THINK TANK tutoring program that operates out of several academic buildings and residence halls for academic support.

Arizona's Office of Student Engagement and Career Development helps connect students with real-world learning experiences, whether through courses that involve experiential learning components or through out-of-classroom opportunities like internships, fieldwork, and research or service projects. The Honors College offers one of the nation's largest and most selective honors programs, serving more than 5,500 students. In addition to offering a variety of honors courses, the college features smaller classes, personalized advising, special library privileges, and great research opportunities. The Undergraduate Biology Research Program also has a national reputation. For those seeking new vistas, there are study abroad programs available in more than 60 countries; 4 percent of undergrads take part.

> **"Most of my professors are very well versed in their fields and continue to do research."**

"The vast majority of UA students are outgoing and openhearted," says one student. Despite—or possibly because of—tougher admissions standards, the administration cites a sharp increase in freshman applications over the past few years, especially from out-of-staters, who constitute 31 percent of the undergraduate student body; another 7 percent hail from foreign countries. Hispanics account for 27 percent, African Americans 4 percent, Asian Americans 5 percent, and multiracial students 5 percent. A diversity action council, a student minority advisory committee, and cultural resource centers help promote positive race relations. A senior reports that, with a mix of political views on campus, activism is not unheard of but is "always respectful and peaceful." Twenty-six percent of students qualify for Pell Grants. Merit scholarships averaging $8,000 and hundreds of athletic scholarships are available to qualified students. Arizona also guarantees that incoming students' tuition and fees won't increase for four years.

A junior says the quality of residence halls is "all over the board," but all are generally well maintained: "Dorms range from brand new with every amenity to a 1920s women-only dorm with sleeping porches that's a historical landmark." Only 20 percent of undergraduates live in the dorms; some freshmen and most older students flock to the abundant and inexpensive apartments near the school. Several restaurants are located in the student union and sprinkled around campus, and although options are varied, some students complain that there aren't enough healthy choices. "UA has an initiative called 'I Will,' which emphasizes consent and aims to prevent sexual assault," explains a sophomore. "It is well known on campus and students seem to take the issue seriously."

> *Students praise the THINK TANK tutoring program that operates out of several academic buildings and residence halls for academic support.*

> **"Tucson is a hippie town and offers a different local vibe and a fun atmosphere for a college town."**

Despite the high percentage of off-campus residents, students stream back to campus on weekends for parties, sports, and cultural events. Five percent of the men belong to fraternities, and 10 percent of the women join sororities. The campus is technically alcohol-free, though some question whether the frats have realized that yet. "Tucson is a hippie town and offers a different local vibe and a fun atmosphere for a college town," says a junior. Students enjoy Tucson's shops, restaurants, bars, and various dance clubs, not to mention easy access to hiking and other outdoor activities. Phoenix is less than two hours away. One of Arizona's most time-honored traditions is Spring Fling, said to be the largest student-run carnival in the country. On Dead Day, the day before final exams begin, the university offers free snacks and stress-relieving activities like yoga, meditation, and coloring, and seniors have been known to relax by jumping into the Old Main fountain after midnight and splashing around—a ritual that may or may not be related to preceding hours of drinking.

The university is home to 500 athletes who compete in 17 sports as a member of the Division I Pac-12 Conference. The Wildcats women's golf team won the national championship in 2018, while the men's basketball team took home the conference title in 2017 and 2018. Football and baseball enjoy national prominence and provide great weekend entertainment, especially when the opposing team is big-time rival Arizona State. As one Wildcat points out, "Every time we play against ASU in any sport, there are T-shirts, stickers, and people asking, 'A-S-who?'" Arizona's battle cry, "Bear Down!"—frequently heard at sporting events—dates back to 1926, when a campus football hero, fatally injured in a car crash, whispered his last message to his teammates: "Tell them, tell the team to bear down." More than ninety years later, the enigmatic slogan still appears all over campus.

The University of Arizona offers a wide variety of academic opportunities along with spectacular weather. Prospective students are warned to honestly evaluate how that will affect their ability to concentrate. "Professors and advisors urge us to get involved in any way possible and get as many experiences as we possibly can under our belts before we finish our four years," says a marketing major. Indeed, the UA is a place to go in pursuit of knowledge, experience, and a good tan.

Arizona guarantees that incoming students' tuition and fees won't increase for four years.

Overlaps

UC Davis, UCLA, University of Florida, U of I at Urbana–Champaign, University of Iowa, Arizona State, Michigan State, Ohio State

If You Apply To ›

Arizona: Rolling admissions. SATs or ACTs: optional (required to be considered for merit scholarships and admission to engineering, nursing, architecture, and Honors College). Subject Tests: optional. Accepts the Common Application with supplement.

Arizona State University

Box 870112, Tempe, AZ 85287

ASU is the largest university in the nation—with ambitions to grow even larger, enhance interdisciplinary applied research, and increase socioeconomic diversity. Location in the Valley of the Sun attracts plenty of out-of-staters who like the idea of seeing the sun every day. Administration's relentless emphasis on growth makes the professional schools and Barrett, The Honors College, the best bets. Strong student support services.

Arizona State University has transformed itself over the last decade into the nation's largest public university. With no pretense of modesty, this mega-university, situated in a desert oasis that is one of the nation's fastest-growing metro areas, describes itself as the model for a New American University—one where "massive innovation" is the norm and where an interdisciplinary culture is seen as the best means of developing "world-changing ideas." ASU's stated goal is to serve any Arizona student qualified for college-level work and, in the process, it has become a national model of how to navigate the emerging demographics of U.S. higher education. Research spending is up, as are student retention and graduation rates. Not surprisingly, ASU can seem overcrowded and overwhelming at times, but it provides motivated students who can find a manageable niche with countless opportunities for work and play.

The most populous of ASU's four locations, the Tempe campus offers a beautiful blend of palm-lined walkways and contemporary urban architecture. It is home to the College of Liberal Arts and Sciences and engineering. Fifteen minutes by light rail brings you to the Downtown Phoenix campus, which looks like it sounds. It houses journalism, nursing, and public service programs and has a young professionals feel. The Polytechnic campus, a converted Air Force base, specializes in science and technology and boasts a desert arboretum, while West campus has the feel of a liberal arts learning community, with a large central lawn and a focus on interdisciplinary, collaborative studies. Each of the four campuses has a Pat Tillman Veterans Center, which brings together academic and student support services that serve the university's continually growing enrollment of veterans and their dependents—currently more than 3,000 undergraduate and graduate students. The new Greek Leadership Village, housing more than 950 students, and adjacent Greek Leadership Community Center opened on the Tempe campus in 2018.

> "[Many professors are] excited and passionate about what they do."

The academic star at ASU is Barrett, The Honors College, a selective school-within-a-school that serves more than 7,200 students from every school and college across all four campuses. The overwhelming majority of participants reside in a cloistered complex on the Tempe campus that was designed by students, faculty, and staff working with nationally renowned architects. It features multiuse classrooms and meeting spaces, a dining hall, a fitness center, numerous outdoor courtyards, and a central amphitheater. The nation's first four-year residential honors college within a major public university, Barrett has more than 40 dedicated faculty members who oversee students' ambitious honors projects.

ASU has 16 undergraduate schools and more than 350 undergraduate programs. Regardless of major, all students must fulfill distribution requirements that include courses in three awareness areas: global, historical, and U.S. cultural diversity. The most popular majors are in business, management, marketing, biological and biomedical sciences, social sciences, and engineering. The School of Sustainability emphasizes the study of land use and planning models that minimize environmental harm. The Walter Cronkite School of Journalism and Mass Communication enjoys state-of-the-art facilities and a growing national reputation, while the Herberger Institute for Design and the Arts features an innovative child drama program and nationally recognized majors in art, design, music, and dance. The sciences (including biochemistry, chemistry, geology, and biology) and social sciences boast first-class facilities, notably the largest university-owned meteorite collection in the world. The School of Earth and Space Exploration is a leading center for research in astronomy and astrophysics. Anthropology benefits from its association with the Institute of Human Origins' Donald Johanson, who

> "Sun Devils buckle down and focus on what needs to get done."

discovered the 3.2-million-year-old fossil skeleton named Lucy. ASU also offers the largest teacher preparation program of any university in the nation. Other unique, interdisciplinary options include majors in forensic science, innovation in society, and global management.

Engineering programs, especially microelectronics, robotics, and computer-assisted manufacturing, are sure bets; the facility for high-resolution microscopy allows students to get a uniquely close-up view of atomic structures. The Fulton Schools of Engineering, composed of six discipline-specific schools, has a presence on the Tempe and Polytechnic campuses and offers a traditional engineering education with an emphasis on designing and creating innovative and entrepreneurial solutions. Future engineers can opt for a B.S. degree or, for those with broader interests, a B.A. The Fulton Undergraduate Research Initiative provides engineering students with hands-on lab experience, independent and thesis-based research guided by faculty mentors, and travel to national conferences.

"It is mostly freshmen who choose to live on campus, but our dorms are so nice!"

Faculty members are expected to do both teaching and research, preferably with a practical emphasis. As one administrator explains, "We don't do 30-year longitudinal studies." And while, according to a geological sciences major, many professors are "excited and passionate about what they do," students say the university's emphasis on research can have a negative impact on the classroom experience when professors put their research first. Forty-three percent of undergraduate classes have fewer than 20 students, and one senior says the academic climate is "mostly relaxed, but focused." The university has made serious efforts to provide students with strong support services. The First-Year Success Center connects new students with upperclassmen and graduate students for weekly coaching sessions on topics like time management, finances, and health and wellness. Incoming freshmen who are undecided on a major participate in the Major and Career Exploration program, which involves seven-week courses offering opportunities for hands-on career exploration. ASU has drawn national attention for its innovative and patented eAdvisor system that keeps students on track to meet degree requirements and is backed up by a corps of full-time professional advisors. It also guarantees that students will find a place in any required course. The 9 percent of students who study abroad have access to more than 250 programs in more than 65 countries.

The academic star at ASU is Barrett, The Honors College, a selective school-within-a-school that serves more than 7,200 students.

"Sun Devils buckle down and focus on what needs to get done," says a senior. "We love to have fun, but we also love to succeed." Sixty-seven percent of ASU students are Arizona residents, while 10 percent come from abroad. Twenty-three percent of the undergraduate student body is Hispanic; African Americans contribute 4 percent, Asian Americans 7 percent, and multiracial students 4 percent. Students here can be divided in their politics, but a sophomore says that "classes embrace political discussion in a healthy manner." ASU offers merit scholarships averaging $8,600 to qualified students and awards more than 450 athletic scholarships annually to athletes in 24 sports. It also guarantees to meet the demonstrated need of any student from Arizona. One-third of incoming students qualify for the Pell Grant.

"ASU has an incredible amount of school spirit."

Only 21 percent of ASU students live in the co-ed dorms. "It is mostly freshmen who choose to live on campus, but our dorms are so nice! I've visited several other schools, and ASU has some of the largest rooms," says one junior. Students don't have to buy a meal plan, no matter where they live, which many say is a good thing. "Dining is subpar, with the exception being the honors dining hall, and that is still only average," grumbles one student. Some complain about the campus's "walk-only zones" that prevent students from using bikes (of which there are 14,000),

The First-Year Success Center connects new students with upperclassmen and graduate students for weekly coaching sessions.

skateboards, or other modes of transportation in certain high-traffic areas. Students say campus security is sufficient, and the Devils in the Bedroom student group helps promote awareness regarding sexual assault prevention.

"Sometimes I feel there is so much stuff going on that I have to pick between two or three things on a day or night or weekend," says one junior. "But, hey, that's a good problem to have!" ASU's Greek system attracts only 8 percent of the men and 12 percent of the women, and "small kick-backs in dorms are just as common as huge house parties," says a sophomore. The campus is officially dry, so many students head off campus on weekends—often far off campus. Many have cars, giving them access to the mountains of Northern Arizona, the lakes on the outskirts of town, and the natural beauty of the Grand Canyon. Tempe gets generally positive reviews from students. "It has great restaurants nearby, different shopping centers, and a street called Mill Ave that has stores, food, and bars/nightclubs for the 21-and-over set," says a communication major. Devils in Disguise, an annual, student-run day of service, sends students out to complete various volunteer projects in the community.

"ASU has an incredible amount of school spirit," says a junior. Arizona State's Division I athletics department—supported by a fee required of all students—is consistently ranked among the nation's best, and the Sun Devil Fitness Complexes are first-rate. Men's wrestling won its second consecutive Pac-12 Conference title in 2018, and men's and women's basketball reached their respective national tournaments. Baseball, softball, and women's golf are also competitive. Teams are known as the Sun Devils after a meteorological phenomenon, and the biggest rival is the University of Arizona, normally referred to simply as "that school down south."

Arizona State may seem like an overwhelmingly big school with a reputation for rowdiness, but that's not the full story. "ASU has gotten away from its party school reputation in recent years," says a senior. To its credit, ASU likes to pride itself on how many students it accepts, not how many it turns away, and on its strong student support services. Despite common college complaints ("Parking, parking, parking!"), the university gives students much to appreciate. For those not intimidated by its sheer immensity, ASU may be a good place to earn a degree while enjoying a four-year relationship with the sun.

ASU guarantees to meet the demonstrated financial need of any student from Arizona.

Overlaps

UCLA, Michigan State, University of Minnesota, Ohio State, UT Austin, University of Arizona, Northern Arizona, San Diego State

If You Apply To ›

Arizona State: Rolling admissions. SATs or ACTs: optional (required for merit-based scholarship consideration and some majors). Subject Tests: required for some programs. Accepts the Common Application.

University of Arkansas

200 Hunt Hall, Fayetteville, AR 72701

University of Arkansas rates in the second tier of Southern public universities alongside Alabama, LSU, and Ole Miss. Though conservative by national standards, Fayetteville is progressive by those of Arkansas. With traditional strength in agriculture, U of A has also developed programs in business, engineering, and other professional fields. Its most popular program takes the field on Saturday afternoons in the fall.

The flagship public institution for the state of Arkansas, the University of Arkansas is a nationally competitive, student-centered research institution. Freshman class enrollment has increased 75 percent in the last 10 years, and the university has grown to keep pace. A $300 million cash gift from the family of Walmart founder Sam Walton—one of the largest ever made to an American public university—created the undergraduate Honors College and endowed the graduate school. More recently, a $120 million gift from the Walton Family created the School of Art.

The Arkansas campus is nestled among the mountains, lakes, and streams of the Ozarks, in the extreme northwest corner of the state. "Come to a Razorback game in the fall when the leaves are changing," says one student, "and you will be totally won over." The community is friendly and safe, and the moderate climate means recreational opportunities abound. Architectural styles range from modern concrete to buildings that date from the Depression. The center of campus is the stately brick Old Main, which once housed the entire university. Recent construction includes the Art and Design District and the Brewer Family Entrepreneurship Hub.

> "Even if you aren't in a Greek organization, chances are you're attending something put on by one."

Established as a land grant institution in 1871, with agricultural and mechanical roots, U of A serves more than 20,300 undergraduates and includes 10 colleges, as well as more than 50 research and outreach centers. U of A's core requirements include credits in English, history, math, humanities, fine arts, science, and social sciences. The more than 3,500 undergrads who join the Honors College complete research or creative work culminating in an honors thesis; the College awards more than $1 million in research and study abroad grants each year. The Walton College of Business offers two of the most popular majors on campus: marketing and finance. Other popular disciplines here include engineering, nursing, kinesiology, social sciences, biology, and English, particularly creative writing. The Bumpers College of Agricultural, Food, and Life Sciences includes the Center of Excellence for Poultry Science, a national leader in research on poultry epidemiology. The Jones School of Architecture and Design's architecture program is also notable.

Students are quick to point out that U of A's academic climate is "laid-back, but still demanding a high standard of excellence," says a senior. To help ease into the college transition, students recommend ROCK Camp, an optional summer orientation weekend, as well as the tutoring services of the Center for Learning and Student Success. While there is a healthy portion of large, TA-taught lecture classes, 48 percent of classes enroll fewer than 20 students. Professors are said to be knowledgeable and accessible. Undergraduates in all disciplines are encouraged to conduct research, and about a third do so, often with generous funding. "Getting involved in campus research is very easy and often just requires talking to an enthusiastic professor with room in their lab," says a biology major. Study abroad programs are available in 26 countries across six continents; 15 percent participate.

"U of A is a very accessible school for students, which means it has people from diverse walks of life," explains a childhood education major. Fifty-one percent of undergraduates are Arkansas residents, while 3 percent are international. African Americans make up 4 percent of the student body, Hispanics 9 percent, Asian Americans 2 percent, and multiracial students 4 percent. Students tend to lean right, and although there are pockets of politically engaged students, a senior calls the political climate "very mild." Arkansas awards thousands of merit scholarships each year, averaging $5,200. There are also roughly 400 athletic scholarships available in 19 varsity sports. Additionally, the New Arkansan Non-Resident Tuition

Website: www.uark.edu
Location: Small City
Public
Total Enrollment: 22,068
Undergraduates: 20,399
Male/Female: 47/53
SAT Ranges: ERW 560–640,
    M 550–640
ACT Ranges: 23–29
Financial Aid: 41%
Pell Grant: 19%
Expense: Pub $
Student Loans: 47%
Average Debt: $ $
Applicants: 21,715
Accepted: 66%
Enrolled: 35%
Grad in 6 Years: 62%
Returning Freshmen: 82%
Academics: ✑ ✑ ✑
Social: 🎭 🎭 🎭 🎭
Q of L: ★ ★ ★
Admissions: (479) 575-5346
Email Address: uofa@uark.edu

Strong Programs:
Marketing
Finance
Engineering
Nursing
Kinesiology
Social Sciences
Biology
Poultry Science

The Center of Excellence for Poultry Science is a national leader in research on poultry epidemiology.

The New Arkansan Non-Resident Tuition Award gives scholarships to incoming students from neighboring states.

Award gives scholarships to incoming students from neighboring states with GPAs of 3.30 or higher and ACT scores of at least 24.

Roughly one-quarter of all undergrads at Arkansas live in the residence halls; most move to Greek houses or other off-campus digs after their first year. About 250 students participate in the nine living/learning community options. Campus dining is described as adequate. Campus police are said to be effective, and a presence at Greek parties.

Arkansas's Greek chapters attract 21 percent of the men and 38 percent of the women, and Greek parties are the most visible outlet for weekend social life, aside from the revelry that accompanies Razorback football and basketball. "Even if you aren't in a Greek organization, chances are you're attending something put on by one," notes a sophomore. School-sponsored Cardinal Nights offer alternative programming on Fridays, and students look forward to the annual Springtime of Youth music festival. Dickson Street, the main drag in the town of Fayetteville (population 84,000), is full of restaurants and bars that are popular with upperclassmen; the town also offers drive-in movies, live music at local clubs, and touring Broadway shows at the Walton Arts Center. Students are big on community service, especially through programs like Full Circle Campus Food Pantry, Make a Difference Day, and Hogs Care Week. Those with cars will find Dallas, Tulsa, Oklahoma City, Memphis, and St. Louis all within a six-hour drive.

"No matter the time, place, or situation, it is always considered appropriate to call the hogs."

Varsity teams are the Razorbacks (wild hogs), and the beloved Hog Call "Wooo! Pig sooie!" rings out during football and basketball weekends, although according to one senior, "No matter the time, place, or situation, it is always considered appropriate to call the hogs." Red Razorback logos are all over town—on T-shirts, napkins, book covers, license plates, and on game day, the cheeks of ecstatic fans. Powerhouse teams include men's and women's track and field and golf, men's baseball, and women's gymnastics. Recreational sports are hugely popular and include everything from flag football and sand volleyball to ballroom dance and bass fishing.

At the University of Arkansas, "Everyone is friendly, and we love our campus a lot, which creates a sense of unity and belonging," says a sophomore. This kind of Southern hospitality means poultry science students aren't the only ones flocking to Arkansas for a solid education at a bargain price. Northerners may feel out of their element, and those who frown on football should keep their feelings to themselves. But all students here look forward to graduation day, when their names will join forever those of 186,000 other alumni, etched into the nearly four-mile network of sidewalks on campus.

Overlaps

University of Oklahoma, Louisiana State, University of Missouri, University of Nebraska–Lincoln, Iowa State, Texas A&M, Texas Tech, UT Austin

If You Apply To ›

Arkansas: Early action, rolling admissions. SATs or ACTs: required. No Subject Tests. Does not accept the Common Application.

Atlanta University Center

Atlanta is viewed as the preeminent city in the country for bright, talented, and successful African Americans. It became the capital of the civil rights movement in the 1960s—a town described by its leaders as "too busy to hate."

At the heart of this extraordinary culture is the Atlanta University Center, the largest African American educational complex in the world, replete with its own central library and computer center. The four component institutions have educated generations of African American leaders. The Reverend Martin Luther King Jr. went to Morehouse College; his grandmother, mother, sister, and daughter went to Spelman College. Graduates spread across the country in a pattern that developed when these were among the best of the few colleges to which talented African Americans could aspire. Even now, when the options are almost limitless, alumni continue to send their children back for more.

The center consists of two undergraduate colleges (Morehouse and Spelman) and two offering graduate degrees (Clark Atlanta University and the Morehouse College of Medicine) on adjoining campuses in the center of Atlanta, three miles from downtown. Two other institutions, Morris Brown College and the Interdenominational Theological Center, are no longer members. Students at the affiliated schools can enjoy the quiet pace of their beautiful magnolia-studded campuses or plunge into all the culture and excitement of this most dynamic of Deep South cities. The six original schools—all but the medical school—became affiliated in 1929 using the model of California's Claremont Colleges, but the remaining members are fiercely independent. Each has its own administration, board of trustees, and academic specialties, and each maintains its own dorms, cafeterias, and other facilities. There is cross-registration among the institutions (Morehouse students, for example, go to Spelman for drama and art courses) and with Georgia State and Emory University as well. The governing body of the consortium, the Atlanta University Center, Inc., administers a centerwide dual-degree program in engineering in conjunction with Georgia Tech—and it runs campus security, a student crisis center, and a joint institute of science research. There is also a centerwide service of career planning and placement, where recruiters may come and interview students from all four institutions.

Dating and social life at the coeducational institutions tend to take place within the individual schools, though Morehouse, a men's college, and Spelman, a women's college, maintain a close academic and social relationship. The Morehouse–Spelman Glee Club takes its abundance of talent around the nation, and its annual Christmas concert on the Spelman campus is a standing-room-only event.

Morehouse and Spelman (see full write-ups) constitute the Ivy League of historically African American colleges. The following is a sketch of the other institution offering undergraduate degrees.

CLARK ATLANTA UNIVERSITY (WWW.CAU.EDU)

Formed by the consolidation of Clark College, a four-year liberal arts institution, and Atlanta University, which offered only graduate degrees, CAU is a comprehensive coeducational institution that offers undergraduate, graduate, and professional degrees. The university draws on the former strengths of both schools, offering quality programs in the health professions, public policy, and mass communications (including print journalism, radio and television production, and filmmaking). Graduate and professional programs include education, business, library information studies, social work, and arts and sciences. Undergraduate enrollment: 3,200.

Morehouse College

830 Westview Drive SW, Atlanta, GA 30314

Along with sister school Spelman, Morehouse is the most prestigious of the historically black schools. Alumni list reads like a *Who's Who* of African American leaders. Best known for business and popular 3–2 engineering program with Georgia Tech. Built on a Civil War battlefield, Morehouse epitomizes the new South.

Website: www.morehouse.edu
Location: City Center
Private
Total Enrollment: 2,088
Undergraduates: 2,088
Male/Female: 100/0
SAT Ranges: ERW 480–590,
  M 470–570
ACT Ranges: 18–23
Financial Aid: 82%
Pell Grant: 53%
Expense: Pr $
Student Loans: 80%
Average Debt: $ $ $
Applicants: 2,349
Accepted: 74%
Enrolled: 35%
Grad in 6 Years: 55%
Returning Freshmen: 84%
Academics: ✍ ✍ ✍
Social: ☎ ☎ ☎ ☎
Q of L: ★ ★ ★ ★
Admissions: (844) 512-6672
Email Address: admissions@
  morehouse.edu

Strong Programs:
Business Administration
Economics
Biology
Political Science
English
Cinema, Television, and
  Emerging Media Studies
Engineering

Founded in 1867, Morehouse College has the distinction of being the nation's only historically black, four-year liberal arts college for men. Top students come to Morehouse because they want an institution with a strong academic program and a culture that focuses equally on developing global leaders and fostering a sense of brotherhood among students. Notable alumni include the Reverend Martin Luther King Jr., Samuel L. Jackson, and Spike Lee. Says a psychology major, "Morehouse is a college of young, assertive, ambitious black men."

Located near downtown Atlanta, the Morehouse campus was built on 61 acres that were once a Civil War battlefield. The campus is home to 42 buildings, many of them historic, including the Martin Luther King Jr. International Chapel. The college has continued to evolve over the last decade, as it has enriched its academic program, conducted a successful national fund-raising campaign, increased student scholarships and faculty salaries, and improved its physical plant.

Morehouse's general education program includes not only coursework in four major disciplines (humanities, natural sciences, math, and social sciences), but also the study of "the unique African and African American heritage on which so much of our modern American culture is built." A cornerstone of that study is a scheduled series of campuswide assemblies called the Crown Forum, which brings in community leaders and national figures from an array of industries for special presentations, artistic performances, and dialogues on topical issues. Students must attend at least six Crown Forum events per semester for six semesters to graduate. The academic climate at the House can get intense: "Morehouse offers an academic structure that is both competitive and rigorous," states a freshman. Fifty-three percent of the classes have fewer than 20 students, and students say their classmates strive to be the best in the classroom but take time to support each other too. A sense of mentorship pervades the campus, and students consider the school's full breadth of counseling services to be quite strong.

> **"Morehouse offers an academic structure that is both competitive and rigorous."**

Undergraduate programs include the traditional liberal arts majors in the humanities and social and natural sciences, but as a rule of thumb, the more preprofessional your plan, the better Morehouse fits. While STEM fields have been traditionally strong at Morehouse, business and economics have risen in prominence and business administration is now the most popular major. Engineering, another popular choice, is actually a 3–2 program in conjunction with Georgia Tech and other larger universities. Many students major in economics, biology, political science, and English. The cinema, television, and emerging media studies major is growing, and a new major in Chinese studies is available. Notable minors include journalism and sports, sustainability, and neuroscience. Programs that receive less favorable reviews from students are art and drama, and the administration admits that some of the humanities offerings could use strengthening. A four-year honors program is available for the highly motivated, and research opportunities in the sciences abound, including a research partnership with NASA. Sixteen percent of students study abroad in more than 200 programs worldwide.

Seventy-one percent of Morehouse students come from outside the state, with the majority hailing from Southeast and Mid-Atlantic states; 1 percent come from other nations. Ninety-four percent are African American and one student attests, "Many students are here to get a greater understanding of their heritage and to promote it." One percent of students are Hispanic and 2 percent are multiracial; just over half are eligible for the Pell Grant. Morehouse now accepts transgender students who self-identify as male. Merit scholarships averaging $28,800 are available, in addition to 126 scholarships for athletes.

Research opportunities in the sciences abound, including a research partnership with NASA.

Students are required to live on campus for their first three years; seniors find their own off-campus accommodations. Some students grumble that campus housing is "too small" and "not well maintained." For freshmen, students recommend Graves Hall, the college's oldest building, constructed in 1889. Themed residential academic programs are available for students interested in the arts, business, global learning, and STEM. The meal plan at Morehouse is mandatory for

"Many students are here to get a greater understanding of their heritage and to promote it."

students living on campus and draws its share of complaints as well, although dining services has expanded recently to include fast-food options and a coffee shop.

Morehouse's membership in the Atlanta University Center expands students' academic, social, and extracurricular options, particularly with neighboring Spelman College. Homecoming week, for instance, is a joint effort with Spelman and is one of the nation's largest at a historically black college or university, with events like pep rallies, hip-hop and R&B concerts, step shows, and a jazz brunch drawing thousands of alumni and community members. Spelman women have been known to quip, "You can always tell a Morehouse man, but you can't tell him much." Morehouse's four fraternities, which sign up just 3 percent of the students, hold parties, though most students concur that "drinking is not a big deal here." Community service is an important emphasis, through student organizations as well as service-learning courses. Going out on the town in Atlanta is a popular evening activity, and on-campus football games, concerts, movies, and religious programs all draw crowds.

Homecoming week features pep rallies, hip-hop and R&B concerts, step shows, and a jazz brunch drawing thousands of alumni.

In its early years, Morehouse left much to be desired in the area of varsity sports, but the Maroon Tigers now compete well in the Division II Southern Intercollegiate Athletic Conference. The track and field team is a recent conference champion, and the basketball team has also enjoyed success, but it is the intramural program that allows students a chance to become the superstars they know are lurking within them. During football season, students road-trip to follow the games at Howard, Hampton, and Tuskegee universities.

Morehouse is well equipped to serve the contemporary heirs of a distinguished tradition. Morehouse students don't just attend Morehouse. They become part of a prominent and proud network of Morehouse Men who share the bonds of having had the Morehouse experience. Graduates find that alumni stand ready and willing to help them with jobs and other opportunities as they work to effect positive change in their communities and the world.

Overlaps

Spelman, Davidson, Furman, Millsaps, Rhodes, Howard, Clark Atlanta, Georgia State

If You Apply To ›

Morehouse: Early decision, early action, regular decision. SATs or ACTs: required. Subject Tests: optional. Accepts the Common Application. Accepts applications from students who live and self-identify as male.

Spelman College

350 Spelman Lane SW, Atlanta, GA 30314

Comparable to Wellesley in terms of academic excellence, Spelman is a historically black women's college that draws students from all corners of the country. Particularly strong in the sciences with noteworthy emphasis on undergraduate research. Wooded 42-acre Atlanta campus adjacent to brother school Morehouse offers easy access to urban attractions. Has dropped varsity sports to emphasize lifelong physical fitness.

Website: www.spelman.edu
Location: City Center
Private
Total Enrollment: 2,084
Undergraduates: 2,084
Male/Female: 0/100
SAT Ranges: ERW 550–625, M 520–590
ACT Ranges: 22–26
Financial Aid: 89%
Pell Grant: 48%
Expense: Pr $
Student Loans: 80%
Average Debt: $ $ $
Applicants: 8,344
Accepted: 40%
Enrolled: 16%
Grad in 6 Years: 75%
Returning Freshmen: 89%
Academics: ✍ ✍ ✍
Social: ☎ ☎ ☎ ☎
Q of L: ★ ★ ★ ★ ★
Admissions: (800) 982-2411
Email Address: admiss@spelman.edu

Strong Programs:
Biology
Psychology
Political Science
Economics
Mathematics
Engineering
Premed
African Diaspora Studies

As one of only two surviving African American women's colleges in the United States (the other is Bennett), Spelman College holds a special appeal for African American women seeking to become leaders in fields ranging from science to the arts. Students flock here for that something special that predominantly white institutions lack: a supportive environment with first-rate academics where African American women can develop self-confidence and leadership skills before venturing into a world where they will once again be in the minority. Says one student, "Spelman women walk their own path and always strive to be their absolute best in whatever they choose to do."

Spelman was founded in 1881 by Sophia B. Packard and Harriet E. Giles, two pioneers in women's education from New England who were concerned with the lack of educational opportunities for African American women. John D. Rockefeller was an early funder, and the school was named in honor of his wife, Laura Spelman Rockefeller, and her parents, who were longtime activists in the antislavery movement. Spelman was traditionally the starting point for teachers, nurses, and other African American female leaders. Today's emphasis is on getting Spelman grads into courtrooms, boardrooms, and engineering labs. Honing women for leadership is the main mission, and that nurturing takes place on a classic collegiate-green campus with a $367 million endowment.

These are heady times for Spelman. Although it finds itself competing head-on with the Seven Sisters and other prestigious and predominantly white institutions that are eager to recruit talented African American women, the college is holding its own. Spelman offers a well-rounded liberal arts curriculum that emphasizes the importance of critical and analytical thinking and problem solving. Usually, by the end of sophomore year, students are expected to complete 40 credit hours of core requirements, including English composition, foreign language, wellness and health, mathematics, African diaspora and the world, international or comparative women's studies, and computer literacy. In addition, freshmen are required to take First-Year Experience, and sophomores must take Sophomore Seminar.

> **"Spelman women walk their own path and always strive to be their absolute best."**

Spelman's established strengths lie in the natural sciences (especially biology) and the humanities, both of which have outstanding faculty. Biology is among the most popular majors, as are psychology, political science, and economics. Over the last decade, the college has greatly strengthened its offerings in math and the natural sciences; extensive undergraduate research programs in these areas provide students with publishing opportunities, and many end up attending grad school. In fact, Spelman leads the nation in the number of African American women who go on to earn Ph.D.s in STEM fields. Premed and prelaw programs are strong, and the 3–2 dual-degree program in engineering in cooperation with Georgia Tech is also a standout. The Women's Research and Resource Center specializes in women's studies and community outreach.

"The academic climate is very competitive," says an English major. "The school is made up of the top students from around the country, and the courses are designed to be a challenge for the best of the best." Individual attention is the hallmark of a Spelman education. Many faculty members are African American and/or female—and thus, excellent role models, ones the students find very accessible. Except for some of the required introductory courses, classes are small; 60 percent have fewer than 20 students. Through the Spelman MILE (My Integrated Learning Experience), all students complete internships or undergraduate research projects in their majors. Students who want to spread their wings can venture abroad through a variety of programs, as 21 percent do, or try one of the domestic exchange arrangements with Wellesley, Mount Holyoke, Vassar, or Mills.

Spelman's reputation continues to attract African American women from all over the country, including a high proportion of alumnae children, and the school has become increasingly selective. Twenty-eight percent of the students come from Georgia, and 1 percent come from abroad. Ninety-seven percent are African American, while Hispanic and white students each account for less than 1 percent. The political atmosphere is "moderately liberal," according to a history major, and "hot topics on campus include the gentrification of the city of Atlanta (particularly the West End neighborhood that the campus is located in), women's rights, and issues related to the preservation of black lives." Spelman offers a limited number of merit scholarships, and 48 percent of freshmen receive Pell Grants. There are no athletic scholarships.

> **"Courses are designed to be a challenge for the best of the best."**

Sixty-seven percent of students live on campus, and a junior says that housing "could use some renovations, but the living conditions are adequate." There are 11 dorms, and the older ones add to the school's historical charm; students recommend that freshmen check out Howard-Harreld Hall. The meal plan is mandatory for campus-dwellers and the food gets average reviews. A psychology major says the school's security efforts and Title IX procedures help students "feel protected" on campus.

Largely because of the Atlanta University Center, students have plenty of chances for social interaction with other nearby colleges, especially Morehouse. "Students mingle in the student centers of all four schools all the time, especially on Fridays," a veteran explains. Spelmanites also take advantage of the big-city nightlife; they attend plays, symphonies, and the hot Atlanta nightclubs. "Atlanta is a great college town!" gushes one junior. "If there is any place that a student can be academically enriched, it is here." Lenox Square is popular for shopping. Sororities are present but only in small numbers—just 6 percent of the students go Greek. The attitude on drinking leans toward the conservative. Says one student, "No alcohol on campus—period." The most anticipated annual events include sisterhood initiation ceremonies, homecoming, and the Founders Day celebration. Varsity sports, never all that important, have been replaced with a general fitness and nutrition program that features an extensive list of physical activities such as running and yoga. The college has also introduced an intramural program that includes basketball, flag football, soccer, and volleyball.

Spelman College has spent more than 135 years furthering the education and opportunities of African American women. It has adapted its curriculum to meet the career aspirations of today's youth, built up its bankroll, and successfully met the recruitment challenge posed by affirmative action at other universities. As elite an institution as ever, Spelman is staking its future on its ability to provide a unique kind of education that gives its graduates a competitive edge in the 21st century.

Core requirements include wellness and health, African diaspora and the world, and international or comparative women's studies.

Spelman leads the nation in the number of African American women who go on to earn Ph.D.s in STEM fields.

Overlaps

Agnes Scott, Vassar, Wellesley, Xavier University of Louisiana, Howard, Clark Atlanta, Georgia State

College of the Atlantic

105 Eden Street, Bar Harbor, ME 04609

In today's practical world, COA is as out-there as it gets—a haven for community-minded, environmentally conscious types who would rather save the world than make a buck. Lacks many of the usual trappings of college life, such as sports teams and Greek life. But with just over 300 undergrads, it makes smallness an academic and social virtue. Students have a big voice in running the school.

Website: www.coa.edu
Location: Rural
Private
Total Enrollment: 332
Undergraduates: 328
Male/Female: 25/75
SAT Ranges: ERW 640–700, M 550–650
ACT Ranges: 26–30
Financial Aid: 97%
Pell Grant: 33%
Expense: Pr $
Student Loans: 65%
Average Debt: $ $
Applicants: 474
Accepted: 68%
Enrolled: 28%
Grad in 6 Years: 66%
Returning Freshmen: 76%
Academics: ✐ ✐ ✐
Social: ☎ ☎
Q of L: ★ ★ ★
Admissions: (800) 528-0025
Email Address: inquiry@coa.edu

Strong Programs:
Human Ecology
Marine Science
Field Ecology and Natural History
Zoology
Environmental Science

The College of the Atlantic attracts rugged individualists concerned with the world's most pressing issues, notably climate change, social justice, and food systems. The college's curriculum and sole major is focused on human ecology—the study of the relationship between humans and their natural, social, and built environments. COA bucks the national obsession with growth—seeing smallness as the key to education that cuts across disciplines—eschews academic conventions, and takes a personalized approach to teaching and learning. "I chose COA because I found no other school that gave me as much freedom to create my own educational path," says one sophomore.

The 35-acre campus, covered in lush flowers, vegetable gardens, and lawns, sits on Mount Desert Island, along the shoreline of Frenchman Bay and adjacent to the magnificent Acadia National Park. In addition, the college maintains two offshore island research centers, two agricultural properties, a 100-acre wooded protectorate, wood-pellet-heated "green" dorms, and an oceanside campus center. COA is serious about its mission, and this is reflected in the facilities: sustainability is prized, and the college uses environmentally responsible materials as much as possible. "We believe the most sustainable building is that which isn't built," says an administrator. COA's organic vegetable operation, Beech Hill Farm, recently completed construction of additional housing where student-workers live during the summer season, as well as a greenhouse and a solar-powered electric vehicle charging station.

> "We get one-on-one time with our professors and individualized support."

Most courses focus on a single aspect of humans' relationships with the world. Instead of traditional academic departments, the school has three broad resource areas: environmental sciences, arts and design, and human studies. Many students choose to concentrate on more narrowly defined topics within human ecology, such as climate change and energy, environmental law and politics, educational studies, farming and food systems, or sustainable business. With advisors and resource specialists, each student designs an individual course of study. The natural sciences are stellar, with excellent instruction in marine science, field ecology and natural history, and zoology. Computer science and green chemistry have recently been added to the curriculum. Allied Whale, the school's marine mammal laboratory founded in 1972, offers excellent opportunities for hands-on field research. For the entrepreneurially minded, the Hatchery is COA's sustainable business incubator, offering eligible students academic credit, a variety of resources, and 10 weeks to develop a business venture and build a prototype. The emphasis is on interdisciplinary exploration, and the most compelling ideas get a $5,000 grant from the college along with a year of professional services.

Student life at COA is intense and semicommunal, beginning with an optional, rugged five-day wilderness orientation preceding the first trimester, in which 80 percent of incoming students take part. Before graduating, students must complete a 10-week off-campus internship and a 10-week final project. Other requirements are few: first-years must take the human ecology core course, and two courses are required in environmental sciences, human studies, and arts and design. Sophomores must submit a writing portfolio for evaluation. All students incorporate research into their studies, whether it is a development impact study for the local government or a study on the aggression of fire ants for Acadia National Park.

"COA is an extremely hands-on, participatory, innovative, and collaborative environment," states a sophomore. Some areas only have a professor or two, and 94 percent of all classes have fewer than 20 students. Since the student body is so small, students can become close to faculty members. "We get one-on-one time with our professors and individualized support," says a junior. In lieu of grades, students receive in-depth written evaluations of their work, although they may request grades as well. They must reciprocate with a self-evaluation of their performance.

COA offers regular study abroad programs in Mexico's Yucatán Peninsula and in Vichy, France. In the Yucatán, students do ethnographic, agricultural, or scientific research of their own choosing. In France, they take literature, philosophy, politics, and/or art classes. Both programs include a strong language immersion component. "I am very impressed by the level of fluency students obtain after the program, and for most it is the crowning experience of their time at COA," says one senior. COA also supports student participation in other study abroad programs through partner institutions such as the EcoLeague. Sixty-eight percent of students go abroad during their time at COA.

"Students at COA are open-minded, hardworking, adventurous, flexible, self-motivated, and curious."

"Students at COA are open-minded, hardworking, adventurous, flexible, self-motivated, and curious to explore passions other than their main area of study," says one contented sophomore. Many traveled the world before beginning school and move on to the Peace Corps or AmeriCorps after. Twenty-two percent of students are native to Maine, and another 22 percent are international. The student body is only 1 percent African American, 2 percent Asian American, 5 percent Hispanic, and 2 percent multiracial, and women outnumber men 3 to 1. Thirty-three percent of freshmen are Pell-eligible. The college's governance system gives students and administrators almost equal voices in how it's run; anyone may raise concerns or vote on policy-change proposals or the hiring of new faculty at the All College Meeting. The overtly liberal student body isn't shy about speaking out on more worldly issues either, including "climate change, food justice, biodiversity, and gender rights," says a junior. A limited number of merit scholarships, worth an average of $14,500, are available to top achievers.

Thanks to the college's green waterfront housing village, 46 percent of students live on campus, while the balance find cozy, inexpensive apartments or houses in the nearby town of Bar Harbor. First-years are required to live on campus and tend to form close bonds in their cottage-like houses; one says, "Each house is completely unique and has a very homey feel." Dining fare in the TAB ("Take-a-Break") Dining Hall and the Sea Urchin Café is "like home-cooked meals but with more options," according to one student. Another says COA "is a safe campus situated in a safe town in one of the safest states in the U.S." All students are required to take bystander intervention training once a year.

(continued)

Climate Change and Energy
Environmental Law and Policy
Educational Studies

The College of the Atlantic's curriculum and sole major is focused on human ecology.

First-years are required to live on campus and tend to form close bonds in their cottage-like houses.

Bar Harbor is a tourist community that "nearly shuts down in the winter," according to one student, although students do enjoy the coffee shops, bakeries, restaurants, and movie theaters that stay open. Students get to know the townspeople through the required 40 hours of community service. On-campus activities include open-mic nights, talent shows, concerts, dances, and, during the winter, "weekly Fireside Fridays with free cookies, hot chocolate, and coffee," says a sophomore. There are no fraternities or sororities, and students kick back at small off-campus house parties, which often revolve around potluck meals, since campus dining services are closed on weekends. Drinking is permitted on campus for those of legal age, only in private student rooms, but students agree that alcohol has little influence on the social scene. There are no varsity sports (not even ice hockey), but many students sign up for programs at the local YMCA, which offers sports such as soccer and volleyball. Outdoor programs, which take students hiking, sailing, cross-country skiing, and rock climbing in the wilds of Maine, are very active.

> "You can't escape good conversations, or controversies, or being challenged."

College of the Atlantic is a place where Earth Day really is cause for celebration, where students have been known to cut class to march on Washington, and where everyone who wants to, from students to trustees, jumps into frigid Frenchman Bay on the first Friday of the fall term to swim the stretch of water between the school's pier and the neighboring island. At COA, "You can't escape good conversations, or controversies, or being challenged, or learning something you never thought you'd learn or try," observes a senior. "You can't just play it safe. This community, the professors, your fellow students, won't allow it."

Overlaps

Bennington, Lewis & Clark, Warren Wilson, Hampshire, University of Maine–Orono, University of Vermont, Unity College, University of New England

If You Apply To ›

COA: Early decision I and II, regular decision. SATs or ACTs: optional. Subject Tests: optional. Accepts the Common Application with supplement. Application includes space for applicants to describe their gender identity.

Auburn University

202 Mary Martin Hall, Auburn, AL 36849

Sweet Home Alabama, where the skies are so blue and the spirit of football lasts year-round. Auburn was once called Alabama Polytechnic Institute, and today AU's programs in engineering, agriculture, and the health fields are still among its best. AU's down-home, small-town atmosphere may feel claustrophobic to those from outside the Deep South. As for the role of football, the $14 million scoreboard says it all.

Website: www.auburn.edu
Location: Small City
Public
Total Enrollment: 24,828
Undergraduates: 21,432
Male/Female: 50/50
SAT Ranges: ERW 570–650, M 560–660

Founded in 1856, Auburn University is a public land grant university that excels in professional and technical fields such as architecture, engineering, and agriculture. But the school also welcomes students with frenzied athletics, warm and cozy hospitality, and Southern charm. "It truly is a family atmosphere. We are here to learn and help each other," says one happy Tiger. "That is what makes us such a great university."

The town of Auburn, which grew up amid miles of forest and farmland largely to serve the university, is called the "loveliest village of the plain," a moniker taken from a line in an Oliver Goldsmith poem. The campus stretches for nearly 2,000 acres, graced by mossy trees, lush lawns, and majestic colonnades. Most buildings are redbrick and Georgian in style, with some more modern facilities grouped in a compact central location. Recent construction includes the $44 million Engineering Student Achievement Center, which features classrooms, a wind-tunnel lab, and shop space.

Auburn's core curriculum includes courses in the humanities and fine arts, natural sciences and mathematics, and social sciences. A writing-in-the-disciplines program bolsters every major with significant writing instruction. To ease the transition into college life, freshmen undergo the two-day Camp War Eagle orientation. The academic climate varies by department, and a senior says, "I have found that rather than students competing with each other for higher grades, they are more willing to help their classmates through tutoring or group study sessions." Regardless of the rigor, students say professors generally go the extra mile for them. "Although I have not liked every teacher I've had, every teacher has taught me something new and useful," reasons a junior.

The engineering, architecture, agriculture, and pharmacy programs are stellar. Auburn also boasts a first-of-its-kind program in wireless engineering for students who want to design network hardware or software for cell phones and other mobile devices. The Ginn College of Engineering has an aerospace engineering department, and Auburn has

"It truly is a family atmosphere. We are here to learn and help each other."

produced six NASA astronauts. The most popular majors include biomedical sciences, accounting, mechanical engineering, and finance, and the environmental science and human development and family studies programs also draw attention. Accelerated degree programs in numerous fields allow eligible students to count approved graduate hours toward both a bachelor's and a master's degree, with the goal of completing both in as little as five years. The university has added a new major in neuroscience and a minor in hunger studies.

Many Auburn students are eager to get started on their careers, so the co-op program, which provides pay and credit in several professional fields, is increasingly popular. Five interdisciplinary areas identified as "strategic research clusters" compete for millions of dollars in special funding, which means more opportunities for undergrads to assist faculty with research in areas including health disparities, pharmaceutical engineering, climate and earth systems science, omics and informatics, and scalable energy conversion science and technology. About 30 percent of undergrads have worked with faculty on research by the time they graduate. Thirteen percent of students join the Honors College, which culminates in a six-credit Honors Apogee that may involve a traditional thesis, enhanced study abroad, service learning, or other capstone project. Through the Auburn Abroad Experience, 18 percent of all students study abroad in programs that include more than 50 faculty-led expeditions. Closer to home, the Rural Studio program sends students in the College of Architecture, Design, and Construction to live in economically underserved Hale County, Alabama, to design and build innovative community buildings and homes for local residents.

Auburn students are "mostly Southern people who are from Alabama and who have family that went to Auburn," says a junior. Indeed, 62 percent of Auburn students are Alabama natives, and many are second- or third-generation legacies. African Americans account for 6 percent of the largely homogeneous student body, Hispanics represent 3 percent, and Asian Americans and multiracial students each add 2 percent; 4 percent hail from foreign countries. The conservative tone of this Bible Belt campus makes it hospitable for many Christian groups, and Auburn is home to one of the country's largest chapters of the Campus Crusade for Christ. "Half of Auburn students love politics and enjoy the political process, while the

(continued)

ACT Ranges: 24–30
Financial Aid: 54%
Pell Grant: 12%
Expense: Pub $ $
Student Loans: 40%
Average Debt: $ $ $
Applicants: 18,072
Accepted: 84%
Enrolled: 27%
Grad in 6 Years: 77%
Returning Freshmen: 92%
Academics: ✍ ✍
Social: ☎ ☎ ☎
Q of L: ★ ★ ★
Admissions: (334) 844-6425
Email Address: admissions@ auburn.edu

Strong Programs:
Biomedical Sciences
Accounting
Mechanical Engineering
Finance
Architecture
Wireless Engineering
Environmental Science
Human Development and
    Family Studies

The Honors College culminates in an Honors Apogee that may involve a traditional thesis, enhanced study abroad, service learning, or other project.

other half wouldn't know where their polling place was if you gave them a map," quips one senior. Each year, the university awards merit scholarships averaging $7,200. Gifted athletes vie for 395 athletic scholarships in 21 sports.

The majority of Auburn's 32 residence halls are co-ed by floor, but there are several single-sex halls; 19 percent of undergrads live on campus. First-year students compete for rooms on a first-come, first-served basis with returning students, and the dorms fill up fast. "Get on a waiting list ASAP," advises a junior. The university helps those moving off campus find apartments and roommates. Twenty-five percent of Auburn men join fraternities, and 44 percent of women join sororities, perhaps because chapters get space in the best dorms. Students grumble about the mandatory—and pricey—meal plan, but say the dining has improved considerably in recent years. "The food continues to diversify and get healthier," confirms a student.

Aside from varsity sporting events and off-campus fraternity and apartment parties, students enjoy school-sponsored concerts, free movies, and plenty of intramural leagues. "Social life is great whether you are Greek or not," says a freshman. The campus is officially dry, except on game days, and students say the alcohol policy is enforced. Long-standing traditions include Hey Day, when everyone wears a name tag and walks around saying, "Hey!" Seventy percent of students participate in a variety of community service programs, frequently as part of service-learning courses.

"Social life is great whether you are Greek or not."

Auburn is a football powerhouse with pockets as deep as its location in the South and values to match. The school's $14 million video scoreboard was hailed by the athletic director as "a great asset, not only for our fans but also our students and our prospective student-athletes." On fall Saturdays, nearly 90,000 screaming fans turn the campus into Alabama's fifth-largest city, and the rallying cry "Warrrrr Eagle!" rocks the place each time an Auburn back runs to daylight. The annual Iron Bowl pits Auburn against Southeastern Conference archrival Alabama. In 2018 the equestrian team won its fifth national title; Aubie, the official tiger mascot, has won a record nine titles (yes, mascots compete in national championships too) at the UCA Cheer and Dance competition. Other solid Tigers teams include men's basketball and women's softball and golf. The Auburn Recreation and Wellness Center is a 240,000-square-foot facility containing everything from weight-training areas to a virtual golf simulator and an outdoor leisure pool.

The Auburn Creed, a beloved tradition, states a belief in the value of "work, hard work," and Auburn is working hard to increase the caliber of its students and academic programs. "Auburn has become more focused on the future," one senior says. But students agree that certain key characteristics have stayed the same—and that's a good thing. Says one student, "We just keep getting cooler."

Overlaps

Clemson, Mississippi State, North Carolina State, University of Alabama, University of Tennessee Knoxville, University of Georgia, University of Florida, Georgia Tech

If You Apply To ›

Auburn: Rolling admissions. SATs or ACTs: required. Subject Tests: optional. Does not accept the Common Application. Out-of-state enrollment is capped on a year-to-year basis; there are no set limits.

Austin College

900 North Grand Avenue, Sherman, TX 75090

The second most famous institution in Texas with Austin in its name. Half the size of Trinity (TX), runs neck and neck with Southwestern to be the leading small liberal arts college in Texas. Combines the liberal arts with strong programs in business, education, science, and health, including premed. Don't look for the 'Roos on a map of the city of Austin. The college is just north of Dallas.

For historical reasons over which reasonable persons can and do disagree, the Kangaroo has become the symbol of all things Austin College. All freshmen receive #RooNation T-shirts at orientation, and students hold a trick-or-treat alternative known as 'Roo Boo for local children. AC's preprofessional programs, most notably premed, are among the strongest in the state. Professors here even serve students breakfast at 10 p.m. the night before finals. It's just another example of the personal style that is typical of this charming Southern institution.

Austin College's 100-acre campus is in a residential area in the city of Sherman. The campus is designed in the traditional quadrangle style and comprises beige sandstone buildings, tree-lined plazas, decorative fountains, and an impressive 70-ton sculptured solstice calendar. Residence halls are conveniently located approximately 200 yards from most classrooms, which eases the pain of early morning classes. The IDEA Center for hands-on learning in the sciences features laboratory classrooms as well as a $1 million, 24-inch telescope and astronomical image camera in the building's domed observatory.

The core curriculum begins with a freshman seminar called Communication/ Inquiry. Each professor who teaches the course becomes the mentor for the 20 freshmen in his or her class. Then students select from courses in humanities, social sciences, and natural sciences. Students can combine three of the school's majors into an interdisciplinary degree, and all must complete one major and a minor or a double major to graduate. During the January term, students can focus on just one course, and many use that time to study abroad or undertake off-campus internships. "JanTerms are a must for all students, and traveling abroad during these special instructional periods is an excellent way to expand one's experiential and academic horizons," says an English major.

> "Traveling abroad during [JanTerm] is an excellent way to expand one's experiential and academic horizons."

When it comes time to apply to grad school, premed and predentistry students at this little college have some of the highest acceptance rates of any Texas school, and aspiring lawyers also do well. AC's teaching program grants students both a bachelor's and a master's degree in five years. Science and education receive high marks from students, and business, biology, psychology, and political science are the most popular majors. The Jordan Family Language House is home to 48 students studying Chinese, French, German, Japanese, and Spanish, along with a native speaker of each language, and students speak the language in all common areas. A new major in engineering physics is available, and a cooperative engineering program links the college with other schools.

Of the academic climate, a chemistry major says, "It is competitive enough to push you to do the best work you can, yet very collaborative through working with peers on group projects, lab assignments, research experiences, and other tasks." Sixty-three percent of all classes have fewer than 20 students. "Teachers always make time for students, they're approachable, and the mentor program really helps when

Website: www.austincollege.edu

Location: Small City

Private

Total Enrollment: 1,229

Undergraduates: 1,215

Male/Female: 49/51

SAT Ranges: ERW 590–680, M 570–680

ACT Ranges: 23–29

Financial Aid: 99%

Pell Grant: 38%

Expense: Pr $

Student Loans: 58%

Average Debt: $ $ $ $

Applicants: 3,545

Accepted: 52%

Enrolled: 18%

Grad in 6 Years: 68%

Returning Freshmen: 81%

Academics: ✑ ✑ ✑

Social: ☎ ☎ ☎

Q of L: ★ ★ ★

Admissions: (903) 813-3000

Email Address: admission@austincollege.edu

Strong Programs:
Business
Biology
Psychology
Political Science
Premed
Prelaw
Education
Foreign Languages

it comes to registering for classes and looking for summer research programs or internships," says a student. The college also offers independent study and departmental honors programs. The Posey Leadership Institute offers seminars and courses, and a minor in leadership studies is available. AC also provides five research areas in Grayson County. Forty percent of students conduct undergraduate research, 60 percent study abroad, and about half complete internships. The Global Outreach fellowship program gives 10 to 15 students the chance to volunteer in educational programs around the world.

Eighty-nine percent of AC students hail from the Lone Star State, with 3 percent from abroad. Hispanics comprise 21 percent of the student body, African Americans 8 percent, Asian Americans 13 percent, and multiracial students 4 percent. "Students are thinkers, communicators, debaters, and learners all at once," comments a senior.

"If you need help, often before you need it, people are reaching out to provide it to you."

Students say there is a wide range of political views, but the campus tends to lean liberal. The college was founded by a Presbyterian missionary in 1849, and its continuous ties to the Presbyterian Church (USA) are evident in the emphasis on values in the core courses and high participation in service activities. AC offers merit scholarships worth an average of $22,500, and 38 percent of freshmen qualify for the Pell Grant.

Eighty-six percent of undergraduates live on campus, and all are required to do so for their first three years. "All of the housing on campus is extremely comfortable," a biology major says. Residence halls are co-ed, except for one all-female and one all-male dorm. Juniors and seniors choose from suites, flats, and cottages. Dean Hall is a popular choice for freshmen, despite (or perhaps because of) its reputation as being loud and social. As for campus dining, "The staff here is amazing," cheers one student. "They always have smiles on their faces and aren't afraid to save you an extra cookie." The Pouch Club, an on-campus joint, serves pizza and burgers, as well as beer and wine for those students 21 and over. Students report feeling safe on campus thanks to thorough campus security and sexual assault prevention programs.

Most of the social life is either on or near campus. "There is always something to do on campus, from smaller activities and club meetings to big dinners and guest speakers," a junior says. Fifteen percent of the men and 15 percent of the women belong to local fraternities and sororities, respectively, but the Greeks are not school-funded and are not allowed to advertise off-campus parties without the college's permission. "Greek organizations set the tone for parties but not social life," explains an English major. Students can have alcohol in dorm rooms if they are 21 or older. Mega Texas is a campus carnival in the fall, and Kangapalooza brings a big-name musician to campus in the spring. Popular weekend excursions are a drive to Dallas or to the college's 28-acre recreational spot on Lake Texoma (a half hour north). Sherman is "quaint" and "historic," and is becoming a better college town, students say. "There are lots of restaurants," a junior says, "but for the most part there is nothing to do late at night."

Even without athletic scholarships, varsity sports are generating increasing support. The Kangaroos compete in Division III, and solid teams include men's and women's basketball and swimming and diving, along with football, women's volleyball, and softball. New men's and women's water polo teams debuted for the 2018–19 season. The Mason Athletic/Recreation Complex provides facilities for athletes and the fitness-conscious. There's also a recreational sports program, with basketball, softball, and flag football proving popular; about a third of undergrads participate.

At this college with roots in the Presbyterian Church, students praise the preprofessional programs and the intimate, supportive environment. "Austin College cares for each student, and no one falls through the cracks," says a senior. "If you need help, often before you need it, people are reaching out to provide it to you." And while Sherman may seem to be a sleepy little place, Austin College is definitely hoppin'.

If You Apply To ›

Austin: Early decision, early action I and II, regular decision. SATs or ACTs: optional (test-optional applicants must submit graded expository writing paper). Subject Tests: optional. Accepts the Common Application.

Babson College

Babson Park, MA 02457-0310

The only college in the *Fiske Guide* devoted entirely to business. Babson is the birthplace of entrepreneurial studies—which continue to define the campus ethos. Only 10 miles from College Student Mecca, a.k.a. Boston, and tougher to get into than ever. Has about half as many undergraduates as Bentley, its closest competitor, and more than a quarter of students are international. The one college in Massachusetts where it is possible to be a Republican with head held high.

Babson is a preeminent training ground for budding entrepreneurs and corporate bigwigs. The college is a pioneer in the study of entrepreneurship, dating to the 1970s—a time when people thought it couldn't be taught. Here, hands-on experience is the norm; students get school funding to start businesses during their first year and may hone their stock-picking skills by managing part of the college's endowment. Always the foremost business college in the Boston area, Babson attracts budding tycoons and entrepreneurs from around the globe.

Founded in 1919, the college sits on 370 acres near the sedate Boston suburb of Wellesley. The tract features open green spaces, gently rolling hills, and heavily wooded areas. Buildings are gently shaded and parking lots (filled with expensive foreign cars) are relatively hidden. Architecturally, the campus is mainly neo-Georgian and modern. Park Manor West doubles as a first-year residence hall and the home of the Schlesinger Innovation Center, offering an amphitheater, classrooms, and collaboration spaces. The new Babson Recreation and Athletics Center offers 177,000 square feet of space for varsity and recreational sports and other fitness activities.

> **"[Professors are helpful] especially when you need advice or when they offer you connections to firms."**

Although Babson is a business school, about half of students' classes are in the liberal arts. General education requirements emphasize rhetoric (public speaking); ethics and social responsibility; international and multicultural perspectives; and leadership, teamwork, and creativity. In the required Foundations of Management and Entrepreneurship course, first-year students are split into groups to develop business plans; each group gets up to $9,000 in seed money from the college to get their concept up and running. At the end of the year, the business is liquidated and profits go to charity. Former FME groups have developed Babsonopoly (a Babson-themed version of Monopoly), published children's books, and organized a 5K to raise money for suicide awareness organizations.

All Babson students major in business and then select a concentration, such as management or business analytics—or even identity and diversity studies or literary

Website: www.babson.edu
Location: Suburban
Private
Total Enrollment: 2,783
Undergraduates: 2,342
Male/Female: 52/48
SAT Ranges: ERW 610–680, M 620–730
ACT Ranges: 27–33
Financial Aid: 47%
Pell Grant: 14%
Expense: Pr $ $ $
Student Loans: 40%
Average Debt: $ $ $ $
Applicants: 7,122
Accepted: 24%
Enrolled: 32%
Grad in 6 Years: 92%
Returning Freshmen: 96%
Academics: ✑ ✑ ✑
Social: ☎ ☎
Q of L: ★ ★ ★
Admissions: (781) 239-5522
Email Address: ugradadmission@babson.edu

Strong Programs:
Business
Entrepreneurship

(continued)

Finance
Economics
Marketing
Accounting

and visual arts. (The Sorenson Visual Arts Center has painting, ceramics, and sculpture studios; labs for photography and digital art; a student art gallery; and workspace for artists-in-residence.) Finance, economics, marketing, and entrepreneurship are the most popular concentrations, and the entrepreneurship program is one of Babson's strongest, bringing in venture capitalists and executives from such companies as Dunkin' Donuts and Jiffy Lube for how-to lectures.

In the classroom, Babson relies on the case-study approach more typically employed by M.B.A. programs. Students break into groups or act as officers of pseudo-corporations to address specific business situations and solve marketplace problems. "Even though most of our classes are group project–based, there is still a very intense, competitive atmosphere," says a student. Just 17 percent of classes have fewer than 20 students, but others rarely exceed 50. Students report that professors are accessible and helpful "especially when you need advice or when they offer you connections to firms," says a senior. Accounting students may take graduate classes at Babson in the summer and fall after finishing their bachelor's degrees, letting them sit for the CPA exam about one year earlier than most other programs. The Center for Women's Entrepreneurial Leadership promotes women in business and offers scholarships, special events, and networking opportunities. Babson offers more than 100 semester-long and short-term study abroad programs around the world, in which 46 percent of students participate; students in the Honors Program are required to do so. Not all programs are business focused; the London Theatre Program, for example, focuses on arts appreciation.

In the classroom, Babson relies on the case-study approach more typically employed by M.B.A. programs.

Babson students are go-getters. "We enjoy comparing how full our Google calendars are," says one senior, and another student adds, "No one blinks an eye when a student is walking around campus in a suit." African Americans make up 5 percent of the undergraduate student body, Hispanics 11 percent, Asian Americans 12 percent, and multiracial students 2 percent. Massachusetts residents comprise 27 percent, while 28 percent are foreign. "Babson students generally fit into one of these three classifications: wealthy, white New Englanders, wealthy and international, or diverse scholarship-yielding students," observes a student. "The social classes are very distinct on campus and people often flaunt their money." No one seems to care much about politics, or at least most prefer to avoid political discussions. Merit scholarships averaging $18,600 are available; there are no athletic scholarships.

"No one blinks an eye when a student is walking around campus in a suit."

Babson guarantees housing for four years, and 79 percent of undergraduates live on campus, resulting in high demand for singles and suites. "The suite-style living is awesome," says a freshman. "It allows you to live with a bunch of your best friends but still have separate singles to sleep in." After the first year, rooms are assigned by lottery, with standing based on credits earned. At the main dining hall, you'll find sushi, make-your-own stir-fry, vegan stations, and other options, but the food is often a target of student complaints. Security gets high marks, and the student-led ASAP (Alliance for Sexual Assault Prevention) organization is active in raising awareness about campus sexual assault.

Favorite campus festivals include alumni weekend (great networking opportunities) and Spring Concert.

Social life is centered on campus during the first two years; after that, most students are 21 and have cars, so they head to the clubs and bars of Boston proper, about 20 minutes away. "Because Babson is so close to Boston, many students partake in nightlife activities in the city," confirms one student. The Campus Activities Board brings in comedians and organizes parties, as do Greek organizations, which attract 13 percent of the men and 26 percent of the women. "We never have any Friday classes, so Thursday and Saturday are the big party nights," explains a sophomore. Underage drinking on campus is treated with a three-strike policy, and the third offense gets violators kicked out of the dorms. Favorite campus festivals include alumni weekend (great networking opportunities) and Spring Concert, when bands come to play and parties are thrown. Students also contribute nearly 32,000 volunteer hours annually through the Office of Faith and Service.

The "very affluent" town of Wellesley has shops and restaurants, and there is a subway stop. Students can take the T's Green Line into the city to explore Quincy Market or the campuses of Harvard, Northeastern, Emerson, and Boston Universities. The school sponsors trips to Celtics and Red Sox games. Wellesley is also home to Wellesley College, and it's not unheard of for Babson

"Many students partake in nightlife activities in the city."

students to socialize with Wellesley women; Babson also offers cross-registration at Wellesley and neighboring Olin College of Engineering. Popular road trips include the beaches of Cape Cod and Martha's Vineyard, the ski slopes of Vermont and New Hampshire, and the bright lights of New York City and Montreal.

While making money may be the most popular form of competition at Babson, students recognize the importance of keeping their bodies in competitive condition too. Popular intramural sports include volleyball, rugby, and ice hockey, and on the varsity level, the Beavers play in Division III. Any match against archrival Bentley and soccer games against Brandeis and Colby draw crowds. The men's ice hockey team is a powerhouse, and men's and women's basketball are frequent title contenders, with the men winning the national championship in 2017.

At Babson, students embrace entrepreneurship as an ethos and are willing to work hard for what they want. After all, learning how to balance work with everything else that's important in life is a prerequisite to climbing the corporate ladder. And thanks to small classes, a laser-like focus on all things financial, and plenty of hands-on experience, students leave Babson well equipped to begin scampering up those rungs.

Overlaps

Bentley, Northeastern, Boston University, NYU, University of Pennsylvania, Boston College, University of Southern California, Fordham

If You Apply To ›

Babson: Early decision I and II, early action, regular decision. SATs or ACTs: required. No Subject Tests. Accepts the Common Application with supplement.

Bard College

Annandale-on-Hudson, NY 12504

A dominant presence in the world of nontraditional liberal arts colleges, Bard offers what is arguably the most innovative range of academic programs anywhere. Like Reed on the West Coast, combines unabashed individuality with rigorous traditional academics. Long-standing president Leon Botstein, a polymath known simply as "Leon," is an iconic educator who has championed the liberal arts in countries around the world.

Bard College has come a long way since its 1860 founding by 12 men studying to enter the seminaries of the Episcopal Church. Those pioneers would no doubt be surprised at the eclectic mix of students now running around Annandale-on-Hudson in an ethos once described by the *New Yorker* as one of "quixotic unworldliness." But the idea that Bard is strictly a school for artists and social studies majors has largely disappeared, and the result is a school with lots of intellectual depth. Having expanded its mission beyond undergraduate and graduate education to also

Website: www.bard.edu
Location: Rural
Private
Total Enrollment: 2,095
Undergraduates: 1,809
Male/Female: 42/58

(continued)

SAT Ranges: ERW 630–710,
  M 590–690
ACT Ranges: 28–31
Financial Aid: 66%
Pell Grant: 21%
Expense: Pr $ $ $ $
Student Loans: 55%
Average Debt: $ $
Applicants: 4,922
Accepted: 58%
Enrolled: 16%
Grad in 6 Years: 74%
Returning Freshmen: 82%
Academics: ✍ ✍ ✍ ✍
Social: ☎ ☎ ☎
Q of L: ★ ★ ★ ★
Admissions: (845) 758-7472
Email Address: admission@
  bard.edu

Strong Programs:
Languages and Literatures
Visual and Performing Arts
Photography
Human Rights
Social Studies
Biology
Computer Science

*Students declare
a major through
Moderation, a midway
review of performance
and proposed study
plans discussed with a
board of professors.*

encompass support for the arts, secondary education reform, and the development of partnerships that bring education to underserved areas around the globe, Bard has earned a well-deserved national, even international, profile. To succeed in such a dynamic environment, one student advises, "You don't need perfect grades. You just need an adventurous spirit, an ambitious attitude toward self-improvement, and an ability to evaluate your experiences and capabilities."

Bard's campus occupies 1,000 well-landscaped acres in New York's Washington Irving country, on the shores of the Hudson River. Consistent with everything else at Bard, there's no prevailing architectural theme, so each ivy-covered brick building stands out—especially the dorms, which range from cottages in the woods to Russian Colonial in style. Renowned architect Frank Gehry designed the stunning, $62 million Fisher Center for the Performing Arts, which provides teaching and performance space for everything from opera to improvisation. The Center for Science and Computation, designed by Rafael Vinoly, promotes collaborative, hands-on science. Montgomery Place, a 380-acre estate and National Historic Landmark adjacent to the main campus, provides additional facilities for programs in the arts, humanities, and environmental sciences.

> **"Professors value the students as individuals first."**

Despite Bard's reputation for nonconformism, the list of requirements is extensive, including nine distribution requirements. Classes are small and seminar style, and freshmen show up three weeks before classes start for the Workshop in Language and Thinking, where they read extensively in several genres and meet in small groups to discuss reading and writing. (A literature major calls L&T "the best three weeks of my life.") The First-Year Seminar introduces the intellectual, artistic, and cultural ideas at the core of a liberal arts education. Citizen Science, another three-week workshop in January, examines topics not normally covered in the traditional science curriculum, such as infectious disease; organized into teams, the entire first-year class then teaches science lessons in the local public schools. In the spring of the second year, students declare a major through Moderation, a midway review of performance and proposed study plans discussed with a board of professors in the relevant area. In the junior year preparation for the Senior Project begins. Students create original work as evidence of mastery in their field or fields, and their Senior Project is reviewed by a faculty board.

With authors such as Neil Gaiman, Francine Prose, and Dinaw Mengestu teaching at Bard, literature and written arts are among the school's best programs. Bard was one of the first to grant a B.A. in visual and performing arts and boasts one of the finest studio programs in the country; photography is one of the toughest majors to get into. Bard established what administrators believe is the first collegiate program in human rights. There is also a five-year, dual-degree conservatory program for music students, and although Bard is far from preprofessional, it does offer combined programs of its own and with other schools in sustainability, finance, engineering, public health, and a number of other fields.

Bard's academic climate is "intellectual and consistently challenging," says a senior, but students agree that the atmosphere is collaborative. "Students are more eager to engage in discussions about what they just learned in class than they are likely to discuss what grades they received on the most recent exam," says a sociology and human rights major. Eighty percent of classes have fewer than 20 students, and if students want more individual attention, they can devise a syllabus for their own tutorial and find a professor to sponsor it. There are no teaching assistants here, and professors receive outstanding reviews, for both their expertise and their personal approach. "Professors value the students as individuals first," says a senior.

A semester-long program in New York City lets students study biology and medicine at Rockefeller University, and spots are reserved for Bard students as

Summer Undergraduate Research Fellows. Also located in New York City, Bard's Globalization and International Affairs program merges advanced coursework in global affairs with internships at leading public, private, and nonprofit agencies. Study abroad is available in far-flung locales around the globe; half of the students take part. The Trustee Leader Scholar program provides grants and support for student-run community service projects. In an effort to expand liberal arts instruction overseas and to help nurture emerging democratic societies, Bard has developed partnerships with educational institutions in locations as diverse as Lithuania, Kyrgyzstan, South Africa, and the West Bank, as well as among prison inmates in the U.S.

The Bard Entrance Exam is an early-decision application option in which students submit four 2,500-word essays that are graded by professors.

Bard students tended to march to their own drummer in high school. "Many struggle their first year, when they realize everyone is just as unique as they are," says one senior. But Bardians take pride in diversity, whether racial, geographical (66 percent are from out of state, with 11 percent from foreign countries), or ideological, though they admit the latter can be lacking. "If you're a Republican or conservative, please come and add some dimension to our conversation," implores one student. "I'm sick of agreeing with everyone." While Bard has its

"If you're a Republican or conservative, please come and add some dimension to our conversation."

share of extremely wealthy children of media moguls and Hollywood actors, 21 percent of current freshmen qualify for Pell Grants. African Americans make up 7 percent of the student body, Asian Americans 4 percent, Hispanics 7 percent, and multiracial students 5 percent. Bard offers academic scholarships based on need but no athletic awards. Under the Excellence and Equal Cost program, qualified high school students may apply to attend Bard for the price of a public school education in their home state. Bard offers a unique early-decision application option in which students can take the Bard Entrance Examination, demonstrating their academic ability by submitting four 2,500-word essays on a range of scholarly topics that are graded by professors.

Three-quarters of Bard students live on campus, and freshmen are required to do so. Residence halls vary in style, explains one student: "Some are old Victorian mansions, some are new modern buildings that are eco-friendly, one looks like a castle, and others are big cement monsters from the 1950s." Many upperclassmen move off campus; to help ease their commute, Bard runs a shuttle to the nearby towns of Red Hook and Tivoli, which are home to a variety of restaurants, bars, and other conveniences. Campus dining is described as "decent, but not amazing," but students appreciate that much of the fresh produce comes from Bard's own student-operated farm. Students say they feel safe on their rural campus, but administrative handling of sexual assault has been a point of student activism.

All Bard students are automatically made members of the student government, and cocurricular life is run by students.

All Bard students are automatically made members of the student government, and cocurricular life is run by students; there are more than 140 different clubs. The school offers cultural shows and performances, concerts, and movies, with indie films and alternative rock and hip-hop particularly popular. The Student Activities Board plans Urban Cowboy Night, Welcome Back Weekend, Midnight Breakfast complete with karaoke, the

"There are plenty of pseudo jocks and intellectuals in good shape."

ever-popular Thursday Night Live, and Spring Fling. There are no fraternities or sororities, and when it comes to alcohol, policies are focused on safety and respect, although underage drinking in the dorms is taken seriously. Bard's hometown of Annandale-on-Hudson is 20 miles from the crafts and antiques meccas of Woodstock and Rhinebeck, and not much farther from the ski slopes of the Catskills and the Berkshires. Having a car helps to prevent occasional attacks of claustrophobia, and New York City is just 100 minutes away by train.

The Raptors compete in 18 Division III sports and are members of a number of conferences, including the Eastern College Athletic Conference, the Liberty League, and the College Squash Association. Bard is virtually devoid of dedicated jocks, but one student notes, "There are plenty of pseudo jocks and intellectuals in good shape." Thirty-five percent of the students get involved in intramurals, such as basketball, floor hockey, and bowling, which emphasize participation and fun. Across campus, miles of trails stretch through the woods along the Hudson, perfect for everything from raspberry picking to jogging and hiking. "If you like the woods, it's amazing," sighs an anthropology major. "If you like the city, you'll go stir-crazy."

> **"The one real thing that unites Bard is an ability to be self-driven and independent."**

Thanks to the iconoclastic vision of President Leon Botstein, also conductor of the American Symphony Orchestra, Bard offers strong programs that reach far beyond the arts. Come prepared to work hard and have your mind opened. "The Bard culture is a weird mixture of apathy and activism, arts and sciences, quirkiness and coolness," says a senior. "However, the one real thing that unites Bard is an ability to be self-driven and independent. Bard students are not followers, but establish their own paths."

Overlaps

NYU, Oberlin, Reed, Vassar, Wesleyan, Skidmore, Macalester, Sarah Lawrence

If You Apply To ›

Bard: Early decision, early action, regular decision. SATs or ACTs: optional. Subject Tests: optional. Accepts the Common Application with supplement.

Barnard College

New York, NY 10027

The most selective women's college in the country, Barnard is academically right up there with Wellesley, and the workload is on par with the Ivies. Step outside and you're on Broadway; across the street lies Columbia University, whose academic riches are yours for the taking. Barnard women are a little more artsy and a bit more city-ish than their female counterparts at Columbia.

Website: www.barnard.edu
Location: City Center
Private
Total Enrollment: 2,570
Undergraduates: 2,570
Male/Female: 0/100
SAT Ranges: ERW 660–760, M 650–740
ACT Ranges: 30–33
Financial Aid: 40%
Pell Grant: 15%
Expense: Pr $ $ $ $
Student Loans: 45%
Average Debt: $
Applicants: 7,716

Barnard students get the best of both worlds—the small, close-knit atmosphere of a liberal arts school along with the limitless opportunities of Columbia College, the undergraduate division of the Ivy League research institution just across the street. Whether they are passionate about art and music or urban studies and politics, women seeking a high-energy, empowering environment with top-notch academics are likely to find a niche here.

Barnard's campus is on the Upper West Side of Manhattan, in the Morningside Heights neighborhood. It's just blocks from Riverside Drive, which has a lovely path parallel to the Hudson River for running, biking, or roller-skating. Trees and other greenery shade grand prewar apartment buildings, and grassy medians break up the wide expanse of Broadway itself. Barnard's architecturally diverse buildings are more modern than Columbia's, and in recent years, the college has invested to upgrade labs, classrooms, and the residence halls. The 128,000-square-foot Milstein Center includes a state-of-the-art library featuring interactive technologies and learning spaces.

> **"Students are deeply committed to their studies and their intellectual pursuits."**

Barnard competes head-to-head with Columbia in admissions, an interesting dilemma because Barnard is an affiliate college of Columbia University, along with the engineering school, the medical school, the business school, and, of course, Columbia College. In general, women looking for a more traditional "rah-rah" experience may prefer Columbia. Some students apply to Barnard as a back door to Columbia, which is harder for women to get into, but Barnard's admissions officers have become adept at sniffing out Columbia wannabes. Those who opt for Barnard like the fact that advising and housing are better on their side of Broadway and value its distinctive approach to educating women. Once enrolled, Barnard students share a first-year orientation program with Columbia, where they mix together in small groups and take tours of the campus and city. Students can also take part in a pre-orientation urban volunteer program.

Barnard's Foundations curriculum is designed to enable students to gain general knowledge in a range of academic disciplines, develop critical thinking and communication skills, and spend more of their time exploring other areas of interest or pursuing cocurricular opportunities that enhance their major. First-year students must take a writing course, a first-year seminar, and a physical education class. In addition to standard distribution requirements, students must fulfill Modes of Thinking requirements in six areas, such as Thinking Technologically and Digitally, Thinking Locally, and Thinking about Social Difference. A senior project or thesis ensures academic depth within the major.

Barnard's most popular majors are psychology, economics, political science, English, biology, and neuroscience (there's a healthy contingent of premeds). Architecture and the visual and performing arts, especially dance, are also well regarded. Barnard boasts strong support for budding writers and is a hotbed of new talent. Women's, gender, and sexuality studies and education draw praise, though students in these programs must also choose another major. The Athena Center for Leadership Studies offers workshops, mentoring programs, internships, guest speakers, and other special features. Barnard students may cross-register at Columbia if they find more courses of interest there (including a 3–2 engineering program), or enroll in graduate courses in a number of Columbia's schools. A dual-degree program is available with the nearby Jewish Theological Seminary, and music students may apply to take classes at Juilliard and the Manhattan School of Music. One-third of the students study abroad in more than 35 countries, including Argentina, Australia, China, Morocco, and Spain.

> "From research in labs to internships at the Met, there is no shortage of amazing opportunities."

"The academic climate of Barnard is exhilaratingly rigorous. Students are deeply committed to their studies and their intellectual pursuits," says one senior. Many students come to Barnard because of its low student/faculty ratio. Seventy-three percent of classes have fewer than 20 students. Another plus: Barnard has no graduate teaching assistants. In fact, Barnard professors enjoy Columbia's proximity almost as much as undergraduates, and each year one-third of the full-time faculty teaches in graduate departments throughout the university. Still, faculty members focus on their teaching responsibilities to undergraduates first, and a chemistry major calls the quality of instruction "impeccable." Undergraduate research is also a priority at Barnard, especially in the sciences, and often occurs within guided internships, colloquia, and seminar courses. "From research in labs to internships at the Met, there is no shortage of amazing opportunities outside of the classroom for Barnard students in New York City," cheers a junior.

"Barnard women are not afraid to ask for what they want or to ask for help, and they are interested in the world around them," says a senior. Twenty-seven percent of Barnard students are New York natives, including a sizable contingent from the East

(continued)

Accepted: 15%
Enrolled: 50%
Grad in 6 Years: 93%
Returning Freshmen: 95%
Academics: ✐ ✐ ✐ ✐ ✐
Social: ☎ ☎ ☎
Q of L: ★ ★ ★
Admissions: (212) 854-2014
Email Address: admissions@ barnard.edu

Strong Programs:
Psychology
Economics
Political Science
English
Biology
Neuroscience
Architecture
Visual and Performing Arts

Barnard's admissions officers have become adept at sniffing out Columbia wannabes.

Side of Manhattan, and 9 percent are international. Asian Americans make up 15 percent of the student body, African Americans 6 percent, Hispanics 12 percent, and multiracial students 6 percent. Students are mostly liberal and politically active; according to a history major, "Hot-button topics range from struggles of first-generation students to gender expression to divesting from fossil fuels." Barnard does not offer merit or athletic scholarships, but it does commit to a need-blind admissions process for domestic first-year applicants and meet admitted students' full demonstrated financial need.

Ninety-one percent of Barnard students live in the dorms, which have come a long way in recent years: there's an 18-story Barnard dormitory tower, plus one dorm complex and seven off-campus apartment buildings; nonresidents must be signed in by a resident, and entries are always guarded, so students say they feel safe.

**"Students go out…
maybe once a weekend,
or every other weekend."**

In addition, Barnard shares two co-ed dorms with Columbia. "The dorms and housing at Barnard are amazing," says one senior. "They are clean, comfortable, spacious (mostly!), and very well maintained." Barnard guarantees four years of housing to enrolling first-years, which one student says is "a relief considering how difficult and expensive it can be to find an apartment in New York City." Seniors get the best rooms through a lottery system. Dorm dwellers must buy a meal plan, which may also be used at Columbia's John Jay cafeteria. "The college has created a Step Up program that teaches students how to recognize sexual assault and how to handle it both as a potential victim and as a passerby," explains a junior.

When it comes to social life, students tend to divide their time between the campus and the city. "Most of the social life takes place around campus," a junior says, "but you obviously have all of New York City to explore." Traditions include Big Sub in the fall, when a 700-foot-long sub sandwich is assembled throughout campus and everyone grabs a piece, and Midnight Breakfast the night before finals begin, when deans and administrators serve up eggs and waffles in the student center. Women in the arts are celebrated in the annual Winterfest. Barnard women interested in Greek life are allowed to join sororities at Columbia. Alcohol is permitted in residential spaces for those of legal age, and students seeking parties head next door to Columbia or bars in Morningside Heights, but an English major notes, "This is not a school where students go out every night. Maybe once a weekend, or every other weekend." Many of the city's cultural offerings are free to students with their school ID. Road trips are infrequent, as not many students have cars, but when they happen, destinations range from Washington, D.C., to Boston, easily reached by train and plane, to skiing and snowboarding in Vermont, or spring break on the beaches of South Carolina.

Barnard athletes compete in the Division I Ivy League conference alongside their peers enrolled at Columbia, and basketball, softball, tennis, track and field, and crew are popular and competitive. The fencing team is also strong. Columbia's marvelous gym and co-ed intramurals are also available to Barnard women, but many of them prefer to exercise their minds.

Students see Barnard as having "the supportive community of a small liberal arts women's college, the resources of a large research institution through Columbia, and the infinite opportunities of New York City right outside the gates," in the words of one proud Barnard woman. It's a winning combination that turns out well-rounded students ready to leap toward the future.

Overlaps

**Columbia,
Wellesley,
Brown, Smith,
Northwestern,
NYU, UC Berkeley,
Princeton**

If You Apply To ›

Barnard: Early decision, regular decision. SATs or ACTs: required. No Subject Tests. Accepts the Common Application with supplement. Accepts applications from students who consistently live and identify as women.

Bates College

23 Campus Avenue, Lewiston, ME 04240

Bowdoin got rid of its frats; Bates never had them, and therein hangs a tale. With its long-held tradition of egalitarianism and sense of community, Bates is a kindred spirit to Quaker institutions such as Haverford and Swarthmore. A five-week spring term helps make Bates a leader in studying abroad. Blue-collar Lewiston is not a draw, but New England countryside is within arm's reach.

Founded by abolitionists in 1855, Bates College takes pride in its heritage as a haven for seekers of guidance, freedom, and justice. Its 4–4–1 calendar offers ample opportunity for study abroad, even for just five weeks at year's end. The school's small size also means student/faculty interaction is plentiful, and close friendships are easily formed.

The Bates campus features a mix of Georgian and Federal buildings and Victorian homes spread out over the grassy lawns of Lewiston. The comprehensive Campus Facilities Master Plan, undertaken over several years, has given Bates a new campus core in terms of facilities: Bates has transformed two former student residence halls into key academic buildings, converted a historic Victorian home into a new student residence, and dramatically renovated one of the country's earliest college football fields into a multisport turf field.

Bates emphasizes a broad-based education in the liberal arts that encompasses the humanities, sciences and mathematics, social sciences, and the arts. Although there are no core course requirements, students are expected to select a major and two general education concentrations, each consisting of four interrelated courses structured around a central theme, such as Buddhism, The Human Body, and Popular Culture. More than 75 concentrations are available, and they may fall within one department or program or may be designed by faculty from different disciplines. "One unique part of Bates is that just about all seniors write a thesis," says a chemistry major. "Some are semester-long, while others are yearlong, depending on the department and what you want to do." The Ladd Library is often crowded with the 97 percent of students who write a thesis or produce an equivalent research, service, performance, or studio project. Ladd has almost 600,000 printed volumes, plus an all-night study room, computer labs, and a music composition workstation.

> **"One unique part of Bates is that just about all seniors write a thesis."**

While Bates was a pioneer in not requiring standardized tests for admission, don't expect to coast through. "The academic climate at Bates is extremely rigorous," says one junior. "The academic standard for an institution such as Bates is high, and students are held to that standard in all aspects across all major and minor disciplines." The most popular majors include economics, psychology, politics, history, and environmental studies, and these are also among Bates's best. The music and art departments benefit from the Olin Arts Center, which houses a performance hall, gallery, recording studio, art studios, and practice rooms. Interdisciplinary programs at Bates include American cultural studies, neuroscience, and gender and sexuality studies. Professors teach all courses, including lab and discussion sections, and 69 percent of classes enroll fewer than 20 students. "The professors are always so accessible and make a real effort to get to know their students on a personal basis," one senior states.

For those whose horizons extend beyond the charms of Lewiston, Bates offers study abroad opportunities in more than 80 foreign locations, and 70 percent of

Website: www.bates.edu
Location: Small City
Private
Total Enrollment: 1,787
Undergraduates: 1,787
Male/Female: 49/51
SAT Ranges: ERW 640–730,
   M 630–720
ACT Ranges: 29–32
Financial Aid: 46%
Pell Grant: 11%
Expense: Pr $ $ $
Student Loans: 42%
Average Debt: $
Applicants: 5,316
Accepted: 22%
Enrolled: 42%
Grad in 6 Years: 88%
Returning Freshmen: 95%
Academics: ✐ ✐ ✐ ✐ ½
Social: ☎ ☎ ☎
Q of L: ★ ★ ★
Admissions: (855) 228-3755
Email Address: admission@
   bates.edu

Strong Programs:
Economics
Psychology
Politics
History
Environmental Studies

Bates offers study abroad opportunities in more than 80 foreign locations, and 70 percent of students take advantage of them.

students take advantage of them. Bates's 4–4–1 calendar allows for a five-week short term at the end of the academic year, and students may use this term to focus on a single subject of interest, frequently off campus. Recent examples include geological fieldwork in the Northern Rockies; marine biological studies at stations on the coast of Maine; and art, theater, and music studies in New York City and Europe. A "purposeful work" initiative includes practitioner-taught courses that, in an effort to blend philosophical and pragmatic themes, apply classroom lessons to real-world problems, such as finding mentors and reflecting on career paths that promote personal satisfaction.

Ten percent of Bates students come from Maine, 9 percent arrive from foreign countries, and many others hail from Massachusetts, Connecticut, and New York. "Students at Bates are intelligent, quirky, and eager to try new things," a student says. While the administration has slowly been making Bates more diverse, minorities remain a fragment of the student population, with African Americans accounting for 5 percent, Hispanics 8 percent, Asian Americans 4 percent, and multiracial students 5 percent. Students are drawn to social and political causes, and "Diversity is the biggest social issue on campus," reports a French major. There are no merit or athletic scholarships available, although the college does guarantee to meet the demonstrated need of all students.

"The professors are always so accessible and make a real effort to get to know their students."

Virtually all Bates students live on campus, as housing is guaranteed for four years, and singles, doubles, triples, quads, and suites are available. "Housing is great here," a student raves. Students report that the campus dining hall offers tasty fare, with several stations ranging from brick-oven pizza and pasta to a vegan bar. "We also have over sixty cereals in circulation in the dining hall," adds a politics major. Students say campus security is visible and more than adequate. "Given the nature of a small campus, students know a majority of the officers' names and do not feel intimidated to approach them about a problem," explains a history major.

Bates is home of the famed undergraduate debate organization the Brooks Quimby Debate Council, founded in 1855.

Since there's not much to do in Lewiston, weekend diversions mostly occur on campus. "Whether it is parties, comedians, movies, or bands, there is always something to do for everyone on campus," a freshman says. The Chase Hall Programming Board, run by students, plans many of the social events, including an annual gala. Without a Greek system, college alcohol policies are fairly loose, a student says, and a ban on hard liquor is often ignored. Barbecues and clambakes are big when the weather is nice, and the annual Winter Carnival includes a ski shredding competition, ice skating, and the Puddle Jump, where a hole is

"I came to Bates for the people."

cut in the ice on Lake Andrews and students plunge in. Students with cars can easily road-trip to the outlet stores in Freeport and Kittery, Maine. Other popular destinations include Bar Harbor in Acadia National Park, or "Portland, for great food," says a senior. Montreal and Boston are not far, and neither are the ski slopes of Vermont and New Hampshire. The Outing Club hosts weekend trips into the great Maine outdoors.

Bates's 31 varsity Bobcat teams compete in Division III, except for the ski team, which is Division I. Everyone gets excited for matches against Bowdoin and Colby, especially when it comes to basketball, football, and lacrosse. The women's rowing team won back-to-back national championships in 2017 and 2018. The intramural program, organized by the students, is "strong and spirited" and attracts a large number of participants, with softball, ultimate Frisbee, soccer, and basketball being some of the favorites. Bates is home of the famed undergraduate debate organization the Brooks Quimby Debate Council. Founded in 1855 when completing a public debate was a graduation requirement at Bates, the team was one of the first in the nation to go co-ed and to include African American students. Bates was also the first American institution to debate with foreign universities, and the team continues to achieve national success today.

If you can stand the cold and the silent, starry nights, Bates may be a good choice. With caring professors, a small student body, a focus on the liberal arts, and a free-spirited culture, students quickly become big fans. "I came to Bates for the people," says a sophomore. "The friends you make here will remain your friends well beyond your final days at Bates."

If You Apply To ›

Bates: Early decision I and II, regular decision. SATs or ACTs: optional. Subject Tests: optional. Accepts the Common Application.

Baylor University

Waco, TX 76798

The largest and best-endowed Baptist university anywhere, Baylor has set its sights on becoming a leading research university. Atmosphere is avowedly Christian, but religious image has been tarnished by continuing controversies over how it has dealt with allegations of sexual assault. Strong sense of community, especially when it comes to Saturday afternoon home football games.

Baylor University offers students a solid Christian-influenced education at a bargain price. The university was founded in 1845, 10 months before Texas became a state, and its Baptist tradition fosters a strong sense of community among students and faculty. The school's vision plan promises a slew of strategic changes, such as lowering the student/teacher ratio and building new residence halls while renovating old ones, and it is investing in resources to become a top-tier research university while enhancing its Christian identity. "Baylor's commitment to academic excellence and an incredible alumni network ensures a great education and a chance to get a job," says a junior.

The 1,000-acre Baylor campus abuts the historic Brazos River near downtown Waco, Texas (population 136,000). The architectural style emphasizes the gracious tradition of the Old South, and the central part of campus, the quadrangle, was built when Baylor moved from Independence, Texas, in 1886. The campus has been witness to a number of renovations and new construction, including the Foster Campus for Business and Innovation and an athletic nutrition center.

"The professors are engaging and encouraging."

Core requirements include four English courses and four semesters of human performance. All students also take two religion courses and two semesters of Chapel, a series of lectures and meetings on various aspects of faith and Christian service. Freshmen take a New Student Experience course in the fall. The Honors College oversees the honors program (which offers opportunities for course integration and independent research) and the University Scholars Program (which waives most distribution requirements).

Of Baylor's more than 140 undergraduate degrees, some of the most popular include biology, nursing, accounting, psychology, and finance. Computer science,

Website: www.baylor.edu
Location: Small City
Private
Total Enrollment: 16,350
Undergraduates: 14,085
Male/Female: 41/59
SAT Ranges: ERW 600–680, M 590–680
ACT Ranges: 26–31
Financial Aid: 94%
Pell Grant: 15%
Expense: Pr $ $
Student Loans: 52%
Average Debt: $ $ $ $
Applicants: 37,083
Accepted: 39%
Enrolled: 23%
Grad in 6 Years: 77%
Returning Freshmen: 90%
Academics: ✍ ✍ ✍
Social: ☎ ☎ ☎
Q of L: ★ ★ ★
Admissions: (254) 710-3435

(continued)

Email Address: admissions@
baylor.edu

Strong Programs:
Biology
Nursing
Accounting
Psychology
Finance
Computer Science
Engineering
Communication Sciences and
Disorders

Most of Baylor's more than 330 student organizations involve a community service requirement.

The women's basketball team claimed its eighth straight Big 12 conference title in 2018.

engineering, and communication sciences and disorders are well regarded. More unusual options include institutes focusing on environmental studies and child-hood learning disorders, and a major and minor in Great Texts, an interdisciplinary program exploring "the richness and diversity of the Western intellectual heritage." The archaeology and geosciences departments benefit from fossil- and mineral-rich Texas prairies. Seventeen percent of students travel on study abroad programs, which send them packing to dozens of countries, including China, Spain, Costa Rica, and the Netherlands.

Students say that one of Baylor's greatest strengths is the sense of campus community, fostered by the emphasis on Christianity and the faculty's focus on teaching, along with research. Baylor also strives to keep classes small—52 percent have fewer than 20 students. The university's endowment is hefty and the largest among the nation's Baptist-affiliated schools. "Most of my prerequisite classes tended to be more collaborative and relaxed, but once I started taking the upper-level business courses, the atmosphere became much more competitive," says a senior. Full professors often teach freshman courses, and opportunities for mentored research abound. "The professors are engaging and encouraging," says one sophomore.

"The students at Baylor tend to be kind, involved, and driven," says a finance and economics major. "They differ from some of our closest rivals mainly because of the spiritual influence that many students tend to have and seek out." Sixty-seven percent of undergraduates are Texans and 27 percent are Baptists; 3 percent are international. African Americans account for 6 percent of the student body, Hispanics 15 percent, Asian Americans 6 percent, and multiracial students 5 percent. The university has launched several initiatives to increase and support diversity on campus, including cultural competence training for students, faculty, and staff. Students vie for numerous academic scholarships, averaging $15,000, and 342 athletic scholarships in 19 varsity sports.

As might be expected on such a conservative, religious campus, dorms are single sex and have limited visitation privileges, which is a complaint among many of the 35 percent of students who call them home. Upperclassmen look off campus for cheaper housing with private rooms and fewer rules, but there has been a push for more students to stay on campus with the recent construction of three residence halls with apartment-style rooms. Students say they feel safe, provided they stay on campus. "There are lights everywhere on campus and police cars constantly patrolling the grounds," one student explains. Moreover, "there are people on watch at all times, especially at night." Allegations that Baylor failed to comply with gender-equity laws or to respond properly to incidents of sexual violence led to the resignation of the president and football coach. Under new leadership, the university says that it has implemented "more than 100 improvements to infrastructure, policies, and procedures," including sexual assault training and prevention programs.

Eighteen percent of Baylor's men and 33 percent of the women belong to a fraternity or sorority, and students may also choose from more than 330 other student organizations, most of which involve a community service requirement. With so many students residing off campus, the social life is active but not a party atmosphere. "Alcohol is much less prevalent at Baylor than at most schools," says a senior. It isn't served on campus or at campus-sponsored events. "Common Grounds, an on-campus coffee shop, hosts concerts most weekends," says one student. "The movies are popular (a ticket costs $5 with a student ID)." Easy road trips include Dallas, Austin, San Antonio, Bryan/College Station, and beaches at Galveston, South Padre Island, and Corpus Christi. Most destinations are within a two-and-a-half-hour drive, students say, making a set of wheels a big help, if not a necessity.

Highlights of Baylor's social calendar include the weekly Dr Pepper Hour with free soda floats and Dia del Oso (Day of the Bear), when classes are canceled for a day in April in favor of a campuswide celebration. Christmas on 5th Street, organized by Student Life, gives students an opportunity to enjoy the annual Christmas tree lighting, concert, and other holiday festivities. The school also has the largest collegiate homecoming parade in the nation.

When it comes to football, remember: you're in Texas. The Division I Baylor Bears play in the $266 million McLane Stadium. Freshmen wear special, custom jerseys to games and take the field before the players, then sit together as a pack. "It's a very awesome part of the freshman experience," one student says. The women's basketball team, perennial Big 12 conference champions, dethroned Notre Dame to win the national championship in 2019. In 2018 the acrobatics and tumbling team repeated as national champions. Other recent conference champs include baseball, equestrian, women's track and field, and women's soccer. For weekend warriors, the McLane Student Life Center offers the tallest rock-climbing wall in Texas. The university maintains a small marina for kayaking and paddleboating, and several lakes with good beaches, fishing, and watersports are nearby. Forty-three percent of students play intramural and club sports; popular intramurals include flag football, indoor volleyball, and the country's largest collegiate dodgeball tournament.

"Baylor is a Baptist institution that has been 100 percent commissioned to do God's work in education," states one student. As the university struggles to put its sexual assault scandals in the rearview mirror, students looking to focus on strong academics, community involvement, and discovering their vocational calling may find a good fit here.

> "[Baylor students] differ from some of our closest rivals mainly because of the spiritual influence."

Overlaps

Texas A&M, UT Austin, Texas Tech, Texas Christian, Texas State, UT San Antonio, University of North Texas, University of Oklahoma

If You Apply To ›

Baylor: Early action, regular decision. SATs or ACTs: required. No Subject Tests. Accepts the Common Application with supplement.

Beloit College

700 College Street, Beloit, WI 53511

A small Midwestern college known for freethinking students, international focus, and ever-growing emphasis on practical, hands-on experiences. Wisconsin location makes Beloit easier to get into than comparable schools in sexier places. Well-known anthropology program is among the best in the nation.

Beloit College remains dedicated to the liberal arts and sciences, but encourages students to "practice the liberal arts by integrating knowledge with hands-on experience." Known for attracting liberal freethinkers in the 1960s and '70s, the school has steered back toward the mainstream. What hasn't changed is its emphasis on tolerance, understanding, and the world beyond the United States. "To really enjoy Beloit, you should be open to new ideas, concepts, and people," advises an education and youth studies major. "You will learn how to think critically about your positions and beliefs and work to have a deeper understanding of the world as a whole."

Beloit's 40-acre campus is a Northeastern-style oasis an hour's drive from Madison and Milwaukee and less than two hours from Chicago. Academic and administrative buildings sit on one side, with residence halls on the other. Two architectural

Website: www.beloit.edu
Location: Small City
Private
Total Enrollment: 1,320
Undergraduates: 1,320
Male/Female: 48/52
SAT Ranges: ERW 560–660, M 550–710
ACT Ranges: 24–30
Financial Aid: 98%

(continued)

Pell Grant: 25%
Expense: Pr $ $ $
Student Loans: 65%
Average Debt: $ $
Applicants: 5,400
Accepted: 54%
Enrolled: 11%
Grad in 6 Years: 86%
Returning Freshmen: 85%
Academics: ✐ ✐ ✐
Social: ☎ ☎ ☎
Q of L: ★ ★ ★ ★
Admissions: (608) 363-2500
Email Address: admiss@
beloit.edu

Strong Programs:
Anthropology
Creative Writing
Economics
Theater
Dance
Health and Society
Psychology
Political Science

As part of Beloit's experiential learning and global diversity requirements, students may apply for summer Venture Grants of up to $2,000.

themes dominate, says one student: "1850s colonial and obtuse 1930s." The college's Turtle Creek Bookstore, located three blocks away in downtown Beloit, offers a cozy coffee bar and a patio for relaxing, reading, or studying. Slated for completion in late 2019, the college's newest facility is a 120,000-square-foot student union and recreation center called the Powerhouse; the $38 million project has repurposed a defunct power plant on the Rock River, adjacent to campus.

Beloit does not have core requirements. Instead, students complete a required "beyond the classroom" Liberal Arts in Practice experience, three writing-intensive courses, a quantitative reasoning class, one intercultural literacy course, and a capstone experience. In addition to a First-Year Initiatives seminar in their first semester, Beloiters tackle classes across five domains that focus on systems, arts, behavior, the universe, and texts.

Anthropology is a signature program at Beloit, and the creative writing, economics, theater, and dance programs are also popular and well regarded. Health and society, psychology, and political science enroll high numbers too. Among the more unusual options are a museum studies minor, enhanced by hands-on experience in the college's Wright Museum of Art and Logan Museum of Anthropology, which was established in 1894. The health and society major encourages students to take an interdisciplinary look at health and medical care in the U.S. and around the world. Cross-registration is available with the University of Wisconsin–Madison, as is a 3–2 engineering degree with nine institutions.

> **"Students are expected to do significant work—papers, research, symposiums."**

The academic milieu is described as challenging but not competitive. "Students are expected to do significant work—papers, research, symposiums—but there is also an atmosphere of meaningful collaboration," says one student. Teaching is the faculty's first priority, and 68 percent of classes have fewer than 20 students. "I have always felt that faculty have worked with me to achieve my own goals and have opened themselves to their classes entirely," says an international relations and French double major. "They learn with us much of the time, as opposed to being a font of knowledge—the learning goes both ways."

As part of Beloit's experiential learning and global diversity requirements, students may apply for summer Venture Grants, which offer up to $2,000 for "entrepreneurial, self-testing, or intellectually challenging" activities that engage with outside communities; recent awardees have volunteered with an organic farming and reforesting initiative on the Galápagos Islands and studied women's health issues at tea plantations in Sri Lanka. The Sanger Summer Scholars program provides full funding for students to work directly with a faculty member on a research project, and students may also conduct biological and biomedical research at Northwestern and Rush Universities in Chicago. The Center for Entrepreneurship in Liberal Education at Beloit enables students from any major to plan and execute original entrepreneurial projects. Forty-one percent of Beloit's students study or do research abroad and may choose from programs in 50 countries.

> **"Beloiters like to be different. We like to think of ourselves as iconoclasts."**

"Beloiters like to be different," observes a creative writing major. "We like to think of ourselves as iconoclasts." Eighty-five percent of students hail from out of state, including 16 percent who come from abroad. Hispanics comprise 10 percent of the total, African Americans 7 percent, Asian Americans 3 percent, and multiracial students 4 percent. The Sustained Dialogue program encourages conversations about diversity and identity. Beloit may not be as far-out as it once was, but one history major describes the student body as "aggressively liberal," adding, "If you are conservative, politically or socially, Beloit will eat you alive." Merit scholarships averaging $25,500 are available, although there are no athletic scholarships. Twenty-five percent of freshmen are Pell-eligible.

Eighty-eight percent of Beloit students live in the 37 on-campus housing facilities, where they're required to remain for three years. "The dorms at Beloit will never win an award for beauty, but the rooms are large and comfortable," according to one student. Fraternities attract 19 percent of the men, and sororities draw 20 percent of the women; members may live in their chapter houses. Numerous special-interest houses cater to those interested in foreign languages, music, anthropology, and other disciplines, as well as to student organizations. Food in the Commons dining hall is said to be hit-or-miss at best, but options in D.K.'s Café and Java Joint are better received; co-ops where students cook for each other are an option too. "Our campus security and resident assistants do a great job of keeping an eye out for our campus community," says a student.

Social life is almost entirely campus-based. "On the weekends there are always events going on such as lectures, music groups, movie showings, theater productions, dance shows, and parties," says one junior. Two all-campus festivals liven up the calendar: the Folk and Blues Fall Music Festival brings jazz, reggae, folk, and blues bands to campus, while on Spring Day classes give way to a carnival and everyone kicks back to enjoy the (finally!) warmer weather. Traditional Bell Runs involve running from the quad to a bell and back, disencumbered of clothing. Students describe the party scene as very low-key, and Greek organizations often team up with special-interest houses and other student clubs to throw parties. The school's attitude toward alcohol is relaxed, students say. "We have an alcohol philosophy," says a sociology major. "Beloit would never go so far as to say 'policy.'"

Beloit (population 37,000) is a small, historically industrial city that has been undergoing a revitalization in recent years. "The town of Beloit is in the midst of a change. It was previously in fairly poor economic shape; however the downtown is making a comeback," a student says. Several new restaurants, bars, and shops have popped up, as has a Saturday farmers market, and the city also offers a bowling alley, a movie theater, and a Walmart. "Groups such as Habitat for Humanity, Beloit Interaction Committee, and the Outreach Center work hard to integrate students into the community," says a sophomore. When in need of a change of scenery, Beloiters take off for Chicago or the college town of Madison, easily reached through a cheap regional bus service. For the outdoors-minded, the nearby Dells offer camping and water parks.

Sports at Beloit are played more for fun than glory, unless it's a football game against rival Ripon College. Among the school's 19 Division III Buccaneers squads, standouts include baseball, men's and women's track and field and cross-country, and men's lacrosse. Intramural ultimate Frisbee typically draws hundreds of players and spectators, and more than one-third of students participate in the intramural program, with basketball, volleyball, and soccer also popular.

Beloit is a bundle of contradictions: a small liberal arts college in the heart of Big Ten state university country, and an academic program that has an East Coast rigor but a laid-back classroom vibe reflective of the friendly spirit of the Midwest. Although the school continues to evolve, "the essential core of Beloit has stayed the same," says a senior. "It is still a campus full of artistic creators, unabashed activists, and people who love making dorm-room forts. We're still weird, and we like it that way."

Traditional Bell Runs involve running from the quad to a bell and back, disencumbered of clothing.

"Downtown [Beloit] is making a comeback."

Overlaps

Grinnell, Carleton, Macalester, Lawrence, Kalamazoo, Knox, St. Olaf, College of Wooster

If You Apply To ›

Beloit: Early decision, early action I and II, regular decision. SATs or ACTs: optional (required for homeschooled students). Subject Tests: optional. Accepts the Common Application with supplement.

Bennington, VT 05201-6003

Known for top-notch performing arts and lavish attention on every student. Arts programs rely heavily on faculty who are practitioners in their field. Less competitive than Bard and Sarah Lawrence, comparable to Hampshire. With just over 700 undergraduates, Bennington is one-third the size of most liberal arts colleges. New leadership has revitalized the Bennington brand and reversed an enrollment slump.

Website: www.bennington
 .edu
Location: Small Town
Private
Total Enrollment: 793
Undergraduates: 717
Male/Female: 33/67
SAT Ranges: ERW 620–710,
 M 590–680
ACT Ranges: 27–31
Financial Aid: 86%
Pell Grant: 23%
Expense: Pr $ $ $ $
Student Loans: 65%
Average Debt: $ $
Applicants: 1,465
Accepted: 57%
Enrolled: 26%
Grad in 6 Years: 67%
Returning Freshmen: 78%
Academics: ✐ ✐ ✐
Social: ☎ ☎ ☎
Q of L: ★ ★ ★ ★
Admissions: (800) 833-6845
Email Address: admissions@
 bennington.edu

Strong Programs:
Visual Arts
Literature
Society, Culture, and Thought
Foreign Languages
Anthropology
Dance
Computer Science
Mathematics

Bennington College is a school where architects are teachers, biologists sculpt, and a sociologist might work on Wall Street or in graphic design. It's no wonder they strive to abandon the theory of regimented knowledge. Bennington's focus is on learning by doing. The emphasis on self-direction, fieldwork, and personal relationships with professors sets it apart even from other liberal arts colleges of similar (small) size. Says one junior, "If you want an education you can shape yourself and you want that education to transcend your homework and the classroom, this is a great place to go to school."

Bennington sits on 470 acres at the foot of Vermont's Green Mountains. The campus was once an active dairy farm, and a converted barn houses the main classroom and administrative spaces. But don't let the quaint New England setting fool you. The Dickinson Science Building boasts high-tech equipment for aspiring chemists, biologists, environmental scientists, and geneticists. A 14,000-square-foot student center offers a snack bar, grill, convenience store, and multipurpose spaces.

> "Students here are encouraged to study the things that keep them up at night."

Thanks to its focus on John Dewey–style experiential learning, Bennington's academic structure differs from that of a typical college or university. Rather than selecting from preset majors, students design their own cross-disciplinary course of study (known as their "Plan"). There are some academic requirements, including the Field Work Term, in which students spend seven weeks each January and February conducting an internship in a field of interest and a location of their choice—meaning that all students graduate with at least four internships under their belts. Students receive narrative evaluations instead of grades (although they do have the option to request grades in addition to the evaluations). Even Bennington's application process is nontraditional. In lieu of a standard application, prospective students may choose to submit a "dimensional application"—an open-form application that allows them to choose any materials, in any format, that they believe best convey why they are well suited to attend Bennington. This alternative application seems to have captured the attention of many students; it's just one of the moves the college's president has made to successfully turn around a decline in applications and enrollment.

The most popular areas of study include visual arts; literature; society, culture, and thought; foreign languages; anthropology; and performing arts, especially dance. Computer science and mathematics are strong too, although they attract a smaller number of students than many of the college's programs. "Half of the students here do work in the arts, whether it's theater or dance or studio art. Those are obviously well regarded," says a sophomore. Consistent with Bennington's judgment that traditional academics have become "insular and self-perpetuating," the Center for the Advancement of Public Action invites

> "[Students are] introspective, intelligent, and well-spoken, sometimes to the point of pretension."

students to put the world's most pressing social problems at the center of their education via classwork and hands-on workshops. Closely related are the "pop-up mini-courses" that faculty offer in response to unfolding events or current cultural phenomena. Recent topics of these three-week courses, often suggested by students, have included gun violence and "the semiotics of Trump." Cross-registration options at nearby Williams College expand students' access to course offerings, and 26 percent of Bennington students study abroad.

Rather than selecting from preset majors, students design their own cross-disciplinary course of study (known as their "Plan").

"Students here are encouraged to study the things that keep them up at night, that are important to them personally," explains a literature, music, and drama student. As a result, students tend to bring a certain level of intensity to their classes, "because they genuinely want to be there." Eighty-nine percent of courses enroll fewer than 20 students. Without academic departments, the faculty works to provide students with a well-rounded academic foundation. "Professors work independently with students on their personal trajectory of progress," says a student studying conflict resolution. The First-Year Forum is a yearlong advising program that acclimates students to Bennington's approach to academics.

Curiosity and excitement about exploration and experimentation will take you far here, and if you lean liberal in the voting booth, so much the better. Because of the intense focus on personal development, Bennington students are "introspective, intelligent, and well-spoken," says a senior, "sometimes to the point of pretension." Just 2 percent of undergrads are from Vermont, and a surprising 18 percent are foreign nationals. Other types of diversity are a challenge: African Americans account for only 3 percent of the student body, Hispanics 10 percent, Asian Americans 2 percent, and multiracial students 5 percent. Women outnumber men 2 to 1. Merit scholarships worth an average of $25,600 are awarded to qualified students; there are no athletic scholarships available. Twenty-three percent of freshmen receive Pell Grants.

"Most weekends, one house or several will host dance parties (dark room, loud music, dancing people)."

As Bennington lacks traditional departments, requirements, and even faculty tenure, it's probably not surprising that the school also eschews traditional dorms. Ninety-eight percent of students live in one of the college's co-ed houses; 12 are white New England clapboard, and six are more modern. Each house holds 30 to 40 people with two appointed chairs to govern house affairs. "Each house has a distinct history and personality," says a student, "and exists on a spectrum of social climate, from loud/quiet to party/study." The college's food service provides plenty of options, and a senior says, "As a vegetarian, I have always been satisfied." A literature student states, "Students feel comfortable and safe on campus"; others note that, in response to student complaints, the administration has worked to restructure how it deals with sexual assault cases.

The First-Year Forum is a yearlong advising program that acclimates students to Bennington's approach to academics.

With no Greek system, social life happens in the residential houses. "Most weekends, one house or several will host dance parties (dark room, loud music, dancing people)," says a student, and "there is often heavy drinking on the weekends," adds another. Students say campus alcohol policies focus on keeping students safe rather than punishing them. Annual theme parties always draw raves—themes have included Gatsby's Funeral and Mods vs. Rockers—and twice each year, the college turns part of its huge Visual and Performing Arts complex into an indoor roller rink for a Rollerama party. For 12 hours one day each May, the campus celebrates spring with Sunfest, which includes bands, games, and other events. And during the last week of each term, when (in lieu of final exams) students present their work to faculty, the blaring of fire-truck sirens calls weary students to the dining hall, where professors, staff, and the college president serve up French toast and other breakfast favorites.

Although the vibe on Bennington's campus is liberal and cosmopolitan, the neighboring town of the same name—four miles away—is far more conservative, typical of rural New England. For that reason, one student says, students often avoid it, and "when you combine the hilltop isolation of the campus, the result is a sense of an enclave." Still, the area offers some good restaurants, coffee shops, galleries, and a lake with a public beach. Students also find their way into the community through volunteer work in local schools and homeless shelters, though committing to long-term programs can be tough because of the mandatory midyear internship term, which takes most students away from campus.

Sports aren't a big focus. Bennington has no varsity teams, and intramurals draw just 10 percent of students, but a handful of club teams do compete against other Northeastern colleges. The college has also partnered with Southern Vermont College and the NCAA to allow students to try out and compete with SVC's Division III athletic program. The way one student sees it, "Bennington kids prefer going to a dance performance or poetry reading over playing sports." But, given Bennington's rugged location, hiking, rock climbing, caving, camping, and canoeing keep students moving. Ski slopes beckon in the colder months.

As the first school in the nation to grant the arts equal status with other disciplines, Bennington offers a novel, participatory, and hands-on approach. Whether they're painters or writers, musicians or scientists, sculptors, dancers, or some combination thereof, what Bennington students have in common is self-motivation and a real thirst for knowledge. Says one student, "At Bennington, students have the opportunity to study what they want, but need to be driven to make it happen."

If You Apply To ›

Bennington: Early decision I and II, early action, regular decision. SATs or ACTs: optional. Subject Tests: optional. Accepts the Common Application with supplement. Applicants may submit an alternative "dimensional application" consisting of any materials they choose; under this option, transcripts are preferred but not required.

Bentley University

175 Forest Street, Waltham, MA 02452

Bentley means business—studying it, that is, in the context of strong liberal arts. Now competes on even footing with archrival Babson. Offers both B.A. and B.S. degrees and provides career-oriented internships to 92 percent of its students. Bentley's scenic colonial-style campus is at arm's length from Boston with shuttles to Harvard Square.

Bentley University is a small New England university that excels at turning out men and women who are committed to taking their place among the ranks of future business leaders. "Bentley prepares its students for the workplace by giving them comparable experiences socially, academically, and—most importantly—professionally," says a sophomore. With the university's solid courses in business, state-of-the-art facilities, and a dedication to the liberal arts, students find much to admire.

Bentley is situated on 163 acres in Waltham, Massachusetts, just minutes west of the hustle and bustle of Boston. The dominant architectural style is Georgian, and the majority of campus buildings are classically built in redbrick. The Bentley campus has three tiers. The upper campus revolves around academics and features a library, "smart" classrooms, and high-tech labs and academic centers. Mid-campus centers on student life and is anchored by the 70,000-square-foot student center. Finally, the lower campus focuses on recreation and includes the Dana Athletic Center. Residential housing is spread throughout each tier of the campus. The newest addition to campus is the Bentley Arena, designed to accommodate the school's Division I ice hockey team as well as large-scale special events like guest speakers and concerts.

Bentley has long been committed to producing "liberally educated business students," and this is reflected in the curriculum, which offers both B.A. and B.S. tracks. Although certain requirements vary based on which track a student is on, every student must complete both a general education core covering a broad range of liberal arts disciplines and a general business core. Those pursuing B.S. degrees in business must complete a team project in partnership with an area business or nonprofit group. Freshmen take a mandatory, one-credit First-Year Seminar that is designed to help them with their overall adjustment to college, including academic and social decision-making. Their seminar instructor also serves as their academic advisor for the first three semesters. In addition, freshmen take a six-week Career Development Introduction Seminar, cotaught by career services advisors and professionals from top companies like Fidelity and Liberty Mutual, to get on track early for internships and jobs.

> "[Adjunct professors] bring in real-world examples from their current work and projects."

Not surprisingly, Bentley's most popular majors are finance, economics-finance, marketing, corporate finance and accounting, and management. Students seeking a B.S. degree have their pick of more than a dozen disciplines, including majors in managerial economics and professional sales, while those pursuing B.A. degrees have a slightly more limited selection that includes such fields as English, global studies, sustainability science, and health studies. Motivated students may choose the liberal studies major (LSM), a highly integrated (and optional) second major that must be paired with a business or business-related major and requires a final project in the senior year. About 20 percent of students pursue this option. Current LSM concentrations range from American studies to earth, environment, and global sustainability to quantitative perspectives.

"Bentley is competitive in a sense because we are all career-driven and want to do well in similar fields, but there is also a great sense of camaraderie," says a sophomore. Nineteen percent of classes have fewer than 20 students, but none have more than 50, and group work is routine. Adjunct professors and senior lecturers with professional expertise teach many of the courses, and a finance major says this is beneficial because they can "bring in real-world examples from their current work and projects." Students rave about career services and academic support, which includes "free tutoring centers for almost every subject."

> "Bentley students are wealthy and privileged on average."

As befits the university's focus on the corporate world, approximately 92 percent of undergraduates participate in experiential learning via internships. In keeping with the university's mission to educate students to be active leaders in a global economy, the Cronin Office of International Education offers semester, summer, or week-long faculty-led programs, many of which include internship and service-learning opportunities. Half of the students go abroad before they graduate. The top 10 percent of students in each entering class are invited to participate in the honors program, which tackles a variety of topics—from the ethics of genetic research to analyzing complex financial crises—all in a seminar setting that is designed to promote discussion and debate.

(continued)

Financial Aid: 77%
Pell Grant: 13%
Expense: Pr $ $
Student Loans: 54%
Average Debt: $ $ $
Applicants: 8,867
Accepted: 44%
Enrolled: 26%
Grad in 6 Years: 91%
Returning Freshmen: 92%
Academics: ✍ ✍ ✍
Social: ☎ ☎ ☎
Q of L: ★ ★ ★
Admissions: (800) 523-2354
Email Address:
  ugadmission@bentley.edu

Strong Programs:
Finance
Economics-Finance
Marketing
Corporate Finance and
  Accounting
Management
Managerial Economics
Professional Sales
Global Studies

Freshmen take a Career Development Introduction Seminar cotaught by career services advisors and professionals from top companies.

The liberal studies major is an optional second major that must be paired with a business or business-related major.

"Bentley students are wealthy and privileged on average. Most share a common drive and business savviness," says a marketing major. Although nearly twice the size of rival Babson College, Bentley's undergraduate student body is less diverse. Thirty-six percent of Bentley undergrads are from Massachusetts, and 14 percent are international. African Americans comprise 3 percent of the student body, Asian Americans 8 percent, Hispanics 7 percent, and multiracial students 2 percent. Bentley has a conservative tenor, but for students, social and political issues generally take a back seat to classes and internships. Merit scholarships averaging $19,700 are doled out annually, and talented athletes vie for 107 athletic scholarships in 12 sports.

The university's student residences include apartments, suites, and traditional dormitories and house 78 percent of the student body. "Rooms are large and renovated often, facilities are very accessible, and selecting housing is generally easy," says a senior. A third of students participate in living/learning communities, in which service learning is a big emphasis. The various dining facilities offer the usual college fare, and those on the meal plan are given unlimited meals at the main dining hall, although some say that's not really a perk. Students report feeling safe on campus, thanks to an active police patrol, 24/7 safety escorts, and "Title IX staff who are in constant contact with students and put on various events throughout the year," says a junior.

Students say the social scene begins on campus and spills out into the surrounding areas. "There is so much involvement in Bentley's 100-plus organizations," says one student. "A group is bound to have an event on any given day."

"Waltham does not play a huge role in a Bentley student's daily way of life."

Sponsored events include the annual Back to Bentley and Spring Day festivals, a Boston scavenger hunt, "drive-in" movies on the quad, and activities put on by various cultural groups, like Latin dance night. Practically the entire student body shows up for Super Bingo, "which is like normal bingo, but with awesome prizes like TVs and iPhones," explains a sophomore. The Greek system attracts 16 percent of the men and 19 percent of the women, and Greeks and sports teams host off-campus parties, but neither group dominates the social scene. Students of legal age may have alcohol, but "peer pressure is not an issue" for those who prefer not to imbibe, according to one accounting major.

Students get fired up anytime rival Babson takes the field, and a predictable T-shirt reads, "Friends don't let friends go to Babson."

Waltham may not have the cachet of nearby Boston, but students say it has the basic amenities every college student craves: restaurants, bars, shops, and salons. "Overall, Waltham does not play a huge role in a Bentley student's daily way of life," comments one student. For those seeking a bit more action, the university provides a free shuttle into Harvard Square, where students can mix and mingle with peers from other local colleges and universities. Jaunts to the beaches of New Hampshire, the ski resorts of Vermont, and weekend trips to the Cape make for popular diversions as well.

Competition at Bentley is not confined to the classroom; the university also fields 22 men's and women's varsity teams at the Division II level and a competitive Division I men's ice hockey team. Other solid Falcon teams include men's and women's basketball, women's field hockey, and men's cross-country and golf. The powerhouse women's basketball team has competed in a record 34 NCAA tournaments. Students get fired up anytime rivals Babson and Bryant take the field, and there is the predictable T-shirt reading, "Friends don't let friends go to Babson." Intramurals draw roughly 60 percent of students; popular activities include flag football, soccer, volleyball, and ultimate Frisbee.

"Bentley is a school that will simulate the real world as much as possible so that its students graduate prepared!" says one enthusiastic junior. Like the university

Overlaps

Babson, Boston College, Bryant, Boston University, Northeastern, UMass Amherst, UConn, Fordham

itself, Bentley students have a keen sense of who they are and where they're headed. For those students charting a course into the upper echelons of corporate America, Bentley may be the first step to a long and fruitful career.

If You Apply To ›

Bentley: Early decision, regular decision. SATs or ACTs: required. Subject Tests: optional. Accepts the Common Application with supplement.

Birmingham–Southern College

Box 549008, 900 Arkakelphia Road, Birmingham, AL 35254

One of the Deep South's better liberal arts colleges, BSC is smaller than Rhodes (Tennessee), larger than Millsaps (Mississippi). Strong emphasis on service, and the Greek system is a throwback to the way college used to be. "Tuition reset" initiative aims to mitigate the problem of sticker shock by significantly lowering the price of tuition and fees.

Once an old-school conservative Southern institution, BSC is now striving to prepare students for all aspects of the modern world, with high-tech facilities and a more global curriculum. Affiliated with the United Methodist Church, the college continues to emphasize the value of service: more than half the student body volunteers through the Bunting Center for Engaged Study and Community Action. Attentive faculty add to a sense of commitment to both personal and community growth.

Known as the Hilltop for obvious topographical reasons, BSC is the product of the 1918 merger of two smaller colleges: Birmingham College and Southern University. The 190-acre campus, a green and shady oasis in an urban neighborhood, contains a pleasing hodgepodge of traditional and modern architecture, all surrounded by a security fence for added safety. After a major financial crisis several years ago, student enrollment is back on the rise, and the school has reestablished some previously cut programs and is beginning to introduce new majors.

The Explorations general education curriculum is designed to help students develop effective communication and problem-solving skills, connect with their social and political world, and direct their own learning. It comprises 32 units across several disciplines and includes three global and local citizenship courses. All freshmen take an introductory first-year seminar, and all seniors complete a capstone experience and a public presentation of their work. The Explorations term, a four-week term between the fall and spring semesters, allows students to explore new interests and areas of study, from courses like Bob Dylan in America to teaching English in Uganda.

Business administration, biology, mathematics, and education are the most popular majors. Students interested in medical or law school can participate in special advising programs, and new majors are available in health sciences and architectural studies. The art, theater, and music programs are all among the best in the South, and the college offers a major in musical theater as well. Students stage several major productions each year, often including American and world premieres.

> "[Professors] love to challenge our beliefs and ideas by making us defend what we think."

Website: www.bsc.edu
Location: City Outskirts
Private
Total Enrollment: 1,272
Undergraduates: 1,272
Male/Female: 48/52
SAT Ranges: ERW 520–630, M 510–630
ACT Ranges: 23–29
Financial Aid: 93%
Pell Grant: 24%
Expense: Pr $
Student Loans: 52%
Average Debt: $ $ $
Applicants: 2,559
Accepted: 62%
Enrolled: 23%
Grad in 6 Years: 66%
Returning Freshmen: 75%
Academics: ✍ ✍ ✍
Social: ☎ ☎ ☎
Q of L: ★ ★ ★
Admissions: (205) 226-4696
Email Address: admiss@bsc.edu

Strong Programs:
Business Administration
Biology
Mathematics

Other notable majors include media and film studies and applied computer science. Dual-degree programs in engineering and nursing are offered in partnership with such institutions as the University of Alabama, Auburn, and Vanderbilt.

The courses at BSC are "somewhat competitive" and "challenging but not impossible," according to one senior. Each student is assigned a faculty member who serves as his or her academic advisor from freshman convocation to graduation, an arrangement that students praise for its effectiveness. Equal praise goes out to faculty in the classrooms, where 63 percent of classes have fewer than 20 students. An education major says professors "love to challenge our beliefs and ideas by making us defend what we think." The honors program allows 30 exceptional first-year students to take small seminars with one or more professors. The Krulak Institute coordinates opportunities for experiential learning, such as service-learning projects, study abroad programs, and an entrepreneurial scholars program. Fifteen percent of BSC students study internationally, and 25 percent collaborate with faculty on research projects.

All seniors complete a capstone experience and a public presentation of their work.

Fifty-eight percent of the students are homegrown Alabamians, and practically all the rest hail from Deep South states; many have family ties to BSC. Though moderate by Alabama standards, the student body is quite conservative. "Students at BSC tend to be overcommitted by most standards," says a freshman. Twelve percent of BSC students are African American, 2 percent are Hispanic, 5 percent are Asian American, and 1 percent are multiracial. Just 1 percent of students are international, but, "We have an expanding international student base and multicultural affairs [office]," a student says. "The college is taking steps to diversify." Twenty-four percent of incoming freshmen receive Pell Grants. Beginning with the 2018–19 school year and continuing for 2019–20, Birmingham–Southern has reset tuition and fees back to 2002 levels—decreasing these costs by more than half—in an effort to avoid the sticker shock caused by high published prices that can deter applicants. With this change, merit- and need-based financial aid is still awarded to eligible students, although in smaller amounts.

Eighty-four percent of the students live on campus, including many whose families reside in Birmingham. First-years all live together in four traditional halls that have recently been renovated. Dorms are described as comfortable and convenient. "You can wake up 10 minutes before class, get ready, walk to class, and still have two or three minutes to spare," says a business administration major. Dining facilities have received mixed reviews, but that may improve with the recent switch to a new food service provider. Campus security officials are said to be visible and effective.

"The college is taking steps to diversify."

Nineteen percent of the men and 28 percent of the women are members of Greek organizations, which tend to set the tone. "Social life is good on campus," says a student. "Many people are involved in Greek life, but there is no pressure for others to join or hang out with them. They are very open to having non-Greeks spend time with them and are not exclusive." As for alcohol, it's not allowed on the quad, and elsewhere it must be in an opaque container, a policy most students find reasonable, described by one senior as a "'don't see it, ignore it' policy." The biggest social event of the year is Soco, a two-day festival. Freshmen take part in a square dance during orientation. Other popular events include E-Fest and Halloween on the Hilltop, where students "dress up in costumes and the neighborhood kids go trick-or-treating." When social opportunities on campus dry up, many students take the shuttle to Birmingham for the city's nightlife. Road trips to Auburn, Nashville, and Atlanta are popular, and beaches and mountains are less than five hours away.

Birmingham–Southern has reset tuition and fees back to 2002 levels—decreasing these costs by more than half.

BSC currently fields 22 varsity teams for men and women. The Panthers compete in the Division III Southern Athletic Association, and the baseball, men's track and field, women's basketball, and men's and women's swimming and diving teams have won multiple conference championships in the last few years. Forty-two percent of students take part in the intramural program. Basketball, flag football, and soccer are popular, but less traditional sports, such as dodgeball and inner-tube water polo, are also offered.

Students at BSC continue to focus on academics while balancing community service and an active social scene. Small classes, a caring faculty, and an expanding menu of academic offerings continue to draw attention to this close-knit liberal arts school. A junior says BSC is a good choice for those students who "want to spend four years preparing, maturing, and challenging their minds so that they can make a difference in the world."

If You Apply To ›

Birmingham–Southern: Early decision, early action, regular decision. SATs or ACTs: optional (test-optional applicants must interview and submit academic portfolio). No Subject Tests. Accepts the Common Application with supplement.

Boston College

140 Commonwealth Avenue, Devlin Hall, Room 208, Chestnut Hill, MA 02467

One of the main reasons that Boston is the ultimate college town. Set on a quiet hilltop at the end of a T (subway) line, BC is a close second to Notre Dame in the pecking order among true-blue Catholics (though many students clamoring for a spot are not aware of its religious ties). About 70 percent of students are Catholic, compared to 50 percent at Georgetown and 80 percent at Notre Dame.

Boston College, one of the largest Roman Catholic schools in the country, is a study in contrasts. The academics and the athletic teams are both well respected. The environment is safely suburban, yet barely 20 minutes from Boston, the hub of the Eastern seaboard's college scene. The influence of the Society of Jesus (Jesuits) on the college provides a guiding spirit for campus life, but the social opportunities still seem endless. Despite the paradoxes (or perhaps because of them), students at BC enjoy a rich college experience.

Don't let the modest name fool you. Boston College is actually a research university with nine schools and colleges. It has three campuses: the main campus at Chestnut Hill, the Brighton campus across the street, and the Newton campus a mile and a half away. The dominant architecture of the main campus (known as "the Heights") is Gothic Revival, with modern additions over the past few years. There's lots of grass and trees, not to mention a large, peaceful reservoir (perfect to jog around) right in the front yard. The university is nearing the end of a multiyear master plan intended to double the size of the main campus. A new dorm, a field house, and a variety of athletic fields are the latest facilities to open.

Boston College was originally founded by the Jesuits to teach the sons of Irish immigrants. These days, the college's mission is to "educate skilled, knowledgeable, and responsible leaders within each new generation." To accomplish this goal, the Core Curriculum requires courses not only in literature, natural science, history, philosophy, social science, and theology, but also in writing, mathematics, the arts,

> "The philosophy, theology, and ethics departments are the most important in setting the tone."

Website: www.bc.edu
Location: Suburban
Private
Total Enrollment: 12,872
Undergraduates: 9,358
Male/Female: 47/53
SAT Ranges: ERW 660–760, M 660–730
ACT Ranges: 31–33
Financial Aid: 67%
Pell Grant: 12%
Expense: Pr $ $ $ $
Student Loans: 47%
Average Debt: $
Applicants: 28,454
Accepted: 32%
Enrolled: 26%
Grad in 6 Years: 92%
Returning Freshmen: 95%
Academics: ✎ ✎ ✎ ✎
Social: 🍺 🍺 🍺 🍺
Q of L: ★ ★ ★

(continued)

Admissions: (617) 552-3100
Email Address: N/A

Strong Programs:
Biology
Communication
Economics
Finance
Nursing
English
Physics
Theology

The university is nearing the end of a multiyear master plan intended to double the size of the main campus.

Students in the Undergraduate Faculty Research Fellows Program spend 100 hours per semester assisting faculty with serious research.

and cultural diversity, in addition to specific requirements set by each undergraduate school. "Core Curriculum forces you to take classes you might not want to take but end up enjoying," says a senior. Students in arts and sciences must also show proficiency in a modern foreign language or classical language before graduation. Freshmen are required to take a writing workshop in which each student develops a portfolio of personal and academic writing and reads a wide range of texts. About a quarter of seniors participate in the Capstone Program, choosing one of several seminars that aim to give a "big picture" perspective to the college experience and students' personal development.

The schools of arts and sciences, management, nursing, and education award bachelor's degrees. Biology, communication, economics, and finance are the most popular majors. Programs in nursing, English, physics, and theology are also well regarded. Outside the traditional classroom at the McMullen Museum of Art in Devlin Hall, students find exhibitions, lectures, and gallery tours. The Music Guild sponsors professional concerts throughout the year, and music students emphasizing performance can take advantage of facilities equipped with Steinways and Yamahas. Theater majors find a home in the 600-seat Robsham Theater Arts Center, which produces eight student-directed productions each year.

BC students are serious about their work, but not excessively so, helping to create a collaborative atmosphere. "If you are better at science than your roommate, you will help her out," states one senior, "and perhaps when it comes time to fulfill your philosophy core requirement, her love of Plato will get you through the class." Forty-eight percent of classes have fewer than 20 students, and professors are praised for their passion and knowledge, as well as their accessibility. "I have certainly been challenged by my professors but also supported, since they consistently make themselves available outside of the classroom," says one history major. The Jesuits on BC's faculty (about 35 out of 800) exert an influence out of proportion to their numbers. "The philosophy, theology, and ethics departments are the most important in setting the tone of the campus, because they encourage the students to be open-minded," says a freshman.

Students searching for out-of-the-ordinary offerings will be happy at BC. The PULSE program provides participants with the opportunity to fulfill their philosophy and theology requirements while engaging in social-service fieldwork at any of about 35 Boston organizations. The program reinforces the Jesuit emphasis on community service and sometimes inspires students to major in those areas. Each undergraduate school offers its own honors program, allowing students to work at a more intensive pace and undertake a senior thesis. Fifty-eight percent of Boston College undergraduates engage in an international study or volunteer experience by the time they graduate. BC offers nearly 60 academic programs in more than 30 countries around the world, as well as three-week summer study abroad programs. Under the Undergraduate Faculty Research Fellows Program, participating students spend an average of 100 hours per semester assisting faculty with serious research, for which they are paid an hourly wage.

Twenty-four percent of BC undergraduates come from Massachusetts, and 7 percent come from abroad. Catholics comprise about 70 percent of the student body. African Americans constitute 4 percent, while Asian Americans make up 10 percent, Hispanics 11 percent, and multiracial students 3 percent. "The student body is a socially conscious, environmentally responsible, academically oriented group on the whole," offers one student. "There is a pervasive spirit of compassion that runs through the student body here." Indeed, the Jesuit appeal for tolerance means that students can find support and interaction even when approaching hot-button

> **"There is a pervasive spirit of compassion that runs through the student body here."**

issues that orthodox Catholicism frowns upon, such as homosexuality. More than 300 athletic awards are doled out annually; merit scholarships are worth an average of $22,500. Additionally, BC observes need-blind admissions and meets the full demonstrated need of accepted students.

Eighty-four percent of BC students live on campus. When students are admitted, they are notified whether they will get on-campus housing for three or four years; most juniors with three-year guarantees live off campus or study abroad, then return to campus for their final year. The city of Boston has a fairly reliable bus and subway system to bring distant residents to campus; the few students who drive to school are required to show that they need to park on campus. "The dorms are comfortable and spacious," says an international studies major, "with the exception of forced triples for freshmen." Students pay in advance for a certain number of dining hall meals, served à la carte. "The food is expensive," a student says, "but it is great quality." The Stand Up BC program is intended to combat the issue of campus sexual assault.

BC's reputation as a hard-core party school is diminishing, now that no beer kegs are allowed on campus grounds. Those of legal age can carry in only enough beer for personal consumption. Bars and clubs in Boston ("the college town of all college towns," cheers a junior) are a big draw, along with Fenway Park. On weekends, especially in the winter, the mountains of Vermont and New Hampshire beckon outdoorsy types. The campus is replete with sporting events, movies, festivals, concerts, and plays. As at other Jesuit institutions, there is no Greek system at BC, and "the social life is much more inclusive" as a result, according to a senior. Spiritual retreats occur throughout the year at BC's own retreat center on the Charles River, 30 minutes from campus, and one student says, "Volunteer work is huge."

Boston University is the archrival when it comes to ice hockey.

"[Boston is] the college town of all college towns."

Division I athletic events, especially football games, become social events too, with frequent tailgate and victory parties. The traditional football contest with Notre Dame is jokingly referred to as the "Holy War" and makes for a popular road trip. BC meets fierce competition from Atlantic Coast Conference rivals Duke, Miami, Virginia Tech, and others, and Boston University is the archrival when it comes to ice hockey. Solid teams include men's and women's ice hockey, soccer, fencing, cross-country, golf, and basketball. Intramural sports are huge here. Roughly 45 percent of undergrads participate in more than 40 intramural, recreational, and club sports, from basketball and volleyball to skiing and rugby. Students even get the day off from classes to line the edge of campus and cheer Boston Marathon runners up "Heartbreak Hill."

Since its founding as a Jesuit institution, Boston College has been committed to "educating students who will use their knowledge, talents, and abilities in the service of others." BC students spend four years fine-tuning the art of the delicate balance, finding ways to make old-fashioned morals relevant to life in the 21st century, and finding time for fun while still tending to their academic performance.

Overlaps
Harvard, Boston University, University of Pennsylvania, University of Virginia, Northeastern, Notre Dame, Villanova, Georgetown

If You Apply To ›

BC: Early action, regular decision. SATs or ACTs: required. Subject Tests: optional. Accepts the Common Application with supplement. Apply to particular school or program.

121 Bay State Road, Boston, MA 02215

One of the nation's largest private universities and namesake to a city that boasts 45 four-year colleges. Location adjacent to the Fenway is the promised land for hordes of students from all over the world seeking a funky, artsy, youth-oriented urban setting that is less in-your-face than New York City. More selective than in the past and comparable to NYU and George Washington.

Like The George Washington University and NYU, Boston University is an integral part of the city it calls home. The school's mammoth collection of nondescript high-rises stretches along bustling, six-lane Commonwealth Avenue—and so do thousands upon thousands of students. From aspiring actors, musicians, journalists, and filmmakers, to future doctors, dentists, and hotel managers, BU seems to offer something for everyone. A junior says, "You definitely walk away from BU with a sense of accomplishment and individuality."

The BU campus is practically indistinguishable from the rest of the city that surrounds it. A measure of relief is available on the tree-lined side streets, which feature quaint Victorian brownstones. Facilities include the 35,000-square-foot Hillel House, a multi-level fitness center, and a hockey arena that doubles as a concert hall. The Center for Integrated Life Sciences and Engineering, which features a cognitive neuroimaging center, a satellite vivarium, and six floors dedicated to faculty research, opened in 2017.

> **"[Faculty] bring real-world experiences into the classroom."**

In 2018 BU launched its first ever university-wide general education curriculum, BU Hub, a four-year program intended to create more opportunities for experiential, cocurricular, and interdisciplinary learning. All students must satisfy requirements in diversity, civic engagement, and global citizenship, along with traditional academic areas like communication; quantitative reasoning; philosophical, aesthetic, and historical interpretation; and social and scientific inquiry. The BU Cross-College Challenge, BU Hub's signature feature, gives juniors and seniors the chance to collaborate with a small team of classmates and faculty from across the university on an interdisciplinary project.

BU's 10 undergraduate schools and colleges offer more than 250 majors and minors; business administration, communication, engineering, economics, and psychology are the most popular. "All of the academic programs I've encountered have an accomplished faculty that bring real-world experiences into the classroom," says a political science major. The College of Communication combines theory with hands-on training—some of it by adjunct professors with day jobs at major newspapers and TV networks. It also houses the nation's only center for the study of political disinformation. The School of Music benefits from its own concert hall and from faculty who also belong to the Boston Symphony Orchestra. The College of Arts and Sciences caters to the premed and prelaw students, and BU also offers a highly competitive seven-year program admitting qualified students simultaneously to the undergraduate program and the university's medical school. Many students in the College of Health and Rehabilitation Sciences: Sargent College go on to earn graduate degrees from the college's highly ranked physical and occupational therapy programs.

> **"We can just hop on our Boston trains and be anywhere in the city within minutes."**

The Questrom School of Business, one of BU's top programs, offers an honors program for sophomores and concentrations in such areas as law, health and life

Website: www.bu.edu
Location: City Outskirts
Private
Total Enrollment: 26,402
Undergraduates: 16,349
Male/Female: 39/61
SAT Ranges: ERW 640–720,
  M 660–760
ACT Ranges: 29–32
Financial Aid: 55%
Pell Grant: 18%
Expense: Pr $ $ $
Student Loans: 48%
Average Debt: $ $ $ $
Applicants: 60,825
Accepted: 25%
Enrolled: 23%
Grad in 6 Years: 87%
Returning Freshmen: 93%
Academics: ✑ ✑ ✑ ✑
Social: ☎ ☎ ☎ ☎
Q of L: ★ ★ ★
Admissions: (617) 353-2300
Email Address: admissions@ bu.edu

Strong Programs:
Business Administration
Communication
Engineering
Economics
Psychology
Biomedical Engineering
Health Professions

sciences, and entrepreneurship. Future employers of students in the School of Hospitality Administration offer internships in exotic locales such as Sydney and Shanghai. The College of Engineering boasts a robotics and biomedical engineering lab. Students in the Wheelock College of Education and Human Development can test their ideas for curricular reform in the public schools of nearby Chelsea, while those in the School of Visual Arts may show their work in one of three campus galleries. Sixty-one percent of classes have fewer than 20 students, and students say the academic climate encourages both cooperation and competition. "While I am consistently challenged, I do not feel overwhelmed by the workload," says one senior.

Students rave about the First-Year Student Outreach Project, which brings freshmen to campus a week early to do community service. For a break from brutal Boston winters, BU offers nearly 100 study abroad programs, including internships, field work, research, language study, and liberal arts programs, in 25 countries; 35 percent of students participate. The Kilachand Honors College is a four-year undergraduate program that offers students the small classes, close interaction with faculty, and communal atmosphere of a small liberal arts college along with the resources of a major urban research university.

"The students here are diverse," says a junior. "I feel like that is an overused word, especially when looking at colleges, but it's true. On my freshman floor of 40 girls, seven were from outside the country and 25 were from outside of Massachusetts." Indeed, 80 percent of BU undergrads are from outside the state, including 22 percent who come from foreign countries. Asian Americans are the largest minority group on campus, at 15 percent of the total; Hispanics comprise 12 percent, African Americans 4 percent, and multiracial students 4 percent. "I would consider BU to be a very active and socially aware campus," observes a student. The university offers merit scholarships averaging $20,800 each year; there are also 324 athletic scholarships in 19 sports. Graduates of Boston public high schools receive no-loan financial aid packages that meet their full demonstrated financial need.

"[BU is] a great place…but it's not for the timid student."

Seventy-five percent of BU students live in campus housing, which is guaranteed for four years and selected via a lottery system. "Freshman/sophomore dorms are fairly typical, but housing gets better as you get to be a senior," explains a psychology major. The luxury apartments at 10 Buick Street house 817 upperclassmen on 17 floors in fully equipped apartments with four single bedrooms and two bathrooms each. Meal plans are flexible, and one of the six dining halls on campus is kosher. "BU has great food!" cheers a senior. There's also a farmers market and a food court with national chains like Starbucks and Panda Express. "For being in an urban area, I feel extremely safe on campus," reports one senior. The Sexual Assault Response and Prevention Center provides prevention-based programming and support and advocacy for survivors.

"The social scene at BU has a lot to offer," a student says. "We always have on-campus events every day of the week, including the weekends. If we don't feel like staying on campus, we can just hop on our Boston trains and be anywhere in the city within minutes." Five percent of the men and 15 percent of the women go Greek, and parties at neighboring schools are an option as well. Drinking is fairly common, though not in the dorms, as underage drinkers may find themselves without university housing. Owing to Boston's heavily Irish heritage, St. Patrick's Day is an occasion for revelry. The Splash party in September, homecoming in October, and Culture Fest in March round out the social calendar. Possible road trips include Cape Cod, Cape Ann, and Providence, Rhode Island. Even better, "Fenway Park, downtown, Landsdowne Street, and Boston Common are all within walking distance," says a marine biology major.

BU doesn't field a football team, so hockey season is the athletic high point of the school year. All Terrier teams compete in Division I, and solid teams include men's ice hockey and basketball and women's softball, soccer, field hockey, rowing, and track and field. BU has won 30 of 66 titles in the annual Beanpot men's ice hockey tournament, which pits BU against Harvard, Northeastern, and archrival Boston College. The Head of the Charles regatta, which starts at BU's crew house each fall, draws college crew teams from across the country. Of the dozen or so intramural sports offered, by far the most popular is broomball, which is like ice hockey on sneakers, with a ball instead of a puck and a broom instead of a stick; students may also compete in 34 club sports.

Boston University shamelessly urges students to just "Be You" (ahem) and most are happy to do so, but they warn that being successful here requires a certain degree of initiative. The school is "a great place, with lots of academic and social opportunities, but it's not for the timid student," remarks a geophysics and planetary sciences major. "You have to be proactive about finding out what's going on around campus, so that you can find your niche."

If You Apply To ›

BU: Early decision I and II, regular decision. SATs or ACTs: required (optional for applicants to College of Fine Arts). Subject Tests: optional (required for seven-year accelerated medical program). Accepts the Common Application. Apply to particular school or college. Applicants to fine arts programs must submit a portfolio or audition.

Bowdoin College

Brunswick, ME 04011

Rates with Amherst, Williams, and Wesleyan for liberal arts excellence and pioneered in not requiring the SAT. More selective than Bates and Colby. Bowdoin has strong science programs, and outdoor enthusiasts benefit from proximity to the Atlantic Coast. Smaller than some of its competitors, with less overt competition among students.

Website: www.bowdoin.edu
Location: Small Town
Private
Total Enrollment: 1,811
Undergraduates: 1,811
Male/Female: 50/50
SAT Ranges: ERW 650–750, M 640–760
ACT Ranges: 30–34
Financial Aid: 48%
Pell Grant: 16%
Expense: Pr $ $ $
Student Loans: 25%
Average Debt: $
Applicants: 7,251
Accepted: 14%

For more than two centuries, Bowdoin College has sought to make nature, art, and friendship as integral to the student experience as the world of books. This is, after all, the alma mater of the great American poets Longfellow and Hawthorne. In fact, when they matriculate, new students sign their names in a book on Hawthorne's very desk. Though the New England winter can be frigid, students are quick to point out that good food and friendships that "transcend labels" help make the campus a warm and friendly place. Says one freshman, "If you're passionate about anything, Bowdoin provides you with the resources to explore those passions."

Bowdoin's 207-acre campus sits in Brunswick, Maine, the state's largest town. Hidden amid the pine groves and athletic fields are 120 buildings, in styles from German Romanesque, colonial, medieval, and neoclassical to neo-Georgian, modern, and postmodern. Former fraternity houses now serve as academic and administrative offices and social houses, since Greek groups were phased out. The college recently completed a careful renovation of the historic Harriet Beecher Stowe House, in which the famed author wrote *Uncle Tom's Cabin*, and which now houses faculty offices. The newest addition to campus is the 29,000-square-foot Roux Center for the Environment.

To graduate, Bowdoin students must complete courses in natural sciences and math, social and behavioral sciences, fine arts and humanities, and visual and performing arts. Distribution requirements emphasize issues vital to a liberal education in the 21st century and include courses within interdisciplinary areas such as International Perspectives and Exploring Social Differences. First-years also have their choice of seminars, capped at 16 students each, which emphasize reading and writing; recent topics have included Art and the Environment, The Supreme Court and Social Change, and Performance and Theory in James Bond. "Freshman Seminars are immensely valuable," says one senior. "They can give you a good sense of what you really need to work on to succeed at Bowdoin."

Academic strengths include the sciences, particularly neuroscience, environmental studies, earth and oceanographic science, chemistry, and biology. Making a virtue out of climatic necessity, Bowdoin also offers a concentration in Arctic studies (its mascot is the polar bear), as well as opportunities for Arctic archaeological research in Labrador, Canada, or ecological research at the Bowdoin

> **"Professors make an effort to teach in many different ways in order to reach all types of learners."**

Scientific Station on Kent Island in the Bay of Fundy. The Schiller Coastal Studies Center, just 15 minutes away on Orr's Island, provides additional research opportunities in marine science. Mathematics, Africana studies, and education are also well regarded, and students say the popularity of government and economics—the majors with the highest enrollment—is well deserved. Newer majors include Italian studies and performance arts. Dual-degree programs in engineering are available through Caltech, Columbia, Dartmouth, and the University of Maine, as is a 3–3 law degree with Columbia Law School.

"Students take their schoolwork seriously, and the work is difficult," says a government and economics double major, adding that students "can often be found assisting each other, sharing notes, and studying together." Sixty-six percent of classes have fewer than 20 students. Professors teach all Bowdoin classes—there are no graduate students here, and thus no teaching assistants—and their skills in the classroom are highly praised. "Professors make an effort to teach in many different ways in order to reach all types of learners," says a senior.

Before school begins, the entire entering class takes preorientation hiking, canoeing, kayaking, or community service trips that teach them about the people and landscape of Maine. Indeed, service learning is increasingly an emphasis at Bowdoin; nearly half of all students apply their classroom work to real-world problems faced by local community groups. Undergraduate research is a priority too, and it's common for juniors and seniors to conduct independent studies with faculty members, then publish their results in professional journals. Many seniors complete yearlong honors projects culminating in a written thesis, oral defense, or original creative piece. Fifty-five percent of students study abroad through more than 100 programs, covering six different continents.

Just 10 percent of students hail from Maine, and 6 percent are international. African Americans make up 7 percent of the student body, Hispanics 11 percent, Asian Americans 7 percent, and multiracial students 7 percent. On this liberal campus, "Many students are outdoorsy, athletic, a little preppy—but everyone has an interest and a passion that

> **"The party culture is fun and celebratory but overall safe and controlled."**

might surprise you," a mathematics major says, "and most people have friends from all different social groups on campus." In 1970 Bowdoin became the first leading college to make SAT I scores an optional part of the admissions process, shifting the emphasis to a student's whole body of work. Additionally, Bowdoin employs a need-blind admissions policy, meets the full demonstrated financial need of

(continued)

Enrolled: 51%
Grad in 6 Years: 95%
Returning Freshmen: 96%
Academics: ✍ ✍ ✍ ✍ ✍
Social: ☎ ☎ ☎
Q of L: ★ ★ ★
Admissions: (207) 725-3100
Email Address: admissions@ bowdoin.edu

Strong Programs:
Government
Economics
Biology
Mathematics
Neuroscience
Environmental Studies
Africana Studies
Education

The historic Harriet Beecher Stowe House, in which the famed author wrote Uncle Tom's Cabin, *now houses faculty offices.*

admitted students, and has eliminated loans from its financial aid packages, replacing them with grants.

Ninety percent of Bowdoin students live on campus, where first-years start off in quads, with two double bedrooms and a shared common room, in renovated yet historic halls. After that, students try their luck with the lottery, although members of the social houses, which have replaced sororities and fraternities, can escape by living with these groups. A new 88-bed, apartment-style facility is now an option for upperclassmen. Students give rave reviews to dining services, especially the lobster bake that kicks off each school year and the offerings for vegans and vegetarians. "Bowdoin's food is restaurant quality, and the menu is different every day," cheers a senior. Several student groups are active in raising awareness around issues of sexual violence, and a senior says, "Campus security protects students effectively."

Social life at Bowdoin centers around two groups: sports teams and social houses. "We have a system of eight College Houses that host all types of events—academic,

"Life at Bowdoin involves little anonymity."

cultural, and parties—that are open to all students at the college," explains a junior. "This sense of inclusivity ensures that people do not feel the pressure to drink." Hard liquor is prohibited on campus. "The party culture is fun and celebratory but overall safe and controlled," says a senior. Students look forward to homecoming and Ivies Weekend, one last blast of fun before spring finals. The latter celebrates the fact that Bowdoin didn't join the Ivy League with live music at Whittier Field.

One student says Brunswick (population 20,000) is "a great, quiet college town." Habitat for Humanity and various mentoring programs help build bridges between students and local residents. A car comes in handy for the 15-minute drive to the shopping outlets of Freeport (including L.L. Bean's flagship 24/7 factory store) or the 30-minute trip to Portland for a "real" night out. Students can also opt to take a school shuttle, the bus, or the nearby Amtrak train to these destinations or to Boston, a little more than two hours away. Ski bums will find several resorts within easy reach.

While "the long winters are certainly not a favorite," according to a senior, they do bring out school spirit, and rooting for the ice hockey team is an important strategy for winter survival. Bowdoin's Polar Bears compete in the Division III New England Small College Athletic Conference, and students "get blacked out" to demonstrate support, wearing all black when they attend games. Any sporting event against Colby is exciting, and the annual hockey matchup draws crowds of alumni and Brunswick locals alike. Recent conference champions include men's and women's tennis and women's basketball and field hockey. Also popular are club sports, intramurals, and recreational activities, including those organized by the student-run Bowdoin Outing Club, whose weekend jaunts range from rock climbing and white-water rafting to fireside knitting.

Students who love the outdoors, even when it's cold, will find warm and inviting academics at Bowdoin, where close friendships with peers and professors are easily forged. As a sociology major puts it, "Life at Bowdoin involves little anonymity, and most students enjoy that fact and play active roles in the campus community."

Overlaps

Amherst, Brown, Dartmouth, Middlebury, Williams, Wesleyan, Yale, Harvard

If You Apply To ›

Bowdoin: Early decision I and II, regular decision. SATs or ACTs: optional. Subject Tests: optional. Accepts the Common Application with supplement.

Brandeis University

Waltham, MA 02453

Founded in 1948 by members of the American Jewish community who sought to expand access to education, Brandeis is an elite institution seeking top students of all faiths and backgrounds. Academic specialties range from the natural sciences to business and Near Eastern and Judaic studies. Has one of the top programs in neuroscience at a midsized research university. Competes with Tufts in the Boston area.

Brandeis University, founded to provide educational opportunities to those facing discrimination, has always had a reputation for intense progressive thought. Now it's being recognized as a rising star among research institutions, hosting more than 30 on-campus research centers, and is expanding its experiential- and service-learning offerings. The only nonsectarian Jewish-sponsored college in the nation, Brandeis appears to be focusing less on maintaining its Jewish identity and more on attracting a well-rounded, eclectic group of students from all backgrounds.

Set on a hilltop in a pleasant residential neighborhood nine miles west of Boston, Brandeis's attractively landscaped 235-acre campus boasts many distinctive buildings. The music building, for example, is shaped like a grand piano; the theater looks like a top hat. The 24-hour Shapiro Campus Center includes a student theater, electronic library, and bookstore. The Shapiro Academic Building houses the International Center for Ethics, Justice, and Public Life; the Mandel Center for Jewish Education; conference rooms; and faculty offices.

Undergraduates enter the College of Arts and Sciences, which offers more than 40 majors and 50 minors through its departments and interdepartmental programs. About half of the students graduate with double majors. The Brandeis core curriculum is rooted in a commitment to developing strong writing, foreign language, and quantitative-reasoning skills and an interdisciplinary and cross-cultural perspective. Freshmen must take a writing seminar and attend at least one of several Critical Conversation events held throughout the year, in which professors from different disciplines discuss major issues in a moderated setting, in an effort to "model civil discourse." Other gen-ed requirements include credits in health and wellness; life skills; diversity, equity, and inclusion in the U.S.; and difference and justice in the world.

Neuroscience, biochemistry, chemistry, and physics are top-notch programs; biology, psychology, economics, and business enroll the most students. Premeds are catered to with special advisors, a summer job-shadowing program, and research opportunities. With the largest faculty in the field outside of Israel, the university is virtually unrivaled in Near Eastern and Judaic studies; Hebrew is a Brandeis specialty. The program in Islamic and Middle Eastern studies is strong too. A growing number of interdisciplinary programs are becoming increasingly popular, particularly the international and global studies major and the health: science, society, and policy major. Brandeis also maintains a commitment to the creative arts, with strong theater offerings and a theory-based music program founded by Leonard Bernstein. A major in applied math has recently been added.

"Brandeis takes its academic integrity seriously," says a creative writing and English major, and the climate can be intense. Sixty percent of classes at Brandeis have fewer than 20 students, and a junior says, "Professors are very accommodating and are good lecturers and discussion leaders." A senior praises the university's

> **"Professors are very accommodating and are good lecturers and discussion leaders."**

Website: www.brandeis.edu
Location: Suburban
Private
Total Enrollment: 5,128
Undergraduates: 3,620
Male/Female: 41/59
SAT Ranges: ERW 630–710, M 650–760
ACT Ranges: 29–33
Financial Aid: 60%
Pell Grant: 19%
Expense: Pr $ $ $ $
Student Loans: 54%
Average Debt: $ $ $
Applicants: 11,721
Accepted: 34%
Enrolled: 21%
Grad in 6 Years: 90%
Returning Freshmen: 94%
Academics: ✍ ✍ ✍ ✍
Social: ☎ ☎ ☎
Q of L: ★ ★ ★
Admissions: (781) 736-3500
Email Address: admissions@brandeis.edu

Strong Programs:
Biology
Psychology
Economics
Business
Neuroscience
Chemistry
Near Eastern and Judaic Studies
Islamic and Middle Eastern Studies

advising system for offering "incredibly strong support." All incoming freshmen are assigned a student advisor, an academic advisor, and a faculty advisor in their area of academic interest. The Kraft Transitional Year Program is a one-year academic program for promising students from disadvantaged backgrounds that guarantees small classes, rigorous academics, and strong academic support.

Rising sophomores and juniors have the opportunity to earn credit through study abroad related to their majors. Forty percent of undergrads take advantage of more than 200 off-campus programs in nearly 60 countries, including three university-run programs: an international justice and human rights program in The Hague; an economics program in Copenhagen; and a studio art and art history program in Siena, Italy. Undergraduates have numerous opportunities to conduct original research with faculty, and some even publish their work in academic journals. The Justice Brandeis Semester allows groups of 10 to 15 students to earn credits while focusing on topics of personal interest, such as bio-inspired design, ethnographic fieldwork, or mobile app and game development. The linked courses feature fieldwork, internships, or research under faculty supervision.

Freshmen must attend at least one Critical Conversation, in which professors from different disciplines discuss major issues, modeling civil discourse.

> **"Brandeisians are friendly! Everyone here is very warm."**

"Brandeisians are friendly!" cheers a sophomore. "Everyone here is very warm and always willing to meet new people." Twenty-nine percent of Brandeis undergraduates are from Massachusetts, and the population is heavily bicoastal otherwise, with sizable numbers of New York, New Jersey, and California residents. Twenty-one percent hail from foreign nations. Three chapels on campus—Roman Catholic, Jewish, and Protestant—are placed so that one never casts a shadow on another. It's an architectural symbol that students say reflects the realities of their diverse campus community. Muslim students, with an enrollment of more than 200, have their own dedicated prayer space, as do followers of Dharmic religions. African Americans make up 5 percent of the student body, Hispanics 8 percent, Asian Americans 13 percent, and multiracial students 3 percent. Social justice is a big emphasis on this liberal campus. "Students care a lot about women's rights, LGBTQ+ rights, intersectionality, race relations, and a number of other issues," explains a theater arts major. Even with one of the highest tuition rates in the country, Brandeis does not guarantee to meet each student's full demonstrated financial need. It does offer merit scholarships averaging $14,300 to qualified students, although there are no athletic awards.

Housing options include traditional quadrangle dormitories, where freshmen and sophomores live in singles, doubles, or triples. Juniors and seniors can opt for singles, suites, or apartment-style housing.

> **"The social life is lively, with on-campus productions, events, and activities."**

"Housing on campus improves as you get older," one student observes. Freshmen and sophomores are guaranteed housing, while upperclassmen play the lottery each spring. Seventy-five percent of students live on campus, and the rest find affordable off-campus housing nearby. As for campus dining, a business major says, "Some days the dining halls have pretty good food, and other days it is terrible." The food court in the Usdan Student Center provides decent alternatives, and there are always kosher, vegan, gluten-free, and allergen-safe options. The university has implemented several initiatives, including opening a campus rape crisis center, to address sexual violence on campus.

Brandeis is virtually unrivaled in Near Eastern and Judaic studies, and Hebrew is a specialty.

"The social life is lively, with on-campus productions, events, and activities predominantly occupying students' free time," says an anthropology major. Brandeis hosts more than 280 student clubs; some of the largest include the Waltham Group (a community service organization), Student Events (the campus programming board), and Triskelion (an LGBTQ+ student group). The unofficial fraternities and sororities that have colonized at Brandeis are clamoring for recognition from the school but hardly dominate the social scene. Weekends begin on Thursday, with live entertainment at the on-campus Stein pub. Students can party at will in the dorms, provided they don't get too rambunctious. Annual events include 'DEIS Impact, a weeklong social justice festival; the Springfest outdoor concert; and the 24-Hour Musical, in which students learn and produce an entire musical in just 24 hours ("It's a total disaster, but it's hysterical," says a sophomore). Also well attended are the homecoming soccer match and carnival and the Leonard Bernstein Festival of the Creative Arts.

The possibilities for off-campus diversion are nearly infinite, thanks to the proximity of Boston and Cambridge, which are accessible by the free Brandeis shuttle bus or a nearby commuter train. (A car is more trouble than it's worth.) Brandeis's host town, Waltham, has a diverse selection of restaurants and a cheap movie theater but otherwise receives lukewarm reviews from students. One global studies major asks, "Who needs Waltham for excitement when Boston is a short shuttle ride away?"

Though the school does not field a football team, the Judges athletic program gets a boost from its membership in the Division III University Athletic Association, a neo-Ivy League for high-powered academic institutions such as the University of Chicago, Emory, and NYU. The men's and women's soccer teams make regular NCAA tournament appearances, and women's basketball and softball are also strong. An extensive intramural and club sports program draws 42 percent of students, and contests run nearly every day of the year.

Few private universities have come as far as Brandeis so quickly, evolving from the bare 235-acre site of a failed veterinary/medical school to a modern research university of more than 100 buildings, a $1 billion endowment, and ever-growing academic opportunities. At the same time, it has cultivated a highly supportive atmosphere. One student sums it up this way: "Brandeis is a haven for students who are seeking academic challenge and an environment where social justice is revered, where they can hold leadership roles and collaborate with professors."

For the annual 24-Hour Musical, students learn and produce an entire musical in just 24 hours.

Overlaps

Brown, Cornell University, Tufts, WashU in St. Louis, NYU, Boston University, Harvard, Yale

If You Apply To ›

Brandeis: Early decision I and II, regular decision. SATs or ACTs: optional (test-optional applicants must submit academic portfolio and additional letter of recommendation). No Subject Tests. Accepts the Common Application with supplement.

Brigham Young University

Provo, UT 84602

From the time they are knee high, Mormons all around the world dream about coming to BYU. Most men and some women do a two-year stint as a missionary. Strongest academic programs are all preprofessional. The atmosphere is generally mild-mannered and conservative, but BYU goes bonkers for its sports teams.

Brigham Young University's strong ties with the Church of Jesus Christ of Latter-day Saints means that "BYU has high morals and a wholesome environment, which makes students feel safe and comfortable," a senior says. A sense of spirituality pervades most everything at BYU, where faith and academia are intertwined and life is governed by a demanding code of ethics that has even led to the suspension of star athletes in mid-season. The strict Honor Code covers everything from dating practices to academic honesty; no-no's include men wearing beards; the consuming of

Website: www.byu.edu
Location: Small City
Private
Total Enrollment: 30,037
Undergraduates: 28,156
Male/Female: 51/49

(continued)

SAT Ranges: ERW 610–710,
   M 600–700
ACT Ranges: 27–32
Financial Aid: 68%
Pell Grant: 14%
Expense: Pr $
Student Loans: 26%
Average Debt: $
Applicants: 12,858
Accepted: 52%
Enrolled: 79%
Grad in 6 Years: 83%
Returning Freshmen: 90%
Academics: ✐ ✐ ✐
Social: ☎ ☎ ☎
Q of L: ★ ★ ★ ★
Admissions: (801) 422-4104
Email Address: admissions@
   byu.edu

Strong Programs:
Business
Accounting
Engineering
Nursing
Education
Exercise Science
Prelaw
Public Health Promotion

*BYU's strict Honor
Code covers everything
from dating practices
to academic honesty
and is a point of pride.*

drugs, alcohol, and caffeinated tea and coffee (although caffeine in soda is allowed); and entering the bedroom of a member of the opposite sex. While students elsewhere might find the code burdensome, at BYU it is a point of pride. Indeed, the school's commitment to church values is the reason most students choose it. "The students who attend BYU are unique," says a communications major. "Everyone is clean-cut, shaven, modestly dressed, and proper in their etiquette."

The church's values of prosperity, chastity, and obedience are strongly evident on BYU's 557-acre campus, where the utilitarian buildings, like everything else, are

> **"BYU has high morals and a wholesome environment, which makes students feel safe and comfortable."**

"clean, modern, and orderly." The campus lies on the western edge of the Rocky Mountains, 4,600 feet above sea level, between the shores of Utah Lake and Mount Timpanogos, offering breathtaking sunsets and easy access to magnificent skiing, camping, and hiking areas. Days begin early; church bells rouse students at 8 a.m. with the first four bars of the hymn "Come, Come Ye Saints." (The same bells also peal every hour throughout the day.)

The church's influence continues when students set their schedules; students must take one religion course per term to graduate, and subjects include, of course, the Book of Mormon. In addition to an extensive liberal arts core, BYU requires students to demonstrate proficiency in math, writing (first-year and advanced), and advanced languages, a catch-all category that can be satisfied with coursework in a foreign language or in statistics, advanced math, or advanced music.

BYU's academic offerings run the gamut, from liberal arts and sciences to pre-professional programs in engineering, nursing, business, and law. Students say the strongest offerings include education, exercise science, the Clark Law School, and most departments in the Marriott School of Business, especially accounting. There are also degrees in public health promotion and ancient Near Eastern studies. Brigham Young boasts campuses in Idaho and Hawaii, a center in Jerusalem, and a large study abroad program—nearly 200 programs in more than 50 countries. Approximately 90 percent of the men and 40 percent of the women interrupt their studies—typically after the freshman year—to serve two years as a missionary.

Students agree that the academic climate is demanding. "It is competitive," a senior reports, and "some courses are known for being extremely difficult to pass, such as American Heritage or Econ 110." Freshmen are often taught by full-time professors, who generally get good marks. "Most professors have a passion for their subject and for teaching," says a student. General education courses can be quite large, although 45 percent have fewer than 20 students, and registration can be a chore. The honors program, open to highly motivated students, offers small seminars with more faculty interaction and is "an excellent way to get more out of your college experience," one participant says. The strength of the faculty is one reason BYU has more full-time students than any other church-sponsored university in the United States, almost all of them undergraduates.

Not surprisingly, the typical BYU student is conservative. "The students are very academically and spiritually minded," confides a junior, who further describes students as "intelligent, friendly, and honest." Thirty-three percent of BYU undergraduates are from Utah. Many others hail from California and Idaho, and 3 percent come from more than 100 other countries. Hispanic students contribute 6 percent to the student body, Asian Americans 2 percent, African Americans 1 percent, and multiracial students 4 percent. Tuition for church members is lower than for nonmembers, because Latter-day Saint families contribute to BYU through their tithes. Academic scholarships averaging $4,400 are available, as are roughly 250 athletic scholarships in 21 sports.

Nineteen percent of BYU undergrads—primarily freshmen—live in the single-sex residence halls. "The dorms are small but comfortable and very clean," says a student. Upperclassmen typically opt for cheaper off-campus apartments, which are also single-sex (remember the Honor Code?). When it comes to food, the student dining outlets on campus are described as adequate. "The school provides decent, affordable on-campus meal plans," says a senior. Although it is widely assumed that, because of the Honor Code and the religious tone on campus, sexual violence is not much of a problem, BYU drew national attention in 2016 after female students and alumni spoke out against the school's practice of opening Honor Code investigations of students who report being assaulted. The protests resulted in a new policy of immunity for victims.

Ninety percent of the men and 40 percent of the women interrupt their studies to serve two years as a missionary.

Whether it's work with the homeless or disabled, dances, firesides, concerts, plays, sporting events, or special activities within the campus religious wards (small groups of about 100 students), most of BYU's social life is organized through or linked to the church. Community service is big, with students visiting patients at hospitals and care centers, performing at local festivals, and building and refurbishing houses. Social life is carried out within the church's bounds of propriety and is given a lighthearted feeling with groups that

"The students are very academically and spiritually minded."

encourage "creative dating and lots of dating, period," says a senior. There are no fraternities or sororities to provide housing or parties, which is just fine with most students, since alcoholic drinks are banned. Road trips include Vegas or southern Utah and, with the mountains being so close, you'll find plenty of skiing and camping. Provo itself has plenty of places to eat and shop. "Provo wouldn't really exist without BYU," says a student, and "it's a good college town for people who don't like bustling metropolises."

Physical fitness is big here, and the intramural facilities are some of the country's best, with indoor and outdoor jogging tracks; courts for tennis, racquetball, and handball; and a pool. Also important are varsity sports. The church philosophy of discipline and obedience has worked wonders for Cougar teams, and the football rivalry against the University of Utah provides some serious end-of-season intensity—the ESPN television network has dubbed the BYU–Utah rivalry the "Holy War." One of the most popular courses offered at BYU is ballroom dancing, partly because many participants aspire to join BYU's award-winning dance team.

To most Americans, BYU probably seems old-fashioned or like a step back in time. But for young members of the Church of Jesus Christ of Latter-day Saints, that may be just what the elder ordered. "BYU's dedicated faculty, devout atmosphere, and beautiful, clean campus set it apart from all other universities," a satisfied senior says.

Overlaps

BYU–Hawaii, BYU–Idaho, University of Utah, Utah State, Utah Valley State

If You Apply To ›

BYU: Regular decision. SATs or ACTs: required. No Subject Tests. Does not accept the Common Application. Ecclesiastical endorsement required.

University of British Columbia: See page 357.

Brown University

45 Prospect Street, Providence, RI 02912

To today's stressed-out students, the fantasy of taking every course pass/fail seems like a dream come true. Nobody at Brown actually does this, but the pass/fail option, combined with the school's notable lack of distribution requirements, gives it the freewheeling image that students love. In reality, doing well at Brown is just as tough as at other Ivies. Scorned by conservatives as a hotbed of political correctness.

Brown University is a perennial "hot college," with an overwhelming number of happy students and many more clamoring to join their ranks. Once here, students receive not only a prestigious and quality education, but also a chance to explore their creative sides at a liberal arts and sciences college that does not idolize grades or preprofessionalism and shuns GPAs, required courses, and competitive attitudes among its undergraduates. Brown's environment and policies have drawn both praise and criticism over the years, but its students thrive on this discussion and lively debate. "Brown's open curriculum, though not for everyone, is incredibly liberating," says one student.

Founded in 1764 as the College in the English Colony of Rhode Island and Providence Plantations, Brown was renamed in 1804 after Nicholas Brown Jr., a major benefactor whose father—one of the school's founders—was a businessman with controversial ties to the slave trade. The school recently established a memorial to slaves at Brown and a Center for the Study of Slavery and Justice. The university sits atop College Hill on the east side of Providence, and its 140-acre campus affords an excellent view of downtown Providence. Campus architecture is a composite of old and new—plenty of grassy lawns surrounded by historic buildings that offer students refuge from the city streets beyond. The neighborhoods that surround the campus lie within a national historic district and boast beautiful tree-lined streets full of ethnic charm. Recent construction includes the Engineering Research Center, featuring research labs for multiple disciplines and a large undergraduate teaching lab.

Brown's faculty has successfully resisted the notion that somewhere in their collective wisdom and experience lies a core of knowledge that every educated person should possess. As a result, aside from completing courses in a major and a minimum of 30 courses total, the only university-wide requirement for graduation is "the ability to write well." All students must demonstrate that they have worked at least twice on developing their writing (once during their first two years and again as upperclassmen) by taking approved English or writing-across-the-curriculum classes or by documenting their writing work in any other Brown course. Students can take their classes one of two ways: for traditional marks of A, B, C, or No Credit; or for Satisfactory/No Credit. The NC is not recorded on the transcript, while the letter grade or Satisfactory can be supplemented by a written evaluation from the professor. A habit of NCs, however, lands students in academic hot water.

> **"As far as I know, all our academic departments are super strong (like oxen or Heracles)."**

The most popular majors (or concentrations, as they are called here) are economics, computer science, applied mathematics, and engineering. Neuroscience, classics, and geology are some of the university's best concentrations, and students also praise political science, religious studies, and history—although one says, "As far as I know, all our academic departments are super strong (like oxen or Heracles)." Other top-notch programs include comparative literature, modern languages, and the writing program in the English department. Future doctors can try for a competitive eight-year liberal medical education program where students can earn an M.D. without having to sacrifice their humanity. Fields related to scientific technology have very good facilities, including an instructional technology center, while minority issues are the focus of the Center for the Study of Race and Ethnicity in America.

Those with interests in interdisciplinary fields will enjoy Brown's wide range of concentrations that cross departmental lines and cover everything from cognitive science to public policy to a program in business, entrepreneurship, and organizations. Students can create their own concentration from the array of goodies offered. Brown also offers group independent study projects, a popular alternative for students with the gumption to take a course they have to construct primarily by themselves, and a five-year dual-degree program with the Rhode Island School of Design (RISD), also located on College Hill. Students can cross-register for individual courses at RISD as well. "Brown provides amazing financial support for research opportunities through our UTRAs (Undergraduate Teaching and Research Awards)," says a junior. Adventurous students can choose to spend time in one of Brown's more than 120 study abroad programs in 11 countries. About a third of undergrads study abroad, and others go overseas to complete independent research or internships during the summer. Brown leads U.S. research universities in the number of graduates who win Fulbrights.

> "Brown students are very independent, which is an important quality for navigating our unique curriculum."

"Although the coursework is definitely rigorous, students are mostly only in classes that they really want to be in, and therefore it leads to an enjoyable, relaxed climate," explains a computer science major. Brown prides itself on undergraduate teaching and considers skill in the classroom as much as the usual scholarly credentials when making tenure decisions. An applied math and biology double major says, "Professors come to Brown interested in engaging with undergrads and being part of our experience, so they're really accessible." The advising system reflects the administration's commitment to treating students as adults. It pairs each freshman with a professor and a peer advisor, and a computer science major says, "This duo is great," especially because peer advisors offer "informal advising, social advice, and class advice." Resident counselors in the dorms are also available to lend an ear. "CareerLAB and BrownConnect are super helpful resources for finding jobs and internships," cheers a junior.

Brown does not idolize grades or preprofessionalism and shuns GPAs, required courses, and competitive attitudes among its undergraduates.

Brown offers nearly 90 special freshman seminars annually, capped at 20 students each and taught by faculty in all disciplines. "First-year seminars enable you to experience niche, in-depth seminar classes right away, along with your larger, introductory lecture courses," explains a sophomore. Overall, 70 percent of undergraduate classes have fewer than 20 students. Even so, particularly popular courses are usually jammed with students, and often there aren't enough teaching assistants to staff them effectively. Some, especially writing courses in the English department and studio art courses, can be nearly impossible to get into, although the administration claims that perseverance makes perfect—in other words, show up the first day and beg shamelessly.

> "First-year seminars enable you to experience niche, in-depth seminar classes right away."

"Brown students are very independent, which is an important quality for navigating our unique curriculum," says a sophomore. With a mere 6 percent of undergraduates hailing from tiny Rhode Island, and 11 percent coming from foreign countries, geographical diversity is one of Brown's hallmarks. Consistent with the spirit of openness that defined Rhode Island from the outset and that persists to this day, Brown was the first Ivy League school to accept students from all religious

The advising system pairs each freshman with a professor and a peer advisor.

affiliations. Today, Brown is a hot spot of student activism; nary a semester has passed without at least one demonstration about the issue of the day. African Americans comprise 6 percent of the student body, Hispanics 12 percent, Asian Americans 15 percent, and multiracial students 6 percent. The LGBTQ community is also prominent. "Brown is one of the most conscious schools when it comes to identities, and students take the initiative to create spaces for people of all identities," observes a cognitive science major. Although Brown doesn't offer athletic or academic merit scholarships, it does practice need-blind admissions and guarantee to meet the full demonstrated need of everyone admitted. Brown has also eliminated loans from all university financial aid packages and replaced them with grants.

A favorite tradition involves a beloved music professor performing lively midnight organ concerts in a stately campus hall.

About half the freshmen are assigned to one of eight co-ed Keeney Quad dorms, in "loud and rambunctious" units of 40 to 60 with several sophomore or junior dorm counselors. The other half live in the quieter Pembroke campus dorms or in a few other scattered locations. According to a sophomore, "Freshman accommodations are by and large quite plush; the vast majority of freshman residence halls have been very recently and very handsomely renovated." Options for upperclassmen include apartment-like suites with kitchens, special-interest houses, two social dorms, and Greek housing. Brown guarantees housing for all four years and requires students to live on campus through sophomore year; 74 percent of undergrads reside in university housing. Nearby off-campus apartments are becoming more plentiful—and more expensive—as the area gentrifies. Students appreciate the variety of accommodations offered at the two main dining halls and various smaller locations, one of which is vegetarian only, although the food gets middling reviews. "The larger the eatery is, the less flavorful food you can expect to get," observes a senior. Students say the campus feels safe and one notes, "Brown emphasizes consent education and makes sexual health resources widely available."

"Much of the social life is on campus. I love that! You always feel part of the community," says an American studies major. More than a dozen a cappella groups, daily and weekly newspapers, political organizations, and "even a Scrabble club and a successful croquet team" represent just a few of the ways Brown students manage to keep themselves entertained. The university also sponsors frequent campuswide parties, dances, plays, concerts, and special events. The few residential Greek organizations are generally considered much too un-mellow for Brown's taste—only 10 percent of the men and 9 percent of the women sign up. The nonresidential multicultural fraternities and sororities serve a more comprehensive student-life function, and parties are more likely to be held off campus by sports teams. Students report that alcohol policies focus on safety more than punishment. The biggest annual bash of the year is Spring Weekend, which features plenty of parties and a big-name band on the Main Green. A favorite tradition involves a beloved music professor performing lively midnight organ concerts in a stately campus hall "on the four scariest nights of the year: the night before freshman classes start, Halloween, and the night before finals each semester," explains a denizen.

> **"Brown is one of the most conscious schools when it comes to identities."**

The nationally recognized Swearer Center for Public Service helps place students in a variety of volunteer positions.

Providence, an old industrial city that has undergone a renaissance of sorts, is Rhode Island's capital, so many internship opportunities in state government are available, as are a few good music joints, lively bars, and several fine, inexpensive restaurants, especially along Thayer Street. The city is also home to a number of other colleges, which helps to liven up the social scene. "Providence is a great place to see a concert or attend a festival," says a junior. For those interested in community outreach—and many at Brown are—the university's nationally recognized Swearer Center for Public Service helps place students in a variety of volunteer positions. Brown Community Outreach is, in fact, the largest student organization on campus. For a change of scenery, many students head to Boston or the beaches of Newport, each an hour away.

Brown does not have a reputation as an especially sports-minded school, yet it boasts the third largest collegiate athletic program in the country, with roughly 940 athletes competing on 38 Division I varsity teams. The Bears women's crew team has won multiple NCAA championships. Men's soccer, lacrosse, and water polo have been competitive in the Ivy League Conference. Athletic facilities include an Olympic-sized swimming pool and an indoor athletic complex with everything from tennis courts to weight rooms. Thirty-three club sports, plus intramurals ranging from ice hockey and squash to cornhole and kick-ball tournaments, offer a good mix of competitiveness and fun.

"Providence is a great place to see a concert or attend a festival."

Ever since the days of Roger Williams, Rhode Island has been known as a land of tolerance, and Brown certainly is a 21st-century embodiment of this tradition. "Brown students build themselves up by building others up," says a physics and philosophy double major. "It's cool to be excited about anything here, and Brown students celebrate the talents of all of their peers." The education offered at this university is decidedly different from that provided by the rest of the Ivy League, or for that matter, by other top universities. Brown is content to gather a talented bunch of students, offer a diverse and imaginative array of courses, and then let the undergraduates, with a little help, make sense of it all. It takes an enormous amount of initiative, maturity, and self-confidence to thrive at Brown, but most students feel they are up to the challenge.

Overlaps

Yale, Harvard, Princeton, University of Pennsylvania, Stanford, Columbia, Cornell University, UC Berkeley

If You Apply To ›

Brown: Early decision, regular decision. SATs or ACTs: required. Subject Tests: recommended (any two). Accepts the Common Application with supplement.

Bryn Mawr College

101 North Merton Avenue, Bryn Mawr, PA 19010-2899

Bryn Mawr has the most brainpower per capita of the elite women's colleges. Politics range from liberal to radical, and the honor code shapes the campus culture. Mawrters may take themselves a bit too seriously. The college still benefits from ties to nearby Haverford, though the relationship is not as close as in the days when Haverford was all-male. A train station just off campus offers easy access to Philadelphia.

Leafy suburban enclaves are a dime a dozen around Philadelphia, but only one is home to Bryn Mawr College, a top-notch liberal arts school that happens to be for women. On this campus, students find a range of academic pursuits from archaeology to film studies to physics, and a diverse yet community-oriented student body. Founded in 1885, Bryn Mawr has evolved into a hotbed of intellectualism that prepares students for life and work in a global environment. Although students here abide by a strict academic honor code and participate in a host of long-standing campus traditions, they remain doggedly individualistic. "We are social-justice minded, fiercely independent trailblazers who do not take no for an answer," asserts one sophomore. "I am absolutely certain that we will run the world someday."

Website: www.brynmawr.edu
Location: City Outskirts
Private
Total Enrollment: 1,583
Undergraduates: 1,322
Male/Female: 0/100
SAT Ranges: ERW 650–730, M 660–770
ACT Ranges: 29–33
Financial Aid: 72%

Bryn Mawr's lovely campus is a path-laced oasis set among trees (many carefully labeled with Latin and English names) and lush green hills, perfect for an afternoon walk, bike ride, or jog. Just a 20-minute train ride from downtown Philadelphia, Bryn Mawr provides a country setting with a vital and exciting city nearby. The architecture is predominantly collegiate Gothic, a combination of the Gothic architecture of Oxford and Cambridge Universities and the local material—a style that Bryn Mawr was instrumental in establishing in the United States. Ten of Bryn Mawr's buildings are listed in the National Register of Historic Places. Variations on the collegiate Gothic theme include a sprinkling of modern buildings, such as Louis Kahn's slate-and-concrete residence hall and Bryn Mawr's newest residence hall, which provides housing for 130 students.

> "I am absolutely certain that we will run the world someday."

The general education requirements include one semester of "quantitative" work; one semester in each of four "approaches to inquiry" (scientific investigation, critical interpretation, cross-cultural analysis, and inquiry into the past); an intermediate level of competency in a foreign language; and the requirements of a major. Students are also required to take eight half-semesters of physical education and must pass a swimming test. In addition, all freshmen take a college seminar to develop their critical thinking, writing, and discussion skills.

Most departments are strong, especially the sciences, classics, archaeology, history of art, and the foreign languages, including Russian and French. The growth and structure of cities major is a unique, interdisciplinary program that blends coursework in urban studies, architecture, history, economics, and sociology, among other subjects. Combined degree programs, in which students earn both a bachelor's and a master's degree from Bryn Mawr, are available in a number of fields, ranging from chemistry and physics to classical and Near Eastern archaeology. The most popular majors are mathematics, psychology, biology, and English. Doing serious work in music, fine arts, linguistics, religion, or astronomy requires a hike over to nearby Haverford College, Bryn Mawr's partner in the bicollege system, which allows students at each institution to take courses, use the facilities, eat, and even live in the dormitories of the other. Bryn Mawr and Haverford students cooperate on a weekly newspaper, radio station, orchestra, and other clubs and sports, and a free shuttle bus connects the campuses. Students may also cross-register with Swarthmore and Penn; 95 percent of Mawrters take courses at these institutions or at Haverford at some point during their four years. Five-year dual-degree programs in engineering are offered in conjunction with Caltech, Columbia, and Penn.

> "A lot of people are talking about race at Bryn Mawr, and also transgender issues."

Out of respect for their academic honor code, Mawrters refrain from discussing their grades, but they freely admit that they work hard. "The academic climate of Bryn Mawr is competitive and intense," says one student. Freshmen and transfer students are initiated to the Bryn Mawr experience during Customs Week, which includes a variety of seminars and workshops, and Customs peer advisors support their transition throughout their first year. The quality of teaching at Bryn Mawr is unquestionably high and, thanks in part to small class sizes, "faculty members are very accessible," according to a sociology major, with extensive and flexible office hours.

The growth and structure of cities major blends coursework in urban studies, architecture, history, economics, and sociology.

For those looking ahead to see what the college's steep tuition will buy in the long term, the campus has a career resource center that offers information on interviewing and building a résumé—and there is no lack at Bryn Mawr of special academic programs with which to fill those résumés. The 360° program is an interdisciplinary experience that brings students from a variety of majors together to examine a central theme, like Migrations and Borderlands or Struggles for Global Health Equity, from multiple perspectives. Students take a cluster of two or three courses in a single semester and also complete a hands-on component, such as travel, fieldwork, or lab research. A third of all students study overseas during their time at Bryn Mawr, choosing from more than 70 programs in 30 countries. With easy access to a diverse variety of organizations in Philadelphia, 73 percent of Mawrters complete internships before they graduate.

"Bryn Mawr tends to attract passionate, intelligent, kind, supportive, and involved individuals," says one student. The campus has a strong international flavor, with an impressive 23 percent of undergraduates hailing from abroad; only 13 percent are Pennsylvania residents. African Americans make up 6 percent of the student body, Hispanics 9 percent, Asian Americans 12 percent, and multiracial students 6 percent. "A lot of people are talking about race at Bryn Mawr, and also transgender issues," says one student. There are no athletic scholarships, but merit scholarships averaging $17,300 are available, and the school does guarantee to meet the demonstrated financial need of everyone admitted.

Ninety-one percent of undergrads reside on campus. "Our residence halls are spectacular," says one sophomore. "Each dorm is unique, but they all are very comfortable, and every student is guaranteed housing for all four years." Dorm features include hardwood floors, window seats, and fireplaces. Dining services, which have received national recognition, offer plentiful and tasty choices, according to students. "We have a nutritionist available for students to consult should they have dietary restrictions," says a French major. A classical culture and society major says, "Public Safety are there to help and keep students safe."

> **"[Traditions] play a big role in uniting all four classes."**

Traditions are a very important part of the campus social scene: "They play a big role in uniting all four classes and give students a role in the greater history of the college," says a student. The Elizabethan-style May Day festivities are held the Sunday after classes end in May. Everyone wears white, eats strawberries, watches student plays, and dances around maypoles. Mawrters have been known to skinny-dip in the fountains and drink champagne on the lawn. The presentation of lanterns and class colors to incoming freshmen on Lantern Night, and regal pageants, such as Parade Night and Step-Sing, fill life with a Gothic sense of wonder and school spirit. Bryn Mawr is located on suburban Philly's wealthy Main Line (named after a railroad), and the campus is two blocks from the train station, which provides students with convenient access to cultural attractions, as well as social and academic events at the nearby University of Pennsylvania and elsewhere in the city. "I consider our social life to be hanging out with friends, poetry slams, and watching plays and cultural shows," muses a junior.

As for athletics, the Bryn Mawr Owls compete in the Division III Centennial Conference, and the indoor and outdoor track and field teams are standouts. Intramurals like rugby, cross-country, volleyball, and field hockey are also available, and club sports range from all-female teams to co-ed teams shared with Haverford, such as ultimate Frisbee and fencing. Students in computer science compete in a number of robot competitions, including the international Robocup, which pits colleges against each other in a robo-soccer match.

Bryn Mawr is a study in contrasts: the campus is in suburbia, but steps from a major city. Humanities programs are very strong, but science majors are also enormously popular. The students are independent but revel in college traditions. The result is overwhelmingly positive. Says a student, "The Bryn Mawr experience is one of complete freedom to explore one's interests and individuality without the fear of being ostracized."

With easy access to a diverse variety of organizations in Philadelphia, 73 percent of Mawrters complete internships.

Lantern Night and regal pageants, such as Parade Night and Step-Sing, fill life with a Gothic sense of wonder and school spirit.

Overlaps

Barnard, Mount Holyoke, Smith, Swarthmore, Wellesley, Haverford

Bucknell University

Lewisburg, PA 17837

Bucknell, Colgate, Hamilton, Lafayette—all a little more conservative than the Ivy schools, and all just a little less selective. Bucknell is the biggest of this bunch and, like Lehigh, offers engineering. Bucknell's Greek system is strong, but students don't join until they are sophomores. The central Pennsylvania campus is remote but one of the most beautiful anywhere.

Website: www.bucknell.edu
Location: Small Town
Private
Total Enrollment: 3,623
Undergraduates: 3,581
Male/Female: 49/51
SAT Ranges: ERW 620–700, M 630–720
ACT Ranges: 28–31
Financial Aid: 62%
Pell Grant: 11%
Expense: Pr $ $ $ $
Student Loans: 47%
Average Debt: $ $ $
Applicants: 10,253
Accepted: 31%
Enrolled: 31%
Grad in 6 Years: 90%
Returning Freshmen: 94%
Academics: ✍ ✍ ✍ ✍
Social: ☎ ☎ ☎ ☎
Q of L: ★ ★ ★
Admissions: (570) 577-3000
Email Address: admissions@bucknell.edu

Strong Programs:
Economics
Psychology
Accounting and Financial Management
Biology

The students at Bucknell University strike a healthy balance between hitting the books and hitting the bars or the frat houses of their pastoral central Pennsylvania campus. Yes, they tend to be preppy: "Bucknell students are mostly upper-middle-class, relatively conservative, and materially conscious. However, they are also highly motivated and eager to succeed," says one student. With small classes, engaging faculty, and not a subpar dorm to be found, it's no wonder that students like this junior complain, "Four years at Bucknell go by way too fast."

In addition to being comfortable and friendly, Bucknell is physically beautiful. Located on a hill just south of quaint Lewisburg, the campus overlooks the scenic Susquehanna River valley. Playing fields, shaded by leafy trees, are sprinkled among the Greek Revival buildings. While some structures date from the 19th century, lending a fairy-tale quality, others are far more modern, including an $8 million engineering building. Recent construction includes the 36,000-square-foot Graham Building, which offers a central hub for health and wellness, counseling, and athletic resources.

Students in Bucknell's College of Arts and Sciences and Freeman College of Management must complete general education courses in three areas—Intellectual Skills (including a writing-intensive Foundation Seminar), Tools for Critical Engagement, and Disciplinary Perspectives—and must complete a culminating experience their senior year. In the College of Engineering, students take a common course their first semester that introduces them to all eight of the engineering degree programs, and they must take courses in mathematics, science, social sciences, and arts and humanities. All freshmen, regardless of discipline, participate in the First-Year Integration Series, workshops designed to help them transition to college, featuring topics such as university resources, diverse perspectives, and lifelong learning. And along with major-related requirements, each student must demonstrate competence in writing in order to graduate.

> **"Bucknell students play hard, but work harder."**

While Bucknell is known for engineering, management, and the natural sciences, students say academics are strong across the curriculum, with weaker programs hard to find. The most popular majors are economics, psychology, accounting and financial management, and biology. Other highlights include biomedical engineering; the animal behavior program, which benefits from an outdoor naturalistic primate facility for teaching and research; and environmental studies, which includes not only science courses but also classes in the humanities, social policy, and civil engineering. A major in biophysics was recently added. Management 101 is a favorite course among business students, who work together to create and sell a product and donate their profits to charity.

(continued)

Biomedical Engineering
Animal Behavior
Environmental Studies

Just over half of Bucknell's courses have fewer than 20 students, and the emphasis is on discussion and group work. According to a markets, innovation, and design major, "Students tend to get to know their classmates well and quickly become comfortable working with one another." Professors facilitate the cooperative atmosphere, says a sophomore, and "pay a lot of attention to each student individually."

Forty-nine percent of students study abroad. Semester-long, faculty-led programs take them to England, France, Ghana, Greece, Spain, and Washington, D.C. Relationships with other colleges and universities enable students to choose from more than 400 other programs worldwide. The College of Engineering has one of the highest study abroad participation rates for students in an engineering program, and it also offers a specialized three-week, faculty-taught study abroad course that places engineering concepts into a real-world, global context. The Institute for Leadership in Technology and Management allows a select group of students to learn new ways to solve problems, while building their teamwork and communication skills. Department-specific honors programs attract top scholars, and twenty percent of all undergraduates—in all disciplines—participate in undergraduate research. A political science major points to research as a defining experience at Bucknell: "I got to work one-on-one with a faculty mentor who truly viewed me as an equal and valued my opinions and insights."

The animal behavior program benefits from an outdoor naturalistic primate facility for teaching and research.

"Bucknell students play hard, but work harder," observes an animal behavior major. Twenty-two percent are Pennsylvanians, and 62 percent went to public high school. Racial and cultural diversity have been slow in coming, and many students comment that self-segregation of different groups is noticeable on campus. African Americans account for 4 percent of the student body, Hispanics 7 percent, Asian Americans 5 percent, and multiracial students 4 percent, while international students represent 6 percent. Social and political issues traditionally take a back seat here, although some students say liberal activists are growing more vocal. Each year, Bucknell awards a small number of merit scholarships averaging $11,900, as well as 186 athletic scholarships in 14 sports.

"Friday nights are generally not a time to be in the library."

Ninety-one percent of undergrads live on campus. Thirty-nine percent of each entering class joins the Residential Colleges (which a biomedical engineering major calls "fantastic for first-years"), choosing from among nine themed living/learning communities: Arts, Discovery, Environmental, Food, Global, Humanities, Languages and Cultures, Social Justice, and Society and Technology. A senior notes, "For upperclassmen not in a Residential College, on-campus housing can be tough," yet the university limits the number of seniors allowed to move off campus. Dining facilities offer a wide variety of options, but many students complain that meals are too expensive. Students report feeling safe on campus and well-informed when it comes to issues of sexual assault. "Our school has sexual assault awareness weeks and speakers, as well as groups like Speak UP who are constantly engaging the campus in conversations," says a senior.

The College of Engineering has one of the highest study abroad participation rates for students in an engineering program.

"Greek organizations and sports teams tend to run the social scene," a senior reports. Indeed, Bucknell's robust Greek system draws 32 percent of the men and 48 percent of the women, though rush is delayed until the start of sophomore year. Drinking at frat parties and a few bars close to campus is a weekly pastime for many students of age, but the university offers plenty of on-campus alternatives. Two student organizations arrange everything from carnivals to hypnotists to religious retreats, while the school-run Uptown nightclub offers bands, karaoke, pub nights, and other social events. "Friday nights are generally not a time to be in the library," confirms one student. Favorite traditions include Midnight Mania at the start of the basketball season, the Bison Sound concert with student performers, and the formal Chrysalis Ball in the spring. Also special are the Candlelighting and Convocation ceremonies. "Convocation is an important tradition to Bucknell because you only pass through the Christy Mathewson gates twice in your life: on your first and last days as a student here," explains a senior.

Lewisburg is small and rural, but Market Street has boutiques, restaurants, and an old-style movie theater that serves up first-run flicks as well as student-produced films. "Market Street is a great way to get off campus without having to get in a car to do so," says a senior. Through the Office of Civic Engagement, students have opportunities to volunteer and participate in service learning. When students get claustrophobic, New York, Philadelphia, and Washington/Baltimore are less than three hours away; the main campus of Penn State, in State College, Pennsylvania, is even closer. Bucknell sponsors road trips to these communities for students who lack wheels.

> "Bucknell is a continuous classroom: even when I'm not in the classroom, I learn."

The Division I Bucknell Bison have captured the Patriot League Presidents' Cup, for the league's all-sports champion, 18 times in 28 years. Men's and women's cross-country and track and field are perennially strong, having combined for dozens of Patriot League championships. Other recent conference champions include men's and women's basketball, women's soccer, men's lacrosse, and men's water polo. Basketball is a fan favorite, and Bucknell's biggest rivalries are with Lafayette and Lehigh, though these aren't a tremendous focus. Intramural and club sports draw 43 percent of the students.

"Bucknell is a continuous classroom: even when I'm not in the classroom, I learn from other students and faculty," remarks an accounting major. Bucknell students get the best of several worlds: excellence in engineering and the liberal arts, abundant research opportunities, and a healthy social life. Another perk: "Both students and alumni have a serious amount of pride for their school," says a senior, "and you find that alumni want to give back." The school's rural Pennsylvania location and the preponderance of preppies may seem stifling at times, but if you're seeking small classes and a supportive environment, Bucknell may be a good fit.

Overlaps

Colgate, Lehigh, University of Richmond, Villanova, Washington and Lee, Cornell University, Boston College, Lafayette

If You Apply To ›

Bucknell: Early decision I and II, regular decision. SATs or ACTs: optional. Subject Tests: optional. Accepts the Common Application. Audition required for applicants to music program.

Butler University

Indianapolis, IN 46208

Small, private university with an attractive campus on the outskirts of Indianapolis and a relaxed Midwestern feel. Butler combines a strong liberal arts emphasis with practical learning. Strong in business, dance, and prepharmacy. Classes are small with no teaching assistants. Students are a homogeneous lot who share Indiana's trademark passion for basketball. Larger than DePauw, smaller than Northwestern.

College hoops fans may recognize Butler University as the unheralded outsider who fought its way to the final game of the men's NCAA Division I Basketball Championships not once but twice in the last decade. But those who attend this small Midwestern university know that Bulldogs basketball is representative of the Butler way of life, which emphasizes teamwork, tenacity, and sound fundamentals. Indeed, students here find their school's cozy campus and solid academics to be a slam dunk.

Located five miles from downtown Indianapolis in the city's historic Butler-Tarkington neighborhood, Butler's 295-acre campus is hailed as one of the most attractive in the Midwest for its parklike setting, which includes centuries-old trees, open landscaped lawns, curving sidewalks, fountains, a nature preserve, a prairie, a historical canal, a formal botanical garden, an observatory, and jogging paths. The first building, Jordan Hall, features Gothic architecture and has set the tone for subsequent buildings. Butler's Hinkle Fieldhouse, which opened in 1928, has reigned as one of the nation's great sports arenas for nine decades. A 42,000-square-foot pharmacy building features large, tiered lecture rooms, a pharmacy lab, patient examination rooms, offices, and study spaces. The newest addition to campus is the Irvington House, a 647-bed, apartment-style residence facility.

> **"Butler students want to be the best and be recognized for that."**

As part of Butler's core curriculum, students enroll in two common elements: First-Year Seminar, a two-semester sequence in their first year, and Global and Historical Studies, a sophomore-year sequence of courses. They must also take classes in six general areas of inquiry: analytical reasoning, the natural world, perspectives in the creative arts, physical well-being, the social world, and texts and ideas. In addition to satisfying writing across the curriculum and speaking across the curriculum requirements, students complete the Butler Cultural Requirement, which involves attending eight campus events over four years, and the Indianapolis Community Requirement, which connects students to the local area through off-campus community service. Incoming freshmen hoping to make friends before the start of their first semester can sign up for one of several optional preorientation programs that range from volunteering in Indianapolis to camping in Kentucky to sightseeing in London and Paris.

"Butler students are extremely competitive," says a strategic communication major. "Whether that be for who has the best presentation in a class, the highest grade on a test, and even for internships in the Indianapolis area—Butler students want to be the best and be recognized for that." The university's most popular programs include business administration, marketing, communication, education, and preprofessional tracks in pharmacy and physician assistant studies. Other solid offerings include dance (specifically classical ballet), international business, and English, especially the creative writing track. Students in the risk management and insurance major learn how to mitigate and manage risks through a combination of insurance and financial services techniques and can get hands-on experience through the school's recently established, student-run insurance company. Fifty-two percent of classes have fewer than 20 students, and the majority of classes taken by freshmen are taught by full professors. "Every so often you get a professor that isn't that great, but never are they terrible," says a junior.

The University Honors Program is designed to foster a diverse and challenging intellectual climate; students take four honors courses, participate in special honors events, and research and write a thesis. About 25 students are selected each year for the Butler Summer Institute, where they produce an original research or creative project under the guidance of a faculty mentor and with the support of a $4,500 stipend. For those who wish to travel to far-flung locales around the globe,

The Indianapolis Community Requirement connects students to the local area through off-campus community service.

Butler offers more than 200 study abroad programs in more than 60 countries, including Australia, Ireland, Germany, Ghana, and India. One-third of Butler students participate.

Forty-six percent of Butler students come from Indiana, and are "very bright and very welcoming," according to a freshman. "The school isn't really cliquey." African Americans account for 4 percent of the student body, Hispanics 4 percent, Asian Americans 3 percent, and multiracial students 3 percent; another 2 percent are international. Most students come from middle- to upper-class families and tend not to be overtly political. Still, Butler does receive its share of typical complaints, including the lack of parking and the cost to attend. Merit scholarships averaging $14,300 are available to qualified students, as are numerous athletic awards.

Two-thirds of the students live in university-sponsored housing, with all but seniors and commuters required to do so. "Students are given the opportunity to share very comfortable places with other roommates, either in the dormitories, houses, fraternity houses, or apartments," says a senior. Students may dine in the student union or one of two campus dining halls. "The dining facilities are so-so. The food isn't really that great, but they make up for that by giving a wide variety of options," says a prepharmacy student. And while Butler is "not in the best part of town," students report feeling safe on campus: "Butler is a very tight-knit community and we all look out for each other," says a junior, "but it feels good to know that our campus security is always there."

"Generally, Greek life is social life at Butler," says a student; 22 percent of the men and 36 percent of the women go Greek. Although the university allows alcohol

"It feels good to know that our campus security is always there."

on campus, students say the social scene doesn't revolve around booze. "Butler students think they know how to party, but compared to state schools like IU and Purdue, that's laughable," remarks one senior. Students seeking a change of pace head off campus and into Indianapolis, where bars, restaurants, and cultural events are plentiful. "Students can attend performances by the Indianapolis Symphony Orchestra or a game by the Indiana Pacers, go to Circle Center Mall, or even visit the Indianapolis Children's Museum," says one adventurous sophomore. Favorite traditions include homecoming week, "where students decorate the lawns of the Greek houses, participate in Yell Like Hell, and make a midnight snack run," according to a marketing and finance major.

Butler fields 18 Division I teams (the Bulldogs), and all but one compete in the Big East—the football team is a member of the Pioneer Football League. Aside from men's basketball, the men's tennis and men's and women's soccer teams are strong, having recently won conference titles. Intramurals are popular, especially volleyball, five-on-five basketball, flag football, and soccer, and more serious students may also compete in 18 club sports.

Overlaps

Bradley, Creighton, Drake, Elon, Xavier (OH), DePauw, Marquette, Indiana University

Butler University strives to provide students with a strong undergraduate liberal arts experience and access to professional programs of "local impact and global reach." Students have taken note of the school's revamped programs, improved facilities, and focus on personal attention. "Butler truly becomes a community for our students," says a sophomore. "The students and faculty all work to make Butler life an enjoyable experience for all."

If You Apply To >

Butler: Early action, regular decision. SATs or ACTs: required. No Subject Tests. Accepts the Common Application with supplement. Art applicants must submit portfolio.

California Colleges and Universities

California's three-tiered system of colleges and universities has long been viewed as a model of excellence by other public higher education institutions nationwide and even around the world. The system offers a wealth of educational riches, including world-class research universities, enough Nobel Prize winners to fill a classroom, and colleges on the cutting edge of everything from film to viticulture. Underlying the creation of this remarkable system was a commitment to the notion that all qualified Californians, whatever their economic status, were entitled to the benefits of a college education.

Unfortunately, the well-publicized financial turmoil that has racked the State of California has played havoc with the ability of its public colleges and universities to fulfill their traditional mission. While the state's financial situation has seen some improvement recently, increased spending has not returned funding to the levels seen prior to the crisis. For students, the practical impact is taking the form of larger classes, reduced course offerings, and—surprise, surprise—a big increase in student fees that pushes the cost at a UC university up over the $32,000 mark for California residents (including tuition, fees, room and board, and an allowance for books and supplies). To help offset these budget woes, the UC system has increased its enrollment of out-of-state and international students, who pay much higher rates (more than $55,000). The new policy is controversial within the state, but UC says they need the additional revenue. The Berkeley, Los Angeles, and San Diego campuses now enroll about a quarter of their undergraduates from out of state and other countries.

The California system is composed of the 10 combined research and teaching units of the University of California (UC) and 23 state universities (CSU) that focus primarily on undergraduate teaching. It also includes more than 100 two-year community colleges that offer both terminal degrees and the possibility of transferring into four-year institutions.

ADMISSIONS REQUIREMENTS

Admissions requirements for the three tiers and the institutions within them vary widely. Community colleges are open to virtually everyone with or without a high school diploma. The top third of California high school graduates (as measured statewide by a combination of SAT scores and grade point average) may attend one of the CSU campuses; all applicants must complete a 15-unit pattern of high school courses (referred to as "a-g" courses), including a course in the fine or performing arts, to be considered for admission. The UC system targets the top 12.5 percent of the state's high school graduates. In-state students graduating in the top 4 percent of their high school class who meet regular admissions standards will be guaranteed admission to the UC system, although not necessarily to the campus of their choice. The 4 percent proposal is part of a plan to broaden the representation of California applicants and to give more weight to GPA. Out-of-state students continue to face ferocious competition for a limited number of spots while still paying more. Revised admissions guidelines took effect in 2012, increasing the number of California high school graduates who are considered for undergraduate admission by an estimated 40 percent and reducing the number of students in the state who are guaranteed admission based primarily on grades and test scores.

UNIVERSITY OF CALIFORNIA (UC)

Once a bargain, the University of California system is now one of the priciest of any in the country. This is especially true for out-of-state students, for whom the total cost rivals expensive private institutions. The UC system boasts 238,000 students, 190,000 faculty and staff, and 1.7 million living alumni. Although one university system, the nine undergraduate UC campuses (San Francisco is for upper division and graduate students) each offer a full range of academic programs, and each has its own distinctive character. The most recent addition, Merced, opened in 2005 as the first American research university to be founded in the 21st century. In recent years, UC has moved from relying primarily on statistical academic information for admission to a "comprehensive review" that takes into consideration not only coursework and test scores, but also leadership, special talent, and the educational opportunities available to each student. Subject Tests are no longer required; however, when applying to certain academic colleges or majors, it can be to the student's benefit to submit Subject Test scores. For example, for engineering, it is highly recommended that students submit scores in Math Level 2, Chemistry, and/or Physics. Despite state laws that prohibit the consideration of race in admissions, the system remains dedicated to achieving a diverse student body. UC offers a number of outreach programs designed to assist low-income or educationally disadvantaged students who have promising academic potential with admissions and support services.

To apply for admission to the University of California, students complete the electronic application available at admission.universityofcalifornia.edu. Prospective students may apply to as many as nine UC undergraduate campuses on the application, and students are encouraged to apply broadly to augment their chances of gaining admission to at least one campus. It should be understood that each campus to which a student applies reviews the application using its own methodology and criteria. Decisions are thus campus-unique. (One campus does not know what another campus is planning to do with any given applicant.) There is a $70 application fee for each campus. For each campus selected, students must choose a major and (in some cases) an alternate major.

Profiles of the eight major UC universities follow this overview.

CALIFORNIA STATE UNIVERSITY (CSU)

The California State University system is totally separate from the University of California; in fact, the two institutions have historically competed for funds as well as students. The largest system of senior higher education in the nation, CSU focuses on undergraduate education. Although Fresno, Fullerton, and San Francisco were recently reclassified as doctoral universities, most members offer master's degrees on their own but can only award doctorates in collaboration with a UC institution. Research in the state university system is severely restricted, a blow to CSU's national prestige but a big plus for students. Unlike UC, where the mandate to publish or perish is alive and well, teachers in the state system are there to teach. CSU's biggest problem is the success of UC, and its frequent lament—"Anywhere else we'd be number one"—is not without justification.

The 23-campus system caters to more than 484,000 students a year. And while most of the campuses serve mainly commuters, Chico, Humboldt, Monterey Bay, San Luis Obispo, and Sonoma stand out as residential campuses. While a solid liberal arts education is offered, the stress is usually on career-oriented professional training, and the system produces large numbers of engineers, nurses, and teachers for California's workforce. Size varies dramatically, from more than 30,000 full-time students at Northridge and Long Beach to fewer than 7,000 at several other branches, like Channel Islands and Monterey Bay. Each campus has its own specific strengths, although in most cases a student's choice of school is dictated by location rather than by academic specialties. For those with a wider choice, some of the more distinctive campuses are profiled below.

Chico (enrollment 15,500), situated in the beautiful Sacramento Valley, draws a large majority of its students from outside a 100-mile radius and continues to become more selective in its admissions. The on-campus undergraduate life is strong and the social life is great. **California Polytechnic at San Luis Obispo** (21,000) is the toughest state university to get into. It provides excellent training in the applied branches of such fields as agriculture, architecture, business, and engineering. **Fresno** (21,000), located in the verdant Central Valley, has the only viticulture school in the state outside of UC Davis, and undergraduates can work in the school winery. Yosemite, Kings Canyon, and Sequoia national parks are nearby.

San Diego State (30,000) is the balmiest of the campuses, and since it has a more residential, outdoorsy, and campus-oriented social scene, it appeals more to traditional-age undergraduates. "You could go for the weather alone—some do," says one former student. Contrasted with most other state schools, athletics are very important, and the academic offerings are almost as oriented to the liberal arts as at its UC neighbor in San Diego.

San Jose State (26,400), located in the heart of the Silicon Valley, not only boasts strong programs in computer science and engineering (including aerospace), it also offers amazing internship opportunities for students right in its backyard. **Sonoma State** (8,200), situated just north of San Francisco in the wine-growing capital of the state, has become increasingly popular, with strong programs in computer science, creative writing, and electrical engineering, as well as a concentration in wine business strategies within the business school. Its Hutchins School of Liberal Studies allows students to complete their lower-division general education requirements in small (15 students) seminar-style classes that emphasize critical examination and excellence in written communication. Housing and the new student life building are gorgeous.

Humboldt State (7,600) is perched at the top of the state near the Oregon border in the heart of the redwoods. Humboldt's forestry and wildlife departments have national reputations, and the natural sciences are, in general, strong. Students have the run of excellent laboratory facilities and Redwood National Park. Most in-staters come here to get away from Los Angeles and enjoy the rugged coastline north of San Francisco. **California Maritime Academy** (1,000), located 30 miles northeast of San Francisco, specializes in marine transportation, engineering, and maritime technology, and requires summer cruises on the T.S. *Golden Bear*. **Monterey Bay** (6,400) is one mile from the beach, and 52 percent of students live on campus. It offers an interdisciplinary focus with a global perspective, opportunities for internships, and a unique Capstone Festival featuring the culminating projects of graduating seniors, credential candidates, and master's students.

To apply to a California State University campus, complete the electronic application available at www2 .calstate.edu/apply. There is a single application for all campuses; students must indicate the term they are applying for and their preferred campuses and majors. The filing period is October 1 through November 30. Once this application is completed, the data will automatically transfer to each additional campus. The only screen that must be completed per campus is the Enrollment Information screen (the first screen of the application). Students who apply to Cal Poly–San Luis Obispo, however, must choose a major and complete additional screens. There is a $55 application fee for each campus.

UC Berkeley

110 Sproul Hall #5800, Berkeley, CA 94720-5800

Like everything else at Berkeley, the academic offerings at this flagship of flagship universities can be overwhelming. With more than 29,000 undergraduate overachievers crammed into such a small space, it is no wonder that the academic climate is about as intense as you can get at a world-class public university. Don't expect to be on a first-name basis with your professor in Intro Bio.

Berkeley. Mention the name, and even down-to-earth students get stars in their eyes. Students who come here want the biggest and best of everything, though sometimes that idealism runs headlong into budget cuts, tuition increases, and housing shortages. Never mind. Berkeley is where the action is. If you want a quick indicator of Berkeley's academic prowess, look no farther than the parking lot. The campus is dotted with spots marked "NL"—spots reserved for resident Nobel laureates. The last time anyone counted, Berkeley boasted 22 of them, along with hundreds of Guggenheim fellows, Pulitzer Prize recipients, MacArthur fellows, and Fulbright scholars. Is it any wonder that this radical institution of the '60s still maintains the kind of reputation that makes the top private universities take note? The social climate at this mother of UC schools is not as explosive as it once seemed to be, but don't expect anything tame on today's campus. It has often been at the epicenter of the Free Speech movement. Flower children and granola chompers still abound, as do fledgling Marxists, young Republicans, and body-pierced activists.

Spread across 1,200 scenic acres on a hill overlooking San Francisco Bay, the Berkeley campus is a parklike oasis in a small city. The startlingly wide variety of architectural styles ranges from the stunning classical amphitheater to the modern University Art Museum draped in neon sculpture. Large expanses of grass dot the campus and are just "perfect for playing Frisbee or lying in the

> "This system has allowed me to hear outstanding lectures from amazing professors who write the books we read."

sun." The oaks along Strawberry Creek and the eucalyptus grove date back to Berkeley's beginnings more than 150 years ago. Sproul Plaza, in the heart of the campus, is one of the great people-watching sites of the world.

Of course, Berkeley is not only gorgeous; it's also academically intense. "Everyone was the top student in his or her high school class, so they can't settle for anything less than number one," says one student. Another says bluntly, "Expect very little sleep." Although 54 percent of all undergraduate classes have fewer than 20 students, some introductory courses, particularly in the sciences, have as many as 800, and professors, who must publish or disengage from the university's highly competitive

Website: www.berkeley.edu
Location: City Center
Public
Total Enrollment: 38,948
Undergraduates: 29,351
Male/Female: 48/52
SAT Ranges: ERW 650–750, M 650–780
ACT Ranges: 29–34
Financial Aid: 65%
Pell Grant: 25%
Expense: Pub $ $ $
Student Loans: 35%
Average Debt: $
Applicants: 85,057
Accepted: 17%
Enrolled: 43%
Grad in 6 Years: 91%
Returning Freshmen: 97%
Academics: ✍ ✍ ✍ ✍ ✍
Social: ☎ ☎ ☎ ☎
Q of L: ★ ★ ★
Admissions: (510) 642-3175
Email Address: N/A

Strong Programs:
Engineering
Architecture
Economics

teaching ranks, devote a great deal of time to research. After all, Berkeley has made a large part of its reputation on its research and graduate programs, many of which rank among the best in the nation.

While the undergraduate education is excellent, students take a gamble with the trickle-down theory, which holds out the promise that the intellectual might of those in the ivory towers will drip down to them eventually. As a political science major explains, "This system has allowed me to hear outstanding lectures from amazing professors who write the books we read, while allowing far more personal attention from the graduate-student instructors." Another student opines, "It's better to stand 50 feet from brilliance than five feet from mediocrity." Evidence of such gravitational pull is seen in the promising curricula designed specifically for freshmen and sophomores that include interdisciplinary courses in writing, public speaking, and the history of civilization and an offering of small student seminars (with enrollment limited to 15) taught by regular faculty. Despite these attempts at catering to undergraduates, the sheer number of students at Berkeley makes it difficult to treat each student as an individual. As a result, such things as academic counseling suffer. "Advising? You mean to tell me they have advising here?" asks one student.

"Advising? You mean to tell me they have advising here?"

Each of Berkeley's six undergraduate colleges or schools has its own set of general education requirements, which are generally not extensive, and a set of breadth requirements, which expose students to disciplines outside of their major. All students, however, must take English composition and literature and one term each of American history and American institutions, as well as fulfill an American cultures requirement—an original approach (via courses offered in several departments) to comparative study of ethnic groups in the United States.

Most of the departments at Berkeley are noteworthy, and some are about the best anywhere (like engineering and architecture). Business, sociology, mathematics, physics, chemistry, history, economics, political science, and English are just a handful of the truly dazzling programs. Berkeley offers seven departments and seven interdisciplinary programs in engineering; electrical engineering and computer science is the most popular. Interdisciplinary study and research are common across the sciences, such as the biological sciences department's programs in integrative biology and molecular and cell biology.

Special programs abound at Berkeley, though it's up to the student to find out about them. Students may study abroad on fellowships at one of 50 centers around the world, or spend time in various internships around the country. If all you want to do is study, the library system, with more than 12 million volumes and more than 20 branches, is one of the largest in the nation and maintains open stacks. The Coalition for Excellence and Diversity in Mathematics, Science, and Engineering, which provides women and minorities with undergraduate mentors in these fields, is highly regarded.

Although most Berkeley students are California residents, 16 percent come from out of state, and 12 percent come from foreign nations. Thirty-five percent are Asian American, 2 percent are African American, 16 percent are Hispanic, and 6 percent are multiracial. The university provides a variety of programs to promote diversity and inclusion, including Project DARE (Diversity Awareness through Resources and Education), the Center for Racial Education, and a Sexual Harassment Peer Education Program. Despite Berkeley's liberal reputation, recent trends have inched toward conservatism. Business majors and fraternity members outnumber young Communists and peaceniks, though the school does produce a large number of Peace Corps volunteers. Merit scholarships averaging $8,600 are awarded to qualified students, and athletic scholarships are offered

Sproul Plaza, in the heart of the campus, is one of the great people-watching sites of the world.

too. Twenty-five percent of freshmen are eligible for the Pell Grant. The Berkeley Middle Class Access Plan, a program for in-state students whose families' gross income ranges from $80,000 to $150,000 annually, caps the contribution parents make toward the total annual cost of attendance at a maximum of 15 percent of their total income.

Berkeley's highly prized residence halls have room for only 25 percent of the students, and new students receive housing priority. After that, the Cal Rentals is a good resource for finding an apartment in town. Many students live a couple of miles off campus, where "apartments are cheaper," says one student. A number of student-housing projects have opened in recent years, offering a variety of rooms in low-rise and high-rise settings. In the absence of a mandatory meal plan, everybody eats "wherever and whenever they wish," including in the residence halls.

If the housing shortage gets you down, the beautiful California weather will probably take your mind off it, as will the never-ending social opportunities. "Social life at UC Berkeley is killer!" exclaims one geography major. More than 1,200 student clubs and groups are registered on campus, which ensures that there is an outlet for just about any interest and that no one group will ever dominate campus life. Greek life has become more popular, with 10 percent of the men and 10 percent of the women in a fraternity or sorority. Weekends are generally spent in Berkeley, hanging out at the many bookstores, coffeehouses, and sidewalk cafés, heading to a fraternity or sorority party, or taking advantage of the many events right on campus. Berkeley is a quintessential college town ("kind of a crazy little town," says one anthropology major), and of course, there's always the people-watching; where else can an individual meet people trying to convert pedestrians to strange New Age religions or revolutionary political causes on every street corner? Nearby Telegraph Avenue is famous (notorious?) for such antics every weekend.

"[Berkeley is] kind of a crazy little town."

Many students use the weekend to catch up on studying, but when they want to get away, the BART public transportation system provides easy access to San Francisco, by far one of the most pleasant cities in the world and a cultural and countercultural mecca. The Bay Area boasts myriad professional sports teams as well, including the Golden State Warriors, the Oakland A's, the San Francisco 49ers, and the San Francisco Giants. Get access to a car, and you can hike in Yosemite National Park, ski and gamble in Nevada, taste wine in the Napa Valley, or visit the aquarium at Monterey. But be advised that a car is only an asset when you want to go out of town—students warn that parking in Berkeley is difficult, to say the least.

Division I varsity athletics have always been important here, and the university is a top producer of Olympic athletes. Strengths include men's gymnastics, men's crew, and men's and women's swimming. A surge in popularity for the Golden Bears basketball team probably has to do with its great performance in the Pac-12. And just about everyone turns out for the football team's "Big Game," where the favorite activity on the home side of the bleachers is bad-mouthing the rival school to the south: Stanford. Intramurals and fitness programs are enhanced by an extensive recreational facility and gorgeous weather year-round.

"At Berkeley, it is worse to be dull than odd."

The common denominator in the Berkeley community is academic motivation, along with the self-reliance that emerges from trying to make your mark among upward of 29,000 talented peers. Beyond that, the diversity of town and campus makes an extraordinarily free and exciting college environment for almost anyone. "It makes one feel free to dress, say, think, or do anything and not be chastised for being unorthodox," explains a student. "At Berkeley, it is worse to be dull than odd."

Overlaps

UC Davis, UCLA, UC San Diego, Harvard, Stanford

UC Davis

178 Mrak Hall, Davis, CA 95616

The closest thing to a cow college in the UC system, but with a cultured, upscale feel. Described by the *New Yorker* as "the MIT of American fermentation." Premed, prevet, food science—you name it. If the subject lives and breathes, you can study it here. A small-town alternative to the bright lights of UC Berkeley and UCLA. As is often true at science-oriented schools, the work is hard.

Website: www.ucdavis.edu
Location: Small City
Public
Total Enrollment: 35,592
Undergraduates: 29,201
Male/Female: 40/60
SAT Ranges: ERW 550–650,
   M 570–710
ACT Ranges: 25–31
Financial Aid: 73%
Pell Grant: 36%
Expense: Pub $ $ $
Student Loans: 49%
Average Debt: $
Applicants: 70,214
Accepted: 44%
Enrolled: 19%
Grad in 6 Years: 85%
Returning Freshmen: 93%
Academics: ✍ ✍ ✍ ✍
Social: ☎ ☎ ☎
Q of L: ★ ★ ★ ★
Admissions: (530) 752-2971
Email Address: undergraduate
   admissions@ucdavis.edu

Strong Programs:
Biological Sciences
Economics
Psychology
Animal Science
Engineering
Agriculture

At the University of California Davis, environmental science and most everything that has to do with animals, agriculture, winemaking, or biological science is noteworthy. The Aggies' cup truly runneth over. Originally developed as the University of California Farm, the campus maintains its sprawling, verdant beauty, replete with native and imported forestry, charming bike paths, and mooing cows. But lest you assume this environmentally oriented university is full of quaint country folk right out of *American Gothic*, think again. UC Davis is a major research university and has become an international leader in the agricultural, biological, biotechnical, and veterinary sciences.

Located 20 miles west of Sacramento and 73 miles north of San Francisco, the 5,300-acre campus is located along the Capitol Corridor, skirting the Sacramento–San Joaquin Delta watershed. It features a 100-acre arboretum and hundreds of buildings with a blend of architectural styles, from traditional dairy barn to the modern Sciences Laboratory building with its rooftop greenhouse. The hub of the university is a central area known as the Quad, one of many grassy open spaces on campus outfitted with hammocks, perfect for soaking up the abundant California sunshine. Recent construction includes the 75,000-square-foot Shrem Museum of Art, which devotes one-third of its space to education.

> **"Academics are fairly intense, yet the students are positive and collaborative."**

General education requirements aim to equip students with a breadth of knowledge to complement the expertise they develop in their chosen fields of study. UC Davis students are expected to address four core literacies: quantitative, scientific, and civic and cultural literacy, as well as literacy with words and images.

Biological sciences, economics, managerial economics, psychology, and an interdisciplinary program in neurobiology, physiology, and behavior are among the campus's most popular majors; environmental engineering is the newest. Animal science and engineering are strong, and the agriculture program is one of the best anywhere. The school is "the number 1 choice for any prevet," according to one student, and it's great for premeds too. The food science major is also stellar and not for the faint of heart or those afraid of chemistry. It was Davis scientists who discovered how to optimize grape growing for California's wine industry and devised the method for creating orange juice concentrate. UC Davis's World Food Center is dedicated to innovating food production methods for improved human health and environmental sustainability. Studio art, boasting several internationally known artists, is also among the top in the nation.

"Academics are fairly intense, yet the students are positive and collaborative," says an economics major. Many introductory courses are quite large, and students complain that the average class size is on the rise, but UC Davis also offers more than 200 small freshman seminars taught by the best instructors. The quality of teaching can vary considerably, according to students, although "most professors are willing to hold extra office hours and make time for the students," says a psychology major.

Faculty members here are expected to do top-level research as well as teach, giving 41 percent of undergraduates the chance to work directly with professors and grad students as assistants in first-class research groups. The University Honors Program is for academically talented first-year and transfer students who want to enhance their education through special courses. Roughly 15 percent of students study internationally, frequently through the 50-plus programs designed and led by faculty in more than 30 countries. "You can study abroad essentially wherever your heart desires for as short as one month or upwards of a year," cheers one senior. The innovative UC Center Sacramento and the Washington Program give undergraduates academic credits for courses and internships in state and federal governments, respectively.

"[The party scene] can get dull, so a lot of students like to go out of town."

"Students at Davis are friendly, and you really feel a sense of community when you're here," observes one senior. Eighty-three percent of undergraduates hail from California, and 12 percent come from abroad. African Americans account for 2 percent of the students, Asian Americans 28 percent, Hispanics 21 percent, and multiracial students 5 percent. Thirty-six percent of freshmen are eligible for Pell Grants. The university's Office of Campus Diversity, Cross-Cultural Center, and academic success centers for students of various ethnicities help support diverse populations. Campus hot topics include social justice and sustainability. Davis awards merit scholarships averaging $6,600, and there are 255 athletic awards.

Only a quarter of undergraduates live on campus, although 92 percent of freshmen choose to do so. Campus housing is secure, well maintained, and includes a number of living/learning community options. "Dorms are really nice and new and air-conditioned," a student says. Three meal plans for the three dining halls offer a wide range of options, including vegan and kosher items at every meal. Food trucks are positioned around campus at lunchtime, and a weekly on-campus farmers market provides ready access to fresh produce. A senior notes, "Our fraternities, sororities, and student government have taken steps to address sexual assault and promote a stance against it."

"Bicycles are the norm at Davis. Don't come without one."

"Davis has a good social scene, but you have to put in the effort to find places and events you like," says a design major. Active drama and music departments provide frequent entertainment, and the 1,800-seat Mondavi Center for the Performing Arts features international and local groups. There are more than 800 student clubs, and fraternities and sororities attract 12 percent of the men and 10 percent of the women. While alcohol is allowed in the dorms for those of age, a senior says the party scene "can get dull, so a lot of students like to go out of town" for more vigorous nightlife. Major annual social events include Lawntopia, a student-run music festival; Picnic Day, in which alumni join current students in a massive outdoor shindig; nearly three months of cultural celebrations every spring; and the Whole Earth Festival, "an earthy, tie-dyed sort of event." Health and environmental consciousness run high here, and bicycles are the main form of transportation across the incredible 100 miles of bike paths that crisscross the campus and environs. "Bicycles

(continued)
Food Science
Studio Art

It was Davis scientists who discovered how to optimize grape growing for California's wine industry.

Forty-one percent of undergraduates work directly with professors and grad students as assistants in first-class research groups.

are the norm at Davis. Don't come without one," advises one psych major. The university also sponsors sustainability projects and promotes such novelties as contests between residence halls for the lowest heating and electric bills.

In between quizzes and cram sessions, the surrounding communities offer a welcome change of pace. With its tree-lined streets and quiet nights, the city of Davis itself is small but has enough restaurants, activities, and entertainment to keep those who want to stay close to campus happy. The relationship between the college and town is one of unusual cooperation (partly because the students, who make up half the population, are a significant voting bloc in local elections). A car can come in handy if you are looking for an urban night out in Sacramento (20 minutes) or a big-name show in San Francisco (a little more than an hour). Undergrads who lack wheels of their own can get around town for free on the student-run Unitrans bus system or head to UC Berkeley via an intercampus shuttle. Beaches are a two-hour drive from the campus, and the ski slopes and hiking trails of Lake Tahoe and the Sierra Nevada mountains are a little closer.

Most of UC Davis's 25 Division I varsity teams (the Aggies) compete in the Big West Conference. Men's and women's basketball and men's water polo are recent conference champions, and new programs have been added in women's beach volleyball and equestrian. The annual Causeway Classic football game against rival Sacramento State stirs passions, as do recreational sports: students are active in nearly 40 club sports and more than 25 intramurals. Given the Mediterranean climate, outdoor activities are popular, and almost everyone does something athletic—jogging, softball, tennis, swimming, or Frisbee—if only to break up their studies with a different kind of competition.

Proud of its small-town atmosphere, UC Davis is not for the lazy or faint of heart. As one student says, "There's no free ride. You are going to have to work for everything you get." And most students get a lot out of their four or more years at UC Davis. It's the ideal spot to combine high-powered work in science and agriculture with that famous easygoing California lifestyle.

UC Davis sponsors sustainability projects and promotes contests between residence halls for the lowest heating and electric bills.

Overlaps

UC San Diego, UC Irvine, UC Santa Barbara, UCLA, UC Berkeley, UC Santa Cruz, UC Riverside, UC Merced

If You Apply To ›

Davis: Regular decision. SATs (with essay) or ACTs (with writing): required. Subject Tests: optional. Does not accept the Common Application. Apply to a particular college, school, or program. Application includes optional question about gender/sexual identity.

UC Irvine

260 Aldrich Hall, Irvine, CA 92697

Irvine sits in the midst of one of the nation's biggest suburbs, combining funky, modern architecture with a studious, preprofessional student body. Premed is the featured attraction, along with computer science and engineering. Not quite as close to the beach as Santa Barbara—but close enough for students to enjoy it regularly.

On the surface, UC Irvine's clean, contemporary campus appears to be home to students who study diligently in the busy library, wear sensible shoes to class, and at least try to resist that double shot of espresso at the busy coffee shops around campus. But that image starts to dissipate as soon as you hear that bizarre noise: "Zot! Zot! Zot!" Then a UCI student explains that "it's the sound that an anteater supposedly makes when it swipes an ant with its tongue." Hey, any school that has

Website: www.uci.edu
Location: Small City
Public
Total Enrollment: 34,337
Undergraduates: 28,851

a marauding anteater as a mascot can't be completely straitlaced. The university is, however, serious about its reputation as a school with stellar programs in science, technology, and the arts.

Located in the heart of Orange County and founded in 1965, UCI is among the newest of the UC campuses. While enrollment is up and the administration anticipates further expansion, according to one English major, "It is the perfect size." UCI is liberally supplied with trees and shrubs from all over the world. Futuristic buildings are arranged in a circle around 21-acre Aldrich Park, "giving it the appearance of a relaxed art school," says one observer. Undergraduates have long quipped that UCI stood for "Under Construction Indefinitely." New residential towers housing nearly 500 first-year students opened in 2019 at the Middle Earth community (named after the Lord of the Rings trilogy).

UCI's general education requirements involve three courses each in writing, science and technology, social and behavioral sciences, and arts and humanities. Students also fulfill requirements in foreign language; quantitative, symbolic, and computational reasoning; multicultural studies; and international/global issues. Optional first-year seminars, limited to 15 students each, create a more intimate environment in which to adjust to academic life at a research university. Students may choose from more than 80 majors, and the Campuswide Honors Program is available for top students; several individual departments offer honors programs as well.

A "premed mentality" reigns at Irvine, since the School of Biological Sciences is the best and most competitive academic division; undergraduate degrees in nursing science and pharmaceutical sciences are also notable. The university houses multiple medical research centers focusing on areas like aging and dementia, neurological disorders, and spinal cord trauma. After biology, the most popular majors are computer science, psychology and social behavior, business economics, and political science. The computer science department is bolstered by a fast-growing major in computer game science, and the engineering school is highly competitive. The Claire Trevor School of Arts offers nationally ranked programs in dance, drama, music, studio art, and music theater, and the school's Beall Center for Art and Technology enables students to explore the relationship between digital technology and the arts and sciences. An interdisciplinary major in social ecology combines criminology, environmental and legal studies, and psychology and social behavior, and strongly emphasizes faculty/student relationships. Languages are solid at UCI, and a creative writing program is gaining national recognition.

> "UCI is fairly competitive, and the courses are moderately rigorous."

Like most of the other UC campuses, UCI is on a 10-week quarter system, so the pace is fast and furious. "UCI is fairly competitive, and the courses are moderately rigorous," says a junior, but students are also said to be "surprisingly cooperative." Getting into required classes can be difficult at times, and "Graduate students teach lower-division writing courses," says one student, adding that "many classes are overcrowded, leaving little room for personal attention." Even so, 55 percent of undergraduate classes enroll fewer than 20 students.

Eighty percent of undergraduates are in-staters, the majority from Southern California and many of those from wealthy Orange County—although an impressive 51 percent of incoming freshmen are first-generation college students and 38 percent qualify for Pell Grants. Seventeen percent hail from foreign countries. The campus leans liberal, but students are generally not as active in political or social causes as their peers at some other UC campuses. Minorities account for two-thirds of the student body, with Asian Americans comprising 36 percent, African Americans 2 percent, Hispanics 26 percent, and multiracial students 4

(continued)

Male/Female: 47/53
SAT Ranges: ERW 580–680, M 590–730
ACT Ranges: 25–32
Financial Aid: 76%
Pell Grant: 38%
Expense: Pub $ $ $ $
Student Loans: 55%
Average Debt: $
Applicants: 85,102
Accepted: 37%
Enrolled: 21%
Grad in 6 Years: 85%
Returning Freshmen: 94%
Academics: ✐ ✐ ✐ ✐
Social: ☎ ☎
Q of L: ★ ★ ★
Admissions: (949) 824-6703
Email Address: admissions@ uci.edu

Strong Programs:
Biological Sciences
Computer Science
Psychology and Social Behavior
Business Economics
Political Science
Nursing Science
Engineering
Visual and Performing Arts

New first-year residential towers opened in 2019 at the Middle Earth community (named after the Lord of the Rings trilogy).

percent. One senior notes, "Cultural groups seem to segregate from each other," although several initiatives and events, including the Cross-Cultural Center, the Community Roots Festival, and the Deconstruction Zone Series, are designed to educate and engage the campus community in diversity, social justice, and cultural wellness. Merit scholarships averaging $7,800 are awarded annually, as are 114 athletic awards.

Sixty-one percent of undergraduates live on campus. Condominium-style dorms, both single sex and co-ed, are "exceptional compared to the high-rise dormitories of other institutions," says one senior. Others agree that the homey campus dwellings provide a good experience for freshmen. Although freshmen are guaranteed on-campus housing for two years, 22 percent of them choose to live off campus, which can create a slight commuter-school atmosphere. Most upperclassmen opt for themed housing, fraternity and sorority houses, or off-campus dwellings, often on the beach.

"You have to find the social life on this campus. It won't find you."

One student remarks, "You have to find the social life on this campus. It won't find you." The 18 fraternities and 18 sororities attract 8 percent of the men and 9 percent of the women, and each has something going on every weekend. Students of legal age can unwind at the campus pub. The one event that brings everybody out is Celebrate UCI, a daylong, student-run festival featuring live performances, free food, carnival games and rides, and a car show.

If life on campus is slow, beyond it is not. That's because the campus is located just 50 miles from L.A., five miles from the beach, and a little more than an hour from the ski slopes. Catalina Island, with beaches and hiking trails, is a quick boat trip off Newport Harbor; Mexico is two hours away. While some students treasure the city of Irvine's quiet setting, others lament its "lackluster, homogeneous communities" and conservative feel.

UCI fields 20 Division I Anteater athletic teams. Tennis and cross-country are perennial Big West powerhouses, while men's volleyball and water polo are nationally ranked. There is no football team, but intramurals are extremely popular, as is the state-of-the-art campus recreation center. UCI has also launched an official eSports program—the first of its kind at a public research university—for organized, multiplayer video game competitions, and its coaching staff is actively recruiting top gamers.

What lures students to UCI is its top-name professors, innovative academic programs, and the chance to be a part of its cutting-edge research. For those who come here prepared to keep their heads buried in a book for a few years, the reward will be an exceptional education.

Overlaps

UCLA, UC San Diego, UC Berkeley, UC Santa Barbara, UC Davis, UC Merced, UC Riverside, UC Santa Cruz

If You Apply To ›

Irvine: Regular decision. SATs (with essay) or ACTs (with writing): required. Subject Tests: recommended. Does not accept the Common Application. Apply to a particular college, school, or program. Application includes optional question about gender/sexual identity.

UC Los Angeles

1147 Murphy Hall, Box 951436, Los Angeles, CA 90095

Tucked into exclusive Bel Air with the beach, the mountains, and chic Hollywood hangouts all within easy reach. The adjacent town of Westwood is an ideal student hangout. Practically everything is offered here, but the programs in arts and media are some of the best in the world. Less politically active than Berkeley but just as difficult to get into.

With five Nobel Prizes awarded to alumni and faculty in the past decade, you might think UCLA is an intellectual brain trust. Or with a long list of well-known and highly accomplished alumni in the arts, film, and sports, maybe UCLA is some sort of incubator for truly talented and gifted people. Well, UCLA is all that and more. A superb faculty, a reputation for outstanding academics, and a powerful athletics program make this university an ultimate place to study.

UCLA's prime location—sandwiched between two glamorous neighborhoods (Beverly Hills and Bel Air) and a short drive from the beach, Hollywood, the Sunset Strip, and downtown Los Angeles—makes it appealing for students who want more from their college experience than going to class. The beautifully landscaped, 419-acre campus features a range of architectural styles, with Romanesque/Italian Renaissance as the dominant motif, providing only one of a number of reasons students enjoy staying on campus. A wealth of gardens—botanical, Japanese, and sculpture—add a touch of quiet elegance. The campus is philosophically divided into North and South. North attracts more liberal arts aficionados, while those in math and science tend to favor South. Recent construction includes BFIT—the Bruin Fitness Center, intended exclusively for undergraduate use.

First-year students are encouraged to participate in a three-day summer orientation that provides workshops, counseling, an introduction to the campus and community, and a chance to register for classes. In Fall Quarter, freshmen can begin a yearlong cluster of interdisciplinary courses on topics such as Environment and Sustainability or enroll in small-group seminars such as Student Activism from the Sixties to Present. To graduate, first-year students are required to take (or test out of) quantitative reasoning and English composition courses. Lab science and a language requirement are necessary for a liberal arts degree, and all students must take a course on diversity. Concerned that too many majors have been asking too little of students, the university is now encouraging departments to require capstone projects in which students must use the methodological training of their discipline and integrate what they have learned across topics and fields.

> **"We are spoiled by incredible faculty at UCLA— top researchers in their field and amazing lecturers."**

Strong programs abound at UCLA, and many are considered among the best in the nation. UCLA is well established in the STEM fields; the Samueli School of Engineering and Applied Science is highly regarded and sets the tone on campus, and biological sciences, mathematics, and chemistry are also strong. The School of Theater, Film, and Television is first-rate, and its students have the opportunity to study in Verona, Italy, with the Theater Overseas program. The popular Alpert School of Music offers an institute of jazz performance and boasts legends Herbie Hancock and Wayne Shorter among its distinguished faculty. Economics, sociology, biology, and political science enroll the most students.

UCLA gets more applications than any other college in the country—now exceeding 100,000 per year—and the academic environment is intense and

Website: www.ucla.edu
Location: City Center
Public
Total Enrollment: 42,460
Undergraduates: 30,446
Male/Female: 42/58
SAT Ranges: ERW 630–740, M 610–760
ACT Ranges: 27–33
Financial Aid: 54%
Pell Grant: 29%
Expense: Pub $ $ $
Student Loans: 43%
Average Debt: $
Applicants: 102,242
Accepted: 16%
Enrolled: 37%
Grad in 6 Years: 91%
Returning Freshmen: 97%
Academics: ✍ ✍ ✍ ✍ ✍
Social: ☎ ☎ ☎
Q of L: ★ ★ ★
Admissions: (310) 825-3101
Email Address: N/A

Strong Programs:
Economics
Sociology
Biology
Political Science
Engineering
Mathematics
Chemistry
Theater

competitive, especially in STEM fields. Although 57 percent of undergraduate classes have fewer than 20 students, required core classes, usually taken in the first two years, can be as large as 300 to 400 people, with smaller sections. Students warn that some faculty are mainly interested in their research, but a political science major says, "We are spoiled by incredible faculty at UCLA—top researchers in their field and amazing lecturers." Two undergraduate research centers, one for the sciences and one for the arts, humanities, and social sciences, help students develop research skills and connect them with opportunities. The university regularly ranks in the top 10 in the nation in federal funding for research. Faculty-led study abroad programs are popular, and "financial aid travels with you," according to a junior.

"UCLA is a school of leaders and optimists—people who truly believe they can, and will, change the world," says a global studies major. Seventy-seven percent of undergraduates are California residents, and 12 percent are international. Asian Americans account for 29 percent of UCLA's student population, Hispanics 23 percent, African Americans 3 percent, and multiracial students 5 percent. The political atmosphere is liberal; UCLA is one of the few universities in the nation with a gay fraternity and a lesbian sorority, and students often advocate for social justice issues. Twenty-nine percent of freshmen qualify for Pell Grants. Merit scholarships are available, averaging $5,600 each, as well as nearly 300 athletic scholarships in 21 sports.

> "A lot of social things happen on campus—you always feel like you are a part of something greater."

Forty-eight percent of undergraduates, including almost all freshmen, live on campus in the residential area known as "the Hill"; freshmen are guaranteed three consecutive years of university housing, and the dorms get great reviews. Residential learning communities with a faculty member in residence are an option for those who wish to bond with classmates over shared interests. Fifteen dining halls, restaurants, and snack bars serve meals that students rave about. "I have friends who attend other universities who will visit me just so they can eat UCLA's food," says a senior. UCLA has its own police department that keeps the campus safe, and a junior says, "Our Title IX officer is actively working to spread awareness [of sexual assault] and connect those affected with the right resources."

Consistent with UCLA's huge enrollment, there is no shortage of social options on campus. "Social life is bustling," cheers a junior. "What I love about UCLA is that a lot of social things happen on campus—you always feel like you are a part of something greater because so many students participate in activities going on." Eleven percent of men and 13 percent of women join one of UCLA's nearly 60 fraternities and sororities, and a senior says Greek life "is a fun way to get involved and meet people, but it does not monopolize social life." The university's alcohol policy is similar to that of other UC schools—open consumption is a no-no. Top-name entertainers, political figures, and speakers of all kinds come to the campus; film and theater presentations are frequent, and the air is thick with live music. Spring Sing, a campuswide student talent show presided over by celebrity judges, is a favorite tradition. Volunteer Day is a big deal here too, and attracts more than 8,000 student volunteers annually.

> "Although everyone is striving for excellence, UCLA allows everyone to experience *life*."

With all the attractions of the City of Angels at UCLA's doorstep, social life is hardly confined to campus. "There is constantly a variety of different concerts, plays, art shows, comedy shows, and festivals in L.A. that students can take advantage of," says a junior. The hopping Westwood neighborhood, which borders the university, has at least 15 movie theaters and scores of coffee shops and affordable restaurants, although the shops tend to cater to the upper class. The beach is five miles away, and the mountains are only a short drive. Although public transportation is cheap, it's also relatively inconvenient (although new bus routes have eased this somewhat). The easiest solution is to live close to campus and ride a bike.

UCLA has won a staggering number of collegiate titles, including more than 115 NCAA Division I team national championships. The most recent include men's water polo, women's gymnastics, and women's beach volleyball. UCLA has won more than 260 Olympic medals and has won a gold medal in every Olympics in which the U.S. has competed since 1932. The men's football and basketball teams are the undeniable crowd-pleasers, although beating crosstown rival USC is the name of the game in any sport. UCLA fans regard their intra-city rivalry with enthusiasm. Beat USC Week, the week leading up to the football game between the two, is an event in itself, featuring a bonfire, concert, and blood drive. About a third of students compete in club and intramural sports.

"Although everyone is striving for excellence, UCLA allows everyone to experience *life*," muses a junior. "That means taking time to prepare for exams and do it well, while also making time to play beach volleyball at Sunset Rec with all of your friends." A leading research center, 200 fields of study, distinguished faculty members, and outstanding athletics make UCLA one of the most prestigious universities in the nation. And despite the large size, students still feel they are part of a tight-knit community bubbling with Bruin pride.

If You Apply To ›

UCLA: Regular decision. SATs (with essay) or ACTs (with writing): required. Subject Tests: optional. Does not accept the Common Application. Apply to a particular college, school, or program. Application includes optional question about gender/sexual identity.

UC Riverside

Riverside, CA 92521

Most diverse UC school and the easiest to get into, but offers a more personal touch. UCR's traditional strengths in the sciences are bolstered by expanding opportunities for undergraduate research. Social life is relatively tame, since many students commute. While some complain of a lack of nightlife in Riverside, they readily agree that activities on campus make up for it.

Lacking the big-name reputation and booming athletic programs of the other UC schools, UC Riverside has chosen to place its emphasis on something that not all universities consider to be an important priority: the student. Riverside offers one of the lowest student/faculty ratios in the UC system, strong academic and cocurricular programs, and a richly diverse community. "Students are well taken care of and get personal attention," says one satisfied senior. Though part of the UC system, UC Riverside is a breed apart.

Located 60 miles east of Los Angeles, UCR is surrounded by mountains on the outskirts of the city of Riverside. The beautifully landscaped, 1,200-acre campus consists of mainly modern architecture, with a 160-foot bell tower (with a 48-bell carillon) marking its center. Wide lawns and clusters of oaks create "a veritable botanical garden," where students and faculty enjoy relaxing between classes. Acres of citrus groves form a half-circle on the outer edges of campus and perfume the air. Recent

Website: www.ucr.edu
Location: Small City
Public
Total Enrollment: 22,712
Undergraduates: 19,708
Male/Female: 45/55
SAT Ranges: ERW 550–640, M 540–660
ACT Ranges: 23–29
Financial Aid: 85%
Pell Grant: 51%
Expense: Pub $ $ $ $

(continued)

Student Loans: 66%
Average Debt: $
Applicants: 43,682
Accepted: 57%
Enrolled: 18%
Grad in 6 Years: 75%
Returning Freshmen: 89%
Academics: ✍ ✍ ✍ ½
Social: ☎ ☎
Q of L: ★ ★ ★
Admissions: (951) 827-3411
Email Address: admissions@ ucr.edu

Strong Programs:
Biology
Psychology
Business Administration
Sociology
Plant Biology
Entomology
Computer Science
Computer Engineering

Recent campus additions include the 179,000-square-foot Multidisciplinary Research Building.

campus additions include the 179,000-square-foot Multidisciplinary Research Building, supporting work in the sciences and engineering.

All students are required to meet extensive "breadth requirements" that include courses in English composition, natural sciences and math, humanities, and social sciences. Some majors include a foreign language requirement. The campus libraries have an impressive 3 million volumes, an interlibrary loan system within the UC system, and vast electronic databases. A specialized research collection in science fiction is world-class. UCR's California Museum of Photography, located in downtown Riverside and available on the Web, has grown in stature.

Decades ago, researchers at the Citrus Experiment Station in Riverside perfected the growing methods for the imported navel orange, making discoveries to protect the fruit from disease and pests and saving California's citrus industry. Riverside continues to excel in plant biology and entomology. But the campus has grown since its founding in 1954 to include excellent programs spanning a number of disciplines. Biology, psychology, business administration, and sociology are the most popular majors. The biological sciences program is UCR's most prestigious and demanding, especially the medical biology track, and its most successful students can earn a B.S./M.D. in partnership with the medical school at UCLA. The Bourns College of Engineering, which has strong majors in computer science and computer engineering, is also quite selective, more so than the campus as a whole. One of the few undergraduate environmental engineering programs is at UCR, as is an undergraduate program in creative writing.

> "There is a strong support system that is available to students throughout the campus."

Students say the academic climate is cooperative. "Instead of being super competitive," says a student, "I see more students working together to get the job done." State funding woes have resulted in cuts to some programs and gradual increases in class sizes, although the university is showing signs of recovery. Currently, 30 percent of undergraduate classes have more than 50 students. Research is an institutional priority for faculty, and the quality of instruction can vary. Still, UCR has a tradition of undergraduate and faculty interaction, with a wide range of undergraduate research grants available during the academic year. This may be why one in six graduates goes on to get a Ph.D. "There is a strong support system that is available to students throughout the campus," says a senior. "Even teaching assistants strive to help students." The University Honors Program offers exceptional students further academic challenges, in addition to extracurricular activities and special seminars for freshmen. Talented student singers, dancers, and actors can earn stipends for performing in the community through an arts outreach program. Short-term, faculty-led, summer study abroad options are expanding, and through the UC system, students have access to 120 international programs.

Ninety-six percent of UCR undergraduates are from California, mainly L.A., Riverside, San Bernardino, and Orange County; 3 percent are international. "UCR is one of the most diverse universities in the nation," a political science major says. "Because of this, there is a wide range of students at UCR that make a blended environment of different cultures, nationalities, and social statuses." Indeed, Asian Americans account for 34 percent of the students, Hispanics 41 percent, African Americans 4 percent, and multiracial students 6 percent. A hefty 51 percent of first-time freshmen receive Pell Grants. As part of the UC commitment to diversity, Riverside supports centers for various ethnicities, for women, and for LGBTQ students. Numerous merit scholarships averaging $8,200 are doled out every year, as well as 115 athletic scholarships.

Housing is relatively easy to obtain, but the quality varies greatly. "While West Lothian looks like a prison, Pentland Hills is like a resort," says one student.

Thirty-one percent of undergrads live in the dorms. Five academically oriented living/learning communities are popular with freshmen, who are guaranteed housing for their first year. Campus dining is generally described as adequate. Students say they feel safe on campus; security measures include an escort service, patrolling security officers, and regular training on sexual assault prevention and intervention.

Fraternities and sororities attract 4 percent of the men and 7 percent of the women. "There is always something going on, whether it be a concert, lecture, or sorority/fraternity party," one sophomore says. Campus hangouts, including the Barn, have live bands and comedy nights, and a cultural arts program brings professional shows to campus. Every Wednesday the campus can enjoy a "nooner," where the music department puts on free concerts and lectures during lunch. Returning students are welcomed back every year with a campuswide block party, and the Spring Splash concert brings in

> **"UCR is one of the most diverse universities in the nation."**

Returning students are welcomed back every year with a campuswide block party.

hot bands. University Village is a commercial center offering a movie theater, restaurants, and an arcade right on the edge of campus. Riverside weather is temperate except during the summer months, when the heat and haze combine to make a trip to the ocean look really inviting. The coast is only about 45 minutes by freeway and the desert is an hour east. Big Bear and numerous ski resorts are also within an hour's drive.

The Riverside Highlanders compete in Division I, and men's and women's golf (recent Big West Conference champions), basketball, and softball are especially competitive. A recreational program in men's and women's karate has turned out national champions. A student recreation center offers a health-club atmosphere with sand volleyball, weight and workout machines, and intramural leagues.

All in all, Riverside is expanding and improving, albeit not without some growing pains, including rising tuition and living costs. But it still offers more personal attention to its students than some of its larger, sister UC campuses. UCR is fast becoming a nationally recognized research institution, from which students surely will benefit. "UCR has grown immensely over the past few years," one sophomore says. "The emphasis for the future is to establish a name for UCR, to let the nation know what a wonderful university this is."

Overlaps

UC Irvine, UC Davis, UC Santa Barbara, Arizona State, Iowa State, UC San Diego, Cal State Fullerton, Cal Poly Pomona

If You Apply To ›

Riverside: Regular decision. SATs (with essay) or ACTs (with writing): required. Subject Tests: optional. Does not accept the Common Application. Apply to a particular college, school, or program. Application includes optional question about gender/sexual identity.

UC San Diego

9500 Gilman Drive, MC 0021, La Jolla, CA 92093

Applications have doubled in the past 10 years at this seaside paradise. UC San Diego now rivals better-known Berkeley and UCLA as the Cal campus of choice for top students. Six undergraduate colleges break the university down to a more manageable size. Best known for science, engineering, and the famed Scripps Institution of Oceanography.

Website: www.ucsd.edu
Location: City Outskirts
Public
Total Enrollment: 35,169
Undergraduates: 28,159
Male/Female: 51/49
SAT Ranges: ERW 550–660,
   M 590–720
ACT Ranges: 26–32
Financial Aid: 60%
Pell Grant: 31%
Expense: Pub $ $ $
Student Loans: 53%
Average Debt: $
Applicants: 88,428
Accepted: 34%
Enrolled: 19%
Grad in 6 Years: 85%
Returning Freshmen: 94%
Academics: ✑ ✑ ✑ ✑ ✑
Social: ☎ ☎ ☎
Q of L: ★ ★ ★ ★
Admissions: (858) 534-4831
Email Address:
   admissionsreply@ucsd.edu

Strong Programs:
Engineering
Computer Science
Oceanography
Biology
Chemistry
Economics
Psychology
Cognitive Science

The Scripps Institution of Oceanography is excellent, due to the university's advantageous location.

Some say that looking good is better than feeling good, but at UC San Diego, they're doing a lot of both. Set against the serene beauty of La Jolla's beaches, students catch as much relaxation time as they do study time. But it's not all fun and games around this campus. The research star of the UC system, San Diego's faculty rates high nationally among public institutions in science productivity. And within each of the six undergraduate colleges, a system that offers undergraduates more intimate settings, students are honing their minds with the classics and the cutting edge in academics. Sure, San Diegans tend to be more mellow than the average Southern Californian, and the students here follow suit. But beneath the tanned foreheads and bright smiles, UC San Diego is bubbling with intellectual energy and the healthy desire to be at the top of the UC system.

San Diego's tree-lined campus sits high on a bluff overlooking the Pacific in the seaside resort of La Jolla. The predominant architectural theme is contemporary, with a few out-of-the-ordinary structures, including a library that looks like an inverted pyramid. Another tinge of the postmodern is the nation's largest neon sculpture, which wraps around one of the high-rise academic buildings and consists of seven-foot-tall letters that spell out the seven virtues superimposed over the seven vices. Plans are in the works for a significant campus expansion that will add several new academic and residential facilities.

UC San Diego's six undergraduate colleges have their own sets of general education requirements, their own personalities, and differing ideals on which they are based. Revelle College, the oldest, is the most rigorous and mandates that students become equally acquainted with a certain level of coursework in the humanities, sciences, and social sciences, as well as fulfill a language requirement. Muir allows more flexibility in the distribution of requirements. Thurgood Marshall College was founded to emphasize and encourage social awareness. Like Revelle, it places equal weight on sciences, social sciences, and humanities, but it also stresses a liberal arts education based on "an examination of the human condition in a multicultural society." Warren has developed a highly organized internship program that gives its undergraduates more practical experience than the others do. Eleanor Roosevelt College devotes its curriculum to international and cross-cultural studies. Sixth College focuses on art, culture, and technology, with the aim of preparing students to work collaboratively and enjoy working in their communities. Prospective freshmen apply to the university but must indicate their preferred college.

"We enjoy athletics and extracurricular activities, but academic excellence is our priority."

UC San Diego's programs in science, engineering, and computer science have global reputations and are "not for the faint of heart," says one student. Engineering is particularly competitive, and a limit to the number of students who can declare this major means acceptance into the major usually requires an A average and top test scores in entry-level courses. The Scripps Institution of Oceanography is also excellent, due to the university's advantageous location. Biology (the most popular major) and chemistry are also strengths, but you really can't go wrong in any of the hard sciences. Although the humanities and social sciences are not as solid in comparison, economics, psychology, and cognitive science are popular majors. New interdisciplinary majors are available in business psychology, data science, and oceanic and atmospheric sciences, and students may devise their own majors. Twenty-two percent of students study abroad; San Diego's five-week, faculty-led Global Seminars in the summer are especially popular.

San Diego operates on the quarter system, which means students cram 3 or 4 courses into 10 weeks. Science students in particular find the workload intense. The quality of research done by the faculty, half a dozen of whom are Nobel laureates, is extremely high, and students have ample opportunities to assist with research, sometimes as early as freshman year. Students say the typical scenario of research over teaching seen at most large research universities is not as common at UC San Diego. Even so, given the large class sizes—34 percent of undergraduate courses enroll more than 50 students—"you end up teaching a lot of the material to yourself," according to an anthropology major.

A theater major notes that the university's academic intensity "does not mean that all the students here are nerdy. We enjoy athletics and extracurricular activities, but academic excellence is our priority." A short walk to the beach, however, reveals the student body's wild and crazy half-surfers and their fans, who celebrate the "kick back." Students jumping curbs on skateboards are common on this campus. Yet these beach babies are no scholastic slouches. San Diego ranks highly among public colleges and universities in the percentage of graduates who go on to earn a Ph.D. and in the percentage of students accepted to medical school. Six percent of undergraduates are from states outside of California, and 20 percent are international. Minority representation

> "La Jolla is a rich, conservative, retired, white, snobbish community."

is high, with 38 percent of the student body Asian American, 18 percent Hispanic, and 2 percent African American. Diversity education includes a Cross-Cultural Center for students, faculty, and staff that provides activities, brown-bag luncheons, and programs on race relations. Thirty-one percent of freshmen are Pell Grant recipients. Merit scholarships averaging $11,000 are doled out to eligible undergraduates, and the university has begun to offer athletic scholarships in some sports as it transitions to Division I status.

Each of the university's colleges has its own housing complex, with either dorms or apartments. Most freshmen live on campus and are guaranteed housing for their first two years. "The residence halls are very nice, with all the amenities," says an animal physiology major. Dorm residents are required to buy a meal plan, and their Dining Dollars are good at any of the campus's 13 eateries. Overall, 40 percent of undergraduates live on campus; by junior year, students usually decide to take up residence in La Jolla proper or nearby Del Mar, often in beachside apartments. But that can be costly: the price ends up being inversely proportional to proximity to the beach. If you are willing to relinquish the luxury of a five-minute walk to the beach, a short commute will bring you relatively affordable housing.

"La Jolla is a rich, conservative, retired, white, snobbish community," one sophomore says. "Not a college town!" Cars are, of course, an inescapable part of Southern California life, and owning one—many people do—makes off-campus living even more pleasant. "No car equals no fun," one international studies major says. Unfortunately, trying to park on campus can be difficult. Mexico is a half-hour drive (even nearer than the desert, where many students go hiking), and the two-hour trip to Los Angeles makes for a nice weekend jaunt.

For those looking to stay closer to campus, the Pacific Beach and downtown San Diego, with its zoo, Sea World, and Balboa Park, are all only 12 miles away. Torrey Pines State Natural Reserve is great for outdoor enthusiasts. "Most students hang out at the dance clubs, jazz bars, and great restaurants in the Gaslamp Quarter,"

> "[We have] a beautiful beachfront environment that eases a life of academic rigor."

says a senior. The university offers nearly 600 student-run groups, and 12 percent of the men and 12 percent of the women join a fraternity or sorority. The campus is dry, but some students claim that lax RAs and good fake IDs make for easy underage drinking. Although campus life is relatively tame, everyone looks forward to university-sponsored festivals, including the Open House, UnOlympics, and the Reggae Festival. The biggest annual event pays tribute to a hideously loud and colorful statue of the Sun God, which is the unofficial mascot for this

Each of the university's colleges has its own housing complex, with either dorms or apartments.

The biggest annual event pays tribute to a hideously loud and colorful statue of the Sun God, which is the unofficial mascot.

sun-streaked student body. The Sun God Festival draws such big-name performers as Drake and Wiz Khalifa.

Although San Diego will never be mistaken for a sports-crazed school (à la USC), the university is in the process of transitioning from Division II to the Division I Big West Conference. Triton volleyball, water polo, soccer, basketball, and tennis teams have traditionally been the strongest. The school's club surfing team has won six national championships. For weekend warriors, classes are available in windsurfing, sailing, scuba diving, and kayaking at the nearby Mission Bay Aquatic Center. Most students participate in one intramural league or another, and according to one, if you're not on a team, "you're not a true UC San Diego student."

The students at UC San Diego are exceptionally serious and out for an excellent education. But the pace (study, party, relax, study more) and the props (sun, sand, Frisbees, and flip-flops) give the rigorous curriculum an inimitable flavor that undergraduates would not change. Indeed, many believe they have the best setup in higher education: "a beautiful beachfront environment that eases a life of academic rigor."

If You Apply To ›

San Diego: Regular decision. SATs (with essay) or ACTs (with writing): required. Subject Tests: recommended for engineering, biological sciences, and physical sciences applicants. Does not accept the Common Application. Apply to a particular college, school, or program. Application includes optional question about gender/sexual identity.

UC Santa Barbara

Santa Barbara, CA 93106

Willpower is the word at UC Santa Barbara. On a beautiful day with the sound of waves crashing in the distance, that's what it takes to hang in there with pen, paper, laptop, or book. Fairly or not, Santa Barbara is known as the party animal of the UC system. In the classroom, science is the best bet. Free spirits should check out the unusual College for Creative Studies.

Website: www.ucsb.edu
Location: Suburban
Public
Total Enrollment: 24,641
Undergraduates: 21,776
Male/Female: 46/54
SAT Ranges: ERW 620–710, M 620–760
ACT Ranges: 26–32
Financial Aid: 58%
Pell Grant: 34%
Expense: Pub $ $ $
Student Loans: 51%
Average Debt: $
Applicants: 80,319
Accepted: 33%

For students at UC Santa Barbara, California's famed beaches serve as both classroom and playground. On weekends, sun-worshipping students grab surfboards and don bikinis and head to the water for some serious fun. During the week, those same students can likely be found studying technology rather than tan lines. UCSB provides a comfortable mixture of work and play that is unique to the UC system and draws praise from its students. "On a nice sunny day, the beaches and grassy areas will be flooded with students," says a freshman, "but most of them are there with a book."

Located just a stone's throw from the beach, UC Santa Barbara's 1,000-acre campus is bordered on two sides by the Pacific Ocean, with a clear view of the Channel Islands. On the landward side are a nature preserve and the predominantly student community of Isla Vista, and five miles to the north lie the Santa Ynez Mountains.

> **"On a nice sunny day, the beaches and grassy areas will be flooded with students."**

The campus itself features mainly 1950s Southern California architecture with a Southern California atmosphere to match. An $86 million bioengineering building recently opened, housing offices, research labs, and a 100-seat auditorium.

UCSB's general education program features the usual distribution requirements and coursework in writing, non-Western cultures, quantitative relationships, and ethnicity. Not surprisingly, the marine biology department stands out among the university's best, capitalizing on the school's aquatic resources; chemical engineering, physics, and chemistry are also well regarded. The Bren School of Environmental Science and Management is home to world-renowned faculty, boasting six Nobel Prize winners in economics, chemistry, and physics. The most popular majors include biological sciences, psychology, economics, and communication. The accounting program is strong, and the courses are geared toward taking and passing the CPA exam, so graduation is usually followed by a mass recruitment by California's big accounting firms. The College of Creative Studies offers an unstructured curriculum to about 400 self-starters ready for advanced and independent work in the arts, math, or the sciences. The interdisciplinary global studies major combines language study with global history, culture, economics, and politics.

"It is really easy to get involved and make friends through campus activities."

"The academic climate of UC Santa Barbara is very collaborative," says one sophomore, but "the workload is definitely strenuous at times." Nearly half of all undergraduate classes have fewer than 20 students, but teaching is a hit-or-miss affair, according to one junior: "Many of the professors are more interested in their research than teaching a class." On the flip side, many opportunities are available for undergrads to assist professors, and 55 percent of students get involved in undergraduate research. For those who seek time away, Santa Barbara is the headquarters of the UC system's Education Abroad Program, which sends students to any of 120 host universities worldwide; 17 percent of UCSB students study abroad.

UCSB students, 88 percent of whom are California residents, are traditionally public-spirited and laid-back. "There are some who aren't the most academically focused, but for the most part I'd say the students are great at balancing their academic and social lives while getting involved in helping the community," says one mechanical engineering major. Asian Americans comprise 20 percent of the student body, African Americans make up 3 percent, Hispanics account for 27 percent, and multiracial students add 6 percent; 8 percent are international. The campus vibe is decidedly liberal. "Some of the biggest political issues on campus have to do with the environment. As a coastal area, UCSB is very susceptible to pollution," explains one student. Merit scholarships averaging $8,200 and nearly 200 athletic scholarships in 10 sports are available for those who qualify. Thirty-four percent of freshmen are Pell-eligible.

University housing, which includes both dorms and privately run residence halls, is comfortable, well maintained, and much sought after. "Our on-campus housing is amazing, right in front of the beach," a junior says. "They come fully furnished, with high-speed Internet, cable, telephone lines, and a great atmosphere." Unfortunately, there is a waiting list to get into the dorms—even with the latest student housing addition, Manzanita Village. Only 38 percent of students, most of whom are freshmen, snag on-campus housing. Meals in the dorms are available to residents and nonresidents alike, and are, according to most students, more than simply edible. "Great food and tons of it!" cheers one student. While students say they feel safe on campus, one frequently used motto is "four years, four bikes," because of the frequency of bicycle thefts. Regarding campus sexual assault, "The school has provided as many resources as it can, really," says a chemical engineering major, and it "does its best to prevent it."

"It is really easy to get involved and make friends through campus activities," says a sophomore. "Additionally, the social scene off campus is really thriving in the community of Isla Vista." Neighboring Isla Vista has welcomed its student

(continued)

Enrolled: 17%
Grad in 6 Years: 87%
Returning Freshmen: 93%
Academics: ✍ ✍ ✍ ✍
Social: 🎭 🎭 🎭 🎭
Q of L: ★ ★ ★ ★
Admissions: (805) 893-2881
Email Address: admissions@sa.ucsb.edu

Strong Programs:
Biological Sciences
Psychology
Economics
Communication
Marine Biology
Chemical Engineering
Physics
Chemistry

UC Santa Barbara's 1,000-acre campus is bordered on two sides by the Pacific Ocean.

Santa Barbara is the headquarters of the UC system's Education Abroad Program, which sends students to 120 host universities worldwide.

population—after all, most of its population is UCSB students. As a result, students are very active in the community. The fraternities and sororities, which attract just 4 percent of men and 8 percent of women, are known for their philanthropy. The campus is dry, and one student says, "Drinking alcohol on campus is pretty well regulated and not easy to do." Movies and concerts are also available, and the mountains, Los Padres National Forest, and L.A. are all an easy drive away. The annual Extravaganza is an all-day, free concert, and students are known to go wild on Halloween and dress up for the entire weekend. "Halloween is our claim to fame," boasts one student.

All of UCSB's varsity teams (the Gauchos) compete in Division I, and the most successful include soccer, water polo, baseball, volleyball, swimming, and basketball. A never-ending rotation of intramurals is available on and off the beach, and about a quarter of the students participate. Ultimate Frisbee is also quite popular, as well as nationally competitive.

Sure, UCSB students love to play, but that's not why most come to this coastal institution. "If there was anything that I would like to improve, it would be the lingering reputation UCSB has as a party school," observes one student. "This reputation is more of a relic from times past." Students rave about their professors and the academic challenges they face. But they also know a good thing when they see it: not everyone gets to spend four years on the beach and come away with a degree.

If You Apply To ›

Santa Barbara: Regular decision. SATs (with essay) or ACTs (with writing): required. Subject Tests: recommended for engineering applicants. Does not accept the Common Application. Apply to a particular college, school, or program. Application includes optional question about gender/sexual identity.

UC Santa Cruz

1156 High Street, Santa Cruz, CA 95064

From its flower-child beginnings, UC Santa Cruz has wandered back toward the mainstream. The yoga mats and surfboards still abound and Sammy the banana slug is still the mascot, but the students are a lot more conventional than in its earlier incarnation. The emphasis here continues to be on environmental stewardship, community engagement, and teaching students how to think, not what to think. Relatively small size and residential college system give it a homey feel.

UC Santa Cruz, still a baby in the UC system, was born during the radical '60s when it reigned as the ultimate alternative school, a place that consciously rebelled against the stodginess of educational institutions. The founding vision of an integrated learning environment remains to this day, and every undergraduate affiliates with one of the residential colleges. Progressive thought continues to flourish, as does a strong academic program that strives to focus on undergraduate education. Students still come to UC Santa Cruz to do their own thing.

The campus, among the most beautiful in the nation, is set on a 2,000-acre expanse of meadowland and redwood forest overlooking Monterey Bay. Bike paths and hiking trails wind throughout the redwood-tree-filled campus, and the beach is a quick drive away—or a spectacular bike ride or scenic hike. The buildings range from 1860 Cowell Ranch farm structures to the award-winning, modern residential colleges, whose styles range from Mediterranean to Japanese to sleek concrete block. Thanks to a unique building code, nothing may be built taller than two-thirds the height of the nearest redwood tree. The 26,000-square-foot Digital Arts Research Center serves as a social and intellectual hub for UC Santa Cruz's Arts Division. New additions to campus include the LEED Gold–certified Coastal Biology Building, supporting research and teaching on coastal conservation, ecology, climate change impacts, and similar concerns.

UC Santa Cruz's academic offerings range as widely as its architecture and feature both traditional and innovative programs, but overall, the emphasis is on the liberal arts and sciences, and a majority of the students eventually go on to graduate study. To graduate, students must fulfill a standard set of distribution requirements, in addition to taking one of three "perspectives" courses focused on environmental awareness, human behavior, or technology and society, and a course on creative process, collaborative endeavor, or service learning. A disciplinary communication requirement helps students develop writing skills specific to their chosen field of study. All seniors complete a capstone experience.

"I've been very impressed with how accessible professors are."

Led by marine sciences and biology, the sciences are UC Santa Cruz's strongest suit. Science facilities include state-of-the-art laboratories; the Institute of Marine Sciences, which boasts one of the largest groups of experts on marine mammals in the nation; and the nearby Lick Observatory for budding stargazers. UCSC's Baskin School of Engineering offers strong programs in robotics engineering and computer engineering. The computer game design B.S. is noteworthy as the first such major in the UC system and for its interdisciplinary approach. Students in STEM fields may benefit from research or internship opportunities coordinated through the university's new satellite campus in Silicon Valley. UCSC boasts more than the average number of interdisciplinary programs, including feminist, Latin American/Latino, and critical race and ethnic studies; environmental studies and community studies are standouts. The most popular majors are psychology; molecular, cell, and developmental biology; human biology; and sociology. While most students pursue traditional majors, the possibility is still there for eclectically minded students to pursue "history of consciousness" or just about anything else they can get a faculty member to OK. About a quarter of students engage in faculty-guided undergraduate research, and 13 percent study abroad; field study and internships are also encouraged.

"Courses are very rigorous, in my experience," warns one undergrad. Though the curriculum is demanding and the quarter system keeps the academic pace fast, the atmosphere is emphatically noncompetitive. Classes can be large, with 28 percent enrolling more than 50 students. All UC campuses insist on faculty research, but most professors at UC Santa Cruz are there to teach. "I've been very impressed with how accessible professors are," says a sophomore. "Whether it's via email or regular office hours, I feel very comfortable approaching and talking to all of my professors."

"Before I came here I was told that UCSC was a 'hippie-dippie' college," says one student, "but it's not true at all." Even so, UC Santa Cruz remains the most liberal of the UC campuses and, according to one student, is "still a school with a social conscience." Ninety-one percent of undergraduates are Californians, though the university always manages to lure a few Easterners; 6 percent are international. Asian Americans account for 22 percent, Hispanics 28 percent, African Americans 2 percent, and multiracial students 8 percent. "Racial, ethnic, and cultural diversity is celebrated and strongly encouraged by the majority of the students here," reports a politics major. Thirty percent of incoming freshmen qualify for Pell Grants. Merit scholarships, which average $5,400 each, are available, but there are no athletic scholarships.

(continued)

Expense: Pub $ $ $
Student Loans: 64%
Average Debt: $
Applicants: 52,975
Accepted: 51%
Enrolled: 15%
Grad in 6 Years: 77%
Returning Freshmen: 90%
Academics: ✍ ✍ ✍ ✍
Social: ☎ ☎ ☎
Q of L: ★ ★ ★ ★ ★
Admissions: (831) 459-4008
Email Address: admissions@ucsc.edu

Strong Programs:
Psychology
Molecular, Cell, and
   Developmental Biology
Human Biology
Sociology
Marine Biology
Engineering
Environmental Studies
Community Studies

Thanks to a unique building code, nothing on campus may be built taller than two-thirds the height of the nearest redwood tree.

In an effort to become what one official calls a "near-perfect hybrid" between the large university and the small college, campus life revolves around the residential colleges, each of which has dedicated faculty fellows and support staff. Fifty-two percent of the undergraduate population lives in university-sponsored housing. Freshmen and transfer students are guaranteed on-campus housing for two years. Some dorms have their own dining halls with reasonably good food; students may also opt to join a food co-op. The CARE (Campus Advocacy, Resources, and Education) office provides education on issues of sexual assault and support to survivors.

A dozen fraternities and sororities attract 6 percent of the men and 8 percent of the women, respectively. Students 21 and over are allowed to drink alcohol on campus, although not in public areas, and parties must be registered. More than 150 student organizations on campus—including major-focused clubs, ethnic and cultural groups, hobby clubs, volunteer groups, and honor societies—cover a wide

> **"Before I came here I was told that UCSC was a 'hippie-dippie' college, but it's not true at all."**

range of interests. The beach and resort town of Santa Cruz, with its boardwalk and amusement park, are only 10 minutes away from campus by bike, although pedaling back up the hill takes much longer. Those looking for city lights can take the windy, mountainous highway to San Jose (35 miles away) or the slow, scenic coastal highway to San Francisco (75 miles), or ride a bus to either city. If you have a car, destinations such as Monterey, Big Sur, the Napa Valley, and the Sierras are easily accessible.

Although UC Santa Cruz fields only a handful of varsity teams, which compete in Division III, students love their school mascot, Sammy the banana slug. Men's tennis is strong and makes regular appearances in the NCAA Tournament; women's tennis, basketball, and soccer and men's volleyball have also performed well in recent years. Participation in intramurals ("Friendship through Competition" is the motto) and club sports is widespread, with rugby in particular growing in popularity. Sailing and scuba diving are among the many physical education classes offered, and the student recreation department sponsors everything from white-water rafting to cooking classes.

UC Santa Cruz is a progressive school with a gorgeous campus and innovative academic programs, where the main priority is the education of undergraduates. Many students are concerned that it is growing too fast, and an ambitious proposal for future expansion has threatened its heretofore cozy relationship with local citizens. Still, as long as the university retains its belief in "to each his or her own," it will remain uniquely UC Santa Cruz.

Overlaps

UC Santa Barbara, UC San Diego, UC Irvine, UC Davis, UC Riverside, UCLA

If You Apply To ›

Santa Cruz: Regular decision. SATs (with essay) or ACTs (with writing): required. No Subject Tests. Does not accept the Common Application. Apply to a particular college, school, or program. Application includes optional question about gender/sexual identity.

California Institute of Technology

1200 East California Boulevard, Pasadena, CA 91125

If you're armed with a near-perfect SAT score; a burning desire to study math, science, or engineering; and some independent research or published papers already under your belt, maybe you'll have a fighting chance of getting into and out of Caltech. Best experienced with grit, a propensity for pranks, and wide-ranging intellectual curiosity.

The California Institute of Technology counts 38 Nobel Prize winners among its faculty and alumni, and students' demanding courseload means plenty of opportunities to tap into that brilliance. Expectations are high; "Techers" are fond of saying that "the admissions office doesn't make mistakes," and it's fairly common to take time off to deal with stress and avoid burnout. "The atmosphere promotes a love of science, learning, and discovery that is truly exhilarating," says a biology major. No doubt about it—if you prefer particle physics to partying, Caltech is the place to be.

Caltech's 124-acre campus is located in Pasadena, "a wealthy suburban town about 15 miles outside Los Angeles," says a senior. "It's not a college town at all." The distance from downtown means the school is relatively isolated from the glitz, glamour, and good times that many people associate with La La Land. Outside the classroom, at least, tranquility prevails, with olive trees, lily ponds, and plenty of flowers breaking up clusters of older Spanish mission-style buildings. Leafy courtyards and arcades link these with the more modern, "block institutional" structures. The Beckman Auditorium (affectionately dubbed "The Wedding Cake" due to its round shape and conical roof) features spaces for performing arts, lectures, films, classes, and entertainment events. The $64 million, 212-bed Bechtel Residence opened in 2018.

> "The atmosphere promotes a love of science, learning, and discovery."

Caltech's mission, one official says, is "to train the creative type of scientist or engineer urgently needed in our educational, governmental, and industrial development." After all, it was here that Albert Einstein abandoned his concept of a static cosmos and endorsed the expanding-universe model. This is also where physicist Carl Anderson discovered the positron. With these luminaries as their models, students plunge right into the extensive general breadth requirements, which include math, physics, chemistry, biology, science communication, two introductory lab terms, and 12 terms in the humanities and social sciences to round things out. Students complain about the latter, and "usually take no more than absolutely required," says a biology major. Still, they can be tough to get into come registration time, says a computer science major, since enrollment is limited "to allow for discussion among a small group." The pass/fail grading system in the freshman year goes a long way toward easing the acclimation period for new arrivals. And the honor system, which mandates that "no one member of the Caltech community shall take unfair advantage of any other member," helps discourage unfair tactics to get better grades. Professors give take-home exams, and if violations of the honor code are suspected, "students decide if a violation was indeed made," one student explains.

Caltech made its name in physics, and students say that program remains strong; it's also one of the most popular majors, along with computer science, mechanical engineering, chemistry, bioengineering, electrical engineering, and math. Students praise the geological and planetary sciences department for being "flexible with students and having excellent field trips," says a freshman. "GPS majors are some of the happiest at Caltech." Caltech's endowment is one of the largest among the nation's

Website: www.caltech.edu
Location: Small City
Private
Total Enrollment: 2,238
Undergraduates: 961
Male/Female: 55/45
SAT Ranges: ERW 750–790, M 780–800
ACT Ranges: 34–35
Financial Aid: 58%
Pell Grant: 12%
Expense: Pr $ $ $
Student Loans: 34%
Average Debt: $
Applicants: 7,339
Accepted: 8%
Enrolled: 41%
Grad in 6 Years: 93%
Returning Freshmen: 98%
Academics: ✍ ✍ ✍ ✍ ✍
Social: ☎
Q of L: ★ ★ ★
Admissions: (626) 395-2645
Email Address:
  ugadmissions@caltech.edu

Strong Programs:
Physics
Computer Science
Mechanical Engineering
Chemistry
Bioengineering
Electrical Engineering
Mathematics
Geological and Planetary
  Sciences

tech schools, and regardless of major, students benefit from state-of-the-art STEM facilities, including the Beckman Institute, a center for fundamental research in biology and chemistry. Ninety-five percent of undergraduates participate in research, including 80 percent who receive Summer Undergraduate Research Fellowships, which offer the chance to get a head start on their own discoveries, with help from a faculty sponsor. Many summer fellows publish results from their endeavors in scientific journals. Thirteen percent of students also find time to study abroad.

The pass/fail grading system in the freshman year goes a long way toward easing the acclimation period for new arrivals.

Despite Caltech's reputation for brilliance, "The quality of instruction is variable, since Caltech is a research institution," says a sophomore. "But even the professors who are not stellar lecturers still provide a breadth of knowledge." Another student notes that professors in the humanities and social sciences really shine, since they actually want to teach, rather than hole up in a lab with mass spectrometers and computer simulations of atomic fission. Coursework tends to be heavily theory-based, and one student describes the academic climate as "collaborative, intense, and busy." While teaching assistants do lead some recitation sections affiliated with large lectures, it's not uncommon for professors to lead them too—even for freshmen—and two-thirds of all classes have fewer than 20 students.

"The quality of instruction is variable, since Caltech is a research institution."

"Caltech students are quirky, awkward, extremely passionate, and supportive," says a mechanical engineering major. Twenty-five percent of Techers come from California, and 9 percent hail from foreign nations. Forty-three percent of undergrads are Asian American; other minorities are less well represented, with Hispanics making up 12 percent of the student body, African Americans just 1 percent, and multiracial students 7 percent. Men outnumber women, which has inspired the bittersweet observation among distaff Techers that "the odds are good, but the goods are odd." Students describe their classmates as mostly apathetic when it comes to politics, but a physics major says, "The LGBTQ community is well supported and very present on campus." All financial aid is awarded based on need—meaning no merit or athletic scholarships—and Caltech guarantees to meet the full demonstrated need of all admitted domestic students.

Eighty percent of students receive Summer Undergraduate Research Fellowships, getting a head start on their own discoveries.

While Caltech only guarantees on-campus housing to freshmen, 85 percent of students live in "comfortable and convenient" college-owned or affiliated housing. There are no fraternities or sororities, but the campus's eight co-ed "houses" inspire a loyalty worthy of the Greeks and offer social and emotional support in an academically intense environment. "Housing is the most special thing about Caltech: we are sorted into houses in a fashion similar to rushing, except that everyone gets into a house," explains a computer science major. Freshmen select their house during Rotation Week, after spending an evening visiting each one, and indicating at week's end the four they like the most; resident upperclassmen take the sorting from there. The four older houses, which have been renovated, offer single, double, and triple rooms, while the newer ones have doubles. Each dorm has a dining hall, and those who live on campus must buy a meal plan, which a junior calls "quite expensive for the quality of food." Special plates are prepared daily for those with specific dietary needs. During an annual, student-led Title IX Summit, students plan solutions and strategies to prevent sexual violence.

"The LGBTQ community is well supported and very present on campus."

The houses are the social center of Caltech life, and since each one takes a turn hosting a themed "interhouse" party, students can count on at least eight schoolwide parties throughout the year. Caltech requires any house or organization hosting a party to hire a professional bartender, who checks IDs, and to have students trained in safety and emergency procedures in attendance. Other than house parties, students say, social life is pretty tame, since everyone is so busy with their schoolwork. "Ask any local bartender for a Caltech Cocktail and you will get three ounces of straight water," quips a sophomore. Some students head off campus—to Old Pasadena, nearby schools like USC, Occidental, and the Claremont Colleges, or to downtown L.A., now easily reachable on the Metro's gold line. Disneyland and Hollywood are always options, and road trips to the beach, mountains, or desert—or south of the border, to Mexico—are possible for those with cars.

Even with ample off-campus diversions, many Caltech students still prefer to make their own fun. The annual Pumpkin Drop (on Halloween, of course) involves immersing a gourd in liquid nitrogen, and then dropping it from the library roof, so that it shatters into a zillion frozen shards. On Ditch Day, underclassmen solve complex puzzles, defeat obstacles, and engage in "wild adventures" that have been planned by seniors, who disappear from campus, and then claim a prize at the end of the day. "All classes are canceled, all deadlines are extended, and it's just a day of nerdiness," says a sophomore. During finals week, stereos blast "The Ride of the Valkyries" at seven o'clock each morning, just the thing to get you going after that all-nighter. Caltech also has a storied history of practical jokes. Perhaps the best student prank occurred during the 1984 Rose Bowl game,

"Ask any local bartender for a Caltech Cocktail and you will get three ounces of straight water."

when crosstown rival UCLA played Illinois. A group of Caltech whiz kids spent months devising a radio-control device that would allow them to take control of the scoreboard in the second half, to gain national exposure for Caltech by flashing pictures of their school's mascot, the beaver, and a new version of the score that had Caltech trouncing MIT.

As for Caltech's actual athletic exploits, some of the most successful of the school's 19 Division III teams include men's and women's tennis, swimming and diving, and cross-country. The Beavers' men's basketball team became campus heroes in February 2011 when they ended a conference losing streak that dated back to 1985. The school also offers more unusual sports, such as water polo and fencing. Perhaps more popular than varsity competition, though, are the intramural matches between the houses, in nine sports every year. Also popular is the annual design competition that is the culmination of Mechanical Engineering 72, in which student-built robots must complete tasks while traversing an obstacle course.

Caltech students must learn to thrive under intense pressure, thanks to the school's tremendous workload and somewhat lackluster social life. But students say they appreciate the freedom to think and explore—and the trust administrators place in them through the honor code. "The unique student body, how available professors are (I call almost all of them by their first names), and how much we learn make Caltech a special place," says a sophomore.

Overlaps

MIT, Stanford, Harvard, Princeton, UC Berkeley, Harvey Mudd, University of Chicago, Yale

If You Apply To ›

Caltech: Early action, regular decision. SATs or ACTs: required. Subject Tests: required (math level 2 and either physics, biology, or chemistry). Accepts the Common Application with supplement. Students have the option of submitting published scientific research papers and letters from research mentors.

Calvin College

3201 Burton Street SE, Grand Rapids, MI 49546

An evangelical Christian institution that ranks high on the private college affordability list. One-third of the students are members of the Christian Reformed Church. Archrival of Michigan neighbor Hope and Illinois cousin Wheaton. Best known in the humanities and as one of the few Christian colleges with engineering, Calvin is in the process of changing its name from "college" to "university." Big emphasis on study abroad.

Website: www.calvin.edu
Location: Suburban
Private
Total Enrollment: 3,558
Undergraduates: 3,515
Male/Female: 45/55
SAT Ranges: ERW 560–660, M 540–670
ACT Ranges: 23–30
Financial Aid: 95%
Pell Grant: 20%
Expense: Pr $
Student Loans: 64%
Average Debt: $ $ $
Applicants: 3,221
Accepted: 83%
Enrolled: 33%
Grad in 6 Years: 72%
Returning Freshmen: 87%
Academics: ✍ ✍ ✍
Social: ☎ ☎ ☎
Q of L: ★ ★ ★ ★
Admissions: (800) 688-0122
Email Address: admissions@calvin.edu

Strong Programs:
Business Administration
Engineering
Education
Nursing
Biology
English
Philosophy
Asian Studies

Calvin College takes seriously its mission to equip students to "think deeply, to act justly, and to live wholeheartedly as Christ's agents of renewal in the world." Along with Wheaton College in Illinois, it is regarded as one of the country's top evangelical colleges. Calvin recently announced its intention to change its name to Calvin University in 2020. Though no one is required to attend the school's daily chapel services, classes stop when worship starts, and most students view Christian values as central to the academic experience. "We have a culture here of an eagerness to learn, to see the world, and to get to know people from all different walks of life," says one junior.

Calvin was founded in 1876 as the educational wing of the Christian Reformed Church in North America. After outgrowing one of its first homes, the college bought a tract of land on the edge of Grand Rapids and built its present campus. Calvin spreads out over 400 beautifully landscaped acres that include three ponds and a 100-acre woodland and wetland ecosystem preserve used for classes, research, and recreation. Most facilities are less than 50 years old and were designed by a student of famed architect Frank Lloyd Wright. The east campus includes the DeVos Communication Center, the Gainey Athletic Facility, and the award-winning Bunker Interpretive Center, powered primarily by student-designed solar energy technology.

Calvin's core curriculum, referred to as An Engagement with God's World, has four components: core gateway, core competencies, core studies, and core capstone. All first-year students take two gateway courses, First-Year Seminar and Developing a Christian Mind. Core competencies cover basic skills like written rhetoric and foreign language, while core studies expose students to a broad range of liberal arts disciplines, including two biblical foundations classes. The capstone course is usually taken in the junior or senior year. Calvin LifeWork is an optional program that teaches skills like financial literacy and career readiness, to prepare students for success after college; participants who stay in the program for all four years receive an automatic $3,000 scholarship their senior year.

> "The support services at Calvin have helped me in tremendous ways with grace, patience, and authentic kindness."

Preprofessional programs, such as business, engineering, education, and nursing, tend to be Calvin's best bets, students say—perhaps that's why those programs, along with biology and psychology, are the college's most popular majors. Philosophy, English, and religion are also regarded as strong. Calvin is the only Christian college in the U.S. to offer a comprehensive Asian studies program, which includes courses in Chinese, Japanese, and Korean language, history, and culture. Five-year bachelor-to-master's programs are available in accounting and in speech pathology and audiology.

Calvin is founded on the belief that every subject—even the sciences or mass media and popular culture—can be approached from a Christian perspective, and faculty members work hard to integrate faith and learning. In the absence of teaching assistants, professors are expected to reserve about 10 hours per week for advising and assisting students outside of class. Thirty percent of the classes at Calvin have fewer than 20 students and only a few have more than 50; a social work major says, "Class sizes are small enough that professors will get to know our name, but big enough to offer a variety of opinions in discussions." Students give high ratings to peer tutoring and personal counseling services. "The support services at Calvin have helped me in tremendous ways with grace, patience, and authentic kindness," says a senior.

Learning also takes place outside of the classroom through internships and practicums, and 85 percent of students complete at least one internship before they graduate. Twenty percent collaborate with faculty on research projects. Calvin offers more than 40 faculty-led off-campus programs in such locales as Britain, China, Ghana, and Washington, D.C., in addition to programs offered in conjunction with partner institutions. Eighty-one percent of students participate in study abroad, often during the month-long January interim, and the college is among the top in the nation for the number of students who do so.

"Political views are not a defining characteristic of campus."

Though Calvin still has a strongly Dutch heritage, students who are members of the Christian Reformed Church now account for just a third of the student body. Fifty-one percent are Michigan natives, and 13 percent are international. African Americans constitute 3 percent of the total, Hispanics 5 percent, Asian Americans 5 percent, and multiracial students 3 percent. "Political views are not a defining characteristic of campus, even if they are discussed and argued in various settings," says a junior. Eligible Calvin students receive scholarships based on academic merit, worth an average of $11,700 annually; there are no athletic awards.

Fifty-eight percent of Calvin students live on campus. For their first two years, students bunk in one of seven residence halls—each of which has separate wings for men and women—in four-person suites with two bedrooms connected by a shared bathroom. "The suites are typically set up with two freshmen on one side and two sophomores on the other," explains a nursing major. "It's nice to have an older individual who knows the ropes to guide you in your first year." Most juniors and seniors occupy on-campus apartments or choose to move off campus. Calvin offers three intentional living/learning floors—Creation Care (recreational pursuits/environmental stewardship and sustainability), Grassroots (exploring race and identity in North America), and Honors. Campus dining facilities have recently been renovated, and a junior cheers, "There is always something good to fall back on and something new to try." Safety is highly rated too. "The Sexual Assault Prevention Team is active on campus, and Campus Safety is patrolling 24/7, even during school breaks," notes a sophomore.

"Calvin is a dry campus, and there is no Greek life, but the students aren't uptight—meaning that those who are of legal age take advantage of going to bars and breweries in Grand Rapids for a drink with friends on the weekends," says a senior. The downtown area also offers restaurants, coffee shops, minor-league sports, galleries, and the annual ArtPrize festival and competition. On campus, students find a wealth

"Calvin is a dry campus, and there is no Greek life, but the students aren't uptight."

of entertainment, including movies, speakers, concerts, dances, and dorm banquets. A popular annual event is Chaos Day, which brings the dorms together for a day of athletic contests. The Dance Guild performances in the fall and spring are also a favorite tradition, as is the Rangeela cultural festival. Road trips include the beaches of Lake Michigan (a one-hour drive) or Chicago (three hours distant). Spring break trips see a number of students traveling to places like Mississippi and Louisiana to

All first-year students take two gateway courses, First-Year Seminar and Developing a Christian Mind.

Eighty-one percent of students participate in study abroad, often during the month-long January interim.

complete service projects; Calvin students log more than 50,000 hours of service-learning throughout the year.

Calvin fields a robust Division III athletic program that competes in the Michigan Intercollegiate Athletic Association (MIAA). The women's volleyball team is a recent national champion, and other particularly competitive Knights teams include men's and women's cross-country and soccer. The men's ice hockey program has also seen consistent success and now boasts an ACHA Division I team in addition to its Division III team. Calvin's competition with Hope College is one of the great rivalries in Division III athletics and "makes any sporting event fun," says a sophomore; current students and alumni alike rally together for the annual basketball game. The college's intramural program offers leagues and tournaments in sports ranging from dodge-ball to ultimate Frisbee and fantasy football; half of all undergraduates participate.

Those who come to Calvin College are looking to build community with friends and faculty members who share their already-strong Christian faith. Says one senior, Calvin is a place where "people are intentionally seeking connection with one another, in pursuit of a community where people are welcomed and embraced."

Overlaps

Hope, Wheaton (IL), Taylor, Bethel, Messiah, Grand Valley State, University of Michigan, Michigan State

If You Apply To ›

Calvin: Rolling admissions. SATs or ACTs or Classic Learning Test: required. Subject Tests: optional. Accepts the Common Application with supplement.

Carleton College

Northfield, MN 55057

Less selective than Amherst, Williams, and Swarthmore, mainly because of its out-of-the-way Minnesota location. Yet Carleton retains its position as the premier liberal arts college in the upper Midwest. Predominantly liberal, but not to the extremes of its more antiestablishment cousins, and turns out lots of students who go on to get Ph.D.s. Students at Carleton excel at making their own fun.

Minnesota is many things: the land of 10,000 lakes, home to the massive Mall of America, birthplace of lore from Hiawatha to Paul Bunyan, and proud parent of the Mississippi River. Beyond all that history-book stuff, tucked into a small town in the southeastern corner of the state is Carleton College, arguably the best liberal arts school in the expansive Midwest. Add to this a midwinter carnival complete with human bowling, badminton competitions that raise money to fight cancer, and an expulsion of Coca-Cola from campus for human rights violations, and you have the makings of an engaged, unique institution. "Carleton is quirky, and we're not afraid to embrace our quirk. In fact, we revel in it," says a biology major.

Surrounded by rolling farmland, Carleton's 955-acre campus is in the small town of Northfield, whose one-time status as the center of the Holstein cattle industry brought it the motto "Cows, Colleges, and Contentment." The campus boasts of fragrant lilacs in spring, rich summer greens, red maples in the fall, and a glistening blanket of white in winter. Lakes, woods, and streams abound, and you can traverse them on 15 miles of hiking and cross-country skiing trails. There's even an 800-acre arboretum. Newer facilities include the Kracum Performance Hall. Carleton's architectural style is somewhat eclectic, with everything from Victorian to contemporary, but mostly redbrick.

Website: www.carleton.edu
Location: Small City
Private
Total Enrollment: 2,055
Undergraduates: 2,055
Male/Female: 49/51
SAT Ranges: ERW 680–760, M 680–770
ACT Ranges: 31–34
Financial Aid: 83%
Pell Grant: 14%
Expense: Pr $ $ $ $
Student Loans: 44%
Average Debt: $
Applicants: 6,499
Accepted: 21%
Enrolled: 38%

Carleton's top-notch academic programs are no less varied: the sciences—biology, physics, astronomy, chemistry, geology, and computer science—are among the best anywhere, and scores of Carleton graduates go on to earn Ph.D.s in these areas. Economics, mathematics, and political science/international relations are other popular majors. Engineers can opt for a 3–2 program with Washington University in St. Louis, and for geologists seeking fieldwork—and maybe wanting to thaw out after a long Minnesota winter—Carleton sponsors a program in Death Valley. Closer to home at the "arb," as the arboretum is affectionately known, environmental studies majors have their own wilderness field station, which includes a prairie-restoration site. At the opposite end of the academic spectrum, the arts also flourish. Music and studio art majors routinely get into top graduate programs, and may take advantage of expanded offerings in dance and theater. Carleton offers interdisciplinary programs in Asian, Jewish, urban, African and African American, and women's studies. A minor in cross-cultural studies brings in foreign students to discuss global issues and dynamics with their American counterparts. Seventy percent of Carleton students spend at least one term abroad, and 30 percent conduct undergraduate research.

> "I often joke that the hottest social spot at our school is the library."

Distribution requirements ensure that a Carleton education exposes students not only to rigor and depth in their chosen field, but also to "a wide range of subjects and methods of studying them," administrators say. All students must show proficiency in writing and a foreign language while fulfilling requirements in the areas of humanistic and social inquiry, literary/artistic analysis, the arts, science, and formal or statistical reasoning. There's also a Global Citizenship requirement, under which students must take at least one course dealing with a non-Western culture, and a first-year Argument and Inquiry Seminar. In their final year, all students complete a senior comprehensive project (known around campus as "Comps").

With highly motivated students and a heavy workload, Carleton isn't your typical mellow Midwestern liberal arts college. The trimester calendar means finals may be just three months apart and almost everyone feels the pressure. "I often joke that the hottest social spot at our school is the library," says a linguistics major, and a junior adds, "Everyone is really working diligently, but this breeds a climate of solidarity." The five-week Christmas vacation is Carleton's way of dealing with the cold winters. Seventy percent of classes have fewer than 20 students, so Carls are expected to participate actively. Carleton's faculty members are accessible and committed. "My professors have been unpretentious, caring, and intelligent," says a biology major. As part of its extensive advising program, Carleton assigns a "liberal arts advisor" to work with entering students for their first two years, but a junior comments, "Carleton does not prepare us as well for careers as it does for entering a graduate program."

> "Carleton does not prepare us as well for careers as it does for entering a graduate program."

A philosophy major characterizes Carls as possessing "an endearing blend of quirkiness, awkwardness, geekiness, and humor." Not to be confused with the typically Midwestern students across town at St. Olaf, just 18 percent of Carleton students are Minnesota natives, and 10 percent are international. More than half of the out-of-staters are from outside the Midwest, with both coasts heavily represented. African Americans account for 5 percent of the student body, Hispanics 8 percent, Asian Americans 8 percent, and multiracial students 6 percent. "Students of color here are an active group and a tight-knit community," says a freshman. The Carleton campus is decidedly liberal ("I have watched the conservative minority at this school vanish," remarks a senior), concerned with issues including diversity, gun control, political correctness, LGBTQ rights, and Title IX. Carleton meets

(continued)

Grad in 6 Years: 92%
Returning Freshmen: 96%
Academics: ✍ ✍ ✍ ✍ ✍
Social: ☎ ☎ ☎
Q of L: ★ ★ ★
Admissions: (800) 995-2275
Email Address: admissions@ carleton.edu

Strong Programs:
Biology
Chemistry
Computer Science
Geology
Economics
Mathematics
Political Science/International Relations
Visual and Performing Arts

At the "arb," as the arboretum is affectionately known, environmental studies majors have their own wilderness field station.

the full demonstrated financial need of all enrolled students; the only merit-based awards are granted to National Merit and Hispanic Scholars, and there are no athletic scholarships.

Ninety-six percent of Carleton students live on campus, and housing is guaranteed for all four years; those who wish to live off campus must receive approval to do so. On-campus options range from comfortable old houses to modern hotel-like residence halls. "Even the worst dorms are totally livable and spacious compared to those of friends that I have from other colleges," says a junior. Dorms are co-ed by room, but there are two halls with single-sex floors. Several college-owned "theme" houses, situated in an attractive residential section of town close to campus, focus on special interests such as foreign languages and the outdoors; the Farm House is an environmental studies house located on the edge of the arb. All campus residents must submit to a meal plan, to the chagrin of many. "The meals are usually the same, and bland," says a freshman. Fortunately, students can also use their meal plans at neighboring St. Olaf, where the food gets rave reviews. Students report being "unsatisfied" with administrative treatment of sexual assaults on campus, although one notes, "The school is trying to listen to all of the students' concerns."

> "I have watched the conservative minority at this school vanish."

In their final year, all students complete a senior comprehensive project (known around campus as "Comps").

Absent a Greek system, Carleton's social life tends to be relaxed, informal, and campus-based. "Carleton students have fun and let loose in their own ways," says a freshman. "Parties vary a lot, ranging from packed dorm dancing to bonfires in the woods. I have been to parties with themes such as Limes, Fire, and Illinois." A group called Co-op sponsors dances and Wednesday socials every two weeks, free movies, and special events like Comedy Night. Students say there is no pressure to drink on campus. Popular annual events include the Midwinter Ball, the Spring Concert, and Mai Fete, a gala celebrated on an island in one of the two lakes on campus. Traditions include the weeklong freshman orientation program, where, during opening convocation, students bombard professors with bubbles as the faculty members process. Another distinctive Carleton tradition is the regular liberation and dramatic reappearance—such as dangling from a helicopter over homecoming football games—of a plaster bust of Friedrich Schiller, the Romantic philosopher and buddy of Goethe.

Rotblatt is a marathon softball game played each spring that lasts one inning for each year of Carleton's existence.

Northfield itself is a history-filled town with a population of about 20,000. A favorite town event is the annual reenactment of Jesse James's failed bank robbery in 1876. "Northfield is quaint, but there's not much to do," a sophomore says. There are old-style shops, a beautiful old hotel, and a handful of bars and breweries. Students often frequent St. Olaf's campus and a popular coffee shop called Goodbye Blue Monday. Minneapolis-St. Paul, 35 miles to the north, is a popular road-trip destination. Students aren't allowed to have cars on campus, but daily bus service is available.

> "Carleton students have fun and let loose in their own ways."

The Knights compete in Division III athletics; about a fourth of the students play on varsity teams. Men's and women's soccer have won multiple Minnesota Intercollegiate Athletic Conference titles in recent years, and women's tennis, swimming and diving, and golf and men's tennis are also competitive. The school's ultimate Frisbee club teams have won several national championships. Roughly 80 percent of students compete in intramural and recreational sports, including Rotblatt, which is "the world's longest intramural sport," according to one junior. "Played once each spring, this marathon softball game begins at sunrise and lasts one inning for each year of Carleton's existence. It is Rotblatt tradition for players to both bat and field with a beverage of their choice in one hand."

It can be cold in Minnesota, in a face-stinging, bone-chilling kind of way. And the classes are far from easy. But Carleton is a warm campus where students toe the

Overlaps

Bowdoin, Williams, Amherst, Pomona, Swarthmore, Macalester, Middlebury, Brown

line between individuality and community. At Carleton, says one student, "It isn't about getting the degree; it's about having an impactful experience where students learn more about themselves and the world they live in."

If You Apply To ›

Carleton: Early decision I and II, regular decision. SATs or ACTs: required. Subject Tests: optional. Accepts the Common Application with supplement.

Carnegie Mellon University

5000 Forbes Avenue, Pittsburgh, PA 15213-3890

The only premier university equally strong in technology and the arts, Carnegie Mellon is a national leader in what it calls "liberal-professional" education. Applications continue to increase, so it must be doing something right. Shares its urban neighborhood with a variety of cultural and academic institutions, including the University of Pittsburgh.

Students at Carnegie Mellon don't have to choose between soaking up the high drama of Shakespeare and plunging into the fast-paced tech world. The university is known for both its science offerings and strong drama and music programs. But scholars can't just focus on their own course of study—Carnegie Mellon continues to strive to offer both its technical and liberal arts students a well-rounded education that requires a lot of hard work but promises great results.

Carnegie Mellon was formed by the merger of Carnegie Institute of Technology and the Mellon Institute in 1967, resulting in a self-contained, 152-acre campus attractively situated in Pittsburgh's affluent Oakland section. Next door is the city's second-largest park and its major museum, named after—you guessed it—Andrew Carnegie. Henry Hornbostel, who attended the École des Beaux-Arts in the 1890s, designed the campus using a plan that is a modification of the Jefferson plan for the University of Virginia, with the Beaux-Arts device of creating primary and secondary axes and grouping buildings around significant open spaces. Buildings are designed in a Renaissance style, with buff-colored brick arches and piers, tile roofs, and terra cotta and granite details.

Carnegie Mellon has seven constituent colleges—Heinz College, offering graduate degrees in public policy, management, and information systems—and six others that offer undergraduate and graduate courses: the College of Fine Arts, the Dietrich College of Humanities and Social Sciences, the College of Engineering, the Mellon College of Science, the School of Computer Science, and the Tepper School of Business. Each college has its own distinct character and admissions requirements. All the colleges, however, share the university's commitment to what it calls a "liberal-professional" education, which shows the relevance of the liberal arts while stressing courses that develop technical skills and good job prospects. Humanities and social science types can major in applied history, professional writing, or information systems, for example, instead of traditional disciplinary concentrations.

Most departments at Carnegie Mellon are strong, but exceptional ones include engineering, computer science, and drama. The most popular majors are computer

> "There is absolutely no stigma against tutoring or outside resources."

Website: www.cmu.edu
Location: City Center
Private
Total Enrollment: 13,562
Undergraduates: 6,662
Male/Female: 51/49
SAT Ranges: ERW 700–760, M 730–800
ACT Ranges: 32–35
Financial Aid: 51%
Pell Grant: 15%
Expense: Pr $ $ $ $
Student Loans: 54%
Average Debt: $ $ $
Applicants: 20,497
Accepted: 22%
Enrolled: 37%
Grad in 6 Years: 89%
Returning Freshmen: 96%
Academics: ✍ ✍ ✍ ✍
Social: ☎ ☎ ☎
Q of L: ★ ★ ★
Admissions: (412) 268-2082
Email Address: admission@andrew.cmu.edu

Strong Programs:
Computer Science
Electrical and Computer Engineering

(continued)

Mechanical Engineering
Information Systems
Drama
Music
Design

science, electrical and computer engineering, mechanical engineering, and information systems, and students generally agree that Carnegie Mellon is more of a science-oriented school. Initiatives aimed at connecting art and technology include the Integrative Design, Arts, and Technology network, which offers interdisciplinary minors like game design, animation and special effects, and innovation and entrepreneurship. The Science and Humanities Scholars program allows talented undergrads to develop their own course of study.

Courses are "extremely rigorous with many hours expected outside of the classroom," says one student. Students at Carnegie Mellon work hard, no doubt about it, and many complain that the academic environment encourages a serious culture of stress, but the university has taken steps to try to counteract that. Every day includes a designated "meeting-free" time for students, allowing them time to study or participate in student activities. A mechanical and biomedical engineering double major notes that there is a "mindfulness room" that serves as "a space for students to relax and take a break from schoolwork" (and get weekly visits from trained therapy dogs), and that students are encouraged to use campus counseling services "even if it is just to discuss stress and how to manage a new environment." Students also recommend the Academic Development Office, and one says, "There is absolutely no stigma against tutoring or outside resources." About two-thirds of classes have fewer than 20 students, and professors rate highly with most students. "Some professors are better than others at lecturing, but I have not encountered a professor that doesn't care about the course," says an electrical and computer engineering major.

> "CMU students expect to do well."

Students looking to hone their professional skills will find ample opportunities, including five-year dual-degree options, co-op programs, and advising and other resources within the Career and Professional Development Center. Research opportunities are available across the curriculum, as are several types of grants and fellowships to fund them. Those interested in service learning can get involved with the university's extensive outreach efforts to improve youth STEM education in the local area. Study abroad options are plentiful and include the university's established undergraduate campus in the Arabian Gulf nation of Qatar, but many students have difficulty fitting study abroad into their rigorous schedules.

Despite the university's core emphasis on interdisciplinary, well-rounded education, Carnegie Mellon remains one of the most fragmented campuses in the nation. Students divide themselves between actors, designers, and other artsy types and engineers, scientists, and architects. "CMU is for people who know what they want to do," asserts one student. In any case, students here are all high achievers—74 percent of freshmen graduated in the top 10th of their high school class—and are united in their quest for a good job after graduation. "CMU students expect to do well and are generally confident in their ability to learn and succeed," confirms a business administration major.

> "Financial aid is not the most generous in comparison to peer institutions."

Once a largely regional institution, drawing mostly Pennsylvania residents, Carnegie Mellon now counts 85 percent of its undergraduate students from out of state, including 23 percent from foreign countries. Nearly half are from minority groups, including 29 percent Asian American, 4 percent African American, 9 percent Hispanic, and 4 percent multiracial. Students report that campus politics lean liberal, but most students don't get actively involved in social or political matters. The university says it remains committed to need-blind admissions, but it has stopped guaranteeing to meet the full demonstrated financial need of all students. Most financial aid is need-based, and there are no merit- or athletic-based awards.

Carnegie Mellon has seven constituent colleges, each with its own distinct character and admissions requirements.

The Integrative Design, Arts, and Technology network offers interdisciplinary minors like game design and animation and special effects.

"Financial aid is not the most generous in comparison to peer institutions," remarks a student, in part because Carnegie Mellon's endowment is smaller.

Housing is guaranteed for undergraduates all four years if they stay in the university housing system, and 60 percent do so. Upperclassmen get first pick, so the popular university-owned apartments fill up fast, but there are a number of residence halls specifically for first-year students. The quality of each dorm varies, says a junior, but "the facilities are all very livable." The best dorms for freshmen are Stever House—the first LEED-certified residence hall in the U.S.—Donner, Resnik, and Morewood Gardens. "Instead of buffet-style dining halls, we have several themed eateries that you can pick from," explains a sophomore, and food options are said to be improving in terms of taste and variety. Students report feeling safe on campus, thanks to a comprehensive security program, but one comments, "There is not enough campus conversation or emphasis on the issue of sexual assault."

With all the academic pressure at Carnegie Mellon, it's a good thing there are so many opportunities to unwind, especially with the entire city of Pittsburgh close at hand. "Pittsburgh is a great place to go to college," cheers a junior. "Whatever type of evening you're looking for, Pittsburgh has it." Nearby Oakland has coffeehouses, inexpensive films, dances, and concerts, and the downtown area (just 20 minutes away by bus) offers a rich social scene, with opera, ballet, symphony, concerts, and sporting events. The Greek system provides the most visible form of on-campus social life, with 16 percent of men joining fraternities and 11 percent of women joining sororities, and the school offers late-night events and concerts too. Those of legal age are allowed to have alcohol in their rooms, but according to one student, "Drinking takes place mostly off campus."

One event that brings everyone together is the Spring Carnival, a four-day weekend festival. Student groups build themed booths and design, build, and race buggies made of lightweight alloys. Members of the student-run "Scotch 'n' Soda" theater organization also present a show. "There are lots of social groups like the CIA, the KGB, and Fringe, which participate along with Greek organizations in the yearly Carnival celebrations," says one student. "These groups are a great way to meet upperclassmen and get involved with people outside of your program."

> **"Whatever type of evening you're looking for, Pittsburgh has it."**

As for sports, the Carnegie Mellon Tartans compete in Division III. Men's and women's soccer have made multiple appearances in the national championship tournament. Men's and women's tennis and swimming, men's cross-country, and women's volleyball are also strong. Students also participate in two dozen intramural and club sports.

Carnegie Mellon appeals just as much to those yearning for the bright lights of Broadway as it does to those pursuing the glowing computer screens of the scientific and business worlds. And with a broad range of liberal arts and technical courses available to explore, there's no doubt students leave with a well-rounded education—and an impressive diploma. Students more interested in specializing in one field than being exposed to many may fare better elsewhere, but most who opt for Carnegie Mellon agree that the demanding environment is well worth it.

Spring Carnival is a four-day weekend festival where student groups build themed booths and design, build, and race buggies.

Overlaps

Cornell University, UC Berkeley, MIT, University of Pennsylvania, Stanford, UCLA, Harvard, University of Michigan

If You Apply To ›

Carnegie Mellon: Early decision, regular decision. SATs or ACTs: required. Subject Tests: optional (varies by program). Accepts the Common Application. Apply to particular school or college.

103 Tomlinson Hall, 10900 Euclid Avenue, Cleveland, OH 44106

CWRU has most of the offerings available at Carnegie Mellon or WashU in St. Louis, but somehow it hasn't quite found a niche in the national consciousness. Students in the know sing its praises, especially since CWRU is less difficult to get into than other institutions of comparable quality. Students get an outstanding technical education with solid offerings in other areas.

Website: www.case.edu

Location: City Center

Private

Total Enrollment: 10,412

Undergraduates: 4,966

Male/Female: 55/45

SAT Ranges: ERW 650–740, M 690–780

ACT Ranges: 30–33

Financial Aid: 83%

Pell Grant: 15%

Expense: Pr $ $

Student Loans: 49%

Average Debt: $ $ $

Applicants: 25,380

Accepted: 33%

Enrolled: 16%

Grad in 6 Years: 83%

Returning Freshmen: 93%

Academics: ✍ ✍ ✍ ✍

Social: ☎ ☎

Q of L: ★ ★ ★

Admissions: (216) 368-4450

Email Address: admission@case.edu

Strong Programs:
Biomedical Engineering
Mechanical Engineering
Nursing
Music
Anthropology
Biology
Psychology
Business Management

Cleveland's Case Western Reserve has much in common with Pittsburgh's Carnegie Mellon. Both are the product of mergers between a technical college, known for excellence in engineering, and a more traditional university, focused on the arts and sciences. Both are located in erstwhile Rust Belt cities that have long since reinvented themselves through technology, medicine, education, and advanced manufacturing. And both tend to attract brainy students more concerned with studying than socializing. While CWRU has received less national attention than Carnegie Mellon and WashU, a senior calls it "a university on the rise": applications have doubled since 2010 and the school has become more selective. CWRU has also increased its investment in the arts, humanities, and social sciences, with an aim toward helping students connect these disciplines with their technical studies.

CWRU is located on the eastern edge of Cleveland, at University Circle. This 550-acre area of parks and gardens is home to more than 40 cultural, educational, medical, and research institutions, including the city's museums of art and natural history, its botanical gardens, and Severance Hall, home of the Cleveland Orchestra.

"[CWRU is] a university on the rise."

Campus buildings are an eclectic mix of architectural styles, and several are listed on the National Register of Historic Places. The Peter B. Lewis Building (or "PBL," as it's known around campus), designed by Frank Gehry, is home of the Weatherhead School of Management and features undulating walls similar to those of Gehry's Guggenheim Museum in Bilbao, Spain. The Tinkham Veale University Center ("the Tink") meets LEED Silver standards and serves as a hub for campus dining, special events, and more than 160 student organizations, while the recently expanded Sears think[box] is a fabrication lab designed to support cross-disciplinary entrepreneurial innovation.

The product of the 1967 marriage between Case Institute of Technology and Western Reserve University, CWRU has four undergraduate schools: the College of Arts and Sciences, the Case School of Engineering, the Bolton School of Nursing, and the aforementioned Weatherhead School; all also offer graduate programs. All CWRU students participate in a general education program known as SAGES—the Seminar Approach to General Education and Scholarship. Emphasizing small seminars, critical thinking, and writing, the program requires four seminars, a writing portfolio, and a senior capstone experience that can be an individual or group effort. According to a biomedical engineering major, "CWRU is a collaborative environment that allows students to excel in their own way."

CWRU's strongest programs include engineering, especially the biomedical and mechanical kind, and nursing. The school's polymer science major is one of the few such undergraduate programs in the country. Strengths in the College of Arts and Sciences include music (a joint program with the nearby Cleveland Institute of Music), anthropology (especially medical anthropology), biology, and psychology. Business management is also strong. Combined bachelor's and master's programs are popular, as is the Preprofessional Scholars program, which gives top freshmen conditional acceptance to CWRU's medical or dental schools, assuming satisfactory progress through prerequisite courses. Sixty percent of classes enroll fewer than 20 students, and a biochemistry major says, "While you may run across some professors who are difficult to learn from, there are far more professors who care a great deal about the students." Undergraduate research is highly encouraged, and about two-thirds of students conduct research as part of senior capstone projects or independent studies. Twenty-eight percent of students take part in study abroad; locales include Italy, Israel, Cameroon, and the Netherlands.

A senior says CWRU students are "driven, high achievers" who often "feel the need to prove themselves." Twenty-nine percent of CWRU's students are Ohio natives, and 70 percent graduated in the top 10th of their high school class. International students represent a strong contingent at 13 percent. African Americans make up 4 percent of the student body, Asian Americans 21 percent, Hispanics 7 percent, and multiracial students 5 percent. Diversity 360 is a campuswide training program designed to increase knowledge and awareness about diversity issues. Students describe the political climate

The school's polymer science major is one of the few such undergraduate programs in the country.

"First-year rooms are adequate but nothing special."

as low-key, with liberals and conservatives both well represented on campus. Eligible students receive scholarships based on academic merit that average $23,600, but there are no athletic awards. The university has adopted a need-aware admissions policy that includes a commitment to meet the full demonstrated financial need of incoming freshmen.

Students are required to live on campus for their first two years, and 80 percent of all undergrads stay on campus. Each first-year student participates in one of four residential colleges. "First-year rooms are adequate but nothing special," says one student, but upperclassmen rave about the amenities in the university's apartment-style suites, which also feature music practice rooms, a fitness center, and a cyber café. Some upperclassmen opt for off-campus apartments within walking distance of campus. Dining-hall fare is "not Mom's cooking every night, but it's not bad," reasons one student. A senior notes, "We have a pretty robust Title IX office as well as policies in place to help support students who've been victims of sexual assault."

About two-thirds of students conduct research as part of senior capstone projects or independent studies.

On campus, there are dances and fraternity parties (Greek groups draw 27 percent of the men and 26 percent of the women). "The social life on campus at CWRU is very limited, as students are highly focused on academics. But if a party takes place, it can get pretty wild," one mechanical engineering major says. Popular campus traditions are Greek Week, which includes nearly everyone on campus; the Springfest carnival to celebrate the end of classes; and "Study Overs," where students gather during finals week for free food, massages, study groups, and more. The annual sci-fi movie marathon is a rite of passage, while Engineering Week features a fuel-cell-powered car competition.

CWRU is located five miles from downtown Cleveland, and the city provides ample opportunities for volunteer work. "We're surrounded by museums and cultural institutions, which become a part of our education, and there's lots to do and eat!" enthuses a history major. "It's very budget-friendly," adds a senior. The city features the Rock and Roll Hall of Fame, and—in the warmer

"We're surrounded by museums and cultural institutions, which become a part of our education."

months—Cleveland Indians games at Progressive Field. Convenient RTA train passes are included in student charges for $25 a semester, but having a car can be helpful, especially for road trips to nearby cities in Ohio, or for longer jaunts to Chicago.

Although sports are not a major focus on campus, the Spartans field 17 Division III teams, and the annual football game against Carnegie Mellon is big. Men's and women's swimming and diving, men's cross-country and football, and women's tennis, softball, and track and field all competed in their respective national championship tournaments in the 2017–18 season. About 85 percent of students participate in at least one of the 25 intramural and 17 club sports available, ranging from flag football and floor hockey to crew and kendo. The 26-mile Hudson Relay, held the last week of the spring semester to commemorate CWRU's relocation from Hudson to Cleveland, pits teams of runners from the four classes against one another, with each person running a half mile.

Although a rigorous, science- and engineering-oriented research university, CWRU devotes noteworthy attention to the student experience. "CWRU's personality is friendly and spirited," says a senior. "People can be self-deprecating and make a lot of jokes about Cleveland's bad weather, but the campus community itself is warm and inviting." With challenging academics, preprofessional programs, and research opportunities across all disciplines, students are well-equipped to excel in their future careers.

If You Apply To ›

Case: Early decision I and II, early action, regular decision. SATs or ACTs: required. Subject Tests: optional. Accepts the Common Application. Audition required for artists and musicians.

The Catholic University of America

Washington, D.C. 20064

There are other Roman Catholic–affiliated universities, but this is THE Catholic University. Catholics make up more than 80 percent of the undergraduate student body here (versus roughly half at nearby Georgetown). If you can't be in Rome, there is no better place than D.C. to work and play. CUA even has a Metrorail stop right next to campus. Academic freedom is the norm except in theology.

Founded in 1887 under a charter from Pope Leo XIII, The Catholic University of America was the brainchild of U.S. bishops who wanted to provide an American educational institution where the curriculum was guided by the tenets of Christian thought. Over time, the university has garnered a reputation as a research-oriented school that also provides a strong undergraduate, preprofessional education and an appreciation for the arts. Faced in recent years with the challenges of declining enrollment and changing demographics and social attitudes, top administrators have nonetheless doubled down on the university's image of "cultivating Catholic minds," sparking renewed debate on campus about whether CUA is marketing itself as "too Catholic" and making itself less welcoming to prospective students in the process. "Our authentic Catholic background rules our academics, campus activities, and institutional offices all over campus," says a senior.

Catholic University's campus comprises 176 tree-lined acres, an impressive layout for an urban university, and houses 26 research facilities. Buildings range from ivy-covered limestone and brick to ultramodern, giving the place a true collegiate feel. Over the last few years, the university has renovated many of the residence halls, and a new dining facility is in the works for 2020.

CUA is one of the few colleges in the country that began as a graduate institution (others are Clark University and The Johns Hopkins University), and grad students still account for a respectable portion of the student population. Ten of its

12 schools admit undergrads. Specific graduation requirements vary by program, but all undergraduates participate in the First-Year Experience, an introduction to CUA's brand of liberal arts guided by the Catholic intellectual tradition. Assigned to Learning Communities of about 18 classmates, students take four core classes in philosophy, theology, and English, and they receive one-on-one academic advising throughout the year. First-years also join their Learning Communities for out-of-class activities like an annual Speaker Series, service-learning projects, and group excursions into D.C.

Students have excellent options in almost any department at CUA. In addition to politics, which sets the tone on campus, the psychology, business, and physics departments are strong. The School of Nursing is one of the best in the nation, and nursing is CUA's most popular major. Engineering and architecture are highly regarded and have outstanding facilities; the physics department enjoys a modern vitreous-state lab, a boon for both research and hands-on undergraduate instruction. CUA's Benjamin Rome School of Music offers several bachelor of music degrees, such as composition, music education, and piano pedagogy, as well as a joint degree that combines music with business and economics. The National Catholic School of Social Service offers a bachelor of social work degree.

> **"Our authentic Catholic background rules our academics, campus activities, and institutional offices all over campus."**

"I would describe the academic climate as intense, yet nurturing," says a civil engineering major. "Workloads are manageable when students are proactive." Fifty-six percent of classes have fewer than 20 students, which means special attention from faculty members. According to a sophomore, professors "teach with passion, and it is apparent that they love what they do." About 60 percent of the faculty are Catholic (the Vatican requires that figure to be at least 50 percent). Clergy are at the helm of the School of Theology and Religious Studies and the graduate School of Canon Law. CUA's chancellor is the archbishop of Washington, mass is held on campus daily, and Catholic churches across the country donate a fraction of their annual collections to the university. One downside of being the only Catholic school with a papal charter is that officials in Rome, who do not always warm up to American traditions of academic freedom, keep a sharp eye on who teaches in the theology school and what they write and say.

Top students can enroll in the University Honors Program, which offers challenging seminar-style classes and the option of living in a dedicated honors community. The university offers a wide variety of education abroad programs, including more than 75 semester-long and nearly 50 summer study abroad options available in countries around the globe; 37 percent of students participate. The flagship Rome Center, jointly operated by CUA and an Australian counterpart, emphasizes experiential, on-site learning, with programs for both liberal arts and architecture students, as well as a three-week summer program for the First-Year Experience. For the politically minded, international internships are available with the European Union, British, and Irish parliaments. Students give mixed reviews to CUA's career services but praise the Counseling Center, which offers up to 45 free counseling sessions.

> **"Students embrace the community of respect and service that is present on our campus."**

"Students embrace the community of respect and service that is present on our campus," says a senior. Catholicism is clearly the tie that binds the student body, with 82 percent of students identifying as Catholic. Most students are also conservative, although some socially liberal causes are slowly gaining traction on campus; students report that the administration's insistence on single-sex dorms, refusal to recognize LGBTQ student groups, and ban on speakers who have expressed

(continued)

Academics: ✍ ✍ ✍
Social: ☎ ☎ ☎
Q of L: ★ ★ ★
Admissions: (202) 319-5305
Email Address:
   cua-admissions@cua.edu

Strong Programs:
Politics
Psychology
Business
Physics
Nursing
Engineering
Architecture
Music

About 60 percent of the faculty are Catholic (the Vatican requires that figure to be at least 50 percent).

Students praise the
Counseling Center,
which offers up to
45 free counseling
sessions.

pro-choice views have been controversial among the student body. "It is hard for a lot of students to reconcile their own personal set of beliefs with the Catholic identity of the school, which can be said even for many of the students who are Catholic themselves," remarks a politics major. Ninety-seven percent of undergraduates are from outside D.C., including 6 percent from foreign countries, and most of the rest from the Northeast. Five percent are African American, 13 percent are Hispanic, 4 percent are Asian American, and 5 percent are multiracial. Catholic University maintains a need-blind admissions policy, and all applicants are considered for merit scholarships, which average $19,600. No athletic scholarships are available.

Fifty-eight percent of undergraduates live in the 16 single-sex residence halls, which are intended to foster an environment of virtuous living. All first-year students are assigned to interest communities organized around shared academic or personal interests. On-campus housing offers a variety of options ranging from the traditional to suites and apartments. "Most of the residence halls

> "Most of the residence halls are nice and comfortable enough to make your own impermanent home."

are nice and comfortable enough to make your own impermanent home," says a politics major. Campus fare is a mixed blessing: "The dining is unlimited, which is awesome for big appetites," says one student. "The problem is that it's overpriced and bland." Shuttle buses and escort services are provided as part of campus security, and students agree that they feel safe on campus, as long as they are careful. The Peer Educators Empowering Respectful Students (PEERS) group helps to raise awareness about sexual assault prevention.

When students want to explore the city, they need only walk to the Brookland-CUA Metrorail stop adjacent to campus and then enjoy the ride. Capitol Hill is 15 minutes away and the stylish Georgetown area, with its chic restaurants and nightspots, a half hour. "Because we're in the city, most students would rather get dressed up to go out to a bar than to a house party," observes a senior. Most students agree that school policies are effective in curbing underage drinking. Campus Ministry offers students numerous opportunities to engage in faith and service through regular community service events, student retreats, summer mission trips, and other programs. Annual activities on campus include Fall Festival, the Capital Fest concert featuring a well-known band, Mistletoe Ball, Founder's Day Ball, and Luaupalooza, a popular celebration of the end of the academic year.

Annual campus
activities include the
Capital Fest concert
and Luaupalooza, a
popular celebration
of the end of the
academic year.

CUA's Cardinals compete in Division III. Women's lacrosse has won nine Landmark Conference championships in the last 10 years, and other recent winners include men's basketball, swimming and diving, and baseball. Intramural and club-level programs attract plenty of activity too, especially basketball, indoor soccer, and flag football.

When discussions first raised the idea of a Catholic university, the man who would become the university's first rector, Bishop John Joseph Keane, argued for an institution that would "exercise a dominant influence in the world's future" with a superior intellectual foundation. Now, more than 130 years later, CUA offers students a wealth of preprofessional courses spanning the arts and sciences. Even as it grapples with how best to express and uphold its Catholic identity, the university remains dedicated to its mission of providing "scholarly research, education, and service in the light of the Catholic intellectual tradition."

Overlaps

Notre Dame, Villanova, Fordham, Loyola University Maryland, Saint Joseph's University, University of Maryland, American University, Penn State

If You Apply To ›

Catholic: Early decision, early action, regular decision. SATs or ACTs: optional. Subject Tests: optional. Accepts the Common Application. Music applicants must audition.

Centre College

600 West Walnut, Danville, KY 40422

Centre may not be the most famous institution of higher learning in Kentucky, but it is certainly the best, and it offers college the way it used to be—football games, Greek row, and a decades-old tradition that obliges students to run through campus (in the nude). There is also the closeness between students and faculty that comes with a student body of just over 1,400. Compare to Sewanee, Rhodes, and Davidson.

Centre College, the only independent school in Kentucky with a Phi Beta Kappa chapter, has produced two-thirds of the state's Rhodes scholars over the last 40 years. But the school is not all work and no play. It's also a throwback to the way college used to be, with Friday night parties on Greek row and Saturday afternoon football games. Centre's small size offers an intimate classroom environment. And its liberal arts focus means that despite Centre's southern location, students are progressive, intellectual, and perhaps more well-rounded than their peers at neighboring schools. "We are ready to make what we want happen," says a sophomore. "We are willing to do the hard work."

> "My professors took the time to really get to know me and my learning style."

Located in the heart of Kentucky Bluegrass country, Centre's campus is a mix of old Greek Revival and attractive modern buildings. More than 14 of them are listed on the National Registry of Historic Places, a fact that's less surprising when you know that Centre is the 48th oldest college in the United States. The college is home to four LEED-certified buildings, including two at the Gold level. Recent construction projects include a new 184-bed residence hall.

General education requirements include basic skills in expository writing, math, and foreign language and two courses in four contexts—aesthetic, social, scientific, and fundamental questions. Required first-year seminar courses are offered during the three-week January "CentreTerm." Capped at 15 students each, they offer a chance to explore off-beat topics, such as ethics in science fiction, the history of American holidays, and coffeehouse culture.

Centre's most popular majors are economics and finance, international studies, biology, history, and psychology. Other strong programs include mathematics, politics, behavioral neuroscience, and English. Art is solid too, and glassblowing enthusiasts will find one of the few fully equipped undergraduate facilities for their pursuit in the nation. A 3–2 program sends aspiring engineers on to one of four major universities, including the University of Kentucky and Vanderbilt. Sixty-one percent of classes have fewer than 20 students. "My professors took the time to really get to know me and my learning style," says a politics major. "Our small class sizes allow professors to really feed off of the energy and needs of the class and make it a more personal environment."

> "Athletic contests against Transy are highly attended by students."

The Centre Commitment guarantees students an internship or research experience, a study abroad opportunity, and a degree in four years—or the college will cover the cost of a fifth year of study. Approximately 75 percent of students choose to engage in an internship, 43 percent perform collaborative research with faculty, and 85 percent take advantage of Centre's extensive study abroad programs. Centre runs regular semester-long programs for students in all majors in nine countries, including China, France, and Scotland, in addition to several shorter options offered during the January term. A study-away semester in Washington, D.C., combines

---

Website: www.centre.edu
Location: Small Town
Private
Total Enrollment: 1,440
Undergraduates: 1,440
Male/Female: 49/51
SAT Ranges: ERW 590–680, M 580–730
ACT Ranges: 26–31
Financial Aid: 90%
Pell Grant: 17%
Expense: Pr $
Student Loans: 45%
Average Debt: $ $
Applicants: 2,454
Accepted: 76%
Enrolled: 21%
Grad in 6 Years: 86%
Returning Freshmen: 91%
Academics: ✐ ✐ ✐ ½
Social: ☎ ☎ ☎
Q of L: ★ ★ ★
Admissions: (859) 238-5350
Email Address: admission@centre.edu

Strong Programs:
Economics and Finance
International Studies
Biology
History
Psychology
Mathematics
Politics
Behavioral Neuroscience

coursework with internships. A psychology major highly recommends the college's career services: "They have monthly programs on 'adulting' and provide constant assistance and support in the job-search process."

Fifty-two percent of Centre students hail from Kentucky, and 7 percent arrive from foreign nations. African Americans comprise 5 percent of the student body, Asian Americans 5 percent, Hispanics 5 percent, and multiracial students 3 percent. Politically, the atmosphere is mostly liberal, and a senior says, "Whatever is in the national spotlight definitely gets discussed over dinner or in class." Increasing diversity among faculty and staff has been a particular focus of late. Centre offers merit-based awards averaging $22,500, but no athletic scholarships. Through the Grissom Scholars Program, 10 incoming first-generation students per year are awarded full-tuition scholarships plus $5,000 to support study abroad, research, or an internship.

The Centre Commitment guarantees students an internship or research experience, a study abroad opportunity, and a degree in four years.

Ninety-eight percent of students live on campus, and students say the four-year residential requirement makes for a strong sense of community. "While the dorms aren't the Ritz, they make a pretty nice home away from home," says a junior. Suite- and townhouse-style accommodations are available for upperclassmen, and small Greek houses are an option for some, but most members of Greek life live in the residence halls. Students dine in one main dining hall, Cowan, and two café-style eateries. "We have pretty good food, but it gets old really quickly," says a senior. Centre recently established a bystander intervention program to strengthen efforts to prevent sexual assault.

Greek life is the center of the social scene, with 36 percent of men and 40 percent of women joining up, and their parties are open to all. "Alcohol is a large part of the weekend social life here for many students," says a senior. The Student Activity Council sponsors a variety of alternatives, such as free midnight movies at the local theater and events like comedians, karaoke, and laser tag. Students also get free admission to Centre's separately endowed Norton Center for the Arts, a palatial, 1,500-seat auditorium that brings major musicals, concerts, and other performances to campus. Homecoming in the fall and Carnival in the spring are big annual events. Campus superstitions involve placing pennies on the toe of the Abraham Lincoln statue for good luck on exams, and avoiding stepping on the Centre Seal so as not to fail them. But Centre's most hallowed tradition is "Running the Flame," which has students dashing from their residence halls to a large sculpture of a flame in the center of campus, circling it three times, and running back—"naked, of course." Eighty-five percent of students do community service through the Greek system, Habitat for Humanity, or other organizations. Danville (population 17,000) offers some small-town charm, but there is more to do in Lexington and Louisville, both within an hour's drive, and it's easy to get to the countryside for camping, fishing, and other outdoor pursuits.

> "By the time I reached my senior year, I felt cultivated as a public speaker, a problem solver, and a leader."

Students get free admission to Centre's Norton Center for the Arts, a palatial, 1,500-seat auditorium that brings major performances to campus.

Centre's football team has been around for more than a century, and while it now competes against regional opponents in Division III, that wasn't always the case. In 1921 the Colonels beat then-powerhouse Harvard, six to zero, a triumph that has been called the greatest sports upset in the first half of the 20th century. Nowadays, Rhodes College and nearby Transylvania University are Centre's key rivals. "Athletic contests against Transy are highly attended by students," confirms a senior. The men's and women's soccer and women's cross-country and field hockey teams are recent conference champions, and football and men's basketball are also competitive. A majority of the student body regularly participate in the intramural program, with flag football, softball, and basketball drawing the most players.

Centre College often takes visitors by surprise. Although situated in a quaint, historic setting, much of the campus has a fresh, modern feel. Students come here

Overlaps

Rhodes, Sewanee, Wofford, Kenyon, Davidson, Furman, University of Kentucky, University of Louisville

for a well-rounded liberal arts education yet receive plenty of real-world preparation along the way. "By the time I reached my senior year," recalls a math major, "I felt cultivated as a public speaker, a problem solver, and a leader." With faculty who care about forming lasting friendships with students and a commitment to providing hands-on learning opportunities, this undiscovered gem may be worth a look.

If You Apply To ›

Centre: Early decision, early action, regular decision. SATs or ACTs: required. No Subject Tests. Accepts the Common Application.

Champlain College

251 South Willard Street, Burlington, VT 05401

A small college with a unique "upside-down" approach to blending professional education and the liberal arts. Champlain's major academic strengths are game design, whose students tend to shape the campus culture, as well as business and communication. A good fit for students eager to get started in a career but not a great place to explore options and find yourself. Social life revolves around student-friendly Burlington, and Vermont's nearby ski slopes beckon. Low graduation rate is a problem.

Champlain is an up-and-coming small college, situated on a hill overlooking Vermont's scenic Lake Champlain, that has set out to reinvent the relationship between professional studies and the liberal arts through its so-called upside-down curriculum. Instead of following the traditional academic path—two years of general education courses followed by two years of in-depth study in a major—students at Champlain immediately pursue both their major and a highly structured liberal arts curriculum simultaneously for all four years. This approach appeals to career-minded students who still appreciate the value of a strong dose of the liberal arts. Says one game design major, "We're all driven to find new ways to solve problems and enter the workforce with better ideas and more efficient methods."

The college sits on 22 acres in the historic Hill Section of Burlington, adjacent to the University of Vermont. The core academic campus consists of a mix of lovely restored Victorian mansions and complementary modern structures of brick with slate roofs and green trim. The adjacent "lakeside" campus houses the Leahy Center

> "We're all driven to…enter the workforce with better ideas and more efficient methods."

for Digital Investigation and a variety of administrative facilities, while a "downtown" campus, connected to the academic core by shuttle buses, provides housing and dining for 300 upperclassmen. The recently opened Center for Communication and Creative Media, a 75,000-square-foot facility, offers game and audio labs, studio spaces, and a traditional and digital photo lab.

Champlain's distinctive curriculum is built around three legs ("Education in 3-D," to use the local lingo), starting with professional programs. Students apply to one of four academic divisions—Stiller School of Business; Communication and Creative Media (CCM); Education and Human Studies; or Information Technology and Sciences—and then select a major in that division. For example, CCM, the largest division, offers nine choices, with broadcast media production, creative media,

Website: www.champlain.edu
Location: Small City
Private
Total Enrollment: 2,861
Undergraduates: 2,164
Male/Female: 63/37
SAT Ranges: ERW 560–670, M 530–630
ACT Ranges: 23–29
Financial Aid: 90%
Pell Grant: 26%
Expense: Pr $
Student Loans: 71%
Average Debt: $ $ $ $
Applicants: 5,197
Accepted: 75%
Enrolled: 15%
Grad in 6 Years: 61%
Returning Freshmen: 79%
Academics: ✍ ✍ ✍
Social: ☎ ☎ ☎
Q of L: ★ ★ ★
Admissions: (802) 860-2727
Email Address: admission@champlain.edu

The InSight career and personal finance program is part of the required curriculum.

filmmaking, and professional writing among them. Students disillusioned by their initial choices can easily transfer to another major within their division, but switching to another division is harder. The second leg, the liberal arts component, is a highly structured set of Core courses taught on an interdisciplinary basis by professors from all departments. Students pursue a series of courses over three years that focus in progressive fashion on the nature of the self, concepts of a just and sustainable community in the West, and global themes, such as human rights. Seniors complete a capstone experience that integrates learning from their professional, liberal arts, and out-of-classroom experiences. The school argues that four years of working simultaneously in a professional field and the liberal arts gives students the broad thinking and learning skills that will serve them well beyond their first jobs. The third and final piece of the curricular pie is the InSight career and personal finance program, an array of workshops, company visits, and other activities that teach such real-world skills as developing a résumé and cover letter, setting a budget, and earning a good credit score. "Champlain puts a lot of effort into the thought of 'after college,'" says a junior.

Professors bring "a great deal of passion, dedication, and experience that the students can tap into to expand their own knowledge," says one student. Sixty-nine percent of classes at Champlain have fewer than 20 students, and all are taught on an inquiry basis by professors or adjuncts, with no teaching assistants. A senior says, "From your Core classes to your major-specific classes, you will be engaged in discussions and group projects almost every day." Game design is a particularly popular field, and seniors in game-development-related majors often compete against one another to complete projects for school-sponsored events. The majors with the highest enrollment are business administration, communication, game programming, game design, and graphic design and digital media. Computer and digital forensics is also highly regarded, as is computer networking and cybersecurity, and the recently opened CCM building promises to offer a big boost to writing and the arts. Many students also take minors in areas such as global studies and social justice.

> "You will be engaged in discussions and group projects almost every day."

Virtually all students participate in some sort of internship at some point. Study abroad, which draws 56 percent of the students, plays an important role at Champlain, and the college offers free passports to students who do not already have them. The college maintains international satellite campuses in Dublin, from which students have easy access to the rest of Europe, and Montreal, a major global center for the game industry. Still dozens of other students go abroad through the school's internship sites in Shanghai or through Champlain's service-learning program. There are no honors programs or undergraduate research opportunities, and most graduates—education majors are an exception—head for the job market rather than graduate or professional schools.

Twenty percent of students are native Vermonters, with the rest hailing mainly from the East Coast and Midwest. Champlain students are a fairly homogeneous crowd, with African Americans accounting for 2 percent of the total, Hispanics 6 percent, Asian Americans 3 percent, multiracial students 3 percent, and international students only 1 percent. Largely because of the nature of the curriculum, men outnumber women by a ratio of three to two. "Most of the campus is comprised of geeks and gamers," says a student. "There are many skiers and snowboarders, of course, and a great deal of people who care about the environment or social issues." Twenty-six percent of freshmen qualify for Pell Grants, and the school awards merit scholarships averaging $10,700.

> "Champlain's first-year residence halls are renovated Victorian mansions."

"Champlain's first-year residence halls are renovated Victorian mansions that have modern technology and safety features with the old charm preserved," explains a senior. Sophomores and upperclassmen can choose among well-maintained traditional dorms, some quite new, that feature tuning and repair facilities for bikes, skis, and skateboards, or they can live in an off-campus apartment hall or find their own off-campus digs. Overall, 68 percent of undergrads reside in college-owned housing. Students take their meals at a single dining hall where, this being Vermont, the emphasis is on fresh, local, and healthy foods and sustainable practices: there are no trays, and paper plates or plastic utensils are definite no-nos. One student reports, "Our school's Public Safety department is incredibly friendly and always shows up quickly (even if you just locked yourself out of your room)."

"Because our campus is so small, most of the social life is off campus," says a marketing major, "whether it's downtown on Church Street, by the lake, a friend's apartment, or a concert." The campus is dry and policies are enforced; in the absence of fraternities and sororities, says a sophomore, "hard-core party folks go to our neighbors, UVM." The college sponsors roughly 50 student clubs and organizes a range of activities on and off campus. A small city of 42,000 residents, Burlington is near the top of everyone's list of best college towns. The Church Street pedestrian mall, just below the campus, offers an array of cafés and shops for all tastes, as well as a vibrant music scene and abundant nightlife, and there is a park and bike path that runs along the lake's waterfront.

Champlain maintains international satellite campuses in Dublin and Montreal, a major global center for the game industry.

> "The gaming culture might be a deterrent to those who aren't interested in video games."

No one seems to mind that Champlain has no intercollegiate sports (though it does have a mascot named Chauncey T. Beaver). But there are plenty of intramural options for all skill levels, including soccer, basketball, and dodgeball, as well as a rugby club that competes against other schools; nearly 20 percent of Champlain students participate. Not surprisingly for a school full of gamers, Quidditch and Humans vs. Zombies are popular. Annual traditions include the Rail Jam skiing and snowboarding competition in the fall, the Spring Meltdown carnival just before final exams, and the One World Festival featuring food and music from various countries. The end of the year brings the Game Development Senior Show, where graduating seniors show off their projects to the college community, family members, and company recruiters.

Annual traditions include the Rail Jam skiing and snowboarding competition in the fall.

Administrators at Champlain are sensitive about the fact that only 61 percent of entering students graduate within six years. One contributing factor, students suggest, is the need to plunge immediately into a professional field that may not be a good fit. "Students end up switching out of the program or out of the school, especially if they have trouble deciding what major they want," says a sophomore. Other students point to the heavy workload in some majors and the lack of cultural diversity as possible factors. "The gaming culture might be a deterrent to those who aren't interested in video games," says a game art and animation major. In fact, gaming is so ingrained in the culture here that even one of the college's training programs on sexual assault prevention is delivered through a faculty-developed video game called *Make a Change*.

For gaming enthusiasts, techies, creatives, and other career-oriented students, Champlain is a small school with a big vision of how to refashion the relationship between professional training and the liberal arts. It offers a unique option for students who have a strong, focused interest in its professional majors and who are eager to "press start" on their careers.

Overlaps

Saint Michael's, Roger Williams, Endicott, Worcester Polytechnic, Stonehill, Goucher, University of Vermont, Rochester Institute of Technology

If You Apply To ›

Champlain: Early decision, regular decision. SATs or ACTs: optional. Subject Tests: optional. Accepts the Common Application with supplement. Apply to particular academic division. Some majors require portfolio submission.

Chapman University

One University Drive, Orange, CA 92866

Chapman sits at the hub of Orange County and a stone's throw from L.A. Has parlayed its O.C. location into burgeoning popularity in film, television, and the performing arts. Those without showbiz aspirations can opt for strong programs in business, communication studies, or biology. Disneyland is in the neighborhood, but you need a car or a ride to get there.

Website: www.chapman.edu
Location: Suburban
Private
Total Enrollment: 8,272
Undergraduates: 6,495
Male/Female: 39/61
SAT Ranges: ERW 600–680,
   M 590–680
ACT Ranges: 25–30
Financial Aid: 83%
Pell Grant: 20%
Expense: Pr $ $ $
Student Loans: 59%
Average Debt: $ $
Applicants: 13,170
Accepted: 57%
Enrolled: 22%
Grad in 6 Years: 79%
Returning Freshmen: 91%
Academics: ✎ ✎ ✎
Social: ☎ ☎ ☎
Q of L: ★ ★ ★
Admissions: (888) CU-APPLY
Email Address: admit@
   chapman.edu

Strong Programs:
Business Administration
Communication Studies
Strategic and Corporate
   Communication
Psychology
Film Production
Economics
Health Sciences
Biological Sciences

Although best known as a Southern Californian mecca for budding filmmakers to hone their craft, Chapman University continues to stake its claim as a comprehensive institution that happens to offer one of the nation's best film programs—rather than a film school that also happens to offer other majors. Chapman boasts stellar programs in business and has increased its emphasis on health sciences, technology, and physics. It also facilitates countless internships to send its students out into the workforce with real-world experience.

Founded in 1861, Chapman University is one of the oldest private universities in California. Originally called Hesperian College, the school later merged with California Christian College in Los Angeles. In 1934 the institution was renamed in honor of C. C. Chapman, an Orange County entrepreneur and benefactor of the school. In 1991 the college became Chapman University, reflecting its evolution into a comprehensive institution of higher learning. The beautiful residential campus, situated on 80 tree-lined acres, features a mixture of landmark historic buildings and state-of-the-art facilities. It is located in the historic Old Towne district of Orange, near outstanding beaches, Disneyland, and the world-class cultural offerings of Orange County and Los Angeles. Recent construction includes the 140,000-square-foot Keck Center for Science and Engineering; plans are underway to open a school of engineering in 2020.

Regardless of major, all students complete a four-part general education program: a First-Year Foundations Course taken in the fall; six inquiry categories (natural science, quantitative reasoning, writing, social sciences, values and ethics, and artistic studies); a Global Citizen cluster (two courses in global studies, one in civic issues, and a language course); and a mini-minor, minor, or second major. Chapman's first-year experience program, Fenestra (Latin for "window"), encourages students to approach their first year as a "window of opportunity"; the program involves a weeklong orientation and special workshops, field trips, and social activities held throughout the year.

> **"At Chapman, you are going to have an in-depth and personalized education."**

The most popular majors are business administration, communication studies, strategic and corporate communication, psychology, and film production. Dodge College of Film and Media Arts is a comprehensive, production-based school that offers such majors as creative producing, news/broadcast journalism and documentary, public relations and advertising, and screenwriting, as well as internships and other active learning opportunities. Emerging entrepreneurs can take advantage of a well-stocked portfolio of business programs through the Argyros School of Business and Economics. The Economic Science Institute allows for the study of experimental economics under the direction of Nobel laureate Dr. Vernon Smith and encompasses fields as diverse as finance, engineering, neuroscience, computer science, and philosophy, among others. Notable programs in music, theatre, and dance involve frequent national and international performance components. Additionally, accelerated degree programs that allow students to earn a bachelor's and a master's in five years are available in several disciplines, including pharmaceutical sciences.

"Regardless of the course of study you are taking at Chapman, you are going to have an in-depth and personalized education," says a creative producing major. Forty-five percent of classes have fewer than 20 students. Freshmen are taught by professors—there are no teaching assistants—and professors are praised for being accessible and "genuinely interested in their students," says a senior. Students interested in conducting faculty-mentored research can apply to the SURF (Summer Undergraduate Research Fellowship) program, which awards up to $3,000 in funding to selected fellows. An English and sociology major highly recommends the Honors Program, which allows students to "dive deeply into very niche topics" as well as "build and teach their own classes to their peers." Those seeking a global learning experience can choose from more than 90 preapproved study abroad programs, in addition to short-term, faculty-led travel courses and international summer internships; 42 percent of students avail themselves of these opportunities. As for career services, a junior says, "If I have any question about my résumé or cover letter or need a place to do a phone or Skype interview, I just walk into the Office of Career and Professional Development."

All students complete a mini-minor, minor, or second major.

Chapman attracts a friendly, largely affluent student body. A junior says, "A Chapman student is a leader, someone who wants to be actively involved in their community and consciously making a difference." Sixty-five percent of students hail from California, and 6 percent are international. African Americans comprise 2 percent of the population, Asian Americans 12 percent, Hispanics 15 percent, and multiracial students 7 percent. Chapman's Cross-Cultural Center opened in 2017, and a senior says, "Discussions of diversity, tolerance, inclusion, and safety are common on campus." Eligible undergraduates receive merit scholarships worth an average of $17,000, but since Chapman is a Division III school, there are no athletic scholarships.

"A Chapman student is a leader."

Thirty-three percent of Chapman students reside on campus. First-years are housed in residence halls based on their chosen academic program; one student explains, "This allows for students to know their peers on day one of classes and always have a study partner throughout the semester." Meals at the Randall Dining Commons are described as tasty and diverse. Campus safety receives positive reviews, and the CARES (Creating a Rape-Free Environment for Students) student organization is active in raising awareness about campus sexual assault.

Dodge College of Film and Media Arts is a comprehensive, production-based school that offers internships and other active learning opportunities.

Twenty-five percent of the men join fraternities, and sororities attract 48 percent of the women; all members of the Greek community are required to perform community service, and Greek life doesn't dominate the social scene. A junior describes Chapman's off-campus party culture as "intimate," adding, "Students prefer to keep it to a lower scale, mostly due to the lack of a Greek row." Students also enjoy a plenitude of school-sponsored events. "Our University Program Board hosts hundreds of events throughout the year, including movie screenings; Midnight Breakfast; weekend excursions to the beach, museums, and hiking trails; dances; and many other events," cheers one senior. Every year, students flock to the homecoming celebration's chili cook-off and fireworks, WinterFest, and the Spring Sizzle festival.

"Students prefer to keep [parties] to a lower scale, mostly due to the lack of a Greek row."

The city of Orange (population 140,000) is a college town only in the technical sense of the term. "It's actually a very quiet city," says a junior. The Old Towne district is well known as "the Antique Capital of California," although several trendy restaurants, brew pubs, and boutiques have opened their doors in the last few years. When students grow weary of the area, they take advantage of the pristine Southern California weather to explore the great outdoors or take trips to Disneyland, L.A., or San Diego.

The Chapman Panthers compete in the Division III Southern California Intercollegiate Athletic Conference. Football, men's and women's basketball, and women's volleyball have been competitive in recent years. The Chapman Dance Team has brought home several national championships in the last decade. Intramurals and club sports draw a quarter of the student body.

Students at Chapman are not only expected to hit the books, but also to actively express their creativity through hands-on learning, on-campus involvement, and forays into the real world. In return, they are rewarded with an exceedingly supportive environment that both nurtures and challenges them every step of the way.

If You Apply To ›

Chapman: Early decision, early action, regular decision. SATs or ACTs: required. Subject Tests: optional. Accepts the Common Application with supplement. Talent-based programs require submission of a creative supplement.

College of Charleston

Charleston, SC 29424

A public school one-third the size of the University of South Carolina that blends a small-college feel with the advantages of a midsized, urban university. Offers business, education, and the liberal arts and sciences. Location a feast for history buffs. College of Charleston compares to William and Mary in both scale and historic surroundings but is far less rigorous academically. Addressing its housing crunch to help it reach the next level.

Whether sampling the traditional Lowcountry cuisine or delving into the wide range of courses offered at this strong liberal arts and sciences institution, students at the College of Charleston know they are getting a solid education based on creative expression, intellectual freedom, and hands-on learning experiences. Founded in 1770 as Colonial South Carolina's first college, CofC's original commitment to the liberal arts and sciences and to the citizens of the region has helped it become a well-respected institution throughout the Southeast. And the location only adds to the experience, providing opportunities for research and internships, and a robust social scene.

The 13th oldest college in the country, CofC was founded as a private college and, after a number of identity changes, became a state university exactly 200 years later. Located in Charleston's famous Historic District, the campus features many of the city's most venerable buildings. More than 80 of its buildings are former private residences, ranging from the typical Charleston "single" house to the Victorian, and the clap-clap of horse-drawn carriages bearing tourists is a routine sight. The wooded area in front of Randolph Hall, known as the Cistern Yard, is a student gathering point and the site of May graduation ceremonies. The campus has received countless awards for its design and has been designated a national arboretum and a National Historic Landmark.

CofC has a core curriculum rooted in the liberal arts, sciences, and professional programs. The focus is on the development of problem-solving and critical-thinking skills, as well as "sustainable literacy"—the knowledge and tools to address global issues like climate change, social injustice, and economic inequality. Each student is required to satisfy credits in English, history, mathematics or logic, social science, natural sciences, humanities, and foreign language. All new students attend Convocation, where they are introduced to the college's academic traditions, and freshmen from underrepresented groups can participate in several support programs designed to ensure their successful transition to college. All freshmen take part in the First-Year Experience and choose between seminar and learning community options; sample seminars include Charleston and the Civil Rights Movement, From Russia with Code: Cybersecurity & Russia, and Feminist Jiu-Jitsu for Self-Defense.

> **"I feel surrounded by students, staff, and professors who push me to succeed."**

"The academic climate at College of Charleston is very collaborative. I feel surrounded by students, staff, and professors who push me to succeed," a senior says. Biology and chemistry are two of the strongest programs; many graduates go on to the Medical University of South Carolina, a few blocks down the street. Multiple interdisciplinary programs are available, such as data science, which integrates statistics, social sciences, computer science, learning theory, artificial intelligence, and other areas. The most popular majors are business administration, biology, psychology, and communication, while public health, arts management, and marketing are among the fastest-growing programs. Forty percent of all classes enroll fewer than 20 students, and a public health major describes the quality of instruction as hit-or-miss, adding, "Some professors really care if you are absorbing the content and help you build career goals."

About 700 students enroll in CofC's Honors College, where they are given a more demanding workload, including a culminating Bachelor's Essay that is undertaken with the support of a faculty mentor. The Undergraduate Research and Creative Activities program awards competitive grants to fund student/faculty research projects. Thirty-two percent of undergrads study internationally; CofC sponsors more than 30 faculty-led study abroad programs, as well as several weeklong spring break trips that are tied to First-Year Seminar courses.

> **"Being in the heart of a city can sometimes be overwhelming, but generally, campus feels safe."**

Students may also choose from hundreds of additional options through preapproved providers. Many performing arts majors take advantage of internships with Spoleto Festival USA, Charleston's annual arts festival. The city's growing biomedicine, tech, and aerospace industries also provide opportunities for research and internships.

According to one student, CofC has "a very open-minded and liberal student body." Thirty-three percent of students hail from out of state, and another 1 percent from foreign countries. The administration has been pushing to increase the proportion of students of color; currently, African Americans account for 8 percent of the student body, Asian Americans 2 percent, Hispanics 5 percent, and multiracial students 4 percent. Racial tension in the city of Charleston has sparked "some protests and disagreements" on campus, says a junior, but overall, the political climate is usually relatively calm. The Race and Social Justice Initiative raises awareness of racial injustice through public events, exhibitions, and other projects. Twenty-seven percent of freshmen qualify for the Pell Grant. The college offers merit scholarships averaging $11,800 and 116 athletic scholarships.

"On-campus housing at CofC is very nice, with choices between dormitories, apartments, or historic houses," says a student. Thirty-one percent of students live on campus, and students say more would stay if there were space to accommodate them. One junior grumbles that finding off-campus housing "is kind of a nuisance because to find somewhere that's comparable in price and services, you need to

(continued)

Academics: ✍ ✍ ✍
Social: ☎ ☎ ☎ ☎
Q of L: ★ ★ ★ ★
Admissions: (843) 953-5670
Email Address: admissions@ cofc.edu

Strong Programs:
Business Administration
Biology
Psychology
Communication
Chemistry
Data Science
Public Health
Arts Management

About 700 students enroll in CofC's Honors College, which culminates in a Bachelor's Essay undertaken with the support of a faculty mentor.

go a little farther from campus and find roommates." Parking is limited but food is plentiful; there are options for all types of eaters, including "homestyle, grill, deli, salad bar, Greek, dessert, and cereal bar" selections, as well as vegetarian and kosher fare. "Being in the heart of a city can sometimes be overwhelming, but generally, campus feels safe," says one student.

Students party off campus in local clubs and apartments as well as on campus, where 12 percent of the men and 23 percent of the women belong to fraternities and sororities, respectively. "Campus clubs ensure there is always an event for on-campus fun," explains a junior. A recent crackdown on misconduct among Greek groups has resulted in tightened alcohol policies and the suspension of multiple fraternities. The Medical University of South Carolina and The Citadel Military College, both in Charleston, expand the social opportunities. Students enjoy Charleston's sporting events, concerts, and festivals. As one student puts it, "The city is a social playground for college students. There are tons of restaurants, events to attend, and beautiful architecture to enjoy." On weekends, students can head to beaches such as Folly Beach, Sullivan's Island, and Isle of Palms, which are merely minutes away. For those who don't mind a drive, there's "the Grand Strand," Myrtle Beach, 90 miles north, Savannah and Hilton Head to the south, and Atlanta to the west.

The absence of a football team is a common gripe among students, but other athletic teams are relatively popular, none more so than basketball. The College of Charleston is a Division I school, and several Cougar teams have claimed recent Colonial Athletic Association championships, including men's basketball, women's volleyball, and men's and women's golf. The sailing team is a top performer nationally. The intramural program offers eight team sports throughout the year, and basketball and soccer are the most popular, both in terms of participation and competitive fervor; more than 25 club sports are also available.

The College of Charleston has become the finest public liberal arts and sciences institution in South Carolina, propelled by an honors college, opportunities for internships and study abroad, and a healthy social life. A senior says, "Here, you will find faculty and staff who care for your success and great friends who come from all different backgrounds."

If You Apply To ›

Charleston: Early decision, early action, regular decision. SATs or ACTs: required (SAT essay or ACT writing recommended). Subject Tests: optional. Does not accept the Common Application.

University of Chicago

Rosenwald Hall 105, 1101 East 58th Street, Chicago, IL 60637

Traditionally known as a haven for true intellectuals who enjoy nothing more than the chance to debate a fresh idea. The Common Core remains the intellectual heart of the school, but Chicago has worked hard to shed its reputation as the place where "fun comes to die." Recent investments in dormitory life, the arts, and athletic facilities—coupled with more aggressive recruiting—have helped attract a growing number of Ivy-caliber applicants, including first-generation undergrads. Quarter system can be stressful. Least socioeconomically diverse among elite schools.

The University of Chicago attracts students eager to move beyond the cliquishness of high school and the superficial trappings of Ivy League résumé building—the kids more concerned about learning for learning's sake than about getting a job after graduation, though they're certainly capable of the latter. "'Life of the Mind' is taken very seriously," says a student. "The academic atmosphere extends beyond the class-room, and most people like it that way." Still, administrators have realized that in the 21st century, even the best schools cannot survive on intellectual might alone. To make UChicago more attractive, they've stopped requiring the SAT or ACT for admission, broadened the offerings in the core curriculum, expanded study abroad programs and career advising, and completed a bevy of new facilities. The result? Applications have tripled since 2005 and enrollment is surging. Says a freshman, "The fact that college here is a good time just makes us that much happier."

> **"The academic atmosphere extends beyond the classroom, and most people like it that way."**

The university's 217-acre, tree-lined campus is in Hyde Park, an eclectic community on Chicago's South Side, surrounded by neighborhoods on three sides and Lake Michigan on the other. One of 77 city neighborhoods, Hyde Park "is pretty intellectual," says one student, noting that "two-thirds of our faculty live here." Streets are lined with brownstones, rowhouses, and townhouses, giving way to luxury highrises with beautiful views as you get closer to the lake; the city's Museum of Science and Industry is within spitting distance. The campus itself is self-contained and architecturally magnificent. The main quads are steel-gray Gothic—gargoyles and all—and other buildings were designed by the likes of Frank Lloyd Wright, Eero Saarinen, and Mies van der Rohe. The Regenstein Library (known as "the Reg") is a national treasure, symbolically located in the heart of the campus. Next to the Reg is the Mansueto Library, a geodesic dome. The new Green Line Performing Arts Center opened in Washington Park in 2018.

Historically, UChicago has drawn praise for its graduate programs, but in recent years the undergraduate college has flourished, competing successfully with the likes of Stanford, Harvard, and Princeton. To that end, the university remains unequivocally committed to the view that a solid foundation in the liberal arts is the best preparation for future study or work and, moreover, that theory is better than practice. Thus, music students study musicology, but also learn calculus, along with everyone else. Regardless of major, 15 to 18 of a student's 42 courses fall under general education requirements called the Common Core, which is one of the most comprehensive sets of distribution requirements anywhere. (The precise number of courses in the Core depends on how much foreign language instruction a student needs to reach proficiency.)

Other Core requirements include courses in the sciences and math, humanities, social sciences, and a sequence of study in a specific civilization. There is a required writing tutorial as well. Sound intense? Well, yes, students say it is, especially because UChicago pioneered the quarter system, whereby class material is presented over 10-week periods, with the first term starting in late September and ending in mid-December. In practice, this means that students take more classes than they would on a semester-based system, with virtually uninterrupted work through the year, punctuated by a long summer vacation and three exam weeks. A senior says, "With an intense workload, it is important to practice time management in order to succeed. Once you get into the swing of things, however, everything is manageable (though still intense)." Seniors are also encouraged to do final-year projects. Classes are intimate, with 80 percent enrolling fewer than 20 students, and led by brilliant and distinguished faculty members

> **"[Professors] expect your work to be completed at a very high level."**

who've won Nobel Prizes, Guggenheims, and other prestigious awards. Professors "expect your work to be completed at a very high level, which causes some assignments to take longer than they would somewhere else," says one mathematics major.

The economics department, which has produced numerous Nobel laureates, is known as a bastion of neoliberal economics and is UChicago's main academic claim to fame. Popular majors include economics, biological sciences, English, political science, and mathematics. The university also prides itself on interdisciplinary and area studies programs, such as those focusing on East Asia, South Asia, the Middle East, and the Slavic countries. The Accelerated Medical Scholars Program allows exceptional undergrads to begin medical school during their fourth year, and similar joint-degree and professional options allow undergrads to engage with any of the

"Hyde Park has tons of really cute, cheap apartments."

university's other graduate and professional schools. The cross-subject molecular engineering major—the university's first ever undergraduate degree in engineering—focuses on "solving societal problems at the molecular level"; students delve into such topics as water conservation, quantum computing, and advances in biological immuno-engineering. New offerings include a major in astrophysics and a specialization in business economics.

Students enjoy an abundance of research assistantships and opportunities for publication, even before they graduate. Through the Metcalf Internship Program, students have access to more than 2,500 fully funded internships that are offered exclusively to UChicago students. Established internships are available at the Argonne National Laboratory and Fermilab, both located in nearby suburbs, and at the UChicago-affiliated Marine Biological Laboratory in Woods Hole, Massachusetts. When Chicago gets too cold and snowy, students may take advantage of study abroad programs, which reach most corners of the globe and include study at the university's centers in Hong Kong, Beijing, Delhi, and Paris. Financial aid applies to study abroad programs, and 40 percent of students take part. All students are assigned both an academic and a career advisor, and UChicago has one of the best career advising systems of any school, aimed at assuring that its graduating intellectuals can still get a job.

At UChicago, says a junior, "What brings together the student body is a love for learning and maybe just a bit of geekiness, whether that comes from a love of Plato or

"The city of Chicago is the backyard for UChicago, and students are always exploring it."

an obsession with *The Big Bang Theory*." Sixty-nine percent of undergraduates come from out of state, including many East Coasters with academic parents; another 13 percent are international. Asian Americans represent 18 percent of the total, Hispanics 13 percent, African Americans 5 percent, and multiracial students 6 percent. Students are quick to give voice to opinions and political allegiances. "It would be nice if there was a less hostile political climate on campus," laments one student. In a sign of UChicago's educational philosophy that attracted national attention in 2016, incoming freshmen received a letter reiterating the university's commitment to freedom of speech and thought, rejecting "safe spaces" for the hypersensitive and cancellations of invitations to controversial speakers. Admissions at UChicago are need-blind, and the university meets 100 percent of students' demonstrated need with financial aid packages that include grants instead of loans. The Odyssey Scholarship program offers generous financial aid packages, funding to support internships or study abroad, and other benefits to first-generation and lower-income students. Still, just 10 percent of incoming freshmen qualify for the Pell Grant.

UChicago guarantees on-campus housing for four years, and 54 percent of all undergrads live in the dorms. "Every incoming first-year has to live in a House," explains a student. "Houses here are like Hogwarts in the sense that students form very intense loyalty toward their House and therefore there is competition between Houses." All halls are co-ed, though some offer single-sex floors, and each dorm is different—some house fewer than 100 people in traditional, shared double rooms without kitchens, while another has 700 beds organized into colorful suites. The recently constructed Campus North Residential Commons, complete with a dining commons, replaced a number of off-campus apartment buildings that were scattered throughout the neighborhood. It is part of a long-term campaign to provide more on-campus housing. Still, "Hyde Park has tons of really cute, cheap apartments," reports one student, so many of the more "independent-minded" students move off campus. "The campus feels very safe," says one student. "Not only does UChicago employ its own police force, but security guards are stationed around the neighborhood to help increase the safety." Through the Sexual Assault Dean-on-Call program, students who have experienced assault can reach a trained campus official 24/7 for crisis assistance and continued support.

The Metcalf Internship Program provides access to more than 2,500 fully funded internships that are offered exclusively to UChicago students.

The UChicago social scene is varied, according to a senior. "There is always some sort of event going on around campus, be it a theater performance or an a cappella show, but the city of Chicago is the backyard for UChicago, and students are always exploring it." Indeed, the university's a cappella scene is one of the tops in the country, and the city offers museums galore; world-class symphony, opera, and dance; the Second City comedy improv troupe (invented by University of Chicago undergrads); professional spectator sports; and plenty of clubs and bars. The university provides students with free, unlimited

"Even the varsity athletes are Phi Beta Kappa (that is, very smart)."

access to all parts of the city via public transportation, and Arts Pass offers free or discounted student admission to city art, theater, and cultural events. Cars are a nice luxury (if you can find a parking place). Road trips are infrequent, but one popular destination is Ann Arbor, about five hours away, for concerts and more traditional collegiate fun at the University of Michigan. Greek life has a small presence on campus, with 8 percent of the men and 12 percent of the women joining local fraternities and sororities.

Tradition is a hallmark at UChicago. Students have fond memories of freshman orientation, known as O-Week, an event administrators claim was invented at the university in 1934. In the winter, students head for the outdoor skating rink on the Midway, site of the 1893 World's Fair, for broomball. Students also celebrate the festival of Kuviasungnerk/Kangeiko ("Kuvia" for short), a week of early morning calisthenics and other activities, culminating in a Friday morning yoga session by Lake Michigan and a Polar Bear Run, where naked or seminaked Maroons dash across the academic quad. Each spring, students look forward to Scavenger Hunt ("Scav"), "a pumped-up version of a regular scavenger hunt, with a list of 300 bizarre items," says a sociology major. Campuswide games of Humans vs. Zombies are played once every quarter.

The festival of Kuvia is a week of early morning calisthenics, culminating in a Friday morning yoga session by Lake Michigan and a Polar Bear Run.

UChicago's Maroons compete in Division III, and the school belongs to the University Athletic Association, where rivals include Emory and Washington University in St. Louis. Aside from hitting the gridiron or the basketball court, "even the varsity athletes are Phi Beta Kappa (that is, very smart) and involved with university theater," a junior marvels. In fact, athletes here have a higher overall GPA than the student body as a whole. To everyone's surprise, the football team has had a couple of winning seasons. Consistently solid programs include women's basketball and men's and women's tennis, cross-country, soccer, and swimming and diving. Women's lacrosse was recently added to the Maroons roster. When it comes to intramurals, 70 percent of undergraduates compete on their house teams in sports ranging from the traditional (flag football, soccer, and volleyball) to the offbeat (inner-tube water polo, broomball, and archery).

Although T-shirts lovingly mock the university's rigor ("Where Fun Comes to Die"), the University of Chicago has moved well beyond the Spartan attitudes of former president Robert Maynard Hutchins, who led UChicago from 1929 to 1951 and once told members of the football team that was about to be abolished, "When I feel like exercising, I just lie down until the feeling goes away." A major national force for the liberal arts, he also once declared, "My idea of education is to unsettle the minds of the young and inflame their intellects." UChicago undergraduates today are certainly more social and more heavily involved in extracurricular activities than their predecessors, but the university still occupies its distinctive historical academic niche. The prevailing culture remains highly academic, and the university draws strength from its role as a high-powered haven for "Ivy League orphans"—super-bright students who lack the polished nonacademic credentials favored by admissions committees in places like Cambridge and New Haven. Students at UChicago continue to have a different kind of fun.

If You Apply To ›

UChicago: Early decision I and II, early action, regular decision. SATs or ACTs: optional. Subject Tests: optional. Accepts the Common Application with supplement.

University of Cincinnati

P.O. Box 210091, Cincinnati, OH 45221

In most states, UC would be a big enchilada. But with Ohio State two hours up the road and Miami U even closer, Cincinnati has to hustle to get its name out there. A pioneer in co-op education, it offers quality programs in everything from engineering to art—and a competitive men's basketball team to boot.

Many first-time visitors to Cincinnati are surprised to find an attractive and very livable city. As they traverse the city's hilly roads, they are in for another surprise—its university. Not only has the University of Cincinnati made its mark with its extensive research programs, but its signature cooperative education program, first established in 1906, is also the largest of any public college or university in the country.

The compact campus is a mile uphill from Cincinnati's downtown area. Ultramodern buildings rise up next to traditional ivy-covered Georgian halls. A major $233 million university construction project created a "Main Street" in the center of campus and consolidated all student activities. A renovation of the historic Nippert Stadium was recently completed, and students may also take advantage of the $113 million campus recreation center.

Research has been a UC specialty. Campus scientists have given the world anti-knock gasoline, the electronic organ, antihistamines, and the U.S. Weather Bureau. But the university is perhaps best known for cooperative education, which allows students to earn while they learn. More than 40 programs across the Cincinnati curriculum offer the popular five-year professional-practice option, and more than 7,000 co-op placements are made every year. UC has taken steps to improve the quality of undergraduate education by strengthening its general education requirements to focus on critical thinking and expression and by expanding its honors program. Freshmen must take English and math as well as a contemporary issues class;

other requirements vary by college. All students are required to complete a capstone experience as well.

The colleges of engineering; business administration; and design, architecture, art, and planning (the schools with the most co-op students) are the best bets at UC. The university's music conservatory, one of the best programs in the field, also offers electronic media and broadcasting training. The schools of nursing and pharmacy are well known and benefit from UC's health center and graduate medical school. The most popular majors fall under the fields of business administration and marketing, health professions, engineering, and visual and performing arts. Education students earn two bachelor's degrees: one in education and one in a liberal arts subject. Additional initiatives include a culinary arts and science degree program offered jointly with Cincinnati State, and the state's first baccalaureate program in facilities and hospitality management. UC also sponsors a language-immersion house, a freestanding residence where students are required to live, work, study, and play 24/7 in another language. About a quarter of undergrads choose to study abroad or work in international co-ops in nearly 60 countries.

"We are your traditional hardworking college students."

At UC, the academic rigor is largely a function of the major. Fields such as engineering, business, and nursing require a substantially larger academic commitment. "I would say that the most rigorous courses are those that are nontraditional," offers one student, citing "study abroad, capstones, projects with corporate partners, and advanced topics classes." Some courses end up being quite large (in popular design courses, two people to a desk is not unusual); 37 percent of all classes have fewer than 20 students. A third of the faculty members hold outside jobs, bringing fresh, practical experience to the classroom. "Most of my professors are accessible because they offer office hours, however I have run into difficulty from time to time receiving answers to my emails," says one student.

"We are your traditional hardworking college students," says a sophomore of UC's largely homogeneous student body. Eighty-four percent of undergraduates are native Ohioans, and 5 percent come from abroad. African American, Asian American, Hispanic, and multiracial students comprise a mere 7, 4, 3, and 4 percent of the student body, respectively. Diversity, feminist issues, campus construction, and rising tuition are the hot topics on campus. The school offers merit scholarships averaging $4,500 and 176 athletic scholarships for men and women.

Twenty-three percent of UC students live on campus. Many upperclassmen consider off-campus living far better than dorm life, and inexpensive apartments can usually be found. For meals, "Campus has three dining facilities, multiple fast food restaurants in the university center, and a few cafés located in certain buildings," explains a senior. A marketing major adds, "Living in an urban environment means there are extra safety precautions that keep students safe. Never have I felt unsafe on campus."

Merchants have turned the area surrounding UC, called Clifton, into a mini college town with plenty to do. Although not a major metropolis like Chicago or Boston, the "Queen City" of Cincinnati does offer an urban feel. Nine nearby bus lines take undergraduates into the heart of the city in minutes; there, they find museums, ballet, professional sports teams, parks, rivers, hills, and as many large and small shops as anyone could want. On-campus activities include 550 student clubs, with everything from mountaineering to clubs in various majors. Fraternities and sororities attract roughly 15 percent of the men and women, but are still the most active places to party on campus, usually opening

"Living in an urban environment means there are extra safety precautions that keep students safe."

(continued)

Social: ☎ ☎ ☎
Q of L: ★ ★ ★
Admissions: (513) 556-1100
Email Address: admissions@ uc.edu

Strong Programs:
Business Administration
Marketing
Health Professions
Engineering
Visual and Performing Arts
Architecture and Design
Music
Nursing

More than 40 programs offer cooperative education, and more than 7,000 co-op placements are made every year.

Everyone mentions the football rivalry with Miami (of Ohio) as a game you won't want to miss.

their functions to everyone. "There is a party culture present at the university, but it is by no means dominant," says one senior. The university sponsors some events, such as WorldFest and Greek Week. Cleveland and Columbus make for good road trips.

Seventeen Bearcat teams compete in the Division I American Athletic Conference. The men's basketball team is highly competitive, as are football and women's basketball and volleyball. Everyone mentions the football rivalry with Miami (of Ohio) as a game you won't want to miss, and the same holds true when the men's basketball squad takes on Xavier University. Weekend athletes take advantage of UC's first-rate sports center, and more than 50 club sports and 15 intramurals are an option too.

UC offers students a lively social scene, both on campus and minutes away in downtown Cincinnati. But cooperative education is the name of the game at this Ohio school, where the co-op program allows students to take their degrees out for a test drive before graduation and have a head start on their peers after it.

If You Apply To ›

UC: Early action, rolling admissions. SATs or ACTs: required. No Subject Tests. Accepts the Common Application with supplement. Apply to particular program.

Claremont Colleges

In 1925, James A. Blaisdell had the vision to create a group of colleges patterned after Oxford and Cambridge in England—an "Oxford of the Orange Groves," as he elegantly put it. Nearly a century later, the five schools that comprise the Claremont Colleges thrive as a consortium of separate and distinct undergraduate colleges with two adjoining graduate institutions, a theological seminary, and botanical gardens. Like families, the colleges coexist, interact, and experience their share of both cooperation and tension. Ultimately, however, the Claremont Colleges consortium forms a mutually beneficial partnership that offers its students the vast resources and facilities one might only expect to find at a large university.

The colleges are located 35 miles east of Los Angeles on 560 acres in the suburb of Claremont, a peaceful, tree-lined neighborhood at the foot of the San Gabriel Mountains. The picture-perfect California weather has some-times been marred by smog, courtesy of the neighbors in nearby L.A., but the smog level has declined dramatically in the past few years.

Of the five undergraduate colleges that make up the Claremont Colleges—Claremont McKenna, Harvey Mudd, Pitzer, Pomona, and Scripps—Pomona is the largest, with about 1,670 students. Each school retains its own institutional identity, with its own faculty, administration, admissions, and curriculum, although the boundaries of both academic work and extracurricular activities are somewhat flexible. Each of the schools also tends to specialize in a particular area that complements the offerings of all the others. Claremont McKenna, which caters mainly to students planning careers in economics, business, law, or government, has 11 research institutes located on its campus, while Harvey Mudd is a liberal arts college specializing in engineering, science, and math. Pitzer, a classical liberal arts institution and the most socially progressive of the five, excels in environmental and sustainability studies, and at the all-women Scripps, the top majors include the social sciences, biology, and visual and performing arts. The oldest of the five colleges, Pomona ranks as one of the top liberal arts colleges anywhere and is strong across the board.

Collectively, the colleges share many services and facilities, including a student newspaper, a biological field station, a student health center, auditoriums, a 2,500-seat concert hall, a 350-seat theater, bookstores, a main-tenance department, a business office, and a shared campus safety force. The Queer Resource Center, housed at Pomona but serving the whole community, is a model of collaboration between schools, and the recently established EmPOWER Center provides the community with comprehensive support and educational resources on sexual assault, dating and domestic violence, and stalking. The Claremont library system makes 2 million volumes available to all students. Faculties and administrations are free to arrange joint programs or classes between all or just some of the schools. Courses are open to students from the other colleges (approximately 2,000 courses in all), but each college sets limits on the number of classes that can be taken elsewhere. Perhaps the best example of academic cooperation is the team-taught interdisciplinary courses, which are organized by instructors from the different schools and appeal to a mix of different academic interests.

The Claremont Colleges draw large numbers of students from within California, although their national reputation is growing. These days, about half the students hail from other Western and non-Western states, with a sizable contingent from the East Coast. The tone at the Claremont Colleges is decidedly intellectual, and graduate programs in the arts and sciences are more common goals than business or law school. Anyone who is bright and hardworking can find a niche at one of the five schools.

One student describes the town of Claremont as "a wonderful place if you're married or about to die." Indeed, the quiet local community ("the Village") has its share of senior citizens, but it also offers a flavor reminiscent of Ann Arbor (home to the University of Michigan), with quirky boutiques, coffee shops, truly remarkable candy stores, a Sunday farmers market, and eateries ranging from fine dining to diners and specialty bagel shops. There are even ice cream shops that freeze your ice cream with liquid nitrogen before your eyes—and it's all an easy walk or bike ride from any campus. Students report that the endless list of social activities offered at the colleges makes up for anything Claremont might lack. For hot times, Hollywood's glamour and downtown L.A. are within sniffing distance. The availability of shared Zip Cars and a nearby Metro line make these and other locations easy to access. Nearby mountains and the fabled surfing beaches make this collegiate paradise's backyard complete. Mount Baldy ski lifts, for instance, are only 15 miles away, and you'll reach Laguna Beach before the end of your favorite album. For spring break, Mexico is cheap and a great change of pace.

On campus, extracurricular life maintains a balance between cooperation and independence. Claremont McKenna, Harvey Mudd, and Scripps field joint athletic teams, and the men's teams especially are Division III powers, due to the exploits of CMC athletes. Pomona and Pitzer also compete together with particular strength in water polo, track and field, and soccer. Pomona–Pitzer's football rivalry with Occidental College is purported to be the oldest west of the Mississippi. The popular Claremont Colleges Ballroom Dance Company has won multiple national collegiate championships, as has the perennially successful Claremont Colleges Debate Union.

Each of the five colleges has its own dorms, and since off-campus housing is limited in Claremont proper, the social life of students revolves around their dorms. Large five-school parties are regular Thursday, Friday, and Saturday night fare. "In my opinion, Mudd's parties are the best because they always have themes," says a physics major. Claremont McKenna is said to have the most raucous party scene, while Pitzer hosts multiple music festivals throughout the year. There are no fraternities, except for three local ones at Pomona, where joining is far from de rigueur. All cafeterias are open to all students, and most big events—films, concerts, etc.—are advertised throughout each campus. Day-to-day social interaction among students at different schools, be it for meals or dates, is not what it might be. Occasional political squabbles break out between liberal faculty and students at Pitzer and their conservative counterparts at Claremont McKenna. For the most part, students benefit not only from the nurturing and support within their own schools, each of which has its own academic or extracurricular emphasis, but also from the abundant resources that the Claremont Colleges consortium offers as a whole.

Claremont McKenna College

890 Columbia Avenue, Claremont, CA 91711

Make way, Pomona—this up-and-comer is no longer content with being a social sciences specialty school. CMC is half the size of a typical liberal arts college and smaller than Pomona by about 300 students. Most conservative of Claremont schools. CMC continues to develop its national and global reputation, and Californians now make up less than half the student body.

Website: www.cmc.edu

Location: Suburban

Private

Total Enrollment: 1,341

Undergraduates: 1,334

Male/Female: 52/48

SAT Ranges: ERW 660–740, M 680–770

ACT Ranges: 30–34

Financial Aid: 46%

Pell Grant: 12%

Expense: Pr $ $ $ $

Student Loans: 31%

Average Debt: $

Applicants: 6,349

Accepted: 10%

Enrolled: 53%

Grad in 6 Years: 90%

Returning Freshmen: 97%

Academics: ✍ ✍ ✍ ✍ ½

Social: ☎ ☎ ☎

Q of L: ★ ★ ★

Admissions: (909) 621-8088

Email Address: admission@cmc.edu

Strong Programs:

Economics

Government

International Relations

Psychology

History

Environment, Economics, and Politics

Claremont McKenna College's special niche in the Claremont College pantheon is top programs in government, economics, and international relations. In addition, CMC has 11 research institutes located on campus, which offer its undergraduates ample opportunities to study everything from political demographics to the environment. The arts and humanities are also available, but Claremont McKenna is better suited to those with high ambitions in business leadership and public affairs. "CMC provides students with a pragmatic liberal arts education that will prepare them for grad school and a career," a senior says. "It is a great place to spend four years."

The 69-acre campus is mostly "California modern" in its architecture, with lots of Spanish tile roofs and picture windows that look out on the San Gabriel Mountains. Described by one student as "more functional than aesthetic," the physical layout fits right in with the school's practical attitude. Kravis Center is a state-of-the-art academic center that houses classrooms, seminar rooms, a computer laboratory, and faculty offices. Roberts Pavilion serves as an athletic, fitness, and events center.

CMC's extensive general education requirements include two semesters in the humanities; three in the social sciences; one each in the natural sciences and mathematics; and a senior thesis. All first-years take a Freshman Writing Seminar and a Freshman Humanities Seminar. Claremont McKenna offers top programs in economics and government, but the international relations, psychology, and history programs are also considered strong. A few programs combine these strengths into interdisciplinary majors, such as the environment, economics, and politics major. The biology, chemistry, and physics departments are greatly enhanced through the use of Keck Science Center, an outstanding facility providing students with hands-on access to a variety of equipment. In addition, the 85-acre Bernard Biological Field Station is located just north of the CMC campus and is available to students for field work. The college offers a popular 3–2 program in economics and engineering, a four-year B.A./M.A. program, and a 4–1 M.B.A. program in conjunction with the Claremont Graduate University.

> "CMC provides students with a pragmatic liberal arts education."

The academic climate is fairly strenuous at Claremont McKenna, but not overwhelming. "There are very difficult courses that will push you to the brink of your comfort zone in every major," a junior says. Eighty-four percent of classes have fewer than 20 students ("one of the perks of a small college," says a neuroscience major), and professors are praised for their accessibility. "I have met some of the most incredible teachers at CMC who are both brilliant and devoted to their students," an economics major says. All freshmen take part in a five-day orientation program that includes a Welcome Orientation Adventure (WOA!) trip and a reception with the president and department chairs. Thirty-six percent of Claremont McKenna students take advantage of study abroad programs in 56 countries, including Australia, Brazil, Costa Rica, and Japan. CMC also offers active campus exchange programs with Haverford, Colby, Spelman, and Morehouse. Participants in the Washington Semester can intern with the State Department, the White House, and lobbying groups, and a semester-long Silicon Valley internship program places liberal arts students in technology firms. The college provides stipends to low-income and first-generation students in order to allow them to take unpaid internships.

A senior describes CMC students as "career-oriented, ambitious, and serious about their classes." The CMC student body is 39 percent Californian, with many other domestic students coming from the East Coast, and 17 percent of students coming from other countries. Asian Americans comprise 11 percent of the student body, Hispanics 15 percent, African Americans 4 percent, and multiracial students

A semester-long Silicon Valley internship program places liberal arts students in technology firms.

6 percent. Although CMC is the most conservative of the five Claremont schools, one student notes, "There is a good mix of liberals, conservatives, and libertarians," and different viewpoints are welcomed. The school accepts applicants on a need-blind basis and guarantees to meet the demonstrated need of all admitted students. It also awards merit scholarships, averaging $17,000, to a limited number of eligible students.

Ninety-seven percent of CMC students live on campus, "because of the social life," according to one. All the residence halls are co-ed, and Stark Hall, a substance-free dorm, gives students more living options. A cluster of on-campus apartments equipped with kitchen facilities is a popular option for upperclassmen. Dorm food is said to be quite good, and students can eat in dining halls at any of the other four colleges, though the best bet may be CMC's Collins Dining Hall. "They have a large spread with lots of different options," says one student, including vegetarian, vegan, and organic fare. CMC has expanded its staff dedicated to assisting the campus community with issues related to discrimination, harassment, and sexual misconduct.

The college sponsors an outstanding lecture series at the Cook Athenaeum on Monday through Thursday nights each week.

Most students agree that the social life at CMC is more than adequate, thanks to the five-college system. "There are always parties, club events, barbecues, movie screenings, and other events," says a junior. CMC has a reputation for raucous partying, at least in comparison to its other Claremont counterparts, and is said to have something of a "bro culture" around drinking—an atmosphere that appeals to some students but keeps others away. Aside from

"Leadership pervades almost everything that goes on here."

that party scene, Monte Carlo Night is a favorite annual bash, and Club Claremont plans on-campus events as well as outings for everything from surfing and skiing nearby to day trips to Disneyland and L.A. Ponding, another unusual CMC tradition, involves being thrown into one of the two campus fountains on one's birthday. The college sponsors an outstanding lecture series at the Cook Athenaeum (a.k.a. "the Ath") on Monday through Thursday nights each week. Before each lecture, students and faculty can enjoy a gourmet dinner together and engage in intellectual debates. Students also highly recommend road trips to Joshua Tree, Coachella, San Francisco, and Las Vegas.

Division III athletics are an important part of life at Claremont McKenna, and the school has an overstuffed trophy case to prove it. The men's and women's golf and women's volleyball and tennis teams are recent national champions. Other competitive men's teams (the Stags) include basketball, swimming, and track and field; solid women's teams (the Athenas) include swimming, track and field, and soccer. A third of the students play varsity sports, and CMC students tend to dominate the teams jointly fielded with Harvey Mudd and Scripps. Top rivalries include Pomona–Pitzer, both in athletics and academics, one student claims.

CMC has embraced its mission to produce great leaders by providing students with ample opportunities for research and study abroad, as well as top-notch programs in government and economics. "Leadership pervades almost everything that goes on here," says a junior. "Claremont McKenna builds character, fosters a sense of ambition among its students, and drives them to set their sights high."

Overlaps

UC Berkeley, UCLA, Pomona, University of Southern California, Stanford

If You Apply To ›

Claremont McKenna: Early decision I and II, regular decision. SATs or ACTs: required. Subject Tests: optional (required for homeschooled students). Accepts the Common Application with supplement.

Harvey Mudd College

301 Platt Boulevard, Claremont, CA 91711

Renowned for encouraging women to go into engineering and other STEM fields, Harvey Mudd may rank as the finest institution that few people outside of these areas have ever heard of. Future Ph.D.s graduate from here in greater percentages than at any other school in the nation. HMC rivals Caltech for sheer brainpower and tops it in access to outstanding faculty. Offers more exposure to the liberal arts than most science- and technology-oriented schools.

Website: www.hmc.edu
Location: Suburban
Private
Total Enrollment: 844
Undergraduates: 844
Male/Female: 52/48
SAT Ranges: ERW 720–770, M 750–800
ACT Ranges: 33–35
Financial Aid: 73%
Pell Grant: 14%
Expense: Pr $ $ $ $
Student Loans: 49%
Average Debt: $ $
Applicants: 4,078
Accepted: 15%
Enrolled: 36%
Grad in 6 Years: 96%
Returning Freshmen: 98%
Academics: ✎ ✎ ✎ ✎ ½
Social: ☎ ☎ ☎
Q of L: ★ ★ ★
Admissions: (909) 621-8011
Email Address: admission@hmc.edu

Strong Programs:
Engineering
Computer Science
Physics
Mathematics
Chemistry

A top-ranked liberal arts college with a technical bent, Harvey Mudd College strives to give its students a sense of academic balance. Although it's a leading provider of high-quality programs in science and engineering (Where else can you take an introductory engineering class where you build your own underwater robot?), it also emphasizes a well-rounded education with knowledge in the humanities. "We're characterized as the nerd school of the five Claremonts because the classes are hardest and, yes, we talk about science and math over dinner sometimes," says a junior. Another student adds, "The incredibly intense workload becomes manageable because all of my classmates are happy to help. We will stay up for each other into the wee hours of the morning to make sure that we're all finished with our homework."

HMC's mid-'50s vintage campus of cinder-block buildings even "looks like an engineering college; it's very symmetrical and there's no romance." In addition, the buildings have little splotches all over their surfaces that students have dubbed "warts"—not a very attractive picture. As part of a massive building campaign, however, the college recently completed a 131-bed residence hall and the Shanahan Center for Teaching and Learning, which features technology-rich classrooms, a 300-seat auditorium, and an art gallery.

While most STEM-oriented schools tend to have a narrow focus, HMC has come up with the novel idea that even scientists and engineers "need to know and appreciate poetry, philosophy, and non-Western thought," says an administrator. The extensive Common Core includes coursework in mathematics; physics, chemistry, and biology (each with an associated laboratory); computer science and engineering; college writing (taught by faculty from all departments); and humanities, social sciences, and the arts. Students report that classes are formidable, and the heavy workload is a common complaint. Concerned that the core curriculum has indeed become too onerous and even "soul crushing," the administration has taken steps to relieve student stress without sacrificing rigor, including setting up a multidisciplinary care team to help students struggling with academic or personal issues. "There is a huge focus on getting help if you need it," says a chemistry major. The faculty has also set a goal for the Common Core of nurturing "the joy of learning." The small class sizes and absence of graduate programs means that undergraduates get uncommon amounts of attention, even from top faculty. A physics major says, "Instruction here is excellent, and professors have a really wonderful open-door policy," in addition to regular office hours.

> **"There is a huge focus on getting help if you need it."**

Of the ten on-campus majors, engineering ranks as the most popular by enrollment, followed by computer science, physics, mathematics, and chemistry. HMC has one of the nation's top computer science programs and an award-winning math department, and a combined major in computer science and mathematics is also very popular. Students rave about the Clinic Program, which plops real-life math, science, and engineering tasks (sponsored by major corporations and government agencies to the tune of more than $40,000 per project) into the laps of students. Recent sponsors have included Elon Musk's SpaceX, as well as Pixar, Amazon, and Yelp. All students must either participate in the Clinic Program or complete original thesis-driven research in order to graduate. About 200 students stay on campus in the summer for 10-week research experiences, and a sophomore says, "In research positions, students are working one-on-one with the professors—they aren't washing beakers." Sixteen percent of students pack their bags each year for study abroad programs in more than 20 countries.

The Clinic Program plops real-life STEM tasks into the laps of students; recent sponsors include SpaceX, Pixar, Amazon, and Yelp.

Not surprisingly, these budding technology leaders are also top achievers. "We love to learn, and we love to have fun," says a sophomore. "We take pride in the esoteric and the weird." For a technically oriented school, Mudd boasts a relatively high proportion of female students, at 48 percent, and it is also one of the few colleges strong in engineering and science that has a female president. Forty-three percent of the students are homegrown Californians, and 10 percent are international. African Americans represent 4 percent of the student body, Hispanics 18 percent, Asian Americans 17 percent, and multiracial students 11 percent. A senior notes that while students are often too "wrapped up in schoolwork" to get involved in social and political issues, student groups like FEM Union (Female Empowerment at Mudd) and BLAM (Black Lives and Allies at Mudd) "have created spaces for discussions about issues of diversity and privilege." Merit scholarships averaging $12,700 help some with the hefty tuition bill, but as a Division III college, Mudd offers no athletic scholarships. It does, however, honor policies of need-blind admissions and covering 100 percent of students' demonstrated need with its financial aid packages.

"We take pride in the esoteric and the weird."

Ninety-eight percent of undergrads live on campus, and students speak of a strong "dorm culture" on campus. "Each dorm has a proctor (think: the 'mom' or 'dad' of the dorm, usually a senior) as well as several mentors (the 'older siblings' of the dorm, who are mostly there for freshmen)," explains a computer science major. "The proctor-mentor team helps keep the dorm community strong and safe." Mudd's dining options are said to be decent, and students appreciate their access to dining facilities at the other Claremont Colleges, which vastly expands their options.

Engineering pranks are popular but must be reversible within 24 hours, as established by the honor code.

Despite their heavy workload, most HMC students find abundant social outlets, even if it's just joining the parade of unicycles that has overrun the campus—not to mention skateboards, longboards, scooters, and rollers attached to shoes. Dorms host parties almost every weekend, a favorite being the Wild Wild West party, "where we fill a dorm courtyard with peanut shells and get a mechanical bull," says a physics major. Students describe the party scene as a pressure-free one where classmates look out for each other. While students do frequent the other Claremont campuses to socialize, it's Mudd's many traditions that really get them going. At the end of each semester, Noisy Minutes provide breaks from long hours of studying with loud music, snacks, and activities like a bouncy ball drop, non-Newtonian fluid racing, and battle tie-dye. Engineering pranks are popular and there are "several traditional pranks throughout the year," according to a junior, but they must be reversible within 24 hours, as established by the honor code.

"The proctor-mentor team helps keep the dorm community strong and safe."

Mudd fields varsity sports teams together with Claremont McKenna and Scripps, and the teams do extremely well. Recent national champions include men's and women's golf, women's volleyball, and women's tennis. Intramurals, also in conjunction with Claremont McKenna and Scripps, are even more popular. King among these is inner-tube water polo, which draws huge cheering crowds and, most importantly, removes the most difficult aspect of the sport—treading water.

HMC is right on the heels of Caltech as the best technically oriented school in the West. The college offers a gem of a technical education blended with a worthwhile amount of humanities and social sciences, and the administration seems serious about addressing the common student refrain that the heavy workload comes at the expense of time to reflect on what they are learning. HMC offers a welcoming attitude toward women and other groups traditionally underrepresented in STEM fields. As one student asserts, "Mudd is the college for students to be challenged like they never have been before and have the support to go through it."

If You Apply To ›

Harvey Mudd: Early decision I and II, regular decision. SATs or ACTs: required. Subject Tests: required (Math II and one other). Accepts the Common Application with supplement.

Pitzer College

1050 North Mills Avenue, Claremont, CA 91711

Offers a haven for the otherwise-minded without the hard edge of nonconformity at places like Bard and Evergreen. Traditional strengths lie in the social and behavioral sciences. Far more selective than it was 15 years ago. A national leader in turning out Fulbright Scholars.

As the most laid-back of the Claremont Colleges, Pitzer College offers students a creative milieu, abundant opportunities for intellectual exploration, and a sense of fierce individualism. Founded in 1963, this small liberal arts and sciences school has changed with the times but continues to emphasize progressive thought, social responsibility, environmental sustainability, and open social attitude. In the last 25 years, Pitzer students and alumni have been awarded more than 240 Fulbright fellowships, and the school continues to attract top talent from around the world.

Even Pitzer's campus is, well, different. The classroom buildings are modernistic octagons, and the grass-covered "mounds" that distinguish the grounds "are perfect for sunbathing and Frisbee," says one student, and for lounging in Adirondack chairs beneath the palm trees. Drought-tolerant landscaping pervades the campus,

> "Pitzer people are genuinely socially conscious and academically adventurous."

and there is an organic garden. One interesting campus curiosity is the Grove House, a California craftsman-style house students saved from the wrecking ball decades ago and moved to campus. It houses a dining room, study areas, and art exhibits. Additional facilities include several LEED-certified residence halls, Benson Auditorium, and the recently renovated Gold Student Health and Wellness Center.

In keeping with Pitzer's philosophy of student autonomy, each student has the maximum freedom to choose which classes to take. Instead of traditional academic departments, Pitzer has "field groups," which, as a political studies and Spanish double major explains, "allow for students to major in one subject area, yet receive a holistic education." All students take a sequence of courses on social justice, and a lively freshman seminar program sharpens students' learning skills, especially writing. Students select from more than 40 majors, and they're also encouraged to design their own. Almost anything in the social and behavioral sciences is a sure bet, especially psychology. Environmental analysis, political studies, media studies, biology, organizational studies, and economics are other strong and popular programs. Pitzer is the first college in the country to offer a program in secular studies, with courses such as God, Darwin, and Design in America. Most courses in Pitzer's weaker areas can be picked up at one of the other Claremont schools; on average, Pitzer students take 30 percent of their courses at the other colleges.

The academic climate is "relaxed, interdisciplinary, collaborative, and very discussion-based," according to a sociology major. Class size is generally small, with 71 percent of classes enrolling fewer than 20 students, which promotes close interaction between students and faculty. "The professors I have had are very down-to-earth and incredibly knowledgeable in their fields," says a sociology and gender/feminist studies major. Students play a large role in Pitzer's community government and sit on all policy committees, including those on curriculum and faculty promotion. The environment is a big focus here, and the college boasts the Robert Redford Conservancy for Southern California Sustainability. Pitzer's Firestone Center for Restoration Ecology in Costa Rica is home to programs in science, language, and international studies and provides opportunities for research. Pitzer also runs its own study abroad programs in Botswana, Brazil, Ecuador, Italy, Nepal, and Vietnam and offers students access to 48 exchange programs; in all, 54 percent of Pitzer students go abroad.

Individualism is a prized characteristic among Pitzer students, but one junior says the oft-bandied "hippie" label is unfair: "Pitzer people are genuinely socially conscious and academically adventurous, but do go on to good jobs." Forty-five percent of students are from California, and 9 percent are from foreign nations. Many come from wealthy backgrounds. African Americans comprise 6 percent of the student body, Hispanics 15 percent, Asian Americans 10 percent, and multiracial students 7 percent. Students cite "racism on campus, labor rights, immigration reform, environmental issues, and police brutality" as hot-button social and

"The food is awesome: locally sourced, excellent variety, easy to be vegetarian."

political issues. All financial aid at Pitzer is need-based, and the school is committed to meeting 100 percent of enrolled students' demonstrated need, but it is not need-blind in its admissions.

Seventy-two percent of students live on campus and many find themselves in the new, environmentally friendly dorms; the remainder hang their hats in "old but spacious" rooms. Boarders can choose from a variety of meal plans, and the food gets rave reviews, especially the fresh salad, sandwich, and fruit juice bars in the main dining hall. "The food is awesome: locally sourced, excellent variety, easy to be vegetarian," says a senior. Students say the Pitzer Advocates for Survivors of Sexual Assault student group has been a helpful campus resource.

As for the social scene, "Most students stay on campus to attend events or go to parties," says a senior. Pitzer has no Greek organizations, nor does it want any, and social life tends to be fairly low-key. Kohoutek, an alternative music festival, is the big annual event, featuring bands, food, and a "whole week of hoopla"; there is a rockabilly festival as well. "There is very heavy alcohol and weed usage on campus," says a junior. All parties that serve alcohol must be registered. As much as students enjoy the campus scene, some warn that without a car, things can get claustrophobic.

The Pomona–Pitzer football team has had winning seasons, and the school fields a variety of competitive Sagehens teams within the Southern California

(continued)

Email Address: admission@ pitzer.edu

Strong Programs:
Psychology
Environmental Analysis
Political Studies
Media Studies
Biology
Organizational Studies
Economics
Secular Studies

Pitzer's Firestone Center for Restoration Ecology in Costa Rica is home to programs in science, language, and international studies.

The annual Humans vs. Zombies game is hugely popular, drawing 500 participants across campus.

Intercollegiate Athletic Conference. Men's and women's water polo are recent conference champions, and men's and women's track and field are also strong, along with women's tennis and soccer. Intramurals and club sports thrive, and the annual Humans vs. Zombies game is hugely popular, drawing 500 participants across campus.

Pitzer College attracts open-minded students looking for the freedom to go their own ways. "Pitzer people are really caring and often fight for what they believe in. It is a really loving place," muses one student, "a place that values the silly and the weird parts of yourself."

If You Apply To ›

Pitzer: Early decision I and II, regular decision. SATs or ACTs: optional (required for homeschooled students and applicants to seven-year joint medical program). Subject Tests: optional. Accepts the Common Application with supplement. Application includes optional question on gender identity.

Pomona College

333 North College Way, Claremont, CA 91711

The finest liberal arts college in the West, and one of the few that Easterners will travel west to attend. Offers twice the resources of stand-alone competitors with access to the other Claremonts. A haven for the otherwise-minded, though not to the same extent as nonconformist neighbor Pitzer. Strong across the academic spectrum.

Website: www.pomona.edu
Location: Suburban
Private
Total Enrollment: 1,672
Undergraduates: 1,672
Male/Female: 50/50
SAT Ranges: ERW 690–760, M 680–770
ACT Ranges: 30–34
Financial Aid: 56%
Pell Grant: 18%
Expense: Pr $ $ $
Student Loans: 31%
Average Debt: $
Applicants: 9,045
Accepted: 8%
Enrolled: 55%
Grad in 6 Years: 97%
Returning Freshmen: 98%
Academics: ✑ ✑ ✑ ✑ ✑
Social: ☎ ☎ ☎
Q of L: ★ ★ ★ ★
Admissions: (909) 621-8134

Pomona College, located just 35 miles east of the glitz and glamour of Hollywood, is the undisputed star of the Claremont Colleges and one of the top small liberal arts colleges anywhere. This small, elite institution is the top liberal arts college in the West. But the school's prestigious reputation doesn't go to the heads of Pomona's friendly students. "Students here are very open about different types of people—Pomona prides itself on its diverse community," chirps one Sagehen (the school's mascot).

The architecture is variously described as Spanish Mediterranean, pseudo-Italian, or, as a sophomore puts it, "a perfect mix of Northeastern Ivy and Southern California modern." One certainly notices more than one stucco building topped with a red tile roof on campus, as well as eucalyptus trees, canyon live oaks, and an occasional "secretive courtyard lined with flowers." The numerous open courtyards and gardens are popular study spots. By virtue of its location and beauty, Pomona's campus has served as the quintessential collegiate milieu in various Hollywood movies. Recent campus projects include Andrew Science Hall, which features a host of cutting-edge spaces and equipment, including a digital planetarium, and the new Pomona College Museum of Art, expected to open in 2020.

> "We provide a great deal of support in acclimating students to a college environment."

In order to graduate, students must take at least one course in each of six Breadth of Study areas: criticism, analysis, and contextual study of works of the human imagination; social institutions and human behavior; history, values, ethics, and cultural studies; physical and biological sciences; mathematical and formal reasoning; and creation and performance of works of art and literature. The required Critical Inquiry seminar emphasizes thoughtful reading, logical reasoning, and graceful writing; students choose from more than two dozen offerings, with subjects such as Adventures with Russian Books and Statistics in the Real World. Students must also complete a senior exercise in their final year. A five-day freshman orientation program divides the new arrivals into groups of six to 12 students headed by a sophomore. "We provide a great deal of support in acclimating students to a college environment," says a senior. Economics, mathematics, computer science, neuroscience, and biology are the most popular majors.

"Although classes can be difficult, students help each other out, and the classroom environment is an enjoyable one," offers one economics major. Students often form study groups in an effort to help one another through the demanding curriculum. One undergrad estimates the average student spends 20 to 30 hours a week studying outside the classroom. Classes are small—71 percent have fewer than 20 students—and the faculty makes a point of being accessible. An ever-popular take-a-professor-to-lunch program gives students free meals when they arrive with a faculty member in tow. Better still, "We do not have graduate students or TAs teaching class," says a senior.

Educational enrichment opportunities abound at Pomona. Students can spend a semester at Colby or Swarthmore, pursue a 3–2 engineering plan with the California Institute of Technology, or spend a semester in Washington, D.C., working for a congressperson. Roughly half of the students take advantage of 61 study abroad programs offered in 35 countries. More than half of the students also conduct research mentored by a faculty member, and the Summer Undergraduate Research Program provides funding to more than 200 students to pursue such opportunities each summer. Pomona boasts the highest four-year graduation rate of any private university—92 percent.

Pomona students "tend to be high-achieving, confident, verbal students with a fairly liberal political ideology," says a senior. "Students are laid-back in a very Southern California kind of way," adds another. Twenty-seven percent are Californians, and a growing number venture from the East Coast; 11 percent come from abroad. Nine percent are African American, 16 percent are Hispanic, 15 percent are Asian American, and 7 percent are multiracial. There is a healthy mix of liberals and conservatives on campus, though the leftists, especially the feminist wing, are much more vocal. The student government is active, and the administration is credited with respecting students' opinions. One interesting way students voice their concerns is by painting the Walker Wall. Anyone is allowed to paint any message they want on the wall, and the school will even provide groups with the paint. Pomona is need-blind in admissions and meets the full demonstrated financial need of all those who attend. Although there are no merit or athletic awards, the college has replaced loans with grants in an effort to reduce the debt burden for families. The college also participates in the QuestBridge and Posse programs.

Virtually all Pomona students (98 percent) live on campus all four years. The dorms are co-ed, student-governed, and divided into two distinct groups. Those on South campus are family-like and fairly quiet, offer spacious rooms, and house freshmen and sophomores, while those on the North end have smaller rooms with a livelier social scene and house juniors and seniors. "Pomona's dorms are like palaces," says a student. The two newest residence halls, Dialynas and Sontag, are LEED Platinum and feature suite-style apartments for upperclassmen. Oldenborg Center is a language dorm with wings for speakers of Mandarin Chinese, French, German, Japanese, Spanish, and Russian, and Pomona also has established language tables at lunch. Boarders must buy at least partial meal plans. The food is good, with seafood certified by the Marine Stewardship Council, humanely raised beef and cage-free

(continued)

Email Address: admissions@ pomona.edu

Strong Programs:
Economics
Mathematics
Computer Science
Neuroscience
Biology

Offerings for the required Critical Inquiry seminar include subjects such as Adventures with Russian Books and Statistics in the Real World.

"Students are laid-back in a very Southern California kind of way."

Pomona boasts the highest four-year graduation rate of any private university—92 percent.

eggs, and ice cream for dessert every day. Students generally feel safe on campus. "The worst that usually happens are bike thefts," says a junior.

Social life begins in the dorms, where barbecues, parties, and study breaks are organized. There are movies several nights a week, and students also enjoy just tossing a Frisbee on the lawn. One student wanted to be sure that incoming freshmen and transfers knew of the Coop's (student union) "best milkshakes west of the Mississippi," pool tables, and large-screen TV and gaming system. Students often spend Friday afternoons relaxing with friends over a brew at the Greek Theater. Pomona is unique among the Claremont Colleges in that it has three nonnational fraternities (two co-ed; there are no sororities). As for booze, "I haven't noticed any pressure to drink here," reports one student, but "alcohol is definitely present in the social scene."

"I appreciate the diversity and depth that the five-college community brings to the social life," says a student. "You are guaranteed to meet new and interesting people whenever you step off campus." Five-college parties happen nearly every weekend. During midterms and finals, however, the campus is a "social ghost town."

> **"You are guaranteed to meet new and interesting people whenever you step off campus."**

Harwood dorm throws the five-college costume party every Halloween. Freshman orientation gets interesting too. "First-years have to run through the gates of Pomona with blue and white carnations while upperclassmen throw water balloons and shoot water at them," says a student. It helps to have a set of wheels here because "it's virtually impossible to get around in Southern California without a car," according to one student. Every February or March, hundreds of students spend the morning at a nearby ski resort, then head to a local beach to swim, and end the day with an oceanside cookout.

There once was a time when the Pomona Sagehens were an athletic powerhouse; the football team even knocked off mighty USC on Thanksgiving Day back in 1899. Currently, men's and women's water polo and track and field are strong programs, as are women's soccer and tennis. Intense rivalry exists between the Claremont Colleges; basketball games between Pomona–Pitzer and CMS (Claremont–Mudd–Scripps) are "particularly heated." Pomona–Pitzer enjoys a lively rivalry with Occidental College as well. Intramurals, including hotly contested inner-tube water polo matches, attract many participants, and Pomona's $14 million athletic complex makes its facilities the best of the Claremonts.

"Pomona offers a unique and desirable juxtaposition of rigorous academics and a comfortable social atmosphere," says a student. The strongest link in an extremely attractive chain, Pomona continues to symbolize the rising status of the Claremont Colleges—and the West in general—in the world of higher education. There are few regrets about coming to Pomona. Says a senior, "We're in California. The sun is always shining. What's the problem?"

Overlaps

Brown, Stanford, UC Berkeley, Williams, Yale, Pitzer, Harvard, Dartmouth

If You Apply To ›

Pomona: Early decision I and II, regular decision. SATs or ACTs: required. Subject Tests: optional. Accepts the Common Application with supplement.

Scripps College

1030 Columbia Avenue, Claremont, CA 91711

Scripps is easily the premier women's college on the West Coast, offering a commitment to women's education while interacting with co-ed institutions that are literally next door. Attracts more well-rounded women than either Pomona or Pitzer. Innovative Core Curriculum takes an interdisciplinary approach to learning.

Scripps College offers the best of both worlds—a close-knit women's college, where traditions include weekly tea and fresh-baked cookies, and the size and scope of a major research institution, thanks to its membership in the Claremont Colleges. Founded in 1926 by newspaper publisher Ellen Browning Scripps, the college continues to pursue her mission: "To educate women by developing their intellects and talents through active participation in a community of scholars." Students tend to be outgoing, articulate, and serious about their studies, though they still know how to have fun.

Scripps's scenic 30-acre campus, listed on the National Register of Historic Places, offers a tranquil, safe, and comfortable environment. The architecture is Spanish and Mediterranean, with tiled roofs and elegant landscaping. A performing arts center provides permanent space for the Claremont Concert Orchestra and Concert Choir. In addition to a 700-seat theater, the center offers a music library, recital hall, practice rooms, faculty offices, and classrooms. The Lincoln Ceramic Art Building offers more than 5,000 square feet of work area and kiln yards.

The required Core Curriculum in Interdisciplinary Humanities is a sequence of three courses focusing on ideas about the world and the methods used to generate them. In addition to the Core, everyone takes courses in fine arts, letters, natural sciences, and social sciences—one of these classes must focus on gender and women's studies and one must cover race and ethnic studies. All students also complete a senior thesis or project. First-year students are assigned to Peer Mentor Teams, consisting of six to eight classmates and an older peer mentor, to help ease the transition to college. Mentoring programs specifically for Jewish, Asian American, African American, Latina, international, and LGBTQ students are also available.

> "The students here are diligent, thoughtful, and really down-to-earth."

Popular and well-regarded majors at Scripps include social sciences, biological/life sciences, psychology, and visual and performing arts. The Sheets Art Center offers a state-of-the-art studio and freestanding museum-quality gallery for aspiring painters and sculptors. Premeds benefit from the Keck Science Center, a joint facility for students at Scripps, Claremont McKenna, and Pitzer. Programs in area and ethnic studies, such as Middle East and North Africa studies and Chicanx/Latinx studies, are strong, and the feminist, gender, and sexuality studies major is also popular. The Scripps Humanities Institute offers seminars and lectures open to the general public, along with fellowships for juniors; recently, the institute explored immigration policy and nationalism in the U.S. and abroad. The Scripps Presents event series also brings prominent writers, performers, visual artists, and activists to campus for public lectures as well as student-only discussions and workshops. Scripps students can also take coursework at the other Claremont Colleges.

The academic experience at Scripps emphasizes cooperation. "Scripps is a very supportive community," a junior says. "It is a place where professors encourage you to work in groups because more brains [are] always better." Eighty percent of classes have fewer than 20 students. "My professors are always up for a discussion, always willing to answer questions (even difficult ones), and always up to chat about how

Website: www.scrippscollege.edu
Location: Suburban
Private
Total Enrollment: 1,072
Undergraduates: 1,056
Male/Female: 0/100
SAT Ranges: ERW 660–730, M 630–730
ACT Ranges: 29–33
Financial Aid: 72%
Pell Grant: 12%
Expense: Pr $ $ $ $
Student Loans: 41%
Average Debt: $
Applicants: 2,841
Accepted: 33%
Enrolled: 35%
Grad in 6 Years: 88%
Returning Freshmen: 92%
Academics: ✍ ✍ ✍ ½
Social: ☎ ☎ ☎
Q of L: ★ ★ ★ ★
Admissions: (909) 621-8149
Email Address: admission@scrippscollege.edu

Strong Programs:
Social Sciences
Biological/Life Sciences
Psychology
Visual and Performing Arts
Area and Ethnic Studies
Feminist, Gender, and Sexuality Studies

their day is going," says one student. When they're ready to branch out, typically in the junior year, more than 60 percent of Scripps students study abroad, choosing from more than 120 program options in 47 countries.

Forty-four percent of Scripps women are from California, and 5 percent come from other countries. African Americans account for 4 percent of the student body, Hispanics 13 percent, Asian Americans 16 percent, and multiracial students 4 percent. "The students here are diligent, thoughtful, and really down-to-earth," observes one politics major. "They are usually privileged and have had the opportunity to have really impressive experiences." SCORE, the Scripps Communities of Resources and Empowerment, provides support and funding to student organizations that promote inclusion and social justice. Scripps meets 100 percent of admitted students' demonstrated financial need and has made more grant money available for students with the most need. The college also awards merit scholarships averaging $16,700 to top achievers, although there are no athletic scholarships.

Virtually all of Scripps students live in one of the 10 "spectacular" dorms, where options include singles, suites, and apartment-style living arrangements. A student

"Don't get me started about the hot cookies!"

says, "The dorms are gorgeous. They are well maintained and have lots of charm with French doors, balconies, or the occasional fireplace." Freshmen live in the same halls as sophomores, juniors, and seniors. The dining hall garners rave reviews as well: "The salad bar is gourmet, the bread comes from a local bakery, and the pizza is made in a wood-fired brick oven," cheers a bioethics major. "Don't get me started about the hot cookies!"

Social life at Scripps centers on the residence halls, which take turns throwing parties. "Our social life is very much based on campus," explains a chemistry major. "With five undergraduate colleges literally across the street from each other, it is challenging not to have something to do—from movie screenings, art exhibits, concerts, special events like a carnival or the International Festival, and parties." Alcohol doesn't play a major role in Scripps social life, but the school does have a medical amnesty policy for underage students in need of emergency medical assistance. Traditions are important here, including the Matriculation Ceremony at the start of each year, and the signing of the "graffiti wall" by each class before graduation. For students with cars, popular road trips include Pasadena, Mount Baldy, San Diego, and even Las Vegas and Mexico; students without wheels can hop on the MetroLink commuter train to get to and from Los Angeles.

Athletic rivalries aren't the focus here, but Scripps does field joint teams with Claremont McKenna and Harvey Mudd, and when those teams face off against Pomona and Pitzer, students pay attention. All of the Stag (men's) and Athena (women's) teams compete in Division III, and of the women's teams, golf, volleyball, and tennis are especially strong. Intramural and club sports are also played jointly, and popular options include inner-tube water polo, soccer, flag football, and volleyball.

Scripps offers a winning combination of outstanding academics and personal attention, with a cooperative, nonthreatening feel. Scripps students want to achieve great things, but not if that requires stepping on their classmates' toes. And should the women-only environment begin to feel claustrophobic, the other Claremont Colleges beckon, with parties, intramural sports, and cross-registration privileges for a comprehensive college experience.

Overlaps

Pomona, UC Berkeley, UCLA, University of Southern California, Wellesley

If You Apply To ›

Scripps: Early decision I and II, regular decision. SATs or ACTs: required. No Subject Tests. Accepts the Common Application.

Clark University

950 Main Street, Worcester, MA 01610-1477

Clark has a distinguished history that dates to the late 19th century, and had it been established an hour to the east, it probably would have become a household name. Worcester is not Boston, but Clarkies bring a sense of mission to their relationship with this historic industrial town. Clark is liberal, tolerant, and world-renowned in psychology and geography. Has a less national student body than institutions of comparable quality.

Clark University started in 1887 as an all-graduate school on a German model, excelling in disciplines including psychology and geography, and today welcomes undergraduates of all backgrounds and interests with small classes and no shortage of faculty attention. Clark's Liberal Education and Effective Practice (LEEP) educational model is designed to prepare students for success after college by combining a liberal arts curriculum with "intensive world, workplace, and personal experiences." As a junior explains, "LEEP serves to push students to bring their college education into the real world."

Clark's compact, 50-acre campus has "enough ivy, tall maples, and collegiate brick buildings to make a traditionalist happy," even though it's located in the rather gritty Main South section of Worcester. Buildings range from remodeled Victorian-era residences—former homes of prosperous merchants—to the award-winning Robert Hutchings Goddard Library. Careful restoration has brought a renewed sense of history to the area. Clark is the only American university where famed psychoanalyst Sigmund Freud lectured, and his statue adorns the center of campus. The four-story Shaich Family Alumni and Student Engagement Center is home to the LEEP Center and a venue for special lectures and other events.

> "If you're lagging or unengaged, it will be noticeable."

While Clark now serves primarily undergraduates, its history of graduate education is evident in its classrooms. Most courses are seminars and 58 percent have fewer than 20 students. First-Year Intensives, required of all students, are limited to a small number of students (usually no more than 16) to help introduce them to the intellectual, social, and emotional growth they will experience in college. In most cases, the faculty member teaching the course acts as an academic advisor until students declare a major.

Clark's Program of Liberal Studies promotes the habits, skills, and perspectives essential to lifelong learning. In addition to fulfilling requirements for their major, each student must complete eight courses: one in verbal expression, one in formal analysis, and six in perspectives—aesthetic, global comparative, historical, language, scientific, and values. One class must also satisfy a diversity and inclusion requirement.

> "Clarkies show up for each other."

Many of Clark's course offerings are practice-based, tying in hands-on experiences outside the classroom. Before graduating, all students must also complete a LEEP Culminating Capstone demonstrating the knowledge and capabilities they have honed during their four years.

Clark's historically strong psychology and geography departments continue to burnish their national reputations, the latter having churned out more Ph.D.s in the field than any other school in the nation, plus five members of the National Academy of Sciences (the most of any geography program). Clark is the birthplace of the American Psychological Association and the concept of adolescence as being

Website: www.clarku.edu
Location: Small City
Private
Total Enrollment: 2,941
Undergraduates: 2,187
Male/Female: 39/61
SAT Ranges: ERW 600–700, M 580–680
ACT Ranges: 27–31
Financial Aid: 90%
Pell Grant: 18%
Expense: Pr $ $
Student Loans: 64%
Average Debt: $ $ $ $
Applicants: 8,355
Accepted: 56%
Enrolled: 13%
Grad in 6 Years: 75%
Returning Freshmen: 86%
Academics: ✑ ✑ ✑ ✑
Social: ☎ ☎ ☎
Q of L: ★ ★ ★
Admissions: (508) 793-7431
Email Address: admissions@clarku.edu

Strong Programs:
Psychology
Geography
International Development and Social Change
Environmental Science
Management
Political Science
Biology
Economics

distinct from childhood. International development and social change is another traditional strength, as is environmental science, and the most popular majors include psychology, management, political science, biology, and economics. About a quarter of graduating seniors take advantage of an accelerated B.A./M.A. program that allows them to take a fifth year tuition-free to obtain a master's degree, providing they meet the requirements.

Many of Clark's course offerings are practice-based, tying in hands-on experiences outside the classroom.

While courses at Clark are challenging, students say the small class sizes mean that collaboration is the norm and professors expect regular participation. "If you're lagging or unengaged, it will be noticeable," says a media, culture, and the arts student. "But the atmosphere is supportive; classmates want to see each other succeed, and professors are invested in your progress as well." About a third of Clark students spend at least one semester studying abroad, usually during their junior year, at one of more than 50 programs in 30 countries. Sixty-four percent of students participate in undergraduate research, often assisting with faculty projects or pursuing their own as an independent study.

At Clark, a junior says, "Everyone is really supportive of each other's interests and ready to get involved whenever possible. Clarkies show up for each other." Thirty-two percent of Clark students hail from Massachusetts, and international students from about 65 countries make up another 14 percent. African Americans account for 4 percent of the student body, Hispanics 8 percent, Asian Americans 8 percent, and multiracial students 2 percent. The political climate on campus is decidedly liberal, and a psychology and management major comments that "it is difficult to foster debate" because "most people agree with each other to begin with." Merit-based scholarships average $19,000, but athletic scholarships are not available. The Presidential LEEP Scholarship, awarded to highly motivated students with exceptional academic records, includes full tuition, room, and board for four years.

Clark is the birthplace of the American Psychological Association.

First-year students and sophomores at Clark are required to live in the residence halls. In all, 67 percent of the student body live on campus in accommodations that are described as clean, comfortable, and "surprisingly big." Some upperclassmen looking to save money find apartments and group houses nearby. In addition to accommodating various dietary needs, a senior says, "Dining services are super communicative about the food and are always trying to offer fresh, healthy, and fun options." The school's urban location means that students must be "a little more open-minded and realistic about living in a city," says an environmental science major, but students agree that the campus feels safe.

"Main South Worcester… [has] flavor and spice, and you'll either love it or hate it."

Clark has no Greek life, but more than 130 student-run organizations offer endless concerts, improv and theater shows, games, and other programs. Most students get involved with multiple clubs, and a junior explains, "Your weekend often ends up being a combination of activities that you're involved in and going to events put on by your friends." First-year dorms are dry, but alcohol may be consumed in other dorms by those who are of age, and students say that alcohol policies emphasize safety over punishment. Coping with the frigid New England winters includes quaffing cups of hot chocolate and dreaming about Spree Day, when classes are canceled and students enjoy live music, food trucks, face-painting, rock-climbing walls, mechanical bulls, and other festivities. And according to a geography major, "The newest tradition is Elephant Thursday," in which, every Thursday, a student donning an elephant hat spreads cheer by giving "elephant tickets" to anyone wearing gray; students then redeem their tickets at the end of the year for an elephant-themed prize. "Why, you might ask? No one knows, but it is truly magical."

Coping with the frigid New England winters includes quaffing cups of hot chocolate and dreaming about Spree Day.

Worcester and the vicinity host 12 colleges, and Worcester itself is described as "a city of hidden gems," according to one student, offering movie theaters, restaurants with every conceivable type of cuisine, small clubs with live music, and the DCU Center, a 13,000-seat arena. "Main South Worcester is not the prettiest, quietest locale for a college, but it's got flavor and spice, and you'll either love it or hate it," a biology major says. Students mix with neighborhood residents through extensive volunteer programs coordinated by the Community Engagement Office. To get away, Clarkies head to Boston and Providence (both about an hour away), New York (three hours), or the rural wilds of Vermont, New Hampshire, and Maine.

The Clark Cougars compete in the Division III New England Women's and Men's Athletic Conference (NEWMAC), and the university fields 18 intercollegiate teams. Solid teams include men's lacrosse, baseball, and soccer and women's basketball, volleyball, and rowing. About half of the students participate in intramural and club sports, the most popular of which are Quidditch, ultimate Frisbee, soccer, and basketball.

Like Johns Hopkins and Catholic University, Clark started out serving only graduate students but now offers a dynamic, undergraduate-focused educational environment. Clark continues to challenge convention, pioneering new teaching methods, pursuing new fields of knowledge, and finding new ways to connect thinking and doing. Through all this, community has remained a constant. Says a junior, "Clark is a warm and accepting place with students who hold the door open for others for just a little too long."

> ## Overlaps
>
> **Macalester, Wesleyan, Skidmore, Union, Oberlin, UMass Amherst, American University, UConn**

If You Apply To ›

Clark: Early decision, early action, regular decision. SATs or ACTs: optional. Subject Tests: optional. Accepts the Common Application. Application includes optional field for gender identity.

Clarkson University

Holcroft House, Box 5605, Potsdam, NY 13699

You know you're in the North Country when the nearest major city is Montreal. Clarkson lies over the river and through the woods. With an informal and close-knit atmosphere, Clarkson is one of the few small, undergraduate-oriented technological universities in the nation. Compare to Lehigh, Bucknell, and Union. Out-of-the-way location makes Clarkson easier to get into, but doing well is no easy task.

At Clarkson University, engineering and ice hockey reign supreme. About half of the student body is enrolled in the engineering program, and the hockey teams are a perennial contender for top honors. Students here get a quality technical education in a small-town environment that offers plenty to do, especially during the sled-dog days of winter. At Clarkson, says a senior, "Everyone has a bit of a nerdy side, and it creates an awesome culture that always makes you feel welcome."

The village of Potsdam, New York, is cloistered away between the Adirondacks and the St. Lawrence River. The campus relies mainly on modern architecture and lots of woods and wildlife. Academic buildings are connected by covered walkways that help take the sting out of getting around campus in the cold, snowy winters. Renovations across campus are ongoing, and the university recently opened the Damon Hall Advanced Manufacturing Incubator.

> **Website**: www.clarkson.edu
> **Location**: Small Town
> **Private**
> **Total Enrollment**: 3,600
> **Undergraduates**: 2,979
> **Male/Female**: 70/30
> **SAT Ranges**: ERW 563–650, M 580–680
> **ACT Ranges**: 24–29
> **Financial Aid**: 99%
> **Pell Grant**: 26%

*All students are
required to complete a
capstone professional
experience, like a
co-op or internship.*

The university's general education program (Clarkson Common Experience) emphasizes four components: learning to communicate effectively; developing an appreciation for diversity; recognizing the importance of personal, societal, and professional ethics; and understanding how technology can be used to serve humanity. All freshmen take a first-year seminar that introduces them to project-based learning and involves a culminating research project focused on a social justice issue. All students are also required to complete a capstone professional experience, like a co-op or internship.

Engineering isn't the only academic offering at Clarkson, but it certainly gets top billing, and it includes the four most popular majors: mechanical engineering, civil engineering, engineering and management, and chemical engineering. In the natural sciences, biology, biomolecular science, and environmental health science are the strongest offerings, the latter bolstered by the extensive research and outreach activities of the Institute for a Sustainable Environment. The Reh School of Business is highly praised too and offers several majors, including distinctive programs in global supply chain management and innovation and entrepreneurship. What's more, all business students must have an international study experience in order to graduate, and first-year students actually start and run a business.

> "Everyone has a bit of a nerdy side, and it creates an awesome culture."

Clarkson prides itself on intimacy and personalized instruction; 52 percent of classes have fewer than 20 students, and 28 percent of students conduct research with a faculty mentor. "All professors have had experience in their respective fields and bring their knowledge to the classroom," says a civil engineering major. Some students say Clarkson isn't the academic pressure cooker that many technical institutes can be. "The heavy and sometimes daunting workload is counteracted by the supportive nature of the students and faculty," says an environmental engineering major. "We are encouraged to work together to solve problems." Students recommend taking advantage of the private, small-group, and drop-in tutoring services offered by the Student Success Center, and they uniformly praise the school's career services for contributing to the university's high job-placement rate. "The Career Center is there to help you from day one and will provide assistance on *anything* related to preparing you for your career," enthuses a senior.

Study abroad opportunities are available at more than 50 different schools in 28 countries, although just 9 percent of students participate. The honors program accepts up to 60 first-year students, who undertake an intensive four-year curriculum. Several hundred students from all majors join teams in Clarkson's Student Projects for Engineering Experience and Design program; most compete in collegiate engineering design competitions, but others engage in outreach efforts, such as Clarkson's Engineers Without Borders, which recently implemented a water purification and filtration system in a village in Ecuador. For women interested in STEM fields on this male-dominated campus, the Women in Science and Engineering program enrolls about 25 first-year students into a residential living/learning program.

Clarkson students are "hardworking, driven, attentive to details, and understanding that work comes first," says a senior. Seventy-one percent of the student body is native to New York. Clarkson has trouble luring minorities to its remote locale, although efforts to change that are underway; African Americans currently make up 2 percent of the undergraduate population, Hispanics 5 percent, Asian Americans 4 percent, and multiracial students 3 percent; international students add another 2 percent. Socioeconomically, the school is more diverse, with 26 percent of freshmen eligible for Pell Grants. Students agree that the campus doesn't usually get too vocal about national political issues. Clarkson awards merit

> "The food is very edible. Even professors eat it."

scholarships each year averaging $23,000. Forty-three athletic scholarships are offered, but only men's and women's ice hockey players need apply (it's Clarkson's only Division I sport).

Eighty percent of students live in campus housing. Students are required to reside on campus all four years, unless exempted to live in a Greek house. All freshmen are housed with students in their major areas of study and in some instances in their department, giving them the chance to study and learn together. Students say the quality of the dorms varies, but the university is diligent about updates and renovations, and on-campus apartments offer more gracious living. The dining facilities generally get average marks. "The food is very edible," says a student. "Even professors eat it."

In keeping with Clarkson's "come-as-you-are" atmosphere, the social scene is low-key. Residence halls and student clubs organize plentiful on-campus entertainment, and 14 percent of the men and 12 percent of the women join the Greek system. Drinking is permitted on campus for those of age, and those not into the Greek scene can head to the handful of bars in downtown Potsdam, which one student describes as having "small-town charm with an Adirondack twist." With three other colleges nearby, the town caters to students. The extended snowy winters are great for snowboarders and ice climbers, and many students join the popular Outing Club to enjoy such outdoor adventures year-round. "In the fall and spring students can be found working toward their '46,' or summiting all 46 high peaks in the Adirondack State Park," according to a senior. For those who crave the bustle of city nightlife, Ottawa and Montreal are each about an hour and a half away by car.

> **"[Potsdam has] small-town charm with an Adirondack twist."**

When it comes to sports, Golden Knight ice hockey is first and foremost in the hearts of Clarkson students. The men's and women's teams are perennially competitive in the ECAC conference and nationally, contending for the Division I championship with other blue-chip teams like St. Lawrence and Cornell. The powerhouse women's team claimed the national title in 2014, 2017, and 2018. The annual game against archrival St. Lawrence has evolved into a popular two-day festival called Cold Out Gold Out, featuring live music, ice skating, dogsled rides, and an alumni hockey match preceding the big game. Clarkson also offers 17 Division III sports. Women's volleyball has brought home six consecutive Liberty League championships, and the men's Alpine and women's Nordic ski teams have won recent USCSA national titles. About 80 percent of students take advantage of club sports and intramurals, with soccer, broomball, and volleyball proving to be favorites.

While other majors are offered, Clarkson's bread and butter is its technological programs, particularly its slew of engineering majors. Students here gain ample exposure to the ever-growing variety of specialties in the field. "Our motto is to 'defy convention,'" says one student, "and we take that to heart in all that we do, whether it be how we look at creating the latest technologies and solving the ever-changing problems of our world, or how we treat each other as individuals."

The powerhouse women's ice hockey team claimed the national title in 2014, 2017, and 2018.

Overlaps

Rensselaer, Rochester Institute of Technology, Worcester Polytechnic, Lehigh, Syracuse, University of Rochester, St. Lawrence, Northeastern

If You Apply To ›

Clarkson: Early decision, regular decision. SATs or ACTs: required. Subject Tests: recommended. Accepts the Common Application with supplement. Application includes optional field for gender identity.

Clemson is a technically oriented public university in the mold of Georgia Tech, North Carolina State, and Virginia Tech. Smaller than the latter two and more focused on undergraduates than Georgia Tech, Clemson serves up its education with ample helpings of school spirit and orange paint. Small-town location makes for a tight-knit campus, though also something of a hayseed image next to more sophisticated Carolina locales such as Columbia and Chapel Hill.

Website: www.clemson.edu

Location: Small Town

Public

Total Enrollment: 21,440

Undergraduates: 18,595

Male/Female: 51/49

SAT Ranges: ERW 620–690, M 600–700

ACT Ranges: 27–31

Financial Aid: 87%

Pell Grant: 16%

Expense: Pub $ $ $

Student Loans: 44%

Average Debt: $

Applicants: 25,856

Accepted: 48%

Enrolled: 30%

Grad in 6 Years: 82%

Returning Freshmen: 93%

Academics: ✍ ✍ ✍

Social: ☎ ☎ ☎ ☎

Q of L: ★ ★ ★ ★

Admissions: (864) 656-2287

Email Address: admissions@ clemson.edu

Strong Programs:

Psychology

Biological Sciences

Management

Mechanical Engineering

Nursing

Agriculture

Architecture

History

Nestled in the foothills of the Blue Ridge Mountains, Clemson University is a place where traditional Southern spirit continues to flourish alongside modern academics, big-time athletics, and state-of-the-art facilities. This public university has the ring of a private institution and features quality academics in technical and scientific areas such as engineering and biology. Tiger spirit is as strong as ever, as evidenced by the ubiquitous orange tiger paws that decorate the campus, and students here are happy to make tracks of their own.

CU's 1,400-acre campus is situated on what was once Fort Hill Plantation, the homestead of Thomas Green Clemson. The campus is surrounded by 17,000 acres of university farms and woodlands and offers a spectacular view of the nearby lake and mountains. Architectural styles are an eclectic mix of modern and 19th-century collegiate. Clemson Bottoms, half a mile down the road from the 80,000-seat football stadium, is home to the Calhoun Field Laboratory, a pastoral site dedicated to agricultural research that features a large, student-run organic garden. A fantastic resource for science enthusiasts and history buffs is the library's collection of first editions of the scientific works of Galileo and Newton. Douthit Hills is a $212 million residential village complete with dining and fitness facilities.

General education requirements include courses in advanced writing; oral communications; mathematical, scientific, and technological literacy; social sciences; arts and humanities; cross-cultural awareness; and science and technology in society. An electronic portfolio program allows students to build a collection of their work, demonstrating changes in competencies throughout their experiences at Clemson. Electrical engineering is Clemson's largest department, and computer engineering is among the nation's best in research on large-scale integrated computer circuitry and robotics. The College of Architecture offers intensive semesters at the Overseas Center for Building Research and Urban Study in Genoa, Italy. Psychology, biological sciences, management, mechanical engineering, and nursing are the most popular majors, and the agriculture program is also well regarded. Undergraduate teaching has always been one of Clemson's strong points, and for students interested in pursuing a liberal arts curriculum, the school has degrees in fine arts, philosophy, and languages and enjoys a strong regional reputation for its history program. Because of the prevailing technical emphasis, however, most students interested in the liberal arts head "down country" to the University of South Carolina.

> **"[Professors] make themselves available for tons of extra hours outside of the classroom."**

Academically, the level of difficulty varies. "Classes are very competitive," says one junior. "While challenging at times, the coursework is stimulating and applicable." Professors run the gamut from average to stellar, with most receiving high marks from students. "Professors not only teach the classes but also make themselves available for tons of extra hours outside of the classroom," says a psychology major. Just over half of the classes have fewer than 20 students. Students report some problems finishing a degree in four years, and class registration can be a hassle. Fifty-four percent of undergrads take advantage of research opportunities during their time at Clemson. Highly motivated students should consider applying to the Calhoun Honors College—the oldest honors program in South Carolina. Clemson also offers exchange programs in venues from Mexico to Australia, and 32 percent of students study abroad.

"Students are friendly, kind, academically driven, and are a part of a true family on our campus," says one elementary education major. Clemson's student body has a decidedly Southern air, as 69 percent of undergrads hail from South Carolina, with most of the rest from neighboring states; less than 1 percent come from foreign countries. African Americans make up 7 percent of the student body, Hispanics 4 percent, Asian Americans 2 percent, and multiracial students 3 percent. The average Clemson student is friendly and conservative, and though, as a public institution, the school isn't affiliated with any church, there is a strong Southern Baptist presence on campus. The university offers thousands of merit scholarships averaging $3,700 and nearly 400 athletic scholarships.

Housing gets positive reviews, with several new residence halls opening in the last few years, and 41 percent of the students live on campus, usually during their first two years. Options include single-sex, co-ed, traditional, and apartment-style housing. "The west campus high-rise dorms are awesome," cheers a junior. The dining facilities have been improving, according to students. "They have specials and even ask students to contribute recipes," explains one student. Students say they feel safe on campus: "We have three separate police forces that work on campus at all times, and they truly take care of the students," says a junior.

> *Clemson's computer engineering department is among the nation's best in research on large-scale integrated computer circuitry and robotics.*

"At Clemson, the fun is mostly right outside our windows."

"At Clemson, the fun is mostly right outside our windows," says one student. "Whether it's a football game, a pep rally, an RHA program, or one of our U-Nites Friday night activities, students always find something to do." Fraternities and sororities provide much of the social life, with 16 percent of Clemson men and 33 percent of women going Greek. The administration has introduced measures such as limiting fraternity members to bringing just one six-pack of beer to events, in an effort to curb hazing, alcohol abuse, and other problems related to the Greek scene. The town of Clemson is pretty small, with a few bars and movie theaters, but some students love it. After class, many students hop on their bikes and head to nearby Lake Hartwell. The beautiful Blue Ridge mountain range is also close by for hiking and camping, and beaches and ski slopes are both within driving distance. Atlanta and Charlotte are only two hours away by car, and Charleston is four hours away on the coast.

> *The annual South Carolina game, known as the Palmetto Bowl, has been played for more than a century.*

Clemson has a high-powered sports scene and fields a number of competitive teams in the Division I Atlantic Coast Conference. The football team has won two national championships in the last three years. Football fever starts with the annual First Friday Parade, held before the first home game, and on every game day the campus dissolves into a sea of Tiger orange, with pep rallies, cookouts, dances, and parties for the mobs of excited fans. The roads leading to campus are painted with large orange pawprints. So, too, are half the fans, making the stands in "Death Valley" look like an orange grove. Tiger fans are especially rowdy when the reviled University of South Carolina Gamecocks are in town. The annual South Carolina game, known as the Palmetto Bowl, has been played for more than a century. Baseball is also very competitive, as are men's and women's soccer and golf. Women's softball is debuting for the 2019–20 season. A plethora of intramural and club sports are available too.

Overlaps

Georgia Tech, Virginia Tech, North Carolina State, Auburn, Texas A&M, University of Georgia, University of South Carolina, College of Charleston

Clemson is best at serving those whose interests lie in technical fields. School spirit is contagious, fueled by a love of big-time college sports, and becomes life-long for many Clemson students. Everyone can become part of the Clemson family, from Southern belle to Northern Yankee, as long as they're friendly, easygoing, and enthusiastic about life in general and the Tigers in particular.

If You Apply To ›

Clemson: Rolling admissions. SATs or ACTs: required. Subject Tests: optional. Does not accept the Common Application. Music and theater applicants must audition.

Colby College

Waterville, ME 04901

The northernmost venue for high-quality, private higher education in New England. Colby's picturesque setting is a short hop from the eastern sea coast or Maine's western lakes and mountains. No frats since the college abolished them more than 30 years ago. An active, outdoorsy student body in the mold of Middlebury and Dartmouth, and more buttoned-up than Bates or Bowdoin. Invented the month-long January term. Still requires SAT or ACT, or two SAT subject tests.

Website: www.colby.edu
Location: Rural
Private
Total Enrollment: 1,917
Undergraduates: 1,917
Male/Female: 48/52
SAT Ranges: ERW 670–740, M 670–760
ACT Ranges: 31–33
Financial Aid: 42%
Pell Grant: 14%
Expense: Pr $ $ $ $
Student Loans: 28%
Average Debt: $ $ $ $
Applicants: 11,190
Accepted: 16%
Enrolled: 31%
Grad in 6 Years: 92%
Returning Freshmen: 94%
Academics: ✍ ✍ ✍ ✍ ½
Social: ☎ ☎ ☎
Q of L: ★ ★ ★ ★
Admissions: (800) 723-3032
Email Address: admissions@colby.edu

Colby College draws students who like to push themselves, whether in the classroom or on the ski slopes. The nearby city of Waterville, Maine (population 16,000), offers few distractions, and close friendships with peers and professors help ward off the winter chill. Colby's top study abroad program offers students an opportunity to explore the world, and even those who don't spend a semester or year away can get a taste during the month of January, when Jan-Plan trips send Colby students far and wide.

Colby sits high on Mayflower Hill, with beautiful views of the surrounding city and countryside. Its 714 acres include a wildlife preserve, miles of cross-country trails, and a pond used in winter as an ice-skating rink. Georgian architecture predominates, and the oldest buildings are redbrick with white trim and brass nameplates above their hunter green doors. The more contemporary buildings lend a touch of modernity. One of the most iconic Colby buildings is the library tower, which is topped with a blue light proudly showing off the primary school color. A 350,000-square-foot athletic complex, slated to open in 2020, will feature the state's only Olympic-sized pool.

> **"The professors believe that if you are having difficulty, they aren't doing their job correctly."**

As a small college with a history of innovation and educational excellence, Colby encourages students to learn for learning's sake rather than for a good grade. Students must complete distribution requirements in English composition, foreign language, "areas" (courses in arts, historical studies, literature, quantitative reasoning, social sciences, and natural sciences), diversity, and wellness (five supper seminars over the first two semesters). Colby was the first men's college in New England to admit women, and also the first to establish a special January term. Students must take three such terms for credit to graduate, but almost all take four. Many students use the month off to serve an internship, study abroad, or prepare an in-depth research report.

In all, Colby offers more than 50 majors. Popular and well-regarded programs include biology, economics, environmental studies, global studies, psychology, government, English, and mathematics. Students study oceanography through Colby's partnership with the Bigelow Laboratory for Ocean Sciences in East Boothbay, Maine. For would-be engineers, there is a joint 3–2 program with Dartmouth and a 4–2 program with Columbia, and others may take exchange programs with the Claremont Colleges and Howard. One student says, "Colby is hard and there is no way to sugarcoat that, but hard work and studying is respected here." It helps that Colby's faculty is unusually devoted to undergraduate teaching and easily accessible, with 73 percent of classes enrolling fewer than 20 students. "The professors believe that if you are having difficulty, they aren't doing their job correctly for you and want to fix that in any way possible," a computer science major says.

(continued)

Strong Programs:
Biology
Economics
Environmental Studies
Global Studies
Psychology
Government
English
Mathematics

Study abroad is a serious emphasis at Colby, and the opportunities to do so begin early. Freshmen can apply to the Global Entry Semester program, whisking off to France or Spain with 20 or so classmates for the fall semester. Half of the school's majors have an international component, and 70 percent of Colby students spend some time abroad, taking advantage of more than 200 approved international programs, including Colby-sponsored Jan-Plan trips. A high proportion of graduates enter the Peace Corps and the Foreign Service. Seventy-eight percent of students conduct undergraduate research, and those who stay on campus during the summer as research assistants for faculty are rewarded with a two-day Summer Research Retreat in Forks, Maine, dedicated to short talks, presentations, and white-water rafting or hiking adventures. The recently launched DavisConnects initiative provides funding for off-campus internships, research, and study abroad.

Freshmen in the Global Entry Semester program whisk off to France or Spain with 20 classmates for the fall semester.

Colby students are driven but know how to enjoy themselves too. "You will see the same people in the library Sunday morning who you saw at a party Saturday night," comments a global studies major. Only 11 percent of Colby students are Mainers; the rest learn to act like natives during the COOT program (Colby Outdoor Orientation Trips), required of all first-years. These three-day excursions by bicycle, canoe, or foot introduce them to the beauty of the Maine wilderness or to service or theater

"Every Sunday night, students sit on the steps of the library and a senior tells a story."

experiences. African Americans account for 4 percent of the student body, Hispanics 7 percent, Asian Americans 7 percent, and multiracial students 5 percent. Ten percent are international. "Mayflower Hill is a very liberal space," says a sophomore, and anything related to "hypermasculinity, socioeconomic insensitivity, or racism" is likely to be a hot-button issue. All financial aid at Colby is need-based, the college meets 100 percent of students' demonstrated need, and it has replaced student loans with grants in all its financial aid packages.

Students are required to live in college housing for all four years. On-campus residence halls, which students describe as average, have live-in faculty members. A new residential complex in downtown Waterville offers a living/learning community focused on civic engagement for 200 juniors and seniors. "Colby has three good dining halls, each with their own flair, and makes an effort to source locally and sustainably," says a senior. Freshmen and sophomores take training classes on sexual violence prevention, but some students express a desire for "more trainings for students throughout all four years."

A new residential complex in downtown Waterville offers a living/learning community for 200 juniors and seniors.

When the weekend comes, you'll find most Colby students staying close to campus, though Waterville offers some good restaurants and bars. "Colby does not have Greek life, which definitely sets a more inclusive tone on campus," explains a senior. Parties in the senior apartments are a weekend staple and tend to be driven by sports teams; a senior notes that the school has been attempting to "dial back on a heavy drinking culture" by discontinuing some annual festivities and offering more alternative programming. The first and last weekends of each semester are celebrated with musical acts and other activities. Another favorite tradition, says a sophomore, is Story Time: "Every Sunday night, students sit on the steps of the library and a senior tells a story." The Colby administration likes to share two "big secrets" about Maine winters: they're beautiful, and they're a lot harsher in the telling than in the living. Popular Maine road trips include Augusta, Freeport (home to the L.L. Bean factory and store), and Sugarloaf Mountain. Also easy to reach are the bright lights of Boston and Montreal.

The Colby Mules have come a long way since the first intercollegiate croquet game, played at Colby in 1860. Sports are Division III, except for squash and skiing, which are Division I, and solid programs include women's lacrosse and men's cross-country and ice hockey. Games against Bates and Bowdoin draw crowds, especially the annual Bowdoin hockey match. Nonvarsity athletes are eager participants in 15 club teams and nine intramural sports.

Colby's traditional New England liberal arts college vibe and increasingly global focus extend far beyond its small-city setting and historic buildings. They permeate the air, punctuated by the long-standing traditions, abundant school spirit, and caring faculty members who focus on developing their students' minds.

Overlaps

Brown, Bowdoin, Dartmouth, Middlebury, Williams, Wesleyan, Hamilton, Boston College

If You Apply To ›

Colby: Early decision I and II, regular decision. SATs or ACTs or two Subject Tests: required. Accepts the Common Application with supplement.

Colgate University

13 Oak Drive, Hamilton, NY 13346

With fewer than 3,000 students, Colgate is smaller than Bucknell and Dartmouth but bigger than Hamilton and Williams. Like the other four, it offers small-town living and close interaction between students and faculty. Greek organizations and jocks are still well entrenched despite administrative efforts to neutralize their influence.

Website: www.colgate.edu
Location: Small Town
Private
Total Enrollment: 2,854
Undergraduates: 2,850
Male/Female: 45/55
SAT Ranges: ERW 660–730, M 650–770
ACT Ranges: 31–33
Financial Aid: 48%
Pell Grant: 10%
Expense: Pr $ $ $ $
Student Loans: 35%
Average Debt: $ $
Applicants: 8,542
Accepted: 28%

While you may see the same Canada Goose jackets coming and going (and coming and going) as you stroll across Colgate University's campus, students here aren't all spun from the same cloth. "Most students at Colgate are freethinkers and open to new ideas," says a sophomore. From the herbarium to the Devonian fossils to the plethora of interdisciplinary courses, it's clear that Colgate has more to offer than just its picture-postcard setting. "I think Colgate draws students who want a high level of academic rigor and a top-tier liberal arts education," says one student, "without the competitive air that usually accompanies these."

Colgate's 13 founders started the school with 13 prayers and 13 dollars. Their prayers were answered by soapmaking mogul William Colgate and his sons (now famous for their toothpaste), whose decades of philanthropic gift-giving to the fledgling university were enough to get the name changed in 1890 from Madison to Colgate. Today, the 575-acre campus sits on a hillside in rural New York, overlooking the village of Hamilton. Ivy-covered limestone buildings peek out from tree-lined drives; lush green spaces are perfect for rugby, Frisbee, or other outdoor diversions, at least in the warmer months. Rolling hills and farmland surround the campus, making for stunning vistas during the snowy season, which stretches from mid-October to mid-March. New facilities include two 100-bed residence halls and a career services building.

Aside from blazing a trail to rural New York, Colgate has led its peers in emphasizing interdisciplinary study. The faculty first established an interdisciplinary core program in 1928, and it's been a foundation of the curriculum ever since. Even now, all freshmen take a first-year seminar, capped at 18 students each, that introduces liberal arts topics, skills, resources, and ways of learning. Students choose from more than 40 topics, and seminar instructors double as academic advisors until students declare majors their sophomore year. Students also complete five courses in the liberal arts core—Legacies of the Ancient World, Challenges of Modernity, Scientific Perspectives on the World, Communities and Identities, and Global Engagements—as well as coursework in natural sciences and math, social sciences, arts and humanities, foreign language, and physical education.

> "Colgate draws students who want…a top-tier liberal arts education without the competitive air."

Students give high marks to Colgate's natural and social sciences programs, and economics, political science, history, psychology, and English are the most popular majors. Befitting Colgate's rugged location, there are five interdisciplinary environmental majors: environmental studies, environmental biology, environmental geography, environmental geology, and environmental economics. Two former minors, applied mathematics and film and media studies, are now offered as majors. Seventy-three percent of classes have fewer than 20 students, and an English major says, "Colgate professors do an excellent job of breaking down the professor/student hierarchy that can sometimes make students—especially underclassmen—nervous."

Classrooms and labs devoted to foreign language study help students gain comfort with another tongue—a good thing, since nearly two-thirds of students study abroad. In addition to about 20 semester-long, faculty-led off-campus study programs (called "study groups"), Colgate offers six to eight "extended-study" travel programs that serve as two- or three-week extensions of regular on-campus courses. More than 100 other preapproved study abroad programs offer additional options. The Sophomore Residential Seminars program enables selected students to live together in the same residence hall and take a semester-long course that is capped off with a weeklong trip during winter break; recent participants have traveled to San Francisco for a course on immigrant and sexual cultures and to India for an art and architecture course. Eighty-three percent of students get involved with undergraduate research, many of them working under faculty members as paid summer research assistants. "Colgate offers no classes during the summer because they encourage students to obtain research or professional experience during their college years," says a senior. An economics major adds that the school's "die-hard alumni network" can help with securing internships and jobs.

Interdisciplinary study has been a foundation of Colgate's curriculum since 1928.

"Students at Colgate are ambitious, driven, and intellectually curious," says a senior. "They have a spirit of intensity." Twenty-four percent of students are New Yorkers, while 9 percent are international. African Americans account for 5 percent of the population, Hispanics 9 percent, Asian Americans 4 percent, and multiracial students

> "Professors do an excellent job of breaking down the professor/student hierarchy."

4 percent. Students credit the ALANA Cultural Center with "fostering a comfortable and friendly environment" and describe a left-leaning political climate. A physics major reports, "Several discussion points on campus have been about general inclusivity, the influence of Greek life on campus, and gender and safety issues." Colgate does not award merit scholarships, but nearly 200 athletic scholarships are available in 13 sports. Colgate's need-based financial aid program meets 100 percent of

(continued)

Enrolled: 32%
Grad in 6 Years: 91%
Returning Freshmen: 94%
Academics: ✍ ✍ ✍ ✍ ½
Social: ☎ ☎ ☎
Q of L: ★ ★ ★
Admissions: (315) 228-7401
Email Address: admission@colgate.edu

Strong Programs:
Economics
Political Science
History
Psychology
English
Environmental Studies
Natural Sciences
Social Sciences

enrolled students' demonstrated financial need, and Colgate grants usually represent the largest portion of a typical financial aid award.

Ninety percent of Colgate students live in the residence halls, which range from traditional buildings with fireplaces to newer facilities that seem more like hotels. Students are housed in residential communities called Commons for their first two years and remain affiliated with their Commons throughout their four years. About 250 upperclassmen are allowed to live off campus each year. Students have five dining facilities to choose from, and a junior says, "One amazing thing is that the required meal plan for freshmen gives unlimited 24/7 access to the main dining hall. Whenever hunger strikes, there is food available very close to the freshman dorms." Campus security officers are said to be well respected, and the school recently opened a support center for victims of sexual assault, which a junior says is "making students more aware of the issue and how they can help."

"Colgate has more than 190 clubs and organizations on campus, so there is no end to the opportunities students can have to pursue their interests," says a junior.

> **"Colgate offers no classes during the summer because they encourage students to obtain research or professional experience."**

Partying is the prevailing diversion on weekends, but students say there is no pressure to participate. Eleven percent of the men and 19 percent of the women join the Greek system. "Greek life definitely dominates the party culture," says a senior. "It's also inherently exclusive, which makes it tough at such a small school with a big Greek scene." In an effort to cut down on alcohol consumption, hazing, and other problems that have tended to get out of hand, the administration forced fraternities and sororities to sell their off-campus houses to the university, and recruitment is delayed until sophomore year. Students enjoy free "Take Two" movies on Friday and Saturday nights and open-mic nights at the campus pub, Donovan's. Everyone looks forward to ALANApalooza, Dancefest, and Spring Party Weekend, a last blast before finals that celebrates the thaw with a big concert, barbecues, and fireworks. Given the significance of the number 13 to the school's founding, every Friday the 13th is dubbed Colgate Day, a time to show off school spirit and pride. On the eve of graduation, seniors don their graduation robes, carry lit torches down the campus hill, and throw their torches into a bonfire.

In addition to a required four-day orientation, freshmen may also participate in one of several preorientation programs, such as Wilderness Adventure, where groups

> **"Greek life definitely dominates the party culture."**

of 8 to 12 canoe and hike in the Adirondacks. Hamilton is within walking distance of campus, but there's also a free bus that cycles through every half hour, especially nice in the dead of winter. The Palace draws crowds with music, dancing, and a bar, and the Mexican fare at La Iguana is popular, but students say the quiet village doesn't have much else to offer. For those with wheels, skiing is 45 minutes away in Toggenburg, and the malls and city lights of Syracuse and Utica are roughly the same distance.

About half of Colgate students enjoy facing off in 11 intramural competitions and 40 club sports, but students' most fervent cheers are reserved for Division I men's ice hockey against Cornell. "When Cornell comes to our rink, we throw Big Red gum on the ice, and they throw Colgate toothpaste on the ice," explains a junior. Women's ice hockey is a powerhouse, and the Raiders football and men's soccer teams are recent conference champions. Men's and women's lacrosse, men's basketball, and women's volleyball are also strong. Even weekend warriors may take advantage of facilities like the Sanford Field House, the Lineberry natatorium, and the Seven Oaks golf course, which is ranked among the top five collegiate courses nationally.

Students are housed in residential communities called Commons for their first two years.

Students' most fervent cheers are reserved for Division I men's ice hockey against Cornell.

Overlaps

Middlebury, Boston College, Dartmouth, Tufts, Bowdoin, Cornell University, Brown, Hamilton

Colgate led the way in interdisciplinary work and continues to do so now. What else has remained constant? A senior offers this assessment: "I think Colgate has embraced its identity as different from other liberal arts colleges in that we are not a crunchy granola hippie school and we are not a socially progressive bastion of forward thinking. Colgate is what it is: a hidden gem in the Chenango Valley."

If You Apply To ›

Colgate: Early decision I and II, regular decision. SATs or ACTs: required. No Subject Tests. Accepts the Common Application with supplement.

University of Colorado Boulder

Regent Administrative Center 125, 552 UCB, Boulder, CO 80309

Boulder is a legendary place that draws everyone from East Coast ski bums to California refugees. The scenery is breathtaking and the science programs are first-rate. The University of Arizona is the only public university of similar stature in the Mountain West. Check out the residential academic programs and other living/learning communities.

Wild buffalo may be all but extinct on America's Great Plains, but they're in boisterous residence, proudly wearing gold and black, at the University of Colorado Boulder. A bevy of scholars' programs, residential academic programs, and other learning communities give the campus a community feel, and students choose from a solid menu of academic programs, including research experience, study abroad, and service learning. "There are so many ways to be active and engaged in your learning at Boulder," cheers a sophomore. And with more than 300 days of sunshine a year, is it any wonder that CU Boulder Buffaloes are a happy herd?

Tree-shaded walkways, winding bike paths, open spaces, and an incredible view of the dramatic Flatirons rock formation make CU's 600-acre Boulder campus a haven for students from both coasts and for Colorado residents eager to pursue knowledge in a snowy paradise. The campus includes about 200 classic rural Italian-style buildings and complexes built of Colorado sandstone with red tile roofs. The 45,000-square-foot Gallogly Discovery Learning Center houses 12 advanced labs supporting collaborative research in fields ranging from biotechnology to unmanned vehicle systems. City bus passes are included in the cost of tuition and fees, the campus Environmental Center facilitates sustainable culture and practices, and ongoing renovations and construction projects embody the university's commitment to sustainability and energy efficiency.

Entering freshmen and transfer students at CU Boulder choose from four colleges, one program, and two schools: the College of Arts and Sciences (which enrolls 70 percent of the students); the College of Music; the College of Engineering and Applied Science (the hardest to enter, students say); the College of Media, Communication, and Information; the Program in Environmental Design; the Leeds School of Business; and the School of Education. Each has different entrance standards and requirements. General education requirements cover three skills acquisition areas—written communication, quantitative reasoning and math, and foreign

> "There are so many ways to be active and engaged in your learning at Boulder."

Website: www.colorado.edu
Location: Small City
Public
Total Enrollment: 29,505
Undergraduates: 26,854
Male/Female: 55/45
SAT Ranges: ERW 580–665, M 570–680
ACT Ranges: 25–30
Financial Aid: 59%
Pell Grant: 27%
Expense: Pub $ $ $
Student Loans: 42%
Average Debt: $ $
Applicants: 36,149
Accepted: 80%
Enrolled: 23%
Grad in 6 Years: 69%
Returning Freshmen: 88%
Academics: ✑ ✑ ✑ ✑
Social: ☎ ☎ ☎ ☎ ☎
Q of L: ★ ★ ★
Admissions: (303) 492-6301
Email Address: admissions@colorado.edu

Strong Programs:
Psychology

language—and three distribution categories: arts and humanities, natural sciences, and social sciences.

"Unlike other highly competitive universities, there is a high level of collaboration," says an applied mathematics major. "Your classmates won't refuse to work with you, and you are always comfortable asking questions and asking for help." CU Boulder offers more than 3,900 courses each year in approximately 150 areas of study; psychology, integrative physiology, communication, and finance are among the most popular majors. Outstanding programs include aerospace engineering sciences, physics, chemical and biological engineering, music, astronomy, biochemistry, English, and entrepreneurial business. CU Boulder is consistently among the top universities in the country to receive NASA funding, leading to lots of opportunities for the design, construction, and flight of model spacecraft—and to 18 CU Boulder alumni having worked as astronauts. Concurrent, five-year bachelor's/master's degree programs are available in dozens of fields. Forty-nine percent of undergraduate classes enroll fewer than 20 students, and a freshman says, "In my experience, professors and graduate student instructors alike have taken a keen interest in students' progress, success, and learning."

> "The Residential Academic Program for freshmen is essential for gaining a well-rounded experience at CU."

CU Boulder has tried to make its large campus seem smaller through its 12 residential academic programs (small, specialized living/learning environments) focusing on topics such as leadership, global studies, the arts, and engineering. Participants take one or two courses, each limited to 25 students, in their residence halls. "The Residential Academic Program for freshmen is essential for gaining a well-rounded experience at CU," advises a senior. Six other living/learning communities are also options. The Presidents Leadership Class is a four-year scholarship program that provides the most promising students with leadership training, internships, volunteer opportunities, and visits with influential political, business, and community leaders. The top 10 percent of each incoming class is invited to join the Honors Program, which offers more than 80 honors courses per year. About a third of students undertake undergraduate research, and 31 percent pack their bags for 400 university-sponsored study abroad programs in more than 65 countries around the world.

CU Boulder is consistently among the top universities in the country to receive NASA funding.

"Students are relaxed and explorative, curious and inquisitive, fun-loving and good-natured, focused and committed," says one Buffalo. Fifty-eight percent of CU Boulder's undergraduates come from Colorado, and 7 percent come from abroad. Hispanics comprise 12 percent of the undergraduate population, Asian Americans 6 percent, African Americans 2 percent, and multiracial students 5 percent. Hot topics include "wealth, liberalism, and inequality," according to one student. Qualified undergrads receive merit scholarships worth an average of $9,000, and 264 athletes receive scholarships as well. Additional programs provide debt-free financial incentives for qualified in-state students whose family income is at or below the federal poverty line. Twenty-seven percent of entering students are eligible for Pell Grants. The university offers a four-year tuition guarantee for all of its undergraduates.

> "CU is considered a top party school and people do live up to that expectation."

The Presidents Leadership Class is a four-year scholarship program that provides the most promising students with leadership training.

First-year students are required to live on campus, and 28 percent of all undergrads stay in university housing. "The older dorms are still in pretty good shape but aren't as nice as the newer dorms," a sophomore reports. Most sophomores, juniors, and seniors find off-campus digs in Boulder, and those who want to stay on campus are advised to make early reservations for Farrand, Sewall, or Kittredge halls. An alternative to the main Center for Community dining center and 15 smaller dining locations is the Alferd Packer Restaurant & Grill, which takes its name from a controversial 19th-century folk figure known as the "Colorado Cannibal." *Bon appétit.* Generally, students say the campus is safe. CU Boulder also offers walking and riding escorts at night via a service called CU NightRide.

For the culturally minded, the university and the city of Boulder offer films and plays, the renowned Colorado Shakespeare Festival, art galleries and museums, and concerts by top bands. Denver is only 30 miles southeast, reachable by a free bus service. Most students get involved in community service, and the CU Engage center coordinates service-learning courses and community-based research opportunities. Twelve percent of CU Boulder men and 21 percent of women go Greek, though fraternity and sorority parties have changed dramatically since CU Boulder's sorority chapters became the first in the nation to voluntarily make their houses dry. On campus, the ban on alcohol is taken seriously, and dorms are officially substance-free. Still, "The party scene is fairly large and has a lot going on most weekends," says a political science major. "CU is considered a top party school and people do live up to that expectation." Day trips to ski resorts like Breckenridge and Vail largely replace weekend getaways here, but for those who've got to get out of the cold, Las Vegas isn't so far, says one student.

Physical exercise is a popular extracurricular activity at CU Boulder. The massive Student Recreation Center features four pools, an ice rink, a climbing gym, several multipurpose courts, and 30,000 square feet of strength and cardio space, among other facilities. Varsity teams compete in the Division I Pac-12 Conference, and the Buffaloes skiing and women's cross-country teams are recent national champions. Men's and women's basketball are also strong, as are women's soccer and lacrosse. Ralphie, the live buffalo who acts as CU Boulder's mascot, doesn't miss a game—and neither do many students. Each year, football fans flock to Denver to watch the Rocky Mountain Showdown game against Colorado State. The club sports program, which boasts 30 options, is highly competitive, winning more than 60 national championships in the last 20 years in sports ranging from ice hockey and ultimate Frisbee to cycling and triathlon. Intramurals sign up 28 percent of the students each year.

If you want to flex your muscles as well as your mind, look beyond the ivy-covered bricks and gray city skies endemic to so many Eastern institutions, and consider all the West has to offer instead. "The amount of resources students can utilize to further their education or gain experience in their field at CU and in the city of Boulder is immense and overwhelming," says one student.

Each year, football fans flock to Denver to watch the Rocky Mountain Showdown game against Colorado State.

Overlaps

Colorado State, University of Denver, Colorado School of Mines, Cal Poly–San Luis Obispo, University of Oregon, Penn State, University of Washington, University of Arizona

If You Apply To ›

CU Boulder: Early action, regular decision. SATs or ACTs: required. No Subject Tests. Accepts the Common Application with supplement. Music applicants must audition.

Colorado College

14 East Cache La Poudre Street, Colorado Springs, CO 80903

The Block Plan, a one-course-at-a-time academic schedule, is CC's claim to fame. It is great for in-depth study and field trips but less suited to projects that take an extended period of time. Colorado Springs is an ideal location at the base of the Rockies, which draw outdoor enthusiasts and East Coasters who want to ski. CC is the only top liberal arts college between Iowa and the Pacific.

Website:
   www.coloradocollege.edu

Location: Small City

Private

Total Enrollment: 2,100

Undergraduates: 2,091

Male/Female: 46/54

SAT Ranges: ERW 650–730,
   M 650–760

ACT Ranges: 29–33

Financial Aid: 49%

Pell Grant: 11%

Expense: Pr $ $ $ $

Student Loans: 34%

Average Debt: $ $

Applicants: 8,223

Accepted: 15%

Enrolled: 44%

Grad in 6 Years: 88%

Returning Freshmen: 94%

Academics: ✍ ✍ ✍ ✍

Social: ☎ ☎ ☎ ☎

Q of L: ★ ★ ★ ★

Admissions: (800) 542-7214

Email Address: admission@
   coloradocollege.edu

Strong Programs:
Economics
Political Science
Sociology
Environmental Science
International Political Economy
Geology
Southwest Studies
Race, Ethnicity, and Migration
   Studies

Colorado College is one of the few U.S. schools offering one-course-at-a-time block scheduling. For more than a century, CC's focus on creative approaches to academics and its breathtaking location at the edge of the Rocky Mountains have drawn bright, independent liberal arts enthusiasts who also like to go out and play. "People don't come to CC because they want to make a ton of money or maintain the status quo," asserts a senior. "They come because they want to change the world, help others, and have a little fun."

Founded in 1874, the college campus lies at the foot of Pike's Peak, in the town of Colorado Springs. Many homes in the surrounding neighborhood are on the National Register of Historic Places, as are many CC buildings, including its first, Cutler Hall, and Palmer Hall, named after town founder William J. Palmer, a major force behind the establishment of the college. The prevailing architectural styles are Romanesque and English Gothic, with some more modern structures thrown in. The new East Campus Housing Community includes eight residential facilities for upperclassmen, a community center, and an outdoor courtyard.

> "The students are laid-back, nature-loving hippies."

CC requires students to take courses focused on the Western tradition, non-Western societies, issues of inequality (with respect to nationality, race, ethnicity, gender, class, and/or sexuality), natural sciences, and quantitative reasoning. Foreign language proficiency is also required. What really defines the academic climate, though, is the Block Plan (see also Cornell College in Iowa). Students take eight courses between early September and mid-May, but focus on each one, in turn, for three and a half weeks. Some courses, such as neuroscience or those involving longer-term projects, are two blocks long. Four-and-a-half-day breaks separate the blocks. The plan helps students stay focused, eliminating the temptation to let one course slide so that they can catch up in another. But there are trade-offs. Students say it can be hard to integrate material from courses taken one at a time. There's also the danger of burnout, because so much material on a single subject is crammed into such a short span.

The First-Year Experience program, consisting of a two-block sequence of courses with a student mentor and two advisors, helps students adjust to college-level academics and the fast pace of the Block Plan. "CC is extremely collaborative," notes an environmental policy major, "However, it's extremely intense." Seventy-one percent of classes have fewer than 20 students, and required courses aren't hard to get into, since spots are secured with an auction system. At the beginning of each year, students get 80 points to "bid" on the classes they want. Those who bid the most for a particular class get a seat. If you're going to take only one class at a time, it helps to like the teacher, and students say that's no problem here. "The professors are very accessible, and it is easy to have a good working relationship," says a history and political science major.

> "There is a very large drug and alcohol presence on campus."

The most popular majors at Colorado include economics, political science, sociology, environmental science, and international political economy. Students say that the sciences in general, and particularly geology and environmental science, are strengths. The block schedule permits some classes at unique times and in unique places—for instance, astronomy at midnight, or coral biology work in the Caribbean. The college's popular major in Southwest studies includes time at its Baca campus, 175 miles away in the historic San Luis Valley. Other interesting interdisciplinary programs include Asian studies and race, ethnicity, and migration studies. In addition to giving students the option to pick semester- and yearlong abroad programs in more than 60 countries, Colorado College faculty also teach about 25 off-campus blocks, both domestically and internationally, throughout the school year and summer session. More than 70 percent of students study off campus at least once during their time at Colorado.

Just 16 percent of Colorado College students are in-staters, 9 percent are international, and the rest are from all over the United States. "The students are laid-back, nature-loving hippies," says a student. CC is more selective but less socioeconomically diverse than its closest peer, Cornell College—just 11 percent of Colorado freshmen qualify for the Pell Grant. Three percent of undergrads are African American, 9 percent are Hispanic, 4 percent are Asian American, and 9 percent are multiracial— and the school is trying to attract more diversity. Groups like the Queer Straight Alliance, the Feminist Collective, the Jewish Chaverim, and the Black Student Union provide support to students of varied backgrounds and viewpoints. "The general political orientation is extremely liberal," says a senior. The college meets 100 percent of admitted students' demonstrated financial need, and a limited number of merit scholarships, averaging $14,700, and athletic scholarships are available.

The First-Year Experience program consists of a two-block sequence of courses with a student mentor and two advisors.

Seventy-eight percent of the students call campus housing home, and only seniors are permitted to live off campus. "The underclassmen dorms range from brand-new, almost luxury suites, to pretty old but full of character," says a senior. Four living/learning communities are also available: Enclave, Outdoor Education, PRIDE, and Revitalizing Nations. The "exceptional" dining facilities include a traditional, all-you-can-eat dining hall; a grill with American, Mexican, and sushi options; and an all-natural café and convenience store.

"The intensive and demanding nature of the Block Plan calls for deep but quick thinkers."

When the weekend comes, students unwind at parties in friends' rooms or seniors' off-campus houses. "There is a very large drug and alcohol presence on campus," reports a senior, "though it absolutely is not mandatory." The "low-key" Greek system attracts 11 percent of the men and 11 percent of the women. Favorite traditions include the annual Llamapalooza and Blues & Shoes (bluegrass and horseshoes) music festivals, and the monthly Full Moon Cruisers, where "students gather at 10 p.m. decked out in crazy outfits to ride their bikes downtown and party under the full moon," explains a student. For those seeking a bit of urban culture, Denver and Boulder are a short drive away. Most CC students love heading off campus to ski or hike, either at nearby resorts or in Utah, New Mexico, or the Grand Canyon area. Freshman outdoor orientation trips help newcomers sort out the options, from backpacking and hiking to rafting, bicycling, and windsurfing. Students can even reserve a college-owned mountainside cabin. Service trips are sponsored during block breaks, and the majority of students do some type of community service during their time at CC.

Colorado College faculty teach about 25 off-campus blocks, both domestically and internationally.

The Colorado College Tigers compete in two Division I sports—men's ice hockey and women's soccer—as well as 14 Division III sports. Men's and women's soccer, lacrosse, swimming, and cross-country and women's volleyball all have made national tournament appearances in recent years. The hockey rivalry with the University of Denver is huge. Nearly 70 percent of students partake in 15 intramural sports, and 15 club sports are also available.

The Block Plan made Colorado College what it is today, and the school continues to build on this reputation. As one senior underscores, "The intensive and demanding nature of the Block Plan calls for deep but quick thinkers [and] hard but patient workers." For those who are up to the challenge, CC offers a supportive environment, with a healthy dose of fun, where they can thrive.

Overlaps

Cornell College, University of Denver, University of Colorado Boulder, University of Vermont, Lewis & Clark, Whitman, University of Southern California, Tulane

If You Apply To ›

Colorado College: Early decision I and II, early action, regular decision. SATs or ACTs or three Subject Tests, AP exams, or IB exams: required. Accepts the Common Application with supplement.

Colorado School of Mines

1812 Illinois Street, Golden, CO 80401

Mines is the preeminent technical institute in the Mountain West. Getting in is not all that hard; graduating is another story. One-sixth the size of Texas Tech and best known for mining-related fields but strong in many areas of engineering. Men outnumber women nearly 3 to 1, and Golden provides little other than a nice view of the mountains. Graduates are heavily recruited.

Website: www.mines.edu
Location: Small City
Public
Total Enrollment: 5,631
Undergraduates: 4,546
Male/Female: 70/30
SAT Ranges: ERW 640–710,
    M 670–740
ACT Ranges: 28–32
Financial Aid: 77%
Pell Grant: 11%
Expense: Pub $ $ $ $
Student Loans: 51%
Average Debt: $ $ $
Applicants: 10,619
Accepted: 56%
Enrolled: 19%
Grad in 6 Years: 78%
Returning Freshmen: 93%
Academics: ✍ ✍ ✍ ½
Social: ☎ ☎ ☎
Q of L: ★ ★
Admissions: (888) 446-9489
Email Address: admissions@
    mines.edu

Strong Programs:
Mechanical Engineering
Petroleum Engineering
Chemical and Biological
    Engineering
Electrical Engineering
Computer Science
Metallurgical and Materials
    Engineering
Geophysical Engineering
Engineering Physics

If you're a bit of a geek whose only dilemma is what type of engineer to become, and you want to spend your scarce free time hiking, biking, and skiing with friends, then Colorado School of Mines may be the place for you. This public school's small size and rugged location endear it to the mostly male students who shoulder heavy workloads to earn their degrees. "There are often fun and entertaining conversations that could only be possible with the types of students here," says a mechanical engineering major. Just down the road from Coors Brewing Co., which taps the Rockies for its legendary brews, students at Mines learn to tap the same mountains for coal, oil, and other natural resources.

CSM's 373-acre campus sits in the shadow of the spectacular Rocky Mountains in tiny Golden, Colorado. Architectural styles range from turn-of-the-century gold dome to present-day modern, and native trees and greenery punctuate lush lawns. The $50 million CoorsTek Center for Applied Science and Engineering is the newest addition to campus.

CSM's academics are rigorous. Core requirements include coursework in humanities, social sciences, physical education, and, of course, science and engineering, with extra doses of physics, chemistry, calculus, and differential equations. In the first year, everyone takes the Freshman Success Seminar, an advising and mentoring course. The required two-semester EPIC program—the acronym stands for Engineering Practices Introductory Course—helps develop communication, teamwork, and problem-solving skills with weekly presentations and written reports. Because of CSM's narrow focus, the undergraduate majors—or "options," as they're called—are quite good. There's plenty of variety, as long as you are into engineering; programs range from geophysical, metallurgical, and petroleum to chemical, electrical, and mechanical. Computer science is another popular choice, and the school's fastest-growing program. Mines offers the only B.S. degree in economics in Colorado, and the school has been investing more in humanities and social sciences, offering several minors in these areas. Courses in a student's option start in the second semester of sophomore year, and as seniors, all students complete a capstone requirement.

> "Most of the students would be considered nerds or geeks at other schools, but almost everyone fits in here."

Pass/fail grading is unheard of at Mines, but failing grades are not. "The courses are hard," says a junior, "but good time management and friends" help ease the angst. "We are all working together," another adds. Professors are qualified and helpful, and adjunct professors, who work in the fields they teach, draw raves for their practical knowledge. "Most of the teachers have industry experience and bring that into the classroom," a chemistry major says. Twenty-seven percent of undergraduate classes have fewer than 20 students.

CSM supplements coursework with a required six-week summer field session, enabling students to gain hands-on experience. About 100 undergraduates participate in the McBride Honors Program in Public Affairs, which includes seminars and off-campus activities that encourage them to think differently about the implications of technology. The WISEM program provides training, mentoring, and other support for women in science, engineering, and math. CSM also offers exchange programs with 25 universities worldwide, but only 7 to 10 percent of students study abroad. Each year, 100 to 120 undergraduates participate in research with faculty members or on their own.

Mines is a state school, making it a good deal for homegrown students, who comprise 55 percent of the undergraduate student body. Six percent hail from foreign nations. "Most of the students would be considered nerds or geeks at other schools," a civil engineering major explains, "but almost everyone fits in here." Hispanics comprise 9 percent of the student body, Asian Americans 5 percent, African Americans 1 percent, and multiracial students 6 percent. Students are generally too wrapped up in academics to pay attention to political issues, according to a physics major. Merit scholarships averaging $8,300 are available to qualified students, and athletes may vie for 331 athletic scholarships.

Freshmen are required to live in the residence halls; almost everyone moves off campus after the first year. Most buildings are co-ed, though the preponderance of men results in a few single-sex dorms. "All the residence halls have been refurbished and are looking better than ever," a sophomore says.

"When you leave here, you're prepared for anything."

Options for upperclassmen include fraternity or sorority housing, college-owned apartments, and off-campus condos and houses. There's only one cafeteria, Mines Market, and a junior says, "The vegetarian options are not very good unless you really like cereal and salad" (presumably not during the same meal).

There is life outside of the computer labs here. On campus, a junior says, "There is always a club putting together an event or just students throwing parties." Mines has an active Greek system, with fraternities and sororities attracting 12 percent of the men and 24 percent of the women. Rush is dry, and underage drinking is met with consequences. CU Boulder offers livelier partying 20 minutes away. Mines social life also includes comedy shows, homecoming, and Engineering Days (E-Days)—a three-day party with fireworks, a pig roast, tricycle races, taco-eating contests, and cheap beers. New student orientation features the traditional "M Climb," in which freshmen hike up Mount Zion lugging a 10-pound rock from their hometown, then "whitewash it, and each other," says one participant. The rock is added to an M formation atop the mountain, and at the end of the year, "seniors return to take down a rock, completing the cycle."

CSM's location at the base of the Rockies means gorgeous Colorado weather (make sure to bring sunscreen) and easy access to skiing, hiking, mountain climbing, and biking. Denver is also nearby, and aside from its museums, concerts, and sports teams, the city is home to many government agencies and businesses involved in natural resources, computers, and technology, including the regional offices of the U.S. Geological Survey and Bureau of Mines. Golden hosts the National Earthquake Center, the National Renewable Energy Laboratory, and, of course, the Coors Brewery. (The 3,000-foot pipeline that runs from the Coors plant to campus is there to convert excess steam from the brewery into heat for the school—not to supply the frats with the foamy stuff.) The biggest complaints are too much homework and (among guys) not enough women. Road trips to Las Vegas or Texas provide some respite.

CSM's 16 Division II varsity teams compete in the Rocky Mountain Athletic Conference. The men's cross-country team brought home the school's first ever team national championship in 2015. Other competitive Oredigger teams include men's and women's soccer and basketball, men's track and field, and women's volleyball, all of which are recent conference champs. The intramural and club sports programs have grown dramatically, with 70 percent of students now participating.

Core requirements include extra doses of physics, chemistry, calculus, and differential equations.

The WISEM program provides training, mentoring, and other support for women in science, engineering, and math.

Overlaps

University of Colorado Boulder, Texas A&M, UT Austin, Colorado State, Cal Poly–San Luis Obispo, University of Washington, Purdue, Arizona State

While time spent in the classroom at Mines may not be fun, for those who are focused on engineering, educational options don't get much better than those offered here. "Lots of companies recruit our students," says one senior, thanks to a stellar reputation in the fields of mining and engineering. A junior adds, "When you leave here, you're prepared for anything." Especially if you are an engineer.

If You Apply To ›

CSM: Rolling admissions. SATs or ACTs: required. No Subject Tests. Does not accept the Common Application.

Colorado State University

Fort Collins, CO 80523

It lacks Boulder's glitz and glamour, but Colorado State offers a more complete slice of the Rocky Mountain West. Known throughout the region for its prevet program, CSU turns out more STEM (science, technology, engineering, and math) graduates than any other Colorado campus. Has a traditional college feel with a first-rate student center and strong ties to the local community.

Website: www.colostate.edu
Location: Small City
Public
Total Enrollment: 24,793
Undergraduates: 21,914
Male/Female: 49/51
SAT Ranges: ERW 560–650, M 540–650
ACT Ranges: 22–28
Financial Aid: 47%
Pell Grant: 21%
Expense: Pub $ $
Student Loans: 51%
Average Debt: $ $
Applicants: 23,137
Accepted: 83%
Enrolled: 26%
Grad in 6 Years: 69%
Returning Freshmen: 84%
Academics: ✍ ✍ ✍
Social: ☎ ☎ ☎ ☎
Q of L: ★ ★ ★ ★
Admissions: (970) 491-6909
Email Address: admissions@ colostate.edu

Strong Programs:
Business Administration
Health and Exercise Science

Founded in 1870 as the Colorado Agricultural College, Colorado State University began with five students, two faculty members, and a mission "to serve society through teaching, research, and outreach." Today, the university boasts approximately 1,800 faculty across eight colleges, as well as more than 220,000 living alumni, including state governors, heads of corporations, Olympic gold medalists, teachers, researchers, and artists. Students here enjoy ample research opportunities, a slew of solid academic programs, and an unbeatable location, so it's little wonder they take pride in calling CSU home. "CSU has a great community and a wonderful friendliness about it," says one happy Ram. "It really is a fun and comfortable place to be."

Situated at the foot of the spectacular Rocky Mountains, CSU gives students easy access to abundant natural resources. The open space on the main campus reflects the university's heritage as a land-grant institution. The Oval, a wide expanse of lawn encircled by towering elm trees, anchors the northwest corner of campus. Architectural styles range from Beaux-Arts to Renaissance Revival, and the campus features a spacious outdoor plaza, 32 acres of recreation fields, and stunning views of Long's Peak. The university also boasts a 1,433-acre foothills campus, a 1,575-acre agricultural campus, and the 1,177-acre Pingree Park mountain campus, which provide opportunities for hands-on learning and research. Construction on an 812,000-square-foot multipurpose stadium was recently completed.

"The biggest issues on campus are probably environmental issues."

All CSU students complete a university-wide core curriculum that includes 31 credit hours of coursework in written communication, mathematics, oral communication, biological and physical sciences, arts and humanities, social and behavioral sciences, historical perspectives, and global and cultural awareness. CSU offers 75 undergraduate majors, the most popular of which include business administration, health and exercise science, human development and family studies, psychology, and biological science. "Our science programs are really strong," a sophomore says, and the prevet program is also distinguished. The performing arts have received a boost thanks to improved facilities, but the humanities are not as solid as other departments. Other notable undergraduate majors are available in mechanical engineering, fermentation science and technology, and a dual degree in engineering science and international studies. Unique concentrations include agricultural literacy, sustainable energy, and global tourism.

(continued)

Human Development and
    Family Studies
Psychology
Biological Sciences
Mechanical Engineering
Fermentation Science and
    Technology
Preveterinary Medicine

The academic climate can be competitive—especially in the preprofessional programs. "The courses are hard, but manageable," a junior says. Twenty-seven percent of classes have fewer than 20 students, and one student says, "If you express an interest in their area of study, [professors] may invite you to do research in their lab, write a paper and be published in a major journal, or help you with graduate school applications—who knows!" Freshmen may participate in a midsummer orientation and a variety of first-year seminars designed to ease the transition from high school to college. A sophomore highly recommends the Key Communities living/learning program for first-years: "As a Key student you take three classes with a cluster of 19 people whom you meet before classes start. This is so nice because you immediately have friends and people you know who also live in [the same hall] and can help you study." Qualified students can opt for the honors program or take part in the Honors Undergraduate Research Scholars program, which allows students to conduct long-term research alongside a faculty mentor. Eleven percent of undergrads study abroad via hundreds of programs worldwide.

"The students at CSU are friendly and accepting," says a junior. Seventy-two percent of CSU students are from Colorado, and 4 percent are international. African Americans account for only 2 percent of the student body, Asian Americans 3 percent, Hispanics 13 percent, and multiracial students 4 percent. CSU is a politically active campus, with liberal and conservative viewpoints both well represented. "The biggest issues on campus are probably environmental issues," explains a student, "due mainly to our proximity to the Rocky Mountains." Thousands of merit scholarships averaging $5,000 are handed out each year, and athletes vie for nearly 180 scholarships in 16 men's and women's sports. Twenty-one percent of freshmen are Pell-eligible.

A foothills campus, an agricultural campus, and a mountain campus provide opportunities for hands-on learning and research.

Twenty-six percent of all CSU students live on campus in residence halls and campus apartments; students may move off campus after their first year. "Residence halls are in great condition and more like a resort than the dorms we all picture from movies," says a student. Campus residents may choose from among six meal plans, and the residence hall dining center provides an all-you-can-eat option. "The food is awesome," a student says. "I think it is as good as any restaurant in town." Students also report feeling safe on campus; security measures include a "safe walk" escort program and an active security staff.

"There is a definite sense of community and support for CSU in [Fort Collins]."

The Greek scene attracts 5 percent of the men and 7 percent of the women, so it's not a major force in campus social life. "Campus activities, such as free movies or concerts, draw a large crowd," says one student, "while parties and other gatherings off campus do the same." The Lory Student Center hosts events on a regular basis, and more than 330 active student clubs serve as a social outlet too. The CSU campus is dry and "there is no tolerance for alcohol in the residence halls," a biochemistry major notes. "The policies are enforced."

The Key Communities living/learning program for first-years comes highly recommended.

Fort Collins is "a fun city that revolves around the school," says one junior. "There is a definite sense of community and support for CSU in the town," a senior adds. Students not only frequent the downtown bars, shops, and eateries, but also can be found performing volunteer work or community service alongside the locals. Popular road trips include quick getaways to nearby ski resorts and hiking trails, and longer treks to Utah and Nevada. Back on campus, students enjoy a number of traditions: "We have a huge homecoming," says one student, "with a bonfire, lighting of the 'A,' parade, and football game."

The CSU Rams compete in Division I as members of the Mountain West Conference, and the most competitive teams include football, women's volleyball and basketball, and men's and women's track and field. Women's volleyball has made 24 consecutive trips to the NCAA tournament. The University of Colorado is the hated rival—especially in football—and "the Rocky Mountain Showdown is probably the biggest event of the year," says a family and consumer sciences major. Intramurals and club sports attract roughly 15 percent of the student body; the climbing and polo club teams are recent national champs. The Student Recreation Center features an indoor track, basketball and volleyball courts, cardio machines and free weights, and a host of other facilities for students who want to stay in shape.

Despite ubiquitous complaints about limited parking, rising tuition, and the need for more bike racks, students at Colorado State are quick to say why they appreciate their alma mater: "Because CSU rocks! It is an awesome school to go to and has lots to offer students of all ages and backgrounds," cheers a student. What's more, it's a "fun and beautiful place to be," says a junior, "and you know that your degree will mean something."

Overlaps

Iowa State, Kansas State, Oregon State, North Carolina State, Oklahoma State, Michigan State, University of Colorado Boulder, University of Denver

If You Apply To ›

CSU: Early action, regular decision. SATs or ACTs: required. No Subject Tests. Accepts the Common Application with supplement.

Columbia University

212 Hamilton Hall, New York, NY 10027

Once a high-powered Ivy League afterthought, Columbia now rivals the Ivy League's big three in selectivity. Applications have nearly doubled in the past 10 years for one simple reason: Manhattan trumps New Haven, Providence, Ithaca, and every other Ivy League city, with the possible exception of Boston. The often overlooked engineering program is among the best in the nation for undergraduates. The heart of Columbia is still its Core Curriculum.

Website: www.columbia.edu
Location: City Center
Private
Total Enrollment: 24,061
Undergraduates: 6,231
Male/Female: 52/48
SAT Ranges: ERW 720–780, M 730–800
ACT Ranges: 32–35
Financial Aid: 55%
Pell Grant: 16%
Expense: Pr $ $ $ $
Student Loans: 22%
Average Debt: $ $

Though students entering Columbia will, of course, expect the rigorous academic program they'll encounter at this Ivy League school, they must also be streetwise, urbane, and together enough to handle one of the most cosmopolitan cities in the world. Columbia lets its students experience life in the Big Apple, but serves as a refuge when it becomes necessary to escape from New York, allowing students to immerse themselves in the best academia has to offer, starting with the Core Curriculum. "Students here want a classical liberal arts education but do not want to live in a college bubble," says a freshman. Famous alums can be found in the highest echelons of their chosen professions, whether it be politics, literature, sports, or entertainment. Think Barack Obama.

With a total university-wide enrollment of more than 24,000 students, says one of them, "It's easy to feel lost." Columbia's 6,200 undergraduates are split into two divisions: the flagship Columbia College and The Fu Foundation School of Engineering and Applied Science. (Sister school Barnard College, affiliated with Columbia University but governed by its own board of trustees, has an additional

2,600 students.) Columbia's campus has a large central quadrangle in front of Butler Library and at the foot of the steps leading past the statue of Alma Mater to Low Library, which is now the administration building. The redbrick, copper-roofed neoclassical buildings are "stunning," and the layout, says an undergrad, "is well thought out and manages to provide a beautiful setting with an economy of space."

The undergraduate experience at Columbia centers on its renowned Core Curriculum. While these courses occupy up to a third of the first two years and can become laborious, students generally praise them as worthwhile and enriching. "The Core truly unifies the school in a way that transcends most social limitations," says a freshman. As it has since World War I, the college remains committed to the Core while at the same time expanding the diversity of the canon and requiring Core classes on non-Western cultures. According to a junior, some students find that the Core can "spark some interest in a subject they had never thought of before."

> **"We are mostly content to be liberal artists for as long as possible."**

Two of the most demanding introductory courses in the Ivy League—Contemporary Civilization (CC) and Literature Humanities (LitHum)—form the basis of the Core. Both are yearlong and taught in small sections, generally by full professors. CC examines political and moral philosophy from Plato to Camus, though professors have some leeway in choosing 20th-century selections. LitHum covers about 26 masterpieces of literature from Homer to Dostoyevsky, usually with some Sappho, Jane Austen, and Toni Morrison thrown in for alternative perspectives. One semester each of art and music history is required and, while they are not given the same reverence as their literary counterparts, they are eye-opening all the same. Foreign language proficiency is required, as are two semesters of science, two semesters of "global Core" classes dealing in cultures not covered in the other Core requirements, two semesters of phys ed, and University Writing. Students at the School of Engineering and Applied Science complete approximately half of the Core Curriculum.

Columbia is an intellectual school, not a preprofessional one, and even though a large percentage of students aspire to law or medical school, "we are mostly content to be liberal artists for as long as possible," says an English major. Even students in the School of Engineering and Applied Science pursue "technical education" with a liberal arts base. Almost all departments that offer undergraduate majors are strong, notably English, history, political science, economics, neuroscience, and computer science. Chemistry and biology are among the best of Columbia's high-quality science offerings. The earth and environmental science department owns 200 acres in Rockland County, home to many rocks and much seismographic equipment. The fine arts are improving, thanks to departmental reorganization, newer facilities, and joint offerings with schools such as the Juilliard School of Music. Columbia offers many challenging combined majors such as philosophy/economics and biology/psychology. There are 50 offerings in foreign languages, ranging from Czech to Persian to Urdu, and the East Asian languages and cultures department is one of the best anywhere. There is also an African American studies major and a women's studies major that delves into topics ranging from the Asian woman's perspective to the lesbian experience in literature. Columbia students can take classes at Barnard and graduate-level courses in several departments, notably political science, gaining access to the resources of the School of International and Public Affairs and its multitude of regional institutes.

> **"Prepare to be average and to be happy that you are an average student at Columbia."**

Columbia is tough; the workload is often stressful, and since most students are used to being top achievers, classmates can be competitive. A financial economics major offers this advice: "Prepare to be average and to be happy that you are an

(continued)

Applicants: 37,389
Accepted: 6%
Enrolled: 62%
Grad in 6 Years: 95%
Returning Freshmen: 99%
Academics: ✑ ✑ ✑ ✑ ✑
Social: ☎ ☎ ☎
Q of L: ★ ★ ★ ★
Admissions: (212) 854-2522
Email Address: ugrad-ask@ columbia.edu

Strong Programs:
English
History
Political Science
Economics
Neuroscience
Computer Science
Biology
Engineering

Columbia's renowned Core Curriculum occupies up to a third of students' first two years.

average student at Columbia." Student/faculty interaction is supported by one of the smallest student-to-faculty ratios in the country, and 83 percent of classes have fewer than 20 students. "Some of the professors are real leaders in their fields," says a philosophy major, who also cautions, "Many Core classes are taught by grad students, which has led to some less than ideal experiences for me." Additional interaction stems from professorial involvement in campus politics and forums and from the faculty-in-residence program, which houses professors and their families in spruced-up apartments in several of the residence halls. First-year students are assigned an academic advisor with whom they work for all four years, and they receive a departmental faculty advisor when they declare a major at the end of sophomore year. For students wishing to spend time away from New York, Columbia offers credit through more than 150 programs in more than 100 cities around the world; about a third of students go abroad. Research is big here too, and the university conducts nearly $1 billion of research annually in the sciences, humanities, and social sciences; hundreds of undergraduates participate.

Columbia has 50 offerings in foreign languages, ranging from Czech to Persian to Urdu.

A sophomore says that Columbia is attended by "smart, diverse, individualistic, driven students who tend to contemplate the organization of society and the meaning of life pretty frequently." Twenty-two percent of undergraduates come from New York, and 17 percent come from abroad. Columbia has the largest proportion of students of color in the Ivy League: 8 percent of undergrads are African American, 14 percent are Hispanic, 20 percent are Asian American, and 6 percent are multiracial. Columbia remains one of the nation's most liberal campuses, and an evolutionary biology major comments, "Columbia students are not quiet about their beliefs." The university awards financial aid based on need, meeting the full demonstrated need of all students with grants instead of loans. Students coming from families with annual incomes below $60,000 are not expected to contribute to the cost of tuition, fees, room, or board; the family contribution is reduced for those with incomes between $60,000 and $100,000.

"Columbia students are not quiet about their beliefs."

With the New York housing market out of control, 93 percent of Columbia students live in university housing, which is guaranteed for four years. Many rooms are singles, and it is possible to go all four years without a roommate. Carman Hall, one of three exclusively first-year dorms, is a popular choice for its private bathrooms. "Going into sophomore year, my roommate and I had a very bad lottery number," recalls one student, "but we were still able to get a room in an air-conditioned building with a view of the Empire State Building." First-year students are automatically placed on a 19-meal-a-week plan and take most of those meals at John Jay, where a junior says, "People complain about the meals, but it's buffet style, and I think there is a good variety of options." After the first year, many scale down their meal plans or convert to a buy-what-you-want point system. Several dorms have kitchens, allowing students to do their own cooking. "Columbia's Public Safety makes sure that students feel safe and supported on campus and the surrounding neighborhood at all times of the day," a senior says. One student points out that, despite having introduced several Title IX initiatives, including a comprehensive gender-based misconduct policy and the addition of a second sexual violence support center, "Columbia has taken a lot of heat for the way it handles sexual assault on campus."

First-year students are assigned an academic advisor with whom they work for all four years.

"Columbia has an excellent relationship with its Morningside Heights neighborhood."

The social scene starts on the Columbia campus and spills over into the bustling streets of New York City. "We have the best of both worlds, because Columbia students can be a part of the vibrant on-campus community but also take part in New York's eclectic environment!" cheers one student. The challenge, others say, is finding time to relax and enjoy all the city has to offer. Rarely are there big all-inclusive bashes, the exception being spring's Bacchanal concert. "My favorite tradition is the Varsity Show, a more than 120-year-old tradition of a student-written musical that satirizes Columbia, the Ivy League, and current campus and world events," says a sophomore. Twenty-four percent of the men and 16 percent of the women go Greek; the advent of co-ed houses has raised interest in Greek life, as has the arrival of sororities open to both Columbia and Barnard women. But Columbia is hardly a Hellenocentric campus. "I love that no one activity dominates the social scene," says a freshman. The Community Impact organization coordinates 27 local community service programs, in which nearly 1,000 students participate. "Columbia has an excellent relationship with its Morningside Heights neighborhood," confirms a freshman.

The advent of co-ed houses has raised interest in Greek life, as has the arrival of sororities open to both Columbia and Barnard women.

Columbia athletics don't inspire rabid loyalty. "Columbia students are individualists," according to one sophomore. "This is not a school that rallies together at football games." Still, the Lions field 31 Division I teams. The fencing and women's archery teams are recent national champi-

"This is not a school that rallies together at football games."

ons, while baseball and men's tennis have claimed Ivy League conference titles. As an urban school, Columbia lacks team field facilities on campus; however, 100 blocks to the north is the modern Baker Field, home of the football stadium, the soccer fields, an Olympic track, and the crew boathouse. On campus, the Dodge Gymnasium, an underground facility, houses four levels of basketball courts, swimming pools, weight rooms, and exercise equipment. More than 80 intramural and club sports are available; men's and women's ultimate Frisbee are both nationally competitive.

"Columbia is definitely not a stress-free, friendly community, but it has its own charm," explains a senior. "The university is quintessentially New York: as a student, there are so many experiences to be had, but you really have to engage in the community and seek them out." Columbians are proud to attend college in New York City, and most would have it no other way.

Overlaps

Harvard, Yale, Stanford, MIT, Princeton, University of Pennsylvania, Brown, UC Berkeley

If You Apply To ›

Columbia: Early decision, regular decision. SATs or ACTs: required. Subject Tests: optional. Accepts the Common Application with supplement.

University of Connecticut

2131 Hillside Road, Unit 3088, Storrs, CT 06269

Squeezed in among the likes of Brown, UMass, Trinity, Wesleyan, and Yale—all within a two-hour drive—UConn could be forgiven for having an inferiority complex. But applications have been soaring, with championship basketball teams, both men's and women's, helping to ignite Husky pride and boost selectivity. One of the highest retention and graduation rates among public universities. Storrs is nobody's idea of an exciting destination, but it does offer easy access to beautiful countryside.

The top public university in New England and highly regarded nationally, the University of Connecticut has recently seen billions of dollars poured into new facilities and into expanding educational opportunities and research in STEM disciplines. UConn is the only public university in New England with its own law school, medical school, dental school, and school of social work—and undergraduates benefit indirectly from these resources. What's more, it's one of the few major public

Website: www.uconn.edu
Location: Rural
Public
Total Enrollment: 24,083
Undergraduates: 18,443

(continued)

Male/Female: 49/51

SAT Ranges: ERW 600–680,
 M 610–710

ACT Ranges: 26–31

Financial Aid: 80%

Pell Grant: 18%

Expense: Pub $ $ $ $

Student Loans: 60%

Average Debt: $ $

Applicants: 34,198

Accepted: 48%

Enrolled: 23%

Grad in 6 Years: 83%

Returning Freshmen: 94%

Academics: ✍ ✍ ✍ ✍

Social: ☎ ☎ ☎

Q of L: ★ ★ ★

Admissions: (860) 486-3137

Email Address: beahusky@
 uconn.edu

Strong Programs:

Business

Engineering

Education

Pharmacy

Nursing

Physical Therapy

Agriculture

Coastal Studies

Three-quarters of the freshmen take at least one First-Year Experience course that guides them through the transition to college.

universities that continues to significantly expand their faculty ranks, adding nearly 300 tenure-track positions in recent years. Couple these initiatives with the glow of two championship basketball teams, a wealth of research opportunities, and more than 600 clubs and organizations, and it's clear why UConn has moved well beyond its erstwhile "cow college" image. "I'm incredibly proud to be a UConn student," says a senior.

UConn's 4,000-acre campus is about 23 miles northeast of Hartford. Building styles range from collegiate Gothic and neoclassical to half-century-old redbrick. Dense woods surround the campus, which also boasts two lakes, Swan and Mirror. Ongoing renovations are the norm, sparking jokes about the "University of Construction," but the results are impressive. The 212,000-square-foot NextGen residence hall houses more than 700 students in several living/learning communities and features an innovative makerspace. The five-story, $95 million Engineering and Science Building and the $75 million Student Recreation Center are among the newest additions to campus.

"I'm incredibly proud to be a UConn student."

Students say UConn's strongest offerings are preprofessional—business, engineering, education, pharmacy, and allied health, including nursing and physical therapy. The school's historic focus on agriculture is giving way to an emphasis on environment and ecology, including a strong program in coastal studies. Also notable are neuroscience, linguistics, history, human rights, and, of course, agriculture. (UConn was founded more than a century ago as a farm school; it's where America learned to get more eggs per chicken by leaving the lights on in the coops.) Engineering is demanding, and, as at many schools, it has a relatively high attrition rate, with many students switching to the less rigorous major in management information systems. A special program in medicine and dentistry allows students to earn bachelor's degrees in any of UConn's more than 100 disciplines, and guarantees admission to the School of Medicine or Dental Medicine if they meet all criteria.

UConn's academic atmosphere is described as moderately competitive and challenging, depending on a student's course of study. Core requirements include courses in four basic areas: arts and humanities, social sciences, diversity/multiculturalism, and science and technology. Students must also achieve competency in computer technology, information literacy, and a foreign language. Seminar-style writing classes are available to all freshmen, and three-quarters also take at least one First-Year Experience course that guides them through the transition to college. The Academic Center for Exploratory Students helps freshmen and sophomores who still need to decide on a major. Students generally applaud the enthusiasm of their professors—and the graduate teaching assistants who administer tests, collect assignments, and run labs and discussion groups—but a senior grumbles, "Some lack the ability to connect with students and the skills to teach students effectively."

"Students are very much concerned with what is going on today in our world."

UConn's engineering, business, pharmacy, and honors students are required to undertake research projects, and each year two teams of finance majors run the $1 million student-managed investment fund. Students who aspire to graduate school in academic fields, rather than professional certification, may win grants to work independently under faculty members through the undergraduate summer research program. The 8 percent of students who qualify for the honors program gain access to special floors and dorms; several programs for disadvantaged students are also available. In addition, 15 percent of students participate in the study abroad program, which offers 275 options in more than 60 countries.

UConn students are "hardworking, responsible, intelligent, passionate, and inspirational," according to one psychology major. Seventy percent of UConn undergraduates are from Connecticut, and 8 percent are international. Many students choose to transfer to the Storrs campus after beginning coursework in their chosen major and earning 54 credits at one of UConn's four regional campuses. Six percent of undergrads are African American, 10 percent are Hispanic, 11 percent are Asian American, and 3 percent are multiracial. There are cultural centers for African American, Asian American, Latin American, and Puerto Rican students, as well as the Rainbow Center, a resource for LGBTQ students. "Students are very much concerned with what is going on today in our world," a student says. Eligible UConn students receive merit scholarships averaging $8,300, and hundreds of athletic scholarships are available in 18 sports. Persistence rates are astronomically high for a public flagship university, with 94 percent of freshmen returning for their sophomore year and a graduation rate of 83 percent.

UConn's engineering, business, pharmacy, and honors students are required to undertake research projects.

Sixty-six percent of the students live in university housing, which is available to all undergraduates. "All the dorms are very well maintained," says a senior. Dorms are all co-ed, and the entire campus, including outdoor areas, is equipped with Wi-Fi. Eight dining halls offer plenty of choices, even for vegetarians

"As you get involved, you will be wicked busy!"

and vegans, though many students would just as soon visit the snack bar for some ice cream, freshly made with help from the cows grazing nearby. "The food at UConn each night is diverse, and a student can always find something he or she wants," one student says. A group of students are selected to live on a sustainable farm just off campus where they raise foods that are served in the dining halls. Students report feeling safe on campus. "Crime is so low we think it doesn't exist, the police don't bother anyone unless they have to, and we have a great system of security alerts," says a junior.

"Social life is the best part of college life and includes clubs, frats, sports, and so much more," says one student. "As you get involved, you will be wicked busy!" Students 21 and over are allowed to possess no more than a six-pack of beer, one bottle of wine, or a small bottle of liquor. Underage students caught with booze may be evicted from campus housing. Late-night activities at the student union and other campus events provide a lot of alternatives to alcohol use. Fraternities attract 11 percent of the men, and sororities claim 14 percent of the women; members can live in chapter housing at the Husky Village. On weekends, there are buses to Hartford (only 30 minutes away), Boston, New Haven, New York, and Providence. Cape Cod and the Vermont ski slopes are within weekend driving distance. Favorite annual campus events include the mud volleyball tournament, carnival-style UConn Late Nights, midnight breakfasts during finals, homecoming, Winter Weekend, and Midnight Madness—the first official day of basketball practice. In addition to cheering for the Huskies, "it is good luck to rub the nose of the bronze statue of our mascot, Jonathan," says a sophomore.

Favorite annual campus events include Midnight Madness— the first official day of basketball practice.

The town of Storrs "is basically UConn," says one student. A recent downtown Storrs initiative offers shops, restaurants, and a town green, as well as additional living options available to students. The university provides transportation for students who volunteer in area schools and hospitals. Legend holds that UConn also offers one diversion most other colleges can't: cow tipping—that is, sneaking up on unsuspecting cows, which sleep standing up, and tipping them over. The administration contends that this is a myth, though students always claim to "know someone who did it."

UConn's teams are known as the Huskies (UConn. Yukon. Get it?), and in a state without any major league professional sports teams, the UConn women's basketball team routinely sells out the XL Center. Men's basketball won the national Division I

Overlaps

UMass Amherst, Boston University, Northeastern, University of Delaware, Quinnipiac, Syracuse, University of Rhode Island, Penn State

title in 2014, while in 2016 the women's team brought home its 11th—and fourth-straight—national championship. Women's field hockey claimed the national title in 2017, and men's soccer is also strong. Intramurals are offered at three levels, from recreational to competitive. Popular offerings range from underwater hockey and inner-tube water polo to basketball, volleyball, and flag football.

UConn continues to build on its agricultural roots and adapt them to the 21st century. Those seeking greener pastures will be hard-pressed to find a more dynamic public institution. "We are a well-rounded campus with students from every background," a junior pharmacy student says. And with the campus undergoing a complete face-lift, it's a good time to be at UConn.

If You Apply To ›

UConn: Regular decision. SATs or ACTs: required. No Subject Tests. Accepts the Common Application. Most fine arts programs require a portfolio, audition, or interview.

Connecticut College

270 Mohegan Avenue, New London, CT 06320

Like Skidmore and Vassar, Connecticut College long ago made a successful transition from women's college to co-ed. That means a slightly more progressive campus tenor than at, say, Hamilton or Trinity. The college is strong in the humanities, dance, and drama, and notable for its study abroad programs and funded internships. New London does not offer much, but at least it is on the ocean.

Website: www.conncoll.edu
Location: Small City
Private
Total Enrollment: 1,764
Undergraduates: 1,764
Male/Female: 37/63
SAT Ranges: ERW 640–710, M 630–690
ACT Ranges: 29–31
Financial Aid: 58%
Pell Grant: 16%
Expense: Pr $ $ $ $
Student Loans: 46%
Average Debt: $ $ $
Applicants: 5,434
Accepted: 38%
Enrolled: 22%
Grad in 6 Years: 85%
Returning Freshmen: 91%
Academics: ✍ ✍ ✍ ✍
Social: ☎ ☎ ☎
Q of L: ★ ★ ★ ★
Admissions: (860) 439-2200

Students at Connecticut College follow the example of their mascot, the camel—they take pride in drinking up and storing knowledge. The student-run honor code means finals are not proctored; they're even self-scheduled, whenever students prefer, during a five-day window. "The honor code gives the freedom for the student to be responsible for their actions academically and socially," says an economics major. "It creates a respectful and trustful relationship between professors and students."

Placed majestically atop a hill, the Conn College campus sits within a 750-acre arboretum with a pond, wetlands, wooded areas, and hiking trails. It offers beautiful views of the Thames River (pronounced the way it looks, not like the "Temz" that Wordsworth so dearly loved) on one side and Long Island Sound on the other. The granite campus buildings are a mixture of modern and collegiate Gothic in style, with some neo-Gothic and neoclassical architecture thrown in for good measure. The library underwent a $10 million renovation to enhance space for research, group and individual study, and public talks and meetings.

"A majority of professors at Conn take great personal responsibility in their teaching styles."

Conn was founded in 1911 as a women's college but went co-ed in 1969. The general education program, now cleverly called Connections, has been revamped to span all four years of a student's undergraduate experience. Coursework includes two semesters of foundational courses, including a first-year seminar and an interdisciplinary ConnCourse, followed by a series of thematically linked classes called an "Integrative Pathway." The senior year culminates with an integrative project. Academics are definitely the focus here. "I'd consider the academic climate at Conn to be rigorous and intense, but supportive all the same," says a film studies major. Much of that support comes from professors, who are lauded for their accessibility and thoughtfulness. "I've found that a majority of professors at Conn take great personal responsibility in their teaching styles and try to cater to students' needs as much as possible," observes a psychology major.

Conn's dance and drama departments are superb, and it's not uncommon for dancers to take time off to study with professional companies. Aspiring actors, directors, and stagehands may work on numerous on-campus productions and with the Eugene O'Neill Theater Institute, named for New London's best-known literary son. Chemistry majors may use high-tech gas chromatograms and mass spectrometers from their very first day, and students say Conn also offers excellent programs in biology and physics. Five interdisciplinary centers offer courses and special programming in international studies, arts and technology, public policy and community action, environmental studies, and the study of race and ethnicity; all but the latter administer certificate programs. The most popular majors are economics, psychology, behavioral neuroscience, computer science, and biology.

To escape Conn's small size and occasionally claustrophobic feel, the Study Away/Teach Away (SATA) initiative allows groups of about a dozen Conn students and a faculty member to spend a semester living and working together at an overseas university, in locations as far-flung as Ghana, Iceland, and Vietnam. In fact, 55 percent of Connecticut College juniors study in 40 countries around the world through SATA and other college-approved study abroad programs. All students who participate in a set of career workshops are guaranteed an internship opportunity, including a $3,000 grant to help cover housing or other costs. Opportunities for funded summer research with professors are also available.

"Connecticut College has a reputation for being a 'preppy' school; many of the students are very well-off," says a computer science major. Only 18 percent of Conn College students come from Connecticut, and 8 percent come from abroad. African Americans and Asian Americans each make up 4 percent of the student body, Hispanic students add 8 percent, and multiracial students represent 3 percent. Freshmen must attend a session on issues of race, class, and gender, run by a panel of diverse peers. Students say there is a growing interest in activism on campus, and the political atmosphere is largely liberal. There are no athletic scholarships, but a limited number of merit scholarships are awarded to top achievers, and the college meets all admitted students' full demonstrated financial need. Loan reduction is available for students of highest need.

> "The a cappella groups are the closest thing Conn has to Greek life."

Ninety-nine percent of students live on campus. Options include first-year-only and mixed-class housing, and dorms are run by seniors who apply to be "house fellows." Several specialty houses are dedicated to interests such as environmental awareness, substance-free living, quiet lifestyles, and international languages. "There is a great sense of house pride on campus," says one student. The campus boasts five dining halls that receive generally good reviews; Freeman is devoted exclusively to vegan and vegetarian fare. "Students can make requests to dining staff by writing their thoughts on a 'napkin note' and pinning it to a provided bulletin board," reports a senior. A junior says that life on campus feels safe: "Campus safety officers patrol campus constantly." Another adds, "Conn has a local Green Dot program, which is really successful in educating the community about consent and destigmatizing discussions about sexual assault."

Students keep busy with parties, movie nights, comedy shows, student productions, and dances—sometimes with out-of-town bands and DJs. "The a cappella groups are the closest thing Conn has to Greek life, the only major difference being

(continued)

Email Address: admission@ conncoll.edu

Strong Programs:
Economics
Psychology
Behavioral Neuroscience
Computer Science
Biology
Physics
Dance
Drama

All students who participate in a set of career workshops are guaranteed an internship opportunity, including a $3,000 grant.

Camelympics, when houses compete against each other in a Conn-style Olympics, is a favorite tradition.

their preference for practicing complex vocal arrangements over playing mindless drinking games," quips a sophomore. Students say the absence of Greek groups creates a more inclusive community. The alcohol policy falls under the honor code, so those under 21 can't imbibe at the campus bar, and students take that prohibition seriously. Camelympics, when houses compete against each other in a Conn-style Olympics, is a favorite tradition, as is the Festivus holiday celebration. Students also anticipate the annual Floralia festival in the spring, when "students camp out in tents, eat lots of free food, and dance to music," says a junior.

Many students volunteer at the local schools, aquarium, youth community center, and women's center; a college van makes it easy to get to and from work sites. When students get the urge to roam, the beaches of Mystic and other shore towns are 20 minutes from campus, and the Mohegan Sun casino is also very close. Trains go to Providence, Rhode Island, New York City, or Boston, while Vermont and upstate New York offer camping, hiking, and skiing.

The Conn Camels compete in Division III, and men's ice hockey games against NESCAC rival Wesleyan draw crowds. Women's soccer and men's swimming are among the stronger teams. More than 700 students participate in intramural and club sports, the most popular of which are ultimate Frisbee and broomball. Between classes or at the end of the day, all students may use the natatorium's pool and fitness center and the rowing tanks and climbing walls at the field house.

On its friendly campus, Conn College encourages strong student/faculty bonds and takes pride in its ability to challenge—and trust—students, both in and out of the classroom. "Connecticut College promotes a sense of self-awareness and being able to be yourself in an environment that fosters creativity, acceptance, and community," reasons one junior. A classmate asks, "Who else has a dromedary camel as the mascot?!"

If You Apply To ›

Conn College: Early decision I and II, regular decision. SATs or two SAT Subject Tests or ACTs: optional. Accepts the Common Application with supplement.

The Cooper Union

30 Cooper Square, New York, NY 10003

As college costs skyrocket, so does the popularity of The Cooper Union's low-cost education in art, architecture, and engineering. Expect Ivy-level competition for a place in the class here. Instead of a conventional campus, The Cooper Union has the cool and funky East Village. But be prepared to spend your nights hitting the books rather than the cafés.

Website: www.cooper.edu
Location: City Center
Private
Total Enrollment: 894
Undergraduates: 859
Male/Female: 65/35

Tuition is no longer free at The Cooper Union for the Advancement of Science and Art, but if you manage to get accepted into this technical institute, you get a half-tuition scholarship (with additional aid to those who demonstrate need) and some of the nation's finest academic offerings in architecture, engineering, and art. With the always vibrant East Village in the background and rigorous studying in the forefront, college life at The Cooper Union may seem to be faster than a New York minute. Whatever the pace, though, no one can deny that a CU education is one of the best bargains around—arguably the best anywhere. The only complication is that the number of applicants is booming, and its acceptance rate is comparable to the Ivies.

The school was founded in 1859 by entrepreneur Peter Cooper, who believed that education should be "as free as water and air." With hefty contributions from J. P. Morgan, Frederick Vanderbilt, Andrew Carnegie, and various other fellow robber barons, the school was able to maintain its tuition-free policy and stay afloat in order to recruit poor students of "strong moral character." Trustees ended the famous policy in 2013, citing dire financial straits—although the school has announced plans to reinstate free tuition for all undergraduates by 2029.

In place of a traditional collegiate setting are two academic buildings and one dorm plunked down in one of New York's most eclectic and exciting neighborhoods. The stately brick art and architecture building is a beautiful historic landmark. Built of brick and topped by a classic water tower, the dorm blends right in with the neighborhood. The Great Hall was the site of Lincoln's "Right Makes Might" speech and the birthplace of the NAACP, the American Red Cross, and the national women's suffrage movement. Wedged between two busy avenues in the East Village, Cooper offers an environment for survivors. It also boasts the first academic building in New York City to achieve LEED Platinum status, the highest and most rigorous level of certification.

> **"Cooper Union has a performance-oriented culture. You are expected to produce great work."**

CU's curriculum is highly structured, and all students must take a sequence of required courses in the humanities and social sciences. The first year is devoted to language and literature and the second to the making of the modern world. In some special circumstances, students are allowed to take courses at nearby New York University and the New School for Social Research. The nationally renowned engineering school offers both bachelor's and master's degrees in chemical, electrical, mechanical, and civil engineering, as well as a bachelor of science in general engineering studies. The architecture school is "phenomenal—even unparalleled," in the words of one pleased participant. The art school, rather than offering individual majors, awards a bachelor of fine arts degree that encompasses a broad-based generalist curriculum in graphic design, drawing, painting, sculpture, photography, printmaking, film, and video. All students must fulfill a capstone requirement: engineers complete a senior design project and presentation, architects a yearlong senior thesis and presentation, and artists a senior show.

The academic climate is intense and the workload heavy across all programs, but collaborative group projects and study groups are common. "Cooper Union has a performance-oriented culture. You are expected to produce great work, and you are in an environment that is conducive to that," explains a senior. Academic counseling is available—as are peer mentors—but the school's rigorously structured academic programs largely determine which classes the students take, eliminating a lot of confusion or decision making. Classes are small—73 percent enroll fewer than 20 students—and, with a little persistence, not too difficult to get into. Students report that it's usually easy to build personal relationships with professors, and a civil engineering major says, "There's a good mix of full-time, tenured faculty who are good with the theoretical side of things, and adjunct faculty who have jobs in the 'real world' and put the field into perspective." Ten percent of students—mostly art majors—find time to take their education global, through a variety of study abroad programs. About a quarter get involved in undergraduate research. Engineers in the popular Invention Factory summer program pair up to build their own inventions; prizes

> **"[Students] range from being complete geeks who love math, science, and gaming to artsy and out-of-this-world."**

(continued)

SAT Ranges: ERW 650–740, M 660–790
ACT Ranges: 28–34
Financial Aid: 100%
Pell Grant: 27%
Expense: Pr $ $
Student Loans: 18%
Average Debt: $
Applicants: 2,574
Accepted: 13%
Enrolled: 61%
Grad in 6 Years: 83%
Returning Freshmen: 95%
Academics: ✏ ✏ ✏ ½
Social: ☎
Q of L: ★ ★ ★
Admissions: (212) 353-4120
Email Address: admissions@ cooper.edu

Strong Programs:
Engineering
Architecture
Fine Arts

The Great Hall was the site of Lincoln's "Right Makes Might" speech and the birthplace of the NAACP.

are awarded to the top projects, and all participants file provisional applications for U.S. patents.

Strong moral character is no longer a prerequisite for admission, but an outstanding high school academic record most certainly is. CU students "range from being complete geeks who love math, science, and gaming to artsy and out-of-this-world," one student says, and another adds that "most students stick to their own school." Half of the undergraduates are from New York State, and most of them grew up in the city. Many are the first in their family to attend college; 27 percent of freshmen qualify for Pell Grants. Eleven percent of students are international. Asian Americans account for 20 percent of the student population, African Americans 3 percent, Hispanics 10 percent, and multiracial students 8 percent. Men outnumber women 2 to 1. The political climate depends on who you ask; most students are liberal, but you'll probably find more activism in the art school than elsewhere on campus.

Students love the dorm, a 15-story residence hall that saves its occupants from commuting into the Village or cramming themselves into expensive apartments. The downside is that housing here is not guaranteed, and only 20 percent of the student body (mostly freshmen) reside on campus. The facility is composed of furnished apartments with kitchens and bathrooms and is "in great condition and well maintained," states one resident, even if space can be tight. For those seeking off-campus housing, a freshman assures, "Few students have trouble finding an apartment, as leases are passed down from Cooper student to Cooper student." With no meal plan available, students cook for themselves, eat at the unexciting but affordable school cafeteria, or head for one of the myriad nearby delis and coffee bars. Students are mindful of potential safety concerns, given the urban campus, and Cooper has expanded its education and training programs aimed at preventing sexual assault.

"Cooper Union is extremely intensive."

"Because Cooper Union is extremely intensive, the social life usually takes place on campus," says a junior. Many students belong to professional societies, such as the American Society of Civil Engineers, and cultural groups are active on campus. Students have their choice of more than 90 clubs for everything from fencing and table tennis to religion and drama. Drinking on campus is allowed during school-sponsored parties for students 21 and over—otherwise, no alcohol on campus. Annual events include the Peter Cooper Block Party at the beginning of the year and the Culture Show, featuring multicultural music and dance. Nightlife and other social options are not far: McSorley's bar is right around the corner, and nearby Chinatown and Little Italy are also popular destinations. The heart of the Village, with its abundance of theaters, art galleries, and cafés, is just a few blocks to the west. The Bowery and SoHo's galleries and restaurants are due south; all of midtown Manhattan spreads to the northern horizon.

Cooper teams (the Pioneers) compete in the Division III Hudson Valley Athletic Conference in men's and women's basketball and volleyball, and it also fields a co-ed soccer team. The intramural sports program is held in several different facilities in the city and attracts its fair share of students.

Getting into The Cooper Union is tough, and once admitted, students find that dealing with the onslaught of city and school is plenty tough as well. But most students like the challenge. "The special culture of Cooper Union is built on a foundation of work," says a junior. "It's not simply about going here for half-price tuition, it's about working hard for it." Surviving the school's academic rigors requires talent, self-sufficiency, and a clear sense of one's career objectives. Students who don't have it all can be sure that there are six or seven people in line ready to take their places. That's quite an incentive to succeed.

Cornell College

600 First Street Southwest, Mount Vernon, IA 52314-1098

The One Course At A Time model is Cornell's calling card. The main challenge: trying to lure top students to rural Iowa. Encourages students to do off-campus study in distant corners of the world. More accessible than Colorado College, which follows a similar academic model. Though primarily a liberal arts institution, Cornell has programs in business, engineering, and education.

Cornell College attracts the type of student who seeks an intense yet flexible, self-designed program and a liberal, progressive atmosphere. It suits those who aren't satisfied with easy answers, don't mind heading to the rural Midwest, and do want loads of personal attention while focusing on one class and exercising disciplined study habits. "If you want a normal college experience, don't pick Cornell," warns one student, but "if you want to pour yourself into a class for three and a half straight weeks and feel exhausted but accomplished," Cornell may be just the right fit.

Aside from its distinctive schedule (shared by only one other school, Colorado College), Cornell has one of only two U.S. college or university campuses listed in its entirety on the National Register of Historic Places. The majestic clock tower of King Chapel has been in operation since 1882. A pedestrian mall runs through campus, and other facilities include suite-style residence halls for upper-class students. The school's Cole Library is also the town of Mount Vernon's public library, one of few such libraries in the country. Cornell's student center, Thomas Commons, features an indoor-outdoor fireplace, classrooms and meeting spaces, and a glass-enclosed dining room with panoramic views of campus. The $35 million Russell Science Center opened in 2018.

> **"At Cornell, a semester's worth of work is completed in a month."**

Current general education requirements include courses in humanities, math, natural science, social science, foreign language, and fine arts, as well as at least 124 semester hours to graduate. Freshmen must take a first-year seminar and a writing-intensive course. Block scheduling makes it easier for some students to graduate early; others use the flexibility to finish with a double major. A sophomore explains, "At Cornell, a semester's worth of work is completed in a month. This makes for a fast-paced class that is normally composed of a couple papers, maybe some annotations, a midterm, a final, and a final project." A biology and Spanish double major adds, "Each class is pretty intense." If that sounds intimidating, it can be. But administrators say it also improves the quality of Cornell's liberal arts education by helping students acclimate to the business world, where "what needs to be done needs to be done quickly and done well." The One Course method also helps in academic advising—with grades every four weeks, signs of trouble are quickly apparent.

Cornell awards degrees in more than 50 academic majors, as well as an extensive group of preprofessional programs. The bachelor of special studies, pursued

---

Website: www.cornellcollege.edu

Location: Small Town

Private

Total Enrollment: 1,000

Undergraduates: 1,000

Male/Female: 50/50

SAT Ranges: ERW 610–670, M 625–700

ACT Ranges: 26–29

Financial Aid: 99%

Pell Grant: 22%

Expense: Pr $

Student Loans: 70%

Average Debt: $ $ $ $

Applicants: 2,276

Accepted: 65%

Enrolled: 20%

Grad in 6 Years: 71%

Returning Freshmen: 81%

Academics: ✐ ✐ ✐

Social: ☎ ☎ ☎

Q of L: ★ ★ ★

Admissions: (800) 747-1112

Email Address: admission@cornellcollege.edu

Strong Programs:
Psychology
Kinesiology
Biochemistry and Molecular Biology
Economics and Business

by 3 percent of students, allows students to broaden or deepen their studies by combining courses in an individualized fashion. Among the most popular majors are psychology, kinesiology, biochemistry and molecular biology, economics and business, and education; other strong options include English and creative writing, geology, and theater and dance. The college also offers preprofessional centers for health sciences, law and society, and literary arts. Newer programs include anthropology and musical theater. "Students are deeply involved in their schoolwork and most spend extra time studying and working in the library," observes a biochemistry and molecular biology major. Classes are taught by full professors and are intimate, with 77 percent enrolling fewer than 20 students. Says a senior, "The professors do a great job of teaching practical, hands-on knowledge."

Sixty-four percent of Cornell students study off campus. Cornell faculty teach approximately 20 courses off campus each year; recent international courses have included Geology of New Zealand, Medieval Literature in Florence, Gender and Development in India, and Macroeconomics in Shanghai. Programs are also available in nearly 40 countries through partner providers. During the short breaks between courses, students can take advantage of symposia and athletic events. The Cornell Summer Research Institute offers an eight-week stipend for faculty-directed summer research projects. Career coaches at the Berry Career Institute help each student identify an individual path for their professional development.

> **"There is no singular way to describe a Cornellian other than *unique*."**

"'Cornell weird' is a phrase that gets thrown around a lot and it's accurate," says one student. "With the block plan and a variety of interests to offer to students, there is no singular way to describe a Cornellian other than *unique*." Only 20 percent of students are homegrown, and 5 percent hail from other nations. African Americans represent 6 percent of the student population, Hispanics 9 percent, Asian Americans 3 percent, and multiracial students 2 percent. "Cornell starts with one huge disadvantage in terms of diversity: it's in the middle of a relatively small town in Iowa," admits one student. Politically, Cornell leans liberal. Merit scholarships averaging $21,700 are offered to qualified students, although there are no athletic awards; 22 percent of freshmen qualify for Pell Grants.

The Cornell Summer Research Institute offers an eight-week stipend for faculty-directed summer research projects.

Eighty-eight percent of students live on campus, and first-years enjoy completely renovated residence halls. Six percent of students participate in living/learning communities. Everyone eats together in Thomas Commons, where the food is "usually good," a junior says. Vegetarian options are always available. Student safety is taken seriously, students say, and, "Campus Security is very accessible, with an officer on call and on campus 24/7." The school has enacted programs to deal with sexual assault, including bystander intervention training and risk education.

> **"Students come together to facilitate each other's learning."**

"Most of the social life happens on campus," says a psychology major. "Because everyone lives on campus, there is a lot of effort to make sure that there is always a lot to do and nobody has time to be bored." Fraternities and sororities draw 21 percent of the men and 32 percent of the women, though they are not associated with national Greek systems; some fraternities accept men and women, and most sororities accept students who identify as women. "Some are completely dry or emphasize their commitment to service," explains one student, "while others are notorious for parties and jungle juice (never, *ever* drink jungle juice). The Greek orgs and other social groups set the tone of social life only for those involved." The Performing Arts and Activities Council is in charge of bringing entertainment to campus, which includes bands, comedians, speakers, musicians, and hypnotists. Mount Vernon itself is "small, but very welcoming," says a physical education major. Students

Some fraternities accept men and women, and most sororities accept students who identify as women.

either love the town's idyllic pace—a few local bars; an acclaimed restaurant; some funky shops; and a lot of peace, quiet, and safety—or long for more excitement. The latter is available in Cedar Rapids (home of archrival Coe College) or Iowa City (home to the University of Iowa), each less than half an hour away. Chicago is less than four hours away.

On the field or on the court, Cornell's competition with Coe is always heated, especially when it comes to Rams football and basketball. "'Beat Coe' and 'Coe Sucks' have been emblazoned on Cornell fanwear since the 1920s," says one student. "We have the archival records to back that up." Cornell teams compete in the Division III Midwest Conference, and competitive teams include women's volleyball (recent back-to-back conference champs), basketball, and softball, along with men's cross-country and wrestling. Twenty percent of students participate in intramural sports.

"Cornell is an intense academic community in which professors push their students to excel and students come together to facilitate each other's learning," says a sophomore. Indeed, Cornell offers plenty of opportunities, a top-notch education, and a supportive community. According to one satisfied senior, focusing on just one course at a time "is the most practical and interesting way to learn."

Overlaps

Colorado College, Beloit, Knox, Carleton, Lake Forest, Coe, Kalamazoo, Grinnell

If You Apply To ›

Cornell College: Early action, regular decision. SATs or ACTs: optional (test-optional applicants must submit portfolio and respond to two short-answer questions). Subject Tests: optional. Accepts the Common Application with supplement.

Cornell University

Ithaca, NY 14850

Cornell University's reputation as a pressure cooker comes from its preprofessional attitude and a "we try harder" mentality. Spans seven undergraduate colleges—four private and three public—and tuition varies accordingly. Strong in engineering and architecture, world famous in hotel administration. Easiest Ivy to get into, and also the farthest from an urban center. Once you're there, Ithaca is a great college town.

Cornell University has a long tradition of being the lone wolf among the Ivy League universities—not least for its ambition to become the finest research university for undergraduate education in the nation. The mixture within one institution of private and state-funded colleges and schools, preprofessional programs, and liberal arts results in, as one student says, "a diversity of opportunities in and outside of the classroom."

Perched atop a hill that commands a view of both the city of Ithaca and Cayuga Lake, Cornell is breathtakingly scenic, with ravines, waterfalls, and parks bordering all sides of the campus. (As the saying goes, "Ithaca is gorges.") The Cornell Botanic Gardens, more than 3,500 acres of woodlands, natural trails, streams, and gorges, provide space for walking, picnicking, or contemplation. Cornell's superb library system consists of 20 libraries, including the beautiful underground Carl A. Kroch Library, featuring sky-lit atriums and renowned collections of Icelandic and Southeast Asian materials. The Johnson Museum of Art, designed by I. M. Pei, is one of the best university museums in the nation. The state-of-the-art Bill and Melinda Gates Hall houses high-tech research and teaching labs for the university's computer and information science departments. One of the campus's newest buildings, the

Website: www.cornell.edu
Location: Rural
Private
Total Enrollment: 22,822
Undergraduates: 14,815
Male/Female: 48/52
SAT Ranges: ERW 690–760, M 700–790
ACT Ranges: 31–34
Financial Aid: 56%
Pell Grant: 16%
Expense: Pr $ $ $ $
Student Loans: 41%
Average Debt: $ $
Applicants: 47,039
Accepted: 13%

(continued)

Enrolled: 56%

Grad in 6 Years: 93%

Returning Freshmen: 97%

Academics: ✍ ✍ ✍ ✍ ✍

Social: ☎ ☎ ☎ ☎

Q of L: ★ ★ ★

Admissions: (607) 255-5241

Email Address: admissions@cornell.edu

Strong Programs:

Engineering

Business

Biological Sciences

Agriculture

Hotel Administration

Architecture

China and Asia-Pacific Studies

Industrial and Labor Relations

Cornell is breathtakingly scenic, with ravines, waterfalls, and parks bordering all sides of the campus.

LEED Platinum–certified Klarman Hall is dedicated to teaching, research, and education in the humanities.

At the undergraduate level, the university has four privately endowed colleges: architecture, art, and planning; arts and sciences; engineering; and hotel administration. Cornell is also New York State's land grant university, and as such operates three other colleges under contract with the state: agriculture and life sciences, human ecology, and the school of industrial and labor relations. New York residents at these "contract colleges" pick up their Ivy League degrees at an almost-public price (as tuition at these schools is slightly steeper than SUNY rates). The Cornell College of Business, formed in 2016, houses two undergraduate schools (the privately endowed School of Hotel Administration and the Dyson School of Applied Economics, which it shares with the agriculture college) and one graduate school. Prospective students apply to one of the seven colleges or schools through the central admissions office, and admissions standards vary by school. Each college sets its own general education requirements, but all Cornell undergrads take at least one First-Year Writing Seminar.

Cornell offers more than 4,000 courses in more than 100 fields of study. The most popular majors are in the areas of engineering, business, biological sciences, and agriculture. Cornell's College of Arts and Sciences boasts considerable strength in history, government, and just about all the natural and physical sciences. The English program has turned out a number of celebrated writers, including Toni Morrison, Thomas Pynchon, and Kurt Vonnegut. Foreign languages, required for all arts and sciences students, are strong (try taking Tamil, Zulu, or Nepali), and the performing arts, mathematics, and social science departments are considered good.

"As the years pass, classes become smaller and more intimate, which is a big advantage."

Cornell was early among universities to add women's studies to the curriculum and continues to be an innovator, with programs like China and Asia-Pacific studies, which requires a semester in China and another in Washington, D.C. The College of Agriculture and Life Sciences is highly ranked and a good bet for anyone hoping to make it into veterinary school (Cornell's graduate College of Veterinary Medicine is among the best), while the School of Industrial and Labor Relations is the preeminent school of its kind. The College of Business offers more than a dozen concentrations, including agribusiness management; finance, accounting, and real estate; and business analytics.

"The quality of teaching is top-notch because the majority of professors are regarded as experts in their respective fields," says one student, who also cautions, "Some of the educators struggle to communicate their knowledge." First-year courses in the sciences and social sciences are generally large lectures, but overall, 57 percent of classes have fewer than 20 students. "Freshman year it was difficult to build personal relationships with faculty because the classes are so large," a senior observes, "but as the years pass, classes become smaller and more intimate, which is a big advantage from a student perspective."

Cornell academics are demanding and foster an intensity found on few campuses. "There is a competitive atmosphere, as students who attend Cornell are ambitious and passionate. However, this is a positive and motivating force," says one sophomore. Those who were the class genius in high school should be prepared for a struggle to rise to the top. After a series of well-publicized suicide incidents a number of years ago, Cornell has greatly strengthened its mental health support program. To cope with the anxieties that the high-powered atmosphere creates, the university has one of the best psychological counseling networks in the nation, including an alcohol-awareness program, peer sex counselors, personal-growth workshops, and EARS (Empathy, Assistance, and Referral Service).

A co-op program is available to engineering students, and Cornell-in-Washington is popular among students from all seven undergraduate colleges. Students looking to study abroad can choose from more than 200 programs and universities throughout the world, including those in Indonesia, Belgium, Ireland, and Nepal; 37 percent of students participate. "The number of quality study abroad programs seems inexhaustible," says a sophomore. Roughly 60 percent of undergraduates participate in a faculty-guided research experience during their four years. The Presidential Research Scholars program, open to undergraduates in all disciplines, provides as many as 200 selected students with up to $8,000 in funding to carry out individually designed research programs with the support of faculty mentors. About three-quarters of the students engage in community service opportunities coordinated primarily by the Public Service Center.

Cornell students are "friendly, fun, and balanced," says a sophomore. "We are cooler than the nerdy kids, and nerdier than the cool kids," quips one senior. "We don't quite fit in anywhere else. We by and large didn't get into other Ivies, so compared to those students we feel a need to validate and distinguish ourselves through hard work and a more robust social life." Thirty-one percent of Cornell's undergraduates hail from New York; another 10 percent are international. African Americans constitute 7 percent of the student body, Hispanics account for 13 percent, Asian Americans comprise 19 percent, and multiracial students add 5 percent. All freshmen participate in discussion-based diversity workshops aimed at increasing dialogue and engagement. Upon graduation, nearly one-third of Cornell students attend graduate and professional schools.

> **Roughly 60 percent of undergraduates participate in a faculty-guided research experience during their four years.**

> **"The number of quality study abroad programs seems inexhaustible."**

Cornell is need-blind in admissions and meets the demonstrated need of all accepted applicants, but the proportion of outright grants—as opposed to loans that must be repaid—in the financial aid package varies based on income. Cornell eliminates loans and the parental contribution for students from families with incomes below $60,000 and assets below $100,000 and caps need-based student loans at varying amounts for students whose families have annual incomes between $60,000 and $135,000. The Cornell Installment Plan allows students or their parents to pay a year's or semester's tuition in monthly interest-free installments. The university does not award merit or athletic scholarships.

Just over half of Cornell's students live in university housing; many try their luck off campus in Collegetown, where demand has kept the housing market tight and rents high, although options are increasing. "Housing was one of the main reasons I chose Cornell," says one junior. "I was able to essentially guarantee myself a single room even freshman year. My room was huge, and my dorm was quiet." North Campus residence halls are the home of all freshmen, and about 2,000 students (mostly sophomores) live in the West Campus House System, in five living/learning "houses" with professors in residence, house chefs, and creative programming. There are dorms devoted to everything from ecology to music, and cultural houses include the International Living Center, Latino Living Center, Ujamaa Residential College, and Akwe:kon, a program house focusing on American Indian culture (the only facility of its kind in the U.S.). Cornell's food service is reputedly among the best in the nation, with eight residential dining halls that function independently; one student enthuses, "The food is very diverse and super tasty!"

> **All freshmen participate in discussion-based diversity workshops aimed at increasing dialogue and engagement.**

> **"We feel a need to validate and distinguish ourselves through hard work and a more robust social life."**

Despite the intense academic atmosphere—or maybe because of it—Cornell social life beats most of the other Ivies hands down. Once the weekend arrives, local parties, state parks, and ski slopes are filled with Cornell students seeking a balance between study and play. With 32 percent of men and 31 percent of women pledging fraternities and sororities, these groups play a significant role in the social scene. "Social life at Cornell is really built around Greek life, especially for those under 21. Students who go Greek tend to have busy social schedules, and those who don't really need to find an organization they are passionate about," advises one student. Students have their pick of roughly 1,000 student organizations—including clubs for Japanese drumming and Bhangra dancing—and there are innumerable concerts and sporting events throughout the year. Alcohol is part of the social scene, but one student says the university is "cracking down" on underage and high-risk drinking. Freshmen are not allowed to attend fraternity parties during the fall semester, and after freshmen receive a bid to a house in the spring, there is an eight-week dry period. Big events include Fun in the Sun (a day of friendly athletic competition), Dragon Day (architecture students build a dragon and parade it through campus), and Springfest (a gathering on Ho Plaza). Students celebrate the last day of classes—Slope Day—with a concert on Libe Slope.

Students celebrate the last day of classes— Slope Day—with a concert on Libe Slope.

Cornell has won several Ivy League team titles during the last decade and made a slew of high-profile Division I national championship appearances, most recently in wrestling, women's ice hockey, men's lacrosse, and men's basketball. But men's ice hockey is unquestionably the dominant sport on campus (its chief goal being to defeat Harvard), and camping out for season tickets is an annual ritual. Lightweight rowing has brought home a number of Intercollegiate Rowing Association titles. Cornell boasts the largest intramural program in the Ivy League, with more than a dozen sports, including 100 hockey teams. The "four seasons of Ithaca" (rain, snow, slush, and drizzle) can make walking to class across the vast and hilly campus challenging, but with the first snow of the winter, "traying" down Libe Slope becomes the sport of choice for hordes of fun-loving Cornellians. Students head to Greek Peak Mountain for skiing, Cayuga Lake for boating and swimming, and countless places for hiking and watching the clouds roll by.

> **"Social life at Cornell is really built around Greek life, especially for those under 21."**

Like most other Ivy League universities, Cornell is a premier research institution with a distinguished faculty and outstanding academics. What sets it apart is its focus on preprofessional preparation for undergraduates and a student body that strives for high academic achievement and at the same time a vigorous social life. One junior sums up the Cornell experience like this: "The people are passionate, the academics are rigorous, and the extracurricular activities are empowering."

Overlaps

Harvard, University of Pennsylvania, Princeton, Stanford, Yale

If You Apply To ›

Cornell University: Early decision, regular decision. SATs or ACTs: required. Subject Tests: required for some (varies by program). Accepts the Common Application with supplement. Apply to individual programs or schools. Architecture applicants must interview. Applicants to design programs must submit portfolio.

Irving, TX 75062

Bulwark of academic traditionalism in Big D, with a Core curriculum focused exclusively on Western civilization. Despite being a "university," UD has just 1,400 undergraduates, making small classes and personal attention a priority. The only outpost of Roman Catholic education between Loyola of New Orleans and University of San Diego. A compelling drawing card is the university's program in Rome, pursued by most sophomores.

While many universities around the nation have reexamined their Eurocentric core curriculums, the University of Dallas—the best Roman Catholic university south of Washington, D.C.—remains proudly dedicated to a classic liberal arts education that fosters the study of "the great deeds and words of Western civilization." The campus tenor is conservative, but students say there are plenty of lively happenings to be found. Whether it's discussing Homer and Dante on the campus mall or cutting loose for the school's quirkiest event, a massive Groundhog Day party, one student says, "UD cherishes tradition."

UD's 744-acre campus occupies a pastoral home in a Dallas suburb on top of "the closest thing this region has to a hill." A major portion of the campus is situated around the Braniff Mall, a landscaped and lighted gathering place near the Braniff Memorial Tower, the school's landmark. The primary tone of the buildings is, like the surrounding North Texas landscape, brown, and the architecture, as described by one student, is "post-1950s, done in brick, typical Catholic—institutional." While it may not be a picture-perfect school, it does have a beautiful chapel and a state-of-the-art science building. A $15 million student services and administration building opened in 2018.

Appropriately for a Catholic school, most eyes at UD look to Rome, where 80 percent of undergraduates trek for the unique, semester-long Rome Program, usually during sophomore year. "It sounds cliché to say that a semester could change your life, but the Rome semester does precisely that," enthuses a politics major. The program involves intense coursework, as well

> **"It sounds cliché to say that a semester could change your life, but the Rome semester does precisely that."**

as trips to northern Italy and Greece (not to mention long weekends for individual travel). It is part of UD's four-semester Western civilization Core curriculum, which includes philosophy, English, math, fine arts, science, American civilization, Western civilization, politics, economics, a serious foreign language requirement, and two theology courses (Understanding the Bible and The Western Theological Tradition). All students also complete a senior thesis or project, a comprehensive exam, and/or a senior seminar, depending on their major.

UD students choose from more than 25 majors and 33 concentrations, including a few preprofessional options. Biology, business, English, history, and psychology are the most popular majors. The business program draws on abundant internship opportunities in the Dallas–Fort Worth Metroplex. Politics is another popular major and offers a concentration in political philosophy. Classics is, unsurprisingly, a traditional strength, and a major in human and social sciences tackles 21st-century issues through theory and practical research in areas like anthropology, sociology, and social psychology. Premed students are well served by the biology and chemistry programs. Other students take advantage of 3–2 dual-degree programs in nursing and electrical engineering, as well as 4 + 1 bachelor's/master's programs in a

---

Website: www.udallas.edu
Location: Suburban
Private
Total Enrollment: 1,685
Undergraduates: 1,421
Male/Female: 46/54
SAT Ranges: ERW 590–700, M 550–670
ACT Ranges: 24–31
Financial Aid: 95%
Pell Grant: 24%
Expense: Pr $
Student Loans: 57%
Average Debt: $ $ $ $
Applicants: 3,857
Accepted: 47%
Enrolled: 23%
Grad in 6 Years: 68%
Returning Freshmen: 85%
Academics: ✎ ✎ ✎
Social: ☎ ☎
Q of L: ★ ★ ★
Admissions: (800) 628-6999
Email Address: crusader@udallas.edu

Strong Programs:
Biology
Business
English
History
Psychology
Politics
Classics
Human and Social Sciences

number of fields. The O'Hara Chemical Science Institute offers a hands-on, eight-week summer program to prepare new students for independent research.

"The University of Dallas is very much like a coffeehouse," says one junior. "It is laid-back, but intellectual, it is fun, and all your friends are there with you." The university uses no teaching assistants, and professors are easy to get to know, especially since 60 percent of classes enroll fewer than 20 students. "The professors are brilliant and have chosen to teach at UD because they understand the education the Core entails," says a theology major.

A junior characterizes UD students as "kind, grounded, nerdy, and unpretentious." Seventy-nine percent of UD students are Catholic, and many of them choose this school because of its religious affiliation. Fifty-two percent of undergraduates are homegrown, and 4 percent are international. Twenty-three percent are Hispanic, 6 percent are Asian American, 2 percent are African American, and 3 percent are multiracial. Most students are conservative and "think similarly about social issues such as gender and abortion," says one student, and there is not much political activism on campus. UD offers various merit scholarships averaging $15,300 but no athletic awards, as it is a Division III school. Twenty-four percent of freshmen qualify for Pell Grants.

Sixty-three percent of students live on campus, where tradition and religion govern conduct. Students under 21 who don't reside at home with their parents must live on campus in single-sex dorms with strict visitation regulations. "The freshman dorms are a little old, but there is a great feeling of community there," says a junior. The sole dining hall is spacious and boasts a wonderful view of north Dallas, but the food draws complaints for being too expensive for the quality. The fast food and snacks at the Rathskeller are said to be better. "UD is a small and pretty safe campus, so we have few cases of sexual assault," reports a junior.

"Come here to have fun… and graduate with a deep sense of your place in the Western cultural tradition."

With no fraternities or sororities at UD, the Campus Activities Board sponsors most on-campus entertainment. Free movies, dances, and visiting speakers are usually on the agenda. Church-related and religious activities provide fulfilling social outlets for a good number of students. During Charity Week in the fall, the junior class organizes a variety of fund-raising events. The biggest event of the year is Groundhog, a whole week of events celebrating Groundhog Day and culminating in a huge party at Groundhog Park, featuring "live bands, free food, beer for students over 21, and sports games throughout the day," explains an English major. Smaller off-campus parties happen frequently; on campus, a student warns, "The Office of Student Life runs a tight ship regarding alcohol." Students describe Irving (population 240,000) as "a suburb just like any other," but Dallas offers almost unlimited possibilities, including a full agenda for barhopping on Lower Greenville Avenue and food, craft breweries, and culture in the Bishop Arts District, both about 15 minutes away. The West End and Deep Ellum offer a taste of shopping and Dallas's alternative music scene. And for the more adventurous, Austin and San Antonio aren't too far away.

The University of Dallas is unusual for a Texas school in that its entire population does not salivate at the sight of a football or basketball. But the Crusaders baseball and men's and women's basketball and soccer teams are competitive in the Division III Southern Collegiate Athletic Conference. Club and intramural sports are well organized and sign up about a quarter of the students. The club rugby team (known as the Hoggies, after the school's favorite Groundhog tradition) is particularly popular.

Although some students complain that UD's focus on Western liberal arts and its Catholic emphasis can feel academically limiting, most say they appreciate the sense of shared experience and strong tradition that defines their school. In the words of one senior, "Come here to have fun, build sincere friendships, work hard, and graduate with a deep sense of your place in the Western cultural tradition."

Dartmouth College

6016 McNutt Hall, Hanover, NH 03755

The smallest Ivy and the one with the strongest emphasis on undergraduates. Traditionally the most conservative member of the Ivy League, it has steered toward more student diversity and more serious scholars, but long-standing party culture persists. Ivy ties notwithstanding, Dartmouth has more in common with places like Colgate, Middlebury, and Williams. Great for those who like the outdoors.

Unlike the other seven members of the Ivy League, which trace their roots to Puritan New Englanders or progressive Quaker colonists, Dartmouth College was founded in 1769 to educate Native Americans. The student body has always been the smallest in the Ancient Eight, and the school's focus on undergraduate education differentiates Dartmouth from its peers, though it does offer graduate programs in engineering, business, and medicine. The college attracts plenty of hiking and skiing enthusiasts, and the Dartmouth Outing Club is still the most popular extracurricular organization. But these days, as Dartmouth focuses increasingly on building a warm, inclusive community and emphasizing the importance of global ties, students are just as likely to join a hip-hop dance group or to spend a vacation doing college-sponsored community service in Latin America. According to one freshman, "We strongly value traditions, we like to have fun in our woodsy New Hampshire home, and at the same time, everyone is incredibly academically involved."

Dartmouth's picturesque campus is the most rural of the Ivies, and its winters may be the coldest, with the possible exception of those at Cornell. Set in the "small, Norman Rockwell town" of Hanover, New Hampshire, which is bisected by the Appalachian Trail, the campus is arranged around a traditional New England green. It's bounded by the impressive library at one end and by the college-owned Hanover Inn at the other. Architectural styles range from Romanesque to postmodern, but the dominant theme is copper-topped colonial frame. The nearest big city, Boston, is two hours away, but major artists like Itzhak Perlman routinely visit Dartmouth's Hopkins Center for the Arts, adding to the growing arts culture on campus.

> "We strongly value traditions [and] we like to have fun in our woodsy New Hampshire home."

Dartmouth's status as a member of the Ivy League means academic excellence is a given. First-years must take a writing-intensive seminar that involves both independent research and small-group discussion; about 75 are offered each year across different departments. Students must also demonstrate proficiency in at least one foreign language and take three world culture courses (one non-Western, one Western, and one Culture and Identity), and 10 courses from several distribution areas spanning the liberal arts and sciences. In addition, Dartmouth has a senior culminating

Website: www.dartmouth.edu
Location: Rural
Private
Total Enrollment: 6,343
Undergraduates: 4,360
Male/Female: 51/49
SAT Ranges: ERW 710–770, M 720–790
ACT Ranges: 30–34
Finanoial Aid: 52%
Pell Grant: 14%
Expense: Pr $ $ $ $
Student Loans: 52%
Average Debt: $
Applicants: 20,035
Accepted: 10%
Enrolled: 58%
Grad in 6 Years: 96%
Returning Freshmen: 97%
Academics: ✍ ✍ ✍ ✍ ✍
Social: ☎ ☎ ☎ ☎ ☎
Q of L: ★ ★ ★
Admissions: (603) 646-2875
Email Address: admissions .office@dartmouth.edu

Strong Programs:
Economics
Government
Computer Science

activity—a thesis, public report, exhibition, seminar, production, or demonstration—that allows students to pull together work done in their major with a creative and intellectual twist of their own. Before arriving on campus for their first year, 90 percent of incoming students opt to go on five-day preorientation trips with the Outing Club, getting to know their classmates while exploring the great outdoors.

Though Dartmouth students work hard, the climate is far from cutthroat. "Dartmouth is challenging but supportive," says one junior. Popular majors include economics, government, computer science, engineering sciences, English, and history. Programs in engineering and biological sciences are particularly strong, and the languages are also well regarded; students benefit from the Intensive Language Model developed by the late Professor John Rassias. Computer science offerings are among the best in the nation, thanks in no small part to the late John Kemeny, the former Dartmouth president who coinvented time-sharing and the BASIC language. Indeed, computing has long been a way of life here, and the campus remains a leader in academic wireless connectivity.

Ninety percent of incoming students opt to go on five-day preorientation trips, getting to know their classmates while exploring the great outdoors.

Professors get high marks at Dartmouth, perhaps because of the school's focus on undergraduates. The rural location also helps; faculty make a conscious choice to teach here, leaving behind some of the distractions afflicting their peers at more urban schools. "If you come to Dartmouth for only one thing, it would be the faculty," says an economics major. "The professors are truly the best out there for undergraduates." Sixty-five percent of undergraduate classes have fewer than 20 students, and more than 60 percent of undergrads take advantage of abundant research opportunities. The Presidential Scholars Program provides one-on-one, paid research assistantships with faculty. The Policy Research Shop helps undergraduate public policy students write policy briefs for state legislators and government agencies in New Hampshire and Vermont. Female students interested in STEM fields can participate in the Women in Science Project, which offers mentors, speakers, and even research positions for first-years. Montgomery Fellowships bring well-known politicians, writers, and others to campus for periods ranging from a few days to several months.

The school's most notable eccentricity is the Dartmouth Plan, or "D-Plan"—four 10-week terms a year, including one during the summer. Students must be on

"The professors are truly the best out there for undergraduates."

campus for three terms during the freshman and senior years, and also during the summer after the sophomore year, but otherwise, as long as they're on track to graduate, they can take off whenever they wish. About 60 percent of undergrads use terms away to study abroad, usually signing up for one of Dartmouth's more than 40 faculty-led programs, selecting from options ranging from theater in London to environmental studies in South Africa to biology in Costa Rica.

Ninety-seven percent of undergraduates hail from outside of New Hampshire, including 9 percent from other countries. Dartmouth went co-ed in 1972, and it subsequently became the first major university to award more bachelor's degrees in engineering to women than to men. Women now make up half of the student body. African Americans comprise 7 percent, Asian Americans 15 percent, Hispanics 10 percent, and multiracial students 5 percent. Consistent with its historical roots, Dartmouth continues to have a strong interest in recruiting and supporting Native American students, who currently represent 2 percent of the undergraduate student body. Students here have a "true, true love for this school and a passion for learning not simply for the grade but for the experience," says a senior. Students retain that passion after graduation, as Dartmouth has the most elaborate network of alumni organizations of any college in the country. Politically, an economics major says, "Most students are either liberal or quietly conservative." Admissions are need-blind, even for students admitted from the waitlist, and the school meets the full

The school's most notable eccentricity is the Dartmouth Plan, or "D-Plan"—four 10-week terms a year, including one during the summer.

demonstrated need of all admits. It also offers free tuition and no loans to students from families with incomes below $100,000 a year. No merit or athletic scholarships are awarded; the Ivy League prohibits the latter.

Eighty-five percent of Dartmouth students live on campus in one of more than 30 dorms, which, in an effort to create a greater sense of community among undergraduates, have been organized into six House Communities, each led by a House Professor. "From suites to singles to apartment-style housing, it's easy to find housing on campus that will suit you," says an engineering physics major. Beginning in their freshman year, students can apply to live in one of several living/learning communities, from the Sustainable Living Center to Dartmouth Entrepreneurial Network in Residence to Global Village to various identity-based communities. Housing is guaranteed for freshmen and sophomores. Because of the D-Plan, people are always coming and going, so it may be easier to find a new room or roommate than at schools on the semester system. Seniors may move off campus, where "there's a bunch of cheap, readily available options," says a student. Dining facilities are open until 2:30 a.m. for those needing sustenance during late-night study sessions. Students report feeling safe on campus and say the administration is assertive in dealing with potential issues, including sexual assault. "The Dartmouth Bystander Initiative is a program geared toward educating students about how to intervene in risky situations," explains one psychology major.

> **Dartmouth was the first major university to award more bachelor's degrees in engineering to women than to men.**

> **"[Students have] a passion for learning not simply for the grade but for the experience."**

"Social life primarily occurs on campus," says a senior. "There is college programming every Friday and Saturday night, including everything from roller-skating to pottery nights and comedy shows." Dartmouth's Greek system attracts 44 percent of the men and 46 percent of the women. "What's really unique about our Greek system is that it's open to the entire campus—if you have a Dartmouth ID card, you cannot be denied entry." The Greeks have become less of a force in campus social life because of the Moving Dartmouth Forward plan aimed at bolstering behavioral standards and offering more options for social life. As part of its continuing efforts to reduce binge drinking and other alcohol-soaked misbehavior, the college has banned hard liquor on campus. Parties and kegs must also be registered, and the houses where they're being held are subject to walk-throughs by college safety and security personnel. Alcohol policies are aimed at keeping booze away from those under 21 and reducing the number of students who end up in the emergency room. Indeed, Dartmouth was one of the first schools to develop a counseling and educational program to combat alcohol abuse. Good road trips, although relatively infrequent, include Montreal or Boston, for a dose of bright lights and the big city, or the White Mountains for camping. Dartmouth has a 27,000-acre land grant in the northeast corner of New Hampshire where cabins may be rented for five dollars a night.

> **Winter Carnival includes ski racing at the college's skiway, snow-sculpture contests, and a polar plunge.**

"I was sold on Dartmouth because it is steeped in tradition," says one senior. Weekends bring traditions such as a 75-foot-tall bonfire at homecoming, and Winter Carnival, which includes ski racing at the college's skiway, 20 minutes away, as well as snow-sculpture contests, a polar plunge, and partiers from all over the Eastern seaboard. Spring brings mud as the snow slowly melts, and also Green Key weekend, an annual rite of spring featuring live music and parties. Community service is popular, and the Center for Social Impact sponsors immersion trips to places like New Orleans, Puerto Rico, and the Dominican Republic.

> **"Our Greek system is…open to the entire campus—if you have a Dartmouth ID card, you cannot be denied entry."**

The Dartmouth Outing Club is the oldest collegiate outdoors club in the nation, and the school's love of the outdoors extends to varsity athletics. Dartmouth offers

35 Division I varsity sports. Big Green football and women's basketball teams have each won the most championships in Ivy League history. In recent years, Dartmouth has captured league crowns in men's soccer and tennis; women's lacrosse and softball are also competitive. The school's sports facility boasts a 2,100-seat arena, a 4,000-square-foot fitness center, and the only permanent three-glass-wall squash court in North America. Dartmouth offers 34 club sports including nationally competitive teams in sailing, skiing, figure skating, and men's rugby. There are also 24 intramural sports. Nonathletes beware: Dartmouth does have a nontimed swimming test and a physical education requirement for graduation; you can fulfill the latter with classes such as fencing or ballet, or with participation in a club or intramural sport.

"Dartmouth is really a place for a go-getter," advises one student. The college attracts outdoorsy, down-to-earth students who develop extremely strong ties to the school—and each other—during four years together in this quintessential rural New England setting. It seems as if every other grad has a title like deputy assistant class secretary, and many return to Hanover when they retire, further cementing their bonds with the college, and driving local real estate prices beyond the reach of most faculty members. You'll have to be made of hardy stock to survive the harsh New Hampshire winters. But once you defrost, you'll be rewarded with lifelong friends and a solid grounding in the liberal arts, sciences, and technology.

Overlaps

Brown, Duke, Yale, Stanford, Princeton, Colgate, Middlebury, Williams

If You Apply To ›

Dartmouth: Early decision, regular decision. SATs or ACTs: required. Subject Tests: recommended (any two). Accepts the Common Application with supplement. Submission of a peer recommendation is strongly recommended. Application includes an optional question on gender identity.

Davidson College

P.O. Box 7156, Davidson, NC 28035

Has always been styled as the "Dartmouth of the South." Goes head-to-head with Washington and Lee (VA) as the top liberal arts college below the Mason-Dixon Line, and Division I sports are an advantage. An early leader in the trend to replace loans with grants, it boasts a strong honor system that sets the campus tone. Small-town location is close to Charlotte and prime vacation spots.

Website: www.davidson.edu
Location: Small Town
Private
Total Enrollment: 1,800
Undergraduates: 1,800
Male/Female: 51/49
SAT Ranges: ERW 660–740, M 650–730
ACT Ranges: 30–33
Financial Aid: 70%
Pell Grant: 13%
Expense: Pr $ $ $
Student Loans: 26%

Davidson College boasts the Southern tradition and gentility of neighbors like Rhodes and Sewanee, with the academic prowess more common to Northern liberal arts powerhouses such as Dartmouth and Williams. It turns out more than its share of the region's political, education, legal, and other leaders. Often overlooked because of its small size and Carolina location, Davidson offers students strong interdisciplinary, international, and preprofessional programs, as well as a thriving social scene. As a senior economics major puts it, "Davidson is *the* liberal arts school of the South."

Located in a beautiful stretch of the North Carolina Piedmont, Davidson's wooded campus features Georgian and Greek Revival architecture. The central campus is designated as a national arboretum, and college staff lovingly maintain a collection of the woody plants that thrive in the area. Davidson retains its original quadrangle, which dates from 1837, plus literary society halls built in the 1850s. Recent construction includes the Wall Academic Center, featuring teaching and research labs for the sciences.

Core requirements at Davidson include one course each in historical thought; literary studies, creative writing, and rhetoric; mathematical and quantitative thought; natural science; philosophical and religious perspectives; social-scientific thought; visual and performing arts; and liberal studies. Students must also take coursework in a foreign language, cultural diversity, first-year writing, and physical education. Popular majors are political science, economics, biology, psychology, and English. Those whose academic interests lie outside the mainstream can work closely with select faculty members to pursue one of several majors established by the Center for Interdisciplinary Studies, such as Arab

> **"Davidson is *the* liberal arts school of the South."**

studies, bioinformatics, or global literary theory, or to design a major of their own. The interdisciplinary health and human values minor explores the role ethical values play in defining problems as "medical" and worthy of scientific study. A 3–2 engineering program is available with Columbia University and Washington University in St. Louis.

Davidson's academic climate is rigorous and sometimes grueling. "There are times when I find myself staying up several nights during the week to finish up papers, projects, and tests," says a sophomore. Seventy-five percent of classes have fewer than 20 students. Davidson's Honor Code allows students to take exams independently and to feel comfortable leaving doors unlocked. "The Honor Code is a cornerstone not just for academics, but for all aspects of life at Davidson," says a student. Every entering freshman agrees to abide by the code, and all work submitted to professors is signed with the word "pledged." Professors are highly lauded for being friendly and accessible, and with no graduate students around, opportunities to work with faculty members on research projects are plentiful.

The Sustainability Scholars Summer Program provides students with real-world projects that emphasize sustainability issues; students can be found in locations ranging from skyscrapers to community gardens. Environmental studies majors may apply to the School for Field Studies to spend a month or a semester studying environmental issues in other countries or to work and conduct research at Biosphere 2. Study abroad programs, including 10 faculty-led and more than 100 partner programs, are available in countries from France, Germany, and England to Cyprus and Zambia. About three-quarters of the students graduate with some foreign experience, whether it's coursework, service learning, research, or an internship.

While the school embraces its Presbyterian heritage, Davidson "is alive with an ecumenical spirit, so all students of all religious backgrounds feel comfortable while here," a political science major explains. Twenty-three percent of Davidson students come from North Carolina and 7 percent from abroad. African Americans comprise 7 percent of the student body, Hispanics 8 percent, Asian Americans 6 percent, and multiracial students 5 percent. The college practices need-blind admissions and, thanks to its highly touted Davidson Trust, guarantees to meet 100 percent of admitted students' demonstrated need through grants and student employment—eliminating loans from all need-based financial aid packages. Additionally, a limited number of merit scholarships and 185 athletic scholarships are available.

Ninety-eight percent of Davidson's students live on campus in co-ed or single-sex dorms. "The dorms are generally nice and centrally located," a sophomore says. Freshmen are housed together and eat in Vail Commons, where the "food is great—all you can eat, and lots of options, though it's hard to be a vegan at Davidson." Seniors get apartment-style

> **"[Alcohol] policies are tied into the Honor Code, so they are enforced."**

housing with private bedrooms. Many upperclassmen take meals at one of the fraternity or eating houses, which have their own cooks and serve meals family style. A limited number of upperclassmen receive permission to live off campus.

(continued)

Average Debt: $

Applicants: 5,673

Accepted: 20%

Enrolled: 45%

Grad in 6 Years: 91%

Returning Freshmen: 95%

Academics: ✎ ✎ ✎ ✎ ½

Social: ☎ ☎ ☎

Q of L: ★ ★ ★ ★ ★

Admissions: (800) 768-0380

Email Address: admission@ davidson.edu

Strong Programs:

Political Science

Economics

Biology

Psychology

English

Interdisciplinary Studies

Health and Human Values

Environmental Studies

The Center for Interdisciplinary Studies has established several majors, such as Arab studies, bioinformatics, and global literary theory.

The Alvarez College Union provides a main gathering place, and students have around 200 clubs and organizations at their disposal, but Davidson's eight fraternities, two sororities, and four all-female eating houses are the real center of social life on campus. These nonresidential groups are housed in Patterson Court, which freshmen are not allowed to enter for the first three weeks of school. The dues charged by these clubs cover meals, as well as parties and other campuswide events. The fraternities claim 39 percent of the men, and the sororities and eating houses attract 70 percent of the women. The eating houses, each of which supports a different philanthropic cause, such as cancer and autism research, are not much different from Greek life. Freshmen women simply sign up for the eating house they want to join on Self-Selection Night, with no "rushing" allowed. And even if you don't join up, don't despair; Davidson requires that most parties—"at least two per weekend" at the eating houses—be open to the entire community. "[Alcohol] policies are tied into the Honor Code, so they are enforced," a student says.

Davidson's first-year orientation includes the Cake Race, a tradition since 1930 that provides each runner with a cake they select based on the order in which they finish a (voluntary) 1.7-mile race. Orientation also introduces students to the cozy town of Davidson, which has coffee shops and cafés, and to the college's 110-acre Lake Norman campus, which is ideal for sailing, swimming, and rowing. "Davidson is a great college town," a chemistry major says. The equally quaint town of Cornelius is adjacent to Davidson, so it's a common destination for dinner and a movie or a relaxed night out. When those diversions grow old, North Carolina's largest city, Charlotte, is just 20 miles away, offering clubs and other attractions. A car definitely helps here, as Myrtle Beach and skiing are several hours from Davidson, in different directions. Public transit is an option too, as are the college's shuttle service and fleet of cars that students can check out for personal use.

"Davidson is a great college town."

Davidson fields 21 varsity teams (the Wildcats), 19 of which compete in the Division I Atlantic 10 Conference. The nonscholarship football team plays in the Division I Pioneer Football League, and the wrestling team competes in the Southern Conference. About a quarter of students are varsity athletes. Basketball (one of whose alumni is Stephen Curry), soccer, and wrestling are the most competitive programs. Intramural and club sports are varied and popular.

Despite its North Carolina location, Davidson has the look and feel of a New England liberal arts college and continues to attract top students to its charming neck of the woods. "So many factors contribute to Davidson being such a great place," says a junior. "If it's the right college for you, you can probably tell from the moment you step on campus." From study abroad and independent research to a reception with the college president for graduating seniors, students here combine tradition with forward thinking to make great memories, friends, and intellectual strides.

Overlaps

Williams, Amherst, Swarthmore, Bowdoin, Middlebury, Washington and Lee, UNC at Chapel Hill, Duke

If You Apply To ›

Davidson: Early decision I and II, regular decision. SATs or ACTs: required. Subject Tests: optional. Accepts the Common Application with supplement.

University of Dayton

Dayton, OH 45469

Part of a cohort of Roman Catholic institutions in the Midwest that includes DePaul, Duquesne, Loyola of Chicago, Saint Louis University, and Xavier (OH). Drawing cards include engineering, entrepreneurship, education, and health sciences, as well as a pioneering program in human rights. Medium-size school with larger feel. The city of Dayton, home to the Wright Brothers, is enjoying a resurgence. UD's appeal is largely regional.

Anyone who thinks college students of today subscribe to postmodern cynicism ought to take a peek at Dayton, where optimism and Roman Catholic charity are alive and well. Although its name suggests that it is a public university, Dayton was founded by the Society of Mary (Marianists) and continues to emphasize that order's devotion to service. "If you used one word to describe UD students, it would be 'friendly,'" a senior says. "Everyone on campus is very welcoming. We smile and say hi to people we don't know and hold the doors open for each other." There's good reason for the cheery disposition: Dayton continues to innovate new academic programs and has increased student funding for hands-on experiences like research and study abroad.

Located two miles from downtown Dayton, the 388-acre parklike campus with a riverfront vista is bordered by a quiet suburban neighborhood. The more historic buildings make up the central core of the campus and blend architectural charm with modern technological conveniences. The university has been making substantial investments in student housing, including ArtStreet, an arts-centered living/learning complex; renovation of all existing residential facilities; and construction of two town-house-style residences. The $51 million EPIS Center boasts labs where UD researchers and students work side by side with GE Aviation scientists and engineers to create advanced electrical power technologies. An environmentally friendly, $72 million update to the historic UD Arena—which has hosted more Division I basketball tournament games than any other venue—is the latest campus project.

> **"Career services does an outstanding job of coordinating events with employers."**

The undergraduate curriculum, the Common Academic Program, is designed to equip students with the skills and experience to participate in a complex global society. All students are required to have a notebook computer upon entering UD. The first-year experience course helps incoming students prepare for their academic careers and explore various majors, and all students complete a capstone experience and public presentation their senior year. UD students take full advantage of the strong offerings found in engineering (especially mechanical), entrepreneurship, biology, early childhood education, and premedicine; marketing, communication, and finance are among the most popular majors. Consistent with its religious mission, Dayton offers a major in human rights studies, the first of its kind, and a Human Rights Center. The school has also developed the first undergraduate certificate in Applied Creativity for Transformation, open to students in any major and focusing on creative competencies like complex problem-solving and collaboration with others. The entrepreneurship program dispenses $5,000 loans to participating sophomores to start their own businesses, with any profits going to charity; local entrepreneurs act as mentors. Finance students manage $30 million of the university's endowment.

"Our faculty expects the best from our students, yet with our spirit of collaboration and support, students work in a comfortable environment where they shouldn't

Website: www.udayton.edu
Location: Suburban
Private
Total Enrollment: 9,723
Undergraduates: 8,065
Male/Female: 52/48
SAT Ranges: ERW 550–650, M 550–660
ACT Ranges: 24–29
Financial Aid: 94%
Pell Grant: 14%
Expense: Pr $
Student Loans: 55%
Average Debt: $ $ $ $
Applicants: 15,942
Accepted: 72%
Enrolled: 20%
Grad in 6 Years: 79%
Returning Freshmen: 90%
Academics: ✍ ✍ ✍
Social: 🕿 🕿 🕿 🕿
Q of L: ★ ★ ★
Admissions: (937) 229-4411
Email Address: admission@udayton.edu

Strong Programs:
Mechanical Engineering
Entrepreneurship
Biology
Early Childhood Education
Marketing
Communication
Finance
Human Rights Studies

feel pressured," says a premed major. Thirty-six percent of classes have fewer than 20 students. Students speak highly of professors' enthusiasm about their courses and the quality of their teaching. Career services are described as dynamic and effective in making sure students are well networked upon graduation. "Career services does an outstanding job of coordinating events with employers and prepping students for internships," says a senior.

Qualified freshmen and transfer students may join the University Honors Program, which features special activities and opportunities for fellowships and research. The University of Dayton Research Institute also offers students a chance to gain hands-on experience. Study abroad programs include study at the university's China Institute in the Suzhou Industrial Park or at universities in Ireland and Spain. Dayton offers students $3,000 scholarships to study abroad and lets them do so at no extra cost if they choose a Dayton-organized program; 21 percent study internationally. "Campus ministry provides opportunities for retreats, service-learning trips, cultural immersion, and outreach," adds a senior.

"Students at UD love one word above all," says a sophomore: "community." Forty-four percent of Dayton's undergraduates are from Ohio, while 7 percent come from abroad. The school's minority population, although growing, is still small: 3 percent are African American, 5 percent are Hispanic, 1 percent are Asian American, and 3 percent are multiracial. Just over half of the students are Catholic. A marketing and economics major describes the political atmosphere as "fairly moderate," and overt political activism is not common on campus. Dayton doles out about 100 athletic scholarships each year, and merit-based academic awards average $18,000. In an effort to help students predict future costs, the university does not charge any fees and locks in the net tuition students pay after grants and scholarships for four years.

Seventy-five percent of undergraduates live in university housing; those who live off campus generally live adjacent to it. First-year students live in traditional residence halls, and about 20 percent of them opt to join living/learning communities with their classmates. Sophomores select suites or apartments, while upperclassmen take up quarters in the 400 university-owned houses, apartments, and townhouses that comprise the student neighborhood. The PATH points system determines the order in which returning students select housing; students accumulate points by attending eligible enrichment events like lectures, film screenings, and performances. A sophomore warns, "If you don't have a lot of PATH points, you're screwed." Dining facilities have been renovated and offer full-service, casual restaurant-style menu selections, along with a variety of cafés, delis, and convenience stores spread throughout the campus. "UD prides itself on being a very safe campus, and in my experience I definitely feel safe," says one senior. The Women's Center, which offers support for students, faculty, and staff, is a resource for social and gender justice.

"Students at UD love one word above all: community."

"Students love to stay on campus for the weekends or even for some of our shorter breaks," says a student. The student neighborhood serves as a sort of continuous social center. A lit porch light beckons party-seeking students to join the weekend festivities, and one student says the party scene has "a very communal, open-door kind of feel." St. Patrick's Day celebrations have traditionally been a major event. Greek organizations draw 12 percent of UD men and 21 percent of the women. More than 30 student groups are devoted entirely to service, and Christmas on Campus, when UD students "adopt" about 1,000 local elementary students for a night of crafts, games, and a visit with Santa, is one of the most student-involved activities.

The university is part of Dayton's bike share program, which has five stations on campus and is popular with students. Just a short ride away by bike, bus, or car are attractions like the Dayton Dragons minor-league baseball team, the Dayton Art Institute, the U.S. Air Force's museums, and a symphony or opera in the Schuster Performing Arts Center. Weekend excursions take aim at cities ranging from Louisville to Chicago to Indianapolis, as well as the restaurants, shops, and sports arenas of Cincinnati. But the best road trip is the Dayton-to-Daytona trip after spring finals, a 17-hour trek that draws loads of students each year.

The Dayton Flyers field 17 Division I men's and women's teams, and sports play a big role in campus life. Football competes in the Pioneer League, women's golf plays in the Metro Atlantic Athletic Conference, and all other teams are in the Atlantic 10 Conference. Both the men's and women's basketball teams have reached the Elite 8 in recent years, and the Red Scare student cheering section loves to intimidate opponents. Men's and women's soccer, cross-country, and track and field, baseball, and women's volleyball are also competitive. About half of students participate in one of the many intramural programs, and 35 club sports teams are available too.

"[The party scene has] a very communal, open-door kind of feel."

"UD's community is a great place to form lifelong friendships and prepare yourself for your future career," cheers one senior. The success of Dayton's attempts to provide its students with a high quality of life and a sense of cohesiveness is reflected in the strong social life and family-like atmosphere among both students and faculty. As a midsize university where the undergraduates come first, Dayton has managed to maintain an exciting balance of personal attention, academic challenge, and all-American fun.

Overlaps

American University, Baylor, Fordham, Loyola University Chicago, Xavier (OH), Ohio State, University of Cincinnati, Miami University (OH)

If You Apply To ›

Dayton: Early action, regular decision. SATs or ACTs: required. No Subject Tests. Accepts the Common Application with supplement.

Deep Springs College

Deep Springs Ranch Road, Highway 168, Big Pine, CA 93513

Picture 30 Ivy League–caliber individuals living and learning on a working ranch in a remote desert outpost—that's Deep Springs. DS is the most elite two-year institution in the nation, and also the most unusual—and not just because of its free tuition. Occupies a handful of ranch-style buildings set on 50,000 acres on the arid border of Nevada and California. Students transfer to highly selective colleges after two years. After a century as an all-male school, Deep Springs just went co-ed.

If the thought of spending countless hours under the fluorescent lights of the classroom makes you grimace, you may consider getting your hands dirty at Deep Springs College. This two-year—and newly co-ed—institution doubles as a working ranch. Students enjoy a demanding and individualized education supplemented by the challenges and lessons of ranch life. Both, it seems, demand the same things: hard work, commitment, and pride in a job well done. Deep Springs students are also rewarded for their efforts in other ways: tuition is free and so is room and board. Most Deep Springers have wide-ranging interests in many fields and have shunned acceptance at Ivy League schools to embrace the rigors of a truly unique approach to learning.

Website: www.deepsprings .edu
Location: Rural
Private
Total Enrollment: 30
Undergraduates: 30
Male/Female: 67/33
SAT Ranges: ERW 740–800, M 670–740

(continued)

ACT Ranges: 34–35
Financial Aid: 100%
Pell Grant: N/A
Expense: Pr $
Student Loans: N/A
Average Debt: $
Applicants: 318
Accepted: 5%
Enrolled: 100%
Grad in 6 Years: 100%
Returning Freshmen: 100%
Academics: ✑ ✑ ✑ ✑ ½
Social: ☎
Q of L: ★ ★ ★
Admissions: (760) 872-2000
Email Address: apcom@
    deepsprings.edu

Strong Programs:
Humanities
Environmental Studies
Philosophy
Literature

Deep Springs combines taxing practical work, rigorous academics, and genuine self-government—the three pillars of the school.

For the first time, Deep Springs has admitted women: the class that entered in fall 2018 consisted of 10 women and 5 men.

California's White Mountains provide a stunning backdrop for the Deep Springs campus, set on a barren plain 5,200 feet above sea level, near the only water supply for miles around and 28 miles from the nearest town, a thriving metropolis known as Big Pine, population 1,756. The campus is an oasis-like cluster of trees and a lawn with eight ranch-style buildings that were built from scratch by the class of 1917. The focal point is the Main Building, a venerable ranch-style building with wide eaves that includes a computer room and offices. Faculty houses and the dining facilities are grouped around the circular lawn a few yards away from the sole dorm, and the trappings of farm life surround the tiny settlement. The college has 170 acres under cultivation, mostly with alfalfa, and an assortment of barnyard animals. A solar array produces twice as much energy as the college requires—except during peak summer times when the alfalfa needs irrigating. To accommodate all members of its first ever co-ed class, the college added two private bathrooms in the dorm, as well as an outhouse in one of the vegetable fields.

> **"[Professors have] a deep respect for students as intellectual equals."**

Founded in 1917 by an industrialist who made a fortune in the electric-power industry, Deep Springs today remains true to its charter to combine taxing practical work, rigorous academics, and genuine self-government—the three pillars of the school. In addition to coursework, students are required to perform 20 hours per week of labor, which can include everything from harvesting alfalfa to branding and herding cattle to cooking dinner. Applicants must be committed to the ideals of self-government, reflectiveness, frugality, and community activity. Those who are admitted can truly boast of being handpicked to attend: of the roughly 200 to 300 applications received each year, only a handful of students are accepted. The two-round admissions process is intense, spanning months and involving several essays, letters of recommendation, and an on-campus admissions interview. Admits typically rank in the top 3 percent of their high school class and have near-perfect test scores. More importantly, administrators say, applicants must be able to demonstrate a serious interest in "pursuing a life of service to humanity." For the first time in its 101-year history, Deep Springs has admitted women: the class that entered in fall 2018 consisted of 10 women and 5 men. The school accepts applications from students of all gender identities, and its goal is to achieve an equal male-to-female ratio by 2020.

Students' input carries a lot of weight at Deep Springs. Four student-body committees are an essential part of the school's self-governance pillar: the Applications Committee, the Curriculum Committee, the Review and Reinvitations Committee, and the Communications Committee. These groups play a determining role in admissions and curricular decisions, help choose the college's faculty, and even elect two of their own to be full-voting members on the board of trustees. And they abide by a Spartan community code that bans all drugs, including alcohol, and forbids students from leaving Deep Springs Valley (the 50 square miles of desert surrounding the campus) while classes are in session, except for medical visits and college business. There are no phones and no Internet in the dorm, although there is limited Wi-Fi in all the other buildings on campus, including classrooms and the library. Lest these rules sound unnecessarily strict, keep in mind that these are all decided on and enforced by the student body, not the administration.

> **"Deep Springs students tend to be highly academic [and] curious about a number of disciplines."**

Like almost everything else about it, Deep Springs has an unorthodox academic schedule: two summer terms of seven weeks each, and a fall and spring semester of 14 weeks each. Between 7 and 10 classes are offered every term. All new students arrive in July to complete an intensive summer seminar with some of their older peers. The seminar, often taught by an interdisciplinary team of professors, focuses on issues of ethics and governance and prepares students to read and write effectively for the fall. Currently, the only required courses are public speaking and composition. The students control the academic program and quickly replace courses—and faculty—that do not work out. The humanities, especially literature and philosophy, tend to set the academic tone.

The faculty consists of three "permanent" professors—the humanities chair, the social sciences chair, and the natural sciences chair—who sign on for two years but can stay for up to six. Other courses are taught by the dean, the president, and visiting professors who stay for a single semester or summer term. The quality of particular academic areas varies as professors come and go, but generally, a student says, professors have "a deep respect for students as intellectual equals." With class sizes

ranging from two to 14, there is ample opportunity for close student/faculty interaction—and students must be prepared to discuss their ideas. Close living arrangements have fostered a kind of kinship between faculty and students, who rou-

"The dorm includes a lovely common room with a library and a fireplace (the 'rumpus room')."

tinely continue class discussions over meals. "Faculty are generally accessible most hours of the day or night—as long as their porch lights are on, students can stop by to talk about papers, books they are reading outside of class, or life advice," says a student.

"Deep Springs students tend to be highly academic, curious about a number of disciplines, and excited about learning," a student says. With only 26 to 30 students enrolled in a given year, demographics can fluctuate from year to year. Many Deep Springers are transplanted urbanites; the rest hail from points scattered across the nation or across the seas. Political leanings run the gamut, and there is diversity even among this small population, although that may only translate to a handful of students of color here. Since everyone's tuition, room, and board is covered by a scholarship, students pay only for indirect costs (books, travel, health insurance, and personal items); the average cost of one year at Deep Springs is about $3,500. While most students come from upper-middle-class families, an increasing number qualify for additional, need-based financial aid to help cover these indirect costs. Almost all students transfer to prestigious universities after their two-year program, and 70 percent eventually earn a Ph.D. or law degree.

Rooms in the dorm are said to be spacious and comfortable, and a student explains, "The dorm includes a lovely common room with a library and a fireplace (the 'rumpus room'), as well as a gym, meditation room, multiple porches, and a backyard (with a treehouse!)." Room selection and dorm maintenance is entirely the responsibility of the students, who also pitch in with preparing the meals, from butchering the meat to milking the

"Vegetarians are usually provided for, but we are a cattle ranch."

cows to washing the dishes. "The food is usually five stars," boasts a student. "Vegetarians are usually provided for, but we are a cattle ranch." And what about security? "Unless a tractor runs over you, you're fine," says a freshman. A classmate adds, "Sometimes the bulls get loose."

Social life can be a challenge, and loneliness can be an issue. Still, one student says, "Movies, board games, dance parties, and hangouts are the regular staples of student life and are integral in keeping the community close." Perhaps the most popular social activity on campus is conversation over a cup of coffee in the Boarding House (Deep Springs's dining hall), where the chatter is usually lively until the wee hours of the morning. Other common activities include pick-up soccer games, hikes in the nearby mountains, horseback riding, and competitive gopher-trapping in the winter months. The Turkey Bowl football game, the potato harvest, and Sludgefest (an annual event involving cleaning out the reservoir) are only some of the time-honored Deep Springs traditions.

Critics of Deep Springs charge that DS cultivates arrogance and social backwardness among students who were too intellectual to be in the social mainstream during high school. They argue that students who come here are doomed to be misfits for life. While that charge is debatable, even supporters of Deep Springs confess to a love-hate relationship with the college. Although the interpretations may vary, one common thread winds through the DS mission from application to graduation: training for a life of service to humanity.

Perhaps more than any other school in the nation, Deep Springs is a community where students and faculty interact day-to-day on an intensely personal level. Though the financial commitment is small, the personal commitment is serious—all must quickly learn how to get along in a community where the actions of each person affect everyone. Time will tell what kind of influence coeducation will have on the atmosphere of the place, but one thing is certain: urban cowboys and cowgirls who dream of riding into the sunset are in for a rude awakening. For a select few, however, the camaraderie and soul-searching fostered in this tight-knit community can be mighty tempting.

Overlaps

Brown, Cornell University, Yale, University of Chicago, Harvard, Columbia, Stanford, Princeton

If You Apply To ›

Deep Springs: Regular decision. SATs or ACTs: required. Subject Tests: optional. Does not accept the Common Application. Accepts applications from students of all genders and gender identities.

University of Delaware

116 Hullihen Hall, Newark, DE 19716

Plenty of students dream of someday becoming Nittany Lions or Cavaliers—even Terrapins—but fewer aspire to be Blue Hens. The challenge for UD is how to win its share of students without the name recognition that comes from big-time sports. The state of Delaware is tiny, and only about a third of the students are in-staters. Check out the variety of residential learning options.

Website: www.udel.edu
Location: Small City
Public
Total Enrollment: 20,598
Undergraduates: 17,409
Male/Female: 42/58
SAT Ranges: ERW 580–660, M 570–670
ACT Ranges: 25–29
Financial Aid: 48%
Pell Grant: 13%
Expense: Pub $ $ $
Student Loans: 62%
Average Debt: $ $ $ $
Applicants: 27,803

The University of Delaware is a public gem that boasts solid academic programs, from engineering to nursing. Though lacking a big-time sports program, UD has been gradually attracting more and more students who are looking for strong academics and hands-on experiences. It all adds up to "the small-school feel with the opportunities of a larger university," as one junior says.

Delaware's 970-acre Newark campus has an attractive mix of colonial and modern geometric buildings, set among flowering and native plantings. The hub of the campus is a grassy green mall, flanked by classic Georgian buildings. Mechanical Hall is a climate-controlled art gallery and home to the Paul R. Jones collection of African American Art. Hotel and restaurant management students benefit from classes in a fine dining restaurant and a Courtyard by Marriott right on campus, which doubles as a learning and research facility. A $2 million Innovation Suite recently opened for the electrical and computer engineering department.

As UD has grown in popularity, academic standards have become more rigorous. To graduate, students must pass freshman English (critical reading and writing) and earn at least three credits of discovery-based or experiential learning, such as an internship, research, or study abroad. All incoming freshmen begin with a First-Year Seminar course, and a capstone experience is required during the senior year; other requirements vary by college.

Delaware's academic menu includes more than 135 undergraduate majors, ranging from the liberal arts and sciences to more professional programs like fashion merchandising and new offerings in biomedical engineering and human relations administration. Finance, nursing, marketing, psychology, exercise science, and biological sciences are the most popular majors. Engineering, especially chemical engineering, is one of UD's specialties, and the school benefits from the close proximity of DuPont, the chemical giant that has been a major benefactor of the university. The music department is another attraction, with a 300-member marching band and several faculty members holding impressive professional performance credits.

> "Professors stress the importance of collaboration and working together to succeed."

In the classroom, a senior says, "Professors stress the importance of collaboration and working together to succeed." Classes tend to be on the large side, although 34 percent enroll fewer than 20 students. "Professors go above and beyond to make sure that students are engaged in the material," says a media communication major. Students describe career preparation here as hands-on and useful. "I love how Career Services really wants us as students to experience everything that we might encounter in the real world before we get there," says a biochemistry major.

UD created the nation's first study abroad program in 1923, and today one-third of the students travel to more than 40 countries, mostly for short-term, faculty-led programs during the month-long winter session or summer break. Each year, about 400 UD students receive stipends to do summer research with faculty members. Those wishing to spend their summers serving the local community may apply for the Service Learning Scholars Program, a 10-week immersion program. Overall, 62 percent of students get involved in some form of community service during their time at UD. About 500 new students enter the University Honors Program each year, which offers interdisciplinary colloquia, priority seating in honors sections of regular courses, personal attention, and extracurricular and residence hall programming.

"Students here are positive, friendly, and have a strong social life but also strong career goals," says a senior. Only thirty-six percent of undergraduates at Delaware hail from the First State; many of the rest are from the Northeast. Minority enrollment continues to increase; 5 percent are African American, 8 percent are Hispanic, 5 percent are Asian American, and 3 percent are multiracial. International students, at 5 percent, have a notable presence on campus, and the majority come from China. The campus attracts a mix of liberal and conservative students. Merit and athletic scholarships are offered, with merit awards averaging $7,500. The Commitment to Delawareans initiative is designed to meet the full demonstrated need of state residents.

Forty percent of students live on campus, including all freshmen not commuting from home. After that, dorm housing is guaranteed and awarded by lottery, though many juniors and seniors move into off-campus apartments. Honors students live together in designated residence halls, and certain academic departments require first-year students to reside in living/learning communities. A variety of optional special-interest communities are available as well. Students in traditional residence halls must buy the meal plan; one student advises, "The food courts are excellent and have a range of options for different dietary needs, but the dining halls could be

> "[Students] have a strong social life but also strong career goals."

(continued)

Accepted: 60%
Enrolled: 26%
Grad in 6 Years: 83%
Returning Freshmen: 91%
Academics: ✍ ✍ ✍
Social: ☎ ☎ ☎ ☎ ☎
Q of L: ★ ★ ★
Admissions: (302) 831-8123
Email Address: admissions@ udel.edu

Strong Programs:
Finance
Nursing
Marketing
Psychology
Exercise Science
Biological Sciences
Chemical Engineering
Music

UD benefits from the close proximity of DuPont, the chemical giant that has been a major benefactor of the university.

improved." Campus safety is said to be good, and a senior says, "Our kNOw MORE campaign reaches out to all students on a group and individual level about sexual assault awareness."

"Most of the social life takes place on and around campus. Many students are involved in student organizations, which tend to host events," says a freshman. A classmate adds, "There is a big party culture on campus, but it is not controlled by Greek life." Fraternities attract 18 percent of the men and sororities 23 percent of the women. Aside from parties, common diversions range from concerts and plays on campus to casual gatherings in friends' rooms. Hen Fest welcomes students back to campus every fall, and Resapalooza is the annual spring bacchanal, bringing music and a carnival to the central campus green. Juniors mark their progress in the fall with the Halfway There party, featuring half-legged races, half-lemonade/half-iced-tea Arnold Palmers, and a DJ who plays popular songs—but only halfway through.

Main Street, the heart of downtown Newark, "practically runs right through campus," one student says. "It's easy walking distance from anywhere, and there are tons of coffee shops, pizza places, restaurants, a movie theater, bookstores, and shops—anything you could possibly want." For those seeking further excitement, New York, the Washington/Baltimore area, and Philadelphia are all within a two-hour drive. When the weather is warm, the beaches of Rehoboth and Dewey beckon, and in chilly months, the Pennsylvania ski slopes aren't too far.

Delaware's Division I Blue Hens are becoming more competitive, and on Saturdays in the fall, watch out. "Football is big," says one student. Tailgate picnics are popular before and after the game. The women's field hockey team won a national championship recently, while women's golf and men's soccer have brought home Colonial Athletic Association conference titles. The men's and women's basketball teams enjoy a lively rivalry with Drexel. Recreational sports are popular; students have their pick of more than 35 club sports and 30 intramural programs.

"From our music department to engineering, I have met students from across the board who have had internships, jobs, research opportunities, and other experiences that are very unique and enriching," says a student. Indeed, with UD's traditional emphasis on out-of-classroom experiences, stimulating academic environment, and up-and-coming athletic teams, Blue Hens need never put all their eggs in one basket.

The Commitment to Delawareans initiative is designed to meet the full demonstrated need of state residents.

Overlaps

Penn State, Rutgers, UConn, University of Maryland, University of Pittsburgh, Villanova, Northeastern, Syracuse

If You Apply To ›

Delaware: Regular decision. SATs (with essay) or ACTs (with writing): required (optional for Delaware residents; test-optional applicants must submit supplemental essays). Subject Tests: recommended. Accepts the Common Application with supplement.

Denison University

Granville, OH 43023

Denison draws more Easterners than Wooster and Ohio Wesleyan, and it fashions itself as a sort of Midwestern Haverford. Denison has a middle-of-the-road to liberal student body, fewer preppies than in years past, and one of the most beautiful campuses anywhere. Increasing popularity has helped create a more serious student body.

Denison University, tucked into the "quaint, small, and beautiful" village of Granville, draws "unabashedly curious, down-to-earth, straightforward, and accepting" students from diverse backgrounds, according to one happy matriculant. Thanks to Denison's small size, there's ample opportunity to interact (and do research) with professors and to form close relationships with peers, as everyone focuses on the liberal arts.

Denison's campus is set atop rolling hills in central Ohio. Huge maples shade the sloping walkways, which offer a panoramic view of the surrounding valley. Denison retained park architect Frederick Law Olmsted (designer of New York City's Central Park) for its first master plan back in the early 1900s. The Georgian style of many buildings—redbrick with white columns—also evokes shades of New England and its private liberal arts colleges. The 108,000-square-foot Michael Eisner Center for Performing Arts (named for the former Disney CEO and Denison alum) is the newest addition to campus.

Denison's general education requirements are comprehensive. In addition to a spate of coursework spanning the liberal arts and sciences, students take two first-year seminars and complete an "interdivisional requirement" by selecting a course from one of seven interdisciplinary programs, such as international studies or queer studies. The Power and Justice requirement seeks to give

> "Classes are organized to be very hands-on and professors excel at facilitating rich discussions."

students the ability to question their own place in the structures of power and privilege that constitute human societies. For help navigating the transition to college, most freshmen sign up for optional Advising Circles, meeting weekly with a faculty advisor in groups of around 10 students.

Although economics, communication, biology, and psychology have the highest enrollment, students say some of the best majors are distinctive to Denison. The PPE major is effectively a triple major in philosophy, politics, and economics. The music department features a concentration in bluegrass designed by a faculty member who is an accomplished fiddler. Denison's 350-acre biological reserve is a boon for biology and environmental studies majors, and the computer science and mathematics departments are also strong. The global commerce major is growing, and concentrations have been added in financial economics and narrative journalism. Courses are rigorous, but an English major says, "Classes are organized to be very hands-on and professors excel at facilitating rich discussions." Classes are small—66 percent have fewer than 20 students—and individual attention is the norm. Students rave about the school's Denison Seminars, small, interdisciplinary classes that are team-taught by two professors and involve a travel component. "I've taken two Denison Seminars," says a history major, "and they were defining classes of my time at Denison."

Denison's signature Summer Scholar Program provides scholarships for more than 130 students to stay on campus during the summer, earning a stipend to complete 10 weeks of full-time research in collaboration with faculty members. Typically, more than half of the summer scholars are science students. Those with wanderlust can choose from more than 180 programs in 70 countries; overall, half of the students go abroad, about a third of them in short-term, faculty-led programs. The school has invested $50 million in the Knowlton Center for Career Exploration, which one senior says "has become an incredible asset for students, helping them easily adapt to the ever-changing career landscape." Those considering a run for office may be interested in the Richard Lugar Program in American Politics and Public Service, which includes political science courses on campus and culminates in a House or Senate internship in Washington. (The former senator happens to be a Denison grad.)

Website: www.denison.edu
Location: Small Town
Private
Total Enrollment: 2,319
Undergraduates: 2,319
Male/Female: 45/55
SAT Ranges: ERW 600–690, M 600–690
ACT Ranges: 28–31
Financial Aid: 93%
Pell Grant: 23%
Expense: Pr $ $ $
Student Loans: 53%
Average Debt: $ $
Applicants: 7,540
Accepted: 37%
Enrolled: 22%
Grad in 6 Years: 86%
Returning Freshmen: 91%
Academics: ✐ ✐ ✐ ½
Social: ☎ ☎ ☎ ☎
Q of L: ★ ★ ★
Admissions: (740) 587-6276
Email Address: admission@denison.edu

Strong Programs:
Economics
Communication
Biology
Psychology
Philosophy, Politics, and Economics
Music
Computer Science
Mathematics

Most freshmen sign up for optional Advising Circles, meeting weekly with a faculty advisor in groups of around 10 students.

Twenty percent of Denison's population is homegrown, and 10 percent come from abroad. African Americans constitute 7 percent of the student body, Hispanics 9 percent, Asian Americans 4 percent, and multiracial students 3 percent. According to a junior, "Denison is left-leaning, but not so much that it feels overbearing"; students cite gun control and sexual respect as hot topics of late. Admissions are need-blind, and Denison now commits to meeting the full demonstrated need of all incoming freshmen. Twenty-three percent of freshmen qualify for the Pell Grant. The average merit-based financial aid award is $22,000, and there are no athletic scholarships. The school also funds 80 full-tuition scholarships each academic year for student leaders from Chicago and Boston public high schools.

> **"Denison is left–leaning, but not so much that it feels overbearing."**

Ninety-nine percent of Denison students live on campus; the only ones allowed to live elsewhere are those commuting from home. (Another exception is the dozen Homesteaders, who live in three student-built solar-paneled cabins on a sustainable farm less than a mile away, and grow much of their own food.) Students generally live in dorms for the first three years and campus apartments their senior year, although a chemistry major warns that the lottery system means that "how nice your living arrangements are is definitely random." Dining services staff are described as "wonderful" and the meals as "generally good by college standards." Students report dissatisfaction with administrative handling of Title IX policies: "There are too many rape cases and too many alleged rapists who are not expelled," says one student.

"Naked Week" affords concerned students a chance to run naked through campus to promote healthy body image and acceptance.

Given the residential nature of the campus, social life at Denison tends to revolve around student housing more than anything else. Thirty percent of the men and 49 percent of the women join the Greek system, and a junior explains, "Since fraternities and sororities are not allowed to host parties in their houses, the parties are instead held in the senior apartments, colloquially termed 'the Sunnies.' On Wednesday, Friday, and Saturday nights, students of all class years congregate here." Students characterize campus apartment parties as "overcrowded saunas" where "binge drinking is prevalent." School-sponsored events like guest speakers, plays, and concerts do offer an alternative, and everyone looks forward to three all-campus parties each year: D-Day, Culture Jam, and Aestavalia. There's also "Naked Week" in February, which affords concerned students a chance to run naked through campus to promote healthy body image and acceptance.

Granville is a small, quiet town with four churches on the corners of the town's main intersection, along with "two bars, a coffee shop, a bank, a greasy spoon restaurant, a library, and gift shops," says a student. Most stores and restaurants close by 8 p.m. The Denison Community Association frequently sends students into Granville and nearby Newark to provide tutoring, mentoring, and other volunteer services. Columbus, the state capital and fifteenth-largest city in the U.S., is only 30 miles away, and the school runs trips to the city's Easton Town Center, an outdoor shopping and dining mecca. Pittsburgh, Cleveland, Cincinnati, and Dayton are also close by.

> **"Denison does a great job of crossing over and piecing together academic interests."**

Denison students are enthusiastic supporters of the Big Red, especially when rival Kenyon is in town, and Division III lacrosse games against Ohio Wesleyan always draw large crowds. The men's swimming and diving team claimed the national championship in 2016 and 2018, and the women's team is a top performer too. Men's and women's lacrosse and women's basketball and field hockey are recent conference champions. Intramurals and club sports remain hugely popular, with basketball, volleyball, tennis, squash, and fencing drawing the most interest. Denison recently completed Mitchell Center, a $38.5 million athletics and recreation facility.

Overlaps

Bates, Colgate, Dickinson, Macalester, Trinity College (CT), Kenyon, Franklin & Marshall, Miami University (OH)

Denison University aims to graduate independent thinkers who become active citizens of a democratic society. The school continues to value tradition—woe to the student who steps on the school seal in front of the chapel, for doing so will cause him to fail all his finals—while growing and evolving to emphasize academics and the life of the mind. A recent graduate says, "Denison does a great job of crossing over and piecing together academic interests, and they have tons of connections in the world to help you succeed after you graduate."

If You Apply To ›

Denison: Early decision I and II, regular decision. SATs or ACTs: optional. No Subject Tests. Accepts the Common Application.

University of Denver

2199 South University Boulevard, Denver, CO 80208

The only major midsized private university between Tulsa and the West Coast. DU's campus in residential Denver is pleasant, and admissions brochures tout Rocky Mountain landscapes and healthy lifestyles. Senior faculty teach all core courses. A haven for skiing enthusiasts and business majors, DU has become more selective in recent years.

The oldest private university in the Rocky Mountain region, the University of Denver is where former secretary of state Condoleezza Rice earned her B.A. in political science at age 19 and later returned for a Ph.D. in international studies. Her mentor was Soviet specialist Josef Korbel, father of former secretary of state Madeleine Albright. Thus, it's not surprising that DU boasts strong programs in political science, international studies, and public affairs. Many students, however, opt for DU's business program, and the campus location offers ample opportunities for networking, skiing, and taking in the beautiful Colorado landscape. A freshman says, "DU students share a sense of adventure, risk-taking, and spending time doing what one values."

DU's 125-acre main campus is located in a comfortable residential neighborhood only eight miles from downtown Denver and an hour east of major ski areas. Architectural styles vary and materials include brick, limestone, Colorado sandstone, and copper. Nearby Mount Evans (14,265 feet) is home to the world's loftiest observatory, a DU facility available to both professors and students.

> **"DU students share a sense of adventure, risk-taking, and spending time doing what one values."**

A new facility for the Ritchie School of Engineering and Computer Science recently opened, serving as a hub for interdisciplinary, STEM-related research and scholarship.

Under the general education requirements, undergraduate students choose from a series of courses from the Common Curriculum that emphasize writing and rhetoric, language, analytical inquiry, and scientific inquiry. "At first I thought, 'Who wants to take these science, art, and English classes?'" explains a business major. "But now that I've completed the core, I feel better about myself and my world knowledge." University rules stipulate that all core courses must be taught by senior faculty. Core courses are supplemented by a First-Year Seminar (limited to 20 students) and an advanced seminar, which serves as a capstone to the curriculum model.

Website: www.du.edu
Location: City Center
Private
Total Enrollment: 8,432
Undergraduates: 5,486
Male/Female: 46/54
SAT Ranges: ERW 590–680, M 570–670
ACT Ranges: 25–28
Financial Aid: 84%
Pell Grant: 18%
Expense: Pr $ $ $
Student Loans: 42%
Average Debt: $ $ $
Applicants: 19,904
Accepted: 58%
Enrolled: 13%
Grad in 6 Years: 75%
Returning Freshmen: 87%
Academics: ✏ ✏ ✏
Social: ☎ ☎ ☎ ☎
Q of L: ★ ★ ★ ★
Admissions: (303) 871-2036
Email Address: admission@du.edu

(continued)

Strong Programs:
Finance
Psychology
International Studies
Marketing
Hospitality Management
Music
Chemistry
Computer Science

All juniors and seniors have the chance to study abroad at no additional cost; 71 percent of Pioneers go abroad.

DU is known for its business school—especially the Knoebel School of Hospitality Management. Preprofessional programs are feeders for graduate schools in business, international studies, engineering, and the arts, and undergrads can opt for a five-year program toward a master's degree in business, education, international studies, public policy, or several other fields. A six-year program is available for those pursuing a degree in law. Finance, psychology, international studies, and marketing are some of the most popular majors, and music, chemistry, and computer science have solid reputations.

Since DU operates on a quarter system, classes move quickly and the workload can get intense. "I personally enjoy how rigorous the quarter system can be, because you are constantly learning something new," says an art history major. Students say small class sizes—57 percent have fewer than 20 students—make for a collaborative environment with plenty of support from faculty. "Professors are always open to deep intellectual discussion," says a molecular biology major. DU is also recognized for its strong academic support services. A psychology major says, "The Learning Effectiveness Program has been amazing and given me the accommodations and resources I need to succeed."

DU's Honors Program draws about 350 students who take a sequence of honors courses and complete a thesis or final project. Funded undergraduate research opportunities are widely available. All juniors and seniors have the chance to study abroad at no additional cost; 71 percent of Pioneers go abroad, and they say the 150 available programs are an integral part of the DU experience. "DU fosters a global perspective in which students understand their role in and responsibility to the global community," says a psychology major.

"We have a funky mix of really preppy East Coasters and Midwesterners mixed in with all the laid-back outdoorsy people," says one student. Thirty-four percent of undergraduates are from Colorado, and 7 percent arrive from other countries. African Americans account for 2 percent of the student body, Asian Americans 4 percent, Hispanics 11 percent, and multiracial students 4 percent. Students report that political organizations are active on campus and cite the environment and social justice as issues of particular concern. As one of the few private colleges in the West, DU is also among the most expensive in the region. A majority of undergrads do receive merit scholarships, which average $18,300, and 205 athletic scholarships are also available. "Students have relatively expensive hobbies like skiing, backpacking, and traveling," observes a senior. "I think individuals from low-income backgrounds have a hard time fitting in."

"I personally enjoy how rigorous the quarter system can be."

Half of all undergrads reside on campus; students are required to spend their first two years in the residence halls. "Each residence hall has a leadership development team that plans programming events just for that residence," explains a student. Johnson-McFarlane ("J-Mac") is the favored hall for first-years, though another student says the Towers are a much quieter option. Students praise the five living/learning communities open to first-years: "Being able to come onto campus and already have a structured and supportive group of people who shared a similar interest was incredibly helpful," a senior recalls. Most juniors and seniors opt for the decent quarters found within walking distance. Campus dining receives mixed reviews; while it can be repetitive and occasionally unappealing, a junior says, "There is always a vegetarian option, always a vegan option, as well as gluten-free toasters and allergen-free fridges." Campus police are said to be helpful, and one student comments, "During my four years at DU I have seen a definite change and push in terms of education and advocacy regarding sexual assault."

For the three-day Winter Carnival, administrators, professors, and students all pack off to Keystone or another ski area.

Social life is divided between on-campus activities and off-campus diversions. Twenty-five percent of the men and 30 percent of the women belong to a fraternity or sorority, respectively. "While Greek organizations offer opportunities to party, they certainly do not set the tone of social life on campus," says an international studies major. A classmate adds, "There is more of a bar scene around DU than a party scene, I have found." Students make regular trips into the city, made easy by free access to the nearby light rail. One student cheers, "Campus is minutes from downtown Denver, where there is great shopping, festivals, events, concerts, phenomenal restaurants, and, for students over 21, one of the best microbrewery scenes." With consistently beautiful, sunny weather and great skiing, hiking, and camping less than an hour away in the Rockies, many DU students head for the hills on weekends, often on trips organized by the Alpine Club. Students also explore Estes Park, Mount Evans, and Echo Lake.

> "Students understand their role in and responsibility to the global community."

Students unite when the powerhouse DU hockey team, national champions in 2017, skates out onto the ice, especially against archrival Colorado College. The Pioneers co-ed ski team has won three national championships in the last five years. Other competitive Division I programs include men's lacrosse; men's and women's soccer, swimming, and tennis; and women's gymnastics and volleyball. Intramural and club sports are varied and popular; more than a quarter of students take part. Each February, academics are put aside for the three-day Winter Carnival. Top administrators, professors, and students all pack off to Keystone, Winter Park, or another ski area to catch some fresh powder and see who can ski the fastest, skate the best, or build the most artistic ice sculptures.

Students like the University of Denver for its modest size, its friendly atmosphere, and the flexibility afforded by the albeit sometimes stressful quarter system. As the school pushes for a more ethnically diverse student body and improves its curriculum and facilities, the University of Denver is striving to become better known for its intellectual rigor than for its gorgeous setting in the Rocky Mountains.

Overlaps

American University, Syracuse, Southern Methodist, University of San Diego, Santa Clara, Colorado State, University of Colorado Boulder, University of Vermont

If You Apply To ›

DU: Early decision I and II, early action, regular decision. SATs or ACTs: optional. No Subject Tests. Accepts the Common Application.

DePaul University

Chicago, IL 60604

Few universities have come so far, so fast. DePaul gets the nod over Loyola as the top Roman Catholic university in Chicago. Its Lincoln Park setting is like a Midwestern version of New York's Greenwich Village or Upper West Side. About one-third of undergraduates who report a religion are Catholic. Especially strong in business, public relations, film, and the performing arts.

DePaul University is the largest Roman Catholic university in the nation. Students claim the university's diversity and politically liberal leanings set it apart from rival institutions. Based in the heart of the city, DePaul is a feeder to Chicago's business community. A spate of campus construction has transformed it from the "little school under the El" to Chicago's version of NYU. DePaul inaugurated its first lay president in 2017.

Website: www.depaul.edu
Location: City Center
Private
Total Enrollment: 18,276
Undergraduates: 12,861

DePaul's name is closely associated with Midwestern business and law, and undergraduates can find internships year-round.

DePaul, which was founded by Vincentian fathers in 1898 and is named after the 17th-century French priest Vincent de Paul, has two residential campuses. The Lincoln Park campus, with its state-of-the-art library and student center, is home to the colleges of liberal arts and social sciences, education, and science and health; the theatre and music schools; and residence halls and recreational facilities. Lincoln Park itself is a fashionable Chicago neighborhood with century-old brownstone homes, theaters, cafés, parks, and shops. The Loop (or "vertical") campus is 20 minutes away by elevated train (a.k.a. the El) in downtown Chicago and houses the colleges of business, communication, computing and digital media, and law, as well as the School for New Learning. The DePaul Center, a $70 million teaching, learning, and research complex, is the cornerstone of this campus.

All freshmen take a course called Discover Chicago or its alternative, Explore Chicago, which introduces them to the city. "This class is one of the best things about DePaul. It's really fun and valuable,"

> **"DePaul professors are respectful, intelligent, and don't put up with nonsense."**

says a senior. Other common core courses include composition and quantitative reasoning for freshmen, a sophomore seminar on multiculturalism in the United States, and an experiential learning program that requires an internship, research, study abroad, or service-learning experience. In their senior year, students create a final project.

DePaul's name is closely associated with Midwestern business and law, and undergraduates can find internships year-round with local legal and commercial institutions. The School of Accountancy and MIS is reported to be the most challenging department in the Driehaus College of Business. The College of Science and Health offers a health sciences program that prepares students for a variety of health care professions, and the Pathways Honors Program provides top students with specialized prehealth advising and summer research opportunities. The School of Cinematic Arts has teamed up with Cinespace Chicago, the city's premier movie studio, to create a learning environment that provides students with film and television production experience in the midst of a working studio. Other notable programs include game design and animation. Combined, six-year bachelor's/law degree options are available in several fields, ranging from economics to Islamic world studies, and a number of five-year bachelor's/master's degree programs are also offered. The most popular majors include public relations and advertising, finance, accounting, and psychology.

"The courseload is rigorous at times, but if a student is dedicated to their studies, it is nothing that can't be handled," says a senior. Classes are often small, with 41 percent enrolling fewer than 20 students, and professors teach at all levels. The administration appoints student representatives from each school and college to faculty promotion and tenure committees. "DePaul professors are respectful, intelligent, and don't put up with nonsense," says one senior. Clerics teach some courses and celebrate (voluntary) mass every day. In addition, the University Ministry hosts other religious services and leads programs to teach students about other faiths. The highly selective honors program includes interdisciplinary courses and a senior thesis. Twenty-four percent of students participate in study abroad programs that take them to more than 30 countries around the world, including India, Ireland, Peru, and Switzerland.

Seventy-five percent of DePaul undergraduates hail from Illinois, and less than 1 percent come from foreign countries. Hispanics represent 19 percent of the student body, African Americans 8 percent, Asian Americans 10 percent, and multiracial students 4 percent. Twenty-nine percent of incoming freshmen are eligible for Pell Grants. "The students at DePaul are very diverse," says a sophomore. "There are student organizations to represent all different faiths, ethnicities, and backgrounds."

DePaul has a reputation for being politically liberal, and "it has become more liberal in recent years," says a junior. In addition to academic merit scholarships, DePaul also awards scholarships to students who have artistic talent or strong leadership skills or those who participate in community service; such awards average $13,000 per year. Scholarships for athletes are available too.

One student complains, "Weekends can be boring because many students go home." Traditionally, DePaul has been a commuter school, and just 18 percent of undergraduates live in university housing. Students find the dorms comfortable and well maintained, but they advise applying early to secure a bed, especially after sophomore year. "Housing is in high demand around here," says a junior. The Lincoln Park campus includes six modern co-ed dorms and six townhouse and apartment buildings. At the Loop campus, a 1,700-student residence hall includes a rooftop garden, fitness center, and music, art, and study rooms. Although students like campus housing, some find the food overpriced and limited. "I'm a vegan, and there is not a large or good variety," says a junior. While Chicago may have

> "Housing is in high demand around here."

a high-crime reputation, students say campus security is visible, with officers patrolling in cars and on foot, and dorms require students to swipe ID cards at two or three places before allowing entrance.

Fraternities and sororities draw just 5 percent of DePaul men and 11 percent of the women, respectively. Not surprisingly, with the school's proximity to Chicago's concert venues, restaurants, bars, clubs (especially on Rush Street), and sporting events, most social life occurs off campus. A music major says of the city, "There is everything to do here." In the warmer months, the beaches of Lake Michigan beckon students, while the university's huge annual outdoor Fest concert attracts large crowds from both campuses. Students say that enforcement of alcohol policies doesn't always work when it comes to underage drinking.

DePaul is a member of the Big East Conference, and the Blue Demons compete in Division I in 15 sports. Men's basketball is the headline story, beginning with the Midnight Madness of each fall's first practice in October. The game against Notre Dame always draws a capacity crowd, though Loyola is DePaul's oldest rival. Men's track and field and women's basketball, tennis, and softball have won Big East championships recently. Intramurals and club sports are big draws, and the Campus Recreation department offers a 123,000-square-foot fitness and recreation facility, which includes a four-court gymnasium, a pool, a 200-meter track, and more.

Expanding academic programs, a diverse student body, and all the opportunity of the city of Chicago make DePaul a dynamic university, but students say its popularity is due as much to the special bonds they feel with fellow Blue Demons. "DePaul University provides students a unique atmosphere in which to learn and grow," says a sophomore. "The campus and its students are friendly, open, and always inviting."

The men's basketball game against Notre Dame always draws a capacity crowd, though Loyola is DePaul's oldest rival.

Overlaps

U of I at Chicago, Loyola University Chicago, U of I at Urbana–Champaign, Columbia College Chicago, Illinois State, Northwestern, University of Chicago, Northern Illinois

If You Apply To ›

DePaul: Early action, regular decision. SATs or ACTs: optional (test-optional applicants must respond to additional short essay questions). Subject Tests: optional. Accepts the Common Application with supplement.

204 East Seminary Street, Greencastle, IN 46135

DePauw is a small Midwestern liberal arts institution in the mold of Denison, Dickinson, Illinois Wesleyan, and Ohio Wesleyan. Its Greek system is among the strongest in the nation and full of students destined for careers among business and government elite. DePauw's Fellows and Honors Scholar programs are a major draw for career-oriented students looking to take their liberal arts experience to the next level.

Website: www.depauw.edu

Location: Small Town

Private

Total Enrollment: 2,132

Undergraduates: 2,132

Male/Female: 48/52

SAT Ranges: ERW 560–650, M 550–680

ACT Ranges: 24–29

Financial Aid: 98%

Pell Grant: 21%

Expense: Pr $ $

Student Loans: 66%

Average Debt: $

Applicants: 5,173

Accepted: 67%

Enrolled: 17%

Grad in 6 Years: 81%

Returning Freshmen: 89%

Academics: ✍ ✍ ✍ ½

Social: ☎ ☎ ☎

Q of L: ★ ★

Admissions: (765) 658-4006

Email Address: admission@depauw.edu

Strong Programs:
Biology
Biochemistry
Communication and Theatre
Computer Science
English
Economics
Psychology
Music

DePauw University offers a liberal arts education with an orientation toward experiential learning. The economics and management, natural sciences, and arts departments are strong, and the university produces a high number of Fulbright Scholars. Students here are career-oriented and eager to take advantage of the rigorous classwork and ample real-world experiences. With an undergraduate population of more than 2,100 students, close ties to classmates and faculty are a given.

Founded in 1837 by the Methodist Church, DePauw is set amid the gently rolling hills of west-central Indiana. The lush green campus has a mix of older buildings and more modern redbrick structures. The DePauw Nature Park, about a mile away, is a well-kept, 520-acre park featuring nature trails and the LEED Gold–certified Prindle Institute for Ethics. DePauw has significantly upgraded its main campus in recent years, opening a state-of-the-art dining hall, renovating the student union building, redesigning the East College Lawn as a center of community life, and improving its energy efficiency.

DePauw's first-year program helps students transition into college by combining academically challenging coursework with cocurricular activities and programs. Before arriving on campus, each student is assigned to a mentor-group with 10 to 12 peers, an upperclassman advisor, and a faculty member who will teach their first-year seminar and serve as their academic advisor until they declare a major. By graduation, students must demonstrate competence in writing, quantitative reasoning, and oral communication; pass a course on power, privilege, and diversity; and complete at least two extended study experiences, which may include courses taken during the month-long Winter or May terms, independent study or research, off-campus study, service-learning projects, or internships.

"The classroom environment is highly collaborative and encouraging."

Academically, the DePauw student body is as career-oriented as they come in a liberal arts college. Aspiring business leaders benefit from courses, speakers, and internships offered through the McDermond Center for Management and Entrepreneurship. Future reporters, editors, anchors, and producers will find a home in the Pulliam Center for Contemporary Media, which supplements DePauw's strong student-run newspaper, TV station, and radio stations. Six other centers provide cocurricular opportunities in ethics, technology, diversity and inclusion, civic engagement, student engagement, and 21st-century musicianship. DePauw's School of Music is also worth a mention, offering a five-year dual-degree program in music performance/liberal arts. The most popular majors include biology, biochemistry, communication and theatre, computer science, English, economics, and psychology, and students may also design their own majors. Students say that the classes are rigorous but well supported. "The classroom environment is highly collaborative and encouraging," says one sophomore, "and in many courses the students and professors engage in class discussions that more closely model academic conversations than traditional lectures." DePauw's Gold Commitment guarantees that students will be employed or enrolled in graduate school within six months of graduating; anyone who is not is offered an entry-level job at a university partner or invited back to campus for a tuition-free semester.

For exceptionally motivated students, four Fellows programs in media, management, scientific research, and the environment offer a semester-long internship or research experience and opportunities to interact with top scholars and industry leaders on and off campus. Additionally, the Honor Scholars Program allows high-achieving students to embark on interdisciplinary study and complete a capstone thesis. About 90 percent of DePauw students study off campus, mostly through short, faculty-led programs during the Winter and May terms; semester and year-long options are also available.

One student describes her peers at DePauw as "intellectually curious, philanthropically minded, and socially active." Thirty-eight percent of students are from Indiana, and 10 percent are international. Campus diversity has grown, thanks in part to recruitment of Posse Foundation students from New York and Chicago. African Americans now account for 5 percent of the student body, Hispanics 7 percent, Asian Americans 4 percent, and multiracial students 5 percent. Twenty-one percent of incoming freshmen receive Pell Grants. During the annual DePauw Dialogue event, classes are canceled so students, faculty, and staff can gather to explore issues like bias, privilege, and identity. Merit scholarships averaging $20,600 are available, although there are no athletic scholarships. Three-quarters of DePauw students volunteer with area churches and social service agencies, which can also help them qualify for scholarships.

> "[DePauw students are] intellectually curious, philanthropically minded, and socially active."

DePauw is a 100 percent residential college, meaning all students live on campus for all four years, with few exceptions. Options include homey residence halls, suites, apartments, and college-owned houses, as well as Greek chapter houses. Meals are served in one main dining hall, and there are a few small cafés and grab-and-go options around campus. A whopping 71 percent of DePauw's men and 64 percent of the women go Greek. That's not surprising, given that the first modern-day sorority, Kappa Alpha Theta, began here in 1870, and the university is home to the two longest continually running fraternities anywhere: Beta Theta Pi and Phi Gamma Delta.

"Students love being at DePauw on the weekends," says a student. Perhaps because of the prevalence of Greeks on campus, and spurred by the disciplining several years ago of a sorority accused of purging its overweight members, Greek groups have worked hard to change the negative stereotypes of fraternities and sororities. A community council reviews allegations of misconduct, and rush is delayed until the spring semester so freshmen can first get their feet on the ground academically. Still, students say it's relatively easy for underage drinkers to imbibe, especially at fraternity parties.

The town of Greencastle has a movie theater, a bowling alley, and several pizza places and restaurants, but it "lacks an atmosphere," says a student. "It is fine for sustaining day-to-day living, but doesn't offer many alternatives to the university." In good weather, the DePauw Nature Park and several state parks offer hiking trails and lakes. Indianapolis is only a 45-minute drive, and St. Louis, Chicago, and Cincinnati make for good road trips. A cherished tradition is a takeoff on Indiana University's famed Little 500 bike race, itself a takeoff on the Indianapolis 500 auto race—teams of cyclists compete on a course that circles the heart of the DePauw campus.

Everyone gets excited about varsity athletics, especially the annual football game against Wabash College, which is the oldest small-college rivalry west of the

DePauw's Gold Commitment guarantees that students will be employed or enrolled in graduate school within six months of graduating.

A whopping 71 percent of DePauw's men and 64 percent of the women go Greek.

Alleghenies. The winner of each year's contest claims possession of the much-cherished Monon Bell, hence the popular T-shirt: "Beat the bell out of Wabash." Women's basketball has brought home the Division III national championship twice in the last several years. Other competitive Tigers teams include men's cross-country and baseball, women's golf and softball, and men's and women's swimming. Intramural sports are popular, and students stay fit in the two-story Welch Fitness Center.

For a small school, DePauw offers a multitude of opportunities, balancing strong academics with a healthy dose of school spirit and a wealth of opportunities to lead—whether in one of the abundant extracurricular activities or by blazing a trail through study abroad.

If You Apply To ›

DePauw: Early decision I and II, early action, regular decision. SATs or ACTs: optional. Subject Tests: optional. Accepts the Common Application with supplement.

Dickinson College

P.O. Box 1773, Carlisle, PA 17013

With traditions dating to the 18th century, Dickinson occupies a historic setting in the foothills of central Pennsylvania. Curriculum blends traditional liberal arts values with attention to international studies, foreign languages, study abroad, and sustainable development. With underrepresented minorities, international students, and hippies now more numerous, Dickinson is shedding its image as a preppy haven. Competes head to head with nearby Gettysburg.

Website: www.dickinson.edu
Location: Small Town
Private
Total Enrollment: 2,325
Undergraduates: 2,325
Male/Female: 42/58
SAT Ranges: ERW 620–700, M 610–720
ACT Ranges: 27–32
Financial Aid: 76%
Pell Grant: 12%
Expense: Pr $ $ $ $
Student Loans: 54%
Average Debt: $ $
Applicants: 5,941
Accepted: 49%
Enrolled: 21%
Grad in 6 Years: 83%
Returning Freshmen: 90%
Academics: ✍ ✍ ✍ ✍
Social: ☎ ☎ ☎
Q of L: ★ ★ ★

Dickinson College won its charter just six days after the Treaty of Paris recognized the United States as a sovereign nation in 1783, and this small liberal arts school has been blazing trails ever since. The moving force behind it was Dr. Benjamin Rush, the famous physician and signer of the Declaration of Independence who convinced John Dickinson, the then governor of Pennsylvania, to lend his name to the new school. Now, administrators are focused on diversity, global education, and attracting the best and brightest academic talent. "Dickinson is such a perfect school for students who are looking to find their passion," offers one junior.

Almost all of Dickinson's Georgian buildings are crafted from gray limestone from the college's own quarry, which lends a good deal of architectural consistency. The campus is part of the historic district of Carlisle, an economically prosperous central Pennsylvania county seat nestled in a fertile valley. The newest addition to campus is a $19 million, energy-efficient residence hall housing 129 students in single and double rooms.

To help students understand how the liberal arts fit into the broader world, Dickinson supplements standard distribution requirements with courses in cross-cultural studies, such as comparative civilizations and diversity in the U.S. The required First-Year Seminar introduces new students to college-level writing and critical thinking through interdisciplinary courses such as Digital Culture, Ideas That Have Shaped the World, and The Science of Competition. Eighty-five percent of students also complete a capstone program.

Dickinson is best known for its workshop approach to science education, for its outstanding and comprehensive international education program, and for the depth of its foreign language program, with more than a dozen languages offered, including Arabic, Chinese, Japanese, Hebrew, Italian, and Portuguese. International business and management, one of Dickinson's most popular majors, includes coursework in economics, history, and financial analysis, as well as internships and overseas education. Other popular majors include economics, political science, international studies, and biology.

Consistent with its "Engaging the World" approach, Dickinson has begun offering certificates in food studies as well as in social innovation and entrepreneurship. Other certificates on emerging issues include security studies and health studies. The education program has been upgraded to a major in educational studies, and quantitative economics is now a major too. Students can gain a hands-on understanding of human culture and behavior by studying archaeology in locations such as Mycenae, Greece. Interdisciplinary programs such as neuroscience and workshop physics offer chances to carry out research with faculty members. A 3–3 program with the Dickinson School of Law at Penn State allows students to obtain undergraduate and J.D. degrees in six years.

> "Full professors commonly teach introductory level classes."

(continued)

Admissions: (717) 245-1231
Email Address: admissions@ dickinson.edu

Strong Programs:
International Business and Management
Economics
Political Science
International Studies
Biology
Foreign Languages
Neuroscience
Workshop Physics

Academics are demanding. "The academic climate can become intense during the midterms and finals week. Especially during those times, students come together to support one another," says one junior. Seventy-five percent of classes have fewer than 20 students, allowing freshmen easy access to their professors. A psychology and biology double major says, "Most professors that I have had are experts in their fields and are passionate about the academic growth of their students. Full professors commonly teach introductory level classes."

Dickinson sponsors roughly 40 study abroad programs, many of them faculty-directed, in 24 countries on six continents; 62 percent of students participate. Options include academic year, semester, and summer programs, Globally Integrated courses that include a short-term international field experience, and specialized programs such as the Mosaic Program, which combines domestic study with international study. About three-quarters of all students complete internships, where they may learn about stock trading at a brokerage firm, assist a judge in a common pleas court, or work with the editorial staff of a magazine. Undergraduate research involves 46 percent of students, typically as part of a senior project or an independent study.

Almost all of Dickinson's Georgian buildings are crafted from gray limestone from the college's own quarry.

"Students at Dickinson are highly competitive and very hard workers," says a sophomore. Nineteen percent of the student body hails from the Keystone State. African Americans account for 5 percent of the student population, Asian Americans 4 percent, Hispanics 8 percent, and multiracial students 4 percent; international students comprise 13 percent. Dickinson has been enrolling a growing number of minority and international students, especially through partnerships with the Posse Foundation in New York and Los Angeles

> "You must get involved in something to have a good social life."

and the Philadelphia Futures Foundation, and with schools and foundations abroad, but some students note that the atmosphere on campus does not feel as much like an integrated community as they would like. Dickinson awards four types of merit scholarships but no athletic scholarships.

Given that only seniors are allowed to live off campus and Dickinson guarantees four years of housing, 95 percent of students remain in the dorms. "Freshman dorms have small rooms but they can be made quite comfortable," says a freshman. Additional housing options include small houses and apartments, as well as a formerly abandoned factory that the college transformed into a combination of art studios and loft-style apartments for upperclassmen. About 15 percent of freshmen choose to participate in living/learning communities, as extensions of the First-Year Seminar program. The college farm manages 50 acres and supplies produce to the dining halls and a local food bank. It also serves as a classroom and work-study opportunity for students interested in sustainable development. "Dining services has a rotating menu so that the options always change," says one junior, and aside from the main cafeteria, there are café and snack-bar options. Students report feeling safe on campus, and the Prevention, Education, and Advocacy Center offers comprehensive education and training related to sexual assault.

"Whether it is a club, a sport, or a floor in your dorm, you must get involved in something to have a good social life," advises a political science major. Fraternities and sororities attract 16 percent of the men and 27 percent of the women, and they throw open parties in houses that are owned and maintained by the college.

"[Carlisle has plenty of] cool little shops that you wouldn't find in big cities."

Monitors check IDs at parties, kegs aren't permitted in any college housing, and four underage drinking incidents will get you suspended. "Drinking and parties are a large part of the social culture on campus, especially on the weekends," says a student. At the Quarry, a former frat house, you can grab a cup of coffee, play some video games, or show your moves on the dance floor. In addition to one big concert per semester, each fall brings an arts festival, and a spring carnival gives students one last blast before finals.

Carlisle is 20 miles from the Pennsylvania state capital of Harrisburg, and has plenty of "cool little shops that you wouldn't find in big cities," says a student. "It's a fun place to be," adds a senior. Big Brothers Big Sisters, the Alpha Phi Omega community service fraternity, and other programs help bring the school and community together. In the spring and early fall, Maryland and Delaware beaches beckon; they're just a two- to three-hour drive. Come winter, good skiing is half an hour away. Nature lovers will enjoy hiking the nearby Appalachian Trail. For those craving urban stimulation, the best road trips are to Philadelphia, New York, and Washington, D.C. All are accessible by bus or train—a good thing, since first-years can't have cars.

Dickinson students get riled up for any Red Devils match against top rival Franklin & Marshall, and two annual football battles—the Conestoga Wagon game against Franklin & Marshall and the Little Brown Bucket match against Gettysburg—are favorite traditions. Men's lacrosse recently won the Division III Centennial Conference championship. About 16 percent of students take part in intramurals, where floor hockey, basketball, and soccer are most popular. Students may also organize club teams to compete with other schools in sports like ice hockey and ultimate Frisbee.

Although Dickinson was founded more than two centuries ago, some things remain the same. Seniors still share a champagne toast before graduation. And the steps of Old West, the first college building, are still used only twice a year—in the fall, at the convocation ceremony that welcomes new students, and in the spring, for commencement. Dickinson continues to honor Rush's global vision, with its wealth of study abroad options and its demand that students cross the traditional borders of academic disciplines to grasp the interrelated nature of knowledge.

Overlaps

Franklin & Marshall, Gettysburg, Lafayette, Hamilton, Middlebury, Bucknell, William and Mary, Skidmore

If You Apply To ›

Dickinson: Early decision I and II, early action, regular decision. SATs or ACTs: optional (required for consideration for merit scholarships). Subject Tests: optional. Accepts the Common Application with supplement.

Drew University

Madison, NJ 07940

From Drew's wooded perch in suburban New Jersey, Manhattan is only a 30-minute train ride away, and Wall Street, the UN, and Broadway are common destinations for Drew interns. Drew is the state's only prominent liberal arts college and one of the few in the greater New York City area. Nearly 60 percent of the students are from Jersey, and Drew is still struggling to find a national identity.

Founded more than 150 years ago as a Methodist university, Drew University has grown into a place where an emphasis on hands-on learning, research, and internships is just as important as performance in the classroom. The university encourages theater and the arts to thrive, promotes internships in New York City, and sends its students abroad for month-long educational ventures. As part of its reinforced commitment to global education, Drew has tripled the number of international students on campus in the last four years.

The school occupies 186 acres of peaceful woodland in the upscale New York City suburb of Madison and is known as the "University in the Forest." Fifty-six campus buildings peek through splendid oak trees and boast classic and contemporary styles, a physical reflection of Drew's respect for both scholarly traditions and progressive education. Recent campus renovation projects have included the Hall of Sciences and the International Student Center.

Drew's general education requirements include coursework in six areas: depth of study (courses within the student's chosen major); breadth of knowledge; proficiencies (writing, quantitative literacy, foreign language, and information literacy); local and global citizenship; an off-campus experience; and a first-year experience dubbed the DREW Seminar, the highlight of which is a day-long, faculty-led, course-related field trip to Manhattan. All students also complete a senior capstone experience.

Political science is Drew's strongest undergraduate department, and future politicos can take advantage of off-campus opportunities in New York City, Washington, D.C., and London. Other popular majors include psychology, English, business, and biology; programs in theatre arts, international relations, and neuroscience are also well regarded. Future financiers can follow in the footsteps of the school's founder, Daniel Drew, a financier and railroad tycoon. The theatre arts department works closely with the

> "No student goes unnoticed; everyone bonds with a mentor on campus."

Playwrights Theatre of New Jersey to produce plays that are written, directed, and designed by students. Aspiring doctors can earn a B.A. and M.D. from Drew and the Rutgers New Jersey Medical School in seven years, and dual-degree programs are available with several other universities as well, including Duke and Columbia. Intent on using New York City as a classroom whenever possible, Drew offers six intensive semesters—Wall Street, the United Nations, Social Entrepreneurship, Communications and Media, New York Theatre, and Contemporary Art—that take students into the city two to three days a week for real-world learning experiences.

Students take their academics seriously and rate their professors highly. Small class sizes and extensive enrichment opportunities allow students to develop personal relationships with faculty. "No student goes unnoticed; everyone bonds with a mentor on campus," says a sociology major. The Dana Research Institute for Scientists Emeriti offers opportunities for students to do research with distinguished retired industrial scientists. About 70 percent of Drew undergraduates in all fields undertake research. The Baldwin Honors program includes master classes with guest

Website: www.drew.edu
Location: Suburban
Private
Total Enrollment: 1,650
Undergraduates: 1,389
Male/Female: 41/59
SAT Ranges: ERW 560–660, M 540–640
ACT Ranges: 23–28
Financial Aid: 96%
Pell Grant: 33%
Expense: Pr $
Student Loans: 68%
Average Debt: $ $
Applicants: 3,205
Accepted: 63%
Enrolled: 18%
Grad in 6 Years: 62%
Returning Freshmen: 85%
Academics: ✐ ✐ ✐
Social: ☎ ☎ ☎
Q of L: ★ ★ ★
Admissions: (973) 408-3739
Email Address:
 cadm@drew.edu

Strong Programs:
Political Science
Psychology
English
Business
Biology
Theatre Arts
International Relations
Neuroscience

speakers, special trips, and exclusive activities. Drew's Center for Civic Engagement supports teaching, research, scholarship, art, and other university-based activities that benefit communities. Drew has long been a proponent of study abroad programs and offers 8 to 12 faculty-led TREC (Travel, Rethink, Explore, Connect) courses during winter, spring, and summer breaks each year, in addition to lengthier options through partner programs. Forty-five percent of undergrads go abroad.

Drew has tripled the number of international students on campus in the last four years.

"Drew students are a welcoming bunch; we like new people, we like new ideas, and we like new ideals," observes a junior. Fifty-nine percent of students are from New Jersey and most attended public high schools; 10 percent are international. The school is relatively diverse: 8 percent of students are African American, 13 percent are Hispanic, 5 percent are Asian American, and 5 percent are multiracial. "My favorite thing about Drew is that although people are politically and socially active, they are more interested in listening to what others

"[Madison] is a nice college town according to my parents."

have to say than in projecting their own opinions," says a senior. Thirty-three percent of freshmen are eligible for Pell Grants. Merit awards average $22,600, but there are no athletic scholarships. Drew recently rolled back tuition to 2010 rates, decreasing its sticker price by 20 percent.

Seventy-nine percent of the students live in university housing, which is guaranteed for four years and includes both single-sex and co-ed dorms, theme houses, and, for upperclassmen, townhouses. A lottery gives housing preference to seniors and juniors, making room selection "an easy process," according to a sophomore. Most first-years reside in dorms situated at the back of campus, and 40 percent choose to take part in living/learning communities. Students report that a "massive renovation" to the Commons dining hall has vastly improved the quality of meals; "There's always something that I can look forward to eating," says a junior. Title IX is "actively promoted by the university," says one student, adding that "there is room for improvement" in how sexual assault cases are handled.

Drew recently rolled back tuition to 2010 rates, decreasing its sticker price by 20 percent.

With no Greek life, a sophomore explains, "The athletic teams and theatre groups hold the most vibrant parties on campus," and for those who don't care to party, "Our Office of Student Activities supplements student-run programming by bringing in comedians, musicians, slam poets, and other performers every Thursday to engage the community." There is a 21-and-over pub on campus, as well as two coffeehouses. The Shakespeare Theatre of New Jersey is in residence on campus part of every year and offers both performances and internships. The First Annual Picnic, held on the last day of classes and numbered like Super Bowls (spring 2019 marked FAP XLVI), provides an opportunity to enjoy free food, carnival games, and music. Other traditions include the Holiday Ball, 99 Nights for seniors, and Fern Fest, where students plant native ferns and wildflowers during Earth Week.

Approximately 50 percent of students volunteer in local and international activities such as Mentors at Drew and the Drew Honduras Project. The commuter town of Madison doesn't have the amenities of larger metropolitan areas, of course, but there are several unique shops and restaurants within walking distance of

"[Students benefit from] both a traditional college experience and professional excellence."

campus. One student says the town "is a nice college town according to my parents, but not to students. Everything closes up pretty early." Nearby Morristown is more of a college place. New York City's Pennsylvania Station is less than an hour away by commuter train, and Philadelphia, the Jersey Shore, and the Delaware River are close by.

Interest in the school's 20 Division III varsity teams has grown as the Rangers have become more successful. Men's tennis, women's lacrosse, and men's and women's soccer are consistently strong, with men's soccer taking home a conference title in 2017. The competitive men's and women's fencing teams beat and parry with the likes of Duke and Cornell. Intramural and club sports range from flag football and basketball to dance and eSports, and special recreation events like Hunger Games Dodgeball and the Rock Paper Scissors Tournament are student favorites.

At Drew, students benefit from "both a traditional college experience and professional excellence, due to our proximity to New York City," explains a junior. Indeed, Drew offers its small body of students a wide range of opportunities and plenty of personal attention in a classic liberal arts structure. Above all, says one international relations major, "A culture of understanding, open-mindedness, and accepting others is *the* Drew culture." Not too bad for a school in the forest.

If You Apply To ›

Drew: Early decision I and II, early action, regular decision. SATs or ACTs: optional (required for consideration for honors program and certain merit scholarships). No Subject Tests. Accepts the Common Application with supplement.

Drexel University

3141 Chestnut Street, Philadelphia, PA 19104

Drexel is a streetwise, no-nonsense technical university in the heart of Philadelphia. Like Lehigh, Drexel also offers programs in business and arts and sciences, and its most distinctive offering is the Westphal College of Media Arts and Design. A financial bargain compared to other leading technical schools, Drexel has abandoned its aggressive expansion plans and in-your-face recruitment style of recent years In order to increase yield and graduation rates. Check out the co-op program.

For career-minded students who want to bypass the soul-searching of their liberal arts counterparts, Drexel University offers both solid academics and an innovative co-op program that combines high-tech academics with paying job opportunities—a mix that's particularly appealing in today's economic reality. The school dates to 1891, when Anthony J. Drexel, a Philadelphia financier and philanthropist, set up the Drexel Institute of Art, Science, and Industry in order to prepare young men and women to work in the emerging industrial society. Drexel began offering co-op education in 1919. "If you want a good job, you go to Drexel and you do co-op," asserts a student.

"Drexel's campus is impressive for its downtown Philadelphia location, with gardens and greenery on every block," says a student, "but the campus is woven tightly into the fabric of the city." Drexel's 123-acre campus, which is adjacent to the University of Pennsylvania, is condensed into about a 20-block radius. It lies in a formerly crime-ridden neighborhood that is now one of the most desirable parts of Philadelphia, with plenty of restaurants and stores. A multiphase neighborhood remake will include a $3.5 billion "Innovation Neighborhood" along the Schuylkill River rail yards that will house new research facilities and incubator space. The campus's older buildings are simple and made of brick; most are modern and in good condition. Additional facilities include the Center City Campus for the College of Nursing and Health Professions.

Cooperative education is the hallmark of Drexel's curriculum, which alternates periods of full-time study and full-time employment for four or five years, providing

> **"The campus is woven tightly into the fabric of the city."**

Website: www.drexel.edu
Location: City Center
Private
Total Enrollment: 17,995
Undergraduates: 13,550
Male/Female: 55/45
SAT Ranges: ERW 575–670, M 580–690
ACT Ranges: 24–30
Financial Aid: 94%
Pell Grant: 26%
Expense: Pr $ $ $
Student Loans: 60%
Average Debt: N/A
Applicants: 28,454
Accepted: 79%
Enrolled: 15%
Grad in 6 Years: 71%
Returning Freshmen: 89%
Academics: ✐ ✐ ✐
Social: ☎ ☎

(continued)

Q of L: ★ ★ ★
Admissions: (800) 2-DREXEL
Email Address:
   enroll@drexel.edu

Strong Programs:
Engineering
Computer Science
Finance
Biological Sciences
Nursing
Game Design and Production
Interior Design
Physics

Cooperative education is the hallmark of Drexel's curriculum, providing students with six to 18 months of job experience before they graduate.

students with six to 18 months of job experience before they graduate. The co-op possibilities, which 92 percent of undergraduates take advantage of, are unlimited: students can co-op virtually anywhere in the U.S. or in 51 other countries. Freshman and senior years of the five-year programs are spent on campus, and the three intervening years (sophomore, prejunior, and junior) usually consist of six months of work and six months of school. A 10-week preparatory course, Co-op 101, covers such topics as skills assessment, ethics in the workplace, résumé writing, interviewing skills, and stress management. Most co-ops are paid, and the median six-month salary for co-op students is just over $17,000. And although some students complain that jobs can turn out to be six months of busywork, most enjoy making important contacts in their potential fields and learning while earning.

To accommodate the co-op students, Drexel operates year-round. "I would describe the climate as intense but manageable," says one senior. "Being on a quarter system is rigorous at times." Flexibility in requirements varies by college, but in the first year everyone must take English composition, mathematics, and two one-credit courses: one that introduces students to university resources and one on civic engagement in the local community. Engineering majors must also complete the Drexel Engineering Curriculum, which integrates math, physics, chemistry, and engineering to make sure that even techies enter the workforce well-rounded and able to write as well as they can compute and design. Students enjoy the 700,000-volume library, which offers good hours and lots of room for studying. What's more, each entering freshman is assigned a "personal librarian" charged with helping them make the best use of library facilities. Professors receive high praise from most, and are noted for their accessibility and warmth. Says one student, "The only things that teaching assistants run are labs and study sessions." Fifty-five percent of classes have fewer than 20 students.

"I would describe the climate as intense but manageable."

The most popular majors are mechanical engineering, computer science, finance, and biological sciences. Drexel's greatest strength is its engineering college, which churns out more than 1 percent of all the nation's engineering graduates, B.S. through Ph.D. The materials science, electrical, and architectural engineering programs are particular standouts. Other noteworthy programs include nursing and the Westphal College of Media Arts and Design's majors in game design and production and interior design; the College of Arts and Sciences is well recognized for theoretical and atmospheric physics. An honors college is available for those who seek an even more challenging experience, and about 8 percent of undergrads study abroad.

Drexel has shed its long-standing reputation as an easy-admission commuter college. According to one sophomore, Drexel students are "not afraid of hard work because we do it all the time, even when we're exhausted." The undergraduate student body is 41 percent Pennsylvanian, with another large chunk of students from adjacent New Jersey, and tends to lean right politically. The international student population is 12 percent. Asian Americans comprise 16 percent, African Americans 7 percent, Hispanics 6 percent, and multiracial students 4 percent. Twenty-six percent of freshmen are Pell-eligible. In addition to need-based financial aid, merit scholarships averaging $15,000 and 181 athletic scholarships are awarded to qualified students.

"Drexel graduates are surely among the most capable and motivated individuals I have ever met."

Freshmen live in one of nine co-ed residence halls, including a luxurious high-rise, but most upperclassmen reside in nearby apartments or fraternities houses. Overall, just 22 percent of the students live in the dorms; another third commute to campus from home. Students say the two main dining centers offer a variety of "adequate" food. If all else fails, nomadic food trucks park around campus, providing quick lunches. Students are encouraged to use a shuttle bus between the library and dorms at night, and access to dorms, the library, and the physical education center is restricted to students with IDs, so most say they feel safe on campus.

With so many students living off campus and the city of Philadelphia at their disposal, Drexel tends to be a bit deserted on weekends. Friday-night flicks on campus are cheap and popular with those who stay around, and dorms sponsor floor parties. The dozen or so fraternities, which recruit 14 percent of the men, also contribute to the party scene, especially freshman year; the handful of smaller sororities attract 13 percent of the women. "Greek life is relatively small, so there are plenty of other ways to be involved socially," a senior says. "There's no pressure to drink," adds a communication major, and campus policies are strict; dorms require those of age to sign in alcohol and limit the quantities they may bring in.

Drexel's co-op program often undermines any sense of class unity and can strain personal relationships. Activities that depend on some continuity of enrollment for success—music, drama, student government, athletics—suffer most. "It's hard to get people involved because of the amount of schoolwork and co-ops," says one student. Even so, the university sponsors 18 Division I teams, competing in the Colonial Athletic Association. There is no football team, but the Dragons men's and women's basketball, crew, and soccer teams are strong. "Our biggest rivalry is our feud with Delaware," admits one frenzied student. "We delight in sacrificing blue plastic chickens!"—Delaware's mascot. An extensive intramural program serves all students, and joggers can head for the steps of the Philadelphia Art Museum, just as Rocky did in the movies. Students take full advantage of their urban location by frequenting clubs, restaurants, cultural attractions, and shopping malls in Philadelphia, easily accessible by public transportation.

Aspiring poets, musicians, and historians may find Drexel a bit confusing. But future computer scientists, engineers, and other technically oriented minds could get a fantastic jump-start on their careers, thanks to the university's unique approach to learning inside and outside the classroom. As one satisfied student explains, "The terms are intense, the activities unlimited, but Drexel graduates are surely among the most capable and motivated individuals I have ever met. When I graduate, I will be prepared and proud of it."

With the city of Philadelphia at students' disposal, Drexel tends to be a bit deserted on weekends.

Overlaps

Penn State, Syracuse, University of Pittsburgh, George Washington, Temple, Rochester Institute of Technology, Lehigh

If You Apply To ›

Drexel: Early decision, early action, regular decision. SATs or ACTs or two Subject Tests or two AP Exams or two IB Higher Level Exams: required. Accepts the Common Application. Apply to particular school or program.

2138 Campus Drive, Durham, NC 27708

What fun to be at Duke—face painted blue, rocking Cameron Indoor Stadium as the Blue Devils win again. The most prestigious private university in the South, Duke is academically competitive with the Ivies and Stanford. Strong in engineering as well as the humanities, it offers public policy and economics rather than business. Big emphasis on community service and study across disciplines. DukeEngage service program is special.

Website: www.duke.edu
Location: Small City
Private
Total Enrollment: 15,271
Undergraduates: 6,532
Male/Female: 50/50
SAT Ranges: ERW 680–780,
　M 710–800
ACT Ranges: 31–35
Financial Aid: 44%
Pell Grant: 15%
Expense: Pr $ $ $ $
Student Loans: 33%
Average Debt: $
Applicants: 33,077
Accepted: 10%
Enrolled: 54%
Grad in 6 Years: 95%
Returning Freshmen: 97%
Academics: ✏ ✏ ✏ ✏ ✏
Social: ☎ ☎ ☎ ☎
Q of L: ★ ★ ★ ★
Admissions: (919) 684-3214
Email Address: undergrad
　-admissions@duke.edu

Strong Programs:
Economics
Computer Science
Public Policy
Biology
Biomedical Engineering
Neuroscience
Global Health
English

Duke University is one of the few elite U.S. colleges where strong academics and championship-caliber sports teams manage to coexist. It might be south of the Mason-Dixon Line, and may seem a bit wet behind the ears compared to those ancient and prestigious Northeastern schools known for the erstwhile foliage on their walls, but Duke wins its fair share of intellectually serious superachievers, as well as lots of top athletes. One senior says Duke offers plenty to cheer about, including "a diverse student body, challenging academics, world-renowned professors, research opportunities, and an immense amount of school spirit."

Founded in 1838 as the Union Institute (later Trinity College), Duke University is young for a school of its stature. It sprouted up in 1924, thanks to a stack of tobacco-stained dollars known as the Duke Endowment. Duke's campus in the North Carolina Piedmont is divided into two main sections, West and East, and with 8,300 acres of adjacent forest, offers enough open space to satisfy even the most diehard outdoors enthusiast. West Campus, the hub of the university, is laid out in spacious quadrangles and dominated by the impressive Gothic chapel, a symbol of the university's Methodist tradition. Constructed in the 1930s, West includes collegiate Gothic residential and classroom quads, the administration building, the huge Perkins Library, and the recently renovated student union. East Campus, built in the 1920s, consists primarily of Georgian redbrick buildings. East and West are connected by shuttle buses, though many students enjoy the mile-or-so walk or bike ride between them along wooded Campus Drive.

> **"[Duke offers] world-renowned professors, research opportunities, and an immense amount of school spirit."**

Students opt for one of two undergraduate schools: the Pratt School of Engineering and Trinity College of Arts & Sciences. The school's engineering programs—particularly electrical and biomedical—are national standouts. Natural sciences, most notably ecology, biology, and neuroscience, are also first-rate. The proximity of the Medical Center enhances study in biochemistry and global health. Duke's Sanford School of Public Policy offers an interdisciplinary major—unusual at the undergraduate level—that trains aspiring public servants and future leaders of nonprofit organizations, government agencies, and other bodies that shape public life. Internships and apprenticeships are a big part of the program. Duke's English and dance programs are notable, but students say the language offerings can be weak. Duke has more than 60 interdisciplinary centers, including the Duke Global Health Institute, the Nicholas Institute for Environmental Policy Solutions, and the John Hope Franklin Humanities Institute. Economics attracts the most majors, followed by computer science, public policy, and biology.

Trinity College's curriculum, part of the traditional undergraduate coursework known as Program I, requires courses in five general areas of knowledge: arts, literature, and performance; civilizations; social sciences; natural sciences; and quantitative studies. Students must also fulfill requirements in six modes of inquiry, including foreign language; writing; research; ethical inquiry; science, technology, and society; and cross-cultural inquiry. All students complete three Small Group Learning Experiences: one seminar course during the freshman year, on topics such as Faith and Firearms in America and Environmental Change in the Big-Data Era, and two more as upperclassmen. Those who wish to explore subjects outside and between usual majors and minors may choose Program II, to which they are admitted after proposing a topic, question, or theme for which they plan an individualized curriculum with faculty advisors and deans.

Duke's Sanford School of Public Policy offers an interdisciplinary major—unusual at the undergraduate level.

When college counselors say Duke is hot, they're not referring to the boiling temperatures in the South. "The workload is heavy, but, because of the highly collaborative environment, it is manageable," says a public policy major. Seventy-one percent of classes have fewer than 20 students, and the university focuses resources on undergraduate education and having senior professors teach more classes. A senior says, "Faculty members are accessible, especially through a program called FLUNCH, where you are able to have a meal with a faculty member on Duke's dime." Interdisciplinary work, long part of the Duke culture, is a priority for faculty and students alike. The FOCUS program offers first-year students groups of seminars with 18

"[Through FLUNCH] you are able to have a meal with a faculty member on Duke's dime."

or fewer students clustered around a single broad, interdisciplinary theme, such as biotechnology and social change; participants also live together in the same residence hall. It is "an incredible opportunity to engage with the university's top professors," a senior reports. The Bass Connections program gives undergraduates a chance to work with faculty and graduate students in interdisciplinary, research-based project teams in thematic areas such as global health and energy and environment.

Those who wish to see the world before embarking on their undergraduate career may apply to the Duke Gap Year Program; accepted students receive between $5,000 and $15,000 toward the cost of their chosen gap year program. Fifty-four percent of Duke's undergrads study abroad during their four years in 45 university-administered programs and 150 other partner programs, and there are ample opportunities for those who want a break from campus life without leaving the country. DukeEngage, an ambitious and innovative program backed by a $30 million endowment, supports students willing to spend summers working on projects ranging from building schools in Kenya to working with Gulf Coast flood victims. Nearly a quarter of all undergrads participate in the program, which has become a centerpiece of the school's commitment to "knowledge in service to society."

"Students tend to be extremely driven, upper middle class, and focused on succeeding far after college," says one public policy major. Fifteen percent of Duke students are from North Carolina, and the Northeastern corridor sends a fair-sized contingent, as does California. Ten percent of undergraduates hail from overseas. Duke's Southern gentility is reflected in campus attire, which is generally neatly pressed on guys and maybe a bit outfit-y on women, in contrast to the thrown-together antistatus uniform of jeans and sweats that dominates on many other campuses. Undergraduate women sometimes complain about the pressure they feel to demonstrate, in the words of a former president, "effortless perfection" in all respects. Despite the unmistakable air of wealth on campus, two-thirds of students come from public high schools. Ten percent are African American, 9 percent are Hispanic, 21 percent are Asian American, and 2 percent are multiracial. Students of different ethnicities and races tend to "self-segregate," students say, producing little tension but also little interaction. The Center for Race Relations works to improve the way Duke educates its students about diversity and conflict resolution. Also noteworthy: Duke was among the first universities to include in their admissions

Students in the Duke Gap Year Program receive between $5,000 and $15,000 toward the cost of their chosen gap year program.

application an optional short essay question in which applicants can discuss their sexual, gender, or other identities.

Duke admits students without regard to financial need and meets 100 percent of their demonstrated need. The university has eliminated loans from financial aid packages for families with incomes below $40,000 a year, and families with incomes below $60,000 a year are not expected to contribute to the cost of tuition. Like other Division I universities, Duke hands out lots of athletic scholarships. The university also offers a small number of merit scholarships, including those offered through the Rubenstein Scholars Program, established in 2016 for high-achieving, first-generation students from low-income backgrounds. Incoming Rubenstein Scholars participate in a six-week summer academic program, receive personal mentoring from top faculty, and take special seminars during the academic year.

> **"The dorms look like castles on the outside and feel like Harry Potter."**

Duke undergrads are required to live on campus for three years; overall, 81 percent stay in university-owned housing. Students live in residence halls or quads that house both independent students and members of selective living groups such as fraternities. Freshmen all reside in dorms on the East Campus led by a faculty member and his or her family. "The dorms look like castles on the outside and feel like Harry Potter," says a junior, who adds that the new dorms "are like five-star hotels." Sophomores move to West Campus, where there are also special-interest dorms focused on themes such as women's studies, the arts, languages, and community service. Seniors can move off campus, but "the apartments vary in quality." One student says, "Campus security is nice and makes me feel safe for the most part."

> *Durham includes most of the Research Triangle Park, the largest research center of its kind in the world.*

Duke has been engaged in a massive physical expansion over the last few years aimed at enhancing students' creature comforts, including a 72,000-square-foot, state-of-the-art Health and Wellness Center. The glass-fronted Brodhead Center for Campus Life, recently reopened after a three-year renovation funded by an $80 million grant, is host to an over-the-top collection of dining options operated by local chefs and restaurateurs that, consistent with Durham's reputation as a foodie haven, the university trumpets as offering the most lavish (and, students say, costly) dining on any college campus. Off-campus restaurants—many of which will deliver—are linked to the Duke meal plan.

"Duke students are the type who will start a club if they are interested in something that nobody else is doing, work hard on a paper late into the night, and then go out Thursday, Friday, and Saturday," says a public policy major. Students agree that most social life takes place on campus or in surrounding houses and apart-

> **"[Duke students] go out Thursday, Friday, and Saturday."**

ments. Although it has been pushed away from the center of campus, "the Greek scene dominates," says a history major. Fraternities and sororities attract 29 percent of the men and 42 percent of the women, respectively. Fraternity parties are open to everyone, and the free shuttle bus service that connects the school's various dorm and apartment complexes runs until 4 a.m. "There is a strong drinking and party culture on campus, though students are not pressured to participate," one sophomore reports.

Duke is also a culturally active campus; theater groups thrive, and the Nasher Museum of Art, with its world-class exhibits by Picasso, Calder, and El Greco, among others, has become a popular social hub. The Springternational festival brings in live bands and vendors peddling local crafts and exotic foods each spring, and the traditional Joe College Day has been revived as a daylong fall affair filled with food, arts and crafts, and music. In warm weather, the broad beaches on North Carolina's outer banks are two to three hours away, while winter ski slopes are three to four hours distant.

Durham is a small, working-class city that has had its share of racial tensions but also boasts a vibrant African American middle class and good political leadership. Duke as an institution has been active in the community, especially in public schools, and hundreds of undergrads are involved in service learning, tutoring, and related activities. "Everyone is involved in volunteer work," says one student. Downtown Durham is undergoing a revival, with old tobacco warehouses being converted into restaurants, stores, offices, and apartments. The *New York Times* frequently writes up Durham as a foodie destination. The town is proud of its Durham Bulls, the local minor-league baseball team, which coined the term "bullpen." No one misses the irony of the fact that Durham, once known as the "City of Tobacco," now bills itself as the "City of Medicine." (In another irony, the Duke campus will go smoke-free in 2020.) Durham includes most of the Research Triangle Park, the largest research center of its kind in the world. Duke, North Carolina State, and the University of North Carolina at Chapel Hill created the park for nonprofit, scientific, and sociological research. Many Silicon Valley technology companies have East Coast outposts in the park, which has helped give the area the highest percentage of Ph.D.s per capita in the United States.

Duke's official motto is *Eruditio et Religio* only to a few straitlaced administrators; everyone else knows it as *Eruditio et Basketballio*, which translates more or less as "Go to hell, Carolina"—meaning UNC at Chapel Hill, Duke's archrival in the rough-and-tough Atlantic Coast Conference. At games, students transform into the legendary Cameron Crazies and get the best courtside seats, where they make life miserable

> "Everyone is involved in volunteer work."

for the visiting team. Their efforts paid off in 2015 when the Blue Devils won the national Division I men's basketball championship for the fifth time under fabled coach Mike Krzyzewski. Sports-crazed Blue Devils erect a temporary tent city—dubbed "Krzyzewskiville"—to vie for the best seats. This is far from roughing it—students form groups to hold their places so that some fraction can go to class and keep their peers who hold down the fort on track academically. "There is something magical about Duke basketball, and the feeling of being in the student section with the Cameron Crazies during the Duke–UNC game is something that can't be captured in words," gushes one fan. The women's basketball team has been strong in its own right, and the men's lacrosse team is a national powerhouse. Football has undergone a renaissance under coach David Cutcliffe. The team, which now plays in a renovated stadium complete with luxury boxes for Iron Duke supporters, earns regular bowl bids. Women's softball is new. Duke's stellar debate team brought home the national title recently. Intramurals are big, with roughly 950 teams, and operate on two levels of competitiveness; 40 club sports are available as well.

Meandering around Duke's up-to-date campus, you can see the latest technology, but you can also hear the whisper of the Old South through those big old trees. In addition to blending old and new, Duke also does an impressive job combining sports and academia, producing students who almost define the term "well-rounded." But this may be changing. Says a junior, "It's attracting better students, shifting the focus away from basketball and fraternities, and trying to create a more intellectual environment on campus."

Sports-crazed Blue Devils erect a temporary tent city—dubbed "Krzyzewskiville"—to vie for the best basketball seats.

Overlaps

Brown, University of Chicago, Columbia, Dartmouth, University of Pennsylvania, Cornell University, Harvard, Stanford

If You Apply To ›

Duke: Early decision, regular decision. SATs or ACTs: required. Subject Tests: recommended (any two). Accepts the Common Application with supplement. Additional optional essay invites applicants to share a perspective or experience related to community, family, culture, sexual orientation, or gender identity.

Earlham College

Richmond, IN 47374

BEST BUY

Earlham is a member of the proud circle of liberal colleges in the Midwest that includes Beloit, Grinnell, Kenyon, and Oberlin, to name just a few. Roughly one-third the size of Oberlin and comparable to the other three, but manages to attract a more diverse student body, despite its conservative southern Indiana location. Earlham is distinctive for its Quaker orientation, welcoming environment, and international perspective.

Website: www.earlham.edu

Location: Small City

Private

Total Enrollment: 1,053

Undergraduates: 1,020

Male/Female: 45/55

SAT Ranges: ERW 610–700, M 580–700

ACT Ranges: 25–30

Financial Aid: 95%

Pell Grant: 35%

Expense: Pr $ $

Student Loans: 58%

Average Debt: $ $

Applicants: 2,799

Accepted: 52%

Enrolled: 20%

Grad in 6 Years: 68%

Returning Freshmen: 86%

Academics: ✎ ✎ ✎ ✎

Social: ☎ ☎ ☎

Q of L: ★ ★ ★ ★ ★

Admissions: (765) 983-1600

Email Address: admissions@ earlham.edu

Strong Programs:
Biology
Biochemistry
Psychology
Politics
Visual and Performing Arts
English
Peace and Global Studies
Japanese Studies

Earlham is a study in contradictions—a top-notch liberal arts college in a relatively conservative city that few could place on a map, and an institution that in the 21st century remains true to the traditions of community, peace, and justice that are hallmarks of its Religious Society of Friends (Quaker) heritage. Earlham's curriculum and programs engage students with the world by exposing them to classmates from approximately 55 nations and offering more than 200 academic courses that incorporate an international perspective. Varied study abroad programs provide close faculty involvement and a thoughtful focus on cross-cultural perspectives.

Earlham was established in 1859 in the wake of the Great Migration of Quakers from Eastern states that took place in the first half of the 19th century. The college's 800-acre campus sits in the small, quintessentially Midwestern city of Richmond, just a short distance from Cincinnati and Indianapolis. Georgian-style buildings dominate, surrounded by mature trees and plantings, while the Japanese gardens symbolize the college's long friendship and closeness with Japan. Newer buildings include the Center for Science and Technology and baseball and soccer stadiums.

To graduate, students must complete general education requirements in the arts, analytical reasoning, wellness, scientific inquiry, foreign language, and, not surprisingly, diversity. All students take a reading- and writing-focused first-year seminar and complete a capstone experience. Biology is the most popular major, and biochemistry, the social sciences (especially psychology and politics), the visual and performing arts, and English also garner high enrollment. A wide range of interdisciplinary offerings includes such programs as peace and global studies, global management, Quaker studies, environmental sustainability, and Japanese studies, a field in which Earlham is a national leader. "The Japanese program has high national standing," says one student, "and the sciences have high placement for graduate studies and jobs post-graduation." Preprofessional preparation and integrated learning programs are available in such areas as health sciences, business and entrepreneurship, and law and social justice.

> **"Peace and justice are an Earlhamite's deepest love."**

Challenged to think and meet high academic expectations, students see themselves as capable and eager to learn. An international studies major says the academic climate is "very collaborative, but still leaves room for individual critical thinking." Discussion rather than lecture is the predominant learning style here, facilitated by small classes—76 percent have fewer than 20 students. Earlham faculty members are selected for their excellence in teaching and their ability to cross disciplinary lines. "The faculty is ready and willing to put as much into a student's academic success as that student puts in," says a politics major. Another student explains that, as a matter of Quaker principle, faculty, staff, and students are never addressed by honorifics or social titles like Dr. or Ms., but by their first names: "It's an equality thing."

The new EPIC Advantage program provides every Earlham student with the opportunity to pursue a fully funded internship or faculty-guided research experience, on or off campus, typically during the summer before their junior or senior year. Sixty-five percent of students participate in at least one off-campus study experience. Earlham offers study abroad programs in more than two dozen countries, including Ecuador, Germany, Japan, Jordan, and New Zealand, most of which are managed by the college. In a Border Studies program, students live with families in Tucson, Arizona, and take courses focusing on United States–Mexico border issues. Popular May Term classes send students off campus with faculty for one-month intensive courses in various locations around the world. "One of my friends, only a rising sophomore, is spending several weeks in Germany with a professor studying ancient fossils in one of the most advanced DNA analysis labs in the world," says one sophomore. "His story is not an uncommon one for freshmen and this speaks to the unique availability of great opportunities here." About three-quarters of students eventually pursue postgraduate study, often after taking some time off for a job or to participate in volunteer or service programs.

Only 21 percent of the students are Hoosiers; 22 percent hail from abroad. Eleven percent are African American, with Hispanics adding 7 percent, Asian Americans 5 percent, and multiracial students 2 percent. These days, just 3 percent of students are Quakers, but traditional Quaker values still permeate this liberal campus. "Earlhamites come at all of their endeavors with their whole hearts," says a senior. "Many students walk around barefoot (weather permitting), and peace and justice are an Earlhamite's deepest love." Thirty-five percent of freshmen are Pell-eligible. Merit scholarships averaging $23,000 are available for qualified students; there are no athletic scholarships.

> "Richmond has great opportunities for volunteering or interning with NGOs."

Ninety-two percent of Earlham students live on campus, with first-years occupying eight traditional residence halls. The newest, Mills Hall, offers suite-style accommodations. Upperclassmen can opt to live in the dorms, the Campus Village Apartments, or one of 20 themed college houses. Dining facilities receive average reviews. A senior says safety officers are helpful in all situations: "Once, I had a conversation with a campus security officer about the best places to hide on campus in case of a zombie attack." Some note that the administration has been slow to respond to the issue of campus sexual assault, but that it's making strides in the right direction.

There are no fraternities or sororities at Earlham, but on-campus activities abound. "Most everything happens on campus, which is great because everything is more open and accessible," a student says. Students enjoy improv comedy, a cappella music, equestrian programs, a lip-synch competition, fall and spring festivals, concerts, and sports. Student groups include numerous religious, ethnic, and cultural organizations, some of which also take the lead on throwing campus parties. Students 21 and over can consume alcohol, although only in their residence hall rooms, and a senior expresses the opinion that "Earlham parties are usually regarded as lame." Day trips to Cincinnati, Indianapolis, or Columbus and weekend visits to other nearby universities are also popular diversions.

Though not a college town, the city of Richmond offers standard American and a variety of ethnic restaurants, as well as movie theaters, bowling alleys, golf, and a popular biking and running trail. "Richmond has great opportunities for volunteering or interning with NGOs, but is less exciting if you are looking for a happening night life," reports a politics major. Students fan out into the city, racking up more than 23,000 hours of volunteer service a year.

Earlham's 18 varsity teams (the Quakers) attract nearly a third of the student body and compete in Division III sports. The baseball team recently took home

As a matter of Quaker principle, faculty, staff, and students are never addressed by social titles like Dr. or Ms., but by their first names.

In a Border Studies program, students live with families in Tucson, Arizona, and take courses focusing on United States–Mexico border issues.

a conference title, and the men's and women's tennis and soccer squads are also strong. Men's and women's lacrosse and golf teams have recently been added. Forty percent of the students play intramural sports, and soccer, basketball, and kickball are the most popular.

Earlham students graduate ready to take on the world, thanks to the school's cooperative, can-do spirit, international perspective, and caring student/faculty community—and its commitment to a values-oriented education. Says one student, "Earlham allows an individual to pursue many areas of interest, and the people you meet will be friends for a lifetime."

If You Apply To ›

Earlham: Early decision, early action, regular decision. SATs or ACTs: optional (recommended for applicants who wish to be considered for merit scholarships). Subject Tests: optional. Accepts the Common Application.

Eckerd College

4200 54th Avenue South, St. Petersburg, FL 33711

There are worse places to attend than a college with its own stretch of beach on the shores of Tampa Bay. Eckerd's only direct competitor in Florida is Rollins, which has a business school but is otherwise similar. Marine science, environmental studies, and international studies are among Eckerd's biggest draws. The student body is mainly from out of state, with an abundance of Yankee accents.

Website: www.eckerd.edu
Location: City Outskirts
Private
Total Enrollment: 1,894
Undergraduates: 1,894
Male/Female: 34/66
SAT Ranges: ERW 540–650, M 520–610
ACT Ranges: 23–29
Financial Aid: 96%
Pell Grant: 19%
Expense: Pr $ $
Student Loans: 67%
Average Debt: $ $ $
Applicants: 4,525
Accepted: 73%
Enrolled: 12%
Grad in 6 Years: 70%
Returning Freshmen: 81%
Academics: ✍ ✍ ✍
Social: ☎ ☎ ☎
Q of L: ★ ★ ★ ★ ★
Admissions: (727) 864-8331

Attending Eckerd College demands a special sort of willpower. As an international business major explains, "We are right on the water, and it is like going to college in a resort." With free canoes, kayaks, boats, coolers, and tents always available for student use, it's a wonder anyone finds time to study. But study they do, as administrators continue to lure capable students to Eckerd with small classes, skilled professors, and a thriving social scene. "It's Eckerd's paradise-like setting that seals the deal for most prospective students," says a sophomore.

Founded in 1958 as Florida Presbyterian College and renamed 12 years later after a generous benefactor (of drugstore fame), Eckerd considers itself nonsectarian. Still, the school maintains a formal "covenant" with the major Presbyterian denomination, from which it receives some funds. The lush, grassy campus is on the tip of a peninsula bounded by the Gulf of Mexico and Tampa Bay, with plenty of flowering bushes, trees, and small ponds—it's not unusual to spot dolphins frolicking in the adjacent waters. Campus buildings are modern, and none are taller than three stories. The $25 million, LEED Platinum–rated James Center for Molecular and Life Sciences houses the biology, chemistry, and biochemistry programs, and the Nielsen Center for Visual Arts recently opened.

> **"We are right on the water, and it is like going to college in a resort."**

Autumn Term, Eckerd's version of freshman orientation, is a three-week term before the regular fall semester that introduces new students to the academic expectations and social responsibilities of the Eckerd community. First-years also take a yearlong course called Human Experience, which focuses on topics like justice, power, freedom, and global citizenship. In addition to standard distribution requirements, all students take one course each in environmental and global perspectives and complete at least 40 hours of community service before graduation; service opportunities are built into reflective service-learning courses that are offered in every major. Imagining Justice, the required senior capstone seminar, asks students to draw on what they've learned during college to find solutions to important issues. Seniors present their capstone work at a festival in the spring.

Eckerd students take their coursework seriously, but on the whole, a human development major says, "The atmosphere is relaxed. How could it not be when you can study and sunbathe at the beach?" Popular majors include marine science, environmental studies, biology, psychology, business administration, and international business. Wet subjects are especially strong. "The close proximity to the ocean gives [marine science] majors a great amount of hands-on, close-up experience," a student says. The Eckerd College Search and Rescue, for instance, performs more than 500 marine rescues annually. Eckerd was a pioneer of the 4–1–4 term schedule, in which students work on a single project for credit each January. Every student has a faculty mentor, and there are no graduate assistants; half of all classes have fewer than 20 students. "The faculty here is amazing," says a psychology major. "They are here for us and they want us to do well."

Each year, 20 to 25 top incoming freshmen are selected to participate in First-Year Research Associateships, receiving stipends of up to $1,000 to work side by side with leading professors on active research projects. A four-year honors program is also available. While St. Petersburg isn't exactly a college town, a side benefit to the school's location is the Academy of Senior Professionals, a group of senior citizens who mentor undergrads, work with professors on curriculum development, and lead workshops in their areas of expertise. Two-thirds of Eckerd's students study abroad in more than 300 destinations, including the school's study centers in London and China.

Eckerd's president once referred to the school's quirky students as "intellectuals in sandals," reports a junior. "I like the quote, and it really works." Another student says Eckerd attracts "friendly, liberal, free-spirited, and intelligent" students who enjoy the great outdoors. Seventy-eight percent of the student body hails from out of state, with a large contingent coming from the Northeast; another 3 percent are foreign. Hispanics account for 9 percent of the student body, African Americans 3 percent, Asian Americans 2 percent, and multiracial students 3 percent. Merit scholarships averaging $17,600 and athletic awards are available to qualified students.

> "Residence halls [are] named after Greek letters, making fun of the tradition of having frats and sororities."

Eighty-seven percent of students live in the housing quads. Freshmen usually live in doubles or triples, while townhouse- and apartment-style residence halls are available for upperclassmen. Waterfront views and beach access are a given, and a sophomore notes, "We have many different types of themed housing, including pet-friendly, gender neutral, all-female, and health and wellness housing options." As for the food, a junior says it's "getting better and better" as the staff works with students on improvements, and vegan and vegetarian options are plentiful. A management major explains that, given the school's location near a tourist destination, "a security post at the entrance of the school provides a safer environment for students."

"Eckerd is a primarily student-run campus," says a junior, "and there are usually fun and interactive events that happen every Thursday, Friday, and Saturday." Students can partake in concerts, lectures, shows, and games arranged by the student activity board. There are no Greek organizations (a sophomore comments, "We have residence halls named after Greek letters, making fun of the tradition of having frats and sororities"), and weekend parties are usually held in the Kappa, Nu, and

(continued)

Email Address: admissions@ eckerd.edu

Strong Programs:
Marine Science
Environmental Studies
Biology
Psychology
Business Administration
International Business
International Studies

Autumn Term, Eckerd's version of freshman orientation, is a three-week term before the regular fall semester.

Two-thirds of students study abroad in more than 300 destinations, including Eckerd's study centers in London and China.

Omega dorms. Kegs and glass bottles are prohibited on campus, and students 21 and over must wear wristbands at campus parties. Students and professors gather once a month for Pitchers with Professors to enjoy good conversation and free pitchers of beer (for those of age) and root beer in the campus pub. The last few weeks of the school year bring Springtopia, featuring major events like the Spring Ball, Splash Bash at the waterfront, drag queen bingo, and the Kappa Karnival, with rides, games, and cotton candy galore.

Off campus, students enjoy downtown St. Petersburg's First Friday block parties and Saturday Morning Market. Tampa and St. Pete also offer a Salvador Dalí museum—which Eckerd students get into for free—and professional baseball, football, hockey, and soccer teams. The nightclubs and bars of Latin-flavored Ybor City are about 30 minutes away, and tempting road trips include Orlando's Walt Disney World and Universal Studios theme parks, Miami's South Beach, and that hub of debauchery on the delta, New Orleans.

> **"We have dogs, we have beaches, we have intense science labs, and tons of research opportunities."**

Varsity teams (the Tritons) compete in the Division II Sunshine State Conference. "Men's basketball is the only sport that attracts lots of fans and spectators," a senior says, and for good reasons—the team claimed the conference title in 2016 and 2018, as did the women's team in 2017. A night of Midnight Madness helps kick off the season. The co-ed sailing team has claimed several recent divisional and regional championships. Eckerd doesn't have a football team, but popular intramurals include flag football, soccer, and basketball.

Eckerd is committed to offering "experiential, service, and international learning" alongside the traditional classroom experience. That mission, combined with a focus on social justice and, of course, all the fun to be had in the Florida sun, gives Eckerd its distinctive flavor. As a sophomore puts it, "We have dogs, we have beaches, we have intense science labs, and tons of research opportunities. If you are serious about working hard and studying, and getting tan while doing it, Eckerd is the right place to do it."

Overlaps

Cornell College, Goucher, Saint Anselm, Lewis & Clark, Rhodes, Hampshire, Rollins, Stetson

If You Apply To ›

Eckerd: Early action, rolling admissions. SATs or ACTs: required. No Subject Tests. Accepts the Common Application with supplement.

University of Edinburgh: See page 371.

Elon University

Elon, NC 27244

One of the leading liberal arts colleges in the Southeast and an emerging name nationally, Elon boasts a welcoming environment and a nurturing faculty. Once known for turning on average students to the life of the mind, has become increasingly selective but seemingly at the cost of socioeconomic diversity. Strong emphasis on global perspectives and active, experiential learning. Classic-looking campus adds to the appeal.

Elon University derives its name from the Hebrew word for "oak," which is fitting when you consider the ways in which the school is growing. At each year's opening convocation, entering students are given an acorn. Four years later, they are presented with an oak sapling at commencement. It's a charming tradition and a reminder of how things grow and change. With an emphasis on undergraduate research, internships, service learning, study abroad, and leadership—the five Elon Experiences—the university also provides its students with plenty of opportunities to mature, intellectually and socially. "All schools want students to grow holistically, but Elon is the only one I've heard of that actively pursues that goal on many levels," says a senior.

> "Greek life and club sports support a robust off-campus social life for all students to partake in."

Elon was founded in 1889 and occupies a 656-acre campus in North Carolina's Piedmont region. With apologies to Colby and Miami (OH), it is arguably the most architecturally consistent campus in the nation. Buildings are Georgian-style brick with white trim, and newer buildings have been adapted to modern architectural lines while maintaining this classic collegiate feel. On the north end of campus is Lake Mary Nell, home to an abundance of geese and ducks. Academic buildings are organized in three clusters: a historic quad near a fountain in the older section of the campus; the Lambert Academic Village, complete with an amphitheater; and business and science centers in close proximity to the student center. A spate of recent construction has added new facilities for the School of Communications, a 5,100-seat athletics arena, three new residence halls, and a learning center for academic advising and support services.

To graduate, students must complete a core curriculum that includes a broad range of liberal arts subjects, as well as an interdisciplinary capstone seminar. All students must fulfill an Experiential Learning Requirement (ELR) by completing at least two of the five Elon Experiences. "I've found the critical thinking and reflection that comes from ELRs to be extremely beneficial for discussing my experiences and strengths in job interviews," says a journalism major. The university offers more than 60 undergraduate degrees; business, communications, psychology, and exercise science are the most popular majors. Programs in the performing arts and education are also strong. The School of Communications is nationally recognized and benefits from two ultramodern digital television studios. All undergraduate courses are capped at 33 students, to encourage discussion-based classes and close student/faculty interaction. "Our professors do a great job of inspiring learning," says a human service studies major.

Elon has an elaborate support system designed to ensure that first-year students don't fall through the cracks. Students begin general studies with a first-year course called The Global Experience, a seminar-style interdisciplinary class that investigates challenges facing the world. An optional experiential learning summer program partners more than 120 freshmen with returning students for activities ranging from white-water rafting to volunteer work. Elon 101 serves as an academic orientation for all first-years; students meet weekly in small groups with an academic advisor and an upper-level student.

> "Service is one of the bigger components of life as an Elon student."

"We don't have the same level of academic rigor as other private liberal arts schools in the region," remarks an anthropology major, "but we make up for it with our focus on experiential learning." Approximately one in four undergrads engage in research with faculty and present their work at a research forum in the spring. Seventy-nine percent study abroad, thanks to the 4–1–4 academic calendar and more than 100 study abroad programs. Elon's seven Fellows Programs, to which prospective students can apply alongside their admissions applications, are designed for exceptionally motivated students. They offer faculty support,

Website: www.elon.edu
Location: Suburban
Private
Total Enrollment: 6,539
Undergraduates: 5,885
Male/Female: 40/60
SAT Ranges: ERW 580–670, M 560–660
ACT Ranges: 25–29
Financial Aid: 65%
Pell Grant: 10%
Expense: Pr $
Student Loans: 38%
Average Debt: $ $ $
Applicants: 9,623
Accepted: 67%
Enrolled: 25%
Grad in 6 Years: 84%
Returning Freshmen: 89%
Academics: ✍ ✍ ✍
Social: ☎ ☎ ☎ ☎
Q of L: ★ ★ ★ ★ ★
Admissions: (800) 334-8448
Email Address: admissions@elon.edu

Strong Programs:
Business
Communications
Psychology
Exercise Science
Performing Arts
Education

The five Elon Experiences emphasize undergraduate research, internships, service learning, study abroad, and leadership.

scholarships, and peer networks, and current participants highly recommend them as being "profoundly impactful."

Given Elon's emphasis on out-of-classroom endeavors, students here tend to have a lot going on. "Some might say Elon students are *too* involved," says a finance and marketing double major. Of Elon's predominately female student body, 17 percent come from North Carolina, and most of the rest hail from the Northeast. Six percent are African American, 6 percent Hispanic, 2 percent Asian American, 3 percent multiracial, and 2 percent international. Somewhat surprisingly for a school that was once a top choice for first-generation college students, only 10 percent of undergraduates qualify for Pell Grants. Lack of diversity is a common complaint, but students note that the administration is making efforts to diversify the "fairly rich, white, and preppy campus." Politically, says a senior, the campus "certainly does lean liberal, but there are more conservatives here than you think." The top 15 percent of admitted applicants are automatically awarded the Presidential Scholarship. Students can also vie for merit scholarships averaging $7,900 and 293 athletic scholarships.

Sixty-four percent of students reside on campus; they are required to do so for their first two years, and many choose to say on campus for all four years. "The new dorms and apartments are gorgeous and nicer than where I'll be living after graduation," says a senior. Options include traditional residence halls, university-owned apartments, and the Global and Colonnades neighborhoods, which feature more than 26 living/learning communities, such as Creative Arts, Gender and Sexuality, and Innovation. Designed to bridge classroom learning with social experiences, these communities also serve to bring together diverse groups of students with common interests in a safe space; many participants in the Gender and Sexuality community, for instance, identify as LGBTQIA. Those who move off campus find plenty of options within walking distance. Campus dining consists of three dining halls and almost 20 retail locations, but students say accommodations for special diets can be limited. Campus security programs are said to be effective and include escort services, Safe Rides, and the Live Safe app to help students get home safely. "Elon has quite a few resources to deal with sexual assault and they do not take accusations lightly," says a public health studies major.

When it's time to let off steam, students generally turn to the active Greek scene—which attracts 20 percent of the men and 39 percent of the women. "Greek life and club sports support a robust off-campus social life for all students to partake in," says a senior, and students report that alcohol policies are not well enforced. The Student Union Board hosts events every weekend, like bingo and trivia nights, a cappella concerts, and comedy shows, and, "They almost always serve free food," says a cinema and television arts major. Nearby bars, though few, are popular with students 21 and over, especially The Oak House and Fat Frogg. Road trips to the beach (three hours), the mountains (one hour), and Chapel Hill or Raleigh-Durham (less than an hour) are popular diversions.

The tiny town of Elon is virtually indistinguishable from the university, and students take an active role in the community through volunteer projects. Eighty-nine percent of students participate in community service, both domestically and abroad, and one student confirms, "Service is one of the bigger components of life as an Elon student." The well-known Elon University Poll, which the school runs as a public service, tracks political and public policy issues. Favorite campus traditions include a weekly College Coffee, where students and faculty mingle over free breakfast and coffee—a tradition since 1984. An exercise science major says, "We have a Festival of Lights before winter break, and a holiday party at our president's house is a hallmark of the holiday season."

Elon has an elaborate support system designed to ensure that first-year students don't fall through the cracks.

"Elon's best asset is honestly its commitment to engaged learning."

Favorite campus traditions include a weekly College Coffee, where students and faculty mingle over free breakfast and coffee.

Elon competes in the Division I Colonial Athletic Association and offers 17 Phoenix teams. Women's basketball won conference titles in 2017 and 2018. Men's soccer and baseball and women's tennis, track and field, and softball are also strong. There's also an intramural program covering more than 20 sports, in which 27 percent of students take part, and a successful club sports program that lets students compete with other schools.

"Elon's best asset is honestly its commitment to engaged learning," says one student. By steadily ramping up its educational offerings, increasing and improving its facilities, and becoming more selective, this supportive liberal arts university is quickly outgrowing its local reputation. "Elon is not just a place," says a senior, "it's an experience and a community."

Overlaps

Bucknell, William and Mary, Furman, Villanova, University of Richmond, Lehigh, UNC at Chapel Hill, Clemson

If You Apply To ›

Elon: Early decision, early action, regular decision. SATs or ACTs: required. No Subject Tests. Does not accept the Common Application. Application includes optional field for students who identify as part of the LGBTQIA community.

Emerson College

120 Boylston Street, Boston, MA 02116

Emerson is strategically located on Boston Common in the heart of Boston's Theater District and within walking distance of many of the city's major attractions. Specializes in communication and the arts. With roughly 3,700 undergraduates, Emerson is a smaller alternative to neighboring giants Boston U and Northeastern. Like most Beantown institutions, it is far more selective than it once was.

Those who aspire to a career in film, television, or marketing may want to start with a four-year stint in Boston. There they will find Emerson College, a small liberal arts school that offers strong programs in communication and the arts, as well as top-notch performance and production facilities. At Emerson, students take notes from professors who also happen to be working directors, producers, actors, editors, and writers. It's an approach that helps talented, city-savvy students find their voices. "If you are serious about surrounding yourself with creative people during your college years," says a journalism major, "this is the school for you." Prospective students take note: getting into Emerson requires more than dreams. You'll need a solid academic record as well as plenty of talent.

Founded in 1880, Emerson is located by Boston Common in the middle of the city's Theater District, and much of the surrounding city is accessible by foot. The campus features a mix of traditional and modern high-rise buildings. The historic Cutler Majestic and Colonial theaters, the anchors of Emerson's urban campus, have been restored to their original grandeur. The 11-story Tufte Performance and Production Center features rehearsal spaces, a costume shop, a makeup lab, and television studios. Students here also have access to professional-grade equipment and digital labs, audio postproduction suites, radio stations (Emerson is home to the oldest noncommercial radio station in Boston), a multimedia newsroom, and a marketing research suite featuring eye-tracking technology and a two-way mirror for conducting focus groups. A new dining center and residence hall opened in 2017.

> **"Above all, cocurriculars are the backbone of an Emerson education."**

Website: www.emerson.edu
Location: City Center
Private
Total Enrollment: 4,318
Undergraduates: 3,748
Male/Female: 41/59
SAT Ranges: ERW 620–700, M 580–660
ACT Ranges: 26–30
Financial Aid: 66%
Pell Grant: 15%
Expense: Pr $ $
Student Loans: 63%
Average Debt: $
Applicants: 10,360
Accepted: 46%
Enrolled: 20%
Grad in 6 Years: 81%
Returning Freshmen: 88%
Academics: ✍ ✍ ✍
Social: ☎ ☎
Q of L: ★ ★ ★

(continued)

Admissions: (617) 824-8600
Email Address: admission@
emerson.edu

Strong Programs:
Performing Arts
Visual and Media Arts
Writing, Literature, and
    Publishing
Journalism
Marketing Communication
Film Production
Business of Creative
    Enterprises
Musical Theatre

Core requirements at Emerson consist of a combination of traditional courses and interdisciplinary seminars. All students must take courses in two areas: Foundations, which includes writing and oral communication, and Perspectives, which includes courses in aesthetics, ethics and values, history, literature, quantitative reasoning, diversity, world languages, and scientific, social, and psychological perspectives. Honors students take intensive seminars in their first three years and complete a senior thesis.

Undergraduates may choose from 24 majors in communication and the arts, ranging from stage and screen design technology and business of creative enterprises to communication disorders and journalism. The Interdisciplinary Studies program allows students to design their own major. Performance-related majors, such as acting and musical theatre, tend to be the most popular, along with visual and media arts; writing, literature, and publishing; journalism; and marketing communication. An entrepreneurship minor features a business plan competition known as the Entrepreneurship Exposition; students vie for thousands of dollars in start-up funds. New majors have been added in comedic arts and public relations.

"There is a high amount of collaboration at the college across all majors," explains a sophomore. "For example, if a student is working on a film, they will recruit classmates and friends from different majors to do everything from acting to filming to editing to marketing, and so on." Sixty-seven percent of all classes have fewer than 20 students, and a political communication major says professors "give us real-world perspective and also always have an ear to the ground for those of us looking for internships."

For those seeking a spotlight and stage in a different setting, Emerson offers several global study options, including a semester-long program at Kasteel Well (in the Netherlands), where students are housed in a restored, college-owned, 14th-century castle complete with moats, gardens, and a gatehouse. Each year about 200 students spend a semester at Emerson's Los Angeles Center on Sunset Boulevard in Hollywood, where they can participate in internships with companies such as Interscope Records, CNN, Warner Bros., Dreamworks, and NBC. Another semester-long program sends participants to Washington, D.C., for classes and internships. "Above all, cocurriculars are the backbone of an Emerson education," a film production major says. "Classes are thought-provoking, but nothing prepares you for the real world better than actually getting out into the field to practice as much as possible."

"We have a very large 'hipster' presence at our school."

"The students at Emerson are artistic, passionate, and career-focused," says a student. Adds another, "We have a very large 'hipster' presence at our school." Eighteen percent of undergraduates hail from Massachusetts, and most come from public high schools. Ten percent are international. African Americans account for 3 percent of the student body, Hispanics 12 percent, Asian Americans 5 percent, and multiracial students 4 percent. Despite a noticeable lack of socioeconomic and ethnic diversity, "Emerson is known for being extremely LGBTQ-friendly," says one senior. "Students are always championing liberal social causes." Emerson offers merit scholarships averaging $14,600 to qualified applicants, as well as scholarships to support underrepresented students. There are no athletic awards.

A majority of undergrads reside on campus, since they are required to live in college housing for their first three years. After that, says a junior, "A lot of students take it as a rite of passage to move off campus." Several living/learning communities are available, including Community Outreach, Digital Culture, and Writers' Block, among others. A senior says campus fare passes muster: "The food is fine, but definitely not a highlight." Each building requires an ID to enter, and public safety officers regularly patrol the streets outside the buildings. According to a marketing

The 11-story Tufte Performance and Production Center features rehearsal spaces, a costume shop, a makeup lab, and television studios.

communication major, "The Office of Violence Prevention and Response is incredibly active, especially during orientation events."

"While there is no shortage of on-campus events like comedy shows, performances, and club meetings, a lot of the traditional college nightlife tends to happen in the city or at someone's off-campus apartment," says one sophomore. More than 90 student organizations offer ample opportunity for involvement, including two radio stations, six humor and literary journals, 10 performance troupes, and six production organizations. "Each student is involved in a million different things," says one student. "I have never met a busier student body in my life." Greek life, which attracts 2 percent of Emerson men and 3 percent of the women, is a negligible influence on the social scene. Though the campus is considered "dry," a sophomore reasons, "Drugs and alcohol are as easy to find as they are to avoid, and it is up to the students' discretion to be responsible." Popular annual festivities include the EVVY Awards, the largest student-run awards show in the country. When students tire of on-campus events, they can step off campus into Boston. A student says, "Emerson students live, study, work, and volunteer in almost every major neighborhood and area of the city." There are plenty of diversions, including museums, the Franklin Park Zoo, the Boston Public Garden, the Freedom Trail, the Boston Symphony Orchestra, and major league baseball at Fenway Park.

Several living/learning communities are available, including Community Outreach, Digital Culture, and Writers' Block.

"Emerson students live, study, work, and volunteer in almost every major neighborhood [of Boston]."

Emerson fields 14 Division III athletic teams, and the Lions compete as a member of the Eastern College Athletic Conference and the New England Women's and Men's Athletic Conference. Solid teams include baseball, softball, basketball, cross-country, lacrosse, and soccer. Students also enjoy an active intramural program and take advantage of the 10,000-square-foot fitness center featuring state-of-the-art equipment, classes, and wellness workshops.

"Emerson prepares creative thinkers to get out into the workforce and make a difference," says one senior. While you are not guaranteed to become the next Oscar-winning director, the possibility is not out of the question at Emerson. And even if a lifestyle of fame is not for you, the excellent education, small classes, and attentive professors may teach you how to be the "star" of your own life story.

Overlaps

Bentley, Chapman, Columbia College Chicago, Butler, Rollins, Elon, NYU, Northeastern

If You Apply To ›

Emerson: Early action, regular decision. SATs or ACTs: optional (test-optional applicants must submit an additional essay or a major-related portfolio). No Subject Tests. Accepts the Common Application with supplement. Additional materials required for applicants to performing arts, media production, comedic arts, and honors programs.

Emory University

200 Boisfeuillet Jones Center, Atlanta, GA 30322

Often compared to Duke and Vanderbilt, Emory may be most similar to Washington University in St. Louis. Both are in major cities and both tout business and premed as major draws. Emory's suburban Atlanta location is tough to beat. Attracts a larger contingent from the Northeast than more Southern competitors such as Vanderbilt. Also consider Oxford College, Emory's two-year, small-town liberal arts campus.

Website: www.emory.edu
Location: Suburban
Private
Total Enrollment: 12,519
Undergraduates: 6,714
Male/Female: 41/59
SAT Ranges: ERW 670–740,
    M 680–780
ACT Ranges: 30–33
Financial Aid: 56%
Pell Grant: 19%
Expense: Pr $ $ $
Student Loans: 36%
Average Debt: $ $
Applicants: 23,747
Accepted: 22%
Enrolled: 27%
Grad in 6 Years: 91%
Returning Freshmen: 93%
Academics: 🖉 🖉 🖉 🖉
Social: ☎ ☎ ☎
Q of L: ★ ★ ★ ★
Admissions: (404) 727-6036
Email Address: admiss@
    emory.edu

Strong Programs:
Business Administration
Biology
Economics
Nursing
Neuroscience
Political Science
English and Creative Writing
Irish Studies

Emory University offers two distinct campuses: Emory College in Atlanta, GA, and Oxford College in Oxford, GA.

Emory University may lack the liberal arts prowess of the Northeastern schools with which it competes, but it's a favorite of preprofessional students from both U.S. coasts and around the globe. They come for its size (big, but not too big), location, national reputation, and, increasingly, for its diversity. One sophomore says, "Probably the best part of Emory [is] meeting people from all over the world and all different kinds of backgrounds." Regardless of where they come from, students are challenged, not coddled, in the classroom; they form study groups and work together to succeed. An atmosphere of Southern friendliness enhances the vibrant campus life.

Set on 631 acres of woods and rolling hills in the Druid Hills suburb of Atlanta, Emory's campus spreads out from an academic quad of marble-covered, red-roofed buildings. Contemporary structures dot the periphery of the lush, green grounds. In recent years, Emory has expanded science and math research facilities, added a performing arts center, and updated freshman housing. The three-story Emory Student Center, opened in 2019, houses the campus's main dining facilities, student organizations, and various multipurpose spaces.

Emory University offers applicants the choice between two different undergraduate experiences at two distinct campuses: Emory College in Atlanta, GA, and Oxford College in Oxford, GA. Emory College may be best for students who seek a four-year undergraduate experience at a research institution that values academic independence and intellectual engagement. Oxford College is suited for students who seek a small liberal arts college experience and early opportunities for leadership; it is also easier to get into. Following two years of study at Oxford, all students continue as juniors at Emory's Atlanta campus. Emory's distribution requirements aim to develop competence in writing, quantitative methods, a second language, and physical education, and include exposure to the humanities, social sciences, and natural sciences. Other required coursework helps broaden students' perspectives on national, regional, and global history and culture. All freshmen take a first-year seminar that is limited to 15 students each and participate in PACE (Pre-Major Advising Connections at Emory), which brings together faculty, staff, and student leaders to mentor them on all aspects of college life.

> "[Faculty members] set aside a significant amount of time for mentoring and helping students."

Sixty-three percent of classes have fewer than 20 students. Just as Emory has invested in its physical plant, the school has spent lavishly in the past to add star faculty members to key departments, such as Archbishop Desmond Tutu in the school of theology, the Dalai Lama, and Salman Rushdie. "Faculty members make teaching a priority and set aside a significant amount of time for mentoring and helping students with both the course material and with life in general," says one student. Opportunities for mentored research are available in all fields, and a chemistry major says, "Many students find research opportunities through professors they had during their freshman year."

The most popular majors include business administration, biology, economics, nursing, and neuroscience. Biology and chemistry benefit from physical proximity to the federal Centers for Disease Control, while many political science professors have ties to the Carter Center (named for the former president, who holds a town hall meeting on campus each year) and serve as regular guests on nearby CNN. The English and creative writing program is strong too. Emory has received a significant portion of Nobel laureate Seamus Heaney's archive, and its Irish studies program is said to rival those of Notre Dame and Boston College. A 3–2 dual-degree program allows students to earn a bachelor's degree at Emory and a bachelor's degree in engineering at Georgia Tech. The Center for International Programs Abroad offers more than 100 study programs on six continents. The 37 percent of students who participate earn Emory credit and Emory grades, and they can receive Emory financial aid, scholarships, and grants.

"Though Emory is definitely not an easy school, and you have to work hard to earn your grades, overall, everyone manages to find a good balance between classwork, extracurriculars, and socializing," says a senior. Twenty-one percent of Emory undergraduates are from Georgia, and 16 percent are international. New York, New Jersey, California,

> "We are so close to Atlanta nightlife that many students choose to explore the area."

and Florida are also well represented. African Americans make up 8 percent of the student body, Asian Americans 20 percent, Hispanics 9 percent, and multiracial students 4 percent. Politically, the campus is left-leaning, but according to one sophomore, political activism "is not a huge part of campus life." That's not to say students aren't concerned about social issues; in fact, 85 percent do service work through Volunteer Emory. Emory meets the full demonstrated need of all admitted students; merit scholarships worth an average of $27,000 are awarded annually, but there are no athletic scholarships. Furthermore, university financial aid packages replace loans with grants for students from families whose income is $50,000 or less, and cap loans at $15,000 over four years for families with incomes between $50,000 and $100,000.

Sixty-five percent of Emory students live on campus; freshmen and sophomores are required to do so. Each first-year dorm has a special living theme, such as social innovation and global cultures, and a theater studies major reports, "The accommodations for first-years are really nice because all of the rooms have been renovated recently, but the sophomore residence halls aren't as nice." Lucky juniors and seniors may hang their hats in the one- to four-bedroom Clairmont Campus apartments, which boast such luxuries as private bedrooms, a washer-dryer in each unit, a rec center, and a heated, outdoor, Olympic-sized pool. In addition to the dining halls, there are small cafés, grills, and food courts on campus. Meals get fair reviews, but a nursing major cautions that "a disproportionate amount of tofu and catfish is served." When it comes to combating sexual violence, one student says, "Emory is very big on education and prevention."

"Most social life takes place on campus, but we are so close to Atlanta nightlife that many students choose to explore the area," says a student. Fraternities and sororities attract 26 percent of Emory's men and 29 percent of the women so, of course, Greek parties are prevalent. Other options include concerts, Theater Emory shows, and other events organized by the

> "[Emory] still has the hospitality and charm of a Southern school."

Student Programming Committee. Alcohol isn't allowed in the freshman dorms, and "anyone caught will definitely suffer consequences," a freshman says. A very popular highlight of the social calendar is Dooley's Week, a spring festival in honor of the "Spirit of Emory" (the school's unofficial mascot), Dooley, a skeleton who reportedly escaped from the biology lab more than 100 years ago. If Dooley walks into your class, the class is dismissed, and the week culminates with a costume ball in his honor. Freshman halls also have Songfest, a competition where residents make up spirit-filled song-and-dance routines.

Just 20 minutes from campus, downtown Atlanta offers a multitude of diversions, from Braves baseball and Falcons football to plays at the Fox Theatre, exhibits at the High Museum of Art, marine wildlife at the Georgia Aquarium, and shopping at Underground Atlanta or the Lenox Square, to which Emory provides a free shuttle every Saturday. Upperclassmen enjoy the Atlanta bar scene, and some local dance clubs host college nights. Popular road trips include Stone Mountain, Athens, Savannah, and the beaches of Florida and the Carolinas.

Emory doesn't field a varsity football team, but the Eagles have produced a number of Division III national champs, including men's and women's swimming

The Carter Center is named for the former president, who holds a town hall meeting on campus each year.

Dooley's Week is a spring festival in honor of the school's unofficial mascot, Dooley, a skeleton who reportedly escaped from the biology lab.

and diving and women's volleyball and tennis. Emory competes against such academic powerhouses as the University of Chicago and Carnegie Mellon in the University Athletic Association conference, and recent conference winners include men's golf and women's softball. Many students join at least one intramural sports team at either a competitive or a recreational level. Popular intramurals include flag football, volleyball, and ultimate Frisbee.

While many Southern schools suffer from a regional provincialism, that isn't true at Emory, which blends a focus on teaching and research to nurture creativity and turn out leaders who are highly sought after in the working world—and by postgraduate law, medical, and business programs. As one satisfied student concludes, Emory offers "high academic quality and rigor," yet "still has the hospitality and charm of a Southern school."

If You Apply To ›

Emory: Early decision I and II, regular decision. SATs or ACTs: required. Subject Tests: optional. Accepts the Common Application with supplement.

Eugene Lang College of Liberal Arts

65 West 11th Street, New York, NY 10011

Home to roughly 1,700 street-savvy, freethinking urbanites, Eugene Lang College is becoming increasingly popular as an alternative to much larger neighbor NYU in Manhattan's chic Greenwich Village. Emphasis on progressive critical inquiry pursued in seminar settings. With the city as its campus, Lang offers a less cohesive sense of community than traditional small liberal arts schools. Long-standing international perspective and strength in arts and humanities still predominate.

Students seeking a typical college experience—large lectures, rowdy football games, and rigid academic requirements—would do well to steer clear of Eugene Lang College of Liberal Arts, The New School's undergraduate liberal arts college. That's because Lang offers small seminars instead of traditional lectures, individualized academic programs with minimal required coursework, and not a single varsity sport—not to mention an urban campus that reflects the quirky and kinetic atmosphere of Greenwich Village. "We don't want to become business leaders, but instead teachers, community organizers, thinkers, professors, and writers," a junior says. "Students here want to change the world."

Lang fits right in amid the brownstones and trendy boutiques of one of New York's most vibrant neighborhoods. Lang's main hub is a single five-story building between Fifth and Sixth avenues on West 11th Street, although students make use of all 16 of the buildings that The New School occupies along Fifth Avenue. The New School's library is small, but students have access to the massive Bobst Library at NYU, which is just a few blocks away, as is the excitement of Greenwich Village and Washington Square Park. The 16-story University Center offers state-of-the-art facilities, including "smart" classrooms, design studios, a residence hall, and an auditorium.

"[The focus is on] communal and collaborative learning."

The New School was founded in 1919 by a band of progressive scholars that included John Dewey, Charles Beard, and Thorstein Veblen. A decade and a half later, it became a haven for European intellectuals fleeing Nazi persecution, and over the years it has been the teaching home of many notable thinkers, including Buckminster Fuller and Hannah Arendt. Created in 1975, the undergraduate college was renamed ten years later for Eugene Lang, a progressive philanthropist who made a significant donation to the school. In addition to Lang, today's New School includes a graduate program in social research, a school of management, and various arts programs, most notably Parsons School of Design. At night, the Schools of Public Engagement are host to a huge assortment of lectures and continuing education courses.

The two most distinctive features of Lang are the small classes—90 percent have fewer than 20 students—and undergraduates pursuing their own path of study with minimal general education requirements. As freshmen, students take one year of writing and choose one required first-year seminar from a broad-based menu; the seminar also incorporates workshops on nonacademic concerns and study skills and is taught by a professor who serves as students' faculty advisor. Additionally, all students take two University Lecture courses, choosing from three categories: Tools for Social Change, Introductions to Social Research, and Interdisciplinary Approaches to the Arts and Humanities. In their final year, students take on a senior capstone through a seminar or independent project that synthesizes their educational experience.

Lang's most popular majors include culture and media, literary studies, psychology, and the arts; economics, journalism and design, and politics are other strengths. Its city location enhances the urban studies program, and the writing concentration is highly praised. While introductory language courses are plentiful, upper-level language offerings are limited. The college has, however, beefed up its offerings in global studies and added new majors in screen studies and contemporary dance. More than 40 joint B.A./M.A. and B.S./M.S. programs are available, including international affairs, nonprofit management, and psychology. "The coursework and expectations are demanding," a senior says, but the focus is on "communal and collaborative learning." Professors are well versed and engaging, according to many students. "I appreciate the way that class discussions are so well planned and thought out," says one student.

"We are nontraditional college students who relish in this difference."

The main academic complaint is the limited range of seminars, but outside programs and partnerships offer more variety. Students may enroll in approved classes in other divisions of The New School, including Parsons, and more than 50 minors offered across the university provide opportunities to study topics like sustainable cities, creative entrepreneurship, and data visualization. Exchange programs with Sarah Lawrence College, the University of Amsterdam, and John Cabot University (among others) provide motivated students with additional academic opportunities. Lang's Civic Liberal Arts program offers courses that are cotaught by faculty and visiting fellows from community partners, the likes of which have included the *New York Times*, the Whitney Museum of American Art, and Brooklyn Grange. Sixteen percent of students study abroad, and Lang has designed a Global Immersion program that gives freshmen a chance to spend their second semester abroad, undertaking coursework, fieldwork, and an internship focused on issues of development, social justice, and sustainability.

Lang attracts a disparate group of undergraduates, but most of them can be described as idealistic and independent. "We are nontraditional college students who relish in this difference and exciting uniqueness that sets us apart from conforming NYU students," a junior says. Some are slightly older than conventional college age and are used to looking after themselves; 79 percent are female.

The Global Immersion program gives freshmen a chance to spend their second semester abroad, focusing on issues of social justice and sustainability.

(continued)

Academics: ✍ ✍ ✍
Social: ☎
Q of L: ★ ★ ★
Admissions: (800) 292-3040
Email Address:
  lang@newschool.edu

Strong Programs:
Culture and Media
Literary Studies
Psychology
The Arts
Economics
Journalism and Design
Politics
Urban Studies

Twenty-four percent of Lang's students are from New York, and 9 percent come from abroad. Eight percent are African American, 18 percent are Hispanic, 6 percent are Asian American, and 6 percent are multiracial. Lang admits students regardless of their finances, and 27 percent of freshmen qualify for Pell Grants. A handful of merit scholarships averaging $11,200 are offered, but no varsity teams means no athletic awards.

Roughly one-third of the students sign up for dorm life at Lang, and the rooms are reported to be in good shape. Stuyvesant Park and University Center are the newest dorms; the former caters predominantly to first-year students. A gender-inclusive housing policy assigns housing based on students' preferred gender pronouns. Off-campus dwellers live in apartments in the Village (if they can afford it) or in Brooklyn (if they can afford it), or elsewhere in the New York City area. A meal plan is available, but most students opt for the hundreds of delis, coffee shops, and restaurants that line Fifth and Sixth Avenues.

A gender-inclusive housing policy assigns housing based on students' preferred gender pronouns.

Indeed, many students cite the school's location as one of its best features. "Whatever is desired can be found somewhere in New York City," says a junior. "It's a nice place to be if you want to party or be a stone-cold intellectual." The social network at Lang is quite small and, like many things, is left up to the student.

"Our lack of campus kind of makes all activity 'off campus.'"

"Our lack of campus kind of makes all activity 'off campus,' though we do have dances and club activities within the school facilities themselves," a junior says. On-campus activities tend to involve intellectual pursuits, such as poetry readings, open-mic nights, and working on the student newspaper and the literary magazine. A multitude of cultural events, like Bollywood Night and Gospel Night, enhance campus diversity. Students generally avoid drinking on campus, and when they do imbibe, alcohol is "far from the central focus of activity," says a junior. Fifty-seven percent of students get involved in community service. Athletics barely register here, although the school does field three teams: men's basketball, and men's and women's cross-country.

Despite the seeming lack of tradition and typical sense of college community, Lang's stock continues to rise. Students relish the freedom and independence they have here. For a student who yearns for four years of "traditional" college experiences, Lang would likely be a disappointment. But for those desiring an intimate education in America's cultural capital, Lang offers all the stimulation of the city it calls home.

Overlaps

Sarah Lawrence, Bard, NYU, Hampshire, Oberlin, Pace, Fordham, Emerson

If You Apply To ›

Eugene Lang: Early action, regular decision. SATs or ACTs: optional. Subject Tests: optional. Accepts the Common Application.

The Evergreen State College

Olympia, WA 98505

There's no mistaking Evergreen for a typical public college. Never mind its unconventional students; Evergreen's interdisciplinary, team-taught curriculum is unique. To find anything remotely like Evergreen, you'll need to go private and travel east to places like Hampshire or Sarah Lawrence. Accepts just about anyone who applies, and graduation rate is modest.

In "La Vie Bohème," the anthem of Jonathan Larson's rock opera *Rent*, one of the characters asks, "Anyone out of the mainstream / Is anyone in the mainstream?" At The Evergreen State College, the answer has always been a vehement "No!" The school's unofficial motto is *Omnia Extares*, Latin for "Let it all hang out." Founded in 1967 as Washington State's experimental college, Evergreen has narrative evaluations instead of grades and lacks formal majors, and even departments. This system may sound strange, but it works for those seeking the freedom to chart their own course. Where else will you find a criminologist and a theater professor teaching a class together?

Evergreen lies in a fir forest at the edge of the 90-mile-long Puget Sound. The peaceful, 1,000-acre campus includes an organic plant and animal farm as well as 3,300 feet of saltwater beach. Most of Evergreen's buildings are boxy concrete-and-steel creations, though the Longhouse Education and Cultural Center is designed in the Native American style typical of the Pacific Northwest. In keeping with Evergreen's progressive nature, all new building projects strive to comply with LEED standards.

At first glance, Evergreen's wide-open curriculum looks like Easy Street: it's based on nine "planning units"—Native programs; critical and creative practices; culture, text, and language; environmental studies; expressive arts; sustainability and justice; scientific inquiry; consciousness studies; and society, politics, behavior, and change.

> "[Evergreen] gives space for both self-directed learning and small learning communities."

The college operates on 10-week quarters, but the structure of learning is different. Instead of signing up for unrelated classes to fulfill distribution requirements, students enroll in a single coordinated, 12- to 16-credit "program" spanning several disciplines that are often team-taught by multiple professors. Recent program offerings include Clones and Mutants: Genetics and Photography and Business: Innovation, Stewardship, and Change. Programs designed specifically for first-year students combine academics with weekly cocurricular experiences that focus on developing skills for college success. In addition to professor and self-evaluations, students must write an annual Academic Statement, reflecting on their academic experiences and goals. Upperclassmen may fulfill an Individual Learning Contract developed in partnership with a faculty sponsor, and many complete some form of capstone experience, such as a senior thesis.

Students praise Evergreen's environmental and sustainability studies offerings, which span agriculture, ornithology, and marine science, among others. To supplement their coursework, environmental scientists may also study marine animals while sailing in Puget Sound, spend seven weeks at a bird sanctuary in Oregon, or trek to the Grand Canyon or the tropical rainforests of Costa Rica. The Native American and indigenous studies program is notable, and various arts programs—dance, writing, visual arts, and media arts—also get high marks. Regardless of what they study, students warn that while the integrated approach to learning may improve comprehension and deepen understanding, it likewise means a lot of work. "The academic climate at Evergreen is robust, collaborative, and engaging," says a junior. "It gives space for both self-directed learning and small learning communities." Many academic programs include a service-learning component, and several faculty-led study abroad programs are available; 8 percent of undergrads study abroad.

Because Evergreen attracts many nontraditional students and students who are older than the typical college freshman, administrators take advising and career counseling seriously. In hopes of improving retention and graduation rates, they've also asked faculty members to do more to help students adjust to life on campus. "A goal of the faculty here is to get to know each student personally and to understand

Website: www.evergreen.edu
Location: Small City
Public
Total Enrollment: 3,618
Undergraduates: 3,321
Male/Female: 42/58
SAT Ranges: ERW 500–630, M 460–560
ACT Ranges: 19–27
Financial Aid: 62%
Pell Grant: 36%
Expense: Pub $
Student Loans: 57%
Average Debt: $
Applicants: 1,772
Accepted: 96%
Enrolled: 31%
Grad in 6 Years: 57%
Returning Freshmen: 61%
Academics: ✍ ✍ ✍
Social: ☎ ☎ ☎
Q of L: ★ ★ ★ ★
Admissions: (360) 867-6170
Email Address: admissions@evergreen.edu

Strong Programs:
Environmental Studies
Sustainability Studies
Native American and Indigenous Studies
Visual and Media Arts
Cultural Studies
Biology
Chemistry

Instead of signing up for unrelated classes, students enroll in a single coordinated, 12- to 16-credit "program" spanning several disciplines.

their interests and goals," explains a political economy student. Another bonus: because Evergreen doesn't award formal tenure, there's less pressure for professors to conduct research and publish their findings—and less to distract them from teaching undergraduates. Professors who do engage in research often involve students in their work, and students may apply for competitive Summer Undergraduate Research Fellowship stipends.

"Greeners want to be open-minded, intelligent, and actually meaningful to the world in which they live," says a student. Three-quarters of Evergreen's students are Washington residents, and just 1 percent come from foreign countries. African Americans account for 5 percent of the student body, Hispanics 11 percent, Asian Americans 3 percent, and multiracial students 8 percent. Thirty-three percent of students self-identify as LGBTQ, and 38 percent are of a nontraditional age. Liberal views and student activism dominate the campus; "If you are someone who doesn't like high energy debate, you may find yourself struggling to connect with the school,"

> **"If you are someone who doesn't like high energy debate, you may find yourself struggling."**

says a media studies major. Feminists in Solidarity Together, Food Not Bombs, T-Rex (a transgender group), and Black Cottonwood Collective (an anarchist group) represent just a small sampling of the student activist groups on campus. Several Evergreen faculty and staff members resigned in the wake of student protests in 2017 related to issues of free speech and institutional racism; 80 students were disciplined for their role in those protests. A newly hired vice provost for equity and inclusion is working to address campus culture and climate. An impressive number of incoming freshmen (36 percent) are eligible for the Pell Grant, and the proportion of first-generation students has risen to 30 percent. A limited number of merit scholarships are available for qualified students, as are athletic scholarships in five sports.

Twenty-four percent of Evergreen students, mostly freshmen and sophomores, live on campus. Students appreciate the amenities in the school's apartment complexes but say the dorms need sprucing up. "Housing is a really fun time for first-year students excited to become a part of the Evergreen community, but it is expensive and only really makes sense for the first year," reasons a junior. There's an efficient bus system to get nonresidents to class on time, though it helps to have a car. Evergreen's food service offers a wide variety of dishes. "We have the amazing student-run café, the Flaming Eggplant. They serve delicious, locally sourced food that caters to special diets," cheers one student. Students say campus security is good and although instances of sexual assault are uncommon, one student says, "Evergreen needs to work on reconciling its progressive, liberal image with the way that assaults are actually handled."

Given the pervasive individualism that flavors Evergreen, it's little surprise that the college lacks a Greek system. Still, the housing and student activities offices organize plenty of events—including open-mic nights, soccer and other field games, and

> **"Housing is a really fun time for first-year students."**

parties. Student musicians are often at the center of the social scene, hosting on-campus performances or playing popular "house shows" off campus. "We are in a marijuana-legal state, but you cannot have pot on campus. As you can imagine, this is the most violated rule on campus," quips a religious studies student. The fall Harvest Festival on the college's organic farm is a favorite annual event.

Olympia (the state capital) doesn't really qualify as a college town, but it is progressive and open-minded, with art walks through local galleries, coffee shops, clothing stores, co-ops, and a thriving music scene. "It's a rad little town with its own personality," says a junior. The college's outdoor program organizes mountaineering, backpacking, and rock-climbing trips and offers a wide range of gear for rent. Seattle (just over an hour away) and Portland and the rugged Oregon coast (two to three hours away) provide changes of scenery; everything is kept green and lush by the (interminable) rain, which stops in time for summer break and resumes by November.

You may chuckle at Evergreen's mascot, an eight-foot clam named "Speedy" (a nod to the large geoduck clams found in Puget Sound), but the school has an active intercollegiate athletics program. Geoduck teams compete in the NAIA Division II Cascade Conference, and men's soccer, men's track and field, and women's volleyball have enjoyed recent success. About a quarter of students choose to participate in recreational or intramural sports.

Evergreen remains one of the best choices for students who see traditional academic structures as too restrictive. Freed from requirements and grades, Greeners delight in exploring the connections between disparate disciplines at their own pace. It's a challenging task that requires an ability to focus, but for Greeners, the rewards lie in an education that is personally meaningful and that allows them to develop and express their own identities. "Here you can truly be whoever you want to be," says a junior. "There's really nothing to fit into. There is no box at Evergreen; there's just the experience of being here."

If You Apply To ›

Evergreen: Rolling admissions. SATs or ACTs: required. Subject Tests: optional. Accepts the Common Application with supplement.

Fairfield University

Fairfield, CT 06824

Strategically located on Long Island Sound near New York City, Fairfield offers a classic Jesuit-style Roman Catholic education. Nursing and business are the biggest academic draws. Lack of big-time sports keeps Fairfield from enjoying the visibility of Boston College or Holy Cross. Lack of diversity, socioeconomic and otherwise, is both a problem and an issue on campus. Explosive party scene.

Fairfield University is still trying to move into the same class as older, more revered East Coast institutions founded by the Society of Jesus (Jesuits), such as Boston College to the north and Georgetown to the south. It offers a dynamic living/learning environment that combines solid academics, real-world opportunities in and outside of the classroom, and an abundance of community service projects. Priests and lay faculty alike promote traditional Jesuit religious and humanistic values to the largely preprofessional (and privileged) student body, and the lack of Greek organizations is never an obstacle to organizing a good party.

The physical beauty of the university's scenic, tree-lined campus just 60 minutes from Manhattan is a source of pride. The administration takes pains to preserve a lush atmosphere of sprawling lawns, ponds, and natural woodlands. Buildings are a blend of collegiate Gothic, Norman chateau, English manor, and modern. Students enjoy a 24-hour computer lab and a Geographic Information Systems lab. A brand-new building for the business school includes a big data analytics lab, an entrepreneurship center, a gaming lab, and other high-tech tools.

Students may have difficulty finding time to savor the beautiful facilities. A demanding class schedule requires everyone to complete the classic Jesuit-style liberal

Website: www.fairfield.edu
Location: Suburban
Private
Total Enrollment: 4,355
Undergraduates: 3,879
Male/Female: 40/60
SAT Ranges: ERW 590–660, M 590–660
ACT Ranges: 27–29
Financial Aid: 90%
Pell Grant: 11%
Expense: Pr $ $
Student Loans: 75%
Average Debt: $ $ $
Applicants: 11,218
Accepted: 61%

(continued)

Enrolled: 15%

Grad in 6 Years: 81%

Returning Freshmen: 90%

Academics: ✍ ✍ ✍

Social: ☎ ☎ ☎ ☎

Q of L: ★ ★ ★ ★

Admissions: (203) 254-4100

Email Address: admis@
   fairfield.edu

Strong Programs:

Nursing

Finance

Management

Accounting

Marketing

Psychology

Irish Studies

Humanitarian Action

The liberal arts core curriculum constitutes almost half of a student's total courseload.

arts core curriculum over four years, with coursework in math, natural sciences, history, social and behavioral sciences, philosophy and religious studies, applied ethics, English, visual and performing arts, and modern and classical languages. The core constitutes almost half of a student's total courseload. Freshmen are introduced to Fairfield with a thorough orientation program that includes a series of seminars and events throughout the fall term. A formal academic convocation in the first week of classes includes a speaker chosen to reflect the school's Jesuit values.

Fairfield's main academic strengths—and most popular majors—are nursing, business (finance, management, accounting, and marketing), and psychology. Students enrolled in the Dolan School of Business have access to the state-of-the-art Business Experiential, Simulation, and Trading Floor classroom. Irish studies has strong ties to the University of Galway, and Italian studies features links to the Florence University of the Arts. A minor in humanitarian action has been created as an outgrowth of Fairfield's involvement as a founding member, along with Fordham and Georgetown, of the Jesuit Universities Humanitarian Action Network (JUHAN). Students can also join the JUHAN club to organize campus events raising awareness for humanitarian issues, participate in alternative spring breaks, and serve as delegates to the UN Youth Assembly.

> **"The good professors I had were wonderful and helped me shape my future."**

"Some courses and majors are challenging and do require you to put in that extra time and effort," says an international studies major, although core courses are generally described as "relaxed." There are no teaching assistants at Fairfield, and 44 percent of classes have fewer than 20 students. Students report that the quality of teaching varies. "For every great professor, there was a terrible counterpart," says a biology and psychology double major. "That being said, the good professors I had were wonderful and helped me shape my future and change my life."

Thirty-five percent of students study abroad through their choice of more than 80 programs. Fairfield administers its own programs in Australia, France, Ireland, Italy, Nicaragua, and Spain, and several professors lead short educational tours for credit during the winter intercession, spring break, and the summer. Eight percent of students join the four-year honors program, and while participants give it mixed reviews, most agree that its best feature is the team-teaching from professors across departments, which lends an interdisciplinary perspective that "challenges you to think critically," according to a senior. A quarter of the students carry out undergraduate research projects, and qualified students in biology, chemistry, and physics are guaranteed the opportunity to do so.

Twenty-six percent of Fairfield undergraduates are from Connecticut, and 3 percent come from abroad. Hispanic students constitute 8 percent of the student body, while African American, Asian American, and multiracial students each represent just 2 percent. Two-thirds of students are Catholic, and the vast majority come from conservative, relatively wealthy families; a senior says, "Any students of diversity have a hard time." Race and diversity became a topic of reflection on campus in 2016 after students held an off-campus "ghetto"-themed party that attracted the attention of the *New York Times* and went viral on social media. According to a junior, "There is a high level of entitlement," and others note that a predominant spending culture can make it difficult for students from lower-income backgrounds to fit in. To help students with Fairfield's price tag, the school offers merit scholarships annually, averaging $15,000, as well as athletic scholarships in 20 sports.

> **"Any students of diversity have a hard time."**

Fairfield's residence halls house 71 percent of the student body, and housing is guaranteed for all four years. Several living/learning communities are available for undergrads of all levels and come highly recommended. "Living in a tight-knit community and making wonderful friends while having important discussions about the state of the world and giving back to the community was very rewarding," says a junior. Seniors can apply to live off campus, and among the most popular options are the privately owned beach houses and apartments on Long Island Sound made available to students off-season. In the recently renovated main dining hall, a junior says, "The food is not impressive, but it is palatable."

In an effort to enhance the residential nature of the school and at the same time curb the number of beach parties along the Sound, the university has added more on-campus townhouses and apartments for upperclassmen—but students say their school still parties hard. "The level of alcohol consumption is just a culture at this point and is almost expected," says a sophomore. A junior notes that strict policies and penalties for underage drinkers "encourage binge drinking" among those trying to "avoid being caught"; a medical amnesty policy protects violators from punishment when reporting emergency situations. Despite

> "The level of alcohol consumption is just a culture at this point."

increased educational programming aimed at preventing sexual assault, students indicate that reported cases "have not been dealt with as effectively as they could have been." Counseling services in general receive mixed reviews.

Party culture notwithstanding, students find plenty of on-campus activities to keep them busy, including a growing number of student organizations to meet just about any interest. Sponsored events range from dances to hanging out at the campus coffeehouse to concerts. The Presidential Ball in the fall and Dogwoods Weekend in the spring provide relief from the stress of studying, and Clam Jam is an annual beach party with live music, kegs, and food trucks. The Campus Ministry draws a large following, with daily masses, annual retreats, and regular community service work, including two weeks of programs in the Caribbean and Latin America.

As for the surrounding area, some students say the quaint, wealthy town of Fairfield can feel a bit "snobby," and though they enjoy frequenting the many shopping centers, boutiques, and restaurants, relations with local residents are sometimes strained. "Community members are not often comfortable participating in university events and vice versa," a student says. Even so, volunteerism abounds, with nearly three-quarters of the student body performing community service, often in

> "[Fairfield] really allows students to make mistakes and learn from their experiences."

the troubled nearby city of Bridgeport. "The influence of Bridgeport on my Fairfield experience has been profound," says a student. Road trips to New York (an hour by train) and Boston (two hours away) are popular.

The Stags compete in Division I, and men's and women's swimming and diving, men's soccer, and women's lacrosse, field hockey, volleyball, and softball are all recent Metro Atlantic Athletic Conference champions. Men's and women's basketball both draw crowds, and the boisterous home-court fans, who come to games in full Fairfield regalia, have been dubbed the "Red Sea." Living up to the Jesuit commitment to sound mind and body, 45 percent of the students play on one of 25 intramural and 25 club sports teams.

"Fairfield focuses on self-improvement and really allows students to make mistakes and learn from their experiences, both good and bad," comments a junior, an observation that seems to suit the circumstances of the university itself as of late. Although Fairfield is wrestling with issues of diversity and is reflecting seriously on how to create a safe, inclusive social atmosphere on campus, it remains committed to its Jesuit ideals and to offering an undergraduate experience defined by close bonds with faculty, challenging academics, an emphasis on community involvement, and the holistic development of each student.

Business students have access to the state-of-the-art Business Experiential, Simulation, and Trading Floor classroom.

Volunteerism abounds, with nearly three-quarters of the student body performing community service.

Overlaps

Providence, Loyola University Maryland, Bentley, Fordham, College of New Jersey, UConn, Quinnipiac, Sacred Heart

University of Florida

Gainesville, FL 32611

It should come as no surprise that UF is a world leader in citrus science. Add accounting, engineering, and Latin American studies to the list of renowned programs. Among Deep South public universities, only the University of Georgia rivals UF in overall quality. Top-shelf varsity sports teams are a year-round draw, and UF's party-school reputation remains intact.

Website: www.ufl.edu
Location: Small City
Public
Total Enrollment: 43,224
Undergraduates: 30,887
Male/Female: 43/57
SAT Ranges: ERW 620–700, M 620–710
ACT Ranges: 28–32
Financial Aid: 90%
Pell Grant: 23%
Expense: Pub $
Student Loans: 38%
Average Debt: $
Applicants: 32,747
Accepted: 42%
Enrolled: 46%
Grad in 6 Years: 87%
Returning Freshmen: 96%
Academics: ✑ ✑ ✑ ✑
Social: ☎ ☎ ☎ ☎ ☎
Q of L: ★ ★ ★ ★
Admissions: (352) 392-1365
Email Address: freshman@admissions.ufl.edu

Strong Programs:
Engineering
Business
Social Sciences
Biology
Accounting
Citrus Science
Entomology
Latin American Studies

Set on 2,000 acres of rolling, heavily forested terrain in north-central Florida, the University of Florida is an athletic powerhouse, and administrators are working hard to gain the same level of national recognition for their academic offerings as well. With roughly 30,000 undergraduates, the school is already massive and continues to become more so as it adds scores of new faculty in areas such as food security, big data, drug discovery, and neuroscience. While some students certainly get lost in the shuffle, those who can navigate the bureaucratic red tape will find ample resources at their fingertips, including the world's largest collection of butterflies and moths, an $85 million Cancer and Genetics Research Complex, and extensive facilities for agriculture education. The state's flagship university has become more selective in its admissions and continues to wage an aggressive campaign against its long-standing tradition of free-flowing alcohol.

UF's campus has more than 20 buildings on the National Register of Historic Places. Most are collegiate Gothic in style—redbrick with white trim. They're augmented by more modern facilities, including a 173,000-square-foot complex for nursing, pharmacy, and the health professions, and a 110,000-square-foot chemistry building that opened in 2017. UF's research capabilities and equipment are likewise impressive and a boon to aspiring physicians. Cypress Hall is one of only five residence halls in the nation designed specifically to accommodate students with severe physical impairments.

> **"Prospective students should definitely look into a course called First Year Florida."**

Academically, UF's strongest programs are those with a preprofessional bent, including engineering, accounting, and pharmacy. To balance students' preprofessional coursework, UF's general education program requires helpings of liberal arts, including classes that focus on themes of internationalism or diversity, as well as multidisciplinary courses focused on topics of current importance. "Prospective students should definitely look into a course called First Year Florida," one student suggests. "It is equivalent to a semester-long orientation to our university." Popular majors include engineering, business, social sciences, and biology, and entomology and Latin American studies are specialties. Students also give high marks to the College of Journalism and Communications, which boasts the lavish Innovation News Center that houses the college's news, weather, and sports operations. The Graham Center for Public Service trains students in languages, culture, and other skills vital to careers in public service.

Students admitted to UF's freshman class with super-high GPAs and test scores are invited into the Honors Program, where they live together in a residential college and take honors sections of standard academic subjects and special interdisciplinary courses, most of which are limited to 25 students. The Innovation Academy offers another distinct living/learning opportunity for undergraduates with a spring-summer schedule, offering options for internships and research in the fall. It draws students from more than 30 majors with one common minor: innovation. Overall, half of UF's undergraduates do research, while about 6 percent study abroad through university-sponsored, exchange, and affiliate programs in more than 70 countries.

UF's academic climate is intense and collaborative. "Closer to midterms and final exams, campus feels constricted and very tense, with everyone huddled in libraries. However, around football season, campus tends to be more relaxed," says one political science major. Despite the university's huge size, nearly half of all undergraduate classes have fewer than 20 students. Some students say they have to climb a mountain of bureaucracy if a course they need is full, but the administration reports that UF is in the process of hiring 500 new faculty to further reduce class sizes and improve undergraduate student/faculty ratios. Professors often have deep professional experience and bring enthusiasm to their work, though students often find teaching assistants behind lecterns. A junior says, "The quality of instruction is somewhat low in introductory classes but ramps up significantly in more specialized courses."

"Around football season, campus tends to be more relaxed."

Students describe their classmates as "very outgoing and friendly" and "leadership-oriented." UF is Florida's flagship university, and 91 percent of undergraduates hail from the Sunshine State, while 2 percent come from overseas. African Americans represent 6 percent of the student body, Asian Americans 8 percent, Hispanics 22 percent, and multiracial students 3 percent. Students say there is a mix of political views on campus and racial tensions can occasionally flare up. One first-generation minority student remarks, "It's great to be a Gator, but it's hard to not be represented on this campus." UF offers more than 450 athletic scholarships as well as thousands of merit scholarships averaging $2,700. UF has also raised special funds for financial aid for students from low-income families; 23 percent of freshmen are Pell eligible.

Undergrads typically live on campus during their freshman year but then move out after that, for the sake of more space and privacy; overall, 22 percent of students stay on campus. Dorms are described as comfortable, and a senior advises, "It is great to live on campus for at least one year to really immerse oneself in the UF experience and for simple convenience." Dining halls get mixed reviews, but students agree that suitable provisions are made for vegetarians and vegans. Campus security draws praise, thanks to a robust police presence and a late-night "Later Gator" transportation system. "The STRIVE center works to educate the student body against sexual assault and other sexual violence on campus," notes a sociology and women's studies major.

Students at UF have more than 1,100 student organizations to choose from, and a psychology major says, "Getting involved on campus takes time, but it's a surefire way to find a mini-community in a university that can be dauntingly massive." Eighteen percent of UF's men and 23 percent of the women go Greek; rush is held before classes start in the fall and again in the spring. Students report that "elitism" of Greek groups and the outsize influence they have on campus life, especially student government, are common complaints. UF students have a well-deserved reputation for knowing how to party, but the binge-drinking rate has fallen sharply as a result of tough enforcement of zero-tolerance campus policies, including a ban on drinking games. A senior points out that "off-campus parties are certainly a fixture" of the social scene, especially in the Midtown area across from the football stadium.

Cypress Hall is one of only five residence halls in the nation designed specifically to accommodate students with severe physical impairments.

UF is in the process of hiring 500 new faculty to improve undergraduate student/faculty ratios.

Students at UF have more than 1,100 student organizations to choose from.

Gainesville, a city of about 130,000 between the Atlantic Ocean and the Gulf of Mexico, largely revolves around the university. "Gainesville is an awesome, young town that is perfectly suited for college students who wish to relax and unwind," a student says. There are plenty of stores, restaurants, and bars, as well as a sports arena and the Center for Performing Arts, which brings in world-class symphony orchestras, Broadway plays, opera, and large-scale ballet productions. The university owns a nearby lake, which is "great for lazy Sundays" and more vigorous water sports, and there's a plethora of parks, forests, rivers, and streams for backpacking, camping, and canoeing. Orlando and the beaches of St. Augustine and Jacksonville are also popular destinations.

> "It's great to be a Gator, but it's hard to not be represented on this campus."

Sports are a year-round obsession here, and the students go wild anytime the Division I Gators take to the court, field, or gridiron, especially when they're squaring off against rivals Florida State or the University of Georgia. The annual homecoming extravaganza, known as "Gator Growl," is billed as the biggest student-run pep rally in the country. The university has one of the top intercollegiate programs in the nation, with varsity competition (in the ferocious Southeastern Conference) for men and women in 19 sports. Baseball, softball, men's track and field, and women's tennis and gymnastics are all recent national champions. More than 40 intramural leagues and tournaments are offered, as well as more than 50 club sports, and for those who don't want to join a team, the 60,000-square-foot fitness park offers aerobics classes, martial arts, strength training equipment, and squash and racquetball courts.

For some students, Florida's sheer size is overwhelming. For others, it's a drawing card that means plenty of opportunities to pursue their interests or find new ones. Combine great weather with nationally recognized programs in engineering and business, and nationally ranked athletic teams, and it's easy to see why Sunshine State natives clamor to study here.

Overlaps

UC Berkeley, UCLA, University of Virginia, University of Michigan, UNC at Chapel Hill, University of Georgia, Florida State, University of Central Florida

If You Apply To ›

Florida: Regular decision. SATs or ACTs: required. No Subject Tests (required for homeschooled students). Does not accept the Common Application. Apply to particular school within UF.

Florida Institute of Technology

Melbourne, FL 32901

FIT is practically a branch of the nearby Kennedy Space Center, so aeronautics and aviation are popular specialties. The Atlantic Ocean is close at hand, making the school an ideal spot for marine biology. Only drawback to otherwise ideal location is the occasional early-fall hurricane evacuation. FIT is the smallest of the major technical institutions in the Southeast.

Website: www.fit.edu
Location: Small City
Private
Total Enrollment: 4,561
Undergraduates: 3,262

Students at the Florida Institute of Technology can explore the endless depths of the ocean or shoot for the stars. Located just 40 minutes from one of NASA's primary launch pads, Florida Tech is a child of the nation's space program and the only independent technological university in the Southeast. The school's subtropical setting is perfect for scientific research and study in oceanography, meteorology, marine biology, and environmental science. It comes as no surprise that some of the most cutting-edge work in space and water-related sciences happens here. The combination of academic excellence and a convenient central Florida location—just an hour from the dizzying bustle of Walt Disney World—draws students to this high-flying and innovative school.

Founded in 1958 to meet the academic needs of engineers and scientists working at what is now the Kennedy Space Center, Florida Tech's 130-acre contemporary campus features a botanical garden, an aquatic center, and a textile art museum. Campus architecture ranges from modern to Georgian Gothic. The university has opened a number of new facilities in recent years, including the Harris Student Design Center, also referred to as "the PantherWorks," a high-tech space that serves seniors working on capstone projects in engineering and science.

If you're considering Florida Tech, make sure you have a strong background in math and science, especially chemistry and physics. Few students major in the less practical sciences. Everyone must take courses in communication, physical or life science, mathematics, humanities, and social sciences and demonstrate proficiency in the technologies pertinent to their chosen major. All majors include hands-on projects and capstone requirements.

"Florida Tech is very competitive because of the nature of the majors."

Incoming freshmen are welcomed with a weeklong orientation program highlighted by trips to Disney World and the beach, just three miles away. Almost all freshmen take part in the University Experience course, which helps them adapt to college life. Popular majors include mechanical engineering, aerospace engineering, aviation management, computer science, chemical engineering, and electrical engineering. Prospective aviation students can major in aviation management, aviation meteorology, or human factors and safety as well as aeronautics with or without a flight option. The flight school has a modern fleet of 30 airplanes and three flight-training devices.

The academic climate at FIT is challenging. "Florida Tech is very competitive because of the nature of the majors," says one junior. Forty-three percent of classes have fewer than 20 students, and the majority are taught by full professors. In a move designed to elevate its national standing, FIT has begun to offer faculty tenure for the first time. Research opportunities are available at the Indian River Lagoon or on the *RV Delphinus*, a 60-foot research boat owned by the school. Marine research has included manatee preservation, beach erosion, and sea turtle studies. Established in 2017 in partnership with Apollo 11 astronaut Buzz Aldrin, the Aldrin Space Institute conducts research and development intended to support an eventual human settlement on Mars. The ProTrack cooperative education program allows students in the College of Engineering to complete three semester-long paid work experiences. Students graduate with their employers' names on their final transcripts. Study abroad options are available in Oxford, England, and other locales, although only 3 percent of undergrads study internationally while at FIT.

Thirty-three percent of Florida Tech students are Florida natives, and at 32 percent, the school's international population is huge. "It is a microcosm of intelligent people representing 100 countries," says a sophomore. "It's like traveling the world in four years." African Americans comprise 6 percent of the student body, Asian Americans 3 percent, Hispanics 9 percent, and multiracial students 2 percent. The proportion of women is low even by techie school standards. Florida Tech offers merit scholarships averaging $15,400 and 160 athletic scholarships; 22 percent of freshmen qualify for the Pell Grant.

Florida Tech's dorms are modern and well maintained. Forty-one percent of students make their home on campus. "Residence Life takes a holistic approach to making every resident feel right at home," says a junior. Freshmen are required

(continued)

Male/Female: 71/29
SAT Ranges: ERW 550–640, M 580–680
ACT Ranges: 24–29
Financial Aid: 86%
Pell Grant: 22%
Expense: Pr $
Student Loans: 47%
Average Debt: $ $ $
Applicants: 8,898
Accepted: 63%
Enrolled: 12%
Grad in 6 Years: 60%
Returning Freshmen: 80%
Academics: ✍ ✍ ✍
Social: ☎ ☎ ☎
Q of L: ★ ★ ★
Admissions: (800) 888-4348
Email Address: admission@fit.edu

Strong Programs:
Mechanical Engineering
Aerospace Engineering
Aviation Management
Computer Science
Chemical Engineering
Electrical Engineering
Marine Biology
Oceanography

The Aldrin Space Institute conducts research and development intended to support an eventual human settlement on Mars.

to live on campus in large double rooms. Four-student apartments are available to a small percentage of qualifying upperclassmen by lottery. Students who live off campus are drawn by cheap rent and not much else, because Melbourne is "quiet and is not a typical college town," reports an aerospace engineering major. The meal plan is an open, unlimited arrangement, and students report the food is fair to middling. FIT's thorough Title IX program includes the Stop It Before It Starts campaign, developed by students as a senior design project.

Watching space shots from campus with a trained eye and a cold brew is a treasured pastime. The campus bar, the Rat, is a popular hangout, and there are more than 100 active clubs and organizations on campus; gaming, sci-fi, and performance-oriented groups such as Pep Band are student favorites. Fraternities and sororities are becoming slightly more popular at Florida Tech, claiming 3 percent of the men and 3 percent of the women, respectively. Underage students can manage to access alcohol at frat parties, according to students. The annual International Festival is a much-anticipated event. Students also spend their downtime surfing, fishing, sailing, hanging out at the beach, shopping, or going for a "Sunday drive" (in the sky) with a flight school student. Bikes and skateboards are popular modes of transportation around campus; dining halls and other common areas are equipped with skateboard racks. "If you don't have a car of your own, it may be hard because public transportation is limited," cautions one student. Diversions can be found in Orlando (with Epcot, Disney Hollywood Studios, and Animal Kingdom abutting Disney World) or at the Kennedy Space Center, each within an hour's drive. Students also hit the road for other Sunshine State cities, including Tampa, Key West, Miami, Daytona, and St. Augustine. Every April, students brace for the invasion of other collegians on spring break.

"Residence Life takes a holistic approach to making every resident feel right at home."

The Florida Tech Panthers field 22 varsity teams that compete in Division II. Men's and women's rowing are highly competitive nationally, and softball, baseball, men's and women's golf, men's swimming, and women's basketball have also been successful. The university's Precision Flight Team, the Falcons, regularly wins awards from the National Intercollegiate Flying Association. About a third of students participate in the expanding intramural program in sports like soccer, volleyball, flag football, and cricket.

Whether it's surveying the sky 30,000 feet above or marine coral 50 feet below the surface of the sea, students at Florida Tech get hands-on experience that serves to sharpen the school's already specialized, high-quality academics—all in a small, more personal setting. The administration continues to focus on capital improvements, sponsor cutting-edge research, and embrace diversity. And with beaches and amusements close at hand, students can have some real fun in the sun while they prepare for high-flying or low-lying careers.

Overlaps

Worcester Polytechnic, Stevens Institute of Technology, Rochester Institute of Technology, Rensselaer, Drexel, Embry-Riddle Aeronautical, University of Central Florida, University of Florida

If You Apply To ›

Florida Tech: Rolling admissions. SATs or ACTs: required. Subject Tests: optional. Accepts the Common Application with supplement.

Florida Southern College

111 Lake Hollingsworth Drive, Lakeland, FL 33801

FSC combines top-ranked Division II athletics, strong career-oriented programs, an active Greek system, and a picturesque campus that doubles as a Frank Lloyd Wright museum. Centrally located between Tampa and Orlando. Competes with Rollins and Eckerd among leading liberal arts schools in the Southeast.

Founded in 1883, Florida Southern College remains committed to providing students with a solid liberal arts foundation and exceptional signature programs. The college is affiliated with the United Methodist Church, to which less than 10 percent of students belong. Students enjoy a bevy of academic choices, including outstanding preprofessional programs, extensive internship opportunities, and a vigorous study abroad program. They also appreciate the college's attractive setting and its mission to develop well-rounded graduates.

Situated on 113 acres overlooking pristine Lake Hollingsworth, Florida Southern encompasses one of the world's largest concentrations of buildings designed by famed architect Frank Lloyd Wright. The campus features 12 original Wright structures, as well as the Usonian Faculty House, which the college

> **"The Career Center is the *best* resource on campus."**

constructed based on one of Wright's 1938 Usonian home designs to serve as a museum and welcome center for the college's architectural tourism. Wright's Annie Pfeiffer Chapel is a popular meeting and performance venue. The campus is also home to several buildings designed by Robert A. M. Stern, dean of the Yale School of Architecture, including the Becker Business Building.

Florida Southern's core curriculum is based on student learning outcomes in eight areas that range from critical and creative thinking to effective communication to personal and social responsibility. Most classes meet for four hours a week, with at least one of those hours fully devoted to engaged learning techniques such as debate, small-group discussions, case studies, and research. First-year students are assigned a faculty mentor who meets with them on a regular basis. As part of the required Passport Program for student involvement, students attend a minimum of 10 events every year, choosing from more than 350 eligible events across five Passport categories: school pride, learning beyond the classroom, fine arts, service and diversity, and health and wellness.

In all, FSC students may choose from more than 50 undergraduate majors and 40 minors. The most popular majors include business administration, biology, elementary education, accounting, nursing, and computer science; all are among the college's strongest programs. The premed program boasts an exceptional placement rate in medical, dental, and pharmacy schools nationwide. Unique at the

> **"The school is mostly conservative (as one might expect of a school in central Florida)."**

undergraduate level, a major in citrus and horticultural science includes plenty of hands-on experience, thanks to FSC's on-campus collection of citrus trees. FSC's Center for Free Enterprise offers a major in business and free enterprise that blends political science and economics, preparing students to "analyze business decisions from a social perspective." Dual-degree programs are available in engineering with Washington University in St. Louis and in pharmacy with Lake Erie College of Osteopathic Medicine.

"We have a very relaxed academic climate," says a senior. "FSC is a huge advocate for engaged learning, so we always end up working in groups, creating a very

Website: www.flsouthern.edu
Location: Small City
Private
Total Enrollment: 2,621
Undergraduates: 2,363
Male/Female: 36/64
SAT Ranges: ERW 540–640, M 530–610
ACT Ranges: 23–28
Financial Aid: 99%
Pell Grant: 25%
Expense: Pr $
Student Loans: 86%
Average Debt: $ $
Applicants: 5,983
Accepted: 51%
Enrolled: 24%
Grad in 6 Years: 63%
Returning Freshmen: 80%
Academics: ✎ ✎ ✎
Social: ☎ ☎ ☎
Q of L: ★ ★ ★
Admissions: (863) 680-4131
Email Address: fscadm@flsouthern.edu

Strong Programs:
Business Administration
Biology
Elementary Education
Accounting
Nursing
Computer Science
Premed
Citrus and Horticultural Science

collaborative culture." Sixty percent of classes enroll fewer than 20 students. "From the time I was a freshman, I have had extraordinary professors who do their best to cover their material in depth and who genuinely want to see their students succeed," a psychology major says. Students are bullish about FSC's career services. Says an interpersonal and organizational communication major, "The Career Center is the *best* resource on campus. They offer résumé building, [mock] interviews, and many more things to help you with your future career."

The Junior Journey program guarantees all full-time undergraduates a short-term travel-study experience, often at no additional cost.

All FSC students are guaranteed an internship in their fields of study, and 60 percent avail themselves of this opportunity. Students have interned with Charles Schwab, the Kennedy Center, OPEC, Fox News, the Walt Disney Company, NASA, and scores of other organizations. Sixty-nine percent of students go abroad, mostly through the Junior Journey program, which guarantees all full-time undergraduates a short-term travel-study experience, often at no additional cost. Students may embark on faculty-led trips during May term or academic breaks to domestic and international locales such as Alaska, the Bahamas, Spain, and Japan. Traditional study abroad options are available as well through preapproved partner programs. Qualified students may enroll in the highly selective honors core, which offers specialized gen-ed courses. Thirty-nine percent of students carry out undergraduate research projects during their time at FSC, usually as part of a senior capstone course.

Florida Southern students are "very down-to-earth and easy to get along with," says one student. Fifty-eight percent of the student body hail from Florida; 4 percent of students are international. African Americans account for 4 percent of the population, Asian Americans 3 percent, and Hispanics 10 percent. "While the school is mostly conservative (as one might expect of a school in central Florida), students are generally tolerant of their peers' political opinions," reports an environmental studies major. The college awards merit scholarships averaging $21,700, as well as talent awards and more than 250 athletic scholarships. Twenty-five percent of freshmen qualify for Pell Grants.

"Greek life definitely defines the party culture, but parties are often very inclusive."

Ninety-two percent of FSC undergrads reside in student housing. First-year students live together in dedicated residence halls, while upperclassmen may choose from a variety of living arrangements, including college-owned apartments within walking distance of the campus. Overcrowding has been an issue of late, due to growing freshman enrollment, and according to one student, some residential buildings "could be updated to be more modern or less moldy." The cafeteria serves up "average" fare, including special options for vegetarians. Students report feeling safe on campus, and the "Just Ask" initiative aims to educate the community on preventing sexual assault and gender-based discrimination.

The annual Winter Wonderland festival features a Christmas tree lighting and temporary Florida-style snow.

The social scene is active on campus, with frequent cookouts, concerts, sporting events, and activities organized by more than 100 student clubs. "The school sponsors various bimonthly wellness trips that vary from paintball to snorkeling with manatees," adds a student. Thirty percent of the men and 33 percent of the women go Greek, and a junior says, "Greek life definitely defines the party culture, but parties are often very inclusive." Alcohol is prohibited on campus, and a senior notes that alcohol policies "are not always obeyed but are enforced." FSC offers a number of traditions, including Southern's Got Talent, Flapjack Fling during finals week, the Winter Wonderland festival (complete with a Christmas tree lighting and temporary Florida-style snow), and the end-of-year Fair-Well Festival.

Lakeland (population 108,000) offers eateries, malls, movie theaters, and a historic downtown district with unique shops and attractions. "Lakeland is a great college town!" cheers a junior. "There are plenty of hip stores and restaurants." Many students venture out into the local community to volunteer, often through Greek life programs, or to take part in off-campus church services. For those with access to wheels, popular road trips include excursions to Tampa's sandy beaches, Orlando's famed theme parks, or the Florida Keys.

The Florida Southern Moccasins ("Mocs") field 20 varsity teams that compete in Division II as a member of the Sunshine State Conference. Men's golf won the national championship title in 2017, as did women's lacrosse in 2016. Other competitive teams include men's and women's cross-country, men's basketball, baseball, and women's volleyball. "Our athletes dominate Division II sports every year," boasts one student, and the University of Tampa is the Mocs' chief rival. Intramural sports and activities sign up 40 percent of undergraduates; the most popular activities include volleyball, basketball, floor hockey, and flag football.

Florida Southern has a lot going for it. Despite the ubiquitous college student laments of limited parking and so-so food, most are quick to point out that they have access to strong academic programs, championship athletics, and all the sun and fun a person could want. "Florida Southern College is a great community where students can grow academically, socially, and emotionally," says one senior.

If You Apply To ›

Florida Southern: Early decision, rolling admissions. SATs or ACTs: required. No Subject Tests. Accepts the Common Application with supplement.

Florida State University

A2500 University Center, Tallahassee, FL 32306

Located in Florida's down-home panhandle, FSU is far from the glitz of South Beach or Daytona. The motion picture college is among the best around, and business and the arts are also strong. Notable programs include several living/learning options for freshmen.

At Florida State University, you could have a Nobel laureate for a professor, study in one of the finest science facilities in the Southeast, or network at the state capitol. While the choices are plentiful here, the pace of life makes it possible to taste a little of everything: a wide array of solid academic options, blistering Florida sunshine, and plenty to do, from football to Tallahassee hangouts. "There is a relaxed feel to campus that makes FSU the cool, laid-back friend of the Florida university system," says a junior.

FSU is located in the "Other Florida": the one with rolling hills, flowering azaleas and dogwoods, and a canopy of moss-draped oaks. Glistening Gulf of Mexico waters are only half an hour away. The main campus features collegiate Jacobean structures surrounded by plenty of shade trees, with some modern facilities sprinkled in. Situated on 450 compact acres, the campus is the smallest in the state university system—it's just a 10-minute walk from the main gate on the east side to the science complex on the west side. Construction on a new 130,000-square-foot building housing the earth, ocean, and atmospheric science department was completed in 2019.

FSU offers nearly 200 undergraduate degrees, the most popular of which are business-related majors (especially finance and marketing), international affairs, biological sciences, and psychology. Outstanding programs include music, drama, art,

Website: www.fsu.edu
Location: Small City
Public
Total Enrollment: 35,050
Undergraduates: 29,286
Male/Female: 43/57
SAT Ranges: ERW 600–670,
  M 590–660
ACT Ranges: 26–30
Financial Aid: 48%
Pell Grant: 26%
Expense: Pub $
Student Loans: 47%
Average Debt: $
Applicants: 35,334
Accepted: 49%
Enrolled: 37%
Grad in 6 Years: 80%

(continued)

Returning Freshmen: 94%
Academics: ✍ ✍ ✍
Social: ☎ ☎ ☎
Q of L: ★ ★ ★ ★ ★
Admissions: (850) 644-6200
Email Address: admissions@
fsu.edu

Strong Programs:
Business
International Affairs
Biological Sciences
Psychology
Fine and Performing Arts
Engineering
Health Sciences
Communication

Freshmen take an E-Series course that explores a particular question or issue from multiple perspectives.

The Seminoles women's soccer and softball teams won national championships in 2018.

and dance, and engineering and the sciences are solid, particularly health sciences, physics, ecology and evolutionary biology, and computer science. Communication, statistics, and business have strong reputations in the Southeast, and a new major has been added in entrepreneurship. The English department and the College of Motion Picture Arts have consistently won national and international awards. The economics department has been controversial because of funding it received from the aggressively free-market Koch brothers.

Students report that the academic climate varies by department and depends on how much students choose to challenge themselves. As part of FSU's liberal studies curriculum, freshmen take an E-Series course that explores a particular question or issue from multiple perspectives. Students must also fulfill a diversity requirement and take two Scholarship in Practice courses, in which they apply their learning to produce an original project. Forty percent of undergraduate classes have fewer than 20 students, and a psychology major says, "Professors and graduate instructors are amicable, welcoming, and express genuine interest in the success of their students." Freshmen can take advantage of living/learning communities (where students with similar interests or majors live together in the same residence hall) and freshman interest groups (clusters of high-demand freshman courses that have been linked by a theme or academic program).

> **"FSU [is] the cool, laid-back friend of the Florida university system."**

Honors courses, usually limited to 25 students, give gifted students the opportunity to rub shoulders with top faculty. Certain students can even earn their degrees in three years. About a quarter of undergrads conduct some sort of out-of-class research, and students highly praise the Undergraduate Research Opportunity Program, which connects freshmen and sophomores to faculty research projects for two semesters. Internships and political jobs abound for tomorrow's politicians, since the state capitol and Supreme Court are nearby. For those with wanderlust, FSU offers extensive study abroad programs, in which 15 percent of students take part. Options include time at branch campuses in England, Italy, Spain, and Panama and faculty-led programs in several other countries.

Perhaps not surprisingly, FSU's student body has a distinctly Floridian flavor: in-staters comprise 87 percent of the group and international students just 2 percent. Eight percent of undergraduates are African American, 2 percent are Asian American, 20 percent are Hispanic, and 4 percent are multiracial. Seminoles are a mixture of friendly small-towners and city dwellers, and students say political tastes tend to be somewhat conservative compared to other universities, but more liberal than the surrounding town. "Politically minded students have many opportunities to join marches, protests, and campaigns," says a sophomore. Merit scholarships averaging $5,000 are available to qualified scholars, and athletes vie for 246 scholarships in 20 sports. Twenty-six percent of current freshmen qualify for Pell Grants.

> **"Professors and graduate instructors are amicable, welcoming, and express genuine interest."**

Twenty percent of FSU's undergrads live in the university dorms, some of which have just been built in the last few years. The dorms get mixed reviews from students, but a junior says that on-campus living makes for "a fun, smooth first-year experience." After freshman year, students generally move into the ample apartments and houses located within walking distance of campus; the city and campus bus systems are useful for those who live farther away. The university has switched to a new food provider, which students say should improve the dining options. Students cite FSU's student-driven "kNOw MORE" campaign as helping to educate the community about preventing sexual assault.

When they're not studying, FSU students keep busy with films, concerts, and parties in the dorms or off campus. Nineteen percent of the men and 24 percent of the women belong to Greek life, but new guidelines and limitations for Greek social activities have been enacted in response to the 2017 death of a pledge at one fraternity. The school's president has called for "a new normal for Greek life at the university." With roughly 800 student organizations, there are plenty of other activities for students to get involved in. Many head out to Tallahassee's "beautiful bar patios, art parks, and cafés," says one junior, or to its hopping club scene for nightlife.

The Seminoles compete in the Division I Atlantic Coast Conference. School spirit runs high during football season, and each game is heralded by the beating of the campus spirit drum. The football team won two national titles in the '90s and another in 2013 but attracted national attention in 2016 when it settled a lawsuit alleging sexual assault by a star quarterback. The women's soccer and softball teams won national championships in 2018. Recent conference champs include baseball and beach volleyball. About a third of students participate in the school's more than 40 intramural sports and 40 sports clubs.

Florida State remains a solid choice for those seeking knowledge under the blazing Florida sun. The school's laid-back, cheery atmosphere is appealing to many, but make no mistake: students here take their learning and their futures seriously. As one freshman comments, "At FSU, the only limiting factor to your success will almost always be your own motivation."

Overlaps

Indiana University, Michigan State, Iowa State, Kansas State, Missouri State, University of Florida, University of Central Florida, University of South Florida

If You Apply To ›

Florida State: Regular decision. SATs or ACTs: required. No Subject Tests. Accepts the Common Application.

Fordham University

Rose Hill Campus: 441 East Fordham Road, Bronx, NY 10458
Lincoln Center Campus: 113 West 60th Street, New York, NY 10023

New York City's Fordham is riding the wave of euphoria for colleges in New York. Though still operating in the shadows of places like NYU and Boston College, Fordham is coming on strong. There is no better location than Lincoln Center in Manhattan, where the performing arts programs are housed. The Bronx location is less appealing but home to larger programs and adjacent to the New York Botanical Garden and Bronx Zoo.

At Fordham University, the tradition of the Society of Jesus (Jesuits) pervades all aspects of life, from the quality of teaching, to the emphasis on personal relationships, to the pursuit of both "wisdom and learning," which also happens to be the school's motto. Students benefit from two campuses: the gated Bronx community of Rose Hill and the Lincoln Center facility, just a short subway ride away from the heart of midtown Manhattan. Though half of the student population is Roman Catholic, there's plenty of variation in ethnic background and in students' political, social, and religious views. Fordham is "more diverse than Boston College, less funky than NYU," says a German and English double major.

The 85-acre Rose Hill campus is an oasis of trees, grass, and Gothic architecture; it's close to the New York Botanical Garden and Yankee Stadium and had cameo appearances in films such as *A Beautiful Mind*. Rose Hill is home to Fordham College

Website: www.fordham.edu
Location: City Center
Private
Total Enrollment: 13,294
Undergraduates: 9,061
Male/Female: 43/57
SAT Ranges: ERW 620–700, M 610–710
ACT Ranges: 27–31
Financial Aid: 81%
Pell Grant: 18%

(continued)

Expense: Pr $ $ $
Student Loans: 60%
Average Debt: $ $ $ $
Applicants: 45,147
Accepted: 46%
Enrolled: 11%
Grad in 6 Years: 80%
Returning Freshmen: 91%
Academics: ✑ ✑ ✑
Social: ☎ ☎ ☎
Q of L: ★ ★ ★
Admissions: (718) 817-4000
Email Address: enroll@
   fordham.edu

Strong Programs:
Communication
Finance
Economics
Business Administration
Biological Sciences
Theater
Dance
Global Business

Freshmen can participate in Urban Plunge, three days of exploring the city and working on a team service project.

at Rose Hill, the largest liberal arts school at the university, as well as the primary programs of the Gabelli School of Business. The Lincoln Center campus benefits from its proximity to the Juilliard School, to the CBS and ABC television studios between 10th and 11th Avenues, and to Lincoln Center itself, Manhattan's performing arts hub. In addition to its own liberal arts college, the campus also houses some business programs, Fordham's law school, and three other graduate schools. Shuttles run between the two campuses.

Undergraduate requirements include coursework in English, social and natural sciences, philosophy, theology, history, math/computer science, fine arts, and foreign languages. Students also complete four *Eloquentia Perfecta* seminars, including a capstone senior seminar on values. Freshmen can opt to participate in Urban Plunge, three days of exploring the city's diverse neighborhoods and working on a team service project before the start of the fall semester.

No matter where at Fordham you study, humanities are a good choice. Strengths at Rose Hill include history, philosophy, psychology, and economics, while at

> **"[Fordham is] more diverse than Boston College, less funky than NYU."**

Lincoln Center theatre, English, and communication shine. The most popular majors across the university are communication, finance, economics, business administration, and biological sciences. The B.F.A. in dance is offered along with the Alvin Ailey American Dance Theater; students must be accepted both by Fordham and by the Ailey audition panel. Fordham's public radio station, WFUV, offers hands-on experience for aspiring deejays and radio journalists, and there is a TV production studio in Rose Hill. The global business program at Lincoln Center engages students in courses about the global dimensions of business and requires a study abroad experience. Rose Hill offers 3–2 engineering programs with Columbia and Case Western Reserve, and both colleges have a 3–3 program with Fordham Law School and a teacher-certification program.

"The academic climate at Fordham is one of rigor and depth," says a junior, but students frequently work together on homework and group projects. Fifty-two percent of all undergraduate classes have fewer than 20 students, and professors are praised for bringing much-appreciated professional experience and real-world perspective to the lectern. What's more, "Every department has tutors at no cost to the students," says a sociology and urban studies major. Helped by alumni connections, business students often obtain internships on Wall Street or elsewhere in the Manhattan financial community. Forty-two percent of undergrads study abroad in 52 countries, choosing from 110 programs, including those offered by the university's London Centre.

A political science major says Fordham students are "open-minded and eager to learn about different cultures and perspectives," but are also "opinionated, assertive, and outspoken." This is, after all, New York City. The atmosphere is less intellectual than at nearby Columbia and NYU. Thirty-five percent of undergraduates hail from New York State, and many of the rest are from elsewhere on the East Coast; 8 percent come from abroad. African Americans comprise 4 percent of the student body, Asian

> **"Every department has tutors at no cost to the students."**

Americans 10 percent, Hispanics 14 percent, and multiracial students 3 percent. The university supports a vibrant LGBTQ community, and while it leans left, there is a healthy variety of political views. Hundreds of merit scholarships averaging $17,000 are available to eligible students, and the university now awards scholarships to those who demonstrate athletic gifts.

Half of Fordham undergrads live in the dorms, and all are guaranteed university housing for four years. Those who snag rooms in the two high-rise residence halls near Lincoln Center are saved from the borough's unscrupulous brokers and unconscionable rents. Both campuses offer living/learning communities; all Lincoln Center freshmen participate in the first-year experience integrated learning community, while first-years at Rose Hill can apply for the Manresa Scholars Program, which offers access to academic live-in tutors and a Jesuit priest-in-residence. Students across the university complain about strict guest policies that require sign-ins and restrict overnight passes to visitors of the same sex. Campus dining is said to need "more dietary options and extended hours," according to a marketing major. Despite its Bronx location, the Rose Hill campus is safe, students say. "The entire campus is gated, with security guards at each entrance," notes one junior.

Fordham's Campus Activities Board sponsors events like movies, concerts, and dances on both campuses; there is no Greek system. Says one student, "Parties with alcohol are practically unheard of on campus." Students are far more likely to head to nearby bars, clubs, performances, festivals, and cultural events. "The slogan 'Fordham is my school. New York is my campus' is often quite accurate," says a junior. The Rose Hill campus backs up against the Bronx Zoo and it's around the corner from Arthur Avenue, the Little Italy of the Bronx. Both provide welcome weekend diversions. Students look forward to homecoming and Spring Weekend, which features a major concert and the Under the Tent dance on Martyr's Lawn at Rose Hill. Fordham's Dorothy Day Center for Service and Justice helps connect students with local community service opportunities.

> "The slogan 'Fordham is my school. New York is my campus' is often quite accurate."

The Fordham Rams compete in Division I and the Atlantic 10 Conference (and the Patriot League for football), and its location near the Hudson River has helped to produce the women's rowing Metropolitan champs. Women's softball has brought home six consecutive conference titles, and men's soccer is also a recent conference champ. The Lombardi Memorial Athletic Center (named for Vince, an alumnus) supports club sports and intramurals. Perhaps Fordham's most unusual athletic endeavor is Riding the Ram. "Students are expected to climb on the granite blocks and sit on the bronze statue of the Fordham Ram at least once in their time here," explains a computer science major. "However, ride the Ram at your own risk, as you will be reprimanded if caught in the act."

Consistent with its Jesuit tradition, Fordham fancies itself a family. Some things are changing—including its admissions and academic standards, which are inching up, and its national profile, which is also far higher than in years past. What hasn't changed is the idea that diversity and community can coexist, instilling confidence and pride in Fordham students and loyalty in the expanding alumni base. "Fordham University is the Jesuit university of New York," asserts one student. "The bustle of New York City is unlike anywhere else on the planet, and our students graduate as experts of the city and have their Jesuit ideals to guide them for the rest of their lives."

Half of Fordham undergrads live in the dorms, and all are guaranteed university housing for four years.

Overlaps

Boston University, Villanova, George Washington, Syracuse, Santa Clara, NYU, Boston College, SUNY–Binghamton

If You Apply To ›

Fordham: Early decision, early action, regular decision. SATs or ACTs: required. Subject Tests: optional. Accepts the Common Application. Apply to particular school or program. Theatre and dance applicants must audition.

F&M is known for churning out hardworking preprofessional students. Faces tough competition from the likes of Bucknell, Dickinson, Gettysburg, and Lafayette for Pennsylvania–bound students. Known for natural sciences, business, government, and emphasis on civic engagement. Bases all financial aid on need and meets the demonstrated need of every student.

Website: www.fandm.edu
Location: Small City
Private
Total Enrollment: 2,263
Undergraduates: 2,263
Male/Female: 46/54
SAT Ranges: ERW 620–700, M 640–720
ACT Ranges: 28–32
Financial Aid: 56%
Pell Grant: 21%
Expense: Pr $ $ $ $
Student Loans: 57%
Average Debt: $ $
Applicants: 6,720
Accepted: 34%
Enrolled: 28%
Grad in 6 Years: 85%
Returning Freshmen: 92%
Academics: ✐ ✐ ✐ ✐
Social: ☎ ☎ ☎
Q of L: ★ ★ ★
Admissions: (877) 678-9111
Email Address: admission@fandm.edu

Strong Programs:
Business, Organizations, and Society
Economics
Government
Psychology
Biology
Natural Sciences
Computer Science
Premed

At Franklin & Marshall College, set in the serene hills of Pennsylvania's Amish country, you might come nose-to-nose with a horse and buggy, but you can still enjoy the perks of being in one of the country's 50 largest metro areas. While the city of Lancaster has modernized beautifully, parts of this historic town look much the same as they did when two acclaimed but struggling colleges decided to pool their resources. Marshall College (named for Chief Justice John Marshall) merged with Franklin College (started with a donation of 200 English pounds from Ben himself) in 1853. These days, F&M is trying to modernize too, particularly by bringing a more international and service-oriented bent to the curriculum. "At F&M you have the chance to really explore and find yourself," says a junior.

F&M's 220-acre campus is surrounded by a quiet residential neighborhood shaded by majestic maple and oak trees. The campus itself is an arboretum and boasts 65 buildings of mainly Gothic and colonial architecture. The Blue Line Café and nearby Hartman Green appeal to students seeking a study respite. Other notable facilities include the Life Sciences and Philosophy Building and Martin Library of the Sciences. As part of a decade-long urban renewal project, the college has developed 28 acres of land that was once home to aged industrial buildings and rail yards into a new North Campus for athletic fields and facilities, including the $19 million Shadek Stadium, which opened in 2017.

First-year students are introduced to F&M's academic community through two required Connections seminars, intimate courses that teach the skills of critical analysis, research, writing, and civil debate. First-years also live together in seminar-based living/learning communities. Additional general education components include writing and language requirements and distribution requirements in the arts, humanities, social sciences, natural sciences, and non-Western cultures. Collaborations are optional opportunities to get course credit for an experience that includes working with others. F&M has long been known for being strong in the natural sciences, its computer science program is on the rise, and the school is now placing more emphasis on service-learning courses in many disciplines. A preprofessional college in line with Lafayette and Bucknell, F&M has an excellent reputation for preparing undergrads for medical school, law school, and other careers. The major in business, organizations, and society is the most popular, followed by economics, government, psychology, and biology. F&M also offers several cooperative-degree and domestic-exchange programs.

> **"At F&M you have the chance to really explore and find yourself."**

Students uniformly describe the coursework as demanding, but say the environment is supportive. "The courses are challenging, as professors aim to push students to new levels," a senior says. The relatively small student body and intimate class sizes help create a strong sense of community between students and professors. A business major says the professors are caring and "make Franklin & Marshall an exciting and comfortable place to learn." More than a third of F&M students engage in directed research under the guidance of faculty, including students in the Hackman Summer Research Scholars program. In the summer, faculty-led study abroad programs head to countries such as China, Italy, Russia, and South Africa, and about half of the students study in locations around the world during their time at F&M.

"Students here are open-minded and very free-spirited," says a sophomore. Twenty-two percent of students hail from Pennsylvania, and 16 percent come from foreign nations. African Americans comprise 6 percent of the student body, Hispanics 10 percent, Asian Americans 5 percent, and multiracial students 2 percent. Perhaps because most of the community shares a liberal point of view, "intense political debate is uncommon," according to a senior. Fummers do, however, take an interest when it comes to extracurricular activities and social opportunities. The 140 clubs on campus attest to that, as does a notably high level of participation in community service activities (70 percent). There are no athletic scholarships, and the school has eliminated merit scholarships in order to redirect the funds toward need-based financial aid, guaranteeing to meet 100 percent of admitted students' demonstrated need. Twenty-one percent of freshmen qualify for the Pell Grant.

The college requires students to live in college-affiliated housing all four years, and housing options include residence halls organized into five College Houses, apartments, lofts, townhouses, and special-interest housing. The faculty-led College House system "provides a strong academic and social structure within living spaces," says a music and math double major. Boarders eat most of their meals in the campus dining hall under a flexible meal plan, but students are issued debit cards that they may use at a number of different food stops on campus. Campus security is described as "efficient and friendly," and students report feeling safe.

Six fraternities attract 20 percent of the men, and five sororities attract 26 percent of the women. They are integral to much of the nightlife, although the residence halls and student organizations such as the College Entertainment Committee offer a range of alternatives, including concerts and comedians. "Off-campus parties dominate the lives of students on the weekends," one student says. Ben's Underground, a popular student-run nightclub, and Hildy's, a tiny local bar, are also favorite meeting places. The biggest annual event is the Spring Arts Festival, held the weekend before finals, which includes live concerts, student air-band contests, art exhibits, games, booths, and barbecues. Another highlight is the Flapjack Fest, when professors serve pancakes to students.

Lancaster is a historical and well-to-do city located in a larger metro area of more than 500,000. Lancaster offers a 16-screen cinema, scores of shops and art galleries, a historic farmers market, brick-and-cobblestone streets, and a plethora of quaint restaurants and cafés. Students have a measured, realistic appreciation of its urban amenities and rural ambiance. "Lancaster is a lot of fun," says one student. "There are great restaurants and bars." The Amish culture, although not as visible as some newcomers might expect, draws the interest of some students too. Those with a hankering for contemporary action take road trips to Philly, Baltimore, Washington, D.C., and New York City.

With the exception of wrestling, which is Division I, F&M teams compete in Division III. The college boasts recent Centennial Conference championships in women's field hockey, lacrosse, and softball and men's soccer and golf. Varsity squads are called the Diplomats, a moniker that gained currency in 1935 when the football team nearly upset national powerhouse Fordham. The annual football game against Dickinson for the Conestoga Wagon trophy is always a crowd-pleaser. The college also offers a selection of five co-ed intramural sports and 11 club sports, such as cycling, rugby, and ultimate Frisbee, which sign up 28 percent of students.

As part of a decade-long urban renewal project, the college has developed 28 acres of land into a new North Campus for athletic fields and facilities.

"Intense political debate is uncommon."

F&M has eliminated merit scholarships in order to redirect the funds toward need-based financial aid.

Overlaps

Dickinson, Gettysburg, Davidson, Lafayette, Skidmore, Penn State, Muhlenberg, Lehigh

One senior likens Franklin & Marshall's personality to that of "the sexy librarian. During the day, we're extremely studious and outwardly boring, but then if given the opportunity, we go nuts." While the college's illustrious namesakes might raise an eyebrow at that, they would no doubt be proud of the quality academics and ever-evolving opportunities at the institution that bears their names.

If You Apply To ›

F&M: Early decision I and II, regular decision. SATs or ACTs: optional. Subject Tests: optional. Accepts the Common Application with supplement.

Furman University

3300 Poinsett Highway, Greenville, SC 29613

Furman's campus is one of the most gorgeous anywhere, with the swans being a particularly nice touch. With just under 2,700 undergraduates, Furman is larger than Davidson and half the size of Wake Forest. Academic life includes a strong emphasis on off-campus experiences. Benefiting its Baptist heritage, Furman is conservative, and the student body is still largely regional.

Website: www.furman.edu
Location: Suburban
Private
Total Enrollment: 2,704
Undergraduates: 2,655
Male/Female: 41/59
SAT Ranges: ERW 600–690, M 590–690
ACT Ranges: 26–31
Financial Aid: 97%
Pell Grant: 15%
Expense: Pr $ $
Student Loans: 39%
Average Debt: $ $ $
Applicants: 5,002
Accepted: 61%
Enrolled: 23%
Grad in 6 Years: 84%
Returning Freshmen: 93%
Academics: ✍ ✍ ✍ ½
Social: ☎ ☎ ☎
Q of L: ★ ★ ★
Admissions: (864) 294-2034
Email Address: admissions@furman.edu

Strong Programs:
Health Sciences

Furman University has been called the "Country Club of the South." And if you're Southern, white, and Christian, you're likely to feel like a member. Beyond the country club vibe, though, students find small classes led by caring faculty and plenty of opportunities for independent research. Prominent alums include the late Nobel Prize–winning physicist Charles Townes and Keith Lockhart, director of the Boston Pops Orchestra.

Furman's 750-acre campus is one of the country's most beautiful, with tree-lined malls, fountains, a formal rose garden and Japanese garden, and a 30-acre lake filled with swans and ducks. Flowering shrubs dot the well-kept lawns, which surround buildings in the classical revival, Colonial Williamsburg, and modern architectural styles. Many have porches, pediments, and other Southern touches, such as hand-made Virginia brick. Recent campus projects include a renovation of the Lakeside Housing complex.

Furman operates under the "semester-plus" system. The school year begins in late August, and the first semester ends prior to the December holiday break. Students begin the second semester in January and then have the option of attending a three-week Maymester in (guess when). General education requirements include a first-year seminar and a series of core requirements that fulfill the following "ways of knowing": empirical studies; human cultures; mathematical and formal reasoning; foreign language; ultimate questions; and body and mind. Finally, students must fulfill global awareness requirements. The most popular majors include health sciences, business administration, politics and international affairs, and communication studies. Chemistry, biology, and psychology are strong too. Students in the health sciences program have access to the innovative international health and nutrition program as well as a human performance laboratory. Internships and research opportunities are available through the recently established Institute for the Advancement of Community Health.

> **"As someone who is not a part of Greek life, I've had to seek out activities on my own."**

Furman's academic climate is challenging. "Furman students all understand that the courses are difficult and seem to commiserate with one another," says one junior. Sixty percent of classes have fewer than 20 students, helping students get to know faculty members well, and the new Pathways advising program helps freshmen and sophomores stay on track. "All classes are taught by professors, and only a handful of labs are taught by teachers' assistants," says one senior. The Furman Advantage ensures that every undergraduate will have the opportunity to participate in research, an internship, or study abroad. Twenty-eight percent of undergrads assist professors with research, many through paid Furman Summer Research Fellowships. Furman typically sends one of the largest student delegations to the annual National Conference on Undergraduate Research. Internships are popular, with 66 percent of students taking part. Fifty-three percent of students study abroad through one of two dozen Furman-sponsored programs on five continents, including programs in Iceland, Japan, Jordan, Belize, and Botswana. Entering freshmen have the opportunity to travel in small groups to an island off the coast of Charleston, the mountains of North Carolina, or even China during the summer before they enroll.

(continued)

Business Administration
Politics and International
 Affairs
Communication Studies
Chemistry
Biology
Psychology

Furman broke with the South Carolina Baptist Convention in 1992, but it remains in South Carolina, where religion ranks second only to football; 79 percent of freshmen identify as Christian. Three-quarters of undergrads hail from Southeastern states, including 28 percent from South Carolina; 5 percent are international. Most come from well-off, conservative backgrounds. A political science major says, "Students here tend to be sheltered and ignorant of real-world issues. They are very image-conscious." Another student adds, "Bow ties and button-downs are expected for guys on game day at tailgates, and girls wouldn't be caught dead without their Longchamp totes and Tory Burch flats." The administration has committed to diversifying the school, but those efforts have been slow to bear fruit. African Americans make up 6 percent of the student body, Hispanics 5 percent, Asian Americans 2 percent, and multiracial students 3 percent. The recently created Task Force on Slavery and Justice seeks to examine and help the community understand Furman's historic ties to slavery. Every year, Furman awards hundreds of merit scholarships averaging $18,600, plus 189 athletic scholarships in 20 sports.

Sixty-six percent of students take part in internships, and 53 percent study abroad.

Furman is a residential campus, with 89 percent of students living in university housing, and students enjoy the resulting camaraderie. "The residence halls undergo cyclical renovations such that no one dorm is in disrepair," says a junior. Furman is no longer a dry campus, although the alcohol policy is strictly enforced in freshman and sophomore dorms, where most students shouldn't be imbibing anyway. The atmosphere is more relaxed for students of legal drinking age, who may consume alcohol in North Village, a university-owned apartment complex of 10 buildings for juniors and seniors. Meal plan credits can be used in the dining hall or food court, and, overall, students say campus fare is tasty and diverse. Campus security helps provide a relatively safe environment.

"Downtown [Greenville] is booming and is a really fun place to visit."

"Greek life does tend to dominate life on Furman's campus," reports one student. "As someone who is not a part of Greek life, I've had to seek out activities on my own. There are a lot of interesting cultural and religious programs on campus, and great outdoor/sporting facilities." When the weekend comes, Furman's Student Activities Board sponsors "free movies, weekend trips, restaurant deals, and huge concerts," says a communication studies major. Fraternities claim 30 percent of the men and sororities 58 percent of the women, and off-campus Greek parties draw crowds.

Furman's athletic teams are the Paladins (after the toughest warrior in Charlemagne's court).

"Greenville is a great city that is seeing a large amount of growth," says a senior. "The downtown is booming and is a really fun place to visit." The Peace Center for the Performing Arts, located downtown, brings in touring casts of Broadway shows and other top-rated acts. Sixty-eight percent of Furman's students devote spare time to the Heller Service Corps, which provides volunteers to more than 50 community agencies and organizes the annual Exceptional Adults Valentine's Day Dance for special-needs adults. The best road trips are to the mountains of Asheville (only 45 minutes away), Atlanta (for the big city and shopping, about two hours), and Charleston or Myrtle Beach (four hours).

Furman's athletic teams are the Paladins (after the toughest warrior in Charlemagne's court), and they compete in the Division I Southern Conference. Recent conference champs include men's and women's cross-country, men's basketball and lacrosse, and women's tennis, golf, and softball. Students happily yell out the school's tongue-in-cheek cheer ("F.U. one time, F.U. two times, F.U. three times, F.U. all the time!") during football games against archrivals Wofford and The Citadel. Two-thirds of the student body plays intramural and club sports, and Greek groups compete annually for the coveted All Sports Trophy. Furman's debate and mock trial teams are both nationally ranked and regularly compete in intercollegiate tournaments.

Nearly three decades after severing its religious ties, Furman is still a largely homogeneous institution, although it continues to evolve. It may call itself a university, but its educational approach is closer to that of a liberal arts college, emphasizing broad exposure to many fields, problem solving, and experience-based learning.

Overlaps

Sewanee, Rhodes, Washington and Lee, Davidson, Wake Forest, Clemson, Wofford, University of South Carolina

If You Apply To ›

Furman: Early decision, early action, regular decision. SATs or ACTs: optional. No Subject Tests. Accepts the Common Application.

George Mason University

4400 University Drive, Fairfax, VA 22030

The largest public research university in Virginia, George Mason is the antithesis of UVA—a place where traditions are still in their infancy and inclusive growth is a dominant value. A bastion of conservative political and economic thought and recipient of considerable Koch brothers largesse, Mason takes full advantage of location in job- and internship-rich northern Virginia. Big focus on overall student well-being. Nearly half of students start out in community colleges.

Website: www.gmu.edu
Location: Suburban
Public
Total Enrollment: 24,196
Undergraduates: 20,001
Male/Female: 49/51
SAT Ranges: ERW 560–650, M 540–640
ACT Ranges: 24–30
Financial Aid: 68%
Pell Grant: 31%
Expense: Pub $ $ $

Located in the middle of greater Washington, D.C.'s budding high-tech corridor, George Mason University features a suburban campus and symbiotic relationship with the surrounding region that contrasts starkly with Virginia's two other major universities, which have held classes for many years in the relative isolation of Charlottesville and Blacksburg. Well-established as a center of conservative thinking on social issues, Mason has grown by leaps and bounds for most of the past two decades, largely because of its commitment to extend the benefits of higher education to as many Virginians as possible. As one sophomore puts it, "The university's biggest drives are for diversity and innovation."

Founded in 1957 as a sleepy outpost of the University of Virginia, Mason became independent in 1972. It sits on a 677-acre wooded campus 20 miles southwest of Washington, D.C., in suburban Fairfax, Virginia. Campus architecture is modern and homogeneous, with lots of brick, glass, and metal, and just about everything is within a 15-minute walk. The campus observatory is second in the area only to that of NASA. The 100,000-seat Eagle Bank Arena hosts both sporting and entertainment events. Although Mason's campus doesn't have the colonial ambiance or tradition of William and Mary or UVA, its namesake does have the same Old Virginia credentials. George Mason drafted Virginia's influential Declaration of Rights in 1776, and he later opposed ratification of the federal Constitution because there was no Bill of Rights attached.

Though it is growing up fast, Mason shows its youth in a number of ways. First, programs taken for granted at more established universities are just hitting their stride here. Its physical plant is expanding, thanks largely to a small but growing endowment, funding from the State of Virginia, and some public-private partnerships. One notable addition is the Peterson Family Health Science Hall, which opened in 2018. Through the university libraries, which are also growing, students have access to electronic resources and borrowing privileges of the Washington Research Library Consortium.

> "The university's biggest drives are for diversity and innovation."

Mason has standard general education requirements, but students who prefer to find their own way can design a major under the bachelor's in integrative studies, which teams small groups of faculty and undergraduates on projects that can be easily connected to the world outside the campus. Nontraditional students who enter Mason have the option of creating their own degree in the bachelor of individualized studies program. All students must complete a capstone or synthesis course in their major. Mason has had two Nobel Prize laureates in its libertarian-oriented economics department, which is probably its strongest. The extent to which the Koch brothers and other conservative donors have influenced hiring and other decisions is a matter of continuing controversy. Not surprisingly, given the school's location, the Schar School of Policy and Government also receives accolades. Business-related majors are popular, along with psychology; criminology, law, and society; information technology; and biology. Other notable majors include the nation's first conflict analysis and resolution major, a fast-growing computer game design major, and forensic science. Recently added programs include statistics, atmospheric sciences, and cybersecurity engineering.

Academically, a community health major says, "I have never felt extrinsically pressured to be better than anyone else." Classes are often fairly large; 31 percent have fewer than 20 students. All faculty members are required to teach, although some do better than others. For the most part, though, says an English major, "Professors are helpful and encouraging, while asking students to contribute their best at all times." Mason's Center for the Advancement of Well-Being is a national leader in encouraging students, faculty, and staff members to live more mindful and meaningful lives.

> "I have never felt extrinsically pressured to be better than anyone else."

Students here are decidedly career focused: 83 percent enter the working world after graduation and 26 percent proceed to graduate and professional schools, although Mason does offer its undergrads 51 accelerated master's degree programs. The Smithsonian-Mason School of Conservation allows students to live on-site at the Smithsonian Conservation Biology Institute of the Smithsonian's National Zoo and study global conservation issues and civic concerns. About half of students conduct undergraduate research, and an Honors College is available to top achievers. For those seeking adventure in faraway places—as about 9 percent of undergraduates do—the Global Education Office offers more than 140 different study abroad programs in more than 50 sites around the world, including Mason's new campus in South Korea.

"A great deal of our students are older in age, work full time, and attend classes in the evening," says a student, and as such, many commute. Eighty-five percent of Mason undergraduates are from Virginia, and 5 percent are international; the

(continued)

Student Loans: 56%
Average Debt: $ $ $
Applicants: 18,993
Accepted: 81%
Enrolled: 23%
Grad in 6 Years: 71%
Returning Freshmen: 88%
Academics: ✐ ✐ ✐
Social: ☎ ☎
Q of L: ★ ★
Admissions: (703) 993-2400
Email Address: admissions@ gmu.edu

Strong Programs:
Economics
Business
Psychology
Criminology, Law, and Society
Information Technology
Biology
Conflict Analysis and Resolution
Computer Game Design

The Smithsonian-Mason School of Conservation allows students to live on-site at the Smithsonian Conservation Biology Institute.

university boasts students from 49 states and more than 130 countries. Nearly half of incoming undergrads start out at Northern Virginia Community College or other two-year institutions, while 31 percent of incoming freshmen are Pell-eligible. African Americans account for 11 percent of the student population, Hispanics 14 percent, Asian Americans 20 percent, and multiracial students 5 percent. One senior says of the campus's diversity, "I've learned about many different cultures here, and I don't ever feel singled out." Students are politically aware and, being so close to D.C., have plenty of opportunities to get involved. Merit scholarships averaging $4,000 are available to those who qualify, as are 150 athletic scholarships in 22 sports.

George Mason's status as a commuter school is changing. On-campus housing is guaranteed for the first two years; 24 percent of students live on or around campus in university-sponsored housing, including 67 percent of first-time freshmen. "Housing is competitive but the residence halls are generally nice," says a global affairs major. Those who want an active campus social life should definitely consider a stint in the dorms, but freshman dorms are dry, and you can get the boot if you're caught having a party with alcohol. Freshmen live together in Presidents Park, while other students get rooms on a first-come, first-served basis prioritized by class status. Eleven academic- and lifestyle-focused living/learning communities are available for those seeking tighter-knit relationships with their classmates. Campus dining facilities are plentiful and operate around the clock but receive mixed reviews. "GMU has many different security officers patrolling the area at all times," says an English major, and students agree that the university responds quickly and effectively to incidents of campus sexual assault.

> **"A great deal of our students are older in age, work full time, and attend classes in the evening."**

"Due to the fact that the majority of our students are commuters, weekends are pretty dead," says a junior, and students advise that getting involved is key to a good social life. Mason's Johnson Center, with its food court, movie theater, library, classrooms, computer labs, student support offices, and study areas, is the center of on-campus social life. Two student unions, the Student Union Building and the HUB, offer additional options for socializing and studying. Seven percent of the men and 9 percent of the women go Greek. With barely two generations of history under its belt, Mason is still developing traditions and annual events: "Come here and invent one!" a student urges. Patriots Day, Gold Rush, and Mason Day are major bashes, in addition to homecoming and International Week. On the weekends, students find a predictable assortment of malls and shopping centers in Fairfax, but off-campus parties and the sights and sounds of downtown D.C., Georgetown, and Old Town Alexandria beckon when the sun goes down. Best of all, these are only a short commute away via a free shuttle bus to the Metro. Those searching for alternative collegiate scenes take road trips to James Madison and UVA.

Mason competes in the Division I Atlantic 10 conference, and the basketball team is the marquee program—any game against Virginia Commonwealth University draws a big crowd. Students are proud of the colorful pep band, known as the Green Machine and directed by a tuba professor known as Doc Nix. Patriots teams that have recently brought home conference titles include men's and women's track and field and men's volleyball. Club sports and intramurals are growing in popularity, with 13 percent of students participating.

"Nearly every aspect of Mason is developing at breakneck speed. We haven't hit our best yet," says one student. The name of George Mason may not have the cachet of George Washington, James Madison, or the other luminaries of Virginia history who have had universities named for them, but with improving academics, an ever-expanding physical campus, and the rich cultural and economic resources of Washington, D.C., Mason's namesake may be set to follow in their footsteps.

Overlaps

Virginia Commonwealth, Arizona State, Temple, UMBC, Virginia Tech, James Madison, University of Virginia, Old Dominion

The George Washington University

Washington, D.C. 20052

Not so long ago, GW was a backup school maligned for its lack of identity. But the allure of Washington, D.C., coupled with ambitious leadership and an intellectually stimulating educational environment, has made it increasingly selective. Located steps away from the State Department. One of the most expensive private schools in the country, it is also the nation's leader in internships per capita.

Like Washington, D.C., itself, the George Washington University draws students from all over America—and 130 countries around the world. Upon arrival, they find a bustling campus in the heart of D.C., enriched with cultural and intellectual opportunities. Students often have rare access behind the scenes of the Smithsonian Institution museums, the U.S. Capitol, the Library of Congress, and other national treasures. GW offers a front-row seat to history as top political officials and influential leaders serve as frequent guest speakers and visiting professors—and it is the only school in the country to hold its commencement on the National Mall. "We are the students who will make change in the world and we are at the center of the important things that are going on right now," says one confident junior.

GW was established in 1821 by an act of Congress as a testament to George Washington's dream of a national institution of higher learning in D.C. Today, undergraduates experience life at GW on primarily two campuses—the Foggy Bottom campus on Pennsylvania Avenue near the State Department and the Mount Vernon campus, three miles away in the Foxhall neighborhood. (A few other satellite campuses in the area serve mostly graduate students.) The Foggy Bottom campus has a mix of renovated federal row houses and modern buildings and is virtually indistinguishable from the rest of the neighborhood, while the wooded Mount Vernon campus spans 23 bucolic acres near Georgetown and includes athletic fields, tennis courts, and an outdoor pool. Students live and take classes on both campuses and travel between the two on the "Vern Express," a shuttle that runs 24/7 during the academic year. The 500,000-square-foot Science and Engineering Hall is the largest academic building in D.C. dedicated to STEM fields.

Freshmen may enroll in the School of Engineering and Applied Science, the School of Business, the Elliott School of International Affairs, the Milken Institute School of Public Health, and the largest undergraduate division, the Columbian College of Arts and Sciences (which also houses the School of Media and Public Affairs and the Corcoran School of the Arts and Design). All undergraduates are required to complete a 19-credit core curriculum in the following areas: writing, natural or physical science, mathematics or statistics, social science, and the humanities, plus two writing-in-the-disciplines courses. During their first year, all

> **"[GW is] less competitive than you would expect, with definite space for collaboration."**

Website: www.gwu.edu
Location: City Center
Private
Total Enrollment: 18,568
Undergraduates: 10,803
Male/Female: 39/61
SAT Ranges: ERW 640–720, M 640–720
ACT Ranges: 29–32
Financial Aid: 74%
Pell Grant: 14%
Expense: Pr $ $ $ $
Student Loans: 49%
Average Debt: $ $ $
Applicants: 26,987
Accepted: 41%
Enrolled: 24%
Grad in 6 Years: 81%
Returning Freshmen: 91%
Academics: ✑ ✑ ✑ ½
Social: ☎ ☎ ☎
Q of L: ★ ★ ★
Admissions: (202) 994-6040
Email Address: gwadm@gwu.edu

Strong Programs:
International Affairs
Political Science
Finance
Psychology
Political Communication
Public Health

(continued)

Geography
Archaeology

undergraduates take a University Writing course. The most popular majors are international affairs, political science, finance, and psychology. GW's political communication major, which combines political science, journalism, and communication technologies, is one of the few undergraduate programs of its kind and benefits from its Washington location. Programs in public health, geography, and archaeology are also well regarded. A number of accelerated undergraduate/graduate degree programs are available. Students warn that recent budget cuts have impacted several humanities and arts programs, including women's studies, music, and dance.

The workload at GW tends to be heavy, and a human services and social justice major says the climate is "less competitive than you would expect, with definite

"Students intern at Capitol Hill (we call it hill-terning because of how common it is)."

space for collaboration (at least in liberal arts classes)." Fifty-two percent of the classes taken by undergraduates have fewer than 20 students; professors handle lectures and seminars, and TAs facilitate discussions or labs. Almost half of GW's faculty members divide their time between the halls of academia and real-world positions, many of them governmental, but the quality of teaching is said to be "hit or miss."

For about 500 highly motivated and capable students in all majors, the University Honors Program offers special seminars, independent study, and a university symposium on both campuses. Thirty-one percent of students study abroad in more than 300 programs in more than 60 countries, including GW-run programs in England, France, Spain, and Chile. The Center for Career Services connects students with more than 12,000 internship opportunities. "Students intern at Capitol Hill (we call it hill-terning because of how common it is), the Kennedy Center, the Smithsonian, and many other local organizations," says a junior. Volunteering is big too, and more than 70 GW courses combine academics with service work in the D.C. community.

The 500,000-square-foot Science and Engineering Hall is the largest academic building in D.C. dedicated to STEM fields.

"Students who go to GW are driven by success," says an economics major. "They know what they want and they will go after it." Ninety-seven percent of undergraduates come from outside D.C., including 11 percent who hail from foreign countries. Seven percent are African American, 10 percent are Hispanic, 10 percent are Asian American, and 4 percent are multiracial. Many students come from wealthy backgrounds (and pricey nights out on the town are a common diversion), and a

"[GW students] know what they want and they will go after it."

senior comments that the campus "remains fairly segregated according to race and cultural background." Diversity training is now mandatory for all incoming students. As you might expect, political issues of all sorts are important here. A fixed-rate plan guarantees that tuition will not increase for up to five years of full-time undergraduate study. Merit scholarships are available, averaging $19,800, and athletes vie for 175 awards. GW is need-aware, not need-blind, in its admissions.

GW's political communication major is one of the few undergraduate programs of its kind.

Sixty-one percent of GW undergrads live in campus housing, which is required for the first three years, although rising juniors interested in living off campus can enter a lottery that grants a limited number of exemptions. "The conditions and popularity of the dorms are varied," reports one junior. Those who move off campus typically find group houses in Foggy Bottom or go to fashionable nearby neighborhoods like Dupont Circle and Georgetown, just a short walk from campus. GW's meal plans allow students to dine at on-campus cafés or at more than 100 off-campus vendors, which means there are a "variety of options ranging from fast food, to food trucks, to nice sit-down dinners at fancier restaurants," according to one sophomore. Given GW's open, urban campus, safety can be a concern, but one student says, "There are many services to ensure security." A junior adds, "Student organizations like Students Against Sexual Assault (SASA),

Allied in Pride, the Feminist Student Union, and others work very diligently to increase awareness of sexual assault and provide students with the tools to protect themselves and others."

"If you're bored at GW, you're doing something wrong," states one business administration major. "Whether it's on campus or off campus, there's always something to do." Fifteen percent of GW men and 19 percent of the women go Greek, and there are more than 475 student organizations on campus. Alcohol consumption is allowed on campus for those of legal age. Major annual events include the Fall Fest and Spring Fling carnivals, with free food and nationally known musical performers. And every four years, GW celebrates the beginning of the new U.S. presidential term with a formal Inaugural Ball of its own in January. Popular road trips include the beaches of Ocean City, Maryland, and Virginia Beach, Virginia. Philadelphia and New York City are easily accessible by bus or train, a boon because most GW students don't have cars.

GW doesn't field a football team, but its 27 varsity teams (the Colonials) are competitive in Division I Atlantic 10 Conference play. Men's and women's basketball make regular NCAA tournament appearances, and recent conference champions include women's basketball, gymnastics,

GW's meal plans allow students to dine at on-campus cafés or at more than 100 off-campus vendors.

"If you're bored at GW, you're doing something wrong."

men's swimming and diving, and men's water polo. Sailing and men's and women's squash are also competitive. Approximately 20 percent of undergraduates participate in the recreational sports program, which offers 25 intramural activities throughout the year, in addition to 34 club sport options. And while the school's official mascot resembles a certain Founding Father, its quirky, unofficial one is the hippopotamus.

Perhaps it's fitting that a university located in the nation's seat of government would generate complaints about red tape: "Stop with the bureaucracy," grumbles one student. "The simplest of problems for students could be fixed if we didn't have to go through so many hoops to just get an answer." Still, despite the bureaucratic annoyances, GW continues to build its reputation by putting its location to good use. "The opportunities are endless," says a student. "Picking and choosing what you want to do is the hardest part." For students interested in urban living in the heart of the nation's political establishment, GW may fit the bill. But that bill will be hefty.

Overlaps

Boston University, NYU, Northeastern, University of Miami (FL), University of Southern California, American University, Penn State, University of Maryland

If You Apply To ›

GW: Early decision I and II, regular decision. SATs or ACTs: optional (required for applicants to accelerated programs, homeschooled applicants, and recruited varsity athletes). No Subject Tests. Accepts the Common Application. Art and design applicants must submit portfolio.

Georgetown University

37th and O Streets NW, Washington, D.C. 20057

For anyone who wants to be a master of the political universe, this is the place. Strong international and multicultural environment. In the excitement of studying in D.C., students may pay little attention to the Jesuit affiliation, which adds a slightly conservative tinge to the campus. Occupies a tree-lined neighborhood that is home to many of the nation's most powerful people.

Website: www.georgetown.edu
Location: City Center
Private
Total Enrollment: 14,435
Undergraduates: 6,950
Male/Female: 44/56
SAT Ranges: ERW 680–760,
   M 670–760
ACT Ranges: 30–34
Financial Aid: 56%
Pell Grant: 13%
Expense: Pr $ $ $ $
Student Loans: 38%
Average Debt: $
Applicants: 21,462
Accepted: 16%
Enrolled: 47%
Grad in 6 Years: 95%
Returning Freshmen: 96%
Academics: ✍ ✍ ✍ ✍ ½
Social: 🐎 🐎 🐎 🐎
Q of L: ★ ★ ★ ★
Admissions: (202) 687-3600
Email Address: guadmiss@
   georgetown.edu

Strong Programs:
International Affairs
Government
International Politics
Finance
Nursing
Diplomatic History
International Economics
Theology

Georgetown has worked to atone for its historical ties to slavery and is in the process of developing a new Institute for Racial Justice.

As the oldest and most selective of the nation's Roman Catholic schools, Georgetown University offers students unparalleled access to Washington, D.C.'s corridors of power. Aspiring politicos benefit from the university's emphasis on public policy, international business, and foreign service. The national spotlight shines brightly on this elite institution, drawing dynamic students and athletes from around the world. A senior says, "Georgetown balances academics, social life, and faith in an all-encompassing college experience based on 'care of the whole person.'"

From its scenic location just blocks from the Potomac River, Georgetown affords its students an excellent vantage point from which to survey the world. Established in 1789, the 104-acre campus reflects the history and growth of the first university in the nation to be founded by the Society of Jesus (Jesuits). The Federal style of Old North, which once housed guests such as George Washington and Lafayette and is now home to the McCourt School of Public Policy, contrasts with the towers of the Flemish Romanesque-style Healy Hall, a post-Civil War landmark on the National Register of Historic Places.

Although Georgetown is a Catholic university, the religious atmosphere is by no means heavy-handed, and the student body tends to be liberal. Roughly half of the undergraduates are Catholic, but all major faiths are respected and practiced on campus. That's partially due to the pronounced international influence here. The school's hefty endowment is the largest among the nation's Jesuit colleges and universities. Georgetown has

"The courses are challenging, but it certainly isn't impossible to do well."

worked to atone for its historical ties to slavery by offering preferential admissions status to descendants of 272 slaves who were sold in 1838 to keep its doors open. In addition to offering a formal apology, it has created an African American studies department and is in the process of developing a new Institute for Racial Justice.

Through its broad liberal arts curriculum, GU focuses on developing the intellectual prowess and moral rigor its students will need in future national and international leadership roles. All students must complete requirements in humanities, philosophy, theology, engaging diversity, and writing; other requirements are specific to each school. Optional Ignatius Seminars, which focus on educating the "mind, body, and spirit," give first-years the chance to form close relationships with professors and reflect on their work. Would-be Hoyas may apply to one of four undergraduate schools: Georgetown College for liberal arts, the School of Nursing and Health Studies, McDonough School of Business, and the Walsh School of Foreign Service, which gives future diplomats, journalists, and others a strong grounding in the social sciences. Prospective freshmen must declare intended majors on their applications, and their secondary school records are judged accordingly. This means, among other things, intense competition within the college for the limited number of spaces in Georgetown's popular premed program.

International affairs, diplomatic history, international economics, and regional and comparative studies are among the hottest programs, as evidenced by former secretary of state Madeleine Albright's return to the Walsh School of Foreign Service (SFS). SFS offers several five-year undergraduate and graduate degree programs in conjunction with the Graduate School of Arts and Sciences. The most popular majors include international affairs, government, international politics, finance, and nursing. Of course, the theology department is also strong. The business school balances liberal arts with professional training, which translates into strong offerings in international and intercultural business as well as an emphasis on ethical and public policy issues. Curiously, given its location in D.C., Georgetown does not offer an undergraduate public policy major. The School of Nursing and Health Studies runs an integrated program combining the liberal arts and humanities with professional nursing theory and practice. The Faculty of Languages and Linguistics, the only undergraduate program of its kind nationwide, grants degrees in nine languages, as well as degrees in linguistics and comparative literature.

"Students take their coursework very seriously," says a senior. "The courses are challenging, but it certainly isn't impossible to do well." Sixty-two percent of classes have fewer than 20 students. Georgetown likes to boast about its faculty, and it should. "The professors are outstanding and the teaching is first-rate," says an American studies major, and TAs are used only to lead discussion sections and recitations. That GU views most subjects through an international lens is evidenced by the fact that half of the school's undergraduates study abroad. The Office of Global Education offers more than 190 programs in 55 countries.

A senior says GU students are not the stereotypical "pastel polo and pearl-clad preppies from Long Island." Almost half of the undergraduates come from private or parochial schools. Eighty-five percent come from states outside D.C., and another 13 percent are international. African Americans make up 6 percent of undergrads, Hispanics 11 percent, Asian Americans 10 percent, and multiracial students 5 percent. A student committee works with the vice president for student affairs to improve race relations and develop strategies for improving inclusiveness and sensitivity to issues of multiculturalism. Georgetown offers no academic merit

International affairs is among the hottest programs, as evidenced by former secretary of state Madeleine Albright's return to the school.

"Social life is a major part of campus."

scholarships, but it does guarantee to meet the full demonstrated need of every admit, and more than 120 athletic scholarships draw male and female athletes of all stripes. The Georgetown Scholarship Program offers financial and academic support to eligible low-income students.

University-owned dorms, townhouses, and apartments accommodate some 78 percent of undergrads, and "housing is extremely nice," says a senior. All dorms are co-ed, and some have more activities and a stronger community feel than others. Two dining halls serve "steadily improving" but expensive fare. GU students feel relatively safe on campus, thanks to the school's ever-present Department of Public Safety and its walking and riding after-dark escort services.

Jesuits know something about secret societies and frown upon fraternities and sororities at their colleges. The lack of a Greek system and the university's strict enforcement of the 21-year-old drinking age has led to a somewhat decentralized social life, which is not necessarily a bad thing. Alcohol is forbidden in undergrad dorms, and all parties must be registered. The dozens of bars, nightclubs, and restaurants in Georgetown—Martin's Tavern and the Tombs are always popular—are a big draw for students who are legal, but they can get pricey. Bulldog Tavern, a campus pub in the spectacular student activity center, is a more affordable alternative. Popular annual formals such as the Diplomatic and the Blue/Gray Ball inspire students to dress up and pair off. "Social life is a major part of campus," says a student. "Kids can easily find their niche." Georgetown has a reputation as a gay-friendly campus, and regular events include OUTober, a month of LGBTQ pride and awareness events held in October.

Georgetown's chant— "Hoya Saxa Hoya Saxa"—is derived from a Greek and Latin phrase meaning "What rocks!"

Washington offers unsurpassed cultural resources, ranging from the museums of the Smithsonian to the Kennedy Center. "Washington is an ideal place to spend your college years," says a student. "The city has everything students could want, including culture, shopping, museums, monuments, social life, and the clean and convenient Metro for transportation." Given the absence of on-campus parking, a car is probably more trouble than it's worth. Road trips are said to be infrequent.

"Washington is an ideal place to spend your college years."

Should you notice the hills begin to tremble with a deep, resounding, primitive chant—"Hoya Saxa Hoya Saxa"—don't worry; it's probably just another Georgetown basketball game. Hoya is derived from the Greek and Latin phrase *hoya saxa*, which means "What rocks!" Some say it originated in a cheer referring to the stones that formed the school's outer walls. The Hoya men's basketball team has a long history of prominence. Recent Division I Big East champions include men's cross-country and men's and women's soccer and golf. The thrill of victory in intramural competition at the superb underground Yates Memorial Field House is not to be missed, either.

For anyone interested in discovering the world, Georgetown offers an outstanding menu of choices in one of the nation's most dynamic cities. Professors truly pay attention to their undergrads and the diverse students, who are "hardworking, diligent, caring individuals," says one sophomore. "Georgetown is a place where students of all backgrounds, all traditions, and all faiths come together for a common purpose of educating each other and making an impact on the world."

If You Apply To ›

Georgetown: Early action, regular decision. SATs or ACTs: required. Subject Tests: required (any three). Does not accept the Common Application. Apply to particular schools or programs.

University of Georgia

212 Terrell Hall, Athens, GA 30602-1633

What a difference (nearly) free tuition makes. Top Georgia students now choose UGA over highly selective private institutions. Business, engineering, and social and natural sciences head the list of strong and sought-after programs. The college town of Athens boasts a great nightlife and is within easy reach of Atlanta. The university's Center for Undergraduate Research offers rich opportunities.

Website: www.uga.edu
Location: Small City
Public
Total Enrollment: 33,836
Undergraduates: 27,059
Male/Female: 43/57
SAT Ranges: ERW 610–690, M 590–680
ACT Ranges: 26–31
Financial Aid: 43%
Pell Grant: 19%
Expense: Pub $ $
Student Loans: 44%
Average Debt: $
Applicants: 24,165
Accepted: 54%
Enrolled: 45%
Grad in 6 Years: 85%
Returning Freshmen: 96%
Academics: ✎ ✎ ✎

Twenty-six years ago, the state of Georgia began using lottery receipts to fund the HOPE Scholarship program. The program covers 78 percent of tuition at the University of Georgia for all four years for students who finish high school in the state with a B average and maintain that average in college. The impact of the scholarship has been huge. Top Georgia students who in the past would have looked to more prestigious out-of-state universities are opting instead to set their sights on UGA, which is now much tougher to get into. The program has been widely criticized as a somewhat cynical middle-class assistance program, but there is no doubt that it has helped transform a school that was previously known primarily for its dynamite football team and raucous parties into a widely respected research university. Today, "Georgia offers the most complete 'Southern college experience' in the South," says a senior.

> **"The experiential learning requirement has made me explore things outside of what I am predisposed to."**

Founded in 1785, Georgia was the nation's first state-chartered university (UNC was chartered later but wins bragging rights as the first public university to open its doors). Its attractive 706-acre campus is dotted with greenery and wooded walks. The older north campus houses administrative offices and the law school, and features 19th-century architecture and landscaping. The southern end of campus has more modern buildings and residence halls. The new, six-building Business Learning Community complex, featuring such high-tech resources as a trading room, a music business lab, and a business innovation lab, has been a major, multi-year construction project.

UGA's core curriculum includes courses in world languages and culture, humanities, the arts, life sciences, and physical sciences. First-Year Odyssey Seminars allow new students to study under a senior faculty member in a small, personalized setting while earning an hour of academic credit. All students must take part in a hands-on learning opportunity, such as research, study abroad, service learning, and internships, before they graduate. "The experiential learning requirement has made me explore things outside of what I am predisposed to and has expanded my horizons to more professional opportunities," enthuses a psychology major. UGA's Grady School of Journalism is home to the prestigious Peabody

"Hearing the Chapel bell ring is a heartwarming sound."

Awards, and the Terry College of Business is also noteworthy. Ecology, agricultural sciences, public relations, and international affairs are also strengths, and the university's engineering and health-related programs are rapidly expanding. The most popular majors are finance, psychology, biology, and marketing.

A junior describes UGA's academics as "a mixture of individual and collaborative work that encourages both teamwork and competition." As you might expect, large lecture classes are common, but the university recently hired more than 50 faculty members and added roughly 320 new course sections, in an effort to reduce class sizes. "Professors strive to make their lessons not just about grades, but also about developing and growing our minds," says an international affairs major. Students find ample assistance with securing internships and jobs from the hands-on counselors in the Career Center.

The 2,500 students in UGA's highly regarded Honors Program enjoy small classes taught by top professors, as well as special opportunities like Lunchbox Lectures and summer internships in Savannah, Washington, D.C., and New York City. The Center for Undergraduate Research Opportunities allows students to conduct a research or service project, write a thesis, or develop a creative work with close faculty supervision, awarding 500 stipends per semester of up to $1,000 each. The University of Georgia is highly ranked among research universities for the proportion of students who study abroad each year (26 percent). In addition to offering courses at its campuses in Italy, Costa Rica, and Oxford, England, UGA offers more than 100 faculty-led study abroad trips to dozens of countries, exchange programs with partner universities, and independent research and internship opportunities.

Eighty-seven percent of UGA undergrads are Georgians, and 4 percent are international. A political science and psychology double major calls UGA students "driven, charismatic, and a lot of fun." African Americans account for 8 percent of the student body, Asian Americans 10 percent, Hispanics 6 percent, and multiracial students 4 percent. A junior points out that "Athens is a liberal town located in a conservative state," which balances out to a "reasonably moderate" political atmosphere on campus. Merit scholarships are available, and UGA also doles out 426

"Even the city of Athens brags on the Bulldawgs, and we all feel a part of something special."

athletic scholarships in 12 sports. As many as 100 top undergraduates are named Foundation Fellows, netting a full scholarship plus stipends for international travel and research.

Thirty-three percent of Bulldogs live in the 22 residence halls, and freshmen are required to do so. "Each dorm caters to different personality types, bathroom preferences, and social environments," explains a public relations major. There are five campus dining halls—each with its own specialty cuisine—and students drool over the delicious options; many choose to keep their meal plans even after moving off campus. "You don't feel like you're in a dining hall—it's that good," insists a junior.

(continued)

Social: ☎ ☎ ☎ ☎ ☎
Q of L: ★ ★ ★
Admissions: (706) 542-8776
Email Address: adm-info@ uga.edu

Strong Programs:
Finance
Psychology
Biology
Marketing
Journalism
Ecology
Agricultural Sciences
Public Relations

UGA's Grady School of Journalism is home to the prestigious Peabody Awards.

When the weekend comes, students know how to have a good time. "The party scene is alive and well with house parties, frat parties, and downtown Athens," says a senior. Fraternities and sororities attract 20 percent of the men and 31 percent of the women, respectively. Alcohol is prohibited in the dorms, but as at most schools, the determined manage to imbibe anyway. There are also more than 700 student organizations for students to choose from. A favorite campus tradition is ringing the Chapel bell for athletic victories as well as personal accomplishments. "Hearing the Chapel bell ring is a heartwarming sound because you know that regardless of what's going on in your day, there's a Bulldog out there who has something worth celebrating," cheers one happy Dawg.

The funky mix of shops, restaurants, clubs, and various music and cultural events found in downtown Athens is only a 10-minute walk from most residence halls. A senior explains that Athens is "far enough away from Atlanta to maintain the college community, yet close enough to provide an escape." Students enjoy getting involved in mentorship and volunteer programs in the Athens community, and philanthropic organizations like UGA Miracle, UGA HEROs, and CURE are some of the largest student groups on campus. Popular road trips include the Florida and Carolina beaches, and anywhere the Bulldogs are playing on a fall Saturday.

It's no stretch to claim that Athens residents worship UGA's perennially fierce football team. The Georgia–Florida rivalry is the stuff of lore: "The game takes place on neutral ground in Jacksonville, and since it coincides with fall break, 90 percent of the students go," says an accounting major. Teams compete in the tough Southeastern Conference, and men's and women's tennis, women's gymnastics and swimming and diving, and the equestrian team are especially competitive. Georgia's Debate Union enjoys consistent national success as well. Recreational sports are taken seriously too, with 45 clubs and 24 intramural sports available for students to compete in.

UGA's sheer size means you could coast through four years here as nothing more than a number. But with a little effort, that doesn't have to happen. Freshman seminars, research projects, study abroad, and honors courses offer the opportunity to graduate with a solid background in any number of areas and fond memories of Saturdays spent cheering on the Bulldogs—along with 92,000 of your closest friends. "There's a lot of pride at my school," confirms a senior. "Even the city of Athens brags on the Bulldawgs, and we all feel a part of something special."

The 2,500 students in UGA's highly regarded Honors Program enjoy special opportunities like Lunchbox Lectures and summer internships.

Overlaps

University of Florida, Michigan State, Ohio State, UC Davis, Virginia Tech, Georgia Tech, UNC at Chapel Hill, Clemson

If You Apply To ›

Georgia: Early action, regular decision. SATs or ACTs: required. Subject Tests: optional. Does not accept the Common Application.

Georgia Institute of Technology

Atlanta, GA 30332

As the South's premier technically oriented university, Ma Tech does not coddle her young. Students must contend with the sometimes mean streets of downtown Atlanta and fight through a wall of graduate students to talk with their professors. Architecture and big-time sports supplement the engineering focus. Tech's 61/39 male/female ratio is tempered by women from all-female Agnes Scott.

If you're looking for lazy days on the college green and hard-partying weekends, look elsewhere. You won't find those at Georgia Institute of Technology, the South's premier tech university, and a relatively new member of the elite Association of American Universities. What you will find are challenging courses that prepare you for a high-paying job as an engineer, architect, or computer scientist. "Tech is tough," reasons one student. "You have to want to be here." Even those who want to be there are happy to finally arrive at graduation day. What makes Tech a special place? "The fact that I survived it and got out with a degree," says a computer science major, only partially joking. As part of its efforts to become a top technological research university globally, Tech has developed an extensive offering of Massive Open Online Courses (MOOCs), available for free to the general public.

Located just off the Interstate in Georgia's capital city, Tech's 450-acre campus embraces 40 undergraduate residence halls, an aquatic center, a sports performance complex, and an amphitheater. Taking in the campus architecture is like traveling through time: building styles include the Georgian Revival and collegiate Gothic of the historic Hill District (listed on the National Register of Historic

"Tech is tough. You have to want to be here."

Places) and surrounding area, the International Style buildings constructed from the 1940s into the 1960s, the modernist structures of the 1970s and '80s, the post-modern facilities of the '90s, and the newly built high-tech facilities. All these styles coexist comfortably on a tree-filled, landscaped campus that serves as a green oasis in the midst of a dense urban environment.

Regardless of major, students must complete credit hours in social sciences, science, English and humanities, math, U.S. or Georgia history, U.S. and global perspectives, and wellness. Strong programs include math and computer science, as well as most types of engineering, especially industrial, biomedical, aerospace, civil, and mechanical. Students in several disciplines complete a Capstone Design course, in which they work in teams to design, build, and test prototypes of products with real-world applications. Aside from the technical fare, Tech's business college is increasingly popular, and its school of architecture has done pioneering work in historic preservation and energy conservation. Among the architecture program's alumni is Michael Arad, designer of the September 11 memorial in lower Manhattan. The prelaw certificate is a boon to aspiring patent attorneys, as is the minor in law, science, and technology. Tech has plenty of liberal arts courses, but students say history, philosophy, and English aren't the reasons why most students enroll.

Courses at Tech are "extremely rigorous," says a senior, at least in the sciences and engineering. "Grading on a curve creates hypercompetitive situations because your absolute grade is largely irrelevant—you just have to do better than most of the others." Classes tend to be big—26 percent of those taken by undergraduates have more than 50 students—and a computer science major warns that Tech is "absolutely horrible for things like freshman math classes. You're typically taught by TAs. Things get better as you progress and get to know professors." Faculty members have real-world experience; some are Nobel Prize winners and former NASA astronauts.

Tech's demanding workload means it's common to spend five years getting your degree. Students say the course selection process can be frustrating, and getting into required courses can be an issue. One positive factor contributing to delayed graduation dates is the popular co-op program, through which more than 3,000 students earn money for their education while gaining on-the-job experience with more than 700 organizations worldwide. Tech offers more than 90 exchange programs and 30 faculty-led study abroad programs; 52 percent of students have some sort of international study or internship experience by the time they graduate. An honors program

Website: www.gatech.edu
Location: City Center
Public
Total Enrollment: 20,349
Undergraduates: 13,855
Male/Female: 61/39
SAT Ranges: ERW 670–730, M 680–770
ACT Ranges: 30–34
Financial Aid: 62%
Pell Grant: 11%
Expense: Pub $ $ $
Student Loans: 30%
Average Debt: $ $ $
Applicants: 31,467
Accepted: 23%
Enrolled: 39%
Grad in 6 Years: 86%
Returning Freshmen: 97%
Academics: ✑ ✑ ✑ ✑ ✑
Social: ☎ ☎
Q of L: ★ ★
Admissions: (404) 894-4154
Email Address: admission@gatech.edu

Strong Programs:
Industrial Engineering
Biomedical Engineering
Aerospace Engineering
Civil Engineering
Mechanical Engineering
Computer Science
Mathematics
Architecture

Fifty-two percent of students have some sort of international study or internship experience by the time they graduate.

is available for the extremely motivated, and the Center for the Study of Women, Science, and Technology offers a living/learning community and research opportunities for women in STEM fields.

Most Georgia Tech students are too focused on school or their co-op jobs to care much about politics, although improving campus resources for mental health and the LGBTQ community has been a hot topic of late. According to a senior, "There are a lot of left-brain types here—high on the introspection and thinking, low on the social skills," says a senior. And though they may be united in their pursuit of technical expertise, the campus is hardly homogeneous: African Americans account for 7 percent of the student body, Hispanics 7 percent, Asian Americans 21 percent, and multiracial students 3 percent. Fifty-eight percent of undergraduates hail from Georgia, and there are large contingents from California, Florida, and Texas; 9 percent come from abroad. To limit burgeoning enrollment, out-of-state applicants must meet somewhat higher criteria than their Georgia counterparts. Georgia residents who graduated high school with a B average also benefit from the state's HOPE Scholarship, which covers about 74 percent of their tuition over four years, assuming they keep their grades up in college. In addition, Tech has eliminated loans for Georgia residents with family incomes below $33,300 a year—although just 11 percent of freshmen qualify for the Pell Grant. Merit scholarships averaging $5,690 are available, as are 182 athletic scholarships.

> **"There are a lot of left-brain types here—high on the introspection and thinking, low on the social skills."**

> *To limit burgeoning enrollment, out-of-state applicants must meet somewhat higher criteria than their Georgia counterparts.*

Forty-three percent of undergrads live in the dorms, where freshmen are guaranteed a room. A senior says that the quality of residence halls varies widely: "Some dorms are new, apartment-style, and nice. Others are foul dungeons." The campus dining halls offer "little variety and less quality," according to another student. Off-campus housing is generally comfortable, but parts of the surrounding neighborhood are sketchy. "Far too many cars are broken into or stolen," says one student. "There's usually a couple of armed robberies (at least) per semester." Campus police are said to be quick to respond to incidents. VOICE is a campuswide initiative working to address the issue of campus sexual assault.

Being located smack-dab in the middle of "Hot-Lanta" does have its upside: an endless supply of clubs, bars, movie theaters, restaurants, shopping, and museums, both in midtown Atlanta and the Buckhead district. "Atlanta is not a college town," reasons a computer science major. "However, it is the best thing going in Georgia," with friendly, young residents, good cultural activities, beautiful green spaces, and a booming economy. The city also offers plenty of community service opportunities. Fraternities draw 26 percent of Tech's men and sororities attract 30 percent of the women, and members may live in their chapter houses. Alcohol flows freely at frat parties, but otherwise, students say, Tech's policies against open containers and underage drinking are strictly enforced. "There's not much in the way of social life here outside of the frats," says a senior. "You have your group of friends and you do your own thing." The best road trips include Florida's beaches, which are a half-day's drive, and Athens, Georgia, for basketball or football games against the University of Georgia.

> **"Some dorms are new, apartment-style, and nice. Others are foul dungeons."**

> *When the weekend comes, students throw off their lab coats and become wild members of the "Rambling Wreck from Georgia Tech."*

Tech's Division I varsity sports teams (the Yellowjackets) have become as bigtime as any in the South, and when the weekend comes, students throw off their lab coats and become wild members of the "Rambling Wreck from Georgia Tech." Men's swimming, women's basketball, and men's and women's track and golf have been successful in recent years. About 40 percent of students participate in the university's 43 club and 20 intramural sports. Among Tech's many other traditions is "stealing the T," in which students try to remove the huge yellow letter T from the tower on the administration building and return it to the school by presenting it to a member of the faculty or administration. The addition of alarms, motion sensors, and heat sensors on the T has made the task more difficult, but "certainly not impossible for a Georgia Tech engineer," says an electrical engineering major. And then there's the Mini 500, a 15-lap tricycle race around a parking garage with three pit stops, a tire change, and a driver rotation.

Forget fitting the mold; the engineers of Georgia Tech are proud to say they make it. Self-direction, ambition, and motivation will take you far here, as will dexterity with a graphing calculator and a fondness for highly complex software algorithms. And despite their complaints about the workload, the social life (or lack thereof), and the safety of their surrounding neighborhood, Tech students do have a soft spot for their school. Says one student, "I love a good challenge, and Tech is perfect for that."

If You Apply To ›

Georgia Tech: Early action, regular decision. SATs or ACTs: required. Subject Tests: optional. Accepts the Common Application.

Gettysburg College

300 North Washington Street, Gettysburg, PA 17325

The college by the battlefield is strong in U.S. history—that's a given. The natural sciences and business are also popular, and political science majors enjoy good connections in D.C. and New York City. For a small school, participation in undergraduate research and study abroad is notably high.

Whether the reference is to the Pennsylvania town steeped in Civil War history or the small, high-caliber college located in the famed battlefield's backyard, a certain pride and reverence are immediately evident when the name "Gettysburg" is uttered. This feeling is not lost on students at Gettysburg College, who come to southeastern Pennsylvania to acquaint themselves with American history while gearing up for the future. "I have been afforded opportunities inside and outside the classroom that I could not have imagined," says one senior.

Situated in the midst of gently rolling hills, Gettysburg's 200-acre campus is "a historical treasure," an eclectic assemblage of Georgian, Greek, Romanesque, Gothic Revival, and modern architecture, plus several styles not easily categorized. One campus building—Penn Hall—was actually used as a hospital during the Battle of Gettysburg. Rumor has it that ghostly Civil War soldiers can still be seen walking the grounds. Major renovations to the College Union Building and a new addition to the Dining Center are the latest construction projects.

General education requirements cover typical liberal arts disciplines and goals, and students in all majors must complete a capstone requirement. The English department, home of the *Gettysburg Review*, is among the strongest at Gettysburg, as are the natural sciences, especially biology and biochemistry, which are well endowed with state-of-the-art equipment. The fine psychology department offers opportunities for students to participate in faculty research. Political science, organization and management studies, and economics are also popular, as is, of course, the excellent history department, which is bolstered

Website: www.gettysburg.edu
Location: Suburban
Private
Total Enrollment: 2,400
Undergraduates: 2,400
Male/Female: 47/53
SAT Ranges: ERW 640–710, M 630–700
ACT Ranges: 26–30
Financial Aid: 75%
Pell Grant: 28%
Expense: Pr $ $ $ $
Student Loans: 62%
Average Debt: $ $ $
Applicants: 6,384
Accepted: 46%
Enrolled: 25%
Grad in 6 Years: 87%
Returning Freshmen: 90%
Academics: ✍ ✍ ✍ ½
Social: ☎ ☎ ☎

(continued)

Q of L: ★ ★ ★
Admissions: (717) 337-6100
Email Address: admiss@
  gettysburg.edu

Strong Programs:
History
English
Biology
Psychology
Political Science
Organization and Management
  Studies
Economics
Civil War Era Studies

The excellent history department is bolstered by the school's nationally recognized and prestigious Civil War Institute.

The women's lacrosse team won its third national championship in 2018.

by the school's nationally recognized and prestigious Civil War Institute and its minor in Civil War Era studies. Students may choose from three degrees within the Sunderman Conservatory of Music, and a cooperative dual-degree program in engineering is available.

"The academic climate is heavily focused on active discussions and participation in and outside of the classroom," says an economics major. Sixty-nine percent of classes enroll fewer than 20 students, and the small class sizes make for close student/faculty relationships; the academic honor code contributes to the atmosphere of community and mutual trust as well. The popular first-year seminars explore topics such as STEM from the Ground Up and How the White House Works; participants live in the same residence hall and are in the same first-year residential college program.

Undergraduate research is a big emphasis at Gettysburg, with roughly 60 percent participating across all disciplines. The annual Celebration colloquium in the spring allows students to present and showcase their work. The chemistry department offers a summer cooperative research program between students and professors in which they work on a joint publication. Outstanding seniors may participate in the Senior Scholars' Seminar, doing independent study on a major contemporary issue, but all students have a chance to do independent work and/or design their own majors. Most departments offer structured internships, and Gettysburg sponsors a Washington semester with American University and a United Nations semester through Drew University in New Jersey. Participation in study abroad programs is also high, with 60 percent of students traveling to more than 100 programs worldwide for the same price they pay for regular tuition back home.

Gettysburg's "hardworking" and "academically driven" student body is mostly middle- to upper-middle-class. Just 26 percent are native Pennsylvanians, and 7 percent are international. African Americans represent 4 percent of the student body, Asian Americans 2 percent, Hispanics 8 percent, and multiracial students 3 percent. Both sides of the political aisle are well represented on campus. "Everything is a potential hot-button issue these days," comments a sociology major, adding that "the school does an adequate job of providing a respectful conversational environment." No athletic scholarships are available, but merit-based academic scholarships average $13,300. Twenty-eight percent of freshmen are Pell-eligible.

Campus housing at the 'Burg is guaranteed for all four years. "First-years live in traditional dorms, sophomores typically live in dorm or suite-style (bedroom with bathroom) buildings, juniors and seniors are typically in apartment-style housing," explains a student. Student rooms have been added in renovated historical properties on campus (some reputed to be haunted). The top scholars in each class get first crack at the best rooms, and freshmen are required to live in the residence halls. Off-campus apartments lure 6 percent of the student body away. There are a variety of dining options, including the Dining Center, Bullet Hole, and Dive. "All of our food is prepared fresh with many healthy and delicious options," states a junior. Concerning safety, a senior says, "Campus security is very good and very visible."

"The academic climate is heavily focused on active discussions."

"Most of the social life takes place on campus," says one student, and it mostly involves the Greek system and 120 other student groups. Thirty-two percent of the men and 35 percent of the women go Greek. Greek parties are open and attract crowds eager to dance the night away, although students insist they're not the only source of fun on campus. The Campus Activities Board provides alternative social events, including concerts, comedians, bus trips to Georgetown, movies, and campus coffeehouses. Officially the campus is dry, but as on many such campuses, drinking can be done, students report.

The orchards and rolling countryside surrounding the campus are peaceful and scenic, and there is a small ski slope nearby. "The Center for Public Service provides a lot of opportunities to make positive change in our community through volunteer work, immersion trips, and social projects," says an economics major; 86 percent of students actively volunteer. Many participate in the November 19 Fortenbaugh Lecture by noted historians commemorating the Gettysburg Address and in the yearly wreath-laying ceremony to commemorate the birthday of Dwight D. Eisenhower, who lived in Gettysburg after leaving the White House. Students get free passes to the historic attractions in town, though tourist season is a common complaint among students. But those who want to escape can do so—the campus is within an hour and a half of Washington, D.C., and considerably closer to Baltimore, where students enjoy the scenic Inner Harbor area.

> **"Gettysburg students have a network of friends and faculty supporting their every decision."**

Gettysburg sponsors 24 varsity sports—12 for men and 12 for women—that compete at the Division III level as the Bullets. The women's lacrosse team won its third national championship in 2018, and women's golf, women's basketball, and men's swimming claimed Centennial Conference titles the same year. Men's lacrosse and women's softball are also competitive. The annual football game against Dickinson draws a good turnout, and the Little Brown Bucket, mahogany with silver handles, is passed to the team that wins. Intramural and club sports are popular too.

At Gettysburg, students stay true to their slogan: "Do Great Work." A junior says, "Gettysburg students have a network of friends and faculty supporting their every decision." Students wanting personal attention from professors, solid academics, and an area rich with history might consider getting their education with a Gettysburg address.

Overlaps

Dickinson, Franklin & Marshall, Bucknell, Lafayette, Muhlenberg, University of Richmond, American University, William and Mary

If You Apply To ›

Gettysburg: Early decision I and II, regular decision. SATs or ACTs: optional (required for students applying for academic merit scholarships). Subject Tests: optional. Accepts the Common Application.

University of Glasgow: See page 374.

Gonzaga University

502 East Boone Avenue, Spokane, WA 99258-0102

Best known outside the Northwest for its successes on the basketball court, Gonzaga is a medium-sized private university with a picturesque residential campus in an urban setting. Offers classic Jesuit education with rigorous core and emphasis on service, though only half of undergrads are Roman Catholic. Spokane is not as cosmopolitan as Seattle or San Francisco. Less selective than Santa Clara or USD, comparable to USF. Good bet for those who relish school spirit.

Website: www.gonzaga.edu
Location: Small City
Private
Total Enrollment: 5,655
Undergraduates: 5,110
Male/Female: 48/52
SAT Ranges: ERW 590–680, M 590–670
ACT Ranges: 26–30
Financial Aid: 99%
Pell Grant: 12%
Expense: Pr $
Student Loans: 53%
Average Debt: $ $ $
Applicants: 7,613
Accepted: 65%
Enrolled: 25%
Grad in 6 Years: 87%
Returning Freshmen: 94%
Academics: ✍ ✍ ✍
Social: 🐿 🐿 🐿 🐿
Q of L: ★ ★ ★
Admissions: (800) 322-2584
Email Address: admissions@gonzaga.edu

Strong Programs:
Engineering
Nursing
Business
Accounting
Biology
Psychology
Social Sciences

Gonzaga University burst into the nation's frontal lobes in 1999 when its men's basketball team fought its way to the quarterfinals of the Division I tournament. Consistent success in the tournament since then has softened the Zag's image as a midsized David doing battle with Goliaths like UNC at Chapel Hill. What has lingered, though, is the image of a solid regional liberal arts university committed to the Jesuit ideal of educating the whole person: mind, body, and spirit.

Founded in 1887 by the Society of Jesus (Jesuits) as a mission, the school takes its name from St. Aloysius Gonzaga, a 16th-century Italian aristocrat who joined the Society of Jesus and was martyred while serving victims of an epidemic. The campus occupies 152 picturesque acres along the Spokane River, only a 15-minute walk from downtown Spokane. The Centennial Trail, a 37-mile paved bike path, borders the campus and river. Architectural styles range from the Romanesque College Hall to the sleek PACCAR Center for Applied Science. The university's Crosby Collection contains recordings, photographs, and other memorabilia pertaining to Gonzaga's most famous alumnus, crooner Bing. The LEED Gold–certified Hemmingson Center boasts ample space for the student body association, student clubs and organizations, and the main dining hall. Gonzaga opened its 58,000-square-foot Woldson Performing Arts Center in 2019.

> **"[Professors] practically beg their students to get to know them through visiting office hours."**

Consistent with its Jesuit liberal arts tradition, Gonzaga requires undergraduates to complete an extensive core curriculum, beginning with a First-Year Seminar and ending with a Core Integration Seminar. Centered around the question of how students may "educate themselves to become women and men for a more just and humane global community," the core includes courses in English composition, speech communication, and critical reasoning, with doses of philosophy and religious studies, literature, scientific inquiry, and mathematics. Writing, social justice, and global studies are emphasized throughout the core. Although Gonzaga is a Jesuit school and sponsors 16 spiritual retreats annually, there are no requirements to attend mass or chapel.

Gonzaga offers more than 50 undergraduate majors in five divisions: the College of Arts and Sciences and the schools of Business Administration, Education, Engineering and Applied Science, and Nursing and Human Physiology. Students say some of the strongest programs are engineering, nursing, and business, with accounting being a particular strength. Biology majors have the option of adding a research concentration to their degree, while psych students may focus on specialized areas of interest such as child psychology and clinical research. Newly established programs include a minor in solidarity and social justice.

"Most Gonzaga students do not shy away from hard work," says a computer science major, and while the workload can get challenging, students are supportive and often work together. Students say professors are knowledgeable and ready to help, and most "practically beg their students to get to know them through visiting office hours," says a senior. No graduate or teaching assistants teach classes, and one-third of undergraduate courses have fewer than 20 students. Students also praise the school for providing a plethora of resources, including strong support for students with learning disabilities. A criminal justice and philosophy major says the Career and Professional Development staff has "helped me clean up my résumé, research internships, and given me the tips I needed to attend a career fair and not make a total fool of myself."

Top students may apply for the Honors Program, and many of them show off their research projects during Undergraduate Research Week. Other special offerings include the three-year Hogan Entrepreneurial Leadership Program, open to high-achieving first-year students seeking an entrepreneurial leadership minor in addition

The centerpiece program for study abroad is Gonzaga-in-Florence.

to their regular majors, and the Comprehensive Leadership Program, which provides a minor in leadership studies. Gonzaga's Army ROTC program (Bulldog Battalion) ranks as one of the best anywhere. The centerpiece program for study abroad is Gonzaga-in-Florence, which allows students of any major, including engineering, to study at Gonzaga's campus in Florence, Italy, without delaying their four-year path to graduation. A junior calls Gonzaga-in-Florence "one of the most transformative and influential experiences of my college career." Overall, the university offers more than 60 international programs, in which 53 percent of students participate.

Gonzaga offers more than 50 service-learning courses, and 57 percent of undergrads participate in community service.

"Gonzaga students are excited, passionate, service-driven, and open-minded," according to one history major. One percent of Zags are from other countries, with the rest almost equally divided between Washingtonians and out-of-staters. African Americans make up just 1 percent of the student body, while Hispanics represent 11 percent, Asian Americans 4 percent, and multiracial students 7 percent. The lack of diversity on campus is a frequent complaint,

"The downtown Spokane area is full of spunk and character."

and a senior says, "If you are a student of color, I highly encourage and advise you to join a cultural club, because there are a lot of white students and a lot of white voices." Social activism on campus tends to revolve around issues of race, sexual orientation, and religion. The school awards merit scholarships averaging $15,500 and athletic scholarships.

Sixty percent of undergraduates reside in campus housing. Freshmen and sophomores are required to live on campus and purchase a meal plan, but space for upperclassman is limited, so most juniors and seniors find their own housing in the surrounding neighborhood. On-campus residence halls offer a variety of living styles, including both co-ed and single-sex corridors and floors, and several living/learning communities. A senior explains that residence halls "range in how old they are and how nice some of the facilities are. Regardless of this, you will find devout fans of each residence hall." Campus meals are primarily served in the new COG cafeteria, and a secondary education major says, "The dining facilities are amazing and the meals are occasionally great as well." Students say Gonzaga has worked to improve education around issues of sexual assault, promoting increased awareness.

Since Gonzaga's mascot is the Bulldog, the student cheering section is naturally known as the Kennel.

There are no fraternities or sororities at Gonzaga, but students say that their absence has hardly put a damper on social life, either on or off campus. Students agree that while "there is a noticeable party scene off campus in the houses of upperclassmen," they don't feel pressured to drink. Underage students found in possession of drugs or alcohol may be required to take an awareness and safety program. The Hemmingson Center hosts a variety of social activities, and a favorite event is the annual spring music festival, featuring bands, games, food, and a beer garden. With roughly 215,000 residents, Spokane is the second-

"Every Zag should experience [tent city] at least once."

largest city in Washington but has the feel of a much smaller city. "The downtown Spokane area is full of spunk and character," says a public relations major, and it provides plenty of restaurants, outdoor recreation, and community activities.

The culture of Gonzaga places strong emphasis on issues of social justice and service. The school offers more than 50 service-learning courses, and 57 percent of undergraduates participate in some form of community service. "Being involved in the community is a specific Jesuit trait that we all try to live out," says one student. During winter, spring, and summer breaks, nearly 200 students travel to sites across the nation to participate in community service projects, and the university ranks tops in alumni Peace Corps volunteers nationwide.

GU's 14 intercollegiate teams, known as the Zags or Bulldogs, compete in the Division I West Coast Conference. In the absence of football (shut down in 1941 and never resurrected), basketball is both king and queen. The men's team reached the championship game in 2017 and the Sweet 16 in 2018. Men's and women's basketball both won conference titles in 2018, and baseball and women's rowing are also recent conference champs. Intramurals and club sports are popular, attracting 58 percent of undergraduates each year. Outdoorsy types can take advantage of five ski areas within a 90-mile radius, and GU Outdoors sponsors rafting, hiking, and skiing excursions, including trips to Montana and Canada.

School spirit is a big deal at Gonzaga—mainly when it comes to sports and especially when the opponent is St. Mary's College of California. Since Gonzaga's mascot is the Bulldog, the student cheering section is naturally known as the Kennel. Students go through an elaborate process for tickets to big home basketball games that involves strategic tweeting and living in a tent city days before the opening tip. "It's insanity," confesses one sophomore, "but it's so much fun." A junior adds, "Every Zag should experience this at least once."

At Gonzaga, "spirit" takes on multiple meanings. Basketball may inspire the most vocal outpourings of school spirit, but students say that the religious and humanistic values to which the university has long been committed run deep. "Community is a word tossed around quite frequently at all college campuses," says a psychology major, "but at GU, community is almost a belief."

If You Apply To ›

Gonzaga: Early action, regular decision. SATs or ACTs: required. No Subject Tests. Accepts the Common Application.

Gordon College

255 Grapevine Road, Wenham, MA 01984

Gordon is the most prominent Christian college in New England and competes nationally with Wheaton (IL) and Messiah, though it lacks the prestige of the former. Not quite in Boston, but close enough to be within easy reach. Extensive core curriculum shapes the undergraduate experience. Emphasis on integrating faith and learning.

Evangelical Christian values are at the heart of almost all aspects of life at this New England college, where faith sets the tone for campus life inside and outside the classroom. Gordon College is unique in that it is the only Christian college of its type that has no formal denominational ties. Founded as a missionary training school "to prepare the people of God to do the work of God," the college now sees its mission as promoting intellectual maturity and Christian character. Always evolving, Gordon is sharpening its offerings across the board, from international affairs to music education to leadership programs, and looking to increase its diversity. The students revel in the atmosphere. "Gordon is a safe and comfortable place to wrestle with faith and expand our worldview," says a senior.

Gordon is located on Massachusetts's scenic North Shore, three miles from the Atlantic Coast and 25 miles from Boston. The campus sits on more than 480 forested acres, landscaped with flowers and boasting four large ponds. Most campus structures are Georgian-influenced traditional redbrick, except for the administration building, Frost Hall, an old stone structure modeled after a European castle that provides an eye-catching contrast. The Olsen Science Center, an 83,456-square-foot science and technology center at the heart of the campus, is home to a fabrication lab, a vivarium, an aquarium, a human cadaver lab, and a biology greenhouse space.

Religious commitment at Gordon is seen as the foundation of serious academic learning rather than a threat to free inquiry. Gordon's core curriculum includes distribution requirements in Biblical studies and theology, the fine arts, humanities, social sciences, historical perspectives, natural sciences, math, and computer science. Freshmen complete an outdoor education requirement and take The Great Conversation, a writing-intensive first-year seminar that helps them learn how to integrate faith into their academic experience.

Gordon's most popular majors are psychology, business administration, biology, and English language and literature. Biblical studies, physics, theatre arts, and music are also strong programs, although they may draw fewer students. Finance is available as a major—a rarity at small Christian colleges—as is a 3–2 engineering program, and biochemistry is now an option. "The majority of classes are considered difficult and students are pushed to do their best," observes a history and biblical studies major. Sixty-three percent of classes have fewer than 20 students, and students say professors are helpful. "The personal attention I've gotten from my professors is remarkable—even among institutions of our size," says a sophomore.

> "The majority of classes are considered difficult."

The Global Honors Institute encompasses a variety of honors opportunities for high-achieving students, including the Jerusalem and Athens Forum, a yearlong great books seminar; the Pike Honors Program, which allows students to design their own majors; and the four-year Global Honors Scholars program, which offers tuition support and significant travel experiences. The college operates its own study abroad programs in several locations, including its signature program in Orvieto, Italy, and it partners with other programs to offer more than 40 approved study locations; 39 percent of students participate. The recently established Career and Connection Institute is working to expand opportunities for internships, mentorship, and preparation for graduate school and the workplace.

Gordon is one of two top evangelical schools that require applicants to describe how their faith impacts their lives and to affirm that they recognize the Bible as "the Word of God and hence fully authoritative in matters of faith and conduct" (see also Wheaton College in Illinois). Gordon's trustees have reaffirmed the college's policy forbidding "homosexual practice." While observation of the Sabbath is expected, Gordon gives students a bit more latitude than some Christian colleges in determining how they will "separate themselves from worldliness."

Gordon students are interested in "outdoor adventure, spiritual discovery, and overcommitment to both academics and extracurricular activities," says a psychology major. Thirty-two percent of students are native to Massachusetts, and 9 percent are international. Up to 6 percent of students are Roman Catholic. African Americans constitute 6 percent, Asian Americans 5 percent, Hispanics 8 percent, and multiracial students 3 percent. Students say LGBTQ, gender equity, and immigration issues have been hot topics of late, although one notes, "Because it's a Christian school, even the liberals aren't too liberal." Institutional non-need-based scholarships and grants worth an average of $15,600 are offered to qualified undergrads, and 25 percent of incoming freshmen are eligible for the Pell Grant. Each year, the Clarendon Scholars program provides hefty scholarships, as well as mentoring and leadership training, to twelve selected freshmen from urban areas.

> "Because it's a Christian school, even the liberals aren't too liberal."

Eighty-eight percent of Gordon students live in the residence halls, which are clustered either around the central quad or on an area of campus known as The Hill. "Even the oldest residence halls are nice and spacious," says a freshman. Men and

(continued)

Accepted: 89%
Enrolled: 16%
Grad in 6 Years: 70%
Returning Freshmen: 83%
Academics: ✍ ✍ ✍
Social: ☎ ☎
Q of L: ★ ★ ★ ★
Admissions: (866) 464-6736
Email Address: admissions@gordon.edu

Strong Programs:
Psychology
Business Administration
Biology
English Language and
  Literature
Biblical Studies
Physics
Theatre Arts
Music

Honors opportunities include the Jerusalem and Athens Forum, a yearlong great books seminar.

women live in separate wings of the same buildings—separated by a lobby, a lounge, and a laundry room. Persons of the opposite sex may traverse these barriers only at specified times. Permission to move off campus may be granted by petition, but the requirements for doing so are stringent. Students report that meals in the main dining hall, which overlooks a pond and doubles as a study area at night, "have improved significantly" thanks to a change in food service provider. "Our campus police are wonderful individuals who are dedicated to protecting our students," says a senior. Gordon recently revised its sexual misconduct policy, and a junior says it is "taking the issue much more seriously."

Gordon's student-led Campus Events Council organizes activities like movie showings, dances, and coffeehouses held in Chester's Place, a student-run coffee shop with a pub atmosphere, named after a cat. But campus social life can be lacking, since social events are not held every week and the school doesn't have, in the words of one senior, "a pure student center with activities or other things to help students congregate and enjoy each other's company." There is also no Greek system.

> "Gordon strives to keep [the student/faculty] relationship at the forefront of everything."

Still, students highly anticipate annual events like Christmas Gala and the Gordon Globes student film festival, during which students dress up and walk a red carpet. The "hilarious" Golden Goose talent show, which pits all four classes against each other, is another favorite tradition. Drinking and smoking are forbidden on campus (and may result in suspension or expulsion); those who are 21 or older may drink off campus, but are expected to do so responsibly. The town of Wenham offers "cute shops and restaurants along with other oddities—like used bookstores, jewelry shops, and fresh markets."

For those who love the outdoors, Gordon's setting on rugged Cape Ann is ideal, and it attracts its share of tourists. The campus has cross-country ski trails and ponds for swimming, canoeing, and skating. The ocean is a quick bike ride away, nice beaches are available on Cape Cod and in Maine, and students frequently ski New Hampshire's nearby White Mountains. Volunteering through a prison ministry and in soup kitchens and local churches is popular, and domestic and international mission trips take students all over, including West Virginia, Nicaragua, and Northern Ireland. Boston is 25 miles away by a five-minute drive to the T, the city's public transit system, so access to weekend diversions (and excellent internship opportunities) is relatively easy. Gordon students enjoy free entry to the city's Museum of Fine Arts and can also attend Harvard lectures for free.

Gordon's Fighting Scots compete in Division III athletics, and "a good portion of the student body comes out to the games" when the opponent is rival Endicott College, says a history major. Men's soccer, men's basketball, and women's field hockey have won Commonwealth Coast Conference championships. About a third of the student body participates in club and intramural sports. Everyone looks forward to the annual Highland Games, a day of games and traditional Scottish competitions between dorms.

For many students, Gordon's combination of Christian values, strong academics, and a relaxed setting is a winning one. Says one student, "Our school cultivates a great understanding between faculty and students. Gordon strives to keep this relationship at the forefront of everything, something I greatly appreciate."

If You Apply To ›

Gordon: Early action I and II, regular decision I and II. SATs or ACTs: required. Subject Tests: optional. Does not accept the Common Application. Applicants to music or art programs must audition or submit portfolio.

Goucher College

Baltimore, MD 21204

Once a staid women's college, Goucher added men and a more progressive ambience, making it similar to places like Vassar and Skidmore. Strategically located near Baltimore and not far from D.C., Goucher offers an excellent internship program. Unusual requirement that all students spend time studying or working abroad makes for a globally oriented community.

Goucher is the kind of place where quirky students take part in stellar programs ranging from the arts to public policy. The school's mission is to prepare students for a life of inquiry, creativity, and critical and analytical thinking. There's a decidedly international bent to the Goucher experience, including a robust study abroad program that sends students packing for far-flung locales around the globe. Says a senior, "Individuals who truly want to expand their mind and perspective through immersion in different cultures should seriously consider Goucher."

A former women's college that went co-ed in 1987, Goucher has a long-standing history of excellence. Phi Beta Kappa established a chapter on campus only 20 years after the college was founded, and the college ranks among the nation's top 50 liberal arts colleges in turning out students destined for Ph.D.s in the sciences. Set on 287 landscaped acres in the suburbs of Baltimore, Goucher's wooded campus features lush lawns, stately fieldstone buildings (the fieldstone is mined from local quarries), and rare trees and shrubs from all corners of the globe. The Athenaeum is the central gathering place, housing the library, an open forum for performances, exercise spaces, a café, and other vital college facilities. The First-Year Village opened in 2018, featuring three new residence halls and a dining facility near the center of campus.

> **"Goucher has taught me to stop looking at professors as superior beings with infinite knowledge."**

Goucher rolled out a redesigned curriculum in 2017, known as the Goucher Commons, that is intended to give students more freedom to pursue their own interests. While there are no distribution requirements, all students must demonstrate proficiency in writing, data analytics, and foreign language and culture and take coursework focusing on environmental sustainability and race, power, and perspective. First-year students begin with a First-Year Seminar course, juniors study abroad, and seniors synthesize and reflect on their educational experiences by completing a capstone experience or project and an electronic portfolio.

Of Goucher's offerings, the science departments (especially biology and chemistry) are arguably the strongest, bolstered by resources like a nuclear magnetic resonance spectrometer and an observatory with a six-inch refractor telescope. Communication and media studies and computer science are other traditional strengths, and the dance department is recognized as one of the best at a liberal arts school. The psychology, business management, economics, and English majors draw the highest enrollment. Unique minors include Arabic studies, historic preservation, and equine studies. Future engineers can take advantage of a 3–2 program offered in conjunction with the Whiting School of Engineering at The Johns Hopkins University.

According to a psychology major, Goucher academics focus on "growth, meaning that everyone receives individualized suggestions and attention specific to [their] strengths and improvement points." Faculty members here devote most of their time and energy to undergraduate teaching and have a good rapport with students.

Website: www.goucher.edu
Location: Suburban
Private
Total Enrollment: 1,544
Undergraduates: 1,426
Male/Female: 31/69
SAT Ranges: ERW 550–660, M 500–600
ACT Ranges: 23–29
Financial Aid: 93%
Pell Grant: 29%
Expense: Pr $ $
Student Loans: 64%
Average Debt: $ $ $ $
Applicants: 3,474
Accepted: 79%
Enrolled: 15%
Grad in 6 Years: 66%
Returning Freshmen: 78%
Academics: ✍ ✍ ✍
Social: ☎ ☎ ☎
Q of L: ★ ★ ★
Admissions: (410) 337-6100
Email Address: admissions@goucher.edu

Strong Programs:
Psychology
Business Management
Economics
English
Natural Sciences
Communication and Media Studies
Computer Science
Dance

"Goucher has taught me to stop looking at professors as superior beings with infinite knowledge, but instead to see them as fellow intellectuals that can facilitate classroom conversation," says a student. Each first-year has faculty and staff advisors to assist with the academic and overall adjustment to college life, which is made easier by Goucher's trademark small classes and individual instruction. Students roundly praise the Academic Center for Excellence (ACE), which offers academic support services from study-skills workshops and supplemental instruction to stress-reducing meditation sessions. Says a senior, "ACE contains some of the most calming, enlightened souls you'll encounter."

Goucher was the first college in the nation to require all of its undergraduates to study abroad at least once before graduation; more than 60 programs are available in more than 30 countries. Most students head for foreign lands during their junior year, and the experience is expected to complement their major field of study. About half of students embark on semester-long programs, while the other half engage in three-week intensive courses offered during January term or summer. Students may apply their Goucher financial aid packages to study abroad. Some Goucher students are also required to do a three-credit internship or off-campus experience related to their major, in addition to their academic work. Popular choices include congressional offices, museums, law firms, and newspapers.

> "The party scene is not particularly strong on campus."

Thirty-one percent of Goucher's students are homegrown and 4 percent are international; most of the rest hail from Pennsylvania, New York, New Jersey, and California. Women still outnumber men 2 to 1. African Americans make up 14 percent of the student body, Hispanics 9 percent, Asian Americans 4 percent, and multiracial students 5 percent. Twenty-nine percent of freshmen qualify for Pell Grants. The Center for Race, Equity, and Identity supports marginalized populations on campus and creates programming that encourages cross-cultural understanding. Students agree that social activism is prevalent on campus. "I always joke that while many schools bond over football or basketball, Goucher bonds over feminism and black activism," says a senior, adding, "It's nice though—it means our students really care." Goucher offers merit scholarships averaging $19,100 for those who are qualified but no athletic scholarships.

Ninety-three percent of students live on campus. Options range from brand-new residences for first-years to senior apartments. Upperclassmen select housing through lotteries, and a sophomore says, "Housekeeping is friendly, and most students get the rooms that they want. It's a very family-like atmosphere." Campus dining options, which include vegan and vegetarian fare, receive enthusiastic reviews. Says a senior, "We are dining pretty lavishly here." Students note that sexual assault on campus has been an issue in recent years, but, according to a freshman, "We strive every day to make sure that students are educated and those who have been assaulted feel comfortable coming forward."

> "The Goucher Poll is a pretty unique activity that monitors public perception of social issues and decisions."

"The party scene is not particularly strong on campus, but there are plenty of students who get together in each other's rooms to kick back and relax on the weekends," an environmental studies major says. Goucher has no sororities or fraternities, but the close-knit housing units hold periodic events, and the college hosts weekend movies, concerts, and lectures. Alcohol is ever-present but not the hub of the social scene. Major annual events include Gala, Winter Carnival, and Get into Goucher Day, which is "a huge festival held every spring that students look forward to. There are inflatables, great food, live music, and all kinds of other cool stuff," explains a senior. Students frequent the restaurants and bars in Towson, the small

The First-Year Village opened in 2018, featuring three new residence halls and a dining facility.

Goucher was the first college in the nation to require all of its undergraduates to study abroad at least once before graduation.

but bustling college town a five-minute walk away, and a car is useful for visiting Baltimore's Inner Harbor for entertainment. Roughly two-thirds of students volunteer, many through community-based learning programs that tie hands-on service experience in the local area with academic coursework. Students get involved in local politics too, says a senior: "The Goucher Poll is a pretty unique activity that monitors public perception of social issues and decisions via telephone poll."

The Gophers field a number of competitive teams in the Division III Landmark Conference. As Goucher was a women's college for so long, women's athletics are more highly developed than those at many co-ed schools. The co-ed equestrian team is perennially competitive, and men's tennis won its third straight conference championship in 2018. Men's golf, men's lacrosse, and women's field hockey are also frequent conference playoff contenders. Twenty percent of students play on club and intramural teams, with ultimate Frisbee being the most active. Students here can get creative with their recreational pursuits: the Humans vs. Zombies game originated at Goucher in 2005.

Far from a stagnant place, Goucher is constantly rethinking its mission and redirecting its resources to broaden student experiences in a hands-on, global way. "Goucher will force you to engage with challenging topics like sexism, racism, and classism," says a senior, but in a close-knit, supportive environment focused on personal growth for all kinds of learners.

Overlaps

Muhlenberg, Kenyon, Kalamazoo, Ohio Wesleyan, Lewis & Clark, Allegheny, Bard, American University

If You Apply To ›

Goucher: Early decision, early action, regular decision. SATs or ACTs: optional. Subject Tests: optional. Accepts the Common Application with supplement. Applicants may choose the alternative Goucher Video Application option.

Grinnell College

Grinnell, IA 50112

Iowa cornfields provide a surreal backdrop for Grinnell's funky, progressive, and talented student body. With about 1,700 students, Grinnell's population is 1,100 less than Oberlin's. That translates into tiny classes and tutorials. Second only to Carleton as the best liberal arts college in the Midwest. Grinnell's biggest challenge is simply getting prospective students to the campus. The cornfields make for a tight-knit campus community. Turns out lots of future Ph.D.s.

"Go West, young man, go West," Horace Greeley said to Josiah B. Grinnell in 1846. The result of Grinnell's wanderings into the rural cornfields, about an hour from Des Moines and Iowa City, is the remarkable college that bears his name. Despite its physical isolation, Grinnell is a powerhouse on the national scene. Ever progressive, it was the first college west of the Mississippi to admit African Americans and women, and the first in the country to establish an undergraduate political science department. It was once a stop on the Underground Railroad, and its graduates include Harry Hopkins, architect of the New Deal, and Robert Noyce, inventor of the integrated circuit, two people who did as much as anyone to change the face of American society in the 20th century. The school's 120-acre campus is an attractive blend of collegiate Gothic and modern Bauhaus academic buildings and Prairie-style houses. (Architecture buffs should take note of the dazzling Louis Sullivan bank facade just off campus.)

Website: www.grinnell.edu
Location: Rural
Private
Total Enrollment: 1,656
Undergraduates: 1,656
Male/Female: 46/54
SAT Ranges: ERW 640–740, M 670–770
ACT Ranges: 30–34
Financial Aid: 85%
Pell Grant: 16%
Expense: Pr $ $ $

*True to its liberal
arts focus, Grinnell
mandates a first-
semester writing
tutorial but doesn't
require anything else.*

True to its liberal arts focus, Grinnell mandates a first-semester writing tutorial, modeled after Oxford University's program, but doesn't require anything else. The roughly 35 tutorials, limited to about 12 students each, help enhance critical thinking, research, writing, and discussion skills, and allow first-year students to work individually with professors. Recent offerings include Criminal Brains, Icelandic Sagas, and Identity and Belonging in Iowa. "Tutorials are fun, interesting, and a great introduction to the academic possibilities that Grinnell has to offer," one student says. When it comes to declaring a major, students determine their own course of study with help from faculty. In an effort to show the practical relevance of the liberal arts, Grinnell assigns an "explanatory advisor" to each freshman to help her or him develop a sense of direction. They can then join one of seven "career communities," such as Education Professions and Business and Finance.

Departments in the social and natural sciences are strong, the latter bolstered by an influx of research grants. "Due to the college's enormous endowment, the sciences are top-notch, with the best equipment and graduate-level research at the undergraduate level," offers one student. Economics, computer science, political science, and biology are the most popular majors, and students recommend English, foreign languages (including German and Russian) and theater and dance too. Grinnell's

> **"[Tutorials are] a great introduction to the academic possibilities that Grinnell has to offer."**

admissions standards are high, and nearly one-third of graduates move on directly to graduate and professional schools. Students who don't mind studying, even on weekends, will be happiest here. "The academic climate is fairly intense," says one junior, "but not competitive." Sixty-three percent of classes have fewer than 20 students. Teaching is the top priority for Grinnell faculty members, and because the college awards no graduate degrees, there are no teaching assistants hanging around. "In general, profs are here to teach and have generous office hours," a sophomore says.

When the urge to travel arises, students may study abroad in the Grinnell-in-London program or in more than 80 other approved programs. Half of the students spend some time away from campus, and financial aid extends to study abroad. The Grinnell-in-Washington program combines coursework with an internship in the nation's capital. Forty-five percent of students participate in undergraduate research, including the Mentored Advanced Project program, which enables them to work closely with a faculty member on scholarly research or the creation of a work of art. Co-ops in architecture, business, law, medicine, and 3–2 engineering programs are also available.

Grinnell is a bit of Greenwich Village in corn country. Despite the rural environment, the college attracts an urban clientele, especially from the Chicago area. Only 7 percent of Grinnell students are from Iowa, while 20 percent are international. "We're quirky, often hippie and liberal, though increasingly diverse," a student observes. The student body is 7 percent Hispanic, 8 percent Asian American, 6 percent African American, and 5 percent multiracial. Women's rights, gay rights, labor rights, human rights, globalization, the environment, and groups such as the Intersectional Feminism Alliance, Social Entrepreneurs of Grinnell, and Grinnell Advocates (offering support for survivors of gender-based violence) set the tone. Admissions are need-blind, and

> **"In general, profs are here to teach and have generous office hours."**

the college meets 100 percent of admitted students' demonstrated financial need. Merit awards averaging $18,400 are handed out annually, but there are no athletic awards. Grinnell has a policy that at least 15 percent of every freshman class will be students whose parents did not go to college.

The college guarantees four years of campus housing, and 80 percent of students take advantage of the dorms, each of which has kitchen facilities, cable television, and a computer room. All but two dorms are co-ed, and after freshman year, students participate in a room draw, which can be stressful but usually works out. "The dorms are good," a student says, "with no ridiculously small rooms." Students say the area is safe but they are glad to have campus security available.

With no fraternities or sororities, all-campus parties and intramurals revolve mainly around the dorms. "I liken the experience to that of a cruise ship," says one student, "in that the students all stay in one place and entertainment is brought to campus." Each dorm periodically sponsors a party using wordplay from its name in the title. For instance, James Hall puts on the Mary-Be-James party, for which everyone comes in drag. As for alcohol, a senior reports, "Grinnell is not a dry campus, but there are no bars on campus and there is no peer pressure to drink or culture of problematic drinking." Grinnell's social groups and activities range from the SciFi Association and the Queer Rainbow Super Team to improvisational workshops, poetry readings, symposia, concerts, and movies. Highlights of the campus calendar include semiformal Winter

> **"We're quirky, often hippie and liberal, though increasingly diverse."**

and Spring Waltzes, where "most people wear formals and look very nice, not a common occurrence at a school where comfort is the usual standard and women rarely wear makeup," notes one student. At Disco, "everyone dresses up in clothes from the '70s and dances all night," and Titular Head is a festival of five-minute student films. During finals week, the library sponsors study breaks that have been known to feature free milk and cookies, choir sing-alongs, librarians reading their favorite picture books aloud, bubble-wrap-popping sessions, and other stress-relieving activities.

Grinnell (population 9,200), is "a small farming community with a nice downtown." The college's Service Learning and Civic Engagement Program works to bridge the town-gown gap by connecting students with more than 80 area nonprofit and community partners for service opportunities. Nearby Rock Creek State Park lends itself to biking, running, camping, kayaking, and cross-country skiing, and the Grinnell Outdoor Recreation Program sponsors a variety of pursuits, including off-campus trips and open rock-climbing sessions. There are a few bars and pizza joints downtown, but for those craving bright lights, Iowa City and Des Moines are within an hour's drive, and the college runs a shuttle service to them. Chicago and Minneapolis are each about four hours distant.

The Grinnell Pioneers compete in Division III athletics, and the men's basketball team has won national attention for an unusual run-and-gun offense that uses waves of five players like hockey shifts in an effort to wear down opponents. Recent conference champions include men's cross-country, women's golf, and men's and women's tennis and swimming and diving. About 30 percent of students play intramural sports, which offer competitive and noncompetitive options.

Grinnell wouldn't put a grin on every prospective college student's face. "Most of us don't apologize for what at first turns people off about Grinnell," explains a senior. "We like being in the middle of Iowa, we like that you've probably never heard of us, we love that you won't come here because you want a big name." But there's no denying that Grinnell—a first-rate liberal arts college in an unlikely location—is a real gem of a school, and one that is still relatively accessible.

Grinnell has a policy that at least 15 percent of every freshman class will be students whose parents did not go to college.

During finals week, the library sponsors study breaks that feature free milk and cookies, choir sing-alongs, and librarians reading picture books aloud.

Overlaps

Macalester, St. Olaf, Kenyon, Carleton, Colorado College, Vassar, Williams, Oberlin

If You Apply To ›

Grinnell: Early decision I and II, regular decision. SATs or ACTs: required. Subject Tests: optional. Accepts the Common Application.

5800 West Friendly Avenue, Greensboro, NC 27410

One of the few schools of Quaker heritage in the South, Guilford emphasizes a collaborative approach and is among the most liberal institutions below the Mason-Dixon line. A kindred spirit to Earlham in Indiana. With a notably high African American population and strong socioeconomic diversity, Guilford's signature program is justice and policy studies. Substantial number of older students enriches the campus culture.

Website: www.guilford.edu
Location: Small City
Private
Total Enrollment: 1,320
Undergraduates: 1,316
Male/Female: 47/53
SAT Ranges: ERW 440–585, M 463–558
ACT Ranges: 19–25
Financial Aid: 81%
Pell Grant: 49%
Expense: Pr $
Student Loans: 65%
Average Debt: $ $ $ $
Applicants: 1,865
Accepted: 91%
Enrolled: 20%
Grad in 6 Years: 56%
Returning Freshmen: 66%
Academics: ✎ ✎ ✎
Social: ☎ ☎
Q of L: ★ ★ ★ ★
Admissions: (336) 316-2100
Email Address: admission@guilford.edu

Strong Programs:
Business Administration
Biology
Psychology
Sport Management
Health Sciences
Religious Studies
Community and Justice Studies
Criminal Justice

If your idea of a rousing road trip is protesting in Washington, D.C., you'll likely find plenty of like-minded compatriots at Guilford College. Founded in 1837 by the Religious Society of Friends (Quakers), this left-leaning campus loves to debate just about any issue and get involved in the world around it. The student body is becoming more diverse in every respect, and campus inclusiveness is enhanced by a long-standing adult education program. "The students are extremely open to different ideas," says a senior.

Located on 350 wooded acres in northwest Greensboro, Guilford's redbrick buildings are mainly in the Georgian style. The school is the only liberal arts college in the Southeast with Quaker roots and is the oldest coeducational institution in the South and the third oldest in the nation. During the Civil War, Guilford was one of a few Southern colleges that remained open—perhaps because it was also an embarkation point on the Underground Railroad. All of the residence halls have recently been renovated, and 200 solar panels have made the campus more environmentally friendly.

Launched for fall 2019, Guilford's new general education program for traditional students, the Guilford Edge, features a fully redesigned curriculum that emphasizes team-based, interdisciplinary projects. As part of the new curriculum, Guilford has moved to a 12–3 academic calendar, in which every semester includes a twelve-week session as well as a three-week intensive course or off-campus experience. In addition to selecting a traditional, primary major, students also declare a "Q major," a passion or issue of their choosing that they explore in-depth, in the spirit of Quaker queries or questions. Guilford Edge also builds in more comprehensive academic and career advising, campuswide events aimed at enhancing community spirit, and training in ethical leadership development. With these changes, the college hopes to, among other things, boost applications and retention rates.

> **"In most classes, you will be doing some kind of hands-on learning."**

"The college is centered on the Quaker values of community, diversity, equality, excellence, integrity, justice, and stewardship," explains a senior. Students say Guilford's most popular programs are also some of its best: business administration, biology, psychology, sport management, health sciences, and religious studies. The signature justice and policy studies department offers majors in community and justice studies and criminal justice. A unique, issues-based minor in principled problem-solving experience (PPSE) combines interdisciplinary coursework with hands-on learning that addresses a complex social issue. The PPSE topic changes regularly; one recent topic, Every Campus a Refuge, focused on how to mobilize college campuses to provide housing and other support to refugees during their initial resettlement. Classes at Guilford are small, with 65 percent enrolling fewer than 20 students, helping to create a more personal environment. A student says, "As long as students are willing to be challenged, they will be forming strong student and professor relationships."

Guilford believes that experiential learning adds immeasurably to classroom work, so faculty-mentored research and travel are important emphases. "In most classes, you will be doing some kind of hands-on learning, applying the knowledge you're learning to real-life situations," says a health sciences and chemistry double major. In addition to standard laboratory equipment, science students have access to a lake, an organic farm, and 220 acres of woodland property on campus, which provide a rich resource for fieldwork in environmental and sustainability studies. Guilford has several endowed funds that support student scientific research and travel, including an award for Women in Physical Science. The college offers study abroad in 75 nations; 53 percent of students participate. The Brunnenberg Semester gives students a chance to live and learn in a 13th-century castle in the Italian Alps.

A unique minor in principled problem-solving experience addresses a complex social issue; one recent topic was Every Campus a Refuge.

Guilford students come from across the globe and a range of socioeconomic backgrounds; most are liberal and about 3 percent observe the Quaker religious tradition. Sixty-five percent of students are in-staters, and 1 percent are international. African Americans comprise 25 percent of the student body, Hispanics 9 percent, Asian Americans 3 percent, and multiracial students 4 percent; 49 percent of freshmen are eligible for Pell Grants. About 17 percent of full-time undergraduates are 23 or older and benefit from a large selection

"You will be pushed outside of your comfort zone in a lot of ways."

of evening classes and their own adult education orientation and counseling services. A junior says the population of adult students "adds a lot to classes because of their different life experiences." Qualified Guilford students receive merit scholarships, which average $10,000 apiece, but there are no athletic scholarships. The college now offers a four-year tuition guarantee.

All traditional students under the age of 23 are required to live on campus; Guilford's many older students are generally commuters and less involved in campus social life. On-campus apartments for juniors and seniors are comparable in price to off-campus digs. Bryan is the party dorm, while Mary Hobbs is all-female and Shore is gender-inclusive. "The dining options on campus are fantastic and the food is wonderful," cheers a student. Students say incidences of sexual assault have raised some concerns. "There were times when I did not feel safe on campus, especially after midnight," says one psychology major.

Guilford's social life revolves around student clubs and organizations, of which there are more than 50. Greek life is nonexistent, and alcohol is not allowed at college functions, but it remains fairly easy for underage students to drink—despite efforts to impose fines on those who are caught. "When the weather is nice, a lot of events happen outside, and it is easy to find people just lounging in the grass or down by the lake," says one student. Serendipity, a celebration of spring with games, mud wrestling, streakers, big-name musicians, and "a sense of mass disorientation," is a cherished tradition. Beyond the campus gates, students find all of the essentials—Target, Starbucks, some clubs in downtown Greensboro (only 10 minutes away), the ethnic restaurants of Tate Street, and the college's Quaker Village. Popular road trips include UNC at Chapel Hill (one hour), Asheville and the mountains (three and a half hours), and the famous Outer Banks beaches (four and a half hours).

Guilford's Division III athletic teams compete as the Fighting Quakers, and students cheer: "Fight, fight, inner light! Kill, Quakers, kill!"

Guilford's Division III athletic teams compete as the Fighting Quakers, and students cherish the oxymoron, as in their cheer: "Fight, fight, inner light! Kill, Quakers, kill!" Students root for the football team in the annual Soup Bowl against Greensboro College, while the men's golf team has brought home a slew of conference titles in recent years. The men's and women's basketball teams are also recent conference champs. Intramural and club sports draw 40 percent of the students. Because of Guilford's emphasis on developing the whole person, physically, mentally, and spiritually, students are encouraged to participate in school-sponsored outdoor adventures, such as a ropes course, sailing, and white-water rafting.

Overlaps

Earlham, Albright, Augsburg, Eckerd, Elmhurst, Roanoke, Lipscomb, Lynchburg

A popular Guilford mantra is: "How are you going to change the world?" And with students who'd rather get involved than sit back and watch, you can expect some pretty passionate answers to that question. It all goes back to Guilford's traditional Quaker goal of "educating individuals not only to live, but to live well." As one student explains it, "You will be pushed outside of your comfort zone in a lot of ways, but Guilford is also a place for growth."

If You Apply To ›

Guilford: Early decision, early action, rolling admissions. SATs or ACTs: optional (test-optional applicants must submit an additional essay). Accepts the Common Application with supplement.

Gustavus Adolphus College

800 West College Avenue, St. Peter, MN 56082

A touch of Scandinavia in southern Minnesota, GA is a guardian of the tried and true in Lutheran education. With Minnesotans comprising three-quarters of the students, GA is less national than cross-state rival St. Olaf. Extensive distribution requirements include exploring values and moral reasoning. Minnesota location makes for a homogeneous student body.

Website: www.gustavus.edu
Location: Small Town
Private
Total Enrollment: 2,170
Undergraduates: 2,170
Male/Female: 44/56
SAT Ranges: N/A
ACT Ranges: 24–30
Financial Aid: 96%
Pell Grant: 24%
Expense: Pr $ $
Student Loans: 71%
Average Debt: $ $ $ $
Applicants: 4,834
Accepted: 68%
Enrolled: 18%
Grad in 6 Years: 78%
Returning Freshmen: 88%
Academics: ✍ ✍ ✍
Social: ☎ ☎ ☎
Q of L: ★ ★ ★
Admissions:
   1-800-GUSTAVUS
Email Address: admission@ gustavus.edu

Strong Programs:
Biology

Gustavus Adolphus College is named for Sweden's King Gustav II Adolph (1594–1632), who is credited with making Sweden a major European power and defending Lutheranism against the Roman Catholics. While the king's battle victories earned him the title Lion of the North, he was also an advocate of education and culture. Save for the women now attending classes, King Gustav would probably feel at home at the college that bears his name, where a not-so-subtle Swedish influence pervades everything from the buildings to the curriculum. The college is the "epitome of Minnesota nice," says one sophomore admiringly.

The 340-acre GA campus is about 65 miles southwest of the Twin Cities. Not surprisingly, the prevailing architectural theme is Scandinavian, with mostly modern and semimodern brown brick buildings. Highlights include the 134-year-old Old Main and the centrally located Christ Chapel, with spires and shafts resembling a crown. Thirty bronze works by sculptor-in-residence Paul Granlund are strategically placed, and the 135-acre Linnaeus Arboretum and Interpretive Center offers plant study and retreats. The sidewalk running through the middle of campus is nicknamed the Hello Walk, because it's a tradition for students to greet one another as they pass—whether they know each other or not. The $30 million, LEED Platinum–certified Beck Academic Hall features state-of-the-art tools and technologies for the social sciences.

> "Professors expect you to give your best every day, and in return they give you their best."

To fulfill core requirements, Gustavus students have two options. The first, the Liberal Arts Perspective Curriculum, involves fulfilling standard distribution requirements in nine liberal arts areas, plus the First-Term Seminar, which covers critical thinking, writing, speaking, and recognizing and exploring values. The second option, known as the Three Crowns Curriculum, is an integrated 12-course sequence focused on classic works and ideas of the Western tradition, emphasizing connections between different disciplines. Three Crowns is limited to 60 students per entering class, filled on a first-come, first-served basis. In addition to the core courses, students must satisfy a writing-across-the-curriculum requirement, with three courses that have a substantial amount of writing.

In the classroom, students find an academic smorgasbord, as GA aims to offer an education both "interdisciplinary and international in perspective." There are interdisciplinary programs in Scandinavian studies; gender, women, and sexuality studies; and environmental studies, to name a few, and if neither those nor traditional departments suffice, students may design their own courses of study. While biology, psychology, communication studies, nursing, and management are among the most popular majors, physics and classics are also strengths, and students give high marks to GA's premed advising program and its offerings in music. For the professionally minded, Gustavus offers 3–2 engineering programs with the University of Minnesota and Minnesota State in Mankato. Overall, academics at Gustavus are rigorous, but students say small classes make it easy to form dependable study groups, and classmates don't compete for grades. "The courses require a lot of work both inside and outside the classroom," says one junior. "Professors expect you to give your best every day, and in return they give you their best." Students find faculty members not just knowledgeable but also friendly, especially when they're serving up a free meal for students during Midnight Express, which precedes final exams.

"Any time, any sport—if St. Olaf is in town, the event is packed."

During the January term, when winter winds force almost everyone indoors, Gustavus students (appropriately known as Gusties) may take concentrated courses on campus or pursue travel and co-op opportunities. The school sponsors study abroad programs at five colleges and universities in—surprise, surprise—Sweden, as well as in non-Scandinavian haunts such as India, Malaysia, Australia, Russia, and Scotland, and about half of the students participate. Learning opportunities also come from several internationally renowned meetings, such as the Nobel Conference, which brings Nobel laureates and other experts to campus for two days each October. Undergraduate research is a hallmark, and Gustavus Adolphus consistently ranks in the top 10 for papers presented at the National Conference on Undergraduate Research.

The sidewalk running through the middle of campus is nicknamed the Hello Walk, because it's a tradition for students to greet one another as they pass.

"Students are very involved," says one biology major, and they "shuffle about campus from classes, music ensembles, sports practices, interest groups, and community service." For all its good points, though, this liberal arts college is hardly a model of diversity. In fact, the population is more reminiscent of Garrison Keillor's Lake Wobegon: 78 percent of students are Caucasian, 78 percent are Minnesotan, and 48 percent are Lutheran. The school is working hard to increase diversity, but that continues to be a challenge. African Americans currently account for 3 percent of the student body, Hispanics 5 percent, Asian Americans 5 percent, and multiracial students 4 percent; international students add another 5 percent. Politically, the campus has its fair share of both conservatives and liberals, and students debate everything from campus issues to topics of global concern. The merit-based President's Scholarship program offers top students awards of up to $28,500 annually, while Dean's Scholarships range from $17,500 to $25,500. There are no athletic scholarships. Twenty-four percent of incoming students receive Pell Grants.

"Our core values of community, service, faith, justice, and excellence prevail both in and out of the classroom."

On-campus living is required for all four years, and only about 5 percent of students receive permission to live off campus as seniors, but Gusties don't have much to complain about. "The dorms are wonderful," says a student. "They stay full on the weekends and are well maintained." Substance-free floors are available, as is the

(continued)

Psychology
Communication Studies
Nursing
Management
Physics
Classics
Music

Crossroads International House, for students interested in languages and contemporary global issues. Single rooms and apartment-style suites, and some college-owned houses, are reserved for upperclassmen, who get priority at room draw. Students rave about the à la carte meal plan, and especially about the Marketplace dining hall. In response to recommendations from a student task force, the administration has updated its sexual misconduct policies.

Thirteen percent of the men and 12 percent of the women go Greek, but GA's social life does not revolve around fraternities and sororities. "From concerts, to sporting events, to movies and dances, there is never a shortage of things to do on the weekends," says one senior. Because students 21 and older may drink in their rooms—with the door closed—underage students can get alcohol if they want it, but students say drinking isn't a popular pastime here. GA's many musical ensembles all perform together at the Christmas in Christ Chapel concert. The chapel holds 1,500 people and performances usually sell out. Seventy percent of students participate in service projects, volunteering 15,000 hours each semester. Projects include working with children, the elderly, and the local animal shelter, as well as with Habitat for Humanity. The town of St. Peter has coffee shops and bowling, and the college offers periodic trips to Mankato, 10 miles away, and to the Twin Cities, for "real" shopping at the Mall of America or for a professional baseball, basketball, or hockey game.

When it comes to athletics, "Any time, any sport—if St. Olaf is in town, the event is packed," says a lusty Gustie fan. GA competes in Division III, and the men's and women's tennis teams are perennial contenders for the national championship title. Men's and women's swimming and women's ice hockey, basketball, and volleyball have also been successful in Minnesota Intercollegiate Athletic Conference play. The college's forensics team is nationally competitive as well. A majority of Gusties participate in intramural and club sports, including rugby and cross-country skiing.

The Gustavus Adolphus campus may be gorgeous in the spring and fall and too cold in the winter, but it's warmhearted all year long. Small classes, one-on-one academic attention, a plethora of research opportunities, and an active campus social life go a long way toward making St. Peter, Minnesota, seem a lot less isolated. Says one senior, "Our core values of community, service, faith, justice, and excellence prevail both in and out of the classroom, and students commit themselves and their time here to such values."

The school sponsors study abroad programs at five colleges and universities in—surprise, surprise—Sweden.

Overlaps

Luther, Augustana (IL), St. Olaf, College of Wooster, Muhlenberg, Allegheny, Susquehanna, College of St. Benedict and St. John's University

If You Apply To ›

Gustavus Adolphus: Early action, rolling admissions. SATs or ACTs: optional. Subject Tests: optional. Accepts the Common Application with supplement.

Hamilton College

198 College Hill Road, Clinton, NY 13323

Hamilton is part of the network of elite, rural, Northeastern liberal arts colleges that extends from Colby in Maine through Middlebury and Williams to Colgate, about half an hour's drive to Hamilton's south. Hamilton is on the small side of this group and emphasizes close contact with faculty and a senior project requirement. Need-blind admissions with no merit scholarships. Strong commitment to diversity.

Founded in 1793, Hamilton College took its name from Alexander Hamilton, who was an early trustee, and for much of its early life offered its male students a staunchly traditional education rooted in a classical curriculum. In 1978 Hamilton merged with Kirkland College, the artsy, experimental women's college founded under its auspices a decade before. Hamilton is marked by its close sense of community and its commitment to the liberal arts. Particularly dedicated to transforming students into excellent communicators, the college is also gradually increasing opportunities for experiential learning and internships. "Come to Hamilton because you will learn much more than simple facts and data," says an economics major. "You will learn how to think critically, communicate clearly, and lead effectively."

"Most students on our campus are in constant competition with themselves."

The old Hamilton campus features collegiate Victorian architecture rendered in rich, warm brownstone. In fact, the only facility interrupting the rhythmic beauty of campus is the eyesore that houses the library. By contrast, the adjacent Kirkland campus consists mostly of boxy concrete structures of a 1960s "brutalist" vintage, otherwise described as "faux I. M. Pei." Straddling the ravine that divides the campuses and joining them literally and figuratively is a student activities building with a diner, lounges, and areas for student and faculty relaxation. Surrounding the campuses are more than 1,000 college-owned acres of woodlands, open fields, and glens, with trails for hiking or cross-country skiing. The college has invested nearly $250 million over the past decade in new and renovated facilities; the most recent campus additions are an apartment-style residence hall housing 52 students and a new health and counseling center.

In the classroom, Hamilton is pure liberal arts. The general education curriculum has no distribution requirements, but all students must pass at least three writing-intensive courses and a quantitative and symbolic reasoning course. The development of writing skills is a key area of focus in all majors, and more than 100 courses each year require oral presentations. In an effort to reinforce its commitment to inclusion, the faculty has adopted a curriculum requirement that all majors feature relevant, mandatory coursework on diversity. First-year orientation combines on-campus programming with adventure and service trips; more than 65 options are available, from beekeeping to building homes in nearby Utica to kayaking Lake Champlain. First-year students may also participate in an optional series of proseminars—classes of no more than 16 that require intensive interaction through writing, speaking, and discussion. Hamilton requires all students to undertake a senior project in their area of concentration, which may take the form of a research project, a seminar with a presentation and research paper component, or a comprehensive exam.

Economics, mathematics, psychology, government, and biology are the most popular majors. Hamilton's Arthur Levitt Public Affairs Center, named for the former New York State comptroller, is a working think tank where undergraduates focus on leadership and social innovation. The natural sciences are strong too, bolstered by a $56 million science center. Students say that courses are rigorous and the emphasis is on performance. "A lot of students strive to get the best grades they can possibly get, regardless of how other students are doing," says a philosophy major. "Most students on our campus are in constant competition with themselves." You'll always find a professor, not a teaching assistant, at the lectern. Even with the intimate size of most classes—75 percent enroll fewer than 20 students—students report few problems getting needed courses, once they declare a major.

Each year, up to seven academically outstanding juniors are designated as Senior Fellows and allowed to eschew the conventional curriculum in favor of courses or projects that are relevant to their educational goals. At the close of the fellowship

Website: www.hamilton.edu
Location: Rural
Private
Total Enrollment: 1,885
Undergraduates: 1,885
Male/Female: 47/53
SAT Ranges: ERW 680–750, M 680–760
ACT Ranges: 31–33
Financial Aid: 51%
Pell Grant: 18%
Expense: Pr $ $ $ $
Student Loans: 43%
Average Debt: $
Applicants: 5,678
Accepted: 24%
Enrolled: 35%
Grad in 6 Years: 94%
Returning Freshmen: 96%
Academics: ✍ ✍ ✍ ✍ ½
Social: ☎ ☎ ☎ ☎
Q of L: ★ ★ ★
Admissions: (315) 859-4421
Email Address: admission@hamilton.edu

Strong Programs:
Economics
Mathematics
Psychology
Government
Biology
Public Policy
Natural Sciences

More than 1,000 college-owned acres of woodlands, open fields, and glens surround the campus.

year, they submit a written thesis and deliver a public lecture. Stipends are awarded to 140 students each year for summer research, and another 70 students receive stipends to pursue unpaid summer internships. When the town of Clinton gets claustrophobic, students can spend a semester or a year abroad through more than 100 approved programs or through Hamilton's programs in France, China, Spain, and India, or they can study off campus for a term in Washington, D.C., New York City, or the Adirondacks; 66 percent of undergraduates study off campus.

> *The development of writing skills is a key area of focus in all majors, and more than 100 courses each year require oral presentations.*

"It's cool to be passionate about things here," says a psychology major. "Students are so involved in a range of different activities; it's kind of lame if you only go to class and don't have a whole bunch of extracurriculars." Twenty-eight percent of Hamilton students are New York residents, and 6 percent are international. African Americans constitute 4 percent of the student body, Hispanics 9 percent, Asian

> **"It's kind of lame if you only go to class and don't have a whole bunch of extracurriculars."**

Americans 7 percent, and multiracial students 4 percent. Although the campus is no political hotbed, students report that current issues (both local and global) receive ample attention from student activists. Consistent with Hamilton's commitment to socioeconomic diversity, there are no merit or athletic scholarships, but the college has a need-blind admissions policy and guarantees to meet 100 percent of admitted domestic students' demonstrated financial need.

All students reside on campus. Options range from old fraternity houses renovated and turned into dorms to stately mansions with posh amenities, and newer apartments that accommodate three to four students each. "It's possible to get decent housing even as a rising sophomore," says a student. The Hamilton side of campus is the place for party animals; Dunham gets cheers for being social, but some students liken it to a "dungeon." The Kirkland dorms have a more mellow reputation. "The food is surprisingly good for college food," one senior acknowledges. Students say campus security is effective: "Campus Safety is always patrolling the grounds," says one junior. "I have always felt safe on campus."

> *Class & Charter Day marks the last day of classes in the spring with ceremonies, a picnic, a concert, and a triathlon the week before.*

Social life at Hamilton ranges from the campus pub, which occupies an old barn, to programming arranged by the campus activities board, such as comedy shows, a casino night, an award-winning acoustic coffeehouse series, and concerts. There's also the Greek system, which draws 26 percent of the men and 16 percent of the women. Much of the social life does revolve around alcohol, students say, although stiff punishments are meted out to underage imbibers. "Campus parties tend to be dominated by underclassmen. Upperclassmen generally make their own parties in the suites or the quads or they go downtown to the two bars," one student says.

Clinton is "a picturesque village good for pizza and coffee," says a sophomore. The nearest small city, Utica, is only 10 minutes away by car. The college maintains a jitney service and sponsors two Zipcars for student transportation. "On the

> **"[The professors] picked Hamilton because they wanted to be closer to students— to watch them grow."**

weekend, people will sometimes go to the Adirondacks because they are so close and beautiful," a student reports. "This can be a great way to get back in touch with nature and also have a fun weekend excursion." Given the long, snowy winters, such outings are often best enjoyed by skiers and other winter-sports enthusiasts. Other popular road trips include Syracuse and New York City, while Boston, Toronto, and Montreal are each less than five hours away.

In athletics, Hamilton offers 29 varsity sports teams (the Continentals) and is a member of the highbrow New England Small College Athletic Conference. Women's rowing and lacrosse and men's soccer and ice hockey have been the most competitive in recent years. Sixty percent of students compete in the extensive intramurals program, with soccer, basketball, and dodgeball drawing the most participants. Even some school traditions are athletically minded. Class & Charter Day marks the last day of classes in the spring with ceremonies, a picnic, a concert, and a triathlon the week before. "Many students believe this day is better than Christmas," says an economics major.

Hamilton students are, by necessity, hearty. They're used to the cold and the snow—and some may say that's what leads to the strong sense of community evident on campus. But for most, it's the dedicated faculty who foster community spirit as they teach students how to think critically and express themselves effectively. Says a senior, "The professors at Hamilton, from my experience at least, picked Hamilton because they wanted to be closer to students—to watch them grow and to help them grow both inside of the classroom and outside of it."

Overlaps

Amherst, Bowdoin, Carleton, Middlebury, Williams, Colgate, Dartmouth

If You Apply To ›

Hamilton: Early decision I and II, regular decision. SATs or ACTs or three individual exams of student's choice (including one verbal or writing, one quantitative, and one other, selected from SAT Subject Tests, AP or IB exams, or other tests from approved list): required. Accepts the Common Application.

Hampden–Sydney College

P.O. Box 667, Hampden–Sydney, VA 23943

The last bastion of the Southern gentleman and one of three all-male colleges in the nation. Feeder school to the economic establishment in Richmond. Picturesque rural setting evokes the old South. While some would argue that it is out of step with today's world, H–SC holds to its mission of asking what it means to be a "good man" in today's society.

Hampden–Sydney College was founded by Scotch-Irish Presbyterians in 1775 with the University of Edinburgh as its model and was named after two 17th-century English patriots (John Hampden and Algernon Sydney). Seemingly a bit of an anachronism in a society increasingly focused on diversity, the all-male school still aims to expose its small student body to a broad liberal arts education, which is entirely focused on undergraduates. H–SC is one of only three all-male colleges in the nation, and one of only two without a coordinate women's college (see also Wabash). The environment supports "a special sense of brotherhood and community," says one student. Tradition reigns here and students like to call themselves "Southern gentlemen." Of course, says another, there's plenty of not-always-gentlemanly fun to be had when you have roughly 1,000 guys together.

> **"[H–SC supports] a special sense of brotherhood and community."**

Hampden–Sydney's 1,340-acre campus, surrounded by farmland and woods, features mainly redbrick buildings in the Federal style. The $11 million Brown Student Center opened in 2017. The nearby town of Farmville, population 8,000 and home to Longwood University, offers restaurants, stores, and a movie theater; it's just five miles from H–SC, but one student describes the town as "a black hole inside a time warp."

To graduate, students must demonstrate proficiency in rhetoric and a foreign language, along with completing seven humanities courses, three in the social sciences, and four in the natural sciences and mathematics. All freshmen have a

Website: www.hsc.edu
Location: Rural
Private
Total Enrollment: 1,046
Undergraduates: 1,046
Male/Female: 100/0
SAT Ranges: ERW 530–635, M 520–630
ACT Ranges: 21–27
Financial Aid: 99%
Pell Grant: 19%
Expense: Pr $ $
Student Loans: 65%
Average Debt: $ $ $ $
Applicants: 3,573
Accepted: 55%
Enrolled: 16%
Grad in 6 Years: 63%
Returning Freshmen: 84%
Academics: ✐ ✐ ✐
Social: ☎ ☎ ☎ ☎

(continued)

Q of L: ★ ★ ★ ★

Admissions: (434) 223-6120

Email Address: admissions@
hsc.edu

Strong Programs:

Economics and Business

Economics

History

Biology

Government

Physics

Leadership

Rhetoric

special advising program, and 30 percent take freshman seminars linked to living/learning communities. Most majors require a capstone course involving a 20-page research paper. The most popular department is economics and business, which may help explain why more than half of the school's alumni have pursued business careers. The department offers three majors: economics and business, general economics, and mathematical economics. History, biology, government, and physics are also popular. New majors have been added in biochemistry and molecular biology and engineering physics. The Wilson Center for Leadership in the Public Interest puts a public service focus on the study of political science, preparing students for government work and garnering high marks in return. The school's small size offers many opportunities to work closely with professors, but has some academic drawbacks, including limited resources in some departments and fewer than 30 majors.

Students at Hampden–Sydney say there are no free passes when it comes to classwork. "Even though academic competition is a very real part of the experience, that competition is more friendly than anything else," says a biology major. Classes are small; 73 percent have fewer than 20 students and none exceed 50. Most H–SC professors live on campus and make themselves very available to students. Some even make house calls to find out why a student missed class. "I have

"[Farmville is] a black hole inside a time warp."

been invited to numerous dinners at professors' homes, and professors encourage us to contact them whenever we have a question, even if that means at nine o'clock on a Wednesday night," says a junior.

Additional educational opportunities include the honors program, the summer research program (which is particularly popular among students in the sciences), and the Tigerfund, which allows students to manage an equity fund. More than 100 study abroad options are available in 30 countries and revered institutions around the world, including Oxford, Cambridge, and the London School of Economics; 24 percent of students spread their wings in this way. Career services are said to be effective, particularly when it comes to connecting students with alumni for job opportunities.

More than half of Hampden–Sydney's alumni have pursued business careers.

"The prototypical Hampden–Sydney student is a Southern, white, Christian gentleman with conservative political values," says a junior. Sixty-nine percent of students are state residents, and 1 percent come from foreign countries. African Americans make up 4 percent of the student body, Hispanics constitute 4 percent, Asian Americans comprise 1 percent, and multiracial students represent 3 percent. The Office of Inclusion and Intercultural Affairs works to increase tolerance for diversity, and students say diversity is among the hot-button political issues on campus. As a Division III school, Hampden–Sydney offers no athletic scholarships. There are, however, academic awards averaging $17,900 for qualified students.

Ninety-eight percent of students live on campus in traditional and apartment-style residence halls, and housing is guaranteed for four years. "Freshmen are usually

"The prototypical Hampden–Sydney student is a Southern, white, Christian gentleman with conservative political values."

grouped in the larger housing areas in order for them to get the college roommate experience," says one student, and a dozen living/learning communities are available to choose from as well. The spacious dining facilities supply hungry students with "decent," all-you-can-eat fare. Student support services receive good reviews, although one religion major notes, "There is a bit of a stigma [against] using the counseling service, as we all aim to be macho at this boys' school."

Students praise the close-knit atmosphere fostered by Hampden–Sydney's all-male status. "Our code of etiquette requires that we acknowledge people we pass on the sidewalk and reserve our phone calls and headphones for less populated areas, so we get to know each other on a personal level," explains a junior. Hampden–Sydney's social nexus is the Circle, the site of the school's fraternities, which claim 30 percent of the students. "The party culture is huge. Greek organizations absolutely set the tone for the vast majority of our social environment," says one student, who adds, "Alcohol policies are not effective." The annual spring Greek Week brings out the *Animal House* aspect of Hampden–Sydney's budding gentlemen—but students warn that campus security will crack down on underage drinkers if parties get too wild. Student clubs offer another important outlet for socializing, and homecoming and various music festivals are also eagerly anticipated. Nearby women's colleges—Hollins, Sweet Briar, and Mary Baldwin—help mix up the social scene.

Despite its lack of bright lights ("You come here for the school, not the town," one student points out), nearby Farmville does provide numerous community service and outreach opportunities. A campus volunteer group called Good Men, Good Citizens spearheads projects such as tutoring, highway cleanup, and Habitat for Humanity home-building; 75 percent of students perform community service. When rural Virginia gets too insular, H–SC students can be found on road trips to the University of Virginia and James Madison University, Virginia's beaches, or Washington, D.C. The ski slopes of Wintergreen are within a two hours' drive.

Perhaps because of all that testosterone on campus, Hampden–Sydney men are competitive, and that spells excellence in athletics. Tiger football is big; students attend games in coat and tie, and alumni come out in droves for tailgating. H–SC's football rivalry with Randolph–Macon (not the former women's college!) is one of the oldest in the South. At the annual pregame bonfire, the college rallies to sing songs and hear student and faculty leaders vilify the enemy and extol "the garnet and gray." Basketball, baseball, tennis, and lacrosse are also competitive. Sixty-five percent of students participate in intramural and recreational sports ranging from basketball and flag football to clay-target club and water polo.

Hampden–Sydney likes to tell new students that when they enter the campus gates, they're "joining a brotherhood older than America itself." The school's legacy as the 10th-oldest college in the United States may make it largely conservative and rather homogeneous. But two centuries of tradition, an unwavering commitment to the liberal arts, and a tight-knit student body also make for a rich undergraduate experience.

Tiger football is big; students attend games in coat and tie, and alumni come out in droves for tailgating.

Overlaps

Wabash, Randolph–Macon, Roanoke, Austin College, Augustana (IL), Washington College, University of Virginia, UNC at Chapel Hill

If You Apply To ›

Hampden–Sydney: Early decision, early action I and II, regular decision. SATs or ACTs: required. Subject Tests: optional. Accepts the Common Application with supplement.

Hampshire College

P.O. Box 5001, Amherst, MA 01002

Long a leader in nonconformist higher education, Hampshire is facing a serious financial and enrollment crisis. In February 2019 the college suspended regular admissions and accepted only a limited freshman class for the fall. Leaders are now looking for a "long-term partner" to ensure the school's future viability. Stay tuned.

Passion reigns at Hampshire College. It's found in just about everything students do—from devising their own courses to starting new clubs to debating the most current social issues. There's no one way to do things at Hampshire, and the students revel in the freedom they have to direct the path of their education. "We love what we are studying because we get to choose what we are studying," says a junior focusing on sustainable agricultural methods. Without the yoke of traditional majors and the nail-biting stress of regular grades, Hampshire offers a virtually boundary-free exercise in intellectual nirvana.

Located in the Connecticut River Valley of western Massachusetts, Hampshire's 800-acre campus sits amid former orchards, farmland, and forest. Buildings are eclectic and contemporary, and the school is proud of its bio-shelter, arts village, and multisports and multimedia centers. Two nationally known museums—the Yiddish Book Center and the Eric Carle Museum of Picturebook Art—are located right on campus. The innovative Kern Center is the campus's "living building." Constructed entirely with local and regional nontoxic materials, the 17,000-square-foot building generates its own electricity and collects its own water. It's the latest in a series of sustainability efforts that also include converting the campus to 100 percent solar electricity.

> "The academic climate is not competitive because no two students study the exact same thing."

Hampshire was created in 1970 by four nearby colleges—Amherst, UMass Amherst, Mount Holyoke, and Smith—that now make up the Five College Consortium. Instead of grades, Hampshire professors hand out "narrative evaluations," which consist of written evaluations and critiques. The Campus Engaged Learning program requires all students to commit to 40 hours of service or a semester-long equivalent. Degrees are obtained by passing a series of examinations—not tests, but portfolios of academic work, evaluations, and students' self-reflections on their academic development.

The first milestone, known as Division I, begins with a course from four out of five multidisciplinary schools—natural science; critical social inquiry; cognitive science; interdisciplinary arts; and humanities, arts, and cultural studies—plus other coursework. The second milestone, Division II, is each student's "concentration"—the rough equivalent of a major elsewhere. Unlike a major, the requirements of a concentration are unique to each student, emerging from regular discussions with two faculty members, and include courses, independent study, and fieldwork or internships. Division III, or "advanced study," begins in the fourth year, when students complete a sizable independent study project centered on a specific topic, question, or idea, much like a master's thesis. In recent years, students have created smartphone software to monitor blood sugar and examined U.S. military interventions in global conflicts.

Because of the division system, there are as many curricula at Hampshire as there are students. The common denominator is a rigorous workload, an emphasis on self-initiated study, close contact with faculty advisors, and the assumption that students will eventually function as do graduate students

> "[Hampshire] is deliberately unique and experimental."

at other institutions. "The academic climate is not competitive because no two students study the exact same thing," explains a student. The importance of qualified, attentive faculty is not to be underestimated in an environment like this, and students heap praise on their professors. One says, "Professors at Hampshire are truly invested in their students."

Hampshire's flexibility is ideal for artists, and programs in film, video, and photography are dazzling, which is also the reason they are overcrowded. Communications, creative writing, psychology, social sciences, and environmental studies are also good bets, and Hampshire was the first college in the nation to offer an undergraduate program in cognitive science. The Integrated Sciences first-year program gives new students a chance to work together on innovative projects in an interdisciplinary science environment. The college's Farm Center serves as a living laboratory for learning about sustainability, social justice, and community-building. Students also have access to selected courses at sister schools in the Five College Consortium, which are connected by a free bus service; Hampshire students take 1,200 classes per year at the other schools. Internships and other real-world experiences are highly encouraged. Hampshire offers its own study abroad programs in China, Cuba, and Germany, and students may also participate in programs through more than 150 institutions in nearly 50 countries. Befitting Hampshire's entrepreneurial nature, when it comes time for "Div Free" (as students call life after Hampshire), one in four students begin their own businesses, and a large percentage go on to graduate school.

The Campus Engaged Learning program requires all students to commit to 40 hours of service.

"We are not cookie-cutter students," says a sophomore. "We are students who passionately teach ourselves in a school that is deliberately unique and experimental." Just as Hampshire eschews letter grades, it also refuses to consider SAT or ACT scores in the admissions process. Only 15 percent of students come from Massachusetts, and 5 percent come from abroad. The minority community is growing—7 percent of students are African American, 12 percent are Hispanic, 2 percent are Asian American, and 6 percent are multiracial—and most students would like to see these numbers continue to rise. Twenty-seven percent of freshmen receive Pell Grants, and Hampshire's LGBTQ community is visible and vocal. According to a philosophy student, "Political correctness doesn't even begin to describe" the social atmosphere. Take as examples the school's gender-neutral bathrooms and identity-based housing, which allows members of historically marginalized groups to live together. Aside from need-based aid, merit scholarships worth an average of $12,700 are available to qualified students.

"Political correctness doesn't even begin to describe [the social atmosphere]."

Seventy-eight percent of undergraduates live on campus. First-year students live in dorms, while older students may move to one of more than 100 "mods"—apartments in which groups of four to 10 students share the responsibility for cleaning, cooking, and maintaining their space. Campus meals are diverse and include "many great vegan and vegetarian options," says one nanotechnology student, not to mention great ice cream from local cows. Students can also get healthy options from Mixed Nuts, a student-run food co-op that is Hampshire's longest-running student group. Campus safety is good, students say, and sexual assault is addressed up front. "We have a loud and well-known consent culture on campus," says a student concentrating in geology and sustainability. "Students learn about appropriate consent during orientation and it is reinforced consistently throughout all four years."

After Hampshire, one in four students begin their own businesses, and a large percentage go on to graduate school.

Not surprisingly, Hampshire has no fraternities or sororities, and on weekends, some students head for Boston, New York, Hartford, or, in season, the ski trails of Vermont and New Hampshire. But there are plenty of cultural resources within the Five College area, and the free buses to Amherst, Northampton, and South Hadley (all within 10 miles) are always crowded. From edgy record stores to ethnic restaurants and boutiques, the area abounds with diversions. The annual Spring Jam brings live bands to campus, and throughout the year there's almost always a party going on, including the drag ball and the much-anticipated Halloween bash—an intense, all-campus blowout complete with fireworks. A tradition called "Div Free Bell" celebrates the completion of Division III requirements—and graduation—with soon-to-be alumni ringing a bell outside the library, surrounded by friends.

"We have a loud and well-known consent culture on campus."

Hampshire is no place for competitive jocks, since many sports are co-ed and primarily for entertainment (there never was a football team here). Division III Hampshire is affiliated with the United States Collegiate Athletic Association and also is a member of the Yankee Small College Conference. Students organize their own intramural teams and sports clubs (men's and women's soccer, basketball, and fencing are the biggies, and there's also the competitive Red Scare Ultimate Frisbee Team). The outdoors program offers mountain biking, cross-country skiing, and kayaking; equipment may be borrowed for free. The school also has its own climbing wall and cave, a gym with a solar-heated pool, and a co-ed sauna.

Hampshire's six-year graduation rate is low in comparison to other pricey, private liberal arts colleges, though not necessarily for bad reasons. Some students find the culture of individual study unnerving, if not stressful, or miss traditional college life more than they thought they would. Others, however, having taken full advantage of Hampshire's freedom to explore, discover a passion that might be their life's work and move on to pursue it at a larger school with more resources. Hampshire considers the latter situation a success story.

"If you're an independent student and like to think outside the box, then Hampshire is for you," says a student focusing on animal behavior. With the power to make up their own education and the support of devoted faculty members, there's little Hampshire students can't accomplish.

Overlaps

Pitzer, Reed, Antioch, Smith, Eugene Lang, Bard, Bennington, Sarah Lawrence

If You Apply To ›

Hampshire: In February 2019 Hampshire suspended regular admissions. Prospective students should confirm with college officials whether they are accepting applications for 2020 and beyond, as well as specific admissions requirements.

Hartwick College

Oneonta, NY 13820

Hartwick is known for its cozy atmosphere and ability to take good care of students. Combines liberal arts education with experiential learning opportunities. A general education program emphasizes hands-on learning, and a Three-Year Bachelor's Degree Program is an option. Most strong students can get at least a small merit aid award.

Website: www.hartwick.edu
Location: Small Town
Private
Total Enrollment: 1,180
Undergraduates: 1,180
Male/Female: 41/59
SAT Ranges: ERW 460–540, M 460–560
ACT Ranges: 21–26
Financial Aid: 84%
Pell Grant: 37%
Expense: Pr $ $

In recent years, Hartwick College has transformed itself by choosing to better focus on its liberal arts profile. Hartwick emphasizes community-centered learning, crystallizing the school's philosophy that learning isn't about memorization, it's about creating experiential knowledge and developing skills. The students here take full advantage of what's offered and feel at home on this close-knit campus. Says one student, "When coming here, you will feel like you instantly become an active and important member of the community."

Hartwick's campus has a New England feel with its ivy-covered, redbrick buildings and white cupolas, gables, and trim. The campus setting on Oyaron Hill, overlooking the city of Oneonta and the Susquehanna Valley, provides a breathtaking view, though the steepness of the campus may have some wishing for the legs of a mountain goat. Facilities include a greenhouse, an herbarium, a cold room, a biotechnology "clean lab," and a graphics imaging lab. The Wright Observatory,

LEED-certified Golisano Hall, and the state-of-the-art Campbell Fitness Center are other notable campus features.

Hartwick's general education program is divided into seven areas and places emphasis on experiential and integrative learning. Among the requirements are courses in humanities, physical and life sciences, social and behavioral sciences, foreign language, writing competency, and quantitative/formal reasoning. In addition, students must complete a first-year seminar and a senior thesis. Each academic year, a different campus theme is chosen that serves as a foundation for special course offerings, guest speakers, student projects, and campuswide events throughout the year; recent themes have included Fabric of Change, Food and Community, and Health and the Environment.

The most popular majors are business administration, nursing, biology, psychology, and sociology. The English, music, and art programs receive high marks too. The course catalog is necessarily limited by Hartwick's small size, but the Individual Student Program enables students to create their own major dealing with a particular interest, and several new majors have recently been introduced, including criminal justice, global studies, and public health. Students may also broaden their options by taking courses at nearby SUNY Oneonta. The Three-Year Bachelor's Degree Program allows students in most majors to take on a larger courseload in order to earn a B.A. or B.S. within three years—and save significantly on the cost of earning a degree.

> **"You instantly become an active and important member of the community."**

Hartwick's academic environment is described as collaborative and relaxed. "Not only are students encouraged to discuss ideas among each other and work together to learn, but students are also welcomed to work alongside their professors," explains a political science major. "It makes one feel like everyone is on the same team working toward the same goal." Small class sizes are the norm, and a business administration major says, "The professors here are kind and spend a lot of time with students who really need them." Private tutoring and help sessions are offered, along with an innovative freshman early-warning program that identifies struggling students early and offers counseling.

Hartwick's emphasis on learning through real-world experiences is evident in the wide-ranging activities its students have pursued, from working in a Jamaican hospital to interning with the Metropolitan Museum of Art. Seventy percent of students take community-based service-learning classes, which combine academic coursework with service opportunities in the Oneonta area. Participants in the Honors Program carry out four self-selected academic challenges, such as honors seminars, a second major, or independent research. Forty percent of students take part in study abroad courses available in 25 nations around the globe. The four-week January term is a favorite time to explore the world beyond Oneonta.

Hartwick has traditionally attracted a somewhat less academically oriented student body than most of the colleges with which it competes, but it has improved its academic position in recent years, thanks to a focused recruitment program. "The students here are hardworking, well-rounded, driven, and accepting," says a junior. Eighty percent are from New York State, especially upstate, and most of the rest come from New England or the Mid-Atlantic states; 3 percent are international. African Americans make up 12 percent of the student body, Hispanics 9 percent, and Asian Americans 1 percent. Thirty-seven percent of freshmen are eligible for Pell Grants. Students tend to be liberal but not particularly politically engaged; a senior says, "We try not to let outside issues affect our studies." Hartwick awards merit scholarships averaging $24,000, as well as 30 athletic scholarships for its Division I men's soccer and women's water polo athletes. The new Hartwick College Founders' Award guarantees a $10,000 tuition grant to students

(continued)

Student Loans: 82%
Average Debt: $ $ $ $
Applicants: 3,019
Accepted: 89%
Enrolled: 13%
Grad in 6 Years: 54%
Returning Freshmen: 70%
Academics: ✏️ ✏️ ✏️
Social: ☎ ☎ ☎ ☎
Q of L: ★ ★ ★
Admissions:
  (888)-HARTWICK
Email Address: admissions@ hartwick.edu

Strong Programs:
Business Administration
Nursing
Biology
Psychology
Sociology
English
Music
Art

Participants in the Honors Program carry out four self-selected academic challenges, such as honors seminars, a second major, or independent research.

from New York State for each year they are enrolled, provided they remain in good academic standing.

Eighty percent of the student body reside on campus, most in traditional dorms, although limited suite-style options are available. Says a sophomore, "The dorms are all a comfortable size and are maintained properly." Students are required to live on campus through their junior year. Upperclassmen may move into one of the fraternity or special-interest houses or one of the four coveted townhouses. Hartwick's 256-acre Pine Lake Environmental Campus has cabins that are heated by pellet stoves and a lodge where environmentally inclined students can live in rustic style. Students give on-campus dining fair marks but praise campus safety officers; says one student, "It's obvious through their actions that they really care about the well-being of the students at this college."

Hartwick's social scene is found both on and off campus, according to students, and tends to be as mellow or rowdy as one chooses. From campus it's only a short walk, bike ride, or bus ride downhill into the small city of Oneonta, with its tantalizing profusion of bars. Students say the administration is tough about enforcing alcohol policies on campus. The Greek system attracts 4 percent of the men and 7 percent of the women. The school sponsors events like movies, comedians, and lectures every Friday and Saturday night. Popular campuswide traditions include Wicktoberfest, Pine Lake Winterfest, the Last Day of Classes Bash, and the notorious "Wick Wars," a schoolwide sports competition held every spring. There's also the Breakfast of Champions before final exams, when professors and administrators serve students breakfast between 11 p.m. and 2 a.m. Walking to class each day provides great hill workouts for your ski legs, and skiing is popular throughout the region. Oneonta is a "quaint, peaceful town," according to one student. "There aren't very many things to do, but my friends and I haven't gotten bored yet."

> "There aren't very many things to do, but my friends and I haven't gotten bored yet."

Oneonta is big on sports, and the Hartwick Hawks deliver. Hartwick is nationally ranked at the Division I level in men's soccer and women's water polo, both of which have won multiple conference championships in recent years. The remainder of the teams compete in the Division III Empire 8 Conference; women's field hockey is a recent conference champ. Intramurals are popular as well, especially basketball, flag football, and soccer—20 percent of students take part.

Change is good, the sages say, and the folks at Hartwick would definitely agree. By focusing its efforts on recruiting strong students and emphasizing top-notch experiential learning, Hartwick is bolstering its image as a solid liberal arts college. Even some of the T-shirts sold on campus broadcast the students' attitudes about their education: one simply says "Smartwick."

Overlaps

Juniata, Elmira, Moravian, Hobart and William Smith, Lycoming, SUNY–Oneonta, SUNY–University at Albany, Utica

If You Apply To ›

Hartwick: Early decision, rolling admissions. SATs or ACTs: optional (required for nursing applicants and homeschooled students). No Subject Tests. Accepts the Common Application with supplement. Music applicants must audition. Art applicants must submit portfolio of original work.

Harvard University

86 Brattle Street, Cambridge, MA 02138

An acceptance here is the gold standard of American education. Gets periodic slings and arrows for not paying enough attention to undergraduates, some of which is carping from people who didn't get in. It takes moxie to keep your self-image under control in the midst of all those geniuses, but most Harvard students can do it. ("I go to school in Boston.")

Over the past 380 years, the name Harvard has become synonymous with excellence, prestige, and achievement. Harvard University, the nation's first institution of higher learning, is still the benchmark against which all other colleges are compared. Seeking to "educate citizens and citizen leaders," it attracts the best students, the most academically accomplished faculty, and the most lavish donors of any institution of higher education nationwide. Sure, some academic departments at Hah-vahd are smaller than others, but all have faculty members who have made a name for themselves, many of whom have written the standard texts in their fields. Olympic athletes, concert pianists, and Rhodes scholars blend in easily here, ready to embrace the challenges and rewards only Harvard's quintessential Ivy League milieu can offer.

Spiritually as well as geographically, the campus centers on the famed Harvard Yard, a classic quadrangle of Georgian brick buildings whose walls seem to echo with the voices of William James, Henry Adams, and other intellectual greats who trod its shaded paths in centuries past. Beyond the yard's wrought-iron gates, the campus is an architectural mix, ranging from the modern ziggurat of the science center to the white towers of college-owned houses along the Charles River. The Loker Commons student center provides a place for students to meet and philosophize over gourmet coffee or burritos of epic proportions. Construction on a huge, $1 billion science and engineering complex across the river in Allston is slated for completion in 2020.

Harvard's state-of-the-art physical facilities are surpassed only by the unparalleled brilliance of its faculty. Under its "star" system, Harvard grants tenure only to scholars who have already made it—usually somewhere else—and then gives them free rein for research. It seems like every time you turn around, a Harvard professor is winning a Nobel

> **"You can have unlimited contact with professors, but it must be on your initiative."**

Prize or being interviewed on CNN or moving to Washington to hash out national policy. But one of Harvard's finest qualities is also one of its biggest problems. "You can have unlimited contact with professors, but it must be on your initiative," notes a biology major. "This is not a small liberal arts college where people will reach out to you." That's not to say profs are uncaring. Most teach at least one undergraduate course per year, and even the luminaries occasionally conduct small undergraduate seminars (including those reserved for freshmen, which can be taken pass/fail). Harvard also sponsors faculty dining programs, such as Professors & Pastries and Classroom to Table, encouraging professors to chew on ideas and éclairs with students at residential houses and local eateries.

Back in the mid-1970s, Harvard helped launch a major curriculum reform movement. Although it was recently revised, the core curriculum that emerged was for decades regarded as perhaps the most exciting collection of academic offerings in all of American higher education. New general education requirements, implemented in 2018, include one course from each of four perspectives: aesthetics and

Website: www.college
.harvard.edu
Location: City Center
Private
Total Enrollment: 19,618
Undergraduates: 6,699
Male/Female: 52/48
SAT Ranges: ERW 730–790,
M 730–800
ACT Ranges: 32–35
Financial Aid: 67%
Pell Grant: 15%
Expense: Pr $ $ $
Student Loans: 20%
Average Debt: $
Applicants: 39,506
Accepted: 5%
Enrolled: 83%
Grad in 6 Years: 96%
Returning Freshmen: 97%
Academics: ✑ ✑ ✑ ✑ ✑
Social: ☎ ☎ ☎
Q of L: ★ ★ ★ ★
Admissions: (617) 495-1551
Email Address:
college@fas.harvard.edu

Strong Programs:
Economics
Government
Computer Science
Applied Mathematics
History
Biological Sciences
East Asian Studies
African and African American
Studies

culture; ethics and civics; histories, societies, individuals; and science and technology in society. Additionally, students take one quantitative reasoning course and one departmental course from each of the three main divisions of the Faculty of Arts and Sciences: Arts and Humanities; Social Sciences; and Natural Sciences and the School of Engineering and Applied Science. The revised gen-ed program is intended to give students more freedom in the courses they choose and to prepare them to succeed in a diverse, inclusive, and interconnected world.

Harvard's best-known departments tend to be its largest; economics, government, computer science, applied mathematics, psychology, history, and biological sciences account for a large chunk of majors. But many smaller departments are gems as well: East Asian studies is easily top in the nation. And under the leadership of Henry Louis Gates, the African and African American studies department has assembled the most high-powered group of black intellectuals in American higher education. Smaller, interdisciplinary honors majors, to which students apply for admission, boast solid instruction and happy undergraduates too. These programs—social studies, history and science, history and literature, and folklore and mythology—are the only majors that require a senior thesis, although many students in other departments elect to do one. Harvard's visual and environmental studies major serves filmmakers, studio artists, and urban planners, and a major in theater, dance, and media is quickly growing in popularity. Students can also petition for individualized majors, typically during the sophomore year. And should you not find a class you are looking for, Harvard offers cross-registration with several of its graduate schools and MIT.

Freshmen are encouraged to explore a range of disciplines during their first year on campus. Seventy-three percent of classes have fewer than 20 students, but students uniformly complain about the overuse of teaching fellows (graduate students) for introductory courses in mathematics and the languages. TFs aren't all bad, though, says a junior: "They can give good advice, having just been in our position." Besides, it's easier to ask "dumb questions" of mere mortals than of the demigod professors. For many students, the most rewarding form of instruction is the sophomore and junior tutorial, a small-group directed study in a student's field of concentration that is required in most departments within the humanities and social sciences. Teaching of the tutorials is split between professors and graduate students, and the weight of each party's responsibility varies with the subject and the professor. With more than 200 study abroad programs available to choose from, about 60 percent of students have some sort of international experience before they graduate.

The oft-made claim that "the hardest thing about Harvard is getting in" is right on target. Flunking out takes serious and sustained effort. Then again, Harvard can feel indifferent and antisocial. While its resources—including fellow students—are unparalleled, brilliant overachievers who desire the occasional ego stroke might be better off at a small liberal arts college. But for those who are motivated, the possibilities are endless. All incoming freshmen participate in a weeklong orientation, and optional preorientation groups, such as the urban, outdoor, and arts programs, help students acquaint themselves with one another and the Boston area. Although most students feel little competition, the academic climate is still intense. "The courses are difficult, particularly in the beginning as students make the transition from high school to college," says one student. Stressed-out students can count on help from a variety of quarters, including the various deans' offices, the Bureau of Study Counsel, the Office of Career Services ("dedicated to working with Harvard students and alums for the rest of their lives," claims a senior), and counselors

Most profs teach at least one undergraduate course per year, and even the luminaries occasionally conduct small undergraduate seminars.

"[Career Services is] dedicated to working with Harvard students and alums for the rest of their lives."

The high-powered African and African American studies department is under the leadership of Henry Louis Gates.

associated with each residential house. The Radcliffe Institute for Advanced Study, which has evolved from the former Radcliffe women's college, affords undergrads access to a network of professional women, alumnae, and research fellows (both female and male). Sooner or later, all roads lead to Widener Library, where incredible facilities lie in wait (and where snow-covered steps make prime sledding runs in the winter).

Harvard does have one thing its $39.2 billion endowment can't buy: a diverse, high-powered, ambitious, and exciting student body. You will meet smooth-talking government majors who appear to have begun their senatorial campaigns in kindergarten. You will meet flamboyant fine arts majors who have cultivated an affected accent all their own. You will sample the intensity of Harvard's extracurricular scene, where 6,700 of the world's sharpest undergrads compete for leadership positions in a luminous galaxy of extracurricular opportunities.

No one can tell you exactly what it takes to gain admission to Harvard (and if anyone tries, apply a large grain of salt), but here's a hint: 95 percent of incoming freshmen ranked in the top 10th of their high school class and most went to public high school. Though there are old-money types who probably spit up their baby food on a Harvard sweatshirt, their numbers are smaller than one might imagine on this liberal campus. (Many enter as sophomores when no one is looking.) Undergrads come from all 50 states—73 percent are out-of-staters—although the student body is weighted toward the Northeast. Eleven percent are international, representing 70 different countries. African

For students from low-income families who can get in, Harvard is a bargain.

> "It's certainly normal to spend Friday and Saturday nights studying."

Americans account for 8 percent of the student body, Hispanics 12 percent, Asian Americans 20 percent, and multiracial students 7 percent. There are no merit or athletic scholarships to ease the pain of Harvard's hefty tuition, but the university does practice need-blind admissions and it meets the full demonstrated need of accepted students. For students from low-income families who can get in, Harvard is a bargain. The university has eliminated the expected family contribution for students from families with incomes below $65,000 a year; these students also receive a $2,000 "start-up" grant to help cover initial expenses, like dorm-room supplies. Harvard also limits the family contribution for families with incomes between $65,000 and $150,000 to fixed percentages of their incomes, ranging from 1 to 10 percent.

Virtually all undergraduates reside on campus, and every first-year class lives as a single unit in Harvard Yard, dining together at the beautifully renovated Annenberg Hall. The older dorms provide spacious wood-paneled rooms, working fireplaces, and the gentle reminders of Harvard's rich traditions. For their last three years, students live in one of 12 co-ed residential houses, built around their own courtyards with their own dining halls, libraries, and special facilities—from art studios to squash courts. Designed as learning communities, each house holds between 300 and 500 students, plus resident tutors and affiliated faculty members. Each house has a student council that plans social activities. Students are randomly assigned (with up to 15 friends) to a house, but some houses

Every first-year class lives as a single unit in Harvard Yard, dining together at the beautifully renovated Annenberg Hall.

> "Cambridge's Harvard Square is the perfect college town."

still retain a personality from the days of old when each stood for a particular ideology or interest. "The housing is one of the best parts of Harvard!" raves one student. Nine houses lie along the Charles River, while the other three sit a half mile away at the Radcliffe Quad. Some students consider the latter equivalent to a Siberian exile, especially during harsh Cambridge winters—although a shuttle does run regularly to the main campus.

Socializing at Harvard tends to occur on campus and in small groups. "It's certainly normal to spend Friday and Saturday nights studying," says a philosophy major. With the exception of the annual all-school Freshman Mixer and the annual theme festivals each house throws, parties tend to be private affairs in individual dorm rooms. Students report that the legal drinking age is well enforced on campus.

The most distinctive and increasingly controversial aspect of social life at Harvard is the role of the so-called "final clubs." These are exclusive and upscale social clubs that, while occupying their own buildings and in other ways completely separate from the university, play a significant role in the campus social life for the small minority of students who are "punched" for membership. In recent years the Harvard administration, convinced that the exclusive values of final clubs are out of place on Harvard's increasingly diverse campus, has taken steps to weaken their influence. Currently, most of Harvard's final clubs, fraternities, and sororities have succumbed to pressure to go co-ed (or shut down), but the tug of war continues. Stay tuned. For many, the key to happiness in Harvard's high-powered environment is finding a niche, a comfortable academic or extracurricular circle around which to build your life. Outside activities include about 80 plays performed annually, two newspapers and several journals, and plenty of community service projects coordinated through the Phillips Brooks House Association student group.

The possibilities of Harvard's social life are increased exponentially by Cambridge and Boston, where there are many places to have fun. Harvard Square itself is a legendary gathering place for tourists, shoppers, bearded intellectuals, and coffeehouse denizens. The American Repertory Theater, transplanted from Yale in the mid-1980s, offers a season of professional productions and nearly as many professional student shows. Cambridge also enjoys an exceptional selection of new and used bookstores, including, of course, the Harvard Bookstore and the mammoth Harvard Co-op, known universally as "the Coop." Boston boasts Faneuil Hall, the Red Sox, the Celtics, and 45 other colleges. "Cambridge's Harvard Square is the perfect college town," a student cheers. "There are tons of shops, restaurants, and bars."

Harvard has 41 varsity sports (21 men's, 20 women's), which is the most of any Division I school and the most women's sports. The athletic facilities are across the river from the campus, and their incredible offerings often go unnoticed by students buried in the books. Both the men's and women's squash and crew teams are perennial national powers, and

> "I gauge myself by how many allusions in the *New Yorker* I understand."

men's ice hockey and women's lacrosse are also strong. Men's basketball has prospered in recent years under coach Tommy Amaker, a former Duke star. As for football, the team has been doing better in recent years, but the season always boils down to the Yale game, memorable as much for the antics of the spectators and marching band as for the fumbles of the players. Intramural sports teams are divided up by house, and each fall, league champs play teams from Yale the weekend of the game. Another fall highlight is the annual Head of the Charles crew race, the largest event of its kind in the world, where as many as 200,000 people gather to watch the racing shells glide by.

Nowhere but Harvard does the identity of a school—its history, its presence, its pretense—intrude so much into the details of undergraduate life. Admission here opens the door to a world of intellectual wonder, academic challenges, and faculty minds unmatched in the United States—but then drops students on the threshold. "I have quickly gained exposure to major theories in literature, psychology, anthropology, social sciences, and evolutionary biology," says a junior. "I gauge myself by how many allusions in the *New Yorker* I understand." That's the way Harvard is; what other kind of place could produce statesmen John Quincy Adams and John F. Kennedy, pioneers W. E. B. DuBois and Helen Keller, and artists T. S. Eliot and Leonard Bernstein? Even its dropouts are movers and shakers (witness Bill Gates and Mark Zuckerberg). But caveat emptor: it is only the most motivated and dedicated student who can take full advantage of the Harvard experience.

Harvey Mudd College: See page 150.

Haverford College

Haverford, PA 19041

Quietly prestigious college of Quaker heritage. With an enrollment approaching 1,300, Haverford is half the size of some competitors but benefits from its relationship with nearby Bryn Mawr. Close cousin to nearby Swarthmore but not as far left politically. Exceptionally strong sense of community, with parklike campus amid the bustle of suburban Philadelphia. Honor code drives campus culture. Your only option if you want to play varsity cricket.

An overarching honor code covering everything from the classroom to the dorm room defines student life at Haverford College. Students schedule their own final exams, take unproctored tests, and police underage drinking on their own. "The honor code, in some respects, is a self-selecting system which draws many students to Haverford. For this reason, nearly all students who come here share common values of trust, concern, and respect for others as well as academic integrity," says a junior econ major. Haverford may be smaller and less well-known than some of its peers, but it holds its own against the finest liberal arts colleges in the country, especially for students who are willing to put in serious effort.

Founded under the auspices of the Religious Society of Friends (Quakers) in 1833, Haverford functions much like a family. The campus consists of 204 acres just off Philadelphia's Main Line railroad and resembles a peaceful, well-ordered summer camp. The densely wooded campus has an arboretum, duck pond, nature trails, and more than 400 species of shrubs and trees. Architectural styles range from 19th- and early 20th-century stone buildings to a sprinkling of modern structures here and there. The combination enhances the sense of a balanced community, bringing together two traditional Quaker philosophies: development of the intellect and appreciation of nature. The college recently converted the historic Ryan Gym into a new Visual Culture, Arts, and Media building housing multiple academic programs and state-of-the-art studio spaces.

> **"[Students] share common values of trust, concern, and respect for others as well as academic integrity."**

Haverford's curriculum reflects commitment to the liberal arts. General education requirements call for passing a freshman writing seminar and taking three courses in each of three divisions: social sciences, natural sciences, and humanities. Every Haverford student completes a senior thesis, partnering with a faculty mentor to do what amounts to graduate-level research in their major. Biology, English, psychology, and chemistry are among the most popular majors, and the physics, mathematics, and economics programs are also strong. There are more than a dozen areas of concentration—which are different from minors—that are attached to certain

Website: www.haverford.edu
Location: Suburban
Private
Total Enrollment: 1,290
Undergraduates: 1,290
Male/Female: 48/52
SAT Ranges: ERW 700–760, M 690–770
ACT Ranges: 31–34
Financial Aid: 47%
Pell Grant: 16%
Expense: Pr $ $ $ $
Student Loans: 25%
Average Debt: $
Applicants: 4,408
Accepted: 20%
Enrolled: 39%
Grad in 6 Years: 93%
Returning Freshmen: 97%
Academics: 🖉 🖉 🖉 🖉 🖉
Social: ☎ ☎ ☎
Q of L: ★ ★ ★ ★ ★
Admissions: (610) 896-1350
Email Address: admission@ haverford.edu

Strong Programs:
Biology
English

majors, including peace, justice, and human rights; biophysics; and Middle Eastern and Islamic studies.

The bicollege system with Bryn Mawr College, the nearby women's school, allows Haverford students to major in subjects such as art history, growth and structure of cities, and environmental studies. The unique relationship between Bryn Mawr and Haverford dates to the days when Haverford was all-male, and it enables students at each institution to take courses, use the facilities, eat, and even live in the dormitories of the other. Haverford and Bryn Mawr students cooperate on a weekly newspaper, radio station, orchestra, and other clubs and sports, and a free shuttle bus connects the campuses. About half of Haverford students take at least one course at Bryn Mawr. Cross-registration is also available at Swarthmore and the University of Pennsylvania, and joint degree programs are available with a number of institutions, including Penn, Caltech, Claremont McKenna, and Georgetown.

Perhaps because of the intense classroom interaction, the workload is sizable, although students say they don't worry about each other's grades and try to squeeze in nonscholarly pursuits too. "Haverford is very challenging," says one geology major. "As a student, you expect to put in a lot of work." Advising is ever-present: freshmen are matched with professors who work with them from their arrival until they declare majors two years later, while upper-class "Customs people" are resources and mentors for living/learning groups of eight to 16 first-year students. Haverford's biggest strength may be its faculty members, who are described as quite accessible; 61 percent of them live on campus. Most classes are small, with 76 percent enrolling fewer than 20 students, but a political science student recalls that one professor personalized a 90-student class by dividing it up into groups of 10 and having each group over for a pre-exam dessert. "The professors are only here for us. They really enjoy teaching as well as involving us in research." Haverford's Center for Peace and Global Citizenship—appropriate for a Quaker school—offers summer internships that emphasize the study and promotion of social justice and global issues. Nearly 70 study abroad programs around the globe attract just over half of the students.

Through the bicollege system, about half of Haverford students take at least one course at Bryn Mawr.

Haverford's distinctive honor code governs all aspects of campus life. "I can take my final exam at 3 a.m. on Founder's Green," says a junior as an example. The code, administered by students and debated and reratified each year at a meeting called Plenary, helps instill the values of "integrity, honesty, and concern for others." In good Quaker tradition, decisions are made by consensus rather than formal voting, and students play a large role in college policy. While the social honor code encourages students to "voice virtually any opinion so long as it is expressed rationally," this can also mean self-censorship, says a philosophy major. "Sometimes you feel like you are walking on eggshells to avoid offending anyone."

"The professors are only here for us. They really enjoy teaching."

Only 12 percent of Haverford's students hail from Pennsylvania, but many are East Coasters nonetheless; 12 percent are international. Ninety-six percent of freshmen graduated in the top 10th of their high school class. "Students are very academically motivated, but we have a good mix of partiers and shut-ins," a student explains. Twelve percent of students are Asian American, 10 percent are Hispanic, 7 percent are African American, and 3 percent are multiracial. Though the college is nonsectarian, the Quaker influence lives on in the form of an optional silent meeting each week. "Although students tend to be very well informed on political issues and have great concern about these issues, few are very involved in political activism," says a philosophy major. Haverford meets the full demonstrated financial need of every admitted student and, for students from families with annual incomes below $60,000, has replaced loans with grants in its financial aid packages. Merit-based academic and athletic scholarships are not available.

Upper-class "Customs people" are resources and mentors for living/learning groups of eight to 16 first-year students.

Haverford's residence halls are spacious and well maintained, and most rooms are singles—even for freshmen—so it's no surprise that 98 percent of all students live on campus. All dorms are co-ed, but students may request single-sex floors. The school-owned Haverford College Apartments sit on the edge of campus and feature coveted one- and two-bedroom units, each with a living room, kitchen, and bathroom. "Some of the dorms are incredible. The apartments are the best freshman housing anywhere," says an economics major. Upperclassmen in the apartments may cook for themselves, but all others living on campus must buy the meal plan, which includes weekend board. Crime is virtually nonexistent, owing to the school's location in the upscale Philadelphia suburbs. "There is little to worry about coming from the surrounding area," one student says.

Haverford boasts the number-one varsity college cricket team in the country because, well, it's the only school that has one!

While the community spirit at Haverford works well for academics and personal development, it doesn't always carry over to the social scene. Without fraternities and sororities, Haverford and Bryn Mawr hold joint campus parties, but students say these affairs can get tiresome after freshman and sophomore years. The alcohol policy is connected to the honor code. For nondrinkers, there are frequently free movies, concerts, and other activities on campus. Other traditional events include the weekend-

"Sometimes you feel like you are walking on eggshells to avoid offending anyone."

long pre-exams Haverfest—a carnival-like, themed festival with music, food, and games—as well as the winter Snowball dance and the drag ball. Life in the close-knit, introspective environment that is Haverford can get stifling, but there are easy escapes: downtown Philadelphia is 20 minutes away by train. New York City, Washington, D.C., the New Jersey beaches, Pocono ski areas, and Atlantic City are only a couple hours away by car or train. Fifty-five percent of students participate in volunteer projects coordinated by the school's Eighth Dimension organization.

Haverford's rich athletic history dates back more than 100 years, when the soccer team played in its first intercollegiate game. A popular T-shirt boasts that the football team has been "Undefeated Since 1971"—a reference to the year the sport was abolished. The men's cross-country team is a perennial Division III national contender and a recent Centennial Conference champion, and women's basketball and softball are also competitive. Haverford boasts the number-one varsity college cricket team in the country because, well, it's the only school that has one! Despite a lively rivalry with Swarthmore, these Quakers have struggled to reconcile their peace-loving heritage with the desire to bash opponents' brains out on the court or the field. For now, students root for their Black Squirrels and chant, "Fight, fight, inner light—kill, Quakers, kill!" Intramural and club sports are popular too, especially because participation counts toward the required six quarters of athletic credit.

Haverford's student body may be beyond the norm in regards to personal values, but the downside of the honor code, according to one student, is that "students are challenged to meet an ideal set before them of creating the best community possible. For this reason, students are constantly criticizing themselves and the community as a whole to find ways of solving the problems facing them." See? Mom was right. With freedom comes responsibility.

Overlaps

Swarthmore, Hamilton, Davidson, Middlebury, Carleton, Wesleyan, Bowdoin, Amherst

If You Apply To ›

Haverford: Early decision I and II, regular decision. SATs or ACTs: required. Subject Tests: optional. Accepts the Common Application with supplement.

2600 Campus Road, Room 001, Honolulu, HI 96822

One of the most accessible of the public flagships in the U.S.—at least when it comes to admissions—Hawaii at Manoa pursues its research and teaching in a distinctly unique and culturally cosmopolitan setting. While you may be thinking about surfing as much as studying, don't be fooled: it will take more than a great tan and the ability to catch a wave to earn your degree here. Strong on teaching writing.

Website: www.manoa.hawaii
.edu
Location: City Outskirts
Public
Total Enrollment: 13,068
Undergraduates: 10,550
Male/Female: 44/56
SAT Ranges: ERW 530–620,
M 520–620
ACT Ranges: 21–26
Financial Aid: 57%
Pell Grant: 28%
Expense: Pub $ $
Student Loans: 45%
Average Debt: $ $
Applicants: 8,523
Accepted: 83%
Enrolled: 28%
Grad in 6 Years: 60%
Returning Freshmen: 79%
Academics: ✍ ✍
Social: ☎ ☎ ☎
Q of L: ★ ★ ★
Admissions: (800) 823-9771
Email Address: manoa
.admissions@hawaii.edu

Strong Programs:
Nursing
Psychology
Biology
Marketing
Astronomy
Pacific and Asian Studies
Tropical Agriculture
Engineering

One of the goals of the University of Hawaii at Manoa is to "serve as a bridge between East and West." It is one of the few schools that are land, sea, and space grant institutions. Despite—or perhaps because of—the fact that a high percentage of students are in-staters, UHM has more Asian American students than almost any other school. But not everything at UHM is so sunny: the university continues to feel the pain of budget cuts triggered by the state's economic troubles, and students complain of bulging classrooms and outdated facilities in need of upgrades and repairs. Despite these challenges, a plant and environmental protection science major says, "Students, faculty, and community members are friendly and give off the Aloha Spirit."

The UHM campus occupies 300 acres in the Manoa Valley, a residential Honolulu neighborhood. The architecture is regionally eclectic, mirroring historical and modern Asian Pacific motifs, and is enhanced by extensive subtropical landscaping. The campus is also within a few miles of the state capital and the city's major business district, providing excellent opportunities for students to interact with thought leaders, including mentorships and internships.

Core requirements are extensive: all students must take classes in math, humanities, social sciences, natural sciences, world civilization, and a foreign language or Hawaiian. The First-Year program gathers diverse groups of first-year students with similar interests to work and study together in Freshman Seminars, limited to ten students, and in Access to College Excellence residential learning communities. The Manoa Writing Program, founded in 1987, is one of the oldest writing-across-the-curriculum programs in the country. Faculty from more than 70 departments teach writing-intensive (W) courses that use a variety of discipline-specific writing-to-learn techniques, with an emphasis on student/faculty interaction during the writing process. Students are required to take five W courses in order to graduate, but many take more.

> **"Many students are very driven, but others are here to appreciate the island life."**

UHM offers more than 95 bachelor's degrees; among the best are astronomy, Pacific and Asian area studies, languages and the arts, ethnomusicology, and tropical agriculture. Astronomy and astrophysics benefit from the clear Hawaiian skies. It should come as no surprise that ocean-, climate-, and environment-related programs are also first-rate, with world-class facilities. The university takes pride in its programs in engineering, geology and geophysics, international business, political science, and travel industry management. The most popular majors, by enrollment, are nursing, psychology, biology, and marketing. "The courses can be challenging based on what you take and the major you declare," says a senior. Fifty-three percent of undergraduate classes have fewer than 20 students. Desirable classes and times are said to be difficult for freshmen and sophomores to get into, although departmental academic advisors keep close tabs on whether students are on schedule to complete their degrees in four years. The Student Success Center offers academic referrals and support services. Professors receive generally favorable reviews. "Each professor has his or her own style and priorities, but every professor that I have had is knowledgeable," says a biology and music double major. "Most of them are thoughtful and interested in the success of their students."

The two-tier Honors Program offers qualified freshmen and sophomores the opportunity for general education courses in small, intensive classes, while upper-class honors students are guided by faculty through independent, sustained research or creative work and must complete a final Honors thesis. The Undergraduate Research Opportunity Program provides financial support for motivated students to work closely with faculty mentors on research or creative projects across the disciplines. Participants present their work at a semester-end symposium. Students who tire of Hawaii's endless beaches and beatific sunsets can study abroad in locations around the world, including Asia, Australia, Europe, and South America.

It should come as no surprise that UHM's ocean-, climate-, and environment-related programs are first-rate, with world-class facilities.

"Many students are very driven, but others are here to appreciate the island life," says a student. Sixty-seven percent of undergraduates are in-staters, and 3 percent are from other countries. Hawaii stands out among major American universities in that 40 percent of its undergraduates are Asian American, and another 17 percent are of Native Hawaiian or other Pacific Islander descent. African Americans and Hispanics each represent 2 percent of the student body, and 16 percent identify as multiracial. "The climate and diversity in Hawaii allow for a greater and more open dialogue about race and culture," observes an English and history major. Political and social issues often take a backseat to academics and play, but among the more prominent concerns are the environment and Native Hawaiian rights. Twenty-eight percent of freshmen are Pell-eligible, and especially promising students can compete for merit scholarships, which average $12,600 annually. The university also disburses 243 athletic scholarships in 21 sports. The Manoa Service Award offers $1,000 scholarships to current students who volunteer 100 hours of service to the community each semester.

"The climate and diversity in Hawaii allow for a greater and more open dialogue about race and culture."

Twenty-four percent of students live in campus housing, and those who apply by the May deadline are guaranteed a spot. Students recommend the four towers, Ilima, Lehua, Lokelani, and Mokihana; the rooms are small but the hallways are happening. If you're thinking about off-campus housing, take note: housing in Honolulu is scarce and expensive. Cafeterias are located throughout the campus and serve diverse and adequate fare. "The Department of Public Safety has advertised more campus apps to help with safety so students can avoid getting into vulnerable situations," reports a history and economics double major.

The Manoa Service Award offers $1,000 scholarships to current students who volunteer 100 hours of service to the community each semester.

Because many students are commuters, UHM is pretty sedate after dark, especially on weekends. Most social activity revolves around student clubs and, as one student explains, "simply being around the Campus Center, where you can find many students studying, socializing, or hitting the gym." Only 1 percent of the men and 1 percent of the women join the tiny Greek system. Drinking is not allowed in the dorms. A couple of local hangouts provide an escape, and the campus pub, Manoa Garden, is also an option. Many students head off campus to enjoy "more beaches and hikes than one can handle," according to a sophomore. Lest anyone forget, some of the world's most beautiful resorts are less than a 20-minute drive away. Waikiki Beach? Within two miles' reach. And round-trip airfare to the neighboring islands—including Maui, Kauai, and the Big Island—is reasonable. The homecoming dance is one of the most popular campus events of the year. But what students really look forward to is Kanikapila, a festival of Hawaiian music, dance, and culture.

Overlaps

UCLA, Hawaii Pacific, University of Hawaii at Hilo, University of Southern California, University of Washington

UHM's athletic teams compete in Division I; the men's teams are known as the Rainbow Warriors, while the women's teams are the Rainbow Wahine. Men's basketball, football, baseball, and swimming and women's volleyball are among the top draws. Intramural and recreational activities range from soccer and basketball to Tai Chi and snorkeling.

Students seeking warm weather and great surfing won't be disappointed, but mainlanders should think twice about making the leap to UHM unless they are set on one of the university's specialized programs. It's up to you, one student says, to get the best out of Hawaii. "The location allows mainland students to get a different cultural experience," adds another. "You're only young once—might as well be 20 in Hawaii."

If You Apply To ›

UHM: Rolling admissions. SATs or ACTs: required. No Subject Tests. Does not accept the Common Application.

Hendrix College

1600 Washington Avenue, Conway, AR 72032

Hendrix is in the same class of Southern liberal arts colleges as Millsaps and Rhodes. The most progressive of the three, Hendrix has a strong emphasis on international awareness. Arkansas is a tough sell, and the college accepts the vast majority of students who apply. More than half of Hendrix students are from Arkansas, and most of the rest are Southerners.

Website: www.hendrix.edu
Location: Suburban
Private
Total Enrollment: 1,238
Undergraduates: 1,228
Male/Female: 48/52
SAT Ranges: ERW 560–710, M 540–700
ACT Ranges: 24–29
Financial Aid: 100%
Pell Grant: 38%
Expense: Pr $ $
Student Loans: 58%
Average Debt: $ $
Applicants: 1,465
Accepted: 80%
Enrolled: 29%
Grad in 6 Years: 75%
Returning Freshmen: 83%
Academics: ✐ ✐ ✐
Social: 🐿 🐿 🐿 🐿
Q of L: ★ ★ ★ ★
Admissions: (501) 450-1362

For a school in the heart of the Bible Belt and Walton-land, Hendrix College is surprisingly liberal. In fact, it's among the South's most progressive liberal arts colleges. Academics are demanding but the atmosphere is laid-back. Students tend to be liberal—even radical—in their political and social views. Ironically, healthy dialogue about tough issues such as LGBTQ rights, the environment, and capital punishment draws students together. "People here are passionate, intelligent, and fun," says a freshman. "They really want to change the world."

Hendrix's compact and comfortable campus stretches for 180 acres between the Ouachita and the Ozark mountains. College land boasts more than 80 varieties of trees and shrubs, and more than 10,000 budding flowers each spring. The main campus—with its own lily pool, fountain, and gazebo—occupies about one-fourth of the total acreage. The redbrick buildings are a mix of old and new, and a pedestrian overpass connects the main campus to the college's athletic facilities and a wooded fitness trail. An 80,000-square-foot student life and technology center houses state-of-the-art educational technology space as well as a coffee shop and dining facility.

Under Hendrix's general education program, known as Collegiate Center, freshmen take two required courses, The Engaged Citizen and Explorations: Liberal Arts for Life. The Capacities component involves requirements in writing, foreign language, quantitative skills, and physical activity, while the Learning Domains component requires coursework in seven broad liberal arts areas. The Odyssey Program requires students to complete three experiences—which may be coursework, internships, or independent projects—selected from six categories: artistic creativity, global awareness, professional and leadership development, service to the world, special projects, and undergraduate research. Seniors in all majors must complete a capstone experience. Hendrix freshmen also participate in a weeklong orientation program, which includes a two-day, off-campus trip emphasizing outdoor experiences, urban exposure, or volunteer service.

Hendrix is strong in many areas, but natural and social sciences are definitely the school's forte. Popular majors include psychology, biochemistry/molecular biology, biology, economics and business, and English. The chemistry, politics, and international relations programs are also notable. The Murphy Scholars Program in Literature and Language draws participants from a broad range of majors, including the sciences, who are interested in deeper study in these areas of the humanities. Doing well at Hendrix means keeping up with the intense workload. Thankfully, engaging professors are available to help students navigate the coursework. "There are very few bad faculty, and those are usually in temporary positions and are soon weeded out," a senior says. Seventy-three percent of classes have fewer than 20 students, so personal attention is the norm. The school also offers five-year programs with Columbia, Vanderbilt, and Washington University in St. Louis for aspiring engineers.

> **"There are very few bad faculty, and those are usually in temporary positions."**

At Hendrix, undergraduate research takes priority, especially within the sciences, with nearly two-thirds of all students taking part; many get the chance to present original papers at regional and national symposia. Many students get course credit for internships at U.S. embassies and organizations such as the National Institutes of Health and the U.S. Agency for International Development. Thirty-five percent of students participate in a wide variety of opportunities to work, study, and serve abroad. Accademia dell'Arte in Arezzo, Italy, exposes participants to the world of European theater, vocal arts, and dance, while the Heilongjiang program in China focuses on Mandarin Chinese. Hendrix also sponsors programs in Austria, England, Costa Rica, Spain, France, Germany, and Cypress, and students have access to more than 150 partner exchange programs as well. For career preparation, Hendrix offers a three-day Career Term for sophomores during winter break, in which students participate in self-assessments and learn practical skills like interviewing and networking; the school intends to make the course a requirement for all sophomores in 2020.

Hendrix offers a three-day Career Term for sophomores during winter break, in which students learn practical skills like interviewing and networking.

"Most students are liberal and eclectic, but all are respectful of political and social beliefs," says one student. "It seems like everyone is involved in at least something, whether it be athletics, Student Senate, or the informal Dungeons and Dragons club." Fifty-seven percent of Hendrix students are from Arkansas, and 3 percent come from abroad. African Americans represent 7 percent of the student body, Hispanics 6 percent, Asian Americans 5 percent, and multiracial students 4 percent. The recently created Office for Diversity and Inclusion seeks to enhance campus diversity. Thirty-eight percent of freshmen are eligible for the Pell Grant. Hendrix offers a variety of merit scholarships, averaging $26,700, to academically qualified students, but there are no athletic scholarships. Through the Arkansas Advantage Program, the college guarantees to meet the full demonstrated financial need of Arkansas residents who meet certain academic requirements.

> **"Hendrix has such a vibrant social life that students hardly ever leave the campus to party."**

All students are required to live on campus, and only a few are granted exceptions per year, which students say adds to the sense of community. "Hendrix housing is diverse and outstanding," says one student, and all but one of the dorms are single-sex. Sophomores may take advantage of living/learning programs, including Global Issues, Social Justice, Artistic Creativity, and Sustainability. Students generally praise the dining options and report that plenty of choices are available for

(continued)

Email Address:
adm@hendrix.edu

Strong Programs:
Psychology
Biochemistry/Molecular
   Biology
Biology
Economics and Business
English
Chemistry
Politics
International Relations

those with special dietary needs. "Our food rocks!" cheers one student. Students also report feeling safe on campus, due in part to a visible security program and the close-knit nature of the campus. Every member of the Hendrix community is required to complete two comprehensive seminars on issues related to gender, relationship violence, and sexual assault.

"Hendrix has such a vibrant social life that students hardly ever leave the campus to party," a junior explains. Greek life—a staple of most Southern schools—is conspicuously absent at Hendrix, and students are proud of their independence. The student-run Social Committee (SoCo) brings nationally known music and comedy acts to campus and hosts the annual SoCo 54 disco-inspired party. The annual Campus Kitty charity fund-raiser is highlighted by the always memorable Miss Hendrix drag competition. Last but not least is the Shirttail Serenade, a 100-year-old tradition in which first-year men and women from each dorm croon out a song-and-dance routine in their shirts, ties, shoes, and socks for classmates. Judges rate each performance on the basis of singing, creativity, legs, and so on.

Home to three colleges, Conway is undergoing a revitalization and offers a growing number of shops and restaurants, as well as Toad Suck Daze, a rollicking annual carnival downtown featuring bluegrass music. Little Rock, a 30-minute drive, provides more options. Faulkner County, where the school is located, is officially dry, so students must travel to buy booze—or find older peers to help out. Underage drinking is prohibited, but "the alcohol policies could use some work," says one student. Popular road trips are Memphis (two hours by car) and Dallas and Oklahoma City (each a five-hour drive) for concerts and the like. For those who stay in town, the Volunteer Action Center coordinates participation in projects on Service Saturdays.

> "Hendrix is tight-knit with a place for everyone."

The Division III Hendrix Warriors field a number of competitive teams, and recent Southern Athletic Association conference champions include football, men's basketball, and women's volleyball. Rhodes College is the chief rival. For outdoor buffs, the college sponsors trips around Arkansas for canoeing, biking, rock climbing, and spelunking. Most students also compete in intramural or club sports, with sand volleyball, indoor soccer, and basketball proving the most popular.

"Hendrix is tight-knit with a place for everyone," says one student. Musician Jimi Hendrix—whose mug inevitably adorns a new campus T-shirt each year—once asked listeners, "Are you experienced?" After four years at Hendrix College, with small classes, an emphasis on research, and a laid-back atmosphere in which to test their beliefs and boundaries, students here can likely answer, "Yes!"

Overlaps

Austin College, Kalamazoo, Millsaps, Southwestern, Ursinus, University of Arkansas, University of Central Arkansas, Rhodes

If You Apply To ›

Hendrix: Early action I and II, regular decision. SATs or ACTs: required. No Subject Tests. Accepts the Common Application with supplement.

Hiram College

P.O. Box 96, Hiram, OH 44234

The smallest of the prominent Ohio liberal arts colleges. Less nationally known than Denison or Wooster, Hiram draws the vast majority of its students from in state—and sends them around the globe. Lots of classes are taught in seminar format, and under its trademarked "New Liberal Arts" curriculum, offerings ensure a broad education and undergraduate research opportunities.

Hiram College offers students a solid liberal arts education and plenty of opportunities to dive into a research lab, test out the corporate life, or travel the globe. In fact, all students are required to have a hands-on learning experience before they graduate. No matter where they hang their hats, students here enjoy a close-knit environment that ensures every Hiram "Dawg" has his or her day. "Because of its small size, students get noticed, not lost in the shuffle," one junior says.

Set on a charming hilltop campus that occupies the second-highest spot in Ohio, Hiram is blessed with an abundance of flowers and trees as well as a nice view of the valley below. The prevailing architectural motif is New England brick, and many Hiram buildings are restored 19th-century homes. Hiram's biology and environmental studies majors, as well as other students, frequently work, study, and conduct research at the college-owned, 550-acre ecology field study station a few miles away.

The Hiram Plan organizes the academic year into two longer 12-week sessions, each of which is followed by a shorter three-week term. Hiram's core curriculum is extensive. Freshmen take a First-Year Colloquium in the fall and a more advanced First-Year Seminar in the spring. Students are also required to take courses in eight Ways of Knowing, through which they learn various methods for acquiring knowledge, such as experimental scientific methods, social and cultural analysis, and understanding diversity. In addition, students satisfy an experiential learning component by studying off campus, conducting research, or working in an internship, and in the senior year, they complete and present a capstone project. Hiram also requires students to reflect on their career and other goals and on their progress at four points, starting in the spring of their first year. Thanks to the college's Tech and Trek mobile education program, every full-time, traditional student is outfitted with an iPad Pro, an Apple Pencil, a keyboard, and a pair of hiking boots.

> **"Professors are involved and are fun to talk with."**

Hiram has recently trimmed the number of majors while, under the "New Liberal Arts" banner, offering new programs in areas like integrative exercise science and public health, as well as opportunities to focus on societal challenges like climate change. The sciences, especially biology and chemistry, are strong, as is the creative writing program. Hiram has the longest-standing biomedical humanities major in the country, and the Garfield Institute, named after the Hiram educator who went on to become the 20th U.S. president, offers a notable minor in public leadership. The most popular majors include accounting and financial management, business management, nursing, and psychology. Dual-degree engineering programs are available with nearby Case Western Reserve as well as WashU in St. Louis. More than 20 three-year degree programs are available, enabling participants to graduate faster and save tens of thousands of dollars. For most students, however, "The academic climate is relaxed," says a communication major. "Students have time to breathe between classes and an opportunity to thrive without overstressing." Academic resources abound, including tutors, the writing center, and help from peers or profs.

Website: www.hiram.edu
Location: Rural
Private
Total Enrollment: 842
Undergraduates: 838
Male/Female: 47/53
SAT Ranges: ERW 480–610, M 460–590
ACT Ranges: 18–24
Financial Aid: 98%
Pell Grant: 41%
Expense: Pr $
Student Loans: 42%
Average Debt: $ $ $
Applicants: 2,761
Accepted: 64%
Enrolled: 15%
Grad in 6 Years: 56%
Returning Freshmen: 70%
Academics: ✍ ✍ ✍
Social: ☎ ☎ ☎
Q of L: ★ ★ ★
Admissions: (800) 362-5280
Email Address: admission@hiram.edu

Strong Programs:
Accounting and Financial Management
Business Management
Nursing
Psychology
Biology
Chemistry
Creative Writing
Biomedical Humanities

Classes are small, with 82 percent enrolling fewer than 20 students, and students enjoy an impressive degree of faculty accessibility. "Professors are involved and are fun to talk with," says a freshman.

Hiram's unique academic calendar allows ample time for off-campus endeavors of all types. Professors lead five to eight study abroad programs each year in all corners of the globe. Hiram offers several unusual summer opportunities as well, most notably the Northwoods Station up in the wilds of northern Michigan, where students choose courses ranging from photography and botany to geology and writing. Political internships are available in Washington, D.C. A four-year honors program offers further opportunities for networking, independent study, and advanced coursework.

Seventy-eight percent of Hiram students are in-staters, and many of the rest hail from New York and Pennsylvania, though the administration is working aggressively to recruit more students from other states. International students represent 2 percent of the student body. African Americans constitute 16 percent, Asian Americans 1 percent, Hispanics 4 percent, and multiracial students 3 percent. Hiram's Intercultural Forum club is one of the largest and most active on campus, and the Office for Diversity and Inclusion offers peer mentoring and tutoring programs for first-generation students, among other services. A hefty 41 percent of freshmen qualify for Pell Grants. In addition to need-based financial aid, Hiram offers a tuition guarantee to incoming freshmen and awards merit scholarships, luring good students with irresistible financial aid. "My financial aid package at Hiram is unbelievable," says a junior. "After applying to larger, cheaper public universities, I came to realize it would actually cost me less to attend Hiram."

> "Hiram is known for the 'Hiram Hi' because everyone is always greeting one another as they pass."

Most Hiram students—84 percent—live on campus, and everyone who wants a room gets one. "Ours are much better than some I have seen at other schools," says a junior. Most halls are co-ed, and upperclassmen who like their location can stay in the same room year after year. Most students live in two-person suites; the popular (and larger) triple and quad suites, and the townhouse apartments, are scarcer and usually claimed by upper-class students. Dining services receive good reviews, and new educational programming on sexual assault has been well received.

When the weekend rolls around, don't expect to find most Hiram students gathered around a keg; the college has cracked down on underage drinking. "Hiram does a good job of enforcing the alcohol rules when needed, but most of the time there are no problems with parties," says a senior. Only 2 percent of the women go Greek—there are currently no social fraternities at the school. Hiram is a bit isolated, and there are few distractions in town, so students must make their own fun. Typically, that means hanging out in each other's rooms, at the tavern or the pizza place in town, or at other places in neighboring Garrettsville. "We always have tons of things happening on campus," says one student. Every spring on Sugar Day, classes are canceled and the entire student body participates in a day of community service at local nonprofit organizations. The college sometimes offers free tickets to concerts, plays, and ballets in town. Cleveland's Progressive Field is a short road trip, and the city's Rock and Roll Hall of Fame can get students rockin' all year-round. Other diversions include an excellent golf course three miles away and good downhill slopes about an hour distant.

Hiram is hardly a mecca for budding athletic superstars, but it does have a decent Division III sports program. Women's volleyball, men's soccer, and men's and women's basketball have been the most successful Terriers teams. About half of the students play in intramural and club sports, including volleyball, kickball, and dance, and many enjoy the on-campus disc golf course as well.

Overlaps

Baldwin Wallace, College of Wooster, John Carroll, Kent State, Ohio Wesleyan, University of Akron, Notre Dame College (OH), Mount Union

Those looking for a school where anonymity is ensured need not apply. People here are so close that they share an equivalent of a not-so-secret handshake. "Hiram is known for the 'Hiram Hi' because everyone is always greeting one another as they pass," says a senior. Indeed, those seeking a friendly, all-American institution with a touch of internationalism might want to give Hiram a look.

If You Apply To ›

Hiram: Rolling admissions. SATs or ACTs: required (optional for applicants who meet certain requirements). No Subject Tests. Accepts the Common Application with supplement. Submission of a graded writing sample or essay is recommended.

Hobart and William Smith Colleges

Geneva, NY 14456

Two independent, single–gender liberal arts colleges operating under a coordinate college system, overlooking one of New York's picturesque Finger Lakes. An early leader in gender and sexuality studies programs for undergrads, HWS takes pride in personal attention from full professors and a culture of community service. Most social life takes place on campus, especially in the fraternities, but skiing and other outdoor activities beckon.

If you're unsure about a single-sex school, the Hobart and William Smith "coordinate system" may offer the best of both worlds. Students share the same campus, faculty, administration, and curriculum, and even the same residence halls, but each college has its own deans, student government, athletics department, and traditions. Students thus enjoy a close-knit, co-ed community, yet still get to experience the sort of deep brotherly and sisterly bonds that are typically associated with single-sex institutions. If you can tolerate the frigid winters of upstate New York, you'll be rewarded with small classes, caring faculty, and a place where tradition still matters.

Hobart College was founded in 1822 by Episcopal Bishop John Henry Hobart, who conceived it to be an outpost for civilized and learned behavior. William Smith College opened in 1908 and bears the name of a wealthy businessman and philanthropist who wanted to introduce women to opportunities that were largely unrecognized at the time. The HWS campus stretches for 325 tree-lined acres and includes a forest, farmland, and a wildlife preserve. Architectural styles range from colonial to postmodern,

> "The professors here treat serious students as colleagues rather than their students."

with stately Greek Revival mansions and ivy-clad brick residences and classrooms. The nationally ranked sailing team enjoys a boathouse on the shores of Seneca Lake. The LEED Gold–certified Gearan Center for the Performing Arts recently opened, as did the Perkin Observatory.

The HWS curriculum has no distribution requirements. Instead, students start by taking an interdisciplinary seminar in the first year, constructed around a different interest; recent seminar offerings include Earth vs. Humans, Britpop: From the Beatles to Brexit, and Facets of Islam. First-years in each seminar are assigned to the same orientation group, "so they are well acquainted before they start their first class together," explains an economics major. Students must also complete a major and a minor or second major, and all students conduct a senior capstone experience.

Website: www.hws.edu
Location: Small City
Private
Total Enrollment: 2,227
Undergraduates: 2,220
Male/Female: 49/51
SAT Ranges: ERW 610–680, M 600–680
ACT Ranges: 26–32
Financial Aid: 89%
Pell Grant: 19%
Expense: Pr $ $ $ $
Student Loans: 65%
Average Debt: $ $ $ $
Applicants: 4,409
Accepted: 61%
Enrolled: 24%
Grad in 6 Years: 81%
Returning Freshmen: 86%
Academics: ✍ ✍ ✍
Social: ☎ ☎ ☎
Q of L: ★ ★ ★
Admissions: (800) 852-2256
Email Address: admissions@hws.edu

Strong Programs:
Economics

Administrators say the coordinate college system creates "an innovative construct to interrogate gender and difference." Indeed, the Colleges were among the first in the nation to offer full-fledged undergraduate programs in women's studies and LGBTQ studies, in addition to a first-of-its-kind minor in men's studies. The most popular majors include economics, media and society, psychology, and biology, and the long list of minors includes entrepreneurial studies, sustainable community development, child advocacy, and aesthetics. Other solid programs include architectural studies, geoscience, and political science. The Finger Lakes Institute gives students wide opportunities to work in various fields of scientific inquiry, as well as public policy. "I would not describe the academic climate as competitive at all, but that's not to say the workload is not intense," says one student. Small classes are the norm here: 66 percent have fewer than 20 students. Professors are praised for being accessible and engaging. "The professors here treat serious students as colleagues rather than their students," says a sociology and public policy major.

> "One of the most underrated programs on campus is the Centennial Center for Leadership."

HWS students may take a term away from campus, and 60 percent do so, studying abroad on six continents in nearly 50 programs, many of which are faculty led. Each year, about 40 seniors elect to complete an honors project involving research, a critical paper, or an equivalent creative work, in addition to written and oral exams on their projects. At the Senior Symposium each spring, seniors present research findings, discuss theory, display creative works, or present other significant scholarly activities. Students who complete the Pathways Program, a series of workshops and career counseling activities, are guaranteed an opportunity to complete a paid internship or research experience. One student says, "One of the most underrated programs on campus is the Centennial Center for Leadership," which runs programs and workshops throughout the year to promote leadership and entrepreneurship.

The Finger Lakes Institute gives students wide opportunities to work in various fields of scientific inquiry.

According to an international relations major, HWS students are "welcoming, friendly, and excited to try new things." New Yorkers make up 38 percent of the HWS student body and international students 6 percent. African Americans account for 6 percent of undergraduates, Hispanics 5 percent, and Asian Americans 4 percent. The political climate is liberal, but a political science major says that while there are many students who are "active in progressive issues," there are more who "don't engage" with politics. Merit scholarships averaging $16,000 are awarded to qualified students; there are no athletic scholarships.

> "Most parties end early just so people can go downtown."

HWS housing includes nine lakefront residences, as well as theme houses, townhouses, and highly sought-after downtown apartments. Single-sex, co-ed, and gender-neutral options are available. Housing is guaranteed for four years, and only seniors are allowed to apply to live off campus, though few choose to do so: 90 percent of HWS students live in college-owned housing. Thirty percent of first-years opt to participate in living/learning communities. Meal plans are required of all students regardless of where they live, and the food receives mixed reviews. When it comes to safety, a sophomore says campus security officers are "very efficient and helpful at all times." Sexual assault has been a high-profile issue at HSW, but a junior reports that the Colleges "are taking the proper steps and have a come a long way" in educational efforts to prevent and respond to sexual violence.

Collectively, HWS students contribute more than 90,000 hours of service each year.

Eight Hobart fraternities claim 18 percent of the men, who aren't permitted to pledge until sophomore year, and William Smith's sole sorority signs up 2 percent of the women. Much of the social life involves Greek parties and bashes at off-campus houses, although a junior notes that "most parties end early just so people can go downtown." Underage students caught with booze must attend alcohol awareness classes and may face social probation. The Campus Activities Board plans movies, concerts, plays, and other events each weekend. The old industrial city of Geneva has been revitalized in recent years and offers many amenities for students out on the town, including restaurants, bars, shops, concerts, and the Smith Opera House. Because students are actively involved with service in the community, says an English and political science major, "Geneva is more than just a place but a community intimately tied with HWS." Collectively, HWS students contribute more than 90,000 hours of service each year, often through service-learning courses, one-day opportunities like Days of Service, and extended volunteering with groups like the Boys and Girls Club. Rochester, Ithaca, and Syracuse, all about 45 minutes away, make for popular road trips. Seneca Falls, birthplace of the suffrage movement, is also nearby. More adventurous excursions include "skiing with friends or going into New York City or Boston," according to an art history major.

One of the most important ways in which the Colleges have retained their single-gender identities is through their traditions. Hobart students, for instance, sing their alma mater at the end of every formal meeting and celebrate Charter Day in April. William Smith, meanwhile, holds Founder's Day festivities in the fall, and at the end of the year, on Moving Up Day, seniors symbolically hand over their leadership role to juniors. Events that unite the entire campus include the annual Quad-a-Palooza bash and lacrosse matches against rivals Syracuse and Cornell.

HWS teams compete in Division III, except for Hobart lacrosse, which is Division I. Hobart rowing, ice hockey, and soccer and William Smith lacrosse and soccer were all conference champions in 2017–18. The Colleges' co-ed sailing team is also perennially competitive. The HWS Debate Team has had national success recently, as has the club alpine skiing team. Forty-one percent of students participate in intramural and club sports.

At HWS, "The opportunities that students have to engage with each other, with Geneva, and with any field of interest are incredible," says a student. While some may shy away from the coordinate college system, those who come here for the intimate classes, robust service opportunities, and enduring traditions recognize that HWS is a community like no other.

The Colleges' co-ed sailing team is perennially competitive.

Overlaps

Dickinson, Gettysburg, St. Lawrence, Trinity College (CT), Union, Skidmore, University of Vermont, SUNY–Binghamton

If You Apply To ›

HWS: Early decision I and II, regular decision. SATs or ACTs: optional (required for scholarship applicants and home-schooled students). No Subject Tests. Accepts the Common Application. Applicants' gender identity is considered in the admissions process.

Hofstra University

Hempstead, NY 11549

Boasts a combination of suburban setting with ready access to the Big Apple. Hofstra has outgrown its commuter-school origins and offers a broad range of preprofessional and other academic programs. Well known as a lacrosse powerhouse. Has become more selective in recent years, but for many it is still a backup to urban schools like BU and Northeastern.

Website: www.hofstra.edu
Location: Suburban
Private
Total Enrollment: 9,422
Undergraduates: 6,469
Male/Female: 45/55
SAT Ranges: ERW 570–660,
  M 560–650
ACT Ranges: 24–29
Financial Aid: 64%
Pell Grant: 24%
Expense: Pr $ $
Student Loans: 64%
Average Debt: N/A
Applicants: 26,808
Accepted: 64%
Enrolled: 10%
Grad in 6 Years: 63%
Returning Freshmen: 81%
Academics: ✍ ✍ ✍
Social: ☎ ☎ ☎
Q of L: ★ ★ ★
Admissions: (516) 463-6700
Email Address: admission@
  hofstra.edu

Strong Programs:
Business
Communication
Engineering
Health Studies
Accounting
Television and Film
Radio Production
Physician Assistant Studies

Hofstra has hosted U.S. presidential debates for three elections in a row.

Although it sits within easy striking distance of Manhattan concrete, Hofstra University occupies one of the loveliest campuses you'll find anywhere. Its bucolic setting is home not only to an accredited art museum and a nationally recognized arboretum, but also to the school's blossoming preprofessional offerings. Whatever their field, Hofstra students enjoy special learning communities, research opportunities, and first-year programs that help harried freshmen get off to a good start. "It's a friendly environment that allows you to find your special niches, without forcing anything upon you," reflects an accounting and political science major.

Founded in 1935 with one building—the Dutch colonial mansion left in trust by Kate and William Hofstra on their 15-acre estate—the campus is now home to 116 buildings on 244 acres. The suburban campus offers a parklike environment with a variety of architecture, from ivy-covered stone buildings to modern facilities with

"[Hofstra] allows you to find your special niches, without forcing anything upon you."

sleek angles and electronic signage, which surround open green quads. The campus is especially beautiful in the spring, when its 100,000 tulips, a tribute to the Dutch heritage of Hofstra's founders, are in bloom. Several buildings have undergone major renovations, and the Zarb School of Business has a new, 52,500-square-foot building boasting an incubator lab, a market research and behavioral science lab, and other amenities.

With more than 160 academic programs for undergraduates, Hofstra offers students plenty of career paths. Regardless of what major they choose, all undergrad students must complete distribution requirements, including coursework in humanities; natural sciences, mathematics, and computer science; social sciences; cross-cultural studies; and interdisciplinary studies. Everyone must also pass the Writing Proficiency Exam, usually taken in the first year, to demonstrate their competence as writers.

With the recent establishment of the DeMatteis School of Engineering and Applied Science and the Kalikow School of Government, Public Policy, and International Affairs, as well as joint undergraduate programs with its medical school, Hofstra seeks to model itself on much larger and better-known Northeastern universities like NYU and Syracuse. Traditional areas of strength include business, communication, engineering, and health studies; marketing, accounting, journalism, television and film, and radio production are particularly notable. Business students benefit from one of the largest simulated trading rooms in the New York area. A spate of dual-degree programs have recently been introduced (bringing the overall count to more than 15) that pair undergraduate degrees with corresponding master's degrees in such areas as physician assistant studies, labor studies, sustainability studies, and others.

A senior describes the workload as "mostly collaborative, not in the sense that we are working in groups most of the time, but because there is a conversation with the professors." Half of undergraduate classes have fewer than 20 students, allowing for plenty of access to faculty. "The professors are extremely skilled at what they do and have the awards to prove it," says a global studies major. Support services for students with learning disabilities are particularly strong and include accommodations as well as skill-development and coaching programs.

The First-Year Connections program offers new students a combined social and academic experience centered on small seminars (limited to 19 students) taught by senior faculty; recent seminars include Macro Freakonomics, Broadway (and More!), and The Mathematics of Elections. Freshmen may also enroll in clusters of thematically related courses, and several seminars and clusters also have living/learning community options associated with them. The Honors College offers more than 240 qualified entering students a multidisciplinary program with a special housing option. One honors student says, "The added challenge and mentorship have been extremely helpful in preparing me for law school." The university's 17 research centers facilitate opportunities for students to work with professors on scholarly projects. Students with wanderlust can take advantage of study abroad options around the world, including programs in Cuba, India, Italy, and Japan, although only 10 percent of undergrads do so.

"I wanted to make sure I wound up at a school where everyone loved different things and brought something different to the table, and I definitely found it here," says a journalism major. Fifty-eight percent of undergraduates hail from New York, and 6 percent come from abroad. African Americans account for 9 percent of the student body, Hispanics 13 percent, Asian Americans 11 percent, and multiracial students 3 percent. Hofstra has hosted U.S. presidential debates for three elections in a row, and a senior describes the political climate as "semi-intense" but "respectful." The university offers merit scholarships worth an average of $17,500 and 145 athletic scholarships in 17 men's and women's sports. Twenty-four percent of freshmen are eligible for Pell Grants.

Sixty-eight percent of first-year students live in university housing, which is guaranteed for all four years. Many dorms have been renovated in the last few years. Students have nearly 20 different dining options to choose from, and a health science major says, "Most meals are made to order, which ensures freshness and deliciousness." A junior reports, "The school takes safety very seriously, which is why we have five shuttle systems, including a night shuttle."

As for social life, "This is where Hofstra excels," says a sophomore, "offering an incredible number of clubs, in-dorm activities, and departmental organizations." Nine percent of the men and 11 percent of the women go Greek, but they don't dominate the social landscape. Students of legal age are allowed to consume alcohol in their rooms;

"The professors are extremely skilled at what they do and have the awards to prove it."

"parties are there if you're looking for them," says a junior. Hofstra is big on festivals, which include Fall Fest; a spring music festival; Irish, Italian, and Dutch festivals; and a long-running Shakespeare Festival that features performances on a stage that is purported to be the most authentic replica in the U.S. of the original Globe Theatre.

Hofstra's location 40 minutes east of New York City makes it easy to enjoy day trips and nights on the town, and the school organizes Explore Next Door events that take students to various neighborhoods, museums, shows, and sporting events. The two largest community service activities at Hofstra are Shake-a-Rake and Snow Angels, which send students out to do yard work and shoveling for elderly and disabled neighbors.

The Hofstra Pride compete in Division I and play an important role in shaping campus culture—especially the perennially powerful lacrosse teams. Men's and women's soccer and women's softball have won Colonial Athletic Association championships recently. The dance team is nationally ranked, and the forensics team has achieved national success as well. Roughly one-quarter of undergrads participate in the university's 26 club sports and 14 intramural leagues and special events.

Opportunities abound at Hofstra, and the university continues to add resources—both curricular and extracurricular—to serve its diverse, career-oriented student body. Says one senior, "We love our campus, but we know our time here is temporary and serves the purpose of setting up our future careers." Indeed, by offering solid academics and a bevy of programs aimed at first-years, the university seeks to put its students in a New York state of mind.

Overlaps

NYU, SUNY–Binghamton, SUNY–Stony Brook, Syracuse, University of Delaware, Penn State, Boston University, Fordham

If You Apply To ›

Hofstra: Early action I and II, rolling admissions. SATs or ACTs: optional (required for some programs and Trustee Scholarship applicants). Subject Tests: optional. Accepts the Common Application with supplement.

P.O. Box 9707, Roanoke, VA 24020

One of the South's leading women's colleges, Hollins is on the edge of Roanoke, the biggest city in southwest Virginia. Hollins has long been noted for creative writing, the performing arts, and its equestrian program. Social life often involves road trips to Virginia Tech and Washington and Lee, both about an hour's drive, or venturing into the great outdoors.

Website: www.hollins.edu
Location: Suburban
Private
Total Enrollment: 671
Undergraduates: 619
Male/Female: 0/100
SAT Ranges: ERW 580–680,
   M 530–620
ACT Ranges: 23–28
Financial Aid: 100%
Pell Grant: 35%
Expense: Pr $
Student Loans: 74%
Average Debt: $ $ $
Applicants: 2,842
Accepted: 48%
Enrolled: 11%
Grad in 6 Years: 62%
Returning Freshmen: 78%
Academics: ✍ ✍ ✍
Social: ☎ ☎ ☎
Q of L: ★ ★ ★ ★
Admissions: (800) 456-9595
Email Address: huadm@
   hollins.edu

Strong Programs:
English and Creative Writing
Biology
Psychology
Communication Studies
Business
Environmental Studies
Visual and Performing Arts
Leadership Studies

Traditions rule at Hollins University, a private, single-sex college on a lush 475-acre campus in the Virginia mountains. Each fall, students and staff hike up Tinker Mountain for skits, a picnic lunch, and a bird's-eye view of the changing foliage. During the holiday season, faculty and administrators sing carols outside students' residence halls. And after graduation, juniors inherit seniors' decorated gowns during Passing of the Robes. A few male students can now be found on campus, since Hollins offers 11 co-ed graduate programs. "A student should only attend Hollins if they want to be a part of a close-knit community that fosters creative minds and ambitious spirits," says a senior.

Described by the *New York Times* as "achingly picturesque," the neoclassical redbrick buildings at Hollins date back to the mid-19th century. There are some modern structures too, such as the Wetherill Visual Arts Center. Several buildings have been renovated in recent years, including Hollins Theatre, Turner Hall, Presser Hall, Dana Science Building, and Bradley Hall.

Hollins's general education program (known as Education through Skills and Perspectives) teaches real-world skills, including writing, oral communication, applied quantitative reasoning, and applied research techniques, while examining seven perspectives from which people view and understand the world: aesthetic analysis, creative expression, ancient and medieval worlds, modern and contemporary worlds, social and cultural diversities, scientific inquiry, and global systems and languages. Two terms of physical education are mandatory, and those looking to take advantage of Hollins's acclaimed equestrian program can earn PE credits with riding lessons. All freshmen take a required first-year seminar and participate in Orientation Week, which includes academic programming, a day of community service, and plenty of time to form friendships with new classmates.

> **"In general, Hollins women are independent, ambitious, and passionate."**

Academics are the priority at Hollins. "I have been challenged by most of my classes here, but the workload has been manageable enough that I have been able to do a bunch of extracurriculars too," says one senior. Of the school's 28 undergraduate majors, English, biology, psychology, communication studies, and business are the most popular. Students majoring or minoring in creative writing benefit from the nationally recognized Jackson Center for Creative Writing. Environmental studies and the visual and performing arts, especially theatre and dance, have good reputations too. Serious dance students have the opportunity to attend the American Dance Festival at Duke University to study intensively during the summer. Classes are small, with 88 percent enrolling fewer than 20 students and none exceeding 50, and professors are well regarded. "Faculty members are typically accessible and often work hard to make sure they can help any students having trouble," says a senior. Motivated students are encouraged to design their majors or apply to the honors program, which involves interdisciplinary projects carried out through a four-semester sequence of two-credit seminars.

The shorter January Term offers a break for on-campus projects, travel, or internships. A January Term program for first-year students offers local internships in Roanoke, while the Signature Internship Program places upperclassmen in for-credit internships, offered by loyal alumnae across the country, that come with a $300 stipend. Research opportunities are available through the annual Science Seminar, and many seniors undertake independent research projects. The Batten Leadership Institute, open to students of all majors, offers a certificate in leadership studies and opportunities for students to develop skills like effective conflict management, negotiation, and team-building. Participants receive practice sessions with seasoned professionals, videotaped performance reviews, and coaching from senior students. In addition to a Hollins Abroad program in London, students may study through affiliated programs in 20 countries around the world; 48 percent of students study internationally before they graduate.

Each fall, students and staff hike up Tinker Mountain for skits, a picnic lunch, and a bird's-eye view of the changing foliage.

"In general, Hollins women are independent, ambitious, and passionate," a senior says. "There are some significant cliques, but for the most part everyone gets along." Forty-eight percent of undergrads are Virginians, and 5 percent hail from foreign countries. African Americans make up 12 percent of the total, Asian Americans 2 percent,

"Most of the dorms are beautiful historic buildings full of character and comfort."

Hispanics 6 percent, and multiracial students 6 percent. "We have a very active gay and lesbian club called OUTloud, and also an active women's studies department that puts together a lot of rallies and events," says a first-year student. "Our campus has a definite liberal leaning, although there is a small, committed Republican group." The university has made socioeconomic diversity a priority, with a full 35 percent of freshmen qualifying for the Pell Grant. Hollins also hands out merit scholarships averaging $29,500 to qualified students, but no athletic scholarships.

Eighty-seven percent of Hollins students live in the dorms; they have to, unless they're married, older than 23, or living at home in Roanoke with their parents. Options include five traditional residence halls as well as a small apartment complex and seven special interest houses. "Most of the dorms are beautiful historic buildings full of character and comfort," says a student. First-years live in Randolph and Tinker. Upperclassmen make their homes in Main, West, and East, which have 10-foot ceilings and hardwood floors, and some rooms also boast brass doorknobs, walk-in closets, and even fireplaces. Students chow down at Moody Dining Hall, Greenberry's Coffee, or The Hub. While the adjacent Roanoke neighborhood has its rough spots, "the campus is very safe," says one student.

The Batten Leadership Institute offers opportunities to develop skills like effective conflict management, negotiation, and team-building.

"Most social gatherings take place on campus," says a student. "People meet at dinner to talk about their day or hang out until midnight watching movies and talking in their dorm rooms." Hollins shuns sororities, and sporadic student efforts to bring them to campus draw lively debate. To fill the gap, the school organizes mixers, concerts, dances, and second-run movies each weekend. There's also a free shuttle to help students get around Roanoke (population 100,000). "Roanoke is a quaint city, not tall and towering but not small, either," says an English major. "There are local markets, a few clubs, a mall, and curious little local shops." As a result, road-tripping remains the preferred social option—to Hampden–Sydney College, Virginia Tech, the University of Virginia, or Washington and Lee.

Hollins's on-campus stable, in which students can board their own horses, complements the school's top-notch equestrian program, which has brought home the Old Dominion Athletic Conference championship 21 times, most recently in 2017. The university also sponsors eight other Division III sports. Although there are no intramural sports, the popular Hollins Outdoor Program offers hiking, spelunking, and other activities for all skill levels in the beautiful Shenandoah Valley and Blue Ridge Mountains.

Overlaps

Sweet Briar, Roanoke, Mills, Randolph, Salem College, Hampden–Sydney, Virginia Commonwealth, Virginia Tech

As the number of women's colleges continues to dwindle, Hollins remains committed to the virtues of single-sex education. Students leave with confidence, critical-thinking skills, and intellectual depth, thanks to a solid grounding in the liberal arts. And the school's Southern heritage doesn't hurt, either. "Hollins is a great school that empowers women," says one senior. "It has made me independent."

If You Apply To ›

Hollins: Early decision, early action, rolling admissions. SATs or ACTs: required. No Subject Tests. Accepts the Common Application with supplement.

College of the Holy Cross

Worcester, MA 01610

A tight-knit Roman Catholic community steeped in church and tradition, much more so than relatively secularized Boston College. Many students are the second or third generation to attend. Set high on a hill above an evolving Worcester, an hour from Boston. Sports teams compete with (and occasionally beat) schools 10 times HC's size.

Website: www.holycross.edu
Location: City Outskirts
Private
Total Enrollment: 3,020
Undergraduates: 3,020
Male/Female: 48/52
SAT Ranges: ERW 630–700,
  M 640–710
ACT Ranges: 28–31
Financial Aid: 61%
Pell Grant: 15%
Expense: Pr $ $ $
Student Loans: 52%
Average Debt: $ $
Applicants: 6,622
Accepted: 40%
Enrolled: 31%
Grad in 6 Years: 92%
Returning Freshmen: 95%
Academics: ✍ ✍ ✍ ✍
Social: 🍺 🍺 🍺 🍺
Q of L: ★ ★ ★ ★
Admissions: (508) 793-2443
Email Address: admissions@
  holycross.edu

Strong Programs:
English
Sociology

Students at Holy Cross, a Roman Catholic college in the heart of New England, are devoted to the Society of Jesus (Jesuit) tradition of becoming "men and women for and with others." Students on "the hill" are driven to do something for their college or community, whether it's a football player becoming a Big Brother or an upperclassman interning at City Hall. Peers and professors alike offer support and spiritual guidance, and more than 90 community-based learning courses incorporate service opportunities. The classroom focus is critical thinking and writing, but the school's proximity to nine other colleges in the Worcester area means Crusaders can focus on their social lives as well.

Located on one of the seven hills overlooking the industrial city of Worcester, the 174-acre Holy Cross campus is a registered arboretum. The school's landscaping has won national awards, including two first-place prizes as the best-designed and best-planted campus in the nation. Architectural styles range from classical to modern. A $90 million renovation and expansion of the Hart Recreation Center is the college's latest construction project.

Holy Cross's general education requirements comprise 12 courses in 10 areas spanning the liberal arts and sciences. Ideas and thinking are the focus, rather than preparation for a specific vocation. All first-year students participate in Montserrat, a comprehensive program designed to enhance the academic and campus experience by integrating living and learning. The program features small, full-year seminars organized into six clusters, each devoted to a specific theme: contemporary challenge, the divine, the self, the natural world, global society, and core human questions. Students also live in the same residence hall and participate in cluster activities. "It was an eye-opening experience for me, and the friendships I made in my Montserrat class lasted throughout my entire four years," reflects a psychology major.

> **"The friendships I made in my Montserrat class lasted throughout my entire four years."**

HC's health professions advising program boasts a particularly high success rate for getting students accepted to medical school. Students give high marks to the

English, sociology, and chemistry programs, and majors in economics, psychology, political science, and mathematics are popular. One student notes that the classics department is one of the best-kept secrets on campus. As might be expected, philosophy and religious studies are strong, and concentrations in Latin American studies and peace and conflict studies are popular, as these are disciplines central to Jesuit missionary work.

(continued)

Chemistry
Economics
Psychology
Political Science
Mathematics
Religious Studies

Classes are small—58 percent have fewer than 20 students—which helps faculty members keep in touch with undergraduates. Courses are demanding and intense, but professors are praised for being willing to help. "There really is a partnership between professors and students here at HC," says a political science and Spanish double major. And students say the support they receive from each other is exceptional. One senior shares, "I have found notes in the Dinand Library with a positive quote or an encouraging message for the next student who sits there. Someone even attached a honey stick from Cool Beans, our campus coffee shop, to a note that I found!"

HC's popular community-based learning courses require weekly service with local volunteer, education, or health organizations, in addition to time in the classroom; some courses focus on research that benefits local organizations. The honors program enables a small number of juniors and seniors to enroll in exclusive courses and thesis-writing seminars, while the Fenwick Scholar program helps students design and carry out independent projects. Each April, approximately 300 Holy Cross students participate in a four-day conference and present the results of their independent work. Twenty-three percent of students pack their bags for a range of study abroad programs around the world, and the college strongly encourages yearlong programs. Two intensive study away programs, the Washington Semester and the New York Semester, combine an internship with a seminar course and an independent, research-based thesis or capstone project. Counselors in the Center for Career Development "work hard to reach out to students and support them," says a Spanish major.

Each April, approximately 300 students participate in a four-day conference and present the results of their independent work.

"No matter an individual's background, all HC students have a desire to move mountains after graduation," says a junior. The religious influence at Holy Cross is somewhat greater than at other Jesuit schools—about two-thirds of students are Catholic—but students of all faiths are welcomed, and daily mass is not required. The chaplain's office runs numerous types of retreats for all faiths and reflective practices. It also offers an optional five-day silent retreat four times a year, in which student volunteers follow the spiritual exercises of St. Ignatius of Loyola, the founder of the Jesuits. Forty percent of students are in-staters, and 3 percent are international. African Americans make up 4 percent of the student body, Asian Americans comprise 5 percent, Hispanics account for 10 percent, and multiracial students add 4 percent. Social justice issues are a constant focus on campus, and the college sponsors campuswide forums, panel discussions, and other events to "create dialogue between students with different political ideologies," says a political science major. Admissions are need-blind, and HC guarantees to meet accepted students' full demonstrated financial need. A handful of departmental academic merit scholarships are available to top students, and athletes may vie for more than 200 athletic scholarships in 14 sports.

"Volunteering is one way students live out the Holy Cross mission."

Social justice issues are a constant focus on campus, and the college sponsors campuswide forums and panel discussions.

Ninety-one percent of Holy Cross students live in the residence halls, where freshmen and sophomores have double rooms, and juniors and seniors may opt for two- and three-bedroom suites—with living rooms, bathrooms, and kitchens. Floors are single-sex; buildings are co-ed. Most first-years live on "Easy Street," in Hanselman, Clark, and Mulledy (on the college's central hill next to the Hogan Campus Center) or in Wheeler (lower campus). Figge, Loyola, Alumni, and Carlin house mostly upperclassmen. Dorms receive decent reviews, especially for their size and storage space. Dining options include several campus eateries and the main dining hall; students report the food to be tasty and plentiful. "We are more or less a closed campus," says a senior, and students feel safe thanks to regular campus security patrols and a safe-ride program.

Because there are no Greek organizations, dorm life takes center stage. Each dorm has its own T-shirt, and they compete against each other for prizes in athletic and other contests. The Campus Activities Board hosts a variety of events, including karaoke, comedians, casino nights, and movie nights. Underage students caught with alcohol are put on probation and parents are notified. Still, "On the weekends there are always loads of parties going on, which are generally very accessible to all students from all classes," a student says. Tradition is big at Holy Cross, from Reunion to homecoming to Purple Pride Day. Midnight breakfasts provide sustenance as students cram for finals, while the 100 Days weekend begins the senior class countdown to graduation. Spring Weekend brings well-known performers and a carnival. And of course, given the high percentage of Irish Catholic students, St. Patrick's Day is an occasion for celebration.

"Volunteering is one way students live out the Holy Cross mission," a student says, and 45 percent of students get involved in community service. The SPUD (Student Programs for Urban Development) student organization is particularly popular and active in underserved areas of Worcester, which is an underrated college town gradually making a comeback from tough economic times. A school shuttle service takes students to the orchestra, the DCU Center for athletic events and rock concerts, and the Worcester Art Museum. "Shrewsbury Street is an entire street devoted to incredible restaurants where I spend all of my money," says a sophomore. Students are discouraged from having cars, but the college organizes trips to Boston, Providence, and New York City.

"Shrewsbury Street is an entire street devoted to incredible restaurants."

Holy Cross's Crusaders compete in Division I athletics. Men's baseball and basketball are recent Patriot League champions, and men's ice hockey is also competitive. About half of HC students participate in intramural sports. Holy Cross's moot court team, which simulates Supreme Court arguments, won a recent national title at the American Collegiate Moot Court Association's championship tournament.

Holy Cross is keeping the faith—its emphasis on Catholicism and the Jesuit tradition, that is—even as administrators place a renewed focus on academics and small classes. "Holy Cross has prepared me to think critically, challenge the status quo, ask questions, and step outside my comfort zone to make changes in our world," cheers one senior. Indeed, the close-knit atmosphere offers students a multitude of opportunities to grow, serve others, and create lasting friendships.

Overlaps

Boston College, Villanova, Providence, Fordham, UMass Amherst, Northeastern, Fairfield, Colgate

If You Apply To ›

Holy Cross: Early decision, regular decision. SATs or ACTs: optional. Subject Tests: optional. Accepts the Common Application.

Hood College

401 Rosemont Avenue, Frederick, MD 21701

With more than 15 years of coeducation under its belt, Hood has made noteworthy strides toward building a fully co-ed environment while at the same time expanding out-of-classroom opportunities. Male enrollment is now nearly 40 percent. A major asset: Hood's strategic location, one hour from D.C. and Baltimore. Hood's distinctive core curriculum stresses thematic study. Big on technology.

Founded as a women's college in 1893, Hood College undertook a bold reinvention of itself in 2003. That's the year it began admitting men as regular residential students (males had been commuting students since 1971). Now members of all genders have the opportunity to partake of Hood's traditional mix of professional and liberal arts offerings on a campus strategically situated near two major cities. Students see their school's biggest strength in its people: students, staff, and faculty. "There are so many cultures and ethnicities and traditions to be shared," says one junior. "I love living here. I'm having the time of my life."

Hood's strikingly beautiful 50-acre campus features redbrick buildings and lush, tree-shaded lawns. Located at a major crossroads, the town of Frederick saw considerable action during the Civil War. Today, Hood is within an hour and a half of nearly 30 colleges and within minutes of a major National Cancer Institute research complex, high-tech firms, and small and large businesses. On campus, technology programs, which are already important, get a further boost thanks to the Hodson Science and Technology Center. A state-of-the-art trading room allows students to practice using technology and analytical tools similar to what is used on Wall Street.

Hood's core curriculum, designed to expose students to different modes of thinking and critical reflection on global issues, is comprised of two parts, Foundations and Methods of Inquiry. Foundation courses include English composition, quantitative literacy, foreign language, and health and wellness. Methods of Inquiry requires coursework in six traditional liberal arts areas, plus global perspectives. Entering students participate in Hood's First-Year Read program and in a small, writing-intensive First-Year Seminar, which is designed to help build academic skills, confidence, and a sense of belonging.

> **"[Students are] interested in their education and are serious and hardworking."**

"Hood is not extraordinarily competitive," says a sophomore, "although hard work is required to do well." Hood's major strength lies in the sciences, especially the chemistry department and the biology department, with its special emphases on molecular biology, marine biology, and environmental science and policy. A semester-long coastal studies program takes students along the East Coast on a biological educational mission. Education, especially early childhood, is a program of note, as are English and social work. The most popular majors are business administration, psychology, communication arts, and computer science. Five-year bachelor's/master's programs are now available in business, environmental biology, psychology and counseling, and information technology. Only labs are taught by graduate assistants, and 72 percent of classes have fewer than 20 students. "The professors here are extremely intelligent with excellent credentials," raves one student. A math major adds, "The teachers want their students to succeed and are very accessible when students need help."

If you really want to stimulate the brain cells, the four-year honors program features team-taught courses, a sophomore-year seminar on global issues that involves a

---

Website: www.hood.edu
Location: Small City
Private
Total Enrollment: 1,233
Undergraduates: 1,046
Male/Female: 38/62
SAT Ranges: ERW 500–620, M 480–600
ACT Ranges: 18–23
Financial Aid: 98%
Pell Grant: 43%
Expense: Pr $
Student Loans: 73%
Average Debt: $ $ $ $
Applicants: 1,431
Accepted: 81%
Enrolled: 22%
Grad in 6 Years: 61%
Returning Freshmen: 78%
Academics: ✑ ✑ ✑
Social: ☎ ☎ ☎
Q of L: ★ ★ ★
Admissions: (800) 922-1599
Email Address: admission@ hood.edu

Strong Programs:
Business Administration
Psychology
Communication Arts
Computer Science
Biology
Chemistry
Education
English

community service project, and a senior seminar for which students choose both the topic and the professor—not to mention an annual $2,000 scholarship. Internship opportunities include overseas jobs for language and business majors and legislative and cultural positions in Washington, D.C. Study abroad destinations, to which 8 percent of students take flight, include Ireland, Cyprus, Costa Rica, Morocco, and South Korea. The school's strong career resources give students a leg up on their next step in life, whether it be a job or graduate school.

In general, Hood students are "interested in their education and are serious and hardworking," says a sophomore. Nearly three-quarters of undergraduates call Maryland home, while 2 percent come to Hood from other countries. Socioeconomic diversity is stronger, with 43 percent of freshmen receiving Pell Grants. Seventeen percent of students are African American, 11 percent are Hispanic, 2 percent are Asian American, and 6 percent are multiracial. Students say the campus leans slightly left, politically speaking, and key issues include the environment and fiscal concerns. Hood provides merit scholarships worth an average of $17,500.

Hood's co-ed residence halls are well liked, with good-sized, air-conditioned rooms. The lottery system is based on seniority, and just over half of the students live on campus. First-year students live in dedicated freshman residence halls and can expect to be assigned to doubles (seniors and juniors can compete for singles), and Spanish and French majors may apply to live in the language houses. Campus dining options aren't stellar, students say, but campus security receives praise. "I feel very safe on our small, homey campus with lots of lights at night and plenty of officers walking or driving around at all times," says one student.

> "I feel very safe on our small, homey campus."

Social life among the students is centered on the dorms, as each has its own personality as well as its own house council, rules, and social activities. Students report that, although there is no Greek life, there are parties every weekend, along with movies, dances, and other forms of entertainment. The Whitaker Campus Center, with its Ping-Pong and pool tables, grill and sandwich shop, bookstore, and meeting rooms, offers a great gathering place for residents and commuters 24 hours a day. Campus alcohol policies have been tightened, but drinking is generally not a huge part of the social life at Hood. "At parties and events, you have to show ID to get alcohol," one senior says. "If you don't like to stay on campus, there are restaurants, bars, clubs, malls, and coffeehouses within 10 minutes of the college by car," explains an English major. Scenic Frederick is described as small, safe, and beautiful. "Downtown Frederick is a very up-and-coming, artsy town," says one student. A one-hour car ride delivers students to the multiple diversions in Baltimore or Washington, D.C.

With over a century of history, Hood is rife with traditions. Some of the most important ones include the junior class ring dinner and formal, a performance of Handel's *Messiah*, the May Madness festival and crab feast, and a strawberries-and-ice-cream breakfast for seniors the morning of commencement. The Blazers compete in 22 Division III sports, and men's and women's swimming, track, and basketball are among the stronger teams. Recreational and intramural sports attract 20 percent of undergraduates; popular activities include soccer, touch football, and volleyball.

While Hood has undergone the major change from a women's college to a co-ed institution, its mission remains the same: to prepare students to face the challenges of a fast-changing society and professional environment. "The traditions are amazing," boasts a sophomore, "topped only by professors who care and friends you'll have forever."

The four-year honors program features a senior seminar for which students choose both the topic and the professor.

Traditions include the May Madness festival and crab feast and a strawberries-and-ice-cream breakfast for seniors the morning of commencement.

Overlaps

Mount St. Mary's, McDaniel, Towson, University of Maryland, Stevenson, UMBC, Frostburg, Salisbury

Hope College

P.O. Box 9000, Holland, MI 49422

Hope has an in-between size—bigger than most small colleges but smaller than a university. It is evangelical in orientation, but less than 10 percent of the students are members of the founding Reformed Church in America. In addition to the liberal arts, Hope offers education, engineering, and nursing, and makes undergraduate research a priority.

Each fall since 1898, Hope College freshmen have spent three grueling hours engaged in "the Pull," an epic tug-of-war against the sophomores, who stand assembled on the opposite end of a 650-pound rope across the 250-foot-wide Black River. This well-known annual tradition evokes the daily struggle Hope students face: maintaining their faith in a world eager to challenge it at every turn. The heritage of Hope's Dutch founders remains strong and visible on campus. "The academic programs, particularly the research and collaboration opportunities, far surpass those of Hope's rivals," opines a sophomore.

Hope was founded in 1866 with support from the Reformed Church in America and the biblical (Book of Hebrews) mission of becoming an "anchor of hope" for the Dutch church in the West. It is situated on six blocks near downtown Holland, the tulip capital of the nation, and a short bike ride from the shores of Lake Michigan. There's a lush pine grove in the center of campus, which features an eclectic array of buildings in architectural styles ranging from 19th-century Flemish to modern. The $16 million Bultman Student Center opened in 2017.

Among Hope's academic offerings, the sciences (especially biology and chemistry) stand out, with excellent laboratory facilities and faculty who are eager to involve students in their funded research. During the school year, undergraduates often conduct advanced experiments and even publish papers; come summer, about 200 geology, chemistry, mathematics, computer science, physics, and engineering majors receive stipends to participate in research full time. Overall, 40 percent of undergrads get involved with research. Not surprisingly, a large portion of science majors go on to medical and engineering schools and Ph.D. programs. For those otherwise inclined, Hope's offerings in psychology, management, and education are popular, and communication, dance, and English are solid too. One student says, "The sciences get lauded most often, but all four art departments (visual, theatre, dance, and music) are powerhouses in their own right." The modern and classical language departments offer students proficient in a second language the chance to use their skills in volunteer work and research with faculty members, while the Visiting Writers Series gives students an opportunity to interact with noteworthy authors.

The academic climate is demanding yet supportive. "If you're struggling, it's not looked down upon to get assistance," says a junior. Most Hope students select a major from one of the college's fields, but the truly adventurous may design their own composite major. Hope's general education program, designed around the

> "All four art departments (visual, theatre, dance, and music) are powerhouses."

Website: www.hope.edu
Location: Small City
Private
Total Enrollment: 3,012
Undergraduates: 3,012
Male/Female: 39/61
SAT Ranges: ERW 550–660, M 540–660
ACT Ranges: 24–29
Financial Aid: 94%
Pell Grant: 20%
Expense: Pr $
Student Loans: 62%
Average Debt: $ $ $
Applicants: 4,377
Accepted: 74%
Enrolled: 23%
Grad in 6 Years: 80%
Returning Freshmen: 88%
Academics: ✑ ✑ ✑
Social: ☎ ☎ ☎
Q of L: ★ ★ ★
Admissions: (616) 395-7850
Email Address: admissions@hope.edu

Strong Programs:
Biology
Chemistry
Psychology
Management
Education
Communication
Dance
English

themes "knowing how" and "knowing about," includes a first-year seminar, which provides "an intellectual transition into Hope," and a senior seminar. Courses in expository writing, health dynamics, math and natural science, foreign language, religious studies, social sciences, the arts, and cultural heritage are also required; one class must have a focus on cultural diversity and one on international perspectives. Classes are usually small, and one student says, "The faculty are very personable. They love engaging students." Students may study abroad in more than 70 countries, and half do so; options include semester-long exchanges and programs that combine classes with internships.

Students at Hope are "very outgoing, social, and friendly," says a management major. "This is a place where people are involved and love to build community with one another." The student body is a rather homogeneous lot, with 67 percent hailing from Michigan and 3 percent coming from overseas. African Americans account for 3 percent of the student body, Hispanics 8 percent, Asian Americans 2 percent, and multiracial students 3 percent. Politically, according to a junior, "Hope is liberal in comparison to other private, Christian colleges." Merit scholarships averaging $8,800 are available to qualified students, but there are no athletic scholarships.

Seventy-nine percent of Hope students live in university-sponsored housing. Traditional dorms are arranged in freshman clusters by gender or co-ed by suite.

"This is a place where people are involved and love to build community."

"Dorms are fine, and I enjoyed them as a freshman, but most students opt for the college-owned apartment complexes and cottages surrounding the campus area. They're much nicer and better-kept, though it can be difficult to secure one until you're a junior," says a student. On-campus students eat in one of two large dining halls where the fare—especially homemade bread and desserts—is tasty. "The STEP (Students Teaching and Empowering Peers) program focuses on peer education regarding sexual assault," says a senior. "They do a good job but the school could always do more."

"The weekends are full and busy. The Student Activities Committee is the organization that makes the social life at Hope College thrive," says one student. The committee brings in comedians, bands, and hypnotists, shows movies in campus auditoriums, and plans the Spring Fling carnival, held on the last Friday of the academic year. Seven fraternities and eight sororities, all local organizations, claim 14 percent of the men and 18 percent of the women, respectively. Some parties do happen off campus, but those caught drinking on Hope's dry campus must perform community service. Among the 80 student organizations are a variety of active religious life and service organizations, including Hope Way (campus ministry), InterVarsity Christian Fellowship, and Silent Praise, a student group that seeks to praise God through American Sign Language (ASL) and worship music.

Holland (population 33,000) is the site of spring's Tulip Time, one of the largest U.S. flower festivals. When Hope's cozy campus and the quaint town of Holland get too close for comfort, students find relief at the beaches of Lake Michigan ("definitely one of the highlights," says a junior) or drive 30 minutes to Grand Rapids, which offers some large-city amenities and good weekend rental deals at the ski slopes. Chicago and Detroit are other typical destinations for those trying to hit the road.

On the field and on the court, Hope's Flying Dutchmen are talented Division III competitors. Hope teams are frequent conference champions; solid programs include men's and women's golf, tennis, and basketball, as well as women's soccer and softball. The college has won a record number of Michigan Intercollegiate Athletic Association Commissioner's Cups; the trophy recognizes the conference's best cumulative sports program for men and women. Especially important are any competitions against Calvin (a century-old rivalry) and football versus Albion and Kalamazoo for the Wooden Shoes trophy. Sixty percent of students take part in roughly two dozen intramural and club sports, which range from soccer and racquetball to inner-tube water polo.

Hope's mission is "to educate students for lives of leadership and service in a global society." For those seeking an institution with traditional Christian roots and an emphasis on undergraduates, Hope may be worth a look. "Hope is a place where students are challenged to become better students," says one senior, "but, more important, better people."

If You Apply To ›

Hope: Early action, rolling admissions. SATs or ACTs: required. No Subject Tests. Accepts the Common Application.

Houghton College

Houghton, NY 14744

The Mid-Atlantic's leading evangelical Christian college. All students are required to take Biblical Literature and Introduction to Christianity, and most go to chapel three times a week. Perks include three different honors programs and expansive indoor and outdoor equestrian facilities. Rural New York setting fosters an intimate sense of community, but when things gets claustrophobic, students have ample possibilities for a semester away.

Located in the bucolic New York town that shares its name, Houghton College offers a solid, growing academic program and strong athletic teams, while remaining committed to its core mission as a Christian liberal arts school. Sponsored by the Wesleyan Church, Houghton celebrates its Christian heritage and encourages students to do the same. Applicants must explain in their essays why they desire to be a part of a Christian academic community, and current students are expected to attend a set amount of chapel services throughout the semester. These expectations help create true community on campus. One junior says, "Houghton combines academic rigor, athletic excellence, and intentional spiritual formation in a fun-loving and Christ-centered community."

Houghton's scenic hilltop campus covers 1,300 acres of rural beauty, surrounded by vast expanses of western New York countryside. In addition to a 386-acre horseback-riding facility, the college has its own ski trails. The academic buildings are a mix of area fieldstone and brick. Recent construction includes a 115,000-square-foot athletic complex and a 36,000-square-foot indoor equestrian arena.

Houghton students complete general education requirements designed to provide a context and framework for the entire educational program. Freshmen must take Biblical Literature, Writing in the Liberal Arts, and a course titled Transitions, aimed at easing the transition to college. Houghton is known for its equestrian studies program, and the premed, communication, and theology programs are also strong. The school's most popular majors include biology, business, education, and music. A major in music industry gives students plenty of hands-on experience running sound, recording, and lighting for campus events. A new major in electrical engineering, the school's first and only four-year engineering program, was added

Website: www.houghton.edu
Location: Rural
Private
Total Enrollment: 978
Undergraduates: 970
Male/Female: 38/62
SAT Ranges: N/A
ACT Ranges: 22–29
Financial Aid: 99%
Pell Grant: 50%
Expense: Pr $
Student Loans: 74%
Average Debt: $ $ $ $
Applicants: 821
Accepted: 91%
Enrolled: 29%
Grad in 6 Years: 72%
Returning Freshmen: 80%
Academics: ✍ ✍ ✍
Social: ☎ ☎ ☎
Q of L: ★ ★ ★ ★
Admissions: (800) 777-2556

(continued)

Email Address: admission@
houghton.edu

Strong Programs:
Equestrian Studies
Premed
Communication
Theology
Biology
Business
Education
Music

Four-week off-campus Mayterm programs are available in New York City, Alaska, Costa Rica, Europe, and Sierra Leone.

Students eagerly anticipate Christian Life Emphasis Week and Hall Brawl, a week of friendly competitions between dorms.

for fall 2019. Other options include a 3+4 Pharm.D. program with the University of Buffalo and a medical early-acceptance program with the Lake Erie College of Osteopathic Medicine.

Houghton's academic climate is rigorous, but not overwhelmingly so. "Walking into class, I know I will be challenged by faculty and fellow students to become better at what I do," says a student. Sixty-seven percent of classes have fewer than 20 students, and most courses are taught by senior faculty, who students say do an outstanding job of fostering a sense of community. "At Houghton I have coffee with my professors and real conversations. I see them at church and in the dining hall, and I've gotten to know their kids," says an intercultural studies major.

> "At Houghton I have coffee with my professors and real conversations."

Houghton offers three honors programs for incoming freshmen: London Honors, East Meets West, and Science Honors. The London Honors and East Meets West programs offer qualified students an intensive, hands-on experience in the humanities, along with study abroad experiences in the United Kingdom and the eastern Mediterranean, respectively. The Science Honors program allows select students to engage with significant scientific problems in a hands-on, research-oriented environment. Houghton's Summer Research Institute, designed for students in math and the sciences, is also well regarded. Fifty-five percent of all students take advantage of off-campus study in a variety of programs throughout the year, including four-week Mayterm programs in New York City, Alaska, Costa Rica, Europe, and Sierra Leone.

Sixty-three percent of students are from New York, and 5 percent are international, coming from 39 countries. A senior describes Houghton students as "thoughtful and excited about going out and influencing the world in a positive way." African Americans account for 4 percent of the student body, Hispanics 2 percent, Asian Americans 4 percent, and multiracial students 5 percent. "The most noticed and discussed issues are those of race, sexual orientation, and often moral character. As Houghton College is a Christian liberal arts college, these issues are often addressed from a Christian perspective, but all views are welcome," a sophomore says. Qualified undergrads receive merit scholarships averaging $16,500, and half of incoming freshmen are eligible for Pell Grants.

> "[Houghton students are] thoughtful and excited about going out and influencing the world in a positive way."

Houghton's campus houses 83 percent of students. "Housing is fairly limited in terms of options, but all students are guaranteed a spot on campus," says one student. Freshmen and sophomores live in traditional residence halls, while juniors and seniors can apply for campus townhouses and apartments; all accommodations are single-sex. Dining options get good reviews for taste and variety. "Special dishes can be ordered at some stations, and bagged lunches are customizable," says a senior. Students report feeling safe on their rural campus. Houghton's Community Covenant prohibits "premarital sex, adultery, and homosexual behavior," but as one student points out, "Students are able to report sexual assault without facing consequences regarding our Community Covenant."

"Most of the social life takes place on campus," explains an art major. "The surrounding area offers much to do in regards to nature and the outdoors, but not necessarily socially." The Campus Activities Board plans regular happenings, and dorm-identity events, film festivals, and concerts are popular. Seventy percent of students are involved in service projects such as Big Brothers Big Sisters, nursing home visitation, and local church outreach; the area surrounding the college is one of the poorest in New York State. Both the campus and the town of Houghton are dry, and the college's Community Covenant forbids alcohol. As a senior simply puts it, "There is not a party scene on campus." Students eagerly anticipate annual celebrations for homecoming, Christian Life Emphasis Week, the Christmas Prism concerts, and Hall Brawl, a week of friendly competitions between dorms.

Houghton was approved for full Division III membership in 2016, and a $24 million field house accommodates the college's expanding athletic teams. Competitive Highlanders teams include men's and women's tennis and women's basketball and field hockey. About half of the students participate in intramural sports, with co-ed volleyball being the most popular, and the club sports program is growing too.

Students don't come to Houghton for the surrounding town, which is 30 minutes by car from the nearest mall, or for the weather, which can be tough once winter sets in. But they do come, and for good reason: there's little to distract them from their studies, their campus's natural beauty, and their spiritual growth. As one junior observes, "There are few schools that will work so closely with their students, through setting academic goals, [helping them pursue] internships, listening to their passions, and equipping them to work where their deep gladness and the world's deep hunger meet."

Overlaps

Roberts Wesleyan, Messiah, Gordon, Wheaton (IL), Taylor, Grove City, Liberty, Cedarville

If You Apply To ›

Houghton: Rolling admissions. SATs or ACTs: optional (required for consideration for merit scholarships and honors program). No Subject Tests. Accepts the Common Application with supplement. Music majors apply directly to music program.

Howard University

2400 Sixth Street NW, Washington, D.C. 20059

The flagship university of black America and the first to integrate the black experience into all areas of study. Strategically located in D.C., Howard depends on Congress for much of its funding. Preprofessional programs such as nursing, business, and architecture are strong. Only 10 percent of students are an ethnicity other than African American.

Contrary to the advice of early black leaders such as Booker T. Washington, who argued in favor of technical training, Howard has promoted the liberal arts since its inception. This focus has served the school well; Howard's law school counts the late Supreme Court Justice Thurgood Marshall among its alumni, and Nobel Prize–winning author Toni Morrison went here too. In recent years, Howard has strengthened its financial position and has been implementing a strategic plan structured around "Leadership for America and the Global Community." The four-part plan focuses on strengthening academic programs and services, promoting excellence in teaching and research, increasing private support, and enhancing national and community services.

Founded in 1867 by General Oliver Howard primarily to educate freed slaves, the university now operates five campuses and serves roughly 8,600 full-time students. Interestingly, Howard is one of a handful of universities in the nation supported partly by federal subsidies; these days, the school gets about 55 percent of its budget from Congress. The 89-acre main campus houses most classrooms, dorms, and administrative offices, as well as the university center, the Founders, and undergraduate, medical, and dental libraries. The Howard Law Center is on the west campus near Rock Creek Park; the Divinity School is on a 22-acre site in northeast

Website: www.howard.edu
Location: City Center
Private
Total Enrollment: 8,609
Undergraduates: 6,061
Male/Female: 31/69
SAT Ranges: ERW 550–650, M 540–640
ACT Ranges: 22–28
Financial Aid: 78%
Pell Grant: 47%
Expense: Pr $
Student Loans: 78%
Average Debt: $ $
Applicants: 16,815
Accepted: 41%
Enrolled: 30%

(continued)

Grad in 6 Years: 63%
Returning Freshmen: 96%
Academics: ✍ ✍ ✍
Social: ☎ ☎ ☎
Q of L: ★ ★ ★
Admissions: (202) 806-2755
Email Address: admission@
   howard.edu

Strong Programs:
Business
Communication
Physical Sciences
Biology
Political Science
Nursing
Computer Science
Afro American Studies

Washington; and there's also a 108-acre campus in suburban Beltsville, Maryland, and a campus in Silver Spring. Architecturally, the main campus is a blend of old and new, with numerous sculptures and murals created by Jacob Lawrence, Richard Hunt, Elizabeth Catlett, and the late Romare Bearden. Newer facilities include the state-of-the-art, 82,000-square-foot Interdisciplinary Research Building.

All students must complete general education requirements, which vary by school or college but uniformly encompass 18 credits in science, social sciences, humanities, computer literacy, math, languages, and one Afro American studies course. Freshman seminars and various other special programs for first-year students are available in the undergraduate schools, such as communication, engineering, and arts and sciences. Seniors in arts and sciences must weather a comprehensive exam to graduate.

> "Some courses are more rigorous than others. But overall this school is tough."

The school has excellent programs in business, political science, nursing, computer science, and psychology, and it has intensified offerings in Africana and diaspora studies. Other intriguing academic options are jazz studies, architecture, engineering (especially electrical engineering), and accelerated programs for a B.S. on the way to a medical or dental degree. The most popular majors are in the areas of business, communication, physical sciences, and biology. The Howard University Science, Engineering, and Mathematics Program, a multidisciplinary program involving nine departments, is designed to support underrepresented students pursuing degrees in STEM disciplines. Howard students can cross-register for courses at 13 other area schools, including American University, Georgetown, and Corcoran School of the Arts and Design.

In general, students say that the workload at Howard is demanding. "Some courses are more rigorous than others. But overall this school is tough," says a junior. Another student adds, "Come to Howard ready to study." Fifty-five percent of classes have fewer than 20 students. Most students agree that professors are ready and willing to help when asked, though academic advising is not Howard's strength. "Sometimes you may get professors who do not know how to break down anything," explains a psychology major. "Then it is your job to speak up and ask questions. You must ask questions because a closed mouth does not get fed!" Howard's prime D.C. location means internship, co-op, and service-learning opportunities with all manner of government organizations, nonprofits, and corporations are practically limitless. Qualified students can apply for the Junior Experiential Learning Program, which helps them secure internships and other practical work experiences. The program also assigns each participant an alumni career mentor with experience in their field of interest who can assist with networking and career advice. A modest 1 percent of students study abroad at one of the more than 200 institutions in 36 countries where Howard grants credit.

The Howard University Science, Engineering, and Mathematics Program supports underrepresented students pursuing degrees in STEM disciplines.

Ninety percent of Howard undergraduates hail from states outside of the District of Columbia, and another 7 percent are international. African Americans comprise 90 percent of the student body, while Hispanics and Asian Americans each add 1 percent. Many come from decidedly middle-class backgrounds, although 47 percent of students qualify for Pell Grants. Howard seems to be a very cohesive community, but career-minded and highly motivated men and women fit in best, students say, and most are politically liberal. "It's a very competitive school, from grades to fashion," says a junior. A range of renewable merit scholarships are available on a first-come, first-served basis to freshman applicants, and these awards average $29,000 per year. Transfer students are eligible for a separate pool of merit scholarships, and Howard also awards a limited number of athletic scholarships. A deferred-payment plan allows families to pay each semester's tuition in three installments.

> "[Greeks are] an integral part of the university."

Sixty-two percent of Howard's students are accommodated on campus, and facilities receive lukewarm reviews. "Housing at Howard is average in regards to availability, maintenance, and comfort," says one student. Freshmen get room assignments, while upperclassmen take their chances in a lottery. "It is quite difficult to get a room at times," says a sophomore economics major. Many students live off campus purely to avoid the mandatory meal plan.

Weekends bring an assortment of social happenings to campus, many of which take place in the student center. On-campus parties and sports events are always big draws, but the restaurants and clubs in the nearby U Street corridor, the bars of Georgetown and Adams Morgan, and the Capital One Arena (home to the NBA's Wizards and the NHL's Capitals) also beckon and are easily accessible by public transit. Fraternities and sororities do not have their own housing or dining facilities, and only 3 percent of the men and 5 percent of the women go Greek. Though small in numbers, one student says the Greeks are "an integral part of the university."

Athletics are also an important presence on campus, particularly Division I Bison basketball, soccer, football, and swimming and diving. The highlight of the season is always the grudge match with Hampton University to decide which school is the "true HU." Howard's homecoming is one of the best annual events, along with various Greekfests, concerts, and talent shows that current students, alumni, and members of the community enjoy together. Intramurals and club sports attract plenty of students, especially flag football, soccer, basketball, and baseball.

Among America's historically black colleges and universities, Howard stands out as the standard-bearer, a longtime center of excellence and leadership. Its scholarship and collections of artwork, rare books, manuscripts, and photographs are a repository of the African American experience, informing students' intellectual and personal growth. And with an increased focus on providing opportunities for real-world experience and service, Howard is sure to continue its long tradition of turning out African American leaders in all areas of society.

> *Howard's collections of artwork, rare books, manuscripts, and photographs are a repository of the African American experience.*

Overlaps

Morehouse, Spelman, Case Western Reserve, Emory, George Washington, Georgetown, Temple, Hampton

If You Apply To ›

Howard: Early decision, early action, regular decision. SATs or ACTs: required. No Subject Tests. Accepts the Common Application with supplement.

The College of Idaho

Caldwell, ID 83605

Got a map? You'll need a sharp eye to spot C of I, the *Fiske Guide*'s only liberal arts school between the Rocky Mountains and the West Coast. Innovative programs include the PEAK curriculum and leadership studies. Nearly two-thirds of students are from Idaho. Diverse alumni roster includes seven Rhodes scholars, three state governors, and four NFL players.

With an emphasis on education and experiential learning, The College of Idaho, the state's oldest four-year university, offers students an opportunity to earn a solid liberal arts education through small classes in a small town. Outside class, the school's scenic environment allows sports and nature enthusiasts to explore freely before heading back into the classroom. At C of I, you'll be exposed to "hard work, great opportunities, and a healthy amount of fun," says a freshman.

Website: www.collegeofidaho.edu
Location: Small Town
Private
Total Enrollment: 905

*Over four years,
students earn a major
and three minors
spread across four
knowledge "peaks."*

The college is in the small town of Caldwell, where the atmosphere is calm and serene. For those looking for a little excitement, the state capital of Boise is a short drive from campus. Also nearby are some of Idaho's most scenic locations, such as beautiful mountains, deserts, and white-water rivers. The school, originally a Presbyterian college, first planted roots in downtown Caldwell in 1891 and then moved to its present site in 1910, where its nearly 30 buildings now inhabit 43 acres. Construction on a 60,000-square-foot, state-of-the-art library was recently completed.

The school's academic schedule is composed of 12-week semesters, spring and fall, separated by a four-week winter session, during which students can assist professors with research, take an internship, volunteer, or travel abroad. The college's distinctive PEAK program combines a liberal arts education with specialization in multiple fields. Over four years, students earn a major and three minors spread across four knowledge "peaks"—the humanities, social sciences, natural sciences, and a professional field. Students choose among 30 majors and 50 minors. Freshmen sign an honor code and go through a first-year program that involves a common reading book, a junior or senior mentor, a team of advisors, and a weeklong orientation that includes an off-campus overnight stay at a lakeside camp. First-year students demonstrating leadership potential are invited to a series of seminars to draw them into the leadership studies program, a business minor.

"The professors are masters of their craft."

"The workload can be relaxed or intense depending upon a student's desire for success," says one senior. Business, psychology, health sciences, biology, and environmental studies are among the majors recommended by students, and pre-professional programs, such as premed, prenursing, and prelaw are also popular and strong. Sixty-seven percent of all classes at C of I have fewer than 20 students, and faculty are praised for their knowledge and accessibility. "The professors are masters of their craft," a senior says. The college cooperates with the University of Idaho to offer a five-year course of study in engineering. Undergraduate research opportunities are available in all fields, and students present their findings at state and regional conferences. The Center for Experiential Learning coordinates out-of-classroom experiences, such as international education and service learning. For those who want to venture abroad, the college offers options for attending a foreign university or traveling overseas during the summer and winter breaks. Travel has really taken off, with study abroad opportunities in nearly 60 countries around the world.

"Intramurals are huge at our school."

"Everyone seems like some kind of repressed genius trying to figure out their own existence, pursue stability, and create something meaningful," muses one student, adding, "There are also those who are more career-minded." Sixty-one percent of the students are from Idaho and 9 percent come from nearly 50 foreign countries. Fourteen percent are Hispanic, 4 percent are African American, 2 percent are Asian American, and 4 percent are multiracial. Political issues receive plenty of attention on campus, and debates about the school's honor code are not uncommon among students. Of the most recent freshman class, one-quarter qualify for the Pell Grant. The college offers merit scholarships averaging $19,400, as well as roughly 200 athletic scholarships. Not surprisingly, some of those dollars are set aside for skiers.

Sixty-eight percent of students live on campus. "Residences are great, easy to decorate, and relatively big," says one student. Other options include five traditional residence halls, two suite-style apartment buildings, and more than 20 rental houses. For meals, C of I provides "a grill, deli, salad bar, pizza, and vegetarian options" that are "to die for," according to one student. "Campus safety gets a 10 out of 10," says a junior. "There is an officer on duty 24/7 even over breaks and summer vacation."

Twelve percent of men and 16 percent of women participate in the Greek system, which dominates campus social life. Students 21 and over are permitted to have alcohol on campus, in moderation (i.e., no kegs). Annual social highlights include Winterfest, Spring Fling, and homecoming week. Games against rival Northwest Nazarene also attract attention. "We have a fantastic social scene. We host events almost nightly," a student reports. Undergraduates can choose among more than 50 student clubs, and the arts are strong. Students of all majors participate in a wide range of instrumental and choral music, theater, visual arts, and other activities, and the choir has performed at Carnegie Hall and other venues around the country. "Finals breakfasts" offer something for bleary-eyed students to look forward to during finals week; at midnight on Tuesday, faculty and staff cook breakfast for students.

Caldwell, with about 50,000 people, is not a great spot for college students, but students get involved by helping out the local school district. Nearby Boise is a popular destination for shopping, dining, and cultural events, including a symphony orchestra, art museum, zoo, professional baseball and hockey, and the must-see World Center for Birds of Prey. Many students hit the road during a weeklong break taken every six weeks. Outdoor enthusiasts relish the fact that the C of I campus is just minutes away from world-class opportunities for skiing, hiking, camping, fishing, and white-water rafting. The student-run Outdoor Program offers trips, classes, and equipment rentals.

More than a third of students play for one of the college's 20 varsity teams, which compete in NAIA Division II. The Yotes (translation: "We are the Coyotes") have earned national championships in baseball, basketball, and skiing, and recent conference champs include men's basketball and lacrosse. For those who enjoy the game but might not make the team, there is an active intramurals program and the large Albertson Activities Center. "Intramurals are huge at our school," says a sophomore, drawing nearly half the students.

C of I has much to offer its Yotes. They enjoy a well-designed liberal arts education and personal academic attention on a campus striving to keep its offerings on the cutting edge. What's more, students here are encouraged to take an active role in the school's future. From creating traditions to upholding the honor code, a sophomore says, "We are involved in all aspects of campus life."

Freshmen go through a weeklong orientation that includes an off-campus overnight stay at a lakeside camp.

Overlaps

Boise State, University of Idaho, Idaho State, College of Western Idaho, Westminster, Earlham, Northwest Nazarene

If You Apply To ›

Idaho: Early action I and II, regular decision. SATs or ACTs: optional. (Test-optional applicants must complete additional short-answer questions.) No Subject Tests. Accepts the Common Application with supplement.

University of Illinois at Urbana–Champaign

901 West Illinois Street, Urbana, IL 61801

Half a step behind Michigan and neck and neck with Wisconsin among top Midwestern public universities. U of I's strengths include business, communication, engineering, architecture, and the natural sciences. Three-quarters of the undergraduates hail from in state. Huge Greek system.

Like many of its Midwestern neighbors, the University of Illinois has its roots in agriculture. The Morrow Plots, the oldest experimental fields in the nation, still rest in the middle of campus—and when the wind blows the wrong way, students are not-so-subtly reminded of their heritage as a farm school. Like most big, public universities, U of I has a barn full of choices, and with a strong Greek system and

Website: www.illinois.edu
Location: Small City
Public
Total Enrollment: 42,397

(continued)

Undergraduates: 32,210
Male/Female: 54/46
SAT Ranges: ERW 630–710,
   M 710–790
ACT Ranges: 26–32
Financial Aid: 43%
Pell Grant: 22%
Expense: Pub $ $ $ $
Student Loans: 45%
Average Debt: $ $
Applicants: 38,965
Accepted: 61%
Enrolled: 31%
Grad in 6 Years: 85%
Returning Freshmen: 92%
Academics: ✍ ✍ ✍ ✍ ✍
Social: ☎ ☎ ☎
Q of L: ★ ★ ★
Admissions: (217) 333-0302
Email Address: admissions@
   illinois.edu

Strong Programs:
Engineering
Business
Communication
Social Sciences
Architecture
Education
Industrial Design
Agriculture

A new "CS + X"
degree program
allows students to
combine the study
of computer science
with one of 10 other
liberal arts fields.

1,200 clubs, social activities are more than plentiful. Homecoming weekend was invented at the University of Illinois, and whether cheering for the Illini, pledging a Greek organization, or celebrating Moms', Dads', or Siblings' Weekends, students here stir up a vibrant mix of school spirit and good times. This may look and feel like a laid-back Midwestern campus, but make no mistake: Illinois's stellar academics and learning communities are on par with any of the country's public flagships.

Befitting the oldest land grant institution, the Illinois campus was built in farm country between the twin cities of Champaign and Urbana. The parklike campus was designed along a mile-long axis where trees and walkways separate stately white-columned Georgian structures made of brick. Physically challenged students tend to appreciate the campus because it is flat and well equipped with ramps and widened doorways. The impressive Illinois library system, the largest public university collection of its kind worldwide, makes it easier to keep up with classwork. A 225,000-square-foot computer science center and the physical education center are notable. New construction includes the $25 million Siebel Center for Design, opening in 2020.

Illinois has eight undergraduate colleges and one school that together offer more than 150 undergraduate programs; if nothing strikes your fancy, you may design your own. The general education program includes standard distribution requirements across a range of subjects; students may fulfill some requirements by taking recently launched Grand Challenge Learning courses, interdisciplinary classes that explore three main "pathways," or real-world challenges facing today's society: Inequality and Cultural Understanding; Health and Wellness; and Sustainability, Energy, and the Environment.

> **"The school is continuously getting more diverse."**

Partially because of its size, Illinois can afford to support excellent programs across the university, including the expansion of undergraduate minors campuswide. Engineering, business, communication, social sciences, architecture, education, industrial design, and the sciences—especially agriculture and veterinary medicine—get high marks from students and lots of resources from administrators. A new "CS + X" degree program allows students to combine the study of computer science with one of 10 other liberal arts fields, ranging from anthropology and advertising to chemistry and crop sciences, without having to go so far as double majoring. The initiative is a way for students to demonstrate both technical competence and career-related expertise to future employers. The interdisciplinary Beckman Institute for Advanced Science and Technology offers opportunities for undergraduate research in areas like intelligent systems and molecular science and engineering.

"Overall, classes are demanding," says a senior. Freshmen and sophomores, who register last, may have trouble getting into necessary courses, but professors and academic advisors can usually help if classes you need are full, and students appreciate their dedication. Illinois has its share of stellar faculty, including Nobel laureates, National Medal of Science winners, and dozens of members of the National Academy of Sciences. "The quality of teaching is high with few exceptions," says a psychology major. "They are truly invested in our success," adds a senior. Even freshmen stuck in large lectures (750 seats) will find some personal attention in the associated discussion sections, led by graduate teaching assistants. Freshman Discovery Courses, seminars limited to 19 students, enable first-year students to interact closely with full professors. The honors program includes faculty mentoring, intensive seminars, advanced sections of regular courses, and access to special resources. About 7 percent of undergraduates travel and study abroad each year, roaming 45 countries around the globe.

Seventy-three percent of Illinois undergrads are homegrown and "the school is continuously getting more diverse," a sophomore says. Since Illinois stretches from the wealthy north suburbs of sophisticated Chicago to the unspoiled rural hills bordering Kentucky and encompasses classic farm towns as well as factory towns, students do come from multiple backgrounds and fit less into the stereotypical "Midwest" mold than one might think. African Americans make up 6 percent of the student body, Hispanics 11 percent, Asian Americans 18 percent, and multiracial students 3 percent, while international students account for 17 percent. Merit scholarships averaging $5,400 and roughly 200 athletic awards are doled out annually; 22 percent of freshmen receive Pell Grants. The Illinois Commitment program provides free tuition and fees for four years for qualified in-state freshmen or transfer students whose family income is $61,000 or less.

Half of all undergrads live in U of I's co-ed and single-sex residence halls, which range in size from 51 to 660 beds and are arranged in quadrangle-like groups. Some dorms are quite a hike from classrooms, veterans warn. The university offers 11 themed living/learning communities, such as WIMSE (Women in Math, Science, and Engineering) and Innovation LLC (entrepreneurship and creativity), that combine in-hall courses with specialized cocurricular activities. Each residence hall is a mini-neighborhood, with dining halls, darkrooms, libraries, music practice rooms, computers, and lounges creating a sense of community. Chefs keep the food interesting, and campus security maintains a visible presence.

Illinois claims to have the largest Greek system anywhere, with nearly 100 chapters drawing 21 percent of the men and 27 percent of the women. Illinois attracts many socially oriented students who love parties and intramural sports, which may be why the Greek influence is particularly strong. Independents don't have to suffer boredom, though, as there are also nearly 1,200 registered student clubs and organizations, ranging from the ice hockey team to ethnic advocacy groups. "It is a big campus that likes to have a lot of fun," a student says. Though drinking is prohibited in the dorms, the campus policies regarding alcohol are a "token gesture," a business major says. On most weekends, the Illini Union showcases bands, comedians, and hypnotists in its central café. The impressive Krannert Center for the Performing Arts, with four theaters and more than 350 annual performances, serves as the area's cultural center, while Assembly Hall hosts national touring acts. Students get a discount at both facilities. For those who itch for the stimulation of a big city, the campus is just about equidistant from Chicago, Indianapolis, and St. Louis, and Mardi Gras makes for a good road trip in the dead of winter.

"We have a great reputation, and it only grows stronger and stronger."

The Division I Illini compete in the Big Ten, and men's basketball and baseball have winning traditions. Men's golf, gymnastics, and tennis are recent conference champs, and women's gymnastics, tennis, and softball are solid too. The intramural program is extensive, with available facilities that include 16 full-length basketball courts, five pools, 19 handball/racquetball courts, a skating rink, a baseball stadium, and the $5.1 million Atkins Tennis Center. Eighty-five percent of the student body participates in recreational sports. Illinois has a strong athletic program for students with disabilities, including wheelchair basketball, which was invented at the university.

While the University of Illinois may seem mammoth to some students, don't be scared off by this giant institution. Academic and social opportunities are incredibly diverse, and classroom sizes, while growing, are supplemented by smaller group discussions. The breadth of the programs offered combined with an active campus life makes for a well-rounded college experience, students say. "We have a great reputation, and it only grows stronger and stronger."

Illinois has a strong athletic program for students with disabilities, including wheelchair basketball, which was invented at the university.

Overlaps

University of Iowa, University of Michigan, Northwestern, Purdue, UW–Madison, WashU in St. Louis

Illinois Institute of Technology

10 West 33rd Street, Chicago, IL 60616

Forget about cheerleaders, homecoming games, and other traditional trappings of college life. IIT is about learning about technology, getting a degree, and landing a job. Academic focus is on engineering with a bit of architecture thrown in for good measure. If your goal is a technical job in the Chicago area, this is your place. Though private, IIT is relatively inexpensive.

Website: www.iit.edu
Location: City Center
Private
Total Enrollment: 6,051
Undergraduates: 2,586
Male/Female: 69/31
SAT Ranges: ERW 580–680, M 650–730
ACT Ranges: 25–31
Financial Aid: 100%
Pell Grant: 29%
Expense: Pr $ $
Student Loans: 54%
Average Debt: $ $ $
Applicants: 4,708
Accepted: 54%
Enrolled: 19%
Grad in 6 Years: 72%
Returning Freshmen: 93%
Academics: ✎ ✎ ✎ ½
Social: ☎ ☎
Q of L: ★ ★
Admissions: (800) 448-2329
Email Address: admission@iit.edu

Strong Programs:
Engineering
Architecture
Computer Science
Business
Physics
Chemistry
Health Professions

Engineers unite at the Illinois Institute of Technology, where classwork and real-world experience promise to propel students to the top of their fields. After all, when you're engaged in comprehensive undergraduate research and able to take advantage of state-of-the-art labs, you're nearly guaranteed a high-paying job after graduation. IIT programs may be hard, says a junior, but the work "will pay off in the end" as students enter the workforce. Indeed, kids here tend to burn the midnight oil, but frequently escape to downtown Chicago for culture and much-deserved fun.

IIT's home is an urban, 120-acre campus designed by Ludwig Mies van der Rohe, the influential 20th-century architect who directed the architecture school for 20 years. Founded in 1890, the school is just three miles south of Chicago's Loop, and one mile west of Lake Michigan. Guaranteed Rate Field, home of the White Sox, is located directly across from the campus. Miesian-style buildings are adorned by trees and grassy open parks. Crown Hall, home of IIT's College of Architecture, is a National Historic Landmark.

Along with humanities and social science courses, students must fulfill general education requirements that include mathematics, computer science, natural science, and engineering; writing is emphasized across the curriculum. All freshmen take an introduction to the professions seminar, which includes discussion of innovation, ethics, teamwork, communication, and leadership. Incoming first-years also receive Apple iPads; students work with professors to create new applications in order to "enhance their educational experience." Multidisciplinary, group-based learning is big at IIT. Every student must complete two semester-long interprofession projects that sharpen real-world skills.

> **"Professors take an active role in their students' education."**

Engineering is the most popular major, and it sets the tone at IIT. Every engineering department is outstanding. Architecture is also popular and highly regarded; the curriculum emphasizes a team approach that mixes third- through fifth-year students under the supervision of a master professor. "Architecture has a strong faculty," says one student, "and biomedical engineering is very new and well funded." Computer science and business round out the most popular majors, and the sciences, physics in particular, are first-rate. Guided by an academic reorganization, the physical sciences have been bolstered, grouped together with career-oriented fields such as psychology and computer information systems. IIT is the first university to offer a B.S. in bioanalytical chemistry, and recently added majors include environmental chemistry, forensic chemistry, and medicinal chemistry. Dual admissions programs are available in pharmacy, optometry, and osteopathic medicine.

IIT's academic climate is pretty unforgiving, students say. Both the workload and the competition are fierce. "The courses are very difficult," says a junior. Half of the classes have fewer than 20 students, and professors always teach their own classes, while teaching assistants are available for labs and extra help. "Professors take an active role in their students' education," states a biochemistry major.

In addition to meeting outside of class to go over problem sets or for career direction, IIT students and professors often work side by side on research projects. The College of Science awards several $5,000 scholarships to undergrads to perform research work under the supervision of faculty during the summer. Engineering students make use of sophisticated labs and have access to independent research labs in Chicago. Two dozen on-campus research centers, such as the Pritzker Institute of Biomedical Science and Engineering and the Wanger Institute for Sustainable Energy Research, provide additional opportunities. The five-year co-op program—another possibility for hands-on experience—helps lead IIT students into high-paying jobs after graduation. Study abroad programs send students to more than 50 nations around the globe, including France, Greece, Chile, and Singapore; 10 percent of IIT students—mostly architecture majors—participate.

Incoming first-years receive Apple iPads; students work with professors to create new apps.

"Students at IIT are nerds," reports a communication major, but "in a good way." In-state students account for 53 percent of the undergraduate population, and a sizable 21 percent hail from foreign countries. African Americans constitute 6 percent of the student body, Hispanics 16 percent, Asian Americans 14 percent, and multiracial students 3 percent. Students say International Fest is one of the year's most popular events, and IIT sponsors a multitude of cultural awareness workshops and events on different diversity-related topics. Merit scholarships averaging $24,800 are available, and 29 percent of incoming students are Pell-eligible.

As befits the school's urban location, a large chunk of students commute. The 39 percent of students who live in residence halls report that rooms are nice but can be difficult to get. The McCormick Student Village is popular, and students note that Fowler has the biggest rooms but is the only dorm without air-conditioning. The Women in Social Engagement learning community attracts female students who are interested in leadership, civic engagement, and social change. Some students live in apartments in the area; others inhabit one of the eight fraternity houses. The dining hall has several meal plans and a special vegetarian menu. Engineers and architects—notorious late-night studiers—have to hit the library early, since it closes at 10 p.m.

"Chicago provides educational opportunities, internship opportunities, and countless things to do."

IIT's six-block campus is contiguous to Chicago's "Gap" community, where historic but rundown homes are being rehabilitated to form one of the city's hottest new urban residential areas. Most students love exploring Chicago; the city skyline is beautiful and a veritable museum, with buildings designed by the likes of Frank Lloyd Wright, Louis Sullivan, and, of course, Mies van der Rohe. "Chicago provides educational opportunities, internship opportunities, and countless things to do," says one biomedical engineering major. Lake Michigan is within jogging distance, Chinatown is a walk away for lunch or dinner, and the school provides free shuttle bus service to downtown on weekends.

The Women in Social Engagement learning community attracts female students who are interested in leadership, civic engagement, and social change.

Although students who stick around campus on weekends must work hard to find social events, "The social life at IIT has improved over my four years," says a senior. Fraternities claim 10 percent of the men and sororities attract 13 percent of the women, and many students say the social aspect of Greek life is a welcome addition to campus. The Union Board offers movies, concerts, and comedians, and the Bog brings in bands on Thursdays and Saturdays. The annual boat cruise and casino night on the *Odyssey* sightseeing boat is a favorite event, and students can also take advantage of the city's ample nightlife or plan outings to museums or the Chicago Symphony.

In sports-crazy Chicago, IIT's Division III athletic teams (the Scarlet Hawks) are not much of a draw. Still, students praise the men's baseball and basketball teams, and men's and women's soccer and women's volleyball are competitive. Twelve recreational sports, ranging from water polo to Quidditch, are available, but students lament the fact that the facilities close at 5 p.m. on weekends.

Shipping off to Chi-town to take on the mammoth workload at IIT means hitting the books for hours upon hours and a fair share of all-nighters. But the payoff is undeniable. One student says bluntly, "This school is for people who want to make a lot of money after college." Indeed, students who take advantage of this small school's ever-improving engineering departments are likely to have their pick of careers after graduation. And with the innumerable diversions offered in the Windy City, students at IIT revel in the best of two worlds: a challenging academic climate and a great city in which to let off all that steam.

Overlaps

Carnegie Mellon, Loyola University Chicago, Marquette, Rensselaer Polytechnic, U of I at Urbana–Champaign

If You Apply To ›

IIT: Rolling admissions. SATs or ACTs: required. Subject Tests: optional. Accepts the Common Application. Applicants to architecture program may submit optional portfolio.

Illinois Wesleyan University

Bloomington, IL 61701

IWU is a small Midwestern university with a penchant for creativity and the spirit of inquiry. The curriculum is basic liberal arts with additional divisions devoted to fine arts and nursing. An optional three-week term in May allows students to travel or explore an interest. IWU's reputation is limited outside Illinois and surrounding states.

Website: www.iwu.edu
Location: Small City
Private
Total Enrollment: 1,640
Undergraduates: 1,640
Male/Female: 45/55
SAT Ranges: ERW 590–690, M 605–705
ACT Ranges: 24–29
Financial Aid: 99%
Pell Grant: 25%
Expense: Pr $ $
Student Loans: 69%
Average Debt: $ $ $ $
Applicants: 3,697
Accepted: 61%
Enrolled: 17%

Illinois Wesleyan University has its sights set on a special breed of student—the kind who isn't afraid to be many things at once. Students here are encouraged to pursue diverse passions, and IWU is a mecca for students who have preprofessional interests, especially those with unusual pairings like management and music. "What makes Wesleyan really stand out is its care and attention for each student as an individual," says a junior.

Founded in 1850, IWU occupies an 80-acre campus site in a north-side residential district of Bloomington. The heart of campus is the central quadrangle, and tree-lined walkways connect buildings that range in style from gray stone Gothic to ultramodern steel and glass. IWU's main classroom building, State Farm Hall, includes state-of-the-art classrooms and research spaces. A recent expansion of the Shirk Center doubled the size of the university's fitness facilities.

Illinois Wesleyan's general education requirements expose students to a broad array of liberal arts disciplines and are intended to help them develop critical-thinking and writing skills, imagination, intellectual independence, social awareness, and sensitivity to others. All first-year students must take a Gateway Colloquium, a topic-based, seminar-style class of 15 that stresses critical reading, writing, discussion, and analytical skills. Recent topics include What Is Justice?, The Mathematics of Online

Security and Privacy, and Embracing Your Undecidedness. First-years also attend the university's weeklong Turning Titan orientation program, which involves an opening convocation, a common reading program, a day of community service, the Titan Carnival, and other events.

Among the top-notch programs in the College of Liberal Arts are biology, English, chemistry, and math, and some of the most popular majors include business administration, accounting, and psychology. The business administration department offers a Portfolio Management course, in which students buy and sell orders overseen by a client board composed of university trustees. In the design, technology, and entrepreneurship major, students practice all phases of successfully conceiving, developing, and bringing a product to market; administrators say the program aims to turn out "creative people who can actually implement their ideas." IWU's School of Nursing is another big draw. The College of Fine Arts houses three separate schools of music, art, and drama; music is the standout, offering 10 distinct majors and boasting such talented alumni as opera star Dawn Upshaw.

> "[The academic climate] forces you to develop independent critical-thinking skills."

"The academic climate is challenging but rewarding," says a senior. "It forces you to develop independent critical-thinking skills." Seventy-one percent of courses have fewer than 20 students, and professors are "passionate about their subjects, friendly, and approachable," a senior says. In addition to the usual fall and spring semesters, IWU has an optional three-week May term that gives students a chance to focus on a single intensive course, or to conduct a research or service project or an internship. Faculty-led May term travel courses are a particularly popular option. Overall, half of the students take advantage of the university's study abroad program, which sends them packing to more than 70 countries, including England, Denmark, and Japan. Research opportunities are also plentiful, with 60 percent of students taking part, and IWU hosts an annual student research conference that attracts scholars from all disciplines.

Undergraduates at IWU are largely the homegrown variety, with 81 percent hailing from Illinois and 5 percent from outside the country. Students describe their classmates as "down-to-earth" and "easy to talk to." Although IWU began admitting African American students in 1867, they still account for only 5 percent of the student body. Hispanics represent 8 percent, Asian Americans 6 percent, and multiracial students 2 percent. Students here are

> "Some kids from big cities say there is nothing to do in Bloomington–Normal, but in my opinion, they are exaggerating."

generally liberal, socially conscious, and active in groups like Circle K, the Alpha Phi Omega service fraternity, and Habitat for Humanity. Merit scholarships averaging $19,200 are available to qualified students; there are no athletic scholarships. Twenty-five percent of freshmen are Pell-eligible.

Housing is guaranteed for four years, and 79 percent of students live in the dorms. "Other schools have better dorms," says one student, "but after freshman year, housing gets a lot better." Students must be at least 21 to live off campus. Campus food is described as tasty but not as diverse as it could be. Most students say campus security is good, and the university's Consent Is Sexy campaign is helping push awareness of and discussions about sexual violence on campus.

IWU is a mecca for students who have preprofessional interests.

Thirty-two percent of the men and 34 percent of the women go Greek, and fraternities and sororities are the focus of IWU's social life. "Most parties occur at frat houses, but the campus is so small that they are open to everyone," explains an accounting major. Students admit that alcohol policies, which allow drinking on campus for those of legal age, don't always stop underage drinkers. For alternatives, the Office of Student Activities sponsors free events in the student center almost

(continued)

Grad in 6 Years: 78%
Returning Freshmen: 89%
Academics: ✎ ✎ ✎ ½
Social: ☎ ☎ ☎
Q of L: ★ ★ ★ ★
Admissions: (800) 332-2498
Email Address: iwuadmit@iwu.edu

Strong Programs:
Business Administration
Accounting
Biology
Psychology
English
Chemistry
Nursing
Music

every weekend, and academic departments and the Student Senate regularly bring guest speakers to campus. Each fall during homecoming, Greeks and dorm dwellers compete in the Titan Games to get appropriately psyched.

Each fall during homecoming, Greeks and dorm dwellers compete in the Titan Games to get appropriately psyched.

Thanks to the proximity of Illinois State University—less than a mile away in neighboring Normal—IWU offers more than the typical small college town atmosphere. The area's total student population of about 25,000 provides students at tiny IWU with "the best of both worlds," says a senior. "Some kids from big cities say there is nothing to do in Bloomington-Normal, but in my opinion, they are exaggerating," says a freshman. "There may not constantly be ten different events to choose from at any given time, but there is always something." The best road trips are to Peoria or Urbana–Champaign (home of the University of Illinois) or to Chicago or St. Louis, each two and a half hours away.

The IWU Titans compete in the Division III College Conference of Illinois and Wisconsin. Baseball and football are well and good, but Titans basketball really gets students going. The women's track and field team is a recent national champion, and men's and women's basketball, men's golf and baseball, and women's soccer and softball are also strong. The Fort Natatorium houses an impressive 14-lane swimming pool, and the swim team has had its share of stars. The small but active recreational sports program offers about 15 club and intramural sports.

One of the Midwest's better-kept secrets, Illinois Wesleyan is at once cozy and diverse, loaded with opportunities for ambitious students with traditional or offbeat interests. As one junior advises, "The school provides a multitude of paths down which one can travel, and it is up to the student to decide which path to take. IWU allows you to become who you want to be, but only if you let it."

Overlaps

Augustana (IL), Knox, DePauw, Lawrence, College of Wooster, Bradley, U of I at Urbana–Champaign, Northwestern

If You Apply To ›

Illinois Wesleyan: Early action, rolling admissions. SATs or ACTs: required. No Subject Tests. Accepts the Common Application with supplement.

Indiana University

300 North Jordan Avenue, Bloomington, IN 47405

Though men's basketball has traditionally been IU's most famous program, it may not be its best. That distinction could easily go to the world-renowned music school or to the distinguished foreign language program. IU enrolls almost twice as many out-of-staters as the University of Illinois. Bloomington is a great college town, and most students live off campus after freshman year.

With more than 32,000 undergraduates on its enormous campus, Indiana University is the prototype of the large Midwestern school. (And it is emphatically "Indiana University," not "the University of Indiana"—a common mistake.) With strong academics, a thriving social scene, and some of the best sports teams around, this top-notch public institution is a testament to Hoosier determination.

Located in southern Indiana's gently rolling hills, the 1,936-acre campus boasts architecture from Italianate brick to collegiate Gothic limestone to the distinctive style of world-famous architect I. M. Pei. Other unique campus features include fountains, gargoyles, an arboretum of more than 450 trees and shrubs surrounding two reflecting pools, a limestone gazebo, and the Jordan River, a

Website: www.iub.edu
Location: Small City
Public
Total Enrollment: 38,342
Undergraduates: 32,113
Male/Female: 50/50
SAT Ranges: ERW 570–670, M 570–680
ACT Ranges: 25–31

pretty creek that runs alongside a shaded path. Recent construction includes a $42 million, state-of-the-art building for the School of Informatics, Computing, and Engineering, and a $15 million renovation of the cinema that anchors the prominent film studies program.

Indiana prides itself on its liberal arts education—freshmen are admitted not to preprofessional schools but to the "University Division." Majors are declared after one or two years, and the university discourages premature specialization. General education coursework includes math, science, arts and humanities, social and historical studies, English composition, world languages and cultures, and additional requirements that vary by school.

IU's schools and colleges offer many majors and minors, cross-disciplinary study, an individually designed curriculum, and intense honors and research programs. The highly touted Kelley School of Business, with its respected global studies component, is among the most popular on campus, and the School of Education is also strong. Overall, the finance, informatics, marketing, accounting, and media majors enroll the most students. The internationally known Kinsey Institute for the Study of Human Sexual Behavior is housed on IU's campus, and the Jacobs School of Music is top in its field, setting the, ahem, tone for much of the campus. The Media School, lodged in the newly renovated Franklin Hall, gives students the language, communication, research, and technological skills they need to excel in media-related careers, while the School of Public and Environmental Affairs is a top choice for those interested in environmental policy. The School of Global and International Studies brings together language, area studies, and international studies programs to prepare students in the global competencies of the 21st century. For those seeking study abroad opportunities, the university offers more than 380 programs in 52 countries and 17 languages, for students in nearly every field of study; about a quarter of students take part. Recently added academic offerings include majors in environmental health and world languages education.

> "There is a balance with room for both competitive overachievers and laid-back, carefree individuals."

Students describe the academic climate as rigorous but not cutthroat. "With 4,000 different courses per semester, a variety of intensity levels exist," says a marketing major. "There is a balance with room for both competitive overachievers and laid-back, carefree individuals." Students say they regularly share ideas with each other, and group projects are commonplace. Faculty members bring their research results directly to students, and some profs, especially in math and the sciences, bring undergrads into their labs to assist with ongoing projects. "The professors here are remarkable," says an art history major. As for advising, many students seem surprised by the personal attention they receive at such a large university, and they soon learn that many available resources are helpful to those students who seek them out.

Fifty-nine percent of IU undergraduates are from in state, and 10 percent are international, coming from more than 120 countries. African Americans comprise 4 percent of the student body, Hispanics 6 percent, Asian Americans 5 percent, and multiracial students 4 percent. By and large, students do not seem to dwell on political or social issues. And while IU does not guarantee to meet the full demonstrated financial need of every student, it does admit on a need-blind basis. Merit scholarships are awarded to qualified students and average $5,600 annually, and more than 300 athletic scholarships are available for qualified jocks. The Finish in Four program waives any increases in tuition and fees for juniors and seniors who are on track to complete their degrees in four years.

Housing is guaranteed to all incoming freshmen and ranges from Gothic quads (co-ed by building) to 13-floor high-rises (co-ed by floor or unit). One student

(continued)

Financial Aid: 79%
Pell Grant: 19%
Expense: Pub $ $
Student Loans: 45%
Average Debt: $ $ $
Applicants: 41,939
Accepted: 76%
Enrolled: 25%
Grad in 6 Years: 76%
Returning Freshmen: 91%
Academics: ✐ ✐ ✐ ✐
Social: ☎ ☎ ☎ ☎
Q of L: ★ ★ ★ ★
Admissions: (812) 855-0661
Email Address: iuadmit@ indiana.edu

Strong Programs:
Finance
Informatics
Marketing
Accounting
Media
Music
Foreign Languages
Education

About a quarter of students take part in more than 380 study abroad programs in 52 countries and 17 languages.

explains the housing situation this way: "All dorms have laundry facilities, cafeterias, computer clusters, and undergraduate advisors, and some even have special amenities like language-speaking floors." Academic floors are popular with more serious students who are not interested in intense nightlife. Dining options range from buffet-style to food courts with outlets offering international and healthful menus sprinkled among the fast food. Alcohol is prohibited in the dorms, which may help explain why 64 percent of the student body lives off campus. Most off-campus residents choose apartments or small houses with big front porches within walking distance of the campus or the IU bus system. A number of student-driven initiatives, including Culture of Care, MARS (Men Against Rape and Sexual Assault), and Safe Sisters, are working to promote student wellness and safety on campus.

Although campus organizations host numerous events, the most active on-campus groups, in terms of social life, seem to be the Greeks, which attract 24 percent of the men and 21 percent of the women. Some complain of a polarized atmosphere. "There is a large separation between the Greek community and the rest of the student body," says a senior. With concerts, ballets, recitals, and festivals right on campus, students are not lacking for things to keep them busy. The IU student union is one of the largest in the nation, and the range of extracurricular organizations is also impressive. The Little 500 bike race, modeled after the Indianapolis 500, is one of the most highly attended events of the year. Every fall there is a 36-hour Dance Marathon to raise money for Riley's Children's Hospital in Indianapolis. The Office of Diversity Programs, Committee on Multicultural Understanding, and Students Organized Against Racism are a few more ways students can make a difference on campus.

> "Some [dorms] have special amenities like language-speaking floors."

Students say Bloomington is a great college town. There are many excellent bars, shops, and restaurants, including one of the few Tibetan restaurants in the country. Locally, the area offers some impressive rock quarries (often used as illegal but refreshing swimming pools), miles of public forests, and three nearby lakes. Spelunkers will find heaven down below in the many nearby caves. Chicago, Cincinnati, Indianapolis, St. Louis, and even New Orleans are popular road trips.

Although dozens of intramural and club sports are available, recreational sports pale in comparison with Division I varsity athletics here; basketball is an established religion in the state of Indiana. Students and faculty are all eligible for tickets, but they've got to get requests in early—and even those lucky enough to get tickets don't count on going to more than a quarter of home games. In recent years, the Hoosiers men's basketball, track and field, and swimming and diving teams have claimed Big Ten championships, and women's basketball is competitive too. Even the football team draws red-and-white crowds. Purdue is IU's traditional athletic rival, and teams play for the Old Oaken Bucket, found on a farm in southern Indiana in 1925 and alleged to have been used during the Civil War.

Along with IU's reputation as a basketball powerhouse, it also provides committed students with stellar programs ranging from foreign languages to music, and a social scene that's hard to beat. For those not frightened away by throngs of classmates, Indiana University may be a great fit.

If You Apply To ›

Indiana: Early action, regular decision. SATs or ACTs: required. Subject Tests: optional. Accepts the Common Application with supplement.

International Universities

Do you thrive on new experiences? Like to meet new people? Want to learn about different cultures? You can do all that at a college or university in the United States, but if you really want to jump in with both feet, think about attending a school in a foreign country. This section highlights the opportunities available in Canada, Great Britain, and Ireland, by far the most common destinations outside the United States for degree-seeking undergraduates.

The absence of a language barrier is the most obvious reason why these three countries are the preferred destinations for study abroad. Plenty of students do a junior year abroad where the language is Spanish or Swahili, but only a handful can realistically expect to earn an entire degree in a foreign tongue. A growing number of European universities are offering instruction in English, not only to Americans but to students from throughout the world. A smattering of American universities do exist in places ranging from Paris to Cairo, but most are small and the majority of their enrollment is students from other countries seeking an American-style education. If you're willing to venture halfway around the world, Australia is an English-speaking destination that might be worth a look for its combination of beautiful scenery, quality universities, and, at least by American standards, reasonable tuition.

Look for coverage of Australian institutions in a future edition of the *Fiske Guide*. The following sections examine Canada, Britain, and Ireland in more detail, followed by full-length articles on selected institutions.

Canadian Universities

Horace Greeley told ambitious young men of his generation to "go West." Today his admonition to young men and women seeking a quality college education at a relatively modest cost would probably be to "go North"—to Canada. A growing number of American students are discovering the educational riches that lie just above their northern border in this huge land of 35 million people that is known for its rugged mountains, bicultural politics, spirited ice hockey, and cold ale. What's drawing them is easy to discern.

The top Canadian universities are the academic equals of most flagship public universities and many leading privates in the United States. Canadian campuses and the cities in which they are located are safe places and, unless one opts for a French course of study, there are no language and few cultural barriers. Canadian schools are strong on international exchange programs, and their degrees carry weight with U.S. graduate schools.

Canada has 90 institutions of higher learning, ranging from internationally recognized research universities to the small undergraduate teaching institutions in the country's more rural areas. Most of the larger universities are located in highly urban centers, but some are situated in smaller towns where they dominate the life of the community. Most are almost literally next door to the United States, within 100 miles of the Canada–U.S. border. In this guide, we feature four of Canada's strongest universities: the University of British Columbia, McGill University, Queen's University, and the University of Toronto.

Institutions of higher learning in Canada were established from the earliest days of French settlement in the mid-17th century, making them some of the oldest in North America. The precursors to the public universities in Canada were the small, elite, denominational colleges that sprang up in Quebec, in the Maritimes, and later in Ontario. A few private denominational colleges and universities still exist in Canada, but most have been subsumed into affiliations or associations with the larger universities. Education in Canada, including university education, became the exclusive jurisdiction of provincial governments.

One of the key differences between Canadian and U.S. universities is that Canadian universities (and this is what they are, not "colleges") are primarily funded from public monies. Calculating the cost for an American to attend a Canadian university can be tricky. For one thing, the exchange rate between the U.S. and Canadian dollar fluctuates (at this writing, it favors the U.S. dollar). Moreover, tuition and fee rates vary by field of study. The cost of pricey majors such as medicine and other hard sciences can easily be double or triple that of less expensive ones such as social work or theology. Canadian citizens, of course, pay far less than visitors from south of the border. Depending on the factors just described, tuition and fees at the four universities included in the *Fiske Guide* range from less than US $15,000 to more than US $70,000. For many U.S. students, education at one of the top Canadian universities is comparable to out-of-state rates at a flagship public university in the States.

Federal and provincial loans and grants that are readily available to Canadian students are generally not available to students from the United States and other countries. However, the majority of universities with competitive admissions, particularly those featured in the *Fiske Guide*, offer merit-based awards and scholarships to students of all nationalities. American students who attend leading Canadian schools can apply their U.S. student assistance funds, including federal Direct Loans and Pell Grants.

The requirements for obtaining a degree are set by each institution, as are the admissions requirements and prerequisites. Unlike the United States, Canada does not offer nor require its own students to take a Canadian college entrance test. Some Canadian universities admitting students from the United States will require SAT or ACT scores along with high school marks from academic subjects in the last two or three years of high school. In general, top universities are about as selective as their American counterparts.

Application fees vary by institution, as do deadlines. Canadian universities are aware of the May 1 deadline operative in the United States, and they try to accommodate. Applications to the University of Toronto and Queen's University in Ontario are handled centrally through the Ontario Universities' Application Service, although Queen's also accepts the Common Application as an alternative for students applying from the U.S. McGill and British Columbia handle their own applications directly. Canadian universities differ widely in the amount of credit and/or advanced standing they offer for Advanced Placement examinations or International Baccalaureate Higher Level examinations.

The following admissions requirements apply to applicants from an American school system. The University of British Columbia bases admissions decisions on the average of eight full-year academic courses over the last two years of high school. SAT and ACT test results are required, but there is no minimum score requirement. McGill bases its assessment of American high school graduates on the overall record of marks in academic subjects during the final three years of high school, class standing, and results obtained in SAT I and SAT II and/or ACT tests. Queen's wants applicants with a minimum score of 1200 on SAT I (with at least 580 in Evidence-Based Reading and Writing and 520 in Mathematics) and looks at class rank. Toronto's Arts and Science faculties want a high grade point average and good scores on the SAT I and on two SAT II Subject Tests. These universities generally have additional program-specific requirements for STEM fields that may be more stringent. ACT and CEEB Advanced Placement Examination scores are also considered.

It is hard to beat Canadian universities for the quality of student life. Although many students commute, most of the universities in Canada offer on-campus housing; some even guarantee campus housing for first-year students. Universities offer active intramural and intercollegiate sports programs for both men and women, and the usual student clubs, newspapers, and radio stations provide students with opportunities to get involved and develop friendships. As in the United States, student-run organizations are active participants in university life, with leaders serving on university committees and lobbying on issues ranging from creating more bicycle paths to keeping tuition low. Few Canadian campuses are troubled by issues of student safety or rowdiness. In the larger urban centers, Canadian campuses reflect the rich diversity of Canada's cultural mosaic, and most encourage their students to gain international experience by spending a term or a full year abroad.

Americans wondering about the currency of a Canadian degree in the United States should be reassured that top American and multinational companies—the likes of Chase, IBM, and Microsoft—actively recruit on Canadian campuses, as do American graduate schools. According to the Institute of International Education in New York, more than 10,000 Canadians are currently enrolled in graduate schools in the United States.

The one thing that is different for U.S. and other international students intending to study in Canada is that they will have to obtain a Student Authorization, equivalent to a visa, from Canadian immigration authorities, as well as a passport. Getting a Student Authorization is fairly straightforward for American citizens, but this slight bureaucratic hurdle is a reminder that Canada, for all of its similarities in language and culture with the United States, is still another country.

Universities Canada, a nonprofit organization representing Canada's colleges and universities, has more information at www.univcan.ca.

Canadian universities are currently playing host to about 1,600 American students on their campuses and, as a result of funding cutbacks and internationalization policies in the early 1990s, they have become increasingly active in recruiting students from south of the border. This is but one more reason why it makes sense for more young Americans to check out the "Canadian option." Canada, eh?

University of British Columbia

Vancouver, British Columbia V6T 1Z1 CAN

Natural beauty is the first thing that draws Americans to Vancouver—and Canada's premier western university. A similar scale to places like University of Washington but with two major differences—no big-time sports to unite the campus and limited dorm life. The university is active in recruiting overseas, which creates an international ambience.

What do three prime ministers of Canada, three provincial premiers, an astronaut, a world-renowned opera singer, and two Nobel Prize winners have in common? They are all graduates of the University of British Columbia. Founded in 1908, UBC offers students hundreds of solid programs, such as business, science, engineering, the social sciences, and fine arts, as well as ready access to beaches and mountains and a diploma with instant name recognition. Though the massive campus can sometimes feel isolating, students are nevertheless happy to be here in such illustrious company.

Located just 25 minutes from downtown Vancouver, UBC's striking Point Grey campus covers a peninsula that borders the Pacific Ocean and is bounded by an old-growth forest. Mountains—perfect for skiing—loom in the distance. Architectural styles are a mix of Gothic and modern, and students can enjoy a leisurely stroll through the university's botanical gardens. Notable campus facilities include the Kaiser Building (the central hub of engineering), the Barber Learning Centre, the Mitchell Thunderbird Sports Arena, and The Nest (a $106 million student union building). The university also has a smaller campus—UBC Okanagan—located in Kelowna, in the Okanagan Valley.

UBC offers more than 260 undergraduate degree options, and popular majors include psychology, biology, English, and political science. Programs in anthropology, First Nations and indigenous studies, and Asian studies are highly regarded and enhanced by the university's excellent Museum of Anthropology, which features one of the world's best collections of Northwest Coast First Nations art. Music majors benefit from the Chan Centre for the Performing Arts. Economics, geography, international relations, microbiology, and commerce are strong too. One student grumbles about his 8 a.m. philosophy lecture: "Who can focus on the big questions at that time of the morning?" Additional programs include majors in applied animal biology, applied plant and soil sciences, geographical biogeosciences, and zoology.

> "There is a huge diversity here that many smaller schools may lack."

Freshmen benefit from a wide array of first-year programs, including Imagine UBC and Create UBC Okanagan, a first-day orientation. Arts One and the Coordinated Arts programs offer enriched, integrated approaches to broad interdisciplinary themes in arts and humanities. Qualified students can take advantage of Science One, featuring team-taught courses in biology, chemistry, math, and physics. The UBC study abroad program has more than 200 institutional partners in 40 countries, and co-op programs in engineering, science, arts, commerce, and forestry give students an opportunity to earn while they learn. In addition, honors and double-honors programs are available to superbrains and budding geniuses.

The academic climate is exactly what you would expect from a university of UBC's international stature. "Courses can be hard," says one student, "but success is based on your interest and willingness to learn." Most classes have fewer than 50 students, while larger lectures are supplemented with smaller labs and

Website: www.you.ubc.ca
Location: City Outskirts
Public
Total Enrollment: 49,392
Undergraduates: 39,451
Male/Female: 45/55
SAT Ranges: 1150–1450
  (combined)
ACT Ranges: 27–32
Financial Aid: 25%
Pell Grant: N/A
Expense: Pub $
Student Loans: N/A
Average Debt: N/A
Applicants: 34,003
Accepted: 54%
Enrolled: 59%
Grad in 6 Years: 75%
Returning Freshmen: 90%
Academics: ✐ ✐ ✐ ✐ ½
Social: ☎ ☎
Q of L: ★ ★ ★ ★
Admissions: (604) 822-8999
Email Address:
  international@askme.ubc.ca

Strong Programs:
Psychology
Biology
English
Political Science
Anthropology
Economics
Geography
Commerce

discussion groups. Overall, the faculty receives good marks. "The professors are extremely intelligent people who are truly dedicated to their disciplines," says a junior. Academic advising is a mixed bag, with some students complaining that finding a knowledgeable advisor can be time-consuming.

With more than 39,000 undergraduates attending the Vancouver campus, it's no surprise that UBC's student population is a melting pot—24 percent come from outside Canada. "There is a huge diversity here that many smaller schools may lack," says a sophomore. The typical UBC student is bright, hardworking, and gregarious. Minorities are well represented (Asians make up the largest contingency), and the university encourages diversity through a series of special programs and active recruiting. Hot political issues include LGBTQ, women's, and human rights. The International Scholars program offers financial support, as well as special service projects, workshops, and other opportunities, to top international students.

Roughly one-third of the students currently live on campus. A major expansion of on-campus housing is underway, estimated at US $650 million and slated for completion in 2022, and UBC now guarantees a spot to all incoming first-time, first-year students. On-campus options

"Vancouver is one of the most livable cities in the world."

include co-ed complexes (primarily for freshmen), theme houses, university apartments, and family units for upperclassmen. A history major says on-campus living is worth it to "enjoy the community spirit." Those seeking off-campus accommodations must contend with Vancouver's pricey rental market. Hungry students will find an endless variety of meal options at the school's 45 dining locations, including "Japanese, Lebanese, Italian, and vegetarian" plates, according to one student. The Sexual Assault Support Centre provides support services and educational programming related to sexual violence.

On such a large campus, isolation is a real threat. "You need to get in touch with other students quickly when you get here or you could feel lost on such a big campus," says a freshman. Social life happens mostly on campus but largely "depends on the crowd you hang with," according to one student. For partying types, there are the requisite bashes, courtesy of UBC's small but active Greek scene—one of the few places where underage drinkers may sneak a sip of booze. Alternatives include university-sponsored events, such as movies and guest speakers. Popular campus events include Storm the Wall, long-boat racing, and the Arts County Fair.

Vancouver offers students countless opportunities, though one health science major says, "It isn't a college town. It is a well-developed semicosmopolitan city." Another adds, "Vancouver is one of the most livable cities in the world and UBC is located in the nicest, most beautiful part—it's not too hard to imagine what a pleasure it is to go to school here." Beautiful weather draws students outdoors and to nearby beaches and mountains for in-line skating, snowboarding, and swimming. Eleven recreational sports leagues and 16 intramural events are a huge draw for students at the Vancouver campus; popular sports include sailing, skiing, and cycling. UBC has 31 varsity teams (the Thunderbirds), which have brought home more than 120 national championships—the most of any institution in Canada. Men's and women's volleyball and swimming, along with women's ice hockey and field hockey, have been particularly competitive in recent years.

Spending four years at this mammoth university can be intimidating for the shy student. But for those willing to take control of their social lives, UBC offers an impressive academic milieu. A history major offers this point of view: "I think that the school's biggest strength is its size; there are so many opportunities here."

McGill University

Montreal, Quebec H3A 0C8 CAN

The Canadian university best known south of the border. Though instruction is in English, McGill is located in French-speaking Montreal, a world-class city that has it all. Individualism is encouraged, and there's a strong international flavor. Just over 10 percent of students live in university housing, and anyone coming here will be on their own for housing after freshman year.

With such strong preprofessional programs and a diverse student body, it's easy to see why enterprising men and women from around the world flock to McGill University. But beware: this is not a cookie-cutter school, and fitting in actually seems to be discouraged. "McGill is a university where people are allowed to become individuals," a senior says. "Difference and creativity are celebrated here."

Montreal's climate alternates between hot summers and freezing winters. A junior describes McGill's 80-acre main campus as "an oasis in the heart of the city." Located in downtown Montreal amid the hustle and bustle, the campus provides students with ample green space and a welcome respite from the decidedly urban atmosphere of the city. A free outdoor skating rink adds charm in the frigid winter months. Campus buildings range from "Gothic-like" structures with vines growing up the sides to more modern structures. Trees and greenery dot the campus landscape, and the sprawling recreation trails of Mount Royal rise to its immediate north. Notable facilities include a $71 million life sciences research complex. The Schulich School of Music offers an ultramodern symphony and multimedia hall that functions as a recording studio, performance venue, and research studio. A short drive west of downtown, the Macdonald Campus occupies 1,600 acres of woods and fields on the shores of Lac St-Louis, providing unique opportunities for fieldwork and research.

> "McGill treats its students as mature, educated adults."

To fulfill the university's general education requirements, students must first choose which discipline (or faculty) to enter. A senior says, "It is important to consider the university on the basis of which faculty you would be interested in, because they vary greatly and operate almost as independent units." Freshmen must accumulate six to 12 credits in three of four disciplines, including languages, math and science, social sciences, and humanities, and declare a major before their sophomore year. Upon entering their major, students have a menu of course options that includes honors programs and double majors.

Though the most popular majors are psychology, political science, commerce, and education, there is no denying that the university's strengths lie in preprofessional programs such as medicine, law, and engineering. The sciences receive uniform praise, as does the School of Environment. A double-degree interdisciplinary program allows students to combine a bachelor of arts program with one in the sciences. Several programs help freshmen with the transition to college, and some are tailored to international students, which includes those from the United States. For

Website: www.mcgill.ca
Location: City Center
Public
Total Enrollment: 30,380
Undergraduates: 22,895
Male/Female: 42/58
SAT Ranges: 1250 or above (combined)
ACT Ranges: 26 or above
Financial Aid: 24%
Pell Grant: N/A
Expense: Pub $
Student Loans: N/A
Average Debt: N/A
Applicants: 36,304
Accepted: 43%
Enrolled: 42%
Grad in 6 Years: 84%
Returning Freshmen: 92%
Academics: ✐ ✐ ✐ ✐ ½
Social: ☎ ☎ ☎ ☎
Q of L: ★ ★ ★ ★
Admissions: (514) 398-7878
Email Address: N/A

Strong Programs:
Psychology
Political Science
Commerce
Education
Medicine
Law
Engineering

those who want to escape Montreal's brutal winters, there are internships; field studies in Barbados, Africa, and the Smithsonian Tropical Research Institute in Panama; and exchange programs with more than 150 partner universities around the world.

Regardless of major, students can expect classes to be demanding. "McGill has a very stressful and competitive atmosphere," a finance major says. Classes tend to be large—some introductory courses enroll up to 1,000 students—and students must be willing to seek out professors and advisors. "The quality of teaching is generally above average," a student says. "Many of the professors are kind, intelligent, and devoted to their students." Students grumble that academic advising is a bureaucratic tangle. "There is way too much red tape and dealing with the administration can be horrible," says one senior.

Forty-five percent of undergraduates are Quebecers (or Québécois, as Francophones would say), and 28 percent are international, representing more than 135 countries.

"The McGill–Harvard rugby match is a must-watch."

Indeed, McGill students are a diverse lot, and the only common thread among them seems to be their fierce independence. A geography major says McGill students are "hardworking, driven, very intellectual, and research-oriented." Environmental issues are a big concern, and students report that political and social issues receive ample attention on campus. Qualified students are eligible for merit scholarships and a limited number of awards for athletes. There is also a work-study program for those in need of financial assistance.

The university's traditional and alternative residence halls house about 13 percent of undergrads in dorms, apartments, and shared facilities houses. Dorms run the gamut, but one recent acquisition is, according to a senior, a "four-star hotel, turned into a six-star dorm." Party animals will feel free to crank up the stereo in Molson or McConnell, while bookworms might be better suited for Gardner. Off-campus apartments are a popular alternative for upperclassmen, who take advantage of Montreal's clean, affordable housing. "The dining facilities are good," says a sophomore. Despite its urban location, the McGill campus is safe and security receives positive reviews. "There are student organizations like 'Walksafe' and 'Drivesafe' that will walk or drive students to their residences at night regardless of where they are or where they are going," reports one student.

"McGill students are very sociable and love to party!" says one student. Though there are "considerable on-campus social activities, with many clubs and associations," many students venture off campus into Montreal for fun and adventure. "A cultural epicenter, Montreal is home to some of the world's best museums, galleries, restaurants, shops, and music," a senior says. "There are always free concerts and festivals all over the city throughout the year." Drinking is a popular pastime, but underage drinkers are few and far between since the legal age in Quebec is 18 and, a senior says, "McGill treats its students as mature, educated adults." Greek organizations sign up about 2 percent of the students, and McGill boasts Canada's first social fraternity for gay, bisexual, transgender, and progressive men. Well-attended campus events include homecoming, Winter Carnival, and Frosh activities during orientation week. New York City, Ottawa, and Toronto are popular road-trip destinations, and ski slopes are less than an hour away.

Men's and women's basketball and ice hockey, men's rugby, and women's soccer are among the most popular varsity sports; men's baseball and women's basketball and synchronized swimming have captured recent national championships. According to one student, "The McGill–Harvard rugby match is a must-watch." Intramurals offer would-be jocks an opportunity to blow off steam after classes and on weekends, with soccer and ice hockey attracting the most interest.

In recent years the government of Quebec has been less than enthusiastic about funding its English-speaking academic gem, and large classes and mountains of red

Overlaps

University of British Columbia, Concordia, University of Montreal, NYU, Queen's University, University of Toronto

tape are undeniably part of the McGill experience. Nevertheless, most denizens seem happy. "The students who go to McGill are very invested in their academic life and are proud of their school," a student says.

If You Apply To ›

McGill: Rolling admissions. SATs and two Subject Tests or ACTs: required for U.S. applicants. Does not accept the Common Application.

Queen's University

Kingston, Ontario K7L 3N6 CAN

With about 19,000 undergraduates, Queen's is the smallest of the major Canadian universities. It is also the only one set in a metropolitan area of modest size. Engineering and business are the strongest areas of study, followed by nursing. Toronto and Montreal are both about three hours away. With 90 percent of its first-year students in the dorms, Queen's has a more active residential life than other Canadian universities.

Students at Queen's University approach work and play with equal zeal and enjoy a potent mix of school spirit and intellectual drive. Success requires energy and a willingness to get into the thick of things. "People who aren't interested in being a part of the school community are better off at a school that isn't such a big family," warns a sophomore. Solid academics, a pervasive school spirit, and long-standing traditions make life at this storied university unique—and demanding. "Getting into Queen's is just the first challenge," says a senior. "Succeeding at Queen's is another battle."

The 161-acre Queen's campus is located on the north shore of Lake Ontario, just minutes from the heart of Kingston, Ontario ("the limestone city"), and directly between Montreal and Toronto. "Almost all buildings are constructed using limestone," explains a senior. Historically significant buildings have been maintained, and "there are some modern buildings with a lot of glass to provide a bright and welcoming atmosphere." Ample greenery and open spaces provide students a place to stretch out under the sky and hit the books. The 80,000-square-foot Isabel Bader Centre for the Performing Arts features common teaching rooms and shared public spaces designed to encourage interactivity.

> "The courses are often theory-driven and require a substantial amount of work."

Established in 1841 by Royal Charter of Queen Victoria, Queen's University offers undergraduate degrees in a variety of faculties, including science, engineering, commerce, education, music, nursing, and creative arts. Academics are unilaterally solid, but the most demanding are engineering and commerce, and nursing is popular. The bachelor of commerce program was the first of its kind in Canada and provides students with an internationally focused liberal business education, enhanced by leadership modules and the integration of technology. The School of Computing offers bachelor of computer degrees in biomedical computing, cognitive science, and software design, as well as B.A. and B.S. degrees. Computing and the Creative Arts is a multidisciplinary program that allows students to use cutting-edge software programs for music, drama, art, and film production. General education requirements vary by program, but all students can expect to complete a rigorous

Website: www.queensu.ca
Location: Small City
Public
Total Enrollment: 23,072
Undergraduates: 18,935
Male/Female: 40/60
SAT Ranges: 1200 or above (combined)
ACT Ranges: 26 or above
Financial Aid: 58%
Pell Grant: N/A
Expense: Pub $
Student Loans: 34%
Average Debt: N/A
Applicants: 37,066
Accepted: 49%
Enrolled: 28%
Grad in 6 Years: 86%
Returning Freshmen: 95%
Academics: ✍ ✍ ✍ ✍ ½
Social: ☎ ☎ ☎ ☎
Q of L: ★ ★ ★ ★
Admissions: (613) 533-2218
Email Address: admission@ queensu.ca

Strong Programs:
Commerce
Engineering

(continued)

Nursing
Computing
Arts
Sciences

series of core and elective courses. Students participating in programs at the Queen's Bader International Study Centre are whisked away to the university's campus in East Sussex, England, where they enjoy small classes and integrated field studies while residing in a 15th-century castle. In addition, there are exchange programs with 180 universities in 45 countries around the world. Queen's is considered a leader in study abroad; 20 percent of students participate. Opportunities for undergraduate research are abundant as well.

"The academic climate is quite competitive, and the courses are often theory-driven and require a substantial amount of work to prepare for class and complete assignments," says one senior. The general consensus among struggling students is that As are hard to come by. "After working your butt off and reading stacks of textbooks, your grades pale in comparison to the marks of students at other universities," gripes a biology major. The QSuccess program helps orient first-year students academically and socially, and Bounce Back is an opt-in academic support program for first-year students who earn low GPAs in their first term. Participating students are paired with Bounce Back Facilitators, peer mentors who help them set goals and identify strategies for academic success.

The QSuccess program helps orient first-year students academically and socially, and Bounce Back is an opt-in academic support program.

Classes tend to be large for freshmen and sophomores, but dwindle in size as one approaches graduation. The majority of classes are taught by full professors, who receive praise for their accessibility and intelligence. "The teachers I have had have been thorough, challenging, and concerned about my success," says a junior. Office hours and special "wine and cheese" functions give students ample opportunity to mingle with faculty. Students report that there is little trouble getting into desired classes, and "there is lots of counseling available for students who need it."

Queen's students are an industrious, intelligent group, and most are used to academic success. School spirit runs high and campus issues include rising tuition fees—and determining just who is responsible for the cost. Undergraduates come from every Canadian province and 94 countries; 78 percent are from Ontario and 10 percent are international. A sociology major says that "Queen's is very PC and inclusive, regardless of gender, race, religion, or sexual orientation." Though there are no athletic scholarships, hundreds of merit awards averaging $2,000 are handed out annually. "I have had great help through scholarships and financial aid," relates a senior. "There is quite a lot of money for you. You just have to go after it." International students are automatically considered for available merit awards.

"Campus pubs and city pubs have both found their niche."

Ninety percent of undergraduates live in 17 residence halls, and all freshmen are guaranteed a place to hang their hats. Co-ed and single-sex dorms are available, and students say all accommodations are well maintained. A mandatory meal plan gives freshmen a wide variety of foods to choose from, and the surrounding city also offers a plethora of dining options. After freshman year, most students pack their bags and head off campus to the "student village," where comfortable apartments are available. Most Queen's students live within a reasonable walk of campus. Safety is practically a nonissue on campus; students report that they feel quite safe and that security is more than adequate.

The school is steeped in Scottish tradition, and it's normal to see kilt-wearing bandsmen at important campus events.

Make no mistake about it, Queen's students know how to have a good time. One says, "Campus pubs and city pubs have both found their niche." On Thursday nights, students flock to the campus pub, The Underground, for a drink or two, while Saturday nights are reserved for city bars and nightclubs. The legal drinking age is 19, and kiddies will have a tough time skirting the law. "The bouncers in Kingston actually have a couple of brain cells and can spot a fake ID from 90 kilometers away," says a senior. Nonalcoholic alternatives include school-sponsored movies and extracurricular clubs (there are more than 220). "Extracurricular activities are a must, not an option!" says one student. Frosh Week is a favorite event, with "cheers that even the most blasé of students will be shouting out with pride by the end of the week." The school is steeped in Scottish tradition, and it's normal to see kilt-wearing bandsmen at important campus events.

Once the capital of Canada, Kingston is described as "very much a university town." There are several universities in the area (including the Royal Military College), and downtown provides students with shops, clubs, museums, and movie theaters. The city's relative isolation makes it

"There is so much school spirit, sometimes it makes you sick."

the favored stomping ground for students without wheels. Town/gown relations are good, and students are very active in the community. Toronto and Montreal (less than three hours away) are popular road trips.

With 13 varsity teams, 35 varsity clubs, and 30 recreational clubs, Queen's athletic program is not only the largest in Canada, but also ranks with Harvard and MIT for the largest programs in North America. Competitive Gaels teams include men's and women's rugby, ice hockey, soccer, and volleyball. The annual "kill McGill" football game against rival McGill draws pigskin-crazed students from every corner of campus; homecoming is reputed to be a lively affair. Intramural competition is fierce too, and nearly half of the students are involved on some level. A student says, "There is so much school spirit, sometimes it makes you sick."

Life at Queen's University is one of extremes. Though the academic climate can be tough and the winters long, students here find much to praise. "One of the great things about Queen's is that it's constantly growing and expanding to meet the needs of its students," says one senior, "but at the same time, it never loses sight of where it came from or what it stands for."

If You Apply To ›

Queen's: Rolling admissions. SATs or ACTs: required for U.S. applicants. Subject Tests: optional (required for engineering candidates only). Accepts the Common Application. Apply to particular program.

University of Toronto

Toronto, Ontario M5S 1A1 CAN

U of T is one of the largest institutions in the *Fiske Guide* and one of the biggest in the world. If ever there were a place where go-getterism is a necessity, this is it. In the absence of American-style school spirit, U of T students cut loose to find their fun in the city. Toronto is one of the most diverse and cosmopolitan cities in the world, with nearly half of its citizens born outside of Canada.

Students at the University of Toronto avoid getting lost in the shuffle by taking part in a unique residential college system that allows them to model their educational experience after their own personalities. Each college has a distinct character and appeal, yet blends seamlessly into the university's overall academic milieu. And when it comes to academics, the U of T delivers, says a senior: "The students were likely at the top of their class in high school and are very competitive—more so than at Queen's or York universities."

The University of Toronto is so large that it spans three campuses. The St. George campus in downtown Toronto features Gothic architecture and historic buildings.

(continued)

ACT Ranges: 28 or above

Financial Aid: 20%

Pell Grant: N/A

Expense: Pub $

Student Loans: N/A

Average Debt: N/A

Applicants: 47,354

Accepted: 45%

Enrolled: 31%

Grad in 6 Years: 75%

Returning Freshmen: 91%

Academics: ✎ ✎ ✎ ✎ ½

Social: ☎ ☎ ☎

Q of L: ★ ★ ★

Admissions: (416) 978-2190

Email Address: future.students
@utoronto.ca

Strong Programs:

Physical Sciences

Computer Science

Engineering

Commerce

Management

Biochemistry

Forensic Science

Music

Toronto students choose from more than 700 undergraduate degree programs.

The suburban campuses in Mississauga and Scarborough feature more modern structures. Other facilities include the Centre for Biological Timing and Cognition, where researchers study how sleep cycles affect learning and physical and mental health, and the Goldring Centre for High Performance Sport. The Myhal Centre for Engineering Innovation and Entrepreneurship opened in 2018. As befitting such a gargantuan institution, the university's endowment is the largest of any Canadian college or university.

Students apply directly to one of Toronto's nine colleges—seven of which are on the St. George campus—and choose from more than 700 undergraduate degree programs. The most popular programs include physical sciences, computer science, engineering, commerce, and management; majors in biochemistry and forensic science and a minor in food studies are notable as well. The Faculty of Arts and Science offers a wide array of disciplines that span the arts, science, and business, while the Faculty of Music is the oldest in Canada and offers bachelor's, master's, and doctoral degrees in all of their programs. The concurrent education program allows undergraduates to complete the requirements for a bachelor of education, professional teacher certification, and a second undergraduate degree simultaneously. Distinctive learning options include First-Year Learning Communities and a wide range of research opportunities. Optional first-year seminars (called First-Year Foundations: The One Programs) are "a good transition from high school to university," says a senior, and give incoming freshmen the chance to learn from leading faculty members in a less intimidating environment of around 25 to 50 students. Topics range from public policy to urban environments to geological fieldwork.

> "Even in classes of 1,500 students, professors have been consistently engaging and well-versed."

Courses require a great deal of reading outside the classroom and are typically demanding. "During exam periods and the final weeks of each semester, the academic climate can understandably become quite intense," says one senior. Large lecture classes are accompanied by smaller tutorials, facilitating personal attention, and professors get high marks for their teaching skills and their smarts. "Even in classes of 1,500 students, professors have been consistently engaging and well-versed," says a student. Faculty-led Summer Abroad courses are an option for students who wish to venture farther afield.

"Students are from all over the world and represent the full spectrum of values and backgrounds," says an anthropology major. "U of T is very diverse and the student body is generally intelligent, progressive, and open-minded." Twenty-one percent of undergraduates are foreign—from outside Canada, that is—including about 450 Americans. The most significant issues on campus include "tuition fees, unequal pay, the environment, and critical social justice," according to one student. The Ontario Public Interest Research Group and Amnesty International attract sizable followings. A limited number of competitive academic scholarships are available for the most high-achieving international students.

> "Social life here revolves around the very energetic city in which the school is located."

Roughly 11 percent of students live in campus housing, and first-years are guaranteed rooms. "There are new buildings and historic old buildings that are beautiful," says an anthropology major. "They are cozy and comfortable and pretty well maintained." All of the dorms are affiliated with one of the nine undergraduate colleges, which act as "local neighborhoods" and center on specialties, such as Buddhism, Celtic studies, and criminology. "Every cafeteria always has a vegetarian, vegan, halal, kosher, gluten-free, or dairy-free option," a junior reports. "Security is pretty good on campus, and our campus is in a good part of Toronto," a bioethics major says.

"Social life here revolves around the very energetic city in which the school is located," says a sociology and English major. Another student adds, "Social events are balanced between off-campus pubs, clubs, skating rinks, banquet halls, and stadiums to on-campus pubs, event spaces in Hart House, and student lounges." Toronto boasts great culture, super shopping, a clean and safe nightlife district—and the picturesque shores of Lake Ontario, lovely in warmer weather. The legal drinking age here is 19; students who are of age may have alcohol in their rooms but not in common spaces, and anyone caught violating local laws or the open-container policy is reported to the dean of the residence. But according to one student, "There isn't much of a party culture at U of T, because we are much more focused on studying." Students looking to unwind on campus will find plenty of school-sponsored events, such as movies and guest speakers, and while there are no fraternities or sororities, there is a club for nearly every interest. Students turn out in droves to celebrate PRIDE, the largest gay pride event in North America, along with Frosh Week, which includes wacky fun such as bed races between the colleges, and the annual Fireball formal dance.

Nine residential undergraduate colleges act as "local neighborhoods" and center on specialties, such as Celtic studies and criminology.

Varsity sports are not a focus of campus life at Toronto, though hockey, volleyball, and basketball draw something of a following, especially when the opponent is Queen's University or the University of Western Ontario; the Varsity Blues men's and women's water polo teams are recent national champions. The intramural program, however, is another story. It's the largest in Canada, involving more than 10,000 students in 26 sports, with 57 leagues and 20 tournaments each year. Residence halls and groups of friends compete in everything from badminton to indoor cricket, inner-tube water polo, squash, triathlon, ultimate Frisbee, and broomball. Students can also be found cheering the city's many professional teams, including the Blue Jays (baseball), the Raptors (basketball), and the Maple Leafs (hockey).

Toronto's biggest liability, its sheer and sometimes overwhelming size, may also be its biggest asset, students say—as long as they learn to speak up and proactively take advantage of all of the school's resources. Says a senior, "A prospective student should choose the University of Toronto due to its outstanding academic reputation and convenient location in the social hub of Toronto's downtown core."

Overlaps

University of British Columbia, McGill, University of Michigan, University of Pennsylvania, UC Berkeley, Ohio State, University of St Andrews, NYU

If You Apply To ›

University of Toronto: Regular decision. SATs (with essay) or ACTs (with writing): required for U.S. applicants. Subject Tests or AP or IB exams: required for U.S. applicants (any two). Does not accept the Common Application. Apply to specific program.

British and Irish Universities

If going to college in Canada sounds adventuresome, you'll need even more moxie to venture overseas. But give it some thought. As the most popular overseas destination, Great Britain currently has about 4,500 Americans enrolled in undergraduate degree programs, and another 40,000 per year are pursuing shorter study abroad stints. Hundreds more have found their way to the Republic of Ireland. Depending on your course of study, studying in Britain or Ireland may or may not turn out to be less expensive than a flagship public university in the U.S., but the top British and Irish universities offer a richer international experience, infused with historical and cultural perspectives, than you will find on this side of the Atlantic.

Before we go further, here's a word to moms and dads: you may get queasy at the thought of sending your little cherub across a 3,000-mile ocean, but a flight to Dublin or London is quicker than driving 10 hours to get to First Choice U. Once you're there, the cities are at least as safe as those in the U.S., and the small towns have a crime rate roughly equivalent to that of the town of Mayberry on *The Andy Griffith Show*. The best part for parents: you'll need to visit at least once—and preferably more.

For those who are hazy on their geography, England, Scotland, and Wales make up Great Britain; throw in Northern Ireland and the moniker changes to the United Kingdom. The Republic of Ireland, occupying the southern part of the Emerald Isle across the Irish Sea, used to be part of Great Britain, but won its independence in 1921. Ireland is the closest European nation to the East Coast of the U.S., and the only English-speaking country in the eurozone. Britain and Ireland make the most sense for American students interested in studying English literature, history, foreign languages, and anything related to international studies. If medieval history is your passion, why not go to school where the remains of that long-ago world still dot the landscape? If you're looking for a career in international business, perhaps consider a country where the global village has been a way of life and you can make lifelong friends from around the world. Though Britain is an English-speaking country, it offers far better instruction in European and other languages than you can get in the U.S., and Ireland's favorable corporate tax rates have led U.S. companies such as Google, Microsoft, and Facebook to make it their European headquarters (think internships). No matter what your academic interests, your classmates will include a cross section of nationalities that would be the envy of any North American institution. Most importantly, study in Britain and Ireland has the potential to be a life-changing experience that will broaden your horizons and deepen your understanding of our increasingly globalized world. With cheap flights and trains readily available, travel to Continental Europe and beyond becomes second nature.

With all of these benefits come some challenges. American students in Britain need to adjust to a different tenor of academic life than is found at U.S. colleges and universities. Students are treated as adults and expected to behave accordingly. The legal drinking age is 18, which obviates the need for fake IDs but puts the onus on students to behave responsibly. Dorms are generally the domain of first-year students; expect to find a "flat" (apartment) for subsequent years. "Sport" means playing, not watching. The student body will not come out on a Saturday afternoon for the big game for a simple reason: there are no big games. Most faculty members (a.k.a. tutors) are ready to help you if you are struggling with your studies, but only if you take the initiative. There is no Dean of Student Hand-Holding in British universities (nor do they offer landing pads for helicopter parents).

Americans thinking about studying in Britain and Ireland should also be aware of differences in the academic system "across the Pond." Most important: whereas American universities generally require students to sample a variety of fields for two years before choosing a major, British and Irish institutions expect students to identify their field of concentration before they set foot on campus. That's because students take their general education courses in high school. Thus students in Britain and Ireland take only two or three courses at a time, mostly related to their major. American-style distribution requirements are all but unheard of—good news for students who want to get out of those nasty math or foreign language requirements. But keep in mind that since British and Irish students tend to take courses only in subjects that seriously interest them, all classes are taught at a high level, even introductory ones. Moreover, although students get fewer hours in class, they are expected to put in more hours of study per course outside of class. Anyone who wants to change majors after a year or two may encounter difficulty.

Another important academic difference is that British and Irish universities evaluate applicants almost entirely on the basis of academic credentials, with emphasis on demonstrated ability in their field of study. No essays about page 236 of your autobiography or need to present yourself as a well-rounded overachiever who will enrich the campus environment. As one administrator put it, "We don't do social engineering." Along with Trinity College

Dublin, the top British universities, especially the four "ancient" Scottish universities, are thus a good bet for U.S. students who may have the smarts to do Ivy League work, but whose résumés do not include an Olympic medal or building a school in Belize during spring vacation. Standards are high; St Andrews, for example, looks for a minimum score of 1320 on the SAT I, and 28 on the ACT. Institutions tend to prefer the SAT over the ACT, though many will accept either. Scores from SAT II or AP tests may also be required. For the application essay, the British usually ask about commitment to your intended major and why you want to study it. They view American-style personal essays as fluff.

As with Canadian universities, the cost for an American studying at one of the leading Scottish and Irish universities will vary with fluctuating exchange rates. To complicate matters, tuition and fee levels vary not only across universities but also according to the course of study and academic level within each institution. Total tuition and fees among the five universities described in the *Fiske Guide* range from US $20,000 to more than US $50,000 per year—roughly equivalent to the costs for out-of-state students at flagship public universities in the U.S. but less than the sticker price of many highly selective privates. The downside is that the sticker price is also the final price; academic scholarships are scarce and institutional financial aid all but nonexistent. British and Irish students, along with those from the European Union, generally receive government funding. Federal aid such as federal Direct loans and Pell Grants can be transported, but many, if not most, families will find themselves paying the full freight. For a searchable database of the few scholarships available for study in Great Britain, visit the British Council at www.britishcouncil.org/usa. One reason that financially strapped British universities have recently begun showing a greater interest in recruiting U.S. students is that they are a source of much-needed revenue. By and large, the academic bars for U.S. students are slightly lower than for native Brits.

If you are considering a British university, you may be picturing yourself in England, the most populous region of Great Britain that includes London as well as fabled universities Oxford and Cambridge. But here's the rub: the English have a system of higher education that makes degree study impractical in many cases. In England, under-graduate degrees are completed in three years, not four, and students are generally assumed to have completed 13 years of schooling rather than 12. As a result, the most selective English universities are reluctant to admit American high school graduates—some refuse to admit any—and the students who do get in will find themselves navigating a world more appropriate for juniors and seniors in college. One note on terminology: in Britain and Ireland, a program of study is called a "course." The British word for what we call a course is "module."

The University of Cambridge (www.cam.ac.uk) is particularly blunt about "the possible mismatch between the broad liberal arts curriculum of the North American high school and the specialist emphasis of British degree courses." The University of Oxford (www.ox.ac.uk) does offer a glimmer of hope for a select few superachievers; Oxford will consider American students who graduate in the top 2 percent of their class, and it has recently stepped up its recruiting efforts in U.S. high schools. In a recent year it enrolled about 60 U.S. students. Even so, the odds of admission to Oxford are lower than at any college in the U.S., including Harvard. The vast majority of American undergraduates at both Oxford and Cambridge are there for a second bachelor's degree after earning one from an American institution. Students with their hearts set on the Oxbridge institutions should consider them for graduate school, where both welcome Americans (and their dollars) in significant numbers.

Students will hear a similar story at the third-most recognized name in English higher education, the London School of Economics (www.lse.ac.uk), which enrolls about 5,000 undergraduates. The LSE says it will not normally consider U.S. students until they have a year of higher education under their belts. Less selective English institutions are more receptive to Americans, but, once again, only those who feel certain of what they would like to study should apply. If you are in this category, there is one potential benefit to an English degree: the three-year degree program will save you a year of tuition bills.

So what to do? One answer is to cast your gaze on Scotland, England's less populous neighbor, where universities offer four-year degrees that are much better suited to the needs of American high school graduates. Scotland, which lies north of England, was an independent nation until 1706 and has its own parliament that exercises considerable power when it comes to domestic policy. It has an illustrious intellectual history and has produced the likes of David Hume, Adam Smith, Rudyard Kipling, Robert Louis Stevenson, J. K. Rowling, and the world's most famous ogre, Shrek. Scotland is more egalitarian in feel than England—less hung up on social class.

The Scots take great pride in their universities, which are central to their national identity and have deep historical ties with American higher education. The American-style liberal arts institution was imported directly from Scotland in the person of John Witherspoon, a graduate of the University of Edinburgh who was lured to the U.S. in 1768 to head Princeton University. With the model of his alma mater in mind, Witherspoon transformed

Princeton from a small-time school for ministers into a broad-based institution that taught philosophy, history, geography, science, mathematics, and theology. Like their U.S. counterparts, Scottish universities offer four-year programs; thus, they represent something of a middle ground between the American system and that of Oxford and Cambridge with their three-year, entirely specialized programs. Scottish universities expect early specialization, but there is some room to explore fields outside your major during the first two years. One downside of studying in Scotland is its northern location, which makes for long winter nights. Scotland has also been historically regarded as a "dreich" corner of Britain—a Highland term referring to weather variously described as dull, overcast, drizzly, cold, misty, and miserable, or a combination thereof. Scottish higher education is noted for its four "ancient" universities—Aberdeen, Edinburgh, Glasgow, and St Andrews—each of which is profiled in the pages that follow.

There are seven universities in Ireland, but Trinity College Dublin is by far the most distinguished, and it is the only one that operates on a four-year system for undergraduates. TCD was founded in 1592 by Queen Elizabeth as an Irish counterpart to Oxford and Cambridge to train Anglican clergymen. While TCD follows the Scottish system, its cultural ties remain distinctly English, and graduates who subsequently enroll in Oxford or Cambridge are automatically entitled to an "ad eundem" courtesy degree from the English university. TCD was founded as the University of Dublin with the expectation that it would serve as "the mother of a university" and other colleges would grow up around it à la Oxbridge. This never happened, though, so for all practical purposes Trinity College Dublin is the University of Dublin. Roman Catholics make up the overwhelming majority of students despite the fact that up until 1972 they needed special permission from church authorities to attend this bastion of Anglican scholarship.

Students applying to UK institutions should generally use the Universities and Colleges Admissions Service (UCAS, www.ucas.com), which functions like the Common Application group in the U.S. The UCAS form asks you to list all your courses and the grades you received in them, as well as your SAT and/or ACT scores. It also requires an essay and a letter of recommendation. Most institutions will accept applications through the spring, though we recommend that you apply by the deadline for British students, January 15. The deadline for applying to Oxford and Cambridge, or to apply to any program in medicine, is October 15 for entrance the following fall. Many institutions have rolling admissions, another reason to apply early. A few institutions—Aberdeen, Glasgow, and St Andrews—now accept the Common Application as an alternative for American students. Applicants to Trinity College Dublin apply directly to the university, which has rolling admissions.

A high proportion of U.S. students currently enrolled in British universities come from families with international connections, such as close relatives living in other countries or diplomat parents, but prior international experience is by no means required. College in Britain is not for the faint of heart, but it can be richly rewarding for those with the initiative to take the plunge. After college in Britain, students will have the skills and savvy to succeed almost anywhere in the world.

University of Aberdeen

Aberdeen, Scotland AB24 3FX GB

Located in Scotland's third largest city, Aberdeen is the most accessible of the four "ancient" universities. Notable for the flexibility of its curriculum and emphasis on independent learning. Major attractions include engineering, life and health sciences, and anything related to Europe. City of Aberdeen combines charm with the bustle of a small city. Outdoor enthusiasts will love the Scottish Highlands at arm's length.

Website: www.abdn.ac.uk
Location: Small City
Public
Total Enrollment: 15,000
Undergraduates: 12,000

The University of Aberdeen was founded in 1495, three years after a certain well-known explorer sailed from Spain to the New World. Students seeking the flavor of old Europe will not be disappointed. With plenty of cobblestone streets and buildings made of ancient stone (it's the Granite City), the university has a distinctly medieval aura. It offers top-notch academics, a curriculum that is unusually flexible by UK standards, and a slice of life far richer than any U.S. institution can muster. "It's great fun and has a lot of opportunities," says a senior, "both academically and socially."

With a population of 230,000, the port city of Aberdeen is Scotland's third largest city. Once a hub for fishing, shipbuilding, and textiles, it is now a center for the thriving oil extraction business in the North Sea. With two universities—the other is Robert Gordon—it is the educational capital of Northeastern Scotland. Aberdeen is perched at a latitude roughly the same as Juneau, Alaska, but because of the Gulf Stream, winter temperatures are generally milder than those on the East Coast of the United States. December days are short in winter, but sky-gazers are often treated to glimpses of the fabled Northern Lights.

Most university buildings are concentrated in a quiet enclave known as "Old Aberdeen." The campus is crowned, literally, by a 16th-century tower in the shape of an imperial crown. Lightly traveled streets pass through the campus, and the multitude of green lawns and picturesque courtyards are ideal for lounging on sunny days. The university has invested

> "We do a lot of group work, and student interaction is really key."

$450 million in infrastructure and facilities in recent years, including the Sir Duncan Rice Library, the Sports Village, and the Aquatics Centre. Plans are in the works for a $47 million Science Teaching Hub, projected to open in 2021.

Academics at Aberdeen are organized across 12 schools that encompass disciplines in the arts and social sciences, life sciences and medicine, physical sciences, and business. The relative broadness and flexibility of the university's curriculum is more in line with the academic systems of Harvard, Melbourne, Hong Kong, and other top universities around the world than it is with Aberdeen's "ancient" counterparts in the UK. Students are expected to sample a series of interdisciplinary Sixth Century Courses, such as Science and the Media or Oceans and Society, during their first two years. Other curriculum innovations are designed to encourage students to pursue interests outside their core disciplines—what might be called "electives" in an American context. Popular majors include English literature, biology, religious studies, environmental science, and a joint international relations/politics concentration. Engineering is also strong, especially for programs related to the oil industry. The Centre for Learning and Teaching helps faculty members find ways to enhance the learning experience, while the Student Learning Service helps students develop their academic skills.

With approximately 15,000 undergraduate and graduate students, Aberdeen is a medium-sized university by U.S. standards. "The academic climate at Aberdeen is largely collaborative. We do a lot of group work, and student interaction is really key," says a business major. Courses in the first two years

> "We have a very international student body."

generally consist of lectures supplemented by smaller weekly discussion sections. "In my first year I was taught by a mixture of Ph.D. students and lecturers (professors). In my honours years, my lecturers were leading experts in their fields and widely published," says a student. Professors typically team-teach introductory "modules," with each covering the topics that are his or her specialty. As in other Scottish universities, students generally take only three subjects at a time in the first two years, with extensive reading and research outside of class generally taken for granted. "Often we are expected to come to class prepared to discuss certain topics, but given no minimum reading assignment. The professor gives out a list of selected readings from which we can choose," explains a history major. Grades are typically determined by end-of-the-term evaluations with few intermediate assignments. At the end of their second year, students must typically pass exams in order to advance to "honors level," the equivalent of the junior and senior years of college in the States. Upper-level science students typically spend long hours in the lab. One nice

(continued)

Male/Female: 49/51
SAT Ranges: 1250 or above (combined)
ACT Ranges: 26 or above
Financial Aid: N/A
Pell Grant: N/A
Expense: Pub $
Student Loans: N/A
Average Debt: N/A
Applicants: 13,000
Accepted: 27%
Enrolled: N/A
Grad in 6 Years: N/A
Returning Freshmen: N/A
Academics: ✍ ✍ ✍ ✍ ½
Social: ☎ ☎ ☎ ☎
Q of L: ★ ★ ★ ★
Admissions: (+44) 1224 272000
Email Address: ugadmissions@abdn.ac.uk

Strong Programs:
English Literature
Biology
Religious Studies
Environmental Science
International Relations
Politics
Engineering
Health Sciences

Students are expected to sample a series of interdisciplinary Sixth Century Courses during their first two years.

feature: there is generally no limit to the number of students who can enroll in a particular course, thereby giving students the freedom to sign up for anything that strikes their fancy.

Overall, about 56 percent of undergraduates hail from Scotland, 13 percent come from the rest of the UK, and 30 percent arrive from 120 different countries. "We have a very international student body," says one senior. The political climate on campus is described as conservative and relatively subdued. Upon their arrival at the university, students partake of Freshers Week, when student organizations sponsor informational meetings. Aberdeen is a selective institution for U.S. students, though less so than the other three "ancient" universities.

On-campus housing at Aberdeen is varied and guaranteed to all first-year students who apply before the deadline. A majority of the international students live in single rooms in the recently refurbished Hillhead Student Village, a complex of houses and flats that is about a 20-minute walk from the campus. Students may elect catered rooms (two meals per day) or self-catering, wherein they cook their own food with kitchen facilities generally located down the hall from the rooms. Many students choose to move off campus after their first year, and a variety of housing options are available near the campus. Only a few students own cars, as the university is within easy walking distance of the city center and the North Sea and is on a regular bus route.

"Social life is great," raves one student. "There's always something going on." Another adds, "We have around 200 societies and sports clubs, and most students are involved in at least one." Since the drinking age in Britain is 18, social life at Aberdeen entails relaxed, legal consumption. You may find yourself doing what Britons call "the pub crawl," which means sampling the refreshment of several pubs before heading home in the wee hours. Popular campus social events include periodic formal balls, to which the men wear kilts and the women wear evening gowns. Perhaps the biggest event of the year is the Torcher's Parade, which is held every spring and features floats made by various student organizations. Sports are mainly for playing, rather than watching, with more than 50 sports clubs at students' disposal. Individual sports rather than team intramurals are the staple of weekend warriors, and students can purchase passes for various athletic facilities, depending on their interests.

> **"We have around 200 societies and sports clubs, and most students are involved in at least one."**

Aberdeen is described by one student as "a fantastic college town!" The city center offers a variety of pubs and clubs to suit all tastes, as well as inexpensive cinemas, music, and theater. The city has plenty of old-world charm, and outdoorsy types will love the dramatic scenery that is everywhere in northeast Scotland. Picturesque cliffs overlooking the North Sea are within an easy bus or train ride. Fifteen miles south of Aberdeen is breathtaking Dunnottar Castle, a 14th-century ruin set high on a rocky outcrop that was the set for Mel Gibson's film rendition of *Hamlet*. Within a half-hour ride inland is the edge of the legendary Scottish Highlands. Famous castles are in all directions, including the royal family's summer hideaway, Balmoral. For the Scottish version of the big city, Glasgow and Edinburgh are close by and two hours on a plane will get you to most places in Western Europe.

Though Aberdeen may lack some of the conveniences of home, most Americans are happy they came. "Between classes on a sunny day, students will buy something from the bakery and sit on the grass in the midst of 500-year-old buildings and cobblestone streets. It is such a carefree atmosphere with that special touch of Scottish tradition," says a satisfied history major. If you're the kind of person who likes to meet new people and learn about different cultures, you might thrive on the Aberdeen air.

Professors typically team-teach introductory "modules," with each covering the topics that are his or her specialty.

Popular campus social events include periodic formal balls, to which the men wear kilts and the women wear evening gowns.

Overlaps

Dundee, University of Edinburgh, University of Glasgow, University of St Andrews, Harvard

University of Edinburgh

Old College, South Bridge, Edinburgh, Scotland EH8 9JS UK

With close ties to the city that founded it in the 16th century, Edinburgh is the most prestigious of Scotland's major research universities. Combines deep roots in Scottish culture and history with the cosmopolitan flavor and cultural riches of a sophisticated capital city. Competitive admissions for top British students, but better odds for Americans with Ivy-level academic credentials. More diverse student body than St Andrews.

The largest and best-known of the "ancient" Scottish universities, the University of Edinburgh is part and parcel of Scotland's most vibrant urban center. The city of Edinburgh is home to the Scottish Parliament, the national museum, abundant historical sites, winding streets, and countless restaurants and pubs. The university, like the city, has an unmistakable international feel, including long-standing connections across the pond. In addition to the likes of Charles Darwin and J. K. Rowling, eminent graduates include two signatories of the U.S. Declaration of Independence, Benjamin Rush and John Witherspoon. "Students know that by coming to Edinburgh they are attending not only a prestigious university but the city that goes along with it," says a modern language student.

Edinburgh is unique among the major Scottish universities in that it was founded (in 1583) by a municipality rather than under religious auspices. Its buildings are spread throughout the city, which, with nearly 500,000 residents, is really an overgrown town. The two main campus areas are known as the Central Area, home to George Square, the main library, and humanities courses, and King's Buildings, housing science and engineering courses. Public transport is good, but just about everything is within walking distance. The older university buildings are Georgian and tend to bear names from the Scottish Enlightenment (David Hume and Dugald Stewart), while more modern ones date to the '60s and '70s. A $34 million refurbishment of the School of Literatures, Languages, and Cultures was recently completed.

> **"I find the academics very rigorous in comparison to my friends' at American universities, because all the work is independent."**

The university is organized around three colleges: Arts, Humanities, and Social Sciences; Science and Engineering; and Medicine and Veterinary. Edinburgh has traditionally been strong in the sciences, and historical ties to economists like Adam Smith and philosophers like John Locke have contributed to strong programs in those fields. English literature, international relations, international business, art and design, and law attract a lot of U.S. students, and linguistics, sociology, and history (Scottish and otherwise) are strong. Unlike in the U.S., the programs in medicine and veterinary medicine are five-year programs for undergraduates. Veterinary graduates can go on to practice immediately in the U.S. Edinburgh also offers some 250 study abroad programs at leading universities around the world.

Website: www.ed.ac.uk
Location: City Center
Public
Total Enrollment: 30,000
Undergraduates: 22,200
Male/Female: 38/62
SAT Ranges: 1290 or above (combined)
ACT Ranges: 27 or above
Financial Aid: N/A
Pell Grant: N/A
Expense: Pub $
Student Loans: N/A
Average Debt: N/A
Applicants: 59,876
Accepted: 42%
Enrolled: 26%
Grad in 6 Years: 96%
Returning Freshmen: 98%
Academics: ✎ ✎ ✎
Social: ☎ ☎ ☎
Q of L: ★ ★ ★
Admissions: (+44) 131 650 4296
Email Address: international.enquiries@ed.ac.uk

Strong Programs:
English Literature
International Relations
International Business
Art and Design
Law
Economics

(continued)

History
Veterinary Medicine

Applicants apply to study a particular subject, such as physics or English literature, but, unlike the situation in the leading English universities, it is possible to make changes once enrolled. There is no core curriculum, and no one has to endure a class on science or any other subject in which they have little interest. Students normally take three courses for each of their first two years in a variety of fields and then concentrate on one or two subjects the last two years. Most courses involve a combination of lectures, which are taught by full professors, and weekly tutorials, or groups of 10 to 20 students led by tutors. Professors and tutors alike get generally high ratings from students. One student notes, "The faculty is very international."

Coursework throughout the year mostly involves essays, with final exams in late April or May accounting for most of the final grade. In their final year, all undergraduates complete a research project or thesis. The academic system is built around self-study. "As an American student, I find the academics very rigorous in comparison to my friends' at American universities, because all the work is independent even from the beginning of your first year," reports an English literature major. The academic pressure at Edinburgh is said to be intense, with little grade inflation, and although faculty members do not view their role as seeking out students who may need help, "professors and tutors are more than happy to help out when you ask," says one American denizen.

Unlike in the U.S., the programs in medicine and veterinary medicine are five-year programs for undergraduates.

Edinburgh is the leading destination for top-performing Scottish students, who face tighter admissions standards than North Americans. Thirty-three percent of undergraduates hail from Scotland, 30 percent from elsewhere in the United Kingdom, 10 percent from the European Union, and 26 percent from other foreign countries. There are roughly 650 regular American undergrads and 600 postgrads, as well as more than 800 study abroad students. Edinburgh students tend to be more middle class than their counterparts at St Andrews, which is more upper class. Edinburgh is slightly more expensive than the other "ancient" Scottish universities but a bargain compared to the Ivies in the U.S. The university makes scholarships available to international students, and American students can use their U.S. student loans to attend. Given the nature of the student body, there is plenty of discussion of global issues. "Scotland is inherently left-leaning as a country," reports a language student, "but the international students want to share their views while also listening to the opinions of others."

"First-years tend to explore club life in the city center."

Edinburgh guarantees housing to all international first-year students. Many American and international students live in Pollock Halls, a collection of houses with mostly single rooms that are centered around a common cafeteria. Accommodations at Pollack are catered, meaning that residents get 14 meals per week in the cafeteria—breakfast and dinner during the week and brunch on the weekends. Students can also choose self-catered options in which they make their own cooking arrangements. Self-catered flats (apartments) generally consist of three to five students, each with an individual room, sharing a large common living and kitchen area. All university accommodations are described as clean and well maintained. Most students move off campus after their first year; the Student Union Advice Place will help you find a flat. "Edinburgh is a student-oriented city with many cheap flats which are directed especially at students," says a third-year student. Cafeteria food is described as "fine but not that diverse," although several cheap cafés nearby offer alternatives.

Edinburgh students tend to be more middle class than their counterparts at St Andrews, which is more upper class.

Since the university is so closely tied to the city, it's no surprise that social life takes place both on and off campus. "First-years tend to explore club life in the city center," explains an American student, "and as they get into their second and third years, the partying transfers homeward into flat parties." Two student unions, Teviot and Potterrow, offer cafés, coffee shops, and bars; on weekend nights, a large, open study area in Potterrow is converted into a nightclub for dancing. Frequent comedy nights, student productions, and pub crawls are other options. Since the drinking age is 18, the university has no school policy on the serving of alcohol. The city of Edinburgh offers its own menu of ancient and contemporary traditions. The Beltane Fire Festival, with roots in pagan times, celebrates the arrival of spring, and every August the city is host to the huge Fringe Festival, which draws artists and spectators from all over the world. Thanks to affordable trains and low-cost airlines like Ryanair and easyJet, trips throughout Britain and all over Europe are easy to arrange. "You get good at traveling," says one American undergrad.

> *Edinburgh hosts more than 280 societies and 64 sports clubs.*

The Edinburgh University Student Association and the Edinburgh University Sports Union combine to offer what one American describes as "just about every sport, charity, or special interest society/club conceivable." A fair is held during Freshers' Week to give first-year students a sense of the options. Does the Chocolate Lovers Society sound tasty?

> **"The ethereal castle and the wee pubs constantly remind me where I am."**

Edinburgh's sports clubs, which compete against other Scottish and European universities in sports like rugby, soccer, and rowing, do well, but compared to varsity sports in the U.S., one student says, "the competition is laid-back." Most attention goes to the "very strong and popular intramural sports program, which, depending on the sport, has quite a high caliber of play." Many of the teams are co-ed, and there are eight levels of rugby. The Centre for Sport and Exercise boasts sports equipment, studios, weight rooms, a climbing wall, and archery ranges. In all, Edinburgh hosts more than 280 societies and 64 sports clubs.

Much of the fun of going to college in Scotland comes from taking part in centuries-old traditions, of which Edinburgh has an abundance. Various societies and degree programs sponsor weekly or monthly ceilidhs (pronounced "kaylees"), or traditional Scottish Dance Nights. Robert Burns Night is a big deal, as is Guy Fawkes Night on November 5, when students set off fireworks throughout the city. Whereas American commencements feature students moving the tassel of their mortarboards from one side to the other, Edinburgh places a common cap on the head of each student in turn that contains a piece of the trousers of John Knox and a NASA emblem that accompanied an Edinburgh graduate on a space mission.

American students tend to do well at Edinburgh. "They are smart and well-traveled and tend to be independent thinkers," observes a faculty member. An international studies major comments, "This university has allowed me to become an adult and challenge myself because of the independent style of the education." Another American transplant hails the fact that Edinburgh is "incredibly international but still Scottish," adding that "the bagpipes playing in the city streets, the ethereal castle, and the wee pubs constantly remind me where I am."

Overlaps

University of St Andrews, University of Glasgow, King's College London, Oxford, University of Aberdeen, University of Pennsylvania, University of Chicago, NYU

If You Apply To ›

Edinburgh: Rolling admissions. SATs or ACTs or Subject Tests or other exams from approved list: required. Does not accept the Common Application. Apply to particular program.

University of Glasgow

University Gardens, Glasgow, Lanarkshire, Scotland G12 8QQ UK

A major urban research university located in the bohemian section of a working-class city. U of Glasgow is slightly smaller than U of Edinburgh and the atmosphere somewhat more laid-back. The West End is student-friendly, with lots of cafés and shops. Glasgow is a financial and shopping center also known for its nightlife. Locals claim "you can have more fun at a Glasgow funeral than at an Edinburgh wedding." Glasgow students get the point.

Website: www.gla.ac.uk
Location: City Center
Public
Total Enrollment: 27,800
Undergraduates: 19,000
Male/Female: 41/59
SAT Ranges: 1280 or above
   (combined)
ACT Ranges: 27 or above
Financial Aid: N/A
Pell Grant: N/A
Expense: Pub $
Student Loans: N/A
Average Debt: N/A
Applicants: 5,900
Accepted: N/A
Enrolled: N/A
Grad in 6 Years: N/A
Returning Freshmen: N/A
Academics: ✍ ✍ ✍
Social: ☎ ☎ ☎
Q of L: ★ ★ ★
Admissions: (+44) 141 330 2000
Email Address: student
   .recruitment@glasgow.ac.uk

Strong Programs:
Psychology
Business
Politics
History
English Literature
Veterinary Medicine
Nursing
Law

The second oldest of Scotland's major universities, the University of Glasgow shares the history and culture of Scotland's largest city. Glasgow (population 600,000) was a major center of the 18th-century Scottish Enlightenment and the 19th-century Industrial Revolution, and it now ranks as Britain's largest financial center after London. The University of Glasgow was founded in 1451 with quarters in Glasgow Cathedral before moving to its own main campus in Gilmorehill in the city's West End in 1870. In contrast to the elitist traditions of other "ancient" British universities, Glasgow pioneered in serving the educational needs of the growing urban and commercial classes and in 1894 became the first Scottish university to grant degrees to women.

Not surprisingly for a place with more than five centuries of history, the dominant architectural style on campus is neo-Gothic, with a healthy mix of Victorian thrown in. While other sections of Glasgow retain the hardscrabble feel of a depressed industrial area, the West End is a bohemian residential area with an abundance of restaurants, cafés, and shops catering to the college crowd. "The area is very student-oriented, with plenty of venues offering student discounts," reports one student. The city center, a 15-minute walk from the university, offers an abundance of historical sites and museums as well as the best shopping in Britain outside London. Kelvingrove Park and the Botanical Gardens are down the street from the university's main gate. The university has embarked on a $1.2 billion development plan that will expand the campus footprint by more than 25 percent by 2026. The first phase of the plan is underway, with the $115 million Smith Learning Hub opening in 2019.

> **"Professors know their field and are excellent at providing students with an enormous amount of insight."**

Students describe the academic climate as pressured but balanced. "Professors know their field and are excellent at providing students with an enormous amount of insight into the courses and subjects," says a European politics major. But another warns, "Specific assignments aren't given. You're told which books go with the course, and you'd better read them on your own!" The workload is said to increase noticeably in later years, but because students apply to study in a particular field, they "rarely find themselves in courses they would prefer to avoid." All undergraduates complete a dissertation or research project based on independent research, supervised by a faculty member in their major. First-year students go through a Fresher's Week, with tours of the university, concerts, and other events, and special orientation is also provided for international students.

Glasgow is the only Scottish university with the full range of both professional and academic offerings. The university is divided into four colleges: Arts; Social Sciences; Science and Engineering; and Medical, Veterinary, & Life Sciences. Befitting the alma mater of physicist Lord Kelvin, the sciences are strong, notably veterinary medicine, nursing, and geography. The economics department is proud that it turned out Adam Smith, and history is well regarded. English language and literature is a traditional strength, and Glasgow maintains the only department of Scottish literature anywhere. Eastern European languages like Czech and Polish are specialties. For U.S. students, the most popular majors tend to be psychology, business (especially accounting and finance), politics, history, and English literature. A new undergraduate degree in common law is available for students who intend to practice law outside of Scotland.

Students describe faculty members as respected and well published in their fields. Lectures are offered by full professors, and tutorials of about 15 students are occasionally handled by graduate students, whose teaching is described as "hit-or-miss." Fifteen percent of Glasgow undergraduates take advantage of semester-long or yearlong study abroad programs, especially through the Erasmus program, which allows students to take courses at European universities. A year of foreign study is mandatory for foreign language students during their third year. "The university seems to believe that a world culture is very important and values it," says a Scottish literature major.

"Dealing and working with people from different backgrounds is the norm."

Consistent with the university's cosmopolitan setting and traditions, the student body is a diverse lot with regard to nationality, race, religion, and socioeconomic backgrounds. Twenty-six percent of undergraduates are international, hailing from the U.S., the European Union, and dozens of other countries; 59 percent are native to Scotland and the balance come from elsewhere in the UK. Expats include nearly 1,000 American undergrads and grad students. "You don't have an exclusive student body," reports a sophomore. "Dealing and working with people from different backgrounds is the norm." The university offers a fourth-year tuition waiver as a merit scholarship for qualified international students, including those from the U.S., and it also accepts U.S. federal loans, as determined by the FAFSA.

Freshmen usually live in university housing, which is not on campus but spread throughout the northwest sections of the city, and then move into readily available independent housing in later years. Overall, 17 percent of undergraduates live in the dorms, which are generally comfortable, and international students are guaranteed housing. One student recalls, "My first year I was in a student apartment in an old Victorian tenement flat. It was very beautiful. I had friends who stayed in the more modern student flats, and those were nice as well." As for dining, only one of the seven residence halls offers catered food, and it is located away from the main campus. The others are self-catered, which means that students cook for themselves (and save money by doing so) or savor the offerings of dining facilities sprinkled throughout the campus. "The on-campus dining is very good, and they have a range of foods from Indian to Scottish on various days," reports one denizen. Students describe campus security as good. "I always feel safe on campus," says an archaeology major. The university recently launched a campaign, Let's Talk, aimed at educating the community on issues of sexual assault and providing resources to survivors.

"Other than the weather, Glasgow is a great city to live in."

Social life is equally divided between on- and off-campus activities. Glasgow offers an abundance of quality restaurants, clubs, and pubs. There are plenty of ceilidhs (pronounced "kaylees"), or Gaelic social gatherings, and the city sponsors an International Comedy Festival each March. Glasgow has a vigorous music scene, hosting an average of 130 music events every week. Much of the on-campus social life revolves around the two student-run university unions, the Glasgow University Union (GUU) and the Queen Margaret Union (QMU), which host student organizations, provide dining and social activities and, of course, have their own bars. Since most students are above the drinking age of 18, underage imbibing is a nonissue.

GUU favors sports and debates, while QMU is big on music. One popular event is GUU's Daft Friday, a black-tie affair at the end of the first term where the entire building is elaborately decorated around a secret theme.

The Student Representative Council sponsors an annual Raising and Giving week to aid volunteer organizations and raise awareness of volunteer opportunities. Social activism tends to be most vigorous when the issue involves cuts to the university budget and increases in tuition levels, but there are plenty of student groups organized around issues such as the environment, gender equality, and LGBTQ rights. Travel is a major attraction of studying in Scotland. "It's easy to get to visit Europe while studying in Glasgow with cheap flights and accommodations," reports one student.

Intercollegiate debating is taken seriously, and the university has won the world championship several times. A majority of students belong to the Glasgow University Sports Association, and more than 4,000 students play in 50 sports clubs. Competitive team sports include field hockey, rugby, soccer, basketball, American football, cricket, and many others, and recreational clubs are available for everything from cycling to skydiving to surfing. The only athletic rivalry of any consequence in town is the off-campus competition between the two Glasgow soccer clubs, Celtic (Roman Catholic) and the Rangers (Protestant). A student warns, "It's better not to get involved, as the games are just staging grounds for sectarian hatred. Much of the city's police funding goes to monitoring these violent affairs."

The city of Glasgow is shedding its rough reputation, and undergrads describe their experience living and studying in the West End as rewarding. One American sums up her experience as follows: "Glasgow offers a good mix of academics and fun. It's a highly rated school with many good departments, not too competitive, and has all types of students. And other than the weather, Glasgow is a great city to live in."

Overlaps

University of Edinburgh, University of St Andrews, University of Aberdeen, Boston University, NYU, King's College London, McGill, Columbia

If You Apply To ›

Glasgow: Rolling admissions. SATs or ACTs: required. Subject Tests: required (at least two; AP exams also accepted. Subjects relevant to degree program). Accepts the Common Application with supplement.

University of St Andrews

St Andrews, Scotland KY16 9AX

The most international of Scotland's four "ancient" universities and the most popular destination for Americans studying in the UK. Small by British standards and comparable in feel and stature to Brown. Major drawing cards range across English literature, international relations, psychology, medieval history, the sciences, and modern languages. St Andrews is inseparable from the town, which boasts the famed "Old Course." With 600 years to gestate, traditions reign supreme.

Website: www.st-andrews .ac.uk
Location: Small Town
Public
Total Enrollment: 9,140

Harvard likes to brag about the fact that it was founded way back in 1636. Think that's old? Try 1413, the date Pope Benedict XIII issued a Papal Bull recognizing the University of St Andrews as Scotland's first university and the third in the English-speaking world. Set in an ancient town on the North Sea opposite Norway, St Andrews is an ideal spot for adventuresome Americans who want a world-class education and an introduction to life outside North America. It now numbers roughly

1,000 Yankees among its 7,300 undergrads, with the number on the rise. Success here requires a go-getter mentality. Support services are available, but students on this side of the Atlantic are accustomed to being treated like adults. "They don't hold your hand," says one U.S. student.

St Andrews is the only institution in the *Fiske Guide* whose most prominent landmark is the spot where a student was burned at the stake. In 1528, a Protestant reformer named Patrick Hamilton fell victim to a prolonged burning imposed by the local archbishop. Tradition deems that if you step on the stones that mark the spot where he was martyred, you will fail your final exams, unless you submerge yourself in the North Sea just before dawn the first day of May as part of a tradition called the May Dip. Academic buildings are interspersed through the town's narrow medieval streets, and for all practical purposes, says one student, "The university *is* the town." Buildings are constructed of ancient stone and include the ruins of a 13th-century castle and a cathedral. Narrow alleys, called "wynds" by the Scots, lead to secluded gardens and courtyards that add to the old-world charm. A number of academic buildings are perched on cliffs overlooking the North Sea, and white beaches are a two-minute walk from some of the dorms.

Though more flexible than most British universities, St Andrews offers less latitude to explore a variety of subjects than U.S. institutions, and so is best suited to those who arrive with clear academic goals in mind. Students typically take three courses, or "modules," per semester in each of their first two years, continue with two of them in the second year, and then opt for a single or double honors program the final two years. (The course structure and/or number of class hours varies for students in the sciences, medicine, and arts and divinity.) "Pick your courses carefully," counsels one U.S. student. "You can't major in something you haven't taken the first year." Modules generally consist of three lectures per week with 100 or more students and a tutorial with 10 to 20, while honors-level courses are generally taught in seminar format. Fewer courses means less time in class but also significant outside reading. Modules typically end with papers or exams that account for most of the grade.

"The instructors are first-class. They are the ones writing the textbooks we read."

More so than in the United States, the onus is on the students to keep current with their rigorous workload and seek help from faculty when necessary. Nevertheless, the faculty gets high marks, and an international relations major says, "The instructors are first-class. They are the ones writing the textbooks we read." Academic and personal support is also available from Student Services, wardens (RAs) in the residence halls, and ramped-up career services that are, according to a school official, working with American companies to ensure that "U.S. students are returning to the States as competitive in the job market as their peers who studied in the U.S. are."

Signature offerings at St Andrews include international relations, psychology (especially neuroscience), marine biology, English literature, modern languages, and physics, and the university is a world leader in the study of international terrorism. The most popular majors include international relations, medicine, history, and economics and finance. Americans at St Andrews tend to cluster in a few departments, notably psychology and international relations. Standards in foreign language are higher than in the United States, an opportunity but also a challenge. Students in the International Honours joint-degree program spend two years at the College of William and Mary and two years at St Andrews and earn degrees in classical studies, economics, English, film studies, history, or international relations from both institutions.

"St Andrews students are highly motivated, entrepreneurial, curious, and worldly," says a fourth-year student. Indeed, St Andrews is one of the world's most

(continued)

Undergraduates: 7,286
Male/Female: 40/60
SAT Ranges: 1320 or above (combined)
ACT Ranges: 28 or above
Financial Aid: N/A
Pell Grant: N/A
Expense: Pub $
Student Loans: N/A
Average Debt: N/A
Applicants: 18,789
Accepted: 42%
Enrolled: 24%
Grad in 6 Years: 93%
Returning Freshmen: 97%
Academics: ✍ ✍ ✍ ✍ ½
Social: ☎ ☎ ☎
Q of L: ★ ★ ★
Admissions: (+44) 133 446 2150
Email Address: international@ st-andrews.ac.uk

Strong Programs:
International Relations
Medicine
History
Economics and Finance
Psychology
Marine Biology
English Literature
Modern Languages

St Andrews now numbers roughly 1,000 Yankees among its 7,300 undergrads, with the number on the rise.

international universities, with roughly 30 percent of its students from Scotland, another 30 percent from elsewhere in the UK, and 40 percent from the rest of the world, including sizable contingents from Scandinavia, Eastern Europe, Asia, the Middle East, and, of course, the U.S. In fact, Americans represent the largest international group and are typically given a warm welcome, students say. Having friends from around the world is both enriching and convenient because, as one American student explains, "you have lots of choices of places to go on vacation." The international melting pot seems to work, although the upper-middle-class background of many English students lends a more conservative tenor to the campus than some Americans might expect—as is generally true of top universities in the UK.

St Andrews is inviting enough to have attracted the likes of Prince William and Kate Middleton, who met there. While it is competitive for European students, who must be in the top 10th academically, it is more accessible for U.S. students who have the brains to make it into the Ivies but can't throw a football or play a Liszt concerto. Many of the Americans at St Andrews arrive with an international orientation, including "diplo-brats" whose parents have worked in international organizations such as the World Bank or the State Department. Tuition varies depending on the course, but the bill for a year at St Andrews is likely to be roughly $29,000, depending on the exchange rate. The university now fixes rates for each incoming class so that tuition won't increase over a student's four years.

Housing is guaranteed for first-year students only, and students can request a single or shared room; 41 percent of students reside in university housing. They also choose between the university meal plan or self-catering, in which they use kitchens in the dorms to prepare their own food. Catered dorms are the most central and ancient, although students tend to give the food less-than-enthusiastic reviews. Meals are served at specified times with standard portions, so don't expect the glitzy food courts or all-you-can-eat service typical in the States. After their first year, students generally move to one of the many apartments (flats) in town, which can be expensive. "There is a bit of a scramble for flats in February, but most students are able to find good accommodations," reports an international relations and French major.

Given the symbiosis of town and gown, social life "takes place in the town's pubs, the student union, the dorms, and apartments," says an English major. A peek inside the student union reveals something never seen on a U.S. campus: a fully equipped bar with, of course, an ample array of scotch. The drinking age is 18 in Britain, and St Andrews boasts 18 pubs. Though there may not be more alcohol than at an American institution, it is certainly more out in the open and thus less of an issue. Black-tie balls and fashion shows are also staples, as are ceilidhs (pronounced "kaylees"), which feature traditional Scottish dancing akin to square dancing. Like other Scottish universities, St Andrews offers "a society for everything you can think of," says a student. Interested in whiskey tasting? Philosophical debate? Belly dancing? Harry Potter? Tunnocks Caramel

Wafers? Then there's a society just waiting for you, probably with meetings at a pub. The St Andrews debating society was founded in 1793 and continues to do well in international competitions. Political activism is muted, but the annual Charities Campaign is well supported by students.

As befitting a 600-year-old institution, St Andrews is rife with traditions. Red gowns, once the student uniform, are only worn on special occasions, but pubs are still forbidden to serve anyone wearing one. The aforementioned May Dip, aimed at purging oneself of academic bad luck, has roots in pagan times. One student explains that during Raisin Weekend in November, first-year students "equipped with multiple cans of shaving foam and dressed up in costume are taken by their adopted academic parents (older students who will take the first-years under their wing) to a huge shaving foam fight in one of the school squares." Students emerging from their last exam are greeted by their friends and doused with buckets of cold water.

The nearest road-trip destination is the medium-sized city of Dundee, about 20 minutes away, which offers nightclubs, a mall, and movie theaters. "The public transport links in town are really good for students to get around and visit different places in Scotland," notes an English major. Scotland's two largest cities, Edinburgh and Glasgow, are about an hour away, and for outdoorsy types, the legendary Scottish Highlands are within easy reach. The Student Association helps with overseas travel.

Soccer, a.k.a. football, is the national sport, and students congregate to watch pro teams in the pubs or on the big-screen TV at the union. Rugby, tennis, golf, soccer, rowing, and water polo are among the school's most competitive sports teams, although these draw fewer spectators than do varsity sports in the U.S.—"you don't have 40,000 screaming fans," notes one student. Students tend to be much more enthusiastic about their "hall sport" competitions (the equivalent of intramurals in the U.S.), in sports ranging from rugby and ultimate Frisbee to shinty, a violent Scottish mix of field hockey and lacrosse. Students can also join the sports center, which has recently been renovated and upgraded with top-of-the-line facilities and equipment. The fabled Old Course, where golf was invented in the 1500s, offers student discounts, but the sport is not as popular among students here as one might assume.

> **"The public transport links in town are really good for [visiting] different places in Scotland."**

Although St Andrews comes the closest of any of the Scottish universities to having the feel of a liberal arts college, this is not the United States. Those who come here must be ready to adjust to a different way of life, and the tight identification of the university and the town can eventually make for a bit of claustrophobia. But these are small prices to pay for Scotland in all its ancient glory. U.S. institutions may trumpet their diversity, but nothing stateside compares to the richness of living abroad among the best and brightest from all corners of the globe. St Andrews delivers it all against a hauntingly beautiful backdrop that will remain forever etched in the minds of all who come here. And there's always the chance that you will hit it off with a future king or queen of England.

During Raisin Weekend in November, first-year students have a huge shaving foam fight in one of the school squares.

Overlaps

Georgetown, Brown, NYU, Columbia, Tufts, Harvard, McGill, Yale

If You Apply To ›

St Andrews: Rolling admissions. SATs or ACTs: required. Subject Tests: optional. Accepts the Common Application with supplement.

Trinity College Dublin

College Green, Dublin 2, Ireland

The youngest four-year university in Ireland, Trinity College Dublin belongs to a peer group consisting of Oxbridge and the four "ancient" Scottish universities—albeit with a more European feel. Trinity combines rich academic offerings across the curriculum with life in one of the world's youngest and most vibrant capital cities. Traditions abound, academic and otherwise. Where else do honors students get the right to graze their sheep on the college green?

Website: www.tcd.ie
Location: City Center
Public
Total Enrollment: 14,742
Undergraduates: 11,793
Male/Female: 42/58
SAT Ranges: N/A
ACT Ranges: N/A
Financial Aid: N/A
Pell Grant: N/A
Expense: Pub $
Student Loans: N/A
Average Debt: N/A
Applicants: 22,564
Accepted: 14%
Enrolled: 74%
Grad in 6 Years: 90%
Returning Freshmen: 95%
Academics: ✍ ✍ ✍ ✍ ✍
Social: ☎ ☎ ☎ ☎
Q of L: ★ ★ ★ ★
Admissions: (+353) 1 896 4500
Email Address:
academic.registry@tcd.ie

Strong Programs:
Business, Economics, and
    Social Studies
Global Business
English Literature
Political Science
European Studies
International Studies
Molecular Biology
Engineering

Founded in 1592 by Queen Elizabeth as an Irish counterpart to Oxford and Cambridge, Trinity College Dublin is the largest and most distinguished of the seven universities in Ireland and one of the strongest anywhere. Although best known for its offerings in the humanities and social sciences, Trinity is strong across the curriculum, including in new specialties such as nanoscience. The university has produced enough distinguished alumni to fill an encyclopedia (Jonathan Swift, Oscar Wilde, Edmund Burke, Samuel Beckett, and Ernest Walton for starters), and its students bathe in centuries-old academic traditions while enjoying life in one of Europe's most vibrant capital cities.

Trinity College Dublin occupies a 47-acre oasis in the heart of Dublin, within easy walking distance of the national museums, government buildings, and other major cultural attractions. "When you pass under the archway you move from the bustle of the city to a traditional liberal arts setting, complete with rugby and cricket pitches," explains a sophomore. Most of the central buildings are built of light gray Georgian stone, including its iconic Campanile. The Trinity College Library is Ireland's deposit library and home to the Book of Kells, an illuminated Latin manuscript of the Gospels that draws a steady stream of tourists onto the campus. Another

> **"[Trinity] invests some of its best faculty toward teaching undergraduate freshmen."**

library bears the name of James Ussher, the university's first student, who went on to make a name for himself by devising a Biblically based calculation that the world started at 6:00 p.m. on October 22, 4004 BC. A freshman describes Dublin as "a fantastic city in all regards," but cautions, "Let's not go overboard. There is also a lot of rain."

Trinity is organized around three schools in each of the traditional areas: arts, humanities, and social sciences; engineering, math, and science; and health sciences. Unlike other universities in Ireland, Trinity offers a four-year undergraduate program parallel to the four "ancient" universities in Scotland. There are no "core" courses that everyone is required to take, although all students must complete an undergraduate research project in their final year in order to graduate. The college has traditionally been best known for its English and literature courses, along with history, political science, European studies, and international studies. Mathematics and the sciences are also strong, especially molecular biology, genetics, immunology, nanoscience, and chemistry. The Trinity Biomedical Sciences Institute is a state-of-the-art research facility, while the Trinity Long Room Hub accommodates research in the arts and humanities. The BESS program (Business, Economics, and Social Studies) and global business are particularly popular among American students, who are also beginning to pursue the sciences in greater numbers. Trinity has a strong interdisciplinary culture, and the Trinity Elective option encourages students to exercise their curiosity in a module (course) outside their specialty, such as film studies or globalization.

Trinity's academic climate is described as relaxed, and a history and economics double major says, "The vast majority of students are open to collaborative learning and prove helpful to each other outside of the lectures and seminars." The academic year runs for 12 weeks each in the fall and spring, followed by three weeks of exams. Students accumulate 60 credits per year through modules offering various numbers of credits, with strong weight given to final exams, although the balance of continuous and final assessment varies by module. "The major difference between Trinity and American universities is that the onus falls much more on the students," says a junior. Lectures coupled with weekly tutorials are common the first two years but then give way to small seminars the last two years. A junior observes that Trinity "invests some of its best faculty toward teaching undergraduate freshmen." Each entering student is assigned a peer mentor and a faculty tutor, not one of his or her professors, who will be available for personal, academic, and professional advice over four years and, if necessary, become an advocate. American students can also sign up for the weeklong Trinity Smart-Start Program to help them get the hang of the university and its setting.

The Trinity College Library is home to the Book of Kells, an illuminated Latin manuscript of the Gospels that draws a steady stream of tourists.

Trinity students are encouraged to take advantage of the nearly 300 foreign study options, including those with leading institutions in Australia, Canada, India, China, and Singapore; 30 percent take part. Trinity participates in the Erasmus Program with other European universities and has special relationships in the U.S. with such prestigious institutions as Brown, Chicago, and Columbia. Dublin serves as the European headquarters for several major companies, such as Google, Airbnb, Microsoft, and Facebook, which frequently recruit students for internships, summer jobs, and post-graduation careers.

"[Trinity students are] very academic, well-read, and very inclusive."

As the top university in Ireland, Trinity is highly competitive academically. Fifteen percent of undergraduates are international students from more than 120 nations, with the U.S. and Canada making up the largest group. Most U.S. students have no Irish family connections, hail from elite public high schools and prep schools, and have traveled abroad. Trinity is an ideal option for top students who are strong enough academically to qualify for Ivy League schools but who neglected to edit their high school newspaper, star on the soccer team, or do community service in Bujumbura. Trinity draws heavily from New York and New England, but it is attracting an increasing number of Texans and Californians who find access to the University of California frustrating. A neuroscience major describes Trinity students as "very academic, well-read, and very inclusive, especially toward the LGBTQ community."

Each entering student is assigned a peer mentor and a faculty tutor, who will be available for personal, academic, and professional advice.

Trinity offers no institutional financial aid to U.S. students, although it does accept U.S. federal student loans. Nevertheless, all students can try their luck in a series of competitive tests that sophomores can take just after Christmas known as the Foundation Scholarship Exams. More than 400 students typically sit for the exams, with about 90 becoming either "scholars" or "foundation scholars." Scholars become members of the university's governing board. Other benefits include five years of free or heavily discounted tuition, free accommodations and evening meals, and, best of all, the privileges of carrying a sword into an exam and grazing their sheep on the campus green.

"All of Dublin's nightclubs, bars, and pubs are pretty much a stone's throw away."

One drawback of Trinity's self-contained campus is the limited space for housing—only 11 percent of undergrads reside in university-owned facilities. Most first-year students live in Trinity Hall, a modern apartment building about 20 minutes away by bus. After that, preference for on-campus rooms goes to seniors, students with the highest grades, campus leaders, and international students; everyone else finds their own housing. "There is a renting crisis happening in Dublin right now," warns a senior. "It is quite difficult to find affordable accommodations." Trinity offers no university-wide meal plan, so students learn to cook for themselves or head to the two main restaurants or smaller cafés on campus, which provide simple meals. And as a senior points out, given the school's prime location, "Trinity students are spoiled for choice in terms of eating establishments extremely close to the university." Despite its urban setting, the campus is said to be safe, and an engineering major comments, "Trinity has started to introduce sexual consent workshops to incoming students."

Extracurricular activities may not help you get into Trinity, but they play an important role in campus culture once you get there. There are more than 170 student societies devoted to activities from yoga to traditional Irish music to entrepreneurialism. The most famous are the Philosophical Society ("the Phil"), which is the oldest debating club in the English-speaking world (1684), and its rival, the Historical Society ("the Hist"). The two groups share a building, sponsor weekly public debates, and award medals to notable visiting speakers. The Metaphysical Society ("the Metafizz") also gives students a chance to show off how much they know about Plato or Bertrand Russell. The Student Union is active in campaigning for a variety of political and social causes; divestment from fossil fuels has been a hot topic of late.

"You get a top-tier degree that costs less than most private colleges in the U.S."

Social life takes place both on and off campus. Student societies are mandated to throw events once a month, so there is plenty to choose from every day of the week. The drinking age is 18, and most students attend "Pav Fridays," where the lively on-campus Pavilion Bar offers cheap beer and cider. Later in the evening, socializing usually spills out into the surrounding city and its vibrant music and cultural scene. As a senior puts it, "All of Dublin's nightclubs, bars, and pubs are pretty much a stone's throw away." (Where else can you go pub crawling in the footsteps of Bram Stoker, of *Dracula* fame, and James Joyce?) St. Patrick's Day is always a time to celebrate, but unquestionably the biggest event is Trinity Week. It starts on Monday, when the new Scholars are announced, given black robes, and invited to take on current Scholars in a game of marbles on the steps of the chapel. Festivities culminate on Friday with the Trinity Ball, "a massive music festival where many popular Irish and European bands perform," says a recent graduate. "It draws 8,000 students, staff, and alumni in formal dress and takes over the city." Recent headliners have included Bastille and Ellie Goulding. Trinity is ideally located for travel to European and other destinations. "There are cheap buses from Dublin to any corner of Ireland," reports a senior. "It is also possible to fly to continental Europe or the UK for well under 50 euros."

Sports here are for playing, not watching. Says a history major, "There is no school mascot or particular set of colors that students wear. People tend to do sport mainly as an extracurricular activity. It's not really a status symbol." Nevertheless, there are at least 50 club and intramural sports; men's rugby and women's field hockey are the most competitive club teams. Although the English invented rugby, students at Trinity started the first club, and the boat (rowing) club is also one of the oldest. The university does hire coaches for some intercollegiate sports, such as rugby and soccer, and team leaders are eligible for scholarships. The annual dodgeball tournament is also a highlight.

Trinity College Dublin combines strong academics with the benefits of a beautiful campus in the midst of a thriving capital city that is also a gateway to the rest of Europe. "You get a top-tier degree that costs less than most private colleges in the U.S. and gives you the international experience of a lifetime," comments one American denizen. "And I met the nicest, most interesting, and hilarious people—the Irish."

University of Iowa

108 Calvin Hall, Iowa City, IA 52242

A bargain compared with other Big Ten schools such as Michigan and Illinois. Iowa is world-famous for its creative writing program and Writers' Workshop. Other areas of strength include health sciences, social and behavioral sciences, and business. Future scientists should check out the Research Fellows Program. The university is a regional draw, although more students are arriving from outside the Midwest.

At first glance, one might dismiss Iowa as a standard-issue Midwestern State U. But look beyond the state's endless miles of fields and corn and you'll find one of the most dynamic schools in the country—and one of the best values to boot. Iowa is known for breeding stellar nurses, future doctors, and of course, wrestlers. "I feel like I'm at home when I'm here," says a sophomore. "Iowa has a great vibe." Iowa was the first public university in the 19th century to admit men and women on an equal basis and the first to accept theater, music, and the other arts as equal to more traditional areas of academic research. The university has long been a major player in the creative fields, particularly writing, and its small-town atmosphere is just one of many reasons students nationwide flock to this "budget Ivy."

The 1,770-acre campus is located in the rolling hills of the Iowa River valley. Among the 300 major buildings is Old Capitol, the first capitol of Iowa, a national historic landmark, and the symbol of the university. The primary architectural styles of the campus buildings are Greek Revival and modern. Notable facilities include a 216,000-square-foot, state-of-the-art recreation and wellness center. The university spent the better part of a decade recovering from severe flooding that damaged 20 campus buildings in 2008; the recent opening of three new buildings, the Voxman Music Building, Hancher Auditorium, and the Visual Arts Building, marked the completion of those efforts.

> "I feel like I'm at home when I'm here. Iowa has a great vibe."

Seven of Iowa's 11 colleges offer either direct or delayed admission to undergraduates, and requirements vary by college. Liberal arts students must fulfill comprehensive requirements that include general education courses in the areas of communication and literacy; natural, quantitative, and social sciences; and culture, society, and the arts. The three-day On Iowa! program immerses incoming freshmen in the campus culture and introduces them to popular activities and traditions. Optional First-Year Seminar courses help students hone their discussion skills in a small-group setting.

Iowa has a long tradition in creative arts and is also the home of the famed Writers' Workshop, a two-year graduate program for emerging authors whose graduates have included Jane Smiley, John Irving, and Yaa Gyasi. The school also prides itself on its International Writing Program. "The English department is stellar," raves one English major. "It's possibly the best in the country—at least for creative writing." Iowa's on-campus hospital is one of the largest teaching hospitals in the United States. Undergraduates benefit from strong programs in the health professions, such as nursing, physician's assistant, and medical technician. The most popular majors

Website: www.uiowa.edu
Location: Small City
Public
Total Enrollment: 25,796
Undergraduates: 21,079
Male/Female: 47/53
SAT Ranges: ERW 570–680,
  M 570–690
ACT Ranges: 23–28
Financial Aid: 81%
Pell Grant: 22%
Expense: Pub $
Student Loans: 49%
Average Debt: $ $
Applicants: 27,734
Accepted: 86%
Enrolled: 21%
Grad in 6 Years: 74%
Returning Freshmen: 87%
Academics: ✐ ✐ ✐ ✐
Social: ☎ ☎ ☎
Q of L: ★ ★ ★
Admissions: (319) 335-3847
Email Address: admissions@
  uiowa.edu

Strong Programs:
Creative Writing
Finance
Psychology
Communication Studies
Health and Human Physiology
Nursing
Social and Behavioral Sciences
Business

are finance, psychology, communication studies, and health and human physiology. Iowa is also strong in the social and behavioral sciences, business, and paleontology. Combined degree programs permit students to earn degrees in liberal arts and their choice of business, engineering, nursing, or medicine. Agriculture, veterinary medicine, forestry, architecture, and animal science are only taught at Iowa's sister institution, Iowa State.

Just over half of the classes have fewer than 20 students, and "freshmen do tend to spend a majority of their time in large lectures," says a senior. The level of academic rigor tends to depend on the program, and professors are a mixed bag, students report. "I have had a few really amazing teachers become mentors, and I've had more than a few terrible teachers who don't care," a journalism major says. The university's Four-Year Graduation Plan guarantees that students who fulfill certain requirements will not have their graduation delayed by unavailability of a needed course. The University Honors Program provides special academic, cultural, and social opportunities to undergraduates who maintain a cumulative grade point average of 3.3 or higher. About 150 students—across all disciplines—are chosen each year to be ICRU Research Fellows, earning scholarships of up to $2,500 to engage in faculty-mentored research. Roughly 5 percent of undergraduates study abroad in nearly 50 countries worldwide, mostly in UI-sponsored programs.

> "I have had a few really amazing teachers become mentors."

"I think that the students here are more open-minded than at our closest rival," says a premed student. "I think this is because of the strong artistic and performing culture present here." Fifty-nine percent of undergraduates hail from Iowa, with most of the rest coming from contiguous states, especially Illinois; 9 percent are international. African Americans account for 3 percent, Hispanics 8 percent, Asian Americans 4 percent, and multiracial students 3 percent. Students describe the campus as tolerant and supportive of a community atmosphere in and out of the classroom. The university likes to boast that it has the lowest tuition and fees in the Big Ten. Twenty-two percent of freshmen qualify for Pell Grants. In addition to 522 athletic scholarships, there are academic scholarships averaging $5,100 for eligible students. Twenty Carver Scholarships are awarded each year to juniors who have "overcome unusual or debilitating circumstances in life."

Iowa's on-campus hospital is one of the largest teaching hospitals in the United States.

Students say campus residence halls are sociable and therefore not very quiet. "The dorms have a very comfortable atmosphere and are cleaned daily," says a sophomore. All are co-ed by floor or wing, and first-years can opt to live in one of nearly 20 living/learning communities, such as Global Mosaic, Living Literature, and Justice for All. Twenty-eight percent of undergrads live in university housing; most students move off campus after their first year, often to apartments or houses adjacent to the campus. The "very nice" dining halls are "set up like food courts, with numerous options for varying ethnic and special tastes," says a senior. The student union includes a coffee shop, two cafeterias, and the State Room Restaurant.

> "The whole town is basked in black and gold."

The university likes to boast that it has the lowest tuition and fees in the Big Ten.

Students often venture to Iowa City's lively downtown area, across the street from campus, which "is built with the college student in mind," a student says. "There are two university theaters right on campus and many affordable cultural events take place at Hancher Auditorium. The Union Bar and Grill, Mickey's, Sports Column, and George's are all popular hangouts with students." Thirteen percent of the men and 16 percent of the women belong to fraternities and sororities, respectively. Alcohol is not permitted on campus for those under 21. "Students disobey the policy," says a student, "but there are fines and academic ramifications." The university recently suspended more than half of its 23 fraternities for violating a temporary moratorium on alcohol at Greek events that was imposed in the wake of the 2017 death of a freshman. Students look forward to the annual Iowa City Jazz Festival, homecoming, Dance Marathon, and Big Ten football, especially the game against Iowa State. For a change of scene, Chicago, Kansas City, or St. Louis are all within four to six hours by car, a short road trip by Midwestern standards.

Iowa's Hawkeyes compete in the Division I Big Ten Conference. The football team is a national powerhouse and regularly appears in New Year's Day bowl games. Hawkeye fans are serious about their team: "The whole town is basked in black and gold," a freshman says. Men's and women's basketball are especially competitive, as are wrestling, baseball (2017 Big Ten champs), and softball. Sixteen percent of undergrads participate in the extensive intramural program, which offers more than 40 individual, dual, or team sports with a variety of leagues. Among the most popular are flag football, indoor soccer, basketball, volleyball, and spikeball.

Much more than a campus among the cornfields, Iowa is an ever-evolving university where artistic creativity thrives alongside scientific innovation in a relatively progressive college town. "The University of Iowa is continually renovating and improving its facilities to stay modern and keep up with technology," says a sophomore. The scope of its academic programs is broad and social activities abound—especially when it comes to rooting for their Hawkeyes.

Overlaps

UW–Madison, U of I at Urbana–Champaign, University of Minnesota, University of Arizona, Indiana University, Iowa State, Michigan State, Illinois State

If You Apply To ›

Iowa: Rolling admissions. SATs or ACTs: required. No Subject Tests. Accepts the Common Application. Applicants have option of selecting preferred gender pronouns, preferred name, and sexual orientation.

Iowa State University

100 Alumni Hall, Ames, IA 50011

Agriculture and engineering are the twin pillars of Iowa State's curriculum, and the university is a magnet for prevets. Ames is a small city and ISU must still endure barbs from certain snobby people in Iowa City. In truth, ISU is relatively cosmopolitan, with students hailing from more than 100 foreign countries. While others retrench, ISU continues to expand.

Love for Iowa State University runs as deep as its Midwestern roots. Strong programs in engineering, business, and agriculture attract students from around the globe. The close-knit, small-town atmosphere fostered at this school of nearly 29,000 undergraduates keeps them here. At a time when many state universities are tightening the purse strings and retrenching, Iowa State has its eyes set on future growth and has expanded major research initiatives focused on areas like bioeconomics, food safety and security, human/computer interaction, and animal health.

The university has lavished attention on its parklike setting, located on a 1,984-acre tract in the middle of Ames, population 66,000. The campus, which boasts a combination of dignified old buildings and award-winning new ones, is a model of landscape design with numerous shady quadrangles with floral plantings and artwork that create a garden-like quality. History and tradition prevail, from the campanile, which serenades the campus with its carillon bells, to the huge public art collection, including murals by native Iowan Grant Wood (best known for his *American Gothic*) and sculptures by Danish artist Christian Petersen. Much of the

Website: www.iastate.edu
Location: Small City
Public
Total Enrollment: 30,307
Undergraduates: 28,491
Male/Female: 57/43
SAT Ranges: ERW 520–647, M 545–680
ACT Ranges: 22–28
Financial Aid: 78%
Pell Grant: 20%
Expense: Pub $
Student Loans: 59%
Average Debt: $ $

(continued)

Applicants: 19,262
Accepted: 89%
Enrolled: 35%
Grad in 6 Years: 73%
Returning Freshmen: 88%
Academics: ✐ ✐ ✐
Social: ☎ ☎ ☎ ☎
Q of L: ★ ★ ★
Admissions: (515) 294-5836
Email Address: admissions@
iastate.edu

Strong Programs:
Mechanical Engineering
Kinesiology
Finance
Marketing
Animal Science
Agronomy
Biological Systems Engineering
Chemistry

The 1,984-acre, parklike campus features swans (named Sir Lancelot and Lady Elaine) and ducks that reside on Lake LaVerne.

campus is closed to cars, largely for the benefit of walking and bicycling, as well as the swans (named Sir Lancelot and Lady Elaine) and ducks that reside on Lake LaVerne. The free-to-students CyRide bus system delivers students around campus and the city. Howe Hall, home to aerospace engineering, boasts a virtual reality application center and a six-sided virtual reality cave. Construction on an $84 million Student Innovation Center is slated for completion in 2020.

All undergraduates must take two semesters of foundational courses covering written, oral, visual, and electronic communication and demonstrate proficiency in English prior to graduation, in addition to taking a half-credit course on the use of the library and satisfying a three-credit requirement in diversity. Other general education requirements, which vary by college, focus on gaining breadth in the natural and social sciences. When Iowa State opened its doors in 1869 as a land grant university, agriculture and engineering ruled the academic roost, and these colleges still field outstanding programs in animal science, agribusiness, agronomy, and agricultural engineering. These days, though, the liberal arts are nearly as popular, and the College of Liberal Arts and Sciences is actually the largest of ISU's seven undergraduate colleges. Other colleges include business, design, veterinary medicine, and human sciences. Among the university's 100-plus majors, mechanical engineering is the most popular, followed by kinesiology, finance, and marketing. Programs in biological systems engineering, chemistry, and civil engineering are also strong.

> **"We have some world-class profs here who are doing important research."**

One quarter of all undergraduate classes have more than 50 students, and students report that academic intensity varies by program. Despite the university's size, professors teach most classes, with the exception of some freshman English options. "We have some world-class profs here who are doing important research," one senior says. Academic and career counseling draw praise too, and advisors are "always readily available" to help students. Seventy-five percent of freshmen join ISU's 90 highly touted learning communities, taking a common set of classes or living together on the same residence hall floor with other newcomers who share similar academic interests. An honors program enrolls more than 1,400 outstanding students, many of whom live in honors housing. Roughly 6 percent of undergrads study overseas; popular destinations include Italy, the United Kingdom, China, Australia, and Costa Rica. Participation in these programs, as well as undergraduate research and capstone programs, is on the rise.

> **"This is a pretty white campus."**

Sixty percent of ISU's undergraduates are Iowans, though all 50 states and more than 100 countries are represented here. Foreign students comprise 7 percent of the student body. Iowa State was the first co-ed land grant institution, but attracting minorities has proven more difficult: Hispanics comprise 5 percent, Asian Americans 3 percent, African Americans 3 percent, and multiracial students 2 percent. "We have a lot of farmers and small-town Iowans," says a senior. "This is a pretty white campus." To help remedy this situation, ISU launched a $25 million campaign aimed at increasing the number of scholarships available for minority students, athletes, and student leaders. In addition to need-based financial aid and more than 400 athletic scholarships, thousands of merit awards, which average $3,500 annually, are available.

Forty-one percent of students live in on-campus residence halls and apartments, including about 2,000 students who live in college-affiliated Greek housing; most others find their own apartments near campus. Single-sex, co-ed, and suite-style dorms are available, as are special floors for international students, teetotalers, and particularly studious undergraduates, and rooms are said to be well maintained. "The dorms are sterile to begin with but the traditions are very strong here and students transform them into home with their own personal touch," explains a junior.

Students dine at 21 campus locations, including four main dining centers. The university has added several staff members to more effectively respond to the issue of campus sexual assault.

Iowa State is not simply located in Ames—in many respects it *is* Ames, but whether or not it qualifies as a college town depends on whom you ask. Des Moines, the state capital, is about 30 minutes away, and Iowa City, Minneapolis, and Chicago are other easy and enjoyable road trips. Socializing tends to stay on campus, though, with big-name bands playing at Hilton Coliseum and parties always rocking. There are also more than 900 student organizations that cater to just about any interest. Thirteen percent of the men and 21 percent of the women go Greek. The campus is officially dry, but, according to one sophomore, many older students will buy alcohol for minors. Across the street from campus, Campustown offers several bars for those of age, as well as a variety of cafés and ethnic restaurants. One long-held tradition is campaniling, where students must kiss under the campanile at the stroke of midnight to be considered "true" Cyclones. And students have learned not to walk over the zodiac sign in the Memorial Union—it brings bad luck.

In sports, Cyclones basketball is king; the men's and women's teams are usual invitees to the NCAA Division I tournament, and the men's team brought home the Big 12 title in 2014, 2015, and 2017. Football, track and field, men's wrestling, and women's cross-country are also competitive. The Hawkeye rivalry is one of the strongest in the nation. Thirty-eight percent of students participate in nonvarsity sports; the intramural program, which is one of the largest in the country, offers 45 sports—and if that's not enough, students have their pick of 53 club sports too.

From its first class of 28 men and two women in 1869, Iowa State has taken to heart Abraham Lincoln's land grant ideal: to open higher education to all, to teach practical courses, and to share that knowledge beyond the borders of the school. According to one junior, it's this dynamic combination that draws "hardworking, kind students" from near and far.

Seventy-five percent of freshmen join ISU's 90 highly touted learning communities for newcomers who share similar academic interests.

Overlaps

UC Davis, U of I at Urbana–Champaign, Michigan State, University of Minnesota, North Carolina State, University of Iowa, Purdue, UW–Madison

If You Apply To ›

Iowa State: Rolling admissions. SATs or ACTs: required. No Subject Tests. Does not accept the Common Application.

Ithaca College

953 Danby Road, Ithaca, NY 14850

Ithaca offers an unusually wide array of programs for a smallish university. Students looking at Ithaca College also apply to Boston University, NYU, and Syracuse. The common thread? Outstanding preprofessional programs and offerings in the arts and media. Students clamor to get into physical therapy. Crosstown neighbor Cornell adds curricular and social opportunities.

Over South Hill, at the center of the upstate New York Finger Lakes region, sits Ithaca College. The school has a close-knit community, along with strong programs in music, theater, communications, and health sciences. With a "gorges" campus and a size that allows for easy friendships with peers and professors alike, Ithaca draws students from all over the U.S.—and dozens of other countries. Ithaca's special focus on undergraduate education with hands-on learning helps prepare students for the rigors of life outside institutional walls.

Website: www.ithaca.edu
Location: Small City
Private
Total Enrollment: 6,317
Undergraduates: 5,932
Male/Female: 42/58

(continued)

SAT Ranges: ERW 590–670,
   M 560–660
ACT Ranges: 25–29
Financial Aid: 94%
Pell Grant: 21%
Expense: Pr $
Student Loans: 69%
Average Debt: $ $ $ $
Applicants: 14,162
Accepted: 71%
Enrolled: 16%
Grad in 6 Years: 74%
Returning Freshmen: 83%
Academics: ✍ ✍ ✍
Social: ☎ ☎ ☎ ☎
Q of L: ★ ★ ★
Admissions: (800) 429-4274
Email Address: admission@
   ithaca.edu

Strong Programs:
Television-Radio
Business Administration
Integrated Marketing
   Communications
Clinical Health Studies
Music
Theater Arts
Occupational Therapy
Speech-Language Pathology

*Ithaca's campus lies
on the city's southern
hill overlooking
Cayuga Lake.*

Ithaca's campus, midway between Syracuse and Binghamton, in the beautiful Finger Lakes region, lies on the city's southern hill overlooking Cayuga Lake. None of the streamlined, modern campus buildings on the 757-acre plot are more than 60 years old, since the college did not move to its present location until the 1960s. The surrounding area is dotted with forests, waterfalls, rolling hills, and, of course, those ever-present gorges. Author Tom Wolfe dubbed the college "the emerald eminence at the fingertip of Cayuga Lake."

Ithaca has five schools—music, communications, business, health sciences and human performance, and humanities and sciences. Together, they offer nearly 100 undergraduate majors and 70 minors. All students complete the Integrative Core Curriculum (ICC), the centerpiece of which is a Themes and Perspectives sequence that includes courses from a variety of disciplines, all focusing on a common theme, such as Power and Justice or The Quest for a Sustainable Future. All first-year students enroll in a four-credit Ithaca Seminar during the first semester; recent examples of the more than 100 offerings include Farm to Table, Dialogue on Design, and The Right-Brain Revolution. These classes are limited to about 15 students each, and professors and students decide together how to use the fourth hour of instruction each week, covering topics related to the transition to college life, such as personal, social, and academic responsibility. Additional ICC elements include a senior capstone experience and an electronic learning portfolio.

> "The music school has always been lauded and maintained an excellent academic program."

Ithaca is best known for its preprofessional programs—and for its school of music, which dates to 1892, when the college was founded as a music conservatory. "The music school has always been lauded and maintained an excellent academic program," a freshman says. The school requires an in-person audition, making it a destination for already-accomplished musicians, composers, and sound-recording technologists. Professional programs in the School of Health Sciences and Human Performance range from clinical health studies and speech-language pathology to health education and the highly regarded physical therapy program. The Park School of Communications houses two of the college's most popular programs—television-radio and integrated marketing communications—and has added a new major in writing for film, TV, and emerging media. The business school offers undergraduate programs in business administration and accounting. Cross-registration is available at Cornell University and Wells College, and Ithaca also offers a 3–2 physics and engineering program.

"The teaching approach here is discussion-based and hands-on. Students don't learn from simply reading and listening, we learn from applying course material," says a junior. Sixty-one percent of classes have fewer than 20 students, and professors are praised for their knowledge and enthusiasm. A sophomore says, "If you do struggle, as I have, there are lifelines in the form of TAs, free tutoring (in most cases), and persistent professor interaction." The Honors Program offers special, intensive seminars and an array of out-of-class activities to qualified students. Research opportunities in the sciences and psychology are plentiful; students in other departments generally do research as part of an independent study course. Those seeking real-world experience may apply for semester-long programs in New York City or Los Angeles that combine an internship with industry-related courses. Ithaca offers study abroad programs at the Ithaca College London Center and in more than 50 countries; 30 percent of students study off campus.

What are the characteristics of a typical Ithaca student? "Imagine band geeks, jocks, preppy kids, hippies, and every other group you can see sitting at the same table, talking and laughing," says one sophomore. "That—multiplied by about 6,000—is what it feels like to be a student at Ithaca." Forty-three percent of Ithaca students hail from New York State; many of the rest come from elsewhere in New England, and 2 percent come from other nations. African Americans represent 6 percent of undergraduates, Asian Americans 4 percent, Hispanics 8 percent, and multiracial students 3 percent. Politically, the campus is liberal, and according to a biochemistry major, "Some of the very hot topics at the moment are racism and ensuring that all students are treated fairly and equally." Merit scholarships averaging $15,700 are available to top-performing applicants; there are no athletic awards. Twenty-one percent of freshmen qualify for the Pell Grant. In-state residents with annual family incomes of $125,000 or less are eligible to receive an Ithaca College New York State Tuition Award of up to $6,000 per year for four years.

In-state residents with annual family incomes of $125,000 or less are eligible to receive a tuition award of up to $6,000 per year.

Seventy percent of Ithaca's students live on campus, thanks in part to the college's Circle and Garden Apartments, which have full kitchens and space for 630 upperclassmen in units that house two to six students each. First-year students participate in the First-Year Residential Experience, living in communities focusing on themes like multiculturalism and sustainability. A junior recommends learning communities as a way to "meet new people and become more involved in the Ithaca area." Campus residents can eat in any of the three dining halls, each with a different daily menu. "There's a big emphasis on local foods and vendors," says one student, but the meals get mixed reviews. An exercise science major reports, "Our campus police work very hard to keep an overall safe environment on campus."

"Students don't learn from simply reading and listening, we learn from applying course material."

Ithaca recognizes only academic fraternities and sororities, not social ones, but that doesn't slow down the campus social scene. "Between music school concerts, theater performances, Student Activities Board movies, club events, open-mic nights, comedy shows, or athletic events, it is impossible to be bored on campus," one sociology major says. More than 200 student organizations also keep students busy. Students agree that the party scene is low-key; those looking for livelier bashes check out Greek life at neighboring Cornell. The city of Ithaca caters well to college students, with a variety of bars and clubs, a mall, a bowling alley, and movie theaters. Each fall brings Applefest, a local downtown festival that celebrates the harvest, and in the winter, Chilifest helps students warm up. The area's hilly terrain provides abundant opportunities for hiking, biking, sledding, and skiing. Popular road trips include Syracuse and Binghamton (each an hour away), and New York City, Philadelphia, Boston, Washington, D.C., and Toronto, each between a four and six hours' drive.

The biggest annual athletic tradition is the "Cortaca Jug" football game that pits the Ithaca Bombers against rival SUNY–Cortland.

Ithaca fields 27 competitive Division III varsity athletics programs. The Bombers won six Liberty League conference championships during the 2017–18 season, as well as four individual national titles in track and field, swimming and diving, and wrestling. The biggest annual athletic tradition is the "Cortaca Jug" football game that pits the Ithaca Bombers against rival SUNY–Cortland. (The winner gets the jug-shaped "firkin" cask as a trophy, and the game is "the only Division III football game you can bet on in Vegas," boasts a sophomore.) Twenty percent of students sign up for club and intramural sports, and popular options include rugby, ultimate Frisbee, flag football, basketball, and volleyball.

"[Learning communities are a way to] meet new people and become more involved in the Ithaca area."

If you can endure the harsh winters ("Come mid-February or so, we hate the snow!" gripes one senior), you'll appreciate the small size and personal attention characteristic of Ithaca College. "Everybody who is part of the Ithaca College community knows that they are part of something special," observes one student. "At other schools, you're a number. At Ithaca, we know your name."

Overlaps

Marist, Quinnipiac, Elon, Hofstra, Fairfield, Syracuse, NYU, Boston University

James Madison University

Harrisonburg, VA 22807

JMU has carved out a comfortable niche among Virginia's superb public universities. More undergrads than UVA and three times as many as William and Mary, though the city of Harrisonburg gives JMU a more down-home feel. Strong in preprofessional fields such as business, health professions, and education. Undergraduates rule the roost.

Website: www.jmu.edu
Location: Small City
Public
Total Enrollment: 19,871
Undergraduates: 18,860
Male/Female: 41/59
SAT Ranges: ERW 560–640, M 540–620
ACT Ranges: 23–28
Financial Aid: 62%
Pell Grant: 15%
Expense: Pub $ $ $
Student Loans: 50%
Average Debt: $ $
Applicants: 21,099
Accepted: 75%
Enrolled: 29%
Grad in 6 Years: 83%
Returning Freshmen: 90%
Academics: ✑ ✑ ✑
Social: ☎ ☎ ☎ ☎
Q of L: ★ ★ ★ ★
Admissions: (540) 568-5681
Email Address: admissions@jmu.edu

Strong Programs:
Business
Education
Health Sciences
Health Services Administration
Sport and Recreation
    Management
Biology

No doubt about it: students at James Madison University get down to business. In fact, the school's business programs continue to garner national attention and attract top-notch students from coast to coast. The university has been growing at a steady rate, causing some to feel growth pains. But an emphasis on undergraduate teaching, close student/faculty interaction, and a warm and welcoming climate are still business as usual here. "JMU is comfortable—everyone has a place, you just have to find it," says a senior.

JMU is in the heart of the Shenandoah Valley, two hours from Washington, D.C., and Richmond, Virginia. The university straddles Interstate 81, an outlet to several major East Coast cities. Three types of architecture make up the campus. The buildings on front campus have red-tile roofs and are constructed of a distinctive limestone block known as bluestone. Back campus has more modern, redbrick structures. The College of Integrated Science and Technology campus features modern beige buildings. Recent projects include a new, three-story west campus dining hall and a 500-bed residence hall.

The General Education Program requires each student to take courses in several clusters, including Skills for the 21st Century, Arts and Humanities, The Natural World, Social and Cultural Processes, and Individuals in the Human Community. The idea is to give students a basis for lifelong learning by challenging them to become active in their own education and to explore the foundations of knowledge. Freshmen are offered a variety of programs to help smooth their transition into the university. Outdoor Adventures, held before classes begin, give first-year students an opportunity to meet while hiking and climbing in the mountains.

> "You can ask questions, get to know your professors one-on-one, and make connections."

JMU is recognized nationally for its College of Business, while health sciences and education are also strong. Some of the most popular majors include health sciences, health services administration, sport and recreation management, biology, nursing, and psychology. Undergraduates in the biology department have employed recombinant DNA technology to help develop organisms that produce biodegradable plastics, while a mathematical modeling laboratory helps undergrads solve real-world applied math problems. Also worth noting is the geology and geography departments' summer geology field camp for undergraduates.

With undergrads far outnumbering grad students, JMU's main mission is undergraduate teaching, and students say the classroom atmosphere is usually relaxed and supportive. Thirty-four percent of classes have fewer than 20 students, and a political science major reports that "the biggest classroom holds 300 students," so even the largest classes aren't too overwhelming; "You feel like you can ask questions, get to know your professors one-on-one, and make connections." Student support services get high ratings. "The counseling center offers a student oasis and arts center where anyone can go free of charge to do yoga, rest, play relaxing games, make crafts, etc.," notes a senior.

Those looking for a more intense intellectual experience can check out the Honors College, which offers small classes and opportunities for independent study. Many upper-level programs encourage undergraduate participation with faculty research. Thirty percent of students study internationally; JMU runs its own semester abroad programs in Belgium, England, Italy, Scotland, and Spain, as well as dozens of short-term, faculty-led programs in roughly 40 countries.

Students describe their fellow Dukes as cheerful people who hold doors open for each other, and a junior says JMU students are interested in "finding lifestyles that they love instead of just jobs." Most undergrads attended public high schools, and 77 percent are from Virginia. In fact, there's a general effort to keep out-of-state enrollment below 30 percent; international students represent 2 percent. Ethnic diversity, although low, has been slowly on the rise; African Americans currently account for 5 percent of JMU's student body, Hispanics 7 percent, Asian Americans 5 percent, and multiracial students 4 percent. As

"I end up missing my college's food when I'm home."

for political inclinations, both sides of the aisle are represented, but an economics major says most students are "rather apathetic." JMU offers limited merit scholarships averaging $5,200 and 338 athletic scholarships.

Thirty percent of students live on campus, which is a requirement for freshmen. On-campus housing runs the gamut from the old high-ceiling variety to newer, air-conditioned dorms with fitness centers and apartments for sophomores. For upperclassmen, "Off-campus housing is extremely easy to find," reports a senior, "and there is a wide range of prices and amenities available." With 27 dining options on campus serving all sorts of dietary needs and preferences, students rave about the meal plan. "You're supposed to miss your mom's cooking when you go away, but I end up missing my college's food when I'm home," says one student. According to a math major, JMU's Title IX office is "working hard to advance services" and the Campus Assault Response student group "is a great nonreporting resource for students" coping with sexual violence.

"Social life is really fun for a rural area," observes one student. "The students mostly gather at off-campus apartments via a bus system that runs into the late hours." Greek life attracts only 4 percent of the men and 9 percent of the women. The school cracks down on underage drinking on campus, and after three strikes "students are asked to leave," says a student. Favorite traditions include the holiday tree-lighting ceremony, Spring Concert, the Madipalooza music festival, and taking graduation photos with the various campus statues of James Madison (or "JMaddy," as he's been dubbed by students). Most students find Harrisonburg a friendly, if not always lively, Southern town. As for road trips, the University of Virginia, almost an hour's drive to the south, is a top destination, but equally enticing are the many nearby natural delights of the Shenandoah Valley, including hiking, camping, and even skiing.

Sports fans here are known as the JMU Nation, and to say they are enthusiastic about their Division I Dukes teams would be an understatement, especially when it comes to the 2016 FCS national champion football team. Women's cross-country, volleyball, and lacrosse and men's soccer are recent Colonial Athletic Association champions. About half of the students participate in intramurals and

(continued)

Nursing
Psychology

Outdoor Adventures, held before classes begin, give first-year students an opportunity to meet while hiking in the mountains.

JMU makes a general effort to keep out-of-state enrollment below 30 percent.

Overlaps

Appalachian State, Clemson, College of Charleston, Grand Valley State, Illinois State, George Mason, University of Virginia, Virginia Tech

club sports. JMU's debate team rates as one of the top public debate program in the nation.

Though JMU still has a ways to go before establishing itself as a front-rank national university, it is making progress. The school is growing, but not outgrowing its Southern charm. "The school spirit is really what sets us apart," says an elementary education major. "No matter where you go on campus, you are always going to find someone wearing purple and gold."

If You Apply To ›

James Madison: Early action, regular decision. SATs or ACTs: optional. Subject Tests: optional. Does not accept the Common Application.

The Johns Hopkins University

3400 North Charles Street, Baltimore, MD 21218

The Hop's reputation as a top-notch premed factory can be misleading. It's true, but Hopkins also has fine programs in international studies (with D.C. close at hand) as well as in the humanities and social sciences. With total enrollment at the Homewood campus at just over 7,600—5,400 of them undergraduates—Hopkins is smaller than most people think. Major effort underway to diversify the student body.

Website: www.jhu.edu
Location: City Outskirts
Private
Total Enrollment: 7,665
Undergraduates: 5,407
Male/Female: 49/51
SAT Ranges: ERW 720–780, M 740–800
ACT Ranges: 33–35
Financial Aid: 59%
Pell Grant: 15%
Expense: Pr $ $ $ $
Student Loans: 45%
Average Debt: $ $
Applicants: 26,576
Accepted: 12%
Enrolled: 43%
Grad in 6 Years: 94%
Returning Freshmen: 97%
Academics: ✐ ✐ ✐ ✐ ✐
Social: ☎ ☎ ☎
Q of L: ★ ★ ★
Admissions: (410) 516-8171
Email Address: gotojhu@ jhu.edu

One of the few U.S. universities initially founded as a graduate school, The Johns Hopkins University has garnered widespread acclaim for its exceptional professors, extensive resources, and abundant research opportunities. Though the university has a reputation for churning out premed students, the administration has been working for a number of years to make it clear that this midsized Baltimore university has plenty to offer undergrads whose interests are decidedly nonmedical or nonscience based. Students who attend this elite university know they are at the top of the game, and they burn the midnight oil to stay there, but a freshman insists that they also "let loose every once in a while."

The arts and sciences and engineering schools are on the main Homewood campus, 140 picturesque acres just three miles north of Baltimore's revitalized Inner Harbor. Tree-lined quadrangles, open lawns, and playing fields make for an idyllic setting on the edge of a major urban center. The architecture on this woody urban campus is mainly Georgian redbrick, with several recently built, more modern structures scattered throughout. Malone Hall is a state-of-the-art building that houses several collaborative research institutions. Hopkins's medical campus is easily accessible via a crosstown shuttle. Hopkins recently opened a building that combines 157 student apartments with 31,000 square feet of commercial space, to encourage new business development in the Charles Village neighborhood that surrounds the Homewood campus.

> "Intersession is one of the best times of the year. The classes are pass/fail and so much fun!"

Although Johns Hopkins is a firm supporter of traditional and interdisciplinary scholarship, there are no university-wide requirements, other than a four-course writing component. Each major has its own distribution requirements, and there are several creative seminar offerings for freshmen. Freshmen are assigned a premajor advisor, and arts and sciences students are encouraged to wait until at least their sophomore year to declare a major. Hopkins no longer "covers" first-semester freshman grades by recording them as satisfactory or unsatisfactory—ending a policy that had been in place since 1971. Freshmen must now buckle down to a Herculean workload right from the get-go. Even so, the university has developed and strengthened several student support resources over the last few years to help ease the transition to college. Students may also get some relief during the optional January intersession, during which they can take courses or pursue independent study for one or two credits. "Intersession is one of the best times of the year," cheers an international studies major. "The classes are pass/fail and so much fun: everything from profiling mass murderers to a Harry Potter literature class to a chocolate lab!"

(continued)

Strong Programs:
Premed
Public Health Studies
Biomedical Engineering
Neuroscience
International Studies
Engineering
Creative Writing
Music

As much as some try to deny it, students bound for medical school dominate the campus. Public health studies is among the most popular majors, along with biomedical engineering, neuroscience, and international studies. The Johns Hopkins Hospital and Medical School play such a major role in the identity of Hopkins that students sometimes fear it "overshadows the vibrant undergrad life that exists at Homewood." But administrators say the school is paying more attention to the undergraduate programs and emphasizing interdisciplinary, cooperative approaches to the coursework, and students seem to agree. "Hopkins is a rigorous institution, but with its collaborative academic culture, learning is very manageable and enjoyable," says a behavioral biology major.

Engineering majors enjoy strong departments, such as mechanical engineering, chemical and biomedical engineering, electrical and computer engineering, and computer science. Students can receive a B.A. in creative writing through the Writing Seminars program, where they study with authors and poets such as Alice McDermott and Andrew Motion. Musicians can pursue a dual degree in music performance with the university's Peabody Conservatory. There also are broad "area majors," such as natural sciences and romance languages, and students can choose from a cluster of related disciplines to design their own program. Business is now available as a minor, although the major and minor in Russian have been dropped. Students are generally happy with the

Hopkins's medical campus is easily accessible via a crosstown shuttle.

"I feel like I'm part of a conversation, engaged, and enjoying my time in class."

quality of teaching at Hopkins, which is enhanced by small class sizes—74 percent of undergraduate classes enroll fewer than 20 students. "The professors here are *awesome*," enthuses a neuroscience and music double major. "I feel like I'm part of a conversation, engaged, and enjoying my time in class."

The well-developed graduate side of Johns Hopkins proves to be a boon to undergraduates as well. The international studies program, for example, is enriched by its offerings at the university's Bologna Center in Italy, its Nanjing Center in China, and its Nitze School of Advanced International Studies in nearby Washington, D.C. Thirty-nine percent of all undergraduates study abroad in these and other locations across the globe. Undergraduate research is a Johns Hopkins hallmark, with 77 percent of students having at least one research experience. "Without any prior experience, any student can get a meaningful research job," says a political science major. "I was able to secure a research position within my first month as a freshman at JHU." Programs such as the Woodrow Wilson Undergraduate Research Fellowship Program and the Provost's Undergraduate Research Awards offer funding and faculty support for research projects. The Clark Scholars Program offers special academic and networking opportunities to top engineering students. Those interested in service can apply for one of 50 paid summer internships with Baltimore area nonprofits and government agencies through the Community Impact Internships program.

Seventy-seven percent of undergraduates have at least one research experience.

"Students at Hopkins are competitive, motivated, and innovative," says one chemical engineering major, and the campus leans liberal. Geographically, most students come from the Mid-Atlantic states and New England; only 10 percent are

Maryland natives, and another 9 percent are international. Ninety-three percent graduated in the top 10th of their high school class. Twenty-seven percent of students are Asian American, 6 percent African American, 14 percent Hispanic, and 5 percent multiracial. At $3.8 billion, Hopkins's endowment is among the top 25 in the country, and the school recently upped its financial aid game by moving to a fully need-blind admissions process and guaranteeing to meet 100 percent of admitted students' demonstrated need with loan-free financial aid packages. Hopkins rewards the extraordinarily talented with hefty Hodson Trust scholarships worth about two-thirds of tuition annually, regardless of need. Forty-eight athletic scholarships are also awarded in women's and men's lacrosse, where Hopkins is a perennial national powerhouse.

Fifty-one percent of Hopkins students live in student housing; freshmen and sophomores are required to do so. "The freshman-year dorms are classic and encourage social interactions," explains a writing major. "The sophomore-year dorms are spacious, new, and have excellent amenities." Upperclassmen often choose to scope out the row houses and apartment buildings that surround Hopkins, but many stay on campus in the Charles Commons or one of six other residence halls or university-owned "luxury" apartments. Campus dining gets positive reviews, as does security, thanks to the consistent presence of security personnel. The Sexual Assault Resource Unit student organization is active in raising awareness about sexual violence.

> "I was able to secure a research position within my first month as a freshman at JHU."

The image Johns Hopkins students once had as antisocial bookworms is giving way to a more balanced social life. Rowdy dorm parties and all-campus festivities may be few and far between, but fraternity parties can be found on the weekends; 19 percent of the men and 30 percent of the women belong to the Greek system. There are also more than 400 clubs and student organizations to pick from. Students speak fondly of the Lighting of the Quads celebration each winter, but the biggest and most popular undergraduate social event of the year is the student-organized Spring Fair. "Tons of Baltimore food vendors and shops come and line up on the quads, there is a concert, and the campus is generally full of merriment," says an international studies major.

In addition to on-campus events like lectures and performances, says a senior, "You have the whole city of Baltimore and its social scene to explore." Downtown and the famed Inner Harbor are not too distant, and some of the city's best attractions, such as the Baltimore Museum of Art, Wyman Park, and the funky Hampden neighborhood, are right near campus. Trendy Baltimore hot spots—like Canton, Fells Point, and Little Italy—are favorites. Students also head downtown for plays, the symphony, films, clubs, restaurants, the zoo, and major league sports; Camden Yards, home of baseball's Orioles, is the most commodious park in the country. Annapolis is less than an hour away by car, while Washington, D.C., only an hour's train ride, beckons with tourist activities and ample nightlife. In the warmer months, a trek out to the Delaware and Maryland beaches takes the mind off the books.

> "[During Spring Fair] the campus is generally full of merriment."

When the nationally acclaimed Division I men's lacrosse team takes to the road, students often take advantage of the opportunity to road-trip with them and cheer them on. Women's lacrosse is Division I as well, but the rest of the Blue Jays athletic program competes in Division III. Women's cross-country is a recent national champion, and Centennial Conference champs include men's basketball, baseball, and football; women's volleyball; and men's and women's tennis and track and field. The Woodrow Wilson Debate Council has also had national success. Twenty percent of undergraduates compete in intramurals.

With one of the world's premier medical schools, top science programs, and first-rate programs in areas as diverse as writing, international studies, environmental engineering, and philosophy, Johns Hopkins is clearly among the best schools in the country. Students here take pride in the fact that they belong to the cream of the academic crop. "Hopkins students are incredibly passionate about their unique interests," says a senior. "It is a really contagious culture to be a part of, because it inspires you to pursue your passions as well."

If You Apply To ›

Johns Hopkins: Early decision, regular decision. SATs or ACTs: required. Subject Tests: optional. Accepts the Common Application with supplement. Biomedical engineering students must apply to that program.

Juniata College

1700 Moore Street, Huntingdon, PA 16652

Located in the middle of rural Pennsylvania, Juniata boasts one of the best undergraduate science programs among liberal arts colleges. Students are encouraged to design their own education and to think globally. Peace and conflict studies is a specialty. Lots of merit scholarships, but not much diversity among students.

Set amid the ridges and valleys of central Pennsylvania, Juniata College offers students a tantalizing mix of academic flexibility, small classes, and surprisingly solid programs in the natural sciences. Students here chart their own course of study, partner with faculty on research projects, and pack their bags for study abroad opportunities around the world. "The types of students who are attracted to Juniata are those who have a motivation to learn, but are not interested in learning in the conventional way," says a psychology major.

Juniata's quiet 110-acre campus features a central stand of structures reflecting three architectural styles. The college's landmark building, Founders Hall, is a colonial Revival structure, built of brick atop a stone foundation. Halbritter Center for the Performing Arts, Ellis Hall, and the von Liebig Center for Science are all Classical Revival buildings, the prominent pillars on each visible all over campus. The college also boasts a Beaux-Arts building, Carnegie Hall, originally built as a Carnegie library in 1907 and redesigned on the interior to house the college's art museum. Construction was recently completed on a new Integrated Media and Studio Arts building.

> "[Juniata students] have a motivation to learn, but are not interested in learning in the conventional way."

Under Juniata's newly revised general education curriculum, all students complete coursework in five "Ways of Knowing" (creative expression, formal reasoning, humanistic thought, social inquiry, and scientific process), as well as classes focusing on civic responsibility. As juniors or seniors, students take an Interdisciplinary Inquiry course, which is team-taught by faculty from different departments. Every student creates a personal portfolio in their first semester demonstrating their knowledge, skills, and personal reflections, which they continue to build and develop throughout their four years.

In lieu of preset majors, Juniata has flexible Programs of Emphasis (POEs). Each student works with two advisors to either shape an existing POE to fit their academic

Website: www.juniata.edu
Location: Small Town
Private
Total Enrollment: 1,374
Undergraduates: 1,366
Male/Female: 44/56
SAT Ranges: ERW 540–650, M 540–640
ACT Ranges: 23–29
Financial Aid: 98%
Pell Grant: 30%
Expense: Pr $ $
Student Loans: 70%
Average Debt: $ $ $ $
Applicants: 2,289
Accepted: 71%
Enrolled: 21%
Grad in 6 Years: 75%
Returning Freshmen: 81%
Academics: ✍ ✍ ✍
Social: 🐾 🐾 🐾
Q of L: ★ ★ ★
Admissions: (877) 586-4282
Email Address: admissions@juniata.edu

Strong Programs:
Biology

Every student creates a personal portfolio in their first semester that they continue to develop throughout their four years.

On Mountain Day, classes are canceled for the day and students attend outdoor activities at Raystown Lake.

interests or to create an entirely new program. Approximately one-third of students take the latter path, designing their own customized POE. Of the more than 50 established POEs, some of the most popular are biology, business, marketing, chemistry, and integrated media arts. Strong offerings in environmental science and wildlife conservation are enhanced by the college's field station at nearby Raystown Lake. "Juniata has long been known as a school for the natural sciences," confirms a senior. In addition, peace and conflict studies is one of the oldest and most comprehensive programs of its kind in the United States, and includes study abroad opportunities and internships. Museum studies teaches students how to curate art (and provides internships at prestigious galleries around the nation), while the Center for Entrepreneurial Leadership bestows $15,000 in seed capital to budding business leaders.

"Juniata challenges its students to think critically about what they are learning and why it is important," says a secondary education math major. "We work hard, there is no doubt about that, but we are not overworked." Seventy percent of classes have fewer than 20 students, which allows for plenty of interaction between professors and students. The Inbound program allows new students to spend a week on campus as part of a particular club or activity in order to "make their first few days of immersion into college life easier," according to one student. Juniata has international exchange/study abroad agreements with colleges and universities in 22 countries, and 42 percent of all Juniata students go abroad. About 55 percent of students get involved in faculty-guided undergraduate research projects. The annual Liberal Arts Symposium features student research presentations, art exhibitions, and a Multicultural Storyfest, where international students share stories from their home cultures.

Sixty-two percent of Juniata students hail from Pennsylvania, and 8 percent come from foreign nations. African Americans comprise 3 percent of the student body, Asian Americans 4 percent, Hispanics 5 percent, and multiracial students 3 percent. A junior comments that while the school is still working to increase racial diversity, it has also "put a lot more effort into making people of color feel welcome." Although the campus leans left, students report that all viewpoints are represented and respected.

"[Juniata has] put a lot more effort into making people of color feel welcome."

"Compared to schools in New England, we're Bible-thumpers, whereas compared to schools in the South, we're socialists," quips one student. Hundreds of merit scholarships are available, averaging $23,000, but there are no athletic scholarships. Thirty percent of freshmen are eligible for the Pell Grant.

Eighty-two percent of students currently live on campus, although that number is growing as Juniata transitions to a four-year on-campus residency requirement. "Some dorms are newer, some are bigger, but they're all good," says a sophomore. Living/learning communities like the Global Village are a popular option. For grub, Juniata provides two main dining facilities, one buffet-style and one where meals are made to order, as well as several à la carte stops around campus. Students say their rural location feels safe. A sophomore reports that the recently opened SPoT (Safe Place to Talk), which is "one of the first places students go to talk about being a victim of or witness to sexual assault," is proving to be an effective source of support.

"Without barriers such as Greek life, students at Juniata are able to cross different boundaries and interact with those who may be completely different from themselves," says a senior. Social life is mostly on campus, and activities include live bands, trivia shows, poker tournaments, dinners, and dances. Students of legal age may drink on campus, and students say that while the enforcement of alcohol policies is fairly lenient, the drinking and party culture is low-key. Students enjoy a number of traditions, including Madrigal Dinner and Mountain Day, on which classes are canceled for the day and students attend outdoor activities at Raystown Lake ("Food, carnival games, kayaking, Slip 'N Slides, and the president's dog with a GoPro on—it is a great time," says a junior). Students also take part in the "storming of the arch," in which "freshmen attempt to run into an arch defended by the rugby team," explains a student. Huntingdon (population 7,000) is "a relatively small place for a college," says one student, but does provide the basic necessities, as well as several restaurants, a movie theater, and a Mayfest street fair. Community service is popular, as are road trips to Penn State (40 minutes away), Baltimore, Philadelphia, and Pittsburgh.

The Juniata Eagles compete in Division III and have earned 55 conference championships and eight national titles. The most successful sports include men's and women's volleyball, men's tennis, and field hockey. Juniata students also have the chance to participate in a variety of club, intramural, and individual activities; the Quidditch club and men's and women's rugby clubs are among the most popular.

Although students sometimes complain about the limitations of attending a small college in a small town, most seem excited to be part of such an inviting academic institution. Those seeking "big football games, raging frat parties, and a vibrant urban setting" should look elsewhere, a senior observes. However, "if you are more interested in an intensive and personal academic environment with an extremely tight-knit and supportive community, then Juniata is the place for you."

If You Apply To ›

Juniata: Early decision, early action, regular decision. SATs or ACTs: optional. Subject Tests: optional. Accepts the Common Application.

Kalamazoo College

1200 Academy Street, Kalamazoo, MI 49006

Kalamazoo is a small liberal arts school that opens up the world to its students—literally. An impressive 70 percent of students study abroad thanks to the ingenious K-Plan, a curriculum that allows them to study abroad for up to three academic terms. And if you need an extra boost to round out that résumé, there is an extensive career development program.

Kalamazoo College is a small school in America's heartland. But college subsidies enable the majority of students to go abroad during their years here, making the school a launching pad to the world. In addition to international education, the school's K-Plan emphasizes teaching, internships, and independent, faculty-guided research. Students are exposed to a demanding academic schedule and high expectations from faculty, but they say it's well worth the challenge. "Students at K really care about their studies," says an international and area studies major. "We enjoy writing, we enjoy discussion, and we enjoy critical thinking and inquiry."

Life on Kalamazoo's wooded, 60-acre campus centers on the Quad, a green lawn where students ponder their destinies and play ultimate Frisbee with equal ease. With its rolling hills, Georgian architecture, and brick-laid streets, the campus has the quaint look more typical of historic New England than of the nearby city

Website: www.kzoo.edu
Location: Small City
Private
Total Enrollment: 1,406
Undergraduates: 1,406
Male/Female: 43/57
SAT Ranges: ERW 600–690, M 580–690
ACT Ranges: 26–30
Financial Aid: 98%
Pell Grant: 26%

Seventy-one percent of students participate in career development programs like internships, externships, and K-Trek trips.

of Kalamazoo, which, with surrounding communities, has 335,000 residents. The school recently opened a 30,000-square-foot fitness and wellness center.

Founded in 1833 and formerly associated with the American Baptist Churches, Kalamazoo is the oldest private college in Michigan. Many first-years begin the year with a LandSea trip, which includes three weeks of climbing, rappelling, canoeing, and backpacking in the mountains of the Adirondacks. By the end, they're convinced they can survive anything, including the rigors of a Kalamazoo education and the long Michigan winters. Once on campus, they pursue a liberal arts curriculum that includes language proficiency, a first-year writing seminar, sophomore and senior seminars, as well as a senior individualized project—directed research, a creative piece, or a traditional thesis—basically anything that caps off each student's education in some meaningful way.

After their sophomore year, most of Kalamazoo's undergrads meet life's challenges with suitcase in hand, studying wherever their heart takes them, for the regular tuition price. The college offers three-, six-, and nine-month immersive study abroad programs that are available to all students, regardless of major; all credit earned during study abroad transfers back to Kalamazoo. "I studied abroad in Clermont-Ferrand, France, for nine months. I went to a French university, lived with a French family, and was completely immersed in French culture. It was a huge learning and growing experience," says one student. Seventy percent of students study abroad via 45 programs in 22 countries.

> "We enjoy writing, we enjoy discussion, and we enjoy critical thinking and inquiry."

Back on campus, students say the accelerated pace of Kalamazoo's three 10-week terms can make things stressful, but one senior reflects that the academic environment "has taught me to manage my time better and to ask for help when I need it." The natural sciences are exceptionally good—chemistry and biology are among the most popular majors—and interdisciplinary programs in international and area studies, community and global health, and critical ethnic studies are also strengths. Students heap praise on the psychology, economics and business, English, and language departments. Professors, rated highly for their enthusiasm and accessibility, give students lots of individual attention. A junior notes, "Professors here are also doing research or work in their fields, so you may be able to work in a professor's lab during the school year or summer, or hear about their clinical practice in psychology, or learn about the process of writing a book." Seventy-one percent of students participate in career development programs like internships, externships, and K-Trek trips to visit industries around the country.

"Everybody here has a certain amount of weirdness to them, and we love each other for it," says one student. Sixty-one percent of students come from Michigan and 6 percent from foreign nations. The student body is 8 percent African American, 13 percent Hispanic, 8 percent Asian American, and 4 percent multiracial. Many Kalamazoo students crave more diversity on campus. The administration says it is continuing efforts to educate students on intercultural understanding, and the campus has a decidedly progressive tone. "Students here are not afraid to state their opinions and push for what they want and believe the school needs," offers one biology major. Twenty-six percent of incoming students qualify for Pell Grants, and merit scholarships averaging $22,000 are available to qualified students. Athletic scholarships are not available.

> "Professors here are also doing research or work in their fields."

Sixty percent of students live on campus. "The dorms are older and they don't look new on the inside, but they are ridiculously spacious," a student explains. With so many students away each term thanks to the study abroad program, a certain instability pervades all activities, from athletics to student government to living groups in the co-ed residence halls, where suites hold one to six students. Dorms are divided by class year, and three dorms are available for first-year students. Dining services get mixed reviews. For those who tire of campus life, "Off-campus housing is both cheap and located close to campus, so it is a popular option," says a sophomore. While there are no Greek organizations at Kalamazoo, 10 living/learning houses offer a more community-oriented atmosphere, including family-style dinners.

"There are always tons of things to do on campus, like movies, concerts, speakers, and events," an economics major reports. A senior notes that although "drinking and partying does happen at Kalamazoo, I have never felt pressure to do so," and another student describes the school as "a very safe environment." Students look forward to the Monte Carlo casino night, homecoming, Spring Fling, and the Day of Gracious Living, a spring day where, without prior warning, classes are canceled and students relax by taking day trips or helping beautify the campus. (One popular T-shirt: "The end of learning is gracious living.") About two-thirds of students get involved in the community through service-learning courses and student-led

"Students here are not afraid to…push for what they want and believe the school needs."

cocurricular activities, working with local partners to address issues such as neighborhood development, sustainability, prison reform, and migrant rights. The city of Kalamazoo is a "fun city with lots going on," according to one political science major. In addition to the typical collection of restaurants, theaters, and bars, Kalamazoo students benefit from the physical proximity of colleges such as Western Michigan University, where they may use the library or attend cultural events. Lake Michigan's beaches and Chicago's urban playground are easy road trips for students with cars.

For those who equate college with athletics, Kalamazoo has something to offer—even if it's not nationally televised games or tens of thousands of screaming fans. The Kalamazoo Hornets have a long-standing rivalry with Hope College, culminating in the football teams' annual competition for the Wooden Shoes trophy, where the Hornets are cheered on by fans known as "the stingers." Kalamazoo also has an outstanding men's tennis team, which won the conference championship in 2017 and 2018, after enjoying a streak of 74 (!) consecutive conference titles that ended in 2013, as well as seven national championships. The baseball, women's tennis, and men's and women's swimming and soccer squads are also highly competitive. Fifty percent of students participate in intramural sports.

Kalamazoo is best suited for those "looking for a place where everyone is really enthusiastic about learning and thrives in that kind of environment," says one student. A classmate adds that it can be tough for students to "find a balance between the academic life and recreation." The study abroad program may be somewhat disruptive to campus life, but Kalamazoo offers students a truly global education.

Overlaps

Hope, Albion, College of Wooster, University of Michigan, Michigan State, U of I at Urbana–Champaign, Grand Valley State, Western Michigan

If You Apply To ›

Kalamazoo: Early decision I and II, early action, regular decision. SATs or ACTs: optional. Subject Tests: optional. Accepts the Common Application with optional writing supplement.

University of Kansas

1502 Iowa Street, Lawrence, KS 66045

Often overlooked because of its heartland location, KU has the sophistication of the leading Big Ten universities but is much easier to get into. Stereotypes of Kansas to the contrary, Lawrence is not flat as a pancake. Offers a solid slate of professional schools and an honors program that is among the nation's best. Jayhawk basketball is legendary.

Despite its conservative Midwest location, the University of Kansas is a welcoming oasis of progressive activism and tolerance. The school courts extremely dedicated students with an impressive honors program that has helped raise its academic profile. With sound academics and extracurriculars, winning athletics, and a stellar social life, the University of Kansas has a bounty of opportunities for motivated Jayhawks. "You name it, we have it," cheers one satisfied junior.

The 1,000-acre campus is set atop Mount Oread—a hill that was once a crossing point for pioneer wagon trains—and spreads out on rolling green hills overlooking river valleys. Many of the buildings are made of indigenous Kansas limestone and are famed for their red roofs. But the real beauty of the campus lies in its landscape, particularly the breathtaking autumn foliage. The Dole Institute of Politics is home to one of the world's largest congressional archives and a World Trade Center memorial. A massive, $350 million expansion of the campus's Central District was completed in 2018 and features a new Integrated Sciences Building, a student union, and a 700-bed apartment complex, among other facilities.

Prospective KU freshmen may apply to the schools of Architecture, Business, Engineering, Journalism and Mass Communications, and Music, and to the College of Liberal Arts & Sciences. Those not admitted to one of the professional schools will automatically be considered for admission to the College, where nearly 60 percent of the undergraduate population is enrolled. Students wishing to enter the schools of Education, Health Professions, Nursing, Pharmacy, and Social Welfare must pass prerequisite courses and meet the schools' entry requirements. All KU undergraduates must complete a university-wide curriculum as part of their degrees; this curriculum, the KU Core, spans the entire undergraduate experience.

> **"There isn't a time at KU where your academics and instruction are not made a top priority."**

Some of the most notable undergraduate programs offered by KU's 13 schools include architecture, design, education, journalism, music, social work, and health-related majors. The School of Journalism and Mass Communications perpetuates the legacy of famed journalist William Allen White, and the School of Engineering has significantly expanded its resources and facilities, most recently opening the interdisciplinary Earth, Energy, and Environment Center in 2018. Business, health professions, engineering, and journalism are the most popular majors. New accelerated bachelor's/master's programs in several fields, ranging from environmental studies/urban planning to history of art, allow students to earn two degrees in five years.

Forty-seven percent of all undergraduate classes have fewer than 20 students, and a religious studies major says, "I have never felt that I couldn't reach out to other students for help." While TAs do teach some classes, students often have access to leading professors early on. "My calculus course freshman year was taught by the head of the math department—showing that there isn't a time at KU where your academics and instruction are not made a top priority," says an architecture major.

Website: www.ku.edu
Location: Small City
Public
Total Enrollment: 22,783
Undergraduates: 17,046
Male/Female: 49/51
SAT Ranges: N/A
ACT Ranges: 23–28
Financial Aid: 68%
Pell Grant: 23%
Expense: Pub $ $
Student Loans: 50%
Average Debt: $ $
Applicants: 14,538
Accepted: 93%
Enrolled: 31%
Grad in 6 Years: 63%
Returning Freshmen: 83%
Academics: ✍ ✍ ✍ ✍
Social: ☎ ☎ ☎ ☎
Q of L: ★ ★ ★ ★
Admissions: (785) 864-3911
Email Address: adm@ku.edu

Strong Programs:
Business
Health Professions
Engineering
Journalism
Architecture
Design
Education
Social Work

The Office of Student Affairs, run by its own vice provost, wins praise for its academic advising and for its help with internships, disability services, and extracurriculars.

Incoming freshmen can apply to the highly selective University Honors Program, which provides 1,600 academically motivated students with challenging courses, special advising, tutorials, and opportunities for scholarships and research grants. Independent study and certificate programs are also options, and 29 percent of undergrads leave U.S. borders for 165 KU-administered study abroad programs in more than 50 countries, including Costa Rica, Ireland, Italy, Japan, and South Africa. KU provides several region-specific area study programs supported by instruction in more than 40 languages.

The highly selective University Honors Program provides 1,600 students with special advising, tutorials, and opportunities for research grants.

"Proud and passionate. These two words invoke to me what it means to be a Jayhawk," says one student. Sixty-six percent of undergrads are from Kansas, and most of the rest are fellow Midwesterners (many from Chicago), although 6 percent are international. African Americans account for 4 percent, Hispanics 8 percent, Asian Americans 5 percent, and multiracial students 5 percent. KU has a history of progressive attitudes, but conservative views are well represented on campus too. One senior says, "KU allows all voices to be heard, and that has caused tension at times," but students agree that the campus atmosphere is for the most part "welcoming and inclusive," in the words of an engineering student. KU grants four-year renewable merit scholarships to eligible freshmen, and athletes vie for 339 scholarships in 18 sports. Twenty-three percent of freshmen are Pell-eligible, and for those who also meet certain academic criteria, the KU Pell Advantage program provides a combination of scholarships and grants to fund students' tuition and fees.

"Lawrence is *the* American college town. Period."

Twenty-six percent of Kansas students live in KU residence halls, scholarship halls, or on-campus apartments; five new residential facilities have been built since 2015. Most students live off campus in Lawrence apartments, which are considered expensive only by Kansas standards. Three dining complexes provide extended-hour access to food-court-style dining, and the campus also offers 16 retail cafés and snack shops, along with a full-service restaurant. "The food is a good mix of different cuisines and is also healthy and nutritious," says a junior. One student explains, "KU Saferide and Safebus provide transportation for late at night, while Lawrence police and university police constantly patrol the streets." Additionally, the Sexual Assault Prevention and Education Center conducts training on consent and bystander intervention.

Five new residential facilities have been built since 2015.

The Greek system, which attracts 20 percent of the men and 28 percent of the women, is a conspicuous force in the social scene, but doesn't control it. Hard alcohol is not allowed in fraternity properties, and no alcohol of any kind is allowed in sorority properties. According to an accounting major, "The party culture is whatever students want to participate in (big, small, or none at all)." On campus, more than 600 organized groups keep things lively; other activities include movies, poetry readings, and concerts. Scholarship halls, residence halls, and other student groups also sponsor large campus parties and events. The university's bus system is much appreciated by tenderfeet, especially because that great big hill seems to double in size during the cold, windy winters.

"The Rock Chalk chant… creat[es] a sort of bond between all Jayhawks, past and present."

With its myriad boutiques, restaurants, and bars and its active music scene, Lawrence is a favored destination for off-campus fun, and students also enjoy getting involved in the community through KU's Center for Community Outreach. "Lawrence is *the* American college town," says one enthusiastic Jayhawk. "Period." Topeka, the state capital, and Kansas City are each less than an hour's drive, and the area is also served by Amtrak.

After winning its 14th straight conference title in 2018, the men's basketball team advanced to the NCAA Final Four.

KU varsity teams—the only ones in the nation that carry the name Jayhawks—compete in the rough-and-tumble Big 12 Conference. At least nine KU teams have advanced to NCAA postseason competition every year since 2013, including women's volleyball and men's and women's track and field. After winning its 14th straight conference title in 2018, the men's basketball team made its 29th consecutive appearance in the national tournament (an NCAA record), advancing to the Final Four. James Naismith, who invented basketball, was KU's first coach—and the only one with a losing record. Fourteen percent of students take part in 31 sports clubs and 32 intramural sports, the most popular of which is—you guessed it—basketball, which signs up more than 125 teams.

Jayhawk traditions certainly run deep. The school year kicks off with Hawk Week, the official welcome for new students. To demonstrate their loyalty to the Jayhawks, thousands of students show up for the first men's and women's basketball practices of the season. This nocturnal tradition is lovingly labeled "Late Night in the Phog"—an allusion to the late, great coach Phog Allen. The traditional "Rock Chalk Jayhawk" KU cheer and steam whistle signaling the end of every class period are enough to bring a pang of nostalgia to the heart of even the most grizzled Kansas alum. "The Rock Chalk chant is widely recognizable, creating a sort of bond between all Jayhawks, past and present," says one student.

With nearly 50 nationally ranked academic programs, Kansas's reputation (the nonbasketball one) continues to grow. Comprehensive study abroad programs, a distinctive honors program, and a robust sense of school spirit are just some of the reasons students choose to be Jayhawks. "To put it simply," says one proud student, "greatness is our greatest tradition."

Overlaps

University of Missouri, SUNY–Buffalo, Indiana University, Michigan State, University of Oregon, University of Iowa, Kansas State, UT Austin

If You Apply To ›

Kansas: Rolling admissions. SATs or ACTs: required. No Subject Tests. Accepts the Common Application. Apply to particular school or program.

University of Kentucky

100 Funkhouser Building, Lexington, KY 40506

The state of Kentucky is better known for horses and hoops than for higher education, but its flagship public university, located in the heart of the Bluegrass, is working to change that. The University of Kentucky is always a championship contender on the basketball court, but its programs in business, engineering, health, and anything equine are just as competitive. About a third of students come from out of state, mostly from Illinois, Indiana, Ohio, Tennessee, and Georgia.

Website: www.uky.edu
Location: City Center
Public
Total Enrollment: 26,317
Undergraduates: 20,611
Male/Female: 45/55

While the University of Kentucky Wildcats grab the most headlines, the university's claims to excellence stretch into outstanding medical and premedical programs, scientific research involving both professors and students, and a social calendar packed so full of Southern tradition that it would make even the most composed debutante's head spin. Over the last decade, UK has undergone a more than $2.3 billion campus transformation, much of it focused on student life, including more than $450 million in high-tech residence halls and the new Gatton Student Center, complete with dining and a state-of-the-art fitness center. UK is a national leader in efforts to support first-generation college students and has established a dedicated living/learning community for them.

The University of Kentucky campus contains a mixture of old and new, with traditional redbrick buildings that date back to the late 1890s and modern designs using contemporary glass and concrete. The well-maintained grounds are organized around comfortable parklike spaces influenced by Frederick Law Olmsted's design. The campus contains a vast amount of mature trees and lawns set in a natural arrangement of open spaces, typical of the great land grant universities. Of course, UK's location in the heart of one of the finest horse-breeding areas in the world makes it a natural place for the Gluck Equine Research Center, a headquarters for research into horse diseases.

UK's general education program, known as the UK Core, comprises the equivalent of 30 credit hours in 10 course areas that address four broad learning outcomes. Freshmen are encouraged, but not required, to take an academic orientation class called UK101, designed to help them adjust to college life. Students not ready to declare a major may test the academic waters in "Exploratory Programs" in a particular college. Business, engineering, and health, especially nursing and premed programs, tend to be UK's strongest fields, but several unique programs stand out. The equine science and management major prepares students for a wide range of careers in the horse industry by teaching both science and business concepts. Students studying prevet and animal sciences at UK will find coveted slots reserved for them at Auburn and Tuskegee in the advanced veterinary medicine program, at in-state tuition rates. UK's Gaines Center for the Humanities is unusual in its study of public higher education, and the Patterson School of Diplomacy and International Commerce is one of the smallest yet most respected schools of its type in the country. The new Lewis Honors College is housed in a dedicated quad of residence halls.

> "I've had many professors whose lectures made me excited to go to class."

The academic climate is laid-back, but students shouldn't expect easy As. About a third of classes have fewer than 20 students, but lower-level "monster" science classes are common, and one student describes them as "extremely large and not at all personalized." When it comes time for course registration, a marketing major says students "have difficulty if they are freshmen, because most of them have to take the same classes, and sometimes they don't get the right times—or the classes at all." It's hard to complete the engineering, health, business, and architecture programs in four years, students say. Term-time internships, known as co-ops, also complicate— but enliven—the picture. The university recently bolstered its advising services in order to provide more personalized attention and to better coordinate career and academic services. Teaching assistants and full professors teach about the same number of freshman classes, and students praise UK's faculty. "I've had many professors whose lectures made me excited to go to class," says a communication sciences and disorders major. Eighteen percent of students study abroad in more than 200 available programs, including 55 that are directed by UK faculty.

> "Students get really nice amenities, like Tempur-Pedic mattresses, granite countertops, two sinks, and full-size closets."

"UK students are typically self-assured, slightly competitive, and outgoing," says a psychology major, and according to a classmate, "Southern hospitality abounds." UK undergraduates hail from all 120 Kentucky counties and more than 100 countries; 31 percent are from out of state and 3 percent are international. The student body is predominantly white; African Americans account for 8 percent of students, Hispanics 5 percent, Asian Americans 3 percent, and multiracial students 4 percent. Diverse political views are represented on campus, but a senior says UK is "not

(continued)

SAT Ranges: ERW 550–660, M 530–670
ACT Ranges: 22–28
Financial Aid: 78%
Pell Grant: 24%
Expense: Pub $ $ $
Student Loans: 54%
Average Debt: $ $ $ $
Applicants: 18,925
Accepted: 96%
Enrolled: 26%
Grad in 6 Years: 61%
Returning Freshmen: 83%
Academics: ✍ ✍ ✍
Social: ☎ ☎ ☎ ☎
Q of L: ★ ★ ★
Admissions: (859) 257-2000
Email Address: admissions@ uky.edu

Strong Programs:
Business
Engineering
Nursing
Premed
Equine Science and Management
Prevet
Education
International Studies

UK has undergone a more than $2.3 billion campus transformation, much of it focused on student life.

really a politically charged university." Twenty-four percent of freshmen receive Pell Grants. Merit scholarships averaging $9,500 are offered to qualified students, as are more than 500 athletic scholarships.

The university has modernized all of its residence halls and opened 14 new ones in recent years. Dorms are located on three parts of the campus—north, central, and south. The north and central campuses offer suite-style rooms, with no more than four students sharing a bathroom. "Students get really nice amenities, like Tempur-Pedic mattresses, granite countertops, two sinks, and full-size closets," reports a student. The only downside of such plush accommodations, students say, is the cost. Students are not required to live on campus, but 33 percent do so. Dining services get good reviews, and a communication major says, "There are so many options from sit-down, buffet-style to specialty cafés to fast food," as well as "worry-free zones" for students with dietary restrictions. The Green Dot Bystander Intervention program, designed to prevent sexual assault and domestic violence on college campuses, originated at the University of Kentucky and has been adopted by hundreds of colleges and universities across the country.

On campus, students enjoy movies, presentations, seminars, concerts, and athletic events. Nineteen percent of Kentucky men and 31 percent of the women go Greek, and fraternities and sororities offer numerous on-campus social activities, as well as opportunities for volunteer work in the community. Students are not allowed to have alcohol on campus, except for special events that have been registered with the university. Students collaborate to mount one of the largest student-run philanthropies anywhere: DanceBlue. The yearlong fund-raising effort culminates in a 24-hour, no-sleeping dance marathon that benefits local children's health charities. Among the highlights of any student's career at UK are two one-month periods—one in the fall, one in the spring—when students spend afternoons at Keeneland Race Track enjoying the tradition of Kentucky horse racing.

> "[UK] has the competitive energy of the SEC, but it's not an overly Greek-focused campus."

Students collaborate to mount one of the largest student-run philanthropies anywhere: DanceBlue.

Despite the limited diversity on campus, Lexington abounds with a multitude of ethnic eateries, as well as theaters, shops, and nightspots. The downtown area is within walking distance of campus. "Downtown Lexington has a great social scene, so lots of students will venture off-campus for concerts, restaurants, festivals, farmers markets, etc.," says a senior. When it's time for a road trip, UK students head to Cincinnati or Louisville (one hour away), or to Atlanta or Chicago (six hours).

The best road-trip destinations, of course, are anywhere there's a steamy, noisy gym and a basketball team ready to do battle with UK's always-solid Wildcats. Home games at the legendary Rupp Arena—what one student calls "a magical experience"—are consistently packed by the Big Blue Nation. "In Kentucky, basketball is like a second religion," agrees another true-blue Wildcat fan. Football and women's basketball draw crowds too. The school fields 21 Division I teams in all, most of which compete in the Southeastern Conference (SEC). Intramurals range from soccer and basketball leagues to dodgeball tournaments and hot-shot contests.

"The culture of UK is unique because it has the competitive energy of the SEC, but it's not an overly Greek-focused campus and it does a great job of supporting every interest," comments a senior. Indeed, students here find plenty of solid opportunities, from specialties in equine and animal science to support for first-generation students to serious school pride. Whether it's screaming yourself hoarse for five guys hitting the hardwood or for four-legged equines racing around an oval, for many students, the mix of collegiate craziness and old-world Southern hospitality found at the University of Kentucky is just what they want.

Overlaps

Indiana University, University of Louisville, Miami University (OH), Ohio State, University of Tennessee

If You Apply To ›

Kentucky: Early action, regular decision. SATs or ACTs: required. No Subject Tests. Accepts the Common Application.

Kenyon College

Ransom Hall, Gambier, OH 43022

Kenyon is a vintage liberal arts college plunked down in the middle of the Ohio countryside. More mainstream than Oberlin, more serious than Denison, and more selective than Wooster, Kenyon is best known for English and a small but distinguished drama program. Located in a tiny village where faculty and staff are the main residents. Swimming and diving teams make huge splashes.

Kenyon College provides students with an accessible and pure liberal arts experience that rivals those of leading East Coast institutions. Students here are proud of what they see as setting Kenyon apart from other liberal arts colleges. "The one thing that unites us all is that we are passionate about something," explains one student. "Whether it be drama, physics, writing, activism—Kenyon students care!" Though highly selective, the college continues to build on its reputation as a supportive academic environment.

The oldest private college in Ohio, Kenyon's 1,200-acre campus sits on a hillside overlooking a scenic view of river, woods, and fields in a secluded village of roughly 600 residents. The college's original building, Old Kenyon, dating from 1826, is said to be the first collegiate Gothic building in America, and the campus is on the National Register of Historic Places. The campus also includes a 480-acre nature preserve, featuring hiking trails and extensive perennial gardens. Newer facilities include the Wright Center, which houses a state-of-the-art film center and the Office for Community Partnerships.

The hallmark of Kenyon's academic philosophy is a fierce devotion to the liberal arts and sciences. While there is no core curriculum at Kenyon, all students must have proficiency in a second language and complete requirements in quantitative reasoning. A bevy of academic counselors, including upperclassmen and professors, help ensure that freshmen stay on the right track. The culmination of each student's coursework at Kenyon is the senior exercise, which may take the form of a comprehensive examination, an integrative paper, a research project, a performance, or some combination of these. Approximately 12 percent of students graduate with departmental honors.

> "Whether it be drama, physics, writing, activism—Kenyon students care!"

English, a nationally renowned subject at Kenyon since the 1930s, is the most popular major, and it, along with the drama department (which turned out actors Allison Janney and Paul Newman), sets the tone of campus life. Kenyon is the home of the *Kenyon Review*, a prestigious literary quarterly that offers internships to a few lucky students, and is a school about which alum E. L. Doctorow said, "Poetry is what we did at Kenyon, the way at Ohio State they played football." John Green, the giant of young adult fiction, is also an alum. Economics, political science, psychology, and biology round out the list of popular majors, and the modern languages and literatures and mathematics and statistics departments are also strong. Political science draws many undecided majors with its yearlong introductory class, Quest for Justice. The Integrated Program in Humane Studies concentration, the school's oldest interdisciplinary

Website: www.kenyon.edu
Location: Rural
Private
Total Enrollment: 1,661
Undergraduates: 1,661
Male/Female: 44/56
SAT Ranges: ERW 640–730, M 623–730
ACT Ranges: 29–35
Financial Aid: 40%
Pell Grant: 9%
Expense: Pr $ $ $ $
Student Loans: 40%
Average Debt: $
Applicants: 5,603
Accepted: 34%
Enrolled: 24%
Grad in 6 Years: 91%
Returning Freshmen: 93%
Academics: ✎ ✎ ✎ ✎
Social: ☎ ☎ ☎
Q of L: ★ ★ ★
Admissions: (800) 848-2468
Email Address: admissions@kenyon.edu

Strong Programs:
English
Drama
Economics
Political Science
Psychology
Biology
Modern Languages and Literatures
Mathematics and Statistics

program, is also popular. Opportunities for independent study abound, such as a unique farming program that places students on nearby farms for fieldwork each week. Preprofessional opportunities include 3–2 engineering programs with several universities and high access to graduate programs in law, business, and medicine.

"Despite the academic rigor of many classes and departments at Kenyon, I have never felt competitive with my fellow students," says a psychology major. Classes are small, and even the larger introductory courses use a two-part format in which students meet for lectures one week and split up for discussion sections with the professor the next. "Kenyon's professors are active researchers and exemplary teachers," says a math major. "They are passionate about their fields, and they love getting their students excited about the material as well." Many profs live close to campus, which enhances the close-knit environment. On-campus summer research scholarships in the sciences and humanities provide opportunities for collaborative research for aspiring scientists, scholars, and doctors. Roughly half of Kenyon students take part in study abroad, choosing from more than 150 programs in more than 50 countries, including Kenyon-sponsored programs in England and Italy.

> "I have never felt competitive with my fellow students."

The college's original building, Old Kenyon, dating from 1826, is said to be the first collegiate Gothic building in America.

Twelve percent of students are Ohioans, one-third hail from New England and Mid-Atlantic states, and 6 percent come from abroad. African Americans account for 3 percent of the student body, Hispanics 6 percent, Asian Americans 3 percent, and multiracial students 7 percent, and the college is actively working to increase diversity. The liberal, friendly student body is politically engaged, especially when it comes to social justice issues, and a sophomore says, "Students at Kenyon thrive on open conversation and do not silence opinions that contradict theirs." Kenyon meets the full demonstrated financial need of admitted students and awards merit scholarships averaging $16,600, but only 9 percent of incoming freshmen qualify for the Pell Grant. Newman's Own Foundation Scholarships guarantee a loan-free education for 25 selected students with the greatest need who bring the qualities of creativity, community service, and leadership to Kenyon.

All students live on campus, with housing guaranteed for four years. Freshmen start in five dorms at the north end of campus, and most move to the south end the next year. Renovations and expansions are always in the works, but students say some accommodations still need improving. Rooms are selected via a sometimes harrowing housing lottery. Everyone, including those in the apartments with kitchens, must buy the unlimited meal plan. "Kenyon is in an isolated area of Ohio, and is generally very safe," a senior says. The college has adopted a new Title IX policy and hired a civil rights coordinator to enforce it.

> "Kenyon's professors are active researchers and exemplary teachers."

Given the school's rural location, social life happens on campus, with more than 100 student clubs and a Greek system that draws 27 percent of the men and 32 percent of the women. The frats throw lively parties that are open to all, and a senior says, "Every student performance—sports games, public presentations, music recitals, art shows—is incredibly well attended." With its deli, market, coffeehouse, inn, restaurant, couple of bars, bank, and post office, Gambier is at least quaint, even if it is a bit of a culture shock for urbanites. Students enjoy buying real maple syrup, fresh bread, and cheese from Amish farmers with stands on the main street on Saturdays. There are a few more options 10 minutes away in Mount Vernon, to which the college runs a daytime shuttle bus, and two small ski areas lie near campus. Columbus and Ohio State are a 45-minute drive south, and those seeking adventure farther from home sometimes road-trip to Cleveland (home of the Rock and Roll Hall of Fame), Cincinnati, Chicago, or even Canada.

Kenyon is the home of the Kenyon Review, a prestigious literary quarterly that offers internships to a few lucky students.

Kenyon remains defined by its traditions, the most hallowed of which is renewed each year as incoming freshmen sing college songs to the rest of the community from the steps of Rosse Hall. Departing seniors sing the same songs at graduation. On Matriculation Day each October, after a formal ceremony, freshmen sign a book that contains the signatures of virtually every Kenyon student since the early 1800s. Summer Sendoff is an outdoor concert celebrating the end of spring semester classes.

Kenyon's varsity teams are known as the Lords and the Ladies. Men's and women's tennis and soccer are consistently competitive, but the flagship sport is definitely swimming. Kenyon's swimming and diving teams dominate Division III competition, with the men's team having won 34 national titles. Kenyon was instrumental in establishing the North Coast Athletic Conference, which includes a number of academically strong Midwestern schools. The annual hockey game against Denison and soccer games against Ohio Wesleyan draw large crowds. Club and intramural sports attract about a third of the students and sponsor everything from ultimate Frisbee to ballroom dance.

Kenyon students are liberal, global thinkers who are as devoted to one another as they are to their studies and their traditions. The *Kenyon Review*, the legend of alumnus Paul Newman, and national-championship swimming give the college an identity that's hard to match. As one sociology major advises, "It can be tough at times dealing with the location or the intense academics, but if students embrace Kenyon, it is a quirky school that can be extremely rewarding to attend."

Overlaps

Swarthmore, Williams, Hamilton, University of Chicago, Amherst, Oberlin, Middlebury, Brown

If You Apply To ›

Kenyon: Early decision I and II, regular decision. SATs or ACTs: required. Subject Tests: optional. Accepts the Common Application.

Knox College

2 East South Street, Galesburg, IL 61401

This friendly and progressive Illinois college was among the first in the nation to admit African Americans and women. Offers a strong writing program and exceptional sciences. More mainstream than Beloit and Grinnell and smaller than Illinois Wesleyan. With a hugely diverse student body of about 1,300, Knox offers an unusual degree of personal attention, even by the standards of small colleges.

With the unconventional Prairie Fire as its emblem, Knox College has long made a name for itself by breaking away from the conventions of the day. Founded by abolitionists in 1837 as the Knox Manual Labor College, this liberal arts college has a tradition of debate that extends beyond the Lincoln–Douglas event that occurred here in 1858. And through a warm, supportive academic community and emphasis on "putting knowledge into practice through real-world experiences," the college continues to foster a strong sense of individualism.

Located in the heart of the Midwest—almost midway between Chicago and St. Louis—the 82-acre campus has spacious, tree-lined lawns and a dynamic mixture of architecture that reflects the 160-year span of construction dates of existing buildings. Old Main, constructed in 1857, is a National Historic Landmark and the only building remaining from the 1858 Lincoln–Douglas debates. The Whitcomb Art

Website: www.knox.edu
Location: Small Town
Private
Total Enrollment: 1,334
Undergraduates: 1,334
Male/Female: 43/57
SAT Ranges: ERW 560–670, M 580–695
ACT Ranges: 23–30
Financial Aid: 99%
Pell Grant: 32%

(continued)

Expense: Pr $ $
Student Loans: 60%
Average Debt: $ $ $
Applicants: 3,222
Accepted: 72%
Enrolled: 15%
Grad in 6 Years: 76%
Returning Freshmen: 87%
Academics: ✑ ✑ ✑
Social: ☎ ☎ ☎
Q of L: ★ ★ ★
Admissions: (800) 678-KNOX
Email Address: admission@
   knox.edu

Strong Programs:
Creative Writing
Biology
Economics
Psychology
Anthropology and Sociology
Theater
Computer Science

*Every student receives
a Power of Experience
Grant of up to $2,000
to help fund a real-
world experience
of their choice.*

Center, housing art and art history programs, opened in 2017 and features a variety of art studios, metalworking and woodworking shops, and dedicated studio space for seniors.

Students say the academic relationships at Knox are infused with a spirit of cooperation and equality. Knox operates on an honor system that allows students to take tests unproctored in any public area. Beyond the classroom, students, faculty, and administrators make decisions on boards together, each with identical voting power. As part of Knox's Blaze a Trail first-year experience program, incoming students participate in new student orientation and take First-Year Preceptorial, a small seminar taught by professors from across the college that emphasizes critical analysis, writing, and class discussion. They may also join an optional living/learning community associated with their Preceptorial course.

All Knox students apply their learning to a real-world experience of their choice, such as independent research or creative work, an internship, community service, or study abroad, that serves as a capstone experience in the junior or senior year. What's more, every student receives a Power of Experience Grant of up to $2,000 to help fund their chosen experience. The general education curriculum, known as Elements, spans coursework in the arts, sciences, humanities, and social sciences and teaches students how to communicate in a second language, in numbers and symbols, and with people of diverse backgrounds. Creative writing and biology are among the school's strongest programs; the college's biannual literary magazine, *Catch*, has won several national and international awards, while biology attracts lots of research grant money. Other popular majors include economics, psychology, and anthropology and sociology, and the theater and computer science departments are also notable. Knox offers 3–2 or 3–4 programs in engineering, nursing, medical technology, law, and architecture, as well as a cooperative program with The George Washington University School of Medicine and Health Sciences. New majors have been added in business and environmental science.

> "Professors at Knox teach
> [only] two classes per term."

"Knox is challenging but not overwhelming," says a senior. Seventy-seven percent of classes have fewer than 20 students. Knox's trimester system packs a great deal of studying into a short period, but students are only required to take three courses per term and professors are widely available for extra help. "Professors at Knox teach [only] two classes per term, which is intentionally designed to give them time to devote to office hours with students," explains a senior. Immersive terms give students the option of engaging in a hands-on exploration of a single field of study for an entire term; available subjects include clinical psychology, Japanese language and culture, studio art, repertory theater, start-ups, and fieldwork and community-building at the off-campus Green Oaks prairie restoration site. For those interested in service, Knox was the first college in the country to establish an official Peace Corps Preparatory Program. Knox also offers nearly 100 study abroad and off-campus programs in more than 50 countries, and about half of students participate. Students praise Knox's academic advising system for helping them navigate the multitude of options. "Advisors are always available to discuss anything ranging from future plans to personal problems," says a junior.

> "It's not uncommon for
> people to ask you what your
> [gender] pronouns are."

Forty-six percent of students are from Illinois, and 17 percent hail from foreign countries. While Knox is not a hotbed of political protest, students here tend to be progressive and engaged in current events, and a commitment to diversity is evident across campus. African Americans make up 8 percent of the student body, Asian Americans 5 percent, Hispanics 15 percent, and multiracial students 6 percent. Socioeconomically, 32 percent of freshmen qualify for Pell Grants, and a quarter of undergrads are first-generation college students. "We believe we learn the most from students who are different from us," says a senior, and another adds, "It's not uncommon for people to ask you what your [gender] pronouns are." Merit scholarships averaging $21,800 are available, but athletic scholarships are not.

Eighty-nine percent of students reside in campus digs. Most freshmen live in single-sex suites, and a senior describes the dorms as "nothing to write home about" but notes that the apartments and townhouses for upperclassmen are more comfortable. Those who move off campus must obtain permission, which can be difficult. Students say campus dining options are edible if not particularly tasty. The Knox Guardian mobile safety app enhances campus security, and one student says, "Knox fosters the type of community where students feel safe enough to come forward and report cases of sexual assault."

On Flunk Day, a tradition since 1922, classes are canceled to make way for rollicking festivities.

Thirty-five percent of men and 28 percent of women go Greek, and weekends are filled with on-campus club activities, cultural events, and fraternity parties, although all parties must be registered and alcohol-free. Students warn that the administration is quick to deal with underage drinkers. Annual events include the Lincoln Fest music festival and International Fair, but students say Flunk Day, a tradition since 1922, is their favorite. At 6:00 on a spring morning, Old Main's bell rings, whistles blow, and classes are canceled to make way for lawn games, inflatables, karaoke, and other rollicking festivities.

Galesburg is a small Midwestern railroad town, and the Amtrak station makes travel easy and relatively cheap. At one time, this city of about 31,000 was a center of abolitionism, and the honorary degree that the college bestowed on then-presidential candidate Abraham Lincoln was his first. Now, Knox students devote more

"There is a 'freedom to flourish' at Knox."

than 80,000 hours of service to the community every year. A junior says, "Galesburg surprisingly has a lot to offer; you just have to go out and look for it." Nearby Lake Storey offers boating, water slides, and nature trails, and students looking for more excitement can travel to Peoria, about 50 miles southeast, or Chicago, about 200 miles northeast.

Prairie Fire athletics' 20 Division III teams generate a reasonable degree of enthusiasm, boosted by the recent introduction of a new mascot, a fox named Blaze. The men's and women's soccer teams are strong, both having recently earned Midwest Conference titles. Every fall, the football team endures lots of "hard Knox" against archrival Monmouth to bring home the highly prized Bronze Turkey trophy, a throwback to the time when the game was played on Thanksgiving Day. About a quarter of students participate in intramural and club sports; basketball and ultimate Frisbee are the most popular.

Knox may not be a well-known school, but students here have little else to complain about. Academics and hands-on experiences are the priority, and students are encouraged to be individuals, but the close-knit, open-minded atmosphere helps them form strong connections with a diverse group of students and down-to-earth professors. Says a student, "There is a 'freedom to flourish' at Knox. My opportunities are limitless."

Overlaps

Beloit, Lawrence, Kalamazoo, Earlham, Cornell College, Augustana (IL), Grinnell, Illinois Wesleyan

If You Apply To ›

Knox: Early decision, early action I and II, regular decision. SATs or ACTs: optional (required for homeschooled students). Subject Tests: optional. Accepts the Common Application with supplement.

Geographically close to Lehigh, but closer kin to Colgate and Hamilton and boasting a strong global orientation. Does offer engineering, as do Bucknell, Swarthmore, Trinity (CT), and Union. Attracts relatively preppy, athletic students who work hard and play hard. A recent spate of building shows Lafayette's financial health. One of the smallest institutions to play Division I sports.

Lafayette College has become one of the small elite liberal arts colleges with a huge presence abroad. Lafayette is a national leader in undergraduate faculty-mentored research and is ranked among the top colleges in study abroad participation. The liberal arts curriculum mixes nicely with engineering in a small college atmosphere. The number of applications has increased, signaling that the world beyond the Lafayette campus has taken notice. Says one satisfied junior, "Lafayette is a place that believes that we can be leaders, scholars, athletes, and activists and that we don't have to choose just one."

Lafayette is situated on College Hill, a stately hill in Easton, Pennsylvania, just an hour and a half west of New York City and even closer to Philadelphia. The campus has an eclectic blend of architectural styles and more than 125 species of trees. The Skillman Library provides 30,000 square feet of open learning space—a common theme in many Lafayette buildings. The 90,000-square-foot Acopian Engineering Center also features lots of open workspaces and glass walls, and stays open all night and weekends. The environmentally friendly Oechsle Center for Global Education houses programs in international affairs, anthropology, and sociology.

A Common Course of Study (CCS) includes a first-year seminar and courses in lab science, social sciences, mathematics, humanities, writing, global and multicultural proficiency, and a foreign language. "The courses offered at Lafayette are rigorous, but students have time off to do the activities they want to," reasons an international affairs and Spanish major. Lafayette's economics, government and law, mechanical engineering, biology, and psychology majors are among the most popular. Programs in visual and performing arts have grown with the recent opening of the Williams Art Campus. The Economic Empowerment and Global Learning Project allows students from all disciplines to relate classroom lessons to real-world problems in the U.S. and abroad. The Dyer Center for Innovation and Entrepreneurship provides hands-on, multidisciplinary opportunities for collaboration in the liberal arts and engineering. Sixty-one percent of classes have fewer than 20 students. "Professors' passion is contagious, and they're very willing to serve as mentors," cheers a psychology major. The EXCEL program pays students who take research positions with faculty.

> "Professors' passion is contagious, and they're very willing to serve as mentors."

About half of Lehigh students pack their bags for study abroad programs offered in more than 50 countries. Options include several semester-long, faculty-led programs as well as short-term, faculty-led programs for credit during the January and May interim terms. "Study abroad is life-changing," marvels one student. Even engineering students are encouraged to explore foreign cultures; programs led by Lafayette faculty at Jacobs University in Germany and Saint Louis University in Spain allow them to study abroad for a semester while maintaining normal progress toward their degrees.

Lafayette students are friendly and, by and large, come from wealthy backgrounds. They're also loyal. "Students wear Vineyard Vines because the founder

Website: www.lafayette.edu
Location: Small City
Private
Total Enrollment: 2,551
Undergraduates: 2,551
Male/Female: 48/52
SAT Ranges: ERW 630–710, M 630–730
ACT Ranges: 28–31
Financial Aid: 57%
Pell Grant: 11%
Expense: Pr $ $ $
Student Loans: 45%
Average Debt: $ $ $
Applicants: 8,469
Accepted: 31%
Enrolled: 26%
Grad in 6 Years: 90%
Returning Freshmen: 95%
Academics: ✎ ✎ ✎ ✎
Social: 🌮 🌮 🌮 🌮
Q of L: ★ ★ ★
Admissions: (610) 330-5100
Email Address: admissions@lafayette.edu

Strong Programs:
Economics
Government and Law
Mechanical Engineering
Biology
Psychology
Visual and Performing Arts

went to Lafayette," says a sophomore. Seventy-one percent of Lafayette students are from out of state, and another 10 percent are drawn from abroad. African Americans account for 5 percent of the student body, Hispanics 7 percent, Asian Americans 4 percent, and multiracial students 3 percent. A fairly diverse range of political views are represented, and a senior comments, "You can have your own opinions, even unpopular ones, and people will accept you." Roughly 40 incoming freshmen receive merit-based Marquis Scholarships worth $24,000 per year, while 10 top achievers are awarded Marquis Fellowships worth $40,000 per year. Student-athletes vie for athletic scholarships in 11 of the school's 23 varsity sports. Additionally, Lafayette guarantees to meet the full demonstrated need of admitted students, and it reduces or eliminates loans from financial aid packages for students from families with annual incomes less than $100,000.

Ninety-three percent of students live on campus, and housing is guaranteed for all four years. Possibilities include Greek houses as well as independent dormitories and college-owned apartments with a variety of living and eating arrangements. Housing is chosen via a lottery system, but most get into the dorm of their choice. Ruef and South College are more social, while Watson Hall and Kirby House are quieter, students say. The six campus dining facilities get good reviews: "There are definitely a lot of choices and they cater to all those with special needs," says one student. Another remarks, "Lafayette does not ignore the fact that sexual assault happens on campus, but rather works to continuously bring up the issue in order to put a stop to it."

Programs in visual and performing arts have grown with the recent opening of the Williams Art Campus.

> "You can have your own opinions, even unpopular ones, and people will accept you."

Greek life attracts 22 percent of the men and 34 percent of the women. All sororities and some fraternities are dry, at least on campus, and an economics major says, "Parties happen mostly off campus, but there are a lot of events on campus that you can attend." The arts program brings a range of performers to campus, and the most important nonathletic event of the year is Spring Concert, an outdoor event to celebrate the season. The 1,000 Nights dance for freshmen and the 100 Nights dance for seniors mark the number of days remaining until graduation.

For students with cars, or those willing to hop a bus or train, the bright lights of Philadelphia, New York, and Atlantic City beckon on weekends; for a change of pace, there is also hiking the Appalachian Trail. Another popular excursion is touring the nearby Binney & Smith factory, where Crayola crayons are made. Blue-collar Easton "gets a bad rap, but is really nice," says a senior. "A lot of restaurants on the hill, lots of nice shops, great health and beauty salons. I really like Easton." From College Hill and Downtown to the South Side, the city offers plenty of opportunities for volunteer work in schools, prisons, rehabilitation centers, hospitals, and environmental sites, under the auspices of Lafayette's Community Outreach Center.

About half of Lehigh students pack their bags for study abroad programs offered in more than 50 countries.

Division I sports add much flavor to the Lafayette experience. Recent Patriot League champions include men's basketball and women's field hockey. Other competitive Leopard teams include men's soccer, baseball, and lacrosse and women's basketball. The annual football game against nearby Lehigh is intense—dating to 1884, it's the most-played rivalry in college football. For those not up to varsity level, there is an extensive intramural program, buoyed by the state-of-the-art, $35 million Kirby Sports Center.

Students seeking close contact with professors, research opportunities, and a global outlook—and who aren't afraid of some serious study—might take a look at Lafayette. A freshman shares this anecdote: "I was once studying in a lounge area when a student I never met before saw my textbooks, explained that he had taken the course the year before, and proceeded to give me his number in case I had any questions throughout the semester." For those who desire a tight-knit, supportive community, that just about says it all.

Overlaps

Lehigh, Bucknell, Colgate, Villanova, Franklin & Marshall, Union, Boston College, Tufts

If You Apply To ›

Lafayette: Early decision I and II, regular decision. SATs or ACTs: required. Subject Tests: optional. Accepts the Common Application with supplement.

Lake Forest College

555 Sheridan Road, Lake Forest, IL 60045

The only small, selective, private college in the Chicago area, Lake Forest generally attracts middle-of-the-road students. In the exclusive town from which the school takes its name, students can babysit for corporate CEOs at night and get internships at their corporations during the day. Large numbers of Foresters also study abroad.

Website: www.lakeforest.edu
Location: Suburban
Private
Total Enrollment: 1,479
Undergraduates: 1,471
Male/Female: 42/58
SAT Ranges: N/A
ACT Ranges: 24–29
Financial Aid: 98%
Pell Grant: 31%
Expense: Pr $ $
Student Loans: 76%
Average Debt: $ $ $ $
Applicants: 4,303
Accepted: 53%
Enrolled: 16%
Grad in 6 Years: 72%
Returning Freshmen: 85%
Academics: ✍ ✍ ✍
Social: ☎ ☎ ☎ ☎
Q of L: ★ ★ ★
Admissions: (847) 735-5000
Email Address: admissions@
  lakeforest.edu

Strong Programs:
Business
Finance
Psychology
Biology
Communication
Neuroscience
English
Entrepreneurship and
  Innovation

Located just 30 miles north of the downtown Loop, Lake Forest College offers excellent programs in business, communication, and psychology, along with abundant opportunities for study abroad and professional internships at Chicagoland organizations such as the Chicago Blackhawks, the Chicago Board of Trade, and the Shedd Aquarium. Academic improvements at Lake Forest are drawing attention and the school is shedding its image as a haven for spoiled rich kids; applications are up significantly and the school is attracting high-caliber students from around the nation.

With its mixture of century-old Gothic and modern glass structures, Lake Forest's 107-acre campus is storybook beautiful. Located on Chicago's North Shore in a wealthy, quiet suburb of 20,000, the campus has three contiguous parts divided by natural wooded ravines: North, Middle, and South. Each has a mix of residence halls and academic buildings. The state-of-the-art Donnelley and Lee Library offers a 24-hour computer lab, "smart" classrooms, and space where students can work collaboratively on projects. Recent campus projects include the $43 million, interdisciplinary Lillard Science Center.

General education requirements include the First-Year Studies Program, featuring "very small classes designed to help freshmen integrate into the college," says an English major. "These courses are writing intensive and offer a variety of opportunities, including trips to Chicago for plays and museum visits." Students also complete two credits in each of three liberal arts areas (humanities, social and natural sciences, and math), two cultural diversity courses, and a senior studies capstone course.

> **"It's not uncommon to find an entire class sitting in a study room going over material."**

Students say Lake Forest's best and most popular majors include business, finance, psychology, biology, communication, neuroscience, and English. An entrepreneurship and innovation minor has also proven popular. Accelerated and dual-degree programs—including three-year degree programs in philosophy and communication and dual-degree programs in law, engineering, pharmacy, accounting, and international studies—are available. Academic self-starters benefit from the self-designed major program, which allows undergrads to create their own majors outside the boundaries of traditional disciplines.

The academic climate at Lake Forest is described as collaborative. "The small class sizes allow for a lot of group discussion, group projects, and peer mentoring," says a biology major. "It's not uncommon to find an entire class sitting in a study room going over material for an upcoming exam." Foresters especially enjoy the large doses of individual attention that they receive from the faculty. "The professors here know my name, they know what I struggle with, and they know my strengths," confirms a psychology major. The Career Advancement Center is run by the same person who oversees admissions, meaning that the person who brings you to Lake Forest is also looking out for you as you graduate and move into the workforce. The center offers symposia, workshops, and résumé clinics, and students benefit from the college's proximity to downtown Chicago, just an hour away by train. Many pursue term-time internships in the city's business district, known as the Loop, or at nonprofits and other organizations in surrounding communities.

Study abroad is integral to the Lake Forest experience, and 40 percent of students travel via more than 200 programs in approximately 70 nations. Participants in the faculty-led Lake Forest College in Greece program spend half a semester on campus studying the ancient Aegean world, then travel to Athens to take coursework on classical and modern Greece and visit archae-

> **"Absolutely try to do research with your professors. It is the most rewarding thing you can get involved with."**

ological sites and museums. Each year, about 40 students become Richter Apprentice Scholars, living together, working in a 10-week paid research assistantship during the summer before their sophomore year, and taking part in a weekly student/faculty colloquium. "Absolutely try to do research with your professors," urges a communication major. "It is the most rewarding thing you can get involved with."

Sixty-two percent of Lake Forest students hail from the Land of Lincoln. A sophomore counsels that at a small school where everyone knows everyone, "It's important to be open-minded, amiable, and able to get along with others." African Americans make up 6 percent of the student body, Hispanics 15 percent, Asian Americans 6 percent, and multiracial students 4 percent; 8 percent are international. Although the school organizes frequent panels and open-forum discussions on political and social issues, students say political debate is usually mild on this relatively moderate campus. Competitive financial aid packages are helping to bring more students of color and those from less-advantaged backgrounds to Lake Forest. Thirty-one percent of freshmen are eligible for Pell Grants. The college awards numerous merit scholarships averaging $23,100 but does not offer athletic awards.

Seventy-five percent of students live in the dorms, which they are required to do through their junior year. An English major says, "Different halls attract different people. I preferred living in the older buildings because they felt homier than the new buildings, which felt more like a hotel."

> **"The whole place is beautiful, and it feels like you live tucked away in a safe haven."**

Housing selection for upperclassmen is prioritized by seniority and GPA, "so there's a definite incentive to do well in your classes," says a senior. A fair number of students commute from home, and many seniors choose to stay on campus due to high rents in the surrounding area. Everybody eats in the central dining hall, where food is prepared to order at pizza, pasta, stir-fry, and other stations, and helpings are unlimited. "Our dining hall is multicultural, so you can have Mexican food one day and Indian the next," explains a sophomore. A senior says, "We have regular programming events and student panels dedicated to educating the campus on sexual assault."

"The social life on campus is always active because a majority of students live on campus and are involved in multiple organizations," says a biology major. The Campus Entertainment Committee books movies, comedians, and big-name bands, while the Garrick Players also put on several productions per year. The school's three fraternities and five sororities attract 17 percent of the men and 18 percent of the women, respectively, and though they don't have houses, their parties are open to all. Students say the party culture is relatively low-key, and underage students caught drinking on campus are strictly penalized. Everyone enjoys the semiformal

The First-Year Studies Program features small, writing-intensive classes and trips to Chicago for plays and museum visits.

The admissions officer who brings you to Lake Forest is also looking out for you at the Career Advancement Center.

Winter Ball, the annual Forester Day of Service, the Spring Concert, and the Drag Show lip-synch contest planned by PRIDE.

The town of Lake Forest is wealthy and mostly residential, and one student says, "The town is actually in a forest, so the whole place is beautiful, and it feels like you live tucked away in a safe haven." There's a commuter train station five minutes away and the Lake Michigan beach is just as close. The college also offers a weekend shuttle service to local malls and movie theaters, though a car is helpful. Several student organizations are devoted to community service, and Greek organizations sponsor blood drives, bake sales, and car washes. One program sends students to the Appalachian Mountains in Virginia and Tennessee every spring break to help local townspeople repair substandard housing.

Division III Foresters athletics have begun to draw more attention from students. Recent Midwest Conference champions include men's golf and soccer and women's softball. Club and intramural sports programs are plentiful; lacrosse, rugby, and indoor soccer are especially popular.

Although Lake Forest still has its fair share of preppy types, students are quick to emphasize that the college is taking steps to increase diversity, foster a collaborative atmosphere, and encourage school pride. "Lake Forest takes very good care of its students by providing challenging academics, comfortable living, lots of entertainment, and a small-town feel with access to a big city," concludes a senior. "What more could anyone want?"

Overlaps

Knox, Beloit, Cornell College, Luther, Augustana (IL), U of I at Chicago, Loyola University Chicago, DePaul

If You Apply To ›

Lake Forest: Early decision I and II, early action I and II, regular decision. SATs or ACTs: optional (test-optional applicants must have an admissions interview). No Subject Tests. Accepts the Common Application with supplement.

Lawrence University

711 East Boldt Way, Appleton, WI 54911

One of three small colleges in the nation that combines the liberal arts with a first-rate music conservatory (Bard and Oberlin are the others). Lawrence is half the size of Oberlin and comparable to Beloit and Grinnell, though Lawrence's personality is more mainstream than the others. Occupies a scenic bluff in northeastern Wisconsin.

Website: www.lawrence.edu
Location: Small City
Private
Total Enrollment: 1,418
Undergraduates: 1,418
Male/Female: 46/54
SAT Ranges: ERW 620–730, M 600–730
ACT Ranges: 25–32
Financial Aid: 94%
Pell Grant: 23%
Expense: Pr $ $
Student Loans: 60%

Lawrence University is an unpretentious school that can appeal to both the left and right side of students' brains. For those with an analytical bent, there is Lawrence's uncommon physics program. More creative types can take advantage of the school's renowned Conservatory of Music. "I came to Lawrence because I found no other school where I could seriously study music and academics," says a senior. It's this eclectic, individualized approach to learning that attracts interested and interesting students from around the world. "Lawrence allows students to explore individual and intellectual interests in greater depth than most institutions," confirms a neuroscience major.

Lawrence's campus is on a wooded bluff above the Fox River, perfect for long walks, jogging, or simply meditating underneath the trees. It was chosen in 1847 by one of Appleton's earliest settlers. The pristine 84-acre campus reflects several architectural styles of the past 150 years, including classical revival, 1920s Georgian-inspired, and 1950s and 1960s institutional, unified by their limestone color. The award-winning Wriston Art Center and the Conservatory's Shattuck Hall of Music (both designed by Lawrence graduates) bring contemporary architectural touches to the campus.

One of the first coeducational colleges established in the nation, Lawrence was founded to educate German immigrants and Native Americans. While coeducation was shocking enough, innovators at Lawrence didn't stop there. More than 60 years ago, administrators introduced the Freshman Studies program, a required two-term course that focuses primarily on the great works of art, music, science, and literature of both Western and non-Western origin and gives all incoming students a shared intellectual experience. General education requirements at Lawrence include Freshman Studies; distribution requirements; and diversity, foreign language, and writing-intensive courses. All seniors—in all degree programs—are required to produce a final project demonstrating proficiency in their major field of study. As a linguistics major explains, the senior project means that "while everyone is working on something different, the whole senior class is engaged in meaningful discussions and exposed to unique challenges."

> "[The senior project means that] the whole senior class is engaged in meaningful discussions."

At the school's Conservatory of Music, the instrument collection includes an 1815 Broadwood piano identical to Beethoven's Broadwood, and a Guarneri violin. There are first-rate jazz ensembles along with classical and world music programs. The college offers a bachelor of music degree within its liberal arts environment, and students may opt to complete a five-year, double-degree program to earn both a bachelor of music and a bachelor of arts in another field. "Music is the unifying theme at Lawrence," says one student. "Almost everybody plays it or studies it or likes to listen to it and talk about it." Music is also the most popular major, followed by biology, government, psychology, and English. The highly regarded physics department offers 3–2 engineering options with Columbia and WashU in St. Louis, as well as a 4–1 option with the University of Rochester leading to an M.S. in optical sciences. Interdisciplinary areas include museum studies and innovation and entrepreneurship, and a major in ethnic studies has been added.

Lawrentians appreciate their professors' expertise and experience. Small classes—80 percent have fewer than 20 students—make it "easy to connect and work closely with professors for a more personalized and thorough learning experience," says a geology major. Because of the three-term calendar, the academic climate is fast-paced and intense, but also "extremely collaborative," a sophomore says. "As long as you stay on top of reading and notes, it is not overwhelming."

Students are encouraged to spend at least one term of their college career off campus, and 38 percent of undergrads do so. The university is known for its London Centre, which allows students to take classes "across the pond" while taking advantage of the city's many cultural activities. Other off-campus programs include a Francophone seminar in Dakar, Senegal, and a marine biology term in the Cayman Islands. In all, 45 international programs are available in more than two dozen countries. About 65 percent of students participate in research opportunities, especially those in the sciences. The LU-R1 program pairs qualified students with Lawrence alumni who are conducting research at tier-one universities across the country for 10-week research assistantships during the summer.

> "Music is the unifying theme at Lawrence."

Twenty-six percent of Lawrentians hail from Wisconsin, and another quarter come from Illinois and Minnesota. At 12 percent, the international population is sizable and represents more than 40 countries. African Americans make up 5 percent of the student body, Asian Americans 5 percent, Hispanics 9 percent, and multiracial students 3 percent. The political climate on campus is generally liberal, and a junior

(continued)

Average Debt: $ $ $
Applicants: 3,612
Accepted: 61%
Enrolled: 16%
Grad in 6 Years: 79%
Returning Freshmen: 88%
Academics: ✍ ✍ ✍ ✍
Social: ☎ ☎ ☎
Q of L: ★ ★ ★
Admissions: (800) 227-0982
Email Address: admissions@ lawrence.edu

Strong Programs:
Music
Biology
Government
Psychology
English
Physics
Museum Studies
Innovation and
   Entrepreneurship

The Freshman Studies program is a required two-term course that focuses on the great works of art, music, science, and literature.

says, "Students here are very quick to speak their mind and express their opinions, regardless of what they are." There are no athletic scholarships, but top achievers vie for merit scholarships averaging $22,000 each, and 23 percent of freshmen qualify for Pell Grants.

All but 6 percent of students live on campus, as four-year residency is required with few exceptions. "There are tons of options for housing: dorms, theme houses, group houses, lofts, etc.," explains a junior. On-campus students have a choice of meal plans and report that the food is diverse, healthy, and friendly to those with dietary restrictions. "Some of our produce comes from a student-run garden right across the street from the dining hall," says one student. In an effort to enhance campus safety, all on-campus parties hosted by student groups must be attended by at least one member who has been trained in bystander intervention.

Social life at Lawrence is mostly campus-based and as varied and eclectic as the students. Greek life attracts 10 percent of the men and 14 percent of the

"Some of our produce comes from a student-run garden."

women; students say Greek organizations do not set the tone for social life and the party culture tends to be laid-back. Thanks to the Conservatory, students can almost always count on there being some kind of concert or performance on any given day. The President's Ball in the winter and LU-aroo, a music festival in the spring, are favorite annual traditions. The Great Midwest Trivia Contest takes place during January each year; held since 1965, it's the longest running trivia contest in the nation. Octoberfest is also a big weekend event, held in conjunction with the city of Appleton, which draws people in from nearby cities.

Relations between Lawrence and Appleton are good. "The town is safe and has lots to do," says a student, including "cafés, restaurants, shops, nightlife, performing arts, and farmers markets." Downtown Appleton is just one block from campus, but the nearest grocery store is a five-minute drive away; the school provides regular shuttles to help students get around. Volunteerism is popular, and students regularly take part in activities such as tutoring at local schools. The best road trips are to Milwaukee (two hours), Green Bay (half an hour), and Chicago (four hours). There are also weekend seminars at Björklunden, the college's 425-acre estate on the shores of Lake Michigan.

And what would a Midwest fall Saturday be without football? The Division III Lawrence Vikings draw good crowds almost every weekend. Men's cross-country, men's tennis, women's swimming, and men's and women's fencing are among the most competitive teams. The sparkling recreation center helps students fend off midwinter blues. Participating in a rousing game of intramural broomball, a variation of ice hockey played on shoes with brooms and kickballs, is a must for students, even if all you do is watch. Ultimate Frisbee is a popular club sport.

With an outstanding liberal arts curriculum, knowledgeable and caring faculty, an administration that treats students like adults, and a charming country setting, Lawrence University is easily one of the best little-known schools in the country. "Lawrence really does provide the tools and opportunities necessary to become an effective leader. I've always felt that this school is a hidden gem," muses a film studies major. And for students with a musical ear, Lawrence's symphony of offerings strikes just the right chord.

Overlaps

St. Olaf, Oberlin, Macalester, Grinnell, Beloit, UW–Madison, Carleton, Northwestern

If You Apply To ›

Lawrence: Early decision, early action I and II, regular decision. SATs or ACTs: optional. Subject Tests: optional. Accepts the Common Application with supplement. Music applicants must audition.

Lehigh University

27 Memorial Drive West, Bethlehem, PA 18015

Built on the powerful combination of business, engineering, and the humanities, Lehigh occupies a middle ground between techie havens such as Drexel and Rensselaer and liberal arts/engineering institutions such as Bucknell and Union. By graduation, students are primed for the global job market. Hillside campus means that students get plenty of exercise. A wrestling powerhouse.

From the College of Arts and Sciences to the College of Business and Economics, Lehigh University combines the academic resources of a large research university with the collegial atmosphere of a much smaller institution. Because much of Lehigh's reputation rests on its consistently strong engineering program, the school has invested millions of dollars to enhance critical academic programs such as nanotechnology, biotechnology, bioscience, and optoelectronics. And with its robust approach to experiential learning, students are well prepared for life after college. Says one engineering major, "Lehigh students have the know-how to jump right into the workforce and tackle any challenges that they may face."

Grand old oaks shade the buildings on Lehigh's 2,358-acre campus, which is tucked into the side of an eastern Pennsylvania mountain. Architectural styles range from ivy-covered collegiate Gothic to modern glass and steel. In an apt symbol of Lehigh's efforts to link tradition with what it takes to be part of a global workforce, the 1878 collegiate Gothic Linderman Library in the center of campus was completely gutted and rebuilt with attention to computer access, group study areas, and a café. The Goodman Campus provides first-class practice and playing facilities for Lehigh's Division I and recreational sports teams alike.

> "I love the flexibility that I have had with my major."

Distribution requirements are divided into four domains—the mathematical sciences, the natural sciences, the social sciences, and the arts and humanities. First-years take an Evolution Seminar that focuses on the transition to college life. Additionally, some degrees include a mandatory internship or capstone project. Finance, mechanical engineering, accounting, and marketing are the most popular majors. Lehigh is big on connecting traditionally separate disciplines, so students interested in interdisciplinary study will find a wealth of options, including majors in arts and engineering, computer science and business, and environmental engineering and minors in engineering leadership and sustainable development. "I love the flexibility that I have had with my major, and it is really cool that I have been able to study both engineering and psychology," says a senior. Several dual-degree options are available, such as a dental program with the University of Pennsylvania. Plans are in the works for a new college of health. Through the President's Scholars program, top Lehigh students who maintain a 3.75 GPA or better are eligible for a fifth year of study tuition-free.

> "Professors at Lehigh are as good as they get when it comes to professional experience."

Lehigh prides itself on offering innovative special programs. The Technical Entrepreneurship Capstone program brings engineering, business, and arts students together to design and make products for sponsoring companies. The IDEAS (Integrated Degree in Engineering, Arts, and Sciences) and Integrated Business and Engineering programs offer four-year honors curricula that allow students to blend two focus areas into a single course of study. The Mountaintop program gives roughly 175 students a chance to work in teams with faculty mentors on cutting-edge

Website: www.lehigh.edu
Location: Small City
Private
Total Enrollment: 6,220
Undergraduates: 5,000
Male/Female: 55/45
SAT Ranges: ERW 620–700, M 650–730
ACT Ranges: 29–32
Financial Aid: 47%
Pell Grant: 19%
Expense: Pr $ $ $
Student Loans: 51%
Average Debt: $ $ $ $
Applicants: 13,871
Accepted: 25%
Enrolled: 35%
Grad in 6 Years: 86%
Returning Freshmen: 96%
Academics: ✍ ✍ ✍ ✍
Social: ☎ ☎ ☎
Q of L: ★ ★ ★ ★
Admissions: (610) 758-3100
Email Address: admissions@lehigh.edu

Strong Programs:
Finance
Mechanical Engineering
Accounting
Marketing
Arts and Engineering
Computer Science and Business
Environmental Engineering
Integrated Business and Engineering

projects during the summer. Recent Mountaintop projects include Pop-Up Parklets, Health Care for All, and 3-D Concrete Printing. Co-ops allow students to spend eight months working for a major-related company—and getting paid to do so—while still graduating in four years. Twenty-six percent of students participate in more than 250 study abroad options in 60 countries. Faculty-led programs during winter and summer breaks are available in about a dozen countries, including China, the Czech Republic, and Ghana.

Lehigh students are ambitious, and many pursue double majors and multiple extracurriculars, but the atmosphere is by no means cutthroat. "From group projects to late-night study groups in Linderman Library, I have always been able to find a classmate to help me in a variety of subjects," says a journalism major. Forty-five percent of all courses contain fewer than 20 students, and a finance and economics major says, "Professors at Lehigh are as good as they get when it comes to professional experience and the research they are involved in." Students praise the wide range of services made available to them, including career counseling. "Career services is especially good at bringing large numbers of employers at a time to campus," says one junior, "and I think that sort of behind-the-scenes activity is more vital than students realize. Our placement numbers speak for themselves."

"Work comes first, but students love to enjoy themselves."

A computer science major describes his classmates as "hardworking and fun-loving. Work comes first, but students love to enjoy themselves." One-quarter of Lehigh's students come from Pennsylvania, and many others hail from other Northeastern states; 8 percent come from 60 foreign countries. African Americans account for 4 percent of the population, Hispanics 9 percent, Asian Americans 8 percent, and multiracial students 3 percent. Special-interest housing, including the UMOJA House (the Swahili word for "unity") and the PRIDE Community, exists to promote positive cultural exchanges between students. Politically, a senior says, "We have a lot of supporters on both sides of the aisle." Merit scholarships averaging $12,700 are awarded annually, and student-athletes vie for more than 200 athletic scholarships in 25 sports. Lehigh guarantees to meet 100 percent of every domestic student's demonstrated financial need. Additionally, Lehigh caps loans in its financial aid packages at $5,000 per year for students with demonstrated need, and has eliminated loans entirely for students with need whose total annual family income is less than $75,000.

Sixty-five percent of Lehigh students live on campus; first- and second-year students are required to do so. Accommodations are described as "decent." Many upperclassmen choose to live in apartment-style dorms, Greek houses, and off-campus apartments. Other options include Farrington Square, a residential and commercial complex that houses 250 upper-class students. "The dining on campus is great!" cheers one student. "I am an extremely picky eater and can always find something delicious to eat." Campus security draws cheers too, and students note that the Office of Gender Violence Education and Support has done much to educate the campus community, including rallies and prevention-awareness training.

"Bethlehem is an up-and-coming community."

An active Greek scene (38 percent of the men join fraternities and 45 percent of the women belong to sororities) fuels the campus social life. "Students who live off campus often host parties, and it creates a really great social scene," says one student. Although students agree that a drinking and party culture does exist, according to a finance major, "There isn't pressure from anyone to become involved in those activities." Plenty of on-campus social options are available too, says a business information systems major: "Lehigh After Dark events are always a huge hit and range from midnight breakfast bars and a massive carnival to massage therapy sessions and bingo nights." Favorite traditions include the Founder's Day celebration as well as bed races, the Turkey Trot, and other spirit activities during the week leading up to the big football game against Lafayette. Locally and nationally, students volunteer roughly 75,000 hours each year.

The bustling campus has helped revive Bethlehem, a once-great steel town in the heart of the Lehigh Valley. Just five minutes from campus, "Bethlehem is an up-and-coming community," a senior explains; town-gown relations are described as "strained at best." Still, students look forward to some events the city has to offer, including Musikfest in early August, a 10-day music festival that attracts more than one million people and showcases nearly every musical style. For those with wheels, Philadelphia is 50 miles to the south and New York City is 75 miles to the east. Skiers will appreciate the close proximity of the Poconos in the winter, while sun worshippers can enjoy the nearby Jersey Shore in the early fall and late spring.

The Division I Lehigh Mountain Hawks field a number of competitive teams. Lehigh's wrestling program is a powerhouse, having brought home numerous EIWA championships. Football and softball are recent Patriot League champions; other solid programs include men's and women's basketball and men's cross-country and lacrosse. Fans flock to the annual Lehigh versus Lafayette football game, which was first played in 1884 and is the longest-standing rivalry in college football. "Seeing Lehigh beat Lafayette in football is arguably more important to the school than actually winning the Patriot League championship," says a senior. About 80 percent of students participate in the extensive intramural and club sports programs, and weekend warriors make ample use of the expansive facilities in Taylor Gymnasium.

Lehigh students proudly juggle rigorous classes and a packed extracurricular calendar. "The type of student who will do best at Lehigh is the one who prefers to be too involved rather than sit back and observe," advises one senior. They give college life more than the old college try—and expect to succeed (with a little help from others along the way). Enthuses one student, "We are developing the world-changers of tomorrow."

The annual Lehigh versus Lafayette football game was first played in 1884 and is the longest-standing rivalry in college football.

Overlaps

Wake Forest, Boston College, Tulane, William and Mary, Northeastern, Cornell University, Villanova, Bucknell

If You Apply To ›

Lehigh: Early decision I and II, regular decision. SATs or ACTs: required. Subject Tests: optional. Accepts the Common Application with supplement. Apply to particular colleges.

Lewis & Clark College

Portland, OR 97219

The West Coast's leader in international and study abroad programs. Politically liberal, but not as far out as crosstown neighbor Reed. Portfolio Path to admission allows students to finesse standardized tests. With Mount Hood visible in the distance (sometimes), there is a wealth of outdoor possibilities. Located in suburban Portland, within easy reach of the bustle of downtown.

The 19th-century explorers Lewis and Clark struck out from Middle America to find where the trail ended, and their travels took them to Portland, a lush, green paradise by the Willamette River. The college that bears the explorers' names encourages students to explore too. Since 1962, more than 12,000 students and nearly 300 faculty members have participated in study abroad programs in 68 countries.

Website: www.lclark.edu
Location: City Outskirts
Private
Total Enrollment: 2,879

(continued)

Undergraduates: 2,008
Male/Female: 41/59
SAT Ranges: ERW 620–710,
  M 590–680
ACT Ranges: 27–31
Financial Aid: 90%
Pell Grant: 20%
Expense: Pr $ $ $
Student Loans: 50%
Average Debt: $ $
Applicants: 6,305
Accepted: 71%
Enrolled: 12%
Grad in 6 Years: 80%
Returning Freshmen: 83%
Academics: ✐ ✐ ✐
Social: ☎ ☎ ☎
Q of L: ★ ★ ★
Admissions: (503) 768-7040
Email Address: admissions@
  lclark.edu

Strong Programs:
International Affairs
Psychology
Sociology and Anthropology
Biology
English
Entrepreneurship

Sixty percent of students fulfill foreign language and international studies requirements by studying overseas.

Each year, Lewis & Clark offers more than 30 programs on six continents. Without a doubt, Lewis & Clark students receive, as one junior puts it, "an excellent, hands-on education."

Lest students become too enchanted overseas, Lewis & Clark lures them back with a gorgeous campus perched atop fir-covered bluffs overlooking the river. The campus is an old estate, complete with elaborate gardens, fountains, and pools, where cement is almost nonexistent and the roads are paved with cobblestones. The 50,000-square-foot Howard Hall, built as part of the college's commitment to sustainable development, earned a gold certification from the U.S. Green Building Council. Howard is one of several energy-saving, environmentally friendly buildings that also include three residence halls.

Lewis & Clark requires that all students achieve competency in a foreign language and international studies; 60 percent of students fulfill these requirements by studying overseas for a semester or more. Students may travel to such locales as Australia, China, Ecuador, and Morocco—some even study in two or three countries—and may also study in a number of American cities. In addition to the international studies requirement, students must complete courses in scientific and quantitative reasoning, creative arts, and physical educa-

> "Most of the classes are small and discussion-based, so there is a lot of time for personal questions."

tion. Not surprisingly, one of the most popular majors at Lewis & Clark is international affairs; others include psychology, sociology and anthropology, biology, and English. Minors in dance, ethnic studies, and Middle East and North African studies are offered, as are 3–2 programs in engineering and a 4–1 B.A./M.A.T. program in collaboration with Lewis & Clark's Graduate School of Education and Counseling. Honors programs are available in all majors. The Rogers Summer Science Research Program teams students and faculty on research projects ranging from the evolution of spider venom to cybersecurity analysis. The Center for Entrepreneurship encourages collaboration with faculty, mentors, and outside professionals to reframe problems using entrepreneurial thinking.

Lewis & Clark offers a Portfolio Path to admission, where students present a package representing their talents and interests. PP students supply two teacher recommendations and two graded samples of high school work: one quantitative sample and one analytical writing sample. The key to a good portfolio is a "well-rounded approach," administrators say. "The more creative, the better, but be sure it's not solely artwork or writing samples."

Despite this open attitude, L&C students, once enrolled, are expected to follow through with a challenging workload. The required six-week Pioneer Success Institute at the beginning of the year helps ease new students into the college transition, and the yearlong Exploration and Discovery course introduces them to college-level academic work. "Classes are hard but not impossible," says a freshman. Freshmen and graduating seniors get priority in the registration process, helping ensure graduation in four years for those who plan out their requirements and declare majors early. Professors get high marks for being knowledgeable and passionate. "Most of the classes are small and discussion-based, so there is a lot of time for personal questions," says a sophomore.

"Students here are socially conscious, motivated, and involved," says an international affairs major. Twelve percent of undergrads hail from Oregon, and many of the rest are West Coasters seeking an emphasis on the liberal arts; the college is also a haven for well-off Easterners who see L&C as an escape from the social claustrophobia of the typical prep school scene. Five percent of students are drawn from foreign countries. "There is a big divide between athletes and non-athletes," says one student. "This doesn't exactly mean that the two groups don't associate with each other, but the two groups do sit on different sides of the cafeteria. It just feels awkward." The campus is politically active and predominantly left-leaning. The student body is 6 percent Asian American, 3 percent African American, 12 percent Hispanic, and 5 percent multiracial. The college recently appointed its first dean of diversity and inclusion, to promote and expand campus diversity. Non-need-based financial aid awards average $16,700, but there are no athletic scholarships.

Lewis & Clark's residency requirement keeps students on campus their first two years; 66 percent of all undergraduates stay in campus housing, which is described as convenient. "The most common room is a double, but there are also quads and singles, all of which have sufficient room for their

"There is a big divide between athletes and nonathletes."

respective residents," reports a student. Owing to the college's hilltop location, lucky dorm residents have views of Mount St. Helens, Mount Hood, or the Portland skyline—at least when they are not fogged in. Students involved in performing arts, multicultural engagement, outdoor pursuits, and other programs can join living/learning communities. Dining halls cater to different diets and "the food is honestly really good," says a student. Despite L&C's location in a residential section of Portland, safety is a priority—residence halls have card-swipe entry systems and door alarms, and campus security officers are on duty 24 hours a day.

Fun seekers at Lewis & Clark rely primarily on programs offered through Student Activities, such as on-campus movies, contests, dances, and talent shows; there is no Greek life. Yearly events include the Fall Ball and Spring Fling dances and the International Fair. Students 21 and older are permitted to consume alcohol on campus, and alcohol policies for underage drinkers are enforced. "You can get in trouble if you get caught," says a sophomore, "but the repercussions aren't that severe." The neighborhood immediately surrounding the college is pleasant, affluent suburbia, which means a few stores, restaurants, and bars. Students get involved in the local community through Saturdays in Service days and a variety of campus organizations. The activity of downtown Portland—

"We constantly question and search for the answers."

mostly on Hawthorne Boulevard in the southeast section, and in the Pearl District or on 23rd Street in the northwest quadrant—is 15 minutes away on the city's public transit system or the free campus shuttle service, the Pioneer Express. On the weekends and during breaks, College Outdoors sponsors trips to Mount Hood (great skiing, about an hour distant), the eastern Oregon high desert (two hours), or the coastal beaches (an hour and a half). Seattle and Vancouver, BC, three- and six-hour drives, are favorite road trips, as are San Francisco and Las Vegas when there's more time.

Pioneer teams compete in the Division III Northwest Conference, and the most successful teams include men's basketball and men's and women's tennis and rowing. As might be expected at a school in the outdoorsy Pacific Northwest, Lewis & Clark has a well-organized intramural program and plenty of outdoor activities. Ultimate Frisbee, basketball, and volleyball are student favorites. The L&C debate team has won multiple national titles in recent years.

Lewis & Clark's many outdoor enthusiasts and champions of social causes thrive in the college's laid-back atmosphere. Students are knowledge-seeking pioneers—ones who would make the school's namesakes proud. "Students here look outside their lives and experiences in order to find something greater," says a senior. "We constantly question and search for the answers."

The six-week Pioneer Success Institute at the beginning of the year helps ease new students into the college transition.

Overlaps

Willamette, Whitman, Reed, University of Puget Sound, University of Oregon, University of Washington, UC Santa Cruz, UC Berkeley

Louisiana State University

1146 Pleasant Hall, Baton Rouge, LA 70803

In the state that invented Mardi Gras, students come to LSU for a great time as well as a good education. Finding the former is a no-brainer. The latter can be had in business, engineering, and life sciences fields. Administrators are trying to make LSU a more serious place with higher admissions standards and less underage drinking, but they face draconian budget cuts. Aging library contrasts with gleaming new rec center.

Website: www.lsu.edu
Location: City Center
Public
Total Enrollment: 26,093
Undergraduates: 21,949
Male/Female: 48/52
SAT Ranges: ERW 530–640, M 530–650
ACT Ranges: 23–28
Financial Aid: 83%
Pell Grant: 23%
Expense: Pub $ $
Student Loans: 42%
Average Debt: $ $
Applicants: 17,907
Accepted: 74%
Enrolled: 37%
Grad in 6 Years: 67%
Returning Freshmen: 83%
Academics: ✐ ✐
Social: ☺ ☺ ☺ ☺ ☺
Q of L: ★ ★ ★
Admissions: (225) 578-1175
Email Address: admissions@lsu.edu

Strong Programs:
Biological Sciences
Chemistry
Mechanical Engineering
Business
Kinesiology
Landscape Architecture

From abundant azaleas and Japanese magnolias and the smell of Cajun cuisine, to the sororities' antebellum mansions and the "huge and legendary" rivalries with Alabama and Florida, few schools evoke the spirit of the South like Louisiana State University in Baton Rouge. The university continues to offer solid programs in business, engineering, and the life sciences, and admissions standards continue to rise. "I feel that LSU's academic achievements have been underrated," says one senior. "There are so many ways to learn and grow, both in and out of the classroom."

LSU sits on 2,000 acres along the banks of the Mississippi River on the grounds of a former plantation. Most of the 250 buildings are Italian Renaissance in style, with tan stucco walls and red tile roofs. Lakes and huge oak trees dot the landscape, helping to diffuse the strong sun and temper Louisiana's legendary humidity. Recent campus projects include the Brookshire Military & Veterans Student Center and an $85 million expansion of the lavish student recreation center, paid for by hefty student fees.

LSU was once an open-admissions university for state residents, but standards have gone up in recent years, and with them, the caliber of students. Students

"Overall the professors here at LSU love their material and are dedicated to teaching."

must complete a broad core curriculum with coursework in English composition, analytical reasoning, social sciences, humanities, natural sciences, and the arts. Classes can be large, with 18 percent enrolling upward of 50 students, to the chagrin of many. "Some classes can have hundreds of students in an auditorium," says one student. "That changes the dynamic of the classroom experience." Especially motivated students may opt to join the honors college, to enjoy smaller class sizes and produce a senior thesis.

LSU students choose from 73 undergraduate degrees and tend to focus on practical courses of study, which will help them get into graduate school or find jobs after graduation. To that end, popular majors include biological sciences and chemistry—both typical for premeds—as well as mechanical engineering, business, and kinesiology. LSU's programs in landscape architecture, engineering (especially petroleum, civil, and environmental), and English are highly regarded. Given LSU's location and history as a sea grant college, its offerings in coastal environmental science and ecology are notable as well. The multidisciplinary LSU Center for Internal Auditing was the first university-based internal auditing training program to be established. Professors are lauded for their enthusiasm and skill behind the lectern. "Overall the professors here at LSU love their material and are dedicated to teaching," one student says. Research opportunities abound and include the President's Future Leaders in Research Program, which provides undergraduates the chance to work side by side with professors in a research setting, such as a lab or in the field, to learn what a career in that area might be like. Two percent of the student body study abroad and may choose from programs in 51 countries.

(continued)

Petroleum Engineering
Coastal Environmental Science

Eighty-three percent of LSU Tigers are Louisiana natives, and 2 percent come from abroad. "Many of the students here are partiers and social butterflies," says one sophomore. African Americans make up 12 percent of the student body, Asian Americans 4 percent, Hispanics 6 percent, and multiracial students 2 percent. "The biggest political issue is concerning budget cuts in the state and how they affect higher education," says a student. LSU's tuition is below the national average, but, in the face of dwindling support from the state, the university has passed more and more of the cost of education on to students in the form of fees—such as a "student excellence fee"—that function like tuition. Thousands of merit scholarships are available, averaging $4,000, and LSU hands out 510 athletic scholarships each year in 21 sports. Twenty-three percent of freshmen qualify for the Pell Grant. The Pelican Promise Scholarship provides additional financial aid to low-income, Pell-eligible, in-state students.

Given LSU's location and history as a sea grant college, its offerings in coastal environmental science are notable.

Twenty-three percent of students live on campus. Over the past decade, the university has invested more than $150 million in housing facilities, with more than half of the undergraduate housing either newly constructed or renovated. Almost a quarter of first-year students choose to live

"Many of the students here are partiers and social butterflies."

in 8 residential colleges organized by academic interest. Campus dining halls offer a variety of dishes, and students say most are tasty. There are also a variety of eateries near campus that are "delicious and inexpensive," according to one student. Despite Baton Rouge's high crime rate, students report feeling safe on campus. LSU has nearly 100 full-time officers and a transit system so that students don't have to walk alone after dark.

Over the past decade, the university has invested more than $150 million in housing facilities.

Social life at LSU "is never-ending," cheers a student. "Plenty of students enjoy off-campus fun with house parties and plenty of bars nearby in Tigerland," adds another. Sixteen percent of the men and 28 percent of the women go Greek. The administration has instituted several policy changes related to Greek life, including a ban on hard alcohol at all on- and off-campus Greek events, after the alcohol-related death of a freshman fraternity pledge in 2017. As for annual traditions, everyone looks forward to homecoming and festivals such as Groovin', "where big-name bands come play for the students, with lots of food and games—all free!" says a junior. Road trips to the Florida beaches are common during spring break.

Tiger football is king in Baton Rouge. "Tailgating on game day is a big party for everyone," says a senior, and the rowdy LSU contingent at away games has earned a reputation comparable to that of English soccer fans. Many students follow the team (and the fun) to Oxford, Mississippi (home of Ole Miss), or Auburn, Alabama (home of the Auburn Tigers). The Tiger baseball team is a dynasty, having brought home its most recent Southeastern Conference title in 2017. Men's golf and women's gymnastics are also highly competitive. Intramural soccer, flag football, and softball are popular, and even those who don't play may work out at the well-equipped recreation center.

"There is never a boring day at LSU," gushes one psychology major. The trees and traditions date back more than 100 years, but change is the new norm here. LSU is focused on the goals of learning, discovery, diversity, and engagement, and though it may be a while before the school's academic profile matches its athletic prowess, that's what administrators are aiming for. In the meantime, students are happy to *laissez les bons temps rouler*!

Overlaps

Virginia Tech, University of Alabama, University of North Texas, Clemson, Oklahoma State, UT Austin, University of Mississippi, University of Louisiana

If You Apply To ›

LSU: Rolling admissions. SATs or ACTs: required. No Subject Tests. Accepts the Common Application with supplement.

Loyola University Maryland

Baltimore, MD 21210

Vintage Jesuit school with a rigorous liberal arts curriculum, caring faculty, and a strong sense of community. Baltimore location a plus for those with "I don't want to miss anything" attitude. Same size as Providence, smaller than BC, Fordham, and other Roman Catholic schools in urban settings. No varsity football, but top-ranked men's lacrosse team evokes plenty of school spirit.

Website: www.loyola.edu
Location: City Outskirts
Private
Total Enrollment: 4,326
Undergraduates: 3,873
Male/Female: 42/58
SAT Ranges: ERW 580–660,
  M 560–650
ACT Ranges: 25–30
Financial Aid: 73%
Pell Grant: 13%
Expense: Pr $ $
Student Loans: 62%
Average Debt: $ $ $ $
Applicants: 11,600
Accepted: 75%
Enrolled: 12%
Grad in 6 Years: 81%
Returning Freshmen: 85%
Academics: ✐ ✐ ✐
Social: ☎ ☎ ☎
Q of L: ★ ★ ★
Admissions: (410) 617-5012
Email Address: admission@
  loyola.edu

Strong Programs:
Business Administration
Communication
Psychology
Speech-Language-Hearing
  Sciences
Education
Biology
Engineering

Four U.S. universities bear the name of St. Ignatius of Loyola, founder of the Society of Jesus (Jesuits), but this one is the granddaddy of them all. Founded in 1851 (and the one that laid claim to www.loyola.edu), Loyola University Maryland combines the virtues of a residential campus with ready access to a major city on the Amtrak corridor. Loyola jumped up from "college" to "university" status in 2009, and, with a "big enough but not too big" feel, manages to strike a balance between real-world experience and the traditional Jesuit ideals of academic excellence, a liberal arts curriculum, and *cura personalis* (a.k.a. education of the whole person).

Loyola's Evergreen campus, the home to undergraduates, sits on 80 green and wooded acres in a mixed residential area in northern Baltimore, about 15 minutes from the heart of the city. (Graduate students are shunted off to their own campuses in Columbia and Timonium, Maryland.) The academic Quad features the largest collection of collegiate Gothic buildings in Baltimore, including the Alumni Memorial Chapel with its lovely stained-glass windows. Architectural variety is provided by the Tudor-style Humanities Center, built in 1895, and the Sellinger School of Business and Management, a contemporary 50,000-square-foot facility notable for its atrium and five-story glass facade.

Undergraduate academics at Loyola are organized around the triumvirate of the School of Education, the Sellinger School of Business and Management, and Loyola College, the arts and sciences college. Consistent with Jesuit academic tradition, Loyola students pursue a core curriculum that covers "basic knowledge and concepts" and encourages critical thinking across the liberal arts and sciences. Among the requirements are classes in theology and ethics, and the choice of one diversity-designated course—with a focus on global or domestic diversity or justice awareness. Messina is the university's first-year living/learning program, in which students enroll in two small seminar classes, one in the fall and one in the spring, focused on one of four themes: The Visionary, Self and Other, Stories We Tell, and The Good Life. The courses are guided by a professor and an older student (called an "Evergreen") who also lives with the same students, and Messina groups participate in special events and excursions together. "It makes new students feel like they are a part of the Loyola community and realize how many people care about them here," says a biology major.

> **"Professors tend to shy away from boring lectures in favor of engaging discussions."**

The business program is said to be strong, as are most of the humanities. Business administration, communication, psychology, and speech-language-hearing sciences are the most popular majors. Other strong areas, students say, include education, biology, and engineering. Students describe the academic program at Loyola as challenging but supportive. "Students are generally not competing against each other for the best grades, but rather tend to work together on projects or while studying," says a senior. Teaching assistants are an unknown species, and 47 percent of classes have fewer than 20 students. Students praise their professors' emphasis on teaching and getting to know students. "I cannot imagine what it would be like not to have a professor know my name," says a senior. A political science major comments that "professors tend to shy away from boring lectures in favor of engaging discussions."

Each summer, 10 to 12 undergraduates are selected to work side by side with faculty from the six natural science departments to conduct research in the students' area of interest and participate in seminars, journal clubs, and social activities. For top students, the Honors Program provides an interdisciplinary route through a more ambitious core curriculum. A whopping 60 percent of students study abroad, usually for a semester during the junior year. Venues for business students range from Bangkok and Singapore to Melbourne and Accra, while language students set out for Spain, France, China, and elsewhere in search of native speakers. Loyola students are encouraged to do community service while abroad and to submit an Immersion Research Project upon return. "I studied in Cork, Ireland, and it was one of the highlights of my college experience!" cheers a senior.

Messina is a first-year living/learning program in which students are guided by a professor and an older student (called an "Evergreen").

"The passion for service runs very strong through the veins of Loyola."

Students at Loyola tend to be, in the words of one senior, "fairly preppy." Eighteen percent of undergraduates hail from Maryland, and less than 1 percent come from other countries. African Americans represent 5 percent, Hispanics 10 percent, Asian Americans 4 percent, and multiracial students 3 percent. About three-quarters of undergrads describe themselves as Catholics; there are fewer than 10 Jesuits on the faculty. "Religion has a huge impact on campus," says one non-Catholic, who adds, "As a Christian, I love the fact that I can openly talk about my religion and that others accept my beliefs." A political science major says that "social justice is a huge initiative at Loyola, with abortion, immigration reform, gay marriage, homelessness, hunger, and gender equality just some of the issues that students at Loyola are fighting for/against." Merit awards average $17,700, and Loyola offers 114 athletic scholarships in 17 sports.

About three-quarters of undergrads describe themselves as Catholics; there are fewer than 10 Jesuits on the faculty.

Loyola students enjoy the residence halls, which are located west of the main campus and are connected by a pedestrian bridge spanning Charles Street. "We have some of the best dorms in the country," boasts a senior. Facilities, which include traditional dormitories as well as apartments and townhouses for upperclassmen, are spacious and modern. Not surprisingly, 81 percent of students live on campus, at least until their senior year. The main dining facility is Boulder Garden Café, but other options range from the Reading Room to Starbucks. Loyola offers a "meal swipe" or "declining balance" dining plan. Campus security is not an issue. "We are in a relatively dangerous part of the city," says an accounting major, "but the Loyola police do a good job to make us all feel safe on campus."

Loyola has no fraternities or sororities, but given the proximity to Baltimore, this arrangement is just fine with students. "Most of Loyola's social life takes place off campus," says a student. "Bars and clubs are very close to campus, and the penalties for throwing a party in your room are pretty steep." That's not to say that on-campus life is monastic. "The campus is always buzzing with things like concerts and festivals," says an English major. The undisputed high point of the social calendar is Loyolapalooza, the spring festival held on the last weekend before final exams to celebrate the academic year. Students gather on the Quad for a concert, games,

Luck O'Loyola is the annual St. Patrick's Day celebration that features traditional Irish bagpipes, dancing, and music.

and food. A close second is Luck O'Loyola, the annual St. Patrick's Day celebration that features traditional Irish bagpipes, dancing, and music.

Community service also plays a prominent role in campus life. "The passion for service runs very strong through the veins of Loyola," says a senior. The Center for Community Service and Justice helps students find opportunities ranging from one-time volunteer activities to semester-long service-learning courses. The city of Baltimore offers an abundance of sights, including the famed Inner Harbor, with its many restaurants and museums, as well as major league sports. Loyola's neighbors include numerous other colleges and universities, including Johns Hopkins and Towson University. "Loyola students do not regard Baltimore as a 'college town' per se, but it has plenty of young-adult neighborhoods and pockets of entertainment," reports an accounting major. Public transportation is poor in Baltimore, but a "college town" shuttle helps students get around. Washington, D.C., an hour away by train, is a frequent weekend destination.

> "We care for each other, and our Jesuit mission rings true in our day-to-day lives."

Loyola eschews varsity football, but the Greyhounds compete in the Division I Patriot League in eight men's and nine women's sports. Befitting the school's Maryland location, both the men's and women's lacrosse teams are consistently strong. For those with more modest athletic ambitions, Loyola sponsors 25 co-ed and single-sex club sports teams and 30 intramural events that draw about 40 percent of students. Flag football, volleyball, and soccer are popular. The state-of-the-art Fitness and Aquatic Center features a well-equipped 6,000-square-foot fitness center, a rock-climbing wall, an eight-lane pool, and other amenities.

Some Loyola denizens lament the absence of football and the dearth of parties on campus, but such complaints seem a small price to pay for four years as part of a close-knit community that takes its humanistic, academic, and social values seriously. "We care for each other, and our Jesuit mission rings true in our day-to-day lives," says a senior. A classmate adds, "The good food, residence halls, and location don't hurt either."

Overlaps
Boston College, Holy Cross, Fairfield, Fordham, Providence, St. Joseph's, University of Delaware, University of Maryland

If You Apply To ›

Loyola: Early action, regular decision. SATs or ACTs: optional (test-optional applicants must submit additional essay or additional teacher recommendation). Subject Tests: optional. Accepts the Common Application.

Loyola Marymount University

I LMU Drive, Suite 100, Los Angeles, CA 90045

LMU is a Roman Catholic university known for its strategic L.A. location and strong programs in film and television, business, engineering, and communication. Strong international emphasis in film and theatre arts. Compare to Chapman, Santa Clara, and University of San Diego. To take full advantage of L.A., access to a car is highly beneficial.

Website: www.lmu.edu
Location: Suburban
Private
Total Enrollment: 8,334
Undergraduates: 6,119

At Loyola Marymount University, students are treated to ideal weather year-round, a vast array of internship opportunities, and an academic lineup that includes solid programs in film and television, liberal arts and sciences, and business. What's more, LMU has the distinction of being the only Roman Catholic university in Los Angeles. "LMU is more than an academic institution," says a junior. "It is a community dedicated to helping students grow and thrive."

Established in 1911, LMU occupies a 142-acre Westchester campus perched on a bluff overlooking the Pacific Ocean and Marina del Rey in a peaceful residential neighborhood of Los Angeles. The school is sponsored by three religious orders: the Society of Jesus (Jesuits), the Marymount Sisters, and the Sisters of St. Joseph of Orange. Campus highlights include the 24-hour Hannon Library and the $110 million, LEED Gold–certified Life Sciences Building. A downtown campus houses Loyola's law school, and a new Playa Vista campus is home to graduate programs in film and television and business.

LMU offers 58 baccalaureate majors and 53 minors in six colleges and schools. The general education requirements (known as the Core Curriculum) are designed to encourage intellectual breadth, tackling themes such as faith and reason; virtue and justice; culture; art and society; and science, nature, and society. "The nice thing about LMU's academics is that the core requirements encourage students to be open to various studies," says a freshman, "from science to theology to philosophy." Freshmen may take part in a number of programs designed to support first-year students, including an honors program and a first-year seminar.

> "The core requirements encourage students to be open to various studies."

The most popular programs include management, marketing, communication studies, psychology, finance, and film and television production; these are also among the university's strongest. Other solid programs include engineering, theatre arts, political science, English, and economics. Students in the School of Film and Television have access to a number of resources, including a student-run production office, a television stage, and a film soundstage with a professional "green screen" (for those cool CGI effects!). They also benefit from the program's strong international emphasis, including the chance to study in Bonn, Germany, and produce their own documentaries that are exhibited at festivals in Germany and the U.S. Those in the College of Science and Engineering take part in national competitions to design steel bridges and race eco-friendly cars. Thanks to its hip Los Angeles locale, LMU offers a plethora of internships to experience-hungry students, including stints at Disney, MTV, and Warner Bros. LMU offers 55 exchange, semester, and study abroad options on six continents in a wide range of disciplines; 29 percent of students participate during their time at LMU.

Like nearby Tinseltown, LMU manages to be both competitive and relaxed. "Depending on the course, a lot of work might be required or barely any homework could be given," says a freshman. A theology major adds, "Most of the intro classes seem more laid-back and the upper division classes are more rigorous." Fifty-three percent of classes have fewer than 20 students, and students say teacher-student interaction is a given. "Professors truly know their students and take a personal interest in their learning," says a junior.

> "LMU is known for its sense of community and its friendliness."

LMU undergraduates hail from all 50 states and 80 foreign countries; 64 percent come from California and 10 percent from abroad. "LMU is known for its sense of community and its friendliness," says a student. Another adds, "There is an optimistic atmosphere on this campus because students want to be here." Thirty-seven percent of students are Catholic. African Americans comprise 7 percent of the student body, Hispanics 21 percent, Asian Americans 10 percent, and multiracial students 7 percent. Student activism is alive and well on campus and diversity is a perpetually hot issue. Merit scholarships averaging $11,000 are available for qualified students, and the athletically inclined vie for 237 athletic scholarships in 16 sports.

Fifty-three percent of LMU students live on campus, where a student says, "Housing is pretty nice." Many first-years choose to participate in themed living/

(continued)

Male/Female: 44/56
SAT Ranges: ERW 600–680, M 580–680
ACT Ranges: 26–31
Financial Aid: 86%
Pell Grant: 12%
Expense: Pr $ $
Student Loans: 53%
Average Debt: $ $ $
Applicants: 15,381
Accepted: 52%
Enrolled: 18%
Grad in 6 Years: 79%
Returning Freshmen: 91%
Academics: ✍ ✍ ✍
Social: ☎ ☎ ☎
Q of L: ★ ★ ★
Admissions: (310) 338-2750
Email Address: admission@lmu.edu

Strong Programs:
Management
Marketing
Communication Studies
Psychology
Finance
Film and Television Production
Engineering
Theatre Arts

Thanks to its hip Los Angeles locale, LMU offers a plethora of internships to experience-hungry students.

learning communities, including those dedicated to specific academic disciplines, first-generation students, and Ignatian leadership. The university offers a variety of meal plan options and dining facilities and "all types of food are available," according to a political science major. Students describe campus security as good too; "I have never felt unsafe," a junior says.

The social life at LMU takes place "both on and off campus," says one student. Student organizations and clubs frequently host activities, and Greek life influences the scene too, attracting 17 percent of the men and 29 percent of the women. Students say there is little pressure to drink. "If students want to drink, they can find alcohol," says a freshman. "Those that don't want to, don't have to." The university's Jesuit heritage promotes a social atmosphere that "motivates students to improve themselves by helping others," a student says. "Whether it's Greek life, service organizations, or intramurals, students have a number of possibilities." Students volunteer more than 200,000 hours of service every year in after-school programs, homeless shelters, health clinics, and other settings. The area of Westchester is "definitely not a college town," groans a sophomore. Fortunately, Marina del Rey and Santa Monica are a short car or bus ride away, and it's only a mile to the beach. "Since L.A. is a big city, there are plenty of places for a college student to eat, shop, and find entertainment." Popular road trips include San Diego, Santa Barbara, Las Vegas, and Mexico.

Back on campus, LMU's varsity teams compete in the Division I West Coast Conference. Women's water polo is a recent conference champion; men's and women's soccer and women's volleyball are also competitive. The Lions' rivalry with nearby Pepperdine always draws a huge crowd, and the basketball team's annual pep rally—LMU Madness—"is a pretty big event," says a student. Intramurals are popular and include flag football, soccer, and billiards, among others. LMU's debate team is a standout too, having placed first in more than 250 national and international tournaments over the past 40 years.

With its dynamic mix of solid academics, Jesuit and Marymount traditions, and thriving social life, LMU offers students substance and style. "We're very friendly with a gorgeous campus," says a student. Whether you're a budding scientist or a future filmmaker, Loyola Marymount University may be worth a look.

LMU's debate team is a standout, having placed first in more than 250 national and international tournaments.

Overlaps

University of Southern California, UCLA, Santa Clara, Chapman, Cal Poly–San Luis Obispo, UC Santa Barbara, NYU, UC Berkeley

If You Apply To ›

LMU: Early decision, early action, regular decision. SATs or ACTs: required. Subject Tests: optional. Accepts the Common Application with supplement. Applicants to animation, dance, music, and theatre arts are required to submit a portfolio or audition.

Loyola University New Orleans

6363 St. Charles Ave., Box 89, New Orleans, LA 70118

Of the four Loyolas in the nation, this is the only one where you can go to Mardi Gras and then study the music you heard the next morning in class. New Orleans is an ideal setting for this Roman Catholic university with strengths in business, communication, and the arts. New Orleans is the most freewheeling Deep South city, and Loyola's politics are mainly liberal.

Loyola University New Orleans is a liberal arts school founded in 1904 by the Society of Jesus (Jesuits) that continues to enhance its rich tradition through extensive service-learning programs, increasing admissions standards, and a renewed commitment to diversifying the student body. The university has capitalized on its unique NOLA setting to develop excellent programs in artistic and creative fields, with a preprofessional bent. As a Loyola student, "you will be challenged, motivated, and inspired to do more," says one happy senior.

The school's attractive and well-kept 20-acre main campus, in the University section of Uptown New Orleans, mixes Tudor, Gothic, and modern structures. It overlooks acres of Audubon Park and, beyond, the mighty Mississippi River. Two blocks up St. Charles Avenue, Loyola's Broadway campus has an additional four acres. The renovated Monroe Hall features state-of-the-art science labs, high-tech design studios, and a seventh-floor greenhouse. The Monroe Library houses approximately 500,000 volumes, the Boggs National Center for Community Literacy, an art gallery, and the brand-new Student Success Center.

The Loyola Core involves distribution requirements designed to develop skills in critical thinking, effective communication, quantitative reasoning, information literacy, and ethical reasoning. Incoming students take an interdisciplinary First-Year Seminar that introduces them to college-level work and the Jesuit tradition of "thinking critically, acting justly." Other aspects of Loyola's comprehensive first-year experience include a common reading program, a series of lectures and panel discussions, educational excursions, service-learning projects, and a peer mentoring program.

> "I'm a senior, and professors I had in my freshman year still greet me in the halls by name."

The School of Mass Communication, whose students do well in national competitions, wins praise, as does virtually any program in the College of Music and Fine Art, including majors in digital filmmaking, graphic design, jazz studies, and popular and commercial music that are increasingly sought-after in a city where these creative professions are defining specialties. Indeed, music industry studies is one of the most popular majors, along with psychology, management, marketing, and English with a writing concentration. Sociology, biological sciences, and premed advising are also strengths, and minors in entrepreneurship and New Orleans studies are available. Newer majors include food studies and interaction design.

Loyola's academic climate is said to be challenging but supportive. Students point out that retention and graduation rates have been an issue, perhaps in part because "funding is short" in some programs, especially in the humanities, according to a senior. Fifty-three percent of undergraduate classes have fewer than 20 students, and faculty make an effort to get to know their students. "I have connected on a personal level with every professor I've had here. I'm a senior, and professors I had in my freshman year still greet me in the halls by name," says an English major.

The University Honors Program, open to students in all majors, gives 300 high-achieving students access to small seminars, collaborative research projects with faculty, social activities, and other special opportunities. Thirty percent of undergraduates exercise their wings in study abroad programs available in more than 50 countries, from Mexico and Brazil to the Netherlands and South Korea. With the help of the service-learning office, about 500 students make service learning part of their studies, and Loyola is a top producer of Peace Corps volunteers. "As a Jesuit institution, we are very active in the community and social justice," confirms a senior. Many students volunteer their sweat equity with the Loyola University Community Action Program, a student-led coalition of eight organizations that take on issues such as hunger and homelessness.

Website: www.loyno.edu
Location: City Center
Private
Total Enrollment: 2,930
Undergraduates: 2,414
Male/Female: 37/63
SAT Ranges: ERW 560–650, M 520–620
ACT Ranges: 22–28
Financial Aid: 75%
Pell Grant: 35%
Expense: Pr $
Student Loans: 71%
Average Debt: $ $ $
Applicants: 5,112
Accepted: 69%
Enrolled: 23%
Grad in 6 Years: 55%
Returning Freshmen: 80%
Academics: ✍ ✍ ✍
Social: ☎ ☎ ☎
Q of L: ★ ★ ★
Admissions: (800) 456-9652
Email Address: admit@loyno.edu

Strong Programs:
Music Industry Studies
Psychology
Management
Marketing
English
Mass Communication
Digital Filmmaking
Sociology

About a third of undergrads are first-generation college students.

Given Loyola's academic strengths, the student body is an interesting mix of creative types, social justice warriors, career-minded preprofessionals, and "students who are a bit quirky, who see things differently," says one student. Forty-one percent of Loyola undergraduates are Louisiana natives, and many of the remaining students are from the Southeast; 2 percent are international. Sixteen percent are Hispanic, 15 percent are African American, 3 percent are Asian American, and 5 percent are multiracial. Religion—specifically Roman Catholicism—has a significant influence on campus; roughly half of the students are Catholic. Daily mass is voluntary, but many students attend. Even so, the political atmosphere is largely liberal, and students are particularly active in advocating for women's rights and LGBTQ- and gender-related issues. Loyola awards merit scholarships averaging $16,800 each year and 79 athletic scholarships in 9 sports. About a third of undergrads are first-generation college students, and 35 percent of freshmen are Pell-eligible.

Many Loyola students commute from home or off-campus apartments; 54 percent of all undergraduates reside on campus. The transition to college is eased by Themed Living Communities, which house classmates together in a common living space within one of the residence halls. Campus dining in the Orleans Room is described as adequate, and a junior comments, "It's a great benefit to have Tulane University across the street because we can use their dining facilities as well." Students feel safe on campus, according to one junior, who adds that the school is "growing and expanding organizations to improve how it handles campus sexual assault."

"Loyola gives us lots of cool things to do on campus," a philosophy major says, including musical performances and sporting events. Fraternities and sororities are rarities at Jesuit schools, but they make themselves felt at Loyola, with 4 percent of

"[Loyola students] are a bit quirky [and] see things differently."

the men and 13 percent of the women choosing to belong. Major campuswide social events include the annual "Sneaux Day" that blankets Loyola's front lawn with "snow," the senior crawfish boil, family weekend featuring a New Orleans-style jazz brunch, and the musical event Christmas at Loyola, held on the first Sunday in December. Loyola even takes the week of Mardi Gras off as a holiday and allows students to register overnight visitors so they can attend the festivities. With so much nightlife in the surrounding city, students report that not much underage drinking happens on campus. New Orleans is always bustling and offers "tons of live music, bars, clubs, and restaurants all easily accessible to students," says a senior.

Wolf Pack teams compete in the NAIA Division I as a member of the Southern States Athletic Conference. The most competitive teams are men's and women's basketball. Fifteen percent of undergraduates participate in intramural and club sports, and Loyola's wellness program offers a range of fitness classes and recreational activities for jocks and non-jocks alike. Basketball, flag football (no real pigskins at Loyola), and Quidditch are popular pastimes.

Students at Loyola know how to pull together and draw strength from their faith as well as from the distinctive culture of New Orleans. Whether they're working closely with caring professors or relaxing with friends amid the Big Easy's boundless energy, students are satisfied with their choice. A sophomore says, "Loyola is an awesome small Jesuit college with a lot to offer as a community and academic institution."

If You Apply To ›

Loyola: Early action, regular decision. SATs or ACTs: required. Subject Tests: optional. Accepts the Common Application with supplement. Audition or portfolio required for admission to the College of Music and Fine Arts.

Macalester College

1600 Grand Avenue, St. Paul, MN 55105

A small school that punches above its weight, Macalester offers an internationalist and multiculturalist view of the world with a pronounced Scottish flavor. One of a handful of leading liberal arts colleges in a metropolitan setting. Carleton has a slightly bigger national reputation, but Mac has St. Paul, a progressive capital city. Eighty-six percent of the student body hails from outside Minnesota.

Macalester College is an international island in the heart of the Great Plains. Liberal describes both its curriculum and its politics. Students here get riled up over all sorts of issues with local, national, or international import—from LGBTQ rights to immigration policy and fair trade. Mac students come to the school "deeply caring about a social justice issue," says one student, "and throughout their years at Mac, their passions expand and deepen." Bagpipes lead all major processions and are heard frequently on campus as a stirring reminder of the college's historic Scottish roots. Says one senior, "Bagpipes are like the Macalester anthem. They begin all official events, bringing happy tears to my eyes every time."

Macalester takes its name from a Scotsman named Charles Macalester, an advisor to Abraham Lincoln and other U.S. presidents. The college is located in a friendly, family-oriented neighborhood in St. Paul, Minnesota, one mile from the Mississippi River, which divides St. Paul from Minneapolis. Summit Avenue, a tree-lined street with the longest, best-preserved stretch of Victorian homes in the nation, forms the campus's northern boundary. The self-contained, 53-acre campus is arranged around 130-year-old Old Main, a splendid Victorian structure listed on the National Register of Historic Places. The unifying theme is redbrick, the better to set off the octagonal Weyerhauser Chapel, constructed of black glass. The latest addition to campus is a $32 million theater and dance building.

> **"Bagpipes are like the Macalester anthem. They begin all official events."**

Mac's general education requirements span the liberal arts and sciences and include at least two courses that address cultural diversity, in the United States and internationally. Every student also completes a seminar-style First-Year Course and, in the senior year, a capstone experience, such as an independent research project, performance, artistic work, or other original work. In addition to international studies, Mac's academic strengths include geography, chemistry, math and statistics, and computer science. Eleven foreign languages are offered, including Arabic, Portuguese, and Russian. The most popular majors are economics, mathematics, biology, and psychology. Science facilities include an observatory and labs for electronic instrumentation and laser spectroscopy.

A sophomore says, "We take our studies seriously and, as a result, conversations continue outside of the classroom because that's how much of an impact they've had on us." Mac emphasizes small class sizes and working together to handle the challenging workload, and students say most pressure to do well comes from within. Teaching and personal relationships are paramount, with professors often having students over for dinner or dishing off passes on the intramural basketball court. "Professors cater to students' passion for learning by making classrooms safe spaces for discussion and community," says an international studies major.

The late Kofi Annan, former UN secretary general and class of '61, typified one of Macalester's hallmarks: internationalism, not just in its curriculum and its student body, but also in its emphasis on international, off-campus experiences. An

Website: www.macalester.edu
Location: City Center
Private
Total Enrollment: 2,081
Undergraduates: 2,081
Male/Female: 39/61
SAT Ranges: ERW 660–740, M 640–740
ACT Ranges: 29–32
Financial Aid: 85%
Pell Grant: 23%
Expense: Pr $ $ $ $
Student Loans: 61%
Average Debt: $ $
Applicants: 5,900
Accepted: 41%
Enrolled: 23%
Grad in 6 Years: 87%
Returning Freshmen: 93%
Academics: ✏ ✏ ✏ ✏ ½
Social: ☎ ☎ ☎
Q of L: ★ ★ ★ ★
Admissions: (800) 231-7974
Email Address: admissions@macalester.edu

Strong Programs:
International Studies
Geography
Chemistry
Computer Science
Economics
Mathematics
Biology
Psychology

impressive 62 percent of students go abroad to complete traditional coursework, independent research, and internships, choosing from 95 faculty-led, exchange, and partner programs on six continents. Fifty-seven percent conduct undergraduate research, often in stipend-supported positions with Mac professors during the summer. Before graduation, more than three-quarters of the students complete an internship, usually in the Twin Cities area, and almost all students get involved in volunteer work.

An economics major says Mac students tend to fall "somewhere between the quirky intellectual and the globe-trotting activist," adding, "We love discussing political and social issues—sometimes to a fault." Fourteen percent of Macalester students hail from Minnesota, and the rest come from every state, the District of Columbia, and dozens of other countries—the proportion of international students is substantial, at 15 percent. Three percent of students are African American, 8 percent are Hispanic, 7 percent are Asian American, and 6 percent are multiracial. Merit scholarships averaging $15,300 are available to eligible students; there are no athletic scholarships. Macalester guarantees to meet 100 percent of all admitted students' demonstrated financial need, and 23 percent of incoming freshmen qualify for Pell Grants.

> "Conversations continue outside of the classroom because that's how much of an impact they've had on us."

All freshmen and sophomores are required to live in college housing; 60 percent of students dwell in college-owned digs, which include traditional residences with single or double rooms as well as suites for upperclassmen. "Some of the first-year halls are a bit old, but they have so much character and community that it doesn't matter!" enthuses a geography major. Residents of the Interfaith House and the Veggie Co-op prepare their own meals, while others enjoy vittles in the campus center. "It's really easy to hate on Café Mac, the one dining hall here," says a junior, "but honestly the food here is much better than people give it credit for." Students praise campus security and the college's proactive approach to sexual assault awareness. "We are constantly holding dialogues, having discussions, bringing in outside speakers, and addressing policy about this growing issue," reports a junior.

Given the proximity of a major metropolitan area, much of Mac's social life takes place in the city, although there are plenty of events on campus for those loath to leave. "There is no Greek life on campus, which I think is really positive. No one is dictating the party culture on campus and there is no pressure to drink," says one student. Popular events include Founders Day, Winter Ball, Springfest, and the annual Brain Bowl football game against in-state rival Carleton. There are about a dozen other colleges and universities in town, and the Twin Cities are an excellent place to live, with plenty of bookstores, coffee shops, restaurants, bars, and movie theaters, plus dance and jazz clubs and professional sports teams. Public transportation makes it relatively easy to get around. The Mall of America is nearby, though Mac students tend to tire of it quickly. For those with wheels, the best road trips include Chicago, Madison, and Duluth—and Bemidji, Minnesota, "to see Babe the Blue Ox," according to a senior.

Competitive Division III Scots teams include baseball and women's water polo (both recent conference champions), along with football and men's and women's soccer, cross-country, and track and field. Macalester has one of the oldest competitive debate programs in the nation, and the mock trial program is highly ranked nationally. About 60 percent of the students compete in intramural and club sports, including dodgeball, rugby, and ice hockey. "Whenever the weather's nice, students dot the lawns playing Frisbee, soccer, or cricket—yes, cricket!" says one student.

Macalester provides high-powered scholarship and Scottish heritage, pairing academic rigor with global perspective. As the school's story travels, the skill and diversity of the student body are rising. Students here appreciate their freedom to grow within a supportive community. "We are all encouraged to explore ourselves, and we are all encouraged to find our passions and commit to them," says one student. "It is what binds us all."

If You Apply To ›

Macalester: Early decision I and II, regular decision. SATs or ACTs: required. Subject Tests: optional. Accepts the Common Application with supplement.

University of Maine–Orono

Orono, ME 04469

A sleeper choice for out-of-staters amid better-known public universities such as UMass, UNH, and UVM. Not coincidentally, UMaine is the least expensive—and easiest in admission—of the four. A popular marine sciences program flourishes here, as does engineering. UMaine is a global leader in the development of offshore wind power. Offers a solid honors program and one of the top varsity hockey programs in the nation. Aggressively recruiting out-of-state students.

At the University of Maine–Orono, roughly 8,000 undergraduates help themselves to a range of strong academic programs at a reasonable cost. As the state's land grant university and its only sea grant university, UMaine attracts top students to its marine sciences program. "Here at UMaine there seems to be a widely accepted and shared value of the opportunity to further one's education," says a junior.

Situated on an island between the Stillwater and Penobscot rivers, UMaine's campus is 660 acres, centered on a large, tree-shaded grass mall. Architectural themes at this flagship of the state university system range from English academic to contemporary. Newer facilities include the Innovative Media Research and Commercialization Center, which contains a computer-driven 3-D router, a video production lab, and rich-media classrooms, and the $5.2 million Emera Astronomy Center, home to the state's largest planetarium.

As Maine's flagship public university, UMaine offers 100 undergraduate majors and academic programs. The university's colleges are the College of Education and Human Development; the College of Engineering; the College of Liberal Arts and Sciences; the College of Natural Sciences, Forestry, and Agriculture; and the Honors College (which now enrolls approximately 750 students)—as well as the Maine Business School. Specific general education requirements vary from college to college, though all students must demonstrate writing proficiency and earn credits in physical or biological science, human value and social context, math (including statistics and computer science), and ethics. A capstone experience is also mandatory.

"The atmosphere is very relaxed and allows for a more comfortable exploration of your education."

"Unless you're in a very competitive major, the atmosphere is very relaxed and allows for a more comfortable exploration of your education," says a junior. The engineering programs are widely viewed as the most demanding on campus. Other best bets include business, forestry, earth and climate sciences, and nursing. Marine sciences undergrads can spend a semester by the sea at UMaine's prominent Darling

Website: www.umaine.edu
Location: Rural
Public
Total Enrollment: 8,962
Undergraduates: 8,161
Male/Female: 53/47
SAT Ranges: ERW 530–630, M 520–620
ACT Ranges: 22–27
Financial Aid: 92%
Pell Grant: 32%
Expense: Pub $ $
Student Loans: 76%
Average Debt: $ $ $ $
Applicants: 13,231
Accepted: 92%
Enrolled: 19%
Grad in 6 Years: 58%
Returning Freshmen: 75%
Academics: ✐ ✐
Social: ☎ ☎ ☎ ☎
Q of L: ★ ★ ★
Admissions: (207) 581-1561
Email Address: umaine admissions@maine.edu

Strong Programs:
Business Management

Marine Center, and UMaine's Climate Change Institute is renowned. The most popular majors include business management, mechanical engineering, psychology, and kinesiology and physical education. Forty-one percent of all classes have fewer than 20 students, which means a fair amount of personal attention from professors. "Most of my professors have been very thorough, passionate, and enthusiastic about the subject," says a communication major.

Research is a key part of an undergraduate education at UMaine and is woven into many areas of the curriculum, as is real-world experience. SPIFFY, the student investment club, manages a $3 million, real-money portfolio. UMaine's Explorations program lets first-year students work with professionals in different areas before declaring their degree choices, and the First-Year and Transfer Center is the go-to resource for new students seeking academic or personal support. UMaine students may choose from more than 700 study abroad programs in more than 40 countries.

UMaine's Explorations program lets first-year students work with professionals in different areas before declaring their degree choices.

"Students at UMaine are laid-back but also exhibit a love for learning," states one student. Most undergrads hail from Maine and other parts of New England (making them immune to the frigid temperatures). Faced with a declining youth population in Maine, the university has been working hard to lure out-of-state students with several programs, including the Flagship Match program, which allows them to pay the same in-state tuition they would pay at their home flagship university. UMaine has promoted Flagship Match with, among other things, a billboard advertising campaign on highways throughout the region and as far away as California, and their efforts are paying off—out-of-state enrollment is up to 35 percent, double what it was five years ago. African Americans account for 2 percent of the student body, Asian Americans 2 percent, Hispanics 4 percent, and multiracial students 3 percent; international students add 2 percent. "UMaine is pretty homogeneous," admits one journalism major. Socioeconomic diversity is better represented, with 32 percent of students qualifying for Pell Grants. Merit scholarships offer an average of $6,300 a year for qualified students, and 194 athletic scholarships are available in 12 sports.

Forty percent of UMaine students live on campus; the rest seek shelter in Orono, nearby Bangor, or the sparsely populated area in between. "After sophomore year, unless someone is in the Honors College, getting housing on campus is a serious challenge," complains a senior, adding that while off-campus housing is generally more affordable, commuting to campus can be a pain, especially given limited parking and long, snowy winters. Dorms are co-ed; some have gyms, computer labs, or apartment-style suites. First-years may opt to join one of seven living/learning communities organized around themes like wellness, green living, and first-generation college students. Dining options have been overhauled, but students agree that the food could still be improved, especially for the health-conscious. "Campus feels incredibly safe to me," says one student. "The dorms are very well-secured and can only be accessed with our student ID cards."

"The party scene is pretty lively at UMaine."

Out-of-state enrollment is up to 35 percent, double what it was five years ago.

Despite—or possibly because of—UMaine's relatively isolated location, the campus pulses with social life; 200 student groups and organizations plan plays, carnival nights, concerts, and comedy hours, with a different activity offered each night. "Whatever your lifestyle, you can find something to do," one student says. Fraternities draw 8 percent of men, while sororities sign up 5 percent of women. Partiers find their niche off campus at bars, clubs, Greek parties, and house parties. According to a junior, "The party scene is pretty lively at UMaine, with many different parties happening every weekend and sometimes on several weeknights," and underage drinking on campus, though prohibited, is common. The annual Maine Day features a parade, cookout, and campuswide cleanup.

The midsized town of Orono—described by one sophomore as a "great college town"—offers a few bars, a theater, and some other hangouts. Buses to Bangor, a fair-sized city 10 minutes away, run every 15 to 20 minutes. UMaine students tend to be outdoor enthusiasts, and popular road trips include Acadia National Park, skiing at Sugarloaf, L.L. Bean's 24-hour store in Freeport, and the real-life Mount Katahdin, which appears on Bean's logo. More urban types enjoy Boston, just four hours away, or Montreal, with its lower drinking age.

UMaine is the state's only Division I school, and athletic events are a big part of student life. Hockey reigns supreme, especially when played against Boston College, Boston University, or New Hampshire, and the Black Bears are perennial champions. Women's basketball claimed the America East conference title in 2018, and women's softball and men's and women's track and field are also competitive. The popular intramural and club sports programs cover more than 35 sports, from swimming and wrestling to kickball and broomball (ice hockey with a dodgeball and a broom, played with shoes instead of skates).

UMaine is a medium-sized school with a small-school atmosphere. Combine the state's natural beauty with an increased emphasis on top-quality facilities and more intimate student/faculty interaction, and it's no surprise that this campus draws more die-hard "Maine-iaks" each year.

If You Apply To ›

Maine: Early action, regular decision. SATs or ACTs: required. No Subject Tests. Accepts the Common Application with supplement.

Manhattanville College

2900 Purchase Street, Purchase, NY 10577

One of the few small liberal arts colleges in the NYC area, Manhattanville occupies a former estate (complete with a castle) and is a quick train ride into Manhattan. Strong programs include education and psychology, and the distinctive Portfolio System has been rebooted for modern times. Nearly two-thirds of students are women and one-quarter are Hispanic.

Founded in 1841 by the Sisters of the Sacred Heart as an all-women's boarding school, Manhattanville College today is a private, nondenominational, coeducational, liberal arts college with a mission to "educate students to be ethical and socially responsible leaders in a global community." Manhattanville recently overhauled its signature Portfolio System, which had been the college's calling card since 1971. Now known as ATLAS, the new system is currently being piloted as an optional four-year program in which students set goals, reflect on their academic and cocurricular experiences, and showcase their work in e-portfolios. But ATLAS is just one way Manhattanville encourages individuality and personal growth. Personal attention is another.

Manhattanville College pulled up stakes from its original location on Houston Street in New York City in the 1950s for a 125-acre estate in Purchase, New York. The estate is located in wealthy Westchester County, near the town of White Plains—home to several major corporations, and just 28 miles from the excitement of the Big Apple. Overlooking the central Quadrangle, which was designed by Central Park

Website: www.mville.edu
Location: Suburban
Private
Total Enrollment: 1,971
Undergraduates: 1,632
Male/Female: 37/63
SAT Ranges: ERW 480–585, M 430–625
ACT Ranges: 17–27
Financial Aid: 97%
Pell Grant: 39%
Expense: Pr $
Student Loans: 77%
Average Debt: $ $ $ $

(continued)

Applicants: 3,841
Accepted: 82%
Enrolled: 13%
Grad in 6 Years: 55%
Returning Freshmen: 74%
Academics: ✎ ✎ ✎
Social: ☎ ☎ ☎
Q of L: ★ ★ ★
Admissions: (800) 328-4553
Email Address: admissions@
mville.edu

Strong Programs:
Education
Business Management
Finance
Psychology
Communication Studies
Performing Arts
Sport Studies
Studio Art

The President's Cottage, built in 1860, has been converted into a modern Center for Design Thinking.

architect Frederick Law Olmsted, is the focal point of the campus: Reid Castle, a 19th-century replica of a Norman castle. The President's Cottage, built in 1860, has been converted into a modern Center for Design Thinking complete with a high-tech fabrication lab.

Under Manhattanville's general education program, called Inquiry, students must fulfill coursework in four pillars: Investigator (scientific, mathematical, humanistic, and social scientific reasoning), Inventor (creativity and aesthetics), International Citizen (global systems and civilizations, foreign language, and applied liberal learning), and Interpreter (written and oral communication and digital literacy). Freshmen take a first-year seminar and two semesters of first-year writing. Seminar professors serve as faculty mentors, and all incoming students are also assigned academic advisors and peer mentors to help ease the transition to college life.

> "[There is a] strong New York Latino-based community where everyone accepts each other's diversity."

The college's strongest offerings include education, business (particularly management and finance), and psychology, while communication studies and performing arts are also popular. Manhattanville's School of Education boasts a near-perfect passage rate for the New York State Teaching Exam. A popular major in sport studies prepares students for a wide range of careers, such as sports business management, sport psychology, physical education, and sports journalism. Art and design programs are enhanced by the proximity of New York City's many museums and galleries. Students may choose from a bevy of five-year bachelor's/master's degree programs in several fields, cross-register for courses at neighboring SUNY–Purchase, or opt to design their own major.

Undergraduates enjoy regular access to professors, especially since 71 percent of classes have fewer than 20 students. "The academic climate is collaborative, as students often engage with peers and professors," explains an English major. Students give high praise to the academic support services offered by the Academic Resource Center, the Writing Center, the Center for Student Accommodations, and the Valiant Learning Support Program. Qualified freshmen may apply for the Castle Scholars Honors Program for a more intensive curriculum. The college has more than 100 study abroad options in 30 countries, in which 9 percent of students participate. The Center for Career Development is "phenomenal," securing internship placements at more than 350 locations in and beyond the New York Metro area, such as MasterCard, the Metropolitan Museum of Art, and U.S. Senate offices.

A communication studies major characterizes Manhattanville students as "diverse, friendly, and chill," and a classmate adds that there is a "strong New York Latino-based community where everyone accepts each other's diversity." Indeed, most undergraduates (67 percent) are New Yorkers, and Hispanics comprise the largest minority group, at 25 percent. African Americans make up 9 percent of the student body, Asian Americans 2 percent, and multiracial students 2 percent; 7 percent of undergrads come from overseas. Students describe themselves as politically aware, and a senior says, "Our president has held open-school conferences for all students to gather and discuss pressing issues." Thirty-nine percent of freshmen are eligible for Pell Grants. While there are no athletic scholarships, hundreds of merit scholarships averaging $18,600 are awarded to qualified students.

> "The meals are pretty consistent, but it isn't Mom or Dad's homemade cooking."

Sixty percent of Manhattanville's students live on campus in one of four dorms, which have lounges, communal kitchens, and laundry rooms. Freshmen are assigned rooms that are "spacious and very comfortable" according to a student, while upperclassmen hoping to score coveted singles or suites enter a lottery that a senior describes as "a little *Hunger Games*-ish." Campus dwellers can choose from three different meal plans and can use their meal cards at the main dining hall, The Pub (a deli-type eatery), and vending machines. "The meals are pretty consistent, but it isn't Mom or Dad's homemade cooking," a junior says. Students report feeling safe on campus and one notes, "The school as a whole has been promoting more awareness" of campus sexual assault.

The student programming board is working to improve the campus social life with weekend events such as dinners, formals in the castle, comedy and talent shows, movies, plays, and concerts. With no fraternities or sororities, off-campus parties are usually open to all, although students say Manhattanville is no party school. Still, for those of age, one student says, "The social life often takes place at local bars." Every spring, students look forward to Quad Jam, an all-day concert and carnival. There's also a Fall Fest'ville and an International Bazaar, in which students give cultural performances and share ethnic foods.

During the annual International Bazaar, students give cultural performances and share ethnic foods.

Manhattanville students contribute 30,000 hours of community service each year through more than 50 local and global programs. The college's hometown, Purchase, "is not a college town. It is an affluent area with mansions all over," a junior says. Students frequently take the school's free bus to White Plains to enjoy a variety of restaurants, bars, and shops, and as one student points out, "Manhattanville is only 30 miles from New York City, so students can also go to the city for fun." Road trips include Rye Beach in the warmer months and upstate New York or Vermont for skiing in the winter.

Manhattanville has invested heavily in athletics as a way of making the school better known and attracting more males, although some students complain of a lack of school spirit. Even so, Valiant teams have made more than 35 NCAA Tournament appearances. Men's golf and women's softball are recent conference champions, and men's and women's ice hockey are also strong. Men's and women's varsity tennis debuted in the 2018–19 season. Intramural and club sports, ranging from shuffleboard and Ping-Pong tournaments to women's rugby, draw 13 percent of students.

Overlaps

Iona, Pace, Manhattan College, Marist, SUNY–Purchase, St. John's University (NY), Mercy, Sacred Heart

"Manhattanville really feels like a close-knit community," a junior says. The familial atmosphere can get claustrophobic at times, but for those wishing to be part of a close but growing community where values matter, Manhattanville may be worth a look.

If You Apply To ›

Manhattanville: Early action, rolling admissions. SATs or ACTs: optional. No Subject Tests. Accepts the Common Application with supplement.

Marlboro College

Marlboro, VT 05344

Marlboro is a hilltop home to a couple hundred nonconformist souls. Each develops a Plan of Concentration that culminates in a senior project. One of the few colleges in the country that is governed in town-meeting style, where student votes carry the same weight as those of faculty members. Sixty-four percent of the students graduate in six years. Where else can you cheer for the Fighting Dead Trees?

Website: www.marlboro.edu
Location: Rural
Private
Total Enrollment: 241
Undergraduates: 183
Male/Female: 46/54
SAT Ranges: ERW 600–710,
    M 550–630
ACT Ranges: 24–32
Financial Aid: 96%
Pell Grant: 38%
Expense: Pr $
Student Loans: 91%
Average Debt: $ $ $ $
Applicants: 120
Accepted: 97%
Enrolled: 24%
Grad in 6 Years: 64%
Returning Freshmen: 84%
Academics: ✐ ✐ ✐
Social: ☎ ☎ ☎
Q of L: ★ ★ ★ ★
Admissions: (800) 343-0049
Email Address: admissions@
    marlboro.edu

Strong Programs:
Literature
Writing
History
Political Science
Film Studies
Visual and Performing Arts
Environmental Studies
World Studies

Marlboro employs a New England town-meeting style of government, and students can veto Faculty Meeting decisions on academic policy.

Established in 1946, Marlboro College is known far and wide as an innovator in liberal arts education. It was founded on the principles of independent and in-depth study just after World War II, when returning GIs renovated an old barn as the college's first building while living in Quonset huts. And today's Marlboro students are just as trailblazing; they prepare for the future by digging into self-developed Plans of Concentration. With fewer than 200 undergrads and fewer than 30 faculty members, Marlboro is its own little world, which students enter as novices and leave as pros.

Positioned atop a small mountain, surrounded by maples and pines and with a gorgeous view of southern Vermont, Marlboro's physical beauty is striking. Buildings are adapted from barns, sheds, and houses that stood on three old farms that today make up the more than 450-acre campus. Among the renovated structures, many with passive solar heating, are nine dormitories, a science building, a 350-seat theater, and a campus center. Newer facilities include the Snyder Center for the Visual Arts. In the old independent Yankee spirit, Marlboro's library operates on the honor system, where students sign out their own books 24 hours a day. Furthermore, the college employs a New England town-meeting style of government involving students, faculty, and the staff and their spouses in every aspect of policymaking. Students can veto Faculty Meeting decisions on academic policy, and it takes a two-thirds vote of the faculty to override such a veto.

"I consistently find myself saying, 'This is the best class I've ever taken,' every semester."

The cornerstone of a Marlboro education is the Plan of Concentration, which each undergraduate student develops independently. Juniors and seniors "on plan" take most coursework in one-on-one tutorials with their faculty sponsors. Seniors present their thesis or project to their sponsors, who are backed up by outside examiners, experts in the student's field unaffiliated with the college. The administration boasts that by bringing in these outsiders for two- to three-hour oral examinations of its seniors, Marlboro has created its own accountability system, ensuring that neither students nor faculty at this isolated institution are cut off from the most current academic thinking. Faculty members often find the exams as stressful as the students, as it means outsiders are judging their teaching. The only other requirement is the Clear Writing Program, usually completed by the end of the third semester, with a 21-page portfolio reviewed by faculty. Marlboro offers solid instruction in literature, writing, history, political science, film studies, and visual and performing arts, with the physical and natural sciences, especially environmental studies, also well integrated into the curriculum. The world studies program requires students to complete a six- to eight-month internship in a foreign country, as well as a graduate-level course at the nearby School for International Training. Marlboro has direct exchange programs with universities in China, the Czech Republic, Germany, Slovakia, and Mexico, and 25 percent of students do some type of study abroad.

"Most rooms…[have] views straight into the forest."

While some schools see growth as a sign of success, Marlboro intends to remain one of the nation's smallest liberal arts institutions. Academics are modeled after the Oxford system of tutorials and seminars, and administrators believe the college's small size stimulates dynamic relationships between students and faculty, making learning happen both inside and outside the classroom. This isn't a place where students can fade into the background: 85 percent of classes have fewer than 20 students, and the institution relies on everyone to share their talents and skills. Marlboro's flexibility should not be confused with academic flabbiness. Grades are an integral part of the evaluation process, professors are stingy with As, and most students work hard. One student says, "Teachers are very knowledgeable, quick to answer questions, spark discussion, and explore new territory." Another adds, "I consistently find myself saying, 'This is the best class I've ever taken,' every semester."

"Marlboro students are passionate learners with insurmountable curiosity, always excited to see how deep the academic rabbit hole can go," says one religion and dance major. Marlboro remains a liberal-leaning campus, and students are politically active. Eighty-four percent of students hail from outside Vermont and 3 percent from outside the U.S., and minority enrollment continues to be low: African Americans make up 4 percent, Hispanics 3 percent, Asian Americans 1 percent, and multiracial students 5 percent. Socioeconomic diversity is far more present on campus, with 38 percent of freshmen qualifying for Pell Grants. The college offers merit awards averaging $22,800 but no athletic scholarships.

Juniors and seniors take most coursework in one-on-one tutorials with their faculty sponsors.

The "rustic" dorms house 82 percent of Marlboro students and are mostly co-ed. "Most rooms are large and include wood paneling and views straight into the forest," says one dorm dweller. Generally, first-years live in doubles or triples, sophomores live in singles or doubles, and upperclassmen have access to cabins in the woods nearby. Students with the highest number of credits get housing priority. A small percentage of students live off campus in Brattleboro, 20 minutes away, and shuttle to and from campus in a school van. As part of the Real Food Campus Commitment, Marlboro has increasingly been sourcing campus food from local or community-based, fair, ecologically sound, and humane food sources. "The meals are generally very healthy, with many vegetarian/vegan options available," reports a physics major. "On the other hand, if you like Indian food, or really any spices at all, prepare for disappointment."

"The social scene gets strange in the best way."

The college's rural location means plenty of scenic views and a safe campus ("Everyone is out at night and nobody's worried about assault—except maybe by bears," says a freshman). Still, "It's hard to deny that it can feel cramped and isolated," admits a junior. Social life takes place almost exclusively on campus, and as might be expected, Marlboro has no Greek organizations. The school sponsors activities like poetry readings, trips to Boston and New York City, vans to local movie theaters, and pumpkin-carving contests. "The social scene gets strange in the best way," says an economics major. "Students may throw a large punk show on Saturday night and attend a classical pianist performance the next morning." On Work Day, students and faculty skip class and work together to improve the campus through various manual labor projects. The annual Halloween Party and Hogwarts Dinner are popular social events, and regular open-mic nights are always well attended. Students agree that the town of Marlboro, recognizable by little more than a post office, isn't much to write home about. "Marlboro isn't a town so much as a few buildings with a college a mile or so down the road," observes one literature major. Many students head to Brattleboro for its splendid array of restaurants, bookstores, and coffee shops.

The Outdoor Program ensures plenty of opportunities to enjoy the local wilderness.

The school mascot, the Fighting Dead Trees, is emblazoned on the shirts of the ever-popular co-ed soccer team. The annual broomball tournament, offering a variation of ice hockey played using shoes instead of ice skates, brooms instead of sticks, and a kickball instead of a puck, is always popular for athletes and spectators. The rather informal intramural program also offers dodgeball, ultimate Frisbee, and volleyball, among other sports. The "incredibly dynamic" Outdoor Program ensures plenty of opportunities to enjoy the local wilderness, including hiking and cross-country skiing on runs that radiate from the center of campus. Excellent downhill skiing is only a few minutes' drive away.

"Marlboro College is a place for students with a passion for academia, a desire to join and maintain a small democratic community, and an interest in designing their own course of intellectual study," muses one student. This iconoclastic

Overlaps
Bennington, College of the Atlantic, Hampshire, Green Mountain, Sterling, Bard, Warren Wilson, Beloit

school continues to push the academic envelope and remains proud of doing—and being—the unexpected. And that suits its students just fine. Says a freshman, "I feel very empowered here to express and explore different aspects of myself and our community."

If You Apply To ›

Marlboro: Early decision, early action, regular decision. SATs or ACTs: optional. Subject Tests: optional. Accepts the Common Application with supplement. Encourages "nontraditional" students.

Marquette University

Milwaukee, WI 53201

Marquette is an old-line Roman Catholic university that is actively engaged in strengthening its Jesuit character. Service learning is a major emphasis. The student body is mainly from the southern Wisconsin/northern Illinois corridor and is nearly two-thirds Catholic. Relatively inexpensive, in keeping with its middle- and working-class roots. Compare to Saint Louis University and Loyola of Chicago.

Website: www.marquette.edu
Location: City Center
Private
Total Enrollment: 10,110
Undergraduates: 7,961
Male/Female: 47/53
SAT Ranges: ERW 570–660, M 560–650
ACT Ranges: 24–29
Financial Aid: 99%
Pell Grant: 22%
Expense: Pr $
Student Loans: 59%
Average Debt: $ $ $ $
Applicants: 12,957
Accepted: 89%
Enrolled: 18%
Grad in 6 Years: 80%
Returning Freshmen: 89%
Academics: ✐ ✐ ✐
Social: ☎ ☎ ☎
Q of L: ★ ★ ★
Admissions: (414) 288-7302
Email Address: admissions@marquette.edu

Strong Programs:
Biomedical Sciences
Nursing

At Marquette University, students practice what they preach. The college experience at this Roman Catholic institution includes an emphasis on personal growth, civic responsibility, and community service. The university has worked in recent years to strengthen its traditions and values drawn from the Society of Jesus (Jesuits), while at the same time expanding its global focus and connecting students with practical, real-world experiences. Service learning, which helps students put classroom theories to the test through volunteer work, is a cornerstone of campus life, helping to shape well-rounded students who graduate ready, as the school puts it, to "be the difference" in the world.

Marquette occupies more than 80 acres of "concrete with interludes of grass and trees" just a few blocks from the heart of downtown Milwaukee. While offering the advantages of an urban setting, its campus does have plenty of open spaces suitable for throwing everything from a Frisbee to a barbecue. Although most of the buildings are relatively modern, the campus is the site of the St. Joan of Arc Chapel, which was built in France more than 500 years ago and later transported to Wisconsin.

> **"We are the type of students who love debate, and love the free flowing exchange of ideas."**

It is said to be the only medieval structure in the Western Hemisphere dedicated to its original purpose. The university's first new residence hall in 50 years, a $108 million, two-building complex housing 865 freshmen and sophomores, opened in 2018.

Also launched in 2018 was the revised Marquette Core Curriculum, which is structured in three parts. Foundations courses ground students in the theology, philosophy, and rhetoric of a Jesuit perspective. Discovery courses encourage an interdisciplinary approach, as students take four courses all centered around a chosen theme, such as Crossing Boundaries and Exploring the Unknown. A final Culminating course helps students reflect on and apply what they've learned in the Core. Students who want to get a head start on the Marquette experience in a close-knit group can opt to participate in the five-week Freshman Frontier program, which offers credit and noncredit courses, along with intensive assistance from academic advisors.

The most popular majors at Marquette include biomedical sciences, nursing, marketing, and psychology. The social welfare and justice major is well regarded, as are more specialized majors in operations and supply chain management and bioinformatics. Through an affiliation with the Milwaukee Institute of Art and Design, two fine arts minors are available in studio art and graphic design. Marquette has its own art museum and an active theatre program. Among the most popular academic offerings are Marquette's service-learning courses, which draw more than 1,000 students every semester, connecting them with service opportunities in more than 130 community agencies. Roughly 83 percent of students overall take part in some type of community service experience prior to graduation.

Forty-five percent of classes have fewer than 20 students, and students report little difficulty getting into the ones they want. One student says, "Marquette is pretty collaborative. The professors I've had have really instilled the idea of teamwork." The school's Jesuit influence is felt in the classroom, and the Manresa project, named for the Spanish town where St. Ignatius spent a year praying about his vocation, helps professors incorporate Ignatian teaching into their classes—focusing particularly on community-based learning and service, social justice, and personal reflection on faith and vocation.

Twenty-six percent of Marquette students travel to more than 45 countries each year for study abroad programs. The flagship South Africa Service-Learning Program in Cape Town is particularly popular; participants combine their studies at the University of Western Cape with two full days of volunteer work per week in areas like education, literacy, public health, and economic development. The university is also home to the Les Aspin Center for Government in Washington, D.C., which allows students to take courses while participating in an internship with a federal government agency. About 20 percent of students assist faculty members with their research, and approximately 175 top freshmen per year join the University Honors Program, which offers small seminars and an optional living/learning community.

Although Marquette actively recruits in 35 or so states and several U.S. territories, most of the undergraduate student body is from the Midwest, 29 percent from Wisconsin itself. Three percent come from foreign countries. In general, Marquette boasts a friendly collection of traditional, middle-class students. Student religious organizations are active, and students, faculty, and staff can attend mass every day of the week. Catholics are understandably predominant in the student body, at 61 percent, but religious practice is left to the individual. According to one sophomore, "We are the type of students who love debate, and love the free flowing exchange of ideas." African Americans make up 4 percent of the student body, Hispanics 12 percent, Asian Americans 7 percent, and multiracial students 4 percent. Twenty-two percent of freshmen qualify for the Pell Grant. Marquette's successful Educational Opportunity Program enables low-income, disadvantaged students to have the benefit of a college education. Merit scholarships averaging $13,100 are available, as are 325 athletic scholarships in 16 sports.

Fifty-four percent of Marquette students make their home on campus; residency is required for freshmen and sophomores. All but two residence halls are co-ed, and there are more than 400 university-owned apartments (which come with a separate electric bill). Within the residence halls are four different living/learning communities, including the honors, social justice, inclusive leadership, and Spanish language and culture communities. "Marquette has many dining halls, considering the size of the campus, and one is open 24/7," notes a junior. Regarding campus security, a senior says, "Although Marquette is located in an urban environment, public safety does an absolutely outstanding job ensuring that students are safe and know how

(continued)
Marketing
Psychology
Social Welfare and Justice
Operations and Supply Chain
  Management
Bioinformatics
Theatre Arts

Marquette's service-learning courses draw more than 1,000 students every semester, connecting them with more than 130 community agencies.

"A quick bus ride can take you to some of the most booming social spots in Milwaukee."

Sports fans will be impressed with Milwaukee's new Fiserv Forum, home to Marquette basketball and the NBA's Milwaukee Bucks.

to remain safe in the area." The LGBTQ+ Resource Center supports students with an interest in LGBTQ, gender identity, and sexual violence and prevention issues.

Social life takes place both on and off campus. While Milwaukee is hardly a college town, students say there are many good things about being there, including major-league baseball and basketball, plenty of concerts and festivals, and a spate of new downtown developments. "A quick bus ride can take you to some of the most booming social spots in Milwaukee," says a junior. An old advertising slogan once claimed that "Milwaukee Means Beer," and few Marquette students would disagree. Students report that Marquette is stricter than most universities in enforcing the drinking age, especially in the dorms. Fraternities and sororities attract 5 percent of the men and 11 percent of the women, respectively. A well-loved tradition is the Miracle on Westowne Square, the annual lighting of the campus Christmas tree and accompanying mass.

> "Marquette students really are a community. Everyone supports everyone else."

The Golden Eagles Division I men's basketball, golf, and track and field teams are highly competitive, as are women's basketball, volleyball, and soccer. Men's tennis and women's basketball are recent Big East conference champions. Sixty-six percent of students participate in at least one of roughly two dozen intramural sports, and 36 club teams are another option. Sports fans will be impressed with Milwaukee's new Fiserv Forum, close to campus and home to Marquette basketball and the NBA's Milwaukee Bucks. Nature lovers can head to Lake Michigan, a 40-minute walk from campus, or to Kettle Moraine, a glaciated region ideal for hiking and cross-country skiing. Chicago is only 95 miles away.

Students at Marquette are engaged not only in their own personal growth but also in the betterment of their local and global communities through service. Students say it's the supportive, familial atmosphere that makes them excited about those goals, and that makes Marquette what it is. Confirms a senior, "Marquette students really are a community. Everyone supports everyone else."

If You Apply To ›

Marquette: Rolling admissions. SATs or ACTs: required. Subject Tests: optional. Accepts the Common Application.

University of Mary Washington

1301 College Avenue, Fredericksburg, VA 22401

Situated in historic Fredericksburg, Mary Washington could easily be mistaken for one of Virginia's elite private colleges. A public liberal arts college, it offers just as much history and tradition albeit for a much lower price. Named for George Washington's mother and formerly a women's college, it is still about two-thirds female. Administrators failed in an effort to drop "Mary" from the name to attract more men.

Strolling among the University of Mary Washington's elegant buildings of redbrick with white columns has led more than one pleased parent to declare, "Now this is what a college should look like." Indeed, for an aura of history and tradition, few schools stack up to this small college in Fredericksburg, a site of Civil War action and the boyhood town of George Washington. "Tradition is at the heart of UMW and is one of the many things that instills a sense of community here," says a junior.

The campus features classical Jeffersonian buildings, sweeping lawns, brick walkways, and breathtaking foliage. If the campus architecture reminds some people of the University of Virginia, it's no accident: UMW was the all-female branch of that august institution before going co-ed in 1970 and cutting its ties in 1972. The University Center provides dining facilities, a retail bookstore, offices for student services and clubs, and a ballroom, and a major expansion to the Jepson Science Center is underway.

Mary Washington has gained a reputation as one of the premier public liberal arts colleges in the country. The core curriculum emphasizes a strong liberal arts focus, requiring coursework in a broad range of fields. Incoming students must take a first-year seminar, in which classmates live together, receive dedicated advising, and

"Tradition is at the heart of UMW."

participate in a common book reading. Nearly every major requires students to complete a capstone project or experience or to take a senior-level intensive seminar. The program in historic preservation is solid: "It's pretty unique and has great local partners for internships," says a senior. Among the sciences, biology is the clear favorite, and other popular majors include business administration, English, psychology, political science, and international affairs. Newer programs include communication and digital studies, which is growing in popularity, and biochemistry.

The close ties between students and faculty are a great source of pride at Mary Washington, and an economics major describes the academics as "rigorous and hands-on." Forty-eight percent of classes have fewer than 20 students, and instructors are said to be intelligent and accessible. "I never imagined that I would find such a highly engaged and compassionate set of professors my first year of college," says one student. Students are encouraged to take on research projects of their own design, and science students are eligible for a 10-week summer research program. About 230 students participate in the relatively young honors program that was established in 2012. Several departments offer grants for work abroad or in the U.S., and 31 percent of students study abroad. The college's location, roughly an hour from both Washington, D.C., and the state capital, Richmond, is a handy asset for the approximately 350 budding politicos who seek internships every year. A large majority of students continue on to jobs after graduation, rather than graduate school.

At Mary Washington, an unusually strong sense of community characterizes everything from academics to dorm life. "This is a very nerdy, geeky school that often doesn't take itself too seriously," says a women's and gender studies major. "Our student body isn't subdued or isolated." Eighty-nine percent of students are from Virginia and just 1 percent arrive from abroad. African Americans make up 8 percent of the student

"I never imagined that I would find such a highly engaged and compassionate set of professors my first year of college."

population, Hispanics 9 percent, Asian Americans 4 percent, and multiracial students 6 percent. "We have an amazing Multicultural Center that puts a lot of effort into bringing together diverse cultures and backgrounds and blending our community," says a sophomore. The campus is heavily liberal, and a journalism major notes, "I've found that right-wing people have a hard time voicing their opinions, but the climate is far from hostile." Eligible undergraduates receive merit awards averaging $3,100, but there are no athletic scholarships.

Mary Washington has a two-year residency requirement, and, all told, 58 percent of students live in university housing. The residence halls offer a variety of living arrangements, including singles, suites, gender-neutral options, and first-year living/learning clusters. According to one student, "What the halls lack in quality,

(continued)

Male/Female: 36/64
SAT Ranges: ERW 550–650, M 530–610
ACT Ranges: 22–27
Financial Aid: 63%
Pell Grant: 17%
Expense: Pub $ $ $
Student Loans: 54%
Average Debt: $ $ $
Applicants: 5,977
Accepted: 74%
Enrolled: 22%
Grad in 6 Years: 71%
Returning Freshmen: 84%
Academics: ✍ ✍ ✍ ½
Social: ☎ ☎ ☎
Q of L: ★ ★ ★ ★
Admissions: (540) 654-2000
Email Address:
  admit@umw.edu

Strong Programs:
Historic Preservation
Biology
Business Administration
English
Psychology
Political Science
International Affairs
Communication and Digital Studies

Incoming students must take a first-year seminar, in which classmates live together and receive dedicated advising.

they make up for in community and fun." Dining services draw complaints, despite a recent upgrade to the facilities. "Students want more options and a more efficient system," says a political science major. Security is described as good, and a senior adds, "I can attest that UMW has taken many responsible and effective steps to prevent sexual assault, including hiring the right staff members and introducing the Rave Guardian app to our campus."

Although a good number of students go home on the weekends, student involvement in the more than 160 active campus clubs is high. There is no Greek life (aside from a couple of off-campus frats not recognized by the university), but parties can be found both on and off campus, generally thrown by sports teams. "Campus policies regarding alcohol are never punitive and always educational," says a senior. Other student organizations offer special events each Friday, and volunteering is a big part of campus life. Traditions matter here, and several annual outdoor parties, including the homecoming bonfire and Rocktoberfest,

"Our student body isn't subdued or isolated."

never fail to attract a large crowd. All third-year students brace themselves for Junior Ring Week, during which they are the victims of practical jokes prior to receiving their rings from the school's president. The favorite tradition is Devil-Goat Day, an all-day competition pitting odd- and even-year classes against each other in events such as sumo wrestling, jousting, and the Velcro wall. The annual Multicultural Fair draws many residents and vendors from the local community to campus.

Small and friendly, nearby Fredericksburg "has a relaxed social atmosphere. Students are always hanging out downtown at coffee shops or by the Rappahannock River on nice days," according to a senior. While it lacks some of the nightlife of a larger city, there are historic homes to visit, museums with Civil War exhibits, a mall, and restaurants that offer discounts to students. For dance clubs and bars, students drive to Richmond or D.C. Also an hour's drive away is the scenery of the Chesapeake Bay, due east, and the Blue Ridge Mountains, due west.

Mary Washington doesn't have a football team, but its 23 Division III Eagles sports teams are alive and well. Since the inception of the Capital Athletic Conference, UMW has won more conference championships than all other members combined. The men's swim team has won four national championships. Men's and women's tennis, men's soccer, and women's swimming, volleyball, and lacrosse are also top performers. Nonvarsity types also use the 76-acre sports and field complex, complete with an Olympic-size pool, for 21 club sports and a variety of intramurals, ranging from flag football and soccer to indoor Wiffle ball.

"Students looking for an easy pass and wild parties should look elsewhere," advises one student. Instead, the University of Mary Washington offers a first-rate liberal arts education, the feel of a private school, and a public school price tag. "What's more," says one senior, is that "students are connected and feel like a family."

Overlaps

James Madison, Christopher Newport, College of Charleston, Elon, William and Mary, George Mason, Virginia Commonwealth, University of Virginia

If You Apply To ›

Mary Washington: Early decision, early action, regular decision. SATs or ACTs: required for some (optional for applicants with minimum 3.5 GPA who do not seek merit scholarships). Subject Tests: optional. Accepts the Common Application with supplement.

University of Maryland

College Park, MD 20742

The name says Maryland, but the location says Washington, D.C. Students in College Park can jump on the Metro just as they do at American or Georgetown. Maryland is nothing if not big, and savvy students will look to programs such as the Honors College and living/learning communities for some personal attention.

For good luck on exams, University of Maryland students rub the nose of Testudo, the school's terrapin mascot. But even without touching the storied statue, most students here feel lucky to be at a diverse school that offers a multitude of programs, from living/learning communities to special opportunities for freshmen, that make it feel smaller and more personal, despite its daunting size. "With hundreds of different student organizations," says a senior, "students will always be able to find their niche."

Maryland's 1,200-acre campus embraces an array of architectural styles, including the Georgian brick buildings ringing the oak-lined mall at the heart of the campus. The 17,950-seat Xfinity Center hosts Terrapin basketball games and special university events. The Iribe Center for Computer Science, featuring six floors of specialized, high-tech labs, and the St. John Teaching and Learning Center are among the newest additions to campus.

Maryland has earned a strong reputation for its engineering and computer science departments, as well as the Smith School of Business and Merrill College of Journalism. The most popular majors are biological sciences, economics, mechanical engineering, finance, and criminology and criminal justice. General education requirements entail 40 to 46 credits in a number of distribution areas, including professional writing, oral communication, diversity, and others. Students must also take an "i-Series" course that emphasizes "broad, analytical thinking about significant issues." Curricular innovations include an institute that supports technology start-ups and an entrepreneurship center in the business school. For students at the extremes of the academic spectrum, there are departmental honors programs and the Honors College, as well as an intensive educational development and tutoring program. Students participating in individual studies can combine established majors and create their own programs.

> "Dorms are great and an essential part of the freshman experience."

Maryland's coursework is "intense" but "more collaborative than competitive," according to one student. Lower-level courses tend to be large and impersonal ("easy to hide in, even easier to skip"), but the corresponding weekly discussion sections led by teaching assistants offer personal attention. The situation improves by junior year, when classes of 20 to 40 students become the norm. "The quality of teaching here has been pretty good. Faculty members are accessible," a senior says. The university is putting more emphasis on helping students make timely progress toward their degrees. A two-day orientation, seminars, and course clusters are offered for freshmen, and 60 percent of freshmen participate in more than 20 living/learning programs that provide experiential learning opportunities in more intimate settings. The FIRE (First-Year Innovation and Research Experience) program allows qualified freshmen to join faculty-led research groups for research and mentorship experiences. Internships in nearby Washington, D.C., and Baltimore are plentiful, and 22 percent of undergrads study abroad in dozens of countries, such as Costa Rica, Israel, and Sweden.

Seventy-four percent of undergraduates are Maryland natives, while New York and New Jersey are also well represented; 5 percent hail from foreign nations.

Website: www.umd.edu
Location: Suburban
Public
Total Enrollment: 35,623
Undergraduates: 27,538
Male/Female: 53/47
SAT Ranges: ERW 640–720, M 650–750
ACT Ranges: 29–33
Financial Aid: 52%
Pell Grant: 13%
Expense: Pub $ $
Student Loans: 42%
Average Debt: $ $
Applicants: 33,907
Accepted: 44%
Enrolled: 27%
Grad in 6 Years: 87%
Returning Freshmen: 95%
Academics: 🎓 🎓 🎓
Social: ☎ ☎ ☎
Q of L: ★ ★ ★
Admissions: (800) 422-5867
Email Address:
applymaryland@umd.edu

Strong Programs:
Biological Sciences
Economics
Mechanical Engineering
Finance
Criminology and Criminal Justice
Computer Science
Business
Journalism

Diversity is more than just a buzzword: 13 percent of students are African American, 10 percent are Hispanic, 17 percent are Asian American, and 4 percent are multiracial. Major social and political issues on campus revolve around greater awareness of racial and LGBTQ+ issues. Qualified undergrads receive merit awards averaging $6,900, and athletes vie for 437 scholarships in 19 sports.

Forty-one percent of students live on campus in single-sex or co-ed dorms; freshmen are guaranteed housing. While many juniors and seniors seek off-campus accommodations, those who stay on campus all four years will find that their digs improve as they gain seniority—upperclassmen have the option of on-campus apartments and suites. Freshmen generally live in high-rises or low-rises; South Campus is said to be more relaxing than the louder North Campus. "Dorms are great and an essential part of the freshman experience," one senior says. Campus safety features include triple locks on dorm-room doors and walking and riding escort services to transport students after dark. "The area has its rough spots but it is constantly becoming safer," a sophomore says, noting that the campus itself tends to be "extremely safe."

The university's reputation as a haven for those who prefer partying to studying is changing as students with better credentials apply, but there is still always something happening in the dorms and at local pubs. Students enjoy frequent school-sponsored concerts, movies, speakers, and Terp After Dark events, as well as the traditional fraternity parties and football and basketball games. "Social life is epic here," raves one history and education double major. Fifteen percent of men and 20 percent of the women go Greek, but they don't dominate the tone of campus life. As for drinking, "They say no tolerance and in recent years, there have been crackdowns. As a result, policies have increased in effectiveness," says one student. Art Attack is a favorite annual event in which local artists share their crafts and national touring artists perform an evening concert. Other popular events include Maryland Day and homecoming. When Maryland's suburban campus feels too small, a few bucks and a few minutes on the Metro (Washington's subway system) brings Terrapins into downtown D.C. at a hare's pace; downtown Baltimore is a 40-minute drive.

> **"The diversity of the student body and the opportunities afforded are infinite."**

Division I sports are a big deal here, and, in a gesture to the importance of TV revenue, the Terrapins compete in the predominately Midwestern, 12-member Big Ten Conference. The university drew national attention in 2018 following the heatstroke-related death of a sophomore football player, which has resulted in the firing of the football coach, the announced retirement of the university president, and a period of soul-searching about the culture of Maryland's athletics program. Despite the football team's mediocre record on the Big Ten stage, the Terrapins continue to achieve success: men's and women's lacrosse are national powerhouses, and men's soccer, women's basketball, and field hockey are recent conference champs. Basketball fans are intrepid and not always civilized, turning out en masse to disparage opponents. "Students here have a lot of school spirit," a junior says. "Terrapin pride runs rampant." A handful of intramurals and 45 club-level sports draw roughly a third of the students.

The University of Maryland's overwhelming size is both a blessing and a curse for the increasingly capable undergraduates here. On one hand, "the diversity of the student body and the opportunities afforded are infinite," a sophomore says. On the other, largeness can translate into crowded dorms, big classes, parking problems, and other hassles. Still, most students agree that the university's range of academic programs, advantageous location near the nation's capital, and persistent school spirit make the Maryland experience worthwhile.

University of Maryland Baltimore County

Baltimore, MD 21250

A midsize public university with the feel of a private one. Strategically located in a suburban setting between Washington, D.C., and Baltimore, UMBC invests heavily in learning communities and other efforts to ensure that its undergraduates thrive. Nationally known for its selective Meyerhoff Scholars Program and a chess team that routinely bests its Ivy League competition. Working on its commuter reputation.

At the University of Maryland Baltimore County, you can be king or queen of your academic world. Students here are given access to academic and social resources usually reserved for those attending mammoth public institutions or pricey private colleges. "There are so many ways to get involved academically and socially," says a student, "whether it's through clubs, research, internships, or service learning." What's more, the school fields a killer chess team that regularly keeps competitors in check. UMBC encourages exploration and expects students to support one another and the community at large. It's your move.

UMBC's 500-acre suburban campus is located between D.C. and Baltimore, offering students access to an array of cultural attractions including restaurants, art galleries, specialty shops, and museums. In the past decade, the university has invested more than $300 million in new facilities and landscaping, including a LEED Gold–rated performing arts and humanities building, a 5,000-seat event center, and more than 3,000 trees.

All students must complete general foundation requirements, which include courses in the arts and humanities, foreign language, social science, math, and biological/physical science. The university offers a number of programs designed to help freshmen ease into college life. In addition to orientation and a common reading program, First-Year Seminars allow students to partner with faculty members to explore course material in an intimate, active learning environment. Students focus on creative and critical-thinking skills and written and oral communication, and take part in faculty and peer critiques. Additional mentoring is available to freshmen who appear at risk for not completing their degrees.

> "Students here tend to be on the nerdy end of the spectrum, but we embrace it."

UMBC's most popular programs are also its strongest, including biological sciences, computer science, information systems, psychology, and engineering. Programs in bioinformatics, theatre, and visual arts are also well regarded. The individualized study major gives students a chance to create their own majors drawing on a wide range of disciplines; past majors include biomechanics, medical illustration, and intercultural conflict resolution. Students can also take advantage of established programs in Asian studies, Africana studies, and global studies. Thirty-five percent of classes have fewer than 20 students, and students say the environment is more cooperative than competitive. "Some of my professors are very engaged and focused on student success," says a junior, while "others seem to be disinterested. Most are in the middle."

Website: www.umbc.edu
Location: Suburban
Public
Total Enrollment: 10,653
Undergraduates: 9,527
Male/Female: 55/45
SAT Ranges: ERW 550–670, M 590–690
ACT Ranges: 24–29
Financial Aid: 49%
Pell Grant: 22%
Expense: Pub $ $
Student Loans: 44%
Average Debt: $ $
Applicants: 11,201
Accepted: 60%
Enrolled: 26%
Grad in 6 Years: 63%
Returning Freshmen: 88%
Academics: ✐ ✐ ✐
Social: ☎ ☎ ☎
Q of L: ★ ★ ★
Admissions: (410) 455-2292
Email Address: undergraduate@umbc.edu

Strong Programs:
Biological Sciences
Computer Science
Information Systems
Psychology
Engineering
Bioinformatics
Theatre
Visual Arts

The Brown Center for Entrepreneurship sponsors programs and courses to inspire entrepreneurial thinking among students and faculty, while budding researchers may compete for undergraduate research awards through the Provost's Office and via Undergraduate Research and Creative Achievement Day. The highly selective Meyerhoff Scholars Program addresses the shortage of African Americans in the sciences and engineering; today, it is one of the nation's top producers of African American undergrads who matriculate into science, engineering, and math Ph.D. programs. Each year, the Shriver Center places more than 1,200 UMBC students in community-based internship and co-op experiences. Five percent of students participate in study abroad programs in 60 countries worldwide.

Ninety percent of students hail from Maryland, while 4 percent come from abroad. "Students here tend to be on the nerdy end of the spectrum," says one senior, "but we embrace it." African Americans account for 18 percent of the student body, Hispanics 7 percent, Asian Americans 22 percent, and multiracial students 4 percent. "The biggest social and political issues on campus would be Black Lives Matter and a growing awareness of LGBTQIA issues," a senior says. Pell Grant recipients represent 22 percent of freshmen. UMBC awards merit scholarships worth an average of $9,500 and more than 275 athletic scholarships.

"UMBC is not a place where alcohol and partying dictates who is cool."

Thirty-five percent of students live on campus. "Dorms are small, and first priority goes to new students. Housing is also expensive," laments one student. Several living/learning communities connect students with similar interests and house them together in the residence halls; some of the options include the Center for Women in Technology, Intercultural Living Exchange, Honors College, and Discovery Scholars. Students say off-campus housing is plentiful and cheap, although parking on campus can be a chore. Campus dining options include a dining hall and the Commons, which offers a variety of fare, including international cuisine. Campus security is described as "decent" and includes measures like a student ID access system for the residence halls.

Students complain that social life can be slow on campus, so most students head off. "The surrounding area offers a better social scene," one senior reports. On campus, a student says, "Most social groups are formed through the organizations on campus—volunteer, cultural, religious, academic, and others." Only 2 percent of the men and 3 percent of the women go Greek, and you're unlikely to find any alcohol-fueled toga parties here. "UMBC is not a place where alcohol and partying dictates who is cool," says a junior. National acts—including comedians and rock stars—have been known to make an appearance at Quadmania, much to the students' delight. Block Party is "a carnival where all the residential students can win prizes and play games," enthuses a student. "Last year I got to hit my community director in the face with a pie at one of the booths!" For more urban adventures, downtown Baltimore is 10 minutes away and Washington, D.C., 40 minutes.

The UMBC Retrievers compete in Division I and field a number of competitive teams, including men's and women's soccer, men's lacrosse and baseball, and women's volleyball. Swimming and diving have captured multiple America East conference titles in recent years. The men's basketball team earned a footnote to history in 2018 by becoming the first number 16 seed in the NCAA tournament to upset a number 1 seed (Virginia). UMBC is a perennial collegiate chess powerhouse and regularly makes the Final Four of College Chess, and the university lures talented players with a bevy of scholarships. Intramurals are strong too, and offer more than 15 sports and activities each semester. The Retriever Activities Center offers students 18,000 square feet of fitness and recreation space, including a gymnasium, weight room, fitness studio, indoor pool, and tennis courts.

Overlaps

SUNY–Binghamton, New Jersey Institute of Technology, North Carolina State, UC Riverside, UMass Lowell, University of Maryland, Towson, Salisbury

"I would say that UMBC is a school just coming into its own," says a student. Unlike the gargantuan University of Maryland at College Park, UMBC capitalizes on its small size by providing students with intimate learning communities, solid academics, and ample resources on a manageable scale. It's a combination that appeals to a certain kind of student, according to one junior: "We're focused on doing big things and being influential people."

If You Apply To ›

UMBC: Early action, regular decision. SATs or ACTs: required. No Subject Tests. Accepts the Common Application.

University of Massachusetts Amherst

Amherst, MA 01003

A liberal mecca in cosmopolitan and scenic western Massachusetts, UMass boasts strong study abroad programs and an international flavor. Management and engineering are also strong. In addition to the resources of a major research university, offers ready access to privates Amherst, Hampshire, Mount Holyoke, and Smith via the Five College Consortium. Lack of big-time sports makes for a lower national profile than the likes of Michigan or UNC.

A leading flagship and land grant university with more than 150 years of tradition, the University of Massachusetts Amherst offers students a dizzying array of majors, extracurriculars, and social opportunities in a top college town, plus a strong honors program. UMass's membership in the Five College Consortium makes it a good choice for students who want to take advantage of the extensive resources and programs of a large research university, while also getting a taste of the small-school atmosphere and intellectual rigor of four elite private colleges—all without emptying their wallets.

UMass's sprawling 1,463-acre campus is centered on a pond full of ducks and swans, while architectural styles range from colonial to modern. The school is located on the outskirts of Amherst, a city that combines the energy of a bustling cosmopolitan center with the quaintness of an old New England town, while also catering to college life. UMass's library system is the largest of any public institution in the Northeast. The campus is undergoing a spate of new construction, including the Physical Sciences Building, offering flexible labs for research teams, and the state-of-the-art Design Building, housing programs in environmental conservation, architecture, and regional planning. In addition, the historic Old Chapel was recently restored.

> **"I have had some amazing, out-of-this-world professors."**

UMass offers more than 110 undergraduate degree programs, and among them management and engineering are top-ranked. Psychology, finance, biology, and economics are the most popular majors. Accounting, computer science, nursing, and sport management also draw praise, and a new major in informatics has been added. Students seeking to stand out from the masses might consider the interdisciplinary major in social thought and political economy, or the bachelor's degree in individual concentration, a design-it-yourself major. The Exploratory Track Program places undeclared first-years into one of eight academic advising tracks, based on the interests and academic strengths demonstrated in their admissions applications.

Website: www.umass.edu
Location: Small Town
Public
Total Enrollment: 23,993
Undergraduates: 21,481
Male/Female: 51/49
SAT Ranges: ERW 590–670, M 590–690
ACT Ranges: 26–31
Financial Aid: 89%
Pell Grant: 22%
Expense: Pub $ $ $ $
Student Loans: 68%
Average Debt: $ $ $
Applicants: 41,922
Accepted: 57%
Enrolled: 20%
Grad in 6 Years: 77%
Returning Freshmen: 91%
Academics: ✍ ✍ ✍ ½
Social: ☎ ☎ ☎ ☎
Q of L: ★ ★ ★
Admissions: (413) 545-0222
Email Address: mail@ admissions.umass.edu

Strong Programs:
Management

The Center for Student Business allows students to staff and manage nine campus businesses.

All undergraduates must complete courses in writing, basic mathematics and analytic reasoning, the biological and physical world, the social world, social and cultural diversity, and an integrative experience. The writing requirement includes a freshman course taught in sections of 24 or fewer. Commonwealth Honors College offers qualified students special courses and sponsors interdisciplinary seminars, student gatherings, service projects, and a $192 million, 1,500-bed residential complex that includes nine classrooms and space for gathering, advising, and program administration. UMass offers more than 550 study abroad programs in more than 65 countries worldwide and sends 22 percent of its undergrads globe-trotting each year. The Center for Student Business offers one of the most imaginative programs at UMass, allowing students to staff and manage nine campus businesses, learning how to work with others and resolve conflicts professionally.

UMass's intellectual and political climate is extraordinarily fertile for a large state university, and the school lends considerable research might to the Five College Consortium. This special alliance allows students to attend UMass and take courses (for no extra charge) at the other four consortium schools: Amherst College, Hampshire, Mount Holyoke, and Smith. Typically, 30 to 40 percent of the roughly 5,000 courses offered through the consortium are taken at UMass. The university is "definitely competitive," says a student. "The faculty have responded to the demands of serious students by challenging us to learn how to succeed." Nearly a third of undergraduates participate in hands-on research with faculty. Full professors teach most courses, although some of the larger courses are broken down into smaller sections with graduate-level teaching assistants; overall, about half of all undergraduate classes have fewer than 20 students. "I have had some amazing, out-of-this-world professors," says a junior, "and some abysmal ones." Academic and career counseling receive mixed reviews, and it is usually up to students to pursue career help.

"We have nerds, jocks, theater buffs, hippies, and future CEOs," says a senior. Seventy-seven percent of undergrads are in-staters, while 6 percent hail from more than 75 foreign countries. Four percent of UMass students are African American, 10 percent are Asian American, 6 percent are Hispanic, and 3 percent are multiracial. The university has established cultural centers on campus, providing activities and support for students from different backgrounds, but racial equity is still an issue, students report. "There are always rallies about better programs and aid for minorities," says a senior. Twenty-two percent of freshmen are Pell-eligible. Merit scholarships averaging $4,700 are handed out each year, and athletes vie for 400 athletic scholarships in 21 sports.

"[Amherst] is a lively— if small—college town."

UMass has one of the largest on-campus housing systems in the country. Sixty-one percent of students are housed among seven residential areas. The Residential First-Year Experience assigns first-years to living/learning communities with peers who share common interests and experiences. Many freshmen end up in the Southwest Area, a "huge, city-like complex" with five high-rise towers and 11 low-rise residence halls. "It is not a problem for students to get housing on campus, the only trouble is getting the housing that they want," says a student. Dining services get good reviews. A senior comments, "The campus is very self-contained, and so I have felt safe on campus even late at night." The UMatter at UMass program works to address issues of bias, sexual assault, hazing, high-risk drinking, and other community challenges.

Many freshmen end up in the Southwest Area, a huge complex with five high-rise towers and 11 low-rise residence halls.

UMass offers "a vast social life," says a student, with several social dorms, off-campus parties, and more than 400 student organizations of all types. "Most of my social interactions occur on campus during my extracurriculars. On the weekends, we frequent the restaurants and bars in Amherst center, which is a lively—if small—college town," a chemical engineering major says. Both on campus and off, alcohol policies are strict and well enforced; off-campus parties are often registered with the university. First-time underage offenders are sent to alcohol-education programs. Nine percent of the men and 9 percent of the women belong to one of the more than three dozen fraternities and sororities, but they are somewhat out of the mainstream. The Fine Arts Center brings nationally known theater, music, and dance performances to campus year-round. A free public transportation system allows maximum mobility—not only among the Five Colleges, but also to nearby towns, which are graced with a number of exceptional bookshops.

Settled in the Pioneer Valley and surrounded by the Berkshire foothills, Amherst is close to good skiing, hiking, and canoeing areas. It's also 90 miles west of Boston, 150 miles north of New York City, and 25 miles south of Vermont and New Hampshire, making a car very useful (and very expensive if you get too many tickets from overzealous campus cops, students say).

Division I varsity sports are popular, especially football, men's ice hockey, and men's and women's basketball. The UMass Minutemen and Minutewomen compete primarily in the Atlantic 10 Conference; men's soccer and women's field hockey, tennis, rowing, and lacrosse are recent conference champs. With more than 40 intramural offerings and 46 club sports, recreational opportunities are extensive.

UMass is big enough to offer a vast number of academic and extracurricular opportunities, though at times it can feel impersonal and overwhelming. But with special residential programs that group students with similar languages, cultures, and lifestyles, many students will easily find a home in Amherst. And as one junior cheers, "We have so many resources. If we don't have what you want, we'll give you the opportunity to create it!"

Overlaps

Indiana University, Iowa State, UC Santa Barbara, University of Colorado Boulder, University of Delaware, Northeastern, Boston University, UConn

If You Apply To ›

UMass: Early action, regular decision. SATs or ACTs: required (SAT essay or ACT writing recommended). No Subject Tests. Accepts the Common Application.

Massachusetts Institute of Technology

Room 3-108, 77 Massachusetts Avenue, Cambridge, MA 02139

If you're a science genius, come to MIT to find out how little you really know. No other school makes such a massive assault on the ego. Technology is a given, but MIT also prides itself on leading programs in economics, political science, and architecture, with unmatched undergraduate research opportunities. Those who don't study 24/7 can let off steam via the surprisingly extensive athletic offerings or by enjoying MIT's prime location near downtown Boston.

Founded in 1861, the Massachusetts Institute of Technology continues to attract the brightest minds from near and far. MIT teachers and students have discovered many of the technological innovations that we take for granted, from electromagnets and radar to the decoding of the human genome. The school is a magnet for minds like Tim Berners-Lee, the Brit who invented the World Wide Web, to Noam Chomsky, the linguist and antiwar activist. Graduates have formed more than 25,000 companies that, among other things, employ a quarter of the workforce of Silicon Valley. While Harvard stuck to the English model of Oxbridge classical education, with its emphasis on Latin and Greek, MIT looked to the German system of learning

Website: web.mit.edu
Location: City Center
Private
Total Enrollment: 11,107
Undergraduates: 4,456
Male/Female: 54/46
SAT Ranges: ERW 720–770, M 770–800

based on research and hands-on experimentation. This emphasis is enshrined in the school motto—*Mens et Manus,* or Mind and Hand—as well as its muscular logo, showing a gowned scholar standing beside an ironmonger bearing a hammer and anvil. Intellect and craftsmanship pervade the classrooms, and students here are not so much taught as engaged and inspired.

MIT is located on 168 acres that extend more than a mile along the Cambridge side of the Charles River basin facing historic Beacon Hill and the central sections of

> **"Some professors really know how to engage the interest of the student."**

Boston. The main campus of neoclassical architecture carved from limestone was designed by Welles Bosworth and constructed between 1913 and 1920. Since then, more modern designs in brick and glass have been added. The buildings have a utilitarian aura; most are even known by number instead of by name. Athletic playing fields, recreational buildings, dorms, and dining halls are closely arranged on the campus and provide a sense of unity. Sculptures and murals, including the works of Alexander Calder, Henry Moore, and Louise Nevelson, are found throughout the campus. The university's Brain and Cognitive Sciences Complex is the world's largest neuroscience center.

Whatever their major, all students must fulfill a set of General Institute Requirements consisting of a six-course "science core" that includes calculus and a lab and eight courses in the humanities, arts, and social sciences; there's also an eight-credit physical education requirement. Students have a choice of focus in the basic science offerings. A basic biology course, for example, might emphasize either genetics or the environment. To fill much of their science core, many students will join one of four Freshman Learning Communities that offer a coherent freshman curriculum, small classes, and common meeting spaces. In addition to the four learning communities, flexible, small-group alternatives for freshmen include the Experimental Study Group, which allows a self-paced course of study based on tutorials instead of a traditional lecture format. Not only can these offer support, but they can also engage geniuses who excel on exams without attending the lectures.

Once called Boston Tech and now frequently referred to as "the 'Tute," MIT stresses science and engineering studies with a "concern for human values and social goals." Every science and engineering department is superb. The biology depart-

> **"MIT is intense and will take you for quite a ride."**

ment is a leader in medical technology and the search for designer genes. Nevertheless, pure sciences tend to play second fiddle to the engineering fields that, along with computer science, draw the bulk of the majors. Electrical engineering and computer science are almost universally credited as tops in the nation. Students in these two areas may pursue a five-year-degree option, where they can obtain a professional master's degree upon completion of their studies. Biological engineering, chemical engineering, and mechanical engineering; physics; and the aeronautics and astronautics department are also highly praised programs. The most popular majors include computer science and engineering, electrical engineering, mechanical engineering, and biology.

For all of its emphasis on science and technology, MIT takes the arts and humanities as well as the social sciences—especially economics—seriously. Technology is, after all, the point where science and the humanities intersect over matters of values. Beyond that, the administration worries that engineers of the future will need first-rate technical skills coupled with a good understanding of technology's social context and marketplace. As one dean puts it, "Too many MIT graduates end up working for too many Princeton and Harvard graduates." Hence, majors in management, business analytics, and finance are now offered "in response to employers seeking graduates who are better prepared for today's increasingly complex responsibilities." Perhaps to help ensure that they will be able to make their future discoveries known, students must

Many students join one of four Freshman Learning Communities that offer a coherent freshman curriculum, small classes, and common meeting spaces.

take four communication-intensive subjects. Architecture, political science, urban studies, linguistics, graphics for modern art, and holography—and just about anything else that can be linked to a computer—are strong, and the minority who major in these subjects receive enough personal attention to make any college student envious. "Some professors really know how to engage the interest of the student," says a senior.

A pass/no record grading system helps freshmen adjust to "MIT brainstretching": in the first semester, freshmen receive grades of P, D, or F in all subjects they take. P means a C-or-better performance; Ds or Fs do not receive credit or appear on the permanent record. In the second semester, the Ps are replaced by A, B, or C; Ds and Fs do not receive credit and are only noted internally. Grades or not, most MIT students set themselves a breathtaking pace. "MIT is intense and will take you for quite a ride," a biology/premed student says. "The courses demand your full attention and a lot of extra work," another adds. The traditionally humongous introductory physics lectures have been replaced with smaller, hands-on classes that emphasize collaboration. In fact, 70 percent of all undergraduate classes have fewer than 20 students. Along with Harvard, the university has founded an online learning consortium called edX that allows students around the world access to many courses. On campus, students have access to world-renowned professors and the Nobel Prize winners who carry lighter teaching loads to allow them time for research and interaction with students. Faculty advising is "pretty good for freshmen," one student says, but after that, "it's as good as you make it." The vast library system includes some one-of-a-kind manuscripts on the history of science and technology. One library is even open 24 hours a day, and "some students spend the majority of their time (awake or asleep) there," one student reports.

One of MIT's most successful innovations is the Undergraduate Research Opportunities Program, a year-round program that facilitates student/faculty research projects. Considered one of the best programs of its kind in the nation, it allows students to earn course credit or stipends for doing research. Ninety-one percent of students get involved with collaborative or independent research during their time at MIT. Relief from "tooling" (that is, studying) is found through the optional January Independent Activities Period, which offers noncredit seminars, workshops, and activities in fields outside the regular curriculum, as well as for-credit subjects. Participation in the engineering co-op program, junior year abroad (including a major program at Cambridge University in England), or cross-registration at all-female Wellesley College are other helpful ways to get young noses away from the grindstone.

While MIT somewhat justly earned an image as a "conservative, rich, white boys' school" in the past, there is certainly enough racial and ethnic variety to beat that rap today. African Americans account for 6 percent of the undergraduate student body, Hispanics 14 percent, Asian Americans a hefty 27 percent, and multiracial students 7 percent. Women now account for 46 percent of undergraduates. To further welcome diversity, MIT's application includes an optional question regarding gender identity and sexual orientation, including a "straight" option. Ninety-eight percent of incoming freshmen come from the top 10th of their high school class, and average SAT and ACT scores are simply mind-boggling. Just 10 percent of students are residents of Massachusetts, and 11 percent are international. "The average MIT student can be characterized as having a passion and singular drive for what they really want in life," offers a chemical engineering major. Although there are no merit or athletic scholarships, MIT is need-blind in its admissions and meets the full demonstrated financial need of all undergraduates—domestic and international. For students with family incomes less than $90,000 a year, the Institute ensures that scholarship funding from all sources will allow them to attend MIT tuition-free.

The Undergraduate Research Opportunities Program allows students to earn course credit or stipends for doing research.

"[MIT students have] a passion and singular drive for what they really want in life."

MIT is need-blind and meets the full demonstrated financial need of all undergraduates—domestic and international.

Eighty-nine percent of undergraduates live on campus, and all freshmen are required to live in the dorms. Guaranteed housing is either single-sex or co-ed; the dorms are in the middle of campus, and most of the fraternities and living groups are a mile or less away across the Charles. Meal plans are mandatory for dorms that don't have kitchens and optional for equipped quarters. Frat types feast on spreads prepared by their full-time cooks, and the Kosher Kitchen provides some refuge for others. MIT has recently increased its Title IX staffing, training programs, and educational outreach in an effort to combat campus sexual assault.

MIT's social scene is varied. There are special lectures, campus movies, dances, parties, and dorm activities, if one can escape the ubiquitous workload worming its way into the uneasy consciousness of a techie's every waking hour. The Rocket Team, the Guild of Bell Ringers, and a singing group called the Chorallaries are only a few of the diverse interests on this campus.

"[MIT hacks are] practical jokes with technical merit."

Most on-campus drinking for 21-and-over students is relaxed and accepted, "as long as the alcohol does not result in unlawful behavior or cause any problems," a student explains. MIT's alcohol-prevention program is considered a national model, and drug-prevention initiatives are also comprehensive. The Greek scene attracts 48 percent of the men and 30 percent of the women. For those with the urge to roam, the multifaceted greater Boston metropolis sits only a few subway stops away. The student-friendly city boasts many restaurants, clubs, parks, shopping opportunities, and 45 other colleges.

When the MIT megabrains take a break, practical jokes, or "hacks" (described by one student as "practical jokes with technical merit") are sure to follow. In past years, popular hacks have included dismantling a campus police car and reassembling its body at the top of the tower, unscrewing and reversing all the chairs in a 500-seat lecture hall, and, of course, welding shut Harvard's gates. Hacking can also involve Harry Potter–style late-night explorations by students in the tunnels and shafts that run through restricted parts of the campus, a practice that's definitely frowned upon by the school.

When not studying or hacking, these engineering jocks often turn into real jocks. MIT has 33 varsity sports, the most of any Division III school. Teams are known as the Engineers with a beaver named Tim (if you can't figure it out, don't bother to apply) as their mascot. Men's and women's cross-country, track and field, and swimming and diving are among the most competitive teams; MIT is also nationally ranked in crew, sailing, and water polo. Hockey is popular, and even more popular is the extensive, well-organized intramural program (roughly 30 percent participate), with sports ranging from Ping-Pong, billiards, and bowling to the more traditional basketball and volleyball. More than 30 instructional and competitive club sports are also available, and everyone has access to MIT's extensive athletic facilities.

Though students often wonder what life at a so-called typical college would have been like, chances of survival and even satisfaction at MIT are excellent. Students are able to comprehend the incredible experience of attending one of the nation's leading academic powerhouses. A biology major puts it bluntly: "It will take you right up to what you think your limits are, and then MIT will shatter them and make you realize how great your potential is."

Overlaps

Stanford, Harvard, Princeton, Yale, Caltech, Cornell University, Columbia, University of Pennsylvania

If You Apply To ›

MIT: Early action, regular decision. SATs or ACTs: required. Subject Tests: required (one math and one science). Does not accept the Common Application. Application includes optional question regarding gender identity and sexual orientation.

McGill University: See page 359.

University of Miami (FL)

P.O. Box 249117, Coral Gables, FL 33124

Football is a major reason UM is on the map, but it's hardly the only one. Renowned programs in marine science and music are big draws; business is also strong. Housing takes the form of a distinctive residential college system that offers living/learning opportunities. Attracts more Northerners than other leading Florida universities, with geographic reach continuing to expand.

Year-round sunshine and the colorful Miami culture could make even the most dedicated students forget why they are at college. But at the University of Miami, students can have their fun and get a solid education at the same time. The university boasts a boatload of strong programs, including red-hot preprofessional offerings. Sound academics, a diverse and energetic student population, and a subtropical climate create a perfect storm that attracts talented Hurricanes from far and wide. "At UM you will find diversity, tradition, unity, and rivalry," says one senior, "while getting an exceptional education."

Twenty minutes from Key Biscayne and Miami's beaches, and 10 minutes from downtown Miami, the university's 239-acre campus is located in tranquil suburbia and features tall palms, wide lawns, flowering vines, outdoor sculptures, and even a butterfly garden. The campus, with its own lake right in the middle, is architecturally varied, from postwar, international-style structures to modern buildings, most with open-air breezeways to let in the warm winds. A massive, $190 million Student Housing Village, to be composed of 25 interconnected buildings featuring suite- and apartment-style housing for 1,100 students, recreational and dining areas, a 200-seat auditorium, and other facilities, is expected to open in 2020.

UM's Cognates Program of General Education requires students to take at least three courses in each of three areas of knowledge: arts and humanities, people and society, and STEM (science, technology, engineering, and math). With nine undergraduate schools and colleges and more than 180 majors and programs, UM offers a broad range of preprofessional options as well as those across the liberal arts. The university has one of the nation's top programs in marine science, and its architecture program is well regarded. UM was the first American university to offer a four-year undergraduate degree in music engineering. It has also developed a unique program in jazz. The university's dual-degree programs in marine geology, Latin American studies, exercise physiology, law, and biochemistry and molecular biology receive high marks. The most popular majors are nursing, finance, psychology, and biology. The Foote Fellows Honors Program provides high-achieving students with more academic flexibility, opportunities for faculty-mentored research, and additional resources.

UM's academic environment manages to be "both competitive and collaborative," says one junior. "Everyone wants to get into the best graduate programs, but they want their peers to do so as well." Fifty-four percent of the classes have fewer than 20 students, and full professors do teach freshmen. Professors "are extremely accessible through office hours, and teaching assistants often reach out to students to help with workshops and extra study sessions," says a business management

> **"At UM you will find diversity, tradition, unity, and rivalry."**

Website: www.miami.edu
Location: Suburban
Private
Total Enrollment: 15,479
Undergraduates: 10,134
Male/Female: 48/52
SAT Ranges: ERW 610–690, M 610–720
ACT Ranges: 28–32
Financial Aid: 62%
Pell Grant: 12%
Expense: Pr $ $ $
Student Loans: 35%
Average Debt: $ $
Applicants: 30,634
Accepted: 36%
Enrolled: 20%
Grad in 6 Years: 84%
Returning Freshmen: 91%
Academics: ✐ ✐ ✐
Social: ☎ ☎ ☎ ☎
Q of L: ★ ★ ★
Admissions: (305) 284-6000
Email Address: admission@miami.edu

Strong Programs:
Nursing
Finance
Psychology
Biology
Marine Science
Architecture
Music
Latin American Studies

major. Students looking for a change of pace can take advantage of more than 80 study abroad options in dozens of countries, including seven UM semester-on-location programs in Italy, the Czech Republic, Ecuador, South Africa, Argentina, India, and China.

"The students at UM are culturally and academically diverse, with so many interests and passions," says one student. Fifty-five percent of UM's undergraduates come from out of state, including quite a few from the Northeast and upper Midwest, seeking respite from harsh weather. UM's student body is impressively diverse; Hispanics account for a substantial 23 percent of the total, African Americans 8 percent, Asian Americans 5 percent, and multiracial students 3 percent. International students, who represent 15 percent of undergraduates and more than 100 countries, play an integral role in the life of the university. Numerous merit scholarships, averaging $19,200, are available, as are athletic scholarships.

UM offers a distinctive system of five co-ed residential colleges, modeled after those at Oxford and Cambridge. Each residential college has a live-in faculty member who works with staff to organize seminars, concerts, dinners, social events, and lectures, including guest speakers from all walks of life to discuss current issues. Generally, students give the dorms average marks; 39 percent of undergrads live on campus, and others bunk in off-campus apartments or commute. "Housing is slightly dismal in the beginning, but you soon become so engulfed in campus life that you don't mind the dorms at all," says a senior. Scrounging up food on campus is easy. "Our food court is very diverse with just about every food option you can think of," says a senior. Students also report feeling safe on campus, thanks to a robust security program that includes safety escorts and campus shuttles.

> "Miami is an incredible city, so there is always something fun to do with friends."

UM offers a plethora of social opportunities. "Miami is an incredible city, so there is always something fun to do with friends. The university is also constantly hosting activities on campus," says one student. The Rathskeller, a popular student meeting place on campus, offers food, entertainment, a venue for postgame parties, and alcohol to students at least 21 years old. Campus alcohol policies are strict for underage students, but an art history major says, "The drinking and party culture on campus is not something that proves to be a massive issue." Off campus, however, frat parties and Miami's many bars, nightclubs, and festivals keep things lively. Fraternities account for 18 percent of the men, and sororities, with no housing of their own, attract 20 percent of the women. Students anticipate annual events such as International Week and SportsFest, which pits dorms against each other in sports ranging from flag football to obstacle courses. The biggest service event each year is Gandhi Day, during which 1,200 students spend the day doing community service.

Coral Gables is not a college town. "We are a college in a big city," says a junior, which means access to events such as Miami's Art Basel and Ultra Music Festival, as well as professional sports teams (Dolphins, Heat, Marlins). Those who shun sand between their toes head to the boutiques in Coconut Grove, Wynwood, or South Beach. Public transportation and the Hurry 'Cane Shuttle service run in front of the residential colleges, and on-campus parking can be a problem, but most students recommend a car anyway, in order to get "the full Florida effect." The best road trips are Key West, Key Largo, the Everglades, and, of course, UM football games against the University of Florida and Florida State.

> "Students don't have enough time in four years to access all the amazing things available."

The Hurricanes compete in the Division I Atlantic Coast Conference. The most competitive teams are football, baseball, and men's and women's basketball and

> *UM was the first American university to offer a four-year undergraduate degree in music engineering.*

> *Each residential college has a live-in faculty member who works with staff to organize seminars, social events, and lectures.*

diving. Men's diving brought home a recent individual national championship title, while women's track and field is a recent conference champ. In a nod to Harry Potter fans, the extensive club sports program includes Quidditch. The university also has a state-of-the-art recreation facility that includes an 18,000-square-foot fitness room and basketball, racquetball, squash, and tennis courts, plus an indoor pool and a juice bar.

It's hard to imagine a school in the Sunshine State without a generous allotment of fun, and UM is no exception. "Though we're not the number one party school in the nation anymore, we still really love to have a great time," observes a junior. That said, UM students these days are just as likely to search long and hard for the perfect instrumental phrase or mathematical proof as they are to scope out the perfect wave. Says one happy Hurricane, "The biggest complaint is that students don't have enough time in four years to access all the amazing things available."

If You Apply To ›

Miami: Early decision I and II, early action, regular decision. SATs or ACTs: required. Subject Tests: required for some (math and one science required for dual-degree program in medicine and biochemistry/molecular biology). Accepts the Common Application. Apply to particular schools or programs.

Miami University (OH)

301 S. Campus Avenue, Oxford, OH 45056

Rather than disappear into the black hole of Ohio State, top students in the Buckeye state come here to feel as if they are going to an elite private university. MU is the honors public university in one of the nation's largest states. Twice the size of William and Mary, Miami has the same classic look but is much less selective. Miami's top draw is business, and its tenor is preppy/conservative. Bring your best clothes.

This Miami is about 1,000 miles from South Beach, but that doesn't mean it's without sizzle. The academic kind, that is. Miami University is actually tucked into a corner of Ohio and has garnered national recognition as an excellent state university that has the true look and feel of a private, with a picture-perfect campus and high-caliber student body.

The university is staked out on 2,100 wooded acres in the center of an urban triangle of approximately three million people, encompassing Cincinnati and Dayton, Ohio, and Richmond, Indiana. The campus is dressed in the modified Georgian style of the colonial American period, and it remains as impeccably groomed as its sharply attired students. Major renovations have been completed to the East Quad and North Quad housing and dining facilities. A second phase of the recently constructed Armstrong Student Center— the East Wing—has added more dining services and a new home for the Center for Career Exploration and Success.

"Our professors are dedicated to ensuring student growth."

Miami University was founded in 1809 to provide a classical liberal education and has never strayed from its central commitment to the liberal arts. All undergraduates must complete the Global Miami Plan for Liberal Education, which provides them with a background in a range of disciplines and includes requirements in intercultural perspectives, global studies, advanced writing, and experiential

(continued)

Academics: ✍ ✍ ✍ ✍ ½
Social: ☎ ☎ ☎
Q of L: ★ ★ ★
Admissions: (513) 529-2531
Email Address: admission@ miamioh.edu

Strong Programs:
Finance
Marketing
Accountancy
Strategic Communication
Architecture
Interior Design
Nutrition
International Studies

learning. Students must also fulfill a thematic sequence requirement by taking a series of related courses (usually three) outside their major, and they must complete a capstone experience their senior year. University Studies 101 is a one-credit course that helps integrate first-year students into the university community.

Popular majors include finance, marketing, accountancy, and strategic communication. Programs in architecture, interior design, nutrition, and international studies have also been traditional strengths. Students majoring in interactive media studies investigate the impact of a wide range of digital technologies, such as e-commerce, game design, social media marketing, and virtual and augmented reality, and take a consulting course in which they work with a real corporate client. The Center for Social Entrepreneurship helps students put their creativity and business savvy to use in solving persistent social problems. Gerontology is available as a major and a minor, and the Scripps Gerontology Center is one of the oldest of its kind in the country.

In the classroom, "Miami strikes a good balance between intensity and creating a positive working environment for students," says a strategic communication major. Professors are lauded for their knowledge and willingness to help. "Our professors are dedicated to ensuring student growth and have gone above and beyond to help me understand materials and apply them," says a political science major. Thirty-four percent of classes have fewer than 20 students, and most are taught by full professors, though graduate students do appear behind lecterns from time to time.

The three-week Winter Term allows students to take a class, study abroad, conduct research, or participate in an internship. Nearly half of all undergrads head for foreign climes. Miami's Dolibois European Center in Luxembourg offers summer, semester, or yearlong study and the chance to live with a local family. Other opportunities span

> "Students here are ambitious, dedicated, and embody an attitude of success."

more than 90 countries. The Inside Washington program sends students to the nation's capital to meet with high-profile figures and complete an internship. Undergraduate research gets a lot of attention at Miami too. The Undergraduate Summer Scholars Program gives 100 students a stipend, a tuition waiver, and a project allowance to undertake a nine-week, faculty-mentored project. Each year, more than 2,000 Miami undergraduates conduct research, many starting as early as their freshman year.

"Students here are ambitious, dedicated, and embody an attitude of success in the classroom and outside of it," says a political science major. Racial and socioeconomic diversity are lacking, although the university says it is working to boost both; 3 percent of undergraduates are African American, 5 percent are Hispanic, 2 percent are Asian American, and 3 percent are multiracial, while just 12 percent qualify for Pell Grants. Fourteen percent come from foreign countries. Fifty-five percent of students hail from Ohio, and the campus has a long-standing reputation for wealth and conservatism. Paul Ryan, the former Republican Speaker of the House of Representatives, learned his trickle-down economics here. The *New York Times* suggested that Miami appeals to Republican families as "a place unlikely to turn their children against them." The Office of Diversity Affairs, the Center for American and World Cultures, and various student groups regularly hold events designed to encourage awareness of diversity, difference, and privilege. Thousands of merit scholarships, averaging $9,000 each, and hundreds of athletic scholarships in 17 sports are awarded annually. The university also locks in tuition, fees, and room-and-board charges for four years.

Miami is known as the "Mother of Fraternities" because several national ones began here.

Forty-five percent of the student body call the campus home. "Students tend to live off campus after their second year, but the dorms are comfortable and typically well maintained," says one junior. Miami offers 30 theme-based living/ learning communities (LLCs), 25 of which are for first-year students. Eighty-six percent of first-years join the LLCs, which center on interests such as the arts, leadership, premedicine, entrepreneurship, and cultural perspectives, among others. Campus dining options are described as diverse, healthy, and usually tasty, but overpriced. Despite efforts to combat campus sexual assault, like the It's On Us campaign, students say there is more work to be done. "I know people who have gotten in trouble for sexual assault, and I know people who have been victims," comments a senior.

Nineteen percent of the men and 31 percent of the women belong to fraternities or sororities, respectively, and the Greeks have a hard-partying reputation. Miami is known as the "Mother of Fraternities" because several national ones began here. Drinking is a popular pastime and students say alcohol policies don't do much to curb underage consumption, but on-campus activities organized by Late Night Miami,

"The surrounding area of uptown Oxford provides an excellent college social scene."

such as movie screenings, musical performances, craft nights, and casino nights, are a fun alternative. Miami also offers more than 600 student organizations. Annual events include homecoming, Springfest, and continued rivalries with Ohio University. "The surrounding area of uptown Oxford provides an excellent college social scene with various restaurants, bars, stores, and local events," says a psychology major. For students who crave brighter lights and a bigger city, Cincinnati is about 35 miles away.

In the past three years, a number of Miami's Division I RedHawks teams have won championships, including football (MAC East Division championship) and women's volleyball, softball, field hockey, and synchronized skating. Miami Mock Trial consistently ranks in the top 10 nationally and won the American Mock Trial Association national championship in 2018. Intramurals and club sports attract more than 12,000 participants annually, and popular sports include ice hockey, broomball, soccer, and sand volleyball.

Miami University, with its strong emphasis on liberal arts and its opportunities for research, travel abroad, and leadership, is looked upon as a rising star among state universities. The school effectively combines a wide range of academic programs with the personal attention ordinarily found only at much smaller, upscale institutions. Says one premed student, "Every time I step foot on campus, I just want to be a better version of me, and it is amazing that I am able to do that through the resources of the institution."

Overlaps

William and Mary, Indiana University, Southern Methodist, University of Michigan, Ohio State, U of I at Urbana–Champaign, Penn State, UW–Madison

If You Apply To ›

Miami (OH): Early decision, early action, regular decision. SATs or ACTs: required. No Subject Tests. Accepts the Common Application. Applicants may indicate if they are first-generation students or members of the LGBTQ community.

University of Michigan

515 East Jefferson Street, 1220 Student Activities Building, Ann Arbor, MI 48109

The most interesting mass of humanity east of UC Berkeley. UM is among the nation's leaders in most subjects, but undergraduates must elbow their way to the front to get the full benefit. Superb honors and living/learning programs are the best bet for highly motivated students. Out-of-state families may need a second mortgage to cover pricey tuition.

Website: www.umich.edu
Location: Small City
Public
Total Enrollment: 43,334
Undergraduates: 28,519
Male/Female: 50/50
SAT Ranges: ERW 660–730, M 670–770
ACT Ranges: 30–33
Financial Aid: 50%
Pell Grant: 15%
Expense: Pub $ $ $ $
Student Loans: 41%
Average Debt: $ $
Applicants: 59,886
Accepted: 27%
Enrolled: 43%
Grad in 6 Years: 92%
Returning Freshmen: 97%
Academics: ✍ ✍ ✍ ✍ ✍
Social: ☎ ☎ ☎
Q of L: ★ ★ ★
Admissions: (734) 764-7433
Email Address: N/A

Strong Programs:
Computer Science
Business Administration
Psychology
Economics
Foreign Languages
Engineering
Pharmaceutical Sciences
Public Health Sciences

One of the nation's elite public universities, Michigan offers an excellent faculty, dynamite athletics, an endless number of special programs, and the most interesting collection of students east of Berkeley. Boasting more than 780,000 living alumni, it also produces more Fulbright scholars than any other U.S. university. "Michigan is a special place because it has a deep history and reputation," says a senior. "It is an excellent school and no matter what degree you have, it is respected."

Situated on 3,207 acres, Michigan's campus is so extensive that newcomers may want to call on their GPS system to find their way to class. The university is divided into two main sections. Central Campus, the heart of the university, houses most of Michigan's 19 schools and colleges. North Campus, which is two miles northeast of Central, is home to the College of Engineering; the School of Music, Theatre, and Dance; the Stamps School of Art and Design; and the Taubman College of Architecture and Urban Planning. Other campus areas include the Medical Center Complex, containing seven hospitals and 15 outpatient facilities, and South Campus, featuring state-of-the-art athletic facilities. Architecturally, the main drag of campus features a wide range of styles, from the classical Angell Hall to the ultra-contemporary Museum of Art addition. Recent construction includes the Trotter Multicultural Center and Blau Hall, which houses classrooms, workshop space, and support services for the Ross School of Business.

> **"No matter what degree you have, it is respected."**

Michigan offers more than 600 active degree programs, including more than 250 undergraduate majors, as well as individualized concentrations. No courses are required of all freshmen at Michigan, but all students must complete some coursework in English (including composition), foreign languages, natural sciences, social sciences, and humanities. Students in the College of Literature, Science, and the Arts (LSA)—Michigan's largest school, offering the most undergraduate majors—must also take courses in quantitative reasoning and race or ethnicity.

For students with global interests, LSA's menu of 40 foreign languages includes several that can't be found at many other places, such as Dutch, Filipino, Hindi, Persian, Swahili, and Turkish. The screen arts and cultures major balances studies and production, with approximately one-third of a student's coursework devoted to creative, hands-on projects. The College of Engineering and Ross School of Business are well respected, and the university's programs in health-related fields are also top-notch. Preferred admissions programs guarantee top high school students admission to Michigan's programs in architecture, business, education, information, and pharmaceutical sciences, provided they make satisfactory progress during their first years. The most popular majors are computer science, business administration, psychology, and economics.

Students describe Michigan courses as challenging but not cutthroat competitive. "Academics come first, and everybody around you will be putting in the effort required to succeed," says a civil engineering major. Fifty-seven percent of classes have fewer than 20 students, and one student says, "The professors here are intelligent and seem to enjoy teaching." Students report that there is excellent academic and career advising available, but only for those who seek it. The campus Career Center provides individual and group career counseling/planning and works with 950 companies annually in recruiting UM graduating students. The new LSA Opportunity Hub connects LSA students with liberal arts–oriented internships, practical workshops, alumni, and employers.

Michigan's menu of 40 foreign languages includes Dutch, Filipino, Hindi, Persian, Swahili, and Turkish.

Michigan's special academic programs seek to offer the best of both worlds—personalized attention and a large university setting. The First Year Experience is a themed living community, paired with an introductory course taught in the residence halls, designed to support students through the transition to college; past programming has included movie nights, ice cream socials, rock climbing, and a trip to Michigan's Upper Peninsula to learn dog sledding. The university's long-established honors program, considered to be one of the best in the nation, offers qualified students honors courses and seminars, opportunities to participate in individual or collaborative research, and access to dedicated academic advisors. About 1,300 students each year work outside the classroom with a small group of students and a faculty member

"Everybody around you will be putting in the effort required to succeed."

of their choice through the Undergraduate Research Opportunities Program. Service-learning courses are plentiful, and students have the chance to study abroad in nearly 140 countries. Specific programs include a year abroad in a French or German university, a business program in Paris, summer internships in selected majors, and special short-term trips organized by individual departments.

Fifty-five percent of undergraduates hail from Michigan, and 7 percent come from abroad. The student body is notably diverse for a Midwestern state university. African Americans make up 4 percent of the student body, Hispanics 6 percent, Asian Americans 14 percent, and multiracial students 4 percent. Michigan's Program on Intergroup Relations has served as a national model for supporting diversity on college campuses, offering a variety of intergroup dialogues, courses and workshops on social justice, and community outreach programs. There are large and well-organized Jewish and LGBTQ communities here too. While the student body is more conservative today than it was a few decades ago, it is still "most noticeably liberal," says a history major, and political issues flare up from time to time on campus. Students can vie for hundreds of merit scholarships averaging $5,600, as well as 711 athletic scholarships for men and women in 27 sports. Michigan is the only public university in the state that meets the full demonstrated financial need of all in-state students, and Michigan residents with family incomes of $65,000 or less qualify

The new LSA Opportunity Hub connects students with liberal arts–oriented internships, practical workshops, alumni, and employers.

"Ann Arbor is a quintessential college town, with a wide range of cultural opportunities."

for free tuition. At roughly triple the in-state tuition rate, UM charges out-of-state students more for tuition and fees than any other flagship university in the country. It does, however, meet the full demonstrated need of out-of-state admits with family incomes of $90,000 or less.

Dormitories at UM traditionally have well-defined personalities. East Quad, as the home of the Residential College, the Michigan Community Scholars Program, and the Gender-Inclusive Learning Experience, is perhaps the most "open-minded" dorm on campus. North Quad is the newest dorm and the focal point for international and intercultural programming. On-campus housing is said to be mostly comfortable and well maintained, and 32 percent of students reside there. "Freshmen are guaranteed housing, but not every sophomore is lucky enough to secure on-campus housing, and virtually no juniors and seniors get to live in the dorms," reports a student. Alternatives include fraternity and sorority houses, a large number of college-owned and private co-ops, and plenty of off-campus rentals. Campus residents take their meals at the many dining halls located inside dorms. As for concerns about safety on campus, a student says, "Campus security is pretty good and most people I know feel safe." A new Special Victims Unit of the university police deals with instances of interpersonal violence, including sexual assault.

Detroit is a little less than an hour away, but most students become quite fond of the picturesque town of Ann Arbor. "Ann Arbor is a quintessential college town, with a wide range of cultural opportunities and ways for students to get involved," a sophomore says. A surprising variety of visual and performing arts are offered in town and on campus. An art fair held each summer in Ann Arbor draws craftspeople from throughout the nation and Canada. The Huron River and many lakes and swimming holes lay only a short drive away and seem to keep the large summer-term population happy. Michigan winters, though, are known for being cold and brutal. Seventeen percent of the men and 25 percent of the women go Greek. As one sophomore says, "There is a large Greek party scene, and if that is what you are looking for, you won't be disappointed." Campus alcohol policies are described as "moderately effective."

Division I football overshadows nearly everything each fall as students gather to cheer, "Go Blue." Despite a few shaky seasons on the gridiron, the Wolverines are rebounding under new leadership. Attending football games is an integral part of the UM experience, students say, and the Little Brown Jug football competition with Minnesota and games against Ohio State are especially popular. Several teams brought home Big Ten championships in the past year, among them men's basketball, men's and women's cross-country, and women's field hockey and gymnastics. Intramurals, which were invented at the University of Michigan, provide students with a more casual form of athletics, and 30 club sports are also active. The university's Solar Car Team has won numerous American Solar Challenge competitions in recent years.

The University of Michigan strives to offer its students a delicate balance between academics, athletics, and social activities. On one hand, this is an American college with the usual interest in football and fraternities. But it's also a world-class university with a fine faculty and top-rated programs, intent on making America competitive in the 21st century. For assertive students who crave spirit and action as well as outstanding academics, Michigan is an excellent choice.

Michigan is the only public university in the state that meets the full demonstrated financial need of all in-state students.

Overlaps

UC Berkeley, U of I at Urbana–Champaign, Stanford, Cornell University, Ohio State, Michigan State, Northwestern, University of Pennsylvania

If You Apply To ›

Michigan: Early action, regular decision. SATs (with essay) or ACTs (with writing): required. Subject Tests: optional. Accepts the Common Application with supplement. Apply to particular school or program.

Michigan State University

250 Administration Building, East Lansing, MI 48824

Most people don't realize that MSU is the largest institution of higher education in Michigan. Students can find a niche in strong preprofessional programs such as hospitality business management, prevet, and education. MSU's self-contained campus is like a town unto itself, with a bus system available to get from one side to the other. Sexual abuse scandal continues to generate headlines.

Michigan State's roots are agricultural—the school became the state's land grant institution in 1862—and future farmers, plant scientists, and veterinarians still flourish here. So do those with wanderlust, thanks to study abroad programs on each of the world's seven continents. MSU's programs in natural sciences and multidisciplinary social sciences offer students the feel of a small, liberal arts college and the resources of a large research university. "Resources here abound," says a senior.

The heart of the MSU campus, north of the Red Cedar River, boasts ivy-covered brick buildings, some of which predate the Civil War and are listed on the National Register of Historic Places. This area houses five colleges plus the MSU Union and 10 residence halls. Across the river are the medical complex, newer dorms, and two 18-hole golf courses. Most notably, MSU is home to the National Superconducting Cyclotron Laboratory. Current construction includes the $730 million Facility for Rare Isotope Beams, a new facility for nuclear science research that is funded in partnership with the U.S. Department of Energy and the state of Michigan and expected to be completed in 2022. On the southernmost part of campus are farms and animal research and teaching facilities.

Michigan State students tend to be preprofessional and clear about their interests; the premed, prevet, and teacher education programs are strong, and the most popular majors include marketing, communication, journalism, various fields in the social sciences, and biological sciences. Other popular options include supply chain management, environmental science, and hospitality business management; students in the latter program get real-world experience by staffing the university's hotel and conference center. To graduate, all students must satisfy university requirements in math and writing, complete a major, and take a minimum of 26 credits in the integrative studies program, which includes arts and humanities; social, behavioral, and economic sciences; and biological and physical sciences.

> "[We] have a large international population, which is really cool."

Academics at MSU get tougher as students advance through their majors, according to a junior. "Many of our courses are very competitive because they play a part in determining whether or not you are accepted into a specific program," notes a classmate. Classes are often quite large, with 24 percent enrolling more than 50 students, but students say that, for the most part, professors are accessible and dedicated. Hundreds of group-based and individual research opportunities are available to undergraduates. The Honors College offers the intimacy of a small-college atmosphere. MSU has a strong international component as well, with more than 275 study abroad programs in nearly 60 countries; 23 percent of undergrads take part.

"Students here are friendly and diverse," says an elementary education major. "We also have a large international population, which is really cool because it gives you the opportunity to get to know people and cultures from all over the world." Seventy-five percent of undergraduates are Michigan residents, and 12 percent are international. Whether they come from gritty Motor City or pretty Traverse City, or from somewhere outside the Midwest, Michigan State students care about the world around them. Indeed, more than 2,700 alumni have served in the Peace Corps since the school first partnered with the agency in 1961, a milestone reached by only four other universities. African Americans make up 7 percent of the student body, Asian Americans add 5 percent, Hispanics constitute 4 percent, and multiracial students represent 3 percent. Scholarships are offered in 25 Division I sports, and thousands of students also receive grants and awards based on academic merit, which average $10,500 annually.

Forty percent of MSU students—including nearly all freshmen—live in Michigan State's residence halls and apartment communities, which one sophomore describes as "very convenient and well maintained." Those seeking a traditional college

---

Website: www.msu.edu
Location: Suburban
Public
Total Enrollment: 42,914
Undergraduates: 35,249
Male/Female: 49/51
SAT Ranges: ERW 550–650,
  M 550–670
ACT Ranges: 23–28
Financial Aid: 53%
Pell Grant: 19%
Expense: Pub $ $ $
Student Loans: 49%
Average Debt: $ $ $
Applicants: 36,143
Accepted: 72%
Enrolled: 31%
Grad in 6 Years: 79%
Returning Freshmen: 91%
Academics: ✐ ✐ ✐
Social: ☎ ☎ ☎ ☎
Q of L: ★ ★ ★
Admissions: (517) 355-8332
Email Address: admis@msu
  .edu

Strong Programs:
Marketing
Communication
Journalism
Social Sciences
Biological Sciences
Education
Agricultural Sciences
Supply Chain Management

Future farmers, plant scientists, and veterinarians still flourish at MSU, the state's land grant institution.

experience can bunk in one of five huge "neighborhoods," each with three to 10 residence halls plus libraries, advising and tutoring services, health services, cafeterias, and recreation areas. Other living/learning programs, known by their catchy acronyms, include RISE (focus on the environment), MRULE (multiracial unity), and CORE (engineering). All 27 of the school's residence halls are to be updated by 2020. MSU's dining services dish out meals at nine dining halls, two food courts, and one food truck. "All the food is edible," says a senior.

Campus safety measures include walking escorts for those who stay late at the library, and Lansing's bus system offers discounted night-owl rates for those living farther away. Parking places on campus are in chronically short supply, and students complain about the tickets they receive as a result. Once they've earned 28 credits, students may move off campus. Many do so because the city of East Lansing, just outside Michigan's capital, offers all the positive aspects of a large urban area (the population more than doubles when school is in session), along with the safety and community feel of a much smaller town. According to one student, "The social life at MSU is very lively on the weekends." Twelve percent of MSU men and 11 percent of the women go Greek. Other weekend alternatives include bands, dances, and comedians brought in by the Student Activities Board and events held by the more than 900 student organizations. Second-run movies are also shown in Wells Hall—free for campus dwellers, and a couple of bucks for those who live off campus.

Weekends are dominated by Big Ten athletic competitions, with the MSU–Michigan rivalry especially fierce. "Our large campus is filled from end to end with individuals sporting green and white; alcohol-free tailgating is also available," says a junior. "Seeing 150,000 people in a space that usually has about 60,000 is quite an experience." The football, men's basketball, and women's golf teams are recent conference champions. After more than six decades of standing guard at Kalamazoo Street and Red Cedar Road, the school's mascot, affectionately known as "Sparty," was moved indoors to protect him from the elements. However, a replica stands outside and is guarded by students when Wolverines come to town. Students are still able to paint "the Rock," a large boulder donated in the 1960s, to advertise campus events, birthdays, anniversaries, and the like. Eighteen intramurals and 23 club sports, from "spartyball" (a variation of indoor soccer) to competitive cheer, also keep students busy.

> **"Our large campus is filled from end to end with individuals sporting green and white."**

MSU is struggling to deal with continuing fallout from a scandal that erupted in 2017 involving a former faculty member and physician to athletes who was convicted of abusing scores of girls and young women over many years. The scandal attracted national attention and, among other things, led to the resignation of the university president. Administrators say they are working hard to strengthen policies, procedures, training, and community resources to ensure that MSU continues to be a safe, cosmopolitan campus where future leaders, physicians, and financiers happily coexist in what one student calls a "diverse, friendly, and expressive" bunch.

If You Apply To ›

MSU: Early action, regular decision. SATs or ACTs: required (SAT essay or ACT writing recommended). No Subject Tests. Accepts the Common Application.

Middlebury College

Middlebury, VT 05753

Set in the picturesque and ski-friendly Green Mountains of Vermont, Middlebury is a magnet for students with serious interests in environmental and international studies. Known worldwide for its summer foreign language programs. Varsity and intramural sports play a big role in campus culture, which may help explain why Middlebury was the first college to play Quidditch.

For some, Middlebury College's campus, with its picturesque sunsets, excellent skiing, and rural Vermont charm, may bring to mind a resort. Middlebury is indeed a paradise for those interested in the environment, second and third languages, and a tight-knit community. But this school's rigorous workload means four years here is far from a vacation. At Midd, a neuroscience major says, "You have the latitude to ask the questions that you want to investigate, and you are given the resources to answer them."

The college's 350-acre main campus overlooks the village of Middlebury, Vermont, which a junior describes as a "small, quaint Vermont town of 8,700 people and five stoplights." The 1,800-acre mountain campus, site of the Bread Loaf School of English, the famed Bread Loaf Writers' Conference, and the college's Snow Bowl skiing facility, is nearby. Old Stone Row cuts across the campus, where buildings with simple lines and rectangular shapes evoke the mills of early New England. (Middlebury was founded in 1800.) Academic halls and dormitories of marble and limestone sit in quadrangles and feature views of the Adirondack and Green mountains. The Sierra Club rates Middlebury top in the nation for its environmental efforts, which include reliance on a wind turbine and systematic efforts to help students recycle. The 110,000-square-foot, LEED Gold–certified Virtue Field House provides a bevy of athletic facilities and exercise equipment.

Midd students take a discussion-based, writing-intensive First-Year Seminar with only 15 students; the instructor serves as advisor to those enrolled until they declare a major. Students must also satisfy distribution requirements in literature, the arts, philosophical and religious studies, history, physical and life sciences, deductive reasoning and analytical processes, social analysis, and foreign language. Additionally, students take classes in writing, cultures and civilizations, physical education, and, of course, their major. With all of these requirements, it's no wonder students and faculty become close. Students agree that the academic atmosphere is collaborative and the quality of teaching high. An economics major says, "The work is rigorous, but the small class sizes make it so that students form deep connections with their professors and hence receive more personalized help with assignments." Twenty-eight percent of students collaborate with faculty on research projects. During the four-week January term, students can narrow their focus to opportunities like a single intensive course or an internship.

> "You have the latitude to ask the questions that you want to investigate."

Between June and August, Middlebury banishes English from its campus and hundreds of students live, learn, and, hopefully, think only in their chosen language. The language departments continue their excellent instruction during the school year; especially notable are German, Chinese, Japanese, and Hebrew. Although there is no foreign language requirement, just about everyone studies another tongue, if only to take advantage of Middlebury's campuses at 38 universities in 17 countries around the world, from Italy and India to China and Cameroon. In total, there

---

Website: www.middlebury.edu
Location: Small Town
Private
Total Enrollment: 2,511
Undergraduates: 2,511
Male/Female: 49/51
SAT Ranges: ERW 660–750, M 660–760
ACT Ranges: 30–34
Financial Aid: 44%
Pell Grant: 16%
Expense: Pr $ $ $ $
Student Loans: 46%
Average Debt: $
Applicants: 8,909
Accepted: 17%
Enrolled: 42%
Grad in 6 Years: 95%
Returning Freshmen: 96%
Academics: ✐ ✐ ✐ ✐ ½
Social: ☎ ☎ ☎
Q of L: ★ ★ ★
Admissions: (802) 443-3000
Email Address: admissions@middlebury.edu

Strong Programs:
World Languages
International and Global Studies
Environmental Studies
English
Geography
Economics
Computer Science
Political Science

are 90 college-approved study abroad programs, and about 60 percent of students study internationally. Students in the interdisciplinary environmental studies major choose one of 13 areas to focus on, such as conservation psychology, creative arts, and environmental history. Other highly touted Middlebury departments include English (one of the school's most popular majors, bolstered by its connections to the Bread Loaf Writers' Conference) and geography. Economics, computer science, and political science are also popular.

Students say the campus is friendly but can be cliquish, and while there a few typical groups you'll always find in large numbers at Middlebury (preppies, "outdoorsy, granola" types, and athletes), the wide range of opportunities here also means that, in the words of one sophomore, "Whatever your character, you'll find your niche." Just 6 percent come from within the state; 10 percent come from abroad. Six percent of students are Asian American, 10 percent are Hispanic, 4 percent are African American, and 5 percent are multiracial. All first-year students participate in a one-day, student-run program called JusTalks, which facilitates discussions on race and other topics. The campus leans left politically, but a senior says that, for the most part, "Midd is not a huge school for political activism." There are no merit or athletic scholarships, but the college is committed to a need-blind admissions policy and to meeting 100 percent of admitted students' demonstrated financial need. Students say the socioeconomic divide on campus can be noticeable: "It's like a true middle class doesn't exist here," remarks a junior.

> "There can be a work-hard, play-hard attitude here, but the 'play' means different things to different people."

Few Middlebury students live off campus (5 percent), since housing is guaranteed for four years. For the first two years, students live in traditional residence halls grouped into living/learning communities called Commons, each of which is staffed by a dean, a faculty advisor, and a residential advisor. Upperclassmen can choose from a range of options, such as suites, college-owned townhouses, the Environmental House (where residents cook all of their own food), and academic interest houses, while still remaining members of their original Commons. A math major says, "The general trend is that housing improves as you get older." The school's three dining halls get high marks for their tasty victuals, friendly staff, and accommodations for students with dietary restrictions. "Students are allowed to swipe in and out of the dining halls as many times as they want per day," says a senior. Students say they feel safe on campus—"It's hard to feel *unsafe* in rural Vermont," reasons one sophomore—and appreciate the school's responsiveness to sexual assault prevention.

"There can be a work-hard, play-hard attitude here," explains a senior, "but the 'play' means different things to different people—there are groups that party, there are groups that go hiking, etc." Those who stay on campus are treated to school-sponsored dances, plays, dance performances, trivia nights, or parties at the co-ed social houses, which a sophomore describes as "casual" and "much more inclusive" than typical Greek parties at other schools. (Middlebury banned fraternities and sororities in the mid-1990s.) There are more than 170 student organizations, and Middlebury was the first college to play Quidditch. Kegs are prohibited in the dorms but permitted at parties, which must be registered and also offer nonalcoholic drinks and snacks. Despite these measures, alcohol consumption is said to be common among underage students. The three-day Winter Carnival is a major annual extravaganza including parties, a bonfire with fireworks, ski races at the Snow Bowl, snow sculpture, ice-skating at an outdoor rink, and an all-school formal ball.

> "[Middlebury is] the quintessential New England town, straight out of Norman Rockwell."

Middlebury has campuses at 38 universities in 17 countries around the world.

All first-year students participate in a one-day, student-run program called JusTalks to discuss race and other topics.

Off campus, Middlebury is "the quintessential New England town, straight out of Norman Rockwell." It has necessities such as restaurants, grocery stores, drug stores, hardware stores, and clothing shops, and 70 percent of students do volunteer work. "Community service is a big part of who we are here at Midd," says a sophomore. The progressive city of Burlington is 45 minutes away, while Montreal is a three-hour drive, Boston four, and New York City five. Snow comes early here and stays late, but Middlebury's own Snow Bowl and Rikert Nordic Center, not to mention proximity to most Vermont ski slopes, make this a paradise for ski fanatics, a breed Middlebury attracts in appropriately large numbers.

Middlebury athletics draw rabid fans, especially when cheering the powerful Panthers ice hockey teams—men's and women's—to victory against archrival Norwich; townspeople support the hockey games and the teams' members give back by tutoring in local schools. The college offers 31 Division III varsity sports and has won recent national titles in men's tennis, women's lacrosse, and women's field hockey. Recent conference champs include men's track and field and basketball and women's ice hockey and volleyball. About half of the student body is active in the large intramural and club sports program, with soccer, basketball, water polo, crew, and, of course, Quidditch getting the most interest.

Midd students enjoy plenty of student/faculty interaction, tight-knit friendships, and excellent recreational opportunities in a beautiful setting. Add challenging academics to the mix, and Middlebury is a comfortable, yet stimulating, place to spend four years, not just for writers, polyglots, and environmental enthusiasts, but, says a senior, for anyone who is "academically curious and willing to work hard at whatever they do."

Winter Carnival is a major annual extravaganza with ski races at the Snow Bowl and an all-school formal ball.

Overlaps

Amherst, Bowdoin, Brown, Dartmouth, Williams, Yale, Harvard, Princeton

If You Apply To ›

Middlebury: Early decision I and II, regular decision. SATs or ACTs or three Subject Tests: required. Accepts the Common Application.

Mills College

5000 MacArthur Boulevard, Oakland, CA 94613

One of two major women's colleges on the West Coast, Mills is strong in the fine arts, science, and interdisciplinary studies, though it does offer preprofessional programs such as business and health sciences. San Francisco Bay Area location is rich with opportunity, and Mills is working to connect students with more real-world experiences. Student body is highly diverse in every respect. Still the only women's college to turn back coeducation with a massive protest, which it did in 1990.

At Mills College, students receive more than just a liberal arts education. They are expected to dive into hands-on academic experiences, serve their community, and graduate with a deeper understanding of diversity and social issues. The school's dedication to equality is long-standing: Mills was the first women's college in the West to award bachelor's degrees, the first to offer a computer science major, the only women's college to reverse a decision to go co-ed, and the first single-sex college to implement an admissions policy for transgender applicants. "Mills is a magnet for students passionate about social justice and the world around them," says a music major, and "an environment where differences are celebrated."

Website: www.mills.edu
Location: City Outskirts
Private
Total Enrollment: 1,127
Undergraduates: 738
Male/Female: 0/100
SAT Ranges: ERW 530–670, M 500–620

(continued)

ACT Ranges: 23–29
Financial Aid: 79%
Pell Grant: 56%
Expense: Pr $
Student Loans: 75%
Average Debt: $ $ $
Applicants: 965
Accepted: 86%
Enrolled: 21%
Grad in 6 Years: 64%
Returning Freshmen: 77%
Academics: ✍ ✍ ✍
Social: ☎ ☎
Q of L: ★ ★ ★
Admissions: 800-876-4557
Email Address: admission@
   mills.edu

Strong Programs:
English
Psychology
Biology
Economics
Computer Science
Public Policy
Fine Arts
Queer Studies

Mills requires all students to participate in community-engaged learning and complete a faculty-mentored project.

The school's fascinating history started in 1852, when it began as a young ladies' seminary serving the children of California Gold Rush adventurers who were determined to see their daughters raised in an atmosphere of gentility. Troubled recently with enrollment and financial problems, Mills has been forced to reduce its faculty and staff, but it remains dedicated to a combination of student diversity and educational opportunity that helps guarantee that no one will graduate without having her horizons well expanded. The enclosed, parklike 135-acre campus boasts both historic and modern architecture set among rolling meadows, woods, and a meandering creek.

Core curriculum requirements at Mills fall into three main categories: foundational skills, modes of inquiry, and contributions to knowledge and society. As part of the core, all students take a first-year seminar and a course on race, gender, and power. In 2018, Mills launched *MPOWER*, billed as a signature academic experience designed to enhance students' academic coursework with hands-on experiences. The program connects incoming students with a faculty advisor and an "academic navigator" who eases the transition to college, and it requires all students to participate in community-engaged learning, complete a faculty-mentored project such as a creative piece or research-based thesis, and create a digital portfolio to showcase their work to potential employers.

> "Professors want student input and student interactions."

"We are a very collaborative school, always thinking in interdisciplinary terms, and even when the work gets hard, we enjoy working with each other," observes a biology major. The professors are highly regarded and accessible, and since 71 percent are women, there's no shortage of strong female role models. In the classroom, a biopsychology major says, "Professors want student input and student interactions." English, psychology, biology, and economics are some of the most popular majors, and computer science and public policy are also strong. Novel interdisciplinary programs include politics, economics, policy, and law (popular among prelaw students); queer studies; and women, leadership, and social change. The fine arts department is Mills's traditional stronghold, and electronic and computer music specializations within the music program are worthy of note. Mills has concurrent cross-registration agreements with UC Berkeley and many other Bay Area colleges, as well as several five-year bachelor's/master's programs. Mills students are encouraged to explore beyond the Oakland campus, and 17 percent take advantage of programs abroad.

Eighty-one percent of Mills undergraduates are from California, and 1 percent are international. African Americans constitute 9 percent of the student body, Hispanics 29 percent, Asian Americans 9 percent, and multiracial students another 9 percent. An influential subgroup of students consists of "resumers"—women who are returning to college after a break of several years. The LGBTQ community is also strong here; approximately half of a recent incoming class identified as heterosexual and half as other sexual orientations. A substantial 56 percent of first-year students are Pell-eligible, and 32 percent are the first in their families to attend college. A junior cites

> "Everyone has opportunity, and everyone is challenged to reach their own potential."

"gender equality, racial equality, locally sustained foods, water conservation, land conservation, [and] hedging against gentrification," as issues in which students are most engaged. Beginning in fall 2018, Mills lowered its tuition by $16,000—a 36 percent reduction—in an effort to make the school affordable for more students. It also awards merit scholarships to qualified students, but there are no athletic scholarships.

Sixty-four percent of students live on campus; most, even first-years, are housed in single rooms. "The rooms are huge with wood floors and a sink in almost every room," reports a senior. All first-year students are assigned to a living/learning community to form closer bonds with their classmates. Campus dining receives cheers from students for its "endless" variety of tasty options and accommodations for students with all manner of needs and tastes. Mills is a gated campus with one entrance, and students say they feel safe. "We are a small school, but we are not immune to issues of sexual assault," comments a senior. "Our revised policies for dealing with these situations are very strong."

"Party culture is nonexistent on campus. People go off campus to party, stay on campus to study and relax," explains a business economics major. Popular annual events include the Black and White Ball, Midnight Breakfast, and Spring Fling, as well as Latina Heritage Month and a spring powwow sponsored by the ethnic studies department. Most of the time, though, the campus is quiet, and students head to UC Berkeley for parties and to Oakland and San Francisco for culture and urban adventures. Both are accessible via public transportation, beginning with a bus stop outside the front gate. Those with the means can take ski trips to Lake Tahoe or go to the sunny Santa Cruz beaches.

The Cyclones compete in the Association of Division III Independents in six sports: cross-country, rowing, soccer, swimming, tennis, and volleyball; swimming and rowing are the most competitive. A small intramural program draws about 10 percent of students, with futsal (indoor soccer) being the most popular, and students also enjoy college-organized hiking, kayaking, and camping trips.

Despite some complaints about campus life, Mills students enjoy small classes with excellent teaching in one of the country's most desirable locations close to San Francisco. With an educational program that emphasizes skills critical for understanding today's society and succeeding in the real world, Mills students are sure to graduate as independent thinkers capable of making it on their own. At Mills, a senior says, "Everyone has a voice, everyone has opportunity, and everyone is challenged to reach their own potential."

A substantial 56 percent of first-year students are Pell-eligible, and 32 percent are the first in their families to attend college.

Overlaps

Agnes Scott, Sarah Lawrence, Lewis & Clark, Saint Mary's College of California, Whittier, UC Santa Cruz, UCLA, UC Davis

If You Apply To ›

Mills: Early action, regular decision. SATs or ACTs: optional. No Subject Tests. Accepts the Common Application with supplement. Gender nonconforming, genderqueer, and trans students are encouraged to apply.

Millsaps College

1701 North State Street, Jackson, MS 39210

Millsaps is the strongest liberal arts college in the deep, Deep South and by far the most progressive. Its largely preprofessional student body typically has sights set on business, law, or medicine. Usually compared to Hendrix, Rhodes, and Sewanee. Half the students come from out of state, generally from other Southern states.

Millsaps College was once thought of as a finishing school for well-bred Southern belles and gentlemen. Although less well-known outside the Deep South, it has long been one of the region's top liberal arts institutions. Millsaps is affiliated with the United Methodist Church, and the school's motto, *ad excellentiam*, means "promoting excellence"—which the college takes seriously. What characterizes the school is its focus on scholarly inquiry, spiritual growth, and community service. "Millsaps is the perfect package," says a freshman, "strongly academic, small enough to build relationships, yet big-thinking enough to build the mind."

Website: www.millsaps.edu
Location: City Center
Private
Total Enrollment: 830
Undergraduates: 796
Male/Female: 51/49

(continued)

SAT Ranges: ERW 560–660,
  M 550–660
ACT Ranges: 22–28
Financial Aid: 98%
Pell Grant: 16%
Expense: Pr $
Student Loans: 58%
Average Debt: $ $ $
Applicants: 4,276
Accepted: 49%
Enrolled: 11%
Grad in 6 Years: 67%
Returning Freshmen: 75%
Academics: ✐ ✐ ✐
Social: ☎ ☎ ☎
Q of L: ★ ★ ★
Admissions: (601) 974-1050
Email Address: admissions@
  millsaps.edu

Strong Programs:
Business Administration
Accounting
Biology
Psychology
Creative Writing
Sociology/Anthropology
Religious Studies
Prehealth

The college's 100-acre campus sits in the center of Jackson, on the highest point in the city. A mix of modern and traditional buildings is arranged around the Bowl, a sequestered glen surrounded by old-growth trees and shrubs that serves as a main student gathering place. Recent campus projects include a new Visual Arts Center and a major remodel of the McRae Christian Center, completed in 2019, that created new classrooms for the humanities as well as a chapel for students of all faiths and backgrounds.

The Compass Curriculum is built on several learning outcomes: Foundations (covering thinking and reasoning), Communication in Humanities, Integrative and Collaborative Learning, Problem Solving and Creative Practice, Our Human Heritage, and Explorations (covering a range of liberal arts subject areas). A writing across the curriculum initiative ensures that every student develops writing skills, and all students must complete the Major Experience, a capstone learning experience that may involve research, a field- or community-based course, study abroad, an internship, or an honors project.

Millsaps offers more than 30 majors and 40 minors, including the option of a self-designed major. The Millsaps College Writing Program and creative writing are top-notch, and the sociology/anthropology and religious studies programs are well regarded. The most popular majors are business administration, accounting, biology, and psychology.

> "Every professor I've had has used multiple methods for presenting information."

Premed-related courses, including those in biology, chemistry, and neuroscience, are strong, and the college's prehealth mentoring program pairs students with practitioners in their chosen field, allowing them to earn credit for real medical experience. Cooperative agreements allow students to opt for nursing degrees in partnership with the University of Mississippi Medical Center and Vanderbilt University. Millsaps also offers engineering opportunities in cooperation with Auburn, Columbia, Vanderbilt, and Washington universities.

"The courses are rigorous, as the professors continue to push the students' academic boundaries," says a sophomore. Seventy-nine percent of classes at Millsaps have fewer than 20 students, and none exceed 50. "Every professor I've had has used multiple methods for presenting information to help students understand class material," says a biology major. Each year, a few select upperclassmen join the Ford Teaching Fellows Program, letting them work closely with a faculty member to learn about teaching—and paying them for their time in the classroom. For-credit internships are available with local businesses and in state government offices in Jackson. The college also maintains a 4,500-acre biological reserve in the rainforest of the Yucatán Peninsula, which hosts courses exploring Mayan culture and the Mayan coral reef. Nearly 40 percent of Millsaps students study abroad, and courses are offered in more than 50 nations, including Austria, Ghana, Scotland, Peru, and Vietnam.

Millsaps maintains a 4,500-acre biological reserve in the rainforest of the Yucatán Peninsula.

"The student body at Millsaps is friendly and welcoming," says a student. "As a transfer student, I found that the process of making new friends was easier than I expected." Half of the students now come from out of state, the majority being from other Southern states, although 5 percent arrive from foreign countries. Many Mississippians view Millsaps as a hotbed of liberalism, and students report that while there are conservatives on campus, the atmosphere is largely liberal and progressive. "Millsaps has a long history of being responsive to social issues," says a political science major. Indeed, Millsaps was the first college in Mississippi to voluntarily open its doors to minority students, and it recently installed gender-neutral bathrooms on campus. African Americans make up 17 percent of the student body, Asian Americans 4 percent, and Hispanics 5 percent. Qualified students are awarded academic merit scholarships averaging $24,500 each year, but there are no athletic awards.

Eighty-nine percent of students stay in campus housing—mostly, grouses a sophomore, because those who move off campus are subject to a 35 percent reduction in their financial aid. On-campus options include traditional, suite-style, and apartment-style halls, and a psychology major says, "Housing is average." The robust Greek system claims 56 percent of men and 55 percent of women; sophomore, junior, and senior men may live in one of four fraternity houses, but there is no sorority housing. "The caf is clean and offers a large selection of food, including a vegan station," says a senior, but the quality of meals is hit or miss. "Millsaps has really emphasized sexual assault education," notes a biology major, and the issue "has been incorporated into the first-year curriculum."

"Greek life is the center of Millsaps's social life," a student explains, and the fraternity houses are usually open and rocking from Wednesday through Saturday nights. Greek rush is now held after fall midterms instead of during the first hectic week of school, but that hasn't dampened the party spirit. "Campus police are very stringent" when it comes to enforcing alcohol policies, according to a senior. Major Madness is a favorite annual event, offering a week of open-mic nights, hypnotists, and comedians and culminating in a weekend-long festival in the Bowl, with a crawfish boil, carnival games, and live music. The city of Jackson also offers a wealth of options, including professional symphony, opera, and ballet, and the city is a nexus for Mississippi's

> **"Millsaps has a long history of being responsive to social issues."**

legendary blues and "roots rock" musical traditions. The "1 Campus 1 Community" program connects students with local volunteer opportunities. Easy road trips include New Orleans, Memphis, and the riverfront casinos in Vicksburg, Mississippi; closer to campus, 10 miles to the north, is a huge reservoir that is popular for weekend water sports. For students who enjoy the great outdoors, the Natchez Trace offers easy access to wooded trails and bicycling paths.

The Millsaps Majors compete in the Division III Southern Athletic Association, so it isn't nearly as sports crazy as most Southern campuses. Men's and women's tennis, men's soccer and baseball, and women's volleyball and softball have been competitive in recent years. Kickball has been added to the roster of more than 25 intramural sports, and with group exercise classes and sports clubs, all students with recreational interests and abilities can find a game to play. Everyone benefits from the 65,000-square-foot Hall Activities Center, which has facilities for weight training, aerobics, basketball, racquetball, squash, and volleyball.

In a state renowned for blues, barbecue, and the tradition of old magnolia trees and grand plantations, progressive Millsaps College is an anomaly. "Millsaps is a magnet for accomplished students from strong backgrounds and the kind of college not usually found in the South," remarks a junior. Small classes ensure plenty of time to get to know fellow students and faculty members. That's one tradition that never gets old.

Millsaps was the first college in Mississippi to voluntarily open its doors to minority students, and it recently installed gender-neutral bathrooms on campus.

Overlaps

Albion, Austin College, Birmingham–Southern, Eckerd, Hendrix, Rhodes, Sewanee, University of Mississippi

If You Apply To ›

Millsaps: Early action, regular decision. SATs or ACTs: required. No Subject Tests. Accepts the Common Application with supplement.

University of Minnesota

240 Williamson, 231 Pillsbury Drive SE, Minneapolis, MN 55455

Not quite as highly rated as the University of Michigan or the University of Wisconsin, but not nearly as expensive if you happen to be from out of state. In a university the size of Minnesota, the best bet is to find a niche, such as the honors program. Strong programs include engineering, management, and health fields. Pack your woollies.

Website: www.twin-cities.umn
.edu
Location: City Center
Public
Total Enrollment: 39,003
Undergraduates: 29,312
Male/Female: 47/53
SAT Ranges: ERW 620–720,
 M 650–760
ACT Ranges: 26–31
Financial Aid: 48%
Pell Grant: 18%
Expense: Pub $ $ $
Student Loans: 58%
Average Debt: $ $
Applicants: 43,720
Accepted: 50%
Enrolled: 29%
Grad in 6 Years: 80%
Returning Freshmen: 93%
Academics: ✑ ✑ ✑ ✑
Social: ☎ ☎ ☎
Q of L: ★ ★ ★
Admissions: (800) 752-1000
Email Address: admissions@
 umn.edu

Strong Programs:
Psychology
Communication Studies
Journalism
Computer Science
Electrical Engineering
Mechanical Engineering
Entrepreneurial Management
International Business

The University of Minnesota, like the nearby Mall of America, can be overwhelming, given its seemingly limitless variety of offerings and gargantuan size. With 150 undergraduate majors across seven schools and colleges, plus one of the largest study abroad programs in the nation, the U of M offers an abundance of academic choices. Be warned, though—winters can be frigid and it can take a cool customer to navigate the endless choices here.

The vast Twin Cities campus actually consists of two campuses with three main sections. The St. Paul campus encompasses the College of Food, Agricultural, and Natural Resource Sciences; the College of Biological Sciences; the College of Veterinary Medicine; and the College of Continuing Studies. The Minneapolis campus is divided by the Mississippi River into an East Bank and a West Bank that are home to the other colleges and most of the dormitories, as well as most of the fraternities and sororities. Both campuses offer a blend of traditional and modern architecture, with columned buildings seated next to sleek geometric structures. The two campuses are five miles apart and linked by a free bus service. Academic facilities are excellent, beginning with the seven-million-volume library system, one of the largest in North America. Every one of the colleges has its own library, many of which are good places to study. A 695-acre arboretum is used for research and teaching, and the West Bank Arts Quarter makes a lively setting for the university's art disciplines.

> "The classes are relatively difficult [but] it really depends on the subject."

Minnesota's liberal education requirements call for students in all schools and colleges to complete a set of basic distribution requirements and take courses that satisfy four of five themes: civic life and ethics, U.S. diversity and social justice, the environment, global perspectives, and technology and society. Freshmen must take a first-year writing course. The College of Science and Engineering is notable for its tutorial and internship options; the electrical and mechanical engineering programs are particularly strong and well subscribed. The Carlson School of Management is well regarded and offers majors in entrepreneurial management, international business, and other areas. Psychology, communication studies, journalism, and computer science are the most popular majors. Undergraduates also have access to more esoteric fields such as mortuary science.

"The classes are relatively difficult," a junior says, but "it really depends on the subject." The university is on a semester system, and almost all classes have a pass/fail option (limited to no more than a quarter of a student's courses). Efforts to limit class size have been stepped up—37 percent of classes currently have fewer than 20 students—and the university is focusing more on undergraduates. While undergrads have had a difficult time enrolling in courses, one junior reveals, "If a class is closed and somebody really needs it, they can usually get a magic number from the department to be able to register for it." The university also offers a four-year graduation guarantee, provided students follow program requirements, including frequent academic counseling and specific coursework. Helpful teaching assistants are abundant. Professors receive high marks from most students as being approachable and knowledgeable. "The instructors have been exemplary due to their passion for the subject matter and commitment to their students," an archaeology major says.

The excellent honors program in the liberal arts college allows close contact with faculty members as well as leeway to enroll in certain graduate courses and seminars. The Undergraduate Research Opportunities Program provides scholarships of up to $1,500 for students to conduct research with faculty. Students find plenty of internship opportunities at the many corporations and government agencies in the Twin Cities area, and the university pushes its study, work, and volunteer abroad programs in nearly 100 nations. These draw about a third of undergrads, most of whom sign up for short-term programs.

The College of Science and Engineering is notable for its tutorial and internship options.

Most U of M students are "motivated and hardworking," says a junior. Seventy-two percent of undergraduates are from Minnesota, and 9 percent hail from outside the U.S. Five percent are African American, 4 percent are Hispanic, 10 percent are Asian American, and 4 percent are multiracial. Need-based financial aid is available, as are merit scholarships averaging $5,000 and athletic awards in all major sports.

Dorm life at Minnesota follows the big school, wait-in-line mantra. Twenty-three percent of undergraduates live in residence halls; there are nine traditional halls and five university-run apartment facilities. Students can also choose to join one of three dozen living/learning communities, such as Design House, STEM Diversity House, and Lavender House. "Dorms are adequate," says one student, although "some can be a bit cramped." Dorm rooms are hard to obtain, and parking spaces for the school's many commuters are almost as scarce. Students who have rooms get the chance to keep them for the next year, and they're also required to purchase a meal plan. Meals are said to be hit or miss, but, "Fresh fruit and veggies are always available," notes a junior, who also adds (lest anyone fear the campus dietitians are excessively health-obsessed), "they have the best chocolate chip cookies." Campus security includes a free escort system.

"Most social life takes place right off campus."

"Most social life takes place right off campus," says one student, "but there are loads of activities available on campus, such as bowling, theater, late-night activities, and movies." About 12 percent of students go Greek. Students say policies against underage drinking usually work. The union's bowling alley, pool tables, movie theater, and live music dance club are good places to meet people. And there are more than 900 student groups on campus. Spring Jam, a carnival weekend put on by the Greeks each April to raise funds for charity, is a huge event, described by one student as "homecoming in spring—but better." Campus Kickoff Days in the beginning of the fall quarter is also much anticipated.

Women's ice hockey has scored four national championships in the last eight years.

Here, being "under the weather" can be a good thing, as campus designers found a way to get around—or under—wet or wintry conditions by linking many of the campus buildings with tunnels. For those who love winter, happy skiers and skaters become colorful spots all over the state's white backdrop. In the spring and summer, Minnesota's famed 10,000 lakes offer swimming, boating, and fishing. The downtown areas of the Twin Cities are easy to get to by bus, and there are scores of good bars, restaurants, nightspots, and movie theaters.

This is an athletically inclined bunch of students, as both intramural and Division I varsity sports are popular. Students always hope the current season will be one in which the gridiron Gophers take home the roses in a bowl victory, but short of that, a win over Michigan for custody of the Little Brown Jug is cause for celebration. Women's ice hockey has scored four national championships in the last eight years. Men's ice hockey, baseball, and women's soccer, softball, and track and field have all won Big Ten conference titles in recent years. Intramural competition can go on well past midnight.

Overlaps

Marquette, University of Minnesota Duluth, University of St. Thomas, UW–Eau Claire, UW–Madison, University of Michigan

Anonymity is almost a given at a university of this size, but then size does have its virtues in the countless array of campus resources. A senior says, "It offers unparalleled opportunities for students to grow academically, socially, and personally." The University of Minnesota is ideal for those who appreciate an urban setting and a good, old-fashioned, button-up-your-overcoat winter.

University of Minnesota, Morris

600 East 4th Street, Morris, MN 56267-2199

The plains of western Minnesota may seem an unlikely place to find a liberal arts college—and a public one at that. Morris is cut from the same cloth as Mary Washington, UNC Asheville, and St. Mary's College of Maryland. The draw: private college education at a public university price. Remote location pushes students to Minneapolis–St. Paul for city life.

Website: www.morris.umn.edu
Location: Rural
Public
Total Enrollment: 1,494
Undergraduates: 1,494
Male/Female: 44/56
SAT Ranges: ERW 560–680, M 590–710
ACT Ranges: 22–28
Financial Aid: 96%
Pell Grant: 37%
Expense: Pub $ $ $
Student Loans: 72%
Average Debt: $ $
Applicants: 3,211
Accepted: 64%
Enrolled: 17%
Grad in 6 Years: 59%
Returning Freshmen: 80%
Academics: ✐ ✐ ✐ ½
Social: ☎ ☎
Q of L: ★ ★ ★
Admissions: (888) 866-3382
Email Address: admissions@ morris.umn.edu

Strong Programs:
Psychology

The University of Minnesota, Morris is far more comprehensive than the small size of its student body might suggest. The first buildings on its 130-year-old campus were originally home to an American Indian boarding school, which was succeeded in 1910 by an agricultural school. Morris opened its doors in 1960, and since then it has grown into a solid public liberal arts college. Morris "strives to encourage students to push their limits and go out on limbs," says an English and history double major.

The 130-acre Morris campus includes 32 traditional brick-and-mortar buildings, loosely arranged around a central mall. Two high-powered wind turbines generate 60 percent of the power Morris requires each day. The renovated Welcome Center is LEED Gold–certified and is the first building in Minnesota (and the first on the National Register of Historic Places) to use energy-efficient chilled-beam technology.

Everyone at Morris starts their general education requirements with the Intellectual Community seminar, which introduces students to college-level work and active interaction with faculty. Students then move on to as many as five courses under the umbrella of Skills for the Liberal Arts, along with eight courses in Expanding Perspectives. Seniors must participate in a senior seminar or capstone project, and some do both. The most popular majors are psychology, English, biology, management, and economics. Other well-regarded programs include environmental science and environmental studies, as the Morris campus itself serves as a study in renewable energy; Native American and indigenous studies, which benefits from the campus's unique history; and elementary education.

> **"[Morris] strives to encourage students to push their limits and go out on limbs."**

Students describe the academic climate as challenging yet "informally comfortable." "Almost everything at UMM is a collaborative effort," says a biology major, and students are encouraged to reach out to professors for individual help. Seventy-two percent of classes have fewer than 20 students, and professors are respected for their knowledge and real-world experience. "Every professor I've had seems focused on their teaching skills," reports a sophomore.

Morris offers 20 to 30 service-learning courses each year, and 52 percent of students conduct research projects with faculty. Morris's Center for Small Towns, which works with small towns, local schools, and nonprofits to address challenges specific to rural communities, offers opportunities for service projects, internships, and research. The Morris Honors Program allows high achievers to enjoy various honors courses, an honors capstone project, and a core course titled Traditions in Human Thought. Morris continues to integrate study abroad opportunities into the curriculum, offering more than 300 options for students wishing to study overseas; 46 percent of students participate by the time they graduate.

"Being out in rural Minnesota really brings people together to make their own fun."

"Morris tends to be considered the 'nerdy' branch of the University of Minnesota system, and that's accurate both in terms of our interests and our achievements," observes a psychology major. Seventy-four percent of Morris students are Minnesota natives, and 11 percent are international. The campus is more diverse than many other schools in the state: American Indians comprise 8 percent, Hispanics 5 percent, Asian Americans 3 percent, and African Americans 2 percent, and 13 percent of students identify as multiracial. Politically, there can be occasional clashes between liberal and conservative points of view. "Particularly, the rights and treatment of women, ethnic and racial minorities, and the LGBTQ community are of high consideration," notes one student. Merit scholarships averaging $4,000 are available, but there are no athletic awards. Financial incentives for low-income students include the University of Minnesota Promise Scholarship, awarded to Minnesota residents with a family income that does not exceed $120,000. Thirty-seven percent of current freshmen qualify for Pell Grants. Honoring a policy that dates back to the campus's late-19th-century origins, a tuition waiver is available for American Indian students.

Morris's Center for Small Towns offers opportunities for service projects, internships, and research.

Fifty-two percent of Morris students live on campus in one of the six residence halls, which offer several living/learning communities, or in an apartment complex reserved for upperclassmen. It's easy to get a room; students say the environmentally friendly Green Prairie dorm is very nice, but others could use renovations. Many students opt for less expensive apartments and rental homes off campus. Dining options get generally unenthusiastic reviews. Morris's rural campus feels safe, according to students, and a senior says, "People are highly encouraged to speak out about sexual assault and report an incident. This speak-out approach seems to work."

Honoring a policy that dates back to the campus's late-19th-century origins, a tuition waiver is available for American Indian students.

There is no Greek system, but students say there's always something to do on campus, such as concerts, movies, presentations, shows, and campuswide games of Humans vs. Zombies or Hunger Games. "Being out in rural Minnesota really brings people together to make their own fun and recreation," explains a senior. The drinking age is strictly enforced on campus and in local bars. "There is a small party culture on campus. There is zero pressure to drink or do any drugs," says a computer science major. Campus traditions include the annual Circle of Nations Indigenous Association powwow and the tug-of-war competition between the two main freshman dorms; "Hundreds of students show up!" cheers a student. Students also look forward to the Zombie Prom in the fall and the Yule Ball, a holiday dance inspired by Harry Potter.

Morris itself is described as a "small but very friendly" town with a couple of bars, one small music venue, and a bowling alley. For those pining to get away, the nearest retail and restaurant chains are about 45 minutes away in Alexandria. Minneapolis-St. Paul, about three hours southeast, is also a popular destination.

The Cougars compete in the Division III Upper Midwest Athletic Conference. Women's volleyball and basketball are particularly successful, and men's and

Overlaps

St. Mary's College of Maryland, Massachusetts College of Liberal Arts, UNC Asheville, Gustavus Adolphus, St. Olaf, University of Minnesota, University of Minnesota Duluth, St. Cloud State women's soccer and track and field are also strong. In addition, students enjoy access to more than 120 student-led clubs and associations. Basketball, volleyball, and softball are among the most popular intramurals, and students also use the Regional Fitness Center or hiking and biking trails to stay fit.

One of the smaller campuses in the University of Minnesota system, Morris may just epitomize the idea of "Minnesota nice," in a positive sense. Tucked away from the state's big cities, some students might find the campus isolated. But the school's location means fewer distractions—and more time for its happy students to focus on independent reading and research, or just getting to know their peers. "We are the University of Minnesota's gem on the prairie," says a senior. "We have the intimacy of a private school, and the academic excellence of the state's largest educational institution, all for an affordable price."

If You Apply To ›

Morris: Rolling admissions. SATs (with essay) or ACTs (with writing): required. No Subject Tests. Accepts the Common Application.

University of Mississippi

145 Martindale, P.O. Box 1848, University, MS 38677

Located in the progressive town of Oxford, Ole Miss is doing its best to put the state's redneck past behind it. Strong on public policy and international studies, and the honors college is one of the best anywhere. Location near Faulkner's old hangouts is ideal for soaking up Southern literary traditions, and ever-changing mascots continue to stoke school spirit, especially against LSU and Mississippi State. Tailgating remains world class.

Website: www.olemiss.edu
Location: Small Town
Public
Total Enrollment: 20,519
Undergraduates: 17,361
Male/Female: 44/56
SAT Ranges: ERW 550–640, M 520–650
ACT Ranges: 22–29
Financial Aid: 82%
Pell Grant: 24%
Expense: Pub $
Student Loans: 50%
Average Debt: $ $ $
Applicants: 17,416
Accepted: 84%
Enrolled: 25%
Grad in 6 Years: 60%
Returning Freshmen: 85%
Academics: ✍ ✍ ✍

The University of Mississippi (usually known as "Ole Miss" after the nickname of the yearbook) offers students an educational experience steeped in tradition and thick with school spirit. Students have access to a host of academic offerings, including a top-notch honors college and an innovative public policy leadership major, and to a vibrant community of Rebels always ready to have a good time. Whether they're hitting the books, cheering on their teams, or simply hanging out, Ole Miss students exude a love for their school that is hard to miss.

Founded in 1844, the University of Mississippi's central campus occupies 850 acres of rolling land in the center of Oxford. The main campus consists of 200 buildings and a mix of architectural styles, including Greek Revival, Beaux-Arts Classicism, Georgian Revival, and modern. The white-columned Lyceum, which served as a hospital during the Civil War, is the campus's oldest building and now houses administrative offices. Construction on a 200,000-square-foot, $138 million STEM education building is underway, slated for completion in 2021.

> "Our study abroad program is exceptional…[and] offer[s] many different scholarships."

All students at Ole Miss must complete credit hours in English composition, mathematics, laboratory science, humanities and fine arts, and social and behavioral sciences. Approximately 75 percent of first-year students sign up for the Freshman Year Experience, a seminar-style course that helps new students transition from high school into a successful college career. The Center for Writing and Rhetoric administers two mandatory composition courses for freshmen.

Students say coursework is what you make of it and varies by program, but the atmosphere is collaborative. "The classes are definitely challenging at times," says one freshman, "but doable with the right amount of work." The most popular majors include general studies, accountancy, psychology, and elementary education; programs in pharmaceutical sciences, integrated marketing communications, and Chinese language are also strengths. The Lott Leadership Institute is a standout that offers a public policy leadership major and an innovative curriculum that combines the systematic study of public policy with the development of leadership qualities. "The atmosphere of Lott is conducive to learning and team building," says one broadcast journalism major. "Conversational and debate classes are a change from the regular classroom, and Lott offers both." Professors are highly rated across the university. "It is not at all uncommon for full professors to teach freshmen and even offer tutoring to freshmen during their office hours," explains a senior.

"Ole Miss students are ambitious, hospitable, and well-rounded."

For the 10 percent of students who itch to have their passports stamped, Ole Miss offers numerous study abroad options in diverse locations around the world, including China, Greece, Ethiopia, Peru, and Thailand. "Our study abroad program is exceptional," gushes one senior. "Not only do they offer you the opportunity to travel basically anywhere that you want, they offer many different scholarships to make study abroad less costly." Another option is the Croft Institute for International Studies, which accepts 70 students each fall. Participants study international politics, economics, and culture both in the classroom and via study abroad. Gifted students may apply for the highly competitive Barksdale Honors College, where they take part in small, discussion-based honors courses offered in a number of disciplines, engage in community service, complete a senior thesis, and have access to foreign study fellowships. Roughly 1,500 students from 70 majors currently participate.

"Ole Miss students are ambitious, hospitable, and well-rounded," says one public policy leadership major. The student body is fairly homegrown: 54 percent of undergraduates are Mississippi natives and 2 percent hail from abroad. African Americans make up 13 percent, Hispanics 3 percent, Asian Americans 2 percent, and multiracial students 2 percent. "The outside view of UM is that everyone is a sorority girl or a frat guy," a mathematics major complains. "We have people of all categories and cultures." Twenty-four percent of incoming freshmen are eligible for Pell Grants. Merit scholarships averaging $8,800 are awarded annually, as are 330 athletic scholarships in 14 sports.

Roughly 1,500 students from 70 majors currently participate in the Barksdale Honors College.

Twenty-five percent of students live in the dorms, which are a hit-or-miss affair. "Some of the older dorms have seen better days, but there is a new focus on campus to renovate and rebuild housing," a student reports. Options include apartments, traditional residence halls, and residential colleges. According to one student, the residence halls "provide a sense of community and family that makes Ole Miss unique."

"The Grove is a place where people come together regardless of their differences."

Campus dining options are reported to be plentiful and tasty. "We offer several different dining halls," says a student, "some of which are all-you-can-eat and some of which are cafeteria-style." Campus security gets a thumbs-up too. "Ole Miss is the kind of place where people look out for each other," comments a student. "We have a campus police department that works diligently to make sure the campus is safe."

The Ole Miss social scene is dominated by Greek life, which attracts 35 percent of the men and 44 percent of the women, although non-Greeks find plenty to enjoy as well. The Student Activities Association hosts a variety of on-campus activities each week, including movies, pageants, concerts, and multicultural events. Alcohol

(continued)

Social: ☎ ☎ ☎
Q of L: ★ ★ ★
Admissions: (662) 915-7226
Email Address: admissions@ olemiss.edu

Strong Programs:
General Studies
Accountancy
Psychology
Elementary Education
Pharmaceutical Sciences
Integrated Marketing
  Communications
Chinese
Public Policy Leadership

is forbidden on campus, and students say the "two strikes and you're out" policy is effective at curbing consumption. Campus worship organizations have a strong presence, and students can choose among 300 student groups, as well as volunteer opportunities in Oxford. One enthusiastic junior describes the city as "the best college town in the nation." A senior adds, "There are lots of locally owned businesses and restaurants that are unique to the area and very charming."

Famed author William Faulkner grew up here and attended Ole Miss for three semesters before dropping out, and the slew of local cultural events includes the annual Faulkner and Yoknapatawpha Conference, featuring lectures and discussions by literary scholars and critics. Although it lost out to the University of Virginia as repository of Faulkner's papers, Ole Miss operates Rowan Oak, Faulkner's home, and has a sizable collection of Faulkner materials. Blues legend B.B. King gave Ole Miss his personal record collection to help establish its Blues Archive.

The Ole Miss Rebels compete in the gauntlet known as the Southeastern Conference, where they face the likes of Alabama's Crimson Tide, the Florida Gators, and the LSU Tigers. Solid teams include football, baseball, men's and women's basketball, and women's tennis. School spirit is on full display, especially when LSU is in town. After retiring its longtime, problematic Colonel Reb mascot in 2003 and replacing it with Rebel Black Bear in 2010, Ole Miss introduced a new mascot—the Landshark—in 2018. (The "Rebels" nickname remains intact.) The marching band has also stopped playing "Dixie," and the state flag, which includes a Confederate battle emblem, no longer flies on campus. On game days, frenzied fans gather on the Grove—10 acres of oak and maple trees in the center of campus—for tailgating, which draws more than 100,000 loyal supporters who pitch 2,500 tents and drink from red and blue cups (no beer cans allowed). Jackets, ties, and cowboy boots are common, and food is sometimes served on silver trays. Says one happy Rebel, "The Grove is a place where people come together regardless of their differences to support our Ole Miss Rebs and share in a community that we all love." Dozens of intramural and club sports also prove to be popular diversions.

Overall, students at Ole Miss seem to be a contented lot, especially those in the honors college. Despite the administration's continued attempts to reconcile the school's historic roots with a 21st-century visual identity, it's clear that Rebel pride and the sense of community here are as strong as ever. Indeed, Ole Miss students have much to cheer about, including solid academics, game days in the Grove, and a healthy dose of school spirit.

Overlaps

University of Tennessee Knoxville, University of Alabama, University of Kentucky, University of Georgia, Texas Tech, Mississippi State, University of Southern Mississippi, Auburn

If You Apply To ›

Ole Miss: Rolling admissions. SATs or ACTs: required. Subject Tests: required for some. Accepts the Common Application.

University of Missouri

230 Jesse Hall, Columbia, MO 65211

Renowned for having one of the top journalism schools in the nation, Mizzou boasts the country's only commercial university-owned TV station, as well as a National Public Radio outlet. Also strong in agriculture and the health sciences, as well as business and music. Comparable in size to Iowa and Iowa State, smaller than Illinois and Indiana. Recent controversy over racial climate has cut heavily into freshman enrollment.

In 1839, the residents of Boone County, Missouri, raised enough money to create the state university in Columbia. Today, Missouri's flagship university has evolved into a top research institution, yet continues to uphold the belief of its founders in the great value of higher education that is accessible to all. Having recently completed a $1.3 billion development campaign, the university continues to expand programs and facilities in ways that benefit students. It has also become a national leader in generating on-site renewable energy.

The oldest public university west of the Mississippi, Mizzou's 1,262-acre campus is flanked by mansionlike fraternity and sorority houses and features 42,000 plants and trees and numerous thematic gardens. Francis Quadrangle, with 18 National Historic Landmark buildings, is the core of the Red Campus (so named for the predominant color of brick). Central to this area are the 43-foot limestone columns of the original Academic Hall that was destroyed by fire in 1892. To the east of the Columns is the original tombstone of Thomas Jefferson, which the Jefferson family gave to Mizzou (not UVA!) in the 19th century as a symbol of his championing of state-supported education. The White Campus consists of vine-covered limestone buildings by the Memorial Union Tower.

An array of general education requirements includes courses in three content areas: social and behavioral sciences; physical, biological, and mathematical sciences; and humanities and fine arts. Two writing-intensive courses are also required, and all undergrads complete a senior-year capstone course. Full professors teach the lecture courses at Mizzou, supplemented by a weekly discussion session led by a teaching assistant

"Professors use real-world examples to tie heavy topics and theories to reality."

to go over material presented in class. "Professors use real-world examples to tie heavy topics and theories to reality, helping us to make the connection," explains an agribusiness management major. Owing to MU's size, classes can fill up quickly, but the school guarantees the availability of coursework to complete a degree in four years.

With more than 300 degree programs and 19 schools and colleges, Mizzou offers a comprehensive set of choices for basic and advanced study. Aspiring journalists can get hands-on experience working on the *Columbia Missourian*, the local daily paper edited by J-school faculty members and students, or at KOMU-TV, the nation's only university-owned commercial television station. KBIA, MU's National Public Radio station, is popular among journalism students and listeners alike. Agriculture is also nationally ranked, especially in the areas of agribusiness management and applied research for farm communities. The music program is noteworthy, and the College of Engineering maintains several strong undergraduate segments, including biological and civil engineering. The College of Business is competitive and features a five-year bachelor's/master's accounting program.

"The academic climate is relatively competitive, depending on the major," says one senior. "In my experience, there is a nice mix of classes in regards to difficulty." Committed preprofessionals will be glad to know that MU offers ambitious freshmen guaranteed admission to its graduate-level programs in medicine, law, veterinary medicine, nursing, and health professions. Mizzou is also one of the leading public universities for undergraduate research. Twenty-two percent of students study abroad, choosing from programs in more than 50 countries. Additionally, the university sponsors Mizzou Alternative Breaks, service trips in which students work on volunteer projects in the U.S. and abroad during spring, winter, and weekend breaks.

Seventy-three percent of Mizzou students hail from the Show-Me State, though every state in the union is represented; the 3 percent of international students come from more than 100 countries. African Americans account for 8 percent of the

Website: www.missouri.edu
Location: Small City
Public
Total Enrollment: 26,603
Undergraduates: 22,131
Male/Female: 48/52
SAT Ranges: ERW 570–680, M 550–670
ACT Ranges: 23–29
Financial Aid: 80%
Pell Grant: 19%
Expense: Pub $
Student Loans: 52%
Average Debt: $ $
Applicants: 16,373
Accepted: 78%
Enrolled: 32%
Grad in 6 Years: 68%
Returning Freshmen: 87%
Academics: ✍ ✍ ✍
Social: ☎ ☎ ☎ ☎
Q of L: ★ ★ ★
Admissions: (573) 882-7786
Email Address: mu4u@missouri.edu

Strong Programs:
Business
Health Professions
Journalism
Engineering
Agriculture
Agribusiness Management
Music

Agriculture is nationally ranked, especially in the areas of agribusiness management and applied research for farm communities.

undergraduate student body, Asian Americans 3 percent, Hispanics 4 percent, and multiracial students 3 percent. Mizzou experienced a 35 percent decline in freshman enrollment over just two years following protests in 2015 over chronically poor race relations on campus, which attracted national attention, in part because of a strike by the football team, and led to the resignation of the UM system president and the campus chancellor. Since the protests, Mizzou has established several scholarship and support programs designed especially for minorities, created a diversity training program that all incoming students are required to take, and initiated campuswide celebrations of cultural diversity. It has also joined the Common Application and ramped up promotion on social media to boost applications. Enrollment figures are beginning to show signs of recovery, and the number of African American freshmen expected to enroll is rising. Most importantly, says a senior, "Mizzou has become more proactive about making sure every student feels safe and comfortable on campus." Merit scholarships are available averaging $6,300, and student-athletes may compete for 290 awards in 20 Division I sports. Missouri Land Grants cover full tuition and fees for Missouri residents who qualify for the Pell Grant.

> **"Mizzou has become more proactive about making sure every student feels safe and comfortable on campus."**

Twenty-one percent of MU students live on campus, and freshmen under age 20 are required to do so. "I loved my residence hall experience," says one sophomore. "I had a lot of space in my room and the closets were huge!" Residence halls have double rooms and are often crowded and lively—and thus are fun places to call home. Single-sex halls, a few single rooms, and round-the-clock quiet floors are also available. About 30 percent of new students choose from among 100 Freshman Interest Groups, where 15 to 20 students with shared academic interests live in the same residence hall and enroll in three core classes together. All other undergrads living in the dorms participate in general and thematic living/learning communities. Mizzou's all-you-can-eat dining halls, coffee bars, and take-out stands get good reviews for variety and accommodating special needs. The fraternity and sorority houses are livable (the frat houses less so); 25 percent of Mizzou men and 34 percent of women go Greek.

Banning alcohol from all fraternities and sororities, the Greek system is one of the largest in the nation to go dry.

Students say MU's social life is packed with options, including movies, shopping, eating out, the usual fraternity and sorority parties, 500-plus student organizations, and great parks and hiking areas on the outskirts of town. Says a senior, "There is always something going on at Mizzou, whether it be a free event being put on by campus or a social event happening in Greek Town." Mizzou is a champion of tough alcohol policies, and students have agreed to ban alcohol from all fraternities and sororities, making it one of the largest Greek systems in the nation to go dry. (The rule is lifted when alumni come home to visit!) "Columbia is a bustling college town that is high-energy most weekends," says one student. Students support the town by engaging in 210,000 hours of community service each year, and the community caters to them in return. Road trips to St. Louis, Kansas City, and Lake of the Ozarks offer a change of scenery.

> **"We are a school rich in tradition, but looking to the future."**

Mizzou's Tigers compete in the rough-and-tumble Southeastern Conference, and basketball and football games draw big crowds. In fact, the entire town turns out in black and gold for any football game. The women's softball and track and field programs are strong, and the wrestling team took home its seventh consecutive Mid-American Conference championship in 2018. MU's popular intramural program has nearly two dozen sports and two skill divisions, attracting more than a quarter of the student body. "My favorite traditions are our school songs that we sing at all athletic events, Tiger Walk and Senior Sendoff, and yelling 'M-I-Z' and waiting for someone to yell back 'Z-O-U,'" cheers a journalism major.

Overlaps

U of I at Urbana–Champaign, Indiana University, University of Iowa, Iowa State, University of Kansas, Kansas State

Mizzou is working hard to put its racial difficulties in the rearview mirror, support a more inclusive community, and resume its trajectory as a school on the rise. "It is a college that will shape your life and help guide you into the future," says a student. It continues to grow academically and culturally, while sticking with its longtime strengths. One senior reflects, "We are a school rich in tradition, but looking to the future."

If You Apply To ›

Mizzou: Rolling admissions. SATs or ACTs: required. No Subject Tests. Accepts the Common Application with supplement.

Morehouse College: See page 36.

Mount Holyoke College

50 College Street, South Hadley, MA 01075

One of two women's colleges, along with Smith, that are members of the Five College Consortium in the scenic Connecticut River Valley of western Massachusetts. Less nonconformist than Bryn Mawr and Smith. MHC is strongest in the natural and social sciences, and one of few colleges to have a program devoted to leadership.

The women who choose Mount Holyoke College value achievement, leadership, inclusivity, and tradition. Mount Holyoke pioneered women's higher education in 1837 and continues to pave the way as a diverse research liberal arts institution. While students sometimes complain about the heavy workload, most bring that challenge upon themselves as they seek intellectual fulfillment within the supportive, caring environment that MHC fosters. "Mount Holyoke is a sisterhood," says a senior. "I have never before been surrounded by so many amazing, passionate women."

Mount Holyoke is located in the heart of New England on 800 acres of rolling hills dotted with two lakes, miles of hiking trails, and waterfalls. Modern glass-and-stone buildings stand alongside more traditional ivy-covered brick and sandstone structures. Campus highlights include the Japanese Meditation Garden and Teahouse, the Talcott Greenhouse, an art building with studios and a bronze-casting foundry, an 18-hole championship golf course, and an equestrian center. The $33 million science center continues to advance the college's reputation as a leader in science education and houses classrooms, labs, and offices for eight departments. The new Community Center, serving as the main campus destination for student life and dining, opened in 2018.

> "Lynk funding allows students to do work they want to do without sacrificing a summer of making money."

Despite changes to the campus, curriculum at this 182-year-old institution remains rooted in the traditional liberal arts and sciences. All students must take a first-year seminar, and the college offers roughly 36 seminars each fall and 5 in the spring, covering a wide variety of topics and disciplines. The focus of these courses is developing skills in analysis and critical inquiry. Some also include field trips to museums or events in Boston, New York, or Washington, D.C.

Website: www.mtholyoke.edu
Location: Suburban
Private
Total Enrollment: 2,171
Undergraduates: 2,152
Male/Female: 0/100
SAT Ranges: ERW 640–713, M 630–750
ACT Ranges: 29–33
Financial Aid: 66%
Pell Grant: 20%
Expense: Pr $ $
Student Loans: 66%
Average Debt: $
Applicants: 3,446
Accepted: 51%
Enrolled: 30%
Grad in 6 Years: 86%
Returning Freshmen: 91%
Academics: ✍ ✍ ✍ ✍
Social: ☎ ☎ ☎
Q of L: ★ ★ ★ ★
Admissions: (413) 538-2023
Email Address: admission@ mtholyoke.edu

(continued)

Strong Programs:
Chemistry
Biology
Psychology
Economics
English
Environmental Studies
Computer Science
Dance

Chemistry is a traditional strength at Mount Holyoke, bolstered by top-of-the-line labs, a scanning electron microscope, several nuclear magnetic resonance spectrometers, and a linear accelerator. The most popular majors are biology, psychology, economics, English, and environmental studies. The computer science and dance programs are also strong. Five-year dual-degree programs enable students to combine degrees from MHC with B.S. degrees in engineering from the University of Massachusetts Amherst, Caltech, or Dartmouth. Many students find the Five College Consortium one of the school's greatest assets: each year, 74 percent of Mount Holyoke students take at least one course offered through the consortium. A free bus service runs every 20 minutes between MHC and Amherst College, Hampshire, UMass Amherst, and Smith, multiplying a Mount Holyoke student's access to academic, social, and cultural opportunities. As an alternative to pursuing a minor or second major, Mount Holyoke also offers the Nexus program, which builds in opportunities for internships, off-campus research, and public presentations, along with traditional coursework. Participating students select from one of nine preprofessional tracks, such as global business, nonprofit organizations, and data science.

"Mount Holyoke is a simultaneously intense and supportive academic environment," says an environmental studies major. "I feel challenged but not overwhelmed." Students rave about the quality of teaching and the small classes. "Faculty are warm, sensitive, incredibly intelligent, and highly invested in their students," says a psychology and education major. Although some of Mount Holyoke's intro courses have 50 or more students, 73 percent of classes have fewer than 20. Since the required curriculum is so diverse, there is little trouble getting into the smaller classes and finishing in four years. The school's honor code makes possible self-scheduled, self-proctored final exams. Students say the Career Development Center's assistance with résumés, cover letters, and interview preparation is particularly effective. "They even have 40 full suits for students to rent for free!" adds a senior.

The Weissman Center for Leadership offers enrichment programs in leadership and public service and community-based learning.

Many students choose to take advantage of an optional January winter term to take a noncredit, nontraditional course, or do an internship in major cities or points abroad. The Lynk curriculum-to-career experience guarantees all students funding for an internship or research opportunity, domestic or international, and offers students access to special resources, workshops, and networking opportunities with alumnae. "Lynk funding allows students to do work they want to do without sacrificing a summer of making money," cheers a sophomore. The Weissman Center for Leadership can help students hone their rhetorical skills and offers enrichment programs in leadership and public service and community-based learning. For a change of scenery, 39 percent of MHC students spend all or part of junior year in another country. In addition to roughly 100 study abroad programs from approved partners, Mount Holyoke sponsors its own in France, China, Japan, and Costa Rica.

"Social justice and human rights are big issues on campus."

"Mount Holyoke students are all different, and we pride ourselves on our diversity," asserts a senior. Indeed, the college attracts students from 45 states and 69 countries; 19 percent are Massachusetts natives and a substantial 27 percent are international. African Americans make up 5 percent of the student body, Asian Americans 10 percent, Hispanics 7 percent, and multiracial students 4 percent. "Social justice and human rights are big issues on campus," says one student, and others add that transgender rights have been a particular focus recently. CAUSE (Creating Awareness and Unity for Social Equality) is a large and popular campus group dedicated to community-building and student leadership. Mount Holyoke's financial aid packages meet 100 percent of applicants' demonstrated financial need. Merit scholarships are available, averaging $21,000, but there are no athletic scholarships.

All dorms serve milk and cookies (as well as healthier fare like hummus and vegetables) at 9:30 p.m. on school nights.

Ninety-five percent of Mount Holyoke students live in the residence halls. "All the residence halls at Mount Holyoke are great. They all have their own personality, which makes it very difficult to choose sometimes," says a student. Most dorms are also very homey, with living rooms, TV lounges, and baby grand pianos; all serve milk and cookies (as well as healthier fare like hummus and vegetables) at 9:30 p.m. on school nights. Students from all four classes live together, and housing is guaranteed for all four years. Some residence halls also offer apartment-style living. Campus dining gets enthusiastic reviews, as does security. "We are a very safe campus and sexual assault is extremely rare," says a sophomore.

Social life on campus is described as "mellow," consisting of low-key parties, plays, concerts, speakers, and cultural events. "A cappella is the football of Mount Holyoke—we have six different groups who perform every semester and have significant followings in the student body," notes a senior. Students seeking a more "traditional" party scene typically head to UMass or other Five-College schools. Road trips to Boston, Vermont, and New York City are also popular, when students have more time. Closer to campus, the South Hadley Center has eateries, a pub, shops, and a movie theater.

"Traditions are a big part of life at Mount Holyoke," comments a philosophy major. Each class has a color and a mascot, and class spirit is huge, especially for the annual Junior Show and Convocation. Every fall on Mountain Day, students wake up to ringing bells, classes are canceled (even the library is closed), and everyone treks up Mount Holyoke to picnic and see the foliage. "In the spring we have Pangy Day (short for Pangynaskeia, or 'cultivating the total world of women'), where students wrap a maypole, snuggle baby goats, and hang out in the sun with friends," explains a senior. The *Mount Holyoke News* is the oldest continuously running college newspaper in the country, and the campus is also home to the Mount Holyoke College V8s (Victory Eights), the oldest continuing female collegiate a cappella group in the United States. Community service is an important emphasis, and 41 percent of students regularly volunteer.

> **"A cappella is the football of Mount Holyoke."**

In addition to academic pursuits, Division III athletics at Mount Holyoke, such as crew, riding, field hockey, and lacrosse, are popular. The Lyons field hockey, riding, and swimming and diving programs have won team and individual championships recently. The college encourages athletic participation with six club sports and a state-of-the-art fitness center, although intramurals are not offered. Mount Holyoke's Model United Nations team frequently brings home top honors.

Mount Holyoke's diverse student body makes for a globally aware community, and its identity as a women's college promotes a culture where deep, personal relationships are the norm. Academic excellence and easy access to New York and Boston provide a small college atmosphere that's infused with art and culture. As one senior explains, "There is a unique bond and desire for empowerment on campus."

> *The Mount Holyoke News is the oldest continuously running college newspaper in the country.*

Overlaps

Smith, Wellesley, Barnard, Bryn Mawr, Scripps, Brown, Vassar, Tufts

If You Apply To ›

MHC: Early decision I and II, regular decision. SATs or ACTs: optional. Subject Tests: optional (required for homeschooled students). Accepts the Common Application with supplement. Accepts applications from students who are female or who identify as women.

Muhlenberg College

2400 Chew Street, Allentown, PA 18104

There is a definite Muhlenberg type: ambitious, studious, and preprofessional. Takes its Lutheran affiliation and values seriously, but less than 5 percent of students are Lutheran, while one-third are Jewish and another third are Roman Catholic. Strong in premed, prelaw, pre-anything. Has a more humble, middle-class persona than more upscale Dickinson and Lafayette and boasts a nurturing atmosphere.

Website: www.muhlenberg.edu
Location: Suburban
Private
Total Enrollment: 2,278
Undergraduates: 2,278
Male/Female: 40/60
SAT Ranges: ERW 580–680, M 560–660
ACT Ranges: 25–30
Financial Aid: 90%
Pell Grant: 16%
Expense: Pr $ $ $
Student Loans: 59%
Average Debt: $ $ $
Applicants: 4,636
Accepted: 48%
Enrolled: 25%
Grad in 6 Years: 87%
Returning Freshmen: 91%
Academics: ✐ ✐ ✐
Social: ☎ ☎ ☎
Q of L: ★ ★ ★ ★
Admissions: (484) 664-3200
Email Address: admissions@muhlenberg.edu

Strong Programs:
Theater
Business Administration
Media and Communication
Psychology
Biology
Premed
Prelaw
Public Health

When a popular school pseudonym is "The Caring College" rather than some line referring to sun or booze, you know you're in for a different experience. That's the case with Muhlenberg College, a small liberal arts school that takes pride in nurturing its students. School administrators characterize the students as having "Muhlenberg goodness"—meaning that they share a strong sense of community and mutual support. Founded on solid Lutheran roots, the school continues to encourage religious diversity among students and to attract the best and brightest to its top premed program.

Set on 82 parklike acres, the 'Berg campus is a combination of older Gothic stone structures and newer buildings in a variety of architectural styles. Prominent facilities include a lovely chapel, the high-tech Trexler Library, a 40-acre biological field station and wildlife sanctuary, and a 64-acre arboretum with more than 300 species of wildflowers, broadleaf evergreens, and conifer trees. The campus also boasts a football stadium and all-weather track, and the 50,000-square-foot Trexler Pavilion for the Performing Arts that has a dramatic 45-foot glass outer shell and houses a variety of performance spaces.

Muhlenberg's popular First-Year Seminars are small, writing- and discussion-intensive courses capped at 15 students. Other general education requirements include two additional writing-intensive courses, a two-course cluster aimed at helping students connect different disciplines, a two-course diversity and global engagement requirement, and a capstone experience in the major. The fun-filled, four-day freshman orientation program carries just one requirement: learning the alma mater and then hightailing it to the president's house to serenade him.

Muhlenberg's regional reputation rests on its premedical program, which continues to attract large numbers of students. A major in public health is available, as

> **"Sometimes [professors] will tailor their lessons to the interests of the students in the class."**

are joint programs in areas such as physical therapy and occupational therapy with Thomas Jefferson University, medicine with Temple University, and dentistry with the University of Pennsylvania. The college's theater arts program is a national draw, and some alumni have even gone on to star on Broadway. Science lab equipment at Muhlenberg is cutting-edge, and a comprehensive science major allows for a sampling of it all. The Living Writers course, offered once every three years, has brought a number of noted authors to campus, including Neil Gaiman, Jonathan Franzen, and Cristina García. Theater is Muhlenberg's most popular major, followed by business administration, media and communication, psychology, and biology.

A mathematics major says, "I feel that Muhlenberg is competitive in the sense that it urges you to compete with yourself, to question your thinking, and to reach your full potential." Seventy percent of courses have fewer than 20 students, encouraging a cooperative environment, and since there are no graduate students, there are no teaching assistants. "Class sizes are small enough that professors get to know each student, and sometimes they will tailor their lessons to the interests of the students in the class," says a freshman. Advising is strong here too, and seniors may take advantage of the Senior Year Experience program that helps them make the transition from college to "whatever comes next." The program is organized around the concepts of transition, integration, and reflection and includes workshops and seminars.

The college offers three honors programs that provide early opportunities for internships, undergraduate research, and service-learning: the Muhlenberg Scholars Program, the Dana Scholars Program, and the RJ Fellows Program. Each program requires a culminating project or seminar in the senior year; 10 percent of students participate. Students speak highly of the college's array of service-learning course offerings. Muhlenberg sends study groups to Washington, D.C., and there is a semester-long program at the Jewish Theological Seminary in New York City. Those seeking international experiences may study abroad via 160 programs in countries around the globe, and about half do so.

> "Muhlenberg is basically the golden retriever of colleges: everyone is so sweet and friendly."

"Muhlenberg is basically the golden retriever of colleges: everyone is so sweet and friendly, but we are also hardworking and dedicated to our studies," muses a public health major. Muhlenberg draws 23 percent of its students from Pennsylvania, and many from adjacent New Jersey and New York, as well as 4 percent from foreign nations. The student body is more diverse in terms of religion than of race and ethnicity. African Americans account for 4 percent of the student body, Hispanics 7 percent, Asian Americans 3 percent, and multiracial students 2 percent. "There is an open political dialogue where students are encouraged to express their views without worry of backlash," says a junior. Merit scholarships averaging $13,300 are available, but athletic scholarships are not.

Muhlenberg encourages students to live on campus and guarantees housing to all undergraduates except transfers, so 91 percent of students live in campus residences. "Freshmen are required to live in one of three dorms, which is actually nice because it brings them all together in one area of campus," explains a senior. Upperclassmen praise the Muhlenberg Independent Living Experience townhouses and other suite-style options. Two dorms, Robertson and South, house 140 students in single, air-conditioned rooms overlooking Lake Muhlenberg. First-years choose from a seven- or five-day meal plan, and students rave about the food, the staff, and even the dining-hall ambiance. "Our recently renovated Wood Dining Commons is a cross between a ski lodge and Hogwarts," cheers one student. "There's even a fireplace!" A senior says, "With a Title IX coordinator and judicial panel, the college puts a great deal of effort into making sure that students and members of the Muhlenberg community feel safe."

> "Wood Dining Commons is a cross between a ski lodge and Hogwarts. There's even a fireplace!"

Most social life at Muhlenberg takes place on campus, and students say there's something to fit every interest. The Muhlenberg Activities Council provides comedians, current movies in the Red Door Café, live band concerts, and movies on the lawn. Hillel is among the largest of the more than 110 student organizations, as are the theater and dance associations. Allentown offers a decent variety of restaurants, bars, and minor-league sports, and a senior comments, "Muhlenberg's relationship with the surrounding community is definitely growing." Students get involved by volunteering as tutors and with groups such as Habitat for Humanity and America Reads. City buses stop five minutes from campus for trips to Allentown proper and area malls. There also are daily bus runs to New York City (for clubbing and theater), Philadelphia (for nightlife and cheesesteaks), and Baltimore and Washington, D.C. Outdoorsy students can pick up the Appalachian Trail for a little hiking.

The Senior Year Experience program includes workshops and seminars that help students make the transition from college.

Hillel is among the largest of the more than 110 student organizations, as are the theater and dance associations.

*Big social events
include West Fest
in the fall, East
Fest in the spring,
and the Scotty
Wood basketball
tournament.*

Seventeen percent of Muhlenberg men and 21 percent of the women pledge their undergraduate years to fraternities and sororities, respectively, and according to a junior, "Greek life is thriving if you want it but not thrust upon you in any way." Students report that the school takes its policies against underage drinking seriously. Big social events include homecoming, West Fest in the fall, East Fest in the spring, the Scotty Wood basketball tournament, and Midnight Breakfast, when admissions staff serve late-night breakfast to students before finals. There's also a candlelight ceremony where freshmen write down their college goals, to be reopened the day before graduation.

For the athletically inclined, the Muhlenberg Mules compete in the Division III Centennial Conference. Women's basketball, women's lacrosse, and men's soccer have won conference championships recently. Women's soccer and softball are also competitive and popular spectator sports on campus. Students say any contest against Johns Hopkins draws crowds. Muhlenberg's Life Sports Center offers a pool, a basketball court, other all-purpose courts, and a jogging track. Also popular is Frisbee golf; there's an 18-hole course on campus, where play goes on during all seasons and all hours of the day and night.

"It is an unspoken expectation on campus to hold the door for the person behind you, even if they are at a farther distance than would usually warrant such a gesture," explains a student. Small gestures of kindness are just one way in which Muhlenberg earns its moniker as "The Caring College"—it also offers students a warm, intimate academic milieu and plenty of support. It's a winning formula that draws students from far and wide. Put simply, says one senior, "Muhlenberg believes in students and their ability to learn."

Overlaps

Dickinson, Gettysburg, Skidmore, Franklin & Marshall, Ithaca, Lafayette, Ursinus, NYU

If You Apply To ›

Muhlenberg: Early decision I and II, regular decision. SATs or ACTs: optional (test-optional applicants must interview and submit a graded paper). No Subject Tests. Accepts the Common Application with supplement.

University of Nebraska–Lincoln

1410 Q Street, Lincoln, NE 68588

Everybody knows Cornhusker football, but in other areas Nebraska, the smallest public university in the Big Ten, flies under the radar. With less than a third of undergrads coming from out of state, has a corner on the market for Nebraskans without a major competitor like Iowa State. Business administration, psychology, and advertising and public relations top the list of majors. Because of the state's demographic makeup, diversity is a challenge.

On crisp fall weekends, when spirits are high and the Big Red football arcs through the air, Huskers cheer and paint the town of Lincoln red and white in a show of appreciation for their alma mater. In fact, on home-game Saturdays, the stadium is the third largest "city" in the state, holding 5 percent of the population. Away from the stadium, students at the University of Nebraska–Lincoln have more reasons to cheer, with notable programs ranging from software engineering to digital humanities to PGA golf management.

Nebraska spreads across two main campuses. The East Campus is home to the College of Agricultural Sciences and Natural Resources and the College of Law.

Website: www.unl.edu
Location: City Center
Public
Total Enrollment: 22,209
Undergraduates: 19,534
Male/Female: 52/48
SAT Ranges: ERW 550–680, M 550–700

Most entering students end up on the larger City Campus, surrounded by the bustle of downtown Lincoln and home to seven undergraduate colleges: architecture, arts and sciences, journalism and mass communications, business, fine and performing arts, engineering, and education and human sciences. On City Campus, the architectural style ranges from the modern Sheldon Art Gallery designed by Philip Johnson to the architecture building, which is on the National Register of Historic Places. There are also several grassy malls, an arboretum, and a sculpture garden. A third campus location, the Innovation Campus, serves as a research and technological hub where students can test their skills with real-world tools and projects.

Nebraska's 30-credit general education program, known as Achievement-Centered Education, is required of students in all majors and includes a senior-year capstone course. To help freshmen get oriented, Big Red Welcome combines a new student convocation with entertainment, information booths, and food in a carnival setting. Nebraska's College of Agricultural Sciences and Natural Resources is known for its outstanding programs in animal science, food science and technology, and agribusiness. Journalism, actuarial science, and early childhood education are also traditional strengths. The school of music's opera program has received national attention, and the Johnny Carson School of Theatre and Film offers four undergrad degrees, including a new B.F.A. in emerging media arts. The most popular majors are business administration; psychology; advertising and public relations; and nutrition, exercise, and health science.

> "For a university this big, I think that the professors do a good job of making students feel valued."

"The workload is fairly intensive, if you want to get good grades," remarks an accounting major. Getting into courses in the most popular areas, especially education, business, and engineering, can be a problem, students say; preregistration is a must. Although many classes are large, 35 percent have fewer than 20 students. Graduate students teach some freshman courses, but top professors can be found inside the classroom too. "For a university this big, I think that the professors do a good job of making students feel valued," says a prenursing student. "It is hard to be recognized in classes with 100 students, but I don't think that the quality of teaching is any less. And there are always office hours for students."

The University Honors Program offers qualified students challenging coursework and research opportunities. Also, the UCARE (Undergraduate Creative Activity and Research Experience) program provides a stipend for more than 400 students each year to participate in one-on-one research with a professor after freshman year. The Raikes School of Computer Science and Management is a highly selective honors program that focuses on a curriculum in technology, business, and real-world projects, and that awards scholarships to participants. Study abroad opportunities are available in 45 countries and include 40 faculty-led programs; 19 percent of students take part. Career Services shows students how to make a professional résumé, holds mock interviews, and hosts potential employers, among other activities.

> "I feel like my institution has really made an effort to expand diversity."

A junior says Nebraska students' "social etiquette and values are high, embodying 'Nebraska Nice,'" adding, "The political climate is more liberal than the state as a whole." Sixty-nine percent of undergraduates hail from in state, and 9 percent come from abroad. Asian Americans make up 3 percent of the student body, African Americans 3 percent, Hispanics 6 percent, and multiracial students 3 percent. Many students say diversity—or the lack thereof—is an issue, but one notes, "I feel like my institution has really made an effort to expand diversity." Twenty-seven percent of incoming freshmen are eligible for Pell Grants. Merit scholarships

(continued)

ACT Ranges: 22–29
Financial Aid: 76%
Pell Grant: 27%
Expense: Pub $
Student Loans: 52%
Average Debt: $
Applicants: 14,947
Accepted: 64%
Enrolled: 51%
Grad in 6 Years: 68%
Returning Freshmen: 83%
Academics: ✍ ✍ ✍
Social: 🐾 🐾 🐾 🐾
Q of L: ★ ★ ★
Admissions: (800) 742-8800
Email Address: admissions@ unl.edu

Strong Programs:
Business Administration
Psychology
Advertising and Public
  Relations
Nutrition, Exercise, and Health
  Science
Animal Science
Journalism
Actuarial Science
Early Childhood Education

Big Red Welcome combines a new student convocation with entertainment, information booths, and food in a carnival setting.

are available, with an average award of $7,400, in addition to nearly 440 athletic scholarships in 19 sports.

Thirty-seven percent of students live in the university's single-sex or co-ed residence halls, and there's usually no trouble getting a room. "Most of the dorms are up-to-date and are pretty sizable, but there are a few that are smaller," explains a science education major. "There are options, however, for suite-style dorms that are available to everyone, including freshmen." Freshmen must live on campus, and many students move off campus after their sophomore year. Students praise the 26 living/learning communities offered for first-years with common academic interests who live and take classes together. "I was a member of a learning community my freshman year, and it helped make the campus seem smaller and less intimidating," recalls a nutrition and dietetics major. Dining facilities are "new and wonderful," says one student, "and always have a wide variety of food selections." As for campus security, a history major reports, "There are police officers at the Learning Commons in the library who can escort you back to your dorm or car if you aren't comfortable walking alone at night."

"A lot of the social life starts on campus but then moves off," says a communication studies major. "You meet people on your floor or in a club, and then you hang out and go out off campus." Fraternity and house parties, 500-plus student organizations, concerts and theater performances, the movies, eating out, visiting coffee shops and bars, and road trips to Omaha or Kansas City are just some of the activities that keep students busy. For many, the fall semester revolves around football weekends and postseason bowl games. Fraternities draw 17 percent of the men, and sororities attract 24 percent of the women. They offer both social events and a chance to get involved in the Lincoln community. Homecoming, Greek Week, the spring concert, and The Big Event (a major community service occasion) are among the most anticipated campus events.

> **"There is nothing like Game Days in Nebraska."**

"Lincoln is a great college town, especially during football season!" exclaims one business administration major. Another student points out that the "thirty bars within a two-minute walk of campus" are appreciated by those of age, given the school's dry campus. Town/gown relations are good and "the community is always eager for students to return in the fall," according to one premed student. Pachyderm enthusiasts will be delighted by the Nebraska Museum of Natural History's outstanding collection of prehistoric elephant skeletons. Beyond the town's sidewalks are miles of flat trails and plains, ideal for biking and cross-country skiing.

The Cornhuskers have a reputation as a powerhouse in a number of sports and hold consecutive NCAA sell-out attendance records in, of course, football. Women's volleyball and bowling are recent national champions, while baseball, softball, women's soccer, and men's track and field have brought home recent conference titles. Men's and women's hoopsters frolic in the 15,500-seat Pinnacle Bank Arena. And who hasn't heard of the classy Nebraska football? Home football games are not to be missed, and the annual Black Friday bowl game against the University of Iowa is shaping up to be quite the rivalry. "There is nothing like Game Days in Nebraska," says a senior. "The entire city of Lincoln is full of Husker fans." Recreational and intramural sports are popular too, with flag football and basketball drawing the most participants.

At Nebraska, future agricultural experts mingle with techno-whizzes, while teachers-in-training brush elbows with architecture mavens. Whether studying overseas, immersing themselves in internships, launching start-ups, or going wild on Saturday afternoons, students here know how to make the most of their time. Cheers one happy Husker, "UNL is rooted in tradition, kindness, and Husker pride!"

Overlaps

University of Kansas, Iowa State, University of Minnesota, University of Iowa, University of Missouri, University of Nebraska Omaha, University of Nebraska at Kearney, Nebraska Wesleyan

New College of Florida

5800 Bay Shore Road, Sarasota, FL 34243

New College is the South's most liberal institution of higher learning (apologies to Guilford). With a total enrollment of just over 850, New College is about one-third the size of a typical liberal arts college—but has undertaken an aggressive plan to boost enrollment to 1,200. The kicker: it's a public institution and a great bargain. Don't expect to hear many Southern accents; most students are transplants even if they went to high school in Florida.

The mere existence of New College of Florida is proof that it's possible to find success through individualism. This school has done away with grades and GPAs, and the laid-back student body and rigorous academic program "proves to students that learning can be a self-directed, fun, and productive experience," a sophomore says. But New College is not stopping there: the school has announced plans to grow both its student enrollment and its tenure-track faculty by 50 percent, along with spending $45 million on construction of new residence halls and other student facilities, by the fall of 2022. It's just one more move this fast-rising star is making in pursuit of a national reputation.

New College began in 1960 as an alternative private college for academically talented students, but when inflation threatened its existence in the mid-1970s, it offered its campus to the University of South Florida. Today, New College serves as the state university system's honors college but is an academically independent entity. New College's campus is adjacent to Sarasota Bay and consists of historic mansions from the former estate of circus magnate Charles Ringling, abutting modern dorms designed by I. M. Pei. The central quad is filled with palm trees, and sunsets over the bay are spectacular. The college recently completed a $10 million addition to the Heiser Natural Sciences Center Complex, featuring new teaching and research labs.

> "[New College] proves to students that learning can be a self-directed, fun, and productive experience."

All New College undergraduates must complete at least eight courses in the liberal arts curriculum, including courses in humanities, social sciences, and natural sciences, and show literacy in math, computers, and diverse perspectives. The academic calendar is organized around two 14-week semesters separated by a month-long January Interterm, during which students devise and carry out their own research, conduct group projects, or pursue short-term internships. Students work out a "contract" with their advisor each semester and receive written evaluations instead of grades. The seven semester-long contracts and three independent study projects lead to an area of concentration, capped by a senior thesis project that students must defend in an oral examination—excellent preparation for the 80 percent of students who eventually go on to graduate or professional school.

New College doesn't offer the specialized courses of a large university, but there's still plenty to choose from across the academic spectrum. Anthropology wins raves, and many students also gravitate to biology, chemistry, psychology,

Website: www.ncf.edu
Location: Suburban
Public
Total Enrollment: 859
Undergraduates: 835
Male/Female: 37/63
SAT Ranges: ERW 620–710, M 570–670
ACT Ranges: 25–30
Financial Aid: 97%
Pell Grant: 35%
Expense: Pub $
Student Loans: 34%
Average Debt: $
Applicants: 1,353
Accepted: 69%
Enrolled: 21%
Grad in 6 Years: 65%
Returning Freshmen: 79%
Academics: ✏ ✏ ✏ ✏
Social: ☎ ☎ ☎
Q of L: ★ ★ ★
Admissions: (941) 487-5000
Email Address: admissions@ncf.edu

Strong Programs:
Anthropology
Biology
Chemistry
Psychology
Political Science
International and Area Studies
Environmental Studies
Economics

political science, and international and area studies. Academic programs are constantly changing to best suit student needs; an example is the beefing up of offerings in STEM fields, environmental studies, and economics. A 1,100-gallon seawater system is available for lab experiments in animal behavior and physiology. The library makes up for its small size—fewer than 300,000 volumes—with a language lab, digital collections, and an interlibrary loan program with the entire state university system of Florida. "For a small college with limited resources, we have an incredibly thought-provoking and challenging curriculum," says one student. The Cross-College Alliance expands students' options by allowing them to take courses at any of the four other institutions of higher education in Sarasota.

New College serves as the state university system's honors college.

Courses are rigorous, but the focus on individual development and lack of grades negates any competitive airs, and one student says, "The classroom environment is personalized and intimate." Graduate students and teaching assistants don't lead classes here, and 71 percent of classes have fewer than 20 students. A chemistry major says, "Professors are supportive, but they make you work hard in their classes." The shape of any student's program depends heavily on the outlook of his or her faculty sponsor, and students say advising—both academic and career—is readily available. All disciplines provide the opportunity for original research, and students also may conduct field research around the globe. Fifteen percent of students study abroad in roughly 50 countries.

"Professors are supportive, but they make you work hard in their classes."

In keeping with the revolution theme, students on this relatively cosmopolitan campus tend to be, in the words of one sophomore, "barefoot hippies"—creative liberal types with '60s nuances and social habits. "New College does not produce cookie-cutter graduates," asserts a senior. "We are intellects, activists, and sometimes a little self-righteous." Students rally around issues that run the gamut from women's rights to food justice and commercialism. Hispanics account for 18 percent of the student body, while Asian Americans, African Americans, and multiracial students each make up 3 percent; another 3 percent come from foreign countries. Socioeconomic diversity is strong, with 35 percent of freshmen qualifying for Pell Grants. Seventy-nine percent of undergrads hail from Florida, although the college is attempting to attract more out-of-state students by offering them automatic Presidential Scholarships worth $60,000 over four years. All admitted Florida residents are guaranteed automatic scholarships too, in amounts that vary based on academic standing. There are no athletic awards.

Students work out a "contract" with their advisor each semester and receive written evaluations instead of grades.

Seventy-nine percent of students live in campus housing; students wishing to live off campus must apply for permission. The newest residence halls, built to LEED environmental standards, feature lodge and apartment-style accommodations, "which some people like but others think are too stiff," says one student. About 20 percent of students join various living/learning communities, with themes like Global Village, Quiet Community, and Outdoor Adventure. Students report that a recent change in food providers has improved campus dining and increased options for the school's sizable vegan population. Students feel secure on campus, and a junior says, "The college has programs nearly constantly to spread awareness about sexual consent and safe practice."

"We are intellects, activists, and sometimes a little self-righteous."

The campus social scene, sans Greek life, is laid-back and "can range from dance parties, fashion shows, and game nights to listening to NPR under the stars in Palm Court," says a sophomore. Resident advisors organize substance-free events, and a multitude of student organizations also keep students busy, from the New College Student Alliance (the student government) to "Cloud Watching Club (it is what it sounds like)," says a student, adding, "It's a small campus, so it's easy to become involved in new activities." The COUPs (Center of the Universe Parties) are "blow-out-of-proportion" social gatherings that occur during Halloween, Valentine's Day, and graduation. Students also flock to Midnight Breakfast, where faculty and staff serve students free breakfast foods at night during exam weeks; Chocolate Fest, where students bring chocolate-containing dishes to a large potluck; and Queer Pride Week, in which students host events centered on LGBTQ history, awareness, and pride.

Sarasota offers little more than "beaches and old people," according to one sophomore, although 57 percent of students get involved in volunteer work through more than 30 local community organizations. The Ringling Museum of Art and the Asolo State Theater adjoin the campus, and many New College instrumentalists perform with the Sarasota Orchestra, the city's professionally led symphony orchestra. The open road to Tampa, Gainesville, Key West, Orlando, New Orleans, Atlanta, and even Washington, D.C. ("to protest stuff"), beckons when Sarasota becomes too quiet.

New College is definitely no haven for jocks; it fields no varsity teams, although its Intercollegiate Sailing Association sailing team is nationally competitive. The fledgling quiz bowl team has already made a name for itself, recently qualifying for the Academic Competition Federation's national tournament. Roughly 10 percent of students take advantage of club and intramural sports, which range from flag football and fencing to soccer and scuba diving. The annual Ringling College of Art and Design/New College flag football game draws crowds, as does the nearby ocean. "The beaches are gorgeous—white sand and blue water," says a student.

Without a Greek scene, grades, or crazy football games, New College of Florida is definitely not your typical Southern institution. But the eccentricity doesn't impede students' academic motivation; in fact, it encourages an atmosphere that celebrates learning for the sake of curiosity, persistence, and thoughtfulness—whether the subject at hand is biology, belly dancing, psychology, or origami. Major growth is on the way, growth the administration hopes will boost New College's national profile while at the same time opening up even more opportunities for student success.

The COUPs (Center of the Universe Parties) are major social gatherings that occur during Halloween, Valentine's Day, and graduation.

Overlaps

Hampshire, Eckerd, St. Mary's College of Maryland, Agnes Scott, Reed, Brown, Duke, Florida Atlantic

If You Apply To ›

New College: Early decision, rolling admissions. SATs or ACTs: required. Subject Tests: optional. Accepts the Common Application.

University of New Hampshire

Grant House, 3 Garrison Avenue, Durham, NH 03824

UNH is a public university that looks and feels like a private college, and its cost of attendance hits the pocketbook with similar force. Draws half of its students from out of state. Well known for engineering, space science, and life science programs—especially marine biology—and its business school is nationally ranked. With graduate students accounting for less than one-tenth of total enrollment, UNH's focus is squarely on undergrads.

Students at the University of New Hampshire know how to get their hands dirty, and this solid public institution provides them with countless opportunities to do just that. UNH is one of just 17 universities in the nation to receive land, sea, and space grant designations. Its research mission has grown dramatically in the last decade, yet the university remains a moderate-sized institution that emphasizes undergraduate instruction. Unlike many large research universities, faculty members teach all

Website: www.unh.edu
Location: Small Town
Public
Total Enrollment: 14,159
Undergraduates: 12,626

(continued)

Male/Female: 45/55
SAT Ranges: ERW 550–630,
   M 530–630
ACT Ranges: 23–28
Financial Aid: 89%
Pell Grant: 24%
Expense: Pub $ $ $ $
Student Loans: 77%
Average Debt: $ $ $
Applicants: 19,966
Accepted: 76%
Enrolled: 20%
Grad in 6 Years: 77%
Returning Freshmen: 86%
Academics: ✍ ✍ ✍
Social: ☎ ☎ ☎ ☎
Q of L: ★ ★ ★ ★ ★
Admissions: (603) 862-1360
Email Address: admissions@
   unh.edu

Strong Programs:
Business Administration
Psychology
Biomedical Science
Communication
Engineering
Marine Biology
Nursing
Sustainability

Interdisciplinary minors range from leadership to green real estate to beer brewing.

students, including freshmen, and value teaching as much as they do their research. A love of the outdoors is a must, as is the ability to withstand long, cold winters. "Every day is a great day to be a Wildcat!" cheers one student.

The university's wide-open, grassy Durham campus hosts a mix of modern facilities and ivy-covered brick buildings. The sprawling lawns are surrounded by nearly 3,000 acres of farms, fields, and woods. During the past few years, UNH has invested in large-scale construction projects, including new residence halls, a physics building, and a veterinary diagnostic lab. Expansions to the Chase Ocean Engineering Lab and Hamilton Smith Hall, home of the English department, were recently completed.

The university's core curriculum, the Discovery Program, includes general education requirements that apply across the board and mandate coursework in biological science; physical science; historical perspectives; world cultures; social science; fine and performing arts; humanities; and environment, technology, and society. Freshman composition is also mandatory, as part of a four-course writing intensive requirement, as is a class in quantitative reasoning. All first-years take an Inquiry course involving an experiential learning component, and all seniors complete a capstone experience.

"Every day is a great day to be a Wildcat!"

Interdisciplinary programs enhance UNH's emphasis on the traditional academic programs offered by its seven schools and colleges. A dual major allows students to pair a degree in sustainability with any other major, and minors range from leadership to green real estate to beer brewing. Engineering and business are among the most respected programs. The Paul College of Business and Economics is nationally ranked, offering a spate of majors and the opportunity for students to design their own tracks; the college also boasts one of the first student-run angel investment funds. Marine biology is considered stellar, enhanced by UNH's proximity to the ocean and a brackish bay, and ocean engineering, nursing, social work, and a preveterinary advising program are also strengths. The most popular majors are business administration, psychology, biomedical science, and communication.

Students agree that the level of academic intensity varies by school and college, but the atmosphere is always busy. "On a normal day, I see students studying and working everywhere around campus, indoors and outdoors (when the weather permits)," says a business administration major. Classes are relatively small, with just 12 percent enrolling 50 or more students, and teaching assistants only facilitate discussion sections or labs. "We have world-class professors, many of whom participate in research and include students as research assistants," says a senior, and a junior notes that professors are accessible and "easy to speak to."

"[Many professors] participate in research and include students as research assistants."

Research experience is a key emphasis at UNH, and 35 percent of undergraduates get involved with research projects before they graduate. The Hamel Center for Undergraduate Research provides about 100 research awards each year for students to work closely with faculty on original projects. It also hosts the Undergraduate Research Conference, which showcases the scholarly work of more than 1,800 students. Additional opportunities include conducting research on NASA partner projects or at the Isle of Shoals Marine Laboratory, which provides an offshore research setting six miles off the coast. Twenty-two percent of students broaden their horizons through more than 500 approved study abroad and exchange programs. And for the especially motivated, the invitation-only University Honors Program features small classes, personal mentoring, and optional honors-themed housing.

While UNH is New Hampshire's major public institution, it has long been popular with out-of-staters, who make up 51 percent of its undergraduates; international students add another 4 percent. African Americans account for just 1 percent of the student population, Asian Americans 2 percent, Hispanics 4 percent, and multiracial students 2 percent. "We have diversity coalitions for many minorities to try and enhance the cultural diversity of campus," reports a psychology major. Politically, students are "engaged and vocal," says a senior. UNH has the highest published in-state tuition and fees of any flagship university in the country. To ease the pain, the university offers hundreds of merit scholarships, averaging $6,700, and 350 awards are available for gifted athletes. Twenty-four percent of freshmen are Pell-eligible. The Granite Guarantee program gives free tuition to qualifying New Hampshire residents from low-income families.

Fifty-four percent of UNHers live in the school's co-ed dorms. "Some of the freshman dorms are too far away from the main area of campus (Williamson and Christenson)," complains one senior, but accommodations are said to be generally nice. Freshmen and sophomores are guaranteed dorm rooms; most upperclassmen live off campus or in the two on-campus apartment complexes. More than a dozen themed living areas are available and are an increasingly popular option. Campus dining receives rave reviews, and students also give high ratings to campus safety. UNH is a national leader in efforts to prevent sexual assault on campus. In addition to its student-praised training programs and support services, UNH established the Prevention Innovations Research Center to develop evidence-based prevention strategies and policies.

> **"We have diversity coalitions for many minorities to try and enhance the cultural diversity of campus."**

UNH offers more than 250 student organizations covering just about any interest. "Get involved early on, as that will help you become acclimated to the campus," advises a social work and women's studies major. "U Day is a great way to do that." Service organizations are popular, and 55 percent of students get involved with community service activities. The Campus Activities Board organizes weekend social events including dances, movies, bingo, and gatherings at local coffeehouses, and favorite annual events include homecoming and concerts in the fall and spring. Greek groups claim 14 percent of the men and 14 percent of the women. The party culture at UNH is lively, but Greek parties are subject to the university's no-tolerance alcohol policy, which evicts underage students caught with alcohol more than once from on-campus housing.

Less than a five-minute walk from campus is the beautiful little town of Durham, which caters to the student clientele. Its Main Street is lined with restaurants and coffeehouses, a grocery store, an ice-cream parlor, and a few bars, which have been divided into separate sections (for legal consumers of alcohol and everyone else). The Wildcat Transit bus system takes students to cities throughout the state, and the on-campus Amtrak station makes weekend escapes to Boston and Portland, Maine, easy—if students can find time off. (The school's nickname is the University of No Holidays, since an exceptionally generous winter break limits the number of days off during other seasons.) The White Mountains are popular with outdoor enthusiasts, and late nights at L.L. Bean have also become commonplace. Every four years, New Hampshire takes the spotlight when the state holds the nation's earliest presidential primary, making UNH a frequent destination for political campaigners.

UNH has 20 Division I athletic teams, of which ice hockey is a fan favorite. Students celebrate the first Wildcats goal of each game by inexplicably throwing a large fish onto the ice, and during games against its rival, the University of Maine–Orono, students wear white to "white out" the stadium. Women's basketball, cross-country, and volleyball are recent America East conference champions, and other solid teams include football, men's soccer, and men's and women's skiing. Club and intramural sports enlist about half of the student body. Broomball—played with

UNH is a national leader in efforts to prevent sexual assault on campus.

The Northwest Passage program offers adaptive recreation programs for students with disabilities.

Overlaps

UMass Amherst, University of Vermont, University of Rhode Island, UConn, University of Maine–Orono, UMass Lowell, University of New Hampshire–Manchester, Quinnipiac

brooms, balls, and sneakers on the ice—is very popular, as are activities organized by the Outing Club, including skiing, camping, fishing, and hiking. The Northwest Passage program offers adaptive recreation programs for students with disabilities.

New Hampshire's only major public university offers a huge variety of programs in a beautiful natural setting. That's one reason it attracts so many students from out of state. Another reason, a junior says, is that between smaller class sizes, community-oriented dorms, and welcoming student organizations, "You will feel like you're part of a very tight-knit community, even though there are 12,600 undergrads on campus, and you really have the chance to make your experience here whatever you want it to be."

If You Apply To ›

New Hampshire: Early action, regular decision. SATs or ACTs: required. Subject Tests: optional. Accepts the Common Application with supplement. Additional materials required for applicants to music, theatre, and studio art programs.

The College of New Jersey

P.O. Box 7718, Ewing, NJ 08628

A public liberal arts institution in the mold of UNC Asheville or William and Mary. Also offers business and education. With more than nine-tenths of the students homegrown Garden Staters, TCNJ has little draw beyond Jersey. On the other hand, it is now the state's second most selective institution, after a certain school up the road in Princeton. A smaller, more personal alternative to Rutgers.

Website: www.tcnj.edu
Location: Suburban
Public
Total Enrollment: 6,844
Undergraduates: 6,640
Male/Female: 43/57
SAT Ranges: ERW 590–660, M 580–670
ACT Ranges: 25–30
Financial Aid: 58%
Pell Grant: 15%
Expense: Pub $ $ $ $
Student Loans: 62%
Average Debt: $ $ $ $
Applicants: 12,898
Accepted: 48%
Enrolled: 25%
Grad in 6 Years: 87%
Returning Freshmen: 94%
Academics: ✍ ✍ ✍ ✍
Social: ☎ ☎ ☎
Q of L: ★ ★ ★
Admissions: (609) 771-2131

The College of New Jersey is an up-and-coming public institution with special focus on undergraduates, an emphasis more commonly found at a private school. TCNJ offers professors focused on teaching and a campus physically similar to that of nearby Princeton University—without the Ivy League price tag. Formerly a teachers' college, it strives to provide students with opportunities in a host of other fields. The small size makes for closeness among students and faculty. Says one student, "TCNJ is really big on the 'community' feel."

TCNJ is set on 289 wooded and landscaped acres in suburban Ewing Township, six miles from Trenton. The picturesque Georgian colonial architecture centers on Quimby's Prairie, surrounded by the original academic buildings of the 1930s. A flock of Canada geese makes its home in one of the two campus lakes. In partnership with a private developer, the college recently opened Campus Town, a 12-acre, $120 million complex adjacent to the campus that features 612 apartments for upperclassmen, a campus gym, and retail shops and restaurants open to both the campus community and the public.

> **"TCNJ is really big on the 'community' feel."**

Liberal Learning, TCNJ's general education program, requires coursework centered on three fundamental areas: intellectual and scholarly growth, broad areas of human inquiry, and civic responsibility. Freshmen participate in several programs to prepare them for college life and academics, including a summer reading program, welcome week, and a First Seminar course, in which they take a small seminar on a topic outside of their intended major and spend their first year living with their classmates in the same residence hall. Freshmen must also complete at least eight hours of community service.

Consistent with the school's origins as a teachers' college, education programs are well regarded; elementary and special education are particular favorites among students. The business school is strong, as are the natural sciences. Other popular majors include psychology, biology, nursing, and communication studies. The college offers a combined four-and-a-half-year B.S./M.A. in law and justice, taught jointly by TCNJ and Rutgers; a seven-year B.S./M.D. degree program with the University of Medicine and Dentistry of New Jersey; and a seven-year B.S./O.D. degree with SUNY College of Optometry.

Academically, TCNJ is competitive and getting more so. "The academic climate is somewhat intense," confides a sophomore. "Some students and professors try to downplay the competitive nature, but overall it's pretty driven." An honors program is available for those who wish to challenge themselves with an even more rigorous curriculum. Forty-four percent of undergraduate classes have fewer than 20 students. The college has no teaching assistants, and faculty members generally get high marks, though quality is said to vary by department. "My professors are very passionate about their work and field of study," says a psychology major. TCNJ runs foreign study programs in 13 countries, including South Africa, the Czech Republic, and Thailand, and preapproved partner programs give students access to dozens of other countries around the globe. Roughly a third of students get their passports stamped to study, intern, or volunteer overseas. Nearly 100 students spend eight weeks assisting faculty mentors with research and creative projects as part of the MUSE (Mentored Undergraduate Summer Experience) program.

"If you don't leave this school very well educated in political correctness, then you were obviously unconscious."

The typical TCNJ student is "overly book smart," according to one junior. The school has no cap on out-of-state admissions, but only 7 percent of TCNJ's students are non-Jerseyans, including less than 1 percent who are foreign nationals. The college has aggressively pursued minority students, and today, African Americans account for 6 percent of the student body, Hispanics 12 percent, and Asian Americans 11 percent. "If you don't leave this school very well educated in political correctness, then you were obviously unconscious," says a marketing major, who praises the school for its diversity. Merit scholarships averaging $5,100 are available to qualified students. The Educational Opportunity Fund Promise Award covers full tuition and other expenses and provides specialized academic support services for qualifying New Jersey residents from disadvantaged backgrounds.

Dorm housing is only guaranteed for freshmen and sophomores, though 55 percent of students live on campus. "Most of the dorms are really nice," says a student, "but a few are older and outdated." Freshmen hang their hats in one of seven residence halls, two of which, Centennial and Norsworthy, have recently been renovated. After that, students can enter the lottery to secure spots in traditional residence halls, townhouses, or the Campus Town apartments. Many upperclassmen opt for nearby off-campus apartment complexes, which are plentiful.

Although suburban Ewing doesn't really cater to students, funky New Hope, Pennsylvania, and preppy Princeton, New Jersey, are nearby; restaurants, bars, movie theaters—and, this being New Jersey, many malls—are within a short drive. Road trips to Philadelphia and New York, each about an hour away and accessible by train, are also highly recommended. Alcohol policies are strictly enforced; students 21 and over can enjoy adult beverages at the campus restaurant, Traditions, which also features a stage area for performances. Fifteen percent of the men and 13 percent of the women belong to fraternities and sororities, which provide many of the off-campus parties. Campus programming includes dances, concerts, and movies. TCNJers look forward to several annual events, including homecoming, a Family Fest Day, and—the springtime favorite—Senior Week.

(continued)

Email Address: tcnjinfo@ tcnj.edu

Strong Programs:
Elementary Education
Special Education
Business Administration
Psychology
Biology
Nursing
Communication Studies

Campus Town is a $120 million complex adjacent to the campus that features 612 apartments for upperclassmen.

Nearly 100 students spend eight weeks assisting faculty mentors with research and creative projects as part of the MUSE program.

The College of New Jersey's 21 varsity teams (the Lions) are the pride of the New Jersey Athletic Conference and make frequent appearances in national Division III tournaments. Women's lacrosse, tennis, and field hockey, and men's cross-country, swimming and diving, and baseball have claimed recent conference titles. Students rally around the football and basketball squads, especially when archrival Rowan comes to town. The college also offers 14 intramural and 21 club sport programs.

The College of New Jersey is one of the few public liberal arts colleges with reasonable tuition and a location that offers a relaxed suburban haven within shouting distance of big-city opportunities. Not just for teachers anymore, TCNJ prides itself on the personal attention it devotes to students craving both professional preparation and a well-rounded education.

If You Apply To ›

TCNJ: Early decision I and II, regular decision. SATs or ACTs: required. No Subject Tests. Accepts the Common Application. Art applicants must submit portfolio. Music applicants must audition.

New Jersey Institute of Technology

University Heights, Newark, NJ 07102

One of the few public technical institutes in the Northeast. Within New Jersey, NJIT occupies a middle ground between the behemoth Rutgers and smallish Stevens Institute, and 92 percent of undergrads are state residents. Primarily offers engineering, computing, architecture, design, and business, and co-op option is popular. At three to one, NJIT's gender ratio is particularly skewed toward males. Then again, no one comes to NJIT for the social life.

The New Jersey Institute of Technology provides a no-frills STEM education that prepares students for a future in an ever-changing global workplace. NJIT's challenging programs emphasize education, research, service, and (not surprisingly) economic development. The combination is enticing—as is the price tag, relative to some of NJIT's closest competitors.

NJIT's urban 45-acre campus is dotted with 37 buildings of diverse architectural styles, ranging from Elizabethan Gothic to contemporary design. Recent additions include the Life Sciences and Engineering Center and the $110 million Wellness and Events Center, featuring state-of-the-art athletic and fitness facilities. Some of New Jersey's greatest cultural institutions are just blocks away, including the Newark Museum, Symphony Hall, and the New Jersey Performing Arts Center.

> "We have a lot of barbecues that bring people together."

To graduate, students must fulfill general education requirements in areas ranging from English to management. All freshmen take two mathematics courses tailored to their major, English composition, computer science, and First Year Seminar, a course that introduces students to university life. NJIT is composed of five schools and colleges plus the Dorman Honors College, offering 50 undergraduate degree programs. Mechanical engineering, information technology, civil engineering, computer science, architecture, business, and chemical engineering are the most popular majors. Students earning their B.S. in business choose from six concentrations, from financial technology to innovation and entrepreneurship. A new major in forensic science has been added, and NJIT also offers prehealth and prelaw programs with an emphasis on technology.

While some say the atmosphere can be low-pressure in certain fields, most agree that the workload across the board is demanding. The administration assists students if they are having a difficult time, arranging for leaves of absence or extra semesters with a lighter load. One-third of classes have fewer than 20 students; most don't exceed 35. Students report sometimes having problems getting into enrollment-capped classes that are offered only once a year. But one student calculates that if a freshman has all of the prerequisite courses, he or she has a good chance of graduating on time. Academic advising isn't as helpful as it could be, say some students, but professors are given average to high marks. Since most have worked in their industry, they can offer job information along with academic assistance. And students say career counseling services are useful for preparing them for the job hunt.

Perhaps NJIT's most-favored academic option is the co-op program, which enables students to take time away from the classroom in order to gain paid work experience at tech companies and other organizations. Top freshman applicants are offered a spot in the Honors College, and they can stay as long as they keep their grades up; more than 700 undergraduates in all majors are enrolled in the Honors College. Perks include a dedicated honors dorm, research opportunities, and acceptance into the accelerated premed and other prehealth programs. Study abroad is an option, but with their packed schedules, few students find time for it. In the midst of this heavily male-dominated campus, the Murray Center for Women in Technology offers scholarships, networking opportunities, and resources to help female students and faculty alike advance in their chosen fields.

As New Jersey's comprehensive technological public university, NJIT attracts a wide range of students with different interests. "There are students who are very driven and want to achieve their absolute best," observes a sophomore. "However, there are a large number of students who are coasting." In-state residents represent 92 percent of the undergraduate student body, and international students add 5 percent. Eight percent are African American, 21 percent are Hispanic, 22 percent are Asian American, and 3 percent are multiracial. One student praises the Educational Opportunity Program, saying, "If it weren't for them, I would not be here. They make it easy to be a minority." Thirty percent of freshmen qualify for Pell Grants. The university awards merit scholarships averaging $16,200 to qualified students, and more than 100 athletic scholarships are also available.

NJIT's five residence halls can accommodate one-third of the students, and 22 percent live on campus. "I love housing," says a junior. "We get free cable, fast Internet connections. We have very big rooms." Consensus has it that the best freshman dorms are Redwood Hall and Cypress. Upperclassmen move into on-campus fraternity or sorority houses or nearby off-campus apartments. The

"Students here are certainly intelligent and come off as nerds, but everyone has their own niche."

dorms and Greek houses both have kitchen facilities, which many students welcome, as the dining service fare sometimes draws complaints from students. Because of its urban location, safety is always a consideration at NJIT, but, "Public safety officers are always around," says an electrical engineering major.

Newark is hardly a college town, students report, yet it is undergoing something of an urban renaissance, and several good restaurants are within walking distance. On campus, 6 percent of the men and 6 percent of the women join the Greek system. One of the best annual campus events is Spring Fest, which includes bands, intramural games, carnival rides, and a semiformal. Diwali, the Indian festival of lights, and Chinese New Year also give undergrads pause to party. "We have a lot of

(continued)

Q of L: ★ ★
Admissions: (973) 596-3300
Email Address: admissions@ njit.edu

Strong Programs:
Mechanical Engineering
Information Technology
Civil Engineering
Computer Science
Architecture
Business
Chemical Engineering

NJIT offers prehealth and prelaw programs with an emphasis on technology.

More than 700 undergraduates in all majors are enrolled in the Honors College.

barbecues that bring people together," says an architecture major. Another option is the beach, an hour away. Most students agree that the administration's strict alcohol policies are effective.

NJIT students take pride in their athletic prowess, and the school joined the Division I Atlantic Sun Conference in 2015, competing mainly against Southeastern schools like Stetson and University of North Florida. Among NJIT's 17 varsity Highlanders teams, men's and women's basketball and tennis, men's soccer, and baseball are some of the most competitive. Soccer, basketball, and racquetball are the favorites when it comes to intramurals.

"Students here are certainly intelligent and come off as nerds, but everyone has their own niche," says a biomedical engineering student. NJIT students choose their school because they want a top-notch technological education without the topflight price tag. Academics are the priority here, and if the social life is less than electrifying, students deal with it. After all, they know highly skilled jobs will beckon after graduation. Getting through is a challenge, but there's ample compensation available for NJIT alums in the technologically dependent workplaces of today—and tomorrow.

Overlaps

Rensselaer, Case Western Reserve, Virginia Tech, UMBC, Stevens Institute of Technology, Rutgers, Rowan, College of New Jersey

If You Apply To ›

NJIT: Early action I and II, rolling admissions. SATs or ACTs: required. No Subject Tests. Accepts the Common Application with supplement. College of Architecture and Design applicants must submit portfolio of creative work.

University of New Mexico

Albuquerque, NM 87131

UNM gives new meaning to cultural diversity. Studies related to Hispanic and Native cultures are strong, and in a land of picture-perfect sunsets, photography is a big deal. Technical programs are fueled by government labs in Albuquerque and Los Alamos, while the business school produces an outsized percentage of New Mexico's commercial elite.

Website: www.unm.edu
Location: City Center
Public
Total Enrollment: 18,235
Undergraduates: 14,902
Male/Female: 44/56
SAT Ranges: ERW 460–590, M 470–580
ACT Ranges: 19–25
Financial Aid: 74%
Pell Grant: 41%
Expense: Pub $
Student Loans: 39%
Average Debt: $
Applicants: 11,347
Accepted: 49%

The University of New Mexico's heritage stretches back to 1889 when New Mexico wasn't even a state, and the university's strengths are still rooted in the rich history of the American Southwest. New Mexico excels in areas such as Latin American and Southwest studies. Lest you think it is a typical state school, consider that many students are commuters or of nontraditional age. UNM also boasts the state's only law, medical, and architecture and urban planning schools.

Seated at the foot of the gorgeous Sandia Mountains in the lap of Albuquerque, the beautifully landscaped campus sports both Spanish and Pueblo Indian architectural influences, with lots of patios and balconies. The duck pond is a favorite spot for sunbathing, and the mountains, which rise majestically to the east, are visible from virtually any point on campus. Construction was recently completed on the $25 million McKinnon Center for Management.

"For the most part we are focused on school."

UNM offers more than 4,000 courses in 12 colleges and schools, running the gamut from arts and sciences, education, and engineering to management, fine arts, and the allied health fields. Academic and general education requirements vary, but the core curriculum mandates courses in English, humanities, social and behavioral sciences, physical and natural sciences, math, fine arts, and a second language. Those reluctant to specialize can spend a few semesters in the broad University College, which offers a bachelor of liberal arts and a bachelor of integrative studies degree. The Honors College offers a bachelor of arts in interdisciplinary liberal arts. The Tamarind Institute, a nationally recognized center housed at UNM's School of Fine Arts, offers training, study, and research in fine-art lithography. Anthropologists may root around one of New Mexico's many archaeological sites, and engineers may join in major solar-energy projects. Other solid programs include Native American studies, Chicana and Chicano studies, and Latin American studies. Students may also minor in Navajo language.

The academic climate is "very laid-back and depends on what field of study you are going into," according to a senior. Students are quick to help one another study, and competition for grades is the exception rather than the rule. Fifty-four percent of classes have fewer than 20 students. As for professors, "I would have to give them a B," says a student. "There have been some very good ones and some that were very knowl-edgeable but didn't know how to teach." Freshman Learning Communities and academic coaching help ease the transition from high school to the college environment. Many classes, and several complete degree programs, are offered in late afternoon and evening sessions, and about half of the student body takes advantage of these after-hours options. Study abroad programs in such locales as Ecuador, Greece, Mexico, and South Korea beckon to 18 percent of undergrads.

> "People here are serious and accepting, which makes UNM a comfortable environment."

By virtue of its location, UNM enjoys a diverse mix of cultures, even though the vast majority (87 percent) of students are state residents. A large minority student enrollment—49 percent Hispanic, 6 percent Native American, 4 percent Asian American, 2 percent African American, and 4 percent multiracial—reflects this cultural diversity. Two percent of undergraduates are from overseas. UNM hosts a number of centers and student groups, such as El Centro de la Raza and Nations at UNM, that support diversity and cultural activities. "Students here are pretty chill," says a journalism major. "We hang out and stuff, but for the most part we are focused on school." The average merit award is more than $2,000, and athletic scholarships are available as well. Forty-one percent of freshmen qualify for Pell Grants.

UNM has traditionally been a commuter school (and parking is a perennial complaint); currently, a scant 6 percent of students live on campus. But that figure is growing as the university implements a new freshman residency requirement stipulating that first-year students coming from outside a 30-mile radius of campus must live in the residence halls. Students are happy with the variety of food available to them, including a restaurant in the student union that serves food from different cultures every week. An escort service, good lighting, and police who patrol around the clock help students feel safe.

"Social life takes place both on and off campus," a junior says. Alcohol, though banned on the UNM campus, is readily available, according to most students, especially at Greek parties. Just 5 percent of the men and 6 percent of the women join the Greek system. Other students find their fun off campus in Albuquerque's clubs and restaurants. For the more socially conscious, the college sponsors Spring Storm, an outing of roughly 1,000 students who volunteer around the city on a Saturday. Annual social events include Welcome Back Days in the fall and Nizhoni Days, a weeklong celebration of Native American culture. Each spring, the whole campus turns out for a four-day fiesta with food and live music.

Albuquerque—sometimes referred to as ABQ—is New Mexico's largest city, and it offers a variety of cultural attractions, including the nation's largest hot air balloon festival, a growing artists' colony, and concert tours to charm the ears. Santa Fe

(continued)

Enrolled: 57%
Grad in 6 Years: 48%
Returning Freshmen: 80%
Academics: ✐ ✐ ✐
Social: ☎ ☎ ☎
Q of L: ★ ★ ★
Admissions: (505) 277-8900
Email Address: unmlobos@
unm.edu

Strong Programs:
Latin American Studies
Native American Studies
Photography
Business
Anthropology
Education
Health Professions
Navajo Language

The broad University College offers a bachelor of liberal arts and a bachelor of integrative studies degree.

Nizhoni Days is a weeklong celebration of Native American culture held each spring.

is an hour away. Those with cars take advantage of the state's natural attractions: the Sandias, the Carlsbad Caverns, superb skiing in Taos, as well as excellent hiking and camping opportunities. For the historically inclined, numerous Spanish and Native American ruins are within an easy drive.

The UNM Lobos (Spanish for "wolves") compete in the Division I Mountain West Conference, and the men's football and basketball squads usually draw crowds. The women's cross-country team brought home the national championship title in 2017, its second in three years. As a cost-saving measure, the university has cut four varsity sports: men's and women's skiing, men's soccer, and women's beach volleyball. Recreational and intramural sports are popular; students flock to flag football, volleyball, soccer, and basketball.

UNM offers a sun-drenched location that satisfies—precisely because its academic climate is as relaxed as the rolling desert dunes. "People here are serious and accepting," says a senior, "which makes UNM a comfortable environment."

Overlaps

Arizona State, University of Colorado Boulder, Eastern New Mexico, Highlands, New Mexico State, University of Texas at El Paso

If You Apply To ›

UNM: Rolling admissions. SATs or ACTs: required. No Subject Tests. Does not accept the Common Application.

New York University

22 Washington Square, New York, NY 10012

From safety school to global brand, NYU's rise has been breathtaking. The siren song of Greenwich Village now includes the Tandon School of Engineering in Brooklyn, degree-granting campuses in Abu Dhabi and Shanghai, and a dozen global academic centers around the world. Major draws include the renowned Tisch School of the Arts and the best undergraduate business school north of Penn.

Website: www.nyu.edu
Location: City Center
Private
Total Enrollment: 41,967
Undergraduates: 25,175
Male/Female: 43/57
SAT Ranges: ERW 650–730, M 640–760
ACT Ranges: 29–33
Financial Aid: 49%
Pell Grant: 20%
Expense: Pr $ $ $
Student Loans: 43%
Average Debt: $ $ $
Applicants: 64,007
Accepted: 28%
Enrolled: 34%
Grad in 6 Years: 84%
Returning Freshmen: 93%
Academics: ✐ ✐ ✐ ✐ ½

With the world at its doorstep, New York University invites its student body to jump right in. Firmly planted in the heart of Greenwich Village, one of the most eclectic and energizing neighborhoods in New York City, NYU has set its sights on becoming the world's first truly global university. Its growing student body, burgeoning new facilities, and multiple opportunities for high-level internships and research projects have made it a top option for a rising number of students. "NYU is a place to gain street smarts in addition to book smarts," says a senior. "The combination of strong academics and an amazing location give NYU a big advantage."

It doesn't get more real world than the venue that NYU calls home. NYU has campuses and centers throughout the city but is primarily situated on Washington Square. Trendy shops, galleries, clubs, bars, and eateries crowd neighboring blocks;

> "NYU is a place to gain street smarts in addition to book smarts."

SoHo, Little Italy, and Chinatown are just blocks away. Academic buildings—both modern and historic—blend with 19th-century brick townhouses surrounding Washington Square Park (the closest thing NYU has to a quad). Kimmel Center for University Life houses meeting space for NYU's more than 600 student clubs, plus areas for the frequent recruitment fairs and lectures from national and international leaders. It also holds the Skirball Center for the Performing Arts' 860-seat theater, which is the largest performing arts facility south of 42nd Street.

The city scene is central to the NYU experience. So, too, is the wide range of academic programs. Under the Core College Curriculum, freshmen and sophomores take courses including foreign language, expository writing, foundations of contemporary culture, and foundations of scientific inquiry. The language offerings go beyond the typical Spanish-French-German—among the choices are Arabic, Cantonese, Hindi, Modern Irish, Swahili, and Tagalog—and NYU operates a language exchange program with Columbia University as well. The Tisch School of the Arts trained such famed actors and directors as Marcia Gay Harden, Alec Baldwin, Martin Scorcese, and Spike Lee, and current undergrads continue to win many national student filmmaker awards. Tisch also boasts excellent drama, dance, photography, and television departments, and it's not uncommon to see students who haven't yet finished B.F.A. degrees performing in Broadway shows.

Wall Street's future bulls and bears make their home at the Stern School of Business, where they benefit from a business and political economy program. The Leslie eLab provides space for aspiring entrepreneurs. Another favorite department among students (and the New York corporations who recruit them after graduation) is accounting, known for its high job-placement rate. In the College of Arts and Science, economics, English, journalism, history, and politics win highest marks from students. The Tandon School of Engineering, the Steinhardt School, the Silver School of Social Work, the College of Nursing, and the School of Professional Studies offer a bevy of career-based programs, including engineering, education, media, nutrition, hotel and sports management, and real estate. Across the university, the most popular majors are business, economics, nursing, and theater. The Gallatin School of Individualized Study provides flexible schedules and freedom from requirements for those wishing to engage in independent study or develop their own programs. For those tempted to hang around the Village for more than four years, there's a seven-year dental program and several five-year bachelor's/master's programs.

Finding a cheap New York apartment may be easier than sailing through NYU's academics. "The classes can be very challenging," says a senior, "but students have a plethora of resources to help them succeed." Regardless of major, everyone is very focused on career preparation—it's never enough to just concentrate on your classes. "It's hard to avoid the pressure," says a student majoring in drama and politics. At least the NYU library is accommodating—it's one of the largest open-stack facilities in the country, with millions of volumes. And despite the university's mammoth size, 59 percent of classes taken by undergraduates have fewer than 20 students. Graduate students might lead foreign language sections, writing workshops, and the recitations that accompany lectures, but students still say teaching is top-notch and professors are reasonably accessible. "Surprisingly, most of our introductory courses are taught by really great and well-known professors," says one student.

"Surprisingly, most of our introductory courses are taught by really great and well-known professors."

Point to a spot on a world map and you'll likely hit a country hosting undergraduates from NYU, which sends more of them abroad than any other school. In addition to its campuses in Abu Dhabi and Shanghai, NYU has 11 academic sites in cities from Buenos Aires and Prague to Sydney and Tel Aviv, as well as exchange agreements with universities in other locations throughout the world. Roughly 56 percent of undergrads study abroad, and they may do so as early as their freshman year through the University's Core Program in Liberal Studies. Locally, internships range from jobs on Wall Street to assignments with film industry giants. The career center is "amazingly personal and well run," says an econ major, and has thousands of listings for on-campus jobs, full-time jobs, and internships. Students qualifying

(continued)

Social: ☎ ☎ ☎
Q of L: ★ ★ ★
Admissions: (212) 998-4500
Email Address: admissions@ nyu.edu

Strong Programs:
Business
Economics
Nursing
Theater
Dance
Film and Television
Foreign Languages
Accounting

Washington Square Park is the closest thing NYU has to a quad.

It's not uncommon to see students who haven't yet finished B.F.A. degrees performing in Broadway shows.

for freshman honors seminars study in small classes under top faculty and eminent visiting professors. An annual undergraduate research conference at the College of Arts and Science gives students the chance to present findings from their research. Many NYU students graduate in less than four years.

An international politics major says NYU students are "high-achieving individuals, cosmopolitan, independent, self-driven, confident, and able to manage academics, part-time jobs, and internships while having active social lives." Thanks in part to the university's investment in student housing, 66 percent of undergraduates now come from outside New York State, including a substantial 20 percent from outside the United States. In-staters hail primarily from the city and nearby suburbs. African Americans make up 6 percent of the student body, Asian Americans 20 percent, Hispanics 14 percent, and multiracial students 5 percent. Twenty percent of freshmen are Pell-eligible. On this generally liberal campus, social justice, immigration policy, the Israeli-Palestinian conflict, and rights of all kinds—LGBTQ, animal, human, and workers'—are important, students say. "NYU is primarily a pretty liberal university," says a sophomore, "but conservative folks are welcome here too!" Although most financial aid is need based, merit awards averaging $8,000 are available; athletic scholarships are not.

> "[Greenwich Village is] the most exciting, alive, cultural part of New York City."

Whereas NYU students once had to fend for themselves in New York's outrageous housing market, the university now guarantees four years of housing to all freshmen (and most transfers) who seek it. Twenty-two residence halls, ranging from old hotels to a converted monastery, provide a wide range of accommodations. Most rooms have private baths and are larger, cleaner, newer, and better equipped than many city apartments, enticing 43 percent of students to stay on campus. Freshmen are housed largely in freshman residence halls, many of which have theme floors, and rooms are assigned by lottery each spring. Amenities include central air-conditioning, computer centers, music practice rooms, kitchens, and even, in some buildings, small theaters. The university provides free shuttle buses to dorms that are farther uptown or downtown. The dining halls offer extensive choices—from wraps to sushi to a dedicated kosher eatery. "The dining halls really try to accommodate everyone," says one student. Of course, downtown's array of ethnic restaurants also offers a variety of food at cheap prices.

Because NYU is large and fairly decentralized, the Student Resource Center helps students navigate university resources and services. The university's Wellness Exchange provides students with a hotline that connects them with professionals who can help them address daily challenges or crises they may encounter, and S.P.A.C.E. (Sexual Misconduct Prevention, Assistance, Counseling, and Education) provides comprehensive resources and support. Students also meet with academic advisors—usually professors in their major department—at least once a semester. For concerned parents and students, NYU hosts a series of workshops on keeping safe, and programs like the NYU Trolley and Escort Van Service provide door-to-door service for students until 3:00 a.m. "I always feel safe," says a linguistics major. "I can't walk more than one block without seeing an NYU security officer or an NYPD car just patrolling the area."

> "Don't come here if you're not up to working hard and moving fast."

As for NYU's social life, "You're in New York City," says a student. "Why would you bother staying in your dorm at night when you're within minutes of internationally renowned art, world-class theater on Broadway, shopping in SoHo, and dining in Little Italy?" Another adds, "Greenwich Village is full of students, professors, artists, families; it's the most exciting, alive, cultural part of New York City."

Undergrads may study abroad as early as their freshman year through the University's Core Program in Liberal Studies.

The Violet Ball is a dinner/dance held each fall in the atrium of Bobst Library.

On campus, there are concerts, movies, fraternity and sorority events (only 5 percent of the men and 7 percent of the women go Greek), and more than 600 clubs and organizations. The springtime Strawberry Festival includes free berries, cotton candy, outdoor concerts, and carnival amusements. Many students march in the city's Halloween Parade, which takes over Greenwich Village, while most spring and fall weekends find a city-sponsored street fair somewhere nearby. The Violet Ball, a dinner/dance held each fall in the atrium of Bobst Library, offers an excuse to get dressed up. Underage students caught with alcohol in public areas in the dorms may lose their housing. The rest take their chances with the notoriously strict bouncers at bars and clubs around Manhattan. "They card like crazy," warns one junior.

While sports have not traditionally been NYU's strength, successful Violets programs include men's and women's golf (recent Liberty League champions), swimming and diving, and men's wrestling, all of which compete in Division III. Roughly one-third of undergrads participate in intramural sports, which include flag football, bowling, and indoor cricket. The Palladium Athletic Facility boasts a big swimming pool and a 30-foot-high indoor climbing wall.

The heartbeat of New York City thumps day and night; NYU students thrive on all that energy and know how to capture it in their studies and social lives. "To be an NYU student is to be part college student, part New Yorker," a senior says. "Don't come here if you're not up to working hard and moving fast."

If You Apply To ›

NYU: Early decision I and II, regular decision. SATs or ACTs or three Subject Tests, AP exams, or IB exams or IB Diploma: required. Accepts the Common Application with supplement. Portfolio or audition required for some programs.

University of North Carolina at Asheville

I University Heights, Asheville, NC 28804

The "other" UNC happens to offer one of the best educational deals in the country. With 3,200 full-time, degree-seeking students, UNC Asheville is about half the size of fellow public liberal arts college William and Mary and somewhat smaller than Mary Washington. Picturesque mountain location in one of the most livable small cities anywhere. By Southern standards, a progressive university in a progressive city.

Whether it's the lush environment or the money you're saving, the University of North Carolina at Asheville will have you seeing green. This public liberal arts university offers all of the perks that are generally associated with pricier private institutions: rigorous academics, small classes, and a beautiful setting. And it does it for a fraction of the cost. The university continues to integrate experiential learning into its traditional curriculum, emphasizing undergraduate research, internships, and service-learning experiences. Any way you look at it, UNC Asheville is a bargain that may have your friends turning green with envy.

Located in the heart of North Carolina's gorgeous Blue Ridge Mountains, the 360-acre campus lies in the middle of one million acres of federal and state forest near the tallest mountain in the East and the most heavily visited national park in the country. The campus was built in the 1960s, and much of the brick architecture reflects the style of that decade, although many of the buildings have been added within the past several years, including a high-tech science and multimedia

Website: www.unca.edu
Location: Small City
Public
Total Enrollment: 3,202
Undergraduates: 3,201
Male/Female: 43/57
SAT Ranges: ERW 550–650, M 530–610
ACT Ranges: 22–27
Financial Aid: 73%
Pell Grant: 33%
Expense: Pub $
Student Loans: 58%

building. The Botanical Gardens at Asheville, adjacent to the main campus, features thousands of labeled plants and trees, and serves as a wildlife refuge and study center for biology students. The recently renovated Highsmith Union offers modern space for gatherings and student organizations, as well as an Intercultural Center, bookstore, game room, gallery space, and food court. The STEAM Studio, located just off campus, brings together science, engineering, and art students in one collaborative, state-of-the-art makerspace.

Asheville's general education curriculum, the Liberal Arts Core, is required of all undergraduates. In addition to first-year and senior-capstone liberal arts colloquia, students must take courses in eight areas spanning the humanities, sciences, and mathematics, as well as a Diversity Intensive, and must demonstrate competency in information literacy and writing. The most popular majors at Asheville are psychology, environmental studies, management, health and wellness promotion, and English. Students can take advantage of Asheville's strengths as a global source of information for weather forecasting and as a center of digital imaging, music, and fine arts and studio crafts. "UNC Asheville is a very environmentally friendly, artsy school," says a management major. A joint B.S. degree in engineering (with a concentration in mechatronics) with North Carolina State University is the only such program in the state and is one of the fastest-growing majors.

> **"UNC Asheville is a very environmentally friendly, artsy school."**

Courses are challenging, but, "UNC Asheville is laid-back and slower paced, which might be different for students who are used to competition and a faster-paced lifestyle," comments an economics major. Half of all classes have fewer than 20 students, and a number of them have service-learning components. As a French and political science double major points out, "Our faculty's mentorship and close relationships are especially evident in undergraduate research." Research is indeed a key emphasis here: Asheville founded the National Conference on Undergraduate Research and has hosted the conference five times. Two-thirds of Asheville students will have an undergraduate research experience by graduation. The UNC Asheville honors program offers special courses—as well as cultural and social opportunities—to motivated students who can make the grade. Study abroad is an option too, and 15 percent of students participate in programs in more than 50 countries.

The head count at Asheville has risen steadily over the past decade, but only 11 percent of students come from out of state and another 1 percent from abroad. (The state limits its out-of-state admits to 18 percent.) Asheville is moving away from its early reputation as a hippie haven, but students still value individualism: "We encourage everyone to be themselves and pursue their own interests," says a psychology major. Currently, the student body is 5 percent African American, 6 percent Hispanic, 2 percent Asian American, and 4 percent multiracial, but Asheville is making special efforts to bring more students from underrepresented groups to campus. A substantial number of transfer students add their own brand of diversity. Students tend to be progressively minded, and issues of environmental sustainability and racial and gender equity get particular attention on campus. Thirty-three percent of current freshmen are Pell-eligible. Asheville offers 176 athletic scholarships, as well as merit scholarships averaging $2,200.

> **"UNC Asheville is laid-back and slower paced."**

The 360-acre campus lies in the middle of one million acres of federal and state forest near the tallest mountain in the East.

Asheville is working hard to build up its on-campus housing; a new residential complex featuring the university's first apartment-style housing opened in 2018. Thirty-eight percent of the students live in the residence halls. "I would be comfortable living in any of our residence halls on campus and was very glad that none of them have hall-style bathrooms and all of them have nice kitchens, lounges, and study spaces," says a senior. Living/learning communities offer special residential and academic options for students with similar interests, such as LEAD (for leadership and social justice), Wanderlust, and The Cloud (for computer science and atmospheric sciences majors). For meals, students may eat dining-hall fare or grab something quick at retail outlets around campus, including local cuisine and nationally known Argo Tea. A sophomore says, "Our campus security is excellent. We have an on-campus police force that patrols regularly around campus."

Social life at Asheville is fairly low-key, and "everyone finds their friend group and runs wherever there may be something happening," according to a junior. Greek life is not an influential presence, with only 3 percent of the men and 3 percent of the women joining up. Most parties take place off campus, especially since RAs stalk underage drinkers in the dorms. "There is no tolerance for unsafe, underage, or unwise drinking," says a student. There are more than 60 student organizations, including the student newspaper, the *Blue Banner*. Several campuswide events bring the school together each year, including the Turning of the Maples in October, homecoming, a spring lawn party, and a mock casino night with an auction. During Greenfest, explains a student, the campus community gathers to "do outdoor service work on campus and attend informative talks about environmental issues and other events like a farm-to-table dinner."

The city of Asheville, an increasingly popular retirement destination, offers a tame but inviting nightlife, with popular hangouts like the Orange Peel, Ben's Tune-Up, Isis Music Hall, and Tupelo Honey, and the city has been named Beer City USA several times. Asheville is also home to a bevy of street performers, outdoor music festivals, and live entertainment events. For the many Asheville students with a hankering for the great outdoors, the university is surrounded by the Blue Ridge Mountains and the Smokies, where students can hike and rock climb; water buffs can go rafting and kayaking on the nearby rivers. Preorientation wilderness trips help build friendships among freshmen. Those with cars can head to Spartanburg and Charlotte, one and two hours away, respectively. Real big-city action takes extra effort, though, since Atlanta is a four-hour trek.

The Division I Bulldogs boast Big South Conference teams in 16 sports. Men's and women's basketball are the most successful, with each team taking home multiple conference championship titles in recent years. Men's and women's soccer, men's tennis, and women's volleyball are also competitive. "We have a great rivalry with Western Carolina," says a health and wellness major. Intramurals and club sports are at least as popular as the varsity sports, as are outdoor adventure trips and the on-campus challenge course and bike shop.

"Everyone who works here is dedicated to the student experience in some way," says a senior. "That means you won't be a number." Indeed, all the ingredients for a superior college experience lie in wait at Asheville: strong academics, dedicated professors, and an administration that continues to push for excellence. It's a place to get the kind of liberal arts education usually associated with private colleges—but for a lot fewer greenbacks.

Two-thirds of Asheville students will have an undergraduate research experience by graduation.

"Everyone who works here is dedicated to the student experience in some way."

Overlaps

University of Mary Washington, St. Mary's College of Maryland, New College of Florida, UNC Wilmington, Appalachian State, North Carolina State, UNC at Chapel Hill, UNC Greensboro

If You Apply To ›

UNC Asheville: Early action, rolling admissions. SATs or ACTs: required. No Subject Tests. Accepts the Common Application with supplement.

Jackson Hall, CB 2200, Chapel Hill, NC 27599

Close on the heels of UVA as the South's most prestigious public university. With 82 percent of the spots in each incoming class reserved for in-staters, admission is selective but not impossible for out-of-staters who aren't 6'9" with a 43-inch vertical jump. But they keep trying by the thousands. Chapel Hill is a quintessential college town that is morphing into a medium-sized city.

Website: www.unc.edu

Location: Small Town

Public

Total Enrollment: 25,070

Undergraduates: 18,275

Male/Female: 41/59

SAT Ranges: ERW 640–720, M 620–720

ACT Ranges: 27–32

Financial Aid: 53%

Pell Grant: 19%

Expense: Pub $

Student Loans: 40%

Average Debt: $

Applicants: 40,918

Accepted: 24%

Enrolled: 45%

Grad in 6 Years: 92%

Returning Freshmen: 97%

Academics: ✐ ✐ ✐ ✐

Social: ☎ ☎ ☎ ☎

Q of L: ★ ★ ★ ★

Admissions: (919) 966-3621

Email Address: unchelp@ admissions.unc.edu

Strong Programs:

Communication and Media Studies

Chemistry

Sociology

English

Philosophy

Biology

Psychology

Economics

Welcome to "the Southern part of heaven," a place where the sky is Carolina Blue and the academics are red-hot. As the flagship campus of the state university system, the University of North Carolina at Chapel Hill has earned its place among the South's most prestigious universities. The atmosphere here is a unique brand of Southern, a rowdy mixture of hard work, sports fanaticism, progressive social values, and traditions that seems to attract bright, serious, and fun-loving students from everywhere.

Chartered in 1789, UNC was the first public university in the United States to open its doors, and North Carolinians still take pride in Carolina's identity as "the University of the people." UNC's gorgeous and comfortable campus occupies 730 acres lush with trees and lawns and brick-paved walkways. The architecture ranges from Palladian, Federal, and Georgian to postmodern, with redbrick the prevailing motif. The Old Well, the university's symbol, stands at the center of the campus. Recent construction includes a soccer and lacrosse stadium and a field hockey stadium.

> "The majority of professors go out of their way to help students."

The general education curriculum requires all students to complete 38 to 44 credit hours of coursework in three broad themes: Foundations, Approaches, and Connections. Coursework includes physical and life sciences, social and behavioral sciences, humanities and fine arts, composition and rhetoric, foreign language, quantitative reasoning, and lifetime fitness. About two-thirds of first-years participate in the First-Year Seminar program, which allows them to work closely with professors in small classes of up to 24 students each, as an introduction to the university's research-oriented environment. Summer School, including the two-week "Maymester," provides undergraduates with diverse course options, some with off-campus travel or research opportunities not possible during the academic year.

Chapel Hill offers more than 75 undergraduate degree programs. Some of the strongest are communication and media studies, chemistry, sociology, English, and philosophy. Other popular majors include biology, psychology, and economics. The university has developed a broad range of opportunities to help students in business, liberal arts, and sciences become entrepreneurial, including an entrepreneurship minor and the Carolina Challenge, a student-run competition that awards up to $50,000 in prizes each year for the best business plan. Computer science is one of the fastest-growing majors, and a new major in neuroscience is now available. A joint-degree program in biomedical and health sciences engineering with North Carolina State University is an option too.

> "Carolina students are proud to attend this school, and they bleed Carolina blue."

"Although this is a prestigious university, I don't feel a sense of competition at all," says one sophomore. Academic and social life are governed by a student-run honor system. Thirty-eight percent of classes enroll fewer than 20 students, and access to registration is based on seniority. If you get closed out of a class, "be persistent," advises a first-year. The Carolina faculty is, for the most part, top-notch. Professors keep regular office hours, and a history major says, "The majority of professors go out of their way to help students and make sure that they are learning everything they possibly can." Regarding career preparation, a senior cheers, "Our career services department on campus puts effort into each and every student."

More than 60 percent of students in all disciplines take advantage of undergraduate research opportunities, and many present their findings at professional conferences, publish results in academic journals, and win fellowships to support summer research in the United States and abroad. For those tired of the classroom rush, Research Triangle Park, a nearby research and corporate community and home of the National Humanities Center, employs many students as research assistants. UNC offers more than 400 study abroad programs in approximately 70 countries, in which one-third of students participate. Additionally, UNC's honors program is nationally recognized.

"'College town' in the dictionary should show a picture of Chapel Hill."

"Carolina students are proud to attend this school, and they bleed Carolina blue," says one Tar Heel. Out-of-state admission is extremely tough; by statute, 82 percent of undergraduates are North Carolina residents, with 3 percent from foreign countries. Big social and political issues on campus include multiculturalism, gender roles, and religious issues. African Americans account for 8 percent of the student body, Asian Americans 11 percent, Hispanics 8 percent, and multiracial students 5 percent. Women outnumber men on campus, largely because engineering programs are left to NC State. UNC awards a limited number of highly competitive merit scholarships, along with more than 600 athletic scholarships in 28 sports. What's more, the university is need-blind in admissions and commits to meeting the full demonstrated financial need of all admitted students—one of only two public universities in the U.S. to do so (see also University of Virginia). The Carolina Covenant program, which has served as a national model to universities seeking to increase socioeconomic diversity, offers grants and work-study to dependent students below 200 percent of the poverty level, giving eligible low-income students the chance to graduate debt-free. The program offers extensive mentoring and other support to 725 Covenant Scholars, many of whom are the first in their families to attend college.

UNC's honors program is nationally recognized as among the best in the country.

Just over half of the undergraduates live in university housing, which "is an invaluable part of the experience because you are connected to campus resources and also have the ability to make friends and connections easily," according to one student. Housing on the north side of campus offers old and recently renovated dorms; the south side offers several new housing options, which are a 15-minute hike from academic buildings (not to worry—there's a free campus shuttle). "The pickiest of the picky could be happy with Carolina dining services," says a first-year. Campus security is praised for its constant presence, and the university has implemented a number of training and support programs to address the issue of sexual assault.

"[UNC at Chapel Hill has] Southern hospitality blended with a high level of thinking."

"'College town' in the dictionary should show a picture of Chapel Hill," boasts one senior. Franklin Street, the main drag in town that runs across the northern boundary of campus, offers Mexican and Chinese restaurants, ice-cream parlors, coffeehouses, vegetarian eateries, bakeries, a dance club, and a generous supply of bars. Fraternities and sororities may account for only 18 percent of the men and 18 percent of the women, but they exert an influence far beyond their numbers. "Fraternities are a social hub, and many students flock to their off-campus parties," confirms one student. Between Greek life and other campus-sponsored activities, "There are always five or six things happening on any given day," says a political science major. FallFest kicks off the school year with an emphasis on the idea that you don't have to drink to have fun. Students look forward to several annual festivals: the Carolina Jazz Festival and Halloween Celebration on Franklin Street are always,

The Carolina Covenant program supports 725 Covenant Scholars, many of whom are the first in their families to attend college.

shall we say, raucous. The North Carolina Literary Festival is held biannually. About a third of students are involved in community service, many through a service-learning program for which they receive academic credit.

UNC's reputation for balancing high-level athletics and academics took a major hit following reports of long-standing special academic treatment of athletes that have spurred academic and athletic reforms over the past several years. Student and alumni loyalty remains high, and the word "popular" doesn't do justice to the basketball games. A contest between Tar Heel hoopsters and NC State makes any Carolina fan's heart beat faster, but Duke takes the prize as the most reviled of all devils. The Tar Heels play in the 21,750-seat Smith Center, named for the late coach Dean Smith, one of the winningest college basketball coaches of all time. Men's basketball and women's tennis are recent national champions. Men's and women's lacrosse, women's soccer, and women's field hockey are also highly competitive. Extensive intramural and club sports programs draw heavy participation; intramural basketball and soccer alone each boast rosters of more than 200 teams. Those who crave fresh air can take advantage of the Outdoor Education Center's mountain bike trails, rope courses, and one of the longest double zip lines on the East Coast.

As a popular saying goes, "If God is not a Tar Heel, why is the sky Carolina Blue?" It's a cute turn of phrase but also points to something that is well-known in these parts: as one of the best college buys in the country, UNC at Chapel Hill gives students everything they want, both academically and socially. Despite recent budget cuts enacted by Philistine forces in the state legislature, the 230-year history of this school creates an atmosphere of extreme pride, a love of tradition, and monumental school spirit. One first-year, full of that school spirit, says, "Southern hospitality blended with a high level of thinking, an overwhelming dose of friendliness and pep, and a spectacularly gorgeous campus make Chapel Hill my favorite place in the world."

Overlaps

University of Virginia, Duke, UC Berkeley, UCLA, University of Michigan, North Carolina State, Vanderbilt, Wake Forest

If You Apply To ›

UNC at Chapel Hill: Early action, regular decision. SATs or ACTs: required. Subject Tests: optional. Accepts the Common Application with supplement.

University of North Carolina Wilmington

Wilmington, NC 28403

Still overshadowed by Chapel Hill and the other biggies in the strong UNC system, but making a name for itself. Strong in marine biology and other sciences. You won't see the Seahawks in the NCAA Final Four anytime soon, but you will be able to get to know your professors. Seventeen percent of incoming students come from out of state, most of those hailing from Mid-Atlantic, Northeast, and New England states.

Website: www.uncw.edu
Location: Suburban
Public
Total Enrollment: 13,075
Undergraduates: 12,233
Male/Female: 40/60

At the University of North Carolina Wilmington, students enjoy extensive undergraduate research opportunities, a slate of solid sciences, and a close-knit community of like-minded individuals who like their modern academics mixed with a bit of old-fashioned Southern charm. The university's close proximity to the ocean provides motivated students with ample opportunities for fun in the sun and a natural lab for the school's stellar marine biology program. Whether diving into the sea or into their studies, UNCW students are filled with school spirit.

Founded as Wilmington College in 1947, UNCW moved to its present location in the heart of New Hanover County in 1961. The 650-acre campus is only minutes from Wrightsville Beach and historic downtown Wilmington and features Georgian architecture and designated conservation areas. These conservation areas are significant zones of natural beauty with their longleaf pines, oaks, dogwoods, and native magnolias. Notable campus landmarks include the clock tower, the Leutze Hall portico, Chancellor's Walk, and the Campus Life complex, which serves as the hub of the university community. After sustaining $140 million in damage caused by Hurricane Florence in September 2018, the university is moving forward with a spate of new construction to add and enhance academic and residential facilities.

UNCW's University Studies curriculum requires students to complete coursework in three main categories—Foundations, Building Competencies, and Approaches and Perspectives—and to complete one approved Explorations Beyond the Classroom experience, such as an internship or a study abroad program. Freshmen benefit from a slate of special programs, including a required two-day orientation, a common reading, and a first-year seminar. Each seminar is limited to 25 students and has a Seahawk "link": older students who help with the transition into UNCW life. The Cornerstone Learning Communities are home to approximately 225 freshmen, who complete coursework together. "Learning communities are a game changer," says a communication studies major. "They allow freshmen to get used to a college workload, but in a familiar environment where they feel comfortable."

> "UNCW's professors are very welcoming, encouraging, and offer ample amounts of help."

Some of the most popular majors offered are psychology, biology, nursing, education, business, and social work. The university's strengths lie in the natural sciences, especially marine biology, chemistry, ecology, and other disciplines that form the core of the marine sciences. "Our university places a large emphasis on lab and fieldwork," says one geography major. Outside of the sciences, UNCW offers solid programs in film studies and creative writing. Freshmen are taught by full professors, and an accounting and economics major says, "UNCW's professors are very welcoming, encouraging, and offer ample amounts of help." Enrollments in introductory courses sometimes swell to more than 100, but 28 percent of all classes have fewer than 20 students.

A hallmark of the UNCW student experience is known as ETEAL (Experiencing Transformative Education through Applied Learning), which places students in hands-on experiences, such as directed independent study, undergraduate research, internships, and service-learning projects, requiring them to integrate the theories, ideas, and skills they have learned in new contexts. Research opportunities include Undergraduate Research and Creativity Fellowships, which award up to $3,000 for innovative research. For those yearning to experience new vistas, the university offers more than 500 approved study abroad programs in 50 countries; 8 percent of students participate. The UNCW Honors College accepts approximately 125 students each year to participate in living/learning communities, advanced coursework, and experiential seminars; honors students also complete a senior honors capstone research project.

> "How much better can a social scene get than the beach?"

According to a marketing major, UNCW students are "hardworking beachgoers. Every student here is hardworking and motivated but enjoys a little time off as well." Eighty-three percent of undergrads are native to North Carolina, and 1 percent are international. African Americans represent 4 percent of the student body, Hispanics 7 percent, Asian Americans 2 percent, and multiracial students 4 percent. "Our student body is truthfully not very diverse but is working hard to create a sense of community for minorities," says a junior. Students say there is a "relaxed"

(continued)

SAT Ranges: ERW 600–660, M 580–650
ACT Ranges: 23–27
Financial Aid: 54%
Pell Grant: 22%
Expense: Pub $
Student Loans: 60%
Average Debt: $ $
Applicants: 11,677
Accepted: 67%
Enrolled: 28%
Grad in 6 Years: 72%
Returning Freshmen: 87%
Academics: ✍ ✍
Social: ☎ ☎
Q of L: ★ ★ ★
Admissions: (910) 962-3243
Email Address: admissions@uncw.edu

Strong Programs:
Marine Biology
Psychology
Biology
Nursing
Education
Business
Social Work
Film Studies

After sustaining $140 million in damage caused by Hurricane Florence in 2018, UNCW is moving forward with a spate of new construction.

balance of liberal and conservative political views on campus. Outstanding students can vie for merit scholarships averaging $3,100, as well as 129 athletic scholarships. Twenty-two percent of students qualify for Pell Grants, and under UNCW's Support Opportunity Access Responsibility (SOAR) program, high-achieving students from low-income families may receive grants and scholarships equaling the cost of in-state tuition and fees, in addition to federal loans or work-study funding if needed.

Twenty-two percent of undergraduates live on campus, and all freshmen except commuters are required to do so. Options range from traditional freshman dorms to sophomore suites and apartments for upperclassmen. Students report that overpriced rooms and overcrowding can be issues, but plans are in the works for five new residence halls that will add 1,800 beds by 2022. Most students who move off campus stay within a mile or so of the school. Campus eateries include Wagoner Hall, the Hawks Nest food court, and Dubs Café. "For students with allergies, when they swipe their UNCW One Card at a dining location, the employees will be notified of the allergy and a separate meal will be prepared," explains a student. Students praise campus police for keeping the area secure and the CARE office for helping to combat sexual assault on campus.

When it comes to social life, a junior asks, "How much better can a social scene get than the beach?" Indeed, the beach is the place to be for many popular events,

> **"Maybe it's the Southern charm in us, but…it sure helps make this laid-back college an awesome place."**

such as the Beach Blast party the first week of school. Students also look forward to homecoming, the Dub Idol and Hawk It Out singing and dance competitions, and the annual ooze-ball mud volleyball tournament. Additionally, "UNCWeekends puts something on every weekend for students both on and off campus," says a public health major. Fraternities and sororities attract 10 percent of the men and 10 percent of the women, respectively. The party scene is far from raucous, students report, and underage drinkers face stiff penalties if caught. Downtown Wilmington offers its share of restaurants, shops, and bars, and is "a very scenic and beautiful city," says a student. "From the many bars to the many beaches, we have hundreds of social spots to hang out," says a senior. Road trips include jaunts to Myrtle Beach, the Outer Banks, Washington, D.C., and the Appalachian Mountains.

UNCW fields 19 varsity teams that compete in Division I. Recent Colonial Athletic Association conference champions include men's basketball, baseball, golf, and tennis, and women's volleyball and golf are strong. "Seahawk basketball is huge!" raves one freshman. Club and intramural sports are also popular, especially flag football, basketball, and outdoor and indoor soccer, and the sea kayaking and paddleboarding trips organized by Seahawk Adventures are other favorite diversions.

Despite complaints of limited parking and the lack of football, students at the University of North Carolina Wilmington seem to be a happy lot. "Everyone here always seems to be in a good mood and goes out of their way to speak to and help others," says a senior. "Maybe it's the Southern charm in us, but whatever it is, it sure helps make this laid-back college an awesome place to attend."

Overlaps

Appalachian State, East Carolina, North Carolina State, UNC Charlotte, UNC Greensboro, UNC at Chapel Hill, Western Carolina, University of South Carolina

If You Apply To ›

UNC Wilmington: Early action, regular decision. SATs or ACTs: required. No Subject Tests. Accepts the Common Application with supplement.

Box 7103, Raleigh, NC 27695

Although NC State may lack the high national profile of neighbors Duke and UNC at Chapel Hill, it is a major player in North Carolina's Research Triangle and beyond—just ask the thousands of graduates who have moved into jobs in the area. Engineering, business, and biology are the most popular programs. Location in the state capital a big plus. Compare to Clemson and Virginia Tech.

Whether you're looking for a stellar education or a top-rated basketball program, North Carolina State University offers students the benefits of a large school—highly regarded professors, a diverse student body, and plenty to do on weekends—while making sure that no one feels left out. Says an electrical engineering major, "There is definitely a place for everyone here, since there are so many avenues to explore."

The 132-year-old, 2,100-acre campus consists of redbrick buildings, brick-lined walks, and cozy courtyards dotted with pine trees. There is no dominant style, but more of an architectural stream of consciousness that reveals a campus that has grown and changed with time. Holladay Hall has been designated as a historic site by the Raleigh City Council, while the ultramodern, $115 million Hunt Library features a game lab, visualization studio, digital production suites, and more than 100 collaborative spaces. For amusement you can always stroll over and watch its robotic book retrieval system in action. NC State's Centennial Campus is a 1,227-acre, public-private research campus where university researchers work alongside government, corporate, and nonprofit partners.

General education requirements cover a broad range of liberal arts disciplines, in addition to coursework that reflects interdisciplinary perspectives, develops writing skills, and engages students in-depth in an area that is clearly distinct from their major. An Exploratory Studies program provides guidance and counseling for incoming students to

> **"The collective climate of NC State is one of innovation and collaboration."**

introduce them to possible majors. "Overall, the collective climate of NC State is one of innovation and collaboration," says an education major. Many classes at NC State are large, but faculty get high grades for being accessible and helpful during office hours. A biology major comments, "As with any university, NC State employs some outstanding faculty and some less-than-stellar professors who are more effective in the laboratory than in the lecture hall."

NC State excels in the professional areas of engineering, architecture, business, agriculture, and the sciences, which are among the largest and the most demanding divisions. Not surprisingly, given its location in the heart of textile country, the university also boasts the largest and one of the best textiles programs in the country. Engineering tops the list of most popular majors, followed by business, biological sciences, and agriculture. The College of Humanities and Social Sciences is the second largest school in the university, and strong nontechnical areas include communication, English, international studies, and social work. Notable programs are also available in genetics, forest management, biomedical engineering, sport management, and turfgrass science.

An important feature of NC State's approach to education is the cooperative education program, through which students in all schools can alternate semesters of on-site work with traditional classroom time. The university benefits greatly from its relationships with private industry through the state's high-tech Research Triangle

Website: www.ncsu.edu
Location: City Center
Public
Total Enrollment: 27,231
Undergraduates: 21,240
Male/Female: 54/46
SAT Ranges: ERW 610–680, M 620–710
ACT Ranges: 27–31
Financial Aid: 68%
Pell Grant: 21%
Expense: Pub $
Student Loans: 52%
Average Debt: $ $
Applicants: 26,859
Accepted: 51%
Enrolled: 34%
Grad in 6 Years: 79%
Returning Freshmen: 94%
Academics: ✑ ✑ ✑ ½
Social: ☎ ☎ ☎
Q of L: ★ ★ ★
Admissions: (919) 515-2434
Email Address: undergrad-admissions@ncsu.edu

Strong Programs:
Engineering
Business
Biological Sciences
Agriculture
Architecture
Textiles
Communication
Forest Management

Park, located nearby, as well as from cooperative ties with Duke and UNC at Chapel Hill. NC State offers approximately 400 study abroad programs in more than 50 countries, in which 11 percent of undergrads participate. In the University Scholars program, academic standouts live together and participate in weekly activities such as cultural events, honors classes, and outdoor recreation trips. Students in the University Honors Program take small seminars and complete a capstone project, and they can join a dedicated living/learning community.

NC State's star continues to rise as it becomes more selective. The students here are largely "hardworking and humble" North Carolinians; 86 percent are in-state students, and 5 percent are international. Six percent of undergraduates are African American, 5 percent are Hispanic, 6 percent are Asian American, and 4 percent are multiracial. Conservatism is not uncommon, and the largest political organization is the College Republicans, but in general, according to a junior, "political and social activism are not widespread among the student body." Jocks and sports fans are visible, and the university offers 331 athletic scholarships in 23 sports. Those with outstanding academic qualifications can compete for one of hundreds of merit scholarships, which average $5,600. The Pack Promise guarantees that every North Carolina resident admitted to NC State with a family income at or below 150 percent of the federal poverty level will receive an aid package that meets 100 percent of their demonstrated financial need. Pell Grant recipients represent 21 percent of incoming freshmen.

"Living and Learning Villages are a great way to build connections."

Thirty-nine percent of students choose to live on campus, which is a requirement for freshmen. One student quips, "The dorm buildings look like they are from Soviet bloc nations." Rooms range in size from spacious to cramped, and students report that dorm dwelling is more expensive than some off-campus units, which are plentiful. Nearly a quarter of students opt to reside in the school's 16 Living and Learning Villages, where they can live and socialize with others who share their interests, such as entrepreneurship and women's empowerment. "Living and Learning Villages are a great way to build connections and establish a sense of community," cheers a sophomore. The dining halls feed all freshmen and anyone else who cares to join the meal plan, and the food gets good reviews. "University leadership has prominently supported combating sexual assault through the Protect the Pack initiative, which encourages respect of all students," says a junior.

The 28 fraternities and 21 sororities attract 12 percent of the men and 17 percent of the women. The Greek scene provides much of the entertainment, but parties in dorms and at off-campus apartments are also popular. Alcohol policies are enforced, and if you're thinking about grabbing a brew, "don't try unless you're 21," warns a senior. A junior says, "There are always countless free events going on campus: concerts, festivals, free movies, or outdoor activities." Packapalooza, "a huge block party on Hillsborough Street with a free concert at the end," kicks off the academic year, and Wolfstock, a concert on the last day of classes in the spring, closes it. Public transportation affords easy access to downtown, with its shops, restaurants, theaters, and night spots. Many students also like to head to the beach, which is about two hours away, or to the mountains for hiking or skiing, which is about a three-and-a-half-hour trip. Volunteering is popular too.

"[Packapalooza is] a huge block party on Hillsborough Street with a free concert."

Students love to cheer on their Division I teams, which do well in baseball, wrestling, women's gymnastics, and men's and women's swimming and diving. But needless to say, basketball reigns supreme—the Wolfpack plays in the high-powered Atlantic Coast Conference. Some crazy NC State fans storm nearby Hillsborough

Street following game-day victories, especially those over archrival UNC at Chapel Hill. Indeed, the annual State versus Carolina football game always packs the stadium, and the never-ending call to "Beat Carolina!" permeates the campus year-round. Intramurals also thrive; offerings include cricket, team handball, and, for the exceptionally agile, trampoline dodgeball.

North Carolina State has moved well beyond its origins as a land grant school focusing on agriculture and engineering. It has attracted a dedicated and friendly student body lured by an emphasis on learning beyond the classroom and inspired by the university's "Think and Do" slogan. NC State works well for those who can shoot hoops and for those who can calculate the trajectory of the same three-point shot.

If You Apply To ›

NC State: Early action, regular decision. SATs or ACTs: required. Subject Tests: optional. Accepts the Common Application with supplement.

Northeastern University

360 Huntington Avenue, Boston, MA 02115

Northeastern is synonymous with preprofessional education and hands-on experience. By interspersing co-op jobs with academic study, students can help finance their education while getting a leg up on the job market—domestic and global. Aided by a huge spike in applications and an ambitious building program, NU has transformed itself from blue-collar urban into Boston chic. With students always coming and going, campus life is minimal.

Long known for its co-op program and hands-on learning experiences, Northeastern University has set its sights on becoming one of the region's top-tier institutions. More selective than ever, NU has added lavish new facilities and recruited big-name professors while continuing to combine liberal arts requirements with up to 18 months of challenging work placements. "The school has encouraged and empowered me to explore the world through research and study abroad," cheers one mechanical engineering major, "experiences that will stay with me forever."

Northeastern's 73-acre campus is an unlikely oasis located in the heart of Boston, just minutes away from Fenway Park, shopping centers, nightclubs, cafés, Symphony Hall, and the Museum of Fine Arts. The campus's green spaces are interspersed with brick walkways, sculptures, and outdoor art. Older buildings are utilitarian gray-brick, while newer structures are modern glass and brick. During inclement weather, students can be found navigating the underground tunnel system that connects many campus buildings. No longer a commuter college, NU has the rare luxury for an urban institution of having erstwhile parking lots available for new construction. The state-of-the-art Interdisciplinary Sciences and Engineering Complex furthers NU's emphasis on applied—or, to use the local jargon, "use-inspired"—research.

Northeastern's core curriculum (known as NUpath) embraces writing-intensive instruction, mathematical/analytical thinking, and comparative understanding of

> **"[Northeastern has] empowered me to explore the world through research and study abroad."**

Website: www.northeastern .edu
Location: City Center
Private
Total Enrollment: 25,664
Undergraduates: 18,109
Male/Female: 49/51
SAT Ranges: ERW 680–750, M 690–770
ACT Ranges: 32–34
Financial Aid: 70%
Pell Grant: 15%
Expense: Pr $ $ $
Student Loans: N/A
Average Debt: N/A
Applicants: 54,209
Accepted: 27%
Enrolled: 21%
Grad in 6 Years: 87%
Returning Freshmen: 97%
Academics: ✍ ✍ ✍

(continued)

Social: ☎ ☎
Q of L: ★ ★
Admissions: (617) 373-2200
Email Address: admissions@
northeastern.edu

Strong Programs:
Business and Marketing
Engineering
Health Professions
Social Sciences
Biological and Life Sciences

Northeastern's
signature co-op
education program,
which dates to 1909,
places students in
full-time positions
related to their major.

religions and cultures. Students must take part in a first-year learning community, integrated experiential learning, and a capstone experience. Woven into the Northeastern experience is its signature co-op education program—which dates to 1909 and is the second oldest in the country—that places students in full-time positions related to their major and personal interests. Students complete at least two co-ops, four to six months in length, if they seek to graduate in four years and head on to graduate school, or three co-ops if they enroll in the university's traditional five-year bachelor's degree programs. Students may choose from more than 2,900 established co-op locations, including options in more than 80 countries worldwide, or may propose their own co-op. Destinations range from nonprofits in Boston to a digital advertising agency in the Czech Republic, a children's occupational therapy center in Uganda, or even an Antarctic research station. Faculty members prepare students for their co-ops with a special course beforehand, check in with them while they are out in the field, and organize academic reflection on the experience afterward. "Professors want to make sure that you are as attractive as possible to potential employers," says a political science major.

"I feel extremely safe on campus even though it is in the middle of the city."

NU's undergraduate programs are divided among seven colleges and schools: the College of Arts, Media, and Design; the D'Amore-McKim School of Business; the College of Computer and Information Science; the College of Engineering; the Bouvé College of Health Sciences; the College of Science; and the College of Social Sciences and Humanities. The Program for Undeclared Students offers experiential learning opportunities to help students explore potential majors and careers. Students with diverse interests may select from a slew of combined majors that cross disciplines, such as information science and cognitive psychology, political science and communication studies, and international affairs and cultural anthropology. The most popular majors fall under the categories of business and marketing, engineering, health professions, and social sciences. The international business program features an "expat year," in which students spend one semester studying at an overseas university and six months working at an international co-op. Health sciences students may pursue six-year doctor of pharmacy or doctor of physical therapy degrees.

"Students strive to work hard and achieve academically, but also never fail to help a friend out in their time of need," says one student. Sixty-eight percent of Northeastern's classes have fewer than 20 students. Scheduling can be difficult, as students sometimes find that courses they want are offered only when they're scheduled to be away on a job. But dedicated professors help make up for these challenges, according to one senior: "Faculty members make themselves totally accessible via email, face to face for meetings, and phone conferences." Under the Dialogue of Civilizations program, faculty members take about 1,000 students abroad each summer. Overall, roughly 17 percent of students work or study abroad. The Northeastern University Scholars Program, limited to 50 students, offers customized global experiences, personalized advising and mentoring, access to university resources, and financial support. An honors program is also available for the highly motivated.

"We are employees at co-op, students in class, friends and roommates in our free time."

Northeastern was founded as a YMCA educational program and has traditionally served local students from diverse socioeconomic backgrounds. These days, only 27 percent of undergraduates are from Massachusetts, and just 15 percent qualify for Pell Grants. Consistent with Northeastern's efforts to promote a global culture, 18 percent come from overseas. Asian Americans comprise 13 percent of the student body, Hispanics 8 percent, African Americans 4 percent, and multiracial students

4 percent. Merit scholarships averaging $15,200 are awarded annually, as are more than 300 athletic scholarships.

Forty-nine percent of undergraduates live on campus. All freshmen reside in living/learning communities organized around particular interests, and freshmen honors students live together in their own housing. On-campus housing is guaranteed for all four years, though many students find it less expensive to live off campus, where options include privately owned apartments or suites located adjacent to the residence halls. The dining halls offer "a lot of options and good food," according to students, who also speak highly of NU Public Safety: "I feel extremely safe on campus even though it is in the middle of the city," says one senior.

When it comes to Northeastern's social scene, "Most of the social life happens off campus," one student says. Hundreds of clubs and activities abound, but the continuous flow of students on and off the campus for co-ops tends to be disruptive. "I may see a friend one quarter in class and then not again for six months. It's hard to stay connected," a student explains. The upside of this, says an engineering student, is that "you are pushed to meet new people and develop networking skills." Fraternities and sororities attract 10 percent of NU men and 16 percent of women, respectively. Regular traditions include Springfest, an annual concert that draws the likes of Kesha and Kid Cudi, and the annual Underwear Run during Parent Weekend in the fall, when students run through the city at night in their underwear or crazy costumes. Boston is, of course, the "ultimate college town" and offers a seemingly endless array of concerts, museums, clubs, and eateries. In the winter, students head to the ski slopes of Vermont, and in balmier weather, they're off to the beaches of Cape Cod and the North Shore.

Northeastern fields 18 Division I varsity teams (the Huskies) as part of the Colonial Athletic Association and the Hockey East Association. The biggest sports series of the year is the Beanpot Hockey Tournament ("Hockey is king here at Northeastern"), which pits Northeastern against rival teams from Boston College, Boston University, and Harvard. "It is all about bragging rights and pride, and the fans from the schools make it fun," reports a student. One T-shirt reads, "No—we don't want to B.U.," epitomizing the competitive nature of the sports teams in the Boston area. NU's women's rowing team has won multiple conference titles, and the fleet-footed men's and women's track and cross-country teams regularly leave their opponents blinking in the dust. The recreation program offers 30 intramural options, and with 40 club teams, Northeastern is well represented in nonvarsity competition with other schools.

Students gripe about the so-called NU Shuffle, which a junior explains as, "Want to take more than 19 credits in a semester or start a new club? Please track down 14 administrators from your department and get their signatures." Bureaucracy aside, Northeastern is a school on the rise. It has moved well beyond its origins as an open admissions commuter school and—through aggressive fund-raising, an ambitious building program, and unabashed marketing—adapted its decades of experience with co-op education to the emerging global economy. Northeastern students tend to be serious about their studies but learn to wear many hats. "We are employees at co-op, students in class, friends and roommates in our free time," explains one denizen. "We balance work and play while still meeting deadlines." Northeastern students graduate with a broad reservoir of experiences that they know will serve them well once they start scouring those job listings—both in the U.S. and around the world.

Under the Dialogue of Civilizations program, faculty members take about 1,000 students abroad each summer.

The biggest sports series of the year is the Beanpot Hockey Tournament against rivals Boston College, Boston University, and Harvard.

Overlaps

University of Southern California, NYU, Boston College, Boston University, George Washington, Cornell University, University of Pennsylvania, Tufts

If You Apply To ›

Northeastern: Early decision I and II, early action, regular decision. SATs or ACTs: required. No Subject Tests. Accepts the Common Application. Studio art applicants must submit portfolio.

Northwestern University

1801 Hinman Avenue, P.O. Box 3060, Evanston, IL 60208

The Big Ten is not the Ivy League, and NU has more school spirit than its Eastern counterparts. Much more preprofessional than its nearby rival University of Chicago or any of the Ivies except Penn, NU is comparable to Duke and Stanford. World-renowned in journalism. Suburban setting on the shore of Lake Michigan, with quick access to Chicago.

Website: www.northwestern.edu

Location: Suburban

Private

Total Enrollment: 17,562

Undergraduates: 8,271

Male/Female: 48/52

SAT Ranges: ERW 700–770, M 720–790

ACT Ranges: 32–35

Financial Aid: 61%

Pell Grant: 18%

Expense: Pr $ $ $ $

Student Loans: 37%

Average Debt: $

Applicants: 37,259

Accepted: 9%

Enrolled: 55%

Grad in 6 Years: 93%

Returning Freshmen: 98%

Academics: ✍ ✍ ✍ ✍ ✍

Social: ☎ ☎ ☎

Q of L: ★ ★ ★

Admissions: (847) 491-7271

Email Address: ug-admission@ northwestern.edu

Strong Programs:
Economics
Psychology
Political Science
Journalism
Engineering
Visual and Performing Arts
Education
Premed

On Sunday nights before finals begin at Northwestern University, students are encouraged to let off steam with a campuswide "primal scream." The ear-shattering event illustrates two big themes at NU: students work really hard, but they also know how to let loose and enjoy themselves. Regarded as the most elite school in the Midwest, this top-tier university, the only private school in the Big Ten, boasts some of the most well-respected preprofessional programs in the country. Plus, Northwestern is ideally located just outside of Chicago. "I love being at a place where I can learn and have a great social life," says one student.

Northwestern is situated on 231 acres about a dozen miles north of the Chicago Loop. An eclectic mix of stone buildings with abundant ivy, the leafy campus is set off from the town of Evanston and runs for a mile along the shore of Lake Michigan. Students migrate between the North Campus (techy) and the South Campus (artsy). The newer buildings are located adjacent to a 14-acre lagoon, part of an 85-acre lakefill addition built in the '60s. This area provides students with a prime location for picnicking, fishing, running, cycling, roller-skating, or just daydreaming. The Garage, located in a repurposed facility whose origins you can guess, offers meeting and high-tech workshop spaces, classrooms, and a café on a 24/7 basis for entrepreneurs from across the university.

Half of Northwestern's undergraduates are enrolled in arts and sciences, while the other half are spread out among five professional schools, all with national reputations. Indeed, students tend to identify more strongly with their school than with Northwestern as a whole. The Medill School of Journalism, the only such program at a top private university, sends student reporters out with iPads and video cameras as well as spiral notebooks. The curriculum integrates multimedia techniques with the study of "audience understanding" and features internships at dozens of top newspapers, magazines, and television stations across the nation. There's also a four-year accelerated B.S.J./M.S.J. program. A dazzling electronic studio centralizes Medill's state-of-the-art broadcast newsroom and the communication school's radio/TV/film department. The McCormick School of Engineering and Applied Science is strong in all aspects of engineering and pairs students with clients with practical problems. Five-year co-op options are available. The School of Music wants students who can combine conservatory-level musicianship with high-level academics; it offers a five-year program from which students emerge with two B.A. degrees. The School of Education and Social Policy is the only school of its kind in the country and competes with Vanderbilt for education majors. Students and faculty members alike are encouraged to range across traditional disciplinary barriers—a policy that has led to the creation of some entirely new fields such as materials science—and students are free to switch schools once they are enrolled.

> **"I love being at a place where I can learn and have a great social life."**

Consistent with this approach, students say the university's best programs include the Integrated Science Program, the Honors Program in Medical Education, and Mathematical Methods in the Social Sciences, a selective program that gives students the technical skills to move into various areas of the social sciences. Strong arts and sciences departments include chemistry and history, although the humanities as a group are less strong. The social sciences (especially economics, psychology, and political science), journalism, engineering, and visual and performing arts enroll the most majors. Each of the undergraduate schools determines its own general education requirements, but broad outlines are similar. Each school requires a graduate to have coursework in "the major domains of knowledge"—science, mathematics and technology, individual and social behavior, historical studies, values, the humanities, and the fine arts. Incoming students take part in Wildcat Welcome, a weeklong orientation designed to ease the transition into college life.

Students migrate between the North Campus (techy) and the South Campus (artsy).

Unlike most schools on a 10-week quarter system, Northwesterners take four (not three) courses each quarter, except in engineering, where five are permitted. "Students tend to be supportive and collaborative," says a senior, but "the academics are rigorous and will take some adjustment from high school." Virtually all undergraduate courses are taught by regular faculty members. Introductory courses are larger than most, but 79 percent of all undergraduate classes have fewer than 20 students. "The quality of teaching at Northwestern depends on the department and the professor," confides a senior, "but overall I would say it's very high quality." The Office of Undergraduate Research helps students apply for research assistantships and faculty-mentored independent projects, often with the support of grants. One-third of students take a break from campus through 150 study abroad programs in 50 countries.

"Students tend to be supportive and collaborative."

Upon graduating, NU students tend to pursue business fields like consulting and finance, with technology, education, and communication distant followers. "Students at Northwestern are always passionate about something," says a social policy major. "That could be theories of relativity like my roommate, wildlife conservation like myself, or film criticism like one of my good friends. So it's really easy to have interesting conversations and learn from each other." Thirty-two percent of undergraduates hail from Illinois, and 9 percent come from overseas. Minorities represent a sizable contingent of the student body, with Asian Americans accounting for 17 percent, African Americans 6 percent, Hispanics 13 percent, and multiracial students 5 percent. There are no academic merit scholarships, but NU does guarantee to meet the full demonstrated need of every admit and has eliminated need-based loans from its financial aid packages. It also offers hundreds of scholarships for its athletes.

The Medill School of Journalism is the only such program at a top private university.

Fifty-two percent of undergraduates reside in university housing, mostly in double rooms, although there are also singles, triples, and quadruple rooms, as well as suites. "Dorms range from 50 students to 600 students, and some are general dorms while others have themes that the communities are based around," one student reports. Several residential colleges, in areas like engineering, commerce and industry, and communication, bring students and faculty members together during faculty "firesides" or simply over meals. Fraternities and sororities also have their own houses. Students can choose to eat at the coffeehouse or at any one of six dining halls on campus. A variety of meal plans are available, including one that provides Sunday brunch and one offering kosher food, and a dietitian works with students who have food allergies or other special dietary needs. Those who head off campus to apartments are mostly juniors and seniors. Students generally feel safe on campus, but crime has been a concern in Evanston, especially after dark.

"It's really easy to have interesting conversations and learn from each other."

Much of the social life on NU's campus is centered on the Greek system, with 32 percent of the men and 40 percent of the women joining up. Some students say finding a social niche can be tough, especially for those who aren't involved in Greek life, athletics, journalism, or theater. The school's alcohol policy is stiff, but not always effective, "like the vast majority of campuses nationwide," says a student. The student government and Activities and Organizations Board sponsor an array of campuswide events, including theater productions, concerts, and movies. The 30-hour Dance Marathon and Dillo (Armadillo) Day, an end-of-the-year "festival of music, debauchery, and Greek life," in the words of a journalism major, are popular annual events. Another tradition is upheld when representatives of student organizations slip out in the dead of night to paint their colors and slogans on a centrally located rock. In all, there are more than 400 student organizations, ranging from an African drum and dance ensemble to Adshop, an advertising agency that

"[Some dorms] have themes that the communities are based around."

lets students hone their marketing skills by promoting local businesses. Upscale Evanston is "the restaurant haven of Chicago's North Shore," says a junior, and "very quaint with tons of flowers that bloom every spring." A short stroll off campus brings you to the town's myriad restaurant options, trendy bars, and coffee shops with space to plug in a laptop and study. For culture or a night out, of course, Chicago is right across the border.

Football and tailgate parties are a traditional way of bringing alumni back and rousing the students to support the smallest and only private school in the Division I Big Ten. Although the football team's trip to the 1996 Rose Bowl remains the stuff of legend, the Wildcats tend to be strongest in country club sports. In the last few years, wrestling, women's golf, women's soccer, men's swimming, and fencing have brought home team and individual championship titles. As far as facilities, NU is on par with many schools its size and larger, with the beautiful Norris Aquatics Center/Henry Crown Sports Pavilion and the Nicolet Football and Conference Center used for conditioning of varsity athletes. The student-sponsored intramural program provides vigorous competition among teams from dorms and rival Greek groups, and more than 40 club sports are an option too. Northwestern also boasts the winningest debate team in the country.

Northwestern occupies a unique niche in U.S. higher education. It has the academics of the Ivies, the spirited atmosphere of the Big Ten publics, and, along with Duke, Stanford, and perhaps Vanderbilt, combines success in Division I sports with quality instruction. Northwestern students bask in their school's balance of challenging academics, preprofessional bent, and myriad opportunities to get off campus to learn and let loose.

Overlaps

Yale, Stanford, Harvard, University of Michigan, University of Pennsylvania, Princeton, WashU in St. Louis, Duke

If You Apply To ›

Northwestern: Early decision, regular decision. SATs or ACTs: required. Subject Tests: optional (required for applicants to Honors Program in Medical Education and Integrated Science Program). Accepts the Common Application with supplement.

University of Notre Dame

220 Main Building, Notre Dame, IN 46556

The Holy Grail of higher education for many Roman Catholics. ND's heartland location and 80-percent–Catholic enrollment make it a bastion of solid education and equally solid values, religious and otherwise. Offers business, science, architecture, and engineering in addition to the liberal arts. ND's personality is much closer to Boston College or Holy Cross than Georgetown. Only school ever ranked #1 in both football and graduation rates.

Founded in 1842 by the French priest Edward Sorin from the Congregation of Holy Cross, the University of Notre Dame has come a long way from its fledgling days in a rustic log cabin. While described as "a Catholic academic community of higher learning," its students need not be affiliated with the Roman Catholic Church. Notre Dame takes pride in fostering a culture that values open discussion of religious, spiritual, and social issues—witness the willingness of its president to stick by a controversial decision in 2009 to award former president Barack Obama an honorary doctorate even though Obama does not share Catholic views on abortion. The school appeals to non-Catholics who are committed to social justice or seek a broadly spiritual dimension to their education. A soft spot for football doesn't hurt either.

With 1,250 acres of manicured quads, twin lakes, and woods, the university offers a peaceful setting for studying. The lofty Golden Dome that rises above the ivy-covered Gothic and modern buildings and the old brick stadium, where Knute Rockne made the Fighting Irish almost synonymous with college football, are national symbols. The university is in the midst of a $1.1 billion construction spree that will add 20 new buildings by 2020, including several new academic buildings and residence halls. The nine-story Duncan Student Center, which overlooks the football stadium, opened in 2018 and boasts a career services center, dining facilities, a massive rock-climbing wall, and premium new stadium seating for football VIPs. Notre Dame's $13 billion endowment is the largest of any of the country's Catholic colleges and universities.

Liberal education is more than just a catchphrase at Notre Dame. No matter what their major, students must take the First Year of Studies, one of the most extensive academic and counseling programs of any university in the nation. The core of the program is a one-semester writing-intensive university seminar limited to 20 students per section. The remainder of each freshman's schedule is reserved for the first of a comprehensive list of general education requirements covering writing and mathematics, natural science, theology, philosophy, history, social science, and fine arts. Peer advisors are assigned to each student, as are academic advisors and tutors if necessary. Administrators are quick to point out that, due in part to the success of the first-year support program, a whopping 98 percent of freshmen make it through the year and return for sophomore year. (The fact that 91 percent of freshmen are high achievers who graduated in the top 10th of their high school class probably also helps.)

In the College of Arts and Letters, highly regarded departments include English, theology, and philosophy, while physics and chemistry are tops in the College of Science. Within the engineering school, chemical engineering rules. The Mendoza College of Business's accountancy program is ranked among the nation's best, and the chemistry labs in the Nieuwland and Jordan Science Halls have first-rate equipment. The most popular majors overall are economics, finance, political science, and

> **"The workload is very demanding."**

Website: www.nd.edu
Location: Small City
Private
Total Enrollment: 12,127
Undergraduates: 8,509
Male/Female: 53/47
SAT Ranges: ERW 680–750, M 690–770
ACT Ranges: 32–34
Financial Aid: 69%
Pell Grant: 12%
Expense: Pr $ $ $
Student Loans: 46%
Average Debt: $ $ $
Applicants: 19,564
Accepted: 19%
Enrolled: 55%
Grad in 6 Years: 95%
Returning Freshmen: 98%
Academics: ✍ ✍ ✍ ✍
Social: ☎ ☎ ☎
Q of L: ★ ★ ★
Admissions: (574) 631-7505
Email Address: admissions@nd.edu

Strong Programs:
Economics
Finance
Political Science
Mechanical Engineering
English
Theology
Physics
Accountancy

mechanical engineering. Students describe the academic climate as fairly competitive but not cutthroat by any measure. "The workload is very demanding," says a senior. "It requires the student to have very good time-management skills." Faculty members are praised for being dynamic, personable, knowledgeable, and accessible. "The professors here care a great deal about their students, and it shows," says a biology major. Sixty-two percent of classes enroll fewer than 20 students, and students report it can be hard to get all the classes they want during a particular semester, but say it's not difficult to graduate in four years.

Notre Dame offers a variety of special academic programs and options. One of the most popular is the Program of Liberal Studies (PLS), in which students study art, philosophy, literature, and the history of Western thought within their Great Books seminars. The Summer Comprehensive Grant program awards up to $4,500 to students wishing to spend their summer focusing on independent research. Roughly two-thirds of undergrads take part in Notre Dame's extensive international study program, which includes opportunities at the university's Global Gateways in London, Dublin, Rome, Beijing, and Jerusalem.

> **"The professors here care a great deal about their students, and it shows."**

With a predominantly lay board of trustees and faculty, Notre Dame remains committed to "the preservation of a distinctly Catholic community," and it has a more self-consciously Catholic identity than any other major research university, including Boston College and Georgetown. The president and several other top administrators are priests of the Congregation of Holy Cross, and each dorm has its own chapel with daily masses, though attendance is not required. About 80 percent of the students are Catholic. The main social issues discussed on campus include abortion, gender and racial issues, homosexuality, and faith. African Americans make up 4 percent of the undergraduate student body, Hispanics 11 percent, Asian Americans 5 percent, and multiracial students 5 percent. Despite its relative cultural homogeneity, Notre Dame recruits from all over the country; 87 percent of the students are from states outside of Indiana, and 6 percent hail from other countries. Competitive merit awards, averaging $13,500, are offered to students with outstanding high school records, and the university meets 100 percent of accepted students' demonstrated financial need. The Division I powerhouse deals out hundreds of athletic scholarships as well.

Seventy-nine percent of ND students choose to live on campus. "Notre Dame dorm life is extraordinary," says a junior. "The dorm rooms are all very well kept and very comfortable." For their freshman year, students are assigned to a dorm, mixed among the other classes, and they are encouraged to stay in the same one until graduation. Since Greek organizations are banned, the single-sex dorms really become surrogate fraternities and sororities that breed a similar spirit of community and family. Notre Dame has been co-ed since 1972, and parietal rules (midnight on weekdays, 2 a.m. on weekends) are still strictly enforced. Boarders eat in the North Quad or South Quad cafeterias and must buy a 19-meal plan. Students can also reserve their residence hall kitchen to cook their own meals.

> **"The dorm rooms are all very well kept and very comfortable."**

ND's social life isn't as rambunctious as it once was, thanks to policies that forbid alcohol at campus social events. The rules relating to alcohol in the dorms are a bit more relaxed. For those who choose not to indulge, there are several groups dedicated to good times without alcohol. Most activities take place on campus and include parties, concerts, and movies. A popular event is the An Tóstal (Gaelic for "the pageant") festival, which comes the week before spring finals and guarantees to temporarily relieve academic anxiety with its "childish" games, such as pie-eating

The university is in the midst of a $1.1 billion construction spree that will add 20 new buildings by 2020.

Due in part to the success of the first-year support program, a whopping 98 percent of freshmen return for sophomore year.

contests and Jell-O wrestling. The annual Notre Dame Literary Festival is entirely student-run and draws prominent writers and poets from across the country. Students are involved in the community through volunteer work—more than 10 percent of grads enter public service positions. The best outlet for culture is nearby Chicago, about 90 minutes away. South Bend, with a metro area population of 315,000, offers plenty of opportunities for entertainment as well.

Notre Dame competes in the Division I Atlantic Coast Conference for all sports except football and ice hockey. With its proud gridiron heritage, there's nothing like Notre Dame football. From Knute Rockne and the Gipper right on down to modern-day greats such as Joe Montana, the spirit of the Fighting Irish reigns supreme and has regained its former glory under head coach Brian Kelly. It wasn't intentional—at least that's what they say—but the giant mosaic of Jesus Christ on the library lifts his hands toward the heavens as if to signal yet another Irish touchdown. Tailgate parties are celebrated events, occurring before and after the game. Notre Dame offers one of the strongest all-around athletic programs in the country. The women's basketball and fencing teams both won national championships in 2018. Die-hard jocks who weren't recruited for varsity teams will find plenty of company in ND's very competitive club and intramural sports, which attract more than three-quarters of students. The Bookstore Basketball Tournament, the largest 5-on-5, outdoor hoops tournament in the world with more than 700 teams competing, lasts for a month.

Although temperatures here can drop below freezing, few dispute that Notre Dame is red-hot. Everyone at the university, from administrators to students, is considered part of the "Notre Dame family." Traditions are held in high esteem. For those looking for high-quality academics; a friendly, caring environment with a Catholic bent; and an excellent athletic scene, ND could be an answer to their prayers.

The women's basketball and fencing teams both won national championships in 2018.

Overlaps

Vanderbilt, Boston College, Northwestern, Harvard, Duke, Holy Cross, Villanova

If You Apply To ›

ND: Early action, regular decision. SATs or ACTs: required. Subject Tests: optional. Accepts the Common Application with supplement.

Oberlin College

38 E. College Street, Oberlin, OH 44074

The college that invented nonconformity. From the Underground Railroad and coeducation to global learning and the modern peace movement, Obies have long been in the forefront. As at Grinnell and Reed, Oberlin's curriculum is less radical than its students. Oberlin is especially strong in the sciences, and its music conservatory is among the nation's best. The annual Drag Ball is quintessential Oberlin.

New and contrasting ideas are a way of life at Oberlin College, a liberal arts school where nonconformity is a long tradition and student activism continues to make occasional headlines. Tucked away in a small Ohio town, Oberlin was the first American college to accept women and minorities, and it was a stop on the Underground Railroad. That pioneering spirit has not faded. With diverse academic challenges ranging from cinema studies to neuroscience, Obies thrive on higher thinking and exploring their myriad talents. As one junior puts it, "Students here don't sit around during their free time; there's always another activity to be doing, a book to read, a lecture to go to."

Website: www.oberlin.edu
Location: Small Town
Private
Total Enrollment: 2,819
Undergraduates: 2,793
Male/Female: 42/58
SAT Ranges: ERW 670–740, M 650–750

(continued)

ACT Ranges: 30–33
Financial Aid: 80%
Pell Grant: 9%
Expense: Pr $ $ $ $
Student Loans: 42%
Average Debt: $ $ $
Applicants: 7,762
Accepted: 34%
Enrolled: 28%
Grad in 6 Years: 86%
Returning Freshmen: 91%
Academics: ✐ ✐ ✐ ✐ ½
Social: ☎ ☎ ☎ ☎
Q of L: ★ ★ ★ ★
Admissions: (440) 775-8411
Email Address: college
  .admissions@oberlin.edu

Strong Programs:
Music
Biology
Chemistry
Environmental Studies
Politics
History
English
Creative Writing

Oberlin was the first American college to accept women and minorities.

Oberlin's attractive campus features a mix of Italian Renaissance buildings (four designed by Cass Gilbert), late 19th- and early 20th-century organic stone structures, and some less interesting 1950s barracks-type dorms. The buildings rise over flatlands typical of the Midwest, which do little to stop brutal winter winds. The Allen Memorial Art Museum, sometimes mentioned in the same breath as those at Harvard and Yale, is one of the loveliest buildings on campus, with a brick-paved, flower-laden courtyard and a fountain. The Oberlin College Science Center offers state-of-the-art classrooms, a science library, and laboratory space. In a nod to environmental concerns, the college produces half of its energy from renewable resources. Ongoing work on a 13-acre Green Arts District is revamping and expanding performance and other facilities using sustainable technologies.

> **"There's always another activity to be doing, a book to read, a lecture to go to."**

There are no requirements for freshmen at Oberlin, but general education requirements include proficiency in writing and math and coursework in arts and humanities, natural sciences and math, social and behavioral sciences, and cultural diversity. Students must also participate in three January terms during which they pursue month-long projects, traditional or unique, on or off campus. About 40 different First-Year Seminar classes are available every semester, with enrollment limited to 14 students each, and although optional, almost all freshmen sign up because "it's a great way to make friends," says a student. "It also introduces you to the Oberlin academic experience."

Oberlin's Conservatory of Music holds a well-deserved spot among the nation's most prominent performance schools; the voice, violin, and technology in music and related arts programs are especially praised. It is the oldest continuously operating music conservatory in the country, and Oberlin is one of only three liberal arts colleges with a conservatory (see also Bard and Lawrence). The conservatory boasts 150 practice rooms, a substantial music library, and Steinway pianos—one of the world's largest collections. It enrolls about a fifth of Oberlin undergrads, who must audition to gain acceptance. Each year, about 40 students enter the Double Degree Program, which allows them to earn both a B.M. and a B.A. in five (or fewer) years; these students must be admitted to both the college and the music conservatory.

Oberlin has been a leader among liberal arts colleges seeking to promote their science offerings; biology and chemistry are two of the college's strongest departments, and environmental studies is well regarded. Students also flock to the politics, history, and English departments; the latter offers a notable creative writing major. Interdisciplinary and self-created majors, such as Africana, East Asian, Russian, Jewish, and gender studies, are popular—not surprisingly at such a liberal school. One of Oberlin's more unusual offerings is EXCO, an experimental college that offers students and interested townsfolk the chance to learn together. Most classes are taught by students, and topics can range from community organizing to knitting to salsa dancing, and much more.

> **"There are more protests, awareness and advocacy groups, and campaigns here than I can keep track of."**

Oberlin's students are as serious about their schoolwork as they are about politics, justice, and other social causes, and heavy workloads are the norm. "Oberlin is academically rigorous but not competitive between students," says a junior. Seventy-eight percent of classes have fewer than 20 students, and an English major says, "I've been able to form close relationships with many of my professors—both in my major as well as in other departments—which is extremely valuable." Most departments offer group and individual independent study opportunities and invite selected students to pursue demanding honors programs, especially during their senior year. Two-thirds of students conduct undergraduate research, and a whopping 75 percent of students study abroad in Oberlin-directed programs in Italy, Spain, and the UK, or more than 90 other affiliated programs.

Oberlin students are—in a word—*passionate*. "We're all pretty quirky, all pretty dorky. Oberlin students love learning and love talking about the things they're passionate about," says a politics and history major. Eighty-four percent of undergraduates are from states outside of Ohio, primarily from the Mid-Atlantic states, and 10 percent come from abroad. But achieving diversity in rural Ohio has been a challenge: African Americans account for 5 percent of the student body, Asian Americans 4 percent, Hispanics 8 percent, and multiracial students 8 percent. And although Oberlin promises to meet students' full demonstrated financial need, a mere 9 percent of incoming freshmen are eligible to receive Pell Grants. Merit scholarships averaging $16,000 are available to qualified students. "Though the student body is homogeneously liberal," says a junior, "there are more protests, awareness and advocacy groups, and campaigns here than I can keep track of." A popular annual event is the Drag Ball, in which half the student body comes in full drag. "It's very Oberlin, because it's all about challenging social norms," says a student. For all its talk of nonconformity, Oberlin is also a model of political correctness. The director of dining services, for instance, recently issued an apology of sorts for offering "culturally insensitive" items such as inauthentic sushi.

> "Social life is based a lot around live music."

Ninety-three percent of Oberlin students live in campus housing, including several program houses focusing on various foreign languages and cultural backgrounds. "Some of the dorms are beautiful (Talcott, Asia House) and some are large concrete blocks (Dascomb)," says one East Asian studies major. For five dollars, students can rent up to two original works of art to decorate their rooms. A small number of upperclassmen are allowed to live off campus every year, and those who wish to do so must try their luck in a random lottery. Students may eat in any of five dining halls and cafés. Appetizing alternatives to institutional fare can be found at the eight co-ops that comprise the Oberlin Student Cooperative Association, a nearly $3-million-a-year corporation run entirely by students. Regarding campus safety, a senior says, "Unlike many schools concerned with their reputation, Oberlin doesn't try to hide it when sexual assault occurs. I think this generally makes students feel more comfortable speaking up because they know that someone will listen."

> *Interdisciplinary and self-created majors are popular—not surprisingly at such a liberal school.*

Social life, like so much of the Oberlin experience, is what you make of it, students say. "Social life is based a lot around live music—we go to a lot of concerts, and parties usually book at least one campus band," explains a junior. The monthly midnight Organ Pump concerts in Finney Chapel combine serious classical music with musical oddities, such as the school police blotter performed as Anglican chant. House parties, plays, movies, and conservatory performances are planned every other night. And since there's no Greek system, nothing is exclusive. As for drinking, underage students can finagle booze, and of-age students are allowed to imbibe in their rooms. "I think the rules work well," a chemistry major says. "Not too many students get into trouble."

> "Our motto is 'Think one person can change the world? So do we!'"

The small town of Oberlin offers some good restaurants and local shops, although they tend to close early. "There's only really two square blocks of downtown," says one student, "but within it is basically everything that you need." When the urge to wander strikes, Cleveland is only 30 miles away. And Obies are always enthusiastic about giving back to the community through volunteer activities at local schools, hospitals, and nursing homes. "Our motto is 'Think one person can change the world? So do we!'" says a student.

> *Two-thirds of students conduct undergraduate research, and a whopping 75 percent study abroad.*

The Yeomen and Yeowomen, terms that originated with British warriors of old, appear to be building a loyal fan base: the women's cross-country team is a perennial powerhouse, and women's track and field has produced three individual national champions in the last two years. Baseball and men's soccer are competitive as well. As for intramural and club sports, one-third of students compete, and "as soon as the rain stops in the spring, there are students on every green area between the dorms, playing ultimate Frisbee," says a sophomore. Fencing and Quidditch are other student favorites.

Oberlin may be small, but its emphasis on global learning, undergraduate research, and a vibrant liberal arts education helps it burst those statistical seams. Students are more likely to discuss local poverty than the quality of cereal choices in the dining halls, and can be found playing a Steinway or plugging away at astronomy. One Obie sums it up this way: "Oberlin is a place where you can be yourself, but also learn and grow as a person in a diverse environment enhanced by people equally interested in personal growth."

If You Apply To ›

Oberlin: Early decision I and II, regular decision. SATs or ACTs: required. Subject Tests: optional. Accepts the Common Application with supplement. Applicants to Conservatory of Music must audition.

Occidental College

1600 Campus Road, Los Angeles, CA 90041

Oxy is a streetwise cousin to the more upscale and suburban Claremont Colleges. Plentiful internships and study abroad give Oxy students real-world perspectives. Oxy's innovative diplomacy and world affairs program features an internship at the UN. Strong focus on diversity and social justice.

Occidental College is one of a handful of small colleges located in a big city, in this case La La Land. But unlike the sprawling and impersonal City of Angels, Oxy emphasizes a strong sense of community and a decidedly diverse student population. Notable alums include former president Barack Obama. "Students dream big at Oxy," says a senior. "Whether a student wants a career in Hollywood or on Wall Street, everyone knows that it starts in the classroom."

Set against the backdrop of the San Gabriel Mountains, Oxy's self-contained Mediterranean-style campus is a secluded enclave of flowers and trees between Pasadena and Glendale, minutes from downtown Los Angeles. A renovated and expanded career center opened recently, while the McKinnon Center for Global Affairs features a two-story, LED-lit wall of sculpted glass with embedded interactive screens that display a shifting array of student and faculty research and coursework.

"Professors' office doors are always open for students."

Inside this urban oasis resides a thriving community of high achievers who don't for a moment believe that the liberal arts are dead, or even wounded. Required first-year cultural studies seminars include topics in human history and culture, with an emphasis on writing skills. Each seminar has 16 students, and first-years are assigned to residence halls based on their seminar. In addition, all Oxy students must show proficiency in a foreign language and complete coursework in world cultures, fine arts, the preindustrial-era, science, and math. In their final year, all students complete a senior comprehensive, or "comp," such as a project, paper, or exam that shows mastery in their field. Many of Occidental's academic departments are excellent; economics, diplomacy and world affairs, biology, psychology, urban and environmental policy, and politics are among the strongest and most popular majors. New offerings include a major in computer science and a major and minor in Black studies. There are also 3–2 engineering programs with Caltech and Columbia University and a 4–2 biotechnology program with Keck Graduate Institute (of the Claremont Colleges).

Academics at Oxy are challenging, but the atmosphere is not competitive. Faculty members are readily available in and out of the classroom, and students say the teaching, in general, is excellent. Sixty-seven percent of classes have fewer than 20 students, and as academic advisors are responsible for about four students per class (16 total), personal relationships develop quickly. "Professors' office doors are always open for students if they need help in class or in life," confirms a senior.

Oxy encourages diverse learning experiences through independent study, internships, and study abroad—including one of only a few undergraduate programs to offer internships with UN-related organizations in New York City. The Campaign Semester, offered every two years, gives students a chance to work full time on political campaigns and then return to campus for a seminar where they reflect on their experiences. The California Environment Semester is a team-taught, interdisciplinary course for freshmen that involves extended field trips throughout the state. Forty-one percent of students broaden their horizons in study abroad programs in more than 50 countries. The Summer Research Program supports about 120 student research projects in the sciences, social sciences, and humanities every summer, and many students publish and present their work.

"Students at Oxy are generally creative, smart self-starters and politically and socially engaged/opinionated," says a sociology major. Forty-five percent of the students are from California, and 7 percent hail from foreign nations. African Americans make up 5 percent of the student population, Hispanics 14 percent, Asian Americans 14 percent, and multiracial students 8 percent. Perhaps not surprisingly, students tend to be liberal, and the raging social concerns are "racial and social inequalities, environmentalism, and gender issues," according to one student. Merit scholarships are doled out to qualified students each year—averaging $11,600—but there are no athletic scholarships. Occidental typically meets the full demonstrated need of admitted students and has increased the amount of grant aid awarded to middle-class students. Special financial packages are available to low-income students as well. Launched in 2017, the Barack Obama Scholars Program provides top achievers who have demonstrated serious commitment to public service with a four-year scholarship covering the full cost of attendance, as well as funding for three summer experiences, such as internships or service projects.

The residence halls are small—almost all house fewer than 150 students—and co-ed by floor or room. Eighty-one percent of students live on campus, but what you get depends on your luck in the housing lottery. Students from all four classes live together, many in special-interest housing like the Multicultural Hall, the Food Justice House, or the Global Diversity Floor in Newcomb Hall. Freshmen, sophomores, and juniors are required to live on campus and purchase a meal plan. "The food is fresh and yummy!" cheers a student. "It's always changing and they bring in locally sourced produce." Resources related to sexual assault include the Project SAFE student group, which a senior says "has been absolutely wonderful in creating a safe and respectful campus."

While the bustle of L.A. often beckons on weekends, the Oxy campus provides its share of fun too, whether it be a "basketball game, concert, dance, or party," says

(continued)

Q of L: ★ ★ ★ ★
Admissions: (800) 825-5262
Email Address: admission@ oxy.edu

Strong Programs:
Economics
Diplomacy and World Affairs
Biology
Psychology
Urban and Environmental
    Policy
Politics

New offerings include a major in computer science and a major and minor in Black studies.

"Students at Oxy are generally creative, smart self-starters and politically and socially engaged/opinionated."

The Campaign Semester, offered every two years, gives students a chance to work full time on political campaigns.

one student. Fraternities and sororities, though declining on the Oxy social ladder, attract 16 percent of the men and 22 percent of the women, but they are neither selective nor exclusive; students choose which to join, rather than being chosen, and the frats must invite everyone to their functions. As for alcohol, "like most other colleges, there is underage drinking even though this is illegal," says a junior. Dance Production—a decades-old tradition in which student dancers perform works by student choreographers—sells out both performances each year. Other big events include Apollo Night (a talent contest) and the Fall Fest and Spring Fest concerts, featuring big-name performers. You may want to keep your birthday a secret, or on that unhappy day a roaring pack of your more sadistic classmates will carry you out to the middle of campus and mercilessly toss you in the Gilman Fountain. It's a tradition, after all.

A student characterizes the surrounding neighborhood of Eagle Rock as "a quaint little community with an eclectic combination of 'ma and pa' restaurants and plenty of hole-in-the-wall stores." Community outreach is important at Occidental and dates back to the mid-1960s, when the college opened its Community Literacy Center and one of the country's first Upward Bound programs for underserved students. Today, Oxy's Upward Bound is one of the largest in the country, and half of Oxy students participate in some kind of community project, most through the Center for Community Based Learning. When students become weary of the social life in the "Oxy fishbowl," they head for the bars, restaurants, museums, and theaters of downtown Los Angeles and Pasadena, where, one student notes, "You can find almost anything except snow." But the ski slopes of the San Gabriel Mountains are not far away, and neither is Hollywood nor the beautiful beaches of Southern California. A car (your own or someone else's) is practically a necessity, though the college runs a weekend shuttle service to Old Town Pasadena. The weather is warm and sunny, but the air is often thick with that infamous L.A. smog.

> **"We are pushed to take our writing and critical thinking to the next level."**

Oxy's sports teams (the Tigers) compete in Division III and draw a modest following. Football is the most popular, while baseball, men's and women's cross-country and track and field, and women's lacrosse are some of the most successful. Oxy's football rivalry with Pomona–Pitzer is said to be the oldest west of the Mississippi, and the school's *Io Triumphe* ("Hurrah, O Triumph") Latin chant, a tradition since 1905, has been mocked for nearly a century by rival Redlands, which made up a gibberish chant of its own in 1921. L.A. is, of course, also home to the NBA's Lakers, the NHL's Kings, and the MLB's Dodgers. Oxy has a small intramural program, in which 20 percent of students take part; popular club sports include rugby and ultimate Frisbee.

Occidental's creative, motivated, and diverse students are not here for the bright lights and beautiful people of Los Angeles; those are just fringe benefits. Instead, students are drawn to this intimate oasis of learning by professors who hate to see anyone waste one whit of intellectual potential. "We are pushed to take our writing and critical thinking to the next level," says a sociology major. And students here are only too happy to live up to these lofty expectations.

Overlaps

Whitman, Colorado College, Macalester, Hamilton, Trinity College (CT), Pomona, Pitzer, Oberlin

If You Apply To ›

Oxy: Early decision I and II, regular decision. SATs or ACTs: required (SAT essay or ACT writing recommended). Subject Tests: optional. Accepts the Common Application with supplement.

4484 Peachtree Road NE, Atlanta, GA 30319

Small wonder that brochures for Oglethorpe trumpet Atlanta as the college's biggest drawing card. In a region where most liberal arts colleges are in sleepy towns, Oglethorpe has the South's most exciting city at its fingertips. Highly diverse student body and extensive financial aid. Oglethorpe Idea stresses broad academic values, while interdisciplinary Core Program gives shape to the curriculum.

Founded in 1835, Oglethorpe University is named for the visionary founder of the state of Georgia, James Edward Oglethorpe. His idealism is well captured in the school's motto, *Nescit cedere* (He does not know how to give up), and in its ambition to become the first-choice university for high-achieving students in a region where it faces tough competition from much bigger names. Even as it seeks to boost enrollment, the university remains committed to the Oglethorpe Idea and to connecting students with real-world experiences. Says a junior, "Although few outside of the Southeast have heard of it, this school provides a top-notch education."

Oglethorpe's 118-acre campus is strategically located in Brookhaven, one of Atlanta's most popular inner suburbs, with a picturesque Gothic campus that gives a traditional college feel. The heavily wooded, slightly rolling terrain is perfect territory for walks or long runs, and the beautiful campus has served as the backdrop for several movies and TV shows. Oglethorpe's academic buildings and some residence halls are in the English Gothic style. The Cousins Center for Science and Innovation, featuring laboratory-classrooms and workshops, opened in 2019.

The university's guiding principle is the Oglethorpe Idea—a philosophy based on the conviction that education should help students make both a life and a living. All students take the sequenced, interdisciplinary Core Curriculum program at the same point in their college careers, providing them with a model for integrating information and gaining knowledge.

> "I have never breezed through a class. The academics are so rigorous."

In addition to requiring several liberal arts and sciences courses that help develop students' ability to reason, read, and speak effectively, the core asks them to reflect on and discuss matters fundamental to understanding who they are and what they ought to be.

Oglethorpe's most popular majors—business administration, psychology, biology, and communication studies—are some of its strongest, along with English, accounting, theater, and preprofessional advising for a variety of health and medical fields. Weaker bets are the fine arts and foreign language departments, though the latter does offer courses in Japanese, French, and Spanish. Aspiring engineers may take advantage of dual-degree programs with Auburn, Georgia Tech, and other universities. The school also offers cross-registration with other schools in the Atlanta area.

"I have never breezed through a class," says an art history major. "The academics are so rigorous." Oglethorpe's faculty may be demanding, but they're also friendly and helpful. "They really do care for you intellectually and personally," says one junior. Classes are generally small—55 percent have fewer than 20 students. The new Compass advising program guides students through all aspects of their first year, while the "A_LAB" (Atlanta Laboratory for Learning) coordinates opportunities like internships, research, service, and study abroad. Ten percent of students sign up for a wide variety of study abroad programs, including short-term and faculty-led options.

What's an Oglethorpian like? "We tend to be open-minded, thoughtful, and intellectual," explains one student. Most come from public schools and 70 percent

Website: www.oglethorpe.edu
Location: City Outskirts
Private
Total Enrollment: 1,166
Undergraduates: 1,166
Male/Female: 41/59
SAT Ranges: ERW 570–670, M 540–640
ACT Ranges: 22–27
Financial Aid: 97%
Pell Grant: 43%
Expense: Pr $
Student Loans: 69%
Average Debt: $ $
Applicants: 2,159
Accepted: 58%
Enrolled: 27%
Grad In 6 Years: 48%
Returning Freshmen: 77%
Academics: ✍ ✍ ✍
Social: ☎ ☎ ☎
Q of L: ★ ★ ★ ★
Admissions: (404) 364-8307
Email Address: admission@oglethorpe.edu

Strong Programs:
Business Administration
Psychology
Biology
Communication Studies
English
Accounting
Theater
Premed

are Georgians; 8 percent hail from abroad. "Our campus is pretty small—cliques do form," says a student. Oglethorpe prides itself on being one of the first Georgia colleges to admit African American students, and students report that there's a level of comfort with racial differences. Twenty-four percent of students are African American, 4 percent are Asian American, 11 percent are Hispanic, and 2 percent are multiracial. Socioeconomic diversity is also strong, with 43 percent of freshmen receiving Pell Grants. Notably, every admitted student who completes the FAFSA form receives a $1,000 grant, regardless of financial need. Merit scholarships are also available, averaging $21,500. In an effort to earn more national name recognition, Oglethorpe's new Flagship 50 program pledges to match the in-state tuition rate of each U.S. state's flagship institution for incoming freshmen who meet certain academic requirements.

Fifty-nine percent of Oglethorpe's students choose to live on campus—and most love it. "The dorms are big and have nice furniture," says an accounting major. Most rooms are suites with private bathrooms, and some singles are available. Some students commute to campus; many live in Atlanta—not a college town, but where the wild life is. "Some weekends, everyone stays around and life is great, and then there are others when campus is deserted," one student explains. Fraternities and sororities, which claim 41 percent of the men and 59 percent of the women, respectively, throw parties that draw big numbers. Officially, the campus is dry, but underage students can find alcohol if they try, students agree. The campus celebrates its origins once a year during Oglethorpe Day. Named after a 1742 battle in which James Oglethorpe defeated Spanish troops in southern Georgia, the annual Battle of Bloody Marsh is a tug-of-war game between students and faculty. Each Christmas brings a particularly unique tradition: the Boar's Head Ceremony celebrates a medieval scholar who halted a stampeding wild boar by ramming his copy of Aristotle down the animal's throat.

"We tend to be open-minded, thoughtful, and intellectual."

It's rumored that Oglethorpe barflies do more hopping than Georgia bullfrogs, and bars, clubs, and cafés abound within 10 minutes of campus. Students can also find excitement on the campuses of the dozen or so other colleges in the area or in downtown Atlanta, which one student describes as "the heart of Atlanta and a few minutes from Buckhead, a party district." Atlanta proper offers everything you can imagine—arts, professional sports (including basketball's Hawks, football's Falcons, and baseball's Braves), and entertainment (ride the Great American Scream Machine at Six Flags). Oglethorpe always has a big contingent going to Savannah for St. Patrick's Day and to New Orleans for Mardi Gras, and sunny Florida beckons too.

Oglethorpe's mascot, the Stormy Petrel, is a sea bird that flies in the face of storms. James Oglethorpe was inspired by them on his first visit to Georgia in 1733. Intramurals are important at Oglethorpe, sometimes more so than varsity sports. Still, the men's golf team is a Division III powerhouse, making regular NCAA Tournament appearances, and men's soccer and women's basketball are recent Southern Athletic Association champions. Basketball games against cross-city rival Emory are popular. The Georgia landscape makes possible a plethora of outdoor activities, including hiking at nearby Stone Mountain and boating or swimming in Lake Lanier (named for Georgia poet Sidney Lanier—Oglethorpe Class of 1860).

Though Oglethorpe is still working to achieve widespread name recognition, its diverse group of students get all the attention they need from a caring faculty on a close-knit campus. And being in a large city like Atlanta provides anything else that might be lacking, ranging from great nightlife to internships and postgraduate employment with big-name corporations. In a sea of large Southern state schools, Oglethorpe stands out as a place where students come first.

Overlaps

Berry, Agnes Scott, Birmingham–Southern, Emory, Millsaps, University of Georgia, Georgia State, Kennesaw State

Ohio State University

Student Academic Services Building, 381 West Lane, Columbus, OH 43210

The biggest school in the Big Ten, Ohio State lacks the prestige of a Michigan or a Wisconsin, in part because it competes with two other Ohio publics, Miami and Ohio U, for top students. Operates the mother of all college sports programs that consistently claims multiple national titles. Check out the top-notch honors program. Columbus is a major city and the capital of Ohio.

Envision a campus with 52,000 students and too many opportunities to count. What might come to mind is Ohio State University, located in the heart of the state's capital, offering 15 colleges and 12,000 courses in more than 200 undergraduate majors. If those numbers aren't staggering enough, consider the fact that OSU has 36 varsity sports, 30 intramural sports, nearly 60 sports clubs, and the third largest campus in the nation. It also has an operating budget larger than that of the state of Delaware. While students cite the school's size as both a blessing and a curse, all seem to agree that at OSU, the sky is the limit for those with a desire to sample its academic and other resources.

This megauniversity stands on 1,777 acres in the middle of the city, just two miles north of downtown Columbus. Across the Olentangy River from campus is a teaching and research farm associated with the College of Food, Agricultural, and Environmental Sciences. "One part of the campus maintains a nostalgic air while another is relatively modern," observes a student. The grounds are nicely landscaped, and a centrally located lake provides a peaceful setting for contemplation and a break from all the surrounding activity. OSU's rich array of academic resources includes 15 libraries, all linked electronically, with seven million volumes. The Recreation and Physical Activity Center (RPAC) is the nation's largest facility dedicated to student fitness, wellness, and recreation. Since 2016, eight new residence halls, a dining hall, and a recreation facility have been added to the campus's North district.

> "Students are generally willing to work together and help each other."

The university's commitment to liberal arts learning means all undergrads must satisfy rigorous general education requirements that include courses in math, writing, foreign language, social science, natural science, and arts and humanities. Some of the school's most celebrated departments include business, engineering, neuroscience, dance, and design; political science and education are also strong. OSU bills itself as the place to go for computer graphics and has a supercomputer center to back up its claim. The strong African American and African studies program, which grew out of the civil rights movement of the 1960s, offers the most extensive offering of African languages of any U.S. university. Furthermore, the university has the nation's only programs in welding engineering and geodetic science, the state's only program in medical communications, and the nation's first undergraduate program in data analytics. The majors that enroll the most students include psychology, finance, communication, and biology. A personalized study program enables students to create their own majors.

Website: www.osu.edu
Location: City Center
Public
Total Enrollment: 51,856
Undergraduates: 41,824
Male/Female: 52/48
SAT Ranges: ERW 610–700, M 650–750
ACT Ranges: 27–31
Financial Aid: 70%
Pell Grant: 17%
Expense: Pub $ $
Student Loans: 53%
Average Debt: $ $
Applicants: 47,782
Accepted: 48%
Enrolled: 31%
Grad in 6 Years: 83%
Returning Freshmen: 94%
Academics: ✍ ✍ ✍ ½
Social: ☎ ☎ ☎ ☎
Q of L: ★ ★ ★
Admissions: (614) 292-3980
Email Address: askabuckeye@osu.edu

Strong Programs:
Psychology
Finance
Communication
Biology
Business
Engineering
Neuroscience
Dance

Freshmen may take advantage of numerous first-year programs, including the First Year Success Series covering topics like study skills and career exploration, and pre-enrollment programs like the Leadership Collaborative and Buckeyes First (for first-generation students). Once the academic year is underway, they experience a variety of class formats and sizes, ranging from intimate freshman seminars to large lectures; 22 percent of all undergraduate classes have more than 50 students. Teaching assistants hold smaller recitation sections of large lecture courses and deal on a personal level with students. Class sizes generally whittle down as students continue in their fields of study. At such a large institution, the quality of instruction can vary greatly, and students report this to be the case. But, according to a welding engineering major, "Students are generally willing to work together and help each other in courses that they share."

OSU's honors program allows selected students to learn from top professors in small classes averaging about 25 students each. "The whole system of honors classes, priority scheduling, honors housing, and cocurricular activities really adds to the overall experience at OSU," a biology major says. Twenty percent of undergraduates participate in research opportunities coordinated by the Office of Undergraduate Research and Creative Inquiry. Columbus affords students access to internships with the state government, Fortune 500 companies, and major tech and research organizations, including the IBM Analytics Solutions Lab and Battelle. Roughly 5 percent of students study abroad through 200 programs in more than 70 countries.

> **"The accommodations are adequate and sometimes excellent, depending on the age of the building."**

"Most students are extremely well-mannered, ambitious, open-minded, and obsessed with the Buckeyes," says a loyal sophomore. Seventy-five percent of Ohio State's undergraduates come from Ohio, and most out-of-staters come largely from Illinois, Pennsylvania, California, New York, and New Jersey—many of them lured by one of the most generous merit aid programs of any public university in the country. Eight percent come from foreign countries. The student body is 6 percent African American, 4 percent Hispanic, 7 percent Asian American, and 3 percent multiracial. Several programs aim to attract and retain minority students, including a statewide Young Scholars Program that begins working with students when they start the seventh grade. Qualified students compete for merit scholarships averaging $7,200, and hundreds of athletic scholarships go to talented athletes each year. For incoming, in-state freshmen, the Ohio State Tuition Guarantee freezes tuition, fees, and room and board for four years.

The residence halls, which house 32 percent of the Ohio State masses, are located in three areas: North, South, and Olentangy (that is, those closest to the Olentangy River). Freshmen and sophomores are required to live in residence halls unless they are commuting from home, and freshmen are scattered among each of OSU's 42 residence halls. "The accommodations are adequate and sometimes excellent,

> **"Columbus is a vibrant town."**

depending on the age of the building," says a junior. The South campus section is said to be among the most desirable (it's more sociable, louder, and full of single rooms). A system of variable room rates based on frills (air-conditioning, private bath, number of roommates), as well as a choice of four meal-plan options, give students flexibility in determining their housing costs. "The food at OSU is fantastic," chirps one student. Buckeyes ACT is a comprehensive program intended to combat sexual misconduct and relationship violence on campus.

OSU is a bustling place on weekends. "Social life is never-ending," cheers one student. Various social events are planned by on-campus housing groups—floors, dorms, or sections of the campus. The student union runs eateries, a tavern, movies,

---

The Recreation and Physical Activity Center is the nation's largest facility dedicated to student fitness, wellness, and recreation.

Twenty percent of undergraduates participate in research opportunities coordinated by the Office of Undergraduate Research and Creative Inquiry.

and other activities. Thirteen percent of OSU men and 14 percent of the women go Greek. By one account, these students make the Greek system "a way of life and isolate themselves from the rest of the student population." But with nearly 1,400 other student organizations to choose from, it's hardly difficult for those not interested in the Greek scene to find something to get involved with.

Such a large student market has, of course, produced a strip of bars, fast-food joints, convenience stores, bookstores, vegetarian restaurants, and you-name-its along the edge of the campus on High Street, and downtown Columbus is just a few minutes away. "Columbus is a vibrant town," says a junior. The fine public transportation system carries students not only throughout this capital city but also around the sprawling campus. In addition to the usual shopping centers, restaurants, golf courses, and movie theaters, Columbus boasts a symphony orchestra, a ballet, and professional hockey and soccer teams; OSU's D-Tix program offers students discounted or free tickets to cultural and sporting events. The city's central location in

"Everything stops on game day."

the state makes it easily accessible to Cleveland and Cincinnati. Outdoor enthusiasts can ski in nearby Mansfield, canoe and sail on the Olentangy and Scioto rivers, hike the city's 19 metro parks, or camp in nearby Hocking Hills.

Ohio State operates perhaps the most lavish—and successful—college sports program in the nation. The Buckeyes field 16 men's, 17 women's, and three co-ed varsity teams, from golf to gymnastics to riflery. (A buckeye, incidentally, is a small, shiny nut that falls from Ohio's official state tree.) Recent national champions include women's synchronized swimming, men's volleyball, and men's pistol, and the school has claimed 18 conference championships in the last two years. "Football is somewhat like religion," says one student. "As hard as students may work during the school week, everything stops on game day." Rivalries abound, and nonrecruited students should not expect to make any varsity team as walk-ons. Many take advantage of an ambitious intramural program that boasts a dozen basketball courts and 26 courts for handball, squash, and racquetball.

OSU's sheer size is sometimes overwhelming to be sure, but students here seem to thrive on the challenge and excitement of a big university, not to mention Buckeye spirit. For those who really want to be Buckeyes, be prepared to jump in with both feet and be assertive about your goals. "Knowing what you want is great, but to get it, you'll need to work hard," warns one student. "Because if you want it, there are likely hundreds of other people who want it too."

Overlaps

University of Michigan, U of I at Urbana–Champaign, Penn State, UW–Madison, University of Maryland, Miami University (OH), University of Cincinnati, Purdue

If You Apply To ›

OSU: Early action, regular decision. SATs or ACTs: required. Subject Tests: optional. Accepts the Common Application with supplement.

Ohio University

Chubb Hall 120, Athens, OH 45701

OHIO is roughly one-third the size of Ohio State and plays up its homey feel compared to the cast of tens of thousands in Columbus. The Honors Tutorial College is a draw for top students who want close contact with faculty. Communication and journalism top the list of prominent programs, and residential learning communities are plentiful. OHIO is not in the Big Ten, but the Mid-American Conference has begun to generate excitement.

Website: www.ohio.edu
Location: Small Town
Public
Total Enrollment: 20,824
Undergraduates: 17,714
Male/Female: 47/53
SAT Ranges: ERW 550–640, M 530–620
ACT Ranges: 22–26
Financial Aid: 82%
Pell Grant: 34%
Expense: Pub $ $ $
Student Loans: 67%
Average Debt: $ $
Applicants: 26,263
Accepted: 74%
Enrolled: 21%
Grad in 6 Years: 64%
Returning Freshmen: 80%
Academics: ✍ ✍ ✍
Social: ☎ ☎ ☎ ☎
Q of L: ★ ★ ★
Admissions: (740) 593-4100
Email Address: admissions@ohio.edu

Strong Programs:
Nursing
Communication Studies
Journalism
Psychology
Business
Engineering
Education
Visual Communication

With top-notch programs in journalism, business, and engineering, Ohio University has become a competitive public research institution without shedding its small-town roots. Faculty interests range from dinosaur anatomy to rural diabetes rates. Students here love to hit the town for fun but are quick to hit the books too. Those who choose to attend OHIO receive ample returns, says a senior, including "a quality education, lifelong friends, supportive faculty, and a beautiful campus."

Established in 1804 as the first institution of higher learning in the old Northwest Territory, Ohio University is located in Athens, which lies about 75 miles southeast of Columbus, the state capital, and was named after a certain ancient center of learning in Greece. Encircled by winding hills, the campus features neo-Georgian architecture, tree-lined redbrick walkways, and white-columned buildings all clustered on "greens," which are like small neighborhoods. Long walks are especially nice during the fall foliage season. The Living Learning Center is a multipurpose building with classrooms, meeting rooms, and offices for residential housing staff.

The general education program at OHIO involves a standard set of distribution requirements, plus a senior-level interdisciplinary capstone course. Students enroll in nine undergraduate colleges and one center, and the Scripps College of Communication contains five distinct schools: the schools of journalism, information and telecommunication systems, communication studies, media arts and studies, and visual communication. The most popular majors are nursing, communication studies, journalism, and psychology. The highly regarded journalism program offers tracks in news and information and strategic communication, in addition to an emphasis on learning to use current and emerging technology. Business, engineering, and education are also strengths. The innovative food studies program focuses on global food systems and sustainable health choices.

> "I would like to see the OUPD and student government take sexual assault cases more seriously."

OHIO students work hard, but a communication major says the academic environment is "open and inviting." Freshmen are often taught by full professors with TAs handling study sessions. Classes of 100-plus students do exist, and budget cutbacks have limited access to some courses, but 31 percent of undergraduate classes have fewer than 20 students, and faculty make themselves as available as possible. "The professors are more than willing to help you learn if you are willing to ask," says a junior.

One of the advantages of an Ohio University education, and something that sets the school apart from run-of-the-mill state institutions, is the Honors Tutorial College. Founded in 1972, it's the nation's first multidisciplinary, degree-granting honors program modeled on the tutorial method used in British universities, notably Oxford and Cambridge. Ranked as one of the best programs on campus, it is highly selective: only around 60 to 70 freshmen get in every year. Students take an individualized curriculum in a major field and spend much of their time in one-on-one weekly tutorials with profs. Special opportunities abound for those not in the honors program too. Co-op programs are available for engineering students, and nearly anyone can earn credit for an internship. The Provost's Undergraduate Research Fund provides financial support for undergraduate research, and students showcase more than 650 research and creative projects at the university's annual Student Research Expo. The Office of Global Opportunities offers worldwide destinations for anywhere from one week to one year; 12 percent of students study abroad.

Students in the Honors Tutorial College spend much of their time in one-on-one weekly tutorials with profs.

"Students at Ohio University are accepting, motivated, and enthusiastic about being Bobcats," says a communication studies major. Eighty-six percent of undergraduates are Ohioans, and 2 percent are international. Students express a desire for greater diversity on campus: "While we do have a strong Multicultural Center, they are representing such a small population of students," says a senior. Five percent of undergraduates are African American, 3 percent are Hispanic, 1 percent are Asian American, and 4 percent are multiracial. Thirty-four percent of freshmen are Pell-eligible. The student body's liberal leanings are pronounced in comparison to the conservatism of southeast Ohio. The OHIO Signature Awards program provides merit scholarships and need-based grants for outstanding students, and the athletically gifted can vie for 232 scholarships in 16 sports. The OHIO Guarantee initiative sets fixed rates for each incoming class for tuition, housing, dining, and most other fees that are guaranteed not to increase for four years.

"We all love Athens—it has a special place in our hearts."

Forty-three percent of students live in campus housing, and the university is in the midst of an extensive renovation effort. Five LEED-certified residence halls have been built since 2015. OHIO supports more than 250 residential learning communities, in which 97 percent of first-year students participate. "Learning communities are paired with a professor in your area of study, so you can make connections in your program in your very first class," explains a journalism major. Juniors and seniors usually move to fraternity or sorority houses, nearby apartments, or rental houses. All three campus dining halls have been renovated and receive positive reviews; one location now accepts food stamps. A senior comments, "I would like to see the OUPD and student government take sexual assault cases more seriously."

Five LEED-certified residence halls have been built since 2015.

Campus social life includes guest speakers and performers, plays, midnight movies, and other events. Approximately 12 percent of the men and 16 percent of the women choose to participate in Greek life. The administration has attempted to curtail underage drinking with a strict alcohol policy, and many students complain that OHIO's party-school image overshadows the school's academic quality, but an accounting major concedes that "there is definitely a large party atmosphere." Students look forward to university events such as homecoming and the International Street Fair, as well as the so-called fest season in Athens. "We are known for our street fests," says a journalism major. "Almost every Saturday in the spring has a party on a street." Court Street is dotted with bars and clubs, and the city's fabled Halloween celebration is a huge block party that draws people from all over the Midwest. Volunteer opportunities, such as Habitat for Humanity and a local homeless shelter, are available through the Center for Campus and Community Engagement. Students also love to hike and camp at the nearby state parks and national forest or trek to Columbus for shopping.

Division I sports are a big draw at OHIO. The Bobcats field 16 varsity teams, and football, baseball, and softball are recent conference champions. The Bobcat football team has made nine bowl game appearances in a row. The university also has a nationally ranked forensics program. Twenty-two intramural and 32 club sports draw 21 percent of students; popular choices include basketball, rugby, and crew.

Students say Ohio University has a lot to offer, from quality professors to a vibrant social life and a sense of community. "We are always looking out for one another," says a sophomore, "and we all love Athens—it has a special place in our hearts."

Overlaps

University of Cincinnati, Miami University (OH), Colorado State, Oregon State, University of South Carolina, Ohio State, Bowling Green State, Kent State

Ohio Wesleyan University

South Sandusky Street, Delaware, OH 43015

OWU serves up the liberal arts with a popular side dish of business-related programs. In a region of beautiful campuses, Ohio Wesleyan's is nondescript. Like Denison, OWU is working hard to make its fraternities behave. Attracts middle-of-the-road to liberal students with preprofessional aspirations. Offers a variety of research, travel, and internship programs, notably New York Arts and Wesleyan in Washington.

Website: www.owu.edu
Location: Small Town
Private
Total Enrollment: 1,549
Undergraduates: 1,549
Male/Female: 47/53
SAT Ranges: ERW 530–640, M 510–630
ACT Ranges: 22–28
Financial Aid: 97%
Pell Grant: 29%
Expense: Pr $ $
Student Loans: 70%
Average Debt: $ $ $ $
Applicants: 4,160
Accepted: 71%
Enrolled: 15%
Grad in 6 Years: 70%
Returning Freshmen: 78%
Academics: ✏ ✏ ✏ ½
Social: 🐦 🐦 🐦 🐦 🐦
Q of L: ★ ★ ★
Admissions: (800) 922-8953
Email Address: owuadmit@owu.edu

Strong Programs:
Psychology
Economics
Zoology
Health and Human Kinetics
Business
Communication
Botany
Microbiology

Ohio Wesleyan University is a small school with a big commitment to providing its students with a well-rounded education. Affiliated with the United Methodist Church, OWU hallmarks include strong preparation for graduate and professional school, a solid grounding in the liberal arts, real-world experience, and an emphasis on having fun outside the classroom. Once known for its raucous students, this small university has overcome its hard-partying past and now offers students a complete academic experience.

Situated in the center of the state and on the outskirts of Columbus, OWU's spacious 200-acre campus is peaceful and quaint. Several buildings are on the National Register of Historic Places. The architecture ranges from Greek Revival to colonial to modern, with ivy-covered brick academic buildings on one side of a downtown thoroughfare and dormitories and fraternities on the other side. Stately University Hall, with its majestic spire and bell tower, is the main campus landmark and houses the president's office and the 1,100-seat Gray Chapel, home to the largest Klais organ in the United States. The university recently built four new residential duplexes to house living/learning communities.

> "OWU professors are diverse in both their backgrounds and teaching styles."

To graduate, OWU students must take an introductory first-year course, as well as coursework in the social sciences, natural sciences, arts, humanities, cultural diversity, and foreign language. Students must also pass three mandatory writing classes to sharpen their written communication skills, but these aren't burdensome. In fact, more than a quarter of students find time to complete double or triple majors. The most popular majors are psychology, economics, zoology, and health and human kinetics. Preprofessional education has always been Ohio Wesleyan's forte; the curriculum includes majors in business administration, communication, and data analytics, and the highly popular zoology and botany and microbiology departments are interesting alternatives to the traditional premed route. Dentistry, optometry, veterinary medicine, law, public administration, and theology round out the list of preprofessional offerings. The Woltemade Center for Economics, Business, and Entrepreneurship caters to budding entrepreneurs, and the music and fine arts programs offer both professional and liberal arts degrees. Classes are small, with 76 percent enrolling fewer than 20 students, and a senior says, "OWU professors are diverse in both their backgrounds and teaching styles."

All students participate in the OWU Connection, supplementing their major with interdisciplinary learning, global perspectives, and practical experiences; students may fulfill these expectations by choosing from a number of pathways, such as special courses, study abroad, internships, and independent projects. Students seeking financial support for these endeavors may apply for a Theory-to-Practice Grant. OWU's most prominent cocurricular program is the Sagan National Colloquium, a series of lectures, classes, events, and projects around a theme that unites the liberal and civic arts. The honors program offers qualified students one-on-one tutorials and a chance to conduct research with faculty members in areas of mutual interest. Students who desire careers in public policy and service may choose to pursue a semester-long internship through the Wesleyan in Washington program, while others may join the New York Arts program to spend a semester in Manhattan in apprenticeships with working professionals in the arts and creative industries. Thirty percent of students study abroad, and the university's travel-learning courses, which append one to two weeks of travel to a regular semester-long class, are particularly popular.

More than a quarter of students find time to complete double or triple majors.

Forty-six percent of students come from Ohio and 5 percent are international. Students agree that diversity could be improved but is valued on campus; African Americans make up 10 percent of the student body, Hispanics 6 percent, Asian Americans 3 percent, and multiracial students 5 percent. Liberals and conservatives

"Members of [themed] houses do house projects every semester for the campus."

are well represented on campus and hot topics include racial, gender, and sexual equality. Merit scholarships averaging $23,400 are available for qualified students, and 29 percent of freshmen qualify for Pell Grants.

Eighty-six percent of OWU students live in university-sponsored housing. All but one of the dorms are co-ed, and rooms are mostly doubles or apartment-style, four-person suites. All fraternities offer a residential option, and there is a Panhellenic House for women in sororities. "We have small-living units or SLUs, which are essentially themed houses," says a senior. "The members of these houses do house projects every semester for the campus and are an extremely important part of the OWU community." Students enjoy numerous culinary choices, from 24/7, all-you-can-eat in the main dining hall to snacks from the college grocery store, although the price of meals is a common complaint. A sophomore reports, "We have a Safewalk program at night, so students do not have to walk alone."

"There are many social events on campus to keep students busy and entertained. The school hosts many functions, like laser tag or roller-skating or different events with free food," says a sophomore. Does the buttoned-down seriousness of recent years mean that OWU has forsaken its heritage of raucous partying? Administrators certainly hope so. Part of OWU's commitment to mend its partying ways includes dry rush for all fraternities and an armband policy at parties—and two fraternities have been shut down since 2015 for various violations. Still, Greek membership attracts 36 percent of men and 33 percent of women. "There is definitely pressure to drink, because so many people do it every weekend," says one student. Among OWU's best-loved traditions are homecoming in the fall and Alumni Weekend in the spring, as well as the President's Ball in December.

The Sagan National Colloquium is a series of lectures, classes, events, and projects around a theme that unites the liberal and civic arts.

Delaware is "adorable," says one junior. "There are several small shops and restaurants that are also relatively diverse from Greek to Cajun to just regular pizza and burger joints." The Little Brown Jug, one of harness racing's Triple Crown events, takes place each autumn, bringing thousands of people to the city of Delaware. Two-thirds of students are involved in service, either through mission trips or local service projects like Habitat for Humanity, Delaware Reads, and the Delaware County Humane Society. "Because of the high amount of volunteering that OWU students do in Delaware, we have a fairly good relationship with the town," one student says. Ohio's capital and largest city, Columbus, is only 30 minutes away by car and offers many internship and job opportunities. Lakes, farms, and even ski slopes are within a few hours' drive.

OWU's Division III Battling Bishops are a North Coast Athletic Conference powerhouse. Men's soccer consistently dominates, and men's basketball and men's and women's track and field are recent conference champions. Varsity programs in women's rowing and men's wrestling debuted in the 2018–19 season. Sports fever carries over into intramural and club sports (roughly a third of students take part), and a massive annual game of Capture the Flag begins at 11:00 at night and lasts until the wee hours.

Ohio Wesleyan offers a solid liberal arts education focused not on bells and whistles, but on practical, career-related experience. "Ohio Wesleyan is a place where the education goes well beyond the classroom," says one student. "The family atmosphere and the opportunities that the college provides you enrich the entire college experience."

If You Apply To ›

OWU: Early decision I and II, early action, regular decision. SATs or ACTs: required (optional for students with minimum qualifying GPA). Subject Tests: optional. Accepts the Common Application with supplement.

University of Oklahoma

1000 Asp Avenue, Room 127, Norman, OK 73019

Tops among public universities in attracting National Merit Scholars, OU is strong in engineering and geology-related fields. Check out the nationally recognized Honors College and the growing variety of living/learning options. Football aside, OU has traditionally lacked the visibility of rival UT Austin. Counseling program is a national model.

The University of Oklahoma has more to boast about than its powerhouse football program. Founded in 1890, OU has capitalized on its Great Plains location by cultivating strengths in petroleum and geological engineering, meteorology, and the history and culture of the American West. It has also worked to make itself, in the words of one freshman, "a large university with a small-town vibe" by capping the size of freshman comp courses, housing faculty members in residence halls, and establishing residential colleges for upperclassmen. Couple that with a genuine friendliness among the student body, and it's easy to understand this favorite saying: "Sooner born and Sooner bred, when I die, I'll be Sooner dead!"

Located about 20 miles south of Oklahoma City, OU's 3,500-acre Norman campus features tree-lined streets and predominantly redbrick buildings. Many are historic in nature and built in the Cherokee Gothic or Prairie Gothic style. The Norman campus houses 16 colleges; six medical and health-related colleges are located on the OU Health Sciences Center campus in Oklahoma City, and programs from colleges on both campuses are also offered at OU's Schusterman Center in Tulsa. OU is home to the 10 million artifacts of the Sam Noble Oklahoma Museum of Natural History, which is famous for having the oldest work of art ever found in North America—a lightning bolt painted on an extinct bison skull—and the largest

Apatosaurus on display in the world. Recent campus construction includes the $194 million Cross Neighborhood, a mixed-use housing complex for upperclassmen that includes theater and performance venues, workout facilities, restaurants, and a coffee shop.

OU's general education requirements consist of coursework in symbolic and oral communication (including English composition), natural science, social science, and humanities, as well as an upper-division general education course outside the major, a diversity experience, and a senior capstone experience. All OU freshmen start out in University College before choosing among OU's degree-granting colleges. The most popular majors include nursing, finance,

"[OU is] a large university with a small-town vibe."

petroleum engineering, and psychology. The Gallogly College of Engineering offers aerospace, civil, mechanical, and environmental engineering, among others. The Mewbourne College of Earth and Energy provides resources related to petroleum and geological engineering, geology, and geophysics. In fact, OU's petroleum engineering program ranks among the best in the nation. OU is home to the largest meteorology department in the country and the National Weather Center. In the College of Arts and Sciences, the natural sciences, notably chemistry, are strong. The Price College of Business offers a major in entrepreneurship and venture management. Other well-recognized programs at OU include majors in Western American history, Native American studies, and energy management and a minor in Constitutional studies. The Rainbolt College of Education's rigorous five-year teacher-certification program, Teacher Education Plus, incorporates field experience, mentoring, and instruction from 30 full-time professors.

"I have never had a course that is impossible," comments a psychology major, "but I have also never been in a class that requires little effort." Study groups are common, and students recommend University College's academic tutoring and advising services. OU has worked to address large classes and is one of the nation's few public universities to cap first-year English comp courses at no more than 19 students; overall, 46 percent of undergraduate classes have fewer than 20 students. In the past two decades, increased private support has helped OU more than quadruple its endowed faculty positions, helping the school attract and retain talented professors. "Professors do a great job of engaging students and making the material easy to understand and fun to learn," says one sophomore. OU's newly expanded advising service offers support on topics ranging from financial and mental health issues to life skills.

The rigorous Honors College offers small classes with outstanding faculty members and independent study, along with its own dorm. Top students may also apply for the Scholar-Leadership Enrichment Program, under which well-known lecturers give seminars at the university for academic credit. Students across the university compete for Undergraduate Research Opportunities Program grants of up to $1,000 to support faculty-mentored research and creative work. Study abroad opportunities are

"Eating at the Caf is like eating dinner with the whole freshman class every night."

available in 80 countries, including programs at OU's study centers in Italy, Brazil, and Mexico. Students are often able to apply their financial aid to study abroad, and special scholarships are available for qualified students as well.

A nursing major says OU students create a "lively, energetic, young, and studious" atmosphere on campus. Sixty-three percent of undergraduates hail from the Sooner state, and 5 percent come from abroad. African Americans account for 5 percent, Asian Americans 6 percent, Hispanics 10 percent, American Indians 4 percent, and multiracial students 8 percent. A meteorology major describes the political climate as "open and accepting," with greater diversity of views than one tends to

(continued)

Grad in 6 Years: 67%
Returning Freshmen: 92%
Academics: ✍ ✍ ✍
Social: ☎ ☎ ☎
Q of L: ★ ★ ★
Admissions: (405) 325-2151
Email Address: admissions@ ou.edu

Strong Programs:
Nursing
Finance
Petroleum Engineering
Psychology
Meteorology
Entrepreneurship and Venture Management
Western American History
Native American Studies

Recent campus construction includes the $194 million Cross Neighborhood, a mixed-use housing complex for upperclassmen.

find in the rest of the very red state. Qualified students receive scholarships based on academic merit, with awards averaging $2,500, and there are also 256 athletic scholarships in 12 sports. OU offers a variety of special aid programs aimed at making the university more affordable for low-income students; 24 percent of incoming students are eligible for the Pell Grant.

Thirty-one percent of students live on campus, and the university is making living/learning communities a major focus. The residence halls are mostly occupied by freshmen, who can choose to live on specific academic floors or at the Honors College, and a faculty-in-residence program has been established. New residential colleges for upperclassmen opened in 2017; modeled after those at Yale and Oxford, the residential colleges also serve as living/learning communities. The OU Traditions Square apartment community is another option for upperclassmen, featuring fully furnished units, fitness areas, and other amenities. Come mealtime, one student says, "Eating at the Caf is like eating dinner with the whole freshman class every night." Students say they feel safe on campus and praise programs like OU Advocates and Step In, Speak Out for their efforts in combating sexual assault.

The OU social scene is vibrant and well balanced with on-campus activities and off-campus fun. Greek life sparked controversy in 2015 when two fraternity brothers were videotaped saying a racist chant, but initiatives like a required five-hour training on diversity are helping the university put the scandal behind it. Twenty-five percent of men and 31 percent of women go Greek. Although the dorms and Greek houses are dry, off-campus fraternity parties are the highlight of weekends at OU. The "three-strikes" alcohol policy "has greatly cut down on alcohol incidents" on campus, says one student. Campus Corner, located right across the street from campus, is another source of nightlife, with several restaurants and bars, as well as coffee shops and boutiques. The town of Norman, population 123,000, is Oklahoma's third-largest city, and Oklahoma City is just 20 minutes away. The Big Event sends thousands of students into the community for a day of service each year. Favorite traditions include the University Sing talent show, tailgating, and, of course, the annual road trip to Dallas for the OU–Texas football game.

OU has a reputation for powerhouse Division I athletic teams. Sooner football has brought home the Big 12 Conference title multiple times in recent years. "Every football game day, the town swells to over 500,000 people, and I consider game days an all-day festival," says a letters major. Softball, men's and women's golf, and men's and women's gymnastics captured national titles in 2017 and 2018. Baseball and men's and women's basketball make regular NCAA Tournament appearances too. Recreational and intramural programs attract 22 percent of the undergraduate population, and flag football and basketball are especially popular.

"OU offers the classic college experience," says a senior. Indeed, students at Oklahoma have a lot to brag about. "The educational opportunities are top-notch," says one junior, and "a student can come from anywhere and find that they are part of something special." If you're searching for a school with plenty of spirit and a feeling of family, OU may be worth a look—sooner, rather than later.

In the past two decades, increased private support has helped OU more than quadruple its endowed faculty positions.

OU operates its own study centers in Italy, Brazil, and Mexico.

> "Every football game day, the town swells to over 500,000 people."

Overlaps

UT Austin, Texas A&M, University of Kansas, University of Colorado Boulder, Texas Christian, Oklahoma State, Texas Tech, Baylor

If You Apply To ›

OU: Rolling admissions. SATs or ACTs: required. No Subject Tests. Accepts the Common Application with supplement.

Olin College of Engineering

Olin Way, Needham, MA 02492

Olin opened its doors in 2002 with an innovative project-based curriculum and a commitment to turning out "technologists with soul." Already an elite institution that competes with Caltech and MIT. Every enrolled student gets a hefty merit scholarship. Located in Needham, near Wellesley, on the outskirts of Boston.

In the mid-1990s, leaders of the F. W. Olin Foundation began daydreaming about what "state-of-the-art" engineering education for the 21st century would look like. Two decades and $470 million later they have their answer: the Franklin W. Olin College of Engineering. This elite engineering school aims to turn out Elon Musk-style graduates who are not only technically competent but who can "come up with innovative ideas and products." The curriculum is project-based, and students become as comfortable in the machine shop as in labs and classrooms. The founders also decided that, rather than gradually building up the quality and reputation of their new school, they would invest in excellence from the get-go. By offering every enrolled student a half-tuition scholarship worth more than $100,000 over four years, Olin has succeeded in luring superbright students away from Caltech, MIT, and other engineering highfliers. Sure, the college lacks the rich tradition and reputation for research of more established institutions. But that doesn't seem to bother the nearly 350 students who have latched onto perhaps the best deal in U.S. higher education.

Olin's 70-acre campus is located adjacent to Babson College in a pleasant suburb less than 15 miles west of Boston. The campus design is an innovative blend of the traditional and futuristic. Five buildings curve around a central green space, creating a sense of community and echoing the design of the traditional New England college. The classrooms make use of state-of-the-art instructional media, and there are plenty of meeting and public spaces to encourage the kind of collaboration called for in modern-day engineering.

Olin's innovative curriculum emphasizes science and engineering, as well as business and entrepreneurship. Students choose from three majors—electrical and computer engineering, mechanical engineering, or a self-designed major in engineering with a concentration, such as bioengineering, computing, design, or robotics. In addition, students must complete 30 credits of math and science (10 of which must be in math) and 28 credits of arts, humanities, social sciences (AHS), and entrepreneurship, 12 of which must be in AHS. The course catalog is thin, especially in liberal arts subjects, but students can and do take courses at nearby Babson, Wellesley, and even Brandeis.

"The professors value feedback from the students very highly."

The hands-on nature of Olin's curriculum means that students start out with relatively simple projects, building mechanical systems intended to mimic animals that hop, crawl, and swim (such as a wall-climbing gecko) in the first-semester Design Nature course. They then progress to more sophisticated challenges like Principles of Engineering, in which they build a project involving electronic, mechanical, and software components (such as an automatic cake decorator or a light-seeking flower pot). Concern for "engineering design" is built into every subject. Each student also completes one of two options—SCOPE (Senior Capstone Program in Engineering) or ADE (Affordable Design and Entrepreneurship)—for a yearlong, team-based senior capstone project, in which they apply their knowledge to solving real-world problems, in partnership with outside organizations or communities.

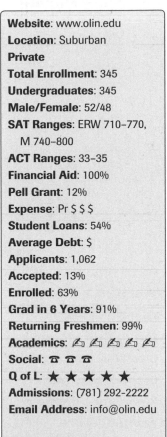

Website: www.olin.edu
Location: Suburban
Private
Total Enrollment: 345
Undergraduates: 345
Male/Female: 52/48
SAT Ranges: ERW 710–770, M 740–800
ACT Ranges: 33–35
Financial Aid: 100%
Pell Grant: 12%
Expense: Pr $ $ $
Student Loans: 54%
Average Debt: $
Applicants: 1,062
Accepted: 13%
Enrolled: 63%
Grad in 6 Years: 91%
Returning Freshmen: 99%
Academics: ✐ ✐ ✐ ✐ ✐
Social: ☎ ☎ ☎
Q of L: ★ ★ ★ ★ ★
Admissions: (781) 292-2222
Email Address: info@olin.edu

Strong Programs:
Engineering
Electrical and Computer Engineering
Mechanical Engineering

Courses are rigorous, but working in teams and across disciplines is the norm for faculty as well as students. "We work very hard, and we work a lot," says one senior, "but there's no real feeling of anything but the friendliest competition." Grading starts after the first semester. Forty-nine percent of classes have fewer than 20 students, and all are led by professors, with whom students are on a first-name basis. Prospective faculty members must go through an extensive interview and audition process, and once hired, none are ever granted tenure. Like their students, many of them have been lured from the likes of MIT because they like the challenge of helping to create what one of them termed "the model of engineering for the future." A sophomore explains, "The professors value feedback from the students very highly—courses are often altered halfway through the semester with suggestions from the students."

First-year students participate in an interactive, weeklong orientation program that includes team-building exercises, meetings, and meals with faculty and advisors, as well as a trip into Boston. The college also encourages students to engage in "Passionate Pursuits" by enabling them to pursue personal interests via faculty-guided projects, for which they receive nondegree academic credit and, often, funding. A sampling of student projects includes rock climbing, guitar making, marathon training, gelato making, and Bhangra (Indian folk dancing). Olin offers several direct-exchange options, as well as preapproved programs at approximately 40 institutions around the world; 28 percent of students study away from campus.

"We're all engineers, but we have social skills!" asserts a senior. Only 12 percent of students hail from Massachusetts, and 8 percent come from abroad. African Americans comprise a mere 3 percent of the student body, Asian Americans 12 percent, Hispanics 9 percent, and multiracial students 8 percent. "Students are generally liberal, but not particularly active in promoting political issues," according to a sophomore, and while students appreciate the balanced male/female ratio as "very uncommon" for an engineering school, many express a desire to see their campus become more racially diverse. To make sure that it selects students who are a good fit for Olin's unique approach to engineering, the admissions office invites 220 applicants to attend one of three "candidates' weekends" in the spring, where they learn about the school, take part in team projects such as building a weight-bearing bridge out of Styrofoam, and go through a 25-minute interview with a team that may include faculty, staff, students, and alumni. About 130 of these students are accepted, and about 30 are placed on a waiting list. In addition to awarding half-tuition scholarships, Olin guarantees to meet 100 percent of any remaining demonstrated financial need for all enrolled domestic students.

All students live on campus in Olin's two residence halls, first-years and sophomores in doubles in West Hall and upperclassmen in either doubles or suites in East Hall. Meal options in Olin's sole dining hall have recently been updated with a change in dining-service provider. Olin operates with a student-designed honor system that makes for unlocked rooms and take-home exams. "You can leave your laptop in the lounge, and it won't walk off," says a senior. Campus security is good and "students do feel physically safe," says one student. A senior adds, "The college continues to refine its [sexual assault] policies at the behest of vocal students and the student government."

When students aren't laboring over the latest Modeling and Simulation assignment, they tend to congregate on campus for fun. "There are parties in the residence halls, and the Student Activities Committee hosts some sort of schoolwide event

Each student completes a yearlong, team-based senior capstone project in partnership with outside organizations or communities.

Prospective faculty members must go through an extensive interview and audition process, and once hired, none are ever granted tenure.

"You can leave your laptop in the lounge, and it won't walk off."

"Olin is pretty quirky, and we like to think we're different—passionate, weird, and doing fun things."

every weekend," says a junior. There are no Greek organizations, and students say the social scene does not revolve around alcohol. "The campus alcohol policies are quite reasonable," says a student, "relying largely on student responsibility." The student orchestra has no conductor—or, as the joke goes, "not even a semicon-ductor." When the campus scene grows tiresome, students often travel to nearby Babson (on foot) or Wellesley (by shuttle bus) to mingle. Aside from frequent visits to Boston, students enjoy road trips to Vermont or the beaches of Maine.

The surrounding town of Needham "isn't a great college town, but does have some good restaurants," says a sophomore. Students take advantage of volunteer opportunities, and the college organizes community-oriented events, such as a Halloween labyrinth for local school children and a charity auction where students offer up everything from original artwork to haircutting services. Campus traditions, however, are few and far between. "I think our healthy disregard for tradition makes life a little more interesting," says a senior, adding, "We do have a traditional spring formal and an academic exposition at the end of each semester."

Although Olin does not offer varsity sports, "a number of pick-up leagues have evolved for soccer, Frisbee, football, and basketball," says a junior, and students are allowed to participate in intramural sports at Babson and Wellesley. Many students join extracurricular project teams that participate in competitions like Formula SAE, SAE Baja, the ASME Human-Powered Vehicle competition, and robotic sailing.

For those who have what it takes, Olin College offers a top-notch engineering degree at a bargain price. Olin students have watched their school grow up and blos-som before their eyes, frequently taking part in shaping its innovative approach to engineering education. Students here value interdisciplinary, project-based instruc-tion, and the importance of "learning to learn," and they graduate inspired to shake up the workforce. As one junior comments, "Olin is pretty quirky, and we like to think we're different—passionate, weird, and doing fun things."

> *Students often travel to nearby Babson (on foot) or Wellesley (by shuttle bus) to mingle.*

Overlaps

MIT, Stanford, Caltech, Harvey Mudd, UC Berkeley, Yale, Carnegie Mellon, Rose–Hulman

If You Apply To ›

Olin: Regular decision. SATs or ACTs: required. Subject Tests: optional. Accepts the Common Application with supplement.

University of Oregon

1585 E 13th Ave, Eugene, OR 97403-1226

A flagship university of manageable size in a great location, UO is notable for its emphasis on the undergraduate educational experience. Liberal arts are more than just a slogan, and programs in the sciences, business, and communication are strong. Splashy sports program plays a big—faculty members say too big—role in shaping the vibrant campus life and culture. Lagging state funding assures that it lacks the academic range of larger flagship universities.

Blend two vegetarians, one track star, one fraternity brother, two tree huggers, three hikers, and one conservative. What have you got? Ten UO students. Sure, the joke's hokey, but its offbeat humor is typical of the laid-back, slightly eccentric attitude that prevails here in Eugene, where bicycling is the main form of transportation, recycling is a requirement, and littering is déclassé. As the most accessible of the West Coast flagship universities, the University of Oregon attracts brainy students who are proud of their quirky ways.

Website: www.uoregon.edu
Location: Small City
Public
Total Enrollment: 20,920
Undergraduates: 17,788
Male/Female: 46/54

*First-Year Interest
Groups take three
courses together
around a common
theme, such as Edible
History and Science
for Social Change.*

UO's buildings date from as early as 1876 and are surrounded by the university's lush 295-acre arboretum-like campus, which boasts more than 4,000 trees representing nearly 500 species. Most academic buildings were built before World War II and represent a blend of classical styles, including Georgian, Second Empire, Jacobin, and Lombardic. In a move to make undergraduate life more pleasant, major renovations were recently completed to the Student Recreation Center and the Erb Memorial Union. Construction is underway on the ultramodern Knight Campus for Accelerating Scientific Impact, a multiphase project made possible by a $1 billion capital campaign (including a $500 million donation from UO alum and Nike cofounder Phil Knight and his wife). The first phase, a 160,000-square-foot, glass-and-steel facility, is expected to open to students and researchers in 2020.

> "[UO students] find what they love and work hard for it."

While a liberal arts emphasis underlies Oregon's entire curriculum, general education requirements are not highly structured. The calendar is composed of quarters, and in addition to distribution requirements in several disciplines, students must take two courses exploring American or international culture, identity, pluralism, and tolerance. Each summer, the university offers IntroDUCKtion to new students, featuring opportunities for orientation, registration, and advisement. First-Year Interest Groups (FIGs) help new students develop close working and advising relationships with faculty members and other students. Each FIG consists of 20 freshmen who take three courses together around a common theme, such as Edible History and Science for Social Change.

Due to a decline in state funding, UO has a relatively modest array of academic offerings for a major research university and a higher ratio of tenured faculty members to students than many of its peer institutions. UO's professional schools—journalism, design, education, law, business, and music and dance—are highly regarded, and considered to be more accessible to entry-level students than similar programs elsewhere. The most popular majors include business administration, journalism, general social science, psychology, and economics. The College of Design is the home of Oregon's only accredited degrees in architecture, landscape architecture, and interior architecture. In the College of Arts and Sciences, the science departments enjoy advanced resources and offer many opportunities for research in fields like nanotechnology, optogenetics, and neuropsychology. In keeping with Oregon's eco-friendly reputation, the Green Chemistry Laboratory and Instrumentation Center was the first in the nation to use nontoxic materials in experiments. Pine Mountain Observatory, a field-study resource for astronomy and physics students located high in the Cascade Mountains, and the Oregon Institute of Marine Biology give students a chance for hands-on studies in their major.

> "[Every home football game] thousands of students whoop and holler and scream their lungs out."

"I would say that the academic climate at the University of Oregon is collaborative yet challenging," says an accounting major. "Above all else, it is what you make of it." Thirty-eight percent of classes have fewer than 20 students. The quality of instruction varies, and it's not uncommon to find teaching assistants handling some of the teaching duties, but a math major says most professors are knowledgeable and will "check in on students' progress." A senior adds that it is possible to find "supportive and encouraging mentors" among the faculty.

Highly motivated undergraduates may apply to the Clark Honors College, a small liberal arts college with its own four-year curriculum that includes a senior thesis and opportunities for exclusive research assistantships. The student-run community internship programs provide credit for community volunteer work. About a quarter of undergrads study or complete internships abroad during their time at UO, and more than 250 programs are offered in more than 90 countries.

UO students "find what they love and work hard for it," says a journalism major. Only 53 percent of undergraduates are native Oregonians, largely because the university has increasingly relied on revenue from full-paying outsiders to balance the budget. "There are a lot of people from California," says a freshman, and "a lot of artsy hipsters." There is also a noticeable contingent of international students, who account for 12 percent of the student body. Asian Americans comprise 6 percent, African Americans 2 percent, Hispanics 12 percent, and multiracial students 8 percent. "The political climate is skewed liberal all across campus," notes a sophomore. Numerous merit scholarships worth an average of $6,100 are awarded to qualified students, as are about 350 athletic scholarships in 20 sports. Twenty-four percent of freshmen are eligible for the Pell Grant.

Twenty-one percent of UO students live in the university's 10 residence halls, which are a mix of traditional halls and modern high-rises. Freshmen are required to reside on campus. A student says of the rooms, "They are pretty small, but I love the cozy feeling." There are a number of thematic living arrangements, including the Global Scholars Hall, which provides an immersive language environment for students learning Chinese, Japanese, French, German, and Spanish, as well as the Clark Honors College. Student can choose from five meal plans, and nine dining facilities serve up fresh, diverse menus. "The food on campus is actually amazing," says a sophomore. Regarding sexual violence on campus, a junior comments, "I think that the university is working hard to create a safer campus community," citing several administrative initiatives and student groups dedicated to the issue.

Sixteen percent of UO men and 21 percent of the women join Greek organizations, which provide living space, interesting social diversions, and a wealth of leadership and community service opportunities. "The university plays host to a variety of concerts, culture nights, film viewings, guest lecturers, sporting events, and dances," a journalism major says. Students 21 and over may have alcohol in their rooms, but only with the doors closed. A junior says, "There are large parties happening around campus most nights of the week for people who would like to spend their time on such activities," but there is no pressure to do so. University Day, which happens each spring, offers students, faculty, and staff an opportunity to clean up campus. Other major events include the Willamette Valley Music Festival, where big-name artists perform for students on campus, and, of course, every home football game, where "thousands of students whoop and holler and scream their lungs out" for their Ducks.

Eugene is "the best college town ever! Everything about Eugene is based around the Ducks!" one student raves. Popular hangouts include Taylor's and Rennie's Landing. The one drawback to all this fun is Oregon's weather: it rains and rains. "Eugene gets some sunny days in early fall, late spring, and summer," reports a veteran. Still, the moist climate rarely dampens enthusiasm for the many expeditions available through the university's well-coordinated outdoor program, from rock climbing to skiing. An hour to the west, the rain turns to mist on the Pacific Coast; an hour to the east, it turns to snow in the Cascade Mountains.

UO's official mascot is a whimsical yellow-and-green likeness of Donald Duck. The athletic program is financially independent of the university, and the Ducks continue to dominate their Division I athletic rivals. The women's program made NCAA history in 2017 by becoming the first to win national titles in women's cross-country, indoor track, and outdoor track in the same season—the "triple crown." Football, men's golf and basketball, women's acrobatics and tumbling, and softball have had impressive successes as well. Duck fans love cheering on their teams,

Pine Mountain Observatory and the Oregon Institute of Marine Biology give students a chance for hands-on studies in their major.

"[Eugene is] the best college town ever!"

UO's official mascot is a whimsical yellow-and-green likeness of Donald Duck.

Overlaps

University of Arizona, CU Boulder, University of Iowa, University of Georgia, University of Maryland, Cal Poly–San Luis Obispo, University of Washington, UCLA

especially during the Civil War football game against Oregon State, a rivalry that has been playing out since 1894. Intramurals are another time-honored pastime here, and roughly 43 percent of students take part.

A recent University of Oregon Orientation Week T-shirt sported a picture of a duck and a simple exhortation: "Let your future take flight." UO offers ample opportunities for those with lofty ambitions to succeed. Indeed, UO's accessible academics, expert faculty, and abundance of social activities reveal that UO is all it's quacked up to be.

If You Apply To ›

UO: Early action, regular decision. SATs or ACTs: required. Subject Tests: optional (required for homeschooled students). Accepts the Common Application with supplement.

Oregon State University

Corvallis, OR 97331

The biggest dilemma facing the typical 18-year-old Oregonian is whether to be a Beaver or a Duck. Choose Duck and hang with the ex-hippies in cosmopolitan Eugene. Choose Beaver and get small-town life with professional programs in business, engineering, and life sciences in Corvallis. Strong STEM focus, along with global emphasis.

Website: www.oregonstate.edu
Location: Small City
Public
Total Enrollment: 21,729
Undergraduates: 18,394
Male/Female: 54/46
SAT Ranges: ERW 540–650, M 530–650
ACT Ranges: 22–28
Financial Aid: 60%
Pell Grant: 25%
Expense: Pub $ $
Student Loans: 58%
Average Debt: $ $
Applicants: 14,888
Accepted: 79%
Enrolled: 33%
Grad in 6 Years: 65%
Returning Freshmen: 85%
Academics: 🖊 🖊 🖊
Social: ☎ ☎ ☎
Q of L: ★ ★ ★
Admissions: (541) 737-4411
Email Address: osuadmit@ oregonstate.edu

Once known as Moo U, there's much more to Oregon State University than fruits and vegetables. The most accessible West Coast public university, OSU is strong in many departments, including biotechnology, forestry, and engineering. It's also one of just two universities in the country with land, sea, space, and sun grant designations. Research opportunities and co-op work experiences abound, especially for students in STEM fields. Says one satisfied student, "Anyone would be lucky to be at Oregon State."

Located in the pristine but rainy Willamette Valley, OSU's campus is a mix of older, ivy-covered buildings and more modern structures. In addition to the 500-acre main campus, OSU owns 13,000 acres of forestland near campus and numerous agricultural tracts throughout Oregon. Thousands of azalea and rhododendron bushes welcome springtime on campus with their colorful blooms, and summers are unfailingly sunny. A bevy of newly renovated, LEED-certified facilities have been added over the past few years, and the $65 million Oregon Forest Science Complex opened in 2018.

"The best way to describe students at Oregon State? Two words: 'Go Beavs!'"

OSU's extensive Baccalaureate Core requires courses in a variety of areas, including skills; perspectives; and difference, power, and discrimination. One writing-intensive course is required as well. Perhaps the core's most innovative facet is its "synthesis" requirement, in which upperclassmen take two interdisciplinary courses on global issues in the modern world. The level of academic pressure varies by major, but even those in the various honors programs say they don't feel overworked. Although classes can be large, a senior says, "Professors make sure to get to know each individual and work with them, so that we as students gain the most from our education."

OSU's College of Liberal Arts ranks with business and engineering as the largest on campus, but there are many more preprofessionals than poets. With the exceptions of history and English, the liberal arts—including such standard fare as sociology, economics, and philosophy—play second fiddle to more practical, technical fields. The business school offers some of the finest business-related programs in the state, and majors in forestry, natural resources, marine biology, and engineering are strong drawing cards. Even though agriculture doesn't lure as many students as it used to, those who do come find excellent programs, including agricultural sciences, animal sciences, and food science and technology. Computer science, human development and family sciences, public health, and psychology are among the most popular majors.

Students in the Honors College participate in small seminars with top professors and hands-on research, culminating in a senior thesis. The university's small-town location makes it difficult to find much career-oriented part-time employment, and internships are hard to come by. (OSU operates on a quarter system.) Students in almost all majors, however, can participate in the cooperative education program, which allows them to alternate terms of study with several months of work in a relevant job. About a quarter of undergraduates get involved in research. The 9 percent who choose a semester abroad may select from 200 study abroad programs or research and internship opportunities in 70 countries around the world.

"The best way to describe students at Oregon State? Two words: 'Go Beavs!'" cheers a senior. Indeed, school spirit runs high on this friendly campus. Sixty-nine percent of undergraduates are from Oregon, and 9 percent hail from foreign countries. One percent are African American, 10 percent are Hispanic, 8 percent are Asian American, and 7 percent are multiracial. The Office of Diversity and Cultural Engagement sponsors several cultural resource centers, conferences, social justice retreats, and other diversity initiatives to support students from underrepresented backgrounds. Most Oregon Staters are conservative and "very all-American—not cowboys and not city slickers, but very middle-of-the-road in all respects," a business major observes. Merit scholarships averaging $5,000 are awarded annually, as are 379 athletic awards in 17 sports. Twenty-five percent of freshmen qualify for Pell Grants, and the Bridge to Success program allows roughly 3,000 in-state students per year to attend the university tuition-free.

Freshmen are expected to live in college housing, though fraternity pledges have the option of living in their houses. Co-ed and single-sex options are available in the dorms, which house 17 percent of the students. "I loved living in my hall because it is where I made many friends; however, I much prefer living off campus because it is not as expensive," a student says. In addition to standard rooming situations, eight living/learning communities in areas like engineering, health, and mindfulness are also options. "The meals in the dining facilities are good with lots of variety," says a kinesiology major, and campus security gets good reviews too.

"Most social events happen on campus or close to campus," says a student. Ten percent of the men and 16 percent of the women join fraternities and sororities, and Greek events offer a social scene but don't dominate campus life. Administrative efforts to make Greek parties safer include a ban on hard alcohol, a training program for students who wish to serve as sober party monitors, and a medical amnesty policy. Favorite campus traditions include the All-University Sing (featuring musical numbers staged by fraternity and sorority members) and the annual Fall Festival. A popular student activity is complaining about the Willamette Valley weather: "People in the valley don't tan, they rust," warns one native. One reward for all the rain, however, is the abundance of flowers that bloom in every color and shape each May. Many students consider Corvallis a good-size town, with enough bars and cheap theaters to cater to their entertainment needs. Beautifully rugged beaches are less than an hour away, and some of the best skiing in the country can be found

(continued)

Strong Programs:
Computer Science
Human Development and
   Family Sciences
Public Health
Psychology
Business
Forestry
Engineering
Agricultural Sciences

Oregon State is one of just two universities in the country with land, sea, space, and sun grant designations.

"People in the valley don't tan, they rust."

About a quarter of undergraduates get involved in research.

in the Cascade Mountains, two hours east. Hiking and rafting are nearby too, and camping on the coast provides more good times.

Cheering for Beavers athletic teams demands a lot of students' time and energy here, as does participation in the well-rounded intramural and club sports programs. Benny Beaver, the school's former (and somewhat benign) mascot, has been replaced by a more aggressive beaver that students have dubbed the "angry beaver." The baseball team took home the national title in 2018, and recent Pac-12 conference champs include women's basketball and men's wrestling. The men's basketball team has one of the top-10 winningest programs of all time among Division I schools. As for rivalries, one student says, "Civil War games between OSU and U of Oregon are a big part of every season."

While still a leader in agricultural education, OSU has expanded its reputation as a university that prepares students for successful futures in ever-evolving scientific, technical, and business fields. OSU doesn't scream for attention. Instead, it's content to be a "nice" college, in "a safe and pleasant little town," where professors are "helpful" and, even if everyone doesn't know your name, they'll let you stand under their umbrella whenever the skies open up.

Overlaps

Colorado State, Washington State, University of Nebraska–Lincoln, Oklahoma State, Montana State, University of Oregon, University of Washington, Cal Poly–San Luis Obispo

If You Apply To ›

Oregon State: Early action, regular decision. SATs or ACTs: required (SAT essay recommended). Subject Tests: optional. Accepts the Common Application. Applicants have the option of identifying their gender, preferred name, and sexual orientation.

University of the Pacific

3601 Pacific Avenue, Stockton, CA 95211

The university's name dates from a time when there were no other universities near the Pacific. Still the only small, independent university in California north of L.A., it offers an eye-popping array of programs for an institution its size, including business, engineering, pharmacy, and education. The student body is just as diverse.

Website: www.pacific.edu
Location: Suburban
Private
Total Enrollment: 5,419
Undergraduates: 3,447
Male/Female: 45/55
SAT Ranges: ERW 540–650, M 530–680
ACT Ranges: 22–30
Financial Aid: 73%
Pell Grant: 33%
Expense: Pr $ $
Student Loans: 67%
Average Debt: $ $ $
Applicants: 13,064
Accepted: 65%

University of the Pacific was established in 1851 by Methodist ministers as California's first institution of higher education. Perhaps that's why it looks like 175 acres of New England plunked down in California wine country. With its stately combination of redbrick and ivy, it could be mistaken for an East Coast liberal arts college. But instead of a blanket of snow, Pacific is surrounded by the lush greenery of the San Joaquin Valley. On campus, this increasingly competitive bastion of learning offers its 3,400 undergrads a solid and diverse academic program and scores of things to do when not hitting the books.

With majestic evergreens and flowering trees, Pacific is home to six undergraduate schools and the College of the Pacific, the university's liberal arts and sciences division. There is also a school of law in Sacramento and a superlative school of dentistry in San Francisco. A biological sciences building provides 56,000 square feet of space for the biological sciences program, and a four-story, apartment-style residence hall recently opened.

The university-wide general education program has three components: the Pacific seminars, the breadth program, and fundamental skills. All students complete three Pacific Seminars, starting with a two-course sequence (What Is a Good Society? and

Topical Seminars on a Good Society) in their first year, followed by What Is an Ethical Life? in their senior year. In addition, students must complete six to nine courses in the breadth program and must demonstrate competence in writing, math, and reading. Strong departments abound in the schools of engineering, pharmacy, education, and business (with specialty concentrations in arts and entertainment management, business law, and entrepreneurship). The sciences, English, communication, and international studies are also strong. A freshman says, "The best academic departments tend to be prepharmacy, predentistry, and the health, exercise, and sport science programs, because they do an astounding job of preparing students for their future professions." Students may also design their own majors with faculty approval.

Students report that studying accounts for anywhere from 10 to 40 hours a week, but the atmosphere is relaxed. "Instead of students who do whatever it takes to be at the head of the class, everyone works together," says an international relations major. Fifty-seven percent of classes have fewer than 20 students, and teaching assistants teach labs only. "The faculty members are very accessible and always willing to help," says one sophomore. The university guarantees graduation in four years (assuming the student follows all university guidelines), or it will pay for the extra schooling. Students are also guaranteed to have the opportunity for some type of experiential learning, and a number of internship and co-op programs are available. An extensive study abroad program offers 200 choices in dozens of countries; international studies majors are required to participate.

"The faculty members are very accessible and always willing to help."

Pacific students are "genuinely nice and friendly," says one freshman. Eighty-seven percent of undergraduates are California residents, and 6 percent hail from foreign countries. As for ethnic diversity, Asian Americans account for 36 percent, African Americans 3 percent, Hispanics 20 percent, and multiracial students 7 percent. The school is middle-of-the-road to conservative, though politics in general play a small role on campus. "We're very open to all political, religious, sexual orientations, etc.," says a senior. Though not unusually expensive by national standards, the university price tag can seem steep when compared to the University of California system. So Pacific has stepped up efforts to compete, using merit scholarships, which average $14,000 annually, as well as athletic scholarships in several sports. One-third of freshmen qualify for Pell Grants.

Freshmen and sophomores are required to live on campus, and 44 percent of all undergrads make their home on campus. "Housing is generally pretty clean and the sense of community is felt all across the halls," says one student. With three meal plans, two dining halls, and one fast-food-type facility, residents are well fed. A senior reports, "Campus security is pretty effective."

"The social life happens on campus, whether it is at sporting events, going to events for different fraternities, sororities, or clubs, or simply playing games out on the UC Lawn," says a student. Four percent of the men and 6 percent of the women go Greek, and the majority of Greek houses are designated substance-free. "I only recently attended my first party where there was alcohol," one student says. "There was no pressure for me to drink." Students caught violating the alcohol policy must take an online course in alcohol education. Other social opportunities are offered by the Residence Hall Association, intramural and club sports, conservatory and drama/dance programs, campus movies, and more than 150 student clubs. Annual campus festivities include the Lip Sync competition during homecoming, the popular Fall Festival, Diversity Week, and International Spring Festival. For weekend excitement, Pacific students love to hit the road: within about two hours, they can be skiing, shopping in San Francisco, or surfing in Monterey. Stockton itself

"You instantly feel like you are surrounded by very friendly and loving people."

(continued)

Enrolled: 11%
Grad in 6 Years: 66%
Returning Freshmen: 85%
Academics: ✍ ✍ ✍
Social: ☎ ☎ ☎
Q of L: ★ ★ ★ ★
Admissions: (209) 946-2211
Email Address: admission@ pacific.edu

Strong Programs:
Engineering
Prepharmacy
Education
Business
English
Communication
International Studies
Health, Exercise, and Sport Science

University of the Pacific looks like 175 acres of New England plunked down in California wine country.

The university guarantees graduation in four years, or it will pay for the extra schooling.

(population 310,000) offers shopping and plenty of fast-food joints, as well as numerous volunteer opportunities.

Pacific dropped its football program in 1995, but the Tigers field a number of other competitive Division I teams. The women's volleyball team makes regular NCAA Tournament appearances, and men's and women's basketball, water polo, and golf are also strong. The university also sponsors a solid speech and debate team.

Pitted against the state's immense public university system, Pacific stands out for offering major university opportunities in a small-college setting. The administration is striving to place more focus on its student body, which is becoming more top-notch and diverse. A political science major says, "When you come here, you instantly feel like you are surrounded by very friendly and loving people."

If You Apply To ›

Pacific: Early action, regular decision. SATs or ACTs: required. Subject Tests: recommended. Accepts the Common Application.

University of Pennsylvania

1 College Hall, Philadelphia, PA 19104

An Ivy League institution in name, Penn has more in common with places like Georgetown and Northwestern—where the liberal arts share center stage with preprofessional programs. At Penn, that means business, engineering, and nursing. Penn has something else other Ivies don't: school spirit. It's a good idea to apply early decision if Penn is your first choice.

Website: www.upenn.edu
Location: City Center
Private
Total Enrollment: 20,259
Undergraduates: 9,782
Male/Female: 49/51
SAT Ranges: ERW 700–770,
 M 720–790
ACT Ranges: 32–35
Financial Aid: 43%
Pell Grant: 13%
Expense: Pr $ $ $ $
Student Loans: 27%
Average Debt: $
Applicants: 40,413
Accepted: 9%
Enrolled: 65%
Grad in 6 Years: 96%
Returning Freshmen: 98%
Academics: ✍ ✍ ✍ ✍ ✍
Social: ☎ ☎ ☎
Q of L: ★ ★ ★

Benjamin Franklin would be proud of the way his university has surged in recent years. Once relegated to the bottom of the Ivy League (and occasionally confused with Penn State), the University of Pennsylvania is now the first choice for top students who see no conflict between high-level academics and having a life. The undergraduate College of Arts and Sciences—once on the university's back burner—is now central not only to its undergraduates, but also to three other undergraduate schools that tap into its programs and course offerings. Penn established the nation's first medical school, the first business school, the first journalism curriculum, and the first psychology clinic, and is a pioneer in service learning and service research. In her inaugural address, a former president paid tribute to Franklin as "the ultimate visionary and pragmatist. Franklin thought education should be for the body as well as for the soul—that it should enable a graduate to be a breadwinner as well as a thinker, that it should produce socially conscious citizens as well as conscientious bankers and traders."

"Penn" is the university's traditional informal name. In recent years "UPenn" has also emerged as a nickname; although this alternative is used more by outsiders than by students themselves, it is gaining currency. Penn's campus is situated in a tree-shaded, self-contained, 299-acre nest called University City, which is adjacent to downtown Philadelphia. Its 217 buildings range from Victorian Gothic to postmodern. There are very old structures, such as College Hall, and newer ones, such as Wharton's Huntsman Hall and Skirkanich Hall, home to Penn's bioengineering programs. Recent construction projects include an overhaul of Hill College House, home to first-year students.

Penn's reputation is primarily wrapped up with its 12 graduate schools, especially the prestigious Wharton School of Business; the Annenberg School of Communication; and the well-known law, medical, and veterinary schools. Three of the four undergraduate schools—engineering, nursing, and the undergraduate division of Wharton—are also professionally oriented and offer an education that's hard to beat anywhere. The undergraduate College of Arts and Sciences (a.k.a. "The College") has come into its own in recent years and provides students with high-quality instruction as well as the chance to run into a Nobel laureate here and there.

Finance is among the most popular undergrad majors, followed by economics and nursing. Penn's anthropology department ranks with Chicago's as perhaps the best in the country, while the management and technology program is also outstanding. Penn has earned applause in the field of cognitive and computer sciences because of its special program linking psychology, linguistics, and computers with philosophy. Another popular crème-de-la-crème interdisciplinary major, biological basis of behavior, combines psychology, biology, and anthropology. Students are allowed to design their own individualized majors, and they can hop from school to school—undergraduate or graduate—in doing so. Students in the Vagelos Program in Life Science and Management pursue studies in both the College of Arts and Sciences and the Wharton School, exposing them to research and development, biotech start-ups, managed care, and other related issues.

At the Wharton School, the Joseph Wharton Scholars program (named after the 19th-century industrialist who founded the school) emphasizes breadth in the arts and sciences. Another added plus that comes with a Penn undergraduate education is the opportunity for early entry (submatriculation) into the university's graduate programs. Juniors may apply to any master's program (continuing into the Wharton M.B.A. program is especially popular) and begin completing graduate requirements during their senior year. Penn offers no co-op programs and discourages full-time internships for credit, remaining true to the Ivy League belief that learning should be based in academic settings. Those who want to explore more exotic classrooms may study abroad at Penn's programs in Italy, Scotland, Japan, China, Nigeria, and Russia, among others. Freshmen are

"Most departments have fantastic professors who are top in their field."

encouraged (but not required) to participate in a seminar program that explores various areas of academic interest, and also in the Penn Reading Project, which involves student and faculty discussion of a common text.

Sixty-eight percent of undergraduate classes have fewer than 20 students, and while professors at Penn take their research responsibilities seriously, they are surprisingly accessible to freshmen. "Most departments have fantastic professors who are top in their field," says one student, "and have developed a great teaching style." The academic program at Penn is well supplemented by its huge and busy library, which houses more than six million volumes.

Despite all the preprofessional programs, Penn never lets its undergraduates stray too far from the liberal arts. The general education requirements in the College of Arts and Sciences mandate that students take at least one course in each of seven "sectors": society; history and tradition; arts and letters; living world; physical world; humanities and social sciences; and natural sciences and mathematics. Students must also complete one course in each of six "foundational approaches" areas, including writing, foreign language, quantitative data analysis, formal reasoning and analysis, cross-cultural analysis, and cultural diversity in the U.S. Strict academic policies and demanding professors exacerbate the academic pressure. "Penn is a competitive university," says one nursing major, "but is also intellectually stimulating."

Thousands of faculty and students give expression to Benjamin Franklin's adage that service to humanity is "the great aim and end of all learning." To wit, Penn is

(continued)

Admissions: (215) 898-7507
Email Address: info@ admissions.upenn.edu

Strong Programs:
Business
Engineering
Nursing
Finance
Economics
Anthropology
Management and Technology
Cognitive Science

Penn is a pioneer in service learning and service research.

Juniors may apply to any master's program (continuing into the Wharton M.B.A. program is especially popular).

a national leader in service learning and service research. Students work with local public school students as part of academic coursework in disciplines as diverse as history, anthropology, and mathematics. There are tons of opportunities to volunteer—from tutoring to Big Brothers Big Sisters to the Ronald McDonald House. "Penn students have historically been extremely involved with the local community and have taken the experiences they've had in the neighborhood with them to the real world," an economics and history double major says.

Nineteen percent of Penn undergraduates are Pennsylvania natives, and 13 percent are international. "There are all kinds of people with all kinds of personalities,

Freshmen participate in the Penn Reading Project, which involves student and faculty discussion of a common text.

"Penn students have historically been extremely involved with the local community."

interests, and backgrounds," says a student, "all of which makes Penn a vibrant place to live and study." Seven percent of undergrads are African American, 10 percent are Hispanic, 21 percent are Asian American, and 5 percent are multiracial. Penn admits students regardless of need—and meets full demonstrated need with loan-free financial aid packages—but does not offer any merit or athletic scholarships. Outreach programs target hundreds of schools and thousands of students from low- and middle-income families in an effort to improve socioeconomic diversity.

Fifty-two percent of all undergraduates live on campus and enjoy a wide range of living options in Penn's 12 co-ed "College Houses." The Quad, home to three of the 12 houses, seems to be the hot spot, described as "well maintained and incredibly comfortable." There are living/learning programs in most College Houses for those who are interested in the arts, Asian studies, etc., and want to be surrounded by others with the same interests. Some upperclassmen reluctantly move to the high-rises across campus that look like "prefabricated, 24-story monsters" but do offer more space, as well as kitchens. Most head to nearby off-campus houses and apartments—"for the freedom, plus it's a lot cheaper," a junior says. Meal plans are required for freshmen, and the food isn't all that bad for institutional fare. "The best kept secret on campus is the kosher cafeteria," a finance and management major says.

Undergraduates may work hard during the week, but in contrast to most Ivy League achievers, they leave it behind them on weekends. "Social life at Penn centers around frats," a junior explains. "Parties

"There are all kinds of people with all kinds of personalities, interests, and backgrounds."

freely serve alcohol to underage drinkers," according to another student, despite school policies dictating otherwise. More than two dozen fraternities attract 30 percent of the men and provide "your basic meat-market scene"; sororities claim 29 percent of the women. The frats' exclusive claim to the houses along Locust Walk, the main artery on campus, has been undone: after some controversy, it was determined that non-Greeks, too, must be able to live at the social nexus of the campus. Two big annual events at Penn are Spring Fling, a weekend "nothing short of absolutely incredible fun," and Hey Day, a century-old tradition where juniors, donning Styrofoam hats and thin wooden canes, march down Locust Walk to officially become seniors, taking chomps out of each other's hats as they go.

Hey Day is a century-old tradition where juniors, donning Styrofoam hats, march down Locust Walk to officially become seniors.

Downtown Philadelphia is only a few minutes away by foot, Lyft, or public transportation. Penn is located in the western part of town, once considered to be dangerous, but nowadays, as a senior explains, "There are a wealth of cultural resources at the tip of your fingers, and more and more students are able to find jobs in the Philadelphia area after graduation." Students frequent sporting events, malls, South Street ("a miniature Greenwich Village"), and, of course, myriad bars and dancing joints. The city is home to several other colleges, and a student says, "There is a lot of social intermingling among the schools, and university students dominate the nightlife." Road trips include New York City, Washington, D.C., Atlantic City, and even Maine and Florida.

Penn is more sports-minded than most Ivy schools, and Division I football is the biggie. The team has grown accustomed to sitting on the top of the Ivy League and has sparked a widespread boost in school spirit. Tickets are free for those with a student ID. The Penn–Princeton rivalry is always a crowd-pleaser. At the end of the third quarter of each home game, everyone in

> "There are a wealth of cultural resources at the tip of your fingers."

the stands begins belting out the lyrics of the Penn fight song, and when they get to "Here's a toast to dear old Penn," the students shower the field with burnt toast, "a moment that makes all Penn students proud," according to a senior. Aside from football, solid Quakers teams include men's and women's basketball, men's lacrosse, and women's field hockey and fencing. A bevy of intramurals and 36 club sports bring thousands of less-seasoned athletes out to play each year, and all types of athletes benefit from the swanky track and weight-lifting facilities. Each spring, Penn hosts the prestigious Penn Relays, a track-and-field extravaganza that attracts the nation's best track athletes.

While its students work hard, Penn lacks the intellectual intensity of some of the other top Ivies, and you can detect preprofessional undercurrents. But most accept it for what it is: a first-rate university where you can live a relatively normal life. Penn is one Ivy League university where no one apologizes for having fun. Says one sophomore, "There is a great balance between academics and social activities, which is rare in such highly competitive institutions."

Overlaps

Brown, Columbia, Cornell University, Harvard, Stanford, Yale, Georgetown, Northwestern

If You Apply To ›

Penn: Early decision, regular decision. SATs or ACTs: required. Subject Tests: recommended (varies by program). Accepts the Common Application with supplement.

Pennsylvania State University

201 Old Main, University Park, PA 16802

Although its athletic programs have tended to grab most of the headlines, Penn State remains one of the premier public universities academically. With a student body the size of a small city, the university is strong in fields from meteorology to film and television. The 1,800-student Schreyer Honors College is one of the nation's elite programs.

Once viewed as the model of how the values of big-time football and academic excellence could coexist, Penn State's image took a major hit seven years ago with the conviction of a former assistant football coach as a sexual predator. Since then a new administration has enacted governance and other changes aimed at shoring up institutional values. Fortunately, the legendary school spirit of the 40,000 undergraduate denizens of what sportswriters have long called Happy Valley is still alive, as are Penn State's stellar choices in engineering, the sciences, and other fields appropriate to a land grant university.

With an eclectic architectural mix, including white-columned brick, stone, and some modern apartments, Penn State continues to experience growth as major renovation and expansion projects proceed. New facilities are added every year, and

Website: www.psu.edu
Location: Small City
Public
Total Enrollment: 45,218
Undergraduates: 39,683
Male/Female: 53/47
SAT Ranges: ERW 580–660, M 580–680
ACT Ranges: 25–30
Financial Aid: 54%

(continued)

Pell Grant: 13%

Expense: Pub $ $ $ $

Student Loans: 54%

Average Debt: $ $ $ $

Applicants: 56,114

Accepted: 50%

Enrolled: 28%

Grad in 6 Years: 85%

Returning Freshmen: 93%

Academics: 🖎 🖎 🖎 🖎 ½

Social: 🕿 🕿 🕿 🕿 🕿

Q of L: ★ ★ ★

Admissions: (814) 865-5471

Email Address: admissions@
   psu.edu

Strong Programs:

Business

Engineering

Computer and Information
   Sciences

Social Sciences

Meteorology

Food Sciences

Agricultural Sciences

Forensic Science

*The College of
Agricultural Sciences'
food sciences program
is one of the best
in the nation.*

renovations and other improvements are constantly underway. The $144 million Chemical and Biomedical Engineering Building was completed in 2019. "Penn State just keeps growing and improving itself," says one student.

Penn State's general education requirements consist of 45 credits that include several communications and quantification courses as well as humanities, arts, natural sciences, social and behavioral sciences, and health and physical education courses. The incorporation of critical-thinking skills has been a priority in redesigning the general curriculum. In addition, undergrads must enroll in courses on U.S. and international diversity. One helpful program offered to freshmen is LEAP (Learning Edge Academic Program), which gives new students the benefit of a big university while making it seem small. Students in LEAP take a team approach by taking classes and living together. About 1,800 of the university's best and brightest are invited to participate in the Schreyer Honors College, which offers opportunities for research and an honors thesis, as well as honors options in regular courses.

The most popular majors at Penn State fall under the categories of business, engineering, computer and information sciences, and social sciences. The university maintains strong programs in the scientific and technical fields such as earth sciences, engineering, forensic science, and life sciences, as well as nutrition and family studies. The meteorology program boasts alumni worldwide, including the founder of AccuWeather, an internationally renowned private forecasting firm. The College of Information Sciences and Technology is designed to prepare students for the digital age. The College of Agricultural Sciences has extensive facilities that include huge livestock barns. Its food sciences program is one of the best in the nation. Dairy products from the school's cows are sold at an on-campus store, and courses are offered in the production of its famous ice cream. Students can choose from more than 160 undergraduate majors and more than 160 graduate fields spread over 24 locations statewide, including the College of Medicine and Dickinson Law, both located near Harrisburg, and Penn State Law on the University Park campus. Combined undergraduate/graduate degree options are available, as are engineering co-op programs, distance learning, and student-designed majors.

> "Your academic experience is completely what you make it."

According to one student, "The one thing about Penn State is that your academic experience is completely what you make it." Some of the intro-level lecture courses draw up to 400 students at University Park, yet most students seem to agree that classes are excellent and require your full attention. Students report that professors are accessible and engaging—when they are teaching; grad students frequently take on that responsibility. For cramming outside of class, the Penn State library system contains 7 million volumes. A large number of students study abroad through more than 300 summer, semester, and full-year programs in roughly 50 countries.

"Penn State students are active, fun, and open-minded," says one student. Fifty-eight percent of undergraduates are residents of Pennsylvania, with 12 percent hailing from foreign nations. More than half of Penn State's undergrads who finish at University Park began their education at one of the university's 19 undergraduate campuses across the state. Many students note that race and diversity issues can be pronounced on a campus that is still pretty homogeneous for a public university: Asian Americans make up 6 percent of the undergrad population, African Americans 4 percent, Hispanics 7 percent, and multiracial students 3 percent. A whopping 535 athletic scholarships are available in 29 varsity sports, as are thousands of merit awards, averaging $5,200.

> "Penn State students are active, fun, and open-minded."

Freshmen must live in the dorms, which students say are comfortable and located near classroom buildings and dining facilities. Overall, 35 percent of students live on campus; the rest find a home off campus, often in downtown apartments. "I loved living in the dorms," reports one public relations major. "I think it's part of the whole college experience and I made some great friends along the way." The meal plan operates on a point system where you pay for what you eat. Stand for State is a comprehensive bystander intervention program covering sexual assault, drug and alcohol use, acts of bias, and mental health concerns.

"Social life at Penn State is huge," says a freshman. Seventeen percent of men and 20 percent of women go Greek. Partying at Penn State mostly happens at fraternities, but Greek life became a matter of serious concern following the death of a sophomore involved in a fraternity initiation event in 2017. One fraternity was permanently banned from campus, and the administration has been focusing on measures to increase student safety and reduce dangerous drinking, hazing, and sexual assault, including imposing new rules for social events sponsored by Greek organizations. A new Greek Chapter Scorecard tracks conduct violations and disciplinary actions, as well as academic performance, community service hours, and philanthropic fund-raising efforts, for every Greek chapter on campus. For social alternatives, the recently renovated HUB (the campus union building) offers nonalcoholic entertainment, and more than 950 student organizations keep students busy too. Favorite annual events include the mid-July arts festival, the Dance Marathon, and, of course, homecoming.

A new Greek Chapter Scorecard tracks conduct violations, as well as academic performance, community service hours, and philanthropic efforts.

University Park students take advantage of the picturesque and peaceful locale by engaging in outdoorsy activities, including skiing and snowboarding at a nearby slope, and sailing, canoeing, hiking, and renting cabins in Stone Valley. State College offers restaurants, bars, cultural events such

"A majority of the students get involved in community service."

as symphonies, theatrical shows, and ballets, while the Bryce Jordan Center hosts top-notch performers. The town may be small, but according to a biochem major, "a majority of the students get involved in community service to maintain and constantly improve town relations."

When thousands of alumni converge to cheer on their Nittany Lions in blue and white, the festivities include tailgating replete with pregame parties and postgame revelry. As a member of the Big Ten, Penn State's foes include Michigan and Ohio State, both of which make great road trips. Nittany Lions teams have won more than 75 national team championships in a wide variety of sports; the men's wrestling team has brought home seven national titles in the last 10 years. Men's ice hockey, women's field hockey and soccer, and men's and women's track and field are recent conference champions. There are three large gyms, a competitive-size pool, an indoor ice rink, and an extensive program of intramural and club sports for the recreational athlete, including a large angler's club.

After a period of agonizing soul-searching about what led to its football scandal several years ago and its more recent Greek life troubles, Penn State's sense of pride and community spirit are reasserting themselves. As one proud Lion explains, "Imagine a family of 40,000—the excitement, compassion, and sense of belonging, which is unparalleled at any institution."

Overlaps

University of Pittsburgh, Temple, University of Maryland, University of Delaware, Rutgers, Indiana University of Pennsylvania

If You Apply To ›

PSU: Early action, rolling admissions. SATs or ACTs: required. No Subject Tests. Accepts the Common Application. Apply to particular school or program.

Pepperdine University

24255 Pacific Coast Highway, Malibu, CA 90263

Pepperdine has arguably the most beautiful campus setting in America. The buildings are nothing special, but the views of the Pacific Ocean are incomparable. With L.A. nearby, small wonder its popularity is soaring. Students should come to Pepperdine ready to embrace an evangelical Christian emphasis.

Website: www.pepperdine.edu
Location: Suburban
Private
Total Enrollment: 5,685
Undergraduates: 3,299
Male/Female: 40/60
SAT Ranges: ERW 600–690,
    M 600–700
ACT Ranges: 25–30
Financial Aid: 52%
Pell Grant: 19%
Expense: Pr $ $ $
Student Loans: 56%
Average Debt: $ $ $
Applicants: 11,704
Accepted: 40%
Enrolled: 19%
Grad in 6 Years: 80%
Returning Freshmen: 90%
Academics: ✍ ✍ ✍
Social: ☎ ☎
Q of L: ★ ★ ★ ★
Admissions: (310) 506-4392
Email Address: admission
    -seaver@pepperdine.edu

Strong Programs:
Business Administration
Communication
Management
Psychology
Sports Medicine
Economics
Biology

With picturesque surroundings, it's easy to confuse Pepperdine University with its nickname—Pepperdine Resort. Surrounded by the beautiful Southern California seashore, Pepperdine University might seem like paradise for students seeking sunshine rather than studies at this conservative, Christian-affiliated university, though students take their work and their worship seriously. "The philosophy of the school is that God and the academic experience must be married," says a senior communication major. "This creates an intimate learning environment that prides itself on moral integrity and a high academic standard." Business and communication are the most blessed programs, though other departments deserve recognition too. Undergrads praise their educational opportunities, the strength of their school's spiritual community, and the vast sandy beaches beckoning below their hilltop campus.

There's no denying that Pepperdine's location—high in the Santa Monica Mountains, about 25 miles northwest of Los Angeles—is a strong selling point. The 830-acre Malibu campus, to which the school moved in 1972, overlooks the Pacific Ocean and features fountains, hillside gardens, mountain trails, and a 20-minute walk to the beach. Cream-colored, Mediterranean-style buildings topped with red terra-cotta roofs dot the landscape. A 125-foot-tall white stucco cross stands near the center of campus, reminding students and faculty of the school's affiliation with the Churches of Christ (to which 12 percent of students belong). Pepp's 10-facility library system boasts nearly 500,000 volumes.

> "[Pepperdine offers] an intimate learning environment that prides itself on moral integrity and a high academic standard."

Pepperdine was founded in 1937 by George Pepperdine, a lifelong member of the Churches of Christ who had amassed a fortune through his mail-order auto parts supply company. The church's continued influence on the school pervades many aspects of campus life, from the prohibition of overnight dorm room visits by members of the opposite sex to the requirement that students attend convocation—similar to chapel—14 times each semester. Students at Seaver College, Pepp's undergraduate school, must also take three religion courses. While drinking is officially prohibited on campus, the administration has lifted the ban on dancing and now allows students to choose their own seats at convocation. Though restrictions like this would drive the average American kid up a wall, most at Pepperdine like the "highly moral" atmosphere. Says one student: "In comparison to other schools, Pepperdine students generally have a more religious foundation and thus have high standards of moral integrity."

Seaver's academic programs aim to provide students "with a liberal arts education in a Christian environment and relate it to the dynamic qualities of life in the 21st century." Individual classes are demanding, as is the required General Studies program, which includes a freshman seminar and courses in physical education, Western heritage, American heritage, English composition, foreign language, and non-Western culture. However, faculty members are said to be accessible and responsive—not surprising when 71 percent of classes have fewer than 20 students. One student says, "Because it is a small school, professors don't accept excuses or laziness. They demand a lot from their students and expect a high standard and quality of work."

The business administration department is unequivocally the strongest and most popular at Pepperdine, and it tends to set the tone on campus. Those seeking advanced business education can enroll in a B.S./M.B.A. program that allows them to earn a bachelor's degree in business administration or international business from Seaver College and an M.B.A. from the university's graduate business school in five years. The communication department, with majors including advertising, public relations, and journalism, is also highly touted, and boasts radio and television broadcasting studios. Management, psychology, sports medicine, economics, and biology are also popular. Dual-degree engineering programs are available in partnership with the University of Southern California and Washington University in St. Louis. The well-organized Career Center allows students

Students are required to attend convocation—similar to chapel—14 times each semester.

"Pepperdine tends to shy away from political activism."

to sign up for job fairs, interviews, and individual and group career-counseling sessions. Juniors interested in international culture may spend a year at Pepperdine's own facilities in Buenos Aires, Florence, Heidelberg, Lausanne, London, or Shanghai. Locations for summer study have included East Africa, the Galapagos Islands, Madrid, and Oxford. Roughly two-thirds of Pepperdine's undergraduates participate in short- and long-term study abroad programs.

One might expect students at this religiously oriented school to be politically conservative, and they most definitely are. Many come from well-to-do California Republican families; there are also quite a few wealthy international students. Students joke that there's never a shortage of Porsches and BMWs on campus, but there is a shortage of places to park them. Overall, 54 percent of undergraduates are California natives, and 11 percent come from abroad. Hispanics account for 14 percent of the students, Asian Americans 10 percent, African Americans 5 percent, and multiracial students 6 percent. The Republican influence is felt far and wide. Pepperdine has received millions of dollars from conservative donors, including the late Pittsburgh financier Richard Mellon Scaife. One student sums up the political climate gently: "Pepperdine tends to shy away from political activism." The university awards merit scholarships averaging $17,800 to top achievers, in addition to about 100 athletic scholarships in 16 sports.

Students joke that there's never a shortage of Porsches and BMWs on campus, but there is a shortage of places to park them.

Fifty-two percent of undergraduates live on campus. A senior declares that Pepperdine's single-sex dorms are "comfortable, convenient, and really quite nice." Rooms are assigned on a first-come, first-served basis, and the housing stock consists of more than 20 dorms, including the new, suite-style Seaside Residence Hall. Freshmen are typically assigned to suites with bathrooms, living rooms, and four double bedrooms. Some consider these arrangements crowded, but a junior says they "connect freshmen instantly to seven suitemates and friends." Despite the above-average cost of living in the Malibu area, many upperclassmen choose to live off campus.

"Parties on weekends… probably draw a larger portion of students than church on Sunday."

Some say flashy student vehicles fit into the small, very wealthy community of Malibu better than the students themselves. Because the social scene in Malibu is pretty slack, with a 10 p.m. noise curfew and high price tags for everything, students typically head to L.A., Hollywood, Westwood, and Santa Monica for fun. "For a large proportion of students, academics and their social lives take priority over religious matters," says a public relations major. "Parties on weekends are well attended, and probably draw a larger portion of students than church on Sunday." Twenty-three percent of the men and 32 percent of the women join one of six national fraternities or eight national sororities, which are playing a larger role in social life. Along with student government, they sponsor dances, movies, and other typical college activities, including the occasional illicit drink. "Pepperdine enforces a 'dry' campus, but 'damp' would be a better way of describing the residential community," says one student. The student union serves as the main campus social center, and annual events including Songfest, Waves Weekend, and Midnight Madness draw crowds.

Sports receive a lot of attention at Pepperdine. The Waves compete in the Division I West Coast Conference. Recent conference champions include baseball, men's and women's golf, and women's tennis and beach volleyball. Thirteen club and intramural sports keep students busy, as does the physical education department, with classes in everything from surfing to ballet. A tennis pavilion and recreation center serves varsity jocks and weekend warriors alike.

Pepperdine has taken up the challenge of trying to marry the Christian focus of a Bible college with the academic rigor of a secular university—all in a location not known for the strength of its moral fiber. Students love to tease their well-manicured university with T-shirts proclaiming, "Pepperdine. 8-month party. 50K cover charge." But most seem to think the solid, values-oriented education they receive is worth the stiff price tag.

Overlaps

Baylor, Calvin, Loyola Marymount, Macalester, Occidental, Southern Methodist, University of San Diego, Wheaton (IL)

If You Apply To ›

Pepperdine: Early action, regular decision. SATs or ACTs: required. Subject Tests: optional. Accepts the Common Application with supplement.

University of Pittsburgh

Alumni Hall, 4227 Fifth Avenue, Pittsburgh, PA 15260

As its home city has risen in stature, Pitt has become a hot commodity along with next-door neighbor Carnegie Mellon. A state-related university in the mold of the University of Cincinnati—not the state flagship, but strong in a host of preprofessional programs, especially in health fields. Curiously, Pitt is among the nation's best in philosophy. Admissions is rolling, so apply early.

Website: www.pitt.edu
Location: City Center
Public
Total Enrollment: 25,735
Undergraduates: 18,352
Male/Female: 48/52
SAT Ranges: ERW 620–700, M 620–720
ACT Ranges: 27–32
Financial Aid: 50%
Pell Grant: 16%
Expense: Pub $ $ $ $
Student Loans: 62%
Average Debt: $ $ $ $

Pittsburgh has joined the ranks of the most livable cities in the United States. The University of Pittsburgh has matured too, becoming a formidable public research institution. The school offers numerous opportunities for students pursuing business, medical, and engineering careers, but leaves a great deal of room for exploration in the liberal arts. Students are encouraged to be individuals and carve out their own academic niche, either with multiple majors or with certificate programs. "The great thing about Pitt is they are always adding and adapting programs to fit the students' needs and interests," says a junior.

Pitt began as a tiny, private educational academy in the Allegheny Mountains in 1787. Oh, how times have changed. The university, which became state-related in 1966, is adjacent to Carnegie Mellon and is now part of the landscape of shops, museums, and galleries that make up Oakland, the heart of Pittsburgh's educational and medical center. Spacious, light-filled, contemporary buildings and generic modern office buildings make up the Pitt campus, but the architectural delight is the fabled 42-story, neo-Gothic academic building, appropriately called the Cathedral of

Learning, a national historic landmark. The stately and towering cathedral, with its unique Nationality Rooms, attracts 30,000 visitors annually. And contrary to images you may hold of inner-city Pittsburgh, the campus borders a 456-acre city park.

Academic requirements in the Dietrich School of Arts and Sciences include writing, quantitative and formal reasoning, and foreign languages, as well as coursework in the humanities, social and natural sciences, and foreign cultures. First-year students undergo an extensive orientation that includes one and a half days in the summer focused on academics, another five days before the term starts, and a one-credit freshman studies seminar. Pitt offers guaranteed admission into a wide variety of graduate programs for outstanding freshman applicants. The Outside the Classroom Curriculum is an optional cocurricular program in which students participate in activities in 10 goal areas, such as leadership development, sense of self, service to others, and arts appreciation, in order to round out their college experience.

> "Students are constantly trying to make the best grades, but most study in groups in order to do so."

With 16 undergraduate, graduate, and professional schools and nearly 100 undergraduate majors across its five-campus system, Pitt rightfully claims to accommodate students with diverse needs. The engineering and nursing schools are excellent and attract high-caliber students. Premed students can watch transplants at the famed University of Pittsburgh Medical Center, one of the world's leading organ transplant centers. Pitt's highly competitive physical therapy program is the top one in the country, and bioengineering is also a strength. The most popular majors include psychology, finance, biological sciences, and nursing. The interdisciplinary politics and philosophy major is a unique offering, and an undergraduate degree in gender, sexuality, and women's studies was recently added.

Coursework at Pitt is described as intensive but manageable, and a molecular biology major says, "Students are constantly trying to make the best grades, but most study in groups in order to do so." Forty-three percent of classes have fewer than 20 students. Pitt faculty members are often at the top of their fields, leading the way in areas like astronomical discoveries and medical advances. "The quality of instruction from freshman through senior year is excellent," reports a history and philosophy of science major.

The academically motivated can take advantage of the excellent University Honors College, and those who do graduate with a distinctive bachelor of philosophy degree. Pitt is one of the top 10 institutions in the nation in terms of annual research support awarded by the National Institutes of Health. Fifty-nine percent of undergrads pursue research projects, facilitated by the university's 400 centers, institutes, laboratories, and clinics.

> "The It's On Us campaign has been very prevalent on campus."

For those who want to travel, the university boasts 350 study abroad options in 82 countries; one-quarter of undergrads participate. Closer to home, Pitt is a partner with Carnegie Mellon and Westinghouse Electric Company in the Pittsburgh Supercomputing Center. Students praise the career center's internship guarantee program, which places students in local internships after they've completed a set of workshops and other requirements.

Sixty-eight percent of undergraduates are from Pennsylvania, including a substantial number from the Pittsburgh area, and 4 percent hail from more than 100 other countries. African American students account for 5 percent of the student body, Asian Americans 10 percent, Hispanics 4 percent, and multiracial students 4 percent. "From the Black Action Society to the Rainbow Alliance, there is an organization or group for students of any identity and background at Pitt," says a junior. When it comes to political and social issues, students say the campus is "very vocal"

(continued)

Applicants: 27,679
Accepted: 58%
Enrolled: 25%
Grad in 6 Years: 82%
Returning Freshmen: 93%
Academics: ✍ ✍ ✍ ½
Social: ☎ ☎
Q of L: ★ ★
Admissions: (412) 624-7488
Email Address: oafa@pitt.edu

Strong Programs:
Psychology
Finance
Biological Sciences
Nursing
Premed
Rehabilitation Science
Bioengineering
Politics and Philosophy

Premed students can watch transplants at the famed University of Pittsburgh Medical Center.

but also respectful. Pitt offers merit awards averaging $11,000, and 248 athletic scholarships are available in 19 varsity sports.

Living/learning communities are popular, with 17 options for first-years and nine for upperclassmen.

While student housing may have been scarce in the past, Pitt continues to increase the amount of on-campus living space and guarantees housing for three years. Forty-three percent of students live on campus in 20 co-ed dorms with all kinds of rooming situations, from singles to seven-person, apartment-style suites. Students say the quality varies, but "for the most part, students tend to be really happy with wherever they end up," says a junior. Living/learning communities are popular, with 17 options for first-years and nine for upperclassmen. Hungry students may choose from nearly 20 dining spots, and the food gets generally high marks. Campus safety is bolstered by a consistent police presence, and a history major notes, "The It's On Us campaign has been very prevalent on campus."

Within minutes of Pitt's campus are shops, parks, museums, professional sporting events, and performing arts venues, and Pitt Arts provides students with low-cost tickets to attend cultural events in the city. The university also grants students fare-free access to city buses. "Exploring the city has been one of my favorite parts of my Pitt experi-

"Exploring the city has been one of my favorite parts of my Pitt experience."

ence. There's so much more to do and see outside of Oakland," says a senior. Another adds that, for students of age, "Bars tend to be big here." On campus, students have nearly 600 clubs and organizations to choose from, and 10 percent of the men and 12 percent of the women belong to the Greek system. "Greek life is small on campus, so they don't take over the scene like at other schools," says one senior. Fall Fest and Bigelow Bash are favorite annual concerts that bring recognizable performers like OneRepublic and Kesha to campus. Adjacent Schenley Park offers jogging trails and facilities for outdoor recreation. Ski slopes and mountain trails are not far away, and road trips to Penn State and Philadelphia, Boston, and New York City are popular.

The Pitt Panthers compete in the Division I Atlantic Coast Conference, and solid teams include baseball, softball, gymnastics, women's volleyball, men's and women's swimming and diving, and men's and women's track and field. Approximately 39 percent of undergrads take part in intramurals and club sports; basketball, football, soccer, and volleyball are the most popular. The Pitt Sports Dome opened in 2017 to accommodate recreational sports.

Pitt is a large university made to feel small. Its flexibility in adapting to students' needs and its commitment to community breed a kind of loyalty and pride that students say can't be found elsewhere. Case in point, one senior declares, "I have two separate friends who have our unofficial slogan, 'Hail to Pitt,' tattooed on them." Now *that's* commitment.

Overlaps

Boston University, NYU, University of Southern California, University of Maryland, Georgetown, Penn State, Ohio State, Carnegie Mellon

If You Apply To ›

Pitt: Rolling admissions. SATs or ACTs: required. Subject Tests: optional. Does not accept the Common Application.

Pitzer College: See page 152.

Pomona College: See page 154.

Presbyterian College

503 S. Broad Street, Clinton, SC 29325

A South Carolina liberal arts college that competes head-to-head with Wofford for students who want their education served up with plenty of personal attention. Programs in business and engineering complement those in the liberal arts. Lacks the urban allure of Furman or Oglethorpe, but Scottish heritage adds flavor. Nearly two-thirds of PC students are from South Carolina.

Presbyterian College students live up to the motto *Dum Vivimus Servimus* ("While we live, we serve."). Virtually all students participate in some kind of community service while at PC. Current students seem a far cry from the orphans for whom William Plumer Jacobs founded the school way back in 1880. And although today's matriculants largely come from stable, economically secure families, they continue to pursue personal, spiritual, and academic growth.

The Presbyterian campus sits on 240 acres in the South Carolina piedmont. The redbrick buildings are largely Georgian in style, with tall, white columns and lots of shade trees; many structures are listed on the National Register of Historic Places. The campus resembles Thomas Jefferson's University of Virginia, with buildings grouped around three plazas just perfect for reading, studying, or throwing a Frisbee. A major renovation and expansion to the campus's most recognizable building, Neville Hall, was recently completed, and a 144-bed, suite-style residence hall opened in 2019.

Presbyterian's curriculum emphasizes the traditional liberal arts, with a range of required courses, as well as experiential learning: all students either study abroad, do independent research, or complete an internship before graduation. The required Compass program extends from freshman through senior year, beginning with a First-Year Exploration course that focuses on critical thinking, academic skills, and personal exploration of vocation and calling. Sophomores take a course that helps them explore potential career paths. Students must also develop an electronic portfolio and participate in a senior capstone course.

> **"[Coursework] is not so intrusive that it devours all of a student's time."**

"The coursework is intense at times but is not so intrusive that it devours all of a student's time," says a political science major. An honor code holds students accountable for their work and creates an atmosphere of mutual respect. Classes are small, with 66 percent enrolling fewer than 20 students, encouraging personal relationships with faculty. "My professors have been so much more than just teachers to me—they have become my friends, travel partners, mentors, and role models," enthuses an English and history double major. The most popular majors are business administration, psychology, English, biology, and political science. History and music are strong, and biochemistry is one of the fastest-growing majors. High-achieving students desiring a degree in pharmacy can apply to the Early Entry Pre-Pharmacy Program, which allows them to earn a doctorate degree in six years through the PC School of Pharmacy.

Options for off-campus study, in which 40 percent of students partake, include semester-long exchange programs as well as highly popular, short-term Maymester trips, led by faculty, to destinations such as Australia, Greece, South Africa, India, and, of course, Scotland. For eight weeks each summer, 10 to 25 Summer Fellows receive stipends to live on campus, undertake independent research guided by faculty, and present the findings of their work. The president and provost work with

---

Website: www.presby.edu
Location: Small Town
Private
Total Enrollment: 1,198
Undergraduates: 943
Male/Female: 50/50
SAT Ranges: ERW 510–620, M 510–630
ACT Ranges: 21–27
Financial Aid: 99%
Pell Grant: 34%
Expense: Pr $
Student Loans: 54%
Average Debt: $ $ $
Applicants: 2,277
Accepted: 63%
Enrolled: 19%
Grad in 6 Years: 69%
Returning Freshmen: 82%
Academics: ✐ ✐ ✐
Social: ☎ ☎ ☎
Q of L: ★ ★ ★ ★
Admissions: (864) 833-8230
Email Address: admissions@presby.edu

Strong Programs:
Business Administration
Psychology
English
Biology
Political Science
History
Music
Biochemistry

10 to 12 Presidential Fellows in an academic seminar; Fellows also intern with various campus offices to gain leadership experience.

Fifteen percent of students are Presbyterian, but a Christian atmosphere permeates the campus. "Our students practice servitude and Christian love in their daily lives," a senior says. Thirty-two percent of undergraduates hail from states outside South Carolina, and 5 percent come from nations abroad. Minorities are a small but increasing presence on campus: African Americans make up 12 percent of the population, Hispanics 3 percent, Asian Americans 1 percent, and multiracial students 5 percent. Thirty-four percent of freshmen qualify for the Pell Grant. Politically, according to a sophomore, "Both extremes of the spectrum are active, but the majority who fall in the center are pretty quiet or nonchalant about their views." Merit scholarships worth an average of $16,800 are handed out to eligible students, as are roughly 200 athletic awards.

Sophomores take a course that helps them explore potential career paths, and students also develop an electronic portfolio.

Ninety-nine percent of Presbyterian students live on campus, where accommodations range from traditional rooms with hall baths to suites and apartments. Where you live is determined by lottery based on academic standing. "I really enjoy the dorm life. I believe it allows everyone to stay close and connected," says a student. The two dining facilities on campus, a buffet-style dining hall and a dining center with a Starbucks, Boar's Head Deli, and Moe's Southwest Grill, receive good reviews from students and locals alike. "The Sunday buffet is awesome—after church, people from the community pay to eat in our cafeteria," says an English major. A senior notes that the school's strict honor code means that "you can trust your neighbors at PC."

"Although PC is a small campus, there are great opportunities for expanding your worldview."

Thirty-three percent of PC's men and 50 percent of the women join Greek groups, and "social life is very active," says one student. "Fraternity Court is the popular spot on weekend nights." The school has taken a firm stand against underage and unsafe drinking: all frat parties must be registered and attended by sober party monitors, while staff check IDs and distribute under-21 wristbands at the door. For an alternative, "Student Activities Board is always hosting fun events on campus like laser tag and movie nights," says a senior. Many students join clubs, and owing to PC's aforementioned motto, Student Volunteer Services is the largest organization on campus, routinely sending students to local orphanages, nursing homes, schools, and other facilities where their time and talents can be helpful. Favorite annual traditions include Shuckin' and Shaggin', an oyster roast and dance in the fall, and Spring Fling, a weekend carnival featuring four or five bands. Students also look forward to the Christmas at PC concert and to the outdoor graduation ceremony under the oaks, with bagpipes heralding students and faculty in full academic regalia. Students with cars enjoy heading to Greenville, Columbia, or Spartanburg for a bite to eat or some shopping—or, if there's more time, to Charleston or Atlanta. PC is equidistant from South Carolina's mountains and beaches, providing many opportunities to enjoy the outdoors.

Favorite annual traditions include Shuckin' and Shaggin', an oyster roast and dance in the fall.

PC's 19 varsity sports teams, including new programs in men's and women's wrestling, compete in Division I. The college's mascot is the Blue Hose, a reference to the stockings of their Scottish ancestors. (While some students wear kilts during athletic events, most are more restrained, says a junior.) Men's tennis is a recent Big South Conference winner, and other strong programs include baseball, softball, and men's and women's golf. Recreational sports are divided into three divisions, depending on how competitive you are. All students may take advantage of PC's 31-acre recreational facility, with lighted softball, football, and soccer fields, volleyball courts, a basketball court, a track, and an amphitheater.

Overlaps

Wofford, Furman, Mercer, Samford, Sewanee, Rhodes, Centre, College of Charleston

Presbyterian College students take pride in the school's history and traditions, including its very own tartan. PC's church affiliation keeps them focused on service, and on bettering the broader world, giving their classroom experiences added dimension. Says one Blue Hose, "Although PC is a small campus, there are great opportunities for expanding your worldview."

If You Apply To ›

Presbyterian: Early action, regular decision. SATs or ACTs: optional (required for applicants with GPA below 3.25). No Subject Tests. Accepts the Common Application with supplement.

Prescott College

220 Grove Avenue, Prescott, AZ 86301

With its commitment to environmental studies in a liberal arts context, Prescott attracts students who love the outdoors and are looking for an alternative college experience. Has ready access to northern Arizona and southern Utah, the nation's most exotic outdoor playground. College of the Atlantic is the only remotely comparable college in the *Fiske Guide*. If you loved Outward Bound, consider Prescott.

Future *Hunger Games* contestants take note: this tiny outpost in the wilderness of central Arizona is a perfect spot for the nature lover who seeks adventure, wants to learn survival skills, and likes studying outdoors. Where else but Prescott College could you major in adventure education or take courses like Backcountry Skiing and Avalanche Training, Ecopsychology, and Geology through Bikepacking? Before any Prescott student sets foot in a classroom, the college sends him or her to the outback for three weeks of hiking and camping. Wilderness Orientation is an introduction to everything Prescott stands for: hands-on experience, personal responsibility, cooperative living, and stewardship of the environment.

Founded in 1966 and still the only private liberal arts college in Arizona, Prescott retains the air of a 1960s commune. Surrounded by national forest, the college's "campus" consists of a two-block-long handful of buildings in the small town of Prescott. The architectural style of the campus ranges from the historic to the modern. The largest of the college's buildings is the Crossroads Center, an all-green building, which houses the library, computer labs, classrooms, conference centers, and the Crossroads Café. The administrative building was once a convent; its chapel is now used for meetings, art shows, and performances.

> **"People are inspired to work hard because their projects reflect their passions."**

Prescott's requirements for graduation are characteristically unorthodox. Instead of grades, faculty members give narrative evaluations, although students may elect to receive grades. And rather than accruing credits, students design individualized "degree plans" that outline the competence (major) and breadth (minor/concentration) areas they will pursue, and the Senior Project (thesis) they will complete to demonstrate competence (graduate). Students must obtain two levels of writing certification (college level and thesis level) and math certification, showing knowledge of college-level algebra. Students also take a set of required interdisciplinary Core Curriculum courses, which are cotaught by faculty from multiple fields. Prescott's personal touch even extends to graduation, a unique experience where a faculty

Website: www.prescott.edu
Location: Small City
Private
Total Enrollment: 358
Undergraduates: 282
Male/Female: 44/56
SAT Ranges: ERW 570–615, M 490–570
ACT Ranges: 19–27
Financial Aid: 68%
Pell Grant: 43%
Expense: Pr $
Student Loans: 63%
Average Debt: $ $ $ $
Applicants: 394
Accepted: 94%
Enrolled: 17%
Grad in 6 Years: 44%
Returning Freshmen: 72%
Academics: ✐ ✐ ✐
Social: ☎ ☎
Q of L: ★ ★ ★ ★
Admissions: (877) 350-2100
Email Address: admissions@ prescott.edu

Strong Programs:
Environmental Studies

member speaks about each student personally and then the student speaks on his or her own behalf.

Prescott bills itself as a college "for the liberal arts and the environment," and most students envision themselves becoming teachers, researchers, park rangers, or wilderness guides. To design their degree plans, students start by selecting one of six areas of study: adventure education, arts and letters, cultural and regional studies, education, environmental studies, and psychology and human development. Each area of study offers several concentrations. In the standout environmental studies program, for instance, concentrations cover impressive breadth and depth, ranging from earth science and marine studies to natural history and ecology. Adventure education, in which students learn everything from alpine mountaineering to sea kayaking, is also a specialty. The program in psychology and human development—a hodgepodge of sociology, psychology, and New Age mysticism—includes such offbeat courses as Life Centering. Among the college's few concessions to practicality is the teacher preparation program, which offers students teaching credentials in elementary and secondary education. Several programs have accelerated pathways in which undergrads can earn a master's degree tuition-free. Prescott does not offer a comprehensive program in advanced math, chemistry, physics, or foreign languages other than Spanish.

> "There is a 'hippie' stereotype of PC students, but I think that image is slowly shifting."

"People are inspired to work hard because their projects reflect their passions, not because they're worried about getting an A," observes one senior. A human consciousness major adds, "Because you're not cramming for the next test (I never took one here), you can interact with your coursework in a way that's more meaningful to you." There's no tenure track at Prescott, so publishing and research take a backseat to teaching, although students warn that the quality of instruction can be inconsistent. With 95 percent of classes having fewer than 20 students, the academic atmosphere is intimate, to say the least.

Prescott's calendar is divided into three periods, each with one 10-week quarter and one four-week block. During the quarters, students follow a traditional schedule, studying liberal arts and spending time doing fieldwork and student teaching. During the blocks, students pursue intense immersion in one course, most likely in the field, perhaps the backcountry of Baja California, the alpine meadows of Wyoming, or a local service clinic. Students can even take a one-month rafting trip down the Colorado River for credit. Though Prescott does not offer a traditional study abroad program, students are encouraged to take courses in marine biology and cultural studies at the Kino Bay Center for Cultural and Ecological Studies in Mexico, as well as a social justice course in Kenya; about half of Prescott students have an international experience by the time they graduate. Paid internships are available through partnerships with AmeriCorps and other organizations.

Before any Prescott student sets foot in a classroom, the college sends him or her to the outback for three weeks of hiking and camping.

> "If you love the outdoors, Prescott is great. Do not come here for a social experience."

"There is a 'hippie' stereotype of PC students, but I think that image is slowly shifting," remarks a senior. Environmental issues still predominate among the liberal student body. Despite the challenges of declining enrollment and a low graduation rate, Prescott's unconventional approach continues to entice students well beyond Arizona. Sixty percent of undergraduates are out-of-staters; less than 1 percent come from other countries. The minority population is small but growing, with African Americans making up just 2 percent of the total, Hispanics 7 percent, Asian Americans 1 percent, American Indians 3 percent, and multiracial students 11 percent. Pell Grant recipients represent 43 percent of freshmen, and merit scholarships are available. The new Changemaker Scholarship, an effort to boost enrollment, awards a half-tuition scholarship to every incoming student from Arizona and seven other southwestern and western states; recipients must agree to "support relationship-building and outreach" in their home state communities.

Twenty-five percent of students call the housing units home. "The Village is a series of eight-person townhouses," explains a senior. "Each townhouse has two single rooms and three double rooms." The vast majority of students fend for themselves in the town of Prescott, a rapidly growing community of approximately 43,000 where almost everything is accessible by bicycle. The college assists with the apartment hunt by providing lists of available properties and by cosigning leases when necessary. The Crossroads Café, the only dining facility, draws praise for being tasty and fresh. "Omnivores, vegetarians, vegans, and gluten-free folk all love the food in the café," cheers one student. Additionally, "The café staff offer cooking lessons throughout the semester. There's also free community lunch every Wednesday."

Social life at Prescott is informal and spontaneous, often consisting of small, "mellow" off-campus parties. With fewer than 20 student organizations and no strong traditions to speak of, students say the campus doesn't offer much in the way of a social scene. "If you love the outdoors, Prescott is great. Do not come here for a social experience," advises an adventure education major. As for the townsfolk, students describe them as "a mix of artists, activists, students, locals, retirees, and ranchers." Aside from environmental activities, Prescott offers a nationally recognized literary magazine, *Alligator Juniper*. Those looking for nightlife can hit Whiskey Row, the town bar scene, or drive to Flagstaff (90 minutes) or Phoenix (two hours).

The college offers just one sport—cycling—which competes as a Division II USA Cycling collegiate varsity team and has won titles in road cycling, mountain biking, and cyclocross. For other sports, students often participate in city leagues. "Our school has bike jousting, juggling, barefoot soccer, ultimate Frisbee, and capoeira—none of which involve competing against other schools," says one student.

Prescott may not have the huge campus or financial resources that are typically associated with larger schools; however, the small classes and specialized programs appeal to a student who would not be interested in your "typical" college. As a senior explains, "Our passion and dedication to education springs from a deep inner desire to effect positive change in the world."

During four-week blocks, students pursue intense immersion in one course, most likely in the field.

Overlaps

Alaska Pacific, Green Mountain, College of the Atlantic, Warren Wilson, Dickinson, Northern Arizona, Arizona State, Fort Lewis

If You Apply To ›

Prescott: Rolling admissions. SATs or ACTs: optional. Subject Tests: optional. Accepts the Common Application with supplement.

Princeton University

110 West College, Princeton, NJ 08544

Princeton is the smallest of the Ivy League's Big Three, which means more attention from faculty and plenty of opportunity for rigorous independent work. Offers engineering but no business major. The affluent suburban location contrasts with urban New Haven and Cambridge. Residential college system modeled on Yale's provides a social alternative to long-standing eating clubs.

Website: www.princeton.edu

Location: Suburban

Private

Total Enrollment: 8,273

Undergraduates: 5,260

Male/Female: 51/49

SAT Ranges: ERW 700–770,
  M 730–790

ACT Ranges: 32–35

Financial Aid: 60%

Pell Grant: 20%

Expense: Pr $ $

Student Loans: 17%

Average Debt: $

Applicants: 35,370

Accepted: 6%

Enrolled: 68%

Grad in 6 Years: 97%

Returning Freshmen: 98%

Academics: ✐ ✐ ✐ ✐ ✐

Social: ☏ ☏ ☏

Q of L: ★ ★ ★

Admissions: (609) 258-3060

Email Address: uaoffice@
  princeton.edu

Strong Programs:

Public and International Affairs

Economics

History

Mathematics

Philosophy

Computer Science

Engineering

Molecular Biology

Princeton occupies a distinctive niche among America's super-elite universities. It is a major research university with a world-class corps of professors who, in the absence of lots of graduate and professional students, lavish their attention on a relatively modest number of undergraduates. Princeton has an engineering school as well as programs in applied science, architecture and public planning, public policy, and an Entrepreneurial Hub near campus, but it is basically an "arts and sciences university." The academic atmosphere across campus is dominated by commitment to the liberal arts—with a carefully structured set of core requirements and a heavy emphasis on independent study, including a mandatory senior thesis. "Many schools brag about great buildings and great professors, but it's really your fellow students that end up making or breaking your college experience," says one sophomore. "What sets Princeton students apart is that they come here not just for an excellent education, but they come to share knowledge with others."

For better or worse, Princeton has been known as a bastion of exclusivity, although its undergraduates are just as racially and ethnically diverse as any other Ivy League school. Still, university leaders are looking to make Princeton's particular brand of high-powered undergraduate liberal arts education available to an even more diverse group of students. Sensitive to faculty complaints that Princeton enrolls too many bright students whose main claim to fame is that they have learned to work the system, the admissions office is on the look-

> **"[Students] come here not just for an excellent education, but they come to share knowledge with others."**

out for more students with demonstrated intellectual curiosity—including more STEM majors, creative types, and high-ability/low-income students. The administration has made major investments in the sciences, engineering, and creative and performing arts to enhance these efforts. Support for first-generation and low-income students is offered through the Freshman Scholars Institute, which offers an academic and social introduction to Princeton over the summer before classes start, and the Scholars Institute Fellows Program that covers all four years.

Cloistered in a secluded but upscale New Jersey town, Princeton's architectural trademark is Gothic, from the cavernous and ornate university chapel to the four-pronged Cleveland Tower rising majestically above the treetops. Interspersed among the Gothic are examples of colonial architecture, most notably historic Nassau Hall, which served as the temporary home of the Continental Congress in 1783 and has defined elegance in academic architecture ever since. A host of modern structures, some by leading American architects Robert Venturi, Frank Gehry, and I. M. Pei, add variety and distinction to the campus, but the ambiance is still quintessential Ivy League at its best. The outstanding library facilities embrace five million volumes and provide 500 private study carrels for seniors working on those mandatory theses; there are another 700 enclosed carrels in other parts of the campus. Princeton's campus is self-contained, but those who venture outside its walls will find the surroundings quite pleasing. One side of the campus abuts quaint Nassau Street, which is dominated by chic (and pricey) boutiques and restaurants, as well as coffee shops and more affordable eateries. The other side of campus ends with a huge man-made lake that was financed by Andrew Carnegie so that Princetonians would not have to forgo crew. Recent campus projects include the Andlinger Center for Energy and the Environment and the 22-acre Lewis Arts Complex, which opened in 2017 and significantly expanded teaching and performance spaces for art and music programs.

Princeton became the model for American-style liberal arts colleges after John Witherspoon was lured from the University of Edinburgh to become president in 1768. Today, Princeton is distinctive in its modest scale and its emphasis on undergraduates. Each student's Princeton experience begins with a week of orientation;

800 each year participate in Outdoor Action, a few days of wilderness activities immediately preceding orientation. All first-year students are also assigned a faculty advisor. Seventy-six percent of undergraduate classes have fewer than 20 students. With fewer graduate students to siphon off resources or consume faculty time than at large research universities, undergraduates get the lion's share of both; at last count, 70 percent of Princeton's department heads taught introductory undergraduate courses. An economics major says, "I can open the newspaper and read my professor's article or turn on the TV and see him giving a speech, then go to a lecture to hear him speak, then go to his office to speak with him one-on-one." Special opportunities to work closely with senior faculty members include the optional freshman seminar program, taken by two-thirds of new students, which offers the opportunity to go deep into dozens of topics ranging from the Physics of Music to the Search for Life in the Universe. Lovers of literature can study with Tracy K. Smith, Paul Muldoon, or Jhumpa Lahiri, and nearly every other department has a few stars of its own. "We have some of the most brilliant professors in the world here," confirms a junior. Senior professors lead at least one or two of the small discussion groups that accompany each lecture course.

Princeton places heavy emphasis on independent study, including a mandatory senior thesis.

Every student must fulfill distribution requirements in epistemology and cognition, ethical thought and moral values, historical analysis, literature and the arts, quantitative reasoning, social analysis, and science and technology. Students also take a first-year writing seminar, choosing from more than 70 options offered annually. During their junior year, liberal arts students work closely with a faculty member of their choice in completing two junior papers—about 30 pages of independent work each semester in addition to the normal courseload. Princeton also requires every graduate to complete a senior thesis—an enterprise that serves as a culmination of their work in their field of concentration. As a result, "seniors develop close personal relationships with their thesis advisors," says one student. Alumni often note the thesis as one of their best experiences at Princeton.

"I can open the newspaper and read my professor's article... then go to his office to speak with him one-on-one."

Naturally, given Princeton's small size, the number of courses offered is smaller than at other Ivies, but students still have many high-quality options. Princeton's math and philosophy departments are among the best in the nation, and economics, history, public policy, English, physics, molecular biology, and romance languages are right on their heels. As part of a major effort to become a national center in the field of molecular biology, the university supports a sizable laboratory for teaching and research. Princeton is one of the few top liberal arts universities with equally strong computer science and engineering programs, most notably chemical, mechanical, electrical, and aerospace engineering. Operations research and financial engineering is one of the fastest-growing majors. There is also a five-year program that leads to a B.S.E. and M.E. in mechanical and aerospace engineering. One of Princeton's best-known programs is the prestigious Woodrow Wilson School of Public and International Affairs ("Woody Woo" to the students). The school's name recently survived a well-publicized campaign to change it, in protest of former president Wilson's strong advocacy of racial segregation. Fifty-five percent of students study abroad in more than 100 programs in 43 nations. For those wishing to postpone their entry into the university in favor of an international experience, Princeton's Bridge Year program covers the full cost of one-year service abroad programs in Bolivia, China, India, Indonesia, and Senegal.

A huge man-made campus lake was financed by Andrew Carnegie so that Princetonians would not have to forgo crew.

"The courses are very challenging and rigorous," a junior reports, "but perhaps because of that, people are very cooperative. They realize that no one can really succeed alone." Princeton's semester system gives students a two-week reading period before exams in which to catch up, with first-term exams postponed until after New Year's, much to the dismay of many ski buffs and tropical sun worshipers. The university honor code, unique among the Ivies, allows for unproctored exams. A limited number of courses can be taken on the pass/fail option, and the University Scholars program provides especially qualified students with what the administration calls "maximum freedom in planning programs of study to fulfill individual needs and interests." Although the faculty gets high ratings for its academic advising, students are rather cool on the university's nonacademic counseling programs.

The university honor code, unique among the Ivies, allows for unproctored exams.

"Our students are tight-knit, extremely hardworking, highly cooperative, and supportive of one another's activities," says an economics major. Eighteen percent of undergraduates are New Jersey natives, and 12 percent are international. African Americans account for 8 percent of the student body, Hispanics 10 percent, Asian Americans 21 percent, and multiracial students 4 percent. While diversity is present, the social atmosphere can be somewhat stratified. "As an African American, I can say that even the African Americans are subdivided based on economics, place of origin, and whether you went to public or private school," explains one senior. Although students report that there can be a general air of apathy around campus, administrators are quick to point to the numerous political organizations on campus as evidence of students' interest in political and social issues. Princeton undergraduates are admitted to the university without regard to their financial need, and those who qualify for aid receive generous support that covers their full demonstrated need. In fact, Princeton was the first university in the U.S. to replace loans with grants for all aid recipients. Twenty percent of freshmen qualify for Pell Grants—the highest proportion in the Ivy League.

"Seniors develop close personal relationships with their thesis advisors."

Twenty percent of freshmen qualify for Pell Grants—the highest proportion in the Ivy League.

In an attempt to improve campus life and broaden the social options for freshmen and sophomores, Princeton has grouped many of its dorms into six residential colleges, each with its own dining hall, faculty residents, and an active social calendar. Under this system, nearly all freshmen and sophomores live and dine with their residential college unit. Some students complain that the system "creates a gulf between underclassmen and upperclassmen." All upperclassmen maintain an affiliation to their residential colleges, however, and can choose to continue living in them, although most prefer to move into separate, upperclassmen dorms. Just 4 percent of all undergraduates live off campus. The university's turn-of-the-century Gothic dorms may look like crosses between cathedrals and castles, and some halls have amenities like living rooms and bay windows. But conditions on the inside are sometimes less glamorous. The modern and roomy Spelman dorms, which come complete with kitchens, are the best on campus and fill up quickly every year with seniors who do not belong to eating clubs.

Princeton's eating clubs are its most firmly entrenched bastions of tradition. Run by students and unaffiliated with the school, they line Prospect Avenue, and have, for more than a century, assumed the dual role of weekday dining hall and weekend fraternity. Of the 11, five admit members through an open lottery, but the others still use a controversial selective admissions process called bicker (because of the wrangling over whom to admit), to the chagrin of the administration and most students. While many of the clubs opened their doors to women back when Princeton went co-ed, two of the oldest and most exclusive—the Ivy Club and the Tiger Inn—remained all-male until 1991, when a court decision compelled them to admit women. Now, all the clubs are co-ed.

"Our students are tight-knit, extremely hardworking, highly cooperative, and supportive."

Catering exclusively to upperclassmen, the eating clubs provide a secure sense of community for their members. More than half of all sophomores join one of the clubs at the end of the year, becoming full-fledged members by the fall of their junior year. Annual dues vary; the most expensive is the Ivy Club, which charges its members almost $10,000 a year. Financial aid covers eating costs for those who qualify and want to join. Unfortunately, the social options for those who choose not to join may feel limited. All too often the upper-level eating clubs steal the thunder from college-sponsored social events. As a result, "the underclassmen spend too much time pining for the day when they, too, can join the closest thing Princeton has to cliques," says one student. Some opt for life in independent dormitories or join the handful of Greek fraternities and sororities (not sanctioned by the administration) that have sprung up on campus over the past few years and have become feeders to particular eating clubs.

Princeton's 11 eating clubs assume the dual role of weekday dining hall and weekend fraternity.

"Virtually all social life takes place on campus, both at the eating clubs and at dorm parties," says a sophomore. Princeton has the oldest licensed college radio station in the nation, plenty of journalistic opportunities, a prestigious debating and politics society (Whig-Clio) whose ranks have included James Madison and Aaron Burr, and a plethora of arts offerings. McCarter Theatre, adjacent to campus, houses Princeton's Triangle Club, which counted Jimmy Stewart and Brooke Shields as members. The roundup of annual campus events includes Communiversity Day, an international festival, and lawn parties in the spring. Each year about 3,000 students engage in volunteer activities such as tutoring, working in soup kitchens, or helping the elderly. Few students complain about boredom, and many praise the affluent town of Princeton for the parks, woods, bike trails, and, most important, the quiet and safety it offers students. Students rarely venture much farther than New York or Philadelphia, each one hour away (in opposite directions) on the train.

"Virtually all social life takes place on campus."

Athletics are a big deal at Princeton, both varsity and intramural. Eleven of the Tigers' 38 Division I teams took home Ivy League conference titles in 2017–18, among them men's cross-country and track and field and women's lacrosse, basketball, and soccer. Dozens of club and intramural sports are available, ranging from rugby to ballroom dancing to wallyball, and the eating clubs and residential colleges offer recreational athletic programs too. Every fall the freshman and sophomore classes square off in Cane Spree, an intramural Olympics that has been a tradition since 1869.

Princeton's unofficial motto is "Princeton in the nation's service and the service of humanity," and the oft-repeated notion that with privilege comes responsibility lives on as part of its culture. It's easy to be humbled at Princeton. Even the most jaded students must be awed and inspired when they think of those who've traversed the campus paths before them. While some may find the ambiance too insular, not many turn down membership in this very rewarding club.

Overlaps

Harvard, Yale, Columbia, University of Pennsylvania, Stanford

If You Apply To ›

Princeton: Single choice early action, regular decision. SATs or ACTs: required. Subject Tests: recommended (any two; engineering applicants required to take either physics or chemistry and math I or II). Accepts the Common Application with supplement.

Principia College

Elsah, IL 62028

Prin is a tiny college in a tiny town about an hour from St. Louis. All students, faculty, and staff are practicing Christian Scientists. Prin is mainly liberal arts, though one of its most popular programs is business administration. Sixty-five percent of students study abroad. Campus tenor is similar to places like Pepperdine and Wheaton (IL).

Students come to Principia College with a common bond—Christian Science. They shun smoking, drinking, drugs, and sex in favor of God and learning. Prin graduates are culturally, spiritually, and intellectually well-rounded, the product of a liberal arts education that promotes critical thinking and a broad worldview. As the only college anywhere for Christian Scientists, Prin attracts a lot of international students. The historic campus is reminiscent of Harry Potter's Hogwarts, but the fictional school of wizardry never had a woolly mammoth to unearth as Prin once did. Says one senior, Prin "has a warm, calm, and cozy atmosphere that reminds me of a second home."

Principia's 2,600-acre campus, on limestone bluffs above the mighty Mississippi River, is a designated National Historic Landmark. The dominant architectural influences are colonial American, Tudor, and medieval, and many buildings—including most student housing—were designed by California architect Bernard Maybeck. A contemporary of Frank Lloyd Wright, Maybeck urged Principia trustees to bring the college to its current spot when they relocated from St. Louis in 1935. The College Chapel, whose bells ring out hymns every Sunday evening, is the symbolic center of campus. A full renovation of Morey Field House was recently completed.

In addition to coursework in their major, students must complete a broad range of distribution requirements in the arts, humanities, social sciences, and natural sciences, as well as two physical education courses. All freshmen participate in a first-year experience program their first semester, and all seniors must complete a capstone course or project. Of the 25 majors offered, the most popular are educational studies, business administration, mass communication, biology, environmental studies, and programs in visual and performing arts. Students say political science and religious studies are also strong. A sustainability major has been added, and a dual-degree program is available in engineering science, in conjunction with the University of North Dakota.

> **"Most classes take advantage of group work in small teams."**

Academics are challenging, but students can count on each other and their professors for help. "Most classes take advantage of group work in small teams, and this helps you develop teamwork, leadership, and collaborative skills," says a senior. Most professors receive high marks. "Due to the small classroom style, faculty members are extremely accessible," says a business administration major. Sixty-five percent of Principia students participate in the five or six study abroad programs the school organizes each year. Each program enrolls 18 to 22 students, and sites are determined by academic subject and focus. Recent locations have included Greece, Croatia, the Czech Republic, Nepal, and Ireland. Others participate in a prairie restoration program, gather data for the study of the Mississippi River's aquatic life, or build solar cars to be entered in races around the world.

"We are all Christian Scientists who strive to be the most moral people we can be," says one junior. The minority population is minuscule—2 percent of students are African American, 2 percent are Hispanic, and 2 percent are Asian American. Still, an impressive 18 percent of students arrive from abroad, and only 12 percent are from Illinois. One international student says, "I've found that diversity positively impacts me. I've learned that there are more good things that bind us than negative things that divide us as human beings." Principia does not accept any governmental financial aid, so Pell Grants and the typical federal loans are not available to students, but the school does offer merit scholarships averaging $22,700, grants, and private, institutionally funded loans. No athletic scholarships are available.

All students live on campus, except for the few who are married or live locally with their parents. "The housing at Principia is superb, in the form of large, historical houses rather than the typical dormitory," says a senior. Students are expected not to be in wings where the opposite sex lives during "house hours" every night. Freshmen live in two modernized Maybeck houses with upperclassmen resident advisors trained to help new students adjust to college life. "Each house has its own sense of culture and traditions, and houses have brother-sister relationships as well as rivalries," explains a business administration and mass communication major. A sit-down pub and restaurant on campus provides a nice alternative to traditional dining-hall fare. "Dining facilities are improving, but vegetarians and vegans are still struggling," reports a junior. Students agree that they feel safe on campus, citing the rural location and a strong security presence.

> **"It's a wonderful thing not to have to deal with alcohol on campus."**

In addition to eschewing alcohol, tobacco, and drugs, students are also asked to sign a pledge of abstention from premarital and extramarital sexual relationships. "Those who sign the contract are committed to those morals for religious reasons," a political science major says. "It's a wonderful thing not to have to deal with alcohol on campus," says a senior. It goes without saying that Greek organizations are nonexistent; instead of partying, students keep busy at school-sponsored concerts, movies, dances, or intramural sporting events that pit one house against another. "Prin is remote enough where people stay on campus during the weekends to attend our awesome social events," says one student. Each house organizes its own annual celebration, international students show off their native cuisines at the Whole World Festival, and everyone looks forward to Spring Formal. The Public Affairs Conference is the oldest student-run event of its type, bringing in big-name speakers to give talks, lead workshops, and provide networking opportunities to students. "Elsah is not a college town," says a junior, complaining that "not much has changed" since the town was founded in 1853. Stores, restaurants, and movie theaters are about 20 minutes away, and St. Louis is about an hour's drive.

Principia's Panthers compete in Division III, and baseball, men's and women's soccer, and women's indoor and beach volleyball are especially competitive. Nearly two-thirds of students play intramural and club sports; the men's rugby and women's lacrosse club teams are strong. Campus athletic facilities include a four-court indoor tennis center, a field house with gym and pool, and outdoor courts and running trails.

Prin students embrace the conservative environment at their Christian Scientist school. Gone are the pressures that take hold of most college students, and a political science major says it "promotes character development and personal growth." A strong international presence and study abroad opportunities give students a taste of what lies beyond this quaint rural campus, but in the meantime, a junior says, students enjoy the comfort of Prin's "supportive community of like-minded thinkers."

Principia does not accept any governmental financial aid, so Pell Grants and the typical federal loans are not available to students.

The Public Affairs Conference is the oldest student-run event of its type, bringing in big-name speakers.

Overlaps

Wheaton (IL), Pepperdine, Northwestern, Purdue, University of Southern California, Stanford, William and Mary

If You Apply To ›

Principia: Rolling admissions. SATs or ACTs: required. Subject Tests: optional. Accepts the Common Application. Only college in the world that admits only Christian Scientists.

Providence College

Providence, RI 02918

Strong Roman Catholic atmosphere makes Providence more comparable to Notre Dame than to Boston College or Holy Cross. Liberal arts emphasis rooted in a required two-year interdisciplinary Western Civilization sequence, though more than a third of the students opt for business disciplines. Friars athletic teams do well in small but high-profile Big East Conference. No fraternities or sororities, but Providence is a vibrant oollege town.

Website: www.providence.edu
Location: City Outskirts
Private
Total Enrollment: 4,269
Undergraduates: 4,040
Male/Female: 45/55
SAT Ranges: ERW 580–660,
    M 580–670
ACT Ranges: 26–30
Financial Aid: 71%
Pell Grant: 14%
Expense: Pr $ $ $
Student Loans: 68%
Average Debt: $ $ $ $
Applicants: 11,251
Accepted: 52%
Enrolled: 18%
Grad in 6 Years: 84%
Returning Freshmen: 92%
Academics: ✍ ✍ ✍
Social: ☎ ☎ ☎
Q of L: ★ ★ ★
Admissions: (401) 865-2535
Email Address: pcadmiss@
    providence.edu

Strong Programs:
Marketing
Finance
Accountancy
Management
Biology
Psychology
Education
Chemistry

As the nation's only college or university operated by the Dominican Friars, Providence College wears its Roman Catholic and Dominican identities on its sleeve. Nearly three-quarters of students are Catholic, friars in habits walk the campus grounds, crucifixes adorn the walls of classrooms and offices, and St. Dominic Chapel stands tall in the heart of the campus. The school's mission is grounded in these identities, as it aims to "provide an education for the whole person—body, mind, and soul—that bridges the common divides between matter and spirit, God and creation, faith and reason." Students here enjoy solid offerings in the sciences and liberal arts—including a unique and rigorous two-year Western Civ course—and a tight-knit community of like-minded men and women.

Located only an hour's drive from Boston and just a few hours' drive from New York City, Providence College's 105-acre campus is situated in Rhode Island's capital city. The campus boasts open spaces, beautiful lawns, and student-centered facilities. The traditional brick and stone academic buildings, residence halls, and campus chapel coexist with several contemporary structures. In 2018 the college completed a massive, five-year campus transformation project that added several new facilities, among them the Ruane Center for the Humanities, a four-level addition to the Science Complex, and the $30 million Ryan Center for Business Studies.

> **"Professors here go the extra mile for their students. They are enthusiastic and available to us."**

The heart of Providence's Core Curriculum is a sequence of seminar-based classes that comprise the Development of Western Civilization (DWC). This 16-credit course spans students' freshman and sophomore years and introduces them to the seminal ideas and primary texts in history, literature, theology, and philosophy, as well as the music and visual arts that shaped the Western world and other civilizations. Aside from DWC, students take additional coursework in theology, philosophy, natural science, social science, quantitative reasoning, and fine arts, and they must demonstrate proficiency in intensive writing, oral communication, diversity, and civic engagement.

Providence comprises four schools: arts and sciences, business, professional studies, and continuing education. The School of Business draws 38 percent of the students and offers some of the most popular majors, include marketing, finance, accountancy, and management. All School of Business majors share a common set of core courses to ensure that business graduates have a broad understanding of all essential business disciplines. Biology, psychology, and education are also popular choices, and the chemistry program is strong. The biology department has added a new major in environmental biology and also offers a combined degree program with the New England College of Optometry, which allows for completion of the B.A. and doctorate in seven years.

"The academic climate at Providence College is rigorous but supportive," says a junior. Fifty-four percent of classes have fewer than 20 students and are taught by tenured or junior faculty. A Spanish and global studies double major says, "Professors here go the extra mile for their students. They are enthusiastic and available to us." The Liberal Arts Honors Program offers students of high academic ability and initiative a more in-depth and rigorous version of PC's core curriculum, and small, seminar-style honors courses are offered in virtually all areas. Students have ample opportunity for experiential learning through internships and faculty-directed laboratory or field research. PC's Center for International Studies sends 33 percent of students to more than 40 countries, including Argentina, Italy, New Zealand, and South Africa.

Nine percent of PC's undergraduates come from Rhode Island, and the remainder are mostly from the Northeast. In addition, most students are "preppy, white, Catholic, and generally upper middle class," according to a sophomore. Two percent are foreign nationals. African Americans account for 4 percent of the student body, Hispanics 9 percent, Asian Americans 1 percent, and multiracial students 2 percent. Many students are vocal about social and political issues, particularly when it comes to religion and race.

> *The heart of Providence's Core Curriculum is a 16-credit sequence of classes that comprise the Development of Western Civilization.*

"We have Division I school spirit but in a small-school atmosphere."

"We have a lot of outspoken liberals and closet Republicans at PC," observes a senior. The lack of diversity on campus draws near-universal concern: "I think it is felt very strongly among the minority students that we need more diversity on campus, even with all of our cultural clubs," says a junior. Merit scholarships averaging $17,400 are available to qualified students, and gifted athletes may vie for 185 awards.

Eighty percent of students live in the dorms, where conditions are said to be adequate and well maintained, if not spacious. Options include eight traditional halls, five apartment buildings, and a suite-style residence. Many seniors move off campus into the surrounding neighborhoods. Campus dining is "good and constantly getting better," says a global studies major. "We have a good line of communication between administration and students, and I feel as if PC has implemented all that they can to keep students safe," says an English major.

A junior says the social life is varied and, "There are free events for students to attend almost every day of the week, including weekends." Absent a Greek presence, students find other ways to let off steam. Owing to the college's strong Catholic identity, community service and volunteer work are popular pastimes. Annual traditions include a spring concert featuring top national acts and Civ Scream, held at midnight on the eve of Western Civ finals: "The entire sophomore class circles around the quad and screams to let out their frustration over Civ. People do crazy things and it is always something to remember," says a student. And although the college is located in "kind of a rundown area," an English major says the city of Providence "is full of opportunities," including a mall, a movie theater, and a cultural district with all sorts of shops and eateries. The city is also home to six other colleges, which enhances the social scene. Popular road trips include treks into Boston and New York City.

> *Owing to the college's strong Catholic identity, community service and volunteer work are popular pastimes.*

The Providence Friars field 19 varsity teams, most of which play in the competitive Division I Big East Conference (hockey is part of the Hockey East Association). Highly ranked teams include men's and women's ice hockey and cross-country, men's basketball and soccer, and women's lacrosse. "Basketball and hockey games are very important to PC students because we can show our school spirit," says a sophomore. Students get especially rowdy when rivals UConn and URI are in town. A majority of students get involved in intramurals and club sports, with flag football, softball, and rugby proving to be particularly popular.

Providence College appeals primarily to those students who want to challenge themselves academically without compromising their faith. Despite frequent complaints about the length and rigor of the Western Civ requirement and the lack of

Overlaps

Notre Dame, Boston College, Villanova, Holy Cross, Fairfield, Loyola University Maryland, Fordham, Northeastern

diversity, students here seem content with what the college has to offer and are proud to be part of the PC community. "PC is preppy and a great place to be," says a senior. "We have Division I school spirit but in a small-school atmosphere."

If You Apply To ›

Providence: Early decision I and II, early action, regular decision. SATs or ACTs: optional. Subject Tests: optional. Accepts the Common Application.

University of Puget Sound

1500 North Warner, Tacoma, WA 98416

Ask anyone in Tacoma about Puget Sound and they'll tell you that UPS (the college, not the package service) delivers solid liberal arts programs with a touch of business. Within easy reach of the Sound and Mount Rainier, the university specializes in all things Asia, including a nine-month university-sponsored trip. Compare to Whitman and Willamette.

Website: www.pugetsound.edu
Location: Small City
Private
Total Enrollment: 2,591
Undergraduates: 2,390
Male/Female: 40/60
SAT Ranges: ERW 580–690, M 570–680
ACT Ranges: 25–31
Financial Aid: 99%
Pell Grant: 16%
Expense: Pr $ $
Student Loans: 49%
Average Debt: $ $ $ $
Applicants: 5,958
Accepted: 84%
Enrolled: 12%
Grad in 6 Years: 78%
Returning Freshmen: 86%
Academics: ✍ ✍ ✍ ½
Social: ☎ ☎ ☎
Q of L: ★ ★ ★ ★
Admissions: (253) 879-3211
Email Address: admission@pugetsound.edu

Strong Programs:
Business
Psychology
Biology

An ambitious building program and revised core curriculum have raised the profile of the University of Puget Sound, transforming it from a regional liberal arts college in Tacoma to an undergraduate institution with growing national reach. What hasn't changed is the school's close-knit community and its emphasis on Asia. "People don't come here because they have heard of us before," says one contented senior. "They come here because they visit and they don't want to leave."

Founded in 1888, Puget Sound is cradled by the Cascade Range and the rugged Olympics, with easy access to the urban energy of Seattle and the natural beauty of Mount Rainier. The 97-acre campus boasts carefully maintained lawns, native fir trees, and plenty of other greenery, thanks to the moist climate. Most buildings, with distinctive arches and porticos, were built in the 1950s and '60s. Additional facilities include a recently opened athletics and aquatics center and a 3,850-square-foot Sculpture House, with facilities for welding, woodwork, and painting.

Puget Sound students must complete a core curriculum that includes a freshman seminar in writing and rhetoric, and another in scholarly and creative inquiry; they must also demonstrate foreign language proficiency and take a course on knowledge, identity, and power. In their first three years at Puget Sound, students also study five Approaches to Knowing—fine arts, humanities, math, natural sciences, and social sciences. An upper-level capstone course, Connections, challenges traditional disciplinary boundaries and examines the benefits and limits of an interdisciplinary approach to learning.

After navigating UPS's requirements, students may pursue a B.A., B.S., or B.M. (bachelor of music) degree. Some of the most popular majors are business, psychology, biology, economics, and international political economy. "I would recommend the environmental policy and decision making classes; you're often able to go on field trips with professors and working professionals," notes a senior. The university has developed a reputation as a jumping-off point to Asia—both literally and figuratively. Its curriculum stresses two of the fastest-growing fields in the region: Asian studies and Pacific Rim economics. Nearly one-third of Puget Sounders take at least one Asian studies course, and once every three years, there's a nine-month, school-sponsored trip through Japan, Thailand, Korea, India, China, and Nepal, where participants study art, architecture, politics, economics, and philosophy. In all, more than 100 study abroad programs are available in more than 40 nations; 28 percent of students participate. Other special offerings include a classics-based honors program, the Business Leadership Program, and residence-based humanities programs.

Students say that while their peers are academically motivated, the atmosphere at Puget Sound is relatively relaxed. "Most students recognize that their Puget Sound experience is more than just inside the classroom," explains a studio art major. Sixty-two percent of classes have fewer than 20 students, and you won't find grad students leading classes. "Our professors are here because they value small class sizes and genuine relationships with their students," says an art history major. Students also praise the plentiful opportunities for under-

"Our professors are here because they value small class sizes and genuine relationships with their students."

graduate research, which recently have ranged from examining bacteria on lizard eggs to summer fieldwork studying graffiti in Europe. Advising, which includes both academic and peer advisors, and career services receive positive reviews.

"Students at Puget Sound are definitely outdoorsy," says a Hispanic studies junior. "Lots of Birkenstocks and plaid. Politically liberal, for the most part." Most UPS students come from western states, with 21 percent hailing from Washington; less than 1 percent come from abroad. African Americans make up only 1 percent of the student body, Hispanics 9 percent, Asian Americans 6 percent, and multiracial students 9 percent. According to a junior, "There is a big push for more diversity on campus," and students are also concerned with LGBTQ rights, gender equality, and environmental issues. There are no athletic scholarships, but merit awards averaging $16,400 are doled out annually.

Once every three years, there's a nine-month, school-sponsored trip through Japan, Thailand, Korea, India, China, and Nepal.

Sixty-five percent of Puget Sound students live on campus, and freshmen and sophomores are required to do so. First-year students all live together, and after that students may live in Greek chapter housing, pursue a single room in the dorms, or apply for one of 60 university-owned theme houses, which focus on interests like outdoor leadership and entrepreneurship. "The surrounding neighborhood is happy to rent out houses to students who choose to live off campus their junior and senior years," reports a computer science major. Aside from the main campus dining area, students can chow down at three campus cafés and the Cellar, and meals get good reviews for freshness and variety. "We have a strong security team that takes sexual assault very seriously and has been good at communicating with the campus about situations that have happened," comments a junior.

Twenty-eight percent of Puget Sound men and 27 percent of the women go Greek, though fraternities and sororities don't dominate the social scene and all Greek parties are alcohol-free. "Social life at UPS is fairly intimate. In my experience, people tend to hang out more off campus on the weekends, at people's houses and such," a

"Students at Puget Sound are definitely outdoorsy. Lots of Birkenstocks and plaid."

philosophy major says. Popular school-sponsored activities include the Log Jam BBQ and club fair that kicks off the school year, the Foolish Pleasures festival of short student-produced films, and the Lumbershoot music festival in the spring (a play on Seattle's Bumbershoot). An active Hawaiian student organization sponsors a luau each spring, with "great food and lots of traditional dances." The Repertory Dance Group and Puget Sound Outdoors are among the most popular campus organizations. A few Tacoma bars and restaurants are within walking distance, and a junior says the university is working "to give students pipelines to the local community through volunteering and social justice programs, free and discounted

Popular school-sponsored activities include the Log Jam BBQ and club fair and the Lumbershoot music festival.

museum passes, and more." With the mountains and beaches so close—Seattle is 30 minutes away by car, Portland two hours south, and Vancouver, British Columbia, three hours north—road trips are *de rigueur*. That's especially true during ski season, and the school rents out all the necessary equipment.

Students are fond of saying that Puget Sound's Division III varsity teams, the Loggers, "Kick Axe." Solid teams include men's and women's soccer and women's basketball (recent Northwest Conference champs), crew, and volleyball. The school's archrival is Pacific Lutheran University; "football and basketball games against PLU are a big deal and always packed," says a fan. About half of the students sign up for intramural and club sports.

Don't let UPS students' slacker-chic clothes and casual demeanor fool you. Puget Sound means business and serious study for students seeking immersion in the liberal arts and the natural beauty of the outdoors. As a molecular and cellular biology major explains, "The vibe is laid-back, but purposeful at the same time. People who come to this school are passionate and love to share those passions with others."

Overlaps

Lewis & Clark, Reed, Whitman, Willamette, University of Washington, University of Oregon, Pomona, Kenyon

If You Apply To ›

Puget Sound: Early decision, early action, regular decision. SATs or ACTs: optional (test-optional applicants must submit two short-answer essay questions). No Subject Tests. Accepts the Common Application with supplement.

Purdue University

1080 Schleman Hall, West Lafayette, IN 47907

Purdue is Indiana's STEM university—with side helpings of business, health professions, and liberal arts. Compare to Kansas State and Big Ten rival Michigan State. Does better than most large universities in giving students hands-on opportunities such as internships and co-ops. Flight technology and aerospace—and turning out future astronauts—are longtime specialties.

Website: www.purdue.edu
Location: Small City
Public
Total Enrollment: 36,052
Undergraduates: 29,622
Male/Female: 57/43
SAT Ranges: ERW 570–670, M 580–710
ACT Ranges: 25–31
Financial Aid: 55%
Pell Grant: 16%
Expense: Pub $
Student Loans: 42%
Average Debt: $ $
Applicants: 48,912
Accepted: 57%
Enrolled: 27%

Successful Indiana colleges typically have three things in common: a solid agricultural program, a powerhouse basketball team, and a conservative student body. Purdue University has all of these—plus one of the nation's strongest engineering programs, and the distinction of having awarded more bachelor's degrees in the field than any other institution. Purdue is also home to the nation's first computer science department, and its programs in pharmacy, nursing, and management are top-notch. Budding classicists, dramatists, and literary critics might want to look elsewhere, but those seeking small-school friendliness with big-school spirit may be very happy to join the ranks of Boilermakers.

Purdue is the main attraction in the small industrial town of West Lafayette, where the population triples when students return each fall. The campus features redbrick and limestone buildings arranged around lush shaded courtyards. Recent construction includes the $90 million Honors College and Residences facility. Purdue is also home to Amazon.com's first ever brick-and-mortar location, where students can have textbooks shipped overnight for no cost.

Students apply to and enroll in one of Purdue's 10 colleges, and academic requirements vary by school and major. Typically, they include English, math, a lab science, and foreign language proficiency. Management is the most popular major, followed by mechanical engineering, computer science, and industrial engineering. Students flock to the five-year engineering co-op program, one of the most competitive on campus, because it marries classroom study with real-world work. Additionally, Purdue offers a strong undergraduate program in professional flight technology, which includes hands-on training at the university's own airport. Purdue has produced more than 20 astronauts, including pioneers Neil Armstrong and Gus Grissom. A four-year program in retail management is available in partnership with the Fashion Institute of Technology (FIT) in New York. For those seeking to save money on their degree and pursue their post-graduation plans sooner, Purdue offers nearly 20 "Degree in 3" programs in the colleges of Liberal Arts and Education through which students can earn a bachelor's degree in three years; options range from communication and history to sociology and special education.

> **"Everyone knows the reason we are here is to get a degree to be successful in the future."**

"The academic climate is fairly competitive and intense," says a sophomore. Despite the university's size, 38 percent of classes have fewer then 20 students and many freshman classes are seminar-style, taught by graduate students and academic advisors who help answer students' questions and provide career advice. "I've had some teachers who were phenomenal at connecting with the students and having them understand the concepts," one student confides, "and other teachers act like they are presenting to an empty room." Twenty-three percent of students study abroad, and options are available for students in all majors in more than 60 countries. Undergraduates also participate in more than 2,000 research projects each year.

"The students here are very academically focused and driven," says a junior. "They have fun and relax on weekends, but everyone knows the reason we are here is to get a degree to be successful in the future." Fifty-three percent of undergraduates are from Indiana, although there is a healthy proportion of international students, at 16 percent. Four percent are African American, 9 percent are Asian American, 6 percent are Hispanic, and 3 percent are multiracial. A tuition freeze has been in place since 2013, helping to keep costs down. Thousands of merit scholarships averaging $5,300 are awarded annually; athletes vie for 216 scholarships in 18 sports. The Purdue Promise program grants financial assistance and specialized academic and leadership coaching to eligible Indiana residents from lower-income backgrounds.

Forty percent of students live in Purdue's residence halls; the numbers may be so low because of rules governing male and female visitation hours. (The notion of a "co-ed dorm" here means that both sexes share a lobby.) Almost all freshmen live on campus, though they aren't required to, and Harrison Hall is said to be a good pick for newbies. "Some are definitely nicer

> **"[Purdue has] an awesome sense of community. Boiler Up!"**

than others," a sophomore admits. "Many of them still do not have air-conditioning." Most upperclassmen find inexpensive housing just off campus. Those with a grumbling stomach are treated to tasty options on campus. "Our food is fantastic," cheers one junior. "It's all-you-can-eat." Walking and riding escorts and a visible security presence help students feel safe.

"The social life typically takes place on campus," reports one philosophy major. Alcohol is prohibited in dorms, and "people have been kicked out of the residence halls for being caught with alcohol," says a sophomore. Still, as at other schools, underage students can find ways to get served. Greek life draws 21 percent of Purdue men and 23 percent of the women and offers many social opportunities. But there are other options too, including sports games and more than 1,000 student organizations, ranging from the BBQ society to professional development clubs. "Outside of class, you can do anything from skydiving, paintball, choir, rock

(continued)

Grad in 6 Years: 79%
Returning Freshmen: 92%
Academics: ✑ ✑ ✑ ½
Social: ☎ ☎ ☎
Q of L: ★ ★ ★
Admissions: (765) 494-1776
Email Address: admissions@purdue.edu

Strong Programs:
Management
Mechanical Engineering
Computer Science
Industrial Engineering
Pharmacy
Nursing
Professional Flight Technology
Aeronautical and Astronautical
  Engineering

The five-year engineering co-op program is one of the most competitive, because it marries classroom study with real-world work.

A tuition freeze has been in place since 2013, helping to keep costs down.

climbing, salsa dancing—anything. It's up to you," encourages a senior mechanical engineering major.

As far as college towns go, West Lafayette "would not exist if it weren't for Purdue," one student says. Another adds, "The surrounding area has a good social scene for those 21 [and over], with excellent bars and nightlife. There are also many great nearby restaurants within walking distance for all students." Harry's Chocolate Shop—a bar, not a candy store—is a longtime student favorite. Chicago and Indianapolis are favored weekend destinations for students with cars, and each spring, a week of fun and parties leads up to the Grand Prix go-kart races. Students also look forward to the Bug Bowl, an annual event sponsored by Purdue's entomology department, including cricket-spitting and cockroach races.

Purdue's "Boilermaker" moniker was coined by a sportswriter in 1891 describing how "the Burly Boiler Makers from Purdue" defeated Wabash College's football team 44–0. Boilermaker pride manifests itself at Division I games of all types, especially when the opposing team is Indiana University, known derisively as "that school down south," in the annual struggle for the Old Oaken Bucket. Every year, the winner adds a link to a chain on the bucket in the shape of either an "I" or "P." Men's basketball, women's golf, and men's and women's swimming and track and field are among the most competitive sports on campus. Thirty-four club sports and more than 40 intramurals are a big draw for those looking for friendly competition. Solar car racing and Rube Goldberg machine contests are some of the more popular activities among STEM students.

Happy students here have discovered that learning is fun when academics are mixed with real-world experience and a healthy dose of school spirit. "Purdue has great academic programs, incredible organizational and social opportunities, and an awesome sense of community," says one enthusiastic sophomore. "Boiler Up!"

Overlaps

U of I at Urbana–Champaign, Indiana University, Ohio State, University of Michigan, Penn State, Georgia Tech, UW–Madison, UC San Diego

If You Apply To ›

Purdue: Early action, regular decision. SATs or ACTs: required. Subject Tests: optional. Accepts the Common Application with supplement. Apply to particular schools or programs.

Queen's University: See page 361.

Quinnipiac University

275 Mount Carmel Avenue, Hamden, CT 06518

Aggressive expansion of programs and facilities has put Quinnipiac on the map of New England liberal arts colleges with a preprofessional bent. Less selective than Fairfield and Ithaca, with more dual-degree options. Business and health sciences are big attractions, though Quinnipiac is best known to the public for its political polling. Midway between NYC and Boston.

Website: www.qu.edu
Location: Suburban
Private
Total Enrollment: 8,522

Over the last three decades, Quinnipiac University has grown from a small liberal arts college of 2,000 full-time undergraduates to a full-fledged university with nearly 7,000 undergrads, three dozen graduate programs, and eight professional schools spread out over three campuses—a massive expansion that has helped to increase the school's national prominence. With enrollment now leveling off and its strengths in health, business, and communications well established, the university has begun to carve out a niche for itself as a place where talented, preprofessional undergraduates can get on a fast track to advanced degrees and jump-start their careers.

Quinnipiac's 250-acre Mount Carmel campus sits adjacent to Sleeping Giant State Park, with its 1,700 acres of hiking and walking trails, 90 minutes from New York City, and two hours from Boston. Traditional New England redbrick dominates, and a large central quad is surrounded by the library, the student center, the admissions and financial aid office, and academic buildings. The three-building College of Arts and Sciences Center features a spacious quad that overlooks Clark's pond and its family of swans. The campus also houses one of the world's largest collections of art and literature dealing with the Great Irish Famine. The 250-acre York Hill campus is just across Whitney Avenue and features the cozy Rocky Top Student Center, which

> "[Professors] want you to leave the class feeling confident about what you've learned."

resembles a European ski lodge and boasts panoramic views of the region. The 104-acre North Haven campus, located four miles from the Mount Carmel campus, serves as home to the Center for Medicine, Nursing, and Health Sciences, the School of Law, and the School of Education.

Quinnipiac's liberal arts philosophy is evident in its general education curriculum, which includes foundational courses in the sciences, social sciences, humanities, fine arts, writing, and intercultural understanding, as well as a capstone requirement in the senior year. All freshmen take a First Year Seminar based on a common reading—"It gives the student an idea of how he or she fits into the community," a math major says.

Quinnipiac offers nearly 60 undergraduate majors; the newest include four flavors of engineering (civil, industrial, software, and mechanical), and 17 engineering labs have recently been completed to accommodate them. The most popular majors include nursing, psychology, biology, and marketing. The Lender School of Business offers strong programs in entrepreneurship and finance, while students in the School of Communications benefit from several university-owned media outlets, including two radio stations and a television station. A spate of combined undergraduate/graduate degree programs are available in such fields as business, communications, law, and social work; the physician assistant, physical therapy, and occupational therapy combined degree programs are particular specialties. The university's career-oriented student body makes the most of these opportunities: nearly a third of undergrads stay at Quinnipiac to complete an advanced degree in their chosen profession.

"Students will find courses challenging but reasonable," says a junior. Forty-three percent of all classes have fewer than 20 students, and "there are no massive lecture halls," says one journalism major. There are no teaching or graduate assistants, either; all classes are taught by professors. "Professors are interested in teaching you the material and want you to leave the class feeling confident about what you've learned," says an occupational therapy major. Each school and college provides its own career services center, which students rate highly for assisting with internship and job placements.

Gifted students may enroll in the University Honors Program, which features special seminars, close relationships with professors, and a slew of enrichment and leadership opportunities. Internships and clinical experiences abound: communications students may elect to spend their summer on production sets or on-air, while political science majors have the opportunity to assist elected officials at the state capital or in Washington, D.C. The university is home to the renowned Quinnipiac Polling Institute, which regularly surveys residents of nine key swing states about

(continued)

Undergraduates: 6,959
Male/Female: 39/61
SAT Ranges: ERW 550–630, M 530–630
ACT Ranges: 23–27
Financial Aid: 96%
Pell Grant: 17%
Expense: Pr $ $
Student Loans: 68%
Average Debt: $ $ $ $
Applicants: 22,071
Accepted: 74%
Enrolled: 12%
Grad in 6 Years: 75%
Returning Freshmen: 86%
Academics: ✍ ✍ ✍
Social: ☎ ☎ ☎
Q of L: ★ ★ ★ ★
Admissions: (203) 582-8600
Email Address: admissions@qu.edu

Strong Programs:
Nursing
Psychology
Biology
Marketing
Physician Assistant
Physical Therapy
Business
Communications

Nearly a third of undergrads stay at Quinnipiac to complete an advanced degree in their chosen profession.

political races, state and national elections, and issues of public concern. Study abroad options include a highly popular semester program at University College Cork in Ireland; 30 percent of students take part in programs in 32 countries across the globe. "With so many different ways to go abroad (semester program, 10-day service trip, three- or six-week seminar), there is no reason not to take advantage and explore the world," urges a physical therapy major.

The university is home to the renowned Quinnipiac Polling Institute, which regularly surveys residents of nine key swing states.

Twenty-five percent of Quinnipiac's undergraduates come from Connecticut, and students say there is something of a preppy New England vibe on campus. "A lot of students come here for a very specific program or a dual degree, which makes them very focused on maintaining high grades," observes a biomedical sciences major. The student body is 4 percent African American, 9 percent Hispanic, 3 percent Asian American, and 3 percent multiracial; 1 percent of students are international. Political and social issues aren't a huge concern on campus, students say. Qualified undergraduates receive merit awards averaging $16,900, and gifted athletes vie for 348 athletic scholarships in 21 sports.

Housing is guaranteed for three years to incoming freshmen, and 75 percent of students reside in school-owned housing. Most freshmen and sophomores live on the Mount Carmel campus, while upperclassmen live on the York Hill campus in suite-style accommodations or in nearby houses or an apartment complex owned by the university. About a quarter of the students join the eight available living/learning communities. Students are required to purchase a meal plan, and food options at the main dining hall (Café Q) and the Bobcat Den get positive reviews, especially for variety. Campus security maintains a visible patrol on campus, and an occupational therapy major says, "Students are required to learn about sexual assault during their freshman orientation, and it's a serious topic that is reinforced throughout their time here."

"Greek organizations are more philanthropy-oriented than party-oriented."

The Quinnipiac social scene is bustling. The campus hosts a variety of events, including guest speakers, comedians, and film screenings; there are also more than 150 student clubs to whet the appetite of those seeking a good time. The university sponsors two fraternities and three sororities, but there is no dedicated Greek housing; 24 percent of the men and 30 percent of the women join. "Greek organizations are more philanthropy-oriented than party-oriented," notes a sophomore. Quinnipiac is a "wet" campus—students 21 or older are allowed to possess alcohol in the dorms—but underage drinkers face stiff penalties. Two annual concerts, Fall Fest and Wake the Giant, bring big headlining performers to campus.

Nothing brings out the Bobcat faithful like the annual hockey match versus rival Yale.

When students tire of the campus scene, they trek into surrounding towns in search of fun. Hamden offers the usual mix of chain restaurants, movie theaters, and bowling alleys, and the university provides a free shuttle to New Haven (home of Yale University), where students enjoy the food and nightlife. Eighty percent of students choose to get involved in the local community through volunteer work. The great outdoors beckon too. "It's a rite of passage to hike Sleeping Giant State Park at least once during your time here," says an English major.

"It's a rite of passage to hike Sleeping Giant State Park at least once during your time here."

The Quinnipiac Bobcats field 21 Division I teams—seven for men and 14 for women—and most compete in the Metro Atlantic Athletic Conference. Men's and women's ice hockey play in the powerful Eastern College Athletic Conference, and field hockey competes in the Big East. Women's rugby is a recent national champion, while conference champs include women's basketball, women's tennis, and men's ice hockey. Nothing brings out the Bobcat faithful like the annual hockey match versus rival Yale. "The Yale rivalry is fierce, and student pride comes alive," says a student. Eighty percent of students join Quinnipiac's intramural program, which includes competition in more than a dozen sports.

"The feeling of community is why I chose Quinnipiac University, and why I would recommend it to prospective students," says one junior. Expanding academics, flexible degree options, and increased selectivity are all part of the university's continuing mission to attract bright students. It's an expensive gamble that administrators and students feel will pay off. "There are more resources here than I can think of," says one satisfied student. "Any student who wants to succeed will succeed."

If You Apply To ›

Quinnipiac: Early decision, rolling admissions. SATs or ACTs: optional (required for health sciences and nursing applicants). No Subject Tests. Accepts the Common Application with supplement. Apply to particular program.

Randolph College

2500 Rivermont Avenue, Lynchburg, VA 24503

Co-ed since 2007, Randolph College continues to pursue its traditional mission of strong liberal arts programs in the spirit of its motto *Vita abundantior* (the life more abundant). Males now make up more than a third of undergrads. Its suburban location on the James River is rich in history, though of limited appeal to most students.

With rich traditions, cozy dorms, and challenging, seminar-based classes, Randolph College has preserved the best elements of its past while evolving into an institution that remains relevant today. The college, formerly known as Randolph–Macon Women's College, offers men and women a place to be themselves. "Fitting in isn't what Randolph is about," says a sophomore. "One of our mottoes is 'Be an Original,' and you can see that throughout the school."

The college's 100-acre campus sits in the historic neighborhood of Lynchburg, on the banks of the James River. Graceful old buildings are covered with purple wisteria and linked by glass corridors called trolleys; the surrounding trees burst into riotous bloom each spring. Main Hall, dating from 1893, houses dorm rooms, classrooms, and faculty and administrative offices. The Maier Museum of Art has one of the best college collections of American art in the country. The school's Riding Center offers indoor and outdoor arenas in the nearby Blue Ridge foothills.

> "[The workload is] just heavy enough to promote academic growth, but still reasonable enough to keep you sane."

Randolph's general education requirements are reflected in a matrix of study areas, with core competences (writing, quantitative reasoning, and language) on one axis, and ways of knowing (artistic expression, human experience, culture and identity, social and natural science, and physical education) on the other. "It forces you to explore different areas and take classes in almost every department," explains a sophomore. "I never thought I would major in psychology, but I took a psych class my spring semester and loved it!" All freshmen take the First-Year Seminar, which examines how to maximize academic success, and participate in the Passport Program, which orients them to campus resources and events. Every major culminates in a senior-year capstone experience, with an honors option available for highly motivated students.

Website:
  www.randolphcollege.edu
Location: Small City
Private
Total Enrollment: 661
Undergraduates: 643
Male/Female: 36/64
SAT Ranges: ERW 490–610, M 460–580
ACT Ranges: 19–25
Financial Aid: 100%
Pell Grant: 46%
Expense: Pr $
Student Loans: 69%
Average Debt: $ $ $ $
Applicants: 1,696
Accepted: 86%
Enrolled: 14%
Grad in 6 Years: 59%
Returning Freshmen: 67%
Academics: ✍ ✍ ✍
Social: ☎ ☎
Q of L: ★ ★ ★ ★
Admissions: 800-745-7692

(continued)

Email Address: admissions@
randolphcollege.edu

Strong Programs:
Biology
Psychology
History
English
Sport and Exercise Studies
Physics
Global Studies
Dance

Biology, psychology, history, English, and sport and exercise studies are some of the most popular majors at Randolph—and among the school's best departments. Programs in physics, global studies, and dance are also well regarded. A program in American culture combines classroom study with guest speakers and travel to historic sites; in past years, topics have focused on the Deep South, American capitalism, and Native lands in the American West. SUPER (Step Up to Physical Science and Engineering at Randolph) is an immersive STEM scholarship program for first-year students that includes a two-week residential academic program in the summer and specialized academic services and mentoring.

According to a senior, the workload at Randolph is "just heavy enough to promote academic growth, but still reasonable enough to keep you sane." The student-run Honor System has been in effect for more than a hundred years. Since 86 percent of classes enroll fewer than 20 students, and there are no TAs, it's easy for students to form friendships with their professors. "Professors know what interests you," says a senior, "and are always open to helping out with finding jobs or internships."

> **"[Professors] are always open to helping out with finding jobs or internships."**

All Randolph students are eligible to apply for a $2,000 RISE grant, which they can use to fund research, international travel, and other academic pursuits. Those interested in research may compete to assist professors with ongoing projects during an eight-week summer session, and many present their findings at the National Conference on Undergraduate Research. Thirty-seven percent of students study abroad, many in the school's flagship program at the University of Reading in England, and others in programs that are thematic in nature, such as examining peace studies in Nagasaki and Hiroshima. More than half of Randolph students secure off-campus internships, with organizations from the Chicago Lyric Opera to the National Gallery in London.

All Randolph students are eligible to apply for a $2,000 RISE grant to fund research, international travel, and other academic pursuits.

Seventy-one percent of Randolph students hail from Virginia, and 80 percent graduated from public schools; 4 percent are international. Minorities have a notable presence, with African Americans comprising 15 percent of the student body, Hispanics 6 percent, Asian Americans 3 percent, and multiracial students 6 percent. Socioeconomic diversity is strong, with 46 percent of freshmen qualifying for Pell Grants. The student body is largely liberal, but students say there is a respectful exchange of political views on campus. "Gender and race are two topics frequently discussed as the college strives to be inclusive and transparent," observes a senior. Randolph awards merit scholarships averaging $23,400 each year, but there are no athletic awards.

Seventy-six percent of Randolph students live in the dorms, which a global studies major calls "pretty nice and comfy," although students gripe about the lack of air-conditioning in some dorms. Main Hall, a.k.a. "the Hilton," is the largest dorm, and its central location makes it the most convenient. After the first year, housing is selected by lottery, and college-owned apartments across the street from campus are the preferred option among upperclassmen. As for campus dining, a biology major says, "The actual dining hall is very nice; the food is mediocre at best." Security officers patrol continuously and take pride in knowing students by name, and a sophomore says, "Effective programs around the issue of sexual assault are promoted throughout the school year."

> **"The real social scene is inside the Red Brick Wall."**

"The real social scene is inside the Red Brick Wall," says a sophomore. "We have a number of secret societies, clubs, and other social organizations." The Macon Activities Council makes sure no one is bored by hosting comedians, bands, and other entertainers, as well as talent shows and outdoor parties. Randolph's close-knit community can get too close at times (a junior warns, "You may learn things about your personal life from other people before you knew them yourself"), so students occasionally escape to other nearby colleges like Hampden–Sydney, Washington and Lee, and the University of Virginia, for those seeking frat parties and football. Underage drinkers face consequences, in accordance with the honor code. There is no Greek life, but sports teams and other organizations offer a moderate party scene.

The town of Lynchburg (population 80,000) hosts two other colleges and has a shopping mall and some retail chains like Target and Barnes & Noble, but is otherwise "less than exhilarating," says a biology major. Most clubs in the area are 21 and over, and the restaurants, stores, and movie theaters are closed by 10 p.m. Thankfully, the college's coffee bar satisfies students' caffeine cravings. "We also have a lot of hiking and recreation options that are close by and affordable," offers a junior. Students often get involved in the local community via volunteering.

Randolph's WildCats compete in Division III, and the school's top rival is the University of Lynchburg. Recently, the equestrian and women's tennis teams have been most competitive, along with men's soccer, basketball, tennis, and track and field. But more than athletic contests, students look forward to Randolph traditions, such as the Even/Odd class rivalry, Ring Week (in which a freshman anonymously decorates the door of a junior and leaves small gifts all week, culminating with a scavenger hunt for their class ring), and the Pumpkin Parade (during which sophomores present lit jack-o'-lanterns to seniors, who show them off in an evening parade). The Never-Ending Weekend each fall includes both a formal and the annual Tacky Party, for which tasteless attire is *de rigueur*.

The students of Randolph aren't shy about their academic goals, career drive, or sense of campus unity. "The college went co-ed years ago and so the population changed," says one student. "But the core dynamic and value system did not. Students still value respect and responsibility."

During Ring Week, a freshman anonymously leaves a junior small gifts all week, culminating with a scavenger hunt for their class ring.

Overlaps

Hendrix, Millsaps, Wells, Eckerd, Elmira, Randolph–Macon, Centre, Washington College

If You Apply To ›

Randolph: Early action, regular decision. SATs or ACTs: required. Subject Tests: optional. Accepts the Common Application with supplement.

University of Redlands

1200 East Colton, P.O. Box 3080, Redlands, CA 92373

If you like the thought of palm trees against a backdrop of snow-covered peaks, Redlands may be your place. As a "university," Redlands is double the size of Occidental and Whittier. The Johnston Center for Integrative Studies, an alternative living/learning program, makes an odd contrast to the buttoned-down preprofessionalism of the rest of Redlands.

Amid the dozens of gigantic and well-known universities in the state of California stands the University of Redlands. With its innovative, alternative living/learning option and strong preprofessional emphasis, this versatile school is one of higher education's better-kept secrets, and a place where students receive all the personal attention and intellectual stimulation they could want. As one junior puts it, "All the staff want you to succeed, and the school is designed to help you learn and grow according to your needs."

Website: www.redlands.edu
Location: Suburban
Private
Total Enrollment: 4,353
Undergraduates: 2,439
Male/Female: 41/59

(continued)

SAT Ranges: ERW 540–630,
    M 530–620

ACT Ranges: 23–28

Financial Aid: 95%

Pell Grant: 36%

Expense: Pr $ $

Student Loans: 68%

Average Debt: $ $ $ $

Applicants: 4,776

Accepted: 75%

Enrolled: 20%

Grad in 6 Years: 77%

Returning Freshmen: 82%

Academics: ✎ ✎ ✎

Social: ☎ ☎ ☎

Q of L: ★ ★ ★

Admissions: (909) 748-8074

Email Address: admissions@
    redlands.edu

Strong Programs:
Business Administration
Psychology
Communication Sciences and
    Disorders
Biology
Education
Music
Global Business
Integrative Studies

*All students must
take a first-year
seminar, participate
in community service,
and complete a
capstone requirement.*

The University of Redlands's 160-acre campus, covered in majestic oak trees, is designed around "The Quad," a group of dorms that face one another. The two main landmarks are the Memorial Chapel and the Administration Building. Redlands's facilities are a mixture of older, historical columned buildings and more modern, renovated ones. The view from campus can only be described as breathtaking. Mountain ranges form the backdrop, and neighboring Big Bear Lake and Arrowhead ski resorts give endless getaway opportunities. Also nearby are the San Gorgonio Wilderness and Joshua Tree National Park.

Redlands's most distinctive attribute is the Johnston Center for Integrative Studies, an experimental living/learning community where students create their own course of study and are assessed by professor and self-evaluations rather than grades. The Johnston Center was established in 1969 to function as an alternative college within a traditional setting; it's now a program within the College of Arts and Sciences, rather than a separate college. With about 200 participants, it's one of the university's largest programs and offers unusual academic freedom: there are no departments, majors, or distribution require-ments. Instead, students design contracts with professors for their entire plan of study. At the beginning of each course, students make up the syllabus by consensus and then set their own research and writing goals. Each student develops four-year goals—which are reviewed by a student/faculty board for direction and breadth—within one or more broad areas: the social sciences, behavioral sciences, humanities, and fine and per-forming arts. One student explains, "Johnston Center students tend to be indepen-dent thinkers, self-motivated, and [don't] take classes just because they have to." Recent participants have designed degrees such as urban agriculture, social behavior across cultures, and neuroscience of oneirology.

> "Education becomes a conversation, and students' original ideas are not only allowed but encouraged."

Aside from Johnston, Redlands is unusual among liberal arts institutions mainly in that it also offers preprofessional programs. The schools of education and music provide strong career training, as does the excellent program in communication sci-ences and disorders. Premed/prehealth and prelaw students receive advising on requirements for graduate school, and 3–2 engineering degrees with Columbia University and WashU in St. Louis are available. Redlands has emerged as a national leader in science curriculum reform with innovative interdisciplinary offerings like the new health, medicine, and society program, which combines the study of natu-ral science, medical humanities, public policy, global health, and more. Business administration is the most popular major, and the university also offers majors in global business and theater business. Psychology, communication sciences and dis-orders, and biology are popular too. Regardless of major, all students must take a first-year seminar, participate in community service, and complete a capstone requirement, such as an internship or academic research, in order to graduate.

"I love Redlands's small, discussion-based classes," says a Johnston Center stu-dent. "Education becomes a conversation, and students' original ideas are not only allowed but encouraged." Sixty-four percent of classes have fewer than 20 students, meaning "interaction with professors is common and camaraderie is abundant," says a psychology and Spanish double major. Professors are said to be very acces-sible outside of class too, even occasionally coming by the dorms for "fireside chats." With its 4–4–1 calendar, Redlands affords students the option to take one intensive course each May, and some use this time to study abroad. Students may embark on Redlands's signature program in Salzburg, Austria, or choose from among 100 other options worldwide; 48 percent study abroad. The Redlands Promise guarantees that if incoming students are unable to graduate in four years with the help of faculty advising, Redlands will cover the cost of additional courses needed for graduation.

"Redlands has a very personal, small-town sort of feeling," says a sophomore. "Everyone is so friendly and supportive." Seventy-two percent of undergraduates come from within the state, creating a mellow, Southern California atmosphere on campus. The climate is a definite plus, with temperatures rarely below 50 degrees. The typical Redlands student tends to be fairly conservative, although the student body as a whole "is not the most politically engaged," according to one senior. Two percent of students are international, and the racial makeup of the school is diverse, with Hispanics representing 30 percent, Asian Americans 6 percent, African Americans 4 percent, and multiracial students 6 percent. Redlands annually awards a variety of merit scholarships averaging $27,000. There are talent awards in art, writing, music, and theater, but there are no athletic scholarships. Thirty-six percent of incoming students are Pell-eligible.

The "Och Tamale" school chant—a string of complete gibberish invented in mockery of Occidental's Latin chant—is a beloved school tradition.

Sixty-three percent of students live in the residence halls, most of which are co-ed. Other housing options include on-campus apartments and student-run co-ops. Students enjoy their food at the Irvine Commons or Plaza Café, part of the Hunsaker University Center, which has a "town square" atmosphere. Students praise Redlands's safety and its approach to sexual assault prevention; says one, "My school has taken measures to protect students by being very transparent with them."

> **"Redlands has a very personal, small-town sort of feeling."**

Social life is well balanced between on-campus activities and off-campus fun. Local fraternities and sororities claim 10 percent of the men and 15 percent of the women, respectively, and their generally well-controlled parties are open to all. Alcohol is accessible but "there is no pressure to drink or party," according to one senior. Students look forward to the Spring Fest concert every year. The nearby city of Redlands offers a variety of coffee shops and restaurants, and students are highly involved in the local community, contributing more than 120,000 hours of service each year. Road trips to Los Angeles, Palm Springs, and San Francisco are common.

The University of Redlands sponsors 21 intercollegiate Bulldog teams, all of which consistently vie for spots among the top of the Division III Southern California Intercollegiate Athletic Conference (SCIAC). Football, men's soccer, and women's basketball, track and field, and swimming and diving are competitive. Games against rival Occidental always draw crowds, and the "Och Tamale" school chant—a string of complete gibberish invented in 1921 in mockery of Oxy's Latin chant—is a beloved school tradition ("Och tamale gazolly gazump!"). Half of students participate in at least one intramural or club sport, and weekend adventurers strike out on regular excursions organized by Outdoor Programs.

The University of Redlands is a lot of different things to a lot of different people. With roughly 170 full-time faculty members, it manages to be a preprofessional institute, a liberal arts college, and an alternative school all in one. The Johnston Center is clearly a path to travel for the innovative individualist, but even those who don't join Johnston can find what they want and need at Redlands.

Overlaps

Chapman, Loyola Marymount, University of San Diego, Whittier, California Lutheran, Cal Poly–San Luis Obispo, San Diego State, UC Irvine

If You Apply To ›

Redlands: Early decision, early action, regular decision. SATs or ACTs: required. No Subject Tests. Accepts the Common Application. Applicants to music program must audition.

3203 S.E. Woodstock Boulevard, Portland, OR 97202

Reed is a West Coast version of Grinnell or Oberlin, mixing nonconformist students with a traditional and rigorous curriculum. Sends huge numbers of grads on to Ph.D.s. Students who were square pegs in high school often find Reed a square hole. Annual springtime Thesis Parade symbolizes Reed's culture of quirky intellectualism.

Website: www.reed.edu
Location: City Outskirts
Private
Total Enrollment: 1,402
Undergraduates: 1,402
Male/Female: 46/54
SAT Ranges: ERW 670–740, M 640–760
ACT Ranges: 30–33
Financial Aid: 50%
Pell Grant: 12%
Expense: Pr $ $ $ $
Student Loans: 50%
Average Debt: $
Applicants: 5,652
Accepted: 36%
Enrolled: 21%
Grad in 6 Years: 80%
Returning Freshmen: 88%
Academics: ✍ ✍ ✍ ✍ ½
Social: ☎ ☎ ☎
Q of L: ★ ★ ★ ½
Admissions: (503) 777-7511
Email Address: admission@reed.edu

Strong Programs:
Biology
English
Mathematics
Art
Psychology
Environmental Science
Physics

Reed College is one of the most intellectual colleges in the country. It's the place where the late Steve Jobs—cofounder of Apple—attended for a semester before dropping out to rule the world and where students complain that the library, which closes its doors at midnight on Fridays and Saturdays, shuts down too early. Letter grades are de-emphasized as a form of evaluation. Instead, students receive lengthy and detailed commentaries from professors, which fosters continued dialogue and eliminates grade inflation. "Reed is the absolute best place for someone who likes to think, to read, to question, and to work," says a student. "It's a community of scholars."

Located in Southeast Portland, Reed's 116-acre campus boasts rolling lawns, winding lanes, a canyon creek, and protected wetlands. A fish ladder was installed to help salmon reach their spawning grounds, and nonnative plants are being removed from the area to protect the natural habitat. Two thousand majestic arbors shade a mix of original campus buildings, constructed of brick, slate, and limestone in the Tudor Gothic style, as well as lodges in the homey Northwest Timber style and some more modern facilities, such as the Performing Arts Building. New construction includes a $27 million, 180-bed residence hall—the college's largest—on the north end of campus.

Although Reed emphasizes personal freedom and responsibility, especially through its Honor Principle, the curriculum and academic requirements are remarkably traditional. Freshmen must complete Humanities 110, a yearlong interdisciplinary course focused on society and culture from classical Greece and the ancient Mediterranean to the Harlem Renaissance. The course, which has been taught for more than 50 years, was updated in 2018 in response to student protests to make it "less Eurocentric and more inclusive," according to a junior. Designed to create a shared intellectual experience for new students, the class draws on instruction from 25 professors, including some of Reed's most senior and distinguished faculty. Students must also take courses in three "breadth" areas: literature, arts, and languages; history and social sciences; and mathematics and laboratory sciences (including psychology). Seniors must submit a research-based thesis to graduate. On the due date, just after spring classes have ended, seniors march from the library steps to the registrar's office in the Thesis Parade. This marks the beginning of Renn Fayre (originally "Renaissance Fayre"), a weekend-long celebration that involves a bug-eating contest, Glow Opera, live human chess, music, and fireworks.

> **"[Reed is] a community of scholars."**

"The academics here are very rigorous, but not highly competitive," says an economics major. Reed's most popular majors include biology, English, math, art, and psychology. A new major in comparative race and ethnic studies draws from sociology, anthropology, history, and the arts. Dual-degree (3–2) programs are offered in engineering and forestry/environmental science. Students take full advantage of the range of academic options, which often keep them tethered to their computers and study carrels. You'll never find a TA at the lectern here or leading a group discussion, so students rarely attend class unprepared for the lively intellectual banter that typically ensues between inquiring and active minds. Reed has "the best profs from anywhere around," says a psychology major. "They want to be at Reed, meaning that their top priority is teaching." Reed has improved its retention and graduation rates considerably in the last decade or two by becoming more selective in admissions, increasing on-campus housing for a stronger residential community, and bolstering student support services, including a popular peer tutoring program.

Despite Reed's small size—76 percent of the courses taken by undergraduates have fewer than 20 students—the school offers excellent research opportunities in the liberal arts and sciences. Budding physicists and environmental scientists can work with college staff at the 250-kilowatt Triga nuclear reactor after passing an Atomic Energy Commission examination. "It's grueling, but physics here is legendary," says a junior. Reed also has a tradition of respect for calligraphy that, among other things, inspired Steve Jobs to build first-rate graphics into Apple computers. Fifty-two exchange programs attract 25 percent of each graduating class, taking students to 23 countries, from Germany and China to Ecuador and Russia. Reed also offers domestic exchange programs with Howard, Sarah Lawrence, and the Woods Hole Oceanographic Institute. Over the years, a quarter of Reed's grads have gone on for Ph.D.s—the highest percentage of any liberal arts college in the country.

Reed's 116-acre campus boasts a canyon creek and protected wetlands.

"Students who attend Reed are ridiculous, silly, cerebral, passionate, critical, and questioning."

"Students who attend Reed are ridiculous, silly, cerebral, passionate, critical, and questioning," says one observant Reedie. "If we have one thing in common, we are people whose lives center on learning." While Reed is located in Oregon, its quirky brand of intellectualism means only 7 percent of the students are in-staters. Eleven percent hail from other nations. Six percent are Asian American, 10 percent are Hispanic, 2 percent are African American, and 8 percent are multiracial. "The Multicultural Resource Center provides resources—guest speakers, lecturers, Tuesday Talks, and more—to keep diversity an ongoing discussion on campus," says an English major. When it comes to political and social issues, a linguistics major says, "The school is pretty rigidly liberal, and students have very strong opinions on fighting discrimination." All financial aid at Reed is need-based, and the school covers 100 percent of admitted students' demonstrated need.

Humanities 110, which has been taught for more than 50 years, was updated in 2018 in response to student protests to make it more inclusive.

Sixty-five percent of Reed students live on campus in comfortable rooms, some of which feature such homey touches as fireplaces or balconies. Freshmen are guaranteed housing and usually get divided doubles; upperclassmen get singles. There are six language houses (French, German, Russian, Spanish, Chinese, and Arabic), each of which is staffed with a native speaker. Those who lose out in the housing lottery, or upperclassmen seeking a taste of post-college independence, contend with Portland's pricey rental market. On-campus students must buy the meal plan. "The food is surprisingly good and diverse," one student says, "and the kitchen is happy to help with any particular dietary needs." As for campus security, "I know the community safety officers on campus," says one student. "They aren't uniformed nameless entities patrolling dorms." Another adds, "Our student body really promotes a strong culture of [sexual] consent."

"Portland, Oregon, is one of the coolest, weirdest places in America."

"There's always a ton going on, both on campus and off. On campus, there are always small parties, or plays, or giant Student Union dances, or fire-dancing shows, or bands playing," says one student. Students describe Reed's drug and alcohol policies, guided by the college's Honor Principle, as effective and well enforced, but something of a drug culture persists on campus—although in a pressure-free way. "I have never been pushed to use substances I am not comfortable using," says a junior. Students look forward to Paideia (which means "education" in Ancient Greek), a weeklong program of wacky, noncredit alternative classes before spring semester begins. Past Paideia workshops have ranged from Bollywood dance and the history of Batman to how to speak with a French accent. "Other traditions are…hard to explain," muses a junior. "You've got to see them to believe them."

"Portland, Oregon, is one of the coolest, weirdest places in America, so of course it's a good social scene," raves a senior. The city boasts a diverse range of live music, literary events, and film screenings, as well as an array of quirky shops, bars, and restaurants. Many students get involved in community service projects organized by SEEDS (Students for Education, Empowerment, and Direct Service). The mammoth Powell's bookstore downtown is about a 15-minute drive, and Oregon's coastal beaches, mountains, or high desert are all about two hours away—although finding time for road trips can be a challenge. The school also owns a ski cabin on Mount Hood that sleeps 15.

The closest thing Reed has to a school mascot is the Doyle Owl, a 300-pound concrete sculpture that dorms regularly plot to steal from one another. While Reed doesn't have varsity athletics, club teams in basketball, rugby, soccer, and ultimate Frisbee do compete with other clubs in the area. A variety of intramural and recreational sports are available for the less competitive, such as mountaineering, rowing, and curling.

Reed attracts seriously intellectual, unconventional students, but it is not without a sense of humor—the school's unofficial, tongue-in-cheek slogan is "Atheism, Communism, Free Love." If you're a lover of learning who prefers to start Saturday nights with your nose in a book and end them at an all-school dance party, this Portland school is definitely worth a look.

Overlaps

University of Chicago, Oberlin, Pomona, Carleton, Swarthmore, Brown, Lewis & Clark, UC Berkeley

If You Apply To ›

Reed: Early decision I and II, early action, regular decision. SATs or ACTs: required. Subject Tests: optional. Accepts the Common Application with supplement.

Rensselaer Polytechnic Institute

110 Eighth Street, Troy, NY 12180

If you can spell Rensselaer, you've already got a leg up on many applicants. RPI is one of the nation's great technical universities—along with Caltech, Harvey Mudd, MIT, and Worcester Polytech—and one of the most innovative. The beauty of RPI is the chance for hands-on learning and synergy between technology and management. Building boom and faculty hiring spree have raised its profile, and it's now much more selective in admissions than a few years ago.

Website: www.rpi.edu
Location: Suburban
Private
Total Enrollment: 7,425
Undergraduates: 6,305

It would be an exaggeration to say that technology is god at RPI, though the school's conversion of a Gothic chapel into a computer lab does hint in that direction. Even if it's not deified, technology remains omnipresent at this school, which pioneered the teaching of calculus via computer in the early '90s. Students attend class in high-tech studio classrooms where they work on team projects and collaborate to solve real-world problems, and the institute continues to ramp up its research funding. For students who may have been known as geeks in high school, coming to Rensselaer is like coming home.

Set high on a bluff overlooking Troy, New York, Rensselaer's 275-acre campus mixes modern research facilities and classical, ivy-covered brick buildings dating to the turn of the century. The cutting-edge Center for Biotechnology and Interdisciplinary Studies houses more than 400 researchers in biotechnology and related disciplines who work in such areas as regenerative medicine, bioinformatics, biocatalysis, and metabolic engineering.

In order to graduate, all students must complete extensive coursework in humanities, social sciences, and physical, life, and engineering sciences; a minimum of 30 credits in their majors; and two communication-intensive courses, including one writing-intensive course. RPI made its reputation as one of the nation's premier engineering schools and continues to excel in traditional favorites such as mechanical and aeronautical engineering, as

> **"Most professors have spent multiple years in the industry before coming to teach, so they have real-world experience."**

well as newer specialties like environmental and computer systems engineering. Engineering majors tend to be the most popular, followed by computer and information sciences, business and management, and biological sciences. Architecture is also a strength. The nuclear engineering department has its own linear accelerator, while graduate and undergraduate students participate in research at the Center for Industrial Innovation. The Center for Computational Innovations is among the world's most powerful university-based supercomputers and is designed to advance semiconductor technology to the nanoscale.

RPI's Lally School of Management combines elements of a business school with the latest technical applications. Entrepreneurship is one of its specialties; budding entrepreneurs from all majors may participate in a business incubator program, a support system for start-up companies run by Rensselaer students and alumni. RPI is a national leader in the study and application of electronic media and offers a B.S. degree in electronic arts. Students in the information technology program select one of 20 concentrations ranging from cognitive science to economics. Majors in the humanities and social sciences are limited, and their quality is directly related to their applicability to technical fields. Students with long-term professional goals may enter a seven-year dual-degree program in medicine; a six-year program in law; or five- and six-year master's programs in business, sciences, or engineering.

"The workload does get pretty intense," says one junior, "but everybody helps each other out to be as relaxed and prepared as possible." Eighty-five percent of Rensselaer students are undergraduates, a high percentage for a top engineering school; because of this, RPI has worked hard to ensure that classes are smaller

> **"Politics? Not so much on this campus."**

and more attention is paid to individual needs. Fifty-two percent of classes enroll fewer than 20 students. "Most professors have spent multiple years in the industry before coming to teach, so they have real-world experience that they draw on to build tests and projects," says an aeronautical engineering major. Students also give high ratings to the drop-in tutoring services offered by the Advising and Learning Assistance Center.

Juniors and seniors enjoy self-paced courses and occasionally paid positions helping with faculty research. For students who can't wait to start working, popular co-op programs in more than a dozen fields help them earn both money and credit. Although most engineering schools discourage studying abroad, Rensselaer expects and encourages undergrads to participate in some sort of international study, internship, or service-learning experience, offering programs in more than 15 countries on four continents.

(continued)

Male/Female: 68/32
SAT Ranges: ERW 640–730, M 680–770
ACT Ranges: 28–32
Financial Aid: 85%
Pell Grant: 18%
Expense: Pr $ $ $
Student Loans: 65%
Average Debt: $ $ $ $
Applicants: 19,505
Accepted: 43%
Enrolled: 20%
Grad in 6 Years: 83%
Returning Freshmen: 93%
Academics: ✍ ✍ ✍ ✍
Social: ☎ ☎ ☎
Q of L: ★ ★ ★
Admissions: (518) 276-6216
Email Address: admissions@rpi.edu

Strong Programs:
Engineering
Computer and Information Sciences
Business and Management
Biological Sciences
Mechanical Engineering
Aeronautical Engineering
Architecture
Electronic Arts

The Center for Biotechnology and Interdisciplinary Studies houses more than 400 researchers in biotechnology and related disciplines.

Thirty percent of RPI students are New Yorkers, and 12 percent are international. RPI is fairly diverse, with Asian Americans comprising 12 percent of the student body, African Americans 4 percent, Hispanics 9 percent, and multiracial students 7 percent. "The students at RPI are driven and motivated. They want to get ahead and change the world," says one student. Despite that ambition, RPI is far from a center of political activism; students say they're just too busy. "Politics? Not so much on this campus," says a student. The biggest campus issue may be choosing the Grand Marshal, who oversees a boisterous weeklong carnival celebrating campus elections, during which professors are barred from giving tests. Merit scholarships averaging $19,300 are available, as are 41 athletic scholarships for men's and women's ice hockey.

Fifty-seven percent of students live in university housing; freshmen and sophomores are required to live in the residence halls, where they are supported by a team of faculty and peer advisors intended to create smaller, more tightly knit student communities. "The freshman dorms are pretty typical, but the upper-class residence halls are great," one senior says. Most upperclassmen choose to move into less expensive off-campus apartments. Meals served in the four campus dining halls get lukewarm reviews. Students say they receive thorough education regarding personal safety and sexual assault prevention, and one reports, "I've never had to use any of the skills and techniques taught."

"Hockey at RPI equals insanity."

A senior says, "There are things to do on campus, but a majority of the social students go to celebrations in the Greek houses and off-campus apartments." Thirty percent of men and 16 percent of women go Greek and, other than Greek parties, weekend options at RPI include sporting events, live entertainment, concerts, movies, and a half-dozen local pubs—some of which students find easily accept fake IDs. The campus is not dry, but fraternities aren't allowed to have "containers of mass distribution" (i.e., kegs) at parties; students say alcohol isn't an issue on campus. More than 200 student-run extracurricular clubs are on offer, organized around such interests as chess, dance, judo, multiculturalism, and philanthropy.

Free shuttle buses run regularly from campus to downtown Troy, a former industrial revolution town. "Troy is not a college town," says a senior, "but it does have good places to eat and some beautiful parks." Students and Greek groups get involved with community service projects, and the town offers opportunities for internships. Rensselaer has helped generate economic growth in Troy by investing in the downtown area and providing grants to homebuyers. A six-screen movie theater is within easy reach, and for a taste of bigger-city nightlife, Albany is a half-hour drive. For scenic excursions, the Berkshires, Catskills, Adirondacks, Lake George, Lake Placid, the Saranac Lakes, Montreal, and Boston are popular destinations.

The athletic scene at Rensselaer revolves around hockey, hockey, hockey—the school's only teams playing in Division I. One of the biggest weekends of the year is Big Red Freakout, when all festivities center around cheering on the beloved Big Red. "Hockey at RPI equals insanity," one student says. "If you go to one hockey game all season, go to the men's hockey season opener. The place is packed with rowdy RPI students who scream and chant in unison." Other varsity teams play in Division III, and the football, baseball, men's and women's basketball, and women's field hockey teams are most successful. There are many intramural sports to choose from, but the most popular may be the D-level hockey team (meaning "I really don't know how to play this," says a junior).

Rensselaer provides cutting-edge technology to students constantly wondering how things work. Computer geeks and video game junkies aren't the only ones who will find a home at RPI—students who thrive on teamwork and collaboration will also find it to their liking. RPI students work hard, sometimes to the detriment of a social life, but they don't seem to mind. Says a computer engineering major, "Students at RPI are all a little bit nerdy, and proud of it."

If You Apply To ›

RPI: Early decision I and II, regular decision. SATs or ACTs: required. Subject Tests: optional (required for applicants to accelerated programs). Accepts the Common Application with supplement. Apply to particular program.

University of Rhode Island

14 Upper College Road, Kingston, RI 02881

URI is a smallish alternative to UConn and UMass. With Boston, Providence, and vacation hot spot Newport within easy reach, there is plenty to do. Strong programs include engineering, marine sciences, nursing, and pharmacy. Nearly half of URI's students are out-of-staters.

No longer an unabashed party school, the University of Rhode Island has earned a reputation for challenging academics with an emphasis on innovation and interdisciplinary learning. URI offers an environment in which students engage in service learning, do research with top faculty, and find a much heavier emphasis on alternative styles of learning. "Our college is an amazing place to learn, prosper, and have fun," boasts one sophomore.

URI's 1,200-acre campus is located in the small town of Kingston. Surrounded by farmland and only six miles from the coast, it is also within easy driving distance of cities such as Providence—the Renaissance City and home to Brown, the Rhode Island School of Design, and several other colleges and universities—Boston, and New York. The main academic buildings at URI, a mixture of modern and "old New England granite," surround a central quad on Kingston Hill. At the foot of Kingston Hill lie the athletic buildings and agricultural fields. Dozens of construction projects have been completed in the last five years, including a new, $125 million facility for the College of Engineering.

New students initially enroll in the University College, which offers academic and career guidance, as well as advice on selecting from among required general education courses. All new students take URI 101, a one-credit course intended to acquaint them with support services, cocurricular activities, and academic majors and career options. After a year or two in University College, students choose more specialized colleges, such as the well-regarded College of Pharmacy, which offers a six-year Pharm.D. program. Programs in engineering, business, and marine sciences are also strong, and the most popular majors include psychology, communication studies, kinesiology, and nursing. The five-year international engineering dual-degree program combines degrees in engineering and a foreign language with a year abroad. Students can earn up to four academic credits during the recently introduced Winter J Term session in January. New undergraduate degrees include criminology and data science.

Academic intensity at URI tends to vary by program. Professors receive generally good marks for their teaching, but their accessibility can be hit or miss. "At times, it can be difficult to work with faculty," says a marine affairs major, who encourages

> "Our college is an amazing place to learn, prosper, and have fun."

Website: www.uri.edu
Location: Small Town
Public
Total Enrollment: 14,407
Undergraduates: 12,578
Male/Female: 44/56
SAT Ranges: ERW 550–630, M 530–620
ACT Ranges: 23–27
Financial Aid: 84%
Pell Grant: 30%
Expense: Pub $ $ $
Student Loans: 76%
Average Debt: $ $ $
Applicants: 22,667
Accepted: 69%
Enrolled: 22%
Grad in 6 Years: 66%
Returning Freshmen: 85%
Academics: ✍ ✍
Social: ☎ ☎ ☎ ☎
Q of L: ★ ★ ★
Admissions: (401) 874-7000
Email Address: admission@uri.edu

Strong Programs:
Psychology
Communication Studies
Kinesiology
Nursing

(continued)

Pharmacy
Engineering
Business
Marine Sciences

students to "[find] a professor or faculty member who is invested in you and your studies." Forty-two percent of classes enroll fewer than 20 students. The Academic Enhancement Center, along with its Writing Center, provides peer tutorials, course-specific collaborative learning projects, supplemental instructional sessions, and special programs for high-risk students.

URI offers nationally recognized international exchange programs with universities in such diverse locales as Chile, France, Korea, and Norway, as well as domestic exchange programs with state colleges and universities. Twenty percent of undergraduates participate in the more than 200 available programs in 60 countries. Students interested in research can collaborate on projects with multidisciplinary teams of faculty through established research partnerships, such as the Partnership for the Coastal Environment. The Center for Student Leadership Development offers for-credit leadership development classes, as well as conferences, retreats, and workshops.

The five-year international engineering dual-degree program combines degrees in engineering and a foreign language with a year abroad.

Although URI gives preference to in-state students, 46 percent of undergrads are from outside Rhode Island, including 2 percent from foreign countries. "Students here are involved and outgoing," one junior says. Minority enrollment stands at 5 percent African American, 10 percent Hispanic, 3 percent Asian American, and 3 percent multiracial. "There is no doubt about it that URI is a predominantly white institution," says one student of color, "but diversity comes in many shapes and forms. We are diverse when it comes to socioeconomic status, nationality, sexual orientation, political affiliation, gender, and many other ways." The university has been investing in resources to support diversity in recent years, and a senior says, "URI has great women's services as well as LGBTQ services." The academic profiles of the incoming class have risen steadily over the past 10 years, in large measure due to the Centennial and Merit Scholarship Programs for outstanding freshmen. Merit awards average $6,700, and athletes vie for 340 athletic scholarships in 16 sports. Thirty percent of freshmen qualify for the Pell Grant.

Though most freshmen live on campus, 59 percent of all undergraduates choose to find off-campus digs near the beach. The majority of residence halls have recently been renovated, and the new Brookside Apartments residence hall has added 500 beds for upperclassmen. "Some of the fresh-man dorms are gorgeous," one student reports, although "housing isn't the best aspect of URI." About half of freshmen participate in living/learning communities in a variety of disciplines. Dining options include two dining halls, and students say the staff is accommodating of various dietary needs. "Campus security does rounds around campus throughout the night," notes a student.

"There is nothing in Kingston, but we are 10 minutes from the beach and 30 minutes from Providence."

"Most of the social life takes place off campus," a senior says. "There is not much for underage students to do at night on campus." Greek life attracts 16 percent of the men and 22 percent of the women. The student newspaper that covers it all has one of the most original names anywhere: *The Good Five Cent Cigar* (as in, "what this country needs is a really good five-cent cigar," a quip uttered by U.S. vice president Thomas R. Marshall in 1914). The campus coffeehouse hosts open-mic nights, and movie theaters, clubs, and malls beckon just off campus, but a fair number of students choose to head home on weekends. As for Kingston, it's a sleepy New England college town, although students do get involved in the community through clubs or URI 101, which requires volunteer work. "There is nothing in Kingston," complains one student, "but we are 10 minutes from the beach and 30 minutes from Providence." Newport's thriving social scene is just 20 minutes away, and other fun road trips include Boston (90 minutes) and New York City (four hours). Travel is facilitated by the Amtrak stop on campus.

The student newspaper has one of the most original names anywhere: **The Good Five Cent Cigar.**

Division I sports are big at Rhode Island, and basketball games are especially exciting. Midnight Madness (the team's first sanctioned practice of the year) is always well attended, and URI fans love it when the Rams defeat archrival Providence College. Recent Atlantic 10 conference champs include women's rowing and men's basketball and track and field. A favorite student tradition is oozeball, an April volleyball tournament played in about two feet of mud. As befits the school's locale, sailing draws much interest, and the team regularly produces All-Americans.

URI offers students a large-school feel in a small state. Consistent efforts by the administration to invest in campus upgrades and new educational opportunities have paid off, as evidenced by the changing face of the student body and their accomplishments. Although URI was once ground zero for wild drinking and carousing, students here now work hard to achieve good grades and lay the foundation of lifelong learning.

If You Apply To ›

URI: Early action, regular decision. SATs or ACTs: required. No Subject Tests. Accepts the Common Application with supplement.

Rhode Island School of Design

2 College Street, Providence, RI 02903

The nation's best-known art and design school, RISD sits on a hillside adjacent to Brown. The campus offers easy access to downtown Providence, but it can't match the location of rival Parsons in New York's Greenwich Village. Offers 16 undergraduate majors in architecture, fine arts, and design. Industrial design is a specialty, and athletics are quirky.

Founded in the late 19th century to address the country's need for more artisans and craftsmen, Rhode Island School of Design has grown into a premier arts incubator. It's a place where today's artists and designers gather to share ideas and create tomorrow's masterpieces and architectural icons. In fact, the cofounders of Airbnb, Brian Chesky and Joe Gebbia, met and developed their creative instincts here. RISD (pronounced "Rizdee") grants degrees in virtually every design-related topic, and like the varied curriculum, the students and their creations are as diverse as the colors on an artist's palette. The one thing everyone here shares is an intense workload and a highly competitive spirit. "RISD students are masochists," says one freshman.

Though you might expect an art school like RISD to occupy funky, futuristic buildings, the predominant look here is colonial New England. Set on the upgrade of College Hill, RISD sits at the edge of Providence's beautifully preserved historic district, adjacent to Brown University. Many campus buildings date from the 1800s and early 1900s; the mostly redbrick-and-white-trim group includes converted homes, a bank, and even an old church. Perhaps RISD's most prized facility is the RISD Museum, a superlative collection of roughly 100,000 works that includes everything from Roman and Egyptian art to works by Monet, Matisse, and Picasso. Recent campus projects include a new first-year residence hall.

While RISD looks traditionally New England on the outside, behind its historic walls lies something else entirely. First-year students take a common curriculum called Experimental and Foundation Studies, which acclimates them to RISD's

Website: www.risd.edu
Location: Small City
Private
Total Enrollment: 2,440
Undergraduates: 1,976
Male/Female: 32/68
SAT Ranges: ERW 570–660, M 560–710
ACT Ranges: 25–31
Financial Aid: 39%
Pell Grant: 14%
Expense: Pr $ $ $
Student Loans: 41%
Average Debt: $ $ $
Applicants: 3,420
Accepted: 29%
Enrolled: 46%
Grad in 6 Years: 90%
Returning Freshmen: 95%
Academics: ✍ ✍ ✍ ✍

(continued)

Social: ☎ ☎
Q of L: ★ ★ ★ ★
Admissions: (401) 454-6300
Email Address: admissions@
risd.edu

Strong Programs:
Illustration
Industrial Design
Graphic Design
Film/Animation/Video
Painting
Architecture

First-year students take a common curriculum that acclimates them to RISD's approach to studio learning and group critiques.

approach to studio learning and group critiques. In addition to courses in their major, students must complete coursework in the liberal arts (theory and history of art and design; literature; and history, philosophy, and social sciences) and a final-year project to graduate.

The most popular majors include illustration, industrial design, graphic design, film/animation/video, painting, and architecture. Students may choose to supplement their degrees with one of six concentrations in computation, technology, and culture; drawing; theory and history of art and design; history, philosophy, and the social sciences; literary arts and studies; and nature-culture-sustainability studies. The Nature Lab allows for examining, exploring, and understanding patterns, structures, and interactions of design in nature. RISD also offers cross-registration and a dual-degree option with Brown, for students seeking more diverse courses.

> **"Sometimes there is not even one male–identifying person in the classroom."**

Hands-on studio courses abound at RISD, and 83 percent of classes have fewer than 20 students. "The academic atmosphere is competitive because we are passionate and collaborative because we need others' input for our work to be successful," explains a textiles major. Though highly selective, RISD will sometimes take a chance on students who did not perform well in high school by the usual academic criteria but who make up for that with special artistic talent. Still, while students at RISD don't "hit the books" in the traditional sense, the in-studio workload is considerable, and students warn that organizational and time-management skills are essential. Teaching here is said to be generally good, although it can be a mixed bag. "For the most part, I have had positive and supportive professors, but I have also had professors who lacked a sense of criticality," says a senior.

During RISD's Wintersession, five weeks between the first and second semesters, students are encouraged to take courses outside their major. Each year, about 40 juniors and seniors venture to Rome for the semester-long European Honors Program, which offers self-directed studio work with RISD faculty and visiting artists, special study tours, immersion in Italian culture, and a chance to savor the likes of Michelangelo, Bernini, and Caravaggio firsthand. An international exchange program provides opportunities to study abroad at approved art institutions in 25 countries worldwide. In all, 11 percent of students study abroad.

RISD students (referred to as "RISDoids") come to Providence to form a distinctly urban mix of styles and personalities. "We are the lost misfits who have found each other," says a senior. A mere 5 percent of students are native Rhode Islanders, not surprising given the state's small size, while an impressive 30 percent hail from foreign countries. The racial makeup of the campus is fairly mixed, with Asian Americans representing 19 percent of the student body, African Americans 3 percent, Hispanics 8 percent, and multiracial students 5 percent.

> **"Given the high level of commitment at RISD, there is not a large social life."**

Students say the campus is liberal, open-minded, and inclusive. Some complain about the skewed male/female ratio, since "sometimes there is not even one male-identifying person in the classroom," according to an illustration major. Low socioeconomic diversity can be an issue as well; one senior remarks, "I cannot afford to be as elaborate in my projects as most people can, wasting materials and going all out, but I find other ways." Tuition and fees here are steep, and the school does not guarantee to meet students' full financial need. Need-based scholarships are available, but merit and athletic scholarships are nonexistent.

Sixty percent of undergraduates reside on campus, and all RISD housing is gender inclusive. Freshmen live together in a group of co-ed dorms known as the Quad. "All on-campus housing is well maintained, comfortable, and damn luxurious for dorms, with plenty of security," says one film major. "It's just grossly overpriced." Most upperclassmen move off campus to nearby apartments, many of which occupy floors of restored homes; RISD also owns an apartment building and some renovated colonial and Victorian houses. All boarders buy the meal plan, but campus dining receives mixed reviews. Some students criticize the administration for handling sexual assault cases too lightly.

Despite a student body that looks like it could have been plucked from the streets of New York's Greenwich Village, RISD is not the place to come for a wild and funky nightlife. "Given the high level of commitment at RISD, there is not a large social life," laments an architecture major. "Many students are consumed by their studios, working until very late." The Tap Room inside Memorial Hall went dry years ago, and each year, those 21 and over vote on whether to allow drinking in their residences. There is no Greek life, and a painting major comments, "A RISD party is usually a group of five to seven friends drinking wine, listening to good music, and cooking together." Students head to Brown for more adventuresome parties, and Providence

The semester-long European Honors Program in Rome offers self-directed studio work with RISD faculty and visiting artists.

"If you are a student who thrives under pressure…then RISD is the place for you."

provides some social outlets too. Though RISD isn't much for traditions, one big annual event is the Artist's Ball, a festive October dance party featuring eclectic and over-the-top student-made costumes. When claustrophobia sets in, students can flee to the RISD farm, a 33-acre recreation area on the shores of nearby Narragansett Bay. Boston and New York City are one and four hours away by train, respectively.

Though jocks are an endangered species at RISD, recreation opportunities are plentiful. There is no intercollegiate sports program in the ordinary sense, though there is a co-ed club ice hockey team, called the Nads (which, of course, inspires RISDoids to holler "Go Nads!") and a mascot named Scrotie (use your imagination). The school also boasts strong men's and women's cycling teams that compete at the varsity level. Other recreational sports range from football and soccer to sailing and skiing.

"If you are a student who thrives under pressure, under constraints that are meant to fortify your critical skills, then RISD is the place for you," says one senior. Indeed, students come to RISD committed to their crafts, and most march to the beat of their own drums as they rush from studio courses to gallery openings to exhibitions. Students here can be confident that their endless studio hours are starting them on the path to future success.

Overlaps

Maryland Institute College of Art, School of the Art Institute of Chicago, Pratt Institute, Parsons School of Design, California College of the Arts, Carnegie Mellon, Savannah College of Art and Design, UCLA

If You Apply To ›

RISD: Early decision, regular decision. SATs or ACTs: required. No Subject Tests. Accepts the Common Application with supplement. Portfolio with 12–20 examples of recent visual work plus two art assignment responses required.

Rhodes College

2000 North Parkway, Memphis, TN 38112

Goes head-to-head with Sewanee for the top spot in the pecking order of mid–South liberal arts colleges, with Rhodes the more progressive of the two. While Sewanee has a gorgeous rural campus, Rhodes has Memphis and its red-hot music scene. Natural and social sciences head the list of solid programs, and undergraduate research opportunities are plentiful. Strong honor system.

Website: www.rhodes.edu
Location: City Center
Private
Total Enrollment: 1,990
Undergraduates: 1,969
Male/Female: 44/56
SAT Ranges: ERW 620–720,
    M 600–690
ACT Ranges: 27–32
Financial Aid: 93%
Pell Grant: 14%
Expense: Pr $ $
Student Loans: 48%
Average Debt: $ $
Applicants: 4,733
Accepted: 51%
Enrolled: 21%
Grad in 6 Years: 83%
Returning Freshmen: 91%
Academics: ✐ ✐ ✐ ½
Social: ☎ ☎ ☎
Q of L: ★ ★ ★ ★
Admissions: (901) 843-3700
Email Address: adminfo@
    rhodes.edu

Strong Programs:
Business
Biology
Psychology
Neuroscience
Economics
English
International Studies
History

Since 1848, Rhodes College has been instilling the timeless values of truth and honor in Southern sons and daughters, and today increasing numbers of students from the rest of the country are discovering its charms. The school's honor code means exams are not proctored and backpacks are left unattended in the cafeteria. Its small size gives everyone an opportunity to take on leadership roles in campus clubs and organizations, and people are generally friendly. Throw in the college's proximity to Memphis's world-famous Beale Street, barbecue, and the blues, and it's clear that Rhodes offers a winning combination.

Rhodes was founded as a Presbyterian school in Clarksville, Tennessee, and it moved to a 100-acre campus in Memphis in 1925. Located in the residential mid-town section of the city, Rhodes sits across from a 175-acre park housing the city's largest art museum, a golf course, and the Memphis Zoo, which has two giant pandas. Whether new or old, all campus buildings are Gothic in style, constructed of Arkansas fieldstone with leaded-glass windows and slate roofs. Thirteen of the original buildings are on the National Register of Historic Places. Robertson Hall, a $34 million science facility, opened in 2017.

The Rhodes general education curriculum features highly regarded three-course sequences known as The Search for Values in the Light of Western History and Religion, and Life: Then and Now. The Search sequence has been part of the Rhodes curriculum for nearly 75 years. To receive a Rhodes degree, students must select one of the two sequences and demonstrate proficiency in 12 areas that form the foundation of the liberal arts. These include being able to critically examine questions of meaning and value, developing excellence in written communication, and understanding how historical forces have shaped human cultures. A yearlong first-year seminar is also required of freshmen.

> **"Every professor I've had has been very personable, available, interesting, and invested in the students."**

Rhodes is especially strong in the natural and social sciences, thanks to labs with state-of-the-art equipment. Business, biology, psychology, and neuroscience enroll the most students, but economics, English, international studies, history, and chemistry are also well respected. Aside from traditional lecture-style classes, the college offers seminars, honors programs, one-on-one Directed Inquiry tutorials, and interdisciplinary majors. Rhodes also participates in a dual-degree program for engineers with Washington University in St. Louis. The academic climate at Rhodes is "demanding and challenging," according to one student. "Professors expect quality contributions." Sixty-eight percent of classes have fewer than 20 students, which means professors are more than talking heads. "Every professor I've had has been very personable, available, interesting, and invested in the students," says a junior. Though students can get the courses they need to graduate on time, "we often cannot get classes with certain professors until senior year," a junior says.

Students who can't find what they want on campus may tap into the European Studies program, a joint program with Sewanee that offers students a 17-week semester with coursework in England and travel in Western Europe. Sixty percent of students participate in a variety of study abroad programs around the world. The Buckman International Fellows program offers summer internships in Madrid, Hong Kong, and Johannesburg. A partnership with St. Jude Children's Research Hospital lets students conduct research there in the summers and continue their projects during the next school year; half of Rhodes students take part in undergraduate research, often with the support of fellowships.

Like Davidson and Hendrix, Rhodes tends to attract white, Southern, middle- and upper-middle-class students, although minority enrollment is on the rise and students hail from 46 states. Twenty-eight percent of students are Tennessee natives,

Whether new or old, all campus buildings are Gothic in style, constructed of Arkansas fieldstone.

and 4 percent are international. "Students tend to be friendly and motivated," a sophomore says. African Americans comprise 8 percent of the student body, Asian Americans 6 percent, Hispanics 6 percent, and multiracial students 4 percent. "Representation for minority students is always a hot topic," a student says. Eligible students receive scholarships based on academic merit, and the average award is $22,600. There are no athletic scholarships.

Seventy percent of Rhodes students live on campus, where all dorms are air-conditioned and clean. "While expensive, Rhodes dorms are pretty well maintained," one student says, and most are single sex. Freshmen live in Glassell or Williford, and upperclassmen vie for rooms in the East and West Village apartments during the yearly lottery. Twenty percent of first-year students opt to join living/learning communities. Students eat in the Refectory (known as "the Rat") or the Lynx Lair; the former has hot food lines and the latter offers fare such as wraps, sandwiches, and burgers, along with a well-stocked salad bar. "Our two campus dining facilities serve very edible food," reports one student, "and there is typically something for all tastes, preferences, and lifestyles." Students report feeling safe on campus thanks to helpful campus security officials.

Fraternities draw 32 percent of the men and sororities sign up 42 percent of the women. "Most of Rhodes's social life is centered around Greek life," says a student. Chartered buses provide rides to off-campus parties, many of which are sponsored by the Greeks, though independents are welcome to attend. While it's illegal for students under 21 to drink, students say those who are determined can usually find booze—if not at parties, then in other students' rooms. In

The Buckman International Fellows program offers summer internships in Madrid, Hong Kong, and Johannesburg.

"Service is an integral part of the Rhodes experience."

April, everyone looks forward to the three-day Rites of Spring concert and to the preceding Rites of Play carnival, which brings underprivileged kids to campus for a day of food, fun, and games.

Lively and energetic Memphis has its fair share of college students, with three other four-year institutions in the area and a number of community colleges as well. There are plenty of clubs and bars, along with live music and arts organizations, volunteer opportunities, and internships. "Service is an integral part of the Rhodes experience," a student says, and 80 percent of students get involved in community service.

Rhodes fields 11 women's and 10 men's varsity Lynx teams, which compete in Division III. The women's golf team drove its way to national championship titles in 2014, 2016, and 2017, and men's and women's lacrosse, men's cross-country and golf, and women's field hockey are among the recent Southern Athletic Conference championship winners. A quarter of all students participate in intramurals and club sports, the most popular being five-on-five basketball and crew, respectively. The Bryan Campus Life Center boasts squash and racquetball courts and a suspended indoor track. Rhodes's mock trial team holds the record for consecutive appearances in the national championship tournament (31).

Rhodes College students adore the school's solid academics and rich Southern tradition. "The Rhodes community is incredibly friendly and helpful," says a sophomore. The school's reputation is rising, within and outside the Southeast, and it is slowly becoming more diverse. What hasn't changed is the friendly vibe on campus and the eagerness of students, faculty, and staff to welcome you to the community.

Overlaps

Sewanee, Furman, Centre, Tulane, Trinity University (TX), WashU in St. Louis, Vanderbilt, Hendrix

If You Apply To ›

Rhodes: Early decision I and II, early action, regular decision. SATs or ACTs: required. Subject Tests: optional. Accepts the Common Application.

Rice University

6100 Main Street MS-17, Houston, TX 77251

One of the few elite private colleges that keeps tuition relatively affordable. Rice is outstanding in engineering, architecture, the sciences, and music, and it is a national leader in entrepreneurship studies. With nearly 4,000 undergraduates, Rice is smaller than many applicants realize. In lieu of frats, Rice has a residential college system like Yale and Princeton.

Website: www.rice.edu
Location: City Center
Private
Total Enrollment: 6,676
Undergraduates: 3,902
Male/Female: 53/47
SAT Ranges: ERW 730–780, M 760–800
ACT Ranges: 33–35
Financial Aid: 57%
Pell Grant: 17%
Expense: Pr $ $
Student Loans: 25%
Average Debt: $ $
Applicants: 18,063
Accepted: 16%
Enrolled: 37%
Grad in 6 Years: 91%
Returning Freshmen: 97%
Academics: ✐ ✐ ✐ ✐ ✐
Social: ☎ ☎ ☎
Q of L: ★ ★ ★ ★
Admissions: (713) 348-7423
Email Address: admission@rice.edu

Strong Programs:
Engineering
Biosciences
Social Sciences
Computer Science
Architecture
Economics
Music
Entrepreneurship Studies

Founded in 1912 by Texas cotton mogul William Marsh Rice, Rice University has stayed true to its mission of providing unsurpassed programs in science, engineering, the arts, and humanities—with a price tag most families can afford. With its top-notch programs in the liberal arts and sciences and huge endowment (used to keep tuition modest), Rice is a good deal among top schools. It is the dominant university in the Southwest and second only to Duke in the entire South. Thanks to an aggressive growth plan and generous financial aid, the university continues to attract more and more top talent from around the country.

Rice was modeled after such disparate institutions as progressive, low-tuition Cooper Union and the more traditional Princeton University. Today, Rice boasts plenty of distinctive characteristics all its own. The predominant architectural theme of the campus, situated three miles from downtown Houston, is Spanish Mediterranean, and it's surrounded by a row of hedges—the singular buffer between the quiet campus and the sounds of the city. A particular standout is the colorful Duncan Hall, designed by British architect John Outram.

> **"The political climate at Rice is pretty liberal, especially for a Texas school."**

Rice has traditionally excelled in the sciences and engineering, and SEs (as these students are called) still dominate the student body. Architecture here is one of the finest undergraduate programs in the nation, and the space physics program works closely with NASA. Programs in engineering, biosciences, social sciences, and computer science are popular, and economics and music are highly regarded. An "entrepreneurship initiative" is fueling more undergraduate courses and programs in this area, drawing from the resources of Rice's well-established graduate program. Rice has a long tradition of encouraging double and even triple majors in such seemingly opposite fields as electrical engineering and art history. Under the area-major program, students can draw up proposals for independent interdisciplinary majors. All freshmen participate in a freshman writing program that is tailored, in part, to individual disciplines. Other distribution requirements are flexible: student take three courses each in the humanities, social sciences, and applied sciences/mathematics, choosing the courses that interest them most.

Courses are challenging, and competition in the engineering and premed programs can be intense. For the most part, though, says a senior, "Students are almost always willing to help each other, creating a caring and supportive atmosphere." Everyone operates under the honor system, and most exams go unsupervised. Class size rarely presents a problem; 70 percent have fewer than 20 students. Faculty members receive high marks, and full professors often teach freshmen. "One of my favorite things about Rice is how the professors are so invested in my learning," says a kinesiology major. Under the Mellon Fellow program, selected humanities and social sciences majors may work with a faculty mentor on an academic project that offers a summer research stipend. Sixty-two

> **"Rice has improved low-income accessibility."**

percent of undergrads complete at least one research experience by the time they graduate. About a quarter of students participate in 150 study abroad programs offered in 60 countries.

Students describe their classmates as friendly and quirky, and a senior says Rice students are "intellectual, but not navel-gazing." Rice was founded to serve "residents of Houston and the state of Texas," and 43 percent of undergraduates still hail from the Lone Star State. Most of the out-of-staters are transplanted from California, Florida, the Northeast, and other Southern states; 12 percent come from other countries. Twenty-six percent of undergraduates are Asian American, 15 percent are Hispanic, 7 percent are African American, and 4 percent are multiracial. "The political climate at Rice is pretty liberal, especially for a Texas school," notes an engineering major.

Rice has a long tradition of encouraging double and even triple majors.

In addition to keeping tuition relatively low, Rice practices need-blind admissions and guarantees to meet the full demonstrated need of every admit. Merit scholarships averaging $21,000 are available to qualified students, and 273 athletic scholarships are awarded each year. The university has rolled out an ambitious new

"Rice is a welcoming place with an openness to new ideas and a willingness to explore."

financial aid program, the Rice Investment, that makes tuition free for low-income and middle-class students. Undergraduates with an annual family income of up to $130,000 receive full-tuition grants, and those whose annual family income does not exceed $65,000 also qualify for grants that cover room, board, and mandatory fees. Additionally, students with family incomes between $130,001 and $200,000 are awarded half-tuition grants, and need-based loans have been eliminated for all students who qualify for the Rice Investment. A junior points out that "Rice has improved low-income accessibility by training faculty and staff on how to support first-generation and low-income students."

Rice's founder did not approve of elitist organizations, which means fraternities and sororities are forbidden on campus. Their functions are largely assumed by the 11 residential colleges, Rice's version of dorms, which 72 percent of students call home. The housing system is based on the British residential college model. Every undergraduate is assigned to a residential college in the first year, and they remain a member of that college for all four years—even if they choose to live off campus at any time. Students praise the residential college system for giving everyone a sense of belonging to a relatively small community. The quality of housing "varies from OK to super nice," according to one senior. Each residential college is connected to a "servery" (a.k.a. dining hall), and students can eat anywhere they please. "There's a wide variety of options, so you can be as indulgent or as healthy as you want," says a senior. Another student comments that "Campus security is about as good as it can be in a big city like Houston." A five-week, one-credit Critical Thinking in Sexuality course is mandatory for all incoming freshmen.

An ambitious new financial aid program, the Rice Investment, makes tuition free for low-income and middle-class students.

Social life is campus-based and revolves around the residential colleges, which frequently host themed, campuswide parties as well as private gatherings. "While Rice students can write algorithms and social commentary, they still know how to throw a good party," boasts one junior. Students 21 and over are allowed to have alcohol on campus. Other student organizations host activities like shows, dinners, and dances too. Halloween brings a massive naked run, but the favorite annual tradition by far is Willy Week, which features a variety of festivities put on by the residential colleges, a university-wide water-balloon fight, and the highly anticipated Beer Bike, a relay race in which co-ed teams must speed around a bicycle track and chug water ("which used to be beer, before the drinking law changed," a student explains).

Houston has a bustling nightlife, but you'd better bring a car to enjoy it. The light-rail system makes it easier to get to the city, but it's still a challenge to get

Social life revolves around the residential colleges, which frequently host themed, campuswide parties.

around—even with free transportation passes. The city offers ample opportunities for volunteerism, in which three-quarters of students get involved, and internships. Galveston's beaches on the Gulf of Mexico are only 45 minutes away, and heading for New Orleans, especially in February, can make a great weekend trip.

Ardent football fans abound at Rice; tearing down the goalposts after home victories remains a happy Owls tradition. Baseball is a powerhouse, and women's basketball and tennis are strong too. All teams compete in the Division I Conference USA. Rice students go really wild for intramurals, which pit the residential colleges against each other—75 percent participate.

William Marsh Rice never lived to see the fruits of his bequest (he was chloroformed by his valet in an ill-fated conspiracy to claim his estate), but he would certainly be proud of the university that he created and that bears his name. "Rice is a welcoming place with an openness to new ideas and a willingness to explore," says an economics major. As the university grows, it remains to be seen whether it will be able to maintain the close relationships with faculty and the intimate quality of the residential experience that has made it special. But when students venture outside the hedges for the last time, their Rice diplomas open doors to the corporate world. And thanks to Rice's efforts to keep tuition affordable, their wallets haven't been emptied.

If You Apply To ›

Rice: Early decision, regular decision. SATs or ACTs: required. Two Subject Tests related to proposed area of study recommended. Accepts the Common Application with supplement.

University of Richmond

28 Westhampton Way, Richmond, VA 23173

Offers students a preprofessional climate rooted in the liberal arts. Though located in the former capital of the Confederacy, there are plenty of Yankee and international voices on UR's forward-looking campus. Business and a unique school for leadership studies are featured offerings, along with a strong global emphasis. Compare to Bucknell but with urban proximity.

Students at the University of Richmond enjoy a healthy mix of Southern ambiance and intellectual rigor that includes small classes, close friendships, and lots of teamwork. A force for progressive liberal arts, UR describes itself as "a private university for the public good." It was a pioneer in leadership studies and continues to expand its international emphasis. Under its unique coordinate system, a holdover from the days of single-sex education, men and women take advantage of separate student governments and traditions.

UR's 350-acre campus is nestled amid rolling hills about 15 minutes from downtown Richmond, the state capital. The campus, notable for its stately pines and consistently redbrick collegiate Gothic buildings, wraps around 10-acre Westhampton Lake. The $20 million Weinstein International Center features an open courtyard with a fountain, surrounded by a cloistered walkway with spiral columns and balconies. Recent campus additions include the Queally Center, a $27 million facility combining admissions, financial aid, and career services.

All Richmond undergraduates complete general education requirements in communications (including writing and a foreign language) and in six other fields:

historical studies, literary studies, natural science, social analysis, symbolic reasoning, and visual and performing arts. Everyone takes a First-Year Seminar in the fall and spring of their first year, with faculty drawn from across the university, on topics ranging from bioethics to consumer culture. Enrollment is capped at 16 students in order to ensure that faculty members can focus on their students' writing.

Among more than 60 academic majors is one in philosophy, politics, economics, and law (PPEL) that combines disciplines from the School of Arts and Sciences, Business School, and Law School. Business administration is the most popular major—UR boasts a top undergraduate business school lodged within a liberal arts institution. Other popular options include accounting, leadership studies, biology, and international studies. The Jepson School of Leadership Studies, founded in 1986 and still unique, draws on the liberal arts to educate students about how they can best serve society. About half of UR students take the foundation leadership course. An interdisciplinary major in healthcare studies examines the business, legal, interpersonal, and sociopolitical aspects of health care. UR is at the forefront of the movement called "digital humanities," and the Digital Scholarship Lab allows students to mine huge databases in order to look for and generate new knowledge on topics.

"Every student here has at least one professor that they have this special kind of mentorship with."

Students describe the academic climate as intense but collaborative. Classes are usually small; 70 percent have fewer than 20 students. Richmond students enjoy close relationships with professors and the absence of TAs in the classroom. "My anthropology professor from my freshman year has been like my second mom for the last three years," says a senior, adding, "I know it's hard to believe, but every student here has at least one professor that they have this special kind of mentorship with." Students are also enthusiastic about career-related programs, such as Spider Road Trips, which take students to major cities to learn firsthand about various industries and network for potential jobs and internships. A junior points out that students have access to the Office of Alumni and Career Services for life: "I am a fourth-generation Spider, and if tomorrow my grandpa woke up and decided he wanted to switch careers, he could go to Career Services and they would help him."

Spider Road Trips take students to major cities to learn firsthand about various industries and network.

About 20 percent of sophomores participate every year in what one student calls the "especially sought-after" Sophomore Scholars in Residence program, a living/learning program that combines a yearlong interdisciplinary course, a group capstone project in the spring, and various opportunities for community-based activities and domestic or international travel. The Richmond Guarantee program offers traditional undergrads guaranteed funding of up to $4,000 for at least one summer research or internship experience. Sixty percent of undergrads study abroad for credit at one of Richmond's 70 partner institutions in more than 30 countries. To encourage globe-trotting, the university ponies up the cost of passports and, as one participant notes, "provides students with a cultural stipend to reimburse us for museum entrance fees, cooking classes, and other cultural activities" while overseas.

"The newest apartments are way nicer than anything I will be able to afford after school."

"Students are UR are generally friendly, academically driven, and very involved," according to a business administration major. Nearly half of UR students hail from the Northeast, and only 18 percent are native Virginians. Foreign students account for 9 percent of the student population. Seven percent of students are African American, 9 percent Asian American, 9 percent Hispanic, and 5 percent multiracial. The Office of Common Ground is working to foster diversity and inclusion on campus, although students report that it could use more resources. A political science major comments, "Students in nonelection years are generally apathetic

(continued)

Accepted: 33%
Enrolled: 24%
Grad in 6 Years: 88%
Returning Freshmen: 93%
Academics: ✎ ✎ ✎ ½
Social: ☎ ☎ ☎
Q of L: ★ ★ ★
Admissions: (804) 289-8640
Email Address: admission@ richmond.edu

Strong Programs:
Business Administration
Accounting
Leadership Studies
Biology
International Studies
Philosophy, Politics, Economics, and Law
Healthcare Studies

and are not very politically involved." Despite its high sticker price, UR prides itself on being accessible, mainly because it practices need-blind admissions and guarantees to meet the demonstrated financial need of all domestic students. Richmond's Promise to Virginia program gives qualified in-state residents whose total family income is $60,000 or less grant assistance equal to full tuition, room, and board. The Richmond Scholars program awards 25 full-tuition merit scholarships for every entering class, and student-athletes vie for 176 athletic awards.

Ninety-two percent of Richmond students live on campus. Freshmen typically live in traditional doubles and can choose from suite- or apartment-style options after that. "The newest apartments are way nicer than anything I will be able to afford after school," says a senior. Freshmen can apply for the new Richmond Endeavor living/ learning program, which combines two academic courses with advising from a faculty mentor and a peer advisor. The Heilman Dining Center offers hot entrées as well as made-to-order paninis, pizza, pasta, and such. "I am convinced that the dining center offers the best brunch in Richmond," cheers one gourmand. Students say they generally feel safe at UR, and initiatives like the Spiders for Spiders peer network are educating students on how to "prevent potentially bad situations and listen to survivors [of sexual violence] in the proper ways," according to a senior.

> **"Fraternities host 'lodges,' which are on-campus events that are essentially huge dance parties."**

Students agree that Richmond is "a very social campus" with plenty of options for entertainment during the week and on weekends. Nonresidential fraternities and sororities attract 21 percent of men and 28 percent of women, and they throw most of the parties. "Fraternities host 'lodges,' which are on-campus events that are essentially huge dance parties that are open to any student who attends UR," explains a junior. The Campus Activities Board sponsors regular movie nights, karaoke, and concerts. The school provides an hourly shuttle to downtown Richmond, which boasts good restaurants, art galleries, beautiful historic neighborhoods, and plenty of internship opportunities at local corporations and government agencies. For those wishing to get away, Williamsburg, Virginia Beach, and Washington, D.C. are not far, and nature buffs also like the river and the nearby backpacking, thanks to the proximity of the Blue Ridge Mountains.

Eager to shed its past image as a privileged enclave, UR has made a strong commitment to the city of Richmond. Seventy-two percent of students are engaged in volunteer programs, donating more than 100,000 hours a year. Through programs at UR Downtown, undergraduate students partner with nonprofit organizations to support children and families in the community. First-year students have Proclamation Night for women and Investiture for men, during which they sign the honor code and write a letter to themselves, which is not opened until senior year. Other traditions range from the Ring Dance, a soiree for junior women at the elegant Jefferson Hotel, to Pig Roast, a campuswide cookout hosted by fraternities.

The school's 17 varsity teams spin their webs in Division I. The Spiders are members of the Atlantic 10 Conference, with the exception of football, men's lacrosse, and women's golf, which play in the highly competitive Colonial Athletic Association, Southern Conference, and Patriot League, respectively. The women's swimming and diving team has won 15 conference titles in the past 17 years. Other recent conference champs include men's and women's lacrosse and golf. Football Saturdays find throngs of students throwing tailgate parties. Nearly 30 club sports offer various levels of competition, as do a variety of intramurals.

Students at Richmond certainly find plenty of programs to like. From first-of-their-kind academic programs to innovative out-of-classroom learning and networking opportunities, Richmond is working hard to push its vision of preprofessional education shaped by commitments to the liberal arts, leadership, and community involvement.

Ripon College

300 Seward Street, P.O. Box 248, Ripon, WI 54971

Located where the Republican Party was born in 1854, Ripon is more conservative than Beloit and Lawrence and similar in atmosphere to places like DePauw and Knox. With fewer than 800 students, Ripon is the smallest of the five. Strengths are science, education, and communication. Offers a three-year degree option. Nearly three-quarters of the students are in-staters.

Everything about Ripon College is small, aside from perhaps its academic ambitions. The school is in a tiny Wisconsin town, and there are fewer than 800 students, meaning "if you don't go to class, your professor will know," a freshman says. The weather can be a downer, with bitter cold and lots of snow come winter, but the warmth of personal relationships with peers and professors helps to compensate for the frigid temperatures. Says one happy student, "Ripon is friendly and familiar."

Ripon's 250-acre campus sits in a town of 7,800, about 20 miles west of Highway 41 between Fond du Lac and Oshkosh. It features tree-lined walks, wetlands, prairie, and woods, and a mixture of 19th- and 20th-century architecture lends a majestic feel. The Willmore Center, the campus's main health and wellness facility, opened in 2017 after a $24 million renovation and expansion.

Ripon's Catalyst curriculum calls for students to complete five required seminar courses. Two courses in the first year and two in the sophomore year focus on developing basic academic skills that will prepare students for the Applied Innovation Seminar their junior year, in which they work in small teams with a faculty member to research, develop, and present solutions to large questions facing society. "The Catalyst curriculum enhances skills that employers are looking for," explains a sophomore. All Ripon students graduate with a concentration in applied innovation, and their academic transcripts attest that they have acquired skills in oral communication, writing, critical thinking, collaboration, quantitative reasoning, information literacy, interdisciplinary integration, and intercultural competence. In addition to the Catalyst courses, most students complete a senior seminar or thesis in their major.

> **"The Catalyst curriculum enhances skills that employers are looking for."**

A politics and government major describes the academic climate as "moderately relaxed" and the workload as "very reasonable." Ripon students delight in their small classes, which have fewer than 20 students on average. There are no teaching assistants, and student-initiated study groups are common. "Professors spend a lot of one-on-one time with students and really get to know them," says a theater major.

Ripon's strengths include the sciences, education, communication, and history; the most popular majors are psychology, education, English, and biology. Students also give high marks to exercise science, sports management, the arts, and the premed and health sciences advising program. New offerings include a major in finance and minors in coaching, adapted physical education, and American studies.

Website: www.ripon.edu
Location: Small Town
Private
Total Enrollment: 756
Undergraduates: 756
Male/Female: 46/54
SAT Ranges: ERW 520–610, M 520–650
ACT Ranges: 20–26
Financial Aid: 100%
Pell Grant: 44%
Expense: Pr $
Student Loans: 84%
Average Debt: $ $ $ $
Applicants: 2,504
Accepted: 68%
Enrolled: 14%
Grad in 6 Years: 68%
Returning Freshmen: 71%
Academics: ✍ ✍ ✍
Social: ☎ ☎ ☎
Q of L: ★ ★ ★
Admissions: (800) 947-4766
Email Address: adminfo@ripon.edu

Strong Programs:
Psychology
Education
English
Biology
Communication
History
Exercise Science
Sports Management

Motivated students with AP credits—or just the stamina to take an extra class each term—may finish in three years, thanks to Ripon's accelerated degree program. A 3–2 dual-degree program in engineering with WashU in St. Louis is now an option, as is a 3–3 law program with multiple partner universities. About 15 percent of students take terms away from campus, in the U.S. or abroad, through 30 programs organized by Ripon or partner providers.

Ripon students are "laid-back, friendly, and positive people," says a student. Seventy-one percent come from Wisconsin, and most of the rest hail from elsewhere in the Midwest. Five percent come from foreign nations. African Americans comprise 3 percent of the student body, Asian Americans make up 1 percent, Hispanics add 8 percent, and multiracial students represent 2 percent. The college organizes a social justice retreat every February and a student diversity conference every April. Ripon's claim to fame is its status as the birthplace of the Republican Party, founded on campus on February 28, 1854, to be exact. Students say these days all political views are represented on campus. "One day a week during lunch, students have the option of participating in a 'table talk' where students discuss a current issue," says a freshman. The school offers merit scholarships, worth an average of $18,800, but no athletic awards. Forty-four percent of incoming freshmen are eligible for Pell Grants. The Access Ripon College program covers full tuition and room and board, without loans, for qualified students of low-income families.

"Downtown Ripon offers many great restaurants, little shops, and a movie theater."

Ninety-five percent of Ripon students live on campus, since they must petition to live off campus. Freshmen are housed together; students may choose co-ed or single-sex halls, with doubles, singles, or suites. "The dorms are comfortable, clean, and large enough to suit their purpose," offers one student. Ripon has three dining halls—the café-style Terrace; the Pub, with a grill and à la carte options; and the Commons, with a traditional hot-food line. "The food is pretty decent, and they will make food to order daily for those with special needs or food allergies," explains a psychology major.

Students report feeling safe on Ripon's small-town campus but say the social life could be more robust. Forty percent of the men join fraternities and 26 percent of the women pledge sororities. Members of Greek life are grouped together in the dorms and host parties in their rooms or lounges, where alcohol is permitted for those of age, but one student likens this to "having a party at your parents' house. You're allowed to do it, but you're constantly being watched." Underage drinkers face fines. The Ripon College Project Space, located a couple of blocks away in downtown Ripon, hosts art shows, poetry readings, special lectures, and other events, while across the street, Bovay's Study Bar offers space for late-night studying and barista coffee service. Favorite annual traditions include homecoming and the Springfest concert and carnival. The best road trips include nearby Oshkosh and Appleton, or even Milwaukee and Madison. Chicago is a three-hour drive.

"We are interactive. We are tight-knit. We are a community."

"Downtown Ripon offers many great restaurants, little shops, and a movie theater," says a freshman, but most places close down early. About 81 percent of students get involved in community service in the local area, and at the start of each year, all the churches in Ripon come together to host a home-cooked potluck dinner for students. Though Ripon's winters can be bitterly cold, the college's location means frozen lakes and a blanket of snow are a natural part of the winter landscape, and cross-country and downhill skiing, tobogganing, and ice skating are regular diversions. There is even some fervent cheering for dogsled and iceboat races. And when it's not winter ("for one month during the year," warns one student), nearby Green Lake offers boating, fishing, and other water sports.

Ripon's varsity teams (the Red Hawks) compete in Division III, and matches against Lawrence University usually draw excited crowds, as the Lawrence–Ripon rivalry is one of the oldest in Wisconsin. Men's basketball, baseball, and women's soccer and volleyball have been competitive recently, and the men's and women's cycling teams are Division II powerhouses. Seventy percent of students participate in the intramural program, which offers varying levels of competitive sports as well as fun activities like snowman building and a board game night. The forensics team, which dates to 1913 and offers $5,000 scholarships, consistently ranks in the nation's top 20.

Ripon College offers a strong grounding in the liberal arts, along with a peaceful, quaint, historical, and friendly community where you'll be much more than a number. "I am on a first-name basis with our dean and president, and it's not because I'm in trouble," a junior says. Though being at such a small place can be stifling, Ripon students aren't complaining. "We are interactive. We are tight-knit. We are a community," one student says. "We are Ripon."

If You Apply To ›

Ripon: Rolling admissions. SATs or ACTs: optional. No Subject Tests. Accepts the Common Application with supplement.

University of Rochester

Rochester, NY 14627

The name may conjure up a nondescript public university, but Rochester, located in an up-and-coming city, is a quality private university in the orbit of Carnegie Mellon, Case Western Reserve, Johns Hopkins, and Washington University in St. Louis. The university has a scientific bent and a strong reputation for churning out premeds. Music is another strength. Has half as many undergraduates as neighboring RIT.

The University of Rochester is not afraid of change. This distinguished private university implemented its unique Rochester Renaissance Plan in the mid-1990s, and since then it has never looked back. The plan included reducing class size; making new investments in the library, classrooms, and computer networking facilities; and launching a curriculum that eliminates entry-level general education courses to allow students to design their own paths. Today, ever-expanding academic opportunities ensure that students have freedom to explore while getting plenty of hands-on experience in the process.

Founded in 1850, the University of Rochester occupies a snug little 90-acre campus, which nestles up to a bend in the Genesee River. One student acknowledges that the university lives under "perpetually gray [read: winter] skies," but finds comfort that "it's great for winter sports or studying or even sleeping late on a snowy Saturday." Although a few buildings are modern—the Wilson Commons student center designed by I. M. Pei, for example—most of the older structures come in Greek Revival and Georgian colonial styles. There is an aesthetically pleasing contrast between old and new, and the Eastman Quadrangle, with the library and original academic buildings, adds to Rochester's stately look. Wegmans Hall, a 58,000-square-foot building designed for interdisciplinary work in data science, opened in 2017.

> "[The weather is] great for winter sports or studying or even sleeping late on a snowy Saturday."

Website: www.rochester.edu
Location: Suburban
Private
Total Enrollment: 9,726
Undergraduates: 6,227
Male/Female: 51/49
SAT Ranges: ERW 630–710, M 650–770
ACT Ranges: 29–33
Financial Aid: 52%
Pell Grant: 18%
Expense: Pr $ $ $
Student Loans: 51%
Average Debt: $ $ $
Applicants: 18,066
Accepted: 33%
Enrolled: 23%
Grad in 6 Years: 85%
Returning Freshmen: 97%

There are no general education course requirements at Rochester, but academic offerings are designed to expose students to the full range of liberal arts. The curriculum—appropriately but unimaginatively known as the Rochester Curriculum—focuses on three classic divisions of learning: humanities and arts; social science; and natural science, mathematics, and engineering. Students choose a major from one of these areas and also complete a cluster of three courses in each of the remaining two divisions. Freshmen have the option of taking seminar-style Quest courses, which involve collaborative work with faculty and classmates on original materials and data. Orientation Rochester-style is a week long and includes a fall festival called Yellowjacket Weekend, designed to help new students "become fully integrated in the university community."

The university's 200 degree programs span the standard fields of study, but Rochester takes special pride in its famed Eastman School of Music, which is open to undergraduates. It also excels in the engineering and scientific fields, including biomedical engineering. Optics has long been a strength—naturally, given that the city of Rochester is home to Kodak, Xerox, and Bausch & Lomb. The university's Institute of Optics, the nation's first center devoted exclusively to the subject, is a leader in basic optical research and theory, and it awards about half of all optics degrees in the U.S. The most popular majors include psychology, financial economics, economics, biomedical engineering, and business. Rochester's Combined-Admission Programs offer exceptional undergraduates simultaneous admission to both undergraduate and graduate degree programs in medicine, engineering, and education.

> **"Teaching is dynamic—incorporating guest speakers, videos, lecture slides, and discussions."**

Students admit the academics are challenging but describe the atmosphere as helpful. "There are many study spaces used primarily for group work, and many professors explicitly encourage working together on assignments and projects," says a brain and cognitive science major. Sixty-nine percent of classes have fewer than 20 students. Professors are praised for their skills behind the lectern as well as their passion. "Teaching is dynamic—incorporating guest speakers, videos, lecture slides, and discussions," notes one senior. Students also highly rate the Greene Career and Internship Center for its vigorous preparation of seniors for the job market.

To help enhance students' résumés, Rochester's Take Five program offers a tuition-free fifth year that allows students to explore interests outside their major. The Kaufman Entrepreneurial Year enables qualified students to take up to a year, tuition free, to pursue internships, special projects, or the development of entrepreneurial plans. Students selected for the Senior Scholars Program undertake a capstone project that can range from a piece of scholarly research to a work of artistic creativity. Seventy-seven percent of students are involved in undergraduate research programs; opportunities include Research and Innovation Grants, which provide funding of up to $4,500, and the *Journal of Undergraduate Research*. More than 70 Rochester-sponsored study abroad options are available in more than 35 countries, and about a third of students take part. Options include "on-location" courses taught by Rochester faculty in locales such as Israel, France, Peru, and Russia.

Freshmen have the option of taking seminar-style Quest courses, which involve collaborative work with faculty and classmates.

"Students can be intense," says an economics major. "Most of the people here are high achievers, go-getters, and hard workers." Thirty-one percent hail from New York State. Many also come from New England, and there's been a large jump in the numbers from Florida, the Midwest, California, and overseas, with 28 percent coming from foreign countries. Asian Americans make up 9 percent of the student body, while African Americans account for 5 percent, Hispanics

7 percent, and multiracial students 3 percent. A senior says, "There is always an active dialogue" about current social and political issues. Eligible undergraduates receive merit scholarships averaging $13,000. The Rochester Promise initiative offers a $25,000 tuition benefit annually to graduates of local high schools.

Freshmen and sophomores are required to live on campus, and 90 percent of students choose to remain on campus all four years. "Dorms are comfortable, modern, high-tech, very generously sized, and well maintained," a senior says. New students are assigned to rooms—usually doubles—and upperclassmen can usually get suites or apartments through the lottery. The Susan B. Anthony residence halls come highly recommended. In addition to a variety of co-ed and single-sex options, special-interest floors are available for enthusiasts of music, computers and technology, anime, green space, and interclass living. For those who live off campus, a shuttle bus runs to and from the major off-campus living areas. Fare served in the dining halls receives high ratings from students. "Security officers patrol all the time," says one student, "and if ever you feel unsafe, they will pick you up and take you where you need to go, any time of the day." The university recently implemented an "affirmative consent" policy, and several student groups have been involved in promoting awareness of sexual assault issues.

Rochester's Take Five program offers a tuition-free fifth year that allows students to explore interests outside their major.

"Most of the people here are high achievers, go-getters, and hard workers."

Twenty percent of the men and 26 percent of the women go Greek, and fraternities contribute heavily to the social life of Greeks and independents alike by sponsoring parties and concerts. Students of legal age are allowed to drink in designated areas of the campus, but students agree that Rochester is not much of a party school. "While there are many things to do in the city of Rochester, it seems that most of the social life occurs right on campus," observes one student. UR has its own set of movie theaters, and a cappella concerts always draw a crowd. Favorite annual events include Meliora Weekend during homecoming, the holiday Boar's Head Dinner, and a spring fling known as Dandelion Day. Wilson Day is an annual day of community service that places incoming students in more than 50 agencies throughout the city of Rochester to paint houses, landscape, and play bingo in nursing homes.

Special-interest floors are available for enthusiasts of music, computers and technology, anime, green space, and interclass living.

Many students take the free campus shuttle into the greater Rochester area, where they may entertain themselves on the beaches of Lake Ontario, in the International Photography Museum at the Eastman House, or at the Rochester Philharmonic Orchestra. An unofficial Rochester tradition calls for each student to eat a "garbage plate" at Nick Tahou's, an infamous local dive, before graduating. In addition to frequent ski trips, favored out-of-town destinations include Niagara Falls, about 70 miles west, and, for the more venturesome, Toronto, 125 miles farther westward.

The 23 varsity sports are coming of age at Rochester, and Yellowjacket teams compete in the Division III University Athletic Association. Rochester athletic teams have captured recent conference or regional championships in men's soccer and basketball, women's field hockey and softball, and men's and women's swimming and diving. About a quarter of students participate in intramurals each semester. If intramural competition isn't your bag, Rochester has group fitness classes and an $8 million sports complex, complete with lighted rooftop tennis courts, a Nautilus fitness center, an eight-lane pool, and an indoor track.

In the past, students bemoaned the fact that their university didn't have a wider academic reputation, but that has changed, due, in part, to the Rochester Renaissance Plan. Improvements have been made in the curriculum, the facilities, and just about anywhere you look on campus. Rochester seems to be winning its battle for a spot among the nation's leading private universities. Now if they could only do something about all that snow.

Overlaps

Cornell University, Carnegie Mellon, Brown, Tufts, University of Chicago, Boston College, Northeastern, WashU in St. Louis

Rochester Institute of Technology

60 Lomb Memorial Drive, Rochester, NY 14623

RIT is the largest of New York's three major technological universities—about double the size of Rensselaer. The school is strong in anything related to computing, art and design, and engineering. In the city built by Kodak (remember them?), photography, imaging science, and film and animation are among the tops in the nation. Big focus on connecting students with careers.

Website: www.rit.edu
Location: Suburban
Private
Total Enrollment: 14,901
Undergraduates: 12,435
Male/Female: 67/33
SAT Ranges: ERW 590–680, M 600–700
ACT Ranges: 26–32
Financial Aid: 74%
Pell Grant: 30%
Expense: Pr $ $
Student Loans: 76%
Average Debt: $ $ $ $
Applicants: 20,451
Accepted: 57%
Enrolled: 24%
Grad in 6 Years: 70%
Returning Freshmen: 90%
Academics: ✎ ✎ ✎
Social: ☎ ☎ ☎
Q of L: ★ ★ ★
Admissions: (585) 475-6631
Email Address: admissions@rit.edu

Strong Programs:
Mechanical Engineering
Electrical Engineering
Computer Science
Game Design and Development
Photography
Film and Animation

Unlike many liberal arts colleges that prefer that students test the academic waters before deciding on a major or future job plans, RIT focuses on career-oriented and technology-based academics from the get-go. And unlike many big universities where the academic luminaries shine from research-oriented graduate schools, RIT's spotlight is very definitely on undergraduates. RIT is more accessible than many of its closest competitors too. Students who are geared up and ready to "go professional" will be more than satisfied with RIT's extensive co-op program.

While the town of Rochester may sometimes seem like a reluctant host to weekend fun-seekers, it can hardly deny that it is, in fact, a college town; RIT shares the city with six nearby colleges. RIT's main campus, located on 1,300 suburban acres six miles from downtown Rochester, has its own distinctive style—redbrick buildings with sharp, contemporary lines. A new MAGIC Spell Studios facility housing a state-of-the-art production studio for the RIT MAGIC (Media, Arts, Games, Interaction, and Creativity) Center opened in 2018.

RIT's general education program offers students considerable flexibility. The number of required liberal arts credits has been reduced and more than 80 academic minors have been added within the past few years. Unlike many universities, RIT allows freshmen to schedule significant coursework in their majors early on, and spreads out liberal arts requirements over a more extended period.

RIT specializes in carving out niches for itself with unusual programs, and majors are offered in more than 200 fields, from basic electrical and chemical engineering to packaging science and bioinformatics. Fortunately, applicants narrow the range of choices to a manageable size by applying to one of nine undergraduate colleges: Art and Design; Saunders College of Business; Golisano College of Computing and Information Sciences; Gleason College of Engineering; Engineering Technology; Health Sciences and Technology; Liberal Arts; Science; or the National Technical Institute for the Deaf. RIT is a leader in providing access and support services for deaf and hard-of-hearing students. Many hearing students choose to learn sign language as well.

> **"People wear bathrobes to class and knit during lectures and do interpretive dances on the quad."**

Predictably, majors in engineering and engineering technology are among the most popular at RIT, particularly mechanical engineering and electrical engineering; computer science and game design and development also enroll high numbers of students. Photography is a signature program, and the film and animation, industrial design, and business administration/marketing programs are well regarded. The College of Art and Design offers excellent programs in ceramics, furniture design, glass, and metals and jewelry design, and students have the run of Bevier Gallery, where visiting artists provide firsthand instruction. Undergraduates being the school's top priority, classes are kept relatively small—47 percent have fewer than 20 students—and the faculty develops new academic programs to fit career needs. A biology major says, "Professors have a passion for what they teach, and it shows."

Students come to RIT to prove themselves, both in the classroom and through real-world experiences, so it's no surprise that students' schedules are demanding. "RIT makes me want to work harder, without making me feel like I won't succeed," says a biomedical engineering major. Through RIT's co-op program, more than 4,400 juniors and seniors each year take one to two terms away from campus for full-time, paid positions that give them practical experience in their field, key networking opportunities with potential employers, and, often, inspired ideas to bring back to campus. The Simone Center for Student Innovation and Entrepreneurship helps students learn how to take an idea from conception to commercialization through coursework, consulting opportunities, and workshops. Students showcase their research and creative projects every year during Imagine RIT. Although 400 study abroad programs are available in 50 countries, including RIT's global campuses in China, Croatia, Kosovo, and the United Arab Emirates, only 2 percent of students find time to go abroad.

RIT students are quirky and comfortable in their own skin. "People wear bathrobes to class and knit during lectures and do interpretive dances on the quad," says a junior. "Whatever quirk you have, bring it here, because it makes us fun." Forty-eight percent of undergraduates are from New York State, the remainder coming largely from New Jersey, Pennsylvania, and Connecticut; 7 percent are international. Five percent of students are African American, 7 percent Hispanic, 9 percent Asian American, and 4 percent multiracial. "The male-to-female ratio is still not where it should be," says one woman, "but this is a tech school, and 2 to 1 really isn't that bad." Socioeconomic diversity is strong, with 30 percent of incoming freshmen qualifying for Pell Grants, and the large number of deaf students also helps create a unique atmosphere. Politically, students tend to be aware of global issues, if not overtly active in them. RIT admits students without regard to financial need and offers merit scholarships averaging $10,200 to eligible students, but there are no athletic scholarships.

Fifty-two percent of RIT students live on campus; freshmen are required to live in the dorms, while upperclassmen sign up for the numerous campus apartments on a first-come, first-served basis. RIT offers a variety of special-interest houses and lifestyle floors, including "mainstream" floors where both deaf and hearing students live. Those who choose to live off campus take advantage of areas serviced by the school shuttle bus. Vegetarians, vegans, and carnivores alike will find on-campus meal options to be reasonably diverse. Four percent of the men and 2 percent of the women choose to go Greek and live and eat in RIT's fraternity and sorority houses. Campus security is "all over campus all of the time," says one student.

RIT's buzzing campus may seem at odds with its sedate suburban surroundings. The only facilities within walking distance are a variety of shopping plazas. Downtown Rochester has more to offer, and students also take road trips to Buffalo, Syracuse, and Canada. For those without transportation, there's always something to do on campus, courtesy of the more than 300 student clubs and organizations, including a fine jazz ensemble and a chorus that perform regularly. "Campus policies on alcohol are very strict," warns a senior, adding, "The policies work because

(continued)

Industrial Design
Imaging Science

Unlike many universities, RIT allows freshmen to schedule significant coursework in their majors early on.

"This is a tech school, and [the male-to-female ratio of] 2 to 1 really isn't that bad."

RIT is a leader in providing access and support services for deaf and hard-of-hearing students.

there isn't a lot of partying on campus." Brick City Homecoming, FreezeFest, and SpringFest are favorite annual celebrations.

RIT fields 21 Division III athletic teams. In addition, the Tigers men's and women's hockey teams compete in Division I, and both have won conference titles in recent years. Men's lacrosse, baseball, and women's basketball are recent conference champions as well. Approximately half of RIT undergrads participate in more than a dozen intramural sports.

RIT students are dedicated and career-oriented, yet they don't take themselves too seriously, which gives this demanding techie school a surprisingly relaxed feel. And best of all, says an imaging science major, thanks to an abundance of co-op education opportunities, "we graduate with lots of lab/field/hands-on experience." Indeed, self-motivated and focused, RIT students have their eye on the future and are well prepared to meet it.

If You Apply To ›

RIT: Early decision, regular decision. SATs or ACTs: required. Subject Tests: optional. Accepts the Common Application with supplement. Applicants to art, design, and film and animation programs must submit portfolio.

Rollins College

1000 Holt Avenue, Box 2720, Winter Park, FL 32789

Rollins is the marriage of a liberal arts college and a graduate business school that operates under the mantra of "applied liberal arts." A haven for Easterners who want their ticket punched to Florida, Rollins attracts many conservative and affluent students, as well as world-class water-skiers. Strong Greek system ensures active, if not diverse, social life. Just over half of the undergrads come from the Sunshine State.

Website: www.rollins.edu
Location: Suburban
Private
Total Enrollment: 2,374
Undergraduates: 1,977
Male/Female: 39/61
SAT Ranges: ERW 605–680, M 590–670
ACT Ranges: 25–30
Financial Aid: 85%
Pell Grant: 23%
Expense: Pr $ $
Student Loans: 46%
Average Debt: $ $ $
Applicants: 5,297
Accepted: 64%
Enrolled: 16%
Grad in 6 Years: 75%
Returning Freshmen: 83%
Academics: ✐ ✐ ✐

Move over, Mickey Mouse. Hold up, Harry Potter. You're not the only attractions in central Florida. For students looking to hit the books under the ever-present Florida sunshine, there's also Rollins College. Located in Winter Park, a quiet suburb of Greater Orlando, Rollins offers students plenty of places to have fun when making the grade gets to be too much. "Rollins is close to hundreds of internships and job opportunities just waiting for the next ambitious student," says one satisfied senior.

Capitalizing on its location along the shores of Lake Virginia, Rollins's campus combines the natural beauty of the lakeside with consistent, Spanish Mediterranean architecture. The Bush Science Center is a state-of-the-art, LEED-certified facility featuring 19 research labs, 18 student-faculty lounges, and 15 instructional labs. Construction is underway on a new residential complex aimed at housing juniors and seniors.

The general education curriculum, known as Rollins Foundations in the Liberal Arts, seeks to help students develop skills relevant to any major or career, while preparing them for global citizenship and responsible leadership. Students are required to demonstrate competency in foreign language, mathematical thinking, writing, and health and wellness. They must also take five courses within a given "neighborhood"—related courses that address a broad theme, exposing students to the arts, humanities, sciences, and social sciences. Students choose one of four neighborhoods: Innovate, Create,

"Rollins is close to hundreds of internships and job opportunities."

Elevate; Identities: Mirrors and Windows; When Cultures Collide; and Mysteries and Marvels. Additionally, first-year students must take a fall-semester Rollins College Conference course, a small class of no more than 15 students, led by a professor-advisor who is assisted by two upperclassmen peer mentors.

The most popular of Rollins's more than 50 academic programs include business, communication studies, psychology, and biology. Economics, English, and political science draw large numbers too. A minor in Australian studies is a particular specialty and involves travel Down Under. The chemistry department turned out a Nobel Prize winner, and the Annie Russell Theatre hosts productions staged by the active theater department. A 3–2 accelerated management program allows qualified freshmen to gain guaranteed admission to Rollins's top-ranked Crummer Graduate School of Business, leading to B.A. and M.B.A. degrees in five rather than six years. The international business dual-degree program offers students a chance to graduate with a B.A. from Rollins and a B.S. from Reutlingen University in Germany.

The workload at Rollins varies by major. "It is a laid-back environment without too much pressure. However, there are opportunities for students to pack on more rigorous courseloads depending on personal preferences," says a music major. Students find there's always help from their professors, with whom they have close relationships. There are no TAs here; teaching is the responsibility of professors, who "only want to see you succeed and find your passion," according to one student. Rollins offers many opportunities to collaborate on research with faculty or pursue independent projects, participate in internships, and volunteer through service-learning classes. Fifty-five percent of students study abroad at least once while at Rollins, taking off for programs in more than 50 countries all over the world.

According to one student, many Rollins students are "very wealthy and enjoying the campus for the extracurricular activities, Greek life, or entertaining classes," but many others are "hardworking" and "shaping the campus by leading organizations." Fifty-three percent of Rollins undergraduates are from Florida, and 10 percent hail from outside the United States. The student body is 4 percent African American, 16 percent Hispanic, 3 percent Asian American, and 4 percent multiracial. For students not hailing from affluent families, adequate financial aid is available, with merit scholarships averaging $25,300 for qualified students and more than 100 athletic scholarships given to male and female standouts. Twenty-three percent of incoming students qualify for the Pell Grant.

"It is a laid-back environment without too much pressure."

Sixty percent of the college's students live on campus in spacious co-ed dorms. "Dorms are really nice," a student says, and feature "big rooms and hardwood floors." Another adds that, for those who prefer to live off campus, "there are plenty of houses and apartments near the campus that can be rented at a reasonable cost." Dining facilities are located throughout campus and food is charged on a credit-card system, so students pay only for what they eat. A nautically themed, pub-style restaurant treats diners to views of the lake. One student says, "The food is a little on the pricey side, but it is delicious." A senior says, "Campus security is top of the line and super friendly."

The high-octane Greek scene claims 33 percent of the men and 33 percent of the women, so there's always a party somewhere. "It's a great idea to join fraternity and sorority life," recommends one recent grad. "You'll get that social experience, find your own good group of friends, and become more involved on campus." The administration has clamped down on social excesses, with party monitors checking IDs and a student activity director attending each on-campus party. Underage students caught drinking alcohol will be referred to Rollins's judicial affairs. A senior warns, "If you get caught, you're in major trouble!" Students can paddleboard, sail, or wakeboard on Lake Virginia between classes, and there are also movies on Mills

(continued)

Social: ☎ ☎ ☎ ☎
Q of L: ★ ★ ★
Admissions: (407) 646-2161
Email Address: admission@ rollins.edu

Strong Programs:
Business
Communication Studies
Psychology
Biology
Economics
English
Political Science
Australian Studies

A minor in Australian studies is a particular specialty and involves travel Down Under.

Every freshman participates in SPARC, Rollins's annual day of service held during orientation.

Lawn or "dive-in" movies at the pool, lip-synch contests, live bands in the campus center, and more than 100 student organizations. Fox Day in the spring is "a sacred tradition"—the president cancels classes for the day by placing a fox statue on the front lawn, and almost everyone heads for the beach.

"Winter Park isn't a typical college town," says one student. "It is one of the oldest cities in Florida, has a charming restaurant and shopping street known as Park Avenue, and is family friendly." Every freshman participates in SPARC, Rollins's annual day of service held during orientation, and many students volunteer with community partners such as Habitat for Humanity and local schools. Orlando's offerings include entertainment complexes and theme parks such as Walt Disney World, Epcot Center, Universal CityWalk, and Islands of Adventure. Popular road trips include Cocoa Beach, Miami, and Tampa.

Athletics are an integral part of the Rollins experience. Division II Tars teams have claimed 23 national championships and more than 90 Sunshine State conference titles. Competitive teams include men's and women's soccer, men's basketball, and women's lacrosse and golf. The water ski team is a perennial national powerhouse. Intramural sports are popular too, with more than 20 leagues and events during the school year. Teams have been formed for everything from Quidditch and wakeboarding to table tennis and dance.

Rollins students enjoy sand and sun, as well as a diverse academic climate. As the oldest recognized college in the state of Florida, Rollins offers a rich legacy and smooth-as-silk Southern character. Says one senior, "Students can expect to find a safe haven [and] a real college experience," not to mention plenty of practical career preparation.

Overlaps

Furman, Roanoke, Eckerd, Rhodes, University of Puget Sound, Florida State, Stetson, University of Central Florida

If You Apply To ›

Rollins: Early decision I and II, regular decision. SATs or ACTs: optional (required for applicants to honors program and accelerated management program). Subject Tests: optional. Accepts the Common Application.

Rose–Hulman Institute of Technology

5500 Wabash Avenue, Terre Haute, IN 47803

Co-ed since 1995, Rose–Hulman offers that rare combination of technical education and personal attention. Only Caltech, Clarkson, and Harvey Mudd offer comparable intimacy and a technical academic environment. Nearby Indiana State and Saint Mary-of-the-Woods help mitigate the skewed gender ratio. RHIT is among the few engineering schools that encourage study abroad and boast significant athletic opportunities.

Website: www.rose-hulman.edu
Location: Suburban
Private
Total Enrollment: 2,182
Undergraduates: 2,133
Male/Female: 75/25
SAT Ranges: ERW 610–690, M 650–760

Rose–Hulman Institute of Technology may not be as well known as Caltech, MIT, or even Carnegie Mellon, but it was the first private college to offer an undergraduate degree in chemical engineering, and it continues to innovate today. If you can handle the lopsided male/female ratio and the limited list of majors (all in engineering and the sciences, with the exception of econ), Rose–Hulman offers an outstanding technical background and bright prospects for future employment. Students are smart, motivated, and highly competitive, and love using their computers for work and play. "We are all dorks," says a senior. "Some of us just hide it better than others."

Established in 1874, Rose–Hulman is the oldest private engineering school west of the Alleghenies. Its benefactors were Chauncey Rose, an entrepreneur who brought the railroad to Indiana, and the Hulman family, owners of the Indianapolis Motor Speedway, who gave their fortune to the institution in 1970. (A member of the Hulman family starts the Indianapolis 500 race every year with the famous words, "Drivers, start your engines.") The 200-acre campus includes numerous trees, rolling hills, and a lake. A $25 million expansion and renovation of the student union was completed in 2018.

General education requirements at Rose–Hulman include math, physics, chemistry, and humanities and social sciences. Humanities professors "are very eager to educate and expose science- and engineering-oriented people to a different way of thinking," an applied biology major says. In the first quarter, freshmen must take a Foundations for Success course that covers such topics as time management and study skills. Students in any major can enroll in multidisciplinary senior capstone projects, often completing projects for outside organizations.

"Being on a quarter system, the academics are fast-paced and challenging, but still manageable," says a junior, especially because students are so willing to work together. Thirty-nine percent of classes have fewer than 20 students. Mechanical engineering, chemical engineering, computer science, and electrical engineering are the most popular majors, and biomedical engineering, math, and physics are also strong. A new major in engineering design gives students a chance to work on projects with real clients through all phases of the design process. Regardless of which discipline you choose, odds are you'll find faculty members eager to help. "Our professors love to teach," one student explains. "Research and side projects come in as a distant second to teaching."

> **"[Career services] helped me make lots of decisions when I had multiple offers at hand."**

Since only a few dozen graduate students are enrolled, teaching assistants don't teach classes and opportunities to get involved with faculty research abound. The Interdisciplinary Research Collaborative gives selected students the chance to work on ongoing research projects for 10 weeks during the summer. The school is increasing its emphasis on global education and offers, in addition to exchange programs, a number of courses that combine traditional on-campus coursework with a two- to three-week trip at the end of the quarter. Still, with their demanding schedules, only 4 percent of students go abroad. When it comes time to start the job search, Rose–Hulman students are in good hands. "Career services works with every student individually to assist them in finding the right job for them," cheers a senior. "They helped me make lots of decisions when I had multiple offers at hand."

A chemical engineering major says Rose–Hulman students "are always tinkering, and their hands can't move as fast as their minds do." Thirty-one percent of students are Indiana natives, and 15 percent come from abroad. African Americans comprise 3 percent of the student body, Asian Americans 5 percent, Hispanics 5 percent, and multiracial students 5 percent. "Students are conservative but don't really get involved politically," one senior explains. Merit scholarships are available, averaging $12,300, but there are no athletic awards.

Fifty-eight percent of students live on campus; freshmen and sophomores are guaranteed rooms in the residence halls. "We're allowed to do almost anything to the rooms, like add lofts or decks to gain space," says a civil engineering major. (At an engineering school, would you expect anything less?) The HERE living/learning community for freshmen focuses on sustainability topics and design projects. Most upperclassmen move into Greek houses or find other off-campus digs, students say. There's a traditional cafeteria, as well as a restaurant-style

(continued)

ACT Ranges: 27–32
Financial Aid: 98%
Pell Grant: 13%
Expense: Pr $ $
Student Loans: 60%
Average Debt: $ $ $ $
Applicants: 4,473
Accepted: 61%
Enrolled: 21%
Grad in 6 Years: 81%
Returning Freshmen: 91%
Academics: ✐ ✐ ✐
Social: ☎
Q of L: ★ ★
Admissions: (800) 248-7448
Email Address: admissions@ rose-hulman.edu

Strong Programs:
Mechanical Engineering
Chemical Engineering
Computer Science
Electrical Engineering
Biomedical Engineering
Mathematics
Physics

Students in any major can enroll in multidisciplinary senior capstone projects, often completing projects for outside organizations.

dining facility, and a senior reports that meals are usually tasty with "lots of good options." As for safety, "there is essentially zero crime on campus," according to one student, and the school has introduced new training programs to prevent sexual assault.

The town of Terre Haute has some restaurants and bars, a mall, a couple of Starbucks locations, and two movie theaters, but generally, it's "sleepy and lacking in nightlife, so we create our own," says a physics major. Various groups, including the Greek organizations and Habitat for Humanity, help the town out with service projects. There are eight fraternities and three sororities, which draw 36 percent of the men and 34 percent of the women, respectively. "Fraternities host most parties, and since Rose is such a small school, most people attend," says a biomedical engineering major. When it comes to alcohol, Rose–Hulman allows students 21 and over to imbibe, provided it's behind closed doors. Students say the best weekend activities are usually road trips to Chicago, Cincinnati, Indianapolis, or St. Louis, all within a few hours' drive. Everyone looks forward to the homecoming bonfire, and to basketball games against DePauw. "Homecoming is very big," says a sophomore. "Freshmen build up and guard the bonfire the week preceding homecoming while upperclassmen try to sabotage it," explains a junior.

> "[Students] are always tinkering, and their hands can't move as fast as their minds do."

Varsity teams (the Engineers) play in Division III, and recent conference champions include men's and women's basketball, cross-country, and tennis. Competitive tech teams like the Human Powered Vehicle Team, Team Rose Motorsports, and Cyber Defense Team are strong, but if you're envisioning Rose–Hulman students as pasty-faced lab dwellers, you're sorely misinformed. Just over half of the student body participates in 32 intramural sports, with flag football, basketball, and ultimate Frisbee the most popular.

Students committed to careers in engineering or the sciences will find a top-flight education at this Midwestern technical school. While Rose–Hulman "doesn't have that big-school pride" so common in this part of the country, students appreciate the community feel created by the small classes and the school's small size, balanced with a bit of healthy competition. "The atmosphere makes you want to try to do your best and stand out," says a junior, "but everyone is here to help you do that."

Just over half of the student body participates in 32 intramural sports.

Overlaps

Harvey Mudd, Kettering, Lawrence Tech, Milwaukee School of Engineering, Olin College of Engineering, Purdue, U of I at Urbana–Champaign, Ohio State

If You Apply To ›

Rose–Hulman: Early action, regular decision. SATs or ACTs: required. No Subject Tests. Accepts the Common Application.

Rutgers–The State University of New Jersey

65 Davidson Road, Piscataway, NJ 08854

One of only nine American universities founded during the Colonial period, Rutgers is the dominant public university in the Garden State. Originally chartered as Queens College but subsequently renamed for Revolutionary War hero and benefactor Henry Rutgers. Everything is available: engineering, business, pharmacy, the liberal arts, and the nation's largest women's college. Well known as the birthplace of football.

Proud of traditions that extend back to its founding in 1766, this flagship public university of New Jersey likes to compare itself to a city with multiple neighborhoods, each with its own particular identity. With 45,000 full-time undergraduate students spread across three regional campuses in New Brunswick, Newark, and Camden, Rutgers is all about choice. Choices between more than 100 undergraduate majors and 4,000 courses. Choices about which of the more than 500 student organizations catch your fancy. Even choices about which of its 18 computer centers or six student centers to frequent. "Rutgers is a place that gives students opportunities to do and be whatever they want," says a senior.

Seventy-five percent of undergraduates (about 34,000) enroll in Rutgers–New Brunswick, which is itself a collection of five residential sub-campuses strung out along the Raritan River and linked by a free university bus system that allows students to move easily among the various units for classes, housing, and social life. The historical core is the College Avenue campus, which boasts architectural gems dating to the American Revolution and is home to the huge School of Arts and Sciences. In addition to the football stadium, the Busch campus hosts the engineering and the newly expanded pharmacy schools, while Cook offers a bucolic setting for the School of Environmental and Biological Sciences. Douglass, with its Georgian Colonial architecture, is home to the Douglass Residential College, the largest women's college in the country. Livingston, with its extensive array of solar panels, is home to the business school and the basketball arena.

"The sense of community in classes is very strong."

Among the more than 100 undergraduate majors offered, the most popular include psychology, nursing, communication, and exercise science and sport studies. Philosophy is internationally renowned, and students universally praise fine arts, agricultural sciences, business, and the six-year pharmacy program. The "incredible resources and opportunities" at Douglass Residential College make the women's and gender studies major a good bet, according to an English major. Workloads vary across disciplines, and students generally find them ambitious but manageable. "The sense of community in classes is very strong," says one senior. "Students like to help each other out, and professors understand that you are at Rutgers to do more than take classes." Faculty members all have office hours, and first-year students are taught by regular professors. As at any big state university, classes can be large, but a sophomore reports that "even in those 200-person lecture halls, my professors know my name and are super flexible when it comes to finding time to meet with struggling students."

In an effort to reverse the long-standing exodus of New Jersey high school superstars from the state, Rutgers offers a wide range of special academic programs, including the new state-of-the-art (and highly selective) Honors College, whose members pursue specialized courses, fulfill service requirements, and complete a cumulative capstone project during their senior year. Interdisciplinary living/learning communities offer live-in faculty that draw students with common interests ranging from French to meteorology. Biology students have the run of the 360-acre Rutgers Ecological Preserve and Natural Teaching Area, and the Aresty Research Center supports students seeking to engage in research as early as the summer after their freshman year. Entering students have the option of a first-year seminar where they work closely with a faculty member. A junior singles out the Road to Wall Street Program that "provides finance majors with one-on-one mentoring with people currently working on Wall Street." Rutgers is home to more than 175 specialized research centers and institutes dedicated to topics ranging from ancient Roman art to mountain gorillas. Rutgers also offers undergraduate study abroad in more than 40 countries, from France and Greece to Thailand. As for career, health, and other student support services, an English major reports, "The services are strong, but students have to reach out for them."

Website: www.rutgers.edu
Location: Small City
Public
Total Enrollment: 42,103
Undergraduates: 33,619
Male/Female: 50/50
SAT Ranges: ERW 590–680, M 600–720
ACT Ranges: N/A
Financial Aid: 53%
Pell Grant: 28%
Expense: Pub $ $ $
Student Loans: 55%
Average Debt: $ $ $
Applicants: 38,384
Accepted: 58%
Enrolled: 28%
Grad in 6 Years: 80%
Returning Freshmen: 94%
Academics: ✐ ✐ ✐ ✐
Social: ☎ ☎ ☎
Q of L: ★ ★ ★
Admissions: (732) 932-4636
Email Address: admissions@ugadm.rutgers.edu

Strong Programs:
Psychology
Nursing
Communication
Exercise Science and Sport Studies
Philosophy
Fine Arts
Agricultural Sciences
Pharmacy

Rutgers–New Brunswick is a collection of five residential sub-campuses strung out along the Raritan River.

Although the administration has been attempting to increase the number of out-of-staters, 85 percent of Rutgers students hail from the Garden State. Nevertheless, the student body reflects the substantial diversity of the state itself, with a good mix of students from cities, suburbs, farms, and seaside communities, and students take pride in their heterogeneity. "Our diversity spans interests, race, gender, class, sexual orientation, religion, and politics," says a management major. "It is the best part of Rutgers." Minorities account for half of undergraduates, including 7 percent African American, 13 percent Hispanic, 27 percent Asian American, and 3 percent multi-racial. Nine percent of undergrads come from abroad, and 28 percent of freshmen are Pell-eligible. More than 450 students receive athletic scholarships in 24 sports; merit scholarships average just over $10,000.

The Aresty Research Center supports students seeking to engage in research as early as the summer after their freshman year.

On-campus housing in New Brunswick accommodates 43 percent of full-time students and is readily available on all five sub-campuses. "The rooms are large, and every room comes with a microwave and fridge/freezer combination," reports a music education major. Other on-campus housing options include the aforementioned living/learning communities and apartment complexes with kitchens and living rooms. The university also offers a special dormitory for students who are trying to overcome addictions to drugs and alcohol. "We have four dining halls, and there are many cafés and food vendors on campus that accept meal swipes," notes one sophomore. "Most people can find a place they are happy eating at regularly." In part because of its Office for Violence Prevention and Victim Assistance, Rutgers has become a national leader in confronting sexual assault on campus.

"Even in those 200-person lecture halls, my professors know my name."

Social life happens both on and off campus. The Greek scene is located off campus near College Avenue, and a sophomore notes, "Only 11 percent of students are involved in Greek life, so we are definitely not 'go Greek or go home.' People party in apartments, bars, houses, and dorms, and there is no single party culture." Another reports, "The RAs are really effective about enforcing alcohol policies." Each sub-campus has its own student center with pinball machines, pool tables, bowling alleys, and a snack bar, and the Rutgers University Programming Association sponsors films, performances, and other events. As a major city, New Brunswick offers an array of nearby restaurants and theaters. For those who want to hit the road for fun, New York City and Philadelphia are each only about an hour's drive or train ride, and students flood the Jersey Shore in springtime.

Funky social rituals include Beats on the Banks, which brings a major rapper or other artist to campus.

Funky social rituals include Hot Dog Day, which features rides and free hot dogs, and Beats on the Banks, which brings a major rapper or other artist to campus. Given that Rutgers likes to remind the world that it was the birthplace of college football, homecoming is a big deal—with tailgate parties in the stadium parking lot, tons of food (including roast pigs and whole sides of beef), continuous music, and thousands of revelers. Students participating in the Homecoming Bed Races decorate twin beds on wheels and race them down College Avenue for charity.

"Our diversity…is the best part of Rutgers."

Varsity, intramural, and club sports fill whatever gap is left by the social scene. In an effort to move from relative athletic obscurity to instant national prominence, Rutgers in 2014 became the 14th (sic) member of the powerhouse Big Ten, which appreciated its proximity to New York City and other East Coast media markets. The transition, however, has been marred by NCAA rules infractions and costly settlements to former coaches. On a more positive note, the Scarlet Knights compete in 10 men's and 14 women's Division I sports, and men's lacrosse, wrestling, and women's soccer are nationally ranked. "Rutgers likes to pretend that Penn State is our rival, even though they don't care about us," confesses a management major.

Overlaps

Penn State, University of Maryland, University of Pittsburgh, Ohio State, University of Minnesota, College of New Jersey, NYU, Boston University

"So that is fun." Nonvarsity athletes can take their pick of 57 club sports and dozens of intramural leagues and tournaments.

Rutgers has the usual abundance of people and programs characteristic of a large state university coupled with loyal support from the state's legislature and private sector and tuition that is relatively affordable. Students express irritation about the bus system ("not enough buses," "they leak when it rains"), but most appreciate the fact that, as a public land grant university, Rutgers offers them a huge range of professional and other academic options from which to choose. If all this choice seems a bit overwhelming, a senior counsels that the school has somehow figured out how to "feel big and incorporate a lot of the student body while simultaneously feeling small and allowing niche groups to form."

If You Apply To ›

Rutgers: Early action, regular decision. SATs or ACTs: required. No Subject Tests. Does not accept the Common Application. Apply to particular school.

University of St Andrews: See page 376.

College of Saint Benedict and Saint John's University

37 South College Avenue, St. Joseph, MN 56374

The College of Saint Benedict (CSB) and Saint John's University (SJU) are throwbacks to the way colleges were 50 years ago: women and men on separate campuses and copious amounts of school spirit. Founded by Benedictines, and monastic communities are still active on both campuses. Nearly 80 percent of students are from Minnesota, but global perspectives and study abroad are big emphases.

Remember when women's colleges had nearby brother schools, when dorms were single-sex, and when visitors of the opposite gender were only welcome at certain times? Doesn't ring a bell? Well, you might ask your grandparents. Or you could visit the College of Saint Benedict and Saint John's University. These two single-sex campuses—all-female CSB and all-male SJU—are five miles apart and have their own presidents, but they share a common heritage and mission: students and faculty join together in a shared liberal arts education, guided by Benedictine principles. The schools' small sizes and respect for tradition give rise to a tight-knit community.

Founded by what is now one of the largest men's Benedictine monasteries in the world, Saint John's now operates as an independent entity. It occupies 2,600 pristine acres in rural Minnesota, an area filled with forests, lakes, and the wide-open spaces perfect for out-doorsy types. The two colleges are connected by a free and frequent shuttle bus. Alongside a 130-year-old quadrangle erected by monks is a strikingly modern church designed by Marcel Breuer. Saint Benedict is a cohesive 800-acre campus comprised of redbrick buildings and cobblestone walks. Together, the colleges have invested millions in facilities in recent years, including a major renovation of the SJU library that added a new Learning Commons.

> **"Many of the classes are flipped classrooms or centered on discussion."**

Website: www.csbsju.edu
Location: City Outskirts
Private
Total Enrollment: 3,667
Undergraduates: 3,619
Male/Female: 47/53
SAT Ranges: ERW 530–630, M 480–590
ACT Ranges: 22–28
Financial Aid: 96%
Pell Grant: 25%
Expense: Pr $ $
Student Loans: 73%
Average Debt: $ $ $ $
Applicants: 3,642
Accepted: 80%
Enrolled: 34%
Grad in 6 Years: 78%

(continued)

Returning Freshmen: 88%
Academics: ✍ ✍ ✍
Social: ☎ ☎ ☎
Q of L: ★ ★ ★
Admissions: (800) 544-1489
Email Address: admissions@
  csbsju.edu

Strong Programs:
Global Business Leadership
Biology
Communication
Accounting
Political Science
Music
Nursing
Chemistry

Saint Benedict and Saint John's share a joint academic program through which students take classes together on both campuses. A new core curriculum is set to go into effect in fall 2020. The new program, called the Integrations Curriculum, is intended to give students a more cohesive, interdisciplinary, and hands-on education and features components like a first-year seminar, experiential learning such as study abroad or service learning, and an electronic portfolio that ties together their four years.

The global business leadership program prepares students to be leaders in a global economy and is the most popular major, followed by biology, communication, and accounting. Programs in political science, music, nursing, and chemistry are also well regarded. The interdisciplinary environmental studies program is enhanced by access to the area's natural resources and one of the largest solar farms in the upper Midwest. The theology program benefits from abundant resources, including the Hill Museum & Manuscript Library, one of the foremost microfilm collections of centuries-old handwritten manuscripts. "Many of the classes are flipped classrooms or centered on discussion, so everyone is playing a critical role in the learning process," says a chemistry major. Very few classes have more than 30 students, and some fill up fast. The small classes encourage a community atmosphere and strong student/faculty ties. "Faculty members encourage students to ask them questions and will go out of their way for the success of their students," says a nursing major.

For those who tire of the Minnesota winters, which can start in November and occasionally run until April, the colleges offer faculty-led, semester-long international study programs in 15 countries on six continents. Each program is limited to about 30 students, and 64 percent of students take part. Numerous shorter trips are also offered during semester and summer breaks. "Study abroad is a big part of our culture here," says a biology major, "and your scholarships will transfer over to your study abroad, making it affordable." The McNeely Center for Entrepreneurship provides classes, coaching, and assistance to budding entrepreneurs from a range of disciplines. The program's Entrepreneurial Scholars travel to Silicon Valley and China/Hong Kong, and all of them start their own entrepreneurial ventures. Undergraduate research is becoming more prevalent at CSB/SJU (41 percent of students participate), and there is an endowed summer research program in the health and medical areas. Exceptional first-years students are invited to join the colleges' honors program, and upper-class students may also apply.

> **"The progression to nicer housing as you get older is a rite of passage."**

"We are a very social and friendly campus with an upbeat personality," says a sophomore. Fifty-two percent of students, known as "Bennies" and "Johnnies," are Roman Catholic, 79 percent are from Minnesota, and most are white. African Americans constitute 4 percent of the student body, Hispanics 8 percent, and Asian Americans 4 percent. International students account for 4 percent of the student population. A senior notes that despite the lack of diversity on campus, the schools offer "a lot of programming events encouraging students to learn about diversity." Politically, a junior says, "We encompass all viewpoints, from ultraconservative to ultraliberal," and a senior adds that the atmosphere is "becoming more polarized." In an effort to become more inclusive, CSB and SJU have both recently adopted policies allowing for the admission of transgender students. Merit scholarships averaging $18,600 are available, and 25 percent of first-year students qualify for the Pell Grant, but there are no athletic scholarships.

Through a four-year residential program, 91 percent of students live on campus; seniors wishing to move off campus must apply for permission. "The progression to nicer housing as you get older is a rite of passage," says a senior. The residence

The colleges offer faculty-led, semester-long international study programs in 15 countries, and 64 percent of students take part.

halls are staffed partly by members of the monastic communities, but students aren't made to feel like a nun is watching their every move. On-campus apartments, such as Flynntown, provide a more independent living area for juniors and seniors, although students complain that there has been a shortage of housing for upperclassmen of late, due to larger incoming classes. Students can choose from four dining halls on either campus, and most report the fare to be tasty and diverse. Campus security gets good reviews, and a sophomore says, "We have bystander intervention training programs on a variety of concerns, such as eating disorders and domestic violence."

The Joint Events Council organizes regular weekday and weekend social events, including student performances, comedians, magicians, and concerts. Students 21 and older are allowed to consume alcohol in their rooms or at SJU's on-campus pub, Brother Willie's; underage drinkers face stiff penalties if caught. There are no fraternities or sororities, and parties tend to be small affairs. Each year, students look forward to the Festival of Cultures, the Fruit at the Finish Triathlon, the Senior Farewell, and spring break trips involving community service. Also popular is the annual Pines music festival, which welcomes the spring with a day of concerts featuring popular Christian musicians. Says a sophomore, "Off campus, there are many things to do in St. Cloud and also in St. Joseph, such as parties, coffee shops, restaurants, shopping, and movies." Seventy-seven percent of students engage in community service, often through Campus Ministry programs. St. Cloud is a few minutes away, and the Twin Cities are 70 miles southeast.

The annual Pines music festival welcomes the spring with a day of concerts featuring popular Christian musicians.

"Once a Bennie or a Johnnie, always a Bennie or a Johnnie."

The CSB Bennies field 11 Division III teams, and the SJU Johnnies boast 12. The football team is a perennial powerhouse (and the winningest Division III team in history), and its rivalry with St. Thomas is as strong as ever. Curiously enough, a team of guys known as the Rat Pack gets students psyched up for games. Men's golf and women's volleyball make regular national tournament appearances, and the men's basketball and baseball teams are recent conference champs. Nonvarsity students can participate in a variety of club and intramural sports, and activities like kayaking and indoor rock climbing, offered through the Outdoor Leadership Center, are popular year-round.

Students who attend CSB/SJU revel in the schools' small-town setting, their traditions, and the grounding that comes from their shared Benedictine values. Perhaps more than anything, they treasure the community spirit that allows them to grow both individually and together. "We have a strong sense of school pride and alumni connection," says one happy student. "Once a Bennie or a Johnnie, always a Bennie or a Johnnie."

Overlaps
Gustavus Adolphus, Pacific Lutheran, St. Norbert, St. Olaf, Linfield, Augustana (IL), Kenyon, Lewis & Clark

If You Apply To ›

St. Benedict and St. John's: Early action I and II, regular decision. SATs or ACTs: required. No Subject Tests. Accepts the Common Application.

St. John's College

Annapolis Campus: 60 College Avenue, Annapolis, MD 21401
Santa Fe Campus: 1160 Camino Cruz Blanca, Santa Fe, NM 87505

Books, books, and more books is what you'll get at St. John's—from Thucydides to Tolstoy, Euclid to Einstein. St. John's attracts smart, intellectual, and nonconformist students who like to talk (and debate) about books and ideas. Easy to get in, not so easy to graduate. One of the few institutions with two coequal campuses. Students admitted to one can spend time at the other. St. John's is a croquet powerhouse.

Annapolis
Website: www.sjc.edu
Location: City Center
Private
Total Enrollment: 499
Undergraduates: 458
Male/Female: 53/47
SAT Ranges: ERW 640–740,
  M 580–690
ACT Ranges: 26–32
Financial Aid: 76%
Pell Grant: 25%
Expense: Pr $ $ $
Student Loans: 74%
Average Debt: $
Applicants: 753
Accepted: 55%
Enrolled: 30%
Grad in 6 Years: 67%
Returning Freshmen: 87%
Academics: ✍ ✍ ✍ ✍ ½
Social: ☎ ☎ ☎
Q of L: ★ ★ ★ ★
Admissions: (800) 727-9238
Email Address: annapolis
  .admissions@sjc.edu

Strong Programs:
The Great Books Program
Liberal Arts and Sciences

Santa Fe
Website: www.sjc.edu
Location: Small City
Private
Total Enrollment: 360
Undergraduates: 309
Male/Female: 56/44

With no majors, departments, or professors (in the traditional sense), and a combined total of fewer than 900 students on its two campuses, St. John's College is about as far from the typical postsecondary experience as you can get. Or maybe it's much closer to what college used to be; the Annapolis campus traces its roots to King William's School—the Maryland colony's "free" school—founded in 1696. More than two centuries later, in 1964, St. John's opened a second campus in Santa Fe, New Mexico, to facilitate a doubling of enrollment and offer its super-serious students a change of scenery. While the campuses may be a thousand miles apart, the Johnnies who populate them share an all-consuming quest for knowledge in the classical tradition. Their true teachers are the Great Books, about 150 of the most influential works of Western civilization. "Students at St. John's College aspire to join the great conversations that began in the primeval forests and have expanded to what we think we know today," says a sophomore. "We appreciate the value of tradition and its role in education."

Physically, the two St. John's campuses are more than just two time zones from one another. The colonial brick structures of the small urban campus in Annapolis, where the central classroom building dates from 1742, are squeezed into the city's historic district. With the Maryland state capitol and the U.S. Naval Academy in the neighborhood, this campus exudes old-world charm, and its location at the confluence of the Severn River and the Chesapeake Bay allows students to participate in sailing, crew, and individual sculling. The Santa Fe campus sits on 250 landlocked acres in the sun-drenched capital of New Mexico, just two and a half miles from downtown. The adobe-style buildings reflect Spanish and Native American traditions, and their perch in the Sangre de Cristo Mountains offers beautiful views of the city below. Students at St. John's in Santa Fe can get back to nature in nearby state and national forests, which offer hiking, mountain biking, kayaking, snowboarding, and skiing. Students may attend both campuses during their academic careers, and about 10 percent do so.

> "We appreciate the value of tradition and its role in education."

The St. John's curriculum, known as "the program," has every student read the Great Books in roughly chronological order. All students major in liberal arts, discussing the books in seminars, writing papers about them, and debating the riddles of human existence that they raise. Classes are led by tutors, who would be tenured professors anywhere else, but here are just the most advanced students. In a snub to the general trend in American academia toward more and more specialization, each tutor is required to teach any subject within the curriculum. As a group, the tutors help students divine wisdom from each other and from great philosophers, writers, scientists, and thinkers, from Thucydides and Tolstoy to Euclid and Einstein. "Because St. John's is not a research institution, the tutor's only job is teaching and engaging with students," says one junior. Both campuses follow a curriculum that would have delighted poet and educator Matthew Arnold, who argued that the goal of education is "to know the best which has been thought and said in the world."

There are no registration or scheduling hassles at St. John's; the daily course of study is mapped out before students set foot on campus. The curriculum includes four years of mathematics, two years of ancient Greek and French, three years of laboratory science, two years of music, and, of course, four years of Great Books seminars. Freshmen study the Greeks, sophomores advance through the Romans and the Renaissance, juniors cover the 17th and 18th centuries, and seniors do the 19th and 20th centuries. Readings are from primary sources only: math from Euclid and Ptolemy, physics from Maxwell, psychology from Freud, and so on. The assumption is that the Great Books can stand on their own, representing the highest achievements of human intellect. Juniors and seniors also take seven-week electives, called preceptorials, where they study a book or topic one-on-one with a tutor. In their final semester, seniors write a 20- to 60-page critical essay on a topic of their choice and must pass an hour-long oral examination by a committee of three tutors.

> "Our class conversations carry over into the dining hall, the quad, the common rooms, and coffee shop."

"There is a real sense of community and a collaborative feel to all of the academic work we do," says one sophomore. "Our class conversations carry over into the dining hall, the quad, the common rooms, and coffee shop." While there are no multiple-choice tests and no formal exams, courses are rigorous with a heavy load of reading every week and lots of writing. Since everyone's doing the same thing, there's a lot of peer pressure not to slack off. Some St. John's students find they need a year off between the sophomore and junior years to decompress; some switch from Annapolis to Santa Fe or vice versa, and a relatively high percentage of students take more than six years to graduate. St. John's prefers that all eight semesters be completed in residence—meaning no heading off campus for internships, study abroad programs, or the like, unless it's during summer vacation. The only exceptions are the 20 lucky students per year (10 from each campus) who are selected for a semester-long, for-credit program in Aix-en-Provence, France, where they are taught the established St. John's junior curriculum in a living European context.

A fifth of St. John's students are transfers from more conventional colleges—a true act of devotion, since St. John's requires everyone to begin as freshmen. Though the reasons students choose St. John's are never simple, the common thread is a fierce love of learning. One student says, "Johnnies are outspoken introverts. We're very thoughtful and self-reflective but unafraid to voice our opinions." The vast majority of students at both campuses are out-of-staters; international students represent 22 percent of the student body in Annapolis and 29 percent in Santa Fe. In Annapolis, 6 percent are Hispanic, 4 percent are Asian American, 2 percent are African American, and 3 percent are multiracial, while in Santa Fe those groups account for 10 percent, 2 percent, 1 percent, and 5 percent, respectively. One student reports that students are "more interested in political philosophy and theory" than in actually engaging in political or social activism. Admissions are need-blind, and limited merit awards are available, but not for athletic prowess. Twenty-five percent of Annapolis freshmen are Pell-eligible, compared to 22 percent at Santa Fe. Qualified international students may take advantage of special financial aid packages.

> "Students most definitely need to find ways to have well-rounded lives."

Seventy percent of students in Annapolis and 83 percent of those in Santa Fe live on campus in the co-ed dorms; freshmen are guaranteed a room. In Annapolis, the six "historic" residence halls are arranged around a central quad, while the two modern halls face College Creek. (Students warn that "historic" is code for "old," and complain about erratic heating and cooling and a lack of hot water for morning

(continued)

SAT Ranges: ERW 580–720, M 540–690
ACT Ranges: 23–32
Financial Aid: 87%
Pell Grant: 22%
Expense: Pr $ $ $
Student Loans: 71%
Average Debt: $
Applicants: 342
Accepted: 63%
Enrolled: 32%
Grad in 6 Years: 65%
Returning Freshmen: 78%
Academics: ✑ ✑ ✑ ✑ ½
Social: ☎ ☎ ☎
Q of L: ★ ★ ★ ★
Admissions: (800) 331-5232
Email Address:
    santafe.admissions@sjc.edu

Strong Programs:
The Great Books Program
Liberal Arts and Sciences

Johnnies' true teachers are the Great Books, about 150 of the most influential works of Western civilization.

showers.) In Santa Fe, the dorms are small, modern units clustered around court-yards. Most students get singles or divided double rooms. Upperclassmen typically live off campus in apartments and group houses; those who stay in the dorms usu-ally get single rooms. Meals at both campuses get average reviews.

"With the amount of reading and thinking done here, students most definitely need to find ways to have well-rounded lives. There are pick-up sports, dance groups, musical ensembles, and many other interest-based clubs to participate in," says one student. A senior adds, "We don't have any Greek organizations (besides study groups for reading ancient Greek!)." Drinking is a favored release for Johnnies, who have, of course, read Plato's Symposium and are familiar with the likes of François Rabelais ("Drink constantly. You will never die."). Still, hard liquor is not allowed on campus, and parties and kegs must be registered. And although college-sponsored events are patrolled to prevent underage drinking, youngsters tip their share of brew at smaller dorm gatherings. According to one student, only those who are extremely rowdy or disruptive are reported to the dean's office to face penalties. Road trips to Washington, D.C., Baltimore, New York, and Assateague State Park are options for Annapolis students with cars. In Santa Fe, nearby blues and jazz clubs are popular, though one student cautions that the town shuts down around 9 p.m.

> **"We don't have any Greek organizations (besides study groups for reading ancient Greek!)."**

Popular annual events on both campuses include Lola's, a casino night spon-sored by the senior class; the Arc party, held to celebrate the sophomores' comple-tion of the Old Testament; and Reality, a three-day festival of food, games, and general debauchery thrown for the seniors the weekend before commencement. Intercollegiate club teams in crew, fencing, croquet, and women's soccer are avail-able. In fact, the Johnnies hold more national croquet titles than any other college, and the match against The Naval Academy each spring is the occasion for a genteel lawn party. Annapolis students relish their intramural teams, with names like the Druids and the Furies. In Santa Fe, the nearby Rio Grande and Chama rivers offer excellent white-water canoeing, kayaking, and rafting, while the Hueco Tanks area offers rock climbing and bouldering; the Taos Ski Valley and Ski Santa Fe are excel-lent in the winter months. The Outdoor Programs Office organizes trips and makes athletic equipment available for use.

Students at St. John's are as passionate about learning as their peers at other schools are about basketball rivalries or blowout parties. And while those larger col-leges and universities try desperately to grow and change, St. John's cherishes its traditions—including the mandate that seniors wear formal academic dress to their oral examinations, which are open to the public. As one happy Johnnie reflects, "A heated discussion about Plato on the grassy knoll is the type of sight that reminds me why I love this place."

Overlaps

Reed, University of Chicago, Thomas Aquinas, Bard, Kenyon, Colorado College, Harvard, Brown

If You Apply To ›

St. John's: Early action, regular decision. SATs or ACTs: optional (required for homeschooled students). Subject Tests: optional. Accepts the Common Application with supplement. Apply to one campus only.

Saint John's University and College of Saint Benedict: See page 615.

St. Lawrence University

Canton, NY 13617

St. Lawrence is perched far back in the north country, closer to Ottawa and Montreal than to Syracuse. Isolation breeds camaraderie, and St. Lawrence students have a special bond similar to that at places like Dartmouth and Whitman. Compare to Allegheny and Hobart and William Smith. Environmental studies is the crown jewel: Where else can you live and work in a Mongolian-style yurt?

St. Lawrence University seeks snow lovers who place equal value on their experiences inside and outside the classroom. Its upstate New York location offers quick access to both pristine ski slopes and rugged hiking trails—and to the bright lights of Ottawa and Montreal. A flood of new facilities has helped to make the campus almost as breathtaking as the natural beauty that surrounds it. And intimate classes mean it's as easy to form friendships with faculty members as it is with fellow students.

Hiking trails, a river, and a golf course surround St. Lawrence's 94 buildings, which sit on a 1,000-acre tract; facilities are clustered, so even the most distant buildings are only 10 minutes from one another. Many buildings date from the late 19th century, and though their exteriors have been preserved, their interiors are fully modernized. The school has invested hundreds of millions of dollars to beautify and better its campus over the past two decades. The LEED Gold–certified Johnson Hall of Science supports the biology, chemistry, biochemistry, neuroscience, and psychology programs.

St. Lawrence offers a classical liberal arts education, placing a premium on small classes and team teaching. General education requirements include courses in the following areas: The Human Experience and the Natural World; Human Diversity: Culture and Communication; Quantitative/Logical Reasoning; Environmental Literacy; and Integrated Learning. Everyone participates in the two-semester First-Year Program (FYP), which emphasizes critical thinking, communication, and interdisciplinary content. "Students are separated into first-year 'colleges' for housing, and each college is enrolled together in a unique course," an economics major explains. There are 32 residential colleges, and FYP professors also serve as academic advisors. "This program creates an instant living and learning community the moment you step on campus, and students within FYPs become like family," says one student. Optional Sophomore Seminars involve intensive advising, teas and coffees with professors, and course-related field trips.

> "The classroom environment is always a place for open discussion where anyone can speak their mind."

Economics is the most popular major, followed by business in the liberal arts, psychology, and government. Programs in conservation biology, mathematics, statistics, and performance and communication arts are notable, and a minor in public health was recently introduced. Students in the signature environmental studies program are encouraged to pursue combined majors that integrate the study of environmental issues with substantial study in one of 10 other fields, such as geology, psychology, English, or sociology. Befitting St. Lawrence's location, Canadian studies is also a specialty. Courses demand that students pay attention and keep up with their work, but competition is hardly a concern. "The classroom environment is always a place for open discussion where anyone can speak their mind," says an English and global studies major. Since there are no teaching assistants, full professors teach even the introductory courses; 64 percent

Website: www.stlawu.edu
Location: Small Town
Private
Total Enrollment: 2,401
Undergraduates: 2,370
Male/Female: 44/56
SAT Ranges: ERW 590–680, M 580–675
ACT Ranges: 25–30
Financial Aid: 99%
Pell Grant: 23%
Expense: Pr $ $ $ $
Student Loans: 60%
Average Debt: $ $ $
Applicants: 5,866
Accepted: 48%
Enrolled: 25%
Grad in 6 Years: 85%
Returning Freshmen: 92%
Academics: ✍ ✍ ✍
Social: ☎ ☎ ☎
Q of L: ★ ★ ★
Admissions: (315) 229-5261
Email Address: admissions@stlawu.edu

Strong Programs:
Environmental Studies
Economics
Business in the Liberal Arts
Psychology
Government
Conservation Biology
Mathematics
Canadian Studies

of all classes have fewer than 20 students. "Teachers value the input of each student," says a junior.

In an effort "to make the world our classroom," St. Lawrence encourages students to spend time away from campus. Sixty-four percent do so, and while some participate in one of the school's 28 international programs, others choose the nearby Adirondack Semester at Saranac Lake, about an hour from campus. Under this program, offered each fall, a small group of students live and study in a yurt village in a park, where they learn wilderness survival skills and take courses on topics such as environmental philosophy and nature writing. Internships are popular too, with 70 percent of students taking part. The St. Lawrence University Fellows Program offers 25 to 30 students housing and $3,750 stipends for summer research.

Optional Sophomore Seminars involve intensive advising, teas and coffees with professors, and course-related field trips.

"Everyone at St. Lawrence smiles. This is easy, as everyone's so good-looking," quips a senior who was probably born in Lake Wobegon. Thirty-six percent of the students are New Yorkers, and 9 percent are international. Three percent are African American, 5 percent Hispanic, 1 percent Asian American, and 2 percent multiracial. Twenty-three percent of freshmen are Pell-eligible. "Politics can be important" on campus, says one student, "although peripherally for most students." The university awards merit scholarships averaging $18,900 to top students and also hands out 43 athletic scholarships for Division I men's and women's ice hockey.

Virtually all students live in the dorms, and seniors definitely have it best, with access to "spacious townhouses that sit along the golf course," says a sophomore. Everyone else makes do in the "adequate" residence halls, which have mostly double rooms featuring Wi-Fi access, cable TV, computer and study lounges, laundry rooms, and kitchens. The dining halls serve up themed dinners once a month, as well as ethnic foods, vegetarian options, and organic items. Twelve percent of the men and 16 percent of the women go Greek; fraternity and sorority members may live and eat in their chapter houses.

"There are always new things being added to the St. Lawrence student experience."

University-sponsored social activities include a campus pub, four different first-run movies each week, and the campus coffeehouse—a great place to hear a live band, acoustic guitarist, or comedian. Students 21 and over are permitted to drink on campus. One sophomore says, "There is a social drinking culture on campus, where students are not raging and binge drinking, but rather having a few beers and hanging out with friends."

The "charming" town of Canton is "a speck on the state map," says one student. "We do not live in a college town at all." Still, Canton does have everything from bagels to handmade jewelry to bars and restaurants, and Potsdam, 10 minutes away, offers more. But students say the most popular pastimes include skiing, hiking, rock climbing, and canoeing down the Grasse River (when it's not frozen over), as well as road trips to Ottawa and Montreal, where there's better shopping and dining, and the drinking age is lower too. "Being in the Adirondacks means you can escape to the mountains, or the river, when you need a break or want to hang out with your friends," says a freshman. Favorite annual traditions include Peak Weekend in the fall, when students, faculty, and staff summit all 46 of the Adirondack High Peaks, and Titus Weekend, when everyone heads to nearby Titus Mountain to celebrate the winter season with skiing, music, and other festivities.

During Titus Weekend, everyone heads to nearby Titus Mountain to celebrate the winter season with skiing, music, and other festivities.

In varsity sports, the Division I Skating Saints hockey teams are the top draw, especially when the opponent is archrival Clarkson. Solid Division III teams include men's lacrosse and squash, men's and women's cross-country and track and field, and co-ed riding. The school's fine athletic facilities include two field houses, one with more than a dozen courts, a pool, a three-story climbing wall, and a ropes course. The golf course doubles as a running route in warmer weather and a cross-country ski trail during the winter. Fifty-six percent of students participate in intra-mural and club sports; available sports range from club hockey to broomball, co-ed soccer, and an annual fall quadathlon.

St. Lawrence makes up for frigid winters with the warmth of a close-knit, caring community. As the frenzied pace of construction winds down and academic standards are ratcheted up, St. Lawrence is a school on the rise, especially for those wanting to get back to nature. "St. Lawrence is always looking for ways to improve," comments a junior. "From changing the meal plan to work better for students to creating Sophomore Seminar programs, there are always new things being added to the St. Lawrence student experience."

If You Apply To ›

St. Lawrence: Early decision I and II, regular decision. SATs or ACTs: optional. No Subject Tests. Accepts the Common Application.

Saint Louis University

221 North Grand Boulevard, St. Louis, MO 63103

SLU is a pleasant oasis in the bustle of midtown St. Louis, and both the campus and the surrounding neighborhood have been spiffed up in the last three decades. In addition to strengths in premed and entrepreneurship, SLU has an unusual specialty in aviation science. Competes with Loyola Chicago and Marquette for bragging rights among Midwestern Jesuit institutions.

Within sight of St. Louis's famed Gateway Arch, the historical gateway to the American West, sits Saint Louis University, the first university established west of the Mississippi River. The school's academic atmosphere is shaped by the tradition of its founders, the Society of Jesus (Jesuits); administrators ensure that each student receives personal care and attention and expect graduates to contribute to society and lead efforts for social change. In return, students find an atmosphere where their faith is encouraged. SLU offers students many nationally recognized programs, from health sciences to business and, of course, theology. "SLU is the type of university that prepares the whole person to go out into the world," says a freshman.

The SLU campus features pedestrian walkways, lush greenery, fountains, and sculptures, as well as the signature Saint Louis University arched gateways at all entrances. Cupples House, a beautiful old mansion in the middle of campus, houses 19th-century furniture and an art gallery—and is just

"This school sets high standards for its students."

a short walk from the modern Busch Student Center. The center is home to a bookstore, eateries, lounges, and conference facilities. Numerous campus renovations and additions have been undertaken in recent years, including two new residence halls, Spring Hall and Grand Hall.

In keeping with SLU's strong Jesuit commitment to education in the broadest sense, all undergrads must complete core curriculum requirements in philosophy and theology, cultural diversity, world history, fine arts, literature, science, social science, mathematics, languages, and foundations of discourse. First-year students participate in a common read, a Fall Welcome program before classes begin, and

Website: www.slu.edu
Location: City Outskirts
Private
Total Enrollment: 10,592
Undergraduates: 6,604
Male/Female: 40/60
SAT Ranges: ERW 590–690, M 580–700
ACT Ranges: 25–31
Financial Aid: 94%
Pell Grant: 18%
Expense: Pr $
Student Loans: 55%
Average Debt: $
Applicants: 13,431
Accepted: 64%
Enrolled: 19%
Grad in 6 Years: 77%
Returning Freshmen: 90%
Academics: ✍ ✍ ✍
Social: ☎ ☎
Q of L: ★ ★ ★

(continued)

Admissions: (314) 977-2500
Email Address: admission@
slu.edu

Strong Programs:
Nursing
Exercise Science
Psychology
Finance
Biology
Entrepreneurship
Theology
Flight Science

small-group University 101 classes. The most popular majors are nursing, exercise science, psychology, finance, and biology. Many students take advantage of premed advising, and five- and six-year direct entry programs allow students to earn advanced degrees in occupational therapy, athletic training, and physical therapy. Business and entrepreneurship majors benefit from the Chaifetz Center for Entrepreneurship, which offers innovation challenges, competitions, and networking events like Billicon Valley. Philosophy and theology are outstanding programs, and SLU attracts scholars from around the globe with one of the world's most complete microfilm collections of Vatican documents. Parks College of Engineering, Aviation, and Technology, America's first certified college of aviation, offers degree programs in aviation management and flight science and is a legacy of the days when St. Louis was an aviation hub. (Remember Charles Lindbergh's "Spirit of St. Louis"?) Engineering offerings are solid too.

The academic climate at SLU is competitive, and one student says, "This school sets high standards for its students, thereby creating opportunities for a good learning environment." Forty-three percent of classes have fewer than 20 students, but the quality of teaching varies greatly, students say. Thirty-one percent of SLU students study outside of the United States in more than 45 approved programs across the globe. In Madrid, Spain, SLU has one of the largest and most charming American campuses in Europe. The Micah Program is a living/learning program integrated around themes of peace, justice, and service—it takes its name from the biblical prophet Micah, who spoke out against social injustice in ancient Israel. The Manresa Program offers interdisciplinary and integrated study in the intellectual and social traditions of the Church from the New Testament period to the present.

Parks College of Engineering, Aviation, and Technology was America's first certified college of aviation.

SLU students tend to be "friendly and pretty laid-back," says a senior, but "most take school seriously." Many undergraduates come from private, religiously affiliated high schools; one-third are Roman Catholic. Forty-one percent hail from the Show-Me State, while 6 percent are international, coming from more than 50 countries. African Americans comprise 6 percent of the student body, Asian Americans 10 percent, Hispanics 6 percent, and multiracial students 3 percent. Consistent with SLU's Jesuit heritage, human rights and inclusion are prominent issues of debate. The school offers athletic scholarships in 18 sports, along with merit scholarships worth an average of $17,600.

Fifty-one percent of undergraduates live on campus, and about half of the freshmen take part in residential learning communities centered on a specific theme or interest. Upperclassmen can move into spacious courtyard-style apartments, but many opt for less expensive apartments off campus. "The dorms are sufficient," one student says. "They're nothing to brag about." The dining options are tasty, but students complain about the lack of healthy options. "The campus isn't really vegetarian/vegan friendly," laments one sophomore. Students say they feel safe on campus thanks to an active public safety department and the continuing improvement of surrounding neighborhoods.

The Micah Program is a living/learning program integrated around themes of peace, justice, and service.

"The social life is very active. Students know how to juggle personal with academic lives."

Social life at SLU includes campus events, such as movies in the Quad, dances, and Greek parties, and the plethora of restaurants and coffee shops in St. Louis, as well as movie theaters, museums, bars, sporting events, and nightlife. A student says, "The social life is very active. Students know how to juggle personal with academic lives." Greek life at SLU—unusual for a Jesuit institution—claims 4 percent of the men and 7 percent of the women. Students say most parties take place in off-campus apartments or at an off-campus fraternity house, and despite the rules limiting alcohol on campus, it's common in the apartments. The homecoming and Spring Fever annual events feature bands, club-sponsored booths, and vendors. Atlas

Week is a weeklong celebration of diversity that includes the Parade of Nations, cultural performances, speakers, and the Billiken World Festival. True to tradition, Sunday evening mass is usually packed with students of all beliefs, and more than 80 percent of students participate in community service and outreach projects. Road trips to Kansas City, Chicago, and schools like the University of Illinois and Indiana University are also popular.

SLU has no varsity football team, but other Billiken squads more than compensate for this deficit. (A billiken was a charm doll and a common good-luck charm in the early 1900s. A popular sportswriter of the time said the charm resembled the then-football coach, and the name stuck.) Teams compete in the Division I Atlantic 10 Conference, and the Billiken's men's soccer and baseball teams and women's basketball, volleyball, and tennis teams are the most competitive. For weekend warriors, the Simon Recreation Center boasts a 40-meter pool, six racquetball courts, and loads of equipment. Sand volleyball and flag football are popular intramural sports.

Saint Louis University is winning students' devotion and increasing its national visibility by offering a slew of strong programs. The Jesuit education prepares students to work for a more just and humane world. "SLU is a good choice for its relatively moderate-sized classrooms, its dedication toward a Jesuit mission, and its enjoyable learning environment," says a senior. "I am very happy that I chose SLU."

If You Apply To ›

SLU: Rolling admissions. SATs or ACTs: required. No Subject Tests. Accepts the Common Application with supplement. Apply to particular programs.

St. Mary's College of Maryland

St. Mary's City, MD 20686

A public liberal arts institution of the same breed as Mary Washington, UNC Asheville, and much larger William and Mary. St. Mary's historic but sleepy environs are 90 minutes from D.C. and Baltimore on Maryland's western shore. With the Chesapeake Bay close at hand, St. Mary's is a haven for sailors and nature enthusiasts. Maryland's public "honors college" is a well-kept secret beyond the state's borders.

Twenty-five years ago, St. Mary's College of Maryland was just another public college, albeit one with a gorgeous waterfront campus in the oldest continuously inhabited English settlement in the New World. In 1992, the state of Maryland decided to make St. Mary's its public "honors college"—and the rest, as they say around here, is history. Students can easily design their own majors, undertake independent research projects, or work closely with professors to investigate whatever interests them. A biology major says, "This place will allow you to try new things, understand yourself better, and open your eyes to the world."

St. Mary's has never been connected with any religious denomination and takes its name from its founding in 1840 in St. Mary's City, the original capital of Maryland. The campus sits on a peninsula in southern Maryland where the Potomac River meets the Chesapeake Bay. Not surprisingly, it has an excellent center for estuary research, as well as a strong working relationship with the Chesapeake Biological Laboratory; the school even has its own marina right on the St. Mary's

Website: www.smcm.edu
Location: Rural
Public
Total Enrollment: 1,536
Undergraduates: 1,508
Male/Female: 42/58
SAT Ranges: ERW 540–650, M 530–630
ACT Ranges: 22–28
Financial Aid: 84%
Pell Grant: 19%
Expense: Pub $ $ $
Student Loans: 53%

(continued)

Average Debt: $

Applicants: 1,655

Accepted: 82%

Enrolled: 25%

Grad in 6 Years: 78%

Returning Freshmen: 87%

Academics: ✍ ✍ ✍ ✍

Social: ☎ ☎ ☎

Q of L: ★ ★ ★ ★

Admissions: (240) 895-5000

Email Address: admissions@
smcm.edu

Strong Programs:
Biology
Psychology
Economics
English
Anthropology
Chemistry
Biochemistry
Music

The land on which the campus is built belongs to a 1,100-acre national historic landmark, commemorating Maryland's first colonial settlement.

River, with a shoreline that gets beautiful sunset views. Architectural styles range from colonial to modern buildings, though the land on which the campus is built belongs to a 1,100-acre national historic landmark, commemorating Maryland's first colonial settlement. For that reason, students may step over archaeological digs as they stroll to class. Anne Arundel Hall is the latest addition to campus, housing classrooms, labs, and research spaces for anthropology, archaeology, and international languages and cultures.

The cornerstone of a St. Mary's education is the small, discussion-focused First Year Seminar, in which students cultivate an area of particular interest while building critical-thinking, researching, writing, and speaking skills. Students may choose from dozens of topics—ranging from The Many Lives of Abraham Lincoln to Ethical Dilemmas of Biotechnology—taught by professors from every discipline at the college. St. Mary's core curriculum also mandates that students complete coursework in arts, cultural perspectives, humanistic foundations, mathematics, natural sciences, and social sciences, as well as demonstrate foreign language proficiency. The Experiencing the Liberal Arts in the World requirement may involve an internship, community service, study abroad, or off-campus research. All seniors complete a capstone requirement, usually in the form of a yearlong research project known as the St. Mary's Project.

> **"Because of the nature of an honors college, all students who attend St. Mary's are academically focused."**

Biology is among the most popular majors, and also one of the more difficult programs; students can spend time on the college's research boat when they tire of the lab. Students also sign up in droves for psychology, economics, and English. Anthropology, chemistry, and biochemistry are traditional strengths, and the standout music department includes prize-winning pianist Brian Ganz. Environmental studies is the school's fastest-growing major, and minors have been added in business and astrophysics. Aside from the 23 established majors and eight cross-disciplinary study areas, more freethinking types may design their own majors.

"Because of the nature of an honors college, all students who attend St. Mary's are academically focused, and there is a common goal to succeed," explains a senior. Seventy-four percent of classes have fewer than 20 students, and graduate students are available for extra assistance but do not teach courses. Professors are said to be accessible and well respected. "Professors at St. Mary's are always engaged in research and like to involve students in the process," says a psychology major.

St. Mary's offers study abroad semesters at Fudan University in China, James Cook University in Australia, Sciences Po in France, and Stellenbosch University in South Africa, among others, as well as short-term study tours in several other countries. Thirty-seven percent of students study internationally. The Washington Program places students in top summer internships with the government, nonprofits, and think tanks in Washington, D.C., and also offers mentoring from alumni.

On this tight-knit campus, says a freshman, "There is never a day where I don't see someone smile and wave at me." Ninety-three percent of St. Mary's students come from Maryland, which gives the campus a homegrown feel; just 1 percent come from foreign countries. Students acknowledge that campus diversity, while growing, is still an area for improvement. African Americans account for 9 percent of the student body, Hispanics 8 percent, Asian Americans 4 percent, and multiracial students 5 percent. A senior points out that the school is located "in a very red county that considers itself the South," but students are said to be left-leaning. St. Mary's is more

> **"There is never a day where I don't see someone smile and wave at me."**

expensive than other publics in Maryland but much less expensive than the private liberal arts colleges with which it also competes. Qualified students receive merit scholarships worth an average of $4,100. There are no athletic awards.

Campus housing is "comfortable and popular among students," and it's also guaranteed for all four years. Eighty-two percent of full-time students live on campus, and most residence halls are co-ed. Attractive apartments and town-houses are reserved for upperclassmen, and students select rooms based on the number of credits they have. Open (gender-neutral) housing is available, as are living/learning centers for women in science, African and African diaspora studies, environmental sustainability, and substance-free living. There are some choices off campus too, including old farmhouses and riverside cottages for rent. Meals served in the main dining hall are "usually decent, with some days being better than others," says a sophomore. Those who tire of the food line may join the veg-etarian co-op.

Biology students can spend time on the college's research boat when they tire of the lab.

St. Mary's doesn't have fraternities or sororities, and its secluded peninsular location means there's little nightlife off campus, but one senior confirms, "The fun that happens on campus is more than enough to make up for that!" The student-run Programs Board organizes events like concerts, comedians, and costume parties, and for the culture-hungry, there are also theaters, an art gallery, lectures, and films on campus. The St. Mary's River offers a wealth of outdoor activities. "Most days if we aren't in class, you'll find us paddleboarding, sailing, kayaking, swimming, or just studying on the docks. On nice days, there's a summer-camp atmosphere to it all," says one stu-dent. Another adds, "It's virtually impossible to graduate without knowing how to sail." The waterfront also becomes the focus of campuswide activities, including the bamboo boat race held each fall, Bay-to-Bay Service Day in April, and the end-of-year One St. Mary's Carnival.

"It's virtually impossible to graduate without knowing how to sail."

St. Mary's fields 19 Division III varsity Seahawks teams; men's and women's soccer, women's lacrosse, and the nationally ranked sailing program are among the most successful. About half of the students at St. Mary's take part in recre-ational sports; floor hockey, dodgeball, and soccer are favorite intramurals, while rugby, ultimate Frisbee, and equestrian are the most popular club sports.

St. Mary's has worked hard to establish itself as one of the nation's premier public liberal arts colleges. Though its small size and remote location can feel confining to some, students leave with a solid grounding in the liberal arts—and the close bonds that they forge with friends during peaceful days on the St. Mary's River. For those looking to be part of an intellectual community in a small-town setting, St. Mary's just might be a place to set sail.

Overlaps

Beloit, Dickinson, Guilford, University of Mary Washington, UNC Asheville, University of Maryland, UMBC, Salisbury

If You Apply To ›

St. Mary's: Early decision, early action, regular decision. SATs or ACTs: required. Subject Tests: optional. Accepts the Common Application with supplement.

Saint Michael's College

One Winooski Park, Colchester, VT 05439

Catholic Edmundite liberal arts college located near a top college town with breathtaking views of the Adirondack and Green mountains. Cheerful academic community with most students being New Englanders. Proximity to Burlington helps make for vibrant social scene. Easy access to Montreal and to some of the best skiing and snowboarding in the East.

Saint Michael's College carries the distinction of being the only Edmundite institution of higher learning in the world. The college was established by the Society of Saint Edmund, a group of Roman Catholic country priests who took Saint Edmund, Archbishop of Canterbury, as their patron and spiritual inspiration. The Society maintains an on-campus presence to this day, and the influence of the patron saint can be found in the college's dedication to meaningful residential experiences, comprehensive liberal arts, and social justice. A junior says, "Saint Michael's teaches students to go out into the world and work to make it a better place."

Founded in 1904, Saint Michael's sits on 440 acres overlooking Vermont's Green Mountains and the Winooski River. Just five minutes from Burlington, the campus features redbrick architecture, themed gardens, and a central quad. To the east, Mount Mansfield—Vermont's tallest peak—provides a spectacular backdrop. The Dion Family Student Center and Quad Commons residence hall overlook the mountains and use geothermal heating and cooling, among other green technologies.

Under the core curriculum, all students take four courses: First-Year Seminar, Fundamental Philosophical Questions, Study of Christian Traditions and Thought, and Junior Seminar. Students also meet requirements in the areas of Intellectual Exploration (liberal arts and sciences), Edmundite Tradition, and Professional Competencies, which encourages experiential learning.

Saint Michael's offers a plethora of solid programs, including business; psychology; biology; media studies, journalism, and digital arts; environmental science; and religious studies. Neuroscience is a top draw too, and new majors in data science and education studies have been added. A 3–2 engineering program with nearby University of Vermont and a prepharmacy program are popular, and there are hybrid summer courses, including an art history course based partly at the Metropolitan Museum in New York City. Students may also take advantage of cross-registration options with Champlain College.

> **"My classroom experiences have ranged from OK to legitimately transformative."**

"My classroom experiences have ranged from OK to legitimately transformative," says an English major. "Most of the time, it just feels like I'm getting a good education." Sixty-one percent of classes have fewer than 20 students, and many are taught in a discussion-based format. Students praise professors for their knowledge and willingness to make themselves available. "Professors build individual relationships with students," says a political science major. "It is quite hard to fail here because there is so much support all over campus."

The Honors Program inducts 14 percent of undergraduates, who take specialized core courses and a colloquium, live in honors housing, and complete a senior honors project. Thirty-one percent of Saint Michael's students take part in undergraduate research, and many receive stipends for full-time work as research partners with faculty during the summer. More than 100 study abroad options include such far-flung locales as Argentina, Ghana, India, Tanzania, and Costa Rica; 43 percent of undergraduates participate.

On campus, says a senior, "I always see people smiling and being generous and helpful to others." Just under half of the student body is Catholic. African Americans account for only 2 percent of the student body, Hispanics 5 percent, Asian Americans 1 percent, and multiracial students 2 percent. Fourteen percent come from Vermont and 4 percent from foreign countries. Student organizations like the Diversity Coalition and Martin Luther King Jr. Society put on events throughout the year to support inclusion on campus. The political atmosphere is heavily liberal, and a senior identifies "white privilege, white supremacy, and gun control" as hot-button issues. Twenty-one percent of freshmen receive Pell Grants. The college offers merit awards averaging $17,700 to qualified students, and a limited number of athletic scholarships are available for basketball players.

Students are required to spend all four years on campus in the residence halls, which a sophomore says "creates a sense of community among the different classes." All first-year students are housed in living/learning communities organized around four main themes: leadership, service, wellness, and approaches to transition. Residence halls include traditional dorms with double and single rooms, suites with shared

Saint Michael's carries the distinction of being the only Edmundite institution of higher learning in the world.

"St. Mike's is a weird mash-up of progressive, traditional, humble, compassionate people."

living spaces, townhouses, and apartment-style accommodations. Campus dining options include an unlimited meal plan at the Green Mountain Dining Room; meals are said to be "decently good" but repetitive. Students report feeling safe on campus, and while there have been instances of sexual assault, says one student, the school "always informs us of what steps they are taking to protect the community and hold those who were responsible accountable."

Socially, says a sophomore, "There's a good mix of hanging out on campus, going downtown, and going skiing or hiking with friends." Despite the lack of Greek life, there is a reliably lively party scene. Apart from senior housing, the campus is dry, and students describe a no-pressure, safety-oriented attitude toward drinking. The Residential Initiative Program delivers a slew of alternative weekend options. Campuswide activities include comedians, coffeehouse music and poetry performances, and talent shows. Every Friday and Saturday night, the college hosts the Weekend Grilling Program, which provides free food between 11 p.m. and 1 a.m. Fall and spring concerts are popular campus events, and students relish the annual P-Day (Preparation Day) tradition, which is "a time for students to relax before finals" with free food, bouncy houses, tricycle races, a movie screening, and other activities, according to an English major. Popular excursions "are to downtown Burlington or to the mountains and great outdoors like Mount Mansfield or Camel's Hump," says one student. Montreal is a popular weekend trip.

The Adventure Sports Center organizes about 75 outdoor outings per semester.

Burlington (population 42,000) is "a great college town, as it contains two other colleges: UVM and Champlain," a sophomore says. "The area consists of young people and entrepreneurs, offering a fun atmosphere to eat, shop, and go out in." Saint Michael's students receive a free bus pass that will take them downtown, and the Saint Michael's Cultural Pass gives students unlimited access to performances at Burlington's Flynn Theater for little or no cost. An unrestricted (and deeply discounted) season pass to Sugarbush Ski Resort is available as well. Seventy percent of students get involved in at least one service program over the course of their college careers; "Volunteering is a huge aspect of life at Saint Michael's," confirms one student.

Saint Michael's fields 21 Division II sports, the majority of which compete in the Northeast-10 Conference. Competitive Purple Knights teams include alpine skiing, men's and women's lacrosse, men's ice hockey, and men's basketball. Recreational

Overlaps

Saint Anselm, Stonehill, Providence, Fairfield, St. Lawrence, University of Vermont, University of New Hampshire, UMass Amherst

and intramural programs are popular too and include the Adventure Sports Center, which organizes about 75 outings per semester, including sea kayaking, rock and ice climbing, white-water rafting, and other outdoor pursuits.

Saint Michael's College attracts students who appreciate the unique vision inspired by Saint Edmund so many years ago—not to mention the beautiful Vermont setting—and who want to use their education for the betterment of the world. An English major reflects, "St. Mike's is a weird mash-up of progressive, traditional, humble, compassionate people who just want to be good for the world and do the right thing."

If You Apply To ›

St. Michael's: Early action I and II, regular decision. SATs or ACTs: optional. Subject Tests: optional. Accepts the Common Application with supplement.

St. Olaf College

1520 St. Olaf Avenue, Northfield, MN 55057

Notable for its deep Lutheran roots and strong international orientation, St. Olaf has more of a Midwestern feel than crosstown rival Carleton. The music program—especially its choir—is world famous, and 73 percent of students study abroad. Daily chapel is not mandatory, but many students go. With about 3,000 students, St. Olaf is on the big side of small.

Website: wp.stolaf.edu
Location: Small City
Private
Total Enrollment: 2,994
Undergraduates: 2,994
Male/Female: 42/58
SAT Ranges: ERW 580–690, M 570–710
ACT Ranges: 25–31
Financial Aid: 96%
Pell Grant: 19%
Expense: Pr $ $
Student Loans: 57%
Average Debt: $ $
Applicants: 5,949
Accepted: 43%
Enrolled: 31%
Grad in 6 Years: 88%
Returning Freshmen: 92%
Academics: ✑ ✑ ✑ ✑
Social: ☎ ☎ ☎
Q of L: ★ ★ ★ ★
Admissions: (800) 800-3025
Email Address: admissions@stolaf.edu

St. Olaf College's home is Northfield, Minnesota, which bills itself as the city of "Cows, Colleges, and Contentment." Founded by Norwegian Lutheran immigrants and affiliated with the Evangelical Lutheran Church in America, St. Olaf provides a solid liberal arts education and plenty of opportunities to study abroad. One Ole describes her peers at St. Olaf as "Minnesota nice." Students differ sharply in this respect from the school's namesake, St. Olaf, a not-so-nice 11th-century Norwegian king prone to violence and brutality. The student also adds, "I feel personally valued and supported by the faculty and administrators. I felt at home here from day one."

St. Olaf's meticulously landscaped 350-acre campus, featured in several architectural journals, is located on Manitou Heights, overlooking the Cannon River valley and Northfield. More than 10,000 trees, native prairie, and a wetlands wildlife area surround the 34 native limestone buildings that form the campus. Regents Hall of Natural and Mathematical Sciences, a 200,000-square-foot science center, is one of the largest and most complex academic facilities in the nation to earn the prestigious LEED Platinum rating. The college recently completed a $13 million renovation of the castle-like Holland Hall, modernizing it with high-tech learning spaces.

> **"I feel personally valued and supported by the faculty and administrators."**

All students at St. Olaf complete a general education program that covers three areas: foundation studies, core studies, and integrative study. Typically, 14 to 16 courses satisfy the general education requirements; some classes may fulfill requirements in more than one area. All first-year students complete a writing seminar and an introductory course in Biblical and Theological Studies.

Biology, mathematics, economics, psychology, and chemistry are the most popular majors and some of the school's best. The music department draws high praise;

it offers many performance opportunities with eight school choirs and seven instrumental ensembles. The choirs perform in major venues around the nation and can be heard singing with the Minnesota Orchestra. The Center for Integrative Studies allows students to form their own majors. The signature Conversation Programs are interdisciplinary, team-taught programs that bring together students and faculty for a critical exploration of specific topics within their historical, cultural, and social contexts. Programs include the Great Conversation, American Conversations, Asian Conversations, Environmental Conversations, the Science Conversation, and the Public Affairs Conversation. These one- to two-year programs, to which students must apply, "take care of a ton of general requirements, but they are extremely rigorous," warns one freshman.

(continued)

Strong Programs:
Biology
Mathematics
Economics
Psychology
Chemistry
Music
Religion

Students hold St. Olaf's faculty members in high regard for their expertise and engaging approaches to teaching. Fifty-four percent of classes have fewer than 20 students, and instructors reportedly have as many as 10 hours of open-office time a week. Academically, Oles have their work cut out for them, but a chemistry and biology double major says, "With every challenge, there are people willing to lend a hand to make sure you succeed." The Piper Center for Vocation and Career receives high ratings, especially for its Connections Program trips, which take students to major cities nationwide to network with alumni. "I had the chance to go on the San Francisco trip and we visited alums at Google, Apple, Cisco, and several start-ups," says a junior.

In the last quarter-century, St. Olaf has cultivated an international agenda for its students and faculty, and it now awards more academic credit for study abroad than any other baccalaureate liberal arts college in the country. Seventy-three percent of students participate. More than 120 programs are available in 50 countries, including St. Olaf's faculty-led Global Semester and Environmental Science

"Conversation Programs take care of a ton of general requirements, but they are extremely rigorous."

in Australia and New Zealand programs. Research opportunities are available in all disciplines, and are especially robust in the sciences; about half of the students take advantage of them.

"The typical St. Olaf student is fairly outgoing, extremely involved, and interested in trying new things," says a freshman. Forty-seven percent of students hail from Minnesota, and 11 percent come from overseas. Asian Americans make up 7 percent, Hispanics 6 percent, African Americans 3 percent, and multiracial students 3 percent, and the college is actively recruiting more students from diverse backgrounds. About a quarter of students are Lutheran; daily chapel services, though not mandatory, are well attended. Most students are high achievers from Midwestern public schools, drawn in part by hundreds of merit scholarships, which average $16,200 each year. St. Olaf has a tradition of meeting the full demonstrated need of all admitted students.

Ninety-four percent of undergrads live in on-campus housing or in college-owned houses available off campus. "Accommodations are very functional and improve each year," says an econ major. All first-years live together in four dedicated dorms, where Junior Counselors on each floor plan fun community activities; upperclassmen enjoy suite-style layouts. Students eat in one large, modern dining hall and rave about the "amazing" meals. They can also use their meal plans at neighboring Carleton's two dining halls (and vice versa). The administration recently expanded its Title IX resources, which a sophomore says "has fostered a more proactive and safe environment on campus."

St. Olaf's social life takes place mostly on campus, and weekend spots include a nightclub called the Pause (beloved for its pizza) and a coffeehouse, the Cage. "The Pause, an entirely student-run organization complete with TVs, hangout areas, food,

St. Olaf awards more academic credit for study abroad than any other baccalaureate liberal arts college in the country.

and a main stage, is the place to go for entertainment," says a junior. The fine arts department provides many music, theater, and dance performances. "Most social life is defined by small dorm parties," adds a sophomore. The campus is officially dry, and there are no fraternities or sororities at St. Olaf, but alcohol can be found by those determined enough to seek it out, students say. The Student Activities Committee sponsors frequent dances, speakers, and cultural events, covered by student fees and at-the-door ticket sales. The most talked-about annual event, which has been running for more than 100 years, is the four-day Christmas Festival, during which five choirs and the St. Olaf Orchestra combine in televised concerts celebrating Christmas.

Northfield is "friendly and intimate" but doesn't offer much of a social scene, although students note that Froggy's and the Contented Cow are decent bars for those of age, and two breweries have recently opened. Each September, the locals

> **"Most social life is defined by small dorm parties."**

reenact the failed 1876 attempt by Jesse James to rob the town bank. Students report a friendly rapport with the community. "Students are actively involved in community mentor, volunteer, and outreach programs," one student says. For those with wanderlust, buses leave regularly for the twin cities of Minneapolis and St. Paul, less than an hour's drive, where one can experience a shopper's paradise at the huge Mall of America.

St. Olaf has outstanding Division III athletic programs. The Oles men's cross-country and soccer teams are recent Minnesota Intercollegiate Athletics Conference champions, and women's cross-country and skiing are also highly competitive. The St. Olaf football team battles rival Carleton for the honor of having the statue in the town's square face the winning campus. The chorus of St. Olaf's fight song is "Um! Yah! Yah!" which has become a popular chant on campus. There is also an extensive intramural program, in which 65 percent of students compete, and broomball—ice hockey played with brooms instead of sticks and shoes rather than skates—is the sport of choice in the winter. The St. Olaf Vortex women's ultimate Frisbee team took home a national title in 2018.

For those yearning for a school where spirituality and scholarship exist on the same exalted plane, St. Olaf could be the right place to spend four years. It's a school where students work hard, are encouraged by good teachers, toughened by Minnesota winters, and nourished by strong moral values—in addition to hearty Scandinavian food.

Overlaps

Macalester, Carleton, Luther, Gustavus Adolphus, Grinnell, Lawrence, University of Minnesota, University of St. Thomas

If You Apply To ›

St. Olaf: Early decision I and II, regular decision. SATs or ACTs: required. Subject Tests: optional. Accepts the Common Application with supplement. Music applicants must submit additional application.

University of San Diego

5998 Alcala Park, San Diego, CA 92110

With a panoramic view of the Pacific Ocean, USD is riding a wave of popularity enhanced by its sun-drenched location. Not to be confused with its UC counterpart across town, USD is now often preferred to Roman Catholic peers the University of San Francisco and Santa Clara. Strong in business, engineering, and study abroad.

Students at the University of San Diego have many reasons to cheer: a beatific oceanside campus, a rich Roman Catholic heritage centered around ethical conduct and compassionate service, and an array of superb academics. "USD is becoming more and more competitive, and the academic programs continue to get better," says one freshman. "There has never been a better time to come to USD than right now."

Founded in 1949, the USD campus occupies 180 acres on a mesa overlooking San Diego's Mission Bay and is only two miles north of downtown San Diego. The buildings are designed in 16th-century Spanish Renaissance architectural style in a nod to San Diego's Catholic heritage and the Universidad de Alcalá in Spain. In a fitting architectural juxtaposition, at one end of campus is the Joan B. Kroc (of McDonald's fame) Center for Peace and Justice; at the other end is the Jenny Craig Athletic Center, where you can work off your Big Macs. The university recently opened the Architecture Pavilion, featuring seminar, lecture, and exhibition areas as well as space for student studios.

USD revised its core curriculum in 2017 to focus more on integrating knowledge and experiences from different disciplines. The core encompasses Competencies, such as writing and critical thinking; Foundations courses in theology, philosophy, ethics, and diversity and inclusion; and Explorations courses in five general liberal arts areas. A fourth component, Integrative Learning, is the focus of the first year, when new students join one of five living/

> **"There has never been a better time to come to USD than right now."**

learning communities (LLCs): Cultivator, Collaborator, Advocate, Illuminator, and Innovator. In addition to taking a fall-semester course related to the theme of their LLC and living together with their classmates in the residence halls, first-years also have access to a "scholastic assistant," an older student who serves as a mentor and organizes out-of-class activities. Students describe the LLCs as integral to their transition to college life. "Being a part of programs such as these really enabled me to find out more about myself and what I am passionate about," says a communication studies major.

USD offers more than 60 degree programs—an impressive number given its relatively small student body—across seven schools: business, leadership and education sciences, law, nursing and health science, arts and sciences, engineering, and peace studies. The most popular undergraduate majors include finance, business administration, communication studies, accountancy, and psychology. Engineering is a traditional strength. Thirty-eight percent of classes have fewer than 20 students, but none exceed 50, which allows for classroom discussions and collaborative projects. "The workload is substantial, but it is also feasible," says a political science major. Professors are said to be knowledgeable and accessible. When it comes to finding employment, one senior comments, "Career services is good, but better for people looking for internships versus actual jobs right out of school."

The Honors Program offers small classes and a core curriculum of innovative courses to qualified students. Those who overdose on Southern California's ubiquitous blue skies and sunshine may take part in USD's robust study abroad program, which sends students to live and study in more than 30 countries and more than 80 programs, including a recently established permanent program at the University of San Diego Madrid Center in Spain. Seventy-seven percent of undergrads participate in yearlong, semester, summer, or intersession programs.

A junior says that USD students are "driven and strive to be successful in all aspects of life, but at the end of the day they know how to enjoy themselves." Fifty-three percent hail from the Golden State, 9 percent are international, and many come from affluent backgrounds. "Low-income students would have a hard time

Website: www.sandiego.edu
Location: City Center
Private
Total Enrollment: 7,238
Undergraduates: 5,539
Male/Female: 46/54
SAT Ranges: ERW 590–670, M 590–680
ACT Ranges: 26–30
Financial Aid: 72%
Pell Grant: 14%
Expense: Pr $ $
Student Loans: 49%
Average Debt: $ $ $
Applicants: 14,739
Accepted: 50%
Enrolled: 16%
Grad in 6 Years: 82%
Returning Freshmen: 90%
Academics: ✍ ✍ ✍
Social: ☎ ☎ ☎ ☎
Q of L: ★ ★ ★ ★
Admissions: (800) 248-4873
Email Address: admissions@sandiego.edu

Strong Programs:
Finance
Business Administration
Communication Studies
Accountancy
Psychology
Engineering

First-years have access to a "scholastic assistant," an older student who serves as a mentor and organizes out-of-class activities.

here because students engage in expensive activities outside of class," remarks a senior. African Americans account for 4 percent of the student body, Hispanics 20 percent, Asian Americans 7 percent, and multiracial students 6 percent. Forty-one percent of students are Catholic, so there is a healthy conservative presence on campus, but one freshman notes, "The university is making a big push toward acceptance and understanding of all people and beliefs." The school offers merit awards averaging $15,400 to qualified students, and there are 195 athletic awards.

Seventy-seven percent of undergrads study abroad in more than 30 countries.

Forty-six percent of undergraduates live on campus, and all but commuters are required to do so for both their first and second year. Residence halls are a mix of singles, doubles, triples, and limited quads, with singles and doubles representing the majority of the units. Apartments range from one room to four bedrooms. When the dinner bell rings, students have plenty to cheer about. "Meals are delicious," says one junior. "Dining facilities are nice, clean, and a hot place to be at all hours of the day." Campus security is excellent, students say, with officers on duty around the clock. "A huge sexual assault awareness task force has done a lot of good things after a few accusations in the past few years," according to a senior.

And how about the campus social scene? "Mission Beach, where most upperclassmen live, has a vibrant social scene. Many USD students congregate in the area on weekends," a finance major explains. For those who choose to eschew the sand and waves, USD offers a slate of on-campus activities, including movies, concerts, and mass (lest you forget, USD is a Catholic university). The Greek scene attracts 23 percent of the men and 31 percent of the women. Alcohol is allowed only in designated areas for those students of legal age, and "this policy is heavily enforced by the RAs," says a marketing major. Downtown San Diego has plenty to offer, including a bevy of bars, eateries, and shopping centers. The USD community is big on giving back too, via more than 300,000 hours of service each year. Popular road trips include Las Vegas and Big Bear. Back on campus, students enjoy annual festivals such as International Week and Greek Week, the Alcalá Bazaar, and the Olé Music Fest.

> **"Mission Beach, where most upperclassmen live, has a vibrant social scene."**

USD sponsors 17 Division I intercollegiate teams and is a member of the West Coast Conference for all sports except football, which competes in the Pioneer League. Students are especially rowdy when the Torero basketball team takes on rival Gonzaga. Football, men's and women's soccer, men's golf and tennis, and women's volleyball and basketball have been competitive in recent years. One-quarter of students participate in intramural and club sports; among the most popular are ultimate Frisbee, climbing, soccer, and lacrosse.

Don't underestimate USD—this small, first-year friendly institution offers a rich variety of academic programs, and its students seem to understand that they are living out their college careers in one of the most beautiful spots in the country. As a sophomore reflects, "The great thing about USD is you can get a great education in a challenging academic environment and in one of the most beautiful cities in the nation."

Overlaps

Loyola Marymount, Pepperdine, Santa Clara, University of San Francisco, Seattle University, UC San Diego, UC Santa Barbara, UCLA

If You Apply To ›

USD: Regular decision. SATs or ACTs: required. Subject Tests: optional. Accepts the Common Application.

2130 Fulton Street, San Francisco, CA 94117

Talk about prime real estate: USF is next door to the legendary Haight–Ashbury district, down the street from Golden Gate Park, and within five miles of the Pacific Ocean. Though USF is a Jesuit institution, less than a third of its students are Roman Catholic. Asia Pacific studies is a standout, along with preprofessional offerings. About a third of the students are from outside California.

In the heart of one of the nation's most liberal cities is a thriving university founded by the Society of Jesus (Jesuits) that has become an integral part of its community. Instead of shunning the city's reputation, the University of San Francisco embraces it with a strong social conscience. With an incredibly diverse student body and an emphasis on programs such as nursing and business, students encounter a broad set of cultures, academic challenges in a liberal arts setting, and the chance to put all that experience to good use.

USF's 55 well-kept acres, spotted with beautiful basilica-type buildings and modern facilities, are, as one student puts it, "wedged into the heart of San Francisco." The campus stands atop one of San Francisco's seven hills, adjacent to Golden Gate Park, overlooking San Francisco Bay and the city skyline. The university recently opened the LoSchiavo Center for Science and Innovation, which features cutting-edge classrooms, laboratories, and community gathering places.

The 44-unit core curriculum requires students to take courses in six major categories: foundation of communication; math and sciences; humanities; philosophy, theology, and ethics; social sciences; and visual and performing arts. A three-part series of success courses emphasizes study skills, critical thinking, and career and major exploration. Optional first-year seminars give students insights into unique topics and a taste of the city through excursions and other enrichment activities; recent topics include Speaking of Bicycles and The Right to the City: Community Movements in San Francisco.

> "Internships and service learning are definitely big parts of the education here at USF."

USF places a strong emphasis on its preprofessional programs, especially nursing, health studies, communications, and business, and these tend to draw the most students. By enrollment, business administration, nursing, psychology, and finance are the most popular majors. Biology, data science, and hospitality management are also strengths. In the School of Nursing's Simulation Lab, nursing students interact with state-of-the-art mannequins, including adult, pediatrics, and obstetrics, that simulate symptoms and conditions specific to real-life patients and scenarios. The Center for Asia Pacific Studies enhances interdisciplinary majors with an Asian focus, as does the Asian studies program. The visual arts program provides courses in art education, graphic and fine art, drawing, painting, art history, and museum studies. Accelerated, three-year bachelor's degree options are available in 21 majors, and there's also a joint B.A./B.S.-J.D. program.

Some of the preprofessional majors are demanding, and "competition for internships and leadership opportunities can get intense," says an advertising major. But students agree that the climate in the classroom is generally more relaxed. Extensive and mandatory academic advising ensures that students' courseloads are manageable. Nearly half of undergraduate classes have fewer than 20 students, and according to a junior, "All USF professors are active in their field" and able to bring real-world experience into the classroom.

Website: www.usfca.edu
Location: City Center
Private
Total Enrollment: 10,026
Undergraduates: 6,567
Male/Female: 37/63
SAT Ranges: ERW 560–640, M 540–650
ACT Ranges: 22–28
Financial Aid: 57%
Pell Grant: 34%
Expense: Pr $ $
Student Loans: 50%
Average Debt: $ $ $ $
Applicants: 16,313
Accepted: 66%
Enrolled: 14%
Grad in 6 Years: 77%
Returning Freshmen: 85%
Academics: ✎ ✎ ✎
Social: 🍷 🍷 🍷
Q of L: ★ ★ ★ ★
Admissions: (415) 422-6563
Email Address: admission@usfca.edu

Strong Programs:
Business Administration
Nursing
Psychology
Finance
Biology
Data Science
Hospitality Management
Asian Studies

"Internships and service learning are definitely big parts of the education here at USF," says one senior. Community-minded students take advantage of volunteer programs, often through University Ministries, and the student body as a whole contributes more than 275,000 hours of community service each year. USF is also the official host of the Human Rights Watch Festival, which is integrated into the curriculum. The St. Ignatius Institute offers an integrated four-year, honors-based curriculum centered on the great books of Western civilization presented in an unusual seminar/lecture combination. The program is not restricted to top students, and participants can spend their junior year studying in Oxford, Rome, or Budapest. Overall, the university offers more than 100 study abroad programs in 45 countries. "USF also has a partnership with UC San Francisco, so a lot of people are able to do research at the various UCSF campuses," notes a junior.

"USF is like a mini San Francisco, with kooky and business-minded students," comments an education and English major. Sixty-five percent of undergraduates are

> **"USF is like a mini San Francisco, with kooky and business-minded students."**

from California, and 17 percent hail from abroad. Asian Americans account for 22 percent of the population, African Americans 4 percent, Hispanics 22 percent, and multiracial students 7 percent. Student groups advocating for LGBTQ rights and racial justice are said to be particularly active on campus. Thirty-four percent of freshmen qualify for Pell Grants. Admission is need-blind, and USF offers merit scholarships averaging $13,800, as well as 137 athletic scholarships.

Just 21 percent of undergrads live in on-campus housing, which is guaranteed for the first year. After that, most students brave San Francisco's budget-busting rental market, which "can be a struggle," says a senior, especially if you don't have a parent or guardian who can cosign a lease. On-campus students say the dining facilities offer a range of vegan, vegetarian, and other choices. "Campus safety officers are constantly roaming the campus making sure that the students are safe," reports a student. And while students say sexual assault has not been a big problem on campus, "USF encourages a lot of dialogue" on the issue.

Notable campus activities include the Hawaiian Club's annual luau, the Barrio Festival held by the Filipino American Club, and the springtime Donaroo music festival. The College Players is the oldest continuously performing college theater group in the West. Fraternities attract 3 percent of the men and sororities draw 11 percent of the women, although they don't have houses. The school's zero-tolerance policy on underage drinking is strictly enforced. USF's greatest social asset is undoubtedly its location, and most social life takes place off campus. San Francisco is a cosmopolitan city where students can take advantage of reliable public transportation, including the famous cable cars, to get to a variety of cultural attractions, ranging from Chinatown to the symphony. "Living in a city like San Francisco, there is no reason to constrict oneself to the confines of a campus, with so many concerts, bars, nightclubs, and other happenings going on literally every single night of the year," says a senior.

Varsity athletics provide a popular diversion as well, and the Division I USF Dons compete in the West Coast Conference. Men's soccer and women's cross-country are perennial powerhouses. The university sponsors two dozen club and intramural sports; the women's club volleyball team won the national title in 2017, and the boxing club is nationally competitive too. Students make ample use of the Koret Health and Recreation Center, which touts an Olympic-size swimming pool, exercise and weight rooms, and a variety of playing courts.

The core mission of USF is to use the Jesuit tradition, which views "faith and reason as complementary resources in the search for truth and authentic human development," as the backdrop for a solid liberal arts and preprofessional education.

Students take advantage of the cosmopolitan setting to get involved and make the most of their time here. "Students at USF truly care about learning and we desire to achieve great things in life," says a kinesiology major. "I haven't met a student who doesn't want to change the world."

If You Apply To ›

USF: Early decision, early action, regular decision. SATs or ACTs: required. No Subject Tests. Accepts the Common Application with supplement.

Santa Clara University

500 El Camino Real, Santa Clara, CA 95053

Santa Clara is a selective midsized California university now drawing increased national attention. Gorgeous Silicon Valley campus is within easy reach of San Francisco, and the large endowment also contributes to an air of prosperity. A well-developed core curriculum keeps students focused on basic academic and other values. Offers engineering and business in addition to the liberal arts.

Steeped in history and tradition, Santa Clara University was founded by the Society of Jesus (Jesuits) with a mission that emphasizes a commitment to academics and the community. The class schedule is based on 10-week quarters, classes stay small and intimate, and the curriculum focuses on an expanding global society. "Santa Clara is progressive, always pushing forward in the atmosphere of Silicon Valley, and excited to be on the cutting edge," says a senior.

SCU's old-world charm includes 106 acres complete with lush green lawns, palm trees, and luscious rose gardens, accented by authentic Spanish architecture. The Mission Gardens, replete with olive trees, are a beautiful escape from the pressures of school. The famous classic mission church was rebuilt in 1926 in the design of the six previous churches that were destroyed by seemingly biblical disasters ranging from fires to floods. Newer facilities include the Dowd Art and Art History Building and the Charney Hall of Law.

The Core Curriculum is designed to express the school's "most basic values." It prescribes courses in three broad categories—Knowledge, Habits of Mind and Heart (skills), and Engagement with the World. The Core Pathways program supplements the major and core curriculum by offering 24 sets of courses with innovative common themes across disciplines, such as design, hunger and poverty, justice and the arts, and values in science and technology; students choose one Pathway and complete three or four courses. It culminates in an integrative Pathway Reflection Essay. All first-year students are members of a Residential Learning Community (RLC) and take two-quarter sequences of Critical Thinking & Writing and Cultures & Ideas linked to their RLC. Students must complete a requirement that involves community service, and most majors require a capstone experience or senior project.

> "Santa Clara is progressive, always pushing forward in the atmosphere of Silicon Valley."

In addition to liberal arts, Santa Clara offers preprofessional programs in engineering and business. Students can opt for the 3–2 engineering program, which allows them to get a bachelor's and master's degree in five years. The Leavey School of Business is renowned along the West Coast, with finance, economics,

Website: www.scu.edu
Location: Small City
Private
Total Enrollment: 7,336
Undergraduates: 5,397
Male/Female: 50/50
SAT Ranges: ERW 630–710, M 640–730
ACT Ranges: 28–32
Financial Aid: 72%
Pell Grant: 9%
Expense: Pr $ $ $
Student Loans: 42%
Average Debt: $ $ $
Applicants: 15,601
Accepted: 54%
Enrolled: 18%
Grad in 6 Years: 90%
Returning Freshmen: 94%
Academics: ✑ ✑ ✑
Social: 🐦 🐦 🐦 🐦
Q of L: ★ ★ ★ ★
Admissions: (408) 554-4700
Email Address: admission@scu.edu

Strong Programs:
Finance
Economics

and marketing all strong. In the College of Arts and Sciences, communication and psychology remain popular. Other notable majors include environmental studies, public health, bioengineering, and computer science and engineering. New minors are available in professional writing and real estate.

While courses are challenging, students say the quarter system gives them more control over the intensity of their workload. "Every 10 weeks you can change your workload to something that fits best for you," explains a public health major. Small classes—47 percent enroll fewer than 20 students—taught by full professors allow plenty of time for one-on-one interaction. The school's Silicon Valley location means that internship and job-recruitment opportunities abound. A junior says, "I work at the Career Center here, and let me tell you, we make things happen for our students" with mock interviews, résumé edits, cover letter help, goal-setting, and more.

For students looking for more of a challenge, the honors program places 45 to 50 selected freshmen in seminar-style classes, and an endowed scholarship sponsors one student's junior year at Mansfield College, Oxford University. The LEAD (Leadership, Excellence, and Academic Development) Scholars Program invites students whose parents did not attend college to join a small community of peers who work closely with faculty and staff to cultivate leadership skills. "LEAD gave me a family that I know will always support me no matter what," cheers one participant. Multiple opportunities are available to all students to engage in research supervised by a faculty member, much of it subsidized by grants. The study abroad program is extensive, with options in more than 55 countries on every continent except Antarctica, and more than a quarter of undergrads study internationally during their four years.

The school's Silicon Valley location means that internship and job-recruitment opportunities abound.

Santa Clara students "create a real community and culture of support," says a junior. Forty-one percent of undergraduates are Roman Catholic, and religion, while not intrusive, is a force in many aspects of campus life. The campus ministry provides counseling and opportunities for spiritual development, and many students are active in local volunteer organizations. Fifty-seven percent of undergraduates hail from California, 5 percent come from foreign countries, and the rest are from 48 states. The student body on this liberal campus is almost evenly split between public school graduates and alumni of religiously affiliated or other private schools. Sixteen percent of the students are Asian American, 3 percent are African American, 18 percent are Hispanic, and 7 percent are multiracial, but socioeconomically, the school is much less diverse, with just 9 percent of incoming freshmen qualifying for the Pell Grant. "Our school is quite posh," concedes an accounting major. "Being located in the heart of Silicon Valley, there is a lot of luxury." Merit-based academic awards averaging $16,200 and more than 100 athletic scholarships are available to those who qualify. The Johnson Scholars Program rewards up to 10 outstanding incoming students with four-year, full-tuition scholarships and special opportunities to develop leadership skills.

"[Students] create a real community and culture of support."

Almost all freshmen and sophomores live on campus before packing up and heading for shared houses or apartments for the last two years. Currently, 56 percent of students reside on campus, but plans are in the works to build more university housing, to combat the rising costs of off-campus living. All first-year students, including commuters, participate in one of the eight Residential Learning Communities, living in themed dorms and taking courses with students who share similar academic or social interests. The campus offers one central dining hall. "The company that does the food for SCU students is the same company that caters Google and Apple events," explains a junior. "Gluten-free, organic, farm to plate, allergen-free. All of that. Here." A marketing major reports, "Campus always

All first-year students, including commuters, participate in one of the eight Residential Learning Communities.

feels safe," and multiple events are held throughout the year to raise awareness for issues of sexual assault.

Santa Clara ended its support of fraternities and sororities, but Greek organizations and a lively off-campus party scene persist, albeit independently. On-campus social life is led by the more than 150 student organizations that coordinate events, making it "easy to join in on the fun," says a senior. The Bronco is a sports and recreation area where students can hang out, play billiards, and enjoy a late-night meal. Bronco **"Our school is quite posh."** Week, the Global Village Festival, the Gonzaga basketball game, and Spring Concert are favorite annual events. The town of Santa Clara is mostly residential. For those who want to bask in the sun, Santa Cruz is only 20 miles away. San Francisco lies within 45 minutes, and other short road trips include Napa Valley, Monterey, and Palo Alto.

The Santa Clara Broncos compete in Division I, and men's and women's soccer, women's volleyball, and men's basketball and golf are among the more successful programs. Thirteen intramural and 17 club sports draw the enthusiastic participation of a third of the undergraduates. "Every patch of grass usually has someone either chucking a Frisbee or kicking a ball around," says a political science major.

Santa Clara University is a warm place in every sense of the word. The physical setting is comfortable and scenic. More important, the SCU community gives meaning to the traditional Jesuit ideals of infusing morality and ethics into strong and coherent academics. Students say they are reminded of all this daily by their school's nickname: "Claradise."

Overlaps

Cal Poly–San Luis Obispo, Loyola Marymount, UC Berkeley, UC Davis, University of Southern California

If You Apply To ›

SCU: Early decision I and II, early action, regular decision. SATs or ACTs: required. No Subject Tests. Accepts the Common Application with supplement.

Sarah Lawrence College

1 Mead Way, Bronxville, NY 10708

A pricey and free-spirited sister of East Coast alternative institutions like Bard and Bennington where individualism reigns supreme. Though co-ed, women significantly outnumber men. Strong in the humanities and visual and performing arts, Sarah Lawrence is nationally known for creative writing. Full of quirky, headstrong intellectuals who hop the train to New York City with ease.

Sarah Lawrence College attracts creative, curious, and highly motivated individuals who are both critical thinkers and devotees of independent learning. They love literature and the arts and take pride in their academic prowess. Indeed, freedom and exploration are valued more highly than any tradition here. And although some students lament Sarah Lawrence's more mainstream elements (including more sports teams than ever), they also appreciate the things that have always been constants here, such as the emphasis on small classes and one-on-one conferences with professors. As a senior studying theater, psychology, film, and community outreach attests, "What makes Sarah Lawrence unique is the ability to make the education system work for you."

Website: www.sarahlawrence .edu
Location: Suburban
Private
Total Enrollment: 1,597
Undergraduates: 1,341
Male/Female: 28/72
SAT Ranges: ERW 650–730, M 590–680

(continued)

ACT Ranges: 27–31
Financial Aid: 68%
Pell Grant: 16%
Expense: Pr $ $ $ $
Student Loans: 37%
Average Debt: $
Applicants: 3,463
Accepted: 53%
Enrolled: 21%
Grad in 6 Years: 79%
Returning Freshmen: 82%
Academics: ✐ ✐ ✐ ✐
Social: ☎ ☎
Q of L: ★ ★ ★
Admissions: 914-395-2510
Email Address: slcadmit@
sarahlawrence.edu

Strong Programs:
Writing
Literature
Visual and Performing Arts
Filmmaking
Foreign Languages
Biology
Computer Science
Psychology

The professor of students' First-Year Studies seminar becomes their "don," guiding their academic development.

Founded in 1926, Sarah Lawrence sits on a quaint, 44-acre tract in the city of Yonkers called Lawrence Park West, a wealthy Westchester County community close to the village of Bronxville, where even the public library boasts Oriental rugs and fireplaces. On campus, the prevailing architectural theme is English Tudor, including the mansion from the founder's converted estate, but more modern structures are present as well. The landscape is hilly and green, with more than a hundred types of trees and abundant rock outcroppings. Because the school's founders believed that there should be as little physical separation as possible between life and work, many classrooms, dormitory suites, and faculty offices are all housed in the same ivy-covered buildings. Though its holdings are small—fewer than 350,000 volumes—the charming library takes the sting out of studying with a café for those wanting a snack or cup of tea.

Regardless of what they choose to focus on, all students at Sarah Lawrence become intimately acquainted with the written word; writing begins in the first year and continues relentlessly "across the curriculum" for the next three. General education requirements include credits in at least three of four academic areas, leaving lots of room for students to dabble in whatever strikes their fancy. Though there are formal grades,

> **"Professors are all integrated almost as colleagues into the work we are doing."**

more important is the student's portfolio of work, accompanied by in-depth, written evaluations from professors, filed twice a year. To ease the transition to college, all first-years take a First-Year Studies seminar. Students choose from more than 30 subjects, and the professor of their chosen course becomes their "don," the person who very often guides their academic development throughout their four years.

The academic climate is "neither particularly competitive, nor incredibly collaborative," according to one student. "Our academics are so independently driven that it's rare for any two students to be working on the same topic." Indeed, every student designs his or her own program of study, and almost no subject is out of bounds. Writing, literature, and visual and performing arts are among the college's traditional strengths, and other popular concentrations include filmmaking, foreign languages, biology, and computer science. Aspiring psychologists—also a significant group on campus—may participate in fieldwork at the college's Early Childhood Center. The premed program, more structured than other offerings, places nearly all eligible graduates into medical school.

Classes are intimate, with 93 percent of them enrolling fewer than 20 students. Everyone takes only three courses per semester, and professors meet one-on-one

> **"[Students are] progressive, a little bohemian, and critical of the status quo."**

with their students weekly or biweekly, in a system modeled after Oxford University's tutorials, so there's no time to slack off—or fall behind. "The quality of instruction is very high because the professors are all integrated almost as colleagues into the work we are doing," says a political economy student. Perhaps because of the college's emphasis on personal relationships with professors, even the registration process requires deep thought: students interview teachers to ensure that courses fit into their academic plans, and that the professor is someone they respect and want to study with.

All students at Sarah Lawrence conduct research as part of their one-on-one work with professors. Ninety percent of all courses include this research, known as "conference work." The Sarah Lawrence Center for the Urban River is a facility on the banks of the Hudson River that affords research opportunities for students pursuing environmental and social sciences. Students are encouraged to study abroad, and the college runs its own semester, yearlong, and summer study abroad programs in such locales as Oxford, London, Paris, Havana, and Shanghai. Forty-five percent of students undertake some sort of international experience. Those interested in service learning may participate in the Intensive Semester in Yonkers, in which they take three classes in Yonkers centered on the history of the city and community empowerment, while also working with local nonprofit organizations.

Ninety percent of all courses include one-on-one work with professors, known as "conference work."

A creative writing student describes Sarah Lawrence students as "progressive, a little bohemian, and critical of the status quo." Nineteen percent of undergrads are natives of New York State—the bulk from nearby New York City—and 13 percent come from abroad. Four percent of students are African American, 5 percent Asian American, 9 percent Hispanic, and 7 percent multiracial. Political and social issues attract much attention here. "Students are very active in fighting against racism, inequality, and sexism, and are more than happy to start a protest," says one student. A sophomore remarks, "I can't think of a time when I met a conservative on campus." Merit scholarships averaging $16,500 are available to qualified students.

Eighty-four percent of students live in the "eclectic" campus housing, which is only guaranteed for first-year students. According to a sophomore, "Some of the dorms are pretty small or run-down." Campus food receives fair reviews, and there are plenty of options for students with special needs. A sociology-focused student says, "Campus security is very attentive and works around the clock" to keep students safe. A senior notes that students and administrators have worked closely together to adjust sexual assault policies, create education around consent and respect, and "fix the reporting process to make it more accessible and simple."

"We have very unofficial rivalries with Vassar and Bard—more ironic than not."

With a plethora of student organizations hosting on-campus activities, and the school's proximity to New York City, social life is varied and active. "Anything you do here will be new, interesting, and fun," cheers one student. Theater fans and aspiring actors flock to discounted Broadway shows, and clubs, bars, museums, and concert halls also beckon. Not surprisingly, Greek life is not part of the Sarah Lawrence scene. College policies require party hosts who serve alcohol to register, and a junior says party culture is "almost nonexistent" on campus. Favorite traditions include Mayfair, the "actually interesting" sex education program called Sleaze Week, fall and spring formals, and midnight breakfast, served during the last week of each semester.

Theater fans and aspiring actors flock to discounted Broadway shows.

The Sarah Lawrence Gryphons, named for a mythical figure that was part lion, part eagle, field 16 teams that compete in the Division III Skyline Conference. Women's cross-country, swimming, and softball and men's swimming are particularly competitive. The men's basketball and co-ed equestrian teams attract the most fans. "We have very unofficial rivalries with Vassar and Bard—more ironic than not," claims a senior. The intramural program revolves around monthly invitational events—squash matches, dodgeball tournaments, fitness challenges—rather than league play.

Sarah Lawrence offers a close-knit community for writers, artists, and creative thinkers in a lush setting just outside the hustle and bustle of Manhattan. "The education students get at Sarah Lawrence is unlike any other. You can truly have it all here," says a writing student. "You can play sports and perform in the theater. You can study botany and poetry at the same time. I think everyone could benefit from the Sarah Lawrence education."

Overlaps

Bard, Vassar, Skidmore, Mount Holyoke, Oberlin, NYU, Wesleyan, Barnard

If You Apply To ›

Sarah Lawrence: Early decision I and II, early action, regular decision. SATs or ACTs: optional. Subject Tests: optional. Accepts the Common Application.

Scripps College: See page 157.

Seattle University

Seattle, WA 98122

Unlike the University of Washington, Seattle U is a stone's throw from downtown and within walking distance of the waterfront. Jesuit tradition guarantees a nurturing environment and student growth both academically and in community service. Transitioning to a national institution but remains true to its humble roots. Out-of-staters are drawn as much by the city of Seattle as by the university itself.

Website: www.seattleu.edu

Location: City Center

Private

Total Enrollment: 5,715

Undergraduates: 4,371

Male/Female: 38/62

SAT Ranges: ERW 570–670, M 560–660

ACT Ranges: 24–29

Financial Aid: 90%

Pell Grant: 20%

Expense: Pr $ $

Student Loans: 60%

Average Debt: $ $

Applicants: 8,576

Accepted: 74%

Enrolled: 15%

Grad in 6 Years: 74%

Returning Freshmen: 84%

Academics: ✍ ✍ ✍

Social: ☎ ☎ ☎

Q of L: ★ ★ ★ ★

Admissions: (206) 220-8040

Email Address: admissions@seattleu.edu

Strong Programs:
Nursing
Finance
Marketing
Accounting
Diagnostic Ultrasound
Criminal Justice
Engineering
Computer Science

Although Seattle has cultivated a reputation based largely on software, Starbucks lattes, and perpetually gray skies, the city is also home to Seattle University, a vibrant institution founded by the Society of Jesus (Jesuits) that attracts 4,400 undergraduates to its urban campus. With strong preprofessional programs and a commitment to social and spiritual engagement, SU continues to express its mission to empower leaders for a just and humane world.

SU's campus is a 45-acre urban sanctuary in the heart of Seattle. Bordered by busy city streets, the diverse campus buildings are united by a recurring theme of redbrick and light-filled atriums. The Chapel of St. Ignatius is a prize-winning building designed by Steven Holl around the concept of a "gathering of different lights." New buildings are designed to meet environmentally friendly standards, and energy efficiency and sustainability are top priorities for renovations. Special areas like the Ethnobotanical Garden and Japanese American Remembrance Garden highlight native plants and local history. The James Tower Clinical Nursing Lab is a state-of-the-art training facility for the school's many nursing students.

The 60-credit University Core Curriculum introduces all students to the "unique tradition of Jesuit liberal education" and aims to develop the whole person for a life of service, provide a foundation for questioning and learning in any major or profession, and provide a common intellectual experience to all SU students. The core features seminars in writing, quantitative reasoning and creative expression, humanities, social sciences, and natural sciences, as well as coursework in philosophy and theology. Freshmen complete a first-year seminar built around a central theme or problem (enrollment is limited to 19 students), and seniors must complete a capstone course. In addition, the writing-across-the-curriculum initiative requires all sophomores to submit a writing sample for assessment.

> **"Professors are more than willing to get students connected with opportunities in the area."**

SU students choose from more than 60 undergraduate degree programs, and popular majors include nursing, finance, marketing, and accounting. The B.S. degree in diagnostic ultrasound is a particular specialty, and criminal justice, engineering, computer science, and biology are also strengths. A six-year, dual-degree program in business and law is available, and the university has added a new major in business analytics. "Being on the quarter system is conducive to fostering academic growth as a community because students are aware that there is no time to slack off," notes a sophomore. Fifty-five percent of classes have fewer than 20 students, making professors easily accessible.

More than 200 service-learning courses are offered each year, and 80 percent of students perform community service during their time at SU. Motivated students may enroll in the University Honors program, which offers three concurrent classes in every term. The program makes extensive use of the seminar format and focuses on the history of ideas, with tracks in Intellectual Traditions; Society, Policy, and Justice; and Innovations. According to a strategic communications major, "Many of our majors require some sort of internship, and professors are more than willing to get students connected with opportunities in the area." When students want to escape Seattle's dreary skies and near-constant drizzle, they can take part in the university's study abroad program. Thirteen percent of students pack their bags for 55 nations around the world, including China, France, Guatemala, Japan, and Sweden. SU also sends approximately 20 students to the National Conference for Undergraduate Research each year as part of a robust undergraduate research program.

The 60-credit University Core Curriculum introduces all students to Jesuit liberal education and provides a common intellectual experience.

"SU students are outgoing, passionate, and very intentional when it comes to how they engage in and outside the classroom," says a social work major. One-quarter of undergraduates are Roman Catholic. Forty-one percent hail from Washington, and 10 percent are from other nations. African Americans comprise 3 percent of the student body, Asian Americans 16 percent, Hispanics 12 percent, and multiracial students 8 percent. The university, like its host

"We're all feminists, agents against racism, and allies."

city, has a reputation for progressive liberalism. "We're all feminists, agents against racism, and allies," says a sophomore, adding, "As a queer student, I feel more than safe—I feel embraced." Merit scholarships worth an average of $14,600 are awarded annually, and athletes vie for more than 200 scholarships.

Forty-five percent of SU students live in university housing. First-year students are assigned to one of 10 theme communities, which focus on common interests like social change and advocacy, interfaith exploration, and global engagement. Students are required to live on campus through their sophomore year; after that, housing is not guaranteed, and students complain that growing enrollment has made getting a room "very competitive." A biology major says, "The surrounding area is very expensive, so most students who move off campus share bedrooms in apartments or townhouses." Dining options, on the other hand, get rave reviews for being local, seasonal, organic, sustainable, made to order, and, in the words of one sophomore, "delicious, Instagram-ready food." Students report feeling safe on campus, day and night.

Dining options get rave reviews for being local, seasonal, organic, sustainable, and made to order.

As for social life, "It often seems like there is too much going on at once," says a senior, with more than 100 student clubs and organizations. Consistent with Jesuit tradition, there are no fraternities or sororities, and one student says, "Not a whole lot of drinking occurs on campus." Instead, students head off campus to enjoy Seattle's vibrant nightlife. "The campus overlooks the urban center of Seattle," explains a student, "and it's a 10-minute walk to the heart of downtown." Once there, students can take advantage of the city's ubiquitous coffeehouses, eateries, and shops, or engage in volunteer work. Everyone anticipates the annual Quadstock festival. "For one Saturday during spring quarter, the campus turns into a huge block party, with live music, games, and food," says a senior; Talib Kweli, OK Go, and Saint Motel have been recent headliners.

SU's Redhawks compete in the Western Athletic Conference (and Division I). Men's and women's soccer and women's basketball are recent conference champs. Basketball, baseball, and soccer games against the University of Washington draw crowds. Intramural and club sports sign up about a third of students; popular options include flag football, softball, crew, and cycling.

With its emphasis on the liberal arts, civic engagement, and Jesuit principles, SU affords students an experience "which focuses on educating the entire person," according to one junior. For those students who are not averse to hard work and overcast skies, Seattle University might be an inspired choice—just be sure to pack a parka.

Overlaps

Gonzaga, University of San Francisco, University of Denver, University of Portland, Santa Clara, Loyola Marymount, University of Washington, Western Washington

If You Apply To ›

Seattle: Early action, regular decision. SATs or ACTs: required. No Subject Tests. Accepts the Common Application with supplement.

Skidmore College

815 North Broadway, Saratoga Springs, NY 12866

Founded in 1903 as a "young women's industrial club," co-ed Skidmore College still excels in the fine and performing arts that were then deemed proper for young ladies—but also in the natural sciences. Little else remains the same. Compare to Connecticut College, Vassar, and Wheaton (MA), all institutions that made the successful transition to coeducation. Unique wooded campus gives the feel of living in a forest.

Website: www.skidmore.edu
Location: Small City
Private
Total Enrollment: 2,629
Undergraduates: 2,629
Male/Female: 40/60
SAT Ranges: ERW 610–700,
  M 595–700
ACT Ranges: 27–31
Financial Aid: 50%
Pell Grant: 13%
Expense: Pr $ $ $ $
Student Loans: 39%
Average Debt: $
Applicants: 10,053
Accepted: 25%
Enrolled: 27%
Grad in 6 Years: 87%
Returning Freshmen: 93%
Academics: ✍ ✍ ✍ ✍
Social: ☎ ☎ ☎
Q of L: ★ ★ ★
Admissions: (800) 867-6007
Email Address: admissions@
  skidmore.edu

Strong Programs:
Business
Psychology
English
Economics
Studio Art
Biology

Skidmore College serves up solid academics with a decidedly nontraditional flair. These politically liberal and free-spirited students seem a happy lot, thanks to small classes and accessible faculty members. "The college has a charm, sort of like a summer camp," says a junior. Thanks to an emphasis on interdisciplinary learning, students can "have diverse interests and be able to dabble in anything," a senior says.

In 1961, as enrollment surged and Skidmore's turn-of-the-century Victorian buildings grew obsolete, Skidmore traded its campus in the heart of Saratoga Springs for 750 acres on the northwest edge of town. Since then, the campus has grown to more than 50 buildings on 1,200 acres, and the student body has doubled in size (men were welcomed in 1971). While contemporary in style, the new buildings on Skidmore's Jonsson campus reflect the Victorian heritage of the school's original Scribner campus. Covered walkways connect the residential, academic, and social centers, and the prevailing views are of surrounding mountains, woods, and fields. Increasingly concerned with sustainability, the college has implemented geothermal heating and cooling in many buildings and generates a portion of its power from a nearby hydroelectric dam and its own solar array.

> **"The college has a charm, sort of like a summer camp."**

Skidmore's First-Year Experience includes a classwide summer reading project and a choice from among more than 40 Scribner seminars. These seminars are capped at 16 students and taught by professors who also serve as mentors and advisors. Seminar topics are broad and varied, in keeping with Skidmore's 43 majors. They range from Galaxies and the Cosmic Web to K-Pop to Sports Analytics. Students in each seminar receive guidance and support from an upper-class peer mentor, and themes raised in the summer reading crop up again during the year in campuswide programming.

The most popular majors at Skidmore are business, psychology, English, economics, studio art, and biology. Not coincidentally, students say these are some of the college's best programs as well. Students majoring in biology, environmental sciences, environmental studies, and geoscience, in addition to students in certain first-year seminars and interdisciplinary classes, may conduct fieldwork in the college's 300-acre North Woods, a natural laboratory. Skidmore augments liberal arts and sciences offerings with preprofessional majors in business, education, exercise science, and social work, not to mention a bevy of cooperative and dual-degree programs in engineering, business administration, accounting, finance, physical and occupational therapy, and nursing, offered in conjunction with such institutions as Clarkson, Dartmouth, Syracuse, and others.

(continued)
Environmental Studies
Social Work

"Skidmore is a very collaborative working environment. Professors challenge students to constantly improve communication skills by working with other students and submitting work in both written and oral forms," says a sophomore. "The professors have a huge passion for whatever they're studying," adds a senior. "They are always accessible." Seventy-three percent of classes have fewer than 20 students, enhancing that accessibility. Students speak highly of off-campus study options, especially Skidmore-run programs in France, England, New Zealand, and Spain, in addition to 118 other approved programs in 45 countries. Nearly 60 percent of students spend at least one semester off campus. Skidmore's Summer Research Program provides roughly 80 students an opportunity to work individually with faculty mentors for up to 10 weeks on original research in disciplines ranging from biology to business. Internships are popular too, with about 70 percent of students doing at least one during their college years.

First-Year Scribner seminar topics range from Galaxies and the Cosmic Web to K-Pop to Sports Analytics.

"Skidmore has a very diverse student body in terms of sexual, religious, geographic, and gender identities. There is also a diverse field of interests," says a student. Many students are well-off. They hail primarily from New York (34 percent), New England, and New Jersey; 11 percent come from foreign countries. Asian Americans constitute 5 percent of the student body, Hispanics 9 percent, African Americans 5 percent, and multiracial students 4 percent. Limited awards for academic merit—up to six annually in music and up to seven annually in math and science (each worth $60,000 over four years)—are available, although there are no athletic scholarships. Additionally, the college commits to meeting the full demonstrated financial need of all enrolled students.

"Professors challenge students to constantly improve communication skills."

Eighty-nine percent of Skidmore students live in the dorms, and most students get singles after freshman year. Dorms are integrated by class and co-ed by floor or suite, with kitchenettes and lounges on every floor. "Housing is great. It's guaranteed all four years, and the on-campus apartments are unbelievably nice," says a student. Most buildings have carpeting, air-conditioning, and cozy window seats. Some upperclassmen move to apartments—whether on campus in the Northwoods Village Apartments or the Sussman Village Apartments, or off campus in Saratoga Springs. The Murray-Aikins Dining Center provides students with fresh food choices in a state-of-the-art facility. "I have friends come and visit me from other schools and demand to be sneaked into our dining hall," says a freshman.

The riding program has won eight Intercollegiate Horse Show Association national championships, most recently in 2018.

"Most of the social life revolves around campus clubs and organizations," says one chemistry major. "Since we don't have Greek Life, we don't have the stereotypical party scene on campus." Skidmore's more traditional activities, which have continued even after nearly a half century of coeducation, include Club Fair, Oktoberfest, Winter Carnival, Spring Fling, Earth Day, and Fun Day in the spring, with games and an inflatable obstacle course on the college green. Newer traditions include the student-run Beatlemore Skidmania tribute concert and the Big Green Scream, which ushers in the men's and women's basketball seasons.

The nearby Adirondacks and Green Mountains make Skidmore a haven for backpackers, skiers, and members of the popular Outdoors Club, while the old resort town of Saratoga Springs, with its healing waters and antique shops, offers plenty of culture, including the Saratoga Performing Arts Center and the country's oldest thoroughbred racetrack. Saratoga is also the summer home of the New York City Ballet, the Lake George Opera, and the Philadelphia Orchestra. Students reach out to the community through BenefAction, a volunteer group connected to several local agencies and schools. The best road trips include Albany, New York City, Boston—and especially Montreal, where you don't need a fake ID to hit the bars at 18.

Skidmore's men's and women's varsity teams (the Thoroughbreds) compete in Division III; the men's basketball, tennis, and golf teams have claimed Liberty League championships in recent years, as have the women's basketball, field hockey, and tennis teams. The riding program has won eight Intercollegiate Horse Show Association national championships, most recently in 2018. Varsity athletes and weekend warriors alike enjoy the 400-meter, all-weather track and the athletic center, which includes a fitness center, a six-lane pool, and an intramural gym.

Skidmore continues to win the hearts of motivated students with gorgeous scenery; caring faculty; and its flexibility, openness, and receptivity to change and growth. Students here are also a bit quirky, says a sophomore, "wearing shorts in the winter, for example." They're more likely to cheer on the fall of a foreign dictator than a goal by the lacrosse team. The point is, there's room for—and encouragement of—all types of students.

If You Apply To ›

Skidmore: Early decision I and II, regular decision. SATs or ACTs: optional (required for homeschooled students). Subject Tests: optional. Accepts the Common Application.

Smith College

College Lane, Northampton, MA 01063

The furthest left-leaning of the nation's leading women's colleges. Liberal Northampton provides sophisticated social life, and membership in the Five College Consortium adds depth and breadth all around. With a total enrollment of about 2,900, Smith is one of the largest top women's colleges, strong in the sciences and the arts, and the first women's college to offer engineering. Compare to Bryn Mawr.

Heaven only knows what Sophia Smith would think of the women's college she founded in 1871 with the hope it would be "pervaded by the Spirit of Evangelical Christian Religion." There are still Evangelicals at Smith, but today they join the rest of their schoolmates in crusading against racism, classism, sexism, and homophobia. Though the all-female school remains strongly committed to its liberal arts mission, it is also focused on placing women at the forefront of science and technology. Students here have the opportunity to become leaders in the male-dominated field of engineering, or pursue interdisciplinary fields such as landscape studies or the study of women and gender. "Smith has an open curriculum, a great college town, and a very strong science program," says one sophomore.

Smith is in the small city of Northampton, an artsy oasis within an hour's drive of the Berkshire Mountains. The 147-acre campus resembles a medieval fortress from the front gate, but inside it sparkles with many gardens, Paradise Pond, and a plant house. Buildings cover a range of styles from late 18th century to modern, and the college has successfully retained its historic atmosphere while keeping facilities up-to-date. The college's science and engineering building, Ford Hall, earned LEED Gold certification and boasts a myriad of high-tech equipment, including two electron microscopes. Smith's four libraries house one of the largest collections of any liberal arts college in the country. Construction on a new, state-of-the art main library, designed by famed architect Maya Lin to replace the historic Neilson Library, is scheduled for completion in 2020.

With the exception of at least one writing course, Smith women have unusual freedom to plan a course of study. They must take half of their credits outside of their major, and first-year students can take small seminars on topics such as Rebellious Women and Exploring Our National Parks. Students can expand their academic options by registering for courses at any of the other Five College Consortium member schools: Amherst, Hampshire, Mount Holyoke, and UMass Amherst.

Economics is among the most popular majors on campus, followed by psychology, government, biological sciences, art, and English. Four in 10 Smith women major in science and thereby enjoy numerous opportunities to assist professors with their research. The Picker Engineering Program is the country's largest and oldest women-only, accredited engineering program and offers students the opportunity to pursue an ambitious

> **"[Smith is] not too competitive because we all want to grow together."**

engineering curriculum taught within the full depth and breadth of the liberal arts. Administrators hope the program will lead to greater gender parity in engineering. Those who complete it are highly sought-after: recent graduates have headed to prestigious graduate programs at Cornell, Harvard, MIT, Princeton, and other colleges; received highly competitive National Science Foundation fellowships; or been quickly snatched up by employers. Smith's art history department is among the best in the nation and enjoys access to the college's superb museum. Landscape studies, which focuses on the relationship between humans and natural and built environments, is a first-of-its-kind undergraduate program among liberal arts colleges.

Be ready to hit the books with your newfound sisters at Smith. Coursework is described as "very intense and very difficult," although the atmosphere is "not too competitive because we all want to grow together," according to one student. Students generally refrain from discussing grades, choosing instead to focus on helping each other. Smith's student-run honor system, which covers everything from exams to library checkout, is widely praised and enforced. All courses are taught by professors, and 68 percent of them have fewer than 20 students. Students seem to be pleased with the quality of teaching. "My professors have all been accessible and supportive as well as open-minded and articulate," says a sophomore.

Qualified students may enter the Smith Scholars program and embark on one or two years of independent study or extra college research for full credit. The STRIDE program allows freshmen and sophomores to become paid research assistants to professors. Students are also enthusiastic about the opportunity to take part in Smith's well-known study abroad program, which usually sends about half of the junior class to a number of countries for at least a semester. The Praxis program allows each student to participate in at least one

> **"[Smith women] know what they want and know how to get things done."**

summer internship funded by the college. About 100 older students are enrolled in the groundbreaking Ada Comstock Scholars program for women going back to college.

Smithies are "women who know what they want and know how to get things done," says a government major. Twenty-one percent of undergraduates hail from Massachusetts, and 14 percent come from abroad. African Americans account for 7 percent of the student body, Asian Americans 11 percent, Hispanics 10 percent, and multiracial students 4 percent. Nobody disputes that Smith is a liberal place, with social issues of the day dominating conversations, though some students are surprised to find themselves in such a freewheeling atmosphere. With an endowment of nearly $2 billion, Smith has deeper pockets than many of its competitors. And though it's got a hefty price tag, the school meets the full demonstrated

(continued)

Grad in 6 Years: 88%
Returning Freshmen: 93%
Academics: ✑ ✑ ✑ ✑ ½
Social: ☎ ☎ ☎
Q of L: ★ ★ ★ ★
Admissions: (413) 585-2500
Email Address: admission@ smith.edu

Strong Programs:
Economics
Psychology
Government
Biological Sciences
Art
English
Engineering
Art History

The Picker Engineering Program is the country's largest and oldest women-only, accredited engineering program.

financial need of admitted students. It also offers a limited number of merit-based awards that average $16,300 annually.

Housing at Smith, which consists of 37 houses (not dorms), is universally adored, and is home to 95 percent of students. "The house system builds strong community, and each house has its own traditions," a student explains. Each house accommodates from 12 to 100 students and functions as a self-governing unit, responsible for everything from visiting hours to weekend parties and concerts. The atmosphere is less that of a sorority than of an extended family. Classes are mixed in each house, and first-year students easily mingle with seniors. Alternative options

"The house system builds strong community."

include food cooperatives, language-themed housing, and an apartment complex. There are 15 dining halls on campus open at specific times for breakfast, lunch, and dinner on the weekdays and brunch and dinner on the weekends, and the food gets good reviews. Some houses even have family-style Thursday dinners to which students invite faculty members.

You will not be greeted with a rocking social scene at Smith, but there are plenty of parties to be had and great places to visit. "The student organizations on campus are pretty good at organizing events like movie nights and sundae parties," says a senior. Meeting men (or non-Smith women) is made easier by the five-college system; a free bus service runs to the other four campuses of the consortium, which offer a broad range of social and cultural opportunities. In addition, each house throws an average of two parties a semester. For special weekends, a whole fraternity may be invited from Dartmouth or another nearby college, an arrangement that is only slightly more civilized than the typical college bar scene. Students say the alcohol policies are getting stricter, and IDs are checked and hands are stamped at campus parties. Smith also offers time-honored traditions like Mountain Day in the fall, when the president cancels class for a day of hiking and female bonding, complete with brown-bag lunches.

Northampton, known as NoHo after New York City's SoHo neighborhood, is a college town of about 30,000 that is known for its freewheeling culture and funky bohemianism. The town is home to multiple subcultures and is generally tolerant of everyone. "Northampton is one of my favorite places," says a senior. "It's small and

"Northampton is one of my favorite places. It's small and artsy."

artsy, has multiple venues for music and dance, a dance club, bowling alley, and a lot of great restaurants. There is never a lack of nightlife." The Community Service Office assists student volunteers with finding long-term placements and short-term projects in Northampton, the surrounding communities, and on campus. The New England countryside has numerous special charms, including ski slopes only an hour away. The best road trips are to Boston (two hours) or New York City (three hours).

Smith has a long tradition of success in Division III athletics; the college was the first women's college to join the NCAA and still places a premium on recruiting scholar-athletes. Top Pioneer teams include crew, basketball, and soccer. The field hockey team won the New England Women's and Men's Athletic Conference title in 2018. Smith's multimillion-dollar sports complex features indoor tennis and track facilities and a six-lane swimming pool. Interhouse competitions include everything from kickball to inner-tube water polo to rugby.

"It can be hard to adapt to the environment of a women's college," acknowledges one senior. "But it's been the most valuable thing I've ever done." The strict evangelism is long gone, and today's Smith women are far from Sophia Smith wannabes. But her namesake and spirit live on at this eclectic, open-minded institution where women don lab coats, power suits, combat boots, and even white dresses at graduation. This "community of close, intelligent, interesting, and compassionate women" readies them to be and do just about anything.

University of the South (Sewanee)

735 University Avenue, Sewanee, TN 37383

Easily mistaken for an Oxford or a Cambridge plunked down in the highlands of Tennessee. Traditions loom large at Sewanee, including its honor code and the wearing of "class dress" and academic gowns. Affiliated with the Episcopal Church, it is more conservative than Davidson and Rhodes and continues to have old-line Southern feel. Burgeoning environmental studies, prebusiness, and study abroad programs. If you have a horse, bring it along.

Tradition is respected at University of the South, known simply as Sewanee. Leonidas Polk, an Episcopal bishop and later a Confederate general, founded the school in 1857, envisioning it as a distinguished center of learning for the region. Before Sewanee could open, its campus buildings and endowment were lost to the Civil War. Anglican parishes in England gave money to restart the school, and Oxford and Cambridge donated the library's first volumes. Sewanee opened its doors for its first convocation in 1868, with nine students and four professors. Many traditions remain alive and well—including calling academic semesters Advent and Easter—even as the school emphasizes inclusivity and a broader national appeal.

Sewanee is located atop Tennessee's Cumberland Plateau, between Chattanooga and Nashville. The atmosphere is like "attending Oxford in England," a freshman says, "only with mountains!" Stately English Gothic buildings are carved from beige-and-pink sandstone native to the region, and each has plenty of space, as the school spreads out over a 13,000-acre forested plot fondly known as "the Domain." Particularly noteworthy structures are St. Luke's and All Saints' Chapel, and Convocation Hall, built in 1886. Three new residence halls have recently been built.

As part of Sewanee's general education program, students pursue six learning objectives in their first two years: Reading Closely, Understanding the Arts, Seeking Meaning, Exploring Past and Present, Observing and Experimenting, and Cross-Cultural Comprehension. An optional Finding Your Place course enhances the first-year experience with lectures, discussions, service opportunities, and field trips before classes begin in the fall. In keeping with European tradition, Sewanee seniors must pass comprehensive exams in their majors to earn their diplomas. While students are tested, friends decorate their cars to celebrate.

> **"[Sewanee professors] are extremely helpful, especially when it comes to one-on-one instruction."**

Economics, English, and psychology are the most popular majors, along with international and global studies, an interdisciplinary program with faculty from 14 departments. The strength of Sewanee's English department is nationally recognized, thanks in part to a bequest from playwright Tennessee Williams. The *Sewanee Review*—the oldest continuously published literary quarterly in the United States—and the Sewanee Writers' Conference enhance the department's reputation. The sciences are also strong, especially variations on environmental studies, given the

Website: www.sewanee.edu
Location: Small Town
Private
Total Enrollment: 1,744
Undergraduates: 1,683
Male/Female: 47/53
SAT Ranges: ERW 620–700, M 590–680
ACT Ranges: 27–30
Financial Aid: 87%
Pell Grant: 16%
Expense: Pr $ $
Student Loans: 40%
Average Debt: $ $
Applicants: 4,218
Accepted: 47%
Enrolled: 23%
Grad in 6 Years: 77%
Returning Freshmen: 88%
Academics: ✐ ✐ ✐ ✐
Social: ☎ ☎ ☎
Q of L: ★ ★ ★ ★
Admissions: (800) 522-2234
Email Address: admiss@ sewanee.edu

Strong Programs:
Economics
English
Psychology
International and Global Studies

campus's rich natural setting. The school's unique major in natural resources and the environment focuses on geology and forestry, and offers cooperative master's programs with Duke and Yale. Premed and preprofessional programs are also highly regarded; students applying to medical, dental, and veterinary schools enjoy high acceptance rates. Although Sewanee does not offer a business major, its prebusiness program, consisting of special experiential learning opportunities and a business minor with finance, managerial, and international tracks, is gaining popularity.

"Sewanee professors are very good at what they do and are extremely helpful, especially when it comes to one-on-one instruction and help during office hours," says a politics major. Most professors wear black academic gowns when they teach, as do many members of Sewanee's signature honor society, the Order of the Gown. Administrators say students and professors voluntarily observe these traditions to demonstrate their commitment to teaching and learning. Women often wear dresses or skirts to class, and many men wear jackets and ties as part of the tradition of class dress. Sewanee also takes its honor code very seriously. Violations—such as lying, cheating, or stealing—usually result in suspension. Sewanee is "steeped in tradition that almost all students abide by, no matter how archaic," a sophomore says. Sixty-four percent of courses enroll fewer than 20 students, and classwork is taken seriously too. "The courses can be quite challenging," says a junior. "They are the perfect fit for the hardworking, motivated, intelligent, and articulate students that Sewanee tends to attract."

> "[Sewanee is] steeped in tradition that almost all students abide by, no matter how archaic."

Many traditions remain alive and well—including calling academic semesters Advent and Easter.

The new Sewanee Pledge initiative promises three benefits to all undergraduates: funding for a summer internship or research opportunity; access to a semester-long study abroad program at no additional tuition cost; and a graduation guarantee that offers an additional year of study tuition-free to students who are unable to complete a single major within four years. Overall, 40 percent of students study abroad in nearly 400 approved programs; the Sewanee Semester in Spain, the semester-long European Studies option, and short-term summer programs tend to draw the most interest.

Twenty-two percent of Sewanee's students are Tennessee natives, though many of the rest come from the Southeast; 3 percent are international. Southern culture is strong here and the atmosphere can be quite familial—almost a quarter of entering freshmen are legacies. Still, one senior argues, Sewanee students are not simply a "large group of privileged preps." The student body is one-quarter Episcopalian and overwhelmingly Christian. Minorities have a small but growing presence on campus, with African Americans making up 5 percent of the student body, Asian Americans 1 percent, Hispanics 6 percent, and multiracial students 3 percent. Politically, both sides of the aisle are represented on campus, according to a history major, and "students grow stronger together through conversation and debate." Each year, the school hands out academic scholarships averaging $13,800, and socioeconomic diversity has gradually risen as the school has shifted more of its financial aid toward need-based aid.

> "Students grow stronger together through conversation and debate."

[Sewanee] spreads out over a 13,000-acre forested plot fondly known as "the Domain."

Ninety-eight percent of Sewanee students live in the dorms, and students report that while the quality of the facilities varies, the community atmosphere is tight-knit and enjoyable. McClurg Dining Hall serves a wide variety of food and accommodates students' requests. Life on the mountain is peaceful and "students most always feel safe and secure," according to one junior. The FOG program sends students who are trained in alcohol and sexual misconduct intervention strategies to parties to mingle with (and monitor) their classmates and step in to offer help when necessary.

Greek life is a huge deal here, with the vast majority of students—70 percent of the men and 80 percent of the women—signing up. "Greek life rules the social scene, but university-funded programs help keep life from becoming one long frat-a-thon," remarks a student. Drinking is a fact of life, but a sophomore reports that with a medical amnesty policy and other measures, "the main focus is safety." Annual Fall and Spring Party weekends draw alumni and friends back to campus, and students also enjoy the Perpetual Motion dance performances and Sewaneroo music festival. Popular road trips include Atlanta, Nashville, and Chattanooga, so it helps to have a car. Nearby lakes, waterfalls, and caverns also offer rafting, hiking, camping, and other active day trips.

Sports are popular at Sewanee, where varsity squads compete in Division III. The most popular Tigers sport on campus is probably football—not so much because the team is good, but because games are important social events. And then there's the cheer: "Sewanee, Sewanee, leave 'em in the lurch. Down with the heathens and up with the Church. Yea, Sewanee's right." The men's and women's tennis teams dominate the Southern Athletic Association, each winning their sixth straight conference title in 2018, and men's and women's lacrosse and golf frequently appear in the NCAA championships. The equestrian team competes in International Horse Show Association events and regularly ranks among the top teams in the country. About two-thirds of students participate in intramural sports and the Outing Program, which sponsors outdoor adventures like bouldering, caving, and kayaking.

Sewanee's small size means it offers students plenty of opportunity to really make a difference. The rich traditions tap into the university's long history and give the campus a life and personality all its own. "Everyone can find their place at Sewanee," says a sophomore. "We promote community with the goal of making all students feel like they have a safe place and a home."

The new Sewanee Pledge initiative promises all undergrads funding for a summer internship or research opportunity.

Overlaps

Rhodes, University of Tennessee Knoxville, Furman, Washington and Lee, University of Georgia, University of Virginia, UNC at Chapel Hill, Wake Forest

If You Apply To ›

Sewanee: Early decision I and II, early action, regular decision. SATs or ACTs: optional. Subject Tests: optional. Accepts the Common Application.

University of South Carolina

Columbia, SC 29208

Among public flagship universities in the South, USC struggles against the image of being one giant step behind UNC at Chapel Hill. The university has paid big money to attract star professors and boasts one of the top international business programs in the nation. Criminal justice is also a specialty. Unlike Clemson, USC is in a major city. Check out the Honors College, which is one of the best anywhere.

Whether it's football or international business, students at the University of South Carolina are game—after all, they're the Gamecocks and, like their mascot, they've got plenty of fighting spirit. Students love to cheer on the school's football and basketball teams, especially if the opponent is longtime rival Clemson. South Carolina is working hard to give its campus a more cosmopolitan feel through programs such as the Student Council on Diversity and Inclusion. "Diversity and loyalty are two words to describe Gamecock students," says a chemical engineering major.

Website: www.sc.edu
Location: City Center
Public
Total Enrollment: 31,071
Undergraduates: 24,578
Male/Female: 46/54

(continued)

SAT Ranges: ERW 590–660,
   M 580–670

ACT Ranges: 25–30

Financial Aid: 75%

Pell Grant: 15%

Expense: Pub $ $ $

Student Loans: 52%

Average Debt: $ $ $

Applicants: 26,019

Aooepted: 72%

Enrolled: 31%

Grad in 6 Years: 73%

Returning Freshmen: 88%

Academics: ✍ ✍ ✍

Social: ☎ ☎ ☎

Q of L: ★ ★ ★

Admissions: (803) 777-7700

Email Address: admissions
   -ugrad@sc.edu

Strong Programs:
Business Administration
Psychology
Nursing
Exercise Science
Biological Sciences
Criminal Justice
Journalism
International Business

The old section of the campus includes the glorious oak-lined Horseshoe.

South Carolina's main campus is located in the heart of Columbia (population 134,000), which also happens to be the state capital. Government buildings and downtown businesses are within an easy walk, allowing students to secure internships or even part-time jobs during the school year. The old section of the campus, which dates to the school's 1801 founding, includes the glorious oak-lined Horseshoe; 10 of its 19th-century buildings are now listed in the National Register of Historic Places. The $250 million Innovista complex integrates public and private sector research in high-tech facilities. Recent campus projects include a new student health center offering expanded health services.

Regardless of the program in which they enroll, students must complete the Carolina Core, a series of distribution requirements that includes courses in problem solving, writing, foreign language, global citizenship and multicultural understanding, and scientific literacy (among others). USC has been a national leader in developing initiatives to support the first-year transition, such as the required three-hour University 101 seminar. According to one student, University 101 is "an incredible class. You learn about student skills, time management, all the resources at USC, and have a ton of fun." To build community, there's the Freshman Reading Experience, in which entering students read the same book before coming to campus then discuss it in small groups upon arrival.

"Diversity and loyalty are two words to describe Gamecock students."

South Carolina offers a slew of undergraduate degree programs; business administration is popular, as are psychology, nursing, exercise science, biological sciences, and criminal justice. Students in the journalism and mass communications program benefit from an excellent film library right on campus, while budding marine scientists may study and do research at a 17,000-acre facility about three hours away. With South Carolina's coastal economy depending on foreign trade, the university has also developed a top-notch international business program. Art students, neglected at many universities, here have access to the latest cameras, editing stations, and computers, as well as pottery kilns and other necessary equipment. Musicians enjoy a four-level building with a music and performance library, rehearsal rooms, recording studios, and a 250-seat lecture hall. The English program benefits from sizable collections of research material on F. Scott Fitzgerald and Ernest Hemingway. An unusual minor in medical humanities gives doctors-to-be an introduction to the ethical, cultural, legal, economic, and political factors that affect medical practice today.

"For the most part, the courses are challenging and the environment is laid-back," says one senior. A classmate adds, "Students share notes, study together, and help out others." Thirty-eight percent of undergraduate classes have fewer than 20 students, and the quality of teaching is generally high: "All my professors are passionate about what they teach and do a great job of sharing their passion with us," one student says. Unlike many honors programs that focus on lower-division education, USC's Honors College provides curricular and research opportunities across all four years. About 600 courses are available annually through the Honors College, which serves more than 2,000 students. Nineteen percent of undergraduates study, intern, volunteer, or conduct independent research abroad in 52 different countries.

"The courses are challenging and the environment is laid-back."

USC draws students from all 50 states and from more than 100 countries; 59 percent of undergrads are in-staters and 3 percent are international. Though the numbers are not huge, the university is more racially diverse than other public universities in the state; 9 percent are African American, 3 percent are Asian American, 5 percent are Hispanic, and 4 percent are multiracial. "It is the norm to be involved with at least two or three student organizations and to be very active on campus," says one student. Another says hot-button issues include education funding and LGBTQ rights, but since there are more than 400 student groups on campus, everyone should be able to find a niche, no matter where they fall on the political spectrum. The university awards merit scholarships averaging $6,600, as well as 513 athletic scholarships. The Gamecock Guarantee promises to cover tuition and fees for low-income South Carolina residents who are the first in their family to attend college.

All first-year students live on campus in nearly two dozen living/learning communities, ranging from academic fields like business and engineering to special interests like sustainability and leadership. "I loved living on campus," recalls one junior. "It was so easy to walk to class from my residence hall." After the first year, housing can be expensive and difficult to get, students say, and only 28 percent of all undergrads reside on campus. Dining options range from fast-food stands to all-you-can-eat lines, with plenty of vegetarian and healthy choices—and of course, some junk food too. "You will never go hungry," promises one student. Students report feeling safe while roaming campus.

About 600 courses are available annually through the Honors College, which serves more than 2,000 students.

"Most social life takes place off campus," says a psychology major. "We have cool bars and restaurants close to campus that are geared toward younger people." Twenty percent of South Carolina's men and 33 percent of the women go Greek, and their chapters provide much of the weekend social life on campus. Despite school policies, some underage students "sneak [alcohol] in, and are not bothered if they behave themselves," says a speech/language pathology major. Still, concerned about binge and underage drinking, administrators have increased funding for alternative activities, such as films, dance performances, theatrical productions, concerts, and comedy shows. Downtown Columbia offers more theaters, a comedy club, a performing arts center, and Five Points, a strip boasting several bars. Outdoorsy types appreciate the beaches an hour and a half away, and the mountain ranges four hours north for hiking, skiing, and camping.

"We have cool bars and restaurants close to campus."

Fall football weekends are always a big deal at South Carolina, which competes in the Division I Southeastern Conference. The enduring USC–Clemson rivalry is one of the oldest and most colorful in college sports, with festivities beginning weeks in advance; their annual game (the Palmetto Bowl) has been played for more than a century. "We do an annual Tiger Burn, where the engineering students build a 30-foot-tall tiger and burn it to the ground before the big game," says one Gamecock. "That's really fun!" Winter weekends welcome another of USC's strong sports, basketball, played in the 342,000-square-foot Colonial Center. The women's basketball team brought home the national title in 2017, to the elation of fans, and reached the Elite Eight in 2018. USC's baseball, equestrian, and women's golf teams are competitive too. Students can also choose from dozens of club and intramural sports, or dip into the indoor and outdoor pools at the Strom Thurmond Fitness and Wellness Center, which also features an indoor track, basketball and racquetball courts, and a climbing wall.

All first-year students live on campus in nearly two dozen living/learning communities.

"Carolina is amazing and Clemson is stuck up and snobby," sniffs one diehard Gamecock. School spirit remains as strong as ever at South Carolina's flagship university, but the pace of change is picking up. Yet even as its academic focus grows increasingly global, USC has a more personal feel than many state universities, thanks to its special emphasis on student support and diversity of all types. Perhaps that's why Gamecocks say no place could be finer.

Overlaps

University of Georgia, UMass Amherst, Auburn, University of Tennessee Knoxville, University of Missouri, Clemson, College of Charleston, Furman

If You Apply To ›

South Carolina: Early action, regular decision. SATs or ACTs: required. No Subject Tests. Does not accept the Common Application.

University of Southern California

University Park, Los Angeles, CA 90089

USC's old handle: "The University of Spoiled Children." USC's new handle: highly selective West Coast university with preeminent programs in cinematic arts and business. The region's only major private university that just happens to have a top football team, USC has been shaken by a series of well-publicized scandals. L.A.'s answer to SMU on the one hand and NYU on the other.

Website: www.usc.edu
Location: City Center
Private
Total Enrollment: 38,335
Undergraduates: 18,465
Male/Female: 48/52
SAT Ranges: ERW 650–730,
    M 650–770
ACT Ranges: 30–34
Financial Aid: 63%
Pell Grant: 17%
Expense: Pr $ $ $ $
Student Loans: 36%
Average Debt: $ $ $
Applicants: 56,676
Accepted: 16%
Enrolled: 37%
Grad in 6 Years: 92%
Returning Freshmen: 96%
Academics: ✐ ✐ ✐ ½
Social: ☎ ☎ ☎
Q of L: ★ ★ ★
Admissions: (213) 740-1111
Email Address: admitusc@
    usc.edu

Strong Programs:
Business
Social Sciences
Visual and Performing Arts
Engineering
Communication
Cinematic Arts

Once dismissed as little more than an academic bastion of privilege, the University of Southern California has come into its own as a West Coast destination for students seeking the advantages of study in a center for the arts, technology, communication, and international trade. The school's lush campus and prime Los Angeles location has led to a flood of applicants, making it continually tougher to win admission. Students cheer on national championship teams and give high marks to the Trojan alumni network as well. Often accused of being elitist, USC continues to populate the next generation of Los Angeles business leaders.

USC's University Park campus has an unmistakably upscale vibe and offers a mix of traditional ivy-covered and modern structures, arranged around fountains and reflecting pools, well shaded from the Southern California sun. Sitting on 226 parklike acres, just minutes from downtown Los Angeles, USC is a veritable urban oasis. The university recently completed the $700 million, 2,700-bed USC Village, a student housing project as well as a neighborhood revitalization effort that includes eight residential colleges, a Gothic-style dining hall, and two dozen retail stores.

> "[USC offers] the flexibility to take classes from different professional schools."

USC's Core Curriculum, aimed at sharpening critical thinking and communication skills, requires nine courses: six general education, two intensive writing, and one diversity. Students with high GPAs and test scores may choose the Thematic Option—a.k.a. the "Traumatic Option"—in place of regular general education courses. The 200 or so who do get smaller classes with some of the university's best teachers and a handpicked group of writing instructors. Freshmen may also join one of the school's Learning Communities, groups of 20 students with common academic interests, such as business, medicine, technology, or languages. Each community takes four common courses during the first year and meets with a dedicated faculty mentor and staff advisor three to six times a semester.

USC offers undergraduates the chance to pursue degrees not only in the Dornsife College of Letters, Arts, and Sciences, but also at any of its 20 professional schools and schools of the arts—an advantage that students appreciate. "The flexibility to take classes from different professional schools really highlights the emphasis here on interdisciplinary studies," says a cinema and media studies major.

> "My professors…are normally my first line of defense when I need advice."

In fact, USC strongly encourages students to pursue double majors or a combination of majors and minors in unrelated academic fields, which means business majors may minor in bioethics or Russian and art history majors may study the music industry or business too. Majors in business, social sciences, visual and performing arts, engineering, and communication enroll the most students. The progressive degree program allows students to apply to a master's-level program during their junior year; depending on the field, one can earn a bachelor's and master's degree in as little as 10 semesters.

The academic climate is challenging, and students report that while there is some "friendly competition," their classmates are mostly supportive of each other. Sixty percent of undergraduate classes enroll fewer than 20 students, but the quality of teaching varies, especially in some introductory courses for freshmen, which can be huge. Advising and career services get mixed reviews. An English major says, "My biggest support system at USC has been my professors, and they are normally my first line of defense when I need advice." The Discovery Scholars program honors original research and creativity among undergraduates, and the Global Scholars program singles out students who excel both at home and abroad. USC offers more than 50 semester- and yearlong study abroad programs in nearly 30 countries, in addition to several short-term options offered during summer and winter breaks and the May term.

USC students are perhaps best characterized by a sense of "ambitious drive," says one senior. Most pride themselves on their ability to maintain decent grades along with an active social life. Forty-three percent of USC undergrads come from within the state, and a high proportion (15 percent) come from foreign countries. Even aside from the international presence, this left-leaning campus is diverse, with African Americans making up 5 percent of the student body, Hispanics 14 percent, Asian Americans 21 percent, and multiracial students 6 percent. Hundreds of merit scholarships, averaging $20,200, are awarded each year, as are more than 380 athletic awards. USC also meets 100 percent of students' demonstrated financial need, and is need-blind in its admissions.

Thirty percent of USC undergrads live on campus. All freshmen are housed in residential colleges, which are led by faculty masters in residence and serve as a hub for social life. Since swimming pools, tennis courts, carpeting, microwaves, refrigerators, and air-conditioning are just some of the luxuries to be found in USC dorms, not to mention the brand-new USC Village, it's no wonder more

> **The $700 million USC Village includes eight residential colleges, a Gothic-style dining hall, and two dozen retail stores.**

> **"The entire Los Angeles area is full of fun things to do if you're willing to hop on a train or take an Uber."**

upperclassmen would like to stay on campus. But because there isn't enough space for everyone, students typically move after their first year to fraternity and sorority houses or apartments, which are just a short walk away. Dining halls offer plenty of options, including an international buffet in the Parkside complex. Some nearby areas are rather rough, but thanks to USC's police department, which regularly patrols the campus and surrounding neighborhood, most students say they've never felt unsafe. "USC has made sure that, with regard to sexual assault, all students know where to seek help and access tools to deal with this issue," notes a senior.

The on-campus social scene revolves around activities organized by student clubs, fraternity parties on "The Row," sporting events, the annual Springfest concert, and the *Los Angeles Times* Festival of Books in the spring. Twenty-six percent of the men and 27 percent of the women go Greek. As a junior points out, "The entire Los Angeles area is full of fun things to do if you're willing to hop on a train or take an Uber." Though L.A. is hardly a college town in any traditional sense, it does offer an endless variety of bars, clubs, shopping, and cultural experiences. Whether you're looking for an internship at a law firm or a movie studio, you want to learn to surf, or you're eager to check out a new band before they get signed to a major label, L.A. delivers. Famous Venice Beach is just a few miles from USC's campus, and in the winter months, students can reach the San Gabriel Mountains (and its ski resorts) in less than an hour (by car, not by skis). USC students are also active in the community, tutoring in 10 local schools through the Joint Educational Project.

Trojan athletics, which compete in the Division I Pac-12 Conference, have won 130 team national championships in more than a dozen men's and women's sports. The football team won the Rose Bowl in 2017, and men's and women's water

> **The progressive degree program allows students to apply to a master's-level program during their junior year.**

polo, women's track and field, and women's beach volleyball are recent national champions. Two of USC's biggest schoolwide traditions center on the ol' pigskin. The first is Troy Week—the week leading up to the UCLA game—which culminates with the Conquest pep rally and concert in the middle of campus. Then there's the Weekender, when USC students take off en masse for northern California to see their beloved Trojans face off against Stanford or Berkeley. Throngs of USC undergrads, alumni, and fans gather in San Francisco's Union Square for a huge pep rally, featuring the band, cheerleaders, and university personalities.

USC is a university on the move, but its remarkable progress has recently been marred by scandals involving athletics, admissions, and sexual abuse. "We are drawing an academically competitive and involved student body," says a geography and communication major. Pack your sunscreen, flip-flops, and some assertiveness, and you'll fit right in. Shrinking violets, on the other hand, should probably look elsewhere.

If You Apply To ›

USC: Regular decision. SATs or ACTs: required. Subject Tests: optional. Accepts the Common Application with supplement.

Southern Methodist University

P.O. Box 750181, Dallas, TX 75275

SMU is best known for business, the performing arts, and an abundance of school spirit. Go-getter mentality is pervasive, and students benefit from internships and other opportunities in nearby Dallas. Picture-book campus on the city outskirts adds to its appeal. Methodist, but mainly in name.

Southern Methodist University is moving well beyond its long-standing characterization as a training ground for the business elite of Dallas. Admissions standards are on the rise, and recent years have brought an updated curriculum, a new residential model, and, in the words of one senior, "tons of new campus buildings." The highly regarded Cox School of Business sets the no-nonsense tone for SMU's success-driven academic climate. Although founded by what is now the United Methodist Church, SMU is nondenominational; less than 10 percent of students are Methodist and all faiths are welcomed.

SMU's well-landscaped campus is located in the toney suburb of University Park, located "five minutes from downtown Dallas and within 30 minutes of everything else," according to one student. Flower beds, fountains, and neatly trimmed lawns surround stately brick buildings, most of them collegiate Georgian. Dallas Hall, with its four-story rotunda, is the centerpiece. The Embrey Engineering Building is one of the first academic buildings in the nation to be designed and constructed to LEED Gold Standards of environmental design. The Meadows Museum houses one of the finest collections of Spanish art outside Spain, and SMU is the only private college in the country to host a presidential library on its main campus, the George W. Bush Presidential Center.

> **"Some of my professors have practically been my life coaches."**

Students describe the academic climate as serious but supportive. "While the classes are extremely challenging and push your intellectual limits, the professors want students to excel," explains an electrical engineering major. General education requirements are laid out in the four-pronged University Curriculum, which combines coursework in a range of disciplines with hands-on experiences. The Office of Engaged Learning supports students who wish to undertake capstone-level projects on campus or abroad, such as extended research, service projects, internships, and entrepreneurial start-ups; participants can apply for fellowships of up to $2,000.

Students hail the Cox School of Business (including its Caruth Institute for Entrepreneurship) and the Meadows School of the Arts, which turns out professional artists, actors, and singers, as SMU's strongest suits. The most popular field of study is economics, followed by finance, accounting, and marketing. Engineers have access to an extensive co-op program, thanks to the proximity of hundreds of high-tech companies, including AT&T and Texas Instruments, that have facilities in the Dallas area. The Tower Center for Political Studies focuses on international relations and comparative politics, while the Tate Lecture Series give students a

> "Most [students] come from upper-middle-class families, but you really do see the whole spectrum."

chance to interact with national and international figures, such as journalist Fareed Zakaria and actress Kathy Bates. The applied physiology and sport management program teaches the biological basis of health while offering the business skills needed in the health and fitness industries. Creative computing, an interdisciplinary major, combines theory and methodology from computer science, engineering, and the arts. As for the humanities, English and history are particularly strong, and SMU publishes *Southwest Review*, the third oldest continuously published literary quarterly in the nation. SMU was the first university in the South to offer a major in human rights.

SMU prides itself on small classes; 59 percent of undergraduate courses have fewer than 20 students. "Some of my professors have practically been my life coaches," says an advertising major. "They've helped me excel in classes and prepare for interviews. They've provided recommendation letters and answered my emails at two in the morning. They never stop caring for their students." Most classes are taught by full-time faculty, and teaching assistants provide extra help. The student-staffed Altshuler Learning Enhancement Center offers tutoring and workshops.

Freshmen have a variety of special programs available to them that "help students to gain experience and knowledge about the university and its programs," including "Mustang Corral, which is an off-campus retreat," explains one student. The Honors Program enables about 800 students to take seminars on topics not offered broadly in classes of 15 to 20 students. Study abroad programs take 28 percent of undergrads around the world; faculty-led options are available in 14 locations. Each year, 20 to 25 exceptional incoming students are named President's Scholars and

> "We still have a blast before home football games…and we have incredible school spirit."

awarded full-tuition scholarships as well as opportunities to study abroad and participate in an annual retreat in Taos. Employers in the Dallas area offer more than 4,400 internships and learning opportunities to SMU students every year.

A marketing major describes SMU students as passionate and driven to succeed, adding, "There's a big go-getter mentality all throughout campus." Forty-one percent of undergraduates are from the Lone Star State, and 9 percent come from outside of the U.S. A majority of undergrads (56 percent) graduated from private or parochial schools, and only 9 percent of incoming freshmen qualify for Pell Grants. Hispanics account for 11 percent of the student body, Asian Americans 6 percent, African Americans 5 percent, and multiracial students 4 percent. A senior reports that "most come from upper-middle-class families, but you really do see the whole spectrum across campus," and there is a "pretty good mix" of political views. SMU offers merit scholarships averaging $25,300, as well as 290 athletic scholarships in 17 sports.

(continued)

Admissions: (800) 323-0672
Email Address:
  ugadmission@smu.edu

Strong Programs:
Economics
Finance
Accounting
Marketing
Performing Arts
Engineering
Applied Physiology and Sport
   Management
Human Rights

The Tate Lecture Series give students a chance to interact with international figures, such as journalist Fareed Zakaria.

Fifty-four percent of undergrads live on campus; first- and second-year students are required to live in one of 11 Residential Commons living/learning communities, each with a resident faculty member, intended to integrate academic, residential, and social experiences. SMU Service House residents engage in community service in disadvantaged neighborhoods across Dallas. All residence halls are co-ed by floor, and options include single and double rooms, some with their own bathrooms. The traditional, all-you-can-eat meal plans include dining dollars that can be used at the two main dining halls and at on-campus Subway and Chick-fil-A outposts. "Now that I live off campus, I actually miss the food in the SMU dining halls," says a student. Campus security is said to be strong, and students praise the Not On My Campus campaign aimed at raising awareness of the issue of sexual assault.

When the weekend comes, the more than 200 student groups sponsor speakers and other diversions. "Social life at SMU is vibrant both on and off campus," says a sophomore. Thirty-five percent of the women join sororities, and 28 percent of the men pledge fraternities. "Greek organizations have off-campus parties, since SMU is technically a dry campus," notes a senior. Dallas has plenty to offer in terms of social life: "Whether it's exploring the Deep Ellum and Bishop Arts districts or going out in Uptown, we never get bored here," says a management major. Hundreds of students volunteer with more than 70 nonprofits in the greater Dallas area, and service trips over spring break are popular too. Highlights of the campus calendar include Perunapalooza, a birthday carnival in honor of the Mustang mascot (a pony). Students mark the end of the fall semester with the Celebration of Lights featuring holiday lights and carols at Dallas Hall. Favorite road trips are to Austin, with its abundance of restaurants, bars, and live music, and South Padre, Texas, a popular spring break spot with a great beach.

Football games are a big deal here—after all, this is Texas—and SMU students get riled up for the annual battle against Texas Christian University for possession of the Iron Skillet. For home games, SMU's answer to tailgating is Boulevarding, with lavish tents, family activities, music, and food on the main quad. When basketball season arrives, students camp out with their friends to get tickets, and "The Mob" spirit group packs into the student section of Moody Coliseum. The SMU Mustangs compete in the Division I American Athletic Conference with considerable success. Men's golf and women's cross-country, swimming and diving, and track and field are competitive. Twenty percent of students participate each year in the intramural program, which offers more than 30 different individual and team sporting activities.

"SMU is a relatively small school that has a big school feel," says a senior. "We still have a blast before home football games, we have big parties, and we have incredible school spirit." Most of all, "We care deeply about our academics." Although known for its striking campus and success-oriented students, SMU offers solid preprofessional training along with an active social life and ample opportunities to give back to the city of Dallas. The result is an environment where future industry moguls, performers, problem solvers, and liberal artists alike can find space to grow.

Overlaps

Vanderbilt, Texas Christian, University of Southern California, Wake Forest, University of Miami (FL), UT Austin, Texas A&M, Baylor

If You Apply To ›

Southern Methodist: Early decision I and II, early action, regular decision. SATs or ACTs: required (optional for applicants to music, theatre, dance, art, and film programs, who must audition or submit portfolio). No Subject Tests. Accepts the Common Application with supplement.

Southwestern University

1001 E. University Avenue, Georgetown, TX 78626

The oldest institution of higher education in Texas, Southwestern is one of its top liberal arts colleges. Compare to more conservative Austin College and much larger Trinity University. Southwestern prides itself on individual attention and down-to-earth friendliness, with emphasis on interdisciplinary and inquiry-based learning. Has now gone native and revived football after 30 years in the Texas athletic wilderness.

In a state known for political conservatism and an assumption that bigger is better, Southwestern University stands out like a monadnock. Small and agile, it pursues a flexible and innovative brand of teaching and learning in a culture where the liberal arts are not always appreciated. "You learn to express and defend your opinions," says one student. "I learned how to think."

Founded in 1840, five years before Texas became a state, Southwestern sits on 700 acres at the edge of the rolling Texas Hill Country, although the city of Austin has expanded to meet Georgetown. The Texas limestone buildings, built in the Romanesque style, date from the early 20th century, and there are plenty of lush lawns and towering oak trees. Southwestern's commitment to sustainability includes two LEED-certified buildings and an agreement with the city of Georgetown that allows it to use 100 percent wind power for the campus's electrical needs. Recent campus projects include a major, two-phase renovation of the Fondren-Jones Science Hall.

To graduate, Southwestern students must complete a First-Year Seminar and satisfy requirements in several liberal arts areas, as well as language and culture, social justice, fitness and recreational activity, and a capstone experience. All students participate in the Paideia program, which gives them a chance to explore interests that may fall outside their major; students pursue a particular theme, such as global health or gender identity, in multiple courses and thus come to see how the various disciplines are interconnected. A sociology and English double major explains, "It's nice to be able to get a taste of how others may see and understand the world in various other disciplines."

> "We are constantly being challenged to… apply [what we learn] to more difficult problems."

The most popular majors include psychology, communication studies, biology, and business, which is taught as one of the liberal arts. In the Sarofim School of Fine Arts, where pottery is a specialty, student work approaches graduate-level quality. Environmental studies and sociology are also strengths. Political science and STEM majors alike benefit from SU's proximity to Austin, the state capital and a hub of tech innovation. New interdisciplinary minors are available in animal science, data science, and health studies. The university offers seven preprofessional programs, among them pre-engineering, prelaw, and premedicine.

"We are constantly being challenged to take what we learn in class and apply it to more difficult problems," says a senior. Sixty-three percent of SU classes have fewer than 20 students, and professors are appreciated for their willingness to help students with course concepts and research opportunities. Academic support and career services are highly praised as well, from departmental student mentors, such as the SCI Guides in the natural sciences, to the comprehensive resources offered by the Office of Career Services, including one-on-one counseling, alumni panels, and campuswide internship and job fairs. "I definitely feel prepared for life after college because everything is a process that has been put in motion since I arrived my first semester," says a junior.

Website: www.southwestern.edu
Location: Suburban
Private
Total Enrollment: 1,363
Undergraduates: 1,363
Male/Female: 43/57
SAT Ranges: ERW 570–670, M 540–650
ACT Ranges: 23–29
Financial Aid: 99%
Pell Grant: 28%
Expense: Pr $
Student Loans: 58%
Average Debt: $ $ $ $
Applicants: 4,133
Accepted: 43%
Enrolled: 20%
Grad in 6 Years: 74%
Returning Freshmen: 86%
Academics: ✍ ✍ ✍ ½
Social: ☎ ☎ ☎
Q of L: ★ ★ ★
Admissions: (512) 863-1200
Email Address: admission@southwestern.edu

Strong Programs:
Psychology
Communication Studies
Biology
Business
Studio Art
Environmental Studies
Sociology

SU encourages undergraduate research (48 percent of students participate), and each year holds a symposium to showcase students' scholarly endeavors. The King Creativity Fund provides grants to support up to 20 "innovative and visionary projects" each academic year. Twenty-two percent of Southwestern's students choose to study abroad, and SU hosts faculty-led programs in England, Spain, Peru, and Argentina, plus a service-learning program in Jamaica. The university also sponsors an internship program in Washington, D.C., and an arts apprenticeship program in New York City.

Nearly nine out of 10 Southwestern students come from Texas, and many are the first in their families to go to college. The university is affiliated with the United Methodist Church, and 35 percent of students are Methodist. Hispanics are the largest minority group at SU, comprising 24 percent of the student body; African Americans add 5 percent, Asian Americans 3 percent, and multiracial students 5 percent. One percent come from foreign countries. Students describe a mix of conservative and liberal political views, and campus diversity has drawn attention recently. "The CDSJ (Coalition for Diversity and Social Justice) is a fantastic umbrella organization that has a place for everyone to get involved and be an activist on and off campus," says a computer science major. Twenty-eight percent of incoming freshmen qualify for the Pell Grant. Eligible students receive scholarships based on academic performance, averaging $21,500 annually; talent awards are also available for fine arts majors, though there are no athletic scholarships.

> "The CDSJ (Coalition for Diversity and Social Justice) is a fantastic umbrella organization."

Seventy-seven percent of SU students live in the residence halls, where the number of stars definitely improves as you get older—juniors and seniors usually get apartment-style facilities with their own bedrooms, bathrooms, and kitchens. "First-year dorms weren't glamorous," says one student, "but I loved everyone in my hall, including the RAs. We were a little family!" All freshmen participate in living/learning communities tied in with their First-Year Seminar. The central, all-you-can-eat Mabee Commons dining hall is said to need improvement, but students enjoy the nearby Cove's coffee bar and late-night grill. Students can also swipe their "Pirate cards" at pizzerias and other local merchants. Students generally feel safe on campus, and SU has launched a Coalition Against Sexual Violence to better inform the student body of issues relating to sexual misconduct.

Almost all the social life at Southwestern takes place on campus. "Wednesday, Friday, and Saturday nights are the main party nights, but there is always something going on," says one political science major. Southwestern has a strong Greek system, drawing 28 percent of the men and 23 percent of the women, "but you do not have to be Greek to have a fabulous social life," says a sociology major. Students 21 and older are permitted to consume alcohol in designated areas on campus. Annual traditions include the Soundwave concert and Late Night Breakfast, in which "faculty and staff serve students breakfast during finals week while karaoke and other fun stuff happens!"

> "Georgetown offers a lot of natural beauty."

Georgetown (population 70,000), the county seat, caters mainly to families, but things are getting more exciting thanks to the expanding bar and restaurant options, weekly farmers markets, and live music on Friday evenings. The city's historic downtown and the popular Blue Hole swimming area are both within walking distance of campus, and students enjoy bike trails along the San Gabriel River. "Georgetown offers a lot of natural beauty," says a communication major. Forty-six percent of students get involved in the community through service-learning and volunteer work. The bars and clubs of Austin's Sixth Street are just a half hour away, and San Antonio, College Station, Dallas, and Houston aren't that much farther.

All students participate in the Paideia program, which gives them a chance to explore interests that may fall outside their major.

SU hosts faculty-led study abroad programs in England, Spain, Peru, and Argentina, plus a service-learning program in Jamaica.

The Southwestern Pirates field 20 Division III varsity sports. The school is a member of the Southern Collegiate Athletic Conference; men's and women's golf are recent conference champions, and men's and women's tennis and women's volleyball are also competitive. The university reintroduced football in 2013, and in just four seasons the team claimed the conference title. Games against archrival Trinity in San Antonio always draw crowds. Sixty percent of students compete in 18 intramural and club sports, with basketball, dodgeball, flag football, and volleyball being the most popular.

With its emphasis on in-depth and student-centered learning, Southwestern is doing its best to push the frontiers of liberal arts instruction in the 21st century. "SU allows you to continue to grow and challenge yourself in a safe and accepting atmosphere," says a freshman. In a state where things tend to be huge and overwhelming, Southwestern University is out to show that good things can come in small packages.

If You Apply To ›

Southwestern: Early decision, early action, regular decision. SATs or ACTs: required. No Subject Tests. Accepts the Common Application with supplement.

Spelman College: See page 38.

Stanford University

Stanford, CA 94305-3005

If you're looking for an Eastern counterpart to Stanford, think Duke with a touch of MIT mixed in. Stanford's big-time athletics, preprofessional feel, and laid-back atmosphere set it apart from Ivy League competitors. In contrast to the hurly-burly of Bay Area rival Berkeley, Stanford's aura is upscale, spacious, and green. Bring your bike and a pair of sunglasses, and leave your ego behind.

You might think the only difference between Stanford and the Ivy League is a couple hundred extra sunny days each year. You'd be wrong. From the red-tiled roofs to the lush greenery and California vibe, Stanford is a world away from the Gothic intellectual culture of the Ivies. Virtually all the great Eastern universities began as places to ponder human existence and the meaning of life, with European institutions as their models. Stanford, by contrast, built its academic reputation around science and engineering, fields characterized by American ingenuity, and only later cultivated excellence in the humanities and social sciences. Stanford is, without a doubt, the nation's first great "American" university. Now the most selective university in the country—turning down 19 of every 20 applicants—Stanford has begun to increase the size of its entering classes and intends to expand its dormitories and number of faculty proportionately until it reaches a new comfort level.

The differences between Stanford and other institutions it competes against for the country's top high school seniors are evident everywhere, from the architecture to the curriculum. The school's mission-style buildings look outward to the world at large, rather than inward to ivy-covered courtyards. And unlike its Colonial-era

(continued)

Accepted: 5%
Enrolled: 82%
Grad in 6 Years: 94%
Returning Freshmen: 98%
Academics: ✏ ✏ ✏ ✏ ✏
Social: ☎ ☎ ☎ ☎
Q of L: ★ ★ ★ ★ ★
Admissions: (650) 723-2091
Email Address: admission@
    stanford.cdu

Strong Programs:
Computer Science
Engineering
Human Biology
Management Science and
    Engineering
Public Policy
Communication
Biology

*Stanford is the most
selective university
in the country—
turning down 19 of
every 20 applicants.*

predecessors, Stanford—founded in 1885 by Leland and Jane Stanford in memory of their son Leland Jr.—has been co-ed from the beginning. During its centennial, the school became the first U.S. university to successfully launch a billion-dollar capital campaign; today Stanford's endowment is $26.5 billion. Some architectural critics say the campus looks like the world's biggest Mexican restaurant, even though Frederick Law Olmsted, designer of New York City's Central Park, planned many of the buildings. The campus stretches from the foothills of the Santa Cruz Mountains to the edge of Palo Alto in the heart of Silicon Valley, smack in the middle of earthquake country. The campus is nationally recognized as "bicycle friendly" and is outfitted with 12 miles of bike lanes, 19,000 bike parking spaces, and free bike repair stations. Recent campus projects include the renovation of the Sapp Center for Science Teaching and Learning.

Stanford requires students to complete one course in Thinking Matters and 11 in a series called Ways of Thinking/Ways of Doing, which includes aesthetic and interpretive inquiry, social inquiry, scientific analysis, formal reasoning, applied quantitative reasoning, engaging diversity, ethical reasoning, and creative expression. Stanford also requires writing and rhetoric courses and one year of a foreign language. More than 200 optional, small-group Introductory Seminars are available to freshmen and sophomores, covering topics like The Aesthetics of Data and Human Rights Advocacy, in which about half of students enroll; one student credits these courses with helping freshmen "develop relationships with really engaging professors."

> "People are always
> working together on
> projects and assignments."

Computer science is the most popular major on campus, followed by engineering, human biology, and management science and engineering. The recently created CS+X program allows students to complete one of 14 joint degrees that combine computer science with disciplines in the humanities, such as foreign languages, history, linguistics, and philosophy. Stanford has also developed a spate of interdisciplinary programs, and a major in aeronautics and astronautics is now available. The Haas Center for Public Service offers more than 130 service-learning courses in a wide range of disciplines, while the communications department offers paid positions at various California media outlets. The Stanford Hopkins Marine Station is located on a mile of coastland in Pacific Grove, next to the Monterey Bay Aquarium, and offers courses in marine and biological sciences.

Don't let Stanford's California location fool you into thinking studying is optional—it's more like a full-time job. "People are always working together on projects and assignments. This might be because it is intense, and many students do take on a heavy workload," one student says. Students sometimes compare themselves to ducks: they look peaceful on the surface, but they're paddling like mad underneath. Stanford's faculty ranks among the best in the nation, with impeccable credentials, and most departments boast a nationally known name or two. Class sizes are generally small, with 68 percent enrolling fewer than 20 students, and 93 percent are taught by faculty, as opposed to graduate students. "Overall, professors do seem to care about the students. They are definitely accessible, almost all having open office hours," says one computer science major. Befitting its location in Silicon Valley, Stanford is pioneering the use of mobile technologies, including replacing paper textbooks with tablet-based digital ones.

> "People are a bit quirky, but
> everyone is generally happy
> and easy to get along with."

For students who are inclined to study abroad, programs are offered at Stanford's campus in Cape Town, South Africa, as well as several other locations around the globe, including Australia, Chile, Japan, and Germany. Fifty-one percent of each graduating class takes advantage of these programs. Closer to home, the Stanford-in-Washington program allows 60 students to live, study, and intern in the nation's capital each quarter, and a similar program is offered in New York City. The Summer Research College is designed to create community among undergraduates engaged in full-time summer research on campus, and there are three honors programs. Three-quarters of students undertake independent study projects with faculty. For those seeking additional academic support, the Schwab Learning Center—named after alum Charles Schwab—offers services for students with learning disabilities and ADHD.

Stanford students may be Olympic champions and future Rhodes scholars, but students say there isn't a sense of elitism on campus. One notes, "People are a bit quirky, but everyone is generally happy and easy to get along with." Fifty-nine percent of undergraduates attended public high school. Thirty-two percent are from California, while international students represent 9 percent of the student population. Minority enrollment is well above average, with Asian Americans accounting for 22 percent of the student body, Hispanics 16 percent, African Americans 7 percent, and multiracial students 10 percent. Students on this liberal campus are keen to be heard, and recent hot topics include "divestment from Israel, divestment from fossil fuels, and race relations," according to one senior. Admissions are need-blind, and the university guarantees to meet the full demonstrated financial need of every domestic admit. Academic scholarships are based on need (meaning no merit awards), and Stanford has eliminated parent contributions for families with annual incomes below $65,000. The university also awards more than 460 athletic scholarships annually in 34 sports.

> **"There is a very innovative and individualistic personality that is also a collective culture on campus."**

The CS+X program allows students to complete one of 14 joint degrees that combine computer science with disciplines in the humanities.

Freshmen must live on campus, and Stanford guarantees housing for four years; 93 percent of students stay on campus, in part because of the lack of affordable off-campus options in extraordinarily expensive Silicon Valley. As students gain seniority, a lottery system decides where they'll live. "Junior year I lived in an old faculty mansion for 30 students that had a Thai chef," one student says. The multimillion-dollar Governor's Corner complex includes all-oak fixtures, homey rooms with views of the foothills, microwave ovens in the kitchenettes, and Italian leather sofas in the lounges. Dorm dwellers must sign up for a meal plan. "Campus security is quite good. We have an AlertSU program that texts emergency messages to the school whenever there is any sort of security violation, and Stanford is extremely well-lit at night," says a freshman.

Ninety-three percent of students stay on campus, in part because of the lack of affordable off-campus options in Silicon Valley.

Like most things at Stanford, social life and activities vary a great deal, although most take place on campus, with a constant lineup of events and performances. Greek organizations claim 19 percent of the men and 27 percent of the women, and provide their share of happy hours and weekend bashes, which are open to all. Underage drinking happens, but is kept under control. As one freshman puts it, "Party culture is not exclusively Greek, and social life is not exclusively partying." As tradition goes, Full Moon on the Quad occurs at the first full moon of the fall quarter, during which freshmen can become "true Stanford students" by kissing a senior at midnight on the quad. The Viennese Ball is a February event that may make you wish you'd taken ballroom dancing lessons, and Halloween finds students partying at the Mausoleum, the Stanfords' final resting place.

> **"Party culture is not exclusively Greek, and social life is not exclusively partying."**

Palo Alto "has a few fun hangouts and is slightly overpriced," a political science major says, and students love to seek refuge in the outdoors—nearby hills are perfect for jogging and biking. Trips to the Sierra Nevada mountains (four hours away) or to the Pacific Coast (45 minutes) are popular, as are jaunts to San Francisco, Los Angeles, or the Napa Valley.

The annual football contest against archrival Cal (Berkeley) is dubbed the "Big Game."

Stanford has a proud athletic tradition. In 2018, Stanford took home its 24th consecutive Directors' Cup, which recognizes the best overall collegiate athletic program in the country. Four Cardinal teams—men's and women's soccer, women's swimming and diving, and women's tennis—won national championships in the 2017–18 season. Men's and women's basketball consistently make it to at least the Sweet 16. The baseball team has been to the College World Series, and the football team has become a powerhouse. The annual contest against archrival Cal (Berkeley) is dubbed the "Big Game." The marching band proudly revels in its raucous irreverence, to the delight of students and the dismay of conservative types. For those not inclined to varsity play, Stanford offers 31 club sports and 20 intramural activities, and its vast sports complex includes 26 tennis courts, two gymnasiums, a stadium, an 18-hole golf course, and four swimming pools.

Stanford University's sunny demeanor and infectious West Coast optimism offer an appealing alternative to the gloom and gray weather that seem to hang over some of its East Coast counterparts, with the same high-caliber academics and deep athletic traditions that have made them great. "Stanford is hard to fit into a box," muses one student, "but there is a very innovative and individualistic personality that is also a collective culture on campus."

If You Apply To ›

Stanford: Single choice early action, regular decision. SATs or ACTs: required. Subject Tests: optional. Accepts the Common Application with supplement.

State University of New York

As the largest university system in the world, the State University of New York provides its 425,000 students with a vast landscape of educational opportunities—both figuratively and literally. Encompassing 64 widely dispersed campuses and 21,000 acres of property, SUNY's staggering physical presence is exceeded only by the scope of its academic offerings. SUNY universities have long been among the most affordable of public universities, and now they are even more so. Under New York State's Excelsior Scholarship program, the first of its kind in the U.S., in-state students from households earning up to $125,000 qualify for free tuition at the state's two- and four-year colleges and universities.

The statistics of SUNY (pronounced "SOOney") are awesome. The university has an annual operating budget of billions, greater than the gross national product of many countries and larger than the budget of more than a dozen American states. It has more than 400,000 undergraduates, about 4,400 undergraduate academic programs, and 33,000 faculty members, and it maintains more than 2,200 buildings. Every year it awards approximately 95,000 degrees (80,000 of which are undergraduate), from associate to Ph.D., in thousands of different academic fields. And—you're not going to believe this one—it has nearly three million living graduates.

Such figures are all the more remarkable considering that until 1948, New York had no state university at all. That year, the legislature created the State University around a cluster of 29 institutions, the best of which focused on the training of teachers, to handle the flow of returning World War II veterans. But a "gentleman's agreement" not to compete with the state's private colleges (which for generations had enjoyed a monopoly on higher education in New York) hindered SUNY's movement into the liberal arts. Not until Nelson A. Rockefeller became governor in 1960 and made the expansion of the university his major priority did SUNY begin its dramatic growth. SUNY has now ripened into a network of four "university centers," 13 arts and sciences colleges, seven technological colleges, 11 statutory and specialized institutions, and 29 locally sponsored community colleges.

Despite this seeming diversity, leaders of the SUNY system are making concerted efforts to improve diversity among the students and to make students of all backgrounds feel welcome. The establishment in 2007 of the Office of Diversity, Equity, and Inclusion has helped to increase minority enrollment, but the student body is still nearly 60 percent white. SUNY's definition of diversity is sweeping and covers not only race and ethnicity but also religion, sexual orientation, gender identity and expression, age, and socioeconomic status. The system has enacted numerous programs aimed at increasing the retention and graduation rates of underrepresented students.

Prospective students apply directly to the SUNY unit they seek to attend. Fifty-one of the colleges use a "common form" application that enables a prospective student to apply to as many as four SUNY campuses at the same time. The central administration runs a SUNY Admissions Assistance Service that helps rejected students find places at other campuses. Students who earn associate degrees at community or other two-year colleges are guaranteed the chance to continue their education at a four-year institution, though not necessarily at their first choice. The level of selectivity varies widely. Most community colleges guarantee admission to any local high school student, but the university centers, as well as some specialized colleges, are among the most competitive public institutions in the nation. Undergraduates at all liberal arts colleges and university centers pay the same tuition, but the rates at community colleges vary (and are lower). Out-of-state students, who make up only 6 percent of SUNY students, pay about double the amount of in-state tuition. Annual costs at institutions like SUNY–University at Albany have traditionally been well below those at such hoary and prestigious publicly supported flagship campuses as UC Berkeley and the University of Michigan, but they are now slightly above the national average.

Mainly for political reasons, the State University of New York chose not to follow the model of other states and build a single flagship campus the likes of an Ann Arbor, Madison, or Chapel Hill. Instead, it created the four university centers with undergraduate, graduate, and professional schools and research facilities in each corner of the state. When they were created in the 1960s, each one hoped to become fully comprehensive, but there has been a certain degree of specialization from the beginning. Albany is strongest in education and public policy, Binghamton is best known for undergraduate arts and sciences, and Stony Brook is noted for its hard sciences. Buffalo, formerly a private university, maintains a strong reputation in the life sciences and geography and comes the closest of any of the four to being a fully comprehensive university.

Critics say that the decision to forgo a flagship campus guarantees that the system won't achieve national prominence, and the lack of big-time Division I football and prestigious Ph.D. programs has affected SUNY's reputation as well. Still, many insist that somewhere in the labs and libraries of these four university centers are lurking the Nobel Prize winners of this century.

The 13 colleges of arts and sciences likewise vary widely in size and character. They range from the 25,000-student University at Buffalo, whose 1,100-acre campus reflects the urban flavor of the state's second-largest city, to the small, rural College at Geneseo. Still others are suburban campuses, such as Purchase, which specializes in the visual and performing arts, and Old Westbury, which began as an experimental institution to serve minority students, older women, and others who have been "bypassed" by more traditional institutions. With the exception of Purchase and Old Westbury, which were started from scratch, the four-year colleges are all former teachers' colleges that have, for the most part, successfully made the transition into liberal arts colleges on the small, private New England model.

SUNY's technical and specialized colleges, while not enjoying the prominence of the colleges of arts and sciences, serve the demand for vocational training in a variety of two- and four-year programs. Five of the seven agricultural and technical colleges—Alfred State, Canton, Cobleskill, Delhi, and Morrisville—are concerned primarily with agriculture but also have programs in engineering, nursing, medical technology, data processing, and business administration. Farmingdale offers the widest range of programs, from ornamental horticulture to aerospace technology. The SUNY Polytechnic Institute, created in 2014 through a merger of two technical schools, offers degrees in nanoscience and nanoengineering at its campuses in Albany and Utica–Rome.

Four of the five statutory schools are at Cornell University—agriculture and life sciences, human ecology, industrial and labor relations, and veterinary medicine—while the internationally known College of Ceramics is housed at Alfred University, another private university. The six specialized colleges consist of the College of Environmental Science and Forestry at Syracuse, the Maritime College at Fort Schuyler in the Bronx, the College of Optometry in New York City, the Upstate Medical University, the Downstate Medical Center, and the Fashion Institute of Technology, whose graduates are gobbled up as fast as they emerge by employers in the Manhattan Garment District.

The 29 community colleges have traditionally been the stepchildren of the system, but the combination of rampant vocationalism and the soaring cost of education elsewhere is rapidly turning them into the most robust members of the family. Students once looked to the community colleges for terminal degrees that could be readily applied in the marketplace. Now, a growing number of students who otherwise would have been packed off to a four-year college are saving money by staying home for the first two years and then transferring to a four-year college—or even a university center—to get their bachelor's degrees.

Following are full-length descriptions of SUNY–Purchase College, which is the liberal arts institution best known beyond New York's borders, SUNY–College at Geneseo, and the four university centers (the University at Albany, Binghamton University, the University at Buffalo, and Stony Brook University).

SUNY–University at Albany

1400 Washington Avenue, Albany, NY 12222

Like the rest of the SUNY system, University at Albany is much better than its relative anonymity would suggest. Strong in anything related to public policy, including criminal justice and social welfare. Study abroad programs in Europe and Asia are also strengths. Only 10 percent of undergrads are from outside New York. Campus is a living reminder of just how bad 1960s architecture could be.

Website: www.albany.edu
Location: Suburban
Public
Total Enrollment: 14,800
Undergraduates: 12,703
Male/Female: 49/51
SAT Ranges: ERW 500–600, M 500–590
ACT Ranges: 22–26
Financial Aid: 69%
Pell Grant: 45%
Expense: Pub $
Student Loans: 67%
Average Debt: $
Applicants: 24,877
Accepted: 54%
Enrolled: 21%
Grad in 6 Years: 65%
Returning Freshmen: 83%
Academics: ✎ ✎ ✎ ✎
Social: ☎ ☎ ☎
Q of L: ★ ★ ★
Admissions: (518) 442-5435
Email Address:
ugadmissions@albany.edu

Strong Programs:
Public Policy and Management
Social Welfare
Criminal Justice

Founded in 1844 to train teachers, UAlbany offers a bevy of outstanding programs in arts and sciences, business administration, and preprofessional programs, and it is placing increased emphasis on technology. Study abroad is solid too, but—consistent with its location in the state capital—it's the university's public policy programs that truly shine.

Designed by Edward Durrell Stone, who also designed the Kennedy Center and Lincoln Center, UAlbany's main uptown campus is stark, modern, and suburban. Almost all the original academic buildings are clustered in the center of the campus, while students are housed in symmetrically situated quads so similar in appearance that it usually takes a semester to figure out which one is yours. (Hint: the quads are named for periods in New York history—Indian, Dutch, Colonial, State, and Freedom—and progress clockwise around the campus. Got it?) The downtown campus primarily houses the university's public policy programs, and the health sciences campus is home to public health programs and research centers. A spate of construction projects has changed the face of the uptown campus over the past decade, and a new, $180 million Emerging Technology and Entrepreneurship Complex, located adjacent to the main campus, is expected to open in 2021.

"There are some superstar professors and a bad apple here and there."

UAlbany's general education program consists of 30 credits of distribution requirements, through which students must demonstrate competency in advanced writing, oral discourse, information literacy, and critical thinking. In addition, all freshmen take a required introductory seminar.

For the career-minded, most of UAlbany's preprofessional programs are among the best of any SUNY branch. Students in the public policy and management, social welfare, and criminal justice programs may take advantage of their proximity to the state government to participate in internships. Psychology, communication, and economics are popular majors, and undergrads are clamoring for admittance to the university's business administration program, which is especially strong in accounting. Students can sign up for one of 30 B.A./M.A. programs or opt for a six-year law degree in conjunction with UAlbany Law School. The New

York State Writers Institute is the least traditional of UAlbany's offerings and has enhanced the university's reputation in creative writing. The university recently established two new colleges: the College of Emergency Preparedness, Homeland Security, and Cybersecurity (the first of its kind) and the College of Engineering and Applied Sciences.

The academic climate is challenging and courses tend to be demanding. Classes can be large, but a third enroll fewer than 20 students. Students form study groups to help one another through the coursework, and professors are always available to offer support. "The quality of teaching is excellent overall," a physics major says. "There are some superstar professors and a bad apple here and there, but usually very good instructors." Qualified students can take part in the Honors College, which allows freshmen and sophomores to enroll in up to six introductory courses that have been designed by distinguished faculty. The courses emphasize research, service learning, and a creative component. Senior honors students design and complete a yearlong research or creative project. About 6 percent of students take advantage of UAlbany's superior offerings in foreign study, which include more than 130 programs in 40 countries, plus hundreds of other options available through the SUNY system and other approved providers.

According to a sophomore, "A great many students come from New York City and Long Island, and it can be difficult for western and upstate New Yorkers as well as out-of-state students to fit in." Just 5 percent of undergraduates come from states outside New York, and another 5 percent come from foreign countries. African Americans comprise 19 percent of the student body, Hispanics 17 percent, Asian Americans 8 percent, and multiracial students 3 percent. "This campus is friendly and welcoming of individuals of every race and sexual orientation," says a sociology major. UAlbany makes available merit scholarships, averaging $4,100, and 181 athletic scholarships in 17 sports. Forty-five percent of first-year students are Pell-eligible. Thanks to New York State's Excelsior Scholarship program, in-state residents whose annual household income does not exceed $125,000 qualify for free tuition.

Fifty-six percent of students live in university housing; freshmen and sophomores are required to live in dorms, where the rooms are described as small but "satisfactory." Each floor is divided into four- to six-person suites. Living/learning communities allow incoming freshmen who share similar interests or majors to live together in the same residence hall and take some courses together. Many students move off campus because "the transportation system to and from campus is convenient and the cost of apartments is as cheap or cheaper than living on campus," explains a junior. Students on the main campus take their meals at the Indian or State quads or at the recently remodeled Campus Center, while most downtowners live and eat at Alumni Quad. "The Advocacy Center for Sexual Violence is a fantastic resource for students and is quite effective," says a sophomore.

"Our school has a vibrant social life on and off campus," says a senior. "There are multiple clubs and events on campus, and downtown Albany also has a good social scene, such as clubs and restaurants." Students have more than 250 clubs and organizations to choose from, many of which are involved in community service. While most people are serious about their work, a UAlbany weekend starts on Thursday night for many, with off-campus parties or barhopping about town. Students warn that alcohol policies forbidding underage drinking are strict and well enforced. Fraternities and sororities attract just 3 percent of the men and 3 percent of the women, yet they have become the school's main party-throwers. Parkfest is a huge all-school concert that brings in well-known as well as up-and-coming bands. The

(continued)

Psychology
Communication
Economics
Business Administration
Emergency Preparedness, Homeland Security, and Cybersecurity

A new, $180 million Emerging Technology and Entrepreneurship Complex is expected to open in 2021.

"This campus is friendly and welcoming of individuals of every race and sexual orientation."

The New York State Writers Institute is the least traditional of UAlbany's offerings and has enhanced the university's reputation in creative writing.

natural resources of the upstate region keep students busy skiing and hiking, and the Student Association owns and operates Dippikill, a wilderness retreat described as UAlbany's "own little Walden" in the Adirondacks. Treks to Montreal and Saratoga are also popular.

As for varsity sports, most Great Danes teams play in the Division I America East Conference. The men's and women's indoor and outdoor track and field teams have dominated the conference, claiming dozens of championships in recent years. Men's and women's basketball, lacrosse, and soccer are also highly competitive. Intramurals and club sports engender a great deal of student enthusiasm, and participation numbers in the thousands.

The University at Albany is not the concrete, sterile diploma mill it may appear to be. It's a place of opportunity for those willing to put in the hours and hard work. As one veteran cautions, "You can find an outlet here for even the most obscure interest, but this is not a school that will educate you when you're not looking."

Overlaps

SUNY–Binghamton, SUNY–Plattsburgh, SUNY–Stony Brook, SUNY–Buffalo, SUNY–Polytechnic Institute, College of Saint Rose, Union, SUNY–Geneseo

If You Apply To ›

SUNY–Albany: Early action, regular decision. SATs or ACTs: required. No Subject Tests. Accepts the Common Application with supplement.

SUNY–Binghamton University

BEST BUY

P.O. Box 6001, Binghamton, NY 13902-6000

If 100,000 screaming fans on a Saturday afternoon tickles your fancy, head 200 miles southwest to Penn State. Binghamton has become one of the premier public universities in the Northeast because of its outstanding academics and commitment to undergraduates. It is writing the rules on how to integrate global awareness and international experiences into undergraduate study.

Website: www.binghamton.edu
Location: Suburban
Public
Total Enrollment: 15,434
Undergraduates: 13,337
Male/Female: 51/49
SAT Ranges: ERW 640–711, M 650–720
ACT Ranges: 28–31
Financial Aid: 74%
Pell Grant: 28%
Expense: Pub $
Student Loans: 51%
Average Debt: $ $
Applicants: 33,467
Accepted: 40%
Enrolled: 20%
Grad in 6 Years: 82%
Returning Freshmen: 91%

Binghamton University offers a private-school experience at a public-school price, even for out-of-staters. With more than 300 clubs and an emphasis on small classes—87 percent of those taken by undergraduates have fewer than 50 students—it's no wonder that students who apply here are also considering schools such as Cornell and NYU. Binghamton offers an intellectually challenging environment with an emphasis on global experiences, including study abroad opportunities in more than 100 countries, area studies programs that focus on specific regions of the world, and the unique Languages Across the Curriculum program. "The biggest complaint," muses one student, "is the one thing that no one can change: the weather."

Binghamton's campus sits on 930 acres of open grassy space and includes a nature preserve, trails, fountains, and a pond. The oldest buildings date from 1958, so the prevailing architectural style is modern and "functional." Some students say that, from the air, the circular campus bears a striking resemblance to the human brain, but administrators say that's merely a coincidence. A slew of recent renovations and construction, including two residential communities, science and technology buildings, and a major renovation of the University Union, is giving the campus a more up-to-date feel. A new, eight-acre Health Sciences Campus, located a short drive from the main campus, includes the new School of Pharmacy and Pharmaceutical Sciences building and plans for a nursing and health sciences building.

Students apply to one of the university's five schools with undergraduate programs: the Decker School of Nursing, the Harpur College of Arts and Sciences, the College of Community and Public Affairs, the School of Management, and the Thomas Watson School of Engineering and Applied Science (named for the founder of IBM). Regardless of the school they choose, students face the same general education requirements, which span five thematic areas: language and communication, creating a global vision, sciences and mathematics, aesthetics and humanities, and physical activity and wellness. All undergraduates must complete one of the global interdependence (or "G") courses offered in all departments as part of the effort to equip students with "a basic understanding of the complex dimensions of contemporary global issues." The Discovery program provides freshmen with peer mentors and assistance in exploring experiential learning opportunities and career paths.

Popular majors include integrative neuroscience, psychology, economics, biological sciences, accounting, and engineering; the minor in global studies is also well regarded. More than 50 combined bachelor's/master's degree programs are available, and the pharmacy school now offers early acceptance to its Pharm.D. program to select top achievers. Students have the option to design their own majors via the Individualized Major Program in Harpur College. Binghamton's academic reputation is enhanced by a tough grading policy, which includes pluses and minuses as well as straight letter grades, and Fs on the transcripts of failing students rather than no credit. "Students are usually self-motivated and cooperative," says a sophomore. "Beating the test is usually more important than beating other students." According to a biology major, "There are some great teachers here and some not so great. All faculty members, however, have made themselves very accessible."

> "The biggest complaint is the one thing that no one can change: the weather."

Binghamton operates student exchanges with universities around the world and directly sponsors more than 40 study abroad programs in locations as diverse as the UK, Costa Rica, India, Ghana, South Korea, and Australia. "Study abroad at Binghamton is huge!" says an English major. Sixteen percent of students study abroad at some point in their undergraduate careers. Undergraduate research is also emphasized here (58 percent of students participate), and the invitation-only Freshman Research Immersion program involves enriched courses, taught by teams of faculty from multiple STEM disciplines, that incorporate authentic research experiences for outstanding freshmen. Faculty-supervised independent research, often culminating in a senior honors thesis, is common in Harpur College. The Binghamton University Scholars Program is a four-year honors program offering special seminars and leadership training to exceptional students, along with opportunities for experiential learning and junior- and senior-year capstone projects.

Although Binghamton offers a top-notch liberal arts and sciences education, word of its excellence has been slow to cross state lines: only 6 percent of undergraduates come from states outside of the Empire State, and another 7 percent hail from foreign nations. By other measures, though, Binghamton's student body is rather diverse: African Americans make up 5 percent of the total, Hispanics 11 percent, Asian Americans 14 percent, and multiracial students 2 percent. Twenty-eight percent of freshmen are Pell-eligible. "The biggest social and political issues on campus relate to social equality," a student reports. "Students at Binghamton are very proactive and we hold meetings that raise questions and provoke ideas." The university is taking several steps to create a more inclusive campus environment, including the recent establishment of an LGBTQ center. Binghamton offers merit scholarships and grants worth an average of $8,000, as well as 343 full or partial athletic scholarships

> "Many students volunteer with local groups, such as food drives and mentoring children."

(continued)

Academics: ✍ ✍ ✍ ✍ ½
Social: ☎ ☎ ☎
Q of L: ★ ★ ★ ★
Admissions: (607) 777-2171
Email Address: admit@ binghamton.edu

Strong Programs:
Integrative Neuroscience
Psychology
Economics
Biological Sciences
Accounting
Engineering
Global Studies

The Discovery program provides freshmen with peer mentors and assistance in exploring career paths.

in 21 sports. Under the state's Excelsior Scholarship program, New York residents from families earning $125,000 or less per year now qualify for free tuition.

Fifty-one percent of Binghamton's students live in the dorms, most of which have traditional double rooms with bathrooms down the hall or suites with common rooms and shared bathrooms. As one student explains, "Binghamton models the housing system after Oxford. We have five different residential communities, comprised of four to five buildings each. This makes a rather large university seem smaller and more comfortable." A sixth community consists of two apartment-style buildings for upperclassmen. Each community is led by a collegiate professor who helps link students' residential and academic experiences. Dining halls have plenty of options, including sushi. Students report feeling safe while trekking around the university grounds. "The university works hard to make our campus feel like a home; students have enough to worry about and safety does not need to be one of those things," a senior says.

When the weekend comes, Binghamton students know how to let off steam. On campus, a senior says, "The options are endless: bowling, concerts, performances, Late Nite Binghamton, sports, and much more." Late Nite Binghamton brings free movies, games, a coffee bar, and other nonalcoholic fun to campus, from 8 p.m. until 1 a.m. every Friday and Saturday. Frat parties occur off campus; 14 percent of the men and 11 percent of the women go Greek. One student emphasizes that Greek Life is "not something that defines you at this school." While some underage students manage to find alcohol, any caught violating the school's policy "will be taken care of accordingly," says a senior. Annual campus traditions include Stepping on the Coat during the Spring Fling carnival (to celebrate the arrival of warm weather) and Picnic in the Park, the annual senior barbecue.

> "Study abroad at Binghamton is huge!"

Binghamton itself is "far from the most exciting place on earth, but the community is still alive and has its own distinct pulse," according to a biomedical engineering major. The downtown area offers restaurants and bars, and "many students volunteer with local groups, such as food drives and mentoring children," says a nursing major. Popular road trips include Ithaca, for parties at Ithaca College and Cornell, and Syracuse, for Destiny USA, as well as Cortland and Oneonta, about an hour away by car. The toughest part about going away may be finding a parking space when you return, as permits currently outnumber spaces by about three to one.

Binghamton teams compete in Division I, but the school doesn't field a football squad. As a result, perhaps the most significant rivalry is with Cornell in men's lacrosse. In recent years, women's volleyball and softball, along with men's cross-country, tennis, and baseball, have brought home America East Conference championships. Binghamton's debate team is among the best in the nation, and computer science students excel in the FAA National Design Competition. Intramurals, club sports, and fitness programs attract about 80 percent of the student body.

With a four-year graduation rate that is among the highest of any public university, Binghamton has a reputation for an excellent education at a reasonable price that continues to draw smart New Yorkers to its vibrant and growing campus. Despite the hubbub of city life, the university maintains a cozy feel. Says one happy senior, "When you walk on the campus, you instantly feel at home and a huge sense of camaraderie."

Six residential communities are led by a collegiate professor who helps link students' residential and academic experiences.

Binghamton's debate team is among the best in the nation.

Overlaps

Clemson, Miami (OH), UC Santa Barbara, UC Santa Cruz, William and Mary, Cornell University, NYU, Boston University

If You Apply To ›

SUNY–Binghamton: Early action, regular decision. SATs or ACTs: required. Subject Tests: optional. Accepts the Common Application with supplement.

SUNY–University at Buffalo

15 Capen Hall, Buffalo, NY 14214

Glamorous it may not be, but the University at Buffalo offers solid programs in everything from business and engineering to geography and English. The majority of students come from Western New York and New York City, and a high percentage commute from home. The largest of the SUNY campuses and the most academically comprehensive, UB is slowly building visibility with bigtime sports.

As part of the mammoth State University of New York system, the University at Buffalo is working hard to ensure it gets noticed. Very few universities share its strength in medicine, engineering, and computer science, and UB is one of the world's leading supercomputer sites. Its resources are large enough to warrant three campuses: North, South, and Downtown. In addition to the sciences, the former private university offers strong professional schools. Students interested in pharmacy find Buffalo has the only accredited school in the SUNY system. "As large as we are, we have a very diverse and welcoming atmosphere," says a senior.

The North Campus of the University at Buffalo, home to most undergraduate programs, stretches across 1,100 acres in the suburbs just outside the city line and boasts buildings designed by world-renowned architects such as I. M. Pei. Meanwhile, the South Campus, along Main Street, favors collegiate ivy-covered buildings and is the home of the schools of architecture, pharmacy, and public health, as well as UB's highly rated dentistry program. The university provides connecting bus service—known as the UB Stampede—between the North and South campuses. The academically oriented student body spends plenty of time in UB's six main libraries, which are, for the most part, comfortable and well stocked at more than four million volumes. The university continues building and renovating at a steady pace and recently completed work on an extensive, state-of-the-art new campus for its medical school in Downtown Buffalo, in the heart of Buffalo's expanding medical corridor.

> **"As large as we are, we have a very diverse and welcoming atmosphere."**

UB's general education program aims to provide cohesion to the undergraduate experience. Components include a small-group UB Seminar for all new students; required coursework in diversity, writing, math, and natural sciences; pathways that allow students to explore interests thematically; and a capstone e-portfolio aimed at integrating their learning. "First-year seminars and classes help make the college transition a successful and enjoyable one," says a sociology major. The engineering and business management schools are nationally prominent, and architecture is solid. Occupational and physical therapy programs are also quite good, while the English department is notable for its emphasis on poetry. Well-known poets visit the campus frequently, and students not only compose and read poetry, but study the art of performing it as well. French, physiology, geography, and music are well regarded, but other humanities vary in quality. The most popular majors are psychology, engineering, business administration/marketing, and social sciences. The university offers more than 40 combined degrees (such as a five-year business administration B.S./M.B.A.) and numerous interdisciplinary majors, as well as opportunities for self-designed majors. Seven percent of undergrads study abroad, choosing from more than 80 UB-sponsored programs and hundreds of other options available through the SUNY system.

Students agree that the academic atmosphere in most disciplines at UB is competitive. "Success through hard work and innovative thinking is really stressed,"

Website: www.buffalo.edu
Location: Suburban
Public
Total Enrollment: 25,428
Undergraduates: 19,316
Male/Female: 58/42
SAT Ranges: ERW 560–640,
   M 580–670
ACT Ranges: 24–28
Financial Aid: 69%
Pell Grant: 33%
Expense: Pub $ $
Student Loans: 45%
Average Debt: N/A
Applicants: 28,088
Accepted: 57%
Enrolled: 26%
Grad in 6 Years: 75%
Returning Freshmen: 87%
Academics: ✍ ✍ ✍ ✍
Social: ☎ ☎
Q of L: ★ ★
Admissions: (716) 645-6900
Email Address:
   ub-admissions@buffalo.edu

Strong Programs:
Psychology
Engineering
Business and Marketing
Social Sciences
Health Sciences
Computer Science
Occupational and Physical
   Therapy
English

says an occupational therapy major. "You are measured against your peers in many classes and labs." Twenty-three percent of courses have more than 50 students, and class size has been a challenge, especially for first-years. At a school where graduate education and research get lots of the attention, the faculty are often experts in their field, but, an international business major says, "Students oftentimes do not build relationships with professors." Given the sheer size of the school and the multitude of opportunities, a junior says, "It's easy to get lost or confused." UB's Finish in 4 program seeks to alleviate these challenges and help students graduate in four years, in part by providing special advising and expanding course availability. Students say the career services office is the most helpful of UB's student support services. Students accepted into the UB Honors College enjoy smaller classes, priority class registration, faculty mentors, and an emphasis on community service.

"Students like to be involved but at the same time are very studious," says one senior. "They also like to party." Eighty-five percent hail from New York State, and

> **"Students like to be involved but at the same time are very studious."**

13 percent come from nations outside the U.S. African Americans account for 8 percent of the student body, Hispanics 7 percent, Asian Americans 15 percent, and multiracial students 2 percent. The campus is socioeconomically diverse as well, with 33 percent of entering first-years qualifying for Pell Grants. UB's considerable efforts in increasing awareness of diversity include the Intercultural and Diversity Center and the Office of Equity, Diversity, and Inclusion. Campus politics tend to lean left. Merit scholarships averaging $4,300 are offered to the top incoming students, and athletes compete for 411 athletic scholarships in 10 sports. In-state residents entering in fall 2019 qualify for free tuition under the state's Excelsior Scholarship program, provided their family's annual income is $125,000 or less.

Thirty-five percent of students live on campus in traditional residence halls or apartments for upper-class students; the rest commute from home or find apartments nearby. "The on-campus apartments are excellent but are quickly becoming pricier than more elegant and affordable off-campus housing," reports an electrical engineering major. Most of the on-campus dwellers reside on the North Campus. Gender-inclusive housing is available for students who wish to live in a mixed-gender housing environment. Students have a smorgasbord of dining choices ranging from three dining halls and two full-service restaurants to a variety of food courts and snack stops, including local favorite Tim Hortons. "Everything is clean, well organized, with great service, and fantastic food," cheers a junior. Students say security on campus is adequate and sexual assault cases are "definitely not taken lightly."

"Most of the social life is really split between on and off campus," explains a social sciences major. School-sponsored events and activities organized by the more

> **"Oozefest is probably our number-one tradition."**

than 300 student organizations keep students busy during the week. The Greek scene is tiny; 2 percent of UB men and 2 percent of women participate.

Alcohol is allowed on campus for students 21 and over. Students tend to gravitate to downtown Buffalo on the weekends; Friday night happy hour centers on beer and the chicken wings that spread the fame of Buffalo cuisine. Also popular are the Albright-Knox Art Gallery, with its world-renowned collection of modern art, and the Triple-A baseball Bisons, who play downtown. The two major pro teams, the Buffalo Bills in football and the Sabres in hockey, are both top draws.

The winters are cold in Buffalo, but students can take refuge inside a series of enclosed elevated walkways that connect most of the North Campus academic buildings. The flip side is that the outlying areas of the city offer great skiing, skating, and snowmobiling—and the ski club even offers free rides to the slopes. Having a car might be a good idea, but students warn that parking can be a problem on campus.

Although most students are content to stay in Buffalo, those who want a change of scenery can drive to Niagara Falls, just a few minutes away, or to Rochester, Cleveland, or Toronto, where the drinking age is lower. "The best road trip is 10 minutes to Canada," says an anthropology and geology double major.

UB has been trying to enhance its visibility by getting its name on the sports pages. It is the only major SUNY unit to field a Division I football team. The Bulls men's and women's basketball teams are the most successful, recently winning Mid-American Conference titles and making NCAA tournament appearances. Men's and women's tennis and women's soccer are also competitive. School spirit is sometimes generated at the student union and UB's impressive sports complex, which boasts a 6,100-seat arena, squash and racquetball courts, and other amenities. Intramural sports are popular, especially soccer and Oozefest—a massive mud-volleyball tournament that draws students, faculty, staff, and alumni. "Oozefest is probably our number-one tradition," says a senior. "Tons of teams sign up, dress in costume, and start playing early in the morning."

At a university as large as UB, students find that they often have to take more initiative with their education, but students here say they appreciate UB's huge range of academic programs, research resources, social events, and people to meet. Yes, students are exposed to the long Buffalo winters, but they also get exposed to some top-notch professors. Says one satisfied senior, "UB is a school that provides people from all walks of life the opportunity to obtain a quality education and experience diversity firsthand."

If You Apply To ›

University at Buffalo: Early action, rolling admissions. SATs or ACTs: required. No Subject Tests. Accepts the Common Application with supplement.

SUNY–College at Geneseo

1 College Circle, Geneseo, NY 14454

Geneseo is a preferred option for New Yorkers who want the feel of a private liberal arts college at a public school price. It is similar in scale to Mary Washington and William and Mary in Virginia, smaller than Miami of Ohio. Offers business and education in addition to the liberal arts and sciences. Less than 5 percent of the students come from outside New York.

The SUNY–College at Geneseo offers a seriously academic environment at an affordable price. This public institution attracts high achievers who "tend to be friendly, liberal, and hardworking," says a junior. Responsive, attentive professors help compensate for the long winters and somewhat isolated location. Excellent preprofessional programs have been making it harder to win admission to this most bucolic campus of the State University of New York system.

Geneseo sits in the scenic Genesee Valley of western New York. Campus architecture ranges from Gothic to modern, and the surrounding community has been designated a National Historic Landmark Community. An elementary education major calls the town "small and inviting" and says the historic storefronts and nearby forests and mountains make for "beautiful scenery." Recent campus improvements include a new outdoor sports stadium and an extensively renovated social sciences building.

Website: www.geneseo.edu
Location: Small Town
Public
Total Enrollment: 5,409
Undergraduates: 5,363
Male/Female: 40/60
SAT Ranges: ERW 570–650, M 550–650
ACT Ranges: 24–29
Financial Aid: 75%
Pell Grant: 30%

Students look forward to the annual GREAT Day, a celebration of student research and creative work.

General education requirements include two courses each in the natural sciences, social sciences, and fine arts; one course each in Western humanities, non-Western traditions, U.S. history, and numeric and symbolic reasoning; and foreign language proficiency. All first-year students take a seminar in persuasive writing and critical reading in a small class, focusing on a theme related to the instructor's discipline. Popular majors include psychology, biology, business administration, and communication. Accounting, physics, geography, and education are strengths. New majors

"Geneseo is challenging but never unreasonable."

are available in neuroscience, applied math, and women's and gender studies. Students interested in medicine may pursue a minor in sociomedical sciences, which studies the social determinants of health and disease. Cooperative programs with other SUNY campuses in dentistry, optometry, engineering, and other fields allow students to finish their graduate degrees a year ahead of schedule.

"Geneseo is challenging but never unreasonable," says a sophomore. Twenty-four percent of classes have fewer than 20 students, and the quality of teaching is said to be generally high, especially in upper-level courses. "Professors are easily accessible and happy to help if you seek them out," says an international relations major. Top students are invited to join the prestigious Edgar Fellows scholarship program, which includes a $2,000 annual scholarship, five honors courses designed specifically for the program, and an opportunity to complete a senior thesis or a research, creative, or service project. The acclaimed Geneseo Opportunities for Leadership Development program, which is open to all students, seeks to prepare students for college and community leadership roles via workshops and symposia. Thirty-seven percent of students study abroad, usually during the summer, and the college offers 68 programs in 36 nations; through other SUNY campuses, students have access to 1,000 programs in 60 countries.

Ninety-six percent of Geneseo students are from New York State, and 2 percent come from abroad. Asian Americans make up 6 percent of the student body, Hispanics 8 percent, African Americans 3 percent, and multiracial students 3 percent. Geneseo is "a blue school in a red town," according to a junior, but the political climate doesn't usually get heated. "Students tend to care about each other and treat each other with respect," says a senior. Geneseo offers merit scholarships averaging $2,800 each, but no athletic awards. Thirty percent of freshmen are Pell-eligible. New York State's Excelsior Scholarship grants free tuition to in-state students whose families earn up to $125,000 in annual income.

Fifty-four percent of Geneseo students live in the residence halls and town-houses, where 13 living/learning communities are available for interested students.

"We do not have a huge nightlife like you would have on a larger campus."

Rooms are guaranteed for four years, although most upperclassmen choose to move off campus. The Red Jacket Dining Hall was recently renovated, and a senior reports, "The quality of meals has been improving every semester." Students say that, given its small-town location, the campus is safe, and an English major notes that Geneseo has "stepped up its educational resources on sexual consent for incoming students."

"We do not have a huge nightlife like you would have on a larger campus, but there is a very charming Geneseo social scene," says a psychology major. "There are a lot of activities on campus as well as great festivals and events in the town itself." Fraternities and sororities, which draw 23 percent of the men and 33 percent of the women, set the social tone and host most of the parties. "Greek life is a loud, influential minority," says one student. If Greek life doesn't appeal, students can get involved in any of the nearly 200 student organizations or partake in college-sponsored late-night activities at the College Union. Students are active in the community, volunteering 200,000 hours of service each year through annual days of service, events like Relay For Life, and numerous student groups. Students also look forward to the annual Spring Fest, GREAT Day (a celebration of student research and creative work), and monthly multicultural club dinners and shows.

Adjacent to campus, the town of Geneseo's Main Street has more than 60 shops, restaurants, and cafés. A campus shuttle takes students to a nearby Wegmans supermarket and Walmart. Outdoorsy types appreciate the nearby Letchworth State Park, often referred to as the "Grand Canyon of the East"; rowers enjoy beautiful Conesus Lake, only a 10-minute drive from campus. Popular road trips include Rochester, 30 miles north, and Buffalo, 60 miles west; don't forget your hat, mittens, and parka!

Almost half of Geneseo students participate in recreational sports; broomball is the most popular intramural, while rugby is the most popular club sport. Geneseo's varsity teams, the Knights, compete in Division III, and the men's ice hockey, women's basketball and tennis, and men's and women's track and field, cross-country, and swimming teams are competitive on the national level. Ice hockey, though, stirs up the most school spirit: "Hockey is huge here," confirms a senior.

The SUNY–College at Geneseo gives students the best of two worlds. Given its size, professors can provide the kind of personal attention normally seen only at private liberal arts colleges; because of its public status, that attention comes at bargain price. These factors have made it more difficult to get in—and, it turns out, getting in is only half the battle. "Students are very serious about their education," says a sophomore. "Once you are here, you must work hard."

Ice hockey stirs up the most school spirit on campus.

Overlaps

SUNY–Binghamton, Ithaca, Syracuse, SUNY–Buffalo, University of Rochester, William and Mary, Skidmore, SUNY–Stony Brook

If You Apply To ›

SUNY–Geneseo: Early decision, regular decision. SATs or ACTs: required. Subject Tests: optional. Accepts the Common Application with supplement. Dance, theater, and music applicants must audition.

SUNY–Purchase College

735 Anderson Hill Road, Purchase, NY 10577

One of the few public institutions that has a strong arts specialty. The visual and performing arts are signature programs, but many students also come to Purchase for a robust range of liberal arts offerings, from environmental studies and psychology to film and creative writing. Campus life offers an active music scene, but NYC is a big draw on the weekends.

SUNY–Purchase College is a dream come true for aspiring artists of all kinds—an academic environment that provides a strong sense of community, yet celebrates individuals for their unique talents and contributions. Liberal artists are well supported here too, with a growing number of academic opportunities. Purchase's location just 30 miles north of New York City is ideal for its creative, socially conscious students, who take full advantage of the endless cultural and professional opportunities the city has to offer. A literature major says, "There's a raw energy that exists on campus—in the students and professors—that I don't think many other colleges have."

Set on a 500-acre wooded estate in an area of upscale Westchester County's most scenic suburbia, Purchase has a campus described by one student as "sleek, modern, ominous, and brick." The college has earned a national reputation for its instruction in music, dance, theater, and visual arts. Almost all the faculty members

Website: www.purchase.edu
Location: Suburban
Public
Total Enrollment: 3,831
Undergraduates: 3,734
Male/Female: 42/58
SAT Ranges: ERW 530–630, M 490–570
ACT Ranges: 20–26
Financial Aid: 74%
Pell Grant: 42%
Expense: Pub $

(continued)

Student Loans: 68%
Average Debt: $ $ $
Applicants: 4,056
Accepted: 74%
Enrolled: 19%
Grad in 6 Years: 67%
Returning Freshmen: 83%
Academics: ✍ ✍ ✍ ½
Social: ☎ ☎ ☎
Q of L: ★ ★ ★
Admissions: (914) 251-6300
Email Address: admissions@
purchase.edu

Strong Programs:
Music
Dance
Theater and Performance
Visual Arts
Environmental Studies
Film
Creative Writing
Psychology

Almost all the faculty members in the School of the Arts are professionals who perform or exhibit regularly in the New York metropolitan area.

in the School of the Arts are professionals who perform or exhibit regularly in the New York metropolitan area, and the spacious, dazzling facilities here rank among the best in the world. The college also boasts the Neuberger Museum, the sixth-largest public college museum. The four-theater Performing Arts Center is huge, and dance students, whose building contains a dozen studios, whirlpool rooms, and a "body-correction" facility, may never again work in such splendid and well-equipped surroundings.

Mingling with highly motivated and talented performers and artists can make some students in the School of Liberal Arts and Sciences feel a little drab and out of place, and the academic atmosphere reportedly varies between programs. "Dancers, actors, visual artists, and music students pull the most weight as far as campus life is concerned," says a student.

> **"There's a raw energy that exists on campus—in the students and professors."**

Even so, about 60 percent of Purchase students pursue liberal arts degrees. Environmental studies, film, creative writing, psychology, and new media have strong reputations, and sociology, biology, and journalism are other popular choices. An arts management major offered through the School of the Arts prepares students to develop, manage, and produce artists and performers.

Regardless of their chosen school or degree program, all Purchase students take the same core curriculum, which requires coursework in eight knowledge areas spanning the arts, humanities, sciences, and health and wellness. When they arrive in the fall, most new students take an introductory First-Year Seminar. Students in the liberal arts and sciences complete a senior project, which is often research-based, while those in the arts divisions undertake a senior recital or show. Purchase students tend to be serious about their own personal achievements, and with 61 percent of classes enrolling fewer than 20 students, professors are said to be accessible and friendly. "The professors are engaged, extremely qualified, and very interested in our education," says a student. Faculty members lead short-term study abroad programs during the summer on such topics as art history and language in Italy and political theater in Prague; affiliated programs in the SUNY system provide access to hundreds of other options.

Purchase attracts "all the students from high school who weren't the cheerleaders and football players," says one student, describing classmates as "artsy, creative, hippies, gay, vegans, and open-minded, liberal activists." Eighty percent of students are from New York State, most from New York City and Westchester County. Others are from Long Island, New Jersey, and Connecticut; 5 percent are international. African Americans account for 12 percent of the student body, Hispanics 22 percent, Asian Americans 4 percent, and multiracial students 5 percent. A hefty 42 percent of freshmen are eligible for the Pell Grant. In addition to need-based aid, merit scholarships averaging $2,300 are awarded each year on the basis of academic achievements, auditions, and portfolios. New York residents from families whose annual incomes are below $125,000 can attend Purchase tuition-free under the state's Excelsior Scholarship program.

Two-thirds of Purchase students live on campus, and a student explains, "There are older and newer dorms and their condition definitely reflects their age." Options are improving, however, with a brand-new, 300-bed residence hall that opened in 2019, and plans are in the works to renovate some of the older facilities. With quirky names like Outback, Farside, and Fort Awesome, the dorms at least sound like fun

> **"[Purchase students are] artsy, creative, hippies, gay, vegans, and open-minded, liberal activists."**

places to live. Housing in the surrounding suburbs is expensive and hard to find, so many students commute from home. The dining facilities are said to offer decent fare, and the college has expanded its resources and educational programming related to student safety.

The campus is a neighbor to the world headquarters of IBM, Texaco, AMF, General Foods, and PepsiCo, and the town of Purchase is by no means student-oriented. A campus shuttle takes students to nearby White Plains and Port Chester, and a student-run van service goes into Manhattan three times a day; the city is also accessible by train. The Big Apple provides a regular weekend distraction, to the extent that it inhibits the formation of a tight campus community, but the school has been working to strengthen campus life. A lively music scene brings indie and up-and-coming bands to campus throughout the year, and the Performing Arts Center is host to at least two student or faculty performances every weekend. New York artists and celebrities also visit for lectures, performances, and other events. Students report that, with about 50 active clubs on campus, there is usually something going on in the Student Center (a.k.a. "the Stood"), and the 21-and-over crowd frequents the Pub. Fraternities and sororities are definitely out. As one artist explains, "Individuality is far more important to the artist than being part of a group." Despite the unconventional aura of the place, Purchase is not without its traditions, including Fall Ball ("a big dance where everyone dresses in drag"), Zombie Prom, and the Culture Shock music festival.

Purchase athletes compete in Division III, and the few competitive Panthers teams include men's basketball, women's volleyball, and women's soccer. Men's basketball and the women's swim team have won the Skyline Conference championship in recent years. Intramural programs draw 30 percent of students, but informal Frisbee-tossing remains more popular than organized sports.

Despite a conspicuous lack of a college-town atmosphere, Purchase is a perfect place to study the arts and still be able to indulge in academics of all kinds, or vice versa. "It's a great place to come and devote yourself to your craft," says a senior. Indeed, the opportunity that Purchase offers for a personalized, diverse education is unique within the SUNY system.

With quirky names like Outback, Farside, and Fort Awesome, the dorms at least sound like fun places to live.

Overlaps

SUNY–New Paltz, Pace, NYU, CUNY–Hunter, SUNY–Albany, Ithaca, SUNY–Binghamton, SUNY–Stony Brook

If You Apply To ›

SUNY–Purchase: Early action, rolling admissions. SATs or ACTs: optional. No Subject Tests. Accepts the Common Application with supplement. Apply to particular school or program. Auditions held for acting, dance, and music. Portfolios required for art and design, creative writing, film, and theater design/technology.

SUNY–Stony Brook University

118 Administration Building, Stony Brook, NY 11794

Strategically located 60 miles east of New York City, Stony Brook has risen a few notches in the SUNY pecking order. The natural sciences, engineering, and health fields are the major drawing cards. Situated in the lap of Long Island luxury, Stony Brook offers easy access to beachfront playlands. Still caters mainly to students from the New York tristate area.

Stony Brook, one of the academic leaders in the SUNY system, aims to be the model of a student-centered research university. The six Undergraduate Colleges provide a small college community experience with all the assets of a leading research university. Since its founding in 1957, the public university has made a name for itself with its top-notch programs in the hard sciences. It has also become known for its competitive learning environment and the high quality of its professors. In short, "Stony Brook is the complete package," boasts one senior.

Website: www.stonybrook.edu
Location: Suburban
Public
Total Enrollment: 21,598
Undergraduates: 16,095
Male/Female: 53/47

(continued)

SAT Ranges: ERW 590–680,
  M 620–730
ACT Ranges: 26–31
Financial Aid: 75%
Pell Grant: 35%
Expense: Pub $
Student Loans: 54%
Average Debt: $ $
Applicants: 35,313
Accepted: 42%
Enrolled: 21%
Grad in 6 Years: 72%
Returning Freshmen: 90%
Academics: ✍ ✍ ✍ ✍
Social: ☎ ☎ ☎
Q of L: ★ ★
Admissions: (631) 632-6868
Email Address: enroll@
  stonybrook.edu

Strong Programs:
Health Science
Biology
Business Management
Psychology
Engineering
Physics
Economics
Anthropology

*The comprehensive
university hospital
offers many
opportunities for
research programs for
undergrads as well as
graduate students.*

The school's location on Long Island's plush North Shore (Gatsby's stomping grounds) is a wonderful drawing point. Sitting on 1,040 wooded acres just outside of the small, picturesque village of Stony Brook, and only 90 minutes from New York City and half an hour from the beaches of the South Shore, the campus is a conglomeration of redbrick buildings interspersed with several modern brick and concrete designs. Campus beautification and sustainability are priorities, and grass and trees have replaced much of the uninspiring campus concrete. Recently completed construction includes two new residence halls and a dining facility.

The Stony Brook Curriculum is based on a series of learning outcomes and is organized into four categories: Demonstrate Versatility, Explore Interconnectedness, Pursue Deeper Understanding, and Prepare for Lifelong Learning. All freshmen—residents and commuters alike—enter the university as members of one of six Undergraduate Colleges. Each college has its own faculty director, as well as both academic and residential advisors. Freshmen participate in theme-based academic and cocurricular programs, which include two small seminar courses.

Coming of age in the high-tech era, Stony Brook quickly became known and respected for its science departments. Facilities are extensive, and the science faculty includes a number of internationally known researchers. The comprehensive university hospital and research center make health sciences strong, especially nursing and physical therapy. The hospital, which has been ranked among the nation's best for teaching, attracts grants and offers many opportunities for research programs for undergrads as well as graduate students. Health science is the most popular major, followed by biology, business management, and psychology. Engineering, physics, economics, and anthropology are also strong, and Stony Brook boasts the only journalism school in the SUNY system. The art program benefits from a fine arts building, complete with studios and a reference library. The building complements Stony Brook's beautiful five-theater Staller Center for the Arts. The Grammy-winning Emerson String Quartet is in residence in the music department. New minors have been introduced in professional writing, ethnomusicology, and health, medicine, and society.

> **"Stony Brook is a fairly competitive place. A solid work ethic is vital for success."**

Students spend a lot of time studying. "Stony Brook is a fairly competitive place," says a senior. "A solid work ethic is vital for success." Classes are often large, with 24 percent enrolling more than 50 students. A recent graduate says, "On the whole, the quality of teaching was excellent. The professors were talented lecturers, passionate about the material, and involved in cutting-edge research."

An Undergraduate Research and Creative Activities program offers undergraduates the opportunity to work on research projects with faculty members from the time they are freshmen until they graduate. The WISE (Women in Science and Engineering) program encourages women entering the university as freshmen to pursue study in the sciences, engineering, and mathematics. The program provides mentoring from women professors in these fields, as well as research experiences during the freshman year. About 3 percent of students take advantage of one of Stony Brook's study abroad programs (England, France, Italy, Japan, and Madagascar are just some of the possibilities), while others choose established internships in the fields of policy analysis, political science, psychology, foreign language, or social welfare. University Scholars is a four-year honors program for students who rank at the top of the incoming freshman class that offers specialized support, programming, and events.

"The majority of the students here are hardworking, ambitious, and well equipped to handle life," says a chemistry major. Eighty percent of Stony Brook undergraduates hail from New York, and a good portion commute from Long Island homes; 14 percent arrive from foreign countries. The student body is 7 percent African American, 12 percent Hispanic, 24 percent Asian American, and 3 percent multiracial. To promote multicultural understanding, students are required to take classes focusing on different cultures. "There isn't much public display of political or social discontent on campus," says a sophomore. Merit scholarships averaging $5,400 are given out each year, in addition to more than 300 athletic scholarships. Thirty-five percent of freshmen receive Pell Grants. As at other SUNY schools, in-state students at Stony Brook whose families earn $125,000 or less in annual income now enjoy free tuition under the state's Excelsior Scholarship program.

Stony Brook, which has one of the largest residential programs in the SUNY system, has a slew of robust facilities that provide students access to state-of-the-art fitness centers, computing centers, and widescreen TVs. Fifty-three percent of undergrads live in university housing. While residential freshmen must take a meal plan, upperclassmen who live in suites on campus either opt for a flexible food-service plan or pay a nominal fee to cook for themselves. Kosher and vegetarian food co-ops keep interested students well supplied with cheap eats. The university has hired several new Title IX staff members, and the Walk Service Program escorts students around campus at night. "We sit through so many sexual assault lectures and workshops and online courses, and it has honestly helped," says one student. "I found it comforting that everyone had to go through this and understand it."

Stony Brook boasts the only journalism school in the SUNY system.

"There is a big social life on campus and a smaller one off campus."

"There is a big social life on campus and a smaller one off campus," notes one senior. Because many students go home on the weekends, Thursday is the big party night. The university has fairly strict policies on alcohol consumption, and "the policies are as effective as possible with young students in college," a student reports. The fledgling Greek system draws 2 percent of the men and 2 percent of the women. Current and classic movies are screened during the week, and student organizations coordinate other entertainment in the form of frequent concerts, plays, and other performances. Annual festivals in the fall and spring, as well as the Roth Pond Regatta and the homecoming football game are among the biggest social events of the year.

The Seawolves women's lacrosse team has won five consecutive conference titles.

"Stony Brook is a wealthy residential town that cannot be categorized as a 'college town,'" one student says. "It doesn't appreciate the large campus located within its limits." Nearby Port Jefferson offers small shops and interesting restaurants. Beachcombing on the nearby North Shore, or on the Atlantic Ocean shore of Long Island, and heading into New York City are popular ways to pass the weekends. "You absolutely need a car if you want to get around the town at all," says a junior. Still, many students make do with trains, and a station is conveniently located at the edge of campus.

"Stony Brook is like its students: we grow and learn quickly."

Stony Brook's 18 Division I teams compete in the America East Conference, except for football, which hits the gridiron in the Colonial Athletic Association. The Seawolves women's lacrosse team has won five consecutive conference titles, and other conference champs include men's cross-country, women's soccer, and women's volleyball. Intramurals, ranging from soccer and flag football to handball and table tennis, provide one of the school's greatest rallying points, and students are also active in more than 40 club sports.

Though Stony Brook is not old enough to have ivy-covered walls, it does offer some of the best academic opportunities in the SUNY system. Students tout their school's diversity and creativity, as well as the feeling of hospitality that pervades campus life. "Though we are a rather new university," says a senior, "Stony Brook is like its students: we grow and learn quickly."

Overlaps
SUNY–Buffalo, UMass Amherst, Rutgers, UConn, Purdue, SUNY–Binghamton, NYU, Cornell University

If You Apply To ›

SUNY–Stony Brook: Regular decision. SATs or ACTs: required. Subject Tests: optional. Accepts the Common Application with supplement.

Stetson University

421 N. Woodland Boulevard, DeLand, FL 32723

The oldest private university in Florida, Stetson keeps company with the likes of Baylor and Furman among prominent Deep South institutions. Established the state's first schools of business, law, and medicine. Business is traditionally the strongest program. More like a small college than a university.

Website: www.stetson.edu
Location: Small City
Private
Total Enrollment: 4,052
Undergraduates: 3,014
Male/Female: 43/57
SAT Ranges: ERW 570–650, M 540–640
ACT Ranges: 23–29
Financial Aid: 99%
Pell Grant: 34%
Expense: Pr $ $
Student Loans: 71%
Average Debt: $ $ $ $
Applicants: 11,732
Accepted: 68%
Enrolled: 11%
Grad in 6 Years: 62%
Returning Freshmen: 78%
Academics: ✎ ✎ ✎
Social: 🕿 🕿 🕿
Q of L: ★ ★ ★
Admissions: (386) 822-7100
Email Address: admissions@stetson.edu

Strong Programs:
Psychology
Business Administration
Health Sciences
Finance
Accounting
Professional Sales
Music
Russian, East European, and Eurasian Studies

Stetson University, named for the maker of the famed 10-gallon hat, draws students from around the Southeast with its small size and emphasis on liberal learning. Once a bastion of conservatism, the school has become more liberal and ecumenical since cutting ties with the Southern Baptists more than 20 years ago. With top-notch business programs and strengths in music and health sciences, this Florida university continues to attract students who aren't afraid to wear a variety of hats during their stay.

Located halfway between Orlando and Daytona Beach, Stetson's 185-acre campus features mainly brick structures in styles from Gothic to Moorish to Southern colonial. While some modern buildings are scattered about, the theme is decidedly Southern, complete with royal palms and oak trees. A major renovation and expansion of the Carlton Union Building, home to dining services and student activities, was recently completed, and a new science and health facility is in the pipeline, funded by an $18 million gift.

Stetson has three undergraduate colleges and schools—music, business administration, and arts and sciences—and its general education requirements apply to all of them. All entering students take a First Year Seminar, which allows them to work closely with Stetson faculty to ease the transition to college. All freshmen who are undecided on a major participate in the Discovery program, and all students take a Junior Seminar that focuses on personal and social responsibility. Students in the college of arts and sciences must complete a faculty-mentored capstone research or creative project, while music students perform a senior recital and business students fulfill internship and experiential learning requirements. Additionally, all students must pass four writing or writing-enhanced courses in order to graduate.

> **"Professors constantly encourage you to take on more projects and research."**

Stetson is known for its business program, particularly majors in accounting, professional sales, and finance. Would-be money managers benefit from the award-winning Roland George Investments program, where they oversee a cash portfolio worth more than $3.5 million. Students who hope to work for themselves can tap into the Prince Entrepreneurial Program, which connects them with successful business owners, while the Family Enterprise Center was one of the first in the nation in educating students for work in family businesses. The most popular majors are psychology, business administration, health sciences, and finance. Russian, East European, and Eurasian Studies is a surprising strength. Stetson's music school is notable (ahem) for choral music and public performances in addition to academic programs. Aspiring lawyers may take advantage of a 3+3 accelerated B.A./J.D. program or a 4+3 direct admission program with Stetson's College of Law.

Of the academic climate, a business major says, "Stetson is a place that understands that to compete at the highest level, you must work together." Sixty percent of classes have fewer than 20 students, and group work is common in many disciplines. Professors are always willing to help, and many have worked in the field they are teaching before stepping in front of the lectern. "The professors constantly encourage you to take on more projects and research, if you are interested, and push you within their classes," says an English major.

Students with wanderlust can choose from more than 100 faculty-led, exchange, or affiliate programs, and international internships are an option too; 20 percent of undergrads study abroad. Stetson's honors program incorporates international study, community service, and a senior colloquium, and also allows students to create their own majors. The Stetson Undergraduate Research Experience program awards funding to students for summer research or creative projects with faculty members, and original student work is celebrated at the annual Stetson Showcase.

Would-be money managers in the Roland George Investments program oversee a cash portfolio worth more than $3.5 million.

Sixty-eight percent of Stetson Hatters are native Floridians, and 6 percent hail from foreign countries. A political science major describes Hatters as "very driven and personable." African Americans constitute 8 percent of the student body, Hispanics make up 16 percent, Asian Americans add 2 percent, and multiracial students comprise 4 percent. Many come from affluent backgrounds, but 34 percent of current freshmen are Pell-eligible. Students of all faiths are welcomed on campus, and the university has three chaplains (Baptist, African Methodist Episcopal, and Buddhist) as well as a professionally staffed Hillel Center. Students describe a mix of political views on campus. Merit scholarships and non-need-based grants averaging $24,100 are awarded each year, and Stetson also hands out athletic scholarships in 17 sports.

"I lived on campus all four years because I loved how connected it made me."

About two-thirds of undergrads live in the residence halls, since everyone is required to do so through junior year, except for commuters who live at home. Accommodations in the residence halls, all of which have been upgraded in recent years, are said to have significantly improved. "I lived on campus all four years because I loved how connected it made me to my campus and my peers," comments a senior. Stetson's traditional, buffet-style cafeteria is known as the Commons, and although the food tends to get so-so reviews, dining offerings have expanded with the recent renovation of the student union. As for campus safety, one student says, "I always feel safe on the central part of campus, but avoid the outer parts of campus at night because there seems to be less patrolling there." Students report a noticeable increase in efforts intended to prevent sexual assault on campus.

The university has three chaplains (Baptist, African Methodist Episcopal, and Buddhist) as well as a professionally staffed Hillel Center.

"Greek organizations are usually the place to find parties or connections to party life," says a junior, adding that "music organizations also offer a type of subculture partying." Fraternities attract 29 percent of the men and sororities draw 32 percent of the women, but students say that tightened alcohol policies have pushed most partying off campus to nearby apartments or bars. The Council for Student Activities offers plenty of on-campus alternatives, bringing in big-name acts, and students also get involved in the more than 100 student organizations. Students look forward to annual events such as Greek Week, when sorority and fraternity chapters compete in a lip-synch contest and other events to raise money for charity, and Greenfeather, aimed at promoting community service. Three-quarters of students participate in volunteer activities, often through service-learning courses. When your birthday rolls around, don't forget to

"If you put the work in, this institution will reward you tenfold."

wear your bathing suit—it's a tradition for fellow students to toss you into the mid-campus Holler Fountain.

As for the "adorable, small Southern town" of DeLand, it boasts "shops, galleries, and cafés," but only a handful of bars, so students often head to Orlando (40 minutes from campus) or Daytona Beach (20 minutes) to eat out, shop, or dance the night away. In addition to the omnipresent beaches, Blue Spring and DeLeon Springs offer canoeing and nature watching. Popular road trips include Miami for clubbing and the Keys for camping.

Stetson's teams compete in Division I, and a football team took the field in 2013 for the first time in 57 years, competing against the likes of Butler, Dayton, and Drake. The women's basketball program has been the standard-bearer for Hatters Athletics, qualifying for NCAA postseason play multiple times in the past several seasons. The beach volleyball team took home its fourth Atlantic Sun Conference title in five years in 2018. Other solid teams include softball, baseball, and women's golf. The Hollis Wellness Center offers a variety of fitness facilities, and about a quarter of students participate in club and intramural sports, ranging from ultimate Frisbee and bass fishing to flag football and pool battleship.

Stetson students tip their hats to the one-on-one attention freely given at this small Sunshine State university with a strong sense of what it is. After four years spent enjoying great weather and forming close friendships with peers and professors, they emerge with solid academic foundations for future work or study. Says one happy student, "Stetson may not be perfect or have the shiniest bells and whistles, but I can promise that if you put the work in, this institution will reward you tenfold."

Overlaps

Baylor, Furman, Baldwin Wallace, Butler, John Carroll, University of Redlands, University of Central Florida, University of Florida

If You Apply To ›

Stetson: Rolling admissions. SATs or ACTs: optional. No Subject Tests. Accepts the Common Application with supplement.

Stevens Institute of Technology

1 Castle Point Terrace, Hoboken, NJ 07030

Stevens ranks with Clarkson and Worcester Polytechnic among East Coast technical institutes that offer intimacy and personalized education. Youth-oriented Hoboken is a major plus and a quicker commute to Manhattan than most places in Brooklyn. Co-op and five-year programs are options. Plan to work hard.

Website: www.stevens.edu
Location: Small City
Private
Total Enrollment: 5,610
Undergraduates: 3,113
Male/Female: 70/30
SAT Ranges: ERW 640–710, M 680–760
ACT Ranges: 29–33
Financial Aid: 92%
Pell Grant: 16%
Expense: Pr $ $ $

At Stevens Institute of Technology, students accept intense classwork, all-nighters, and trips to the Big Apple as givens. The school is located just across the Hudson River from Manhattan, which means that students have the cultural, athletic, and gastronomic resources of New York City at their fingertips. Engineering and the sciences dominate campus life—and even business, arts, and humanities programs are taught through the lens of technology—but students seem prepared to take on the challenge of balancing work and play. "Stevens is a great place to embrace one's inner nerd and party too," says one satisfied student.

An eclectic mix of architectural styles compose Stevens's 55-acre campus. Many of the residence halls and administrative buildings are redbrick; classroom and lab facilities range from traditional, ivy-covered brownstones to modern glass-and-steel structures. The ABS Engineering Center houses five labs designed for robotics, naval engineering, structural engineering, hydraulics, and other research.

Stevens was created in 1870 through the will of 19th-century inventor Edwin Stevens. It is organized into four schools—the Schaefer School of Engineering and Science, the School of Business, the College of Arts and Letters, and the School of Systems and Enterprises—and offers 35 majors. Most programs require calculus, chemistry, physics, humanities courses, and physical education. All entering students are required to participate in the Freshman Experience, which is a sequence of two common courses: Writing and Communication and Knowledge, Nature, Culture. Seniors take a yearlong capstone course culminating in a team-based senior design project.

Engineering has long been king of the hill at Stevens; programs in biomedical, chemical, civil, electrical, and naval engineering are all highly regarded, as is the major in mechanical engineering, not surprising since the program dates to the school's founding. Business programs are growing in number and popularity and include a major in quantitative finance, rare at the undergraduate level. Other notable programs include computer science, cybersecurity, music and technology, and visual arts and technology. A five-year co-op program allows engineering and science students to incorporate full-time internships into their studies. "Classes are competitive, but collaboration is essential when performing experiments, preparing reports, or studying for exams," observes a mechanical engineering major. Thirty-eight percent of classes have fewer than 20 students, and students agree that, despite a few professors more interested in their research than their teaching, the quality of instruction is high. "Professors are often able to provide industry insight," says a senior.

> **"Stevens is a great place to embrace one's inner nerd and party too."**

Professional practice is an important part of the Stevens environment, with nearly all students participating in cooperative education, internships, or mature research and design projects. Men vastly outnumber women, but one junior sees this as an advantage: "As a female at Stevens, I feel this has actually helped me with holding my own and 'vying with the boys,' as I call it. It does not faze me to be the only girl in a group project." The Lore-El Center for Women's Leadership offers events ranging from health and wellness activities to leadership conferences and professional dinners with successful women in industry. Stevens also has an active on-campus recruiting program with major corporations, start-up firms, and government organizations. Hundreds of short- and long-term study abroad and exchange programs are available, although few students find the time to take advantage of them.

"Stevens students are typically more introverted, phenomenally intelligent, and generally kind," boasts one mechanical engineering major. Fifty-nine percent of the students at Stevens are from New Jersey; many others come from the greater New York City portion of New York State, and 4 percent hail from foreign nations. Twelve percent of undergraduates are Asian American, 11 percent are Hispanic, and 2 percent are African American. Politics don't usually receive much attention on campus. Unlike some of Stevens's peer institutions, admissions officers here look more closely at high school grades, especially in math and science, than at test scores. In addition to need-based financial aid, qualified students receive merit-based scholarships that average $18,000.

> **"Stevens has taught me the importance of entrepreneurial thinking and efficiency in everything that I do."**

Stevens guarantees housing for a student's entire four- or five-year stay, but students warn that housing is increasingly becoming a headache as the university continues to grow. After living in the "pretty standard" dorms freshman year, most students are housed in university-leased, off-campus apartments, which a computer science major says are "very nice" but "are distant from campus, cost a lot more, and

(continued)

Student Loans: 69%
Average Debt: $ $ $ $
Applicants: 8,335
Accepted: 44%
Enrolled: 21%
Grad in 6 Years: 83%
Returning Freshmen: 94%
Academics: ✍ ✍ ✍
Social: ☎ ☎
Q of L: ★ ★ ★ ★
Admissions: (201) 216-5194
Email Address: admissions@ stevens.edu

Strong Programs:
Mechanical Engineering
Electrical Engineering
Civil Engineering
Business and Technology
Chemical Engineering
Biomedical Engineering
Quantitative Finance
Computer Science

Seniors take a yearlong capstone course culminating in a team-based senior design project.

do not come with included meal plans." Even so, a regular school shuttle connects all housing with the campus and downtown Hoboken. Sixty-four percent of undergraduates live in housing provided by Stevens, while others find their own, often less expensive, off-campus apartments. Students say the dining hall has improved, thanks to a recent renovation and change in service provider, and campus security officers are visible and friendly. A sophomore notes that a recently introduced bystander intervention campaign "has been very effective because students are more inclined to report a Title IX violation."

Thirty-one percent of Stevens men join fraternities, and 49 percent of the women pledge sororities. "People like to party here, but they keep it in check," says a quantitative finance major. "Greek houses follow campus policies regarding alcohol and usually hold registered parties where bouncers check IDs." An Entertainment Committee plans weekly events, from comedy nights to hypnotists and musical guests. The student-run TechFest is a favorite annual event, and a senior notes that the festival is organized "by proposal only, which makes each year different and unique." Greenwich Village, Times Square, and the bright lights of Broadway are just 15 minutes away on the PATH train, while Hoboken offers popular pubs and clubs right next to campus. Road trips, often taken by train, include Yankee Stadium in the Bronx and Six Flags Great Adventure near Trenton. Beaches and ski slopes are both within a 90-minute drive.

Students cheer enthusiastically when the Division III Stevens Ducks are competing. The men's volleyball team is a national championship winner, while men's and women's soccer and swimming and diving, men's tennis, and women's field hockey have brought home recent conference titles. For those without the time or talent to play at the varsity level, there are intramural and club teams in everything from basketball, soccer, and flag football to archery, crew, and bowling.

Stevens's urban location and relatively small size can make for fun times, but the emphasis here is on hard work and innovation. Stevens graduates go on to make a dent in the world; notable alums include Nobel Laureate Frederick Reines, who detected the subatomic world of the neutrino; Frederick Winslow Taylor, father of scientific management; and Alfred W. Fielding, inventor of bubble wrap. Says a civil engineering major, "Stevens has taught me the importance of entrepreneurial thinking and efficiency in everything that I do."

The Lore-El Center for Women's Leadership offers professional dinners with successful women in industry.

Overlaps

Rensselaer, Worcester Polytechnic, Northeastern, Carnegie Mellon, NYU, Lehigh, Rutgers, Columbia

If You Apply To ›

Stevens: Early decision I and II, regular decision. SATs or ACTs: required (applicants to music and technology or visual arts and technology programs may choose to submit a digital portfolio in lieu of test scores). Subject Tests: optional (required for some accelerated programs). Accepts the Common Application with supplement.

Susquehanna University

Selinsgrove, PA 17870

Susquehanna offers welcome relief from the unimaginative education at many small colleges. Its innovative core curriculum emphasizes personal development and requires students to spend at least two weeks learning off campus. Best known for its business program, and big on study abroad. With a more down-to-earth atmosphere than at upscale competitors like Bucknell and Dickinson, it is a national leader in promoting socioeconomic diversity.

"Susquewho?" That's the question many students ask when they're first introduced to this undergraduate institution. While it may not be a household name, Susquehanna University is earning a reputation as an innovator. Friendly faculty, personal attention, and an increasing emphasis on community make SU a good place to expand your mind. The university's off-campus study requirement makes it an ideal choice for those looking to see more of the world too.

Susquehanna's campus is beautiful and serene, set on 325 lush acres in the small town of Selinsgrove on the Susquehanna River. Most of the 94 buildings on campus are brick, with Georgian the predominant architectural style. Selinsgrove Hall, built in 1858, and Seibert Hall, built in 1901, are on the National Register of Historic Places. The Degenstein Campus Center was recently renovated and now boasts a new student eatery, coffee shop, and bookstore.

Susquehanna's Central Curriculum emphasizes coursework in five areas: Richness of Thought (fine arts and math); Natural World; Human Interactions (history, sociology, ethics, and language); Intellectual Skills (writing, oral presentation, and teamwork); and Connections (an off-campus, cross-cultural experience matched with diversity classes). All

> **"Professors expect students to be active, visit their office hours, and ask questions."**

freshmen must complete a summer Common Reading assignment based on a specific theme, participate in an orientation program, take a Writing and Thinking course, and take a Perspectives seminar that helps them make the transition to college-level work. Finally, all students take a capstone course in their major that involves an extensive research project.

The Weis School of Business is not only one of the most striking buildings on campus, but also a prestigious business program that attracts the most Susquehanna students. Weis also sponsors a semester in London exclusively for its junior business majors. Communications, biology, creative writing, psychology, and music are other popular majors. Susquehanna is increasingly recognized for its science programs, especially biochemistry, environmental science, and biomedical sciences. SU students may also take classes at nearby Bucknell University.

Fifty-four percent of classes at SU have fewer than 20 students, and student/faculty interaction is one of Susquehanna's strong points. Students describe academics as challenging, and a senior says, "Professors expect students to be active, visit their office hours, and ask questions." An assistantship program for outstanding first-year students combines a $16,000 scholarship with hands-on work with a professor or staff member for 10 hours per week. Past recipients have worked on academic research, university publications, the Writers' Institute, and marketing research. Students enjoy a bevy of support services too. "Career services are very helpful in getting you prepared for finding positions after you graduate," says a junior.

To fulfill their curricular Connections requirement, students utilize the Global Opportunities Program, which requires them to study away from campus for at least two weeks and to reflect on their experiences when they return. Students choose from 100 options—many of which are semester-long programs—on six continents, and about 90 percent of students study abroad, while the remaining 10 percent head to locations across the U.S. As a senior explains, "The goal is for students to experience a new culture before they graduate, and this requirement adds to the culture of diversity at Susquehanna." Most students also do summer internships as a crucial part of their education and future job searches. For about 10 percent of students, the academic experience is defined by the Susquehanna Honors Program. The four-year program entails a sequence of special courses and projects, off-campus opportunities like conferences and other events, and an optional living/learning community.

"Susquehanna students generally want to achieve, lead, and serve," observes a senior. Fifty-two percent of SU students are from Pennsylvania, and the majority

Website: www.susqu.edu
Location: Small Town
Private
Total Enrollment: 2,190
Undergraduates: 2,190
Male/Female: 44/56
SAT Ranges: ERW 540–630, M 530–610
ACT Ranges: 22–28
Financial Aid: 99%
Pell Grant: 34%
Expense: Pr $ $
Student Loans: 82%
Average Debt: $ $ $ $
Applicants: 6,033
Accepted: 68%
Enrolled: 15%
Grad in 6 Years: 71%
Returning Freshmen: 87%
Academics: ✐ ✐ ✐
Social: ☎ ☎ ☎
Q of L: ★ ★ ★ ★
Admissions: (570) 372-4260
Email Address: suadmiss@susqu.edu

Strong Programs:
Business Administration
Communications
Biology
Creative Writing
Psychology
Music
Biochemistry
Environmental Science

To fulfill their curricular Connections requirement, 90 percent of students study abroad, while 10 percent head to locations across the U.S.

attended public high school; 1 percent of students are international. Six percent are African American, 7 percent are Hispanic, 2 percent are Asian American, and 3 percent are multiracial; diversity education is an area of emphasis on campus. A political science major describes the political climate as "relatively tame," and the campus is rather moderate. Thirty-four percent of freshmen receive Pell Grants. Merit scholarships averaging $22,100 are available for resident Einsteins, but there are no athletic scholarships.

All Susquehanna students are required to live on campus, except for the 7 percent who are commuters. Freshmen are assigned to four dorms, "each with their own environment and personality," says a junior. After the first year, students partake in a lottery system to choose from a variety of options, including suites, townhouses, on-campus apartments, and Greek houses. One student says food in the main cafeteria "can be hit or miss, but when it's good, it's good." The SAFER program offers monthly educational events covering issues of sexual violence, bystander behavior, and how to build a safe community, and students say the campus feels secure.

"Social life at Susquehanna is very active and gatherings occur throughout the week, typically on campus," explains a student. Charlie's, the school coffeehouse, offers activities like open-mic, trivia, and football-and-wings nights, while Trax, the on-campus nightclub, serves alcohol to those of age. Twenty percent of the men and 19 percent of the women belong to fraternities or sororities, respectively, but Greeks do not set the tone for the social scene. Fall Weekend, homecoming, and Spring Weekend are the big annual events. Favorite campus traditions include a candlelight Christmas service and a Thanksgiving dinner at which faculty members serve students "the best meal of the year."

> "[The Connections] requirement adds to the culture of diversity at Susquehanna."

Outside the university, Selinsgrove is "small and quaint" with several restaurants and stores. SU was originally founded to prepare students for the ministry, and the university's commitment to the community has remained strong. Each year, 71 percent of the student population volunteers on significant community service projects. In the surrounding countryside, "it's not uncommon to see an Amish family go by in their horse and buggy," says a student. Students head outdoors to kayak, hike, and picnic at the Susquehanna River and nearby state parks. For those with cars, Penn State is an hour away.

Division III sports are popular, and the River Hawks (formerly known as the Crusaders) field a number of competitive teams. The women's swimming and diving team brought home its eighth consecutive Landmark Conference championship in 2018, and the baseball and softball teams are recent champs as well. Students also enjoy the recreational sports program, with 45 percent participating in nine club and six intramural sports; crew, rugby, and ice hockey sign up the most students.

At Susquehanna, "Students are challenged to take initiative with their learning" in a friendly, open environment, says a senior. From interning with local organizations to taking classes on the other side of the globe, the firsthand exposure to diverse experiences and perspectives that SU students receive makes Susquehanna worthwhile—and a name worth learning.

Overlaps

Gettysburg, Juniata, Muhlenberg, Ursinus, Washington and Jefferson, Penn State, Ithaca, Dickinson

If You Apply To ›

Susquehanna: Early decision, early action I and II, regular decision. SATs or ACTs: optional. Subject Tests: optional. Accepts the Common Application with supplement.

Swarthmore College

500 College Avenue, Swarthmore, PA 19081

Don't mistake Swarthmore for a miniature version of an Ivy League school. Swat is more intellectual (and liberal) than its counterparts in New Haven and Cambridge. The college's honors program gives hardy souls a taste of graduate school, which is where many Swatties invariably end up. Geekier than Wesleyan, more grounded than Reed, and more collaborative than just about anywhere.

Swarthmore College's leafy green campus may be just 11 miles from Philadelphia, but students often don't have the time or the inclination to make the jaunt. That's because they have opted for one of the country's most self-consciously intellectual undergraduate environments. Swatties are bright, hardworking, and eclectic in their interests, and campus life is fabled for its intensity. But the intensity doesn't come from huge amounts of coursework (à la Yale) as much as the self-imposed drive of talented students who want to do lots of things simultaneously—from academics to social protests to rugby—and do them well. "Swat is a truly intellectual place where people love ideas with all of their hearts," a senior philosophy major says.

Swarthmore was founded in 1864 by the liberal Hicksite branch of the Religious Society of Friends (Quakers) in Philadelphia and named after a 17th-century English manor house that was a center of the early Quaker movement. Swarthmore's 425-acre suburban campus is a nationally registered arboretum, distinguished by rolling wooded hills. Multistory buildings with natural stone exteriors from local quarries, shaped roofs, and cornices are the norm, fostering a quiet, collegiate atmosphere. The Wister Education Center and Greenhouse is LEED Gold–certified and includes classrooms, exhibit areas, and greenhouse space. Construction on the 150,000-square-foot Biology, Engineering, and Psychology Building, featuring state-of-the-art labs and classrooms, is slated for completion in fall 2020.

> **"Each of us in our own way has found a place where our passionate, geekiest interests are validated."**

Students are required to take three courses in each of the college's three divisions—humanities, natural sciences and engineering (unusual for a liberal arts college), and social sciences—and at least two of the three must be in different departments. Swatties must also demonstrate foreign language competency, fulfill a physical education requirement (which includes a swimming test), and take three writing courses from at least two divisions. Optional first-year seminars emphasize close interaction with faculty members; about 86 percent of students participate. The most popular majors are economics, computer science, political science, biology, and mathematics, and students also give high marks to majors in visual and performing arts. Cross-registration is offered with nearby Bryn Mawr, Haverford, and Penn.

Freshmen at Swarthmore are graded on a pass-fail system for their first semester, there is no class rank or dean's list, and there is a big emphasis on group projects. A freshman explains, "While the courses are generally very challenging, the environment of Swat is not competitive at all. You will often see students reminding each other of assignments, giving each other tips on how to succeed, and studying in the library together." Indeed, the administration has encouraged a spirit of collegiality by sprinkling small lounges and cappuccino bars around the dorms and academic spaces. Class sizes are intimate as well, with 74 percent enrolling fewer than 20 students. "All the classes are taught by professors, many of them world-class, and they are always accessible and very, very friendly," says a classics and fine arts double major. Aside from teaching, Swarthmore professors also serve as advisors, and students are also assigned to Student Academic Mentors, who shepherd them through the first year on campus.

Undertaken by about a third of Swat's students, the acclaimed two-year honors program features small seminars or independent study and collaborative relationships between students and professors. Setting it apart from any other program in the United States are the written and oral examinations, which are reviewed by external faculty at the end of the senior year and gauge the students' ability to hold their own with experts in the field. One student describes honors as "like a pre-Ph.D. program"; indeed, Swarthmore is among the top five institutions in the nation for the proportion of graduates who go on to earn Ph.D.s, at 27 percent. Thirty-seven percent of Swarthmore students study abroad in countries such as France, Japan, Poland, and Spain. Roughly two-thirds of students get involved with faculty-guided research or independent creative projects. A sophomore adds, "We have a great group of networked alumni who are always willing to help students, especially with externships, in which students stay with their Swat alum host family one week before winter break and shadow them."

> "We have a *very* active Title IX office that works on prevention and resolution equally."

"Ultimately, we are all nerds here," a history major says. "Each of us in our own way has found a place where our passionate, geekiest interests are validated, appreciated, and celebrated by our fellow Swatties." Swarthmore is home to a diverse student body; 12 percent are Pennsylvania residents and 14 percent are international. Seven percent of students are African American, 17 percent Asian American, 12 percent Hispanic, and 7 percent multiracial. Consistent with its Quaker roots, Swarthmore encourages students to be as educated as possible on issues of cultural, racial, and socioeconomic pluralism, and the entire community is brought into decisions on issues such as socially responsible investments and the pay scale of campus workers. Liberals far outnumber conservatives, students say, but students on both sides are keen to stand up for issues they are passionate about. The Eugene Lang Center for Civic and Social Responsibility has made Swarthmore a national force in the area of service learning. "Swarthmore is characterized by a genuine will to do good in the world," a senior engineering major says. Swarthmore is need-blind in its admissions and meets 100 percent of admitted students' demonstrated financial need. In an effort to reduce the burden of debt, the college has replaced loans with grants in its financial aid packages.

> "We really are dedicated to learning just because we like to learn, not because we want the A."

Freshmen at Swarthmore are graded on a pass-fail system for their first semester, and there is no class rank or dean's list.

Ninety-six percent of undergraduates live on campus, and housing is guaranteed for all four years. "The dorms each have their own personality," says a senior, "and for the most part they are quite comfortable and well maintained." Dining options are said to be diverse and plentiful, if not always outstanding, and a handful of local eateries are also covered by the meal plan. Campus safety personnel are "quick to respond in any circumstance," and a sophomore says, "We have a *very* active Title IX office that works on prevention and resolution equally."

Most social life at Swarthmore takes place on campus, and it often begins late, since students hit the books until 10 or 11 p.m. and then head out for fun. "In order to receive funding from the Social Affairs Committee, an event has to be open to all members of campus," explains an economics major. "Because of this regulation, you don't have to worry about getting in to a party or having to pay for most events." The college allows students of legal age to have alcohol on campus, and one student says, "Campus police are not disciplinarians. They want students to be safe." Swarthmore's two fraternities attract 9 percent of the men; a recently formed sorority draws 4 percent of the women. Annual activities include Primal Scream,

In an effort to reduce the burden of debt, Swarthmore has replaced loans with grants in its financial aid packages.

the tradition where everyone screams at midnight the night before exams, and the McCabe Mile, where everyone decorates the McCabe Library with toilet paper around shelves (the founder of Scott Tissue is an alumnus and donor).

Students' biggest complaints include lack of sleep and too much work, self-imposed or otherwise. If they're not studying, Swatties are volunteering, often in Philadelphia or the nearby smaller city of Chester, or out pursuing a personal whim. The village of Swarthmore, known as the "'Ville," has some stores, a pizza parlor, and a Chinese restaurant. Students say there's not much in the way of off-campus social activity. For that, they hop from the on-campus train station into city-center Philadelphia, where many temptations await, including concerts, dance clubs, museums, and four professional sports teams. The King of Prussia mall, with a movie theater and department stores, isn't far either.

With Swarthmore's focus on academics, athletics aren't a high priority. The school scrapped its football program because the need to recruit enough males to remain competitive in the increasingly intense Division III environment was under-mining efforts to recruit students with other interests and talents. Men's basketball, baseball, and women's volleyball have won Centennial Conference championships in recent years. Other competitive Garnet teams include men's golf, women's track and field, and men's and women's soccer. Any victory over archrival Haverford will have Swatties swelling with pride. Intramurals and club sports enlist 40 percent of students, and Prom Dress Rugby is a beloved annual event. In the Crum Regatta, student-made boats float in nearby Crum Creek—Swarthmore's answer to the America's Cup.

Swarthmore is a place where the administration supports the student body completely, and students are given a voice in a variety of issues ranging from fac-ulty hiring decisions to making campuswide policies. Students who want to take an active role in their education beyond the classroom door may find the right fit here. Says a student, "We really are dedicated to learning just because we like to learn, not because we want the A."

Social life often begins late, since students hit the books until 10 or 11 p.m. and then head out for fun.

Overlaps

Wesleyan, University of Chicago, Brown, Yale, Harvard, Princeton, University of Pennsylvania, Haverford

If You Apply To ›

Swarthmore: Early decision I and II, regular decision. SATs or ACTs: required. Subject Tests: optional. Accepts the Common Application with supplement.

Syracuse University

900 South Crouse Avenue, Syracuse, NY 13244

Syracuse has defined itself as a research university that takes undergraduates seriously. World renowned in the field of communications, its signature program, Syracuse is also strong in architecture, management, the arts, and public affairs. The university has been a national leader in promoting socioeconomic diversity. Basketball provides solace during snowy winter nights.

Anyone who has watched college sports on TV is familiar with the bright orange color associated with Syracuse University. They've seen the screaming fans and the stadiums overflowing with cheering hordes. But beyond all the athletic fanfare is passion of another sort: Syracuse has set out to become a thriving, student-centered research university. In recent years, the university has launched academic programs in emerging areas such as global enterprise technology and sport analytics and

Website: www.syracuse.edu
Location: Small City
Private
Total Enrollment: 18,900
Undergraduates: 14,346

created integrated learning majors in fields such as forensic science and neuroscience. By fostering close working relationships between students and faculty, expanding course offerings, and pouring loads of money into facility upgrades, Syracuse has made its former reputation as an academic assembly line with killer sports teams a thing of the past.

The Syracuse campus is located on a hill overlooking the city of Syracuse in central New York State. The character and mixture of architectural styles depict a continuously changing campus, which is grassy, full of trees, and bordered by residential neighborhoods. Fifteen of the university's 140 buildings are listed in the National Register of Historic Places. Many schools and colleges have restructured facilities to accommodate more faculty/student research, as well as social interaction between the two groups. A $118 million renovation of the Carrier Dome is underway.

General education requirements vary by school and college, but several of them subscribe to the Arts and Sciences core requirements, which include coursework in the sciences, math, social sciences, humanities, and contemporary issues. All entering first-year students participate in a common reading program and take a writing seminar, and each school and college offers a small-group course, known as the First-Year Forum, to share common first-year academic and cocurricular experiences.

The Newhouse School of Public Communications is undoubtedly Syracuse's most prestigious academic program, offering eight majors and opportunities for dual majors. Additionally, programs in architecture, social sciences, management, marketing, visual and performing arts, and life sciences are popular and well regarded. Also well known is the Maxwell School of Citizenship and Public Affairs, whose faculty members teach sought-after undergraduate courses in economics, history, political science, and other social sciences. The College of Arts and Sciences is the largest college at Syracuse and offers recognized programs in writing and rhetoric, philosophy, geography, and chemistry.

> "I have yet to meet a professor who is unwilling to go out of their way to help their students."

A civil engineering major says that "each school at Syracuse has its own academic climate, and some are more competitive than others," but students can expect challenging coursework across the board. Classes are usually small; 59 percent have fewer than 20 students. "Some professors go above and beyond to teach material, while others stick to the old PowerPoint presentations," says a senior, but another student adds that, despite different approaches to teaching, "I have yet to meet a professor who is unwilling to go out of their way to help their students."

Teaming with NASA, the university has a $3 million virtual aerospace engineering facility—one of three in the nation—where students have helped design a reusable space launch vehicle. Syracuse students have also participated in NASA's reduced-gravity student flight programs. The university offers an honors program for a small number of the most motivated students, and a large portion of students participate in undergraduate research. Thirty-two percent study abroad via centers in seven cities around the world, as well as more than 65 World Partner programs and short-term options. Syracuse's centers in Los Angeles and New York City offer semester-long programs for those pursuing careers in the entertainment industry.

Teaming with NASA, the university has a $3 million virtual aerospace engineering facility—one of three in the nation.

"Students on campus are very vocal," says a sophomore. Thirty-five percent of the students are from New York State, and most of those hail from New York City and Long Island; 13 percent are international. The number of students of color has been steadily increasing, with African Americans now comprising 7 percent of the student body, Asian Americans 7 percent, Hispanics 9 percent, and multiracial students 3 percent. Despite pushback from faculty members concerned about the university's academic image—and despite a declining number of Pell Grant recipients—the administration insists that Syracuse remains committed to admissions policies that made the school a national leader in promoting socioeconomic diversity. Sixteen percent of first-year students qualify for Pell Grants. "Two of the current biggest issues on campus are diversity/self-segregation and sexual safety," reports a political science major, noting that the university has sponsored many events to address these concerns. Athletes are well supported with 318 athletic scholarships in 16 sports. Merit scholarships averaging $12,500 are also available.

Seventy percent of undergraduates live in university housing, which is described as comfortable and well maintained. Students are required to live on campus for their first two years; all first-years reside in residence halls on Main Campus, while South Campus houses upperclassmen in apartment-style facilities.

"Greek Life definitely plays a huge role on this campus."

About a third of freshmen participate in more than two dozen living/learning communities. "I was in the engineering learning community, and it was where I met my closest friends," says a senior. "These people were my ultimate support system." The campus offers 18 eateries, including five residential dining centers. As for campus safety, the university has a key-card access system in all dorms and a bus service for students studying late on campus.

Twenty-seven percent of men belong to fraternities, and 40 percent of women join sororities. "Greek Life definitely plays a huge role on this campus. I have never felt pressured to drink, however," a student says. Students 21 and over spend many an evening barhopping on Marshall Street, a lively strip near campus. Orange After Dark puts on late-night activities like movie nights, bowling, and laser tag. Students also enjoy the annual Juice Jam, Mayfest, and Martin Luther King Jr. celebrations.

Students generally enjoy the city of Syracuse, which offers a variety of off-campus retreats, including an excellent art museum, a professional theater, a resident opera company, a symphony, and a string of movie theaters and restaurants. The city's Armory Square is flanked with coffee shops, upscale boutiques, clubs, and eateries. Many students are involved in the community through internships

"On game days we're all bleeding orange."

and volunteer work. If students tire of the life in Syracuse, several quaint country towns, complete with orchards, lakes, and waterfalls, are nearby, as are multiple ski resorts. Destiny USA, about 10 minutes away, is the country's sixth-largest shopping center and has an 18-theater cinema and indoor go-kart track. Popular road trips include Skaneateles Lake, Ithaca, Niagara Falls, Montreal, and Rochester.

"Whether you are a socialite who loves Greek life or a nerd who loves science, on game days we're all bleeding orange," says one senior. The Syracuse Orange football team rocks the spacious Carrier Dome, cheered on by their fruit-inspired mascot, Otto the Orange, and 50,000 fans. Men's and women's basketball are consistently strong, and a new Duke–Syracuse basketball rivalry has been established. Men's lacrosse and track and field have claimed recent Atlantic Coast Conference titles. The "painters" are famous at Syracuse—they are groups of students who each paint a letter of the school's name on their bare chests and run through rain, sleet, or snow to each home game. Syracuse extends its enthusiasm for sports to more than 60 club and intramural programs as well.

From special academic partnerships with NASA to opportunities to study abroad or volunteer right at home, students at Syracuse know they've got something special. The wintry climate may be cold and snowy, but the ubiquitous bright orange paraphernalia all over campus is enough to warm anyone. For many, one senior's words are on target: "You'll never find a school that has more school spirit than we do."

The football team rocks the spacious Carrier Dome, cheered on by their fruit-inspired mascot, Otto the Orange, and 50,000 fans.

Overlaps

Boston University, NYU, Penn State, Northeastern, Cornell University, University of Michigan, University of Southern California, University of Maryland

University of Tennessee Knoxville

Knoxville, TN 37996

UT is in the middle of the pack among its Southeastern rivals—behind Florida, U of Georgia, and UNC; ahead of Alabama, Arkansas, and Ole Miss. As the only major public university in Tennessee, UT comes close to being all things to all students. Strong in business, engineering, and communication. One of the few Southern flagship universities located in a major city.

Website: www.utk.edu
Location: City Center
Public
Total Enrollment: 24,635
Undergraduates: 20,909
Male/Female: 50/50
SAT Ranges: ERW 580–660, M 560–650
ACT Ranges: 24–30
Financial Aid: 80%
Pell Grant: 26%
Expense: Pub $ $ $
Student Loans: 50%
Average Debt: $
Applicants: 18,872
Accepted: 77%
Enrolled: 34%
Grad in 6 Years: 70%
Returning Freshmen: 86%
Academics: ✐ ✐ ✐
Social: 🕿 🕿 🕿 🕿
Q of L: ★ ★ ★
Admissions: (865) 974-1111
Email Address: admissions@utk.edu

Strong Programs:
Business
Supply Chain Management
Architecture
Engineering
Nursing
Psychology

Students at the University of Tennessee put a premium on school spirit, athletics, and academics—typically in that order. In the fall, boisterous fans pack into one of the nation's largest on-campus football stadiums to watch the Volunteers play against national powerhouses like Alabama, Arkansas, and Florida. Also competitive is the SEC-dominating women's basketball team. "Bleeding orange is the only way to go!" cheers one happy Volunteer. Amid this excitement, it's easy to forget that UT also prides itself on a number of strong academic programs.

Set in the foothills of the Great Smoky Mountains, UT is in the heart of east Tennessee's urban hub and only a few miles away from Oak Ridge, Tennessee, home to the prominent Oak Ridge National Laboratory. The 600-acre campus has an array of architectural styles ranging from Gothic to Georgian to modern. Particularly noteworthy is the Hodges Library—the largest one in the state—built in the shape of a ziggurat. The university has spent approximately $1.5 billion in the last five years on new construction, renovations, and landscaping improvements. Streets that once ran through the center of campus have been transformed into landscaped pathways, and several parking lots have been replaced by grassy lawns. Other recent projects include a $167 million student union, a $114 million science and anthropology building, and multiple residence halls; a new West Campus dining facility is in the pipeline, to be completed in 2020.

> **"Bleeding orange is the only way to go!"**

UT's general education requirements are fairly extensive and include courses in written and oral communications, quantitative reasoning, arts and humanities, culture and civilizations, social sciences, and natural sciences, plus a foreign language or multicultural studies. The Life of the Mind program has all freshmen read the same book over the summer and discuss it when they arrive on campus in the fall. Many strong academic programs are in preprofessional fields, most notably business (particularly supply chain management), architecture, engineering, and nursing. On the liberal arts and sciences side, psychology, biology, kinesiology, and sustainability are popular majors. The modern foreign languages and literatures major allows students to combine a concentration in a language, such as German, Spanish, or Japanese, with one in international business.

Academic competition varies, as does course difficulty. "Some classes are harder than anything I could imagine and some require little effort," says one junior. Large lectures are commonplace, and students report occasional problems with registration because preference is given to seniors. Even so, the university has bolstered academic advising, tutoring, and career services in recent years, and graduation rates have been on the rise. Professors receive mixed reviews: "I have had some really good professors and some mediocre ones," a supply chain management major says.

UT is the managing partner of Oak Ridge National Laboratory—the federal government's largest nonweapons lab—which enhances science and technology offerings, and involves 350 students and faculty in disciplines as diverse as English and physics. Up to 10 percent of undergraduates are members of the university-wide Chancellor's Honors program, and most of UT's colleges also offer honors tracks. UT established the Haslam Scholars program for 15 of the nation's top students; selection criteria include scholastic achievement, leadership potential, and special talents. Haslam scholars enjoy such benefits as study groups mentored by top UT faculty, a study abroad experience, and research support. Six percent of students study abroad during their four years, selecting from programs in more than 60 countries on six continents. The most popular options are short-term, faculty-led programs that provide students the opportunity to study under the guidance of a faculty member during the summer terms.

UT students are "levelheaded but tend to get a little crazy on the weekends," says a student. Eighty-five percent of undergraduates are homegrown Tennesseans, and 2 percent are international. Minority enrollment remains low—African Americans account for 7 percent of the students, Hispanics 4 percent, Asian Americans 4 percent, and multiracial students 3 percent—but the university has hired a vice chancellor for diversity and inclusion to promote and support campus diversity. Financial aid opportunities have been generous, with thousands of merit scholarships available (averaging $6,000) and 272 athletic scholarships in 20 sports. Twenty-six percent of freshmen qualify for the Pell Grant.

> "Some classes are harder than anything I could imagine and some require little effort."

One-third of UT students live on campus. Although a few older buildings remain, the university has built seven new residence halls as part of a multiphase housing development plan that concluded in 2019. Each of the dorms has a residence hall association, which for a token fee provides checkout of sports equipment, games, cooking utensils, and other useful items. Freshmen may choose from 16 living/learning communities, where they collaborate with peers on shared academic interests. UT has installed remote alarm units that allow students to report a crime from anywhere on campus and has developed comprehensive sexual assault prevention programs.

Students say that the social life is "very important" and active both on and off campus. Greek life is growing more popular—14 percent of the men and 25 percent of the women join up. The social calendar is dotted with numerous major events, including River Fest on the nearby Tennessee River, Saturday Night on the Town, and the Dogwood Arts Festival. Cumberland Avenue (a.k.a. The Strip), a few blocks away, offers a lively variety of bars and eateries. But nothing compares to the sea of orange that engulfs the campus on Saturday afternoons in the fall. More than 100,000 people jam the football stadium to see the Volunteers (a term dating to the Mexican War) take on their Southeast Conference rivals. Denizens liken football in Knoxville to religion, and according to one, "'Alabama' is a four-letter word" in these parts. UT has claimed 23 team and 255 individual national championships in its history. Recent conference champs include men's and women's basketball and rowing. The intramural program attracts roughly a quarter of undergraduates, and the most popular sports are flag football, indoor and outdoor soccer, basketball, and softball.

(continued)
Biology
Kinesiology

The Life of the Mind program has all freshmen read the same book over the summer and discuss it when they arrive on campus in the fall.

The university has built seven new residence halls as part of a multiphase housing development plan that concluded in 2019.

Overlaps

University of Alabama, University of Tennessee at Chattanooga, University of South Carolina, East Tennessee State, Middle Tennessee State, University of Memphis, Tennessee Tech, Auburn

With its athletic prowess well established, administrators and students are hoping that UT can develop a comparable reputation for its academics. In its quest to climb the ranks of public research universities, UT is transforming its campus with a spate of new construction and ever-increasing academic resources. In the meantime, many will find the growing opportunities here at the "Big Orange" to be well worth the squeezing.

If You Apply To ›

UT: Regular decision. SATs or ACTs: required. Subject Tests: optional. Accepts the Common Application with supplement. Additional essay required for nursing program applicants. Audition required for music applicants.

University of Texas at Austin

Austin, Texas 78712

UT Austin is on anybody's list of the top 10 public universities in the nation. The Plan II liberal arts honors program is one of the country's most renowned. Though it is also the capital of Texas, Austin ranks among the nation's best college towns—a progressive enclave in a conservative state. Boot camp for aspiring political types in the Lone Star State and beyond. Where else can you spend time watching bats?

Website: www.utexas.edu
Location: City Center
Public
Total Enrollment: 47,750
Undergraduates: 37,510
Male/Female: 46/54
SAT Ranges: ERW 620–720, M 610–740
ACT Ranges: 26–33
Financial Aid: 40%
Pell Grant: 27%
Expense: Pub $ $
Student Loans: 43%
Average Debt: $ $
Applicants: 51,033
Accepted: 36%
Enrolled: 44%
Grad in 6 Years: 83%
Returning Freshmen: 95%
Academics: ✍ ✍ ✍ ✍ ½
Social: ☎ ☎ ☎ ☎
Q of L: ★ ★ ★ ★
Admissions: (512) 475-7399
Email Address: bealonghorn@utexas.edu

Strong Programs:
Engineering

The University of Texas at Austin has come a long way from where it began in 1883 as a small school with only one building, eight teachers, two departments, and 221 students. Today, the campus is a Texas-sized home to more than 37,000 undergraduates. From its extensive academic programs to its powerful athletic teams to its location in one of the nation's ultimate college towns, the University of Texas has everything a Longhorn could ask for. "Our university is a diverse community with amazing opportunities for success," says a junior.

A 400-acre oasis near downtown Austin, replete with rolling hills, trees, creeks, and fountains, the campus features buildings ranging from "old, distinguished" limestone structures to contemporary Southwest architecture. The fabled UT Tower

"Our university is a diverse community with amazing opportunities for success."

is adorned with a large clock and chimes (a lifesaver for the disorganized) and is illuminated in Longhorn orange after big athletic wins. From the steps of the Tower, one can see the verdant Austin hills and the state capitol. The outstanding library system at the University of Texas has more than 10 million volumes located in 17 different libraries across campus. Recent construction includes the $310 million Engineering Education and Research Center.

All undergraduates complete a 42-hour core curriculum that requires coursework in English composition, humanities, American and Texas government, American history, social sciences, math, science and technology, and visual and performing arts. Entering freshmen are expected to take a First-Year Signature Course, which is usually small and taught by a senior professor, that introduces them to academic discussion and analysis of issues from an interdisciplinary perspective.

The list of academic strengths at the University of Texas is daunting. Undergraduate offerings in accounting, advertising, architecture, finance, marketing, and social work are first-rate. Engineering and computer science programs are excellent and continue to expand, and engineering, business, communication, and biology represent the most popular majors. The English department is huge (nearly 70 tenure-track professors) and students give it high marks. UT's McDonald Observatory, based in West Texas, boasts one of the world's largest telescopes.

Students say the academic climate is competitive and demanding. "There are many rigorous majors that have accelerated courses or competitive programs," says a student. Many UT classes are quite large—a quarter enroll more than 50 students—and smaller sections fill up quickly. UT is a research university, so the professors are often busy in the laboratories or the library. They do, however, have office hours. "My professors are above and beyond my expectations," says a psychology major. "Their own interest in their topics is obvious, and the determination to aid the students is admirable."

The Plan II liberal arts honors program, a national model, is one of the oldest honors programs in the country and one of the best academic deals anywhere. It offers qualified students a flexible curriculum, top-notch professors, small seminar courses, and individualized counseling, and provides them with all of the advantages of a large university in a small-college atmosphere. Business, communication, engineering, liberal arts, and natural sciences honors programs are also available. Engineering majors can alternate work and study in the co-op program, while education and health majors hold term-time internships. Being in the capital city should have its advantages, and it does. Almost 200 UT undergrads work for lawmakers in the Texas Legislature, only a 10-minute walk from campus. The Sanger Learning Center offers sessions with learning specialists, peer tutoring, coaching on public speaking, and other academic help. Study abroad options are available in 80 countries, and roughly 25 percent of UT undergrads head to foreign locales during their four years.

UT students are "intelligent, involved, and proactive in their education," says a senior. Eighty-nine percent of UT undergraduates are Texans, and 5 percent hail from outside the U.S. Students say there is no dominant political pattern on campus—despite the fact that historically UT has been integral in the careers of big-time (conservative) Texas politicians. The liberals are not exactly hiding out on this huge campus. Political issues, such as human rights, gun control, and abortion, can get students on both sides pretty riled up here. Hispanics account for 23 percent of undergrads, Asian Americans 21 percent, African Americans 4 percent, and multiracial students 4 percent. The university offers special welcome programs, social and educational events, and peer mentoring for African American, Hispanic, and first-generation students. The university also awards merit scholarships averaging $2,400, as well as hundreds of athletic scholarships in 20 sports. Twenty-seven percent of incoming freshmen receive Pell Grants.

"[Professors'] interest in their topics is obvious."

University housing, which accommodates only 18 percent of undergrads, ranges from functional to plush. "Most of the dorms are old," says a student, "but they have nice facilities." Residence halls offer a variety of living options based on common social and educational interests. Apartments and condos close to campus are lovely—and very expensive. More reasonably priced digs can be found in other parts of town. But be forewarned: UT life requires lots of walking, especially for commuters, though free shuttle stops and parking lots are scattered about. As for food, there is a wide variety of options, including healthy, vegetarian, kosher, and vegan fare. Security can be a concern (Austin is an urban area, after all), but students report feeling safe on campus, thanks to active and highly visible campus police. Texas law allows permit holders to carry firearms in designated areas on campus.

The Texas Union sponsors movies and social events, and its Cactus Café is a popular venue for musical acts. It also boasts the world's only collection of orange-topped pool tables in its arcade and bowling alley. For those more interested in

(continued)

Business
Communication
Biology
Accounting
Architecture
Social Work
Computer Science

The Plan II liberal arts honors program, a national model, is one of the oldest honors programs in the country.

Almost 200 UT undergrads work for lawmakers in the Texas Legislature, only a 10-minute walk from campus.

octaves than eight balls, the Performing Arts Center has two concert halls that attract nationally known performers. There are also more than 1,300 student organizations from which to choose. Fifteen percent of the men and 18 percent of the women go Greek. Annual festivals include 40 Acres Fest, a sprawling carnival of the campus organizations. A pep rally gets students psyched before the Longhorns play rival Oklahoma. And Texas Independence Day provides an occasion for celebration in March.

The Texas Union sponsors movies and social events, and its Cactus Café is a popular venue for musical acts.

As the state capital, Austin is hardly a typical college town, but it is one of the best ones. "I love it," exclaims a junior. "It has a great live music scene and is beautiful." Nightlife centers on nearby Sixth Street, full of pubs and restaurants of all types, and the well-known music scene that features everything from blues to jazz to rock to folk, as well as the Austin City Limits and South by Southwest festivals. Along with live music, bat-watching is one of Austin's most popular activities—the city is known as "Bat City" after the colony of Mexican free-tailed bats that lives under the Congress Avenue Bridge in the spring and summer. It's the largest urban bat colony in North America. Halloween draws an estimated 80,000 costumed revelers to Sixth Street (and sometimes up its lampposts). When the weather gets too muggy (quite often in spring and summer), students head for off-campus campgrounds, lakes, and parks. The most popular road trips are to San Antonio or Dallas. For spring break, students travel to Padre Island, if not New Orleans.

Athletics are as vital as oxygen for most Texans, so it's no surprise that UT's athletic department has a budget in excess of $170 million. The Longhorns compete in the Division I Big 12 Conference, and students especially look forward to the annual Texas–Oklahoma football game played in the Cotton Bowl in Dallas. "Football games pull the student body together and give us a chance to show our school spirit," says one student. Bevo XV, the famed UT mascot, is the latest in a long line of live longhorn steer mascots who have at various times been known to bolt loose from their handlers, rip their shirts, and, on one occasion, lie down in the end zone during a game. Basketball and baseball are also popular; the baseball program has many alumni in the major leagues, and the annual spring game between UT's baseball alumni and the current college squad is quite a contest. The men's swimming and diving team claimed its fourth consecutive national championship in 2018, and men's and women's golf, track and field, and tennis, along with women's swimming and diving and rowing, are recent conference champs. UT's extensive intramural program is very popular and offers weekend athletes access to the same great facilities that the big-time jocks use.

> "I love [Austin]. It has a great live music scene and is beautiful."

The University of Texas may seem overwhelming because of its imposing size, but students say the school spirit and sense of community found here make it feel smaller. UT prides itself on having one of the most reasonably priced tuitions in the country for a flagship public research university. It also offers one of the best all-around educational experiences a student could ask for, especially if you make it into Plan II.

Overlaps

Baylor, Duke, University of Houston, MIT, NYU, Rice, Texas A&M, Vanderbilt

If You Apply To ›

UT Austin: Regular decision. SATs or ACTs: required. No Subject Tests. Does not accept the Common Application. Apply either to institution as a whole or particular program. Certain departments have additional requirements.

University of Texas at Dallas

Richardson, TX 75080

A rising star in the Lone Star State, UT Dallas is now the most selective of the regional campuses of the UT system. Has put on a full-court press to attract top students in science and technology. Good living conditions and a serious honors program. Football here is of the flag variety. Slightly less selective than Texas Tech and Texas A&M.

Founded in 1961 as a graduate research center, The University of Texas at Dallas did not begin awarding undergraduate degrees until 1975. It wasn't until 1990 that UT Dallas admitted its first freshman class. Since that time, the university has continued to grow and hone its chops as a four-year university with an emphasis on engineering, mathematics, the sciences, and the management of new technologies. "UTD is a young, vibrant, and promising institution," raves one senior. "Even freshmen have the chance to create new organizations and traditions, work in real labs with full professors, and be in contact with top administrators." Although the university may not fit the typical Texas "frats and football" mold, students here still find plenty of reasons to cheer.

Situated on 700 rolling acres in the Dallas suburb of Richardson, UT Dallas has the feel of a large corporate campus. Most buildings are positioned around an interior mall that features a variety of blooming trees, low flower beds, and fountains. The predominant architectural style is 1970s tilt wall concrete, and many buildings are interconnected by a series of glass sky bridges. The Natural Science and Engineering Research Laboratory provides 192,000 square feet of state-of-the-art labs and is playfully referred to as the "mermaid building" for its iridescent blue, green, and magenta shingles, which resemble fish scales. Recent additions to campus include a $113 million bioengineering and sciences building, and a new building for the physics department is expected to open in 2020.

> **"Even freshmen have the chance to...work in real labs with full professors."**

To graduate, UT Dallas students must complete a general education curriculum consisting of 42 credit hours across eight disciplines: communication, mathematics, life and physical sciences, humanities, creative arts, American history, government, and social and behavioral sciences. As part of the school's new Orbit program for student success, all freshmen take a small-group Freshmen Seminar, learn about campus resources, and receive peer mentoring.

UTD offers budding scientists an especially solid choice of majors, including highly respected programs in speech-language pathology and audiology, information technology, and neuroscience. In fact, all of the hard sciences draw praise from students,

> **"UTD would best fit a nerd."**

especially the engineering and computer science programs. Those seeking to add a pinch of the humanities to their science may opt for the innovative School of Arts, Technology, and Emerging Communication, which offers a B.A. degree and tracks in animation, critical media studies, design and production, games, and mediated communication. The most popular majors are accounting, biology, business administration, and computer science. Students say the academic climate is collaborative, but courses can be grueling. "The workload can be intense, depending on the amount of hours per semester that you take, but it is doable," says one sophomore. Around one in four undergraduate classes has more than 50 students. "Professors do their best to be accessible to students with office hours and review sessions," says

---

Website: www.utdallas.edu
Location: Suburban
Public
Total Enrollment: 21,376
Undergraduates: 15,109
Male/Female: 57/43
SAT Ranges: ERW 600–700, M 620–730
ACT Ranges: 26–32
Financial Aid: 70%
Pell Grant: 24%
Expense: Pub $ $ $
Student Loans: 44%
Average Debt: $
Applicants: 11,791
Accepted: 76%
Enrolled: 35%
Grad in 6 Years: 69%
Returning Freshmen: 87%
Academics: ✐ ✐ ✐
Social: ☎ ☎ ☎
Q of L: ★ ★ ★
Admissions: (972) 883-2270
Email Address: interest@ utdallas.edu

Strong Programs:
Accounting
Biology
Business Administration
Computer Science
Speech-Language Pathology and Audiology
Information Technology
Neuroscience
Engineering

one student. "Many of them are particularly involved in the community and clubs on campus, so it is easy to get to know them."

Qualified first-year students may take part in the Wildenthal Honors College, which houses eight programs that grant students access to personal mentoring and special social and academic opportunities. The program is valuable because it "gets smaller groups together to form real communities and resource networks," according to one junior. The Undergraduate Research Program offers students stipends specifically to pursue short-term research proposals. Study abroad options are available in nearly 60 countries, and roughly 6 percent of undergrads go overseas. The McDermott Scholars program offers a full ride plus stipends for international travel, field trips, and other benefits; approximately 25 freshmen are selected every year.

"Students here are weird, in the best way possible," says a marketing major. "Being called weird is like being called limited edition, meaning you won't see it often." Another student is more direct: "UTD would best fit a nerd." Ninety-two percent of undergraduates hail from the Lone Star State and 4 percent from abroad.

"Sure, UTD is a relatively new university, but there is enough tradition to be proud of."

African Americans account for 6 percent of the student body, Asian Americans add 31 percent, Hispanics comprise 18 percent, and multiracial students make up 4 percent. When it comes to political and social issues, a sophomore says, "UTD seems politically quieter than other universities." The university hands out merit scholarships averaging $12,000 each year, but no athletic scholarships. Twenty-four percent of incoming freshmen qualify for the Pell Grant, and the Academic Bridge Program helps 160 high-potential students from urban schools make the transition to college-level academics with personal advising, mentoring, and tutoring.

Twenty-six percent of undergrads live on campus in apartment-style residence villages. "Dorms are some of the best dorms I've seen at any university," says one student. Freshmen can choose to participate in a living/learning community (LLC); options range from arts and technology and prehealth to first-generation and exploration (for undeclared majors). LLC students live in the same residence hall, attend classes together, and participate in various group activities. A bevy of dining options are available, including choices for the health-conscious. Under Texas law, people with permits may carry firearms on campus; students rate campus security highly.

Students say the social scene is slowly heating up. "There is a decent Greek presence, intramural games are fun to go to, and student government helps create fun student events," according to one senior. There are frequent concerts, dinners, movies, and dances, and the aforementioned Greek scene attracts 5 percent of the men and 7 percent of the women. A math major describes the party scene as "very low-key and generally off campus," and the university is said to be "fairly strict" when it comes to enforcing alcohol policies. Popular traditions include homecoming, the Cometville Carnival, and the oozeball tournament (that's mud volleyball, for the uninitiated). "We're still young and traditions are still forming," explains a sophomore. Richardson is "definitely not a college town, but the surrounding community is pleasant and relaxed," says a senior. Students frequent the neighborhood stores and restaurants and get involved with the locals through volunteering and community service projects. When it's time for off-campus fun, many head into downtown Dallas, which is "lively, artsy, and sophisticated," according to a molecular biology major.

UTD may be one of the few places in Texas where football isn't considered a way of life. In fact, you won't find football listed among the university's 13 varsity teams. Nevertheless, with 24 conference titles since 2002, the UT Dallas Comets are respectable contenders in the Division III American Southwest Conference. The chess team is a juggernaut, having made more than a dozen appearances in the President's Cup (the "final four" of college chess). Many students take part in recreational and club sports. Popular activities include flag football, basketball, and soccer, and students are enjoying a recently built cricket field.

UTD appeals to those students seeking a science- or business-centric curriculum, access to undergraduate research and top-notch facilities, and administrators who value their input. "Sure, UTD is a relatively new university, but there is enough tradition to be proud of," reasons a biomedical engineering major, who adds, "UTD is driven, talented, smart, quirky, and has eclectic interests that truly make the university interesting once you get to know it." Indeed, students here aren't bound by tradition—they're creating it.

If You Apply To ›

UT Dallas: Rolling admissions. SATs (with essay) or ACTs (with writing): required. Subject Tests: optional. Does not accept the Common Application.

Texas A&M University

BEST BUY

College Station, TX 77843

Coming to A&M is like joining an elite club with 58,000 members. In addition to fanatical school spirit, Texas A&M offers leading programs in the natural sciences, engineering, and business. To succeed in this mass of humanity, students must find their academic niche. The student body is 94 percent Texan, and out-of-staters should be prepared for major culture shock.

Known for its top-notch science and engineering programs and its unsurpassed school spirit, Texas A&M opened in 1876 as the state's first public institution of higher education: a land grant college with a military training focus. Today, as one of only 17 universities in the nation to hold federal land, sea, and space grant designations, Texas A&M would seem to have the whole universe covered. This school of nearly 47,000 full-time undergrads boasts a massive endowment and more traditions than Vatican City. When they're not studying for rigorous classes, Aggies may be found at Midnight Yell before each home and away football game or yelling—as the saying around campus goes, "Aggies don't cheer, we yell!"—for their teams at other high-energy athletic events.

Texas A&M is the largest university campus in the country, in terms of acreage (5,200)—something made obvious to students every time they walk to class. The campus combines historic brick buildings from the turn of the 20th century with newer structures in more modern styles, and is pulled together by a heavy cover of live oak trees. The campus is in a constant state of flux, as renovations and new construction take place on a regular basis, the most recent including a $125 million renovation and expansion of the Memorial Student Center.

The general education requirements are standard, but incoming Aggies can expect some heavy coursework. They must also fulfill a cultural diversity requirement and demonstrate computer literacy and proficiency in a foreign language. While Texas A&M is best known for its agriculture and engineering colleges, and for veterinary medicine, the university is cultivating a strong liberal arts program and an even stronger business school. Management, management information systems, psychology, and engineering-related majors are the most popular, although

Website: www.tamu.edu
Location: Small City
Public
Total Enrollment: 58,357
Undergraduates: 46,593
Male/Female: 52/48
SAT Ranges: ERW 570–670, M 570–690
ACT Ranges: 25–30
Financial Aid: 72%
Pell Grant: 22%
Expense: Pub $ $
Student Loans: 43%
Average Debt: $
Applicants: 37,191
Accepted: 70%
Enrolled: 45%
Grad in 6 Years: 82%
Returning Freshmen: 92%
Academics: ✍ ✍ ✍ ✍
Social: ☎ ☎ ☎
Q of L: ★ ★ ★
Admissions: (979) 845-1060

(continued)

Email Address: admissions@
tamu.edu

Strong Programs:
Management
Management Information
   Systems
Psychology
Engineering
Agriculture
Veterinary Medicine
Education
Oceanography

Texas A&M is the largest university campus in the country, in terms of acreage (5,200).

interdisciplinary studies majors in education also garner high enrollment. Aggies stand by their science programs and have done outstanding research in oceanography. Technical programs of virtually all kinds are heartily supported, especially nuclear, space, and biotechnical research.

Students generally agree that while academics are taken seriously here, the climate is, in the words of a junior, "definitely collaborative." Teaching assistants and grad students are often found behind lecterns, and 25 percent of classes have more than 50 students. Some professors may prioritize research over teaching, and a biomedical sciences major rates the quality of instruction as "mostly excellent, sometimes only sufficient." Undergraduate research is, unsurprisingly, important here, and getting involved is "as easy as emailing a professor and starting that conversation," says a biomedical engineering major.

"No matter who you are, you'll be greeted with a smile and a 'Howdy!'"

Highly motivated students also recommend the University Honors Program as a good way to make friends and enjoy perks like "priority registration, access to smaller classes with better professors, and networking with the brightest minds here at Texas A&M," according to one participant. Studying, working, and volunteering sometimes take students far from Aggieland. Roughly one-third of undergrads study abroad during their four years, mostly in short-term programs; more than 100 faculty-led programs are available, along with hundreds of other options through partnerships and exchange programs worldwide.

Ninety-four percent of students are from Texas, and just 2 percent come from other countries. Aggies are known for their friendliness. Says one, "From your first tour on campus to the day you graduate, no matter who you are, you'll be greeted with a smile and a 'Howdy!'" Twenty-two percent of freshmen qualify for the Pell Grant. African Americans comprise 3 percent of the student body, Asian Americans 7 percent, Hispanics 23 percent, and multiracial students 3 percent. The campus is decidedly conservative, and a senior comments that "not many rallies or political protests are organized here." Athletes compete for hundreds of scholarships, while scholars vie for thousands of merit awards averaging $4,000. In-state students can lock in their tuition rate for four years, but out-of-staters are subject to tuition increases.

A&M's single-sex and co-ed dorms range from cheap and not-so-comfortable to expensive and cushy (with private bathrooms and in-unit laundry machines), but they accommodate only 23 percent of undergrads. A communication major recommends the university's freshman living/learning communities as a chance to "meet people with similar interests as you" and because "applying for one can help guarantee a spot

"Applying for living/ learning communities can help guarantee a spot to live on campus."

Roughly one-third of undergrads study abroad during their four years, mostly in short-term programs.

to live on campus." Most upperclassmen live in the numerous apartments and houses in College Station or its twin city, Bryan, and the university runs an extensive bus system throughout the community. Dining halls, fast-food chains, snack shops, and food trucks are all over campus. Out-of-staters may wish to note that Texas law allows permit holders to carry firearms on campus. "I'm never afraid on campus that my things will get stolen or that I will be in danger," says a nonprofit management major. Students report that the Step In, Stand Up campaign has done much to raise awareness about sexual assault.

When it comes to social life, a junior advises, "It is imperative that you join a student organization in order to make A&M feel a little smaller and to really find your niche and purpose." With more than 1,100 student-led clubs and organizations to choose from, students should have little trouble doing so. Greeks attract 8 percent of the men and 17 percent of the women, and students say that, with such a large student body, neither Greek life nor partying define the social scene. Students appreciate the amenities of the surrounding area, especially in the Northgate district, which offers ample restaurants and bars. "College Station is a model college town," asserts a senior. When the school empties out for holidays, the town does too. Students are actively involved in the community, and the Big Event, which draws 21,000 Aggies each year, is the nation's largest student-run day of community service. Those seeking a getaway can drive an hour and a half to either Houston or Austin, and the beaches of the Gulf Coast beckon.

Texas A&M is practically synonymous with tradition. Boasts one senior, "You could write a book—and many have—about all the traditions we have here." Favorites include the Twelfth Man, in which all students stand for the entirety of every football game as a symbol of their loyalty and readiness to take part, and Aggie Muster, held in more than 300 locations around the world to remember alumni who died within the year. There's also the 300-plus member Fightin' Texas Aggie Band and the senior "boot line" at the end of the football halftime performance. The fabled Corps of Cadets is one of the largest uniformed leadership training programs in the country, with more than 2,500 cadets. Although this is just a fraction of the student body, the Corps remains the single most important keeper of the spirit and traditions of Aggieland. Yet another ritual: thousands of seniors join hands and meander through the campus visiting favorite spots for the last time during the Elephant Walk each spring (akin to elephants wandering away from their herds before they die).

Athletics, whether on the varsity level or for recreation, are at the top on anyone's list here. The school's 20 varsity teams compete in the ultracompetitive Division I Southeastern Conference (SEC), where they line up against powerhouses such as Alabama and LSU. Since joining the SEC in 2012, Texas A&M has won four national titles

The fabled Corps of Cadets is the single most important keeper of the spirit and traditions of Aggieland.

"You could write a book— and many have—about all the traditions we have here."

(most recently in men's indoor track and field) and 19 conference championships. Football fans rock Kyle Field with cries of "Gig 'em, Aggies," or "Hump it, Ags," and after touchdowns are scored, Aggie fans kiss their dates. Basketball, flag football, racquetball, and soccer are among the most popular sports in the well-organized and extensive intramural program. Aggie jokes abound, much to the chagrin of A&M students, who don't take too kindly to being the object of ridicule. Example: "How do you get a one-armed Aggie out of a tree?" "Wave."

With undergraduate enrollment increasing by nearly 20 percent in just four years, students express concerns that the university may be getting too large: "There are simply too many students here for the campus and the community to sustain them," remarks a senior, "and our school identity is becoming diluted because of overpopulation." Texas A&M is undeniably gargantuan, yet it is also self-consciously familial. "A great school will challenge and nurture you to become an individual who is ready to conquer any problem in the world—and that right there is Texas A&M," says one satisfied biology major. With varied educational opportunities and memorable traditions worth cheering (that is to say, "yelling") about, it's no wonder students here are so devoted to their "Aggie Family."

Overlaps

UT Austin, UC Berkeley, University of Michigan, UNC at Chapel Hill, Penn State, Baylor, Texas Tech, Texas Christian

If You Apply To ›

Texas A&M: Regular decision. SATs (with essay) or ACTs (with writing): required. Subject Tests: optional. Does not accept the Common Application. Apply to particular schools or programs. Primarily committed to state residents.

Texas Christian University

TCU Box 297013, Fort Worth, TX 76129

The personalized private alternative to Texas-sized state universities. Tuition is less, and the student body less affluent, than that at archrival SMU. Though affiliated with the Disciples of Christ, TCU goes lighter on religion than, say, Baylor. Strengths include business, communication, and the fine arts. Strong sense of community and school spirit.

Website: www.tcu.edu
Location: City Outskirts
Private
Total Enrollment: 10,061
Undergraduates: 8,727
Male/Female: 40/60
SAT Ranges: ERW 570–660,
M 560–670
ACT Ranges: 25–30
Financial Aid: 75%
Pell Grant: 12%
Expense: Pr $ $
Student Loans: 36%
Average Debt: $ $ $ $
Applicants: 19,740
Accepted: 41%
Enrolled: 24%
Grad in 6 Years: 83%
Returning Freshmen: 91%
Academics: ✐ ✐ ✐
Social: ☎ ☎ ☎
Q of L: ★ ★ ★
Admissions: (800) TCU-FROG
Email Address: frogmail@
tcu.edu

Strong Programs:
Nursing
Communication Studies
Finance
Accounting
Biology
Strategic Communication
Education
Fine Arts

You know a school has spirit (if that's the right word) when its students paint themselves purple to cheer raucously for a horny toad. Although outsiders might be baffled by such a display, Texans know these folks are TCU fans cheering for the home team (officially known as the Texas Christian University Horned Frogs) at a Saturday afternoon football game. There's a true sense of school spirit and solidarity here. And while TCU's acceptance rate is about on par with rivals Southern Methodist and Baylor, it has a reputation for being more accessible. Says a senior, "TCU is a community, a real family."

The spacious 277-acre campus is kept in almost perfect condition and features tree-lined walkways and grassy areas. Nearby is a lovely residential neighborhood not too far from the shops and restaurants of downtown Fort Worth. The campus boasts an eclectic mix of architecture, ranging from neo-Georgian to contemporary. Notable facilities include the Walsh Center for Performing Arts, a 56,000-square-foot performance hall and theater complex, as well as a new Greek Village.

Students choose their majors from 114 disciplines, with the core curriculum embodying the base of the liberal arts education. The core emphasizes critical thinking and is divided into three areas: essential competencies; human experience and endeavors; and heritage, mission, vision, and values. There are freshman seminar courses, along with a student orientation and Frog Camp (an optional summer camp that emphasizes team building and school spirit). TCU's standout programs are business, nursing, biology, strategic communication, education, and fine arts. The most popular majors are nursing, communication studies, finance, and accounting. In the Neeley School of Business, some students manage a $1.5 million investment portfolio that is one of the largest student-run investment funds in the nation. The university also offers an innovative dance program with a ballet major, a strong theatre internship program, and majors in comparative race and ethnic studies and ranch management.

> **"[TCU has been] taking a lot more interest in diversity and inclusion efforts."**

The academic climate at TCU is challenging and competitive, but not overwhelmingly so. "TCU students are definitely concerned about academics and grades, but there is also a feeling of support and open cooperation between students," says an English major. Classes are often small, with 44 percent enrolling fewer than 20 students, which according to a senior makes for "an inclusive and comfortable classroom setting." Professors often take on the role of mentors, as do academic advisors. "My advisor is so eager to help," says a student. "I think he really enjoys giving me advice."

Top achievers may be invited to join the Roach Honors College, living together in the honors dorm their first year and pursuing individual research opportunities as part of their honors thesis senior year. "Honors classes are focused more on critical thinking, ethics, and human connections rather than definitions and formulas," explains one participant. Globally minded students can travel to 54 countries to study abroad in more than 250 programs; about a third do so. Career services, which are specific to each college, get high marks, and students also recommend getting involved with leadership opportunities offered through Student Development Services and the Leadership Center.

TCU's student body is fairly homogeneous; 51 percent are from Texas, many from affluent, conservative families. African Americans account for 5 percent of the student body, Hispanics 14 percent, and Asian Americans 3 percent; 4 percent of students are international. Lack of diversity is a top concern among students, but a junior notes that TCU has been "taking a lot more interest in diversity and inclusion efforts within everything from recruitment and admissions to first-year experience programs." This is hardly an activist campus, and although TCU is affiliated with the Christian Church (Disciples of Christ), the atmosphere is not overtly religious. TCU offers merit awards averaging $18,000 and 356 athletic scholarships.

Frog Camp is an optional summer camp that emphasizes team building and school spirit.

Forty-eight percent of the student body lives on campus. Dorm life is a good experience, with up-to-date facilities and helpful staff. "TCU works to make such an amazing community that I would live in Milton, my freshman dorm, forever if I could," enthuses a biology major. Most juniors and seniors, however, move off campus, and fraternity and sorority members may live in their Greek houses after freshman year. Campus meals receive average reviews, except for Sunday brunch. "Wow," says a salivating finance major. "No one misses Sunday brunch. Lobster macaroni and cheese, chocolate fountains, pastries, mountains of fruit, I could go on for days." An evening transportation service, Froggy Five-O, takes you wherever you want to go on campus, and students say they feel safe. The annual, weeklong It's On Us campaign works to raise awareness of sexual assault, and a senior says, "I am proud of TCU for addressing it head-on."

"Wow. No one misses Sunday brunch."

Greek life is important at TCU; 41 percent of the men and 58 percent of the women join Greek organizations. They party in the esprit de corps tradition, but there's plenty of fun left on campus and in Fort Worth to keep the non-Greek Frogs hopping. "Alcohol violations are a big deal," says a student, and involve a three-strike system. Students look forward to the annual fall concert that brings big-name acts like Macklemore and Jason Derulo to campus, and the traditional lighting of the Christmas tree (featuring carols, hot chocolate, cookies, Santa, reindeer, and even fireworks) is always a special event. "Fort Worth is cultured and has plenty of things to do," says a senior. "The stockyards let you get in touch with the inner country in you, and no one should miss a visit to Billy Bob's, the world's largest honky-tonk." Dallas is only 45 minutes to the east, and other road trips include Austin, San Antonio, the Gulf Coast, and Shreveport, Louisiana.

The traditional lighting of the Christmas tree (featuring carols, hot chocolate, reindeer, and even fireworks) is always a special event.

TCU fields 21 athletic programs, which compete in the tough Big 12 Conference. The Horned Frog football, baseball, and men's tennis programs have all won recent conference championships. Eleven TCU teams were nationally ranked in the 2017–18 season, with the equestrian and women's rifle teams performing particularly well. Intramurals are a popular choice with students as well.

From its student-friendly admissions process to its dedication to supporting and developing students once they hop onto campus, TCU is an accessible university offering a personalized educational experience. The school's warm students have no shortage of purple pride. As one junior says, "TCU is full of rah-rah school spirit and a student body that never fails to say, 'Go Frogs!'"

Overlaps

Baylor, University of Southern California, Southern Methodist, Tulane, Vanderbilt, Texas A&M, UT Austin, University of Oklahoma

If You Apply To ›

TCU: Early decision, early action, regular decision. SATs or ACTs: required. Subject Tests: optional. Accepts the Common Application. Optional Freedom of Expression question allows space for any information not included elsewhere in application.

Texas Tech University

Lubbock, TX 79409

A child of the remote West Texas plains, Texas Tech is emerging from the large shadow of Texas A&M as one of the state's top research universities. It takes big-time sports to be on the map in Texas, and the Red Raiders have taken up the challenge. Bills itself as smaller and more personal than UT or A&M.

Website: www.ttu.edu
Location: City Center
Public
Total Enrollment: 31,161
Undergraduates: 27,281
Male/Female: 53/47
SAT Ranges: ERW 540–620,
    M 530–620
ACT Ranges: 22–27
Financial Aid: 54%
Pell Grant: 25%
Expense: Pub $ $
Student Loans: 55%
Average Debt: $ $ $
Applicants: 25,207
Accepted: 69%
Enrolled: 34%
Grad in 6 Years: 59%
Returning Freshmen: 84%
Academics: ✍ ✍ ✍
Social: ☎ ☎ ☎
Q of L: ★ ★ ★
Admissions: (806) 742-1480
Email Address: admissions@
    ttu.edu

Strong Programs:
Mechanical Engineering
Kinesiology
Management
Marketing
Agriculture
Personal Financial Planning
Wind Energy
Music

Texas Tech University has come a long way from its humble beginnings. It opened its doors in 1925 in the West Texas city of Lubbock with fewer than 1,000 students enrolled in four schools: agriculture, engineering, home economics, and liberal arts. Today, Tech hosts more than 27,000 undergraduates, hundreds of academic programs, and schools of medicine and law, and it aspires to become a leading research university on the national level. "We are enjoying increasing emphasis on undergraduate research, service learning and community engagement, personal and professional ethics, and internationalization," administrators say.

Tech's 1,839-acre campus features expansive lawns, impressive landscaping, and Spanish Renaissance-style red-tile-roofed buildings. The school has completed more than $1 billion in construction projects in recent years, including the Maddox Engineering Research Center, an addition to the Rawls College of Business Administration, and a new honors residence hall. Tech also has a slew of other facilities around Texas, such as a 16,000-acre agricultural facility and research farm.

The university's 10 undergraduate colleges and schools boast more than 150 degree programs. Tech's comprehensive general education requirements span all of the colleges and schools, and most majors involve a capstone course as well. The College of Agricultural Sciences and Natural Resources "has the strongest financial foothold on campus, with the largest endowment," says an economics major. "Within the College of Human Sciences lies the department of personal financial planning, the best of its type in the country." Mechanical engineering, kinesiology, management, and marketing draw the most students, and the wind energy and music programs are also well regarded. The university studies major, which allows students to build their own interdisciplinary major by combining any three existing areas of study, is a highly popular option.

> "[Professors] have changed my life and made me think for myself."

Despite Tech's massive size, 79 percent of classes have fewer than 50 students. "Each year that I have been here, the classes have gotten harder and the professors more experienced," says one senior. Those professors "have changed my life and made me think for myself," remarks a communication studies major. Graduate assistants may lead discussion sections or labs, but they aren't the main force at the lectern. An optional one-credit freshman seminar helps with the transition from high school to college, and learning communities provide students with ample service-learning opportunities.

The Program in Inquiry and Investigation (known as Pi Squared) is a two-semester course that prepares interested freshmen to conduct undergraduate research. Between 350 and 400 outstanding first-year students enroll in Tech's Honors College every year, where they sit on committees, help with recruiting, make decisions about course content, and evaluate faculty. They can also work on research projects, either independently (with a professor's guidance) or as part of a student/faculty team. Those yearning to leave the hardscrabble plains of Texas may study abroad in more than 70 countries; Tech also has its own campus in Seville, Spain.

One-quarter of students go abroad, an impressive figure boosted by the requirement that all undergrads enrolled in the Whitacre College of Engineering must have an international experience lasting at least six weeks.

The Tech student body is largely homegrown; 92 percent hail from the Lone Star State and 2 percent come from foreign nations. "'Techsans' are truly down-to-earth and friendly," says one student. "We come from small, West Texas towns and some of the largest cities in the United States." African Americans account for 6 percent of the undergraduate population, Hispanics 28 percent, Asian Americans 3 percent, and multiracial students 2 percent. Tech offers merit scholarships worth an average of $3,600, as well as 328 athletic awards in 17 varsity sports. Elite chess players can vie for a handful of scholarships as well. Twenty-five percent of freshmen are Pell-eligible. The Red Raider Guarantee offers free tuition and fees to qualified freshmen who are Texas residents and whose families earn less than $40,000 per year.

Only 26 percent of the students at Tech live in the dorms, mainly freshmen who are required to do so. "The dorms are the ultimate college experience," says one senior. Co-ed, single-sex, and quiet study dorms are available, as are 19 living/learning communities. Dining options are plentiful, and a junior says, "Whether you're a vegetarian or on a protein diet, you'll eat well here." About 50 restaurants in the area also take the university's Tech Express debit card, and many have student specials one night a week. Under Texas law, people are permitted to carry firearms on campus. A safe-ride shuttle service helps students feel safe, and the recently created Risk Intervention and Safety Education office is working to prevent sexual violence and support personal wellness on campus.

Tech is officially dry and "punishments are quite harsh" for those who attempt to skirt the university's alcohol policies, a senior warns. Since so many students live off campus, that's where most of the weekend action is. Still, the more than 500 student organizations offer plenty of activities to keep students busy on campus. Five percent of the men pledge fraternities and 8 percent of the women join sororities, so a sizable contingent heads to the parties at Greek Circle. The Depot District is also a popular destination, as most bars and clubs admit anyone 18 and over.

The city of Lubbock (population 254,000) offers many opportunities to get involved with the community through work with the Boys & Girls Clubs of America, United Way, animal shelters, or Bible study at local churches. Annual traditions include homecoming, complete with a chili cook-off; the Carol of Lights during the first weekend in December; and Arbor Day, when hundreds of students fan out across campus to plant flowers and trees for the spring. Popular road trips include any of the four nearby lakes (for picnicking, boating, or camping), skiing in New Mexico (four hours away), and anywhere the Red Raiders are playing, especially if it's against the University of Texas Longhorns.

The Division I Red Raiders compete in the Big 12 Conference, and the football, baseball, and men's track and field teams are among the school's best. When the football team takes the field, the Masked Rider, replete with red and black cape and cowboy hat, motivates the crowd by galloping up and down the sidelines. Men's and women's tennis each claimed a regular season conference championship recently. The university's livestock and meat judging teams have won several national championships in recent years. Intramural and club sports, which attract nearly half of undergraduates, include everything from the typical soccer and flag football to mud volleyball, dodgeball, and table tennis.

Texas Tech has come a long way over the past 94 years in carving out its own niche. If you can stand the heat and relative isolation of the West Texas Plains, and the effort it often takes to be more than a number at any school of this size, Texas Tech may be worth a look.

All undergrads in the Whitacre College of Engineering must have an international experience lasting at least six weeks.

"'Techsans' are truly down-to-earth and friendly."

The livestock and meat judging teams have won several national championships in recent years.

Overlaps

Texas A&M, UT Austin, University of Houston, University of North Texas, Texas State, UT San Antonio, UT Arlington, Sam Houston State

University of Toronto: See page 363.

Trinity College

300 Summit Street, Hartford, CT 06106

Long known both for its quality academics and its well-to-do students, Trinity is shaking up its admissions practices and diversifying its student body. Abundant community-based learning and service opportunities take imaginative advantage of the school's troubled urban setting. Trinity joins Lafayette, Smith, Swarthmore, and Union as a small liberal arts college that offers engineering.

Website: www.trincoll.edu
Location: City Center
Private
Total Enrollment: 2,092
Undergraduates: 2,090
Male/Female: 49/51
SAT Ranges: ERW 620–710, M 640–710
ACT Ranges: 28–32
Financial Aid: 49%
Pell Grant: 13%
Expense: Pr $ $ $ $
Student Loans: 45%
Average Debt: $ $
Applicants: 6,085
Accepted: 34%
Enrolled: 28%
Grad in 6 Years: 85%
Returning Freshmen: 89%
Academics: ✑ ✑ ✑ ✑
Social: ☎ ☎ ☎ ☎
Q of L: ★ ★ ★
Admissions: (860) 297-2180
Email Address: admissions .office@trincoll.edu

Strong Programs:
Economics
Political Science
Psychology
Biology

For students at Trinity College, the learning experience doesn't stop at the campus borders. At first glance, the small liberal arts college and the large, gritty city of Hartford, Connecticut, seem like an uneasy match. But instead of insulating itself from outside problems, Trinity takes advantage of its surroundings by using Hartford as its classroom. As part of its recent community revitalization efforts, Trinity partnered with Hartford Public Schools in 2011 to create a public middle/high school designed to prepare students for college-level work. In 2018, Trinity opened its downtown Liberal Arts Action Lab, where community partners team up with students and faculty to research and propose solutions to problems facing the city. On campus, academic standards continue to rise, and students graduate with a strong liberal arts background. "Students are the priority here," says one senior.

Splendid Gothic-style stone buildings behind wrought-iron fences decorate Trinity's 100-acre campus. The large, grassy quadrangle is home to pickup games of hackeysack and lazy relaxation on warm spring and fall afternoons. Along with revitalizing the neighborhood that surrounds it, Trinity's campus is undergoing its own revitalization. Newer facilities include the Gruss Music Center, the Crescent Center for Arts and Neuroscience, and several athletic fields. Classroom facilities in some of the college's original buildings have recently been renovated, and the Crescent Street Townhouses provide accommodations for 340 upperclassmen.

> **"Most professors are distinguished as authorities in their fields."**

Trinity's general education requirements include distribution courses across the liberal arts and sciences, as well as demonstrating proficiency in writing, mathematics, and a foreign language. The First-Year Seminar emphasizes writing, speaking, and critical thinking; the seminar instructor serves as students' academic advisor. Five Gateway programs give selected freshmen a chance to study in-depth topics from interdisciplinary perspectives through a three-semester sequence of courses. Offerings include InterArts, Interdisciplinary Science, Community Action, Humanities: European Cultures, and Cities, which one student calls "phenomenal—very challenging and rewarding." A global engagement requirement can be completed by coursework or study abroad.

(continued)

Modern Languages
Human Rights Studies
Engineering
Neuroscience

Popular majors at Trinity include economics, political science, psychology, biology, and modern languages. Human rights studies is notable, and students say the school's small but accredited engineering program is strong. That department sponsors the Fire-Fighting Home Robot Contest, the largest public robotics competition in the U.S., open to entrants of any age, ability, and experience. Accelerated bachelor's/master's degree programs are available in American studies and neuroscience. Through the BEACON program, biomedical engineering students can take courses at UConn, the UConn Health Center, and the University of Hartford while conducting research at three area health centers. Trinity's close ties to the community also are apparent in the curriculum; students can take courses on urban development and the history of the city of Hartford, or choose from service-learning courses that incorporate opportunities to work with more than 80 local community service organizations.

Faculty/student collaboration is a tradition at Trinity. Two-thirds of students work with professors on research and scholarly papers, and many students join their mentors to present findings at symposia. "The academic climate is rigorous but not overly competitive," says a senior. Seventy-four percent of classes have fewer than 20 students. Students say that professors have high expectations of them, and most go the extra mile to provide support. "Most professors are distinguished as authorities in their fields," says a student.

More than half of the students seek internships in government (including the Legislative Internship Program at the state capital), nonprofit organizations, and businesses in Hartford (the insurance capital of the world). Trinity's study-away program, in which 62 percent of students take part, includes Trinity's own international program sites in nine cities, ranging from Cape Town to Vienna to Shanghai, as well as more than 90 approved and affiliated programs. Trinity's Global Start program offers selected first-year students the chance to spend their first semester studying in Costa Rica. Other enticing choices include the Trinity/La MaMa Urban Arts program in New York City and the Washington Semester in D.C.

Trinity has retreated from its recent policy of consistently increasing freshman enrollment, a practice that undermined the academic quality of entering students and strained faculty resources. Although the school has had a reputation for enrolling, in the words of a sophomore, "prep school students from privileged families," it is moving away from its traditionally heavy recruitment of New England boarding school grads, seeking to diversify the student body. Seventeen percent of Trinity students are Connecticut natives; an increasing number come from California, and 12 percent are international. Asian Americans currently account for 4 percent of the student body, Hispanics 8 percent, African Americans 6 percent, and multiracial students 3 percent. Although no one would mistake the campus for a political hot zone, students remain aware of global issues and local concerns. Athletic scholarships are not available and merit awards are limited, but Trinity does provide special financial packages to replace student loans for students with the most need. The college also guarantees to meet students' full demonstrated need for four years.

Ninety percent of Trinity's students live in the co-ed dorms. Freshmen are assigned housing based on their First-Year Seminar and grouped into "nests" of 60 to 75 students, aimed at creating a more intimate sense of community. Students report that meals at Mather, Trinity's dining hall, are adequate, with options for those with special tastes and needs, and the à la carte and grab-and-go items at the Bistro and the Cave provide alternatives. "Campus safety officers are always around to make sure our students feel safe," says a senior.

"The social life revolves around on-campus activity," a sophomore says. Students praise the Trinity College Activities Council, which brings in comedians and musical

At the Liberal Arts Action Lab, community partners team up with students and faculty to research and propose solutions to problems facing Hartford.

"Campus safety officers are always around to make sure our students feel safe."

Trinity's Global Start program offers selected first-year students the chance to spend their first semester studying in Costa Rica.

performers and organizes parties, study breaks, and community service days. "The campus dances are very popular with the entire student body," says a senior. The Underground Coffeehouse and the Bistro's weekly comedy nights are also student favorites. But the action on Thursday, Friday, and Saturday nights is mostly at the Greek houses (29 percent of the men and 17 percent of the women join up). An effort by the administration to force the single-gender organizations to go co-ed was abandoned after houses failed to attract members of the opposite sex and alumni donors with Greek ties pulled back. Students say alcohol is not hard to come by, but "the campus policies on alcohol are fairly severe on underage drinkers and abusers," says a student. Spring Weekend brings bands to campus for a three-day party outdoors. Popular road trips include Montreal, Boston, New York City, and the beaches and mountains of Maine.

Freshmen are assigned housing based on their First-Year Seminar and grouped into "nests" of 60 to 75 students.

Trinity's location in Hartford has been problematic; some students describe the surrounding area as "scary" and "a terrible college town." In part because the state of Connecticut has not done a good job of investing in its cities, downtown Hartford does not attract visitors from outside the city, and the administration worries about urban problems, such as drugs. Even so, one philosophy major says things are improving: "Hartford has a terrific assortment of restaurants, ranging from cheap but delicious ethnic fare to upscale, parent-friendly places." A college-sponsored "culture van" takes students downtown to catch a show at the Bushnell or visit the Wadsworth Atheneum, the nation's oldest public art museum. A new professional soccer team has debuted for the 2019 season, and a citywide bike-share program was recently introduced. Many see the city's troubles as offering "unique opportunities for internships, mentoring, and community service," according to a sophomore. The Office of Community Service and Civic Engagement helps coordinate such opportunities, and students have created and run organizations that provide housing, tutoring, meals, and other services to youth, families, and senior citizens.

> "Students are pushed to reshape the way they think and tackle challenges."

Trinity's Bantams compete in Division III, and thanks to its international recruits, both men's and women's squash are powerhouses (the men's team has won 17 national titles in the last 20 years). Other solid programs include men's ice hockey, football, and women's lacrosse. Homecoming typically brings Wesleyan or Amherst to campus for a football game, which gets underway after Trinity students burn the opposing school's letter on the quad. Fifty percent of students take part in the intramural and club sports programs.

With its dual emphasis on traditional liberal arts education and civic engagement, Trinity aims to prepare students to be independent thinkers ready to make a difference both locally and globally. And students here have taken their civic responsibility to heart. At Trinity, an English major says, "Students are pushed to reshape the way they think and tackle challenges to make an impact in their community."

Overlaps

Colby, Boston College, Connecticut College, Wesleyan, Boston University, Brown, Tufts, Holy Cross

If You Apply To ›

Trinity College: Early decision I and II, regular decision. SATs or ACTs: optional. Subject Tests: optional. Accepts the Common Application with optional essay supplement that encourages applicants to write about their interest in Trinity.

Trinity College Dublin: See page 380.

Trinity University

One Trinity Place, San Antonio, TX 78212-7200

One of the few quality Southwestern liberal arts colleges in a major city. Trinity is twice as big as nearby rivals Austin College and Southwestern University and offers a diverse curriculum that includes business, education, and engineering in addition to the liberal arts. San Antonio runs neck and neck with Austin as the most desirable city in Texas.

Trinity University is a small school with big bucks. Thanks to that liquid that gushes out of the Texas soil, Trinity has one of the nation's largest educational endowments at a school its size. The wealth is used unashamedly to lure capable students with bargain tuition rates and to entice talented professors from around the nation. The result? A student body composed of smart, ambitious men and women, and a stellar faculty. Students here enjoy challenges but still manage a laid-back Texas attitude. "It's friendly, warm, personal, engaged, and academically stimulating," a senior says.

Trinity was founded in a small central Texas town just after the end of the Civil War. In 1952, the school moved to its current location, a residential area about three miles from downtown San Antonio, one of the most beautiful cities in the Southwest. The 125-acre campus, filled with the Southern architecture of O'Neil Ford, is located on what was once a rock quarry. Everything fits the school's aesthetically pleasing and somewhat well-to-do image, from the uniform redbrick buildings to the stately pathways that wind along gorgeous green lawns and through immaculate gardens spotted with Henry Moore sculptures. Trinity's most dominant landmark is Murchison Tower, which rises in the center of campus and is visible from numerous vantage points throughout San Antonio. The university recently completed a $14 million renovation of the Bell Athletic Center.

> "Students here are eager to take on as many opportunities as they can possibly handle."

Trinity's general education curriculum, called Pathways, contains five signature curricular elements: the First-Year Experience, Core Capacities, Approaches to Creation and Analysis, Interdisciplinary Clusters, and Experiential Learning. Trinity has a highly praised education department, with a five-year master of arts in teaching program, and a good advising program for students interested in health professions. Popular majors include business administration, communication, engineering science, psychology, and finance. The engineering and chemistry departments are strong, and the communication department offers students hands-on training with television equipment or the chance to produce a newscast. The five-year accounting program allows students to serve an internship with the big four accounting firms in offices around the nation while earning a salary and receiving college credit. The Languages Across the Curriculum program features classes such as business, history, and anthropology taught in languages including Chinese, German, Spanish, and Russian.

"Trinity has a relatively intense workload, but that's mostly because the students here are eager to take on as many opportunities as they can possibly handle," comments a neuroscience major. The classes at Trinity are small: 57 percent have fewer than 20 students. Freshmen receive academic counseling from a faculty advisor and peer tutoring from upperclassmen in mentor groups of 10 to 15 students. The professors at Trinity are "available, brilliant, and helpful," according to a junior. "They always hold office hours for students to come in and talk or ask questions."

Website: www.trinity.edu
Location: City Center
Private
Total Enrollment: 2,499
Undergraduates: 2,383
Male/Female: 46/54
SAT Ranges: EBRW 620–710, M 610–700
ACT Ranges: 27–32
Financial Aid: 96%
Pell Grant: 18%
Expense: Pr $
Student Loans: 44%
Average Debt: $ $ $ $
Applicants: 7,663
Accepted: 38%
Enrolled: 22%
Grad in 6 Years: 77%
Returning Freshmen: 89%
Academics: ✑ ✑ ✑
Social: ☎ ☎ ☎
Q of L: ★ ★ ★
Admissions: (800) 874-6489
Email Address: admissions@trinity.edu

Strong Programs:
Business Administration
Communication
Engineering Science
Psychology
Finance
Education
Chemistry
Accounting

Forty-five percent of students participate in research projects with faculty mentors, while 35 percent study abroad in more than 35 countries.

Trinity makes a concerted effort to maintain its admissions standards, keeping enrollment low and recruiting high achievers with greater energy than is possible from larger universities. Seventy-three percent of undergraduates are Texans, and 6 percent are international. The school is fairly diverse ethnically; Hispanics account for 21 percent, Asian Americans 7 percent, African Americans 4 percent, and multiracial students 5 percent. A political science major says the campus leans liberal but the atmosphere is generally accepting rather than ostracizing: "There is a lot of polite political discourse." The proportion of Pell-eligible freshmen has been slowly increasing and currently stands at 18 percent. Merit scholarships averaging $20,500 are available to academically gifted students; there are no athletic scholarships.

> "There is a lot of polite political discourse."

Students are required to live on campus through their junior year. In fact, 80 percent of the students live in the residence halls, which one student describes as "fantastic, with walk-in closets, private balconies, suite-style rooms, and a cleaning service." Residence halls are co-ed by suite, with one single-sex residence hall that is off-limits to freshmen. A university-owned apartment complex is an option for upperclassmen, but most seniors find their own places off campus. Campus dining is "delicious," according to a student. "I've been eating on campus for four years and I'm still not sick of the food." A junior says students feel safe and "the university police are constantly monitoring the campus."

With more than 100 student organizations hosting events every weekend, there is plenty of activity on campus to keep students busy. The university sponsors an excellent lecture series that brings notable politicians and public figures to campus. Beer and wine may be consumed on campus by those of legal age in upper-class residence halls. Seventeen percent of the men and 32 percent of the women join the local fraternity and sorority organizations. "Most students choose to socialize with other students on campus or in Greek houses just off campus," says a sophomore. The school year kicks off with a party at the school's bell tower, which students can climb to get a knockout view of San Antonio. Students look forward to the Tigerfest dance and parade on homecoming weekend and the Chili Cook-Off that pits Greek and other clubs against one another. They also anticipate Fiesta, a weeklong, annual celebration of San Antonio's mixed culture that features bands, dancing, food, and drink.

> "Being part of HOPE Hall grounded and humbled me."

San Antonio, with its famed River Walk replete with interesting restaurants, receives a well-deserved thumbs-up from students. It doesn't hurt that the city is home to several other colleges. "San Antonio is a great place to be, because there are so many things to do. That being said, you need a car to get almost anywhere," says one student. Students frequent the many outdoor shops and cafés in the historic Pearl district, as well as cultural and musical attractions and touristy hangouts such as Six Flags and SeaWorld. Students get involved in city life by contributing more than 88,000 hours of community service every year. Residents of the HOPE Hall living/learning community spend two hours a week volunteering with organizations that serve the city's homeless population; "Being part of HOPE Hall grounded and humbled me," says one participant. The city's beautiful, warm weather provides plenty of activities for the students year-round, but there are also many fun road trips. The funky state capital of Austin is 90 miles north, and students can also road-trip to the Texas Gulf Coast and the Hill Country.

Trinity's varsity sports teams compete in the Division III Southern Collegiate Athletic Conference. One student brags, "There are no rivalries in sports, since we win at everything." The Tigers men's and women's soccer teams have claimed seven

Trinity has one of the nation's largest educational endowments at a school its size.

The school year kicks off with a party at the school's bell tower, which students can climb to get a knockout view of San Antonio.

and ten consecutive conference titles, respectively, and the baseball team is a recent national champion. About two-thirds of students take advantage of intramural and club sports; flag football signs up the most athletes. Country line dancing and outdoor recreation trips are popular too.

A big state and big money give students at this small university many of the advantages of a larger school. But a business analytics and technology major says it's Trinity's sense of community that matters most: "People will ask where you are if you're missing from class and will study with you for hours and will make sure you get home safe." If you are looking for an intimate community feel with quality professors, look no further than Trinity University.

If You Apply To ›

Trinity University: Early decision I and II, early action I and II, regular decision. SATs or ACTs: required. No Subject Tests. Accepts the Common Application with supplement.

Truman State University

100 East Normal, Kirksville, MO 63501

As Missouri's "honors college," Truman has more in common with private institutions than with nondescript regional publics. Occupies a public ivy niche like Miami of Ohio and William and Mary. Rural setting encourages strong focus on academics, including lots of undergraduate research. Just over a quarter of the students are from out of state, mainly from Illinois.

Truman State University, Missouri's only public liberal arts college, attracts overachievers from across the Show-Me State. Founded in 1867 as a regional teacher training institution, the school became a statewide university in 1985 and 11 years later took the name of the only Missourian to serve as a president of the United States. Indeed, since shifting to a liberal arts and sciences mission, Truman has worked to become a "public ivy" on the order of Miami University (OH) or the College of William and Mary. True, the small town of Kirksville, Missouri, is no Williamsburg, Virginia—or even Oxford, Ohio. But the school's relative isolation makes it easier to concentrate on academics. "I would call Truman a nerd school," says one focused physics and mathematics double major. "Nearly everyone at Truman is there to learn first, so education and work take priority over almost everything else."

Truman is located in the northeastern corner of Missouri, about 200 miles from both Kansas City and St. Louis. The flower-laden campus includes approximately 40 buildings on 210 acres, many of which are Georgian in style—in fact, the oldest portion of the campus, dating to 1873, is modeled on Thomas Jefferson's University of Virginia. The Robison Planetarium and Multimedia Theater is the campus's newest facility.

Truman's general education requirements revolve around the liberal arts and sciences. The Liberal Studies Program forms the core of all academic majors; students must complete eight "Modes of Inquiry" that encompass traditional liberal arts disciplines. Students also take an interdisciplinary, writing-enhanced seminar in their junior year and complete a capstone course. All first-year students are required to participate in a one-day orientation session during the summer as well as Truman Days, a five-day program designed to help freshmen adjust to college life.

Website: www.truman.edu
Location: Rural
Public
Total Enrollment: 5,366
Undergraduates: 5,093
Male/Female: 41/59
SAT Ranges: ERW 605–705, M 580–715
ACT Ranges: 24–30
Financial Aid: 89%
Pell Grant: 22%
Expense: Pub $
Student Loans: 57%
Average Debt: $ $
Applicants: 5,263
Accepted: 68%
Enrolled: 37%
Grad in 6 Years: 75%
Returning Freshmen: 86%
Academics: ✏ ✏ ✏
Social: ☎ ☎ ☎
Q of L: ★ ★ ★
Admissions: (660) 785-4114

(continued)

Email Address: admissions@
truman.edu

Strong Programs:
Business Administration
Psychology
Biology
Exercise Science
Nursing
Education
Accounting

The most popular major is business administration; psychology, biology, and exercise science round out the list of programs with the highest enrollment. An interdisciplinary studies major allows students to combine coursework from two or more disciplines to create a specialized major. Nursing is a traditional strength, and there are also five-year programs for students interested in education or accounting, which culminate in the awarding of bachelor's and master's degrees. New offerings include majors in biochemistry and molecular biology and statistics.

Students describe a competitive but worthwhile academic climate. "Students are driven to outdo themselves and their classmates, but we also have to be collaborative, as we usually have a group project in every class," says a communication major. Classes rarely have more than 50 students, which makes access to professors the norm. For the most part, says a student, "Professors work hard to create a valuable and intellectually engaging learning experience." Students praise the career center, and a freshman notes, "There are tons of seminars to talk about practical ways to improve your hirability."

> **"Students are driven to outdo themselves and their classmates."**

The Honors Scholar Program offers a challenging, more sophisticated curriculum to especially motivated students; since Truman State is considered Missouri's "honors college," all students are welcome to participate. Study abroad opportunities are available via roughly 500 programs in more than 65 countries around the world; 19 percent of students study beyond U.S. borders. About 40 percent of students conduct independent research or collaborate with faculty members on research projects, and Truman typically sends one of the largest delegations of undergraduates to the annual National Conference on Undergraduate Research.

All students are welcome to participate in the Honors Scholar Program's challenging, more sophisticated curriculum.

Seventy-one percent of Truman students are native to Missouri, and 6 percent hail from abroad. "International students make a huge impact on campus with festivals and events that share their culture with students who grew up in Missouri," says a history major. Hispanics and Asian Americans each comprise 3 percent of the student body, African Americans add 4 percent, and multiracial students make up 3 percent. Social and political issues are met with much discussion and debate, and a political science major categorizes the campus as "slightly left of center," given its many liberal students but conservative, rural location. Merit scholarships are available to qualified students; the average award is $6,000. The school also hands out 334 athletic scholarships in 16 sports. Twenty-two percent of students are eligible for the Pell Grant. Additionally, the Truman Access Grant provides funding to a limited number of students who have unmet need after their federal financial aid and Truman scholarship award have been packaged.

> **"International students make a huge impact on campus with festivals and events that share their culture."**

Forty-two percent of Truman students live on campus in the residence halls, and "each hallway is decorated so they have more of a warm feeling—not like the feel of a prison," a junior says. Students say it's easy to get a room, but most students seek less expensive options off campus after their sophomore year. Campus dining is described as "tolerable" but "inconsistent" and campus safety as adequate. Several students raise concerns about the stress culture and mental health on campus, and a junior comments that while the school's counselors are "very invested in the student body, there simply aren't enough of them."

The Big Event is a popular one-day service event that brings more than 1,500 campus volunteers to Kirksville.

Social life at Truman is robust, according to students. "Because of Truman's semi-isolated location, the Student Activities Board brings in various musicians, comedians, YouTube stars, speakers, and performers to campus for free," explains a freshman. The Greek system plays an integral part in Truman's social life—23 percent of men and 23 percent of women sign up—but there are also 200 other student organizations to choose from. Since the campus is dry, says an exercise science major, "Most parties take place off campus, where they're hosted by Greek organizations, athletic teams, or one of the five bars in town." Students also venture out on road trips to St. Louis, Kansas City, various destinations in Iowa, and Quincy, Illinois. Everyone looks forward to homecoming and Oktoberfest (featuring free root beer) in the fall and the Final Blowout carnival in the spring, with wacky games, inflatables, free food, and prizes.

The town of Kirksville (population 17,500) grows on you, say students. "All of the essentials of a college town are present, including a Walmart, a bowling alley, a good movie theater, and a beautiful state park," a business administration major says. Two-thirds of students take advantage of various opportunities to get involved in volunteer work and service learning. The Big Event is a popular one-day service event that brings more than 1,500 campus volunteers to Kirksville. Truman hosts 12 service organizations, which provide thousands of hours of service every year.

> "[While counselors are] very invested in the student body, there simply aren't enough of them."

When not competing academically, Truman's Bulldogs, members of the Great Lakes Valley Conference, are succeeding in the pool and on the playing field. The men's and women's swim teams have won multiple Division II titles, and the football, softball, and women's soccer teams are also competitive. Truman's Forensics Team, the school's longest-running cocurricular activity, has brought home several state titles. About one-third of students participate in 35 intramurals, which include everything from basketball and soccer to pickleball and baggo.

"With the highest admissions standards of any public university in the state, Truman has a distinct culture of academic excellence," says a student. Indeed, Truman State offers challenging academics, pursued within a close-knit community. Though its rural Missouri location can feel isolating, its bargain-basement price is certainly worth considering.

Overlaps

SUNY–Geneseo, Creighton, Bradley, College of New Jersey, University of Minnesota Morris, Saint Louis University, Missouri State, University of Missouri

If You Apply To ›

Truman State: Rolling admissions. SATs or ACTs: required. No Subject Tests. Accepts the Common Application with supplement.

Tufts University

Bendetson Hall, Medford, MA 02155

One of the smallest and most undergraduate-focused of the major research universities, Tufts is known for its global focus. Strengths run the gamut from classics and philosophy to engineering and international relations. Located just outside student-friendly Boston, it has more in common with Brown than any other Ivy. Compare to other top urban schools such as Georgetown, Northwestern, and WashU. The Experimental College lets student take nontraditional courses for credit.

Once considered a safety school for those who couldn't get into an Ivy, Tufts isn't so safe anymore. Applications are up dramatically, propelling Tufts into the ranks of the more selective schools in the country. With its strong academics, high-achieving student body, and attractive setting, some might say that not all that much more separates Tufts University from its illustrious neighbors, Harvard and MIT, than a

Website: www.tufts.edu
Location: City Outskirts
Private
Total Enrollment: 10,577

(continued)

Undergraduates: 5,492
Male/Female: 49/51
SAT Ranges: ERW 700–760,
  M 710–780
ACT Ranges: 31–34
Financial Aid: 37%
Pell Grant: 11%
Expense: Pr $ $ $ $
Student Loans: 34%
Average Debt: $ $
Applicants: 21,101
Accepted: 15%
Enrolled: 45%
Grad in 6 Years: 93%
Returning Freshmen: 97%
Academics: ✑ ✑ ✑ ✑ ½
Social: ☎ ☎ ☎
Q of L: ★ ★ ★ ★
Admissions: (617) 627-3170
Email Address: undergraduate
  .admissions@tufts.edu

Strong Programs:
International Relations
Economics
Biology
Computer Science
Engineering
Classics
Philosophy
Child Study and Human
  Development

Tufts has acquired the School of the Museum of Fine Arts in Boston, expanding opportunities for study in fine arts and design.

few stops on the T. Says one senior, "Tufts is a school for people who aren't afraid to speak their mind but are also open to having someone change their mind."

Tufts's 150-acre, tree-lined campus on Walnut Hill overlooks the heart of nearby Boston and is a striking scene. The main campus, with its brick and stone buildings, sits on the Medford/Somerville boundary. Medford, the fifth-oldest city in the country, was a powerful shipbuilding center during the 19th century. Somerville lies adjacent to the Tufts campus, and in 1776, the first American flag was raised on its Prospect Hill. For years, Tufts, founded in 1852 by Universalist businessman Charles Tufts, has devoted resources to traditional areas of graduate strength—medicine, dentistry, veterinary, and diplomacy—as well as new ventures, such as a Nutrition Research Center. Tufts has acquired the School of the Museum of Fine Arts in Boston, expanding opportunities for study in fine arts and design, and recent campus additions include the Science and Engineering Complex.

Undergraduate teaching is what attracts students to Tufts. They get highly personalized attention from faculty, and they enjoy wide freedom to pursue independent study and to complete research and internships for credit. Tufts students also get a healthy diet of traditional academic fare. For liberal arts students, distribution requirements include a World Civilization course in addition to art, English and foreign languages, social sciences, humanities, natural sciences, and math. Engineers must take six courses in the arts, humanities, and social sciences, with one of those fulfilling a writing requirement. The most popular majors include international relations, economics, biology, and computer science. Tufts also boasts strong classics and philosophy departments, and there is an excellent child study and human development program. Interdisciplinary programs such as human factors engineering (or, engineering psychology) are growing in popularity as well.

> **"Tufts is a school for people who aren't afraid to speak their mind."**

Tufts has two popular programs in which students who need a break from being students can develop and teach courses. The first, the Experimental College, annually offers more than 100 nontraditional, full-credit courses on topics ranging from Cryptocurrency and Blockchain to American Witches that are taught by students, faculty, and outside lecturers. The second, Freshman Explorations seminars, are taught by two upperclassmen and a faculty member who doubles as an advisor; these courses are a way for freshmen to get to know each other and ease into the college experience.

"The academics are tough but rewarding," says one junior, and students agree that the atmosphere is supportive. Seventy percent of classes have fewer than 20 students, and most courses are taught by full professors. "Professors are willing to sit with you and explain topics you don't understand, give recommendations on research opportunities, or give you general advice on life," says an economics and international relations double major.

For those looking to get off campus, Tufts offers the Washington Semester, exchanges with Swarthmore and Spelman, and cross-registration at a number of Boston schools. Forty-five percent of undergrads study abroad, and Tufts frequently ranks as one of the top Peace Corps suppliers. Students may choose to spend their summer at Tufts's overseas campus in Talloires, France, embark on a semester or year abroad at one of more than 170 preapproved programs, or select one of Tufts's own full-immersion programs in nine countries around the globe. The Institute for Global Leadership includes the popular, interdisciplinary Education for Public Inquiry and International Citizenship (EPIIC) program. The yearlong intensive experience revolves around a theme and includes a weekly colloquium, international symposium, and a research project or internship. Recent EPIIC themes have been The Future of Europe and Global Health and Security.

"Most Tufts students are charismatic, excited about what they are learning, and very friendly," says a senior. Twenty-five percent of students hail from Massachusetts; California, New York, and New Jersey are also well represented. The university's reputation in international relations attracts a respectable number of international students (10 percent) and Americans living abroad. Asian Americans make up 12 percent of the population, Hispanics 7 percent, African Americans 4 percent, and multiracial students 5 percent. The campus is largely liberal, and many students are enthusiastically engaged in social and political issues, to the point that student activism itself has become a hot-button topic. "The level of social activism has caused a fissure in the student body between those who are fighting for a cause and those who channel their energies elsewhere," remarks a senior. No merit or athletic scholarships are available, but the school does meet the full demonstrated need of all admits. There are additional financial incentives for students from low-income families.

Freshman Explorations seminars are taught by two upperclassmen and a faculty member who doubles as an advisor.

Sixty-three percent of students live on campus. Accommodations in the Uphill and Downhill (the two quads joined by a great expanse of grass and trees) campus dorms vary from long hallways of double rooms to apartment-like suites, old houses, and co-ops—and a good-natured rivalry exists between the two areas. Freshmen and sophomores must live on campus in the dorms, while upperclassmen compete in a lottery or move to affordable apartments just a short walk from campus. "When you're a freshman, go all-freshman housing. Nothing is more special than a community of all freshmen where everyone's looking for a niche to fit in," a student advises. All first-years are required to have the unlimited meal plan, and students give dining services good reviews. The campus police department is said to be effective, and a chemical engineering major says that an ongoing dialogue is "pushing the administration in the right direction for handling sexual assault on campus, and positive changes have been made."

"Professors are willing to sit with you and explain topics you don't understand."

According to a senior, "Partying at a frat is just as acceptable as staying in with your roommate and watching Netflix." Tufts has earned a national reputation for its programs to promote the "responsible" use of alcohol, but Greek culture has been a subject of controversy after a university investigation found that half of the school's 17 fraternities and sororities had violated school policies on alcohol abuse, hazing, and sexual harassment, resulting in suspensions and closings of some organizations. Currently, 10 percent of the men and 9 percent of the women join the Greek system. "Drinking is a significant part of life at Tufts," admits a sophomore, "but it's not overwhelming." University-sponsored activities include concerts, plays (Aidekman Arts Center stages 15 to 20 productions each year), and free movies on weekend nights. Several a cappella groups thrive at Tufts, and a favorite student group is the Tufts Dance Collective, where "groups of students practice goofy dances all semester" and put on two shows per year that draw big crowds. Other major campus events include homecoming and Halloween on the Hill, the latter of which is a carnival for children in the community, as well as Spring Fling, an outdoor concert that helps students relax before final exams.

Major campus events include Halloween on the Hill, a carnival for children in the community, as well as Spring Fling, an outdoor concert.

"Drinking is a significant part of life at Tufts, but it's not overwhelming."

While suburban Medford is not very exciting for those of college age, the T metro system extends to the Tufts campus, so it's easy to make a quick jaunt to "student city" (a.k.a. Boston) for work or play. Davis Square in Somerville is even closer and provides plenty of restaurants, nightlife, and music stores. The largest student organization by far, with more than 1,000 students, is the Leonard Carmichael Society, the umbrella group for volunteer activities ranging from adult literacy and blood drives to work with the homeless and victims of domestic violence.

Tufts fields 29 teams in the Division III New England Small College Athletic Conference (NESCAC). The Jumbos men's soccer team captured national titles in 2014, 2016, and 2018, and men's lacrosse and women's softball are also recent national champs. Sixteen percent of the student body play in intramural and club sports. The Tufts Sabermetrics team, which grew out of the Experimental College, is a national powerhouse in competitions that apply sophisticated statistical techniques to the sport of baseball.

Tufts is in the midst of a modern-day renaissance. This, along with a swelling applicant pool, makes Tufts a much hotter school than it was just a few years ago. And its proximity to Boston, an intellectual and educational mecca, makes it even more attractive. "If you have something that you uncontrollably geek about and love to be able to share that passion," says a senior, "then Tufts is the place for you."

If You Apply To ›

Tufts: Early decision I and II, regular decision. SATs or ACTs: required. Subject Tests: optional. Accepts the Common Application with supplement. Portfolio required for applicants to School of the Museum of Fine Arts. Application includes optional gender identity field.

Tulane University

6823 St. Charles Avenue, New Orleans, LA 70118

The map may say that Tulane is in the South, but it has the temperament of an East Coast institution. Tulane aspires to join Emory and Vanderbilt in the front ranks of Southeastern universities. Has developed a strong emphasis on community service, both academic and practical. High achievers should shoot for the Tulane Honors Program.

Once a staid, genteel choice for students seeking a traditional education, Tulane University has rebranded itself with an emphasis on interdisciplinary research, scholarship, and community service. It now attracts service-minded students from all 50 states who choose from more than 130 service-learning opportunities, many of them existing courses that were revamped to include a service-learning component after Hurricane Katrina, which devastated Louisiana in 2005. Indeed, Tulane promises a solid education to those who are ready to take up residence in the Big Easy.

The school's 110-acre campus is located in an attractive residential area of uptown New Orleans, about 15 minutes from the French Quarter and the business district. Tulane's administration building, Gibson Hall, faces St. Charles Avenue, where one of the nation's last streetcar lines still clatters past mansions. Across the street is Audubon Park, a 385-acre spread where students jog, walk, study, or feed the ducks in the lagoon. The buildings of gray limestone and pillared brick, separated by live southern oak trees, are modeled after the neocollegiate/Creole mixture indigenous to Louisiana institutional-type structures. One particular point of pride is the university's 13 Tiffany windows, one of the largest collections anywhere.

Tulane remains committed to its mission as a major research university that emphasizes undergraduate opportunities. All undergrads enroll in the Newcomb-Tulane College, which coordinates academic experiences and support. Students complete a rigorous set of core curriculum requirements that includes a service-learning course as well as a public service project, which can take the form of a research project, internship, study abroad program, or honors thesis. Several programs help freshmen make the transition from high school to college, such as TIDES (Tulane InterDisciplinary Experience Seminars), where students connect with a peer mentor and take a small-group course on topics as varied as yoga, innovation in chemical engineering, and New Orleans cemetery architecture. Some TIDES courses have associated residential learning communities that encourage closer bonding with classmates.

Together, five schools—architecture, business, liberal arts, public health and tropical medicine, and science and engineering—offer more than 75 undergraduate majors. The most popular include business, public health, social sciences, and biological sciences. Tulane's strength lies in the natural sciences, environmental sciences, and the humanities; international studies in general and Latin American studies in particular are especially strong. The Stone Center for Latin American studies offers more than 150 courses taught by 70 faculty members. An interdisciplinary program in political economy (economics, political science, and philosophy) stands out among the social sciences and is very popular with prelaw students. Environmental studies majors benefit from the ByWater Institute, where faculty members and students work together to study and preserve Louisiana's waterways and coast.

> **"It's impossible to escape the Northern influence that exists on campus."**

Sixty-one percent of classes have fewer than 20 students, and although the majority of those classes are taught by full professors, graduate instructors are most likely to teach the beginning-level classes in English, foreign languages, and math. Overall, students praise Tulane's faculty and say the academic atmosphere can be very intense, depending on the class. Each year the university's highly acclaimed honors program invites about 700 outstanding students to partake in accelerated courses taught by top professors. Tulane offers more than 100 study abroad programs in 40 nations, including one-semester programs in locations such as Thailand to study community public health and Senegal to study international development. In addition, Tulane's Junior Year Abroad program in the UK is one of the country's oldest and most prestigious programs. One-third of undergrads study internationally during their time at Tulane.

Tulane manifests a somewhat Southern feel in a sophisticated and cosmopolitan institution. Says one student, "If you're a Northerner, it's impossible to escape the Southern influence of the city, and if you're a Southerner, it's impossible to escape the Northern influence that exists on campus." Twenty-three percent of undergraduates are Louisiana residents, and 4 percent come from outside the U.S. Despite the diversity of its host city, Tulane's student body is fairly homogeneous: 4 percent are African American, 7 percent are Hispanic, 5 percent are Asian American, 4 percent are multiracial, and just 9 percent of freshmen qualify for Pell Grants. Tulane awards hundreds of merit scholarships, averaging $26,000, and 181 athletic scholarships in 15 sports.

> **"New Orleans itself never stops partying!"**

Forty-eight percent of students live on campus; nonlocal freshmen and sophomores must do so. Many upper-class students opt to move off campus, claiming that it's much cheaper than university housing, but others are concerned about the safety factor of living in New Orleans. Some Greek students live in their chapter houses. Twenty-five dining locations offer a variety of options and are enhanced by a monthly farmers market and food trucks that accept the school's meal plan. A late-night shuttle service transports students safely to and from campus. Tulane has beefed up its counseling staff and programming to combat sexual assault, including a mentoring program to "promote positive men's behavior on campus."

(continued)

Academics: ✍ ✍ ✍ ½
Social: ☎ ☎ ☎ ☎
Q of L: ★ ★ ★
Admissions: (800) 873-9283
Email Address: undergrad.admission@tulane.edu

Strong Programs:
Business
Public Health
Social Sciences
Biological Sciences
Environmental Studies
International Studies
Latin American Studies
Political Economy

All students are required to complete a service-learning course as well as a public service project.

Tulane's Junior Year Abroad program in the UK is one of the country's oldest and most prestigious programs.

Social life at Tulane goes almost without saying. "New Orleans itself never stops partying!" boasts a junior. Fraternities and sororities are a presence—29 percent of the men and 50 percent of the women join—but do not dominate the social life, and there are more than 200 student organizations on campus. Though you're supposed to be 21 to enjoy the bar scene in the cafés and clubs that dot the French Quarter, a sophomore explains that "alcohol is accessible." Mardi Gras is such a celebration that classes are suspended for two days and students from all over the country pour in to celebrate. An annual Jazz Fest in the spring also draws wide participation. Road-trip destinations include the Gulf Coast, Austin, Houston, and the Florida panhandle.

While schoolwork is taken seriously at Tulane, so are sports. Football, women's volleyball, and men's and women's basketball are solid, and the baseball team has a big following. The university fields 16 Green Wave teams that compete in the Division I American Athletic Conference. Club and intramural sports are big, and students can also opt for weight work, squash, or swimming, among other options, at the Reily Student Recreation Center.

Rich in Southern tradition, Tulane is a forward-looking school where the possibilities seem endless. And like its hometown, it is an energetic melting pot of interests and activity. Those seeking a dynamic, service-oriented education in a vibrant city need look no further. *C'est si bon!*

Overlaps

Brown, Duke, Emory, George Washington, Northwestern, Vanderbilt, University of Miami (FL), University of Southern California

If You Apply To ›

Tulane: Early decision I and II, early action, regular decision. SATs or ACTs: required. Subject Tests: optional (required for homeschooled students). Accepts the Common Application with supplement.

University of Tulsa

800 South Tucker Drive, Tulsa, OK 74104

Tulsa is a notch smaller than Texas Christian and Washington U, but bigger than many liberal arts colleges. The university has a technical orientation rooted in Oklahoma oil, but a much more diverse curriculum than Colorado School of Mines. Has an innovative program allowing undergraduates to do research beginning their first semester. English language and literature is an unlikely strength.

Website: www.utulsa.edu
Location: City Outskirts
Private
Total Enrollment: 3,924
Undergraduates: 3,196
Male/Female: 56/44
SAT Ranges: ERW 590–720, M 560–720
ACT Ranges: 25–32
Financial Aid: 95%
Pell Grant: 22%
Expense: Pr $
Student Loans: 50%
Average Debt: $ $ $ $

The University of Tulsa is a small, private liberal arts school with a growing international reputation. Known for its engineering and science programs, including petroleum engineering and geosciences, it attracts students from around the world. With an emphasis on undergraduate research, hands-on work experience, and a diverse array of course offerings, TU has found its niche.

TU's 210-acre campus is just three miles from downtown Tulsa, and there's a striking view of the city's skyline from the steps of the neo-Gothic McFarlin Library. The university's more than 90 buildings run the architectural gamut from 1930s-vintage neo-Gothic to contemporary, all variations on a theme of yellow Tennessee limestone dubbed "TU stone." The Lorton Performance Center is TU's showcase facility for the musical and performance arts. The Helmerich Center for American Research houses the Gilcrease Museum library and archive, which features the 6,000-item Bob Dylan Archive.

In accordance with the Tulsa Curriculum, the cornerstone of the school's emphasis on liberal arts, all undergraduates take at least 25 credit hours of general curriculum classes in aesthetic inquiry and creative experience, historical and social interpretation, and scientific investigation. Coursework in writing, mathematics, and foreign language is also expected. Freshmen participate in a weeklong orientation program prior to the start of the fall semester and are required to take an introductory First Seminar course in the spring. Note: administrators recently rolled out a highly controversial proposal for "reimagining" Tulsa's approach to balancing liberal arts and professional studies that could, if implemented, substantially alter the undergraduate academic experience. Stay tuned.

In addition to its well-established and internationally recognized petroleum engineering and geosciences programs, TU offers solid majors in computer science and English. Tulsa is one of 20 schools in the nation that train America's Cyber Corps, the first line of defense against computer hackers and terrorists. The rapidly growing English department has added a new creative writing major. It also has some impressive resources at its disposal in McFarlin Library's special collections, which boast letters, manuscripts, and other materials by 19th- and 20th-century authors; highlights include a stained necktie that once belonged to James Joyce and more than 50,000 items representing the late Nobel laureate V. S. Naipaul's life and work. Students

"TU is a very academic school that recruits students who care about their grades."

in the new international engineering/science and language program earn both a B.S. in engineering or science and a B.A. in a foreign language in five years, one of which is spent studying abroad. Mechanical engineering, accounting, biology, and psychology are the most popular majors.

Courses are rigorous, and students say the workload can be heavy, but classmates are always willing to help one another out. Sixty-one percent of classes enroll fewer than 20 students, and professors are praised for being approachable and accommodating of student needs. "One time I was struggling with a lab, so I went to talk to my professor," recounts a sophomore. "He ended up clearing all of his meetings for the afternoon so he could redo the entire lab with me step by step. These types of things are not uncommon at TU." Students also give high ratings to the university's academic support resources, including free workshops, subsidized tutoring sessions, and grad students who serve as academic counselors, helping with goal setting, study tips, and time-management skills.

Honors students take exclusive seminars, complete a thesis or advanced project, develop portfolios, and can live together in an honors house. The Tulsa Undergraduate Research Challenge offers outstanding opportunities to conduct cutting-edge research with faculty mentors and has produced dozens of national scholarship winners; research is encouraged in every academic department and often begins as early as freshman year. Twenty-one percent of students travel abroad for programs including global health and society in Ghana, nursing and technology in Scotland, and tropical biology in Costa Rica. "Tulsa puts high emphasis on the vital role summer internships can play in one's academic career," says an enthusiastic senior. "I have had a high-paying internship ever since my freshman year."

"TU is a very academic school that recruits students who care about their grades," comments a freshman. Forty-seven percent of Tulsa's students are from Oklahoma; most others are from the Midwest and Southwest, with many hailing from Dallas and St. Louis. An impressive 20 percent are international. The student body is 5 percent African American, 6 percent Hispanic, 5 percent Asian American, 3 percent American Indian, and 3 percent multiracial. Students describe the campus as "moderately liberal," and a junior says TU is "not a hotbed for political activism." Athletes compete for 306 scholarships in 17 sports. TU also offers merit

"Our worst dorms are nicer than the newest dorms on many state school campuses."

(continued)

Applicants: 7,869
Accepted: 39%
Enrolled: 24%
Grad in 6 Years: 69%
Returning Freshmen: 88%
Academics: ✎ ✎ ✎
Social: ☎ ☎ ☎
Q of L: ★ ★
Admissions: (918) 631-2307
Email Address: admission@ utulsa.edu

Strong Programs:
Petroleum Engineering
Geosciences
Computer Science
English
Mechanical Engineering
Accounting
Biology
Psychology

Students in the international engineering/science and language program earn both a B.S. and a B.A. in five years, one of which is spent abroad.

scholarships averaging $21,500, and 22 percent of incoming freshmen receive Pell Grants.

Sixty-five percent of students reside in campus housing; freshmen and sophomores are required to do so, and while some upperclassmen move off campus, many choose to stay because of the school's six luxury apartment villages. Students enjoy dorm living too, and a marketing major says, "Our worst dorms are nicer than the newest dorms on many state school campuses." The student union food court was recently renovated, and students can also choose from cafeteria and bar-and-grill options, but many students describe the cafeteria food as, simply, "bad." Students give administrators credit for adopting a more transparent approach to the issue of sexual assault. "The president sends an email each Friday addressing facts of college culture, and we are always informed when an assault is reported," notes a media studies major.

The social life at TU is surprisingly robust, if not raucous, thanks to hundreds of student organizations and a healthy Greek life. The university sponsors regular social events, and students enjoy simply hanging with friends at small gatherings too. The Greek organizations claim 18 percent of TU men and 20 percent of the women, and the frats host campuswide house parties. Student-initiated policies govern drinking on campus and are well enforced. Campus traditions include the ringing of the college's cupola bell by each senior after his or her last final exam. Other big events include the homecoming bonfire and football game and the Springfest concert.

Nearby parks, lakes, and a huge recreational water park please outdoor enthusiasts. Downtown Tulsa offers symphony, ballet, opera, museums, and an annual Oktoberfest. "Tulsa is such a vibrant city and is booming every day," says a senior, who recommends the Brookside and Cherry Street districts and concerts at Cain's Ballroom. Fifty-five percent of students take active part in community service opportunities coordinated through the True Blue Neighbors program, volunteering time with groups like Habitat for Humanity and Tulsa's Day Center for the Homeless. The Bricktown section of Oklahoma City and nearby casinos, along with more distant Dallas, St. Louis, and Kansas City, are popular road trips.

"Tulsa is such a vibrant city and is booming every day."

Here in Oklahoma, sports are important (very, *very* important!). The Division I Golden Hurricanes compete in the American Athletic Conference in 17 intercollegiate sports. Students get riled up when the football team is pitted against rivals Oklahoma and Oklahoma State, and when the basketball team suits up against Memphis and SMU. Men's and women's tennis, track and field, and cross-country are also competitive, as is the softball team. Forty percent of undergrads participate in at least one intramural or recreational sport; the most popular by far is flag football.

TU is trying to do some things differently: be a small liberal arts school in a part of the country most known for sprawling public universities, and incorporate professional preparation with an emphasis on broad intellectual challenges. Says one senior, "Tulsa strives to develop well-rounded, highly intellectual individuals who are best equipped to take on the global problems of tomorrow."

Overlaps

Southern Methodist, Texas Christian, Lehigh, University of Richmond, Creighton, Rice, University of Oklahoma, Saint Louis University

If You Apply To ›

Tulsa: Early action, rolling admissions. SATs or ACTs: required. No Subject Tests. Accepts the Common Application with supplement.

Union College

807 Union Street, Schenectady, NY 12308

Union is split down the middle between liberal arts and engineering. That means its center of gravity is more toward the technical side than places like Lafayette, Trinity, and Tufts, but less so than Clarkson and Rensselaer. Schenectady is less than exciting, but there are outdoor getaways in all directions. Relatively anonymous because it does not fit into conventional categories.

Founded in 1795, Union College is one of the oldest nondenominational colleges in the country. Its name reflects the founders' desire to create a welcoming, unifying academic community open to the region's diverse religious and national groups. More than 220 years later, this independent liberal arts college is known for its interdisciplinary studies and its study abroad programs. At Union, engineering and the arts go hand-in-hand. Undergraduate research has deep roots at Union, starting in the mid-20th century when a chemistry professor began involving students in his colloid chemistry investigations. Today, "Union is constantly thinking of ways to better the students' experience," says one satisfied student.

Union's 100-acre campus, designed in 1813 by French architect and landscaper Joseph Jacques Ramée, sits on a hill overlooking Schenectady. Ramée's vision took shape in brownstone and redbrick, with plenty of white arches, pilasters, and lacy green trees; the campus plan also includes eight acres of formal gardens and woodlands. The 16-sided Nott Memorial, a National Historic Landmark and one of the most unusual structures on any U.S. campus, is a meeting, study, and exhibition center—and the site of a naked run each year. Parcels of land adjacent to College Park Hall, a hotel-turned-dorm, have become soccer fields for college and community use. After a two-year expansion and renovation, the interdisciplinary Science and Engineering Center has been transformed into a state-of-the-art, fully integrated complex; the $100 million project was the largest in the school's history.

> "Union is constantly thinking of ways to better the students' experience."

To fulfill Union's general education requirements, students take core courses in their first and second years that promote reading, writing, and analytical skills, including a required, interdisciplinary First-Year Preceptorial. They also take courses spread among social science, humanities, linguistic and cultural competency, quantitative and mathematical reasoning, and natural and applied science or engineering. All students must complete a senior thesis or senior seminar paper in order to graduate.

Among Union's most popular majors are economics, mechanical engineering, political science, and psychology. Students also flock to geology, computer science, English, and history; the latter department is home to Union's most esteemed lecturer, Stephen Berk, whose course on the Holocaust and Twentieth-Century Europe is a hot ticket. Each year, about 50 incoming freshmen are named Union Scholars. The designation extends the First-Year Preceptorial to two terms and gives students access to independent study projects, departmental honors programs, and expanded study abroad options. Eighty percent of all Union students conduct undergraduate research, and each spring, Union cancels classes one afternoon for the Steinmetz Symposium, so that students can present scholarly projects to their peers and professors in a professional conference atmosphere.

Interdisciplinary study is the norm at Union, with established programs in bioengineering, Latin American and Caribbean studies, law and public policy, and Russian and Eastern European studies, to name a few. The college's Kelly Adirondack

Website: www.union.edu
Location: Small City
Private
Total Enrollment: 2,163
Undergraduates: 2,163
Male/Female: 53/47
SAT Ranges: ERW 630–700, M 640–730
ACT Ranges: 29–32
Financial Aid: 77%
Pell Grant: 13%
Expense: Pr $ $ $ $
Student Loans: 56%
Average Debt: $ $ $ $
Applicants: 6,676
Accepted: 37%
Enrolled: 23%
Grad in 6 Years: 85%
Returning Freshmen: 92%
Academics: ✍ ✍ ✍ ✍
Social: 🍻 🍻 🍻
Q of L: ★ ★ ★
Admissions: (518) 388-6112
Email Address: admissions@union.edu

Strong Programs:
Economics
Mechanical Engineering
Political Science
Psychology
Geology
Computer Science
English
History

Center, 10 minutes from campus, features the 15,000-item Adirondack Research Library and is a boon to students interested in environmental research and stewardship. The educational studies program allows aspiring teachers to complete courses and fieldwork required for secondary school certification in a variety of subjects, along with a strong liberal arts grounding. The Leadership in Medicine program, a joint program with Clarkson University's Union Graduate College and Albany Medical College, gives students the opportunity to earn a bachelor's degree, an M.S. in health management or an M.B.A. in health systems administration, and a medical degree in eight years.

Undergraduate research has deep roots at Union, starting in the mid-20th century.

"Union's culture is built around the relationships between students and faculty," says a sophomore. "We are very lucky to have stellar professors who are always looking to be active in the lives of their pupils." Sixty-seven percent of classes have

> **"Union's culture is built around the relationships between students and faculty."**

fewer than 20 students, and students can expect to see full professors at the lecterns rather than teaching assistants. Union operates on a trimester system, which means thrice-a-year exams and a late start to summer jobs—but also the opportunity to concentrate on just three courses a term. More terms also means more opportunities for independent study and internships, either in the state capital of Albany, 20 minutes away, or in Washington, D.C. By the time graduation rolls around, 60 percent of students have studied abroad, many of them in faculty-led, three-week "mini terms" during winter or summer break.

Sixty percent of students study abroad, many of them in faculty-led, three-week "mini terms" during winter or summer break.

Thirty-eight percent of Union students are New Yorkers and 7 percent are international. Four percent of students are African American, 7 percent are Hispanic, 6 percent are Asian American, and 3 percent are multiracial, but the school has been working to boost these numbers. A senior describes the political climate as "rather balanced," and a sophomore says, "I find that there is a great amount of privilege at our school." Union awards hundreds of merit scholarships averaging $11,700, and it meets the full demonstrated financial need of admitted students, but it does not offer athletic scholarships.

Ninety percent of Union students live on campus. The Minerva house system (named after the Roman goddess of wisdom) is aimed at getting students and faculty members to contribute to Union's social, residential, and intellectual life—and, students say, at decreasing the influence of the Greek system, which draws 32

> **"Greek life dominates."**

percent of the men and 41 percent of the women. "The dorms are fine, pretty typical, but the apartments for seniors and all the theme houses are very nice," reports a student. Students recommend West, which is co-ed by room and thus very social, as well as Fox and Davidson, where freshmen and sophomores live in suites. Dining options consist of four main eating areas and the quality of meals "really depends on the day," says a freshman. "Campus police watch out very closely for the safety of students," says a sociology major.

"The majority of social life is on campus," says a student. "There are Minerva events and on-campus movies as well as typical fraternity parties." Campus events also include comedians, concerts, and speakers. Despite these alternatives and strictly enforced alcohol policies, most students agree that "Greek life dominates," and, as one senior explains, "The school is not big enough to counteract the high attendance of Greek parties with school-sponsored events." Favorite annual traditions include the lobster bake (each student gets his or her own crustacean) and Springfest, an outdoor concert. An unofficial graduation requirement is to do a lap around the Nott Memorial—sans clothing.

An unofficial graduation requirement is to do a lap around the Nott Memorial—sans clothing.

Off campus, Schenectady is an old-line industrial city that's a decent—if not great—college town, according to a freshman. Says a sophomore, "There are essentially no college-town amenities—like bookstores—in walking distance. You need a car." What Schenectady lacks can be found in Saratoga Springs, which boasts restaurants, jazz clubs, horse racing, and Skidmore College, or in the nearby Adirondacks and Catskills. Popular road trips include Boston, Montreal, New York, and the ski slopes of nearby Vermont. Students are trying to help Schenectady rebound, through on-campus tutoring programs for local schoolchildren and work with groups like the YMCA and the Boys and Girls Club. There's also a service project during freshman orientation.

Union's athletic teams (the Dutchmen) compete in Division III, aside from men's and women's ice hockey, both of which are Division I. Baseball and men's basketball are recent Liberty League conference champions, and women's basketball, lacrosse, and soccer are also solid. Intramural and club sports include teams in everything from volleyball and broomball to ultimate Frisbee and fly-fishing, and about 60 percent of students participate.

Union's mission is constantly evolving as the college works to meet the needs and interests of students and faculty. It retains its commitment to a strong core liberal arts curriculum while acknowledging the increasing effects of globalization and technology. Union College has plenty to offer—a small, friendly place full of eager intellectual exchange. You just have to seek it out.

> ## Overlaps
>
> **Colgate, Lafayette, Rensselaer, University of Rochester, University of Vermont, Skidmore, Trinity College (CT), Hamilton**

If You Apply To ›

Union: Early decision I and II, regular decision. SATs or ACTs: optional (required for applicants to combined law and medicine programs and for homeschooled students). Subject Tests: optional. Accepts the Common Application with supplement.

Ursinus College

Box 1000, Collegeville, PA 19426

Ursinus is the smallest of the cohort of eastern Pennsylvania liberal arts colleges that includes Franklin & Marshall, Lafayette, and Muhlenberg. The plus side is more attention from faculty and more emphasis on independent and outside-the-box learning. The setting is small town, but Philly is within arm's reach.

Ursinus College takes its name from a 16th-century German Calvinist, Zacharias Ursinus, who directed that students should "examine all things and keep what is good." In recent years, Ursinus has reinvigorated its liberal arts roots—expanding its offerings and restructuring its core curriculum to emphasize questions of human existence and to prepare students "not simply to make a living, but to make a life of purpose." What hasn't changed is the close-knit feel of the school. "Ursinus's culture is one of inquisitive learning through experimentation and discussion with peers that brings students together in a small campus atmosphere," muses a senior.

Ursinus is located in Collegeville, about 40 minutes west of Philadelphia, and 10 miles from the green, rolling hills of Valley Forge National Park. Buildings on the 170-acre campus are mostly constructed of Pennsylvania fieldstone; many have had their interiors upgraded and their exteriors preserved and restored. Actors and dancers benefit from rehearsal and exhibition space in the Kaleidoscope Performing Arts Center. The 42,500-square-foot Innovation and Discovery Center opened in 2018.

> **Website**: www.ursinus.edu
> **Location**: Suburban
> **Private**
> **Total Enrollment**: 1,485
> **Undergraduates**: 1,485
> **Male/Female**: 47/53
> **SAT Ranges**: ERW 560–660, M 550–650
> **ACT Ranges**: 24–30
> **Financial Aid**: 99%
> **Pell Grant**: 20%
> **Expense**: Pr $ $ $
> **Student Loans**: 73%
> **Average Debt**: $ $ $ $
> **Applicants**: 3,488

(continued)

Accepted: 78%

Enrolled: 15%

Grad in 6 Years: 77%

Returning Freshmen: 85%

Academics: ✍ ✍ ✍

Social: ☎ ☎ ☎

Q of L: ★ ★ ★

Admissions: (610) 409-3200

Email Address: admission@ursinus.edu

Strong Programs:
Biology
Applied Economics
Psychology
Health and Exercise Physiology
Neuroscience
Media and Communication
   Studies
Politics
International Relations

The Common Intellectual Experience, taken in the first year, explores works ranging from Plato to Hindu scripture to Ta-Nehisi Coates.

Ursinus's core curriculum, called Open Questions, is intended to engage students in deep inquiry and reflection on four central themes: identifying personal values, living in communities, understanding the world, and making life-shaping decisions. The core begins with the Common Intellectual Experience—a two-semester course taken in the first year that explores works ranging from Plato to Hindu scripture to Ta-Nehisi Coates. Additional components include interdisciplinary coursework, an experiential learning project (an independent research or creative project, an internship, study abroad, student teaching, or civic engagement), and a Core Capstone course in the senior year.

Students choose among nearly 30 majors, with the most popular being biology, applied economics, psychology, health and exercise physiology, neuroscience, and media and communication studies. The college also offers strong programs in politics and international relations and has added a new major in educational studies.

"Ursinus's culture is one of inquisitive learning through experimentation and discussion."

The academic climate is largely dependent on the course of study. Classes are small—68 percent have fewer than 20 students—and an applied economics major says, "You definitely need to put in work outside of class and show up to class—there's no way to sit quietly at the back of a packed lecture." Students are mostly pleased with the quality of teaching, especially since there are no teaching assistants. "The relationships I have with my professors are more personal than I could have ever expected coming into college," says a junior.

Each year, 70 to 80 rising juniors and seniors get fellowships from the school to fund full-time summer research projects with a faculty member. "Many Summer Fellows end up extending their research into honors research senior year," explains a senior. The Parlee Center for Science and the Common Good aims to help students understand and explain the ethical, political, and cultural impacts of their scientific work, offering a speaker series, a student fellows program, internships, and summer research opportunities. The U-Imagine Center for Integrative and Entrepreneurial Studies and the Melrose Center for Global Civic Engagement offer similar programming. Nineteen percent of Ursinus students study abroad, both in programs designed and run by the college and in affiliate programs. The Philadelphia Experience places selected students in a residence hall in Philadelphia for a semester to take courses with Ursinus faculty, along with their choice of an internship or independent research project.

"Our students have many different interests," says an applied economics major. "A football player may also be in the men's a cappella group. A theater star may also do honors biology research." Fifty-eight percent of students are from Pennsylvania and 2 percent are from foreign countries, with most others hailing from New York, New Jersey, and other Mid-Atlantic and New England states.

"Everyone—the students, professors, and staff— is so friendly and open."

African Americans make up 7 percent of the student body, Asian Americans 4 percent, Hispanics 7 percent, and multiracial students 3 percent. One senior describes a "partisan political climate" on campus and another says, "Any liberal social issue is hot-button." Non-need-based scholarships and grants averaging $24,000 are available each year, but no athletic scholarships are offered.

Ninety-four percent of students at Ursinus live in the dorms, which adds to the feeling of community. Upperclassmen quickly grab the Main Street houses, a string of Victorian-era homes across the street from campus, while freshmen are clustered in BPS and BWC (short for Beardwood-Paisley-Stauffer and Brodbeck-Wilkinson-Curtis, respectively), which have generously sized rooms. Reimert Hall is the party dorm. Student-run special interest housing is available too, for those who share social or academic interests. "Although it's easy and commonplace to complain about our only dining hall, Wismer, I think it's good and definitely suits the needs of most students," says a vegetarian. A junior reports, "Campus Safety is always seen around campus mingling with students and gaining their respect and trust."

Much of the social life occurs on campus, including performances, themed cuisine nights, and craft nights organized by the student activities board. Greek life draws 18 percent of the men and 32 percent of the women, and parties hosted by fraternities and sports teams are a popular weekend diversion. Registered on-campus parties are monitored by student "social hosts" who check IDs and make sure things don't get out of hand. "I'm happy we're a wet campus because I think it keeps the students safer. A lot of drinking goes on," reports a junior. Homecoming is a favorite tradition in the fall, and in the spring, students look forward to the annual Bear Bash concert and Airband, "a big charity lip-synching and perform-ing event," says an English major. Sixty-five percent of students perform regular volunteer work.

Ursinus is a well-known stepping stone to post-collegiate careers in coaching.

The town of Collegeville is just 10 blocks long—and Ursinus takes up five of those—but a politics major says it offers "a few good bars and restaurants to enter-tain students." Frequent school-sponsored shuttles take students to the shops, res-taurants, sporting events, and festivals of Philadelphia, less than an hour away. Many students with cars escape to the Jersey Shore during warmer months.

Ursinus students love their Division III sports, and intramural and club sports draw 40 percent of students. For students seeking post-collegiate careers in coach-ing, Ursinus is a well-known stepping stone to those posts, thanks in part to a tight network of loyal alumni-athletes who tap each other for opportunities. The Bears field hockey team is a perennial contender for the national championship, and the women's swimming, men's wrestling, and women's gymnastics teams are also strong. Women's swimming won its fifth-straight conference title in 2018.

Ursinus is on the rise. It may not be in the center of a big metropolitan area, and it doesn't offer big-time sports, but the college compensates for its lack of size with the feeling that students, faculty, and staff are one big family. "The special thing about Ursinus is the people," says a biology major. "Everyone—the students, professors, and staff—is so friendly and open and just wants you to succeed."

Overlaps

Muhlenberg, Washington College, Allegheny, Washington and Jefferson, Wheaton (MA), Gettysburg, Temple, Drexel

If You Apply To ›

Ursinus: Early decision I and II, early action, regular decision. SATs or ACTs: optional (required for homeschooled stu-dents). No Subject Tests. Accepts the Common Application.

University of Utah

Salt Lake City, UT 84112

One of the oldest universities west of the Mississippi, the University of Utah attracts a diverse group of students drawn to the region's only major city. Science and professional programs such as business and engineering are traditional strengths. Has positioned itself as a more accessible alternative to California's public higher education system—with plenty of academic opportunities and school spirit to go around. Applications have doubled in the last five years, and out-of-state enrollment is on the rise.

Website: www.utah.edu

Location: City Center

Public

Total Enrollment: 24,049

Undergraduates: 17,840

Male/Female: 53/47

SAT Ranges: ERW 560–670,
M 550–680

ACT Ranges: 22–29

Financial Aid: 71%

Pell Grant: 26%

Expense: Pub $

Student Loans: 39%

Average Debt: $

Applicants: 22,400

Accepted: 66%

Enrolled: 26%

Grad in 6 Years: 67%

Returning Freshmen: 91%

Academics: ✍ ✍ ✍

Social: ☎ ☎ ☎

Q of L: ★ ★ ★

Admissions: (801) 581-8761

Email Address: admissions@
utah.edu

Strong Programs:

Communication

Psychology

Economics

Nursing

Engineering

Business

Film and Media Arts

Ballet and Modern Dance

LEAP is a learning community committed to civic awareness and service; 13 percent of freshmen participate.

In addition to being the flagship institution of the state's higher education system, the University of Utah is a major national scientific research center. Founded in 1850, the university is unusual in its ability to offer students the advantages of living in a city while at the same time maintaining a connection with nature. Utah has increased its focus in recent years on the undergraduate experience, beefing up academic programs and building new residential facilities, including a $51 million student life center. Applications have surged as a result, and students say enthusiasm for their school is higher than ever. "We have the school spirit, the drive to transform the world, and the resources and connections needed for students to succeed," cheers one senior.

Set in the foothills of the Wasatch Mountains near the shores of the Great Salt Lake, the university enjoys a picturesque location a half-hour drive from "the greatest snow on earth." Occupying 1,500 well-landscaped acres with nearly as many different kinds of trees as undergraduates, the campus doubles as the state's arboretum. The university's structures range from historic 19th-century buildings to state-of-the-art modern facilities. A spate of new construction continues, including a 992-bed freshman residence hall scheduled to open in 2020.

Utah students choose from a comprehensive academic menu, including more than 100 undergraduate majors. Utah is renowned for its research in biomedical engineering, and while the professional degrees in engineering and business are quite popular, the U does not skimp on general education requirements. Students must take classes in writing, American institutions, math, statistics, and intellectual explorations, which includes two courses in the humanities, sciences, social sciences, or fine arts, as well as fulfill international and diversity course requirements. The most popular majors include communication, psychology, economics, and nursing. The film and media arts major offers an emphasis in entertainment arts and engineering, and programs in ballet and modern dance are also strong. The Lassonde Entrepreneur Institute offers training to budding entrepreneurs, 400 of whom get to reside in the $45 million Lassonde Studios, featuring the sort of pods and shared spaces characteristic of high-tech workplaces.

> "We have the school spirit [and] the drive to transform the world."

The academic climate can be challenging, but in general "the workload is fairly manageable," according to one sophomore. Introductory courses often enroll hundreds of students, with smaller discussion sections led by graduate student teaching assistants. Overall, 39 percent of classes have fewer than 20 students. Utah's professors generally receive high marks from the students. "Some professors are clearly more interested in their research than in teaching, but for the most part they'll still do a fair job," says a junior. The LEAP (Learning Engagement Achievement Progress) program is a learning community committed to the principles of civic awareness and service. LEAP features dedicated faculty and peer advisors who mentor new students and challenge them academically through a two-semester sequence of seminars; 13 percent of freshmen participate.

The MUSE (My Utah Signature Experience) Project is an advising program that helps coordinate unique learning experiences, ranging from lunchtime lectures with distinguished professors to internships and service projects, for any interested undergraduate. In addition to enticing leading faculty to Utah, the state-government-backed USTAR (Utah Science Technology and Research) initiative has enhanced opportunities for collaborative student-faculty research, in which about a quarter of undergraduates get involved, often with the support of research grants. Thirteen percent of students study abroad in more than 200 programs in more than 50 countries around the globe.

Utah's students are a mostly middle-class, fairly homogeneous lot; of the 72 percent of undergraduates who are from Utah, nearly all attended public schools. A growing number of students are arriving from out of state, especially Californians who feel shut out by the higher education system in their home state; 7 percent come from abroad. African Americans make up just 1 percent of the student population, Asian Americans 6 percent, Hispanics 13 percent, and multiracial students 5 percent. There is an active student government, and most Utes agree that students here are less conservative than those found at rival Brigham Young, a Mormon institution. A substantial percentage of Utah students are Mormon, though, and, "Diversity and religion are probably the biggest issues on campus," says one student. Utah offers merit scholarships averaging $6,400 and 369 athletic scholarships in 18 sports, while 26 percent of incoming students qualify for Pell Grants.

Only 14 percent of students live on campus, but those who do seem to be pleased with the housing facilities, many of which were built to accommodate visitors during the 2002 Olympics. Students are also generally satisfied with the food, though edibility varies based on which campus eatery you choose. "There are always vegetarian options," says a senior. At lunchtime, local food trucks usually line up around the Marriott Library plaza, a popular gathering place. Students report feeling safe on campus, and the university has increased the number of staff dedicated to Title IX issues.

In the MUSS—Mighty Utah Student Section—cheers are loudest during the "Holy War" rivalry football game against Brigham Young.

Utah has had a reputation as a commuter school, but students say that is changing; much of the off-campus population lives within five blocks of the university, and the on-campus social scene is becoming livelier with the influx of out-of-state students. Participation in Greek life is an increasingly popular option; currently, 6 percent of the men and 7 percent of the women join fraternities and sororities. "From lectures, concerts, dance performances, and late-night Crimson Nights parties, there is something for everyone," a student says.

"Much of the social life is recreational."

Utah's proximity to the mountains means that "much of the social life is recreational," according to one junior. Favorite road trips take students to Las Vegas, Lake Powell, and nearby ski resorts (with slopeside bus service available from the school). Salt Lake City isn't exactly a college town, but a junior says, "The nightlife in SLC downtown is great if you are over 21." Adjacent to campus, the Latter-day Saints Institute of Religion sponsors dances and other social activities with a decidedly conservative bent. There are also centers for other faiths, notably Jewish and Roman Catholic. Cultural activities include the respected Utah Symphony, several dance companies, opera, and, of course, the Mormon Tabernacle Choir.

Utes teams compete in the Division I Pac-12 Conference, and football and basketball bring students together in the MUSS—Mighty Utah Student Section—where cheers are loudest during the "Holy War" rivalry football game against Brigham Young. The co-ed skiing team won the national championship in 2017. Men's basketball and women's gymnastics, softball, volleyball, and soccer also make regular NCAA Tournament appearances. In addition to the university's dozens of club sports and intramurals (canoe battleship, anyone?), the Outdoor Adventure Program offers backpacking, river running, mountain biking, and skiing trips.

Students say that academic quality, diversity, and the residential experience are all on the rise at Utah. "The best thing about students at the U is that they are friendly to all, supportive of each other, and you can do whatever you want," says a computer animation major. It's also one of the few places where you can find nationally recognized professional programs within easy reach of nationally recognized skiing.

Overlaps

Arizona State, University of Arizona, University of Colorado Boulder, University of Washington, University of Iowa, Brigham Young, Utah State, Utah Valley

If You Apply To ›

University of Utah: Regular decision. SATs or ACTs: required. Subject Tests: optional. Does not accept the Common Application.

2305 West End Avenue, Nashville, TN 37240

BEST BUY

Strongest and most selective of schools that still manage to blend Old South gentility with modern ways. Long a preferred choice for Atlanta and Birmingham elites, Vandy has become more diverse, geographically and otherwise. More selective than Emory and now comparable to Duke among leading schools south of the Mason–Dixon line. One of the few major universities where both academics and athletics are top–notch.

Website: www.vanderbilt.edu
Location: City Center
Private
Total Enrollment: 11,753
Undergraduates: 6,791
Male/Female: 49/51
SAT Ranges: ERW 700–760,
    M 700–790
ACT Ranges: 32–35
Financial Aid: 66%
Pell Grant: 15%
Expense: Pr $ $
Student Loans: 21%
Average Debt: $
Applicants: 31,462
Accepted: 11%
Enrolled: 47%
Grad in 6 Years: 92%
Returning Freshmen: 97%
Academics: ✍ ✍ ✍ ✍
Social: ☎ ☎ ☎
Q of L: ★ ★ ★ ★
Admissions: (800) 288-0432
Email Address: admissions@
    vanderbilt.edu

Strong Programs:
Human and Organizational
    Development
Engineering
Biological Sciences
Medicine, Health, and Society
Economics
Education

Once a quiet, conservative school in the heart of the South, Vanderbilt University has diversified its student body and brought a more cosmopolitan atmosphere to campus. Coats, ties, and pearls may be outnumbered by Commodore fan gear at football games these days, but the university has succeeded in marrying Old South gentility with modern attitudes. The result is a relaxed, friendly culture that makes the rigorous academic environment easier to handle. "Students looking for a balance between great academics and a solid social life need to look at Vandy," counsels a history major.

Founded in 1873 by Cornelius Vanderbilt, the university's 330-acre tract in Nashville is an arboretum and includes Peabody College, the central section of which is listed on the National Register of Historic Places. On the main campus, art and sculptures dot the landscape, and architectural styles range from Gothic to modern glass and brick. The Sarratt Student Center is a social hub, with a movie theater, Rand Dining Hall, a pub, and offices for student organizations. Newer additions include the Engineering and Science Building and the Wond'ry, a space designed for innovation and entrepreneurship.

Undergraduates choose one of four schools—College of Arts and Science, School of Engineering, Blair School of Music, or Peabody College of Education and Human Development—but everyone takes their core liberal arts courses in the College of Arts and Science, where the writing program is a standout. Immersion Vanderbilt, a new graduation requirement launched in 2018, calls for every undergraduate to undertake an immersive learning experience (such as internships, fieldwork, or performances) culminating in a final project; students choose from four pathways: civic and professional, creative expression, international, and research. Optional first-year Commons "iSeminars" (project-based Immersion seminars) allow students to explore various topics in small groups with close faculty interaction; recent offerings have included everything from Drug Epidemics: What Lies Beneath? to Electric Power Generation.

> **"[Vandy has] a balance between great academics and a solid social life."**

Popular majors include human and organizational development; engineering (especially mechanical); biological sciences; medicine, health, and society; and economics. Education majors who enroll at Peabody College are required to double major, usually in a liberal arts field. Many students interested in financial careers declare an economics major and pursue a business minor; there's also a 3–2 program with the Owen Graduate School of Business, which lets talented undergraduates save a year on the path to their M.B.A.s.

"The academic climate of Vanderbilt is absolutely collaborative," an elementary education major says. "It provides the academic rigor I was hoping for without any of the cutthroat aspect I was afraid would accompany such an academically challenging school." Two-thirds of courses have fewer than 20 students, and in the classroom, Vanderbilt students are governed by the school's honor system, which dates from 1875. The system governs all aspects of academic conduct and makes it possible for professors to give unproctored exams. Students rave about the faculty. "Many professors go out of their way to encourage students to get involved with research and internship opportunities," comments a junior.

Vanderbilt's study abroad program attracts 44 percent of students and offers the chance to spend a summer, a semester, or a year on one of six continents via more than 120 programs. The optional "Maymester" allows students to spend four weeks on a single project, helpful for double majors or those who'd like to embark on a short-term internship or overseas trip. Roughly half of the students, from all four undergraduate schools, participate in research, and many copublish articles. The campus is home to more than 100 interdisciplinary centers and institutes.

Ten percent of undergraduates are in-state residents, and 8 percent are international, coming from nearly 50 countries. Asian Americans account for 13 percent of the student body, African Americans 10 percent, Hispanics 10 percent, and multiracial students 5 percent. Politically, Vanderbilt students are divided pretty evenly between conservatives, moderates, and liberals. "I would not describe Vanderbilt as an activist campus per se, but in my two years there have been several rallies and protests," observes an English major. Vanderbilt employs a need-blind admissions process, meets full demonstrated need for all admitted students, and offers loan-free financial aid packages for students with demonstrated need. In addition to need-based aid, the university awards approximately 250 merit scholarships, complete with summer stipends, to admitted students through three signature merit scholarship programs. There are also 238 athletic scholarships awarded.

"I would not describe Vanderbilt as an activist campus per se."

Ninety percent of Vanderbilt undergraduates live on campus. All first-year students live together in 10 Commons houses and take part in Vanderbilt Visions, a living/learning initiative designed to foster a sense of community among new students. Each first-year is assigned to a Visions group, which has about 18 students, a faculty advisor, and an upper-class peer mentor. In addition to meeting with their group once a week during the fall semester, students have opportunities to get to know the faculty who live in the various Commons houses. Students also compete in the Commons Cup, which, a junior explains, "is pretty much the House Cup straight out of Harry Potter, and it is a blast. You and your house compete in intramurals, sustainability, community service, and academics over the course of the whole year." Most recently, the school added the Warren, Moore, and Ingram residential colleges for upper-class students. Other options for older students include 10-person townhouses, six-room suites, theme dorms, and school-owned apartments. Seniors may move off campus but must obtain a special waiver.

Vanderbilt has more than 20 dining facilities that "always provide a delicious array of options," according to a junior, and first-years are required to buy a meal plan. The Taste of Nashville program allows students to use their meal money at two dozen local restaurants. Students report feeling safe on campus, thanks to an active security department that "watches out for Vanderbilt students and keeps us safe." As for sexual assault prevention, one student says Vanderbilt "is facing this issue head-on," especially through the efforts of the Project Safe Center.

"[The Commons Cup] is pretty much the House Cup straight out of Harry Potter, and it is a blast."

Fifty percent of the women and 34 percent of the men join the Greek system; while many Greek parties are open to the entire campus, the effort to encourage mixing between the groups is not always successful. "Fraternities and sororities start the social scene," a senior says, "but certainly don't encompass all aspects of Vanderbilt's social life." The first-year Commons campus is dry, but of-age students are allowed to have alcohol elsewhere on campus, although open containers are banned in public and kegs are also taboo. As at many colleges, one student says, "underage students can find loopholes." Students get involved in more than 430 student organizations. Favorite Vanderbilt traditions are the Commodore Quake and Rites of Spring music festivals, Founders Walk, and the Anchor Dash, when all the first-years run onto the football field before the first home game.

Vanderbilt's proximity to Music City USA provides plenty to do. "Nashville is so much fun," cheers one senior. "The list of excellent restaurants, bars, shopping, and live music venues is endless." Country music fans shouldn't miss the Hall of Fame. Beyond Nashville's borders are the Great Smoky Mountains and state parks with picnic facilities, beautiful lakes, and skiing in the winter. The best road trips are to Memphis (home of Elvis), New Orleans (for Mardi Gras), and Louisville (for the Kentucky Derby). Students also engage in the local community through a variety of service-oriented programs. "Alternative Spring Break (ASB) is a very popular program on college campuses across the country, and was actually a student-driven initiative that originated at Vanderbilt," explains an elementary education major. In fact, ASB is Vandy's largest student-run organization.

"Alternative Spring Break (ASB) is a very popular program."

Vanderbilt may be the smallest—and the only private—institution in the competitive and football-crazy Division I Southeastern Conference, but there is no shortage of enthusiasm among Commodore fans. Vandy reconfigured its athletic program some years ago in an effort to cut costs. Instead of losing ground (as many feared), the programs have thrived. The women's bowling team won the school's most recent national championship, and the baseball team is a perennial power-house. The Vanderbilt Aerospace Club has won NASA's annual Student Launch Challenge, an eight-month-long rocketry competition, five times in the last six years. There are 32 club sports for weekend jocks, as well as more than 40 intramural sports leagues.

Vanderbilt sits squarely among the top universities in the nation and has capitalized on its unique blend of Southern charm and scholarly achievement to attract students from around the country and beyond. Four years here do carry a steep before-financial-aid sticker price; witness a tongue-in-cheek campus slogan, "Vanderbilt: It Even Sounds Expensive." But for many, investing in a Vanderbilt education is money well spent.

Overlaps

Duke, Harvard, Yale, University of Pennsylvania, Cornell University, Stanford, WashU in St. Louis, Princeton

If You Apply To ›

Vanderbilt: Early decision I and II, regular decision. SATs or ACTs: required. Subject Tests: optional. Accepts the Common Application. Apply to particular school or program.

Vassar College

Poughkeepsie, NY 12604

It is hard to imagine that Vassar once considered picking up and moving to Yale in the 1960s rather than become a co-ed institution. Half a century after admitting men, still on its ancient and picturesque campus, Vassar is a thriving, highly selective, avant-garde institution where traditional strengths in the fine arts and humanities are matched by robust offerings in the natural and social sciences. At the forefront of national efforts to promote socioeconomic diversity in elite schools.

Are you a scientist who composes music in your spare time? Or perhaps an actor who enjoys dissecting Plato and Aristotle? If so, you may feel at home at Vassar, a distinguished liberal arts college just 70 miles north of New York City. Once known as the most liberal of the Seven Sisters, and still a bastion of the left, Vassar prides itself on curricular flexibility, tolerance, and diversity. A senior characterizes the school this way: "Vassar maintains a connection to the old, Northeastern liberal arts tradition (the connections, prestige, money) but with a creative, alternative, artistic, at times anti-authority student body that makes Vassar a unique institution to be a part of."

Founded by a 19th-century brewer named Matthew Vassar, the college sits just outside Poughkeepsie, New York. Its 1,000-acre campus includes two lakes and plenty of trees. Daffodils bloom in the spring, and foliage is omnipresent in the fall. Encircled by a fieldstone wall, the campus also boasts an astronomical observatory with one of the largest telescopes in the Northeast, a state-of-the-art physics building, a farm with an ecological field station, and an art center with 21,000 works, from Ancient Egyptian to modern times. The architecture is predominantly neo-Gothic, with buildings also designed by notables such as Marcel Breuer, Eero Saarinen, and James Renwick.

Vassar has no core curriculum and no distribution requirements. Indeed, academic flexibility is paramount. That said, all students must choose one first-year writing seminar from more than 50 courses taught across the curriculum, as well as one course that requires significant quantitative analysis. Students must also demonstrate intermediate-level proficiency in a foreign language and can opt to study one of the 20 languages taught at Vassar.

The most popular majors include economics, political science, biology, psychology, and English. The biology building houses two electron microscopes, while music students are spoiled by a grand collection of Steinway pianos spread across the campus. Drama, film, neuroscience, and international studies are also traditional strengths.

> "[Vassar has] a creative, alternative, artistic, at times anti–authority student body."

Regardless of their course of study, students find the academic climate rigorous. "Vassar students are always trying to do their personal best—they're seeking to engage more deeply with each subsequent assignment and each subsequent semester," says a senior. Small classes and tutorials are the norm, and exams are given under an honor system. Since Vassar has no graduate students or research-only faculty, all classes are taught by professors. "I'm really happy with the balance Vassar professors strike between research and teaching, because of how well they know both their fields and how to teach them," says an environmental studies major.

Each year, 45 percent of students study abroad via 240 programs in more than 60 countries. Vassar allows students to use their financial aid packages to support study away from campus. Also highly regarded is the college's Undergraduate Research Summer Institute, which offers stipends for students to work one-on-one with faculty members on scientific projects, either on or off campus. The Ford Scholars program offers opportunities for student/faculty collaboration in the humanities and social sciences. Most students participate in some sort of off-campus internship or community-based fieldwork for credit during the academic year. "Vassar's Career Development Office is deft at leveraging the tremendous alumni network to find students opportunities at all grade levels," says a media studies major.

Other than the obvious chromosomal demographics, coeducation has little impact on the type of student attracted to Vassar—"intellectually curious hard workers," says a senior, who generally share progressive points of view. Vassar's LGBTQ community is visible and active, and a biology major notes, "People usually introduce themselves with their gender pronouns." Twenty-four percent of students are

Website: www.vassar.edu
Location: Small City
Private
Total Enrollment: 2,317
Undergraduates: 2,317
Male/Female: 41/59
SAT Ranges: ERW 690–750, M 680–760
ACT Ranges: 31–33
Financial Aid: 62%
Pell Grant: 23%
Expense: Pr $ $ $ $
Student Loans: 45%
Average Debt: $
Applicants: 7,746
Accepted: 24%
Enrolled: 34%
Grad in 6 Years: 90%
Returning Freshmen: 96%
Academics: ✍ ✍ ✍ ✍ ½
Social: ☎ ☎ ☎
Q of L: ★ ★ ★ ★
Admissions: (845) 437-7300
Email Address: admissions@vassar.edu

Strong Programs:
Economics
Political Science
Biology
Psychology
English
Drama
Film
Neuroscience

Vassar boasts an art center with 21,000 works, from Ancient Egyptian to modern times.

native New Yorkers and 9 percent are international. Asian Americans make up 13 percent of the student body, African Americans 4 percent, Hispanics 11 percent, and multiracial students 7 percent. The school's ALANA Center supports and recognizes students of color and other ethnic and cultural groups. Twenty-three percent of first-year students are eligible for Pell Grants. One senior comments, "While I know Vassar is one of the most socioeconomically diverse private schools in the country, the vibe can still feel pretty rich/entitled at times." Although the college does not award merit or athletic scholarships, it does offer need-blind admissions for all first-year applicants and guarantees to meet the full demonstrated financial need of admits; it also replaces loans with grants for students whose families have annual incomes of $40,000 or less.

Vassar has no core curriculum, and academic flexibility is paramount.

Housing is guaranteed for four years, and 95 percent of students live on campus, where there's an eclectic mix of nine dorms. All but one are co-ed. "Some dorms are really modern and sparkling," says a junior. "Others have a vintage college feel, with traditional wood paneling, trim, and floors." The word is that Lathrop is the best dorm for freshmen, but no halls are reserved strictly for first-year students. Juniors and seniors favor the college-owned townhouses (five-person suites) and the four-person Terrace Apartments, both with kitchens and living rooms. Students report that campus dining has improved considerably with recent renovations, a change in food service provider, expanded options, and late-night hours. Students report that their open campus feels safe, and a psychology major says, "Conversations about consent in all realms of college life are common, and there are multiple systems in place to report sexual assault and help survivors."

"I'm really happy with the balance Vassar professors strike between research and teaching."

Vassar doesn't have a Greek system, so social life revolves around campus films, lectures, concerts, and the like. Small parties are hosted in senior apartments, and students can also party at the on-campus dance club, Matthew's Mug, named for the school's brewmaster-founder. Performing arts groups provide an important social outlet too. "Between student theater, a cappella, comedy troupes, slam poetry, dance groups, and more, students can go see high-quality performances multiple times every weekend," says an economics major. The city of Poughkeepsie has undergone a renaissance in recent years and features the world's longest elevated pedestrian bridge (212 feet tall and 1.28 miles long, in case you're wondering). Restaurants and shops are within walking distance of campus, and malls and movie theaters aren't much farther away, but a junior says, "Poughkeepsie is not explored by students as much as it should be." In warmer weather, Mohonk State Park offers hiking and other outdoor diversions. Also close by are Franklin Roosevelt's Hyde Park (for history) and the Culinary Institute of America (for gourmet meals prepared by students). Popular road trips include New York City and Boston, both easily reached by train.

Students can unwind after a hard day of classes with afternoon tea in the Rose Parlor of historic Main Building.

True to its heritage as one of the Seven Sisters, traditions are big at Vassar. "The year starts with Serenading—a time when the freshmen pay tribute to the seniors by singing them songs," one student explains. On Founder's Day in May, the entire community celebrates Matthew Vassar's birthday with music, carnival rides, food, and a day out on the grass. Fireworks and a movie cap off the festivities. "Founder's Day is easily the most highly anticipated day of the year," says a senior. And students can still unwind after a hard day of classes with afternoon tea in the Rose Parlor of historic Main Building.

"People usually introduce themselves with their gender pronouns."

Vassar's Division III varsity squads (the Brewers) compete in the Liberty League, and the women's field hockey team brought home the conference title recently. Other competitive teams include men's soccer, volleyball, and rugby, and women's volleyball, rugby, and tennis. Intramural sports are offered at two levels, competitive and recreational, and there are also club sports; roughly half the student body participate. Teams face off in everything from basketball and soccer to rowing, kickball, and Quidditch.

While Vassar continues to offer a menu of high-quality liberal arts courses emphasizing interdisciplinary connections, the college has also embraced technology and diversity, helping to create an atmosphere where individual passions shine. Says one contented Brewer, "We take the time to enjoy college for what it is—a serious, but not too serious, time of life for learning and development."

If You Apply To ›

Vassar: Early decision I and II, regular decision. SATs or ACTs: required. Subject Tests: optional. Accepts the Common Application with supplement. "Your Space" section of application allows candidates room to show something else about themselves.

University of Vermont

194 South Prospect Street, Burlington, VT 05401

For an out-of-stater sizing up public universities, there could hardly be a more appealing place than UVM. The size is manageable, Burlington is a fabulous college town, and Lake Champlain and the Green Mountains are on your doorstep. UVM feels like a private university, but, alas, it is also priced like one. Attracts a mix of party animals and serious types.

With its beautiful setting, wide academic offerings, and abundance of clubs and cocurricular pursuits, the University of Vermont draws students from around the country. And, says a math major, they're not all granola types with a penchant for soy milk and snowboarding. While it's a public school, UVM's academics, research opportunities, and price tag are more akin to those of a private institution. Generous financial aid packages, investment in infrastructure, and a growing emphasis on hands-on learning experiences are helping to ensure that Vermont remains both affordable and relevant amid increasing competition from schools of both types.

Chartered in 1791, UVM was established as the fifth college in New England. UVM's picturesque campus sits on the shores of Lake Champlain in Burlington, virtually a stone's throw from the Canadian border. Architectural styles range from colonial to high Victorian Gothic and functional modern; the oldest structures, in the center of the campus,

> "Professors do an excellent job of combining curricula with a sense of purpose."

are recognized on the National Registry of Historic Places. The university has undertaken major construction on a state-of-the-art STEM complex featuring the new Discovery Hall and Innovation Hall lab and classroom buildings.

UVM began as a private university but attained quasi-public status in 1862 with the passage of the Morrill Land-Grant College Act and a merger with a public agricultural college. Today, UVM's seven undergraduate colleges and schools set their own curricula grounded in the liberal arts. All students across the university must take general education courses in sustainability and diversity, and all first-year students must fulfill a three-credit foundational writing and information literacy requirement.

(continued)

Email Address: admissions@
uvm.edu

Strong Programs:
Business Administration
Psychology
Environmental Studies
Nursing
Biology
Political Science
Animal Science
Entrepreneurship

*Special programs for
first-years include
five-day TREK
programs led by
upper-class mentors
before classes start.*

Some of the most popular majors include business administration, psychology, environmental studies, and nursing. Biology, political science, animal science, and entrepreneurship are also strengths, while community development and applied economics, sustainable business, and food systems are among the more unique offerings. Premed, nursing, and prevet students benefit from the research and teaching capabilities of Vermont's fine medical school, as well as from a seven-year program with the vet school at Tufts. How tough is the academic environment? "It really depends on the course of study that you choose," says one student. Just under half of all classes enroll fewer than 20 students, and professors are said to be accessible and supportive. A junior says, "Professors do an excellent job of combining curricula with a sense of purpose. Everything we do here is worthwhile."

Special programs for first-years include five-day TREK programs, in which students, led by upper-class mentors, go hiking or biking, do community service, or take a leadership skills development course before classes start. Students are especially enthused about the Teacher Advisory Program, which places first-years together in groups of 10 to 15 in a writing-intensive, discussion-oriented seminar taught by a professor who is also each student's advisor. Students in the Honors College write a senior thesis, and an environmental studies major notes, "There are lots of opportunities for undergraduates to get involved in professors' research because we have a relatively small population of grad students." Through the Vermont Legislative Research Service, undergraduate public policy students provide state legislators with policy briefs on current issues. Twenty-seven percent of all undergrads go abroad; UVM offers 600 programs in more than 70 countries.

> **"[UVM students are] laid-back, green, and passionate about service."**

A political science major characterizes UVM students as "laid-back, green, and passionate about service." Twenty-seven percent of UVM undergraduates are native Vermonters and 6 percent are international. Hispanics comprise 4 percent of the student body, Asian Americans 3 percent, African Americans 1 percent, and multiracial students 3 percent. The lack of racial diversity is a common complaint, and social justice and environmental issues also receive attention on campus. "UVM is definitely a campus with a conscience," observes an English major. "Students lean left of center, but it is by no means a single-minded institution." The university offers merit scholarships averaging $12,800 and 144 athletic awards in 18 sports. The recently launched Catamount Commitment covers tuition and fees for qualifying in-state students from low-income families.

Fifty-one percent of students reside in campus housing; they are required to do so for their first two years. Eighty-four percent of freshmen opt to join living/learning communities, the most popular of which is the Wellness Environment. "Living in the res hall is a ton of fun and it's an awesome environment to meet new people,"

> **"It's hard to describe the energy that ignites everything we do."**

says an animal science major. A new residence and dining hall opened in 2017, and UVM has three other dining halls and several retail and café options to choose from. Students describe the food as "pretty good" and appreciate the university's efforts to serve local, organic, and sustainable options. An elementary education major notes that UVM has stepped up its education around reporting sexual assault and survivors' rights and says, "Perhaps as a result of these efforts, we are seeing rates of reporting increase on our campus."

Just 8 percent of UVM men and 7 percent of women join Greek groups, so when the weekend comes, college-sponsored movies, dances, craft nights, and coffeehouses help keep things lively. Students enjoy the Fallfest, Winterfest, and Springfest concerts every year, and the Naked Bike Ride is a notable biannual tradition, according to a senior: "On the last day of classes each semester, hundreds of people gather at midnight to run or bike naked around a campus green."

Much of the fun also happens on nearby ski slopes, mountain trails, and waterways, and in Burlington itself, especially the Church Street pedestrian mall, where the music scene draws top talent and is always bustling. "You can spend your Friday night at a gourmet restaurant, an off-Broadway theater production, or barhopping around town, and still be atop a mountain skiing the very next morning," says a junior. Indeed, the energetic downtown boasts symphonies, art galleries, chic shopping, and lively bars and restaurants, and Lake Champlain is only five minutes away. Students are also actively engaged with the local community through volunteer opportunities. As much as they love their little city, students do look forward to getting out of town. A favorite road trip is Montreal—90 minutes away—with its even bigger music scene and a drinking age of 18. The Outing Club is one of UVM's most popular student organizations, as the nearby Green Mountains, White Mountains, and Adirondacks offer prime hiking, backpacking, and rock climbing.

UVM fields a number of highly competitive Division I Catamount ("cat of the mountains") teams. The men's ice hockey team is the school's pride and joy, having ranked as high as second nationally. Students get access to tickets before the general public, a nice perk since games are always sold out. There is no football team, but soccer is competitive and draws crowds in the fall, and the men's basketball team is a recent America East conference champion. The ski team is a perennial powerhouse, winning eight straight Eastern Intercollegiate Ski Association titles and 36 overall. About a third of students participate in intramural and club sports, with broomball, ice hockey, and canoe battleship proving to be popular. Joystick jocks can sign up for intramural video game tournaments.

Students at UVM may be laid-back, but they're also curious, caring, open-minded, active, and willing to work hard. They view extracurricular involvement as critical to the undergraduate experience, and at UVM they find abundant opportunities to engage both inside and outside the classroom. Says one junior, "It's hard to describe the energy that ignites everything we do."

The ski team is a perennial powerhouse, winning eight straight Eastern Intercollegiate Ski Association titles and 36 overall.

Overlaps

Ithaca, University of Colorado Boulder, University of New Hampshire, UMass Amherst, Syracuse, William and Mary, Boston University, UConn

If You Apply To ›

UVM: Early action, regular decision. SATs or ACTs: required. No Subject Tests. Accepts the Common Application. Apply to individual schools or programs.

Villanova University

800 Lancaster Avenue, Villanova, PA 19085

Set in an upscale suburb, Villanova is becoming increasingly respected as Philadelphia's answer to Boston College. As at BC, about 70 percent of the students are Roman Catholic (compared with about half at Georgetown). The troika of business, engineering, and nursing are popular at 'Nova. Downtown Philadelphia is a quick hop away by train.

Villanova University takes pride in its Augustinian heritage, emphasizing intellectual, professional, and spiritual growth as a path to "transforming hearts and minds." The school has all the trappings of a typical Roman Catholic university, from strong academics to deeply rooted traditions and rivalries, and students firmly dedicated to their faith and service to others. Says one junior, "There are times I

Website: www.villanova.edu
Location: Suburban
Private
Total Enrollment: 9,215

(continued)

Undergraduates: 6,525

Male/Female: 47/53

SAT Ranges: ERW 620–710,
M 630–730

ACT Ranges: 30–33

Financial Aid: 64%

Pell Grant: 10%

Expense: Pr $ $ $

Student Loans: 60%

Average Debt: $ $ $ $

Applicants: 21,112

Accepted: 36%

Enrolled: 22%

Grad in 6 Years: 90%

Returning Freshmen: 95%

Academics: ✍ ✍ ✍

Social: ☎ ☎ ☎

Q of L: ★ ★ ★

Admissions: (610) 519-4000

Email Address: gotovu@
villanova.edu

Strong Programs:
Finance
Engineering
Nursing
Economics
Social Sciences
Biology
Communication

*First-year students
take the yearlong
Augustine and Culture
Seminar (ACS).*

walk out of a class at Villanova and just have to stop for a second to take it all in and appreciate what an amazing opportunity I've been afforded."

Founded in 1842 by the community-focused Order of Saint Augustine, Villanova's lush campus of more than 260 acres is situated along Philadelphia's suburban Main Line. Old stone buildings, well-kept lawns, and secluded, tree-lined walkways are a reminder of the campus's historical roots, while several newer buildings are LEED certified. Recent construction includes a major project that has transformed 14 acres of parking lots and asphalt into a bustling area featuring new residence halls, eateries, a bookstore, and a performing arts center, all linked to the campus core by a new pedestrian bridge.

Undergraduates may enroll in the College of Liberal Arts and Sciences, the Villanova School of Business, the College of Engineering, or the Fitzpatrick College of Nursing. All students follow a liberal arts core curriculum. First-year students take the yearlong Augustine and Culture Seminar (ACS) and are housed with their ACS classmates or in optional themed learning communities in the residence halls. In the first semester, they read works from the ancient, medieval, and Renaissance periods—ranging from the Greeks and Saint Augustine to the Middle Ages and Shakespeare. In the second semester, students explore works from the Early Modern, Enlightenment, Romantic, Modernist, and Contemporary eras.

> **"[Students] care about their work, but, more importantly, they care about their community."**

Finance, engineering, nursing, and economics are especially popular at Villanova, as are the social sciences, biology, and communication programs. Additional undergraduate programs include majors in gender and women's studies and Arab and Islamic studies, as well as minors in global health, counseling, and business law and corporate governance. Forty-two percent of undergraduate classes have fewer than 20 students. "The courses are rigorous and are often discussion-oriented and reading- and writing-intensive," says one communication major. Another student says, "Villanova professors go the extra mile for their students through office hours, research, and personal conversations." An honors program is available to about 300 students. Forty percent of students study abroad each year; communication and computer science students can apply for semester-long internships at the Vatican in Rome.

"The students who attend Villanova are passionate and devoted," says a sophomore. "They care about their work, but, more importantly, they care about their community." Many are from the East Coast, and 21 percent hail from Pennsylvania; 2 percent come from foreign countries. African Americans account for 5 percent of the student body, Hispanics 8 percent, Asian Americans 6 percent, and multiracial students 3 percent. "We're not an extremely political campus," one student muses, "although social justice issues like poverty, hunger, and homelessness are all big issues." Merit scholarships are available, averaging $16,500, as are more than 290 athletic scholarships in 24 sports.

Housing on campus is guaranteed for three years, and 66 percent of undergraduates call the residence halls home. "Rooms are great at Villanova," says one senior. "My first and second year I had a sink in my room so I didn't have to walk down the hall to wash my face or brush my teeth." Freshmen live primarily on the South Campus Circle, while upperclassmen choose residence halls on the main campus or apartment-style housing on West Campus via a lottery system. Most seniors move to houses and apartments in the surrounding neighborhoods. The university offers more than a dozen campus eateries, which serve everything from pizza to Chinese food, wraps, and vegetarian and vegan menus. "Food at Villanova is delicious," says a student. "Tons of variety with so many options I sometimes don't know which one to choose." The university has recently expanded its mandatory training programs on sexual assault.

"I have never had a dull weekend at Villanova because there is always something going on. If you are looking to party, you can. If you are looking to just chill, you can do that too," a student explains. Weekend social life centers around campus events and parties, some sponsored by Greek groups, which claim 17 percent of the men and 32 percent of the women. Students get together with friends at the student center on Fridays and Saturdays for Late Night at Villanova events, such as comedians, bands, open-mic nights, and dance parties. Juniors and seniors tend to spend evenings at bars along the local Main Line or in Philadelphia, just 12 minutes away by train. The city's entertainment and cultural opportunities include museums and pro sports, as well as events at numerous other colleges and universities, from La Salle and Temple to Drexel, Penn, and St. Joseph's.

Despite the tough courses, a senior says, "Everyone works hard, plays hard, and still finds time to give back to the community." Indeed, Villanova students volunteer roughly 250,000 hours of service each year. About 400 students participate in service trips over the fall and spring breaks, volunteering for projects like building houses and assisting victims of natural disasters. Each fall, Villanova hosts the largest student-run Special Olympics, which draws people from across campus and the local community.

Each fall, Villanova hosts the largest student-run Special Olympics.

"I have never had a dull weekend at Villanova."

When they are not out socializing or serving their community, Villanova students are cheering for the men's basketball team, which rewarded their enthusiasm by bringing home the Division I national championship in 2016 and repeating the feat in 2018. Recent Big East conference champions include men's and women's track and field and women's cross-country. Club sports and intramurals are a big draw, and popular activities include basketball, flag football, and soccer.

Despite the changes in the world around it, Villanova continues to be a Catholic university devoted to its students, community, and strong traditions, both academic and spiritual. The administration has set its sights on making Villanova one of the premier Roman Catholic institutions, alongside Notre Dame, Georgetown, and Boston College. While the school takes pride in tradition, it recognizes that its continuing improvements to campus facilities and ongoing development of educational and cocurricular programs will help its students remain competitive in the workplace and the world beyond.

Overlaps

Boston College, Fordham, Georgetown, Lehigh, Notre Dame, Northeastern, University of Pennsylvania, University of Virginia

If You Apply To ›

Villanova: Early decision, early action, regular decision. SATs or ACTs: required. No Subject Tests. Accepts the Common Application with supplement. Apply to a particular school or program.

University of Virginia

P.O. Box 400160, Charlottesville, VA 22904

Is it Thomas Jefferson? The Romanesque architecture? The Charlottesville air? Whatever it is, students nationwide go gaga for UVA, where competition for out-of-state admission has hit the Ivy League level. Relatively small for a top-notch public flagship, UVA combines old-line conservatism with high-quality academics and a social scene that is spirited in multiple senses of the word. Charlottesville is a big small town with plenty of culture, just over two hours from D.C.

UVA's campus (the "Grounds") is dotted with historic buildings designed by Thomas Jefferson himself.

Easily one of the most prestigious public schools in the nation, the University of Virginia is known to all in Charlottesville as Mr. Jefferson's University. Not just any Mr. Jefferson, mind you, but *the* Mr. Jefferson, author of the Declaration of Independence. Though he passed away nearly two centuries ago, he is referred to here as if he ran down to the apothecary shop for a bit of snuff and will be back in a moment. Of all his accomplishments, Jefferson was arguably proudest of UVA—he even asked that his epitaph speak to his role in creating the university rather than his presidency of the United States.

Located just east of the Blue Ridge Mountains in central Virginia, UVA's campus (the "Grounds") is dotted with historic buildings designed by Jefferson himself and is still in use today. At the core is Jefferson's "academical village," with majestic white pillars, serpentine walls, and extensive brickwork. The village rises around a rectangular terraced green, known as the Lawn, which is flanked by two rows of identical one-story rooms reserved for undergraduate student leaders. Five pavilions, each in a different style, are arranged on either side of the Lawn; all of them open onto a colonnaded walkway. Behind the buildings are public gardens, while the Rotunda, a half-scale model of the Roman Pantheon, overlooks the Lawn and stands as a symbol of Jefferson's Enlightenment belief in secularism and freedom.

UVA isn't just an elite public school; it holds its own against the best private schools as well. The most popular majors are economics, commerce, biology, psychology, and foreign affairs. Sociology and the life sciences draw praise as well. The vast majority of incoming freshmen enroll in the College of Arts and Sciences, but undergraduates may also enroll in the schools of Engineering, Nursing, or Architecture. After their second year, about 350 students are accepted into the McIntire School of Commerce, UVA's undergraduate business school. Not surprisingly, competition for

> **"[University Seminars] are based on interesting, current topics that provide somewhat of a break from your rigorous, everyday class."**

these spots is tough. A five-year program for aspiring teachers yields a B.A. from the College of Arts and Sciences and a Master of Teaching degree from UVA's Curry School of Education. The Batten School of Leadership and Public Policy trains students for public service careers in both domestic and international arenas and offers a five-year bachelor/master of public policy. Students who qualify for the Distinguished Majors program may pursue independent study during their third and fourth years.

Students agree that the workload at UVA is "intense but manageable," in the words of a commerce major. Virginia requires students in arts and sciences and the business school to master a foreign language before graduation. Arts and Sciences students must also take courses in English composition, humanities and fine arts, social science, natural sciences and mathematics, non-Western studies, and composition. Although 54 percent of classes enroll fewer than 20 students, lower-level classes can be huge, with as many as 500 people. A senior explains that, especially in upper-level courses, "Most professors are willing to schedule appointments as you might need and are excited to connect with their students." Special programs for freshmen include University Seminars, which are limited to 20 students in order to encourage interactive learning and intensive discussion. "These classes are based on interesting, current topics that provide somewhat of a break from your rigorous, everyday class," says a sociology major; they're also taught by some of the university's best faculty.

Highly capable students may win admission to the Echols Scholars program, which allows 225 to 250 top-entering freshmen the chance to pursue academic exploration without the constraints of distribution or major-field requirements. Echols students also live together for their first year. The Rodman Scholars program in the School of Engineering and Applied Science selects its members based on financial need, leadership, and scholarship. An intensive two-week January term provides additional opportunities for research seminars, interdisciplinary course-work, and study abroad. Thirty-five percent of undergrads go abroad to study, con-duct research, or intern in more than 75 countries. UVA boasts the highest four-year graduation rate of any public university, at 88 percent.

Students instituted Virginia's notable honor system in 1842 after no one owned up to shooting a professor on the Lawn. The residence halls, student council, and Judiciary Committee remain student-run to this day—and they really put the brakes on lying, cheating, or stealing. And don't take the policies lightly—breaching the codes means a swift dismissal from campus. After a number of controversial cases recently, discussions continue about the appropriateness of the single-sanction system. But rest assured, some form of the honor code will remain integral to the culture here. A clas-sics major says, "Our honor code is more than just some words scribbled on paper—it's a way of life and a bond of trust between you, your peers, and faculty."

Seventy percent of undergraduates are Virginians, and 4 percent are interna-tional. Admission for out-of-staters gets tougher every year, and many of those stu-dents come from New York, New Jersey, Pennsylvania, and Maryland. Seven percent of UVA students are African American, 14 percent are Asian American, 7 percent are Hispanic, and 4 percent are multiracial. Students describe a mix of political views on campus, and a senior says UVA "by and large feels progressive." Race relations are a perennial hot-button issue that intensified in the wake of a nationally organized white nationalist rally that marched on UVA's campus in 2017. "UVA was badly shaken by the rallies of August 2017, but I think the efforts to recover and heal have shaped a lot of changes," says a junior. "A lot more students are thinking critically and talking about racial inequities and how we can work to eliminate hate." A train-ing program on implicit bias is now required for all incoming freshmen. UVA is one of only two public universities in the nation that practices need-blind admissions and meets 100 percent of all admitted students' demonstrated financial need (see also UNC at Chapel Hill), although achieving socioeconomic diversity remains a challenge. The school hands out hundreds of athletic scholarships each year, along with merit awards worth an average of $4,000 each. Students from families with incomes of less than $80,000 attend tuition-free.

Thirty-nine percent of students at Virginia live on campus, including about 800 who bunk in the three residential colleges: Brown College at Monroe Hill, Hereford College, and International Residential College. Hereford's contemporary architec-ture has been described by the *New York Times* as "proudly, almost defiantly modern," in contrast to most of the other campus buildings. First-year residence halls are said to be the nicest on campus, and freshmen get first pick for housing. Fifty-four top seniors win the honor of living in spartan rooms along the Lawn, and among the outer set of rooms, called the range, students can visit room #13, which was occupied for a semester by Edgar Allen Poe in 1826 before he was suspended for nonpayment of tuition.

"A lot more students are thinking critically and talking about racial inequities."

"Most upperclassmen live off Grounds, and there is a chaotic rush to get good hous-ing beginning as early as September of the year prior," complains a junior. Meal plans are required for first-years and campus fare receives decent reviews.

UVA attracted national attention in 2014 after a *Rolling Stone* article, subsequently retracted, put UVA at the center of a broad national debate about the extent of drink-ing and sexual violence on college campuses, especially at fraternities. Since then, with input from hundreds of students and others, the university has initiated and updated programs aimed at education and prevention. "Our administration is increasing the

UVA boasts the highest four-year graduation rate of any public university, at 88 percent.

"Our honor code is…a way of life and a bond of trust between you, your peers, and faculty."

UVA is one of only two public universities in the nation that meets 100 percent of all admitted students' demonstrated financial need.

normalcy of talking about sexual assault, and I do think it is helping," reflects a junior. As for general safety, a student reports, "We have campus police, Charlottesville police, and an Ambassadors watch program all looking out for the safety of students."

Students say the UVA social scene is dynamic and varied. Fraternities draw 24 percent of Virginia's men, and sororities sign up 28 percent of women; Greek parties happen off campus. Mr. Jefferson founded UVA as a place where students could come together to "drink from the cup of knowledge," and now that fraternity rush is dry and parties must have guest lists, there's less quaffing of other brews going on. Still, determined Virginians haven't stopped metamorphosing into Rowdy Wahoos when the sun goes down—the nickname comes from a school cheer about a fish that can drink twice its weight. "I think a lot of first-years do feel pressured to go out frequently," admits one senior, and another observes that "the drinking culture extends to many organizations outside of Greek life as well." For nondrinkers and those under 21, the student-run University Union and nearly 900 clubs and other organizations offer movies, concerts, social hours, and other booze-free options. Most students are "highly involved" in multiple extracurriculars.

"Almost everything here is a tradition," remarks one student. Favorites include Lighting of the Lawn, featuring a cappella performances and an orchestrated light show on the Rotunda that kicks off the holiday season, and Foxfield, in which students dress up and host catered parties prior to attending a steeplechase horse race each April. Jackets and ties also come out for football games, a relic of when UVA was all male and gridiron contests were an opportunity to meet women. Streaking the Lawn is a rite of passage, students say. We would like to tell you more about the various secret societies, but we won't—they're secret, after all!

> **"The drinking culture extends to many organizations outside of Greek life."**

As for Charlottesville (population 48,000), it's "the perfect college town," says an anthropology major, and often a pleasant surprise for those coming from larger urban areas. There are restaurants; gorgeous vineyards and wineries; and plenty of bars, shops, theaters, and other cultural attractions. Students also immerse themselves in community service in the area; UVA's nationally recognized Madison House coordinates the activities of a host of volunteer groups. Outdoorsy folks can hike, bike, ski, and sightsee in the nearby Blue Ridge Mountains, or simply daydream while strolling Skyline Drive. Popular road trips include Washington, D.C., Richmond, and anywhere the Cavaliers are playing football, basketball, or soccer.

While big-time Atlantic Coast Conference (ACC) basketball has long been an integral part of UVA life, the Cavaliers field a number of competitive Division I teams. Men's basketball claimed the national championship title in 2019. Men's tennis won its third straight national title in 2017, and women's rowing and swimming and diving are recent ACC conference champs. There are also more than a dozen intramural sports leagues or tournaments, in everything from flag football to inner-tube water polo, and more than 60 club sports.

"UVA students are very driven," says a history major. "Instead of waiting for other students or administrators to solve a problem, they step up and take the initiative." The social life is as vigorous as the academics are rigorous, and the friendships that are formed here last far beyond the college years—much as Mr. Jefferson's legacy continues to be felt on campus, long after his death.

Overlaps

William and Mary, Virginia Tech, Duke, UNC at Chapel Hill, University of Pennsylvania, Harvard, Cornell University, Princeton

If You Apply To ›

UVA: Early action, regular decision. SATs or ACTs: required. Subject Tests: optional. Accepts the Common Application.

Virginia Tech

Blacksburg, VA 24061

Offers a unique blend of high tech and Southern hospitality. Engineering has always been its calling card, but business and architecture are popular. Admission is competitive for out-of-state applicants. Blacksburg is a nice college town, but far from the population centers near the coast. Hokie Nation loves its football team. Compare to Clemson, Georgia Tech, and Purdue.

Officially known as the Virginia Polytechnic Institute and State University, Virginia Tech is a land grant university that offers a slate of solid academic programs, competitive Division I athletics, and storied traditions. Engineering, business, and architecture attract top students from around the country who are proud to be part of the "Hokie Nation." A senior says, "Even in a school with 32,000 students, I feel like I'm in a small town with 200 people. Everyone here is so friendly."

Its campus, set on a plateau in the scenic Blue Ridge Mountains, occupies 3,000 acres and comes complete with a duck pond, hiking trails, and a 200-year-old plantation that is a local landmark. Students enjoy unlimited outdoor recreation thanks to the proximity of the Jefferson National Forest, the Appalachian Trail, the scenic Blue Ridge Parkway, and the majestic old New River. The campus buildings are an attractive mix of gray limestone structures, colonial-style brick, and modern cement buildings. The campus continues to undergo renovations and additions, including a new caged drone-testing facility.

Virginia Tech is best known for its first-rate technical and professional training. For undergrads with an appetite for engineering, Tech has programs for every taste, including aerospace, chemical, computer, mining, ocean, and more. The Pamplin College of Business is also prominent, and the five-year architecture program is considered one of the nation's best. The most popular majors include mechanical engineering; business information technology; finance; and human nutrition, foods, and exercise. Though no longer Tech's centerpiece, the College of Agriculture and Life Sciences remains strong, especially in animal science. Students in the College of Natural Resources and Environment can choose from solid majors in forestry, sustainable biomaterials, and wildlife conservation. The humanities tend not to fare as well in the university's high-tech environment, although internationally known poet Nikki Giovanni, who teaches creative writing and advanced poetry, is a bright spot. The university also has a tradition of excellence in the performing arts, and the school's theater group has won numerous awards. Newer majors include international relations, international public policy, and national security and foreign affairs.

A junior describes the academic climate as "rigorous, but very encouraging." All students are required to take courses in English, math, humanities, social and natural science, and foreign language. Introductory class size tends to be large—sometimes well into the hundreds. Most of the big lecture classes are taught by full-time faculty, though discussions and grading are generally handled by TAs. A senior says, "For the most part, my professors seemed to really care about what I was pursuing and how I was learning, not just performing." The nearly 1,700 students who participate in the Honors College are guaranteed access to top faculty and research opportunities.

The nationally acclaimed Small Business Institute enables faculty-led groups of business majors to work with local merchants, analyze their problems, and make suggestions on how to increase profits. Each year, about 500 students (mostly

> **"Even in a school with 32,000 students, I feel like I'm in a small town with 200 people."**

Website: www.vt.edu
Location: Small Town
Public
Total Enrollment: 31,516
Undergraduates: 26,555
Male/Female: 57/43
SAT Ranges: ERW 590–670, M 590–690
ACT Ranges: 25–30
Financial Aid: 53%
Pell Grant: 14%
Expense: Pub $ $ $
Student Loans: 49%
Average Debt: $ $ $
Applicants: 27,423
Accepted: 70%
Enrolled: 36%
Grad in 6 Years: 84%
Returning Freshmen: 93%
Academics: ✑ ✑ ✑
Social: ☎ ☎ ☎
Q of L: ★ ★ ★ ★
Admissions: (540) 231-6267
Email Address: admissions@vt.edu

Strong Programs:
Engineering
Architecture
Mechanical Engineering
Business Information Technology
Finance
Human Nutrition, Foods, and Exercise
Animal Science
Forestry

engineers) take advantage of Tech's co-op program, getting paid for real-world work experience. The Corps of Cadets, a tradition since the university's founding in 1872, offers a unique opportunity for students who wish to combine leadership training with an academic major. The 1,100 Cadets who enroll follow a structured military lifestyle, living together in the Corps' dedicated residence halls and wearing uniforms to class. In addition to choosing between a military/ROTC track and a citizen-leader track, Cadets can earn a minor in leadership. Sixty-nine percent of undergrads conduct research, and for the 28 percent who study abroad, Tech offers more than 200 programs in 60 nations around the globe.

The Corps of Cadets, a tradition since the university's founding in 1872, combines leadership training with an academic major.

Seventy-one percent of undergraduates call Virginia home, and 6 percent arrive from abroad. Not surprisingly, the admissions office is inundated with out-of-state applicants, which means stiff competition for the slots available to non-Virginians. Tech's relative isolation from major cities is a drag on minority recruitment: African Americans represent 4 percent, Hispanics 6 percent, Asian Americans 10 percent, and multiracial students 4 percent. "For a school in southwest Virginia, the political climate on campus is refreshingly balanced," says a sophomore. Students looking at pricey Northeastern technical schools will find Tech a real bargain. The university hands out 420 athletic scholarships, in addition to thousands of merit awards averaging $4,000. The Funds for the Future program aims to offset tuition increases for low-income undergraduates.

Some 25 undergraduate dorms house 35 percent of the students, though only freshmen and the Corps of Cadets are required to live on campus. "Accommodations are getting renovated each year, so the ratio of new-to-old housing is slowly increasing," explains a public relations major. The school's 16 living/learning communities, such as the wellness, leadership, and engineering communities, are increasingly popular. Most upperclassmen live off campus in nearby apartment complexes. Dining services receive enthusiastic reviews for variety, taste, and options for special diets. "Virginia Tech offers many classes to learn how to protect yourself and make yourself knowledgeable about the issue of sexual assault," notes a sophomore.

"My professors seemed to really care about what I was pursuing and how I was learning."

Leisure-time favorites include bowling and billiards in the student center, club activities, and school-sponsored plays, concerts, arts and crafts fairs, and dances. Thirteen percent of the men and 19 percent of the women join fraternities and sororities, and students say Greek groups do not dominate social life. Some of the most important annual events include the Ring Dance (when juniors receive their school rings) and the Corps of Cadets military ball. Service is a big emphasis, and many students get involved in the local community. "Blacksburg has many great restaurants within walking distance of campus, as well as a discount movie theater and the farmers market every weekend," says a neuroscience major. For real big-city action, Washington, D.C. and Richmond are four and three hours away by car, respectively. Given that the school is nestled in the Blue Ridge Mountains, hiking, biking, caving, and water sports are popular pastimes too.

Given that the school is nestled in the Blue Ridge Mountains, hiking, biking, caving, and water sports are popular pastimes.

Virginia Tech competes in the Division I Atlantic Coast Conference, and the football team's multiple appearances in postseason bowl games have cheered alumni and hiked applications by several thousand. The annual big game pits the Hokies against the Cavaliers of the University of Virginia. Men's and women's basketball, men's wrestling, and women's softball have also performed well in recent years. Tech's extensive recreational program boasts more than 30 intramural and 30 club sports, with everything from football to horseshoes and underwater hockey—a recent rage.

Virginia Tech encourages students to "invent the future," and that's just what today's citizens of the Hokie Nation aim to do. By taking advantage of Tech's particular blend of high-tech learning and Southern hospitality, students have countless opportunities to gain industry experience, travel abroad, and spend four years with like-minded peers.

Overlaps

Texas A&M, University of Colorado Boulder, Penn State, Iowa State, UT Austin, University of Florida, Purdue, North Carolina State

Wabash College

301 West Wabash, Crawfordsville, IN 47933

Wabash and Hampden–Sydney in Virginia are the last of the all-male breed. With steady enrollment and plenty of money in the bank, Wabash sees no reason to change. Intense bonding is an important part of the Wabash experience, and few co-ed schools can match the loyalty of Wabash alumni. The Gentleman's Rule says it all.

Wabash was founded in Indiana in 1832 by transplanted Ivy Leaguers who shared the Enlightenment's optimistic view of human nature and envisioned a "classical and English high school rising into a college as soon as the wants of the country demand." Their vision proved to be on target. All-male Wabash has not only prospered but also remained true to its conservative academic and social traditions, including the Gentleman's Rule code of self-responsibility that students continue to live by. "Wabash College has a culture that has not changed for 50 years. It can be a hard school to fit into if you do not meet the status quo, but it also is a brotherhood," says a junior.

The Wabash campus is characterized by redbrick, white-columned, Georgian-style buildings (three are originals from the 1830s). Located in the heart of Crawfordsville, a small town of about 16,000, Wabash is surrounded by grass and tall trees that are part of the gorgeous Fuller Arboretum. The college recently completed a $24 million student housing construction project that added six residential buildings and renovated the flagship dorm, Martindale Hall.

The Wabash educational program has certainly proved itself over the years. This small college has amassed an impressive list of alumni: executives of major corporations, doctors, lawyers, and a large number of Ph.D.s. Wabash alumni are typically faithful to their school in the form of generous donations.

> "Greek organizations *are* the social life on campus."

On a per-capita basis, the school's $340 million endowment makes it one of the wealthiest in the nation. General education requirements include courses from a wide variety of fields—natural and behavioral sciences, literature and fine arts, mathematics, language studies, and a course on cultures and traditions. All freshmen participate in a community service project during orientation and take a tutorial in the fall that is designed to focus them on reading, writing, and class participation, followed by a colloquium titled Enduring Questions in the spring. All seniors complete comprehensive examinations in their final semester, consisting of two days of written exams in their major and an hour-long oral exam on their overall liberal arts experience.

Mathematics, biology, rhetoric, and political science draw the most majors at Wabash, and high accolades go to the political science, history, mathematics, and psychology departments. Religion and theater are also traditional strengths. Many programs have been augmented with cross-cultural immersion learning courses with short-term travel components—at no extra cost to students. Those who can't satisfy their high-tech interests at Wabash can opt for a 3–2 program in engineering

Website: www.wabash.edu
Location: Small Town
Private
Total Enrollment: 864
Undergraduates: 864
Male/Female: 100/0
SAT Ranges: ERW 530–630, M 540–650
ACT Ranges: 23–28
Financial Aid: 99%
Pell Grant: 28%
Expense: Pr $
Student Loans: 94%
Average Debt: $ $ $ $
Applicants: 1,304
Accepted: 63%
Enrolled: 28%
Grad in 6 Years: 71%
Returning Freshmen: 87%
Academics: ✍ ✍ ✍ ½
Social: ☎ ☎
Q of L: ★ ★ ★
Admissions: (800) 345-5385
Email Address: admissions@ wabash.edu

Strong Programs:
Mathematics
Biology
Rhetoric
Political Science
History
Psychology
Religion
Theater

with Columbia, Washington University in St. Louis, or Purdue. With a new major in Hispanic studies and new minors in gender studies, Asian studies, and multicultural American studies, Wabash's curriculum is growing more diverse.

"Wabash prides itself on being very competitive; the classroom atmosphere can be intense at times, and the workload is pretty heavy," says a religion major. Seventy-seven percent of classes have fewer than 20 students. "Most professors prefer active involvement in the classroom and are passionate about what they are teaching," says one student. Students roundly praise the Quantitative Skills Center and the Writing Center for their assistance with classwork, as well as career services for connecting them with internships, jobs, and influential alumni.

Paid, full-time research positions with faculty are a popular summertime pursuit at Wabash, particularly among students in the sciences. Juniors are encouraged to study abroad through programs in 40 countries, and 18 percent do so. Wabash has recently developed a Liberal Arts Plus initiative that provides hands-on experience in four interdisciplinary fields: democracy and public discourse; global health; innovation, business, and entrepreneurship; and digital arts and human values. Participating students engage in such opportunities as academic summits, internships, consulting projects, volunteer work, and travel abroad.

Wabash students "take everything they do very seriously," according to one junior. Most come from public high schools in Indiana, but 22 percent come from other states, and 7 percent come from foreign countries. African Americans comprise 6 percent of the student body, Hispanics 8 percent, Asian Americans 1 percent, and multiracial students 3 percent. A junior reports, "Wabash is predominantly conservative, so very little Black Lives Matter or LGBTQ protesting is present on campus," although the question of whether to admit transgender students to the college has sparked debate. Of the most recent freshman class, 28 percent were Pell-eligible. Merit awards averaging $22,600 are available to qualified students.

"Wabash men have a sense of being in the trenches with one another."

For housing, the college offers five residence halls, two lodges, two duplex-style townhomes, and 10 fraternity houses; students are required to live on campus all four years. "Students often compare the dorms to hotel rooms," says a junior. Dorm residents must eat in the dining hall. "Nine times out of 10, the food is good, but that one time can really stand out," says a sophomore. Wabash addresses the topics of sexual assault and gender-based violence during new student orientation and leadership development activities throughout the year.

The surrounding town of Crawfordsville leaves much to be desired. With few options off campus, the school's 10 fraternities tend to dominate the social scene: 63 percent of the students join up. "Greek organizations *are* the social life on campus. No one else throws parties," says a sophomore. Many students say there is a noticeable divide between fraternity brothers and "independents." Some non-Greeks may feel especially excluded when the fraternities "ship in" sorority members from Butler, DePauw, Indiana, and Purdue for parties. As for drinking on campus, students say that policies are generally loose, as long as students are behaving responsibly, which is to say in a gentlemanly fashion. Traditions are taken seriously at Wabash, from homecoming to not passing beneath certain archways on campus. Chapel Sing, where all the freshmen compete to see who can best sing the lengthy school song, is a favorite ritual, but undoubtedly the biggest is the school's long-standing rivalry with DePauw, which is capped off every year by the football game that decides who gets to keep the prized Monon Bell.

That competitive spirit extends to all of the Little Giants (so named because the 1904 football team was performing above its weight) Division III athletic programs. The wrestling team is a perennial contender for the national title, while the football and track and field teams have recently won conference titles. About half of the students participate in intramural and club sports, including flag football, soccer, bowling, and rugby.

Traditions have not changed much since the school's founding back in the 1830s and still play an important part in the lives of the men at Wabash. Some students complain about the lack of women and culture in the surrounding area, but many are happy with the college's intensive, rigorous programs and expanding opportunities for interdisciplinary study and hands-on experiences. It's a boys club and a brotherhood. Says one senior, "Wabash men have a sense of being in the trenches with one another. I would give a fellow student the shirt off my back because I have every confidence he'd do the same for me."

If You Apply To ›

Wabash: Early decision, early action, regular decision. SATs or ACTs: required. Subject Tests: optional. Accepts the Common Application with supplement.

Wake Forest University

Winston-Salem, NC 27106

Wake Forest's Baptist heritage and Winston-Salem location give it a more down-home flavor than Duke or Emory. With more than 5,000 undergraduates, Wake Forest is small compared with its Atlantic Coast Conference rivals but bigger than most liberal arts colleges. The strong Greek system dominates the social scene. Holds its own in the ACC with universities more than five times its size.

Long one of the top private schools in the Southeast, Wake Forest has transformed its regional recognition into a national reputation. Known for basketball—at least half the student body attends every home game, one junior says—Wake Forest's solid academics are worthy of a look as well. Students work hard, hence the nickname "Work Forest," but the university's size and strong Greek system means it's also easy to establish close friendships. "Wake Forest is the best of both worlds," says a political science major. "Academics are challenging, and you're surrounded by motivated and intelligent peers. At the same time, students pride themselves on being social."

Located in the Central Piedmont region of North Carolina, Wake Forest's 340-acre campus features flowers, wooded trails, and stately magnolias. There are more than 40 Georgian-style buildings constructed of old Virginia brick with granite trim. The campus is bordered by the lush, 148-acre Reynolda Gardens annex, which features a formal garden, greenhouses, and one of the first collections of Japanese cherry trees in the U.S. In 2017 the university opened Wake Downtown, a 115,000-square-foot, STEM-focused space adjacent to Wake's School of Medicine in downtown Winston-Salem. The 180,000-square-foot Wake Forest Wellbeing Center, housing fitness and recreation facilities as well as offices for student health and other support services, was completed in 2018.

> "Academics are challenging, and you're surrounded by motivated and intelligent peers."

To graduate from Wake Forest, students must complete a standard distribution of liberal arts and sciences courses, in addition to taking an introductory first-year

(continued)

Admissions: (336) 758-5201
Email Address: admissions@
wfu.edu

Strong Programs:
Finance
Communication
Psychology
Politics and International Affairs
Business and Enterprise
 Management
Biochemistry and Molecular
 Biology

The Wake Washington Center gives selected undergrads the chance to live, study, intern, and network in the nation's capital for a semester.

The university now offers gender-neutral housing options and has increased the size and visibility of its LGBTQ Center.

seminar and satisfying a cultural diversity requirement. The most popular programs include finance, communication, economics, psychology, and politics and international affairs; the School of Business is highly regarded. Faculty members have expressed concerns about support that the Eudaimonia Institute (which studies the notion of "human flourishing") has received from the free-market fundamentalist Koch brothers. Recently added programs include a B.S. in engineering and a B.S. in biochemistry and molecular biology.

Students agree that courses at Wake Forest are rigorous, but a history and psychology double major says, "I have been impressed by how collaborative Wake students are." Fifty-seven percent of classes have fewer than 20 students. Faculty members get high marks; graduate assistants teach some labs and health classes, but otherwise professors are at the lectern. "I've been told by professors, department heads, and academic advisors that their first goal for me is that I learn the material and have enriching experiences while at school," says a physics major. "It's very refreshing to have faculty who put the emphasis on this rather than grades." The Office of Personal and Career Development takes a four-year approach to helping students prepare for future careers.

Fifty-nine percent of undergraduates receive academic credit for classes that require faculty-mentored research, and Richter Scholarships fund select independent study or research projects that involve travel away from campus. The Pro Humanitate Institute allows students to put their skills and knowledge to work helping the community; the center takes its name from the school's motto, which means "In Service to Humanity." Exceptionally able students may qualify for the Honors in Arts and Sciences distinction by taking three or more honors seminars during their first three years. The Wake Washington Center gives selected undergraduates the chance to live, study, intern, and network in the nation's capital for a semester. And for those who wish to spread their wings internationally, Wake Forest's residential study centers in Copenhagen, London, Vienna, and on the Grand Canal in Venice beckon. Wake Forest offers more than 400 semester, summer, and yearlong study abroad programs in more than 70 countries worldwide; 74 percent of the student body participates.

"Students at Wake Forest are highly driven above all else," says a senior. Seventy-eight percent of undergraduates hail from outside North Carolina, including 10 percent who come from foreign countries. "Students tend to be very conservative," says a sophomore, and a senior adds, "We are not a politically active school." Wake Forest's efforts to boost diversity continue; currently, African Americans make up 7 percent of the undergraduate population, Asian Americans add 4 percent, Hispanics contribute 7 percent, and multiracial students represent 3 percent. Although the university meets 100 percent of admitted students' demonstrated financial need, it is weak on socioeconomic diversity, with just 9 percent of freshmen qualifying for Pell Grants. Merit scholarships averaging $12,800 are awarded to eligible students, in addition to 168 athletic scholarships.

"[Professors'] first goal for me is that I learn the material and have enriching experiences."

Seventy-five percent of students live on campus, as they are required to do for their first three years. "Many of the dorms are getting renovated, which is great because some of them were definitely in need," says a junior. In addition to all-gender restrooms across campus, the university now offers gender-neutral housing options and has increased the size and visibility of its LGBTQ Center. Dining options have improved recently, students say: "There are two standard cafeterias, as well as a Starbucks, Chick-fil-A, Moe's, Subway, and other options." One student complains, "Campus security could be better. There is a fair amount of crime in certain areas of campus." Students say sexual assault is not a prevalent issue, but the Safe Office is an effective resource for those who need it.

Thirty-five percent of men and 60 percent of women go Greek, and Greek life dominates the social scene. Fraternities and sororities do not have houses on campus, but they throw open parties in dorm lounges or in off-campus houses. "Other organizations, such as Student Union, make a huge effort to bring other social options, such as concerts, movies, and events, to campus," says a student. The school's honor code helps to keep rowdy behavior in check; as one student says, "If you are caught with alcohol, and you are under 21, there are strict consequences." Everyone enjoys the annual homecoming festivities, and after the Demon Deacons score big athletic victories, students roll the quad in toilet paper to celebrate. Other favorite events include a midnight concert by the school orchestra every Halloween, with members in full costume, and Lilting Banshees comedy troupe shows. Another Wake Forest tradition is Hit the Bricks, an eight-hour relay race benefitting cancer research that runs along the brick pathways of Hearn Plaza in honor of Brian Piccolo, a Wake Forest alumnus and Chicago Bears running back who died of cancer at age 26. Popular road trips are to the beach or the mountains; Chapel Hill, Durham, and Raleigh are each 100 miles away, and Atlanta and the Washington/Baltimore areas are about a five-hour drive.

The city of Winston-Salem is rich in culture, with a symphony, a Christmastime "Moravian love feast," film festivals, multiple art museums, a thriving arts district, and the well-known University of North Carolina School of the Arts. It's also home to the corporate headquarters of another Southern specialty: Krispy Kreme Doughnuts. "Winston is a very suburban town with a lot of young families and a Southern feel," a student says. The town also has a strong music scene, with live bands playing regularly at downtown venues. Popular volunteer activities include Project Pumpkin, a trick-or-treat night on campus for underprivileged children.

> **"Winston is a very suburban town with a lot of young families and a Southern feel."**

When it comes to sports, basketball is the undisputed king at Wake Forest and is perennially strong in the incredibly tough Division I Atlantic Coast Conference. Men's tennis and women's golf are recent national champions, and other solid teams include baseball and men's and women's soccer. Of course, virtually any contest against in-state rival UNC at Chapel Hill is guaranteed to get students excited. Intramural and club sports are also offered—soccer, basketball, and floor hockey are some of the most popular—and according to a senior, "Fun supersedes talent."

A spirit of involvement and dedication to the community pervades the Wake Forest experience. Whether students are serving the less fortunate or chipping away at their heavy workloads, they benefit from motivated peers, dedicated faculty, and gorgeous surroundings. As one student says, "We are a small school with big school spirit."

Thirty-five percent of men and 60 percent of women go Greek, and Greek life dominates the social scene.

Overlaps

UNC at Chapel Hill, University of Virginia, North Carolina State, College of William and Mary, University of Richmond, Boston College, University of Georgia, Emory

If You Apply To ›

Wake Forest: Early decision I and II, regular decision. SATs or ACTs: optional. Subject Tests: optional. Accepts the Common Application with supplement.

Warren Wilson College

P.O. Box 9000, Asheville, NC 28815

Among a handful of schools where students combine academics, community service, and on-campus work that helps keep tuition down. Roots in the culture of Appalachia combine with a strong international and social justice orientation to give Warren Wilson its distinctive flavor. Setting in the mountains of western North Carolina is tough to beat. Campus atmosphere ranges from liberal to alternative.

Website: www.warren-wilson .edu

Location: City Outskirts

Private

Total Enrollment: 645

Undergraduates: 573

Male/Female: 38/62

SAT Ranges: ERW 610–670, M 530–615

ACT Ranges: 25–29

Financial Aid: 99%

Pell Grant: 35%

Expense: Pr $

Student Loans: 72%

Average Debt: $ $

Applicants: 1,003

Accepted: 79%

Enrolled: 18%

Grad in 6 Years: 53%

Returning Freshmen: 62%

Academics: ✍ ✍ ✍ ½

Social: ☎ ☎ ☎ ☎

Q of L: ★ ★ ★ ★ ★

Admissions: (800) 934-3536

Email Address: admit@ warren-wilson.edu

Strong Programs:
Environmental Studies
Biology
Psychology
Creative Writing
Art
Outdoor Leadership
Appalachian Studies
Global Studies

Warren Wilson is a small liberal arts college flush with engaging little quirks. It promotes global perspectives, puts students to work (including on the campus farm), and makes service learning a central part of the educational experience. The school is also at the forefront of the "green" movement and has partnered with the city of Asheville to purchase offsets for 100 percent of its carbon emission. And at what other college is white-water paddling considered a leading intercollegiate sport? "My school is wild," says a senior. "It is a big old 'take that' to the status quo. It is a group of people who are going to change the world."

Founded by the Presbyterian Church in 1894 as the Asheville Farm School, Warren Wilson College initially provided formal schooling for "mountain boys." In 1967, it transmogrified into a four-year, co-ed liberal arts college that, while still maintaining its Presbyterian heritage, welcomes students of all backgrounds. WWC is located 15 minutes from downtown Asheville in the lush Swannanoa Valley of the Blue Ridge Mountains. Its 1,132-acre campus features formal gardens, fruit and vegetable gardens, a 300-acre farm, and approximately 15 miles of hiking trails. Consistent with campus culture, the wood and stone buildings are small in scale and built in an architectural style that emphasizes natural earth tones accented by extensive stonework by traditional Appalachian stonemasons. The campus is home to one of the most important Cherokee archaeological sites in the Southern Appalachian Mountains, dating from as early as 5000 B.C.

The signature feature of the WWC curriculum is its unique three-part education program, which combines liberal arts coursework, community service, and campus work. To graduate, students have to perform significant community service through organizations such as Habitat for Humanity, Meals on Wheels, or environmental groups. Warren Wilson is also one of only a half dozen four-year colleges in the nation that requires all residential students to work on campus—a practice that helps keep tuition down. To fulfill their weekly 10-hour work requirement, students work in crews that range from blacksmithing, carpentry, and recycling projects to IT services, tutoring, and design and photography, as well as keeping the college farm going. To meet general education requirements, WWC students take a broad range of liberal arts courses aimed at developing four core competencies: critical inquiry, effective communication, civic engagement, and self-awareness. All first-year students enroll in the writing-intensive First-Year Seminar, which includes introductory service-learning experiences that take students and faculty off campus weekly. In addition, every undergraduate major requires a culminating capstone project.

> **"My school is wild. It is a big old 'take that' to the status quo."**

Students may choose from 20 majors, many of which offer concentrations, and 28 minors. The most popular majors are environmental studies, biology, psychology, creative writing, and art. Students give high marks to the natural sciences, especially biology and conservation biology, but say physics could use improvement. Dual-degree programs are available in pre-environmental management, preforestry, prelaw, and pre-M.B.A., and the integrative studies major allows students to develop and complete individually designed majors. The popular outdoor leadership major prepares students to lead outdoor adventure education programs, focusing on both technical skills like backpacking and rock climbing and interpersonal skills like leadership and counseling. Appalachian studies, a minor within the global studies program, serves as a catalyst for local cultural activities, including numerous musical groups. And where else does the music department offer you the choice of "finger-picking" or "flat-picking" guitar?

A biology major says Warren Wilson's study-serve-work program is "challenging and fulfilling, but it requires commitment from the student in order to get the most out of it." All classes are small—90 percent have fewer than 20 students—and a freshman says, "Our faculty members are highly accessible, and many of them live on campus, so home instruction is not unheard of." The college offers honors programs in biology, English, and environmental studies; 6 percent of students enroll. Internship opportunities are available in most programs, and 60 percent of students study abroad during their time at WWC. Faculty-led programs involve a semester-long course on campus, followed by two to three weeks on an international "field experience." Qualified students may also study for a semester or two in countries such as China, Finland, Germany, Japan, and South Korea.

To fulfill their weekly 10-hour work requirement, students work in crews that range from blacksmithing and carpentry to IT services.

"We all care deeply about something, which makes for a chill but intense culture."

Warren Wilson students are "laid-back and at the same time buzzing with excitement and passion," explains a biology major. "We all care deeply about something, which makes for a chill but intense culture." Twenty-five percent of students are native North Carolinians, and 3 percent are international. African Americans account for 5 percent, Hispanics 7 percent, Asian Americans 1 percent, and multiracial students 3 percent. Social justice concerns are big on campus and, upon graduation, most students go into service professions such as teaching or working for environmental or other nongovernmental organizations. The first step for some is into the Peace Corps, for which the school offers a special advising program. In the words of one student, WWC is "liberal to the point that conservative views are demonized by some of the students," but administrators say they are working to change that by actively recruiting more students from rural areas (in hopes of diversifying the political atmosphere) and teaching students strategies for productive dialogue. Thirty-five percent of freshmen are Pell-eligible, and merit scholarships averaging $15,000 are available. Under the school's North Carolina Free Tuition Plan, all North Carolina residents who qualify for federal or state need-based financial aid will have the rest of their tuition covered by the college for all four years.

Administrators are actively recruiting more students from rural areas.

Eighty-two percent of students live in dorms, which a psychology major describes as "simple yet inviting." The 36-bed, LEED Platinum–certified EcoDorm incorporates solar heating and natural ventilation, and is made of hardwoods milled on campus. Other theme housing options are also available. Overall, housing is plentiful and well maintained (unless the "heavy duty" student crew slacks off). Students have two main dining halls and two other cafés to choose from, and the vegetarian and vegan fare at Cowpie is said to be particularly tasty. Students say they feel safe on campus, and the Office for Gender and Relationships provides advocacy, support, and education regarding diverse gender identities and campus sexual assault.

"[Asheville's] downtown scene is amazing for the relatively small size of the town."

Despite the absence of Greek organizations, students find plenty of ways to have fun and blow off steam on campus. The outdoor program is the largest on campus and sponsors weekly hiking, camping, skiing, or other excursions. "The party life is fun, when there actually is a party," remarks a junior. "Because we are a work college, parties can be scarce." Students 21 and over who wish to imbibe must bring their own beer to parties. Popular events include the student-run Warren Wilson Circus and homecoming, which features live bluegrass music, a barbecue, and dancing. On Work Day, classes are canceled so students and faculty can work together on campus projects and enjoy a pig roast, courtesy of the campus farm crew.

"[Asheville's] downtown scene is amazing for the relatively small size of the town," says a student. Museums, cafés, theaters, music clubs, and the symphony are only 15 minutes away. Thanks to the college's service requirement, students take an active role in the community through volunteer work. WWC sponsors short-term service projects during vacation breaks, and popular road trips include Atlanta and the beaches of South Carolina.

In a state famed for its rabid sports fans, Warren Wilson students are decidedly nonchalant about athletics; there are no big sports teams or rivalries, and students say they prefer it that way. The Fighting Owls are members of the U.S. College Athletic Association, and competitive sports include men's and women's basketball and soccer. The cycling team is nationally ranked, and the men's and women's white-water paddling club teams are recent national champs. Twenty percent of WWC students participate in intramural and club sports.

Success at Warren Wilson is measured not only by grades, but by community service and a sense of stewardship. "One of the most beautiful things about Wilson is that it is a college where I can help pull a calf during a winter calving season in a beautiful valley, then head up to my Latin American Cinema class," says a global studies major. Those who aren't afraid to get their hands dirty will see this small liberal arts college as a valuable place that combines the notion of thinking globally with acting locally.

Overlaps

Reed, Hampshire, UNC Asheville, Agnes Scott, Guilford, Appalachian State, Evergreen State, Eckerd

If You Apply To ›

Warren Wilson: Early decision, early action, rolling admissions. SATs or ACTs: optional. Subject Tests: optional. Accepts the Common Application with supplement. Application includes fields to indicate preferred name, gender, and gender pronoun.

University of Washington

1410 N.E. Campus Parkway, Seattle, WA 98195

UDub wows visitors with its sprawling parklike campus in hugely popular Seattle. Washington is tougher than University of Oregon for out-of-state admission but not as hard as UC heavyweights Berkeley or UCLA. Location near both the coast and mountains makes for strong marine and environmental studies programs. Has recently increased its percentage of out-of-staters and international students in an effort to balance the budget.

Website: www.washington.edu
Location: City Center
Public
Total Enrollment: 40,148
Undergraduates: 28,717
Male/Female: 47/53

The University of Washington has cemented its reputation as a solid research institution, and its 29,000 full-time undergraduates benefit from traditional strengths in business, health, and natural sciences. Students here understand that anonymity and size are the prices that must be paid for the wealth of opportunities that await them, although First-Year Interest Groups and a four-year honors program help make the university feel smaller. Those looking for an extra-personal touch might want to investigate UW's two branch campuses in Tacoma and Bothell, where class sizes average 25 students. But if the Seattle campus is your focus, one senior hints, just "learn to work the system."

Washington's Seattle campus blends Gothic architecture and the lush, green landscape of the Pacific Northwest. It features a number of distinctive landmarks. Red Square sits atop the Central Plaza parking garage and features the Broken Obelisk, a 26-foot-high steel sculpture gifted to the university by the Virginia Wright Fund. All of the university's energy comes from renewable resources (including, of course, hydropower) and, despite campus growth, UW has reduced its overall energy use.

Undergraduates in both professional and liberal arts programs must take credits in English composition, writing beyond composition, quantitative and symbolic reasoning, the arts, individuals and societies, and the natural world. Schools and colleges also have their own requirements. Freshmen are given special attention via the First-Year Interest Group (FIG) program, which offers a chance to meet, discuss, and study

> "All of my best experiences and opportunities have been through the Honors Program."

with other first-years who have similar interests. Each FIG consists of 20 to 24 students who share a cluster of classes (which fulfill graduation requirements), and includes a weekly seminar led by a junior or senior peer advisor.

Many of Washington's diverse undergraduate strengths correspond with its excellent graduate programs. The competitive business major, for example, benefits from the university's highly regarded business school and is one of the most popular undergraduate majors, along with communication, psychology, economics, and biochemistry. Students majoring in public health, community medicine, pharmacy, and nursing profit from access to facilities and faculty at the medical school, an international leader in cancer and heart research, cell biology, and organ transplants. English and drama are traditional strengths in the humanities. Also recommended for undergraduates are biological and life sciences and most engineering programs, especially computer science (which is tops in the country in producing female graduates), human centered design and engineering, and bioengineering. Reflecting the focus on natural resources in Washington's economy, the program in fisheries is excellent, as are earth and atmospheric sciences, including oceanography.

UW follows a quarter system, which means academics are challenging and fast-paced. A common complaint about the university is "having to apply to a major. It is already hard to get into UW, but then once you do, you might not even get into your desired major," explains a senior. Entry into preprofessional and STEM-related programs is particularly difficult, and students say you might want to have a backup plan. Like other major state uni-

> "[Students] are go-getters and active in the world around them."

versities, UW faces budget difficulties, resulting in higher demand and larger sizes for many classes; about a quarter of undergraduate classes have more than 50 students. "Faculty members often compensate for large class sizes by making themselves extremely accessible," says a public health major, and many professors are tops in their field.

For those interested in skirting the masses, UW's Honors Program offers small classes on interesting subjects taught by fine professors. "All of my best experiences and opportunities have been through the Honors Program: from scholarships, to the Honors Living Learning Community in the residence halls, to Honors-specific study abroad courses," cheers a sophomore. Roughly 20 percent of all undergrads study abroad in hundreds of programs across the globe. A program in experiential learning encourages students to find internships, and a variety of classes give students the opportunity to volunteer as part of their coursework.

Sixty-nine percent of undergraduates are state residents, and although the university has traditionally preferred to keep its focus on the home folks, it now has

(continued)

SAT Ranges: ERW 590–690, M 600–730

ACT Ranges: 27–32

Financial Aid: 40%

Pell Grant: 22%

Expense: Pub $ $

Student Loans: 35%

Average Debt: $

Applicants: 44,877

Accepted: 46%

Enrolled: 32%

Grad in 6 Years: 84%

Returning Freshmen: 94%

Academics: ✑ ✑ ✑ ✑ ½

Social: ☎ ☎ ☎

Q of L: ★ ★ ★

Admissions: (206) 543-9686

Email Address: apply@uw.edu

Strong Programs:
Business
Communication
Psychology
Economics
Biochemistry
Computer Science
Engineering
English

First-Year Interest Groups consist of 20 to 24 students with similar interests who share a cluster of classes.

a notably large proportion of international students, at 16 percent. It also has an unusually large population of students over the age of 25. The student body is 24 percent Asian American, 8 percent Hispanic, 3 percent African American, and 7 percent multiracial. The school encourages diversity by offering Valuing Diversity workshops on awareness of and sensitivity to individual differences, and the campus, like its host city, is politically liberal. Students, says a senior, "are go-getters and active in the world around them." Scholarships for Washington residents are awarded based on financial need, but merit-based scholarships averaging $4,000 per year are available to high-achieving out-of-staters. The university also doles out more than 400 athletic scholarships every year. The Husky Promise covers full tuition and standard fees for qualifying in-state students from low-income backgrounds, and 22 percent of freshmen receive Pell Grants.

The Husky Union Building offers a dining hall, espresso bar (don't forget, this is Seattle!), writing center, sun deck, and lounges.

Twenty-seven percent of students live in the school's 12 co-ed dorms. Three new residence halls—Madrona, McCarty, and Willow—opened in 2018. "The residence halls are really new and nice facilities for the most part. The main drawback is that they are pretty expensive," says a junior. Most students live off campus in Seattle or other parts of King County. Each dorm has its own cafeteria and fast-food line based on a debit card system. The Husky Union Building also offers a dining hall, espresso bar (don't forget, this is Seattle!), writing center, sun deck, and lounges. A sophomore says, "I have seen an increase in discussion and education on sexual assault, with a focus on the Greek community."

On campus, the social scene tends to be defined by the Greeks and the 800-plus student organizations that sponsor various activities. Sixteen percent of the men

"The residence halls are really new and nice facilities for the most part."

and 15 percent of the women join a combined total of 48 fraternities and sororities. Alcohol is allowed on campus for students 21 and over but marijuana is not (despite being legal in the state of Washington), and students report that policies are strictly enforced. One student says that what the campus lacks in social life "is made up for by the proximity to downtown Seattle." Sooner or later most students hit "the Ave," University Way, where shops and restaurants await them. A 10-minute bus ride connects students to a full array of urban offerings in Seattle. The Seattle Center and other venues host outstanding operas, symphonies, and touring shows, while major league sports are available via the Seahawks (NFL), Mariners (MLB), and Sounders (MLS).

But who needs pro sports with Washington's Division I Huskies around? Husky Fever breaks out on every football weekend, and the stands are always packed for UW's team, especially when Washington State comes to town to vie for the coveted Apple Cup. Women's rowing and golf are recent national champions, while men's rowing, football, and women's volleyball have claimed Pac-12 conference titles. UW offers more than 80 recreational and intramural programs, in which about a third of students compete. More than anything else, the great outdoors defines the University of Washington. The campus offers breathtaking views of Lake Washington and the Cascade and Olympic mountains. Outdoor pastimes for students include boating, hiking, camping, and skiing, all found nearby, and Canada is close enough for road trips to Vancouver. The weather is consistently temperate, and natives insist that the city's reputation for rain is undeserved. Then again, the sports stadium has an overhang to protect spectators from showers.

"UW gives you a reality check that you're not as smart or as special as you think you are, and then shows you all the potential that you still have and gives you the guidance and tools to be successful," says a junior. While some students will not appreciate the occasionally impersonal academics, many students can overlook these obstacles for the big picture of the up-and-coming University of Washington—one that takes in more than just the beautiful scenery.

Overlaps

UC Berkeley, UCLA, University of Southern California, Washington State, U of I at Urbana–Champaign, Boston University, University of Michigan, NYU

Washington and Jefferson College

60 South Lincoln Street, Washington, PA 15301

Premed Central would be as good a name as any for W&J, which has one of the nation's highest proportions of students who go on to medical school. Law school and business school are also popular destinations, and undergraduates in all fields pack their bags to conduct independent research in far-flung locales through the innovative Magellan Project. The Greek system dominates the social life.

Wannabe doctors and lawyers would be well-advised to give Washington and Jefferson College a look. This small Pennsylvania college, founded in 1781 by Presbyterian ministers, is renowned for its preprofessional programs, and graduates are almost guaranteed acceptance into medical or health-related graduate programs. At the same time, the college's curriculum is growing more interdisciplinary and international in scope and putting more emphasis on independent student work. Classes remain small here and, despite the somewhat rural location, students enjoy an active social life thanks to a hearty Greek scene and the nearby city of Pittsburgh.

The campus, like the student body, is tight-knit: more than 50 buildings sit on 60 acres in a small town about 30 miles outside of Pittsburgh. W&J is the 11th-oldest college in the country and houses the eighth-oldest college building, which was built in 1793. The school got its name following the merger shortly after the Civil War of two colleges whose names you can probably guess. The prevailing architectural style is traditional colonial/Georgian, though modern structures have been added at a rapid pace during the past two decades. Recently opened facilities include the Ross Family Recreation Center.

Graduation requirements call for students to take a range of liberal arts and sciences courses and demonstrate proficiency in writing, speaking, reading, quantitative reasoning, foreign language, and use of information technology. Every first-year student enrolls in a First-Year Seminar, selecting from 25 options, many of which involve college-sponsored trips to major East Coast cities and some of which are linked to living/learning communities. All graduating seniors take part in a capstone experience.

> **"Professors don't just read off a slide, they actually teach and engage in discussion."**

Given that W&J is a magnet for students who plan to pursue M.D.s, J.D.s, and M.B.A.s, some of the school's most popular majors are business administration, accounting, psychology, political science, biology, and chemistry. English, communication, and mathematics are also strong. An entrepreneurship minor gives students the chance to interact with founders of Fortune 500 companies, and the interdisciplinary computing and information studies major offers five emphases, in big data, computer science, digital media, interaction design, and web and mobile technologies, from which students choose to concentrate. A thematic major allows students to design their own course of study. Rare among liberal arts colleges are the 3–4 programs with the Pennsylvania Colleges of Optometry and Podiatry. More technically minded students can take advantage of the 3–2 engineering programs with Case Western Reserve, Columbia, and Washington University in St. Louis.

Website: www.washjeff.edu
Location: Small Town
Private
Total Enrollment: 1,374
Undergraduates: 1,374
Male/Female: 53/47
SAT Ranges: ERW 570–650, M 550–640
ACT Ranges: 23–28
Financial Aid: 99%
Pell Grant: 31%
Expense: Pr $ $
Student Loans: 77%
Average Debt: $ $ $ $
Applicants: 5,358
Accepted: 48%
Enrolled: 13%
Grad in 6 Years: 76%
Returning Freshmen: 87%
Academics: ✍ ✍ ✍
Social: ☎ ☎ ☎
Q of L: ★ ★
Admissions: (724) 223-6025
Email Address: admission@washjeff.edu

Strong Programs:
Business Administration
Accounting
Psychology
Political Science
Biology
Chemistry
English
Communication

W&J's formula for success starts with individual attention in small classes; 67 percent of classes have fewer than 20 students, and a sophomore says, "Professors don't just read off a slide, they actually teach and engage in discussion." Students agree that the academic climate is tough, especially for those on the premed and prelaw tracks, but as a business major points out, "Because it is such a small campus, you know everyone in your academic field very well. This makes it very easy to work with others on a problem you have or on a project." Seventy percent of students do internships, and a robust alumni mentorship program ensures that every W&J student who wants an alumni mentor and career coach will have one.

W&J is a magnet for students who plan to pursue M.D.s, J.D.s, and M.B.A.s.

The Magellan Project provides funding for approximately 70 freshmen, sophomores, and juniors to put their liberal arts education to work each year through self-designed summer research projects or internships that involve domestic or international travel. Past projects have studied the migration of great white sharks in South Africa and explored childcare in China. "The Magellan Project is by far the best opportunity that W&J offers," enthuses one participant. The Washington Fellows Program is an honors

"The Magellan Project is by far the best opportunity that W&J offers."

program that provides participating students a bevy of special opportunities to interact with distinguished faculty, alumni, and guests. During the January intersession, students find brief apprenticeships in prospective career areas, take a short-term tour abroad, or engage in nontraditional coursework. Twelve percent of students study abroad, and the Office of Study Abroad offers about 40 approved semester- and year-abroad options in more than 20 countries.

"Students are truly friendly and they care," says one senior. Seventy-four percent of the students hail from Pennsylvania and many are from neighboring states in the Northeast; 4 percent are international. Five percent of students are African American, 5 percent are Hispanic, 2 percent are Asian American, and 4 percent are multiracial. Students report an even split between liberals and conservatives on campus, and one comments that "everyone finds an outlet to talk about their opinions in a free and safe way." Students get something of a bargain if they win an academic scholarship, which averages $21,000. Thirty-one percent of incoming students qualify for the Pell Grant. The college does not award athletic scholarships.

Seventy percent of W&J students do internships, thanks in part to a robust alumni mentorship program.

Students can live in either co-ed or single-sex dorms, and 94 percent of students live on campus. Housing is guaranteed for four years, and students say the freshman dorms are "adequate," but the choices get better with academic rank and include suite-style and apartment options for upperclassmen. Campus meals get a hearty thumbs-up: "I *love* the food here. We have local milk, cage-free eggs, and sometimes local produce," cheers one student. W&J has launched bystander awareness training and a student group of peer advocates to help educate the community on preventing sexual violence.

"[We have] a café where students get free food and milkshakes every weekend!"

The active Greek scene draws 33 percent of the men and 30 percent of the women, and chapter parties are said to be "very inclusive and welcoming" of non-Greeks. The Student Activity Board has worked to offer more on-campus events, such as free movies and cultural events, and a student-run coffeehouse provides another popular diversion. "W&J provides plenty of social options," says a junior. "We have the HUB with flat-screen televisions, Wii, Netflix, pool tables, a Ping-Pong table, and a café where students get free food and milkshakes every weekend!" A nonalcoholic pub called George & Tom's has become a favorite hangout with comedy, musical, and novelty/variety acts. There are also numerous clubs to join, from the equestrian club to the student theater company. During the course of the year, the Spring Street Fair and Spring Concert are the most popular events.

Not all students share the administration's appreciation for "the unique characteristics of the western Pennsylvania milieu." Many complain that there is nothing to do in Washington, a former steel/mining town, now hit by hard times. Relations with the locals can be a bit strained, but students try to assuage this by actively volunteering in the community. One student says, "Most people just make the drive to Pittsburgh," which is 30 minutes away; the University of Pittsburgh and Penn State are popular destinations for more diverse social opportunities.

Just about anyone has a shot at the Division III varsity sports at W&J, where the teams are known, naturally, as the Presidents. Recent conference champions include football, baseball, women's lacrosse, and field hockey; wrestling and women's basketball are also strong. Twenty-two percent of students participate in intramural and recreational sports, with flag football, soccer, and basketball attracting the most interest.

With expanding academic options and the freedom to self-design experiences abroad, the leadership at W&J is opening more and more doors for students. Students praise the education they receive and the school's close-knit environment. As one sophomore sums up, "W&J is a supportive place with lots of opportunities for students who choose to take advantage of them."

Overlaps

Allegheny, College of Wooster, Juniata, Knox, Ursinus, Penn State, University of Pittsburgh, Duquesne

If You Apply To ›

W&J: Early decision, early action, regular decision. SATs or ACTs: optional. No Subject Tests. Accepts the Common Application with supplement.

Washington and Lee University

Lexington, VA 24450

The ninth oldest university in the U.S., tradition-bound W&L is one of the most selective small colleges in the South, rivaled only by Davidson. W&L supplements the liberal arts with strong programs in business and journalism. Picture-postcard campus is three hours from Washington, D.C. Honor System thrives, but diversity has a ways to go.

Washington and Lee University, which shares the town of Lexington, Virginia, with the Virginia Military Institute, has always epitomized Southern gentility. The Fancy Dress Ball is a highlight of each year, the Honor System is revered, and the long-standing "Speaking Tradition" ensures at least casual communication between members of the W&L community when they pass one another on the well-manicured grounds. But this is not your grandfather's W&L. More than three decades after women were first admitted, today's atmosphere is a little less 19th century and a little more 21st century—as befits one of the South's leading liberal arts colleges. Says a senior, "Each individual walks away with a unique sense of what it means to be an honorable, thoughtful, civilized participant in a global society."

W&L's wooded campus sits atop a hill of lush green lawns, sweeping from one national landmark to another. The chapel is the burial site of Robert E. Lee. The Colonnade is the school's most iconic group of buildings—stately redbrick structures with white Doric columns—and the prevailing architectural style is Greek Revival, although the physical face of the campus is changing. The school also

Website: www.wlu.edu
Location: Small City
Private
Total Enrollment: 2,208
Undergraduates: 1,817
Male/Female: 52/48
SAT Ranges: ERW 680–750, M 670–750
ACT Ranges: 31–33
Financial Aid: 51%
Pell Grant: 12%
Expense: Pr $ $ $
Student Loans: 28%
Average Debt: $
Applicants: 5,455

(continued)

Accepted: 22%
Enrolled: 39%
Grad in 6 Years: 92%
Returning Freshmen: 97%
Academics: ✍ ✍ ✍ ✍ ½
Social: ☎ ☎ ☎
Q of L: ★ ★ ★ ★
Admissions: (540) 458-8710
Email Address: admissions@
  wlu.edu

Strong Programs:
Business Administration
Accounting
Economics
Journalism
Politics
History
Biochemistry
Neuroscience

The famous Honor System lends a relaxed feeling to the otherwise rigorous academic climate.

boasts the Elrod University Commons, which contains a dining hall, movie theater, and bookstore, and the $13.5 million Ruscio Center for Global Leaning.

General education requirements account for one-third of a student's coursework and include a first-year writing seminar and courses in literature, fine arts, history, philosophy, religion, science and math, social science, foreign language, and physical education. Students must also be able to swim. The Spring Term has been transformed into a single, four-week experience intended to offer students and faculty more innovative approaches to teaching and learning. Many use the term to study abroad; 57 percent of students spend time abroad at some point, traveling to destinations in more than 50 countries.

Although a standard liberal arts program remains the foundation of W&L's curriculum, the university offers excellent preprofessional programs, particularly in business, accounting, and economics, through the Williams School of Commerce, Economics, and Politics. Journalism, politics, history, biochemistry, and neuroscience are popular choices as well. The Shepherd Program for the Interdisciplinary Study of Poverty and Human Capability offers a minor in poverty that requires students to complete an eight-week summer internship with an organization focused on poverty-related issues.

> "Everyone here has succeeded in the past and everyone wants to keep doing it."

"Students don't compete much with each other, but they work very hard to improve themselves and their grades," explains a business and sociology double major. "Everyone here has succeeded in the past and everyone wants to keep doing it." Classes are small—72 percent have fewer than 20 students—and there are no teaching assistants. Says one student, "There are department heads teaching intro-level classes and senior seminars, and since these classes are small all the way through, the quality of teaching is excellent." Well-qualified students can apply for the Summer Research Scholars Program, which offers students paid fellowships for assisting professors in research or doing their own; 49 percent of undergrads conduct research. The famous Honor System lends a relaxed feeling to the otherwise rigorous academic climate. Tests and final exams are taken without faculty supervision; doors remain unlocked, laptops stay on desks, and library stacks are open 24 hours a day. Counseling and career services are highly praised. "The career counselors make an effort to get to know each student on an individual basis to position students for success," says a junior.

Fifteen percent of W&L students are native Virginians, and students from northeast of D.C. are well represented; international students make up 4 percent of the population. Administrators say they are working to increase diversity of all types; currently, African Americans account for 2 percent of the student body, Hispanics 5 percent, Asian Americans 3 percent, and multiracial students 3 percent. Though the atmosphere is still more traditional than at most leading liberal arts colleges, the days of rock-ribbed conservatism are gone. Middle-of-the-road is perhaps the best way to describe the political leanings of today's student body. A journalism major notes that W&L has made improvements in "acknowledging its institutional history," recently taking measures like renaming certain buildings with ties to slavery and making plans to create a campus history museum.

> "There are department heads teaching intro-level classes and senior seminars."

Merit-based awards averaging $39,000 are available, but athletic awards are not. The university guarantees to meet the full demonstrated financial need—without loans—of all admitted students, and for those whose families earn less than $100,000 annually, the W&L Promise program provides full-tuition grants. With these initiatives, socioeconomic diversity is increasing, but the majority of students still come from wealthy backgrounds. A senior observes, "There are challenges for lower-income students due to implicit expectations, such as appearances and social expenses." Despite such challenges, a first-generation student urges, "We need diverse students at Washington and Lee, and the support system from the university is in place to welcome them."

Seventy-five percent of students reside on campus, as they are required to do for their first three years. Students spend their first year in recently renovated, co-ed dorms. Many sophomores move into Greek houses or theme houses, while upper-classmen opt for apartment- and townhouse-style accommodations. Freshmen must purchase a meal plan, and dining options get good reviews. The Honor System and campus security personnel contribute to the students' feelings of safety on campus. "W&L has several student-run programs aimed at addressing issues of sexual assault, as well as a committee made up of students and faculty called the Healthy Sexual Culture Committee," reports a senior.

"We have the largest percentage of Greek students in the nation, so Greek life definitely sets the tone for the social scene," explains a junior. "Our parties are very inclusive: anyone is allowed to walk into any house on campus when there is a party happening." Seventy-three percent of the men and 75 percent of the women take part in Greek life. A lot of creative energy goes into fraternity bashes, which often feature live bands, although the formal Fancy Dress Ball, or "$100,000 prom," and the Black Ball, sponsored by the Student Association for Black Unity, also draw raves. While underage drinking is banned in the dorms, students insist that their peers "like to party and drink." Friday Underground, a weekly coffeehouse with free food, coffee, and student performances, has proven to be a popular social alternative. W&L's mock political convention for the party out of power, held every four years, has predicted past presidential nominees with uncanny accuracy.

> "The support system from the university is in place to welcome [diverse students]."

The school's scenic location in the midst of the Appalachian Mountains means an abundance of activities for nature lovers, including hunting, fishing, camping, mountain biking, skiing, and tubing on the rivers. The Outing Club, the largest student organization on campus, organizes day trips throughout the year and lengthier excursions during school breaks. Lexington, a "quiet, friendly town that has much history to offer," also offers a few bars, two movie theaters, and several restaurants. Washington, D.C., Richmond, Charlottesville, and Roanoke are easily reached by car for weekend trips.

W&L offers 24 varsity sports at the Division III level, and most teams participate in the Old Dominion Athletic Conference. During the 2017–18 season, the Generals took home conference championships in 11 sports, among them football, men's and women's lacrosse, and field hockey. The university sponsors approximately 25 club and intramural sports, ranging from disc golf and handball to skiing and polo; three-quarters of the student body participate.

"Washington and Lee is an institution with a lot of history, but per our motto, we are 'not unmindful of the future,'" says an English major. A sense of history and tradition does indeed pervade the campus. "W&L has adapted while still preserving the parts of the institution that make it a beloved place for all those who have had the pleasure to attend."

W&L has renamed certain buildings with ties to slavery and is making plans to create a campus history museum.

W&L's mock political convention, held every four years, has predicted past presidential nominees with uncanny accuracy.

Overlaps

Williams, Amherst, Middlebury, Carleton, Davidson, University of Virginia, UNC at Chapel Hill, William and Mary

If You Apply To ›

W&L: Early decision I and II, regular decision. SATs or ACTs: required. Subject Tests: optional. Accepts the Common Application with supplement.

Washington College

300 Washington Avenue, Chestertown, MD 21620

Washington College is among the oldest schools in the country. Small liberal arts college with strengths in creative writing, American history, and environmental science. The college has George Washington rather than Thomas Jefferson as its _éminence grise_. Chestertown is dullsville, so students make their own fun. Best known for the annual Sophie Kerr Prize—worth nearly $64,000 to a graduating senior.

Website: www.washcoll.edu
Location: Rural
Private
Total Enrollment: 1,433
Undergraduates: 1,433
Male/Female: 42/58
SAT Ranges: ERW 550–670,
  M 540–630
ACT Ranges: 23–29
Financial Aid: 93%
Pell Grant: 26%
Expense: Pr $ $
Student Loans: 66%
Average Debt: $ $ $
Applicants: 5,515
Accepted: 48%
Enrolled: 14%
Grad in 6 Years: 73%
Returning Freshmen: 85%
Academics: ✍ ✍ ✍
Social: ☎ ☎ ☎
Q of L: ★ ★ ★
Admissions: (410) 778-7700
Email Address:
  wc_admissions@washcoll.edu

Strong Programs:
English and Creative Writing
History
American Studies
Environmental Science and
  Studies
Business Management
Biology
Psychology
Economics

Chartered in 1782 in the closing days of the American Revolution, Washington College was the first college to be established in the newly independent United States, and the first to adopt a thoroughly secular mission: educating citizens, patriots, and leaders for the new democracy. It takes its name from George Washington, who never slept in any of its dorms but who did make a modest founding grant of 50 guineas and serve as a trustee. His spirit looms over the campus as strongly as that of "Mr. Jefferson" at UVA. One of the first things freshmen do upon arrival is sign the Honor Code (WC students cannot tell lies). The college is now focused on increasing the quality of its academic programs and becoming more affordable for all students, especially those of limited financial means.

Washington College sits on 112 acres adjacent to downtown Chestertown, a quiet community of 5,100 on the Chester River on the eastern shore of Chesapeake Bay. Most buildings are redbrick, Georgian-style structures connected by old brick walkways and enhanced by large shade trees. The historic heart of the campus is the green where commencement is held and where a bronze statue of You Know Who keeps watch. The Gibson Center of the Arts, the Toll Science Center, and the Hodson Commons mix large

> **"The academic climate is by no means easy, but it is not overwhelmingly stressful."**

expanses of glass with traditional redbrick. The college has invested millions in renovations and new facilities in recent years; the latest projects include the state-of-the-art Hodson Boathouse and updates to the Cain Athletic Center and the Casey Swim Center.

First-year students begin their studies with a required Global Perspectives: Research and Writing course in which they consider problems and issues from an international perspective. In addition to standard distribution requirements, students must also complete a senior capstone experience that, depending on their major field, can take the form of a comprehensive exam, thesis, scientific research project, theatrical production, or portfolio of writing or artwork.

While the most popular majors include business management, biology, psychology, and economics, the college's signature academic strengths are English literature and creative writing. Regardless of their disciplines, all students are expected to develop writing proficiency, and the college offers a four-year integrated approach to nurturing good writers. The school has a long-standing tradition of bringing writers such as Alice McDermott, Mark Doty, and Tim O'Brien to campus. The Rose O'Neill Literary House is a cultural hub where students can discuss poetry and literature over a cup of tea and freshly baked cookies. Seniors from all disciplines may submit writing portfolios to vie for the Sophie Kerr Prize. Named after a popular American writer of the early 20th century, it is the largest undergraduate literary prize in the country and inevitably gives the school its annual 15 minutes of fame in the national media. The 2018 winner took home a check for $63,711.

Not surprisingly, WC is a wonderful place to study history and American studies. The Starr Center for the Study of the American Experience, located in the old

Custom House on the Chester River, helps students study the culture of the Native Americans who once populated the area, trace the Revolutionary War campaigns in the Chesapeake region, and explore the area's maritime heritage from aboard *Sultana*, a reproduction 18th-century schooner. WC also takes advantage of its rural setting and nearby waterways to offer a strong program in environmental science and studies. The Center for Environment & Society promotes stewardship of the area's natural resources, including a Chesapeake Semester that offers hands-on experience in the watershed and a trip to Costa Rica for comparative study. The River and Field Campus, located ten minutes from the college's main campus, is a 7,400-acre living laboratory for avian research, local farming, and other environmental research. A 3–2 dual-degree program in environmental studies is now available with Duke University, as is a 3–2 engineering program with Columbia.

The River and Field Campus is a 7,400-acre living laboratory for avian research, local farming, and other environmental research.

With the exception of a few introductory classes, students report that all of their instruction comes from full professors who are easily accessible, and 74 percent of classes have fewer than 20 students. "Professors make an effort to explain material from several perspectives so that all students understand and can engage in it," says a biology major. WC operates on a four-credits-per-course basis, with three hours of classes and students expected to work on their own for the fourth. "The academic climate is by no means easy, but it is not overwhelmingly stressful," observes a freshman. Every freshman is assigned to a Peer Mentor, an older student who is trained to help them adjust to the academic and other sides of college life.

"Integrity runs through as the common character trait among Washington College students."

The Presidential Fellows program offers special academic opportunities to the top 10 percent of entering freshmen. Thirty percent of students study abroad in more than 30 countries. The school's location 75 miles east of Washington, D.C. affords excellent access to internships, which 65 percent of students pursue. In recent years, WC students have interned at the National Archives, the U.S. Congress, and the Smithsonian. A junior notes, "Career advising is really evolving to become a more effective service center for students and alumni, [especially] by having individual appointments."

The school's location 75 miles east of Washington, D.C. affords excellent access to internships, which 65 percent of students pursue.

"Integrity runs through as the common character trait among Washington College students," says a philosophy major. Forty-one percent of students at Washington are from Maryland, and 9 percent hail from other countries. Minority enrollment stands at 8 percent African American, 6 percent Hispanic, 3 percent Asian American, and 1 percent multiracial. The proportion of freshmen eligible for Pell Grants has increased to 26 percent. According to a junior, liberals and conservatives are both well represented, but the campus is generally not too politically active. In an effort to make the school more affordable, tuition is guaranteed not to increase for incoming freshmen who graduate in four years, and merit scholarships averaging $18,100 annually are available; there are no athletic scholarships. The George's Brigade scholarship program awards full funding to high-achieving, high-need students from urban areas. For graduating seniors carrying federally subsidized loans, the college's innovative Dam the Debt program forgives their final-semester debt by paying it off on their behalf at graduation, saving each eligible student an average of about $2,600.

"Not all dorms are created equal, but none of them are completely unacceptable."

All students are guaranteed on-campus housing for all four years, and 85 percent take up the offer. Three co-ed theme houses sit in the historic Hill Dorms complex—international, creative arts, and science—and language suites are available to advanced students of French, German, Japanese, and Spanish. Rooms are assigned through a lottery with numbers based on class year. A sophomore reports that "not all dorms are created equal, but none of them are completely unacceptable." The newest dorm, Corsica, is among the choicest in a cluster of dorms located on what students call the "Western Shore," overlooking the athletic fields. At the recently renovated dining hall, meals are all-you-can-eat and, in the words of one student, "exactly what you would expect from mass-produced food." Students give high ratings to the public safety department, and an environmental science major says, "The school does an excellent job with [sexual assault] prevention and management techniques, including counseling services."

According to a sophomore, WC's social life is "slow-paced compared to other schools." There are occasional off-campus house parties, but the sleepy nature of Chestertown means that most social life takes place on campus, much of it coordinated by the school's 100 student organizations. The Student Events Board sponsors concerts, film series, open-mic nights, silent discos, bonfires, and other entertainment. Fifteen percent of the men belong to fraternities and 17 percent of the women to sororities. The Crab Feast, put on by the frères of Phi Delta

"We love our namesake!"

Theta, is popular, as is the May Day celebration, which gives students an excuse to strip to their birthday suits at midnight and scamper around the quad. By far the biggest social event of the year is the formal Birthday Ball in February in honor of You-Know-Who's birthday. "We love our namesake!" says an English major. Students 21 and over are allowed to imbibe on campus, and students say alcohol policies are focused on student safety. A junior says, "Chestertown is quirky and charming, with historic buildings, music, food, art, and boutique shopping," but students seeking more active nightlife head for Annapolis, Baltimore, Philadelphia, or Washington, D.C.

WC's Shoremen and Shorewomen compete in the Division III Centennial Conference. Men's and women's rowing and the co-ed sailing team have recently become nationally competitive, while women's softball is a recent conference champion. Students turn out in huge numbers for the annual War on the Shore, when the men's lacrosse team takes on its biggest rival, Salisbury University. Sixty percent of students participate in the 20 intramural and club sports, with soccer being the favorite. Offered once a month, Outdoor Adventure trips, like rock climbing, cycling, and crabbing and fishing charters, are also popular.

After managing to be around for more than 235 years without making much of a stir beyond Chesapeake Bay, Washington College now seems bent on carving out a niche for itself in academic areas where it has a comparative advantage, especially creative writing, American history, and the environment. Students describe WC as a "small, tight-knit community" bound by the classic values of a small liberal arts college. George would probably approve.

Overlaps

Allegheny, Muhlenberg, Ursinus, Goucher, Transylvania, University of Maryland, Salisbury, University of Delaware

If You Apply To ›

Washington College: Early decision, early action, regular decision. SATs or ACTs: optional (required for consideration for merit scholarships). Subject Tests: optional. Accepts the Common Application with supplement.

Washington University in St. Louis

Campus Box 1089, One Brookings Drive, St. Louis, MO 63130-4899

No longer simply a backup to the Ivies, WashU has emerged as a nationally competitive university with a wholesome Midwestern feel. Core strength in the biological sciences, but strong across the disciplines. Maintains low acceptance rate—and higher ranking—by favoring early decision and denying top applicants who it thinks will enroll elsewhere. Preprofessional orientation, yet encourages exploration.

Though it's always been well recognized regionally, Washington University in St. Louis long ago established itself as a truly national institution—with a friendly, relaxed Midwestern feel that differentiates it from the high-strung Eastern Ivies. Applications have skyrocketed, and with a hefty $7.7 billion endowment, strong preprofessional programs, and an emphasis on research, it's not hard to see why. An architecture major says, "WashU is a high-end, collaborative research institution dedicated more to the growth of its students than the growth of its own personal brand."

The school's 169-acre campus adjoins Forest Park, one of the nation's largest urban parks. Buildings are constructed in the collegiate Gothic style, mostly in red Missouri granite and white limestone, with plenty of climbing ivy, gargoyles, and arches. The state-of-the-art Knight and Bauer Halls are home to the Olin Business School and include classrooms in tiered lecture configurations as well as "flat" classrooms with mobile furniture, designed to enhance student and faculty interaction. Recent construction projects include the Sumers Recreation Center and a renovation of the Olin Library.

Undergraduates enroll in one or more of WashU's five divisions—arts and sciences, architecture, art, business, or engineering. General education requirements vary by school and program. WashU's most popular majors include business, engineering, biology, and social sciences. The university's offerings in the natural sciences, particularly biology and chemistry, have long been notable, especially among those on the premed track. Biomedical engineering has become a specialty as well. The outstanding medical school runs a faculty exchange program with the undergraduate biology department, which affords bio majors significant opportunities to conduct advanced laboratory research. The University Scholars Program in Medicine allows students to apply for both undergraduate and medical school admission before entering college—though accepted students aren't obligated to attend medical school if their interests change. Double majors are encouraged, and interdisciplinary majors, such as environmental studies and philosophy-neuroscience-psychology, are growing rapidly.

> **"[WashU is] dedicated more to the growth of its students than the growth of its own personal brand."**

Each academic division offers options for incoming freshmen to acclimate to the university environment and explore their options. The freshman FOCUS program in Arts & Sciences, for instance, is a weekly, interdisciplinary seminar that looks at topics of contemporary significance, such as law and society, allowing students to sample offerings from various departments. Similarly, the Olin Business School's Foundations of Business Course, taught by senior faculty, focuses on a different topic each week. Students in the new Beyond Boundaries program take team-taught, cross-disciplinary courses on a range of topics across the university's five divisions in their first year, before moving into the division of their choice as sophomores. Those seeking even broader horizons have the opportunity to study in more than 50 different countries, and roughly a third do so, often through faculty-led programs during the summer.

Website: www.wustl.edu
Location: Suburban
Private
Total Enrollment: 13,159
Undergraduates: 7,021
Male/Female: 47/53
SAT Ranges: ERW 720–770, M 750–800
ACT Ranges: 32–34
Financial Aid: 49%
Pell Grant: 13%
Expense: Pr $ $ $
Student Loans: 29%
Average Debt: $
Applicants: 30,463
Accepted: 16%
Enrolled: 37%
Grad in 6 Years: 94%
Returning Freshmen: 97%
Academics: ✿ ✿ ✿ ✿ ½
Social: 🐘 🐘 🐘 🐘
Q of L: ★ ★ ★ ★
Admissions: (800) 638-0700
Email Address: admissions@wustl.edu

Strong Programs:
Business
Engineering
Biology
Social Sciences
Chemistry
Biomedical Engineering
Philosophy-Neuroscience-Psychology
Premed

Students agree that while academics are rigorous, the university's collaborative atmosphere is a major factor that sets it apart from its Ivy League competitors. "It's not a competitive culture or a weed-out school," reports an English and political science major. Those who are struggling will find plenty of help from teaching assistants (who conduct review sessions), academic advisors, study groups, and even a 24-hour peer counseling service called Uncle Joe's. Sixty-four percent of classes have fewer than 20 students, and undergrads have uncommon access to one-on-one mentoring relationships with top faculty. "The professors are brilliant and extremely accomplished, but they are also extremely down-to-earth and make every effort to get to know each student in their class (even in large lecture classes)," says an economics major.

"Most WashU students are really passionate about something but are rarely pretentious about it," says a junior. Eighty-four percent of undergraduates are out-of-staters, with a large contingent from Eastern states like New York and New Jersey, and another 7 percent are international. African Americans comprise 8 percent, Hispanics 9 percent, Asian Americans 17 percent, and multiracial students 5 percent. "The Center for Diversity and Inclusion has become like a second home to me because of the great study space and the opportunities to have necessary dialogues with excellent professionals and fellow students," says a sophomore. Students are engaged in social and political issues, especially racial justice and renewable energy, and tend to be moderate but left-leaning.

> **"It's not a competitive culture or a weed-out school."**

Academic scholarships averaging $5,300 are awarded each year, but there are no athletic scholarships. The university meets the full demonstrated financial need of admitted students and has replaced loans with grants for students from families with incomes below $75,000 as part of its efforts to become more socioeconomically diverse. A sophomore notes that, socially, "A person who is from a low-income background may have a difficult time fitting in due to the 'spending' culture at WashU."

Seventy-four percent of WashU students live in the school's co-ed dormitories, known as residential colleges. "The rooms are larger than your average dorm room, and we have Tempur-Pedic mattresses," boasts a student. "If that doesn't qualify us as best housing, I don't know what would." Freshmen and most sophomores live on the "South 40" (40 acres located just south of the main campus); freshmen are guaranteed rooms, and gender-inclusive housing is now available as an option. Upperclassmen may live in university-owned apartments, and some choose true off-campus digs in the nearby neighborhoods of University City and Clayton, where apartments are reasonably priced. Meal plans may be used in any of the dining centers, which students say are excellent. "Dining Services offers a wealth of options, with international cuisine, vegetarian, gluten-free, dairy-free, kosher, halal, and more available at each and every dining location," cheers a junior. The university is working to strengthen its Title IX resources and support after student protests criticized the administration's handling of sexual assault cases. "Currently students are unhappy with the Title IX process on campus for taking too long and protecting the rights of the perpetrators instead of the victims," explains a sophomore.

> **"Most WashU students are really passionate about something but are rarely pretentious about it."**

"The social life is as abundant as each student makes it," says a junior, with ample options both on and off campus. WashU students pride themselves on being able to balance work and play, and on weekends, movies, fraternity parties, and concerts tear them away from their books. Every spring, the whole campus turns out for the century-old Thurtene Carnival, the oldest student-run philanthropic festival in the country. Student groups—especially fraternities and sororities, which attract

25 percent of the men and 44 percent of the women—build booths, sell food, and put on plays; profits are donated to a children's charity. Four student-led cultural shows—Diwali, Lunar New Year Festival, Black Anthology, and Carnaval—are always well attended. Another big event is WILD (Walk In Lay Down), held at the beginning and end of the academic year. Everyone brings blankets and inflatable couches to the main quad, assumes a horizontal position, and listens to big-name bands. Alcohol policies emphasize safe and responsible drinking, and students say that, in that regard, they are effective.

WashU offers robust recreational options because of its location abutting Forest Park: a golf course, an ice-skating rink, a zoo, a lake with boat rentals, art and history museums, an outdoor theater, and a science center are all within a short walk. So too are the restaurants, bars, shops, and galleries of the Delmar Loop. The St. Louis Blues and Cardinals attract pro hockey and baseball fans, and the city is also home to the addictive Ted Drewes frozen custard. The school runs a free shuttle service to parts of St. Louis not within walking distance and offers a Metro Pass for free access to the city's bus and light-rail systems. "St. Louis is often described as the largest small town you will ever visit or the smallest big city you will ever see," says a sophomore. "I appreciate St. Louis because there is plenty to do without it being overwhelming." Community service programs such as Each One Teach One, in partnership with the city's schools, attract a sizable number of students. The best road trips include Chicago, Nashville, Memphis, and Lake of the Ozarks, as well as Columbia, Missouri—home of the University of Missouri.

The WashU Bears compete in Division III, and women's soccer and track and field are recent national champions. Women's basketball and volleyball are national powerhouses as well, and the men's basketball and men's and women's track and field teams claimed University Athletic Association conference titles in 2018. Three-quarters of the students play intramural sports, ranging from badminton, racquetball, and flag football to pocket billiards and ultimate Frisbee, and 35 club sports are popular too.

Word among high school guidance counselors is that no one gets admitted to selectivity-conscious WashU through regular admissions—you are either locked in through early admissions or cherry-picked off the waitlist. But however they get there, students find WashU both academically challenging and personally supportive. "The atmosphere is not only about learning academically, but growing as a person," says one senior. "My experiences have taught me to live life to the fullest."

Four student-led cultural shows—Diwali, Lunar New Year Festival, Black Anthology, and Carnaval—are always well attended.

"I appreciate St. Louis because there is plenty to do without it being overwhelming."

Overlaps

University of Chicago, Vanderbilt, Northwestern, Rice, Cornell University, Duke, Stanford, Yale

If You Apply To ›

WashU: Early decision, regular decision. SATs or ACTs: required. Subject Tests: optional. Accepts the Common Application. Apply to one of five undergraduate schools. Portfolio is required for applicants to College of Art and recommended for applicants to College of Architecture.

There is no better recipe for popularity than first-rate academics and a postcard-perfect campus on the outskirts of Boston. That formula keeps Wellesley near the top of the women's college pecking order—along with superb programs in economics and the natural sciences. Among leading women's colleges, only Barnard accepts a lower percentage. Nearly a quarter of the students are Asian American, one of the highest proportions in the East.

Wellesley College is not just the best women's college in the nation—it's one of the best colleges in the nation, period. With an alumnae roster that includes Hillary Rodham Clinton, Madame Chiang Kai-shek, Madeleine Albright, and Diane Sawyer, Wellesley should be at the top of the list for high achievers who are seeking the benefits of an all-women's college. Wellesley women excel in whatever field they choose, including traditional male bastions like economics and the sciences. "Wellesley is an energetic and serious place," says a senior. "When you come on campus, you can just feel that we're doing very important work here."

Nestled in a Boston suburb, the Wellesley campus, one of the most beautiful anywhere, occupies 500 rolling acres of cultivated and natural areas, including Lake Waban. Campus buildings range in architectural style from Gothic (with stone towers and brick quadrangles) to state-of-the-art science, arts, and sports facilities. A 22-acre arboretum and botanical garden features a wide variety of trees and plants. The Davis Museum houses 11 galleries, a cinema, and a café. The five campus libraries, which include an academic art library, boast more than a million volumes. Several facilities have been renovated under the Wellesley Campus Renewal Plan, including the student services building and studio art and performance spaces; a redesign of the Science Center is underway.

> **"When you come on campus, you can just feel that we're doing very important work here."**

Wellesley has distribution requirements that include units in language and literature; visual arts, music, theater, film, and video; social and behavioral analysis; epistemology and cognition; religion, ethics, and moral philosophy; historical studies; natural and physical science; and mathematical modeling and problem solving. In addition, students must take a first-year writing class, a foreign language, and a course on multiculturalism.

With its hefty endowment (the largest among the nation's all-female colleges and universities) and lavish facilities, Wellesley offers a top-of-the-line educational experience. The most popular majors are economics, political science, psychology, biological sciences, and neuroscience. Economics is known as the powerhouse; in fact, Wellesley has produced virtually all of the country's high-ranking female economists. Computer science is also strong, and students in biochemistry work with faculty on DNA research. Two dozen interdepartmental majors are available in fields ranging from astrophysics to peace and justice studies. Anything Wellesley women find lacking in their curriculum can probably be found at MIT, where they have full cross-registration privileges. Wellesley students can also take courses at nearby Babson College, Brandeis University, and Olin College of Engineering.

"Wellesley has a reputation for being competitive, but I find that's not entirely true," observes a mathematics major. "Most students are open to collaboration and willing to support each other." Under the honor system, students may take their finals, unsupervised, at any time during exam week. Class sizes are almost always

---

Website: www.wellesley.edu
Location: Suburban
Private
Total Enrollment: 2,364
Undergraduates: 2,364
Male/Female: 0/100
SAT Ranges: ERW 690–760,
  M 670–770
ACT Ranges: 30–33
Financial Aid: 60%
Pell Grant: 25%
Expense: Pr $ $ $
Student Loans: 49%
Average Debt: $
Applicants: 5,666
Accepted: 22%
Enrolled: 48%
Grad in 6 Years: 90%
Returning Freshmen: 95%
Academics: ✍ ✍ ✍ ✍ ✍
Social: ☎ ☎ ☎
Q of L: ★ ★ ★ ★
Admissions: (781) 283-2270
Email Address: admission@
  wellesley.edu

Strong Programs:
Economics
Political Science
Psychology
Biological Sciences
Neuroscience
Computer Science
Biochemistry
Peace and Justice Studies

small (averaging 18 to 23 students per class). Professors are highly respected and make themselves available through email, voicemail, office hours, and by appointment. "Professors clearly enjoy teaching here and are interested not only in our academic success, but also our well-being," says a philosophy major. First-years (as they are exclusively called here) and upperclasswomen alike have faculty advisors. Students give rave reviews to Wellesley's recently revamped career services but complain that the counseling center is understaffed. In an effort to alleviate first-year students' stress about grades as they adjust to Wellesley's rigorous atmosphere, the college employs a shadow-grading policy, in which their first-semester grades do not appear on their academic transcripts.

Eighty-five percent of students conduct undergraduate research, and grants from private foundations have allowed Wellesley to add innovative programs, including independent research tutorials for advanced science students and fellowship funding for joint student/faculty projects. About 50 percent of juniors study abroad through 160 approved programs, including Wellesley-run programs in France and Germany. Through the Albright Institute, 40 students each year are chosen to be Albright Fellows, attending classes with both Wellesley and visiting professors, then completing a funded summer internship abroad; past Fellows have interned with the U.S. State Department, the European Union Chamber of Commerce, and the Human Rights Education and Monitoring Center.

What are Wellesley women like? A sophomore says, "Think Beyoncé: empowered, smart, and driven." Only 13 percent of students are from Massachusetts, and although the Northeast is the best represented geographical area, students come from every state and more than 75 countries; 13 percent are international. Six percent are African American, 23 percent are Asian American, 12 percent are Hispanic, and 6 percent are multiracial. Politically, the atmosphere is strongly liberal. All financial aid awards are based on need—meaning no merit scholarships—but admissions are need-blind, and Wellesley meets the full demonstrated need of all admitted students. Wellesley has also eliminated loans for families with incomes below $60,000 per year and has reduced loans for others. Twenty-five percent of incoming students are Pell-eligible.

Residence life at Wellesley is a step ahead of most institutions, to say the least. Virtually every student lives on campus, and residence halls feature high-ceilinged living rooms, hardwood floors, fireplaces, walk-in closets, kitchenettes with microwaves, and even grand pianos. First-years are housed in the same halls as upperclasswomen, and juniors and seniors are generally granted single rooms. Peer tutors (called APT advisors) also live in each hall and are trained to tutor in specific subjects, as well as in study skills and time management. Two co-ops, one with a feminist bent, present an educational housing option. Meal cards are valid in all five dining halls and at the campus snack bar, which is stocked with everything from milk and flour to Twinkies. "The meals at Wellesley are awesome," cheers a sophomore. "We have a dining hall that is vegetarian and kosher, as well as one that is nut- and peanut-free." Campus security is strong, and a first-year notes, "Wellesley students are notoriously outspoken about the issue of sexual assault and the importance of educating those around them about it."

Wellesley's social scene tends to be quiet, although as a sophomore explains, "All of the student organizations have to host at least one all-campus event every semester, meaning there is always a dance, mixer, cultural show, or movie being shown." The Lulu Chow Wang Campus Center, referred to affectionately as "the Lulu," is a hub of activity day and night, with its student-run pub, Café Hoop,

Wellesley employs a shadow-grading policy, in which students' first-semester grades do not appear on their academic transcripts.

"Think Beyoncé: empowered, smart, and driven."

Forty students each year are chosen to be Albright Fellows, completing a funded summer internship abroad.

"Wellesley students are notoriously outspoken about the issue of sexual assault."

and coffeehouse. The closest thing Wellesley has to sororities are nonresidential societies, which sometimes host parties, for arts and music, literature, Shakespeare, politics, and general lectures. Service is also a key component of the Wellesley community, dating back to the college's inception. Wellesley's motto, *Non ministrari sed ministrare*, translates to "Not to be served, but to serve."

Wellesley is chock-full of traditions, the most endearing of which include Flower Sunday (where first-years are paired with older students in a welcoming ceremony), step-singing (an all-campus sing-along on the chapel steps), Spring Weekend (with a big-name band and comedian), and a hoop-rolling contest by seniors in their graduation robes. The winner of this contest will supposedly be the first in her class to achieve her goals, whatever they may be, and she gets off to a flying start when her classmates toss her in the lake. The lake is also the site of Lake Day, when students take a break from classes to enjoy a festival held on the lawn.

The town of Wellesley is an upper-crust Boston suburb without many amenities for students. "Be forewarned," cautions a student, "Wellesley is a snobby town of rich people." Still, when it comes to weekend fun, Wellesley is in a prime location. Not even half an hour away, Boston is the place where Wellesley women can mingle with males from Harvard and MIT. Cambridge—with Harvard Square, MIT frat parties, and lots of jazz clubs—is accessible by an hourly school shuttle that runs on weekdays and weekends. There is also a commuter rail station located a short walk from campus. Cape Cod, Providence, and the Vermont and New Hampshire ski slopes are close by car.

> "After just a few years here, all my ideas about… how much I'm truly capable of have changed."

Many students balance their academic schedule with Division III athletics, intramurals, and club sports. The crew team rowed its way to a national championship in 2016. Other top Blue teams include swimming and diving, cross-country, and field hockey. The big athletic rival is Smith College, another of the Seven Sisters group of great women's colleges. The sports center, named the Nannerl Keohane Sports Center in honor of Wellesley's 11th president (who went on to run Duke), offers an Olympic-size pool; squash, racquetball, and tennis courts; dance studios; a weight room; and an indoor track. Harvard's Head of the Charles crew race and the Boston Marathon—Wellesley's "Scream Tunnel" is legendary among runners worldwide—share honors as the most popular spectator sports of the year.

When it comes to academics, Wellesley women are serious. Their school is competitive with all but the top three Ivies. Many of them enjoy the traditions of the school and appreciate the idyllic atmosphere for contemplation, but know they are poised to dominate whatever field they enter. "Female empowerment isn't served with dinner, and we don't get confidence boosts for dessert," muses one student. "But somehow, after just a few years here, all my ideas about what's actually possible and how much I'm truly capable of have changed."

Overlaps

Barnard, Brown, Smith, Swarthmore, Yale, UC Berkeley, Harvard, Columbia

If You Apply To ›

Wellesley: Early decision I and II, regular decision. SATs or ACTs: required. Subject Tests: optional. Accepts the Common Application with supplement. Accepts applications from students who live as women and consistently identify as women. Current students participate on admissions board.

Wells College

Aurora, NY 13026

Founded in 1868 by Henry Wells of stagecoach fame, Wells is a small liberal arts college that shares the fabled "waves of blue" of Cayuga Lake with much larger Cornell. A family atmosphere is its hallmark, right down to the dinner bell that calls everyone to the evening meal. Big on interdisciplinary study and internships during the frosty January term.

Wells College moved beyond its origins as a women's college in 2005 when it began accepting men, but it has by no means abandoned its storied history. Whether it's riding to graduation in an old Wells Fargo stagecoach or showing off in the annual Odd-Even basketball game between freshmen and sophomores, the tradition of Wells is apparent at every turn. Enrollment has been fairly stable over the last decade, and with only about 500 students, anonymity is nonexistent and close relationships with professors and peers come with the territory.

Most of the buildings on Wells's 365-acre campus, which is listed on the National Register of Historic Places, are old, massive, and covered with ivy—the way college ought to look, you might say. The lakeside location affords beautiful sunsets as well as boating and fishing opportunities for those looking for a break from academics. A recent addition to campus is The Grind, a coffee shop operated by the college's Sullivan Center for Business and Entrepreneurship and run entirely by business students.

Wells's recently revamped core curriculum, called Sustainable Community, combines a solid grounding in the liberal arts with hands-on experiences. In addition to a number of distribution requirements, ranging from foreign language to personal wellness, students take four themed seminars, focusing on Crafting Meaningful Lives in the first year, on Local and Global Interconnections in the sophomore year, and on Contemporary Challenges and Ethical Engagement in the junior year. All students also complete two experiential learning activities, one of which must be off campus, such as internships, study abroad, service-learning projects, or student teaching. Additionally, all students complete a senior capstone project in their major.

> "Traditions are the backbone of Wells College."

The most popular majors include psychology, business, biology, health sciences, English, and history; students also give high marks to sociology and anthropology, education, and women's and gender studies. Majors in inclusive childhood education and sustainability have recently been added, and there's an unusual minor in book arts. Individualized majors are available for students whose needs are not met by established programs. There are also dual-degree programs in education with the University of Rochester; in business administration with Clarkson University; and in engineering with Clarkson, Columbia, and Cornell. For a change of pace, students may take one elective course each semester on a pass/fail basis. They may also cross-register for up to four courses each at Cornell and at Ithaca College.

"The academic climate is very collaborative in the sense that there is always someone there to help you achieve your goals," says a psychology major. Eighty-two percent of classes enroll fewer than 20 students, giving students easy access to faculty, and most courses are discussion-based, with the professor present to moderate and focus the conversation. The student-run collegiate association enforces the honor system, and take-home and self-scheduled tests are the rule rather than the exception. Wells uses a semester calendar with elements of the 4–1–4 plan,

Website: www.wells.edu
Location: Rural
Private
Total Enrollment: 491
Undergraduates: 491
Male/Female: 36/64
SAT Ranges: ERW 440–550, M 430–550
ACT Ranges: 19–26
Financial Aid: 100%
Pell Grant: 60%
Expense: Pr $
Student Loans: 97%
Average Debt: $ $ $ $
Applicants: 1,693
Accepted: 80%
Enrolled: 10%
Grad in 6 Years: 53%
Returning Freshmen: 71%
Academics: ✍ ✍ ✍
Social: ☎ ☎
Q of L: ★ ★ ★ ★
Admissions: (315) 364-3264
Email Address: admissions@wells.edu

Strong Programs:
Psychology
Business
Biology
Health Sciences
English
History
Sociology and Anthropology
Education

with internships, research, and study abroad taking place in January. Foreign study draws 30 percent of students; the college's flagship program in Florence, Italy, is especially popular.

"Wells students are polite and humble, and they are led by a sense of being one community," says a business major. Seventy-six percent of Wells students are state residents, while 2 percent are international. African Americans make up 13 percent of the student body, Hispanics 14 percent, Asian Americans 2 percent, and multiracial students 2 percent. Courses, workshops, and a support network for new students help to educate the campus on the importance of multiculturalism. Liberal social and political views are prominent, and women's rights, LGBTQ rights, and immigration policies are key topics of discussion. A notably high portion—60 percent—of freshmen qualify for Pell Grants. Numerous merit scholarships are awarded each year, but not for athletics.

All students are guaranteed college housing, and less than 5 percent live off campus. There are plenty of single rooms, though first-years are typically assigned to doubles, and substance-free and single-sex options are available. "Some of the dorms at Wells are old, but that is what makes them special—they add a nice touch," says a junior. Some residences have bay windows and winding staircases, and most offer lake views. Meals are served in a magnificent Tudor-style dining hall with two working fireplaces, and students report that a recent switch in dining services providers has improved the quality and variety of options. Security is "extremely reliable," says one student.

Though there are no Greek organizations at Wells, the school doesn't need them, given its bevy of other traditions. "Traditions are the backbone of Wells College," confirms a junior. For example, bells are rung every evening to announce dinner, and also to celebrate the first snowfall of the season. Additionally, tea and coffee are served every Wednesday afternoon. Though the long dresses and china cups have long since disappeared, tea is still a great time to hang out with friends, faculty members, and staff, as well as a welcome break from long afternoon seminars. On the last day of classes, there's a celebration around the sycamore tree, where sophomores present roses to seniors. Then, the president of the college and his staff serve breakfast to the graduating class.

"Most students stay on campus to socialize," says a sociology major. The school sponsors comedians, dances, movie and trivia nights, guest speakers, and poetry slams. Students say the campus party scene is very low-key and alcohol policies are well enforced. The town of Aurora has a popular bar and grill and a hotel—and that's about it. "It's a small village, not a college town at all," says a student, but the residents are friendly and on good terms with students, especially since Wells requires student clubs to participate in community service. Those looking for a more traditional college party scene head 30 miles south to Ithaca College and Cornell. Auburn and Syracuse are good for shopping, while New York City and Montreal offer shows and other big-city perks. Given the beautiful, hilly terrain, Wells students also enjoy camping in the warmer months, and cross-country or downhill skiing in the winter, especially with the slopes of Greek Peak less than an hour away.

Varsity teams at Wells compete in Division III, and since the school is so small, virtually anyone interested gets the chance to play. The Express field hockey and men's and women's volleyball and swimming teams have been the most competitive. A fledgling intramural program offers kickball, dodgeball, and ultimate Frisbee, and dance is a popular club sport. Anyone may use the golf course and the college's tennis courts, while the field house offers a pool and other exercise equipment.

All students complete two experiential learning activities, one of which must be off campus.

Bells are rung every evening to announce dinner, and tea and coffee are served every Wednesday afternoon.

"The classes are good, the community is wonderful, and Wells really prepares you for life."

Overlaps

Ithaca, Elmira, Hartwick, Albion, Cornell College, SUNY–Buffalo, City College of New York, SUNY–Oswego

Along with its abundant traditions and close-knit atmosphere, Wells has retained what one student calls a "liberal, progressive, feminist, and independent," spirit, which most students say suits them just fine. "I believe the classes are good, the community is wonderful, and Wells really prepares you for life," says one student. "I already feel more independent having studied at Wells."

If You Apply To ›

Wells: Early decision, early action, regular decision. SATs or ACTs: optional. No Subject Tests. Accepts the Common Application with supplement. Applicants must submit a Unique Expression, any additional material that showcases unique personality and talents.

Wesleyan University

45 Wyllys Avenue, Middletown, CT 06459

Usually compared to Amherst or Williams, Wesleyan is really more like Swarthmore. The key differences: Wesleyan is twice as big and a little more streetwise. Wes students are progressive, politically minded, and fiercely independent. Exotic specialties like ethnomusicology and East Asian studies add spice to the scene. New York and Boston are both two hours away but not easily accessible on public transportation.

Whether they're engrossed in academics, debating and demonstrating over various issues, or engaged in community service, Wesleyan students seem to do things with a passion and intensity that helps set this school apart from tamer institutions. "There's an energy on this campus; for me, it's a spirit of creativity and political energy," a sophomore explains. In recent years, a significant number of Wesleyan alumni have gone on to make their mark in the high-tech world and the entertainment industry, most recently *Hamilton* creator Lin-Manuel Miranda.

Diversity at Wesleyan begins with the campus architecture. The nucleus of this stately university is a century-old row of lovely brownstones that look out over the football field. The rest of the buildings can be described as "eclectic" and range from mod-looking dorms of the '50s and '60s to the beautiful and modern Center for the Arts. Dozens of Wesleyan-owned wood-frame houses serve as senior residences that look freshly plucked from Main Street, USA. The Gordon Career Center is situated in the heart of the campus and features a multipurpose career commons with a broadcast suite. Wesleyan likes to describe itself as "a small college with university resources." The libraries have more than a million volumes, practically unheard of at a school this size. Whenever you happen to walk past the brightly lit, glass-walled study room of Sci-Li (the science library), you're apt to see numerous students huddled over their books.

> "With popular classes, you have to be persistent, but you can get in."

Wesleyan's curriculum renewal program ensures the relevance of liberal arts education in the 21st century by offering seminars for first-year students, requiring an electronic portfolio from each student that allows them to set goals with their advisors and compile their work, and clustering courses to help students reach their academic objectives. Students are expected to take a minimum of three courses in each of three areas—humanities and the arts, social and behavioral sciences, and natural sciences and mathematics. Wesleyan students can choose from among nearly 50 majors, in addition to a number of minors and certificate programs. At the

Website: www.wesleyan.edu
Location: Small City
Private
Total Enrollment: 3,048
Undergraduates: 2,896
Male/Female: 46/54
SAT Ranges: ERW 660–740, M 640–760
ACT Ranges: 29–33
Financial Aid: 44%
Pell Grant: 16%
Expense: Pr $ $ $ $
Student Loans: 39%
Average Debt: $
Applicants: 12,360
Accepted: 16%
Enrolled: 38%
Grad in 6 Years: 90%
Returning Freshmen: 95%
Academics: ✐ ✐ ✐ ✐ ✐
Social: ☎ ☎ ☎
Q of L: ★ ★ ★
Admissions: (860) 685-3000
Email Address: admission@wesleyan.edu

Strong Programs:
Economics

end of their freshman year, students may apply to major in one of three competitive, interdisciplinary seminar colleges: the College of Letters (European literature, history, and philosophy), the College of Social Studies (history, government, political and social theory, and economics), and the Science in Society program (which allows students to do advanced work in a science discipline while studying science and medicine through a philosophical, sociohistorical lens). Other interdisciplinary colleges offering linked majors include the College of the Environment and the College of Integrative Sciences. The College of Film and the Moving Image is first-rate and has an international reputation. The College of East Asian Studies, another strength, offers advanced language courses, study abroad, a focus on cultural fluency, and an authentic Japanese tea room.

Among Wesleyan's strongest programs are economics, neuroscience and behavior, English, music, astronomy, molecular biology and biochemistry, American studies, and earth and environmental sciences; the economics, English, government, and psychology majors enroll the most students. But even the smaller departments attract attention. Ethnomusicology, including African drumming and dance, is a particular specialty; students can be found reclining on the wide, carpeted bleachers at the World Music Hall or watching a dozen musicians play the Indonesian gamelan. The math department emphasizes problem solving in small groups rather than interminable lectures dedicated to theory. Undergraduates in the sciences and psychology work alongside faculty in their research laboratories and frequently earn the opportunity to publish in scientific journals. Students can also take advantage of dual-degree programs in engineering with Dartmouth, Caltech, and Columbia.

"Inclusion—both on and off campus—is always the goal of student activism."

Dozens of Wesleyan-owned wood-frame houses serve as senior residences that look freshly plucked from Main Street, USA.

Despite Wesleyan's rigorous academics and heavy workload, students say the supportive atmosphere makes for a relatively relaxed feel. The university has used its wealth to attract highly rated faculty members who are expected to be scholar-teachers: academic superstars who juggle groundbreaking research, enthusiastic lectures, and personal student attention at the same time—and they seem to pull it off. "Professors aim to engage all of their students and make the classroom a collaborative learning environment. For instance, one of my professors takes notes for each class about what she has learned from our discussions," says an American studies major. Wesleyan strives to keep its classes small, and 74 percent of the courses have fewer than 20 students. "With popular classes, you have to be persistent, but you can get in," a history major says. If beseeching is not your style, studying abroad may be a temporary tonic to registration headaches. Programs are available in all areas of the world, and 44 percent of students take part. Internships are popular too.

"Middletown isn't a bad place for college."

Wesleyan requires an electronic portfolio from each student that allows them to set goals with their advisors and compile their work.

Wesleyan's excellent reputation and strong recruiting network attract students from all over, ensuring the mash-up of viewpoints that makes it such a vital place. "Students at Wesleyan tend to be open-minded, culturally literate, and intellectually curious," says one student, but "people here are not all from the same mold." Just 8 percent of undergraduates are Connecticut natives, and 12 percent hail from foreign nations. The student body is 6 percent African American, 11 percent Hispanic, 8 percent Asian American, and 5 percent multiracial. Students are mostly liberal and vocal about hot social and political issues. "Inclusion—both on and off campus—is always the goal of student activism," says a government major. Approximately 90 percent of freshmen are admitted on a traditional need-blind basis, with the rest admitted with an eye on their ability to pay. The university meets 100 percent of admitted students' demonstrated need and also has a policy of waiving any loan obligation for most families with incomes below $60,000 per year.

For housing, most freshmen are consigned to singles or doubles in the campus dorms. Students say the Butterfield complex is the choice for quiet study, while Clark Hall is where the party people go. Housing is guaranteed for four years; upperclassmen who want to live off campus must apply for permission, and very few do so. "The housing system at Wesleyan is really unique. It's based on a system of progressive independence, so every year you have more freedom and more responsibility," explains a student. Upperclassmen enjoy numerous campus housing options: townhouses for four or five students, college-owned houses and apartments, or special-interest houses organized around concerns such as ecology, feminism, art, community service, or minority student unity. Campus dining gets good reviews: "Vegetarians love Wesleyan and so do meat eaters. There is an option for everyone," one student says. Students report feeling safe on campus and say the university has taken an active role in sexual assault prevention.

Greek membership is nominal, with just 4 percent of men and 1 percent of women joining up. Two former fraternities have turned into co-ed literary societies. As a result of a series of disputes with the administration over single-sex status and allegations of sexual harassment, the remaining fraternities have faced disciplinary actions. Wesleyan's enforcement of the drinking age is rather relaxed compared with most schools. Consistent with the university's

"This is a place that encourages and supports multifaceted learning."

encouragement of independence, students bear a large part of the responsibility for policing themselves. "There is definitely a drinking/party culture, but there is absolutely no pressure to participate," says one senior. Activities abound from comedy performances to a cappella groups, films, plays, bands, lectures, parties, and events planned by the more than 275 student groups. "Most students stay on campus for weekends and other social events," a junior says. Major events on the social calendar include Spring Fling and "the Mash" concert—two outdoor festivals—and Uncle Duke Day and Zonker Harris Day, two similar events with a more psychedelic, '60s flavor, in which students pay tribute to the infamous Doonesbury characters.

Middletown is a small city within easy driving distance of Hartford and New Haven, but it is off the beaten track of steady public transportation. It has undergone a renaissance in recent years, and students cheer the myriad ethnic restaurants available. "Middletown isn't a bad place for college," says a student. "There are bars on Main Street that cater to a college crowd. Plus, there is a diverse collection of restaurants, which is great for when the family comes to visit." Wes students contribute a great deal of time to community service and help maintain a peaceful, beneficial relationship with the town. And Wesleyan's rural surroundings afford the much-appreciated opportunity to jog through the countryside, swim at nearby Wadsworth Falls, or pick apples in the local orchards. Good road trips include New York and Boston, each two hours away, and decent ski areas and beaches just under an hour away.

The Wesleyan Cardinals compete in the Division III New England Small College Athletic Conference (NESCAC) and field 29 varsity teams. Men's lacrosse took home the national title in 2018, and recent conference champions include men's tennis and women's volleyball. Annual encounters with "Little Three" rivals Williams and Amherst get even the most bookwormish student out of the library and into the heat of the action. Recreational sports are extremely popular, and more than half of the students compete in five intramural and 16 club sports. The ultimate Frisbee club (the "Nietzsch Factor," named after a former star player's dog, not a misspelling of the philosopher) almost always whips challengers. Athletics are enhanced by a complex that comes complete with a 200-meter indoor track, a fitness center, and a 50-meter pool.

The key to Wesleyan's success seems to be the fostering of an intellectual milieu where independent thinking and an appreciation of differences are omnipresent.

Overlaps

Brown, Tufts, Vassar, Yale, University of Chicago, Swarthmore, UC Berkeley, NYU

As a junior puts it, "At Wesleyan, you're not solely a STEM kid or a student of history; this is a place that encourages and supports multifaceted learning." Indeed, the Wesleyan experience means liberal learning in a climate of individual freedom—a freedom that requires motivated students who stay on task despite the laid-back atmosphere. Abundant opportunities are open to students willing to take advantage of them, which is precisely what these doers do.

If You Apply To ›

Wesleyan: Early decision I and II, regular decision. SATs or ACTs: optional. Subject Tests: optional. Accepts the Common Application with supplement.

West Virginia University

P.O. Box 6009, Morgantown, WV 26506

Surrounded by the likes of Ohio, Pennsylvania, and Virginia, West Virginia has traditionally exported its best students to other states for college. But WVU also attracts its share of out-of-staters, some drawn to its one-of-a-kind forensics program. The honors program is a must for top students, and the university has solid programs in professional fields ranging from health sciences to engineering.

Website: www.wvu.edu
Location: Small City
Public
Total Enrollment: 25,155
Undergraduates: 20,713
Male/Female: 53/47
SAT Ranges: ERW 510–610, M 510–600
ACT Ranges: 21–27
Financial Aid: 55%
Pell Grant: 27%
Expense: Pub $
Student Loans: 60%
Average Debt: $ $ $
Applicants: 20,594
Accepted: 72%
Enrolled: 35%
Grad in 6 Years: 57%
Returning Freshmen: 80%
Academics: ✍ ✍
Social: ☎ ☎ ☎ ☎
Q of L: ★ ★ ★
Admissions: (304) 293-2121
Email Address:

Strong Programs:
Exercise Physiology

West Virginia University earned the right to be the state's flagship land grant college by being the only one in the state to offer research and doctoral-degree programs. WVU offers more than 120 undergraduate majors, approximately 480 student organizations, and 17 intercollegiate varsity athletic programs. With solid academic programs and student groups, the school has become an increasingly popular choice for scholars, researchers, and athletes, as well as party animals.

WVU is situated in the picturesque mountains of north-central West Virginia, a few miles from the Pennsylvania border and overlooking the Monongahela River. A driverless rail system connects the campus's three areas—the older downtown, the more modern Evansdale, and the health sciences area. Ten of the ivy-covered Morgantown buildings, dating mainly from the 19th century, are listed on the National Register of Historic Places; many of their interiors have been restored or renovated. A 216,000-square-foot business and economics complex that will feature academic, residential, and recreational space is scheduled for completion in 2021.

All WVU students must complete the General Education Foundations program, which consists of coursework in eight areas: English, science and technology, mathematics and quantitative skills, society and connections, human inquiry and the past, artistic expression, global and diversity studies, and a special focus area drawing on a subject of personal interest. For many students, fulfilling the special focus area requirement leads to a minor or even a second major. All incoming students take a First-Year Seminar that covers study skills, university and community support services, goal setting, and career planning.

"Certain classes and a segment of the student population create a competitive climate."

West Virginia's degree programs span 14 colleges and schools, the best of which are engineering (particularly energy-related) and the allied health sciences (medical technology, physical therapy, nursing, and occupational therapy). The most popular majors are exercise physiology, biology, psychology, nursing, criminology, engineering, and business. WVU was the first school in the nation to offer a degree in forensic science and is the only one to offer it at the bachelor's, master's, and doctoral levels. Additional programs of note include undergraduate majors in strategic communications, management information systems, health informatics and information management, physics, and—for those interested in children's theater—puppetry. Thirty-one percent of undergraduate classes have fewer than 20 students, and students say the difficulty of WVU academics depends largely on the classes they take. "The overall academic climate is generally laid-back," says a senior, "but certain classes and a segment of the student population create a competitive climate." The Honors College offers small classes, special housing, and early registration to the top 5 percent of WVU students. Study abroad programs are available in more than 70 countries through a variety of faculty-led, partner, and exchange options.

Though WVU attracts students from all U.S. states and more than 100 countries, its appeal is primarily regional. Fifty-two percent of undergraduates are in-staters, and 7 percent are international; sizable contingents arrive from western Pennsylvania, Maryland, and New Jersey. One student says, "WVU has a unique conglomerate of students" beyond Appalachian natives. African Americans comprise 5 percent of the student body, Hispanics 4 percent, Asian Americans 2 percent, and multiracial students 4 percent. Twenty-seven percent of freshmen are Pell-eligible. The university offers thousands of merit scholarships, worth an average of $3,100, and hundreds of athletic awards.

Just 15 percent of WVU's undergraduates live on campus, where dorms are said to be mediocre but fill up fast because of the limited space. Most are co-ed; the older ones are known for their character, while the newer residential complexes in Evansdale have larger rooms and luxuries like air-conditioning. Living/learning communities are available for first-generation and international students, **"Every football game is a festival in some way."** as well as anyone interested in forensics, innovation and entrepreneurship, or creative arts. Many upperclassmen opt for nearby apartments. All students may buy meal plans regardless of where they live. Students complain that parking on campus can be difficult, but they can also ride the local Morgantown Mountain Line buses, which stop at all university housing, for free.

Morgantown is a small city with a college-town feel and plenty of community service opportunities. "This town revolves around the university and provides so much for the students," says a senior. The school has worked hard to curtail underage drinking, banning alcohol in the dorms and placing restrictions on Greek parties and rush activities. As part of these ongoing efforts, the university recently banned five fraternities from campus for at least 10 years for failing to comply with new rules. Roughly 6 percent of the men and 5 percent of the women go Greek. Social life is still centered on campus, often focused on the free food, movies, bands, and comedians offered Thursday through Saturday by the school-sponsored Up All Night program. The annual Welcome Week offers hundreds of activities, including a free FallFest concert, and Mountaineer Week showcases the customs of Appalachia. For those with cars, road trips to Columbus, Washington, D.C., or Pittsburgh are quick and easy.

Mountaineer football has achieved national prominence, especially with its move to the Big 12, and a senior says, "Every football game is a festival in some way." West Virginia also fields competitive Division I teams in men's and women's basketball and soccer, along with women's gymnastics, men's wrestling, and co-ed rifle. There are hundreds of intramural teams, the most popular being basketball, flag football, dodgeball, and indoor soccer.

As WVU grows, the university continues to be dedicated to research that will improve the lives of citizens not only in West Virginia, but across the globe. At the

(continued)

Biology
Psychology
Nursing
Criminology
Engineering
Business
Forensic Science

For many students, fulfilling the special focus area gen-ed requirement leads to a minor or even a second major.

The annual Mountaineer Week showcases the customs of Appalachia.

Overlaps

Fairmont, James Madison, Marshall, Penn State, Ohio State, Towson, University of Delaware, University of Maryland

same time, WVU's mission is evolving to be more student-centered. And the campus is forever growing and changing. "WVU is a school," says a senior, "that won't look the same for very long."

If You Apply To ›

West Virginia: Rolling admissions. SATs or ACTs: required. No Subject Tests. Accepts the Common Application with supplement.

Westmont College

Santa Barbara, CA 93108

A Christian liberal arts college, Southern California style. Westmont academics are taught from unapologetically Christian perspective, but overall climate is more laid-back than at other evangelical powerhouses like Wheaton (IL) and Gordon. Nationally known for kinesiology. Almost everyone gets financial aid, but student homogeneity is a problem. Shorts and sandals are the norm, and the temptations of Santa Barbara's surf and sand are only five minutes away.

Website: www.westmont.edu
Location: Small City
Private
Total Enrollment: 1,284
Undergraduates: 1,284
Male/Female: 39/61
SAT Ranges: ERW 580–700,
   M 550–680
ACT Ranges: 23–30
Financial Aid: 95%
Pell Grant: 19%
Expense: Pr $ $
Student Loans: 56%
Average Debt: $ $ $
Applicants: 1,826
Accepted: 85%
Enrolled: 23%
Grad in 6 Years: 75%
Returning Freshmen: 81%
Academics: ✍ ✍ ✍
Social: ☎ ☎ ☎
Q of L: ★ ★ ★ ★
Admissions: (800) 777-9011
Email Address: admissions@
   westmont.edu

Strong Programs:
Kinesiology
Economics and Business

Westmont College prides itself on offering students a strong grounding in the liberal arts while remaining faithful to its motto, *Christus Primatum Tenens* ("Christ holding preeminence"). Unlike many Christian colleges, Westmont has never had ties to any particular Protestant denomination and sees itself as part of a worldwide evangelical tradition embracing a range of theological perspectives. Faculty members, all practicing Christians, take pride in presenting competing lifestyles and value systems as a way to challenge and nurture students' faith. "The school's culture is that of a Christian community," says a chemistry major. "It is very cheerful and kind, and there are many hugs!"

Founded in 1937, Westmont sits on a former estate nestled in the foothills of the Santa Ynez Mountains along the Pacific Coast. The campus, which in 2017 was occasionally evacuated due to historic wildfires and flooding, boasts a Mediterranean-style residence, gardens, and buildings crafted of sandstone and other local natural materials. A senior characterizes the academic climate as "fostering a 'we're-all-in-this-together' attitude." All classes are taught by regular faculty members, who are described by one English major as "passionate about teaching and, most importantly, accessible. Any emails I send are usually answered within hours." Students have good things to say about Westmont's career advising and other support services; the psychological counseling center has added staff and expanded its hours.

> **"Christianity is integrated into the curriculum, and there is chapel three times each week."**

Westmont requires all students to undertake an extensive general education program grounded in the Christian liberal arts tradition. The program includes courses in biblical literature and history, standard distribution requirements, and a skills component that includes writing- and speech-intensive courses and foreign language. With their Christian heritage under their belts, students then undertake one of two "Compassionate Action" options aimed at applying their faith to society. Most majors include a capstone or senior seminar course, in which seniors reflect on what they have learned over the previous four years.

One of Westmont's most popular majors is kinesiology. An interdisciplinary science, kinesiology is the study of the art and science of human movement or, as Westmont faculty like to put it, "God's greatest creation: the human body." Students rate the economics and business and English majors as strong, along with chemistry and biology among the hard sciences. The religious studies department boasts a number of respected scholars, which is a good thing, since so many of their courses are required for graduation. Music is well-funded and strong, as is art, which focuses on the fine arts and art history. Students find the computer science offerings underwhelming.

(continued)

English
Chemistry
Biology
Religious Studies
Music
Art

About half of the students engage in undergraduate research independently or with a professor. Students present their work at biannual Research Symposia. The Augustinian Scholars Program offers generous four-year scholarships to 30 to 60 incoming freshmen, who engage in seminars that explore Christian intellectual traditions and higher education as a Christian calling. A semester-long program in social entrepreneurship based in downtown Santa Barbara involves project-based internships. Westmont prides itself on fostering global perspectives, and 58 percent of students receive academic credit for foreign study. Students returning from time abroad can earn a minor in global studies by taking additional seminar and research courses.

A semester-long program in social entrepreneurship based in downtown Santa Barbara involves project-based internships.

Westmont has a lofty acceptance rate of 85 percent, with 40 percent of incoming freshmen hailing from the top 10th of their high school class. Most Westmont students come from California (71 percent) or other Western states, mainly from middle and upper-middle class Christian homes. "Since Christianity is integrated into the curriculum, and there is chapel three times each week, you'd have a rough time fitting in if you were not Christian," says a biology major. Two percent of students come from outside the United States. A sophomore describes fellow students as "generally laid-back, friendly, outdoorsy, and bubbly." The campus political climate is usually low-key, although a junior notes that there have been some "small demonstrations against the college's position on LGBTQ+ relationships." Hispanics make up 18 percent of students, Asian Americans 7 percent, and multiracial students 6 percent, while African Americans account for just 2 percent. A kinesiology major comments, "Although I fit the stereotype, it was more challenging than expected to be in an

"Socializing may look like going swing dancing or to a movie rather than to a party."

environment of people 'just like me.' I genuinely missed having vibrant cultures around me." Westmont is lavish with its financial aid. Ninety-five percent of incoming first-year and transfer students are offered academic scholarships ranging from $6,000 per year to full tuition, and athletic scholarships are available as well.

The dorms at Westmont are clean, well-maintained, and conveniently located. The new Global Leadership Center, where every room has its own bathroom, gives priority to seniors and students who engage in leadership and study abroad programs. All students are required to live on campus for all four years, with only a few limited exceptions. Westmont has a single all-day dining facility, imaginatively known as the Dining Commons, where, as a communication major puts it, "the food is pretty good as far as cafeteria food goes." Fridays are "Farm Fresh," and burgers or salads at El Tejado satisfy late-night hunger pangs.

The new Global Leadership Center, where every room has its own bathroom, gives priority to students who engage in study abroad.

Consistent with their Christian values, almost all Westmont students engage in community service projects. Through the student-run Potter's Clay program, students spend their spring break working with contractors, doctors, and other professionals in Ensenada, Mexico. The Urban Initiative sends teams to work with local nonprofit organizations in U.S. cities. On campus, the Westmont Activities Council sponsors intramurals, dances, and other events. "People at Westmont are usually conservative, so socializing may look like going swing dancing or to a movie rather than to a party," says a chemistry and biology major. Alcohol is banned on campus, but a communication major says that "students are allowed to drink off campus if they are of legal age." A campus shuttle allows ready access to Santa Barbara's many options, ranging from coffee shops and shopping to hiking, surfing, and beach volleyball. Westmont traditions include the annual Spring Sing musical skit competition between dorms and the Fringe Festival featuring theater, dance, and films directed and performed by students.

Athletics at Westmont are low-key, but the school's six men's and six women's varsity teams (the Warriors) do well in competition with eight other Christian colleges in the NAIA Golden State Athletic Conference. Men's and women's track and field and women's basketball are recent conference champions. Popular intramural and club sports include rugby, lacrosse, and—get this!—a polo team that has won two recent national championships.

Westmont students laugh at their stereotypes ("drinking smoothies from the local Blenders store") and occasionally bristle at the chapel requirements ("more a burden than a time with God"), but most welcome these as part of the fabric that makes Westmont's friendly, close-knit, and caring community possible. "While it is very easy to stay within the walls of comfortableness," observes one senior, "there are plenty of opportunities to push the limits of your comfort zone, whether through global travel or local mission work."

Overlaps
Wheaton (IL), Gordon, Point Loma Nazarene, Azusa Pacific, Biola, Pepperdine, Baylor, Whitworth

If You Apply To ›

Westmont: Early action I and II, rolling admissions. SATs or ACTs: required. Subject Tests: optional. Accepts the Common Application with supplement. Applicants must agree to Community Life Statement.

Wheaton College (IL)

501 College Avenue, Wheaton, IL 60187

Wheaton is at the top of the academic heap in Evangelical education, rivaled only by Pepperdine (with its Malibu digs) and traditional competitors such as Gordon and Calvin. Students must not only follow Wheaton's stringent code of conduct but also affirm their personal faith in Jesus Christ. Wheaton's low tuition makes it relatively affordable. The worldly temptations of Chicago are less than an hour away.

Website: www.wheaton.edu
Location: Suburban
Private
Total Enrollment: 2,549
Undergraduates: 2,309
Male/Female: 45/55
SAT Ranges: ERW 630–720, M 600–690
ACT Ranges: 27–32
Financial Aid: 82%
Pell Grant: 22%
Expense: Pr $
Student Loans: 57%
Average Debt: $ $

Wheaton College combines academic rigor and Evangelical orthodoxy with a firm commitment to the liberal arts, preparing students "to help build the church and improve society worldwide For Christ and His Kingdom." It is one of only two Evangelical schools with an admissions process that requires students to be professing Christians (see also Gordon College). The Community Covenant prohibits the use of alcohol, tobacco, or drugs; professors are allowed to drink and smoke, but are discouraged from doing so, especially in front of students. Though most adolescents would chafe under such restrictions, Wheaties take it all in stride. A happy junior says, "Wheaton offers a unique balance of academic excellence, extracurricular activity, and Christian community that simply cannot be found anywhere else."

Wheaton is nondenominational and its verdant, 80-acre campus is an oasis of sorts, in the midst of one of Chicago's oldest and most established suburbs. The castle-like Blanchard Hall, completed in the last century, keeps watch over the community from atop the front campus hill; when couples get engaged, they climb to the top of the tower to share their news by ringing the bell. Nearby is the Billy Graham Center, which houses a museum and the college archives, making it a hub for research on American Evangelicalism. (The late evangelist was a Wheaton alumnus.) An $80 million science center provides 135,000 square feet of research, teaching, and exhibit space. A new Conservatory of Music building recently opened.

Sporting the largest endowment among the nation's Evangelical schools, Wheaton offers students a generous bevy of programs and facilities. General education requirements ("Christ at the Core") include a broad array of thematic coursework, as well as a first-year seminar, an advanced seminar, and a senior capstone experience. Business and economics is Wheaton's most popular major, followed by English, music, applied health science, and biology. Other signature programs include theater and digital media. Motivated students may opt for 3–2 programs that allow them to combine an undergraduate degree in the liberal arts with a master's in nursing or engineering, saving a year in the process. In the classroom, there's an emphasis on teamwork, and a biology major calls the atmosphere "serious but collaborative." The quality of teaching varies, but students get "the benefit of Christian professors who provide a stimulating intellectual experience in light of the Christian faith," according to one junior.

"Study abroad programs are quite common to the Wheaton experience."

Students have the opportunity to perform research at Argonne National Laboratory, just down the road, and for those seeking a truly global experience, there's study abroad in more than 30 countries; 42 percent of students partake. "Study abroad programs are quite common to the Wheaton experience," a student says, describing them as "superb and life-changing." Those concerned with social justice, a definite focus at Wheaton, may be interested in the Human Needs and Global Resources program, which sends students to Third World countries for six months of work on development projects such as building roads and schools. Summer study in several scientific fields is available at the Black Hills Science Station, while leadership training takes place at Honey Rock, Wheaton's campus in the Wisconsin North Woods. For incoming freshmen, the 18-day Wheaton Passage wilderness trek provides "an experience in team building, self-discovery, and physical challenge that should not be missed," says a sophomore; an urban experience is also available at Wheaton's urban studies facility in Chicago's Woodlawn neighborhood.

"The student body is extremely motivated and high-achieving," says one student. "They desire to encourage their peers to pursue excellence in their God-given gifts." Twenty-five percent of Wheaton students hail from Illinois, and 3 percent come from overseas. Nine percent are missionary and third-culture kids. African Americans comprise 3 percent of the student body, Hispanics make up 6 percent, Asian Americans add 9 percent, and multiracial students account for 4 percent. Current events and issues find their way into campus conversation. "The biggest social and political issues would probably be issues tied to faith or race," says one student. Wheaton's Community Covenant shuns "homosexual behavior and all other sexual relations outside the bounds of marriage between a man and woman"; thus, LGBTQ issues—and students—have been controversial on campus. There are no athletic scholarships, but merit awards averaging $7,400 are awarded to qualified students, and 22 percent of freshmen are eligible for the Pell Grant. Wheaton ranks first in the country in the proportion of Pell Grant recipients who succeed in paying back their student loans.

"[Students] desire to encourage their peers to pursue excellence in their God-given gifts."

(continued)

Applicants: 1,693
Accepted: 85%
Enrolled: 40%
Grad in 6 Years: 89%
Returning Freshmen: 93%
Academics: ✍ ✍ ✍
Social: ☎ ☎ ☎
Q of L: ★ ★ ★ ★
Admissions: (800) 222-2419
Email Address: admissions@ wheaton.edu

Strong Programs:
Business and Economics
English
Music
Applied Health Science
Biology
Theater
Digital Media

Wheaton sports the largest endowment among the nation's Evangelical schools.

Eighty-nine percent of Wheaton students live in campus housing, and well-kept accommodations range from single-sex dorms with traditional double rooms and bathrooms down the hall to college-owned houses and apartments. Opposite-sex visitation is limited to certain hours on certain days, though "each semester, dorms are allowed two 'raids' to their opposite floor," says an education major. Everyone eats in Anderson Commons, where one student says, "everything is made from scratch." Students report feeling safe on campus: "Campus security is excellent," says a business major. "They are a phone call away."

Since Wheaton lacks fraternities and sororities, and because students agree to abstain from alcohol, drugs, and tobacco, the social life revolves around other pursuits. "We have a lot of fun here, but all alcohol-free fun," says a psychology major. The College Union plans events like talent shows, roller disco, and an annual President's Ball. A junior says, "The town of Wheaton is a friendly suburb with nice restaurants and a good bike trail, but it's pretty much closed down by 9 p.m." A commuter train near campus whisks students to downtown Chicago in 45 minutes, where restaurants, blues clubs, theaters, museums, shopping, and professional sports are in abundance. Favorite traditions include Missions in Focus week, which brings missionary organizations and Christian speakers to campus, and the individual dorm floors' own traditions, one of which includes an annual root beer kegger.

Wheaton's athletic teams (the Thunder) compete in Division III, and men's and women's soccer, basketball, and swimming are particularly competitive, as are wrestling and women's track and field. Football, basketball, and soccer games "are always exciting and well attended," says one student, especially if the opponent is Augustana College. The debate and chess teams are competitive too. Thirty-eight percent of students play intramural and club sports. And while it's not an athletic competition per se, juniors and seniors do get excited about decorating "the Bench," a reinforced concrete slab that is the subject of an ongoing and often rough-and-tumble game of keep-away.

Wheaton College remains "committed to the principle that truth is revealed by God through Christ, in whom is hidden all the treasures of wisdom and knowledge." Students believe their school's dedication to Christianity only strengthens the bonds they develop with one another and their understanding of the broader world. "The Wheaton education is hard to duplicate," says one student. "Learning at Wheaton truly does prepare you for Christ and His kingdom."

Overlaps

Calvin, Taylor, Biola, Westmont, Hope, Gordon, Pepperdine, Baylor

If You Apply To ›

Wheaton (IL): Early action, regular decision. SATs or ACTs: required. No Subject Tests. Accepts the Common Application with supplement.

Wheaton College (MA)

Norton, MA 02766

Although its address says it's in Massachusetts, Wheaton is actually closer to Providence than to Boston. But getting to either by train is quick and easy. One of the few nationally known institutions in the area that is still relatively accessible. Curriculum includes interdisciplinary, hands-on, and project-based work in addition to traditional courses. Smaller than Skidmore, comparable to Connecticut College.

Wheaton College offers students plenty of opportunities to make their academic marks. Since 2000, more than 220 Wheaton students have received national fellowships, including three Rhodes scholars and four Marshall scholars. The college remains among the top 10 liberal arts colleges for Fulbright scholars as well. Increasingly focused on experiential learning, Wheaton makes sure its students shine outside the classroom too. Says one satisfied senior, "Wheaton's commitment to supporting its students to leverage their liberal arts education and change the world permeates all aspects of life on campus."

Wheaton's rural location offers few distractions from intellectual pursuits. Its 400-acre campus blends Georgian brick buildings and modern structures set among beautiful lawns and shade trees. The two halves of the campus (upper and lower) are separated by Peacock Pond, which probably qualifies as the only heated duck pond on any American campus.

Wheaton's curriculum shows students how to make linkages between disciplines. Rather than simply checking off required courses, all Wheaton students study across the major academic fields, developing a multidimensional view of the world. In practical terms, this means that every student must take a series of Connections courses on a single topic from various departments; recent Connections topics have included Black Aesthetics, Biopharma, and Gender. Core classes include English, quantitative skills, foreign language, natural science, and non-Western history. Students also choose a first-year seminar from among roughly 25 sections, each focused on "controversies" that have generated debate or heralded changes in how people experience or understand the world. The curriculum links experiential learning to each department and requires a capstone senior project.

> "Professors were very encouraging about my future and helped me access new opportunities."

Psychology, business and management, economics, biology, and political science are Wheaton's most popular majors. Programs in the arts are well recognized—impressive given the school's small size—and the chemistry department is also strong. Students interested in interdisciplinary study can choose majors like neuroscience or theater and English dramatic literature, or they may design their own majors. The major in Hispanic studies benefits from its affiliation with a study abroad program in Valencia. Dual-degree programs with Dartmouth, Emerson, and other institutions are available in engineering, business, communication, religion, and optometry. The Center for Global Education offers more than 95 approved study abroad programs in 45 countries around the world; 45 percent of students participate.

According to a psychology major, "Critical thinking, intensive writing, and collaborative projects are part of almost every class, which allows for in-depth exploration of concepts, themes, and lessons." About two-thirds of Wheaton's classes have fewer than 20 students. "Professors were very encouraging about my future and helped me access new opportunities," says a senior. Aside from a faculty advisor, students get a staff mentor and two peer advisors, known as preceptors. The Filene Center for Academic Advising and Career Services gets high marks from students seeking internships—and jobs after graduation. In fact, the center's Wheaton Edge program guarantees each student a $3,000 to $5,000 stipend to pursue unpaid internships, research opportunities, or service projects, ensuring that, in the words of one senior, "students never have to worry about choosing between a paycheck and a professional experience."

Thirty-seven percent of Wheaton's students come from Massachusetts, and 10 percent hail from foreign nations. The student body is largely white and affluent; "I was often the only student in my classes without a MacBook," observes a senior. African Americans account for 6 percent, Hispanics 8 percent, Asian Americans 5 percent, and multiracial students 3 percent. Students are said to be friendly and

Website: www.wheatoncollege.edu
Location: Suburban
Private
Total Enrollment: 1,674
Undergraduates: 1,674
Male/Female: 39/61
SAT Ranges: ERW 590–680, M 560–670
ACT Ranges: 26–30
Financial Aid: 98%
Pell Grant: 17%
Expense: Pr $ $ $
Student Loans: 65%
Average Debt: $ $ $ $
Applicants: 6,089
Accepted: 48%
Enrolled: 17%
Grad in 6 Years: 78%
Returning Freshmen: 88%
Academics: ✎ ✎ ✎
Social: ☎ ☎ ☎
Q of L: ★ ★ ★ ★
Admissions: (508) 286-8251
Email Address: admission@wheatoncollege.edu

Strong Programs:
Psychology
Business and Management
Economics
Biology
Political Science
Fine Arts
Chemistry
Neuroscience

Every student takes a series of Connections courses on a single topic, such as Black Aesthetics, Biopharma, and Gender.

open to differing views; politically, liberals and conservatives are both well represented on campus. "Wheaton's legacy as a former women's college means that people are very attuned to feminist and gender issues," explains a senior. "These are issues that students rally around." Merit awards averaging $20,000 are available, but there are no athletic awards.

As might be expected on this small, suburban campus, virtually everyone (96 percent) lives in one of Wheaton's dorms or theme houses. All students are guaranteed housing for four years; freshmen live in doubles, triples, or quads, and upperclassmen try their luck in the lottery system. "Housing is livable, but some of the facilities are getting old," says a sophomore. The recently renovated dining halls are bright and spacious, and the biggest winners of all are the ducks, which thrive on the leftover bread students toss into Peacock Pond. "There's a big push for local, fresh, and organic produce," says a junior. Students say they feel safe on campus and that security is visible and active. A senior notes, "Students are constantly collaborating with the administration to increase discussion, engagement, and education around the issue of sexual assault on campus."

> **"[With Wheaton Edge], students never have to worry about choosing between a paycheck and a professional experience."**

Social life at Wheaton includes dances, concerts, lectures, parties on campus, and other activities organized by the more than 100 student groups. Students unwind at the college's student center, which offers a café, dance studio, and sun deck for afternoon study breaks. There are no sororities or fraternities here. Students say that, as on most campuses, "drinking and partying does occur," but they appreciate the school's "Safety Always Matters Most" policy. Students love to put on their dancing shoes—whether for the Boston Bash party on a boat in Boston Harbor, for the Valentine's Dance, or for any number of events at Rosecliff, a mansion in Newport, Rhode Island. Spring Weekend features live bands, outdoor barbecues, and the Head of the Peacock race, where students build vessels (no boats allowed) and race them across the pond. When it rains, students get dirty as they slide around the craters on Wheaton's lawns, an activity known as "dimple diving."

For the Head of the Peacock race, students build vessels (no boats allowed) and race them across the pond.

The town of Norton, just outside campus, draws more than half of students with services opportunities, such as a Big Brother Big Sister program, hospital visits, and academic tutoring, but there's little to do otherwise, students say. "It's a very quiet town, and most students stay on campus rather than venture off into Norton," says a student. Relatively convenient access to two state capitals livens up the social scene. "We're 20 minutes from Providence and 40 minutes from Boston. If you can't find something to do on the weekend, you're just looking for something to complain about," a student says.

> **"People are very attuned to feminist and gender issues."**

The Wheaton Lyons compete in Division III. The Lyons nickname goes back to Wheaton's days as an all-female school, and it honors Mary Lyon, the 19th-century educational pioneer who established Wheaton's first curriculum and later founded Mount Holyoke. The strongest teams include men's and women's soccer and swimming and diving. Recent conference champs include baseball and synchronized swimming. The athletic facility boasts an eight-lane swimming pool, a field house, and an 850-seat arena for basketball or volleyball. Popular club and intramural sports include rugby, soccer, basketball, and flag football.

Students at Wheaton take an active role and are involved in campus planning and college operations, as well as in their community. "We don't just have coffee in the café," says a political science major. "We text with deans, have lunch with professors, coffee with advisors, a beer with our favorite professor. These kinds of

Overlaps

Bates, Connecticut College, Hobart and William Smith, Colby, Skidmore, Rhodes, UMass Amherst, Clark

relationships are the Wheaton way. They supplement the intellectual energy and debate that takes place among students." Indeed, students here take pride in their achievements inside and outside the classroom, while striving to preserve the school's friendly, small-town feel.

If You Apply To ›

Wheaton (MA): Early decision I and II, early action, regular decision. SATs or ACTs: optional. Subject Tests: optional. Accepts the Common Application with supplement. Application includes question on gender identity.

Whitman College

345 Boyer Avenue, Walla Walla, WA 99362

Whitman has quietly established itself as one of the West's leading liberal arts colleges. Don't bother with the umbrella: Walla Walla is in arid eastern Washington. Whitman's isolation breeds community spirit and alumni loyalty. True to its liberal arts heritage, Whitman has no business program. Combines outdoorsy camaraderie with the slower pace of life in the rural Northwest.

You don't have to own a Frisbee to succeed at Whitman, but if you've got one, bring it along—you'll find a campus full of friendly students eager to toss it back to you. Though it isn't well known outside the Pacific Northwest, Whitman offers a solid liberal arts education, along with plenty of fun for outdoorsy types. Students are down-to-earth and friendly and feel a deep loyalty to one another—and to their school.

Whitman was founded in 1882 and named in honor of Marcus and Narcissa Whitman, missionaries who ministered to the Cayuse Indians and settlers on the Oregon Trail. Even today, everything important is within walking distance of campus, including the main drag of Walla Walla, which once won a national Best Main Street award. The 117-acre campus, where colonial buildings and modern facilities sport New England ivy, sits at the foot of the Blue Mountains, surrounded by golden wheat fields and vineyards. Beyond Walla Walla (which means "many waters" in the Cayuse Indian language) are gorgeous mountains, rivers, and forests. A new residence hall housing 150 sophomores and a 500-seat dining hall opened in 2018.

All Whitman students complete the General Studies Program, which includes both a first-year core and distribution requirements in various disciplines. The first-year program revolves around a yearlong seminar called Encounters that emphasizes analytical reading of common texts—such as Plato's *Symposium*, Darwin's *On the Origin of Species*, and Toni Morrison's *Beloved*—as well as effective writing. Depending on their major, all seniors must either complete a written senior thesis and oral defense or pass comprehensive written and oral exams in their major; Whitman was the first U.S. college or university to require seniors to do so.

Biology, psychology, economics, environmental studies, English, and the interdisciplinary major in biochemistry, biophysics, and molecular biology are some of the best (and most popular) programs at Whitman; the school also boasts an astronomy program, unusual among small colleges. Whitman has an extensive Asian art collection, and additional coursework in Chinese language and Asian

> "Classes are generally difficult, but in a way that encourages cooperation among students."

Website: www.whitman.edu
Location: Small Town
Private
Total Enrollment: 1,455
Undergraduates: 1,455
Male/Female: 43/57
SAT Ranges: ERW 630–720, M 620–730
ACT Ranges: 26–31
Financial Aid: 79%
Pell Grant: 12%
Expense: Pr $ $ $
Student Loans: 46%
Average Debt: $
Applicants: 4,081
Accepted: 52%
Enrolled: 18%
Grad in 6 Years: 88%
Returning Freshmen: 94%
Academics: ✐ ✐ ✐ ✐
Social: ☎ ☎ ☎
Q of L: ★ ★ ★ ★
Admissions: (509) 527-5176
Email Address: admission@ whitman.edu

Strong Programs:
Biology
Psychology

studies is available through a summer program in China. Whitman has 3–2 programs in engineering, oceanography, forestry, and environmental management, offered in partnership with institutions like Caltech, Columbia, Duke, and the University of Washington.

Sixty-nine percent of classes have fewer than 20 students, fostering a collaborative atmosphere. "Classes are generally difficult, but in a way that encourages cooperation among students rather than a malicious competition where grades and rank are most important," says a sophomore. An environmental studies major reports, "Professors are extremely knowledgeable in their fields and are excited to get to know their students."

Forty-five percent of Whitman students study off campus, most packing their bags for the 88 semester- and yearlong programs that are offered in 44 countries. Short-term Crossroads courses, which are led by faculty during the summer, are another option, and financial aid packages can be applied to all approved programs. Students may also take urban studies terms within the U.S. in Philadelphia and Washington, D.C. "Semester in the West is the biggest up-and-coming program," explains a psychology major. "Students travel for one semester along the West Coast, learning from different professors in variable environments." During the day-long Whitman Undergraduate Conference, student scholarship and creativity are celebrated with presentations, posters, and performances. Highly competitive Whitman Internship Grants award $3,000 to selected students to pursue unpaid internships.

Highly competitive Whitman Internship Grants award $3,000 to selected students to pursue unpaid internships.

"No matter how different they may be, most Whitties seem to absolutely love the school," a junior says. "Students are very passionate about what they study, whether it's social justice or poetry." Thirty-two percent of students are from Washington State, and many of the rest hail from the suburbs of Western cities, notably San Francisco and Portland; 7 percent arrive from overseas. Five percent are Asian American, 7 percent are Hispanic, 2 percent are African American, and 7 percent are multiracial. The liberal-leaning student body is "most vocal about" increasing racial diversity, according to one student, but political issues don't generally dominate campus conversation. The Intercultural Center and Glover Alston Center help support diversity and intercultural awareness on campus. There are numerous merit scholarships averaging $11,300 but no athletic awards.

"Whitman security is available 24/7 to support students."

Sixty-four percent of students live in campus housing; freshmen and sophomores are required to do so. "Dorms are very comfortable, especially compared to dorms I have seen at other schools," says one student. Theme houses are available for students interested in foreign languages, fine arts, writing, community service, Asian studies, environmental studies, global awareness, and multiculturalism. "The food is very good, especially at the beginning of the semester, although it is hard not to get sick of it by the end," says a sophomore. A junior notes that "Whitman security is available 24/7 to support students," and measures like safety escorts, bystander intervention training, and "sober roamers" who watch over their classmates at registered on-campus parties help keep the campus community safe.

Hiking, biking, and backpacking are minutes away, and white-water rafting and rock climbing are popular on weekends.

The social life at Whitman revolves around fraternity parties—33 percent of the men and 41 percent of the women go Greek—and other on-campus activities, such as theatrical productions and events held by more than 80 student clubs. "Students at Whitman are very social," says one sophomore. "Most large parties take place either in one of the four fraternity houses or in off-campus houses. Smaller get-togethers and parties are also popular in personal rooms in the residence halls." Big annual events include the spring Renaissance Faire and the Whitsquatch music and art festival, featuring student bands and popular musicians. "Just before finals week in the spring, Whitman students let out some stress by running a naked mile around Ankeny Field at midnight," says a junior; some participants choose to pause every quarter mile to drink a beer.

The town of Walla Walla (population 33,000), located in an arid valley in the center of agricultural southeastern Washington, supports a symphony, community playhouse, art galleries, two rodeos, and a hot-air balloon festival, not to mention a state penitentiary. "Walla Walla is small, but full of culture," says one student. About 70 percent of students get involved in community service opportunities. Outdoor pursuits are important in this part of the country, where autumn is gorgeous, winter sporadically snowy, and spring delightfully warm. Hiking, biking, and backpacking are minutes away, and white-water rafting and rock climbing are popular on weekends. Two ski centers and other recreational areas are within an hour's drive, and Seattle (260 miles) and Portland (235 miles) offer a welcome change of scenery.

The Whitman Blues compete in Division III. Men's tennis has brought home 11 consecutive Northwest Conference championships. Men's and women's basketball are nationally competitive, and men's and women's swimming, women's tennis, and women's golf are solid too. Seventy percent of students play club and intramural sports. Club lacrosse and rugby tournaments draw crowds, as does "Onionfest," a regional ultimate Frisbee tournament. Rock climbers can challenge themselves at the world-class Climbing Center.

"If you're choosing a liberal arts school in the Northwest," says a student, "choose Whitman!" Indeed, students seeking a traditional liberal arts education with a strong sense of community and a healthy dose of outdoor fun would do well to heed this enthusiastic Whittie's advice.

Overlaps

Reed, Colorado College, Occidental, Kenyon, Carleton, Macalester, Lewis & Clark, University of Puget Sound

If You Apply To ›

Whitman: Early decision I and II, regular decision. SATs or ACTs: optional. Subject Tests: optional. Accepts the Common Application with supplement.

Whittier College

13406 East Philadelphia Street, Whittier, CA 90608

Whittier's Quaker heritage brings a touch of the East to suburban L.A. Less selective than Occidental and the Claremont Colleges, Whittier lures ethnically and socioeconomically diverse students with a bevy of academic scholarships and a welcoming community. Whittier's functional campus lacks the opulence of the Claremonts and the panache of Pepperdine. Check out the Whittier Scholars option.

Founded in 1887 by members of the Religious Society of Friends (Quakers), Whittier College is fast becoming a global training ground. Whittier students can be found all around the world, studying in dozens of foreign countries. And when they return to the Whittier campus, they have access to caring faculty and a close-knit environment with "open and friendly" peers, says one student.

Located just 18 miles away from downtown Los Angeles, the college is perched on a hill overlooking the town of Whittier, California, with the San Gabriel Mountains rising up from the horizon. The 73-acre campus is a pleasant mixture of modern buildings tucked between the red-roofed, white-walled Spanish traditionals. Its landmark building, Deihl Hall, includes a digital audio/video computer lab for

Website: www.whittier.edu
Location: Suburban
Private
Total Enrollment: 1,793
Undergraduates: 1,638
Male/Female: 43/57
SAT Ranges: ERW 510–620, M 500–600
ACT Ranges: 21–27

In the college's signature Whittier Scholars Program, students carve their majors out of standard offerings.

languages. A four-foot-high granite monument stands on the north campus lawn honoring Whittier's most famous alum, former president Richard Nixon. The state-of-the-art Science and Learning Center is the latest addition to campus.

Whittier offers its undergraduates two major curricular programs: the traditional Liberal Education Program and the Whittier Scholars Program. Most students take the first option, in which they fulfill distribution requirements that emphasize an interdisciplinary focus, cultural perspectives, and critical and quantitative thinking. They also choose a major from among 31 options, the strongest and most popular of which include business administration, psychology, political science, kinesiology, and English. Biology, child development, and theater are solid too.

The second curricular option, the Whittier Scholars Program, is the college's signature program and a path taken by 12 percent of the undergraduates. They are relieved of most general requirements and start from square one with an "educational design" process. With the help of an academic advisor, Whittier Scholars carve their majors out of standard offerings by taking a bit of this and a bit of that. Recent self-designed majors have included urban community studies, cultural nutrition, and business strategies in film production. The program is highly regarded because of the more active role it allows students to play and the freedom it affords them in pursuing their interests.

> **"[Students] are passionate about social justice and national politics."**

All students, no matter which curriculum they choose, must fulfill a yearlong freshman writing requirement, choosing their preferences from a variety of seminars. First-years also attend a series of speakers who discuss topics relevant to student coursework and take part in the Exploring Los Angeles series, which includes trips to museums and cultural events. Seniors complete a capstone requirement.

Whittier officially ended its affiliation with the Quakers in the 1940s, but the prevailing spirit of community hearkens back to their traditions. A biology major says, "Whittier provides a positive learning environment where students are actively encouraged to get involved." Fifty-eight percent of classes have fewer than 20 students, and freshmen are taught by full professors. "For the most part, the quality of the teaching has been very intense, but very rewarding," says a student. For those looking to add global scope to their college experience, as 45 percent of students do, semester-long and short-term study abroad options include destinations like Paris, Rome, Cape Town, and Beijing; many programs are faculty-led. What's more, every student who studies abroad in a Whittier-approved program receives an automatic Global Poet Scholarship worth $2,000.

"Students at Whittier are mostly liberal and are passionate about social justice and national politics," says a senior. Eighty-one percent of the undergraduates come from California, and the rest are from all over the U.S. and the world—3 percent are international. Half of the student body is Hispanic, while African American, Asian American, and multiracial students constitute 5, 7, and 7 percent, respectively. An on-campus cultural center focuses on diversity programming and resources. "Tolerance is a big watchword on campus," a junior says. "You can get severely disciplined or expelled for being intolerant." Thirty-eight percent of students receive Pell Grants. In addition to need-based aid, the college awards merit scholarships averaging $22,600.

Half of Whittier students seek off-campus housing, but the Turner Residence Hall entices many students to stay on campus and vie for a chance to get a room with a panoramic view of Los Angeles. "The first-year residence halls are older with limited air-conditioning," reports a history and music major. Most freshmen are assigned rooms, while Whittier Scholars, athletes, and members of Whittier's social societies tend to cluster in selected dorms and houses. Campus residents take their meals at the Campus Inn dining hall (known as the CI), where the food is said to be typical college fare. The Spot, Whittier's popular campus coffeehouse, includes a nightclub called—logically enough—the Club. "Whittier is a truly tight-knit community, so tight that it is very easy to spot someone who doesn't belong (which makes Whittier a little safer in this day of sporadic violence on college campuses)," explains a senior.

Nine social societies (they're not called fraternities or sororities here) attract 9 percent of the men and 14 percent of the women but hardly dominate the social scene. Their dances, however, which frequently feature live entertainment, are welcomed by all. Whittier has a fairly strict alcohol policy, students say. Popular annual events include the football game against archrival Occidental College (dubbed the Battle of the Shoes), the Whittfest concert in the spring, the Midnight Breakfast served by professors during second-semester finals, and Sportsfest, which is a campuswide competition in which dorms compete in a variety of athletic, intellectual, and wacky games and events. The most important campus landmark is the Rock, which sits near the front of campus and is given a fresh coat of paint by countless aspiring artists.

For many, a favored diversion is road tripping, everywhere from Disneyland to the California beaches. Other common destinations include Joshua Tree, San Diego, and Las Vegas. For nightlife closer to campus, Los Angeles looms large. The local community, known as Uptown Whittier, offers quaint shops, restaurants, a movie theater, and cobblestone sidewalks, and a senior calls it "a perfect place for a night on the town with friends." It's also a place for community-minded students to get involved. The Center for Engagement with Communities provides course-based service-learning internships and research; 25 percent of students participate.

Johnny Poet is Whittier's pen-wielding mascot (inspired by the school's namesake, Quaker poet John Greenleaf Whittier), and Division III men's lacrosse is the school's most successful team. Men's water polo, basketball, and cross-country and women's water polo, softball, and volleyball are also competitive. Intramurals and club sports are a big draw too, especially the rugby, martial arts, and equestrian clubs.

The students at Whittier have created a supportive, intimate environment where people work together and celebrate their diversity. And with the opportunity to design their own majors, students here are active in their own education but get plenty of support along the way. Says a sophomore, "I have no doubt that I have faculty, staff, and administrators advocating for me and cheering me on toward my personal goals."

Every student who studies abroad in a Whittier-approved program receives an automatic Global Poet Scholarship worth $2,000.

"I have no doubt that I have faculty, staff, and administrators advocating for me and cheering me on."

Overlaps

University of Redlands, Chapman, University of La Verne, California Lutheran, Cal Poly Pomona, California State University–Fullerton, UCLA, UC Riverside

If You Apply To ›

Whittier: Early action, rolling admissions. SATs or ACTs: optional (required for applicants with GPA below 3.0). No Subject Tests. Accepts the Common Application.

Willamette University

900 State Street, Salem, OR 97301

Willamette is strategically located next door to the Oregon state capitol and 40 minutes from Portland. Bigger than Whitman, smaller than U of Puget Sound, and more civic-minded than Lewis & Clark, Willamette offers extensive study abroad enhanced by ties to Asia. Well-known in the West but has yet to develop a national reputation to equal that of competitors such as Lewis & Clark.

Website: www.willamette.edu
Location: Small City
Private
Total Enrollment: 2,240
Undergraduates: 1,752
Male/Female: 42/58
SAT Ranges: ERW 570–680,
  M 550–660
ACT Ranges: 26–31
Financial Aid: 99%
Pell Grant: 25%
Expense: Pr $ $ $
Student Loans: 65%
Average Debt: $ $ $
Applicants: 4,484
Accepted: 89%
Enrolled: 10%
Grad in 6 Years: 73%
Returning Freshmen: 86%
Academics: ✑ ✑ ✑ ½
Social: ☎ ☎ ☎
Q of L: ★ ★ ★ ★
Admissions: (844) BEARCAT
Email Address: bearcat@
  willamette.edu

Strong Programs:
Biology
Economics
Politics
Psychology
Theatre
Chemistry
Japanese Studies
History

Willamette University, founded in 1842, was the first university in the West. Students can take advantage of their proximity to the state's executive and legislative offices as well as a nearby hospital for internships, jobs, or off-campus learning experiences. A comprehensive study abroad program carries students to destinations around the globe. On campus, students find a more personal atmosphere than larger universities nearby and appreciate the low-key yet challenging academic milieu. One satisfied chemistry major says, "This is the place where you can grow as a student, leader, and person as you pursue your passions."

The 61-acre campus is home to abundant trees (thanks to Oregon's frequent rain), small wildlife, and occasionally steelhead salmon that splash around in Mill Stream, which runs between WU's redbrick academic buildings. Zena Forest is a 300-acre outdoor laboratory about a ten-minute drive from campus that hosts regular student and faculty research in biology, sustainability, art, and other fields. The university's LEED Gold–certified Ford Hall features large, collaborative learning spaces and faculty offices. The Sparks Fitness Center and two residence halls were recently remodeled.

All students at Willamette (pronounced "Will-AM-it") complete the freshman College Colloquium seminar, study in a language other than English, and do coursework in six modes of inquiry—the natural world; the arts; arguments, reasons, and values; thinking historically; interpreting texts; and understanding society. Students also take capstone senior seminars, often culminating in research or thesis projects. The most popular majors are biology, economics, politics, and psychology. Other particularly strong programs include theatre, chemistry, Japanese studies, and history. The management and law schools offer 3–2 (B.A./M.B.A.) and 3–3 (B.A./J.D.) programs that integrate the liberal arts and professional education. New minors have been added in management and sustainability.

> **"Tutors are available in every subject, for free, and there is a writing center."**

Academics are rigorous, but students don't compete for grades. "Students are expected to work hard, read copious amounts, and actively contribute in class," says a senior. "That being said, the climate is very collaborative." Classes are small; 65 percent have fewer than 20 students on the roster. "Professors are committed to their students as their first priority," says a math major. And for those seeking additional support, "Tutors are available in every subject, for free, and there is a writing center within which students can arrange appointments for help with papers or academic projects," reports a senior.

When students aren't reading or writing papers, numerous undergraduate research opportunities beckon. Support has more than doubled with the creation of the Carson Undergraduate Research Awards, the Science Collaborative Research Program, and a humanities center. Half of the student body participates in a robust study abroad program that sends them to nearly 40 nations, and Willamette also benefits from its colocation with the U.S. campus of Tokyo International University.

"Willamette students are positive, motivated, smart individuals," says a senior. "They want to give back, but also achieve highly." Twenty-two percent of WU students are native Oregonians, and much of the remainder comes from Western states, notably California and Washington; 2 percent are international. African Americans make up 2 percent of the student body, Hispanics 13 percent, Asian Americans 9 percent, and multiracial students another 9 percent. Social justice issues spark discussion on campus, and the Student Center for Equity and Empowerment supports students from underrepresented groups. Says a sophomore, "Willamette tends to be very involved in state and city political issues." Willamette offers talent and academic merit scholarships each year averaging $21,400; there are no athletic awards. One-quarter of incoming students receive Pell Grants.

Japanese studies is strong, and Willamette benefits from its colocation with the U.S. campus of Tokyo International University.

Sixty-two percent of Willamette students live in campus housing, which is social and convenient to classes and parties. "Willamette's dorms are not remarkable, but they provide incredible experiences for fostering community," says a student. Students may move off campus starting junior year, and "living in Salem is quite cheap," says an upperclassman. The student-owned and operated Bistro offers a coffeehouse atmosphere and is a popular alternative to cafeteria fare. "All of the food is fresh, local, and made on campus by staff that students grow to know personally," explains a senior. Students report that the university has taken a strong stance on responding to and educating the community about sexual assault. One survivor says, "Willamette has hired a number of staff to investigate and build support structures for survivors, and they have generally done a good job of doing so. I was sexually assaulted my freshman year and I feel safe on campus."

"Willamette tends to be very involved in state and city political issues."

Social life tends to center on campus, whether it's free movies and lectures, open-mic nights at the Bistro, dance parties (salsa or swing), or performances by the music and theatre departments. Twenty-four percent of Willamette men and 18 percent of the women go Greek, but students say that Greeks don't dominate the social scene. When it comes to drinking, "Parties happen, but [students] are remarkably well behaved," a student says. The Ram Brewery draws big crowds on Thursdays. Annual social highlights include the spring Wulapalooza festival, celebrating Earth Day, art, and music (and boasting the slogan "It's actually pretty good!"), and the Hawaiian Club Luau, where students chow down on spit-roasted pig. According to a politics major, "Willamette has started a new tradition of breaking a world record every other year. Thus far, both world records have been for the largest game of Red Light/Green Light."

The spring Wulapalooza festival celebrates Earth Day, art, and music (and boasts the slogan "It's actually pretty good!").

Downtown Salem is a short walk from campus, and while students say it's no college town, it does have movies, shopping, restaurants, and coffeehouses. Also nearby are the Cascade Mountains and beaches of Newport and Lincoln City (an hour's drive), skiing and snowboarding on Mount Hood or in the high desert town of Bend (three hours), and the cosmopolitan cities of Portland (40 minutes) and Seattle (about four hours north). Willamette students remain true to the school motto, "Not unto ourselves alone are we born," when they go "Into the Streets" for a day of service each fall.

The Willamette Bearcats compete in Division III, and track and field and baseball are strong. The men's and women's cross-country teams have won numerous West Region Championships in recent years. The annual football game against Pacific Lutheran usually has conference championship implications, and games against Linfield are also well attended. About 30 percent of Willamette students compete in numerous intramural and club sports.

Willamette may be the best little school you've never heard of, at least if you're from outside the California-Oregon-Washington corridor. "Willamette is

Overlaps

Lewis & Clark, University of Puget Sound, Whitman, Reed, University of Portland, UC Davis, UC Berkeley, UC Santa Cruz

unabashedly itself," says one student. "Community members from all backgrounds feel very comfortable being themselves and embracing who they are." The school's close-knit community is strengthened by its emphasis on service and by warm, supportive faculty members who push students to achieve.

If You Apply To ›

Willamette: Early decision, early action, regular decision. SATs or ACTs: optional (test-optional applicants must submit a supplemental essay). No Subject Tests. Accepts the Common Application. Applicants have the option of providing information about their gender and sexual identity.

College of William and Mary

P.O. Box 8795, Williamsburg, VA 23187

Founded in 1693 as a private university, William and Mary is the original public Ivy. History, government, and international relations are among the strongest departments. With 6,200 undergraduates, larger than Mary Washington and Richmond, and smaller but more intellectual than the University of Virginia. Williamsburg is more exciting for tourists than for college students.

Website: www.wm.edu
Location: Small Town
Public
Total Enrollment: 7,958
Undergraduates: 6,192
Male/Female: 42/58
SAT Ranges: ERW 660–740, M 640–740
ACT Ranges: 29–33
Financial Aid: 60%
Pell Grant: 13%
Expense: Pub $ $ $ $
Student Loans: 36%
Average Debt: $ $
Applicants: 14,921
Accepted: 36%
Enrolled: 29%
Grad in 6 Years: 91%
Returning Freshmen: 95%
Academics: ✍ ✍ ✍ ✍ ✍
Social: ☎ ☎ ☎
Q of L: ★ ★ ★
Admissions: (757) 221-4223
Email Address: admission@wm.edu

Strong Programs:
History

Traditions abound at the College of William and Mary, yet this historic university—the second oldest in the nation after Harvard—continues to evolve in its pursuit of academic excellence. "Students at William and Mary choose to attend the college for its intense academic rigor, strong sense of community, rich history, and legacy of traditions," says one senior. It has graduated three former U.S. presidents—Thomas Jefferson, James Monroe, and John Tyler. Rival UVA prides itself on being "Mr. Jefferson's" university, but W&M is quick to remind the Cavaliers that it educated Mr. Jefferson in the first place.

A profusion of azaleas and crape myrtle adds splashes of color to William and Mary's finely manicured campus, located about 150 miles southeast of Washington, D.C. The campus is divided into three sections and includes Lake Matoaka, the oldest human-made lake in Virginia, and a wooded wildlife preserve, which is filled with trails and widely used by the science departments. The Ancient Campus is a grouping of three colonial structures—including the Wren Building, which was constructed between 1695 and 1700 and is the country's oldest college building, and arguably one of the most beautiful—still in use. The Old Campus buildings date from the '20s and '30s, and New Campus, where ground was first broken in the '60s, features a recreation center, the 95,000-square-foot Sadler Center, and the Integrated Science Center. The W&M campus boasts one of the most romantic spots of any in the nation: Crim Dell, a wooded area with a small pond spanned by an old-style wooden bridge.

> "Professors at William and Mary are…mentors, career advisors, and lifelong friends to their students."

William and Mary, which was founded as a private college and did not go public until 1906, created Phi Beta Kappa in December of 1776. The honor code, established by Thomas Jefferson in 1779, demands much from the college's students. W&M's College Curriculum includes two first-year seminars: one "big ideas" course and one reading- and writing-intensive course, both of which are offered in every academic discipline. Students must also take coursework in a range of liberal arts areas, with a particular emphasis on interdisciplinary perspectives, as well as fulfill requirements in global perspectives and foreign language proficiency. All seniors complete a capstone project. The Charles Center for Academic Excellence facilitates honors programs, research opportunities, and interdisciplinary majors like American studies, environmental science, and women's studies.

Fittingly, the history department, which cosponsors the Omohundro Institute for Early American History and Culture with Colonial Williamsburg, is a signature program at William and Mary. Government, kinesiology and health sciences, biology, psychology, and business-related majors are among the most popular, and economics and international relations are well regarded. The accounting program ranks in the top 20 nationwide. A 3–2 engineering program with Columbia University is available, as is a joint degree program with the University of St Andrews in Scotland—one of the few international undergraduate joint degrees available in the U.S. Although academics are rigorous, students agree that the emphasis is on collaboration. They also complain, however, of a "stress culture," in which, a senior explains, "Students will try to one-up each other with their stress levels, lack of sleep, or amount of work left to do." Nearly half of all classes have fewer than 20 students, although a few introductory lectures may have a couple hundred. Teaching assistants are used for grading or lab purposes only. Says a marketing and sociology major, "Professors at William and Mary are not just teachers; they are mentors, career advisors, and lifelong friends to their students."

"Don't come to William and Mary if you're looking for a party school!"

William and Mary is the second oldest university in the nation after Harvard.

W&M offers summer and yearlong study abroad programs around the globe, including 50 faculty-designed programs and hundreds of other exchange and affiliate options. Half of W&M's undergrads receive credit for studying abroad. The top 10 percent of freshmen are designated Monroe scholars and receive summer research stipends to support independent projects, typically used after their sophomore or junior year. Eighty-five percent of students participate in some sort of faculty-mentored research experience. Students cheer the Cohen Career Center, especially its My Active Career Exploration program, which helps freshmen and sophomores identify and pursue career interests.

"William and Mary has three centuries' worth of traditions, legends, and mysteries."

At W&M, "Students are smart, driven, and stressed, but incredibly kind, friendly, and helpful," says a chemistry major, and a public policy major adds that they are "very invested in what they do." Because William and Mary is a state-supported university, 65 percent of its undergraduates are Virginians, hailing largely from wealthier counties in the northern part of the state. Eighty-one percent of freshmen ranked in the top 10th of their high school class, so competition for the nonresident spots—mostly taken by students from the Mid-Atlantic and farther north—is stiff. Six percent of undergrads are international. The college has made a major effort to recruit and retain more minorities; Asian Americans now account for 8 percent of the students, Hispanics 9 percent, African Americans 7 percent, and multiracial students 5 percent. Still, racial and socioeconomic diversity and equity are hot-button topics on this left-leaning campus. Merit scholarships averaging $6,100 are doled out to qualified undergrads, and W&M has its share of eagerly recruited athletes—more than 200 athletic scholarships are offered annually.

The history department cosponsors the Omohundro Institute for Early American History and Culture with Colonial Williamsburg.

Seventy-two percent of the undergraduates live on campus in mostly co-ed dorms that range from stately old halls with high ceilings to modern buildings equipped with air-conditioning. Students are guaranteed housing through their junior year, and a senior says, "Getting a room is very simple, just competitive for the newer buildings." Special-interest housing is available—there are eight language houses, in addition to Africana House, Colonial Williamsburg House, Mosaic House, and others—and life in a fraternity or sorority house is also an option. All freshmen must purchase a meal plan; most students give the three campus cafeterias less-than-stellar reviews. Crime in the surrounding town is not a big concern, and a senior comments that the school "continues to maintain sound safety practices" aimed at preventing campus sexual assault.

On campus, students can enjoy the soothing voices of one of the many a cappella groups, dance the night away at fraternity parties, grab a midnight snack at the Sadler Center, or watch the latest dance or theater performance at Phi Beta Kappa Theater. Twenty-seven percent of the men and 31 percent of the women join Greek organizations, which host most of the on-campus parties. Students also frequent off-campus house parties and the local bars, but a senior warns, "Don't come to William and Mary if you're looking for a party school!" The college has strict policies against underage drinking, but students say as long as they behave safely, they stay out of trouble.

"William and Mary has three centuries' worth of traditions, legends, and mysteries," says one student. Indeed, traditions are the stuff of which William and Mary

> "Eventually, you don't raise an eyebrow when Colonial reenactors are behind you at the grocery store buying beer."

is made, and perhaps the most cherished is the annual Yule Log Ceremony in the Wren Building, where students sing carols and hear the president, dressed in a Santa Claus outfit, read the Dr. Seuss story *How the Grinch Stole Christmas*. On Charter Day, bells chime and students celebrate the distinguished history of their 326-year-old institution. Each year, freshmen walk through the Wren Building for Opening Convocation, where they're greeted by cheering upperclassmen and faculty. Four years later, as they graduate, they walk through the Wren in the other direction. Romantics will be happy to learn that any couple who kisses at the top of Crim Dell Bridge will eventually be married. Multiple secret societies are known to exist; their activities are, understandably, not well documented but generally philanthropic in nature.

Anyone who gets restless can always step across the street to Colonial Williamsburg to picnic in the restored area, walk or jog down Duke of Gloucester Street (a.k.a. "Dog Street"), or study in one of the beautiful gardens. "Eventually, you don't raise an eyebrow when Colonial reenactors are behind you at the grocery store buying beer," quips one senior. Its appeal to tourists notwithstanding, Williamsburg leaves much to be desired as a college town. Nightlife is a hit-or-miss affair (mostly miss), although volunteer opportunities abound and a majority of students participate. Richmond and Norfolk, each an hour's drive, are top road trips; the University of Virginia, although an archrival, is also popular. Virginia Beach, a favorite springtime mecca, is a little farther away.

Each year, more than 500 Tribe athletes compete on 23 Division I teams. Recent conference champs include men's and women's cross-country, swimming, and gymnastics, as well as men's soccer and women's tennis. Intramurals and 45 club sports, such as softball and ultimate Frisbee, attract a large percentage of the student body. The $17 million McLeod Tyler Wellness Center opened in 2018, housing health, counseling, recreation, and other wellness services designed, in part, to combat the stress culture on campus.

From Thomas Jefferson to Jon Stewart, William and Mary has educated some of the nation's most famous and colorful. William and Mary's traditions stretch back to the dawn of this nation, and its grand old campus and stirring history make it a distinguished and cherished part of many students' lives. "I chose W&M for the close-knit community," says one junior. "'One tribe, one family' is not just a saying; it is truly something that can be felt the minute you step onto campus."

Overlaps

University of Virginia, Virginia Tech, UNC at Chapel Hill, Georgetown, Boston College, Notre Dame, WashU in St. Louis, University of Pennsylvania

Williams College

Williamstown, MA 01267

Running neck and neck with Amherst on the selectivity chart, Williams occupies a campus of surpassing beauty in the foothills of the Berkshires. Has shaken the preppy image but still attracts plenty of well-toned, all-around jock-intellectuals who will one day be corporate CEOs. The splendid isolation of Williamstown is either a blessing or a curse.

Williams College vies with rival Amherst for possession of both the color purple—they each use it on team uniforms and in their logos—and the title of most selective liberal arts college in the United States. Nestled in a small hamlet in the Berkshires, Williams is the more isolated of the two, but students say that makes for a more intimate sense of community. "I wanted an environment where I could share ideas and debate with my friends over a meal or a late-night snack, and I've certainly found that at Williams," says a freshman. School spirit abounds, and when not gazing at the purple mountains' majesty, students at Williams are digging into their studies with fervor.

The college's buildings constitute a veritable *omnium-gatherum* of architectural styles, from the elegantly simple Federal design of the original West College to contemporary structures by Charles Moore and William Rawn. The brick and gray stone buildings are arranged in loosely organized quads, which are both enclosed and open to nature. Recent additions include Horn Hall, a 60-bed residence hall, and the new Williams Bookstore.

The Williams curriculum emphasizes interdisciplinary studies and personalized teaching. Distribution requirements include at least three courses in each of the school's three divisions: languages and arts, social studies, and sciences and mathematics. Students must also fulfill requirements in writing and in quantitative and formal reasoning, pick a major from 35 options, pass four quarters of phys ed, spend at least six semesters in residence, and complete four study projects or courses during the January Winter Study.

One of Williams's greatest strengths is in art, which benefits from WCMA (the Williams College Museum of Art—one of the finest college art museums in America), the Clark Art Institute, and MASS MoCA, a nearby center for contemporary visual, performing, and media arts. Popular majors include economics, mathematics, English, psychology, biology, and history. Students in the environmental science program can perform fieldwork in the 2,600-acre, college-owned Hopkins Forest. If the walls of campus threaten to close in, especially during the bitter and blustery winter, students take a term away in more than 250 programs, including relatively inexpensive, faculty-led study tours. There is also an innovative yearlong program organized with Oxford's Exeter College in England. Forty-three percent of students study abroad. Williams turns out more Fulbright winners than any other baccalaureate college.

There are only two small graduate programs at Williams—in art history and development economics—so graduate students are few and far between, and you'll

Website: www.williams.edu
Location: Small Town
Private
Total Enrollment: 2,072
Undergraduates: 2,018
Male/Female: 53/47
SAT Ranges: ERW 710–780, M 690–790
ACT Ranges: 31–35
Financial Aid: 51%
Pell Grant: 22%
Expense: Pr $ $ $ $
Student Loans: 35%
Average Debt: $
Applicants: 8,593
Accepted: 15%
Enrolled: 44%
Grad in 6 Years: 94%
Returning Freshmen: 98%
Academics: ✍ ✍ ✍ ✍ ✍
Social: ☎ ☎ ☎
Q of L: ★ ★ ★ ★
Admissions: (413) 597-2211
Email Address: admission@williams.edu

Strong Programs:
Economics
Mathematics
English
Psychology
Biology
History
Art History
Studio Art

never find them at the lectern. About half of Williams students sign up for courses taught in the Oxford tutorial format: two students and a faculty member meet each week, with the students alternating who has to do independent work, like an essay, lab report, or art piece, and who gets to critique it. "Tutorials are basically all critical engagement all the time," explains a political science major, because students learn to communicate, collaborate, and defend their ideas. And while academics at Williams are rigorous, the environment is supportive. "Professors insist on having a personal connection with the students and always help if needed," a student explains. The college provides a stipend for academic advisors to take their charges out for a bite to eat, and a senior says alumni "go out of their way to help Williams students succeed" by setting them up with internships and other opportunities.

About half of Williams students sign up for courses taught in the Oxford tutorial format.

Students at Williams are accomplished: 88 percent graduated in the top 10th of their high school class. One student says, "I know people who can read Harry Potter in Latin, translate rap songs into Arabic, and sight-read 'Rocket Man' perfectly on the piano." Just 14 percent of students are in-staters and another 8 percent are international. African Americans make up 8 percent of the student body, while Asian Americans and Hispanics each add 13 percent and multiracial students comprise 6 percent. Politically, Williams leans left, and students say there is a small but dedicated group of student activists on campus. Many students come from affluent backgrounds, which according to a junior lends a certain "New England boarding school" vibe to campus, but Williams has a need-blind admissions process, and a respectable 22 percent of freshmen are eligible for the Pell Grant. While there are no merit or athletic scholarships, Williams guarantees to meet the full demonstrated financial need of all admitted students.

"[Williams is] an environment where I [can] share ideas and debate with my friends over a meal."

Ninety-three percent of students live on campus; housing is guaranteed for four years and only seniors are eligible to move out. "You can't go wrong with any housing here," says a student. First-years live in groups of 40 to 50 students each (known as "entries") along with three or four junior advisors, who serve as big siblings, mentors, and sounding boards. Some freshmen luck into large single rooms. After the first year, students have an affiliation with one of four upperclassmen residential neighborhoods and enter their housing draw. Campus dining offers three dining halls with friendly staff and satisfying meals, and small co-ops are available for seniors who want to cook for themselves. "Multiple student groups host events throughout the year to keep up the conversation surrounding the prevention of sexual assault," says a student.

The most beloved tradition is Mountain Day, when students picnic on the campus's main lawn, then choose from a variety of hikes.

Fraternities and sororities were abolished long ago, but that hasn't stopped Williams students from partying. "Since the college is so community-driven and inclusive, parties are often open to anyone who wishes to attend," says a senior. Drinking is a popular pastime on weekends, but most students report no pressure to imbibe. The college has taken steps to make sure that whatever drinking does go on happens safely, such as outlawing drinking games, requiring registration of parties over a certain size, and mandating availability of food and nonalcoholic beverages whenever alcohol is present. Other events like guest speakers, comedians, and concerts keep students busy too, and favorite traditions include homecoming, Winter Carnival, and Spring Fling. The most beloved tradition is Mountain Day, held on a Friday in October. Which day it will be is a well-kept secret, broken only when the college president sends out an email canceling classes, and church bells begin tolling at 8 a.m. Students picnic on the campus's main lawn, then choose from a variety of hikes, including one to the top of Mount Greylock, where hot cider and donuts are waiting on the summit.

"Tutorials are basically all critical engagement all the time."

The small village of Williamstown, adjacent to campus, is "sort of the quintessential New England town," says a student. The Log is a popular hangout for pizza and live performances, and students frequent a few cafés and an independent movie theater, but the town isn't exactly a hot spot for social life. The Clark Art Institute, within walking distance of campus, possesses one of the finest collections of Renoir and Degas in the nation, as well as a great library. The college theater is home to the Williamstown Theatre Festival in the summer, which often features Broadway stars. Nearby slopes and trails beckon, offering skiing, cycling, and backpacking. Civilization—in the form of Albany, New York—is just an hour's drive. Other popular destinations include New York City and Boston (both accessible by train from Albany, or three hours by car).

With 30 varsity teams and an active intramural program, sports are more like an established religion here than an extracurricular activity. The Ephs (short for Ephraim Williams, the school's founder) are a perennial winner of the Division III Directors' Cup, awarded annually to the school with the strongest overall athletic program. Williams competes against Amherst and Wesleyan in the "Little Three," and any

The Ephs are a perennial winner of the Division III Directors' Cup.

"I know people who can read Harry Potter in Latin [and] translate rap songs into Arabic."

contest with archrival Amherst ensures an especially large crowd. After all, Amherst was founded in 1821 by a breakaway group of Williams students, along with the school's then-president. Women's tennis, soccer, cross-country, and golf have all won national championships in the last few years, and the men's and women's swim teams are nationally ranked. The squash and ski teams compete in Division I.

It takes a special kind of student to be happy at Williams. Those who delight in the life of the mind and don't mind trading the creature comforts found at more urban schools for a small, intimate community will no doubt bleed purple by the time they leave. Says a senior, "I've never been more engaged in what I'm learning than here at Williams."

Overlaps

Amherst, Brown, Dartmouth, Harvard, Yale, Middlebury, Princeton, Stanford

If You Apply To ›

Williams: Early decision, regular decision. SATs or ACTs: required. Subject Tests: optional. Accepts the Common Application with supplement.

University of Wisconsin–Madison

BEST BUY

702 W. Johnson Street, Suite 1101, Madison, WI 53715

Madison draws a third of its students from out of state, a higher proportion than some other leading Midwestern public universities. Why brave the cold? Reasons include top programs in an array of professional fields and several innovative living/ learning programs. There's also the pleasure of life in Madison, a combination state capital/college town in the mold of Austin, Texas. Sky-high retention rates.

For more than a century, the University of Wisconsin has been guided by the Progressive-era philosophy of the "Wisconsin Idea" that the purpose of a great state university is to seek truth and apply the resulting knowledge to the benefit of the students and society as a whole. Such a philosophy has turned Wisconsin into one of the world's leading universities—one where nearly 30,000 undergraduates take advantage of high-level academics and a rich array of resources. After five years of

Website: www.wisc.edu
Location: City Center
Public
Total Enrollment: 38,146
Undergraduates: 28,559

(continued)

Male/Female: 48/52
SAT Ranges: ERW 620–690,
 M 660–760
ACT Ranges: 27–31
Financial Aid: 60%
Pell Grant: 12%
Expense: Pub $ $
Student Loans: 45%
Average Debt: $ $
Applicants: 35,615
Accepted: 54%
Enrolled: 35%
Grad in 6 Years: 87%
Returning Freshmen: 95%
Academics: ✍ ✍ ✍ ✍ ½
Social: ☎ ☎ ☎ ☎
Q of L: ★ ★ ★ ★
Admissions: (608) 262-3961
Email Address: onwisconsin@
 admissions.wisc.edu

Strong Programs:
Economics
Biology
Computer Science
Psychology
Education
Agriculture
Communication
Business

Seventy academic programs at Madison are considered in the top 10 nationally.

deep budget cuts enacted by the former governor and other state leaders with little sympathy for the Wisconsin Idea, state funding is back on the rise, and Wisconsin remains a place where professional and other programs are outstanding. Just bring a strong desire to learn—and a very warm coat.

Described by one Madison student as "architecturally olden with a modern touch," the mainly brick campus is distinctive. It spreads out over 936 hilly, tree-covered acres and across an isthmus between two glacial lakes, Mendota and Monona, named by Native Americans who once lived along their shores. From atop Bascom Hill, the center of campus, you look east past the statue of Lincoln and the liberal arts buildings, down to a library mall that was the scene of many a political demonstration during the '60s. Farther east you see rows of State Street pubs and restaurants and the bleached dome of the Wisconsin state capitol. On the other side of the hill, another part of campus, dedicated to the agricultural and health sciences, twists along Lake Mendota. But students from both sides of the hill congregate in the old student union, Memorial Union, where political arguments and backgammon games can rage all night. Outside on the union's veranda, students can look out at the sailboats in summer or iceboats in winter.

Distribution requirements vary among the different schools and academic departments, but they are uniformly rigorous, with science and math courses required for B.A. students, and a foreign language for virtually everyone. All students must fulfill a three-part graduation requirement in quantitative reasoning, communication, and ethnic studies. Students who prefer the academic road less traveled can opt for the Integrated Liberal Studies certificate program, which allows them to fulfill several gen eds with a series of related, interdisciplinary courses, rather than taking electives at random.

> "It's easy to get lost in the crowd here, so you have to be fairly strong and confident."

Madison's academic climate is demanding. "There are a lot of smart people studying here," notes one student. A list of first-rate academic programs at Madison would constitute a college catalog elsewhere. There are 70 programs considered in the top 10 nationally. Some highlights include education, agriculture, communication, biological sciences, and social sciences. The most popular majors are economics, biology, computer science, and psychology. Due to overcrowding, some popular fields, such as business and engineering, have more selective admissions criteria than others. Although many classes are large, 43 percent have fewer than 20 students. Professors at Madison are certainly among the nation's best, with National Academy of Science members and Guggenheim fellows scattered liberally among the departments.

While the university's size can be daunting, harried freshmen aren't left to fend for themselves. The university offers a number of first-year programs designed to ease the transition into college life. A first-year seminar encourages students to examine learning strategies; connect with faculty, staff, and peers; and become familiar with campus resources. First-Year Interest Groups (FIGs) consist of 20 first-year students who may live in the same residence hall or "residential neighborhood" and who also enroll in a cluster of three classes together. Each FIG cluster of courses has a central theme; the central or "synthesizing" course integrates content from the other two classes. After freshman year, many students participate in internships, and 27 percent choose to study abroad in programs all over the world, including France, Brazil, India, Israel, and Thailand. Thirty-eight percent conduct undergraduate research.

If there is a common characteristic among Madison undergraduates, it is assertiveness. "It's easy to get lost in the crowd here, so you have to be fairly strong and confident," declares one student. "No one holds your hand." The flip side is that "anyone can fit in, you just have to find your own niche." Sixty-six percent of undergraduates are from Wisconsin, and 9 percent are international. The school is a heartland of progressive politics, and Madison's reputation as a haven for liberals remains intact. "Students here are called liberal because they are eager and willing to change and are continually looking for newer and better ideas," explains one activist. Asian Americans make up 6 percent of the student body, Hispanics 5 percent, African Americans 2 percent, and multiracial students 3 percent. Academic merit scholarships averaging $5,300 are awarded each year, along with more than 350 athletic scholarships.

First-Year Interest Groups consist of 20 first-year students who enroll in a cluster of three classes with a central theme.

Twenty-five percent of undergrads, mostly freshmen, reside in university housing. Dorms are either co-ed or single sex and come equipped with laundry facilities, game rooms, and lounges. Most also have a cafeteria. The student union offers two meal plans, and there are plenty of restaurants and fast-food places nearby. Escort services for those walking and those needing a ride help keep students safe on campus. A variety of programs and groups, such as U Got This! and We're Better Than That, are working to educate the community on preventing sexual assault and supporting survivors.

One old standby for social life that is still as popular as ever is the student union, which hosts bands, shows, and so forth and provides a great atmosphere in which to hang out. There are more film clubs than anyone can follow, and everyone has a favorite bar. Nine percent of the men and 8 percent of the women go Greek. "Frat parties are a very popular break from the bar scene," quips one expert on both options. Madison (a.k.a. Madtown) is an excellent college town and has been the stomping ground for many fine rock 'n' roll and blues bands on the road to fame. Volunteering is a tradition here; the university consistently tops the list for providing the Peace Corps with the most entrants of any college or university in the nation. Nature enthusiasts can lose themselves in the university's 12,000-acre nature preserve or hit nearby ski slopes.

> "[UW–Madison is] diverse, intellectual, fashionable, and moderately hedonistic."

The students at this Big Ten school show "tons of interest" in sports, especially hockey and football, and especially when the Badgers try to rout the University of Michigan's Wolverines. The Badgers have produced a number of Big Ten champions, most notably men's cross-country, men's and women's soccer, and women's ice hockey. Bucky Badger apparel, emblazoned with slogans ranging from the urbane to the decidedly uncouth, is ubiquitous. However, the much-acclaimed marching band may outdo all the teams in popularity. Recreational sports are another favorite pastime, with 26 intramural and 44 club sports offered at varying levels of competitiveness.

One of the best and most well-rounded state schools anywhere, Madison remains a school that students sum up as "diverse, intellectual, fashionable, and moderately hedonistic." And these are the qualities that attract bright and energetic students from everywhere. "You feel you're accepted for who you are no matter what," says one student. "It's so nice to just be yourself."

Overlaps

Boston University, U of I at Urbana–Champaign, Indiana University, University of Michigan, Northwestern, University of Iowa

If You Apply To ›

Wisconsin: Early action, regular decision. SATs or ACTs: required. No Subject Tests. Accepts the Common Application with supplement.

P.O. Box 720, Springfield, OH 45501

Wittenberg is an outpost of cozy Midwestern friendliness. Less national than Denison or Wooster, Witt has plenty of old-fashioned school spirit and powerhouse Division III athletic teams. Top students should aim for the honors program, which provides a chance for independent research. Witt doles out plenty of merit scholarships to better-than-average students.

Website: www.wittenberg.edu
Location: Small City
Private
Total Enrollment: 1,800
Undergraduates: 1,793
Male/Female: 46/54
SAT Ranges: ERW 540–650,
   M 510–630
ACT Ranges: 22–28
Financial Aid: 99%
Pell Grant: 39%
Expense: Pr $
Student Loans: 74%
Average Debt: $ $ $ $
Applicants: 7,249
Accepted: 72%
Enrolled: 10%
Grad in 6 Years: 67%
Returning Freshmen: 72%
Academics: ✑ ✑ ✑
Social: ☎ ☎ ☎
Q of L: ★ ★ ★
Admissions: (877) 206-0332
Email Address: admission@
   wittenberg.edu

Strong Programs:
Education
Business
Biology
Social Sciences
Nursing
Performing Arts
Russian and Central Eurasian
   Studies
Sport Management

Founded in 1845 by German Lutherans, Wittenberg University remains true to its faith by emphasizing strong student/faculty relationships—and making sure that students don't get too settled in their campus comfort zone. In fact, before granting their diplomas, Wittenberg requires students to complete 30 hours of community service in the surrounding town of Springfield. "The campus is beautiful, it's a great school, and it's so obvious how much everyone here loves it," gushes an education major.

The Wittenberg campus is classic Midwestern collegiate, with a mixture of 1800s and Gothic-inspired buildings on 100 rolling acres in southwestern Ohio. The red-brick Myers residence hall, with picturesque white pillars and an open-air dome dating from the 19th century, stands at the center. Many of the campus's buildings are showing their age, although a brand-new, $40 million Health, Wellness, and Athletics Complex features a full-size indoor turf field surrounded by a running track, among other facilities.

Wittenberg's general education requirements emphasize a solid liberal arts background, with learning goals ranging from experience with writing and research to exercising social and moral responsibility to participating in physical education. Comprehensive first-year programs for new students include a leadership development program, a service-learning course, and a required, yearlong First-Year Seminar that helps students transition from high school to college.

Wittenberg students give high marks to the education program, which is among the most popular majors, along with business, biology, and various offerings in the social sciences. Health-related fields, especially nursing and other prehealth professional programs, are particularly well regarded. Other notable programs include the performing arts, East Asian studies, Russian and Central Eurasian studies, sport management, and a new major in data science. Wittenberg also offers 3–2 engineering programs with Columbia University and Case Western Reserve. The academic climate is described as "challenging but friendly," and study groups are common, according to one junior. Professors are roundly praised for their teaching styles and willingness to make themselves available outside the classroom. "Students take advantage of having professors who are extremely knowledgeable by getting help with class problems or even career advice," one senior says. Fifty-two percent of classes have fewer than 20 students. So long as students declare their major on time and complete all courses with a C or better, the college guarantees a degree in four years—and will pay for any additional necessary courses.

> **"We are constantly championing new causes, whether through community service or fund-raising."**

The new Compass program combines nine different student support services in one collaborative space in the Thomas Library and is intended, in part, to improve the college's retention and graduation rates. In addition to offering academic support, Compass connects students to research, community service, and internship opportunities. A University Honors Program enrolls 13 percent of students, who conduct independent research culminating in a senior thesis, and individual departments offer ample opportunities to work on research with faculty members. In fact, 92 percent of students partake in undergraduate research. Wittenberg encourages students to take a semester or a year away from campus, either in the U.S. or abroad, and about 20 percent do so. Most students pack their bags for the college's own faculty-led semesters in Germany and Costa Rica, although a multitude of other partner programs are also available. Wittenberg's Local Government Management Internship Program is an option for those interested in public service.

"Witt students are proactive," says a junior. "We are constantly championing new causes, whether through community service or fund-raising. We are always on the go!" Three-quarters of Wittenberg students are native Ohioans, and 1 percent hail from other countries. Many others are from nearby states like Indiana, Michigan, and Pennsylvania. African Americans comprise 10 percent of the student body, Hispanics 4 percent, Asian Americans 1 percent, and multiracial students 6 percent. The Diversity Center houses three student awareness organizations to help support minority populations on campus: Concerned Black Students, the American International Association, and the Gender and Sexual Diversity Association. Lutherans represent 11 percent, and students say the campus is fairly evenly split between conservatives and liberals, and both groups are vocal. "Everyone is open to different opinions," a biology major says. Wittenberg is generous in awarding merit scholarships, which average $21,000; there are no athletic scholarships. A hefty 39 percent of

> "[Wittfest] resembles a carnival, and at night there's a big concert on the lawn."

incoming freshmen receive Pell Grants. The Wittenberg College Access Program provides special financial aid packages to academically talented students from low-income families.

Eighty-five percent of students reside on Wittenberg's hilly campus; freshmen and sophomores are required to do so. After that, most upperclassmen choose houses and apartments owned by the school in the surrounding neighborhood—the "Wittenburbs," as students like to say. "Dorms are spacious and air-conditioned," a student says, "with options for all-girl, honors, and substance-free housing." For those in need of sustenance (perhaps to fuel all-night study sessions), there is a variety of dining options, including vegetarian and low-fat items. "The food doesn't taste the best, but is acceptable," says one sophomore. In an effort to mitigate sexual assault on campus, the university has implemented bystander awareness and response training programs.

Students at Wittenberg work hard at their studies, but they are also actively engaged in more than 120 student organizations, performing arts groups, and intramurals. Greek life is a big emphasis, with 29 percent of men and 32 percent of women belonging to fraternities and sororities. When the weekend rolls around, social life centers on parties in houses, dorm rooms, and apartments on or near campus. Greek groups, the Union Board, and the Residence Hall Association bring in guest speakers, movies, comedians, and concerts. Favorite annual events include Greek Week, Homecoming ("the alumni involvement is incredible"), W Day, and Wittfest, a campus festival and concert with games, food, prizes, and socializing before finals. "It is open to the community, but all the students go," a senior says. "It resembles a carnival, and at night there's a big concert on the lawn." Springfield (population 60,000) is a struggling blue-collar city, but it's beginning to show signs of revival. The city offers movie theaters, restaurants, a brewery, a performing arts center, and plenty of service opportunities. Popular road trips include Dayton (30 minutes), Columbus (45 minutes), and Cincinnati (90 minutes).

Wittenberg's athletic teams (the Tigers) are competitive in Division III, and rivalries with Allegheny, Wabash, and The College of Wooster really get students riled up, especially when the football team takes the field. Men's basketball,

Wittenberg requires students to complete 30 hours of community service in the surrounding town of Springfield.

So long as students declare their major on time and complete all courses with a C or better, the college guarantees a degree in four years.

Overlaps

Denison, College of Wooster, Miami University (OH), Ohio State, Ohio University, Ohio Wesleyan, University of Dayton, University of Cincinnati

football, and golf and women's volleyball, softball, and golf are recent North Coast Athletic Conference champions. Intramurals and club sports are a huge draw too, with sports such as crew, ice hockey, and rugby. Nearby state parks offer swimming, camping, biking trails, and picnics in the warmer months, and skiing in the winter.

While not as well known as many of its bigger Midwestern brethren, Wittenberg has plenty to offer those students who decide to attend, including a solid honors program, an active Greek scene, and serious Division III athletics. And with an increased focus on student support and diversifying its academic offerings, the school is slowly broadening its regional reach.

If You Apply To ›

Wittenberg: Early decision, early action, rolling admissions. SATs or ACTs: optional. Subject Tests: optional. Accepts the Common Application with supplement.

Wofford College

429 North Church Street, Spartanburg, SC 29303-3663

Wofford is about half the size of Furman and somewhat larger than Presbyterian. Strong in the life sciences and study abroad. Wofford is one of the smallest institutions to compete in Division I football, and Greek life dominates the traditional social scene. Diversity is a hot-button issue.

Website: www.wofford.edu
Location: Small City
Private
Total Enrollment: 1,571
Undergraduates: 1,571
Male/Female: 47/53
SAT Ranges: ERW 570–660, M 550–650
ACT Ranges: 24–30
Financial Aid: 95%
Pell Grant: 17%
Expense: Pr $
Student Loans: 50%
Average Debt: $ $ $
Applicants: 3,092
Accepted: 70%
Enrolled: 15%
Grad in 6 Years: 81%
Returning Freshmen: 90%
Academics: ✐ ✐ ✐
Social: ☎ ☎
Q of L: ★ ★ ★
Admissions: (864) 597-4130

Wofford students take pride in the Wofford Way, combining a well-rounded curriculum built on traditional strengths in the sciences with career-related internships and study abroad. The college has taken bold steps to increase—and diversify—enrollment while lowering the student/faculty ratio. Students study hard under the "eyes of Old Main" and form lasting friendships with peers and faculty members. "We are bright, driven individuals who learn to utilize our skills to the best of our potential to make the world around us a better place," says a junior.

Wofford is located near the heart of Spartanburg, a midsize city in the northwest corner of South Carolina, and is affiliated with the United Methodist Church. Founded in 1854, it's one of fewer than 200 existing American colleges that opened before the Civil War—and it still operates on its original campus, a National Historic District. Azaleas, magnolias, and dogwoods surround the distinctive, twin-towered Main Building and four original faculty homes on the 170-acre campus, which is also a nationally recognized arboretum. Recent construction projects include a center for the arts and an indoor stadium.

"Many [professors] help students secure research positions, internships, and other opportunities."

Wofford has added dozens of new courses and interdisciplinary programs to its curriculum in the past decade. Courses are required in English, fine arts, foreign languages, humanities, science, history, philosophy, cultural perspectives, math, and physical education. First-years take a required Humanities 101 seminar in the fall that hones their reading, writing, and discussion skills; recent offerings have included Exploring the Middle East, Digital Storytelling, and Truth and Lies. All first-years are also assigned a Student Success Team that includes an academic advisor, a student peer leader, a staff guide, and a personal librarian.

Traditionally, Wofford's strongest and most attractive programs have been in the life sciences, which account for about a third of its graduates and a large share of its Phi Beta Kappas. Every year, two dozen of the school's graduates go on to graduate medical or dental programs; another two dozen go on to law school. Business programs (especially when combined with a second major in Chinese, French, German, or Spanish), and English, with its emphasis on creative writing, are solid, and environmental studies is also strong. Students in the creative writing concentration end by writing a novella, the best of which is given the Benjamin Wofford Prize and is published in paperback. Some of the most popular majors are biology, finance, business economics, accounting, and chemistry. Prospective engineers may apply for 3–2 programs with Clemson or New York's Columbia University. Sixty-five percent of classes enroll fewer than 20 students, and students agree that, across the board, the workload tends to be heavy. "I would say the academic climate at Wofford is very competitive in the sense that students feel pressured to excel," says a sophomore.

"Professors encourage students to come visit their office about both class and personal concerns," says a psychology major. "Many help students secure research positions, internships, and other opportunities." Indeed, special enrichment opportunities abound at Wofford. The Presidential Seminar brings together 20 outstanding seniors from different disciplines to discuss readings from classical and contemporary essays on philosophy, politics, and the complexities of human nature. The Space in the Mungo Center connects

> "Wofford students and alums often show distaste or frustration toward more socially liberal and inclusive endeavors."

students to internships, entrepreneurship opportunities, and other career services. Sixty percent of Wofford students participate in some form of study abroad, embarking on programs in more than 70 countries on all seven continents. Short-term, faculty-led programs are offered during the January term, while semester- and year-long options are available through approved partners; students can often apply financial aid toward program costs. Every year, one lucky student is chosen as the Presidential International Scholar. This student is sent around the world, all expenses paid, to study an issue of global importance for a semester.

Fifty-four percent of students hail from South Carolina, and just 2 percent from abroad. African Americans comprise 8 percent of the student population, Asian Americans 2 percent, Hispanics 4 percent, and multiracial students 4 percent. Conservative white students from middle- to upper-class backgrounds make up the vast majority, and students note that the level of racial diversity has been a source of tension on campus. "Wofford's administration is a lot more liberal and encourages diversity, whereas Wofford students and alums often show distaste or frustration

> "Wofford is interested in creating citizens of our world who will foster improvement."

toward more socially liberal and inclusive endeavors," comments a student. Merit scholarships averaging $17,200 are available to qualified students, and there are also 110 athletic scholarships in 19 sports.

Ninety-three percent of Wofford's students live on campus, where first-years get doubles in Greene and Marsh halls or four-person suites in Carlisle Hall; students report Marsh to be "a bit of a dump," but administrators say renovations are in the works. On the bright side, explains a biology major, "Each year that you are at Wofford, the housing situation gets better and better, culminating in the Village—a fantastic apartment community for the seniors." About a quarter of first-years join the six available living/learning communities so they can live with classmates who share their academic interests. A new food service provider came on board in 2017, and a senior says meals are "getting better each year." Campus security gets mixed

(continued)

Email Address: admission@ wofford.edu

Strong Programs:
Biology
Finance
Business Economics
Accounting
Chemistry
Foreign Languages
English
Environmental Studies

First-years take a required Humanities 101 seminar in the fall; recent offerings have included Digital Storytelling and Truth and Lies.

reviews. "Sexual assault is an issue on Wofford's campus because most cases go unreported," says a junior, who also credits the administration with increasing the visibility of Title IX staff and resources "so more cases will be reported."

The Greek system is a huge force in Wofford's social life, enlisting 50 percent of the men and 55 percent of the women. The Greek Village, which opened in 2016, features individual houses for fraternities, sororities, and multicultural organizations and serves as the social center of campus. Most Greek groups host parties every Friday and Saturday—with some kicking off the weekend on Thursday. "The school wants to shut down underage drinking and they're cracking down on it," warns one student. The Student Affairs Committee offers campuswide events like comedians and music for those uninterested in the Greek system. "Spring Weekend is an event that is always a much anticipated time of the year at Wofford, as there are bands, cookouts, shaving-cream fights, and a beach volleyball tournament," says a student. Off campus, Spartanburg is home to six other colleges. Students say it's not a great college town, but there are some fun hangouts and occasional street fairs and concerts. Almost every Wofford student participates in some type of volunteer work. Terrier Play Day brings kids from the community to campus for a fair with booths and games. For a change of pace, students can head to Greenville, Atlanta, and Charlotte.

The Wofford Terriers compete in the Division I Southern Conference and have produced a number of competitive teams, including football (conference champs in 2017), men's basketball, and women's volleyball; games against rival Furman always draw crowds. The school's quiz bowl and chartered financial analyst teams are nationally competitive. Students are also active in intramural, recreational, and club sports, and some of the most popular programs include Terrier Tag, soccer, basketball, lacrosse, and ultimate Frisbee.

Wofford's former chaplain was fond of saying, "You don't come to Wofford—you join it." And students say that's true, citing the close-knit community and intimate student/faculty relationships fostered by the school's small size. Although administrative efforts to build a more diverse, inclusive campus have been met with some resistance, the status quo here is slowly changing. "Wofford is in a period of transition currently, but I don't think that's a negative," reflects an English major. "Wofford is interested in creating citizens of our world who will foster improvement, and I see Wofford as an institution focused on moving forward while still preserving tradition."

Sixty percent of students participate in some form of study abroad, embarking on programs in more than 70 countries.

Overlaps

University of South Carolina, Furman, College of Charleston, Sewanee, Clemson, UNC at Chapel Hill, Presbyterian, Wake Forest

If You Apply To ›

Wofford: Early decision, early action, regular decision. SATs or ACTs: optional. No Subject Tests. Accepts the Common Application with supplement.

The College of Wooster

Wooster, OH 44691

Though not well known to the general public, Wooster is renowned in academic circles around the world. Access is easy but graduating takes work, with students completing an independent study project in their last two years and earning a coveted Tootsie Roll. More intellectually serious than competitors such as Denison. Prides itself on turning above-average students into real scholars.

Instead of teaching students what to think, The College of Wooster focuses on teaching students how to do it. From the first freshman seminar to the final day when seniors hand in their theses, the college paves each student's path to independence. The emphasis here is on global perspectives, mentored research, and the heritage that stems from its origin as a college founded by Scottish Presbyterians. The one-on-one attention from faculty makes Wooster an intellectual refuge in the rural countryside of Ohio. "Wooster is a school that really celebrates hard work, and one that encourages students to find opportunities that interest them," says a senior.

Located in the city of Wooster, Ohio, COW's hilltop campus is spread over 240 acres, with many campus buildings designed in the English–collegiate Gothic style and constructed of cream-colored brick. More recent buildings are trimmed in Indiana limestone or Ohio sandstone. The central arch and two towers of Kauke Hall (the central building in Quinby Quadrangle,

"Mentorship and collaboration are pervasive across campus."

the square around which the college grew) make it stand out. The Gault Library for Independent Study offers a private carrel for each senior in the humanities and social sciences. The newest addition to campus is the $40 million Williams Hall of Life Science, featuring flexible teaching and lab spaces designed to support student/faculty research.

What goes on behind the facades of Wooster's attractive buildings is more impressive than the structures themselves. The required First-Year Seminar in Critical Inquiry, limited to 15 students per section, introduces students to intensive writing, critical thinking, and interdisciplinary study. Recent section topics include Misogyny, Copycats and Creators, and The Drugs We Drink: Biological and Societal Perspectives. In addition to the first-year seminar, three semesters of Independent Study, and six cross-discipline courses, Wooster mandates coursework in writing; foreign language; global engagement; diversity, power, and privilege; social justice or religious perspectives; quantitative literacy; and seven to nine classes in the student's major.

At Wooster, "students develop specific and deep academic interests," says an English major. The most popular majors are biology, political science, history, psychology, and biochemistry and molecular biology. English and global and international studies are also strengths. The chemistry department has traditionally ranked near the top among private colleges in the number of graduates who go on to earn Ph.D.s. Two-thirds of classes enroll fewer than 20 students, and only a few introductory courses have teaching assistants, who run review sessions and offer extra help. Students praise faculty members for their devotion to teaching, and a history major says, "Mentorship and collaboration are pervasive across campus."

Indeed, mentored undergraduate research is the heart of a Wooster education, highlighted by opportunities in the Applied Methods and Research Experience and the Sophomore Research Program. The Independent Study (IS) required of all seniors lets students explore subjects they're passionate about with one-on-one faculty guidance. "The research skills you develop are second to none," affirms one student. IS has become such a part of COW that each year

"The research skills you develop are second to none."

seniors celebrate IS Monday—the day they turn in their projects—with a campus-wide parade led by bagpipers. Completion of the IS earns you a Tootsie Roll, to eat or keep for posterity next to your diploma. "It's a day all Wooster graduates will always remember!" a senior says. The college even awards nearly $100,000 each year for student research, travel, or materials to support thesis work. The APEX (Advising, Planning, and Experiential Learning) center combines several offices related to student and career services and helps coordinate internships and study abroad. When Wooster's remote locale gets too confining, students may choose

Website: www.wooster.edu
Location: Small City
Private
Total Enrollment: 1,959
Undergraduates: 1,959
Male/Female: 46/54
SAT Ranges: ERW 570–680, M 580–700
ACT Ranges: 24–30
Financial Aid: 99%
Pell Grant: 18%
Expense: Pr $ $ $
Student Loans: 54%
Average Debt: $ $ $
Applicants: 5,615
Accepted: 56%
Enrolled: 18%
Grad in 6 Years: 76%
Returning Freshmen: 86%
Academics: ✏ ✏ ✏ ½
Social: ☎ ☎ ☎
Q of L: ★ ★ ★
Admissions: (330) 263-2322
Email Address: admissions@wooster.edu

Strong Programs:
Biology
Political Science
History
Psychology
Biochemistry and Molecular Biology
English
Global and International Studies
Chemistry

from semester-long programs in more than 60 countries worldwide, or short-term TREK programs led by Wooster faculty during winter, spring, and summer breaks; 30 percent of students participate.

Wooster awards nearly $100,000 each year for student research, travel, or materials to support Independent Study thesis work.

"Students are eclectic, spirited, and incredibly down-to-earth," a student says. As the college's reputation spreads, it's becoming more selective, with acceptance rates dropping and freshman-retention rates improving. African Americans constitute 9 percent of the student body, Asian Americans 5 percent, and Hispanics 5 percent. Wooster has a notable international flavor—13 percent of students hail from foreign nations, while 31 percent come from Ohio. Politically, Wooster "leans left but is not a very far left campus," reports a political science major. Merit awards averaging $24,700 are available, and students are admitted without regard for financial need.

All students live on Wooster's campus in 15 co-ed dorms, where rooms are small but "acceptable," although students comment that some of the older buildings could use renovations. Students seriously committed to service may apply to live in one of the college's 30 residential program houses, each of which is affiliated with a community group. Meals are primarily served in two dining halls, and a sophomore says, "There's enough variety, and the food is always tasty, but nothing special." A senior notes that the college has "responded aggressively" to the national issue of sexual assault by expanding resources for survivors and increasing security measures aimed at prevention. But in general, students say that given Wooster's location "in the middle of cornfields," safety isn't an issue.

"In recent years, the town of Wooster has really taken off."

Despite the school's isolated location, students say they enjoy the "quaint and friendly" town of Wooster, a 10-minute walk from campus. "In recent years, the town of Wooster has really taken off, and a lot of new restaurants and shops have popped up," says a senior. Still, the vast majority of social life is campus-based. "Personally, I do not leave campus very often because there are many events on campus," says an economics and math major. Visiting lecturers and student performances keep students busy on weekdays, and the Wooster Activities Crew organizes events like craft and karaoke nights on weekends. One major weekend hangout is the Underground, a bar and dance club that hosts well-known bands, as well as the campus's bowling alley, pool hall, and game room. The college has no national Greek organizations, but local "sections" draw 14 percent of the men and "clubs" attract 17 percent of the women. Students say the party scene is low-key and no one is pressured to drink alcohol.

When it snows, the student body descends upon the Kauke arch and fills it with snow, a tradition that goes back more than 50 years.

The school's Scottish heritage is on display in its kilted bagpipe band and its Scottish dancers, who trot on stage during Scot Spirit Day in the fall. Other annual traditions include an outdoor music festival and the formal Winter Gala. When it snows—which it does quite often in Wooster—the student body descends upon the Kauke arch and fills it with snow, a tradition that goes back more than 50 years.

Wooster fields a number of competitive Division III teams. Fighting Scots basketball is a spectator favorite, especially when the opponent is rival Wittenberg, and baseball took home its third straight conference championship in 2018. Swimming and diving and track and field have also been strong in recent years. Moot Court has been successful in regional and national competition, and about 60 percent of students compete in intramural sports.

The College of Wooster is nationally recognized for its commitment to mentored research and its international focus. Wooster students are proud to be Fighting Scots and independent thinkers. And as a political science major explains, the college's distinctive Independent Study requirement actively shapes both the individual student experience and the campus atmosphere: "Having that big project on the horizon from the day you enroll changes the way you engage with your education, and I think that brings an element of intensity, dedication, and commitment to the academics at Wooster."

Overlaps

Denison, Dickinson, Lawrence, Rhodes, St. Olaf, Kenyon, Case Western Reserve, Oberlin

Worcester Polytechnic Institute

100 Institute Road, Worcester, MA 01609-2280

Small, innovative, and undergraduate-oriented, WPI is anything but a stodgy technical institute. The WPI Plan is hands-on and project-based and takes a humanistic view of engineering. Emphasizes teamwork instead of competition. Global focus unusual for an engineering school. WPI is smaller than Rensselaer and half the size of MIT.

As a pioneer in STEM education, Worcester Polytechnic Institute has built a solid reputation, particularly for its engineering programs. But with its ever-expanding academic curriculum, surprising devotion to music and theater, and dedication to hands-on undergraduate experiences, WPI has broadened the definition of what it means to be a techie haven. More than anything, it's WPI's humanistic approach to engineering that really sets it apart. As a mechanical engineering major explains, "We all have one common denominator that brings us together: we all love STEM and we all want to design, build, and innovate to make the world better."

WPI is the third-oldest independent science and engineering school in the nation. Its compact 95-acre campus is set atop one of Worcester's "seven hills" on the residential outskirts of town and borders two parks and the historic Highland Street District, where local merchants and students come together to form the neighborhood community. Old English stone buildings complete with creeping ivy are focal points of the architecture, but modern facilities have moved in to claim their own space on the immaculately kept grounds. The $49 million Foisie Innovation Studio, opened in 2018, features high-tech classrooms, makerspaces, and labs, as well as a 140-bed residence hall.

> "[The Great Problems Seminar is] a great way to get one's feet wet with project-based learning."

WPI's curriculum remains remarkably broad and flexible for a high-powered technological university. The intent of WPI's unique educational philosophy is to build self-confidence and social skills, to nurture well-rounded students interested in using their knowledge to improve the world, and, especially, to develop teamwork. First-years have the option of signing up for a two-term Great Problems Seminar, which a junior calls "a great way to get one's feet wet with project-based learning." Standard course distribution requirements vary by major but include classes in engineering, math, and science, as well as a humanities and arts requirement. The Interactive Qualifying Project (IQP) is a distinctive requirement that has students apply technical knowledge to one of society's problems, usually working in teams of two to four students with a faculty advisor. The Major Qualifying Project (MQP) requirement serves as a capstone in which students work on a truly professional-level problem in their major course of study. Many IQPs and MQPs involve corporate, nonprofit, or government sponsors, to whom students present their research findings and recommendations.

The most popular majors are mechanical engineering, computer science, electrical and computer engineering, and biomedical engineering. Aerospace engineering

Website: www.wpi.edu
Location: Small City
Private
Total Enrollment: 5,093
Undergraduates: 4,244
Male/Female: 64/36
SAT Ranges: ERW 620–710, M 660–730
ACT Ranges: 28–32
Financial Aid: 99%
Pell Grant: 12%
Expense: Pr $ $ $
Student Loans: N/A
Average Debt: N/A
Applicants: 10,331
Accepted: 48%
Enrolled: 22%
Grad in 6 Years: 89%
Returning Freshmen: 95%
Academics: ✐ ✐ ✐ ½
Social: ☎ ☎ ☎
Q of L: ★ ★ ★ ★
Admissions: (508) 831-5286
Email Address: admissions@wpi.edu

Strong Programs:
Mechanical Engineering
Computer Science
Electrical and Computer Engineering
Biomedical Engineering
Aerospace Engineering
Interactive Media and Game Development

(continued)

Robotics Engineering
Fire Protection Engineering

and architectural engineering are traditional strengths, as are interdisciplinary programs, such as interactive media and game development, bioinformatics and computational biology, and environmental and sustainability studies. The school launched the nation's first undergraduate robotics engineering program, which has grown to include M.S. and Ph.D. programs, making it the first university to offer all three levels. WPI also offers a rare fire protection engineering combined B.S./M.S. program. Many biomedical engineering majors do their projects at UMass Medical and Tufts Veterinary, as well as at local hospitals. Math and science types can pick up middle or high school teaching credentials through the university's STEM Education Center. Well over 300 students participate in 22 musical and theatrical groups; WPI has one of the largest music programs among technological universities.

An academic year at WPI consists of four terms, each lasting seven weeks, which means courses are fast-paced and intense. When students are not completing their IQP and MQP projects, they take three courses per term. Although some introductory classes enroll more than 100 students, most classes are small—65 percent have fewer than 20 students—and students say teamwork is the norm inside and outside the classroom. Professors are praised for their approachability and willingness to establish relationships, especially when it comes to research opportunities. To further promote cooperation and cohesiveness, the only recorded grades are A, B, C, or No Record. Failing grades do not appear on transcripts, and the school does not compute GPAs or class ranks. "The grading system allows students to take more risks in their curriculum by taking harder classes when they want to," says a chemical engineering major.

> "The grading system allows students to take more risks in their curriculum."

The Interactive Qualifying Project (IQP) has students apply technical knowledge to one of society's problems.

In light of an increasingly interdependent global economy, WPI offers a distinctive Global Projects Program, in which students travel to more than 40 off-campus project centers run by resident faculty advisors across the U.S. and around the world, working in teams to solve a real-world problem for a local sponsor; about 70 percent of students take advantage of the program, most of them to fulfill their IQP or MQP requirements. A new initiative awards a $5,000 Global Project Scholarship to every incoming freshman to support participation in the program. Overall, 48 percent of students take part in some sort of international experience before they graduate. Extremely motivated students can also complete Individually Sponsored Residential Projects, in which they design their own independent, off-campus study project, under the direction of a faculty member, in addition to their other project work. The co-op program enables students to take time away from the classroom to pursue paid, full-time work experience; participants can expect to add on extra time to their degree program.

> "[We are] extroverted nerds: we have the social skills to communicate well and have the ideas to fix problems."

A new initiative awards a $5,000 scholarship to every incoming freshman to support participation in the Global Projects Program.

A junior describes WPI students as "extroverted nerds: we have the social skills to communicate well and have the ideas to fix problems." Thirty-nine percent of undergraduates are Massachusetts natives, and 11 percent come from abroad. African Americans account for 3 percent of the students, Hispanics 9 percent, Asian Americans 3 percent, and multiracial students 2 percent. The dearth of females on campus is a typical complaint, although one woman says, "I have found that women, although underrepresented, are often much more present on campus, more involved." Though students are aware of current events, politics don't factor too much into campus conversations. Merit scholarships averaging $15,800 are doled out annually, but there are no athletic scholarships.

Spots in the university residence halls are only guaranteed to first-years. Co-ed halls offer traditional and suite-style options, while on-campus apartments and smaller houses make for more homelike living. Upperclassmen tend to move to

Greek houses or off-campus apartments; 59 percent of all undergrads live in campus housing. Students can take their meals in the main dining hall, food court, or on-campus restaurant. "Most of the meals are nothing fancy, but they are all staples of a balanced diet," says a sophomore. A junior notes, "Offices that support students dealing with sexual assault have a much greater presence than they did when I started here."

Social life is usually a good mix of on- and off-campus activities. Student-organized coffeehouses, game nights, concerts, improv shows, and movies are popular, as are Greek parties. Twenty-seven percent of the men join fraternities and 45 percent of the women enter sororities. "All fraternity parties are regulated, and a limit is placed on how many drinks an individual will be served," explains a junior. A century-old campus tradition is the Goat's Head Rivalry, a yearlong grudge match between the freshman and sophomore classes that includes the Pennant Rush, a rope pull next to Salisbury Pond, and a WPI trivia competition. The prize? A bronze goat's head trophy with the winning class's year engraved on it.

While not exactly scenic, Worcester does offer a large number of clubs and restaurants, an art museum, and a large multipurpose arena that hosts concerts and sporting events. "WPI is placed in a rather convenient and nice location in the city," a freshman says. Nearby colleges, including Clark and Holy Cross, are linked to WPI through shuttle buses, providing even more social and academic opportunities. Boston and Hartford are both an hour's drive, as are ski resorts and beaches.

The WPI Engineers compete in Division III sports and field a number of competitive teams. Men's rowing claimed a regional championship in 2017, while women's basketball and softball are recent NEWMAC conference champions. Men's and women's swimming and diving and men's cross-country and basketball are also competitive. More than half of the student body participate in intramural and recreational sports, with underwater hockey being a particular favorite.

One of WPI's chants is fittingly mathematic: "E to the x, d-y, d-x, e to the x, d-x; cosine, secant, tangent, sine; 3.14159; e^i, radical, pi; fight 'em fight 'em WPI!" If you know what any of that stuff means, you'll fit right in.

> *Twenty-seven percent of the men join fraternities and 45 percent of the women enter sororities.*

Overlaps

Carnegie Mellon, Clarkson, MIT, Rensselaer, Rochester Institute of Technology, Northeastern, UMass Amherst, Boston University

If You Apply To ›

WPI: Early action I and II, regular decision. SATs or ACTs: optional. Subject Tests: optional. Accepts the Common Application.

Xavier University of Louisiana

1 Drexel Drive, New Orleans, LA 70125

The only historically black college with Roman Catholic ties, Xavier is bigger than a small college but smaller than most universities. Competes with Howard, LSU, Morehouse, and Spelman. Strong in pharmacy and the physical sciences and nationally known for turning out medical students and science teachers. About a quarter of students are Catholic. Location in New Orleans is a big plus.

As the nation's only historically African American Roman Catholic college, Xavier University of Louisiana remains committed to "the promotion of a more just and humane society." This small New Orleans university has a stellar reputation for graduating a wealth of scientists and aspiring medical professionals. Xavier prepares students for their chosen careers while providing a strong foundation in the liberal

Website: www.xula.edu
Location: City Center
Private
Total Enrollment: 2,881

(continued)

Undergraduates: 2,151
Male/Female: 26/74
SAT Ranges: ERW 493–590,
  M 470–590
ACT Ranges: 20–25
Financial Aid: 98%
Pell Grant: 58%
Expense: Pr $
Student Loans: 82%
Average Debt: $
Applicants: 7,164
Accepted: 64%
Enrolled: 16%
Grad in 6 Years: 44%
Returning Freshmen: 72%
Academics: ✐ ✐ ✐
Social: ☎ ☎ ☎
Q of L: ★ ★ ★
Admissions: (504) 520-7388
Email Address: apply@xula.edu

Strong Programs:
Biology
Chemistry
Psychology
Business
Education
Premed
Political Science
African American Studies

Xavier is credited with educating 25 percent of all African American pharmacists nationally.

arts and a supportive community. "If you're actively engaged, faculty and staff will know who you are and look out for you," says a sophomore.

The school was founded in 1915 by Katharine Drexel, a former Philadelphia socialite who devoted her life to the education of African Americans and Native Americans and who was canonized in 2000 by Pope John Paul II. Xavier is located near the heart of New Orleans in a quiet neighborhood dotted with bungalows. The focal point of the campus is the Library Resource Center, which, with its green roof and stately neo-Gothic architectural style, has become a landmark for those traveling by car from the New Orleans airport to the French Quarter. An enclosed campus green mutes the urban feel of the encroaching city, and yellow brick buildings have been erected among the older limestone structures. Xavier was hard-hit in 2005 by Hurricane Katrina (much of the campus was under water), but since then it has gone on a $65 million renovation and building spree that includes the state-of-the-art Pharmacy Pavilion, the Convocation Center, and the stunning St. Katharine Drexel Chapel designed by renowned Argentine architect Cesar Pelli.

The university maintains its reputation as one of the most effective teaching institutions anywhere; the Center for the Advancement of Teaching works to improve pedagogy across the curriculum and encourages African American students to become teachers and researchers, especially in the sciences. Nearly two-thirds of undergraduates major in a science-related field; biology and chemistry are the most popular majors, along with psychology and business. "If you want to go into medicine, I would recommend Xavier," explains a student. "They have one of, if not the best, premed programs for minority students." Xavier has frequently led the nation in the number of African Americans placed into medical school and in the number of undergraduates who go on to earn Ph.D.s in science and engineering. Xavier is also credited with educating 25 percent of all African American pharmacists nationally. Political science is a small but solid department, and minors in African American studies and women's studies are available. In addition to the many internships available, Xavier offers cooperative education programs in all fields and study abroad programs around the world; 3 percent of students sign up for international study.

> **"If you want to go into medicine, I would recommend Xavier."**

"I would describe the academic climate as competitive in terms of obtaining internships," says one student, "but collaborative as well because most students here are willing to help one another with their studies." Xavier's undergraduate curriculum is centered on the liberal arts. All students are required to take a core of prescribed courses in theology and philosophy, the arts and humanities, communications, history and the social sciences, mathematics, and the natural sciences. Freshmen also take a mandatory, two-semester seminar sequence involving a common reading and a service-learning project, to help them adjust to college life. Priests and nuns teach and help run the school, though the notably diverse faculty and staff are composed of laypeople. Fifty-five percent of classes have fewer than 20 students. "Teachers are accessible and give personalized attention," says one senior, "especially in upper-level courses." Academic and career advising are well received, and there is a strong emphasis on community service.

"Most of the students I know tend to be very studious, hard workers, committed to making the grade, but also balancing that studiousness with a weekend social life," says one student. For a historically African American college, Xavier's student body is quite diverse. Seventy-eight percent of undergrads are African American, 7 percent are Asian American, 3 percent are Hispanic, and 4 percent are multiracial. Xavier has achieved a national reputation for its programs to reach out to local high schools to identify and nurture talented minority students. Most students come from the Deep South; 52 percent are from Louisiana, and many are second- or third-generation Xavierites. Two percent are international. Frequent forums and town-hall meetings give students a chance to discuss social and political concerns. A limited number of academic awards, worth an average of $13,000, are available to qualified students, as are athletic scholarships. A substantial 58 percent of incoming freshmen are eligible for the Pell Grant.

Forty-eight percent of Xavier students live in the four contemporary-looking residence halls, three of which are single sex. The freshman dorms have been renovated. Students report being satisfied with, if not enthusiastic about, the campus dining options: "The dining hall gets the job done," says a student. As a major city, New Orleans experiences a fair amount of crime, so campus security is a top priority, with highly visible officers who provide rides back to the dorms after late-night study sessions.

"The on-campus social scene is noticeably lacking," grumbles one computer science major. "Basketball and volleyball games and food and music events at Friday lunch can draw crowds, but each Friday night there is a large exodus of students heading for local bars, clubs, and house parties." Fraternities and sororities play a role in extracurricular and social life, though only 1 percent of the men and 2 percent of the women go Greek. Popular events include Bayou Classic and Spring Fest. But don't get caught drinking—Xavier is a dry campus. "They do room inspections and confiscate prohibited items," explains a sophomore. When it comes to road trips, students head to Baton Rouge, Tallahassee, Houston, and Miami.

> **"Each Friday night there is a large exodus of students heading for local bars, clubs, and house parties."**

Xavier's four Gold Rush (men's) and five Gold Nuggets (women's) varsity sports teams compete in the NAIA Division I and are enthusiastically supported, especially when the opponent is rival Dillard. Competitive teams include men's basketball, women's volleyball, and men's and women's cross-country. Intramural sports are also offered with high participation in basketball, tennis, soccer, Ping-Pong, and flag football.

With a mind for the future, Xavier stays true to its beginnings as a historically black and Catholic university and to a mission of preparing students for a future that will "promote a more just and humane society." Says one English major: "Xavier is where future leaders are made."

Overlaps

Spelman, Tuskegee, Morehouse, Hampton, Clark Atlanta, Southeastern Louisiana, Louisiana State, Florida A&M

If You Apply To ›

Xavier: Rolling admissions. SATs or ACTs: required. Subject Tests: optional. Accepts the Common Application with supplement.

Yale University

38 Hillhouse Avenue, New Haven, CT 06520

Yale is the middle-sized member of the Ivy League's big three: bigger than Princeton, smaller than Harvard. Its widely imitated residential college system helps Yale strike a balance between being a research university and an undergraduate college. New Haven isn't New York, but it has developed a lively urban scene in recent years. Plan to work hard.

Website: www.yale.edu

Location: Small City

Private

Total Enrollment: 12,850

Undergraduates: 5,741

Male/Female: 50/50

SAT Ranges: ERW 710–790,
   M 710–800

ACT Ranges: 32–35

Financial Aid: 64%

Pell Grant: 16%

Expense: Pr $ $ $

Student Loans: 16%

Average Debt: $

Applicants: 32,914

Accepted: 7%

Enrolled: 69%

Grad in 6 Years: 97%

Returning Freshmen: 99%

Academics: ✍ ✍ ✍ ✍ ✍

Social: ☎ ☎ ☎

Q of L: ★ ★ ★

Admissions: (203) 432-9300

Email Address:
   student.questions@yale.edu

Strong Programs:

Economics

Life Sciences

Political Science

Engineering

History

English

Architecture

Modern Languages

Founded in 1701 by Connecticut Congregationalists concerned about "backsliding" among their counterparts at a certain school in Cambridge, Massachusetts, Yale has long been recognized as one of the world's finest private universities, and one of the handful of Ivy League schools focused on undergraduates. Students here remain as focused on their studies as ever and tend to carry their achievements lightly. And thanks to Yale's residential college system, this huge research university feels like more of a home for its students. "Yale students are truly happy to be here," says a sophomore. "Everyone has a massive crush on Yale, and that makes all the difference in living and working here for four years."

Yale's campus looks like the traditional archetype—magnificent courtyards, imposing quadrangles, Gothic buildings designed by James Gamble Rogers, and Harkness Tower, a 201-foot spire once washed with acid to create its aged, stately look. All the residential colleges, most of which date back to the 1930s, have been renovated. The university intends to increase its undergraduate enrollment to 6,200 by 2020 and has opened two new residential colleges, built in the traditional collegiate Gothic style, to accommodate that growth. Kroon Hall is a LEED-certified building that houses the environmental studies program. The Greenberg Engineering Teaching Concourse, opened in 2017, offers state-of-the-art spaces for undergraduate teaching and collaboration.

Inside Yale's wrought-iron gates, academic programs are superb across the board, with arts and humanities programs especially outstanding. With tradition ever-present on campus, the Puritan work ethic remains. Graduating from Yale requires 36 courses—nine a year—rather than the 32 courses required at most other colleges. Students agree that despite all the hard work, the academic environment is not based on competition. "While the workload is challenging, most classes help students collaborate by promoting study groups, facilitating discussions in small, seminar classes, and organizing class section meetings for larger lecture classes," explains a senior.

> "While the workload is challenging, most classes help students collaborate."

Although Yale has 12 professional schools and a Graduate School of Arts and Sciences, Yale College—the undergraduate arts and sciences division—remains the university's heart. Virtually all professors teach undergraduates, and the professional schools' resources—especially architecture, fine arts, drama, and music—are available to them as well. Yale's superb economics department, replete with budding hedge fund managers and management consultants, offers the most popular undergraduate major, followed by life sciences, political science, engineering, history, and English. History offers one of the most demanding programs, including a mandatory 30- to 50-page senior essay. The English department is routinely at the vanguard of literary theory, while an outstanding interdisciplinary humanities major includes the study of the medieval, Renaissance, and modern periods. Most science labs and classrooms are located on Science Hill (the sciences were latecomers to all of the oldest U.S. universities and had to find space outside campus cores). Yale has spent $1 billion on science and engineering facilities and faculty since 2001, and nearly half of incoming students now arrive at Yale with an interest in a STEM major. The biological science departments are excellent, and its students' interests range from biomedical engineering research to preparation for medical school. Architecture and modern languages, especially French and Chinese, are first-rate, and the school's Center for the Study of Globalization is renowned as well. Majors have been added in neuroscience and statistics and data science.

Elite freshmen with a particularly strong appetite for the humanities can enroll in Directed Studies, a three-course program that examines the literature, philosophy, history, and politics of Western tradition. Prospective DSers, who must apply in May or June of their senior year in high school, should be prepared for some serious bonding with their books—they don't call it "Directed Suicide" for nothing. Ninety-five percent of science and engineering majors do research with faculty members in any of the more than 800 labs on campus; many are doing their own research as early as the summer after their freshman year. Yale's Science, Technology, and Research Scholars Program offers research and mentorship opportunities, career planning, and other specialized support for historically underrepresented students, including women, minorities, and those from economically disadvantaged backgrounds.

Ninety-five percent of science and engineering majors do research with faculty members.

Despite its reverence for tradition, Yale doesn't require any specific courses for graduation, and it doesn't have a core curriculum. Instead, students must take two classes in humanities and arts, social sciences, and sciences, along with two courses that emphasize writing and another two that emphasize quantitative reasoning. Yale also mandates intermediate-level mastery of a foreign language. Instead of preregistering, students spend two weeks "shopping" at the beginning of each term, sampling morsels of the various offerings before finalizing their schedules. Sixty-four percent of undergraduates take advantage of hundreds of study, internship, and research opportunities around the world. "Yale works hard to make study abroad affordable for every student," says a political science major. "I spent a summer abroad in Siena, Italy, and, best of all, the entire experience was covered by my Yale financial aid." The Yale in London program is popular, as are summer sessions abroad for intensive language study.

"Yale works hard to make study abroad affordable for every student."

Introductory-level classes at Yale can be large lectures, accompanied by small recitation and discussion sections typically led by graduate teaching assistants, although freshman seminars are offered each year on a wide range of topics, allowing first-year students to interact with professors and peers in small groups. Upper-level seminars are small and plentiful. Of the 1,000 classes offered each semester, 73 percent have fewer than 20 students. The quality of undergraduate teaching at Yale is as high as it gets at elite schools, and "professors are extremely accessible," says one junior. Some of the most popular courses, such as John Gaddis's Cold War history class, seem more like performances, students say. Robert Shiller, winner of the 2013 Nobel Prize in Economic Sciences, teaches introductory economics, and James Rothman, winner of the Nobel Prize in Physiology or Medicine in the same year, lives in one of Yale's residential colleges.

Instead of preregistering for classes, students spend two weeks "shopping" at the beginning of each term, sampling various offerings.

An engineering major says that Yale is a magnet for overachievers "who are passionate about something, whether it be research, community service, music, art, or anything else." Nevertheless, a freshman adds, "The student body is amazingly down-to-earth, especially given the insane accomplishments and talents of the students." Ninety-two percent of undergraduates are from outside of Connecticut, including many from the Northeast and 11 percent from other countries, and the student body is evenly split along gender lines. African Americans make up 7 percent of students, Hispanics 13 percent, Asian Americans 18 percent, and multiracial students 6 percent. Yalies are far less conservative than their counterparts at Harvard

"Yale's dorms are like palaces."

and Princeton, and they aren't shy about expressing their opinions. "Yale students are incredibly active politically and socially and are very conscious of world issues," one history major says. No merit or athletic awards are available, but the university admits students without regard to financial need and meets the full demonstrated need of all its undergraduate students, who are not expected to take out loans. Yale seeks to attract more students from low-income backgrounds; families making less than $65,000 a year don't pay any portion of the cost of their child's education, and these students also receive a $2,000 grant in their first year to help cover expenses like school supplies or winter clothing.

The 14 residential colleges that serve as Yale's dorms are the focal points for undergraduate social life and central to the distinct culture of Yale. "Yale's dorms are like palaces," cheers one student. Endowed by Yale graduate Edward S. Harkness (who also began the house system at Harvard) and modeled on those at Oxford and Cambridge, Yale's colleges provide intimate living/learning communities, creating the atmosphere of a small liberal arts college within a large research university. A senior says they are "similar to the house system at Hogwarts in the Harry Potter series." Each college has a library, dining hall, "butteries" that sell late-night food, and special facilities such as gyms, photography darkrooms, or small theaters. All colleges also have their own dean and affiliated faculty members, a few of whom live in the college, who can help undergraduates struggling to adapt to the rigors of college life. Residential colleges organize social and cultural events, such as teas where prominent public figures meet with groups of students. The dining halls serve good meals and multiple options. A senior notes, "We have an iPhone app that tells you the menu in each dining hall each night. It even tells you how crowded they are in real time."

Much of each residential college's distinctive identity comes from its architecture. Some buildings are fashioned in a craggy, fortress-like Gothic style, while others are done in the more open colonial style, with redbrick and green shutters as the prevailing motif. All colleges have their own special nooks and crannies with cryptic inscriptions paying tribute to illustrious Yalies of generations past.

"Community service is part of the fabric that makes Yale what it is."

Freshmen in 10 of the 14 colleges live together on the Old Campus, the historic 19th-century quadrangle, before moving into their colleges as sophomores; freshmen in the other four colleges live in their college starting their first year. Students generally live in suites with a living room and single or double bedrooms, but many seniors get singles. Some upperclassmen move into New Haven, although 84 percent choose to stay on campus all four years. Despite New Haven's urban character, students say that they feel physically safe. A female biochemistry major adds, "There have been sexual assaults on campus, and, fortunately, the school's administration has been responding swiftly and appropriately to discipline the assailant."

In addition to identifying with their colleges, many Yale students identify strongly with extracurricular groups, clubs, and organizations, spending most of their waking hours outside class at the newspaper, radio station, or computer center. Particularly clubby are the a cappella singing groups, whose members do everything from drinking together on certain weeknights to touring together during spring break. Many of Yale's mysterious secret societies, such as Skull and Bones, have their own mausoleum-like clubhouses and issue invitations to those with the right qualifications (like being a Bush). There are also the Yale Anti-Gravity Society (jugglers), improv comedy groups, and a multitude of other organizations.

Though studying takes the lion's share of their time, students find ways to unwind. About 10 percent of Yalies belong to a fraternity or sorority, and Greek parties are open to all. "There is not pressure to get involved in a party culture," says a freshman. The undergraduate Yale Symphony Orchestra puts on an original show every Halloween that fills Woolsey Hall with students in costume. "The Halloween Show has been home to some of my favorite memories at Yale," says one student. "It is an incredible production." Each year freshmen gather in the Commons for a holiday dinner that features a procession of culinary treats known as the Parade of Comestibles. The evening of the first large snowfall of the season brings the annual snowball fight on Old Campus. Each residential college mounts a spring "fun day" likely to include, in the words of a senior, "a petting zoo, free food, and bouncy castles." For the artistically inclined, there are lots of concerts every weekend and local film societies offer numerous weekend screenings. The Tony Award–winning Yale Repertory Theater depends heavily on graduate school talent but always brings in a few top stage stars each season. For those who want more excitement, the typical Yalie refrain on New Haven—"It's halfway between New York and Boston"—tells it all. Metro North trains run almost hourly to New York, and visiting Boston is nearly as easy.

The Yale campus is in the middle of downtown New Haven, a once-gritty small city that is riding the crest of a resurgence that, in the words of a junior, has made it "the perfect blend of manageable quaintness and urban opportunity." A political science major notes, "There is a movie theater, two world-renowned art galleries, a popular dance club, and countless shops and restaurants within a 10-minute walk from my dorm room." Natural history and art museums on and near campus, especially the Yale University Art Gallery and the British Art Center, are excellent. The city's long-standing theatrical tradition continues at two grand old theater and concert halls a block from campus. Locals will swear that Pepe's on Wooster Street was the first (and best!) pizza parlor in the country, while Louis's Lunch was the first true hamburger joint. Once-testy relations between students and locals are improving. "The city definitely caters to students to make them feel welcome and safe," says a biochemistry major, and 61 percent of Yale undergrads reciprocate by doing volunteer work in town through Dwight Hall, the largest student-run college community service organization in the country. "Community service is part of the fabric that makes Yale what it is," says a senior. "It's a major part of student life and culture."

> **"When I meet other Yalies abroad, we can immediately connect."**

Yale fields a full complement of 33 athletic teams (the Bulldogs), which play in Division I. Recent Ivy League champions include men's lacrosse, baseball, basketball, ice hockey, and crew, as well as women's swimming and diving. The men's squash, men's crew, and co-ed and women's sailing teams also claimed recent national titles. More than half the student body takes part in intramural competition among the residential colleges; the winning college gets the coveted Tying Cup. The annual Harvard–Yale football game—known simply as The Game—is an occasion for tailgating by thousands of blue-clad students, whether it takes place in New Haven or Cambridge. Yale's Mock Trial team won the national championship in 2016.

Yale is one of America's oldest institutions of higher learning, and students and graduates here take seriously the intonation, "For God, for country, and for Yale." For proof, just remember that among its alumni, Yale counts the presidents or former presidents of about 70 other colleges and universities and five U.S. presidents. As the university moves into its fourth century, its past and former students continue to make their marks on the world. "When I meet other Yalies abroad, we can immediately connect by talking about our residential colleges, and other shared Yale traditions, such as the Halloween show," says one student. Yale has found a way to pursue world-class teaching and learning with what one senior describes as "a collegial and relaxed atmosphere that makes your four years here some of the most enjoyable times of your life."

The undergraduate Yale Symphony Orchestra puts on an original show every Halloween that fills Woolsey Hall with students in costume.

Overlaps

Harvard, Stanford, Princeton, MIT, Columbia, University of Pennsylvania, Brown, Cornell University

If You Apply To ›

Yale: Single choice early action, regular decision. SATs or ACTs: required. Subject Tests: recommended. Accepts the Common Application with supplement.

Index

Acknowledgments

FISKE GUIDE TO COLLEGES STAFF

Editor: Edward B. Fiske
Managing Editor: Michelle Lecuyer
Contributing Editor: Bruce G. Hammond
Production Coordinator: Julia Fiske Hogan

The *Fiske Guide to Colleges* reflects the talents, energy, and ideas of many people. Chief among them are Michelle Lecuyer, the managing editor, and Julia Fiske Hogan, the production coordinator. I am also grateful for the support of Bruce G. Hammond, my coauthor on the *Fiske Guide to Getting Into the Right College* and other books about college admissions. Thanks also to Shawn Logue, a longtime colleague, for his continuing interest in the *Fiske Guide* and his help with things technological.

One of the great joys of producing the *Fiske Guide* each year is the opportunity to work alongside the talented and dedicated members of the editorial team at Sourcebooks. They are true professionals who understand that providing college-bound students with accurate information about colleges and universities is an important mission. Among them are Dominique Raccah, Todd Stocke, Anna Michels, Chris Francis, Heather Hall, and Sarah Otterness. Others who played important roles were Bob Lessard, Tina Silva, and Lin Miceli. Thanks also to Michelle Gleeson and Alexis Brooke Redding for their thoughtful editorial suggestions and to Joe Klunder and Matthew Simons for their research assistance. And, as always, I am grateful for the wise guidance of the college counselors who serve on the Editorial Advisory Group.

In the final analysis, the *Fiske Guide* is dependent on the contributions of the thousands of students and college administrators who took the time to answer detailed and demanding questionnaires. Their candor and cooperation are deeply appreciated. While I, of course, accept full responsibility for the final product, the quality and usefulness of the book is a testimony to their thoughtful reflections on the colleges and universities with which they are associated.

Edward B. Fiske
Durham, NC
May 2019

EDITORIAL ADVISORY GROUP

Richard Avitabile, Westport, CT
Gerimae Bassichis, Delray Beach, FL
Nancy Beane, Atlanta, GA
Sam Bigelow, Concord, MA
Eileen Blattner, Shaker Heights, OH
Robin Boren, Englewood, CO
Lauren Cook, San Francisco, CA
Carol Gill, Mount Kisco, NY
Peggy Hoch, Santa Clara, CA
Marcia Hunt, Fort Lauderdale, FL
Marsha Irwin, San Francisco, CA

Matt Lane, Ross, CA
Katrin Muir Lau, Houston, TX
Frank Leana, St. Louis Park, MN
David Miller, Pebble Beach, CA
Judy Muir, Houston, TX
Gay S. Pepper, Naples, FL
William Pruden III, Raleigh, NC
Jan Russell, Moraga, CA
Rod Skinner, Milton, MA
Mark van Warmerdam, Danville, CA

COLLEGE COUNSELORS ADVISORY GROUP

Christine Asmussen, St. Andrew's–Sewanee School (TN)
Greg Birk, The American School in Switzerland
John B. Boshoven, Ann Arbor Public Schools (MI)
Claire Cafaro, Clear Directions (NJ)
Jane M. Catanzaro, College Advising Services (CT)
Ralph S. Figueroa, Albuquerque Academy (NM)
Larry Fletcher, Education Consultant (DE)
Freida Gottsegen, Education Consultant (GA)
Darnell Heywood, Columbus Academy (OH)
Susan Marrs, The Seven Hills School (OH)
Lisa Micele, University of Illinois Laboratory H.S. (IL)
Gunnar W. Olson, Western Reserve Academy (OH)
Stuart Oremus, Wellington School (OH)
Julie Rollins, Episcopal H.S. (TX)
Bruce Scher, Chicagoland Jewish H.S. (IL)

About the Authors

© Sourcebooks, Inc.

In 1980, when he was education editor of the *New York Times*, **Edward B. Fiske** sensed that college-bound students and their families needed better information on which to base their educational choices. Thus was born the *Fiske Guide to Colleges*. A graduate of Wesleyan University, Fiske did graduate work at Columbia University and assorted other bastions of higher learning. He left the *Times* in 1991 to pursue a variety of educational and journalistic interests, including a book on school reform, *Smart Schools, Smart Kids*. When not visiting colleges, he can be found hiking, sailing, or doing research on the educational problems of South Africa and other Third World countries for UNESCO and other international organizations. Fiske lives in Durham, North Carolina, near the campus of Duke University, where his wife, Helen Ladd, is a member of the faculty. They are coauthors of *When Schools Compete: A Cautionary Tale, Elusive Equity: Education Reform in Post-Apartheid South Africa*, and *Handbook of Research in Education Finance and Policy*.

Fiske Guide to Colleges 2020 is the ninth edition of the *Fiske Guide* that **Michelle Lecuyer** has worked on, and her third as managing editor. After serving in a range of editorial roles at Sourcebooks, Inc., the publisher of the *Fiske Guide*, she joined the *Fiske Guide to Colleges* staff as managing editor in 2016. Lecuyer also works as an independent writer and editor for a variety of print and online publishers. She earned a B.A. from Augustana College (IL) and an M.A. from Iowa State University. She lives near Chicago.

Get the Fiske college-prep advantage for all four years of high school!

978-1-4022-6081-0 • $12.99

Matriculate with confidence

Here are the 250 most important words students need to know to be successful in college and beyond, from the former education editor of the *New York Times* and a leading authority on college admissions. Each entry contains information on the word origin, a complete definition, and example sentences, making this book both the perfect gift for high school graduation and an effective tool for expanding a student's vocabulary, increasing word comprehension, and honing writing skills.

978-1-4926-5074-4 • $18.99

Learn—don't just memorize—more than 1,050 words

This amazing new system for building your vocabulary will teach students and word lovers alike to learn—not just memorize—essential words. Readers will learn thousands of new terms in weeks. *Fiske WordPower* includes more than 1,050 words and definitions, example sentences, origins and roots, plus quizzes to determine comprehension.

978-1-4022-6078-0 • $12.99

Discover the words you need to succeed

Starting off with a powerful vocabulary is the best way to prepare for a successful, stress-free time in high school. *Fiske 250 Words Every High School Freshman Needs to Know* will give you the tools to sharpen your writing skills and use language evocatively. Nail your English essays, the SAT and ACT writing tests, and all of your college and scholarship applications.

FISKE'S
College Admission Pledge
for Students

I have accepted the fact that my parents are clueless. I am serene. I will betray not a tremor when they offer opinions or advice, no matter how laughable. My soul will be light as a feather when my mother elbows her way to the front of my college tour and talks the guide's ear off. I am serene.

Going to college is a stressful time for my parents, even though they are not the ones going. I recognize that neurosis is beyond anyone's control. Each week, I will calmly reassure them that I am working on my essays, have registered for my tests, am finishing my applications, have scheduled my interviews, am aware of all deadlines, and will have everything done in plenty of time. I will smile good-naturedly as my parent asks four follow-up questions at College Night.

I will try not to say "no" simply because my parents say "yes," and I will remain open to the possibility, however improbable, that they may have a point. I may not be fully conscious of my anxieties about the college search—the fear of being judged and the fear of leaving home are both strong. I don't really want to get out of here as much as I say I do, and it is easier to put off thinking about the college search than to get it done. My parents are right about the importance of being proactive, even if they do get carried away.

Though the college search belongs to me, I will listen to my parents. They know me better than anyone else, and they are the ones who will pay most of the bills. Their ideas about what will be best for me are based on years of experience in the real world. I will seriously consider what they say as I form my own opinions.

I must take charge of the college search. If I do, the nagging will stop, and everyone's anxiety will go down. My parents have given me a remarkable gift—the ability to think and do for myself. I know I can do it with a little help from Mom and Dad.

FISKE'S

College Admission Pledge
for Parents

I am resigned to the fact that my child's college search will end in disaster. I am serene. Deadlines will be missed and scholarships will be lost as my child lounges under pulsating headphones or stares transfixed at an iPhone for hours at a time. I am a parent and I know nothing. I am serene.

Confronted with endless procrastination, my impulse is to take control—to register for tests, plan visits, schedule interviews, and get applications. It was I who asked those four follow-up questions at College Night—I couldn't help myself. And yet I know that everything will be fine if I can summon the fortitude to relax. My child is smart, capable, and perhaps a little too accustomed to me jumping in and fixing things. I will hold back. I will drop hints and encourage, then back off. I will facilitate rather than dominate. The college search won't happen on my schedule, but it will happen.

I will not get too high or low about any facet of the college search. By doing so, I give it more importance than it really has. My child's self-worth may already be too wrapped up in getting an acceptance letter. I will attempt to lessen the fear rather than heighten it.

I will try not to say "no" simply because my son or daughter says "yes," and I will remain open to the possibility, however improbable, that my child has the most important things under control. I understand that my anxiety comes partly from a sense of impending loss. I can feel my child slipping away. Sometimes I hold on too tightly or let social acceptability cloud the issue of what is best.

I realize that my child is almost ready to go and that a little rebellion at this time of life can be a good thing. I will respect and encourage independence, even if some of it is expressed as resentment toward me. I will make suggestions with care and try to avoid unnecessary confrontation.

Paying for college is my responsibility. I will take a major role in the search for financial aid and scholarships and speak honestly to my child about the financial realities we face.

I must help my son or daughter take charge of the college search. I will try to support without smothering, encourage without annoying, and consult without controlling. The college search is too big to be handled alone—I will be there every step of the way.

Notes